SIXTH EDITION

Child and Adolescent Development:
A Chronological Approach

Megan Clegg Kraynok
Ohio Northern University

Kelvin L. Seifert—Emeritus
The University of Manitoba

Robert J. Hoffnung—Emeritus
University of New Haven

To our families

Joseph, Katie, and Huggins Kraynok **m.c.k.**

Elizabeth Katherine and Michael David Seifert **k.l.s.**

Aaron Hoffnung and David, Graham, and Heather Burbank **r.j.h.**

Cover photo: Rawpixel.com/Shutterstock

Paperback (black/white):	ISBN–13: 978-1-942041-78-8
	ISBN–10: 1-942041-78-0
Paperback (color):	ISBN–13: 978-1-942041-79-5
	ISBN–10: 1-942041-79-9
Loose leaf version (B/W):	ISBN–13: 978-1-942041-80-1
	ISBN–10: 1-942041-80-2
Online version:	ISBN–13: 978-1-942041-81-8
	ISBN–10: 1-942041-81-0

Copyright © 2019 by Academic Media Solutions. All rights reserved.

No part of this work may be reproduced or transmitted in any form or by any means, electronic or mechanical, including photocopying and recording, or by any information storage or retrieval system without the prior written permission of the publisher.

Printed in the United States of America by Academic Media Solutions

Brief Contents

Contents v
Special Features x
Preface xi
About the Authors xv

PART 1 Studying Human Development 1

1. Introduction: Studying Human Development 3
2. Theories of Development 31

PART 2 Beginnings 57

3. Genetics 59
4. Prenatal Development and Birth 79

PART 3 The First Two Years of Life 103

5. Physical Development during the First Two Years 105
6. Cognitive Development during the First Two Years 127
7. Psychosocial Development during the First Two Years 151

PART 4 Early Childhood 181

8. Physical and Cognitive Development during Early Childhood 183
9. Cognitive Development during Early Childhood 199
10. Psychosocial Development during Early Childhood 223

PART 5 Middle Childhood 261

11. Physical Development during Middle Childhood 263
12. Cognitive Development during Middle Childhood 275
13. Psychosocial Development during Middle Childhood 301

PART 6 Adolescence 339

14. Physical Development during Adolescence 341
15. Cognitive Development during Adolescence 363
16. Psychosocial Development during Adolescence 385

Glossary G-1
References R-1
Author/Name Index I-1
Subject Index I-7

Contents

Special Features x
Preface xi
About the Authors xv

PART 1 Studying Human Development   1

1   Introduction: Studying Human Development   3

The Nature of Human Development   4
  Multiple Domains of Development   5
  Development: The Example of Jodi   7
Why Study Development?   10
Focusing On . . . *Wanted: A Child and Family Policy*   11
The Life Course in Times Past   11
  Early Precursors to Developmental Study   12
  The Emergence of Modern Developmental Study   12
Lifespan Perspectives on Human Development   13
  Continuity within Change   13
  Lifelong Growth   14
  Changing Meanings and Vantage Points   15
  Developmental Diversity   16
Methods of Studying Developmental Psychology   16
  The Scientific Method   16
A Multicultural View: *Street Children: Comparing Paraguay and North America*   18
  Researching Questions about Causality   18
  Researching Questions about Association   23
Working with *Marsha Bennington, Speech-Language Pathologist: Communication Difficulties across Development*   24
Ethical Constraints on Studying Development   27
Strengths and Limitations of Developmental Knowledge   29

2   Theories of Development   31

The Nature of Developmental Theories   32
  What Is a Developmental Theory?   32
  How Do Developmental Theories Differ?   33
Psychodynamic Developmental Theories   35
  Freudian Theory   35
Focusing On . . . *Erik Erikson's Identity Crisis: An Autobiographical Perspective*   37
  Erikson's Psychosocial Theory   37
  Applications of Psychodynamic Developmental Theories throughout Development   40
Behavioral Learning and Social Cognitive Learning Developmental Theories   40
  Behavioral Learning Theories   40
  Social Cognitive Learning Theory   42
  Applications of Learning Theories throughout Development   43
Cognitive Developmental Theories   43
  Piaget's Cognitive Theory   44
  Neo-Piagetian Approaches   45
  Information-Processing Theory   45
  Applications of Cognitive Developmental Theories throughout Development   47
Contextual Developmental Theories   47
  Applications of Contextual Developmental Theories throughout Development   48
A Multicultural View: *Street Children: Comparing Paraguay and North America*   49
Working with *Jeffrey Friedman, Clinical Social Worker: The Value of Developmental Theory for Helping Children, Adolescents, and Their Families*   50
  Ethological Theory   51
Developmental Theories Compared: Implications for the Student   52

PART 2 Beginnings   57

3   Genetics   59

Mechanisms of Genetic Transmission   60
  The Role of DNA   60
  Meiosis and Mitosis   60
Individual Genetic Expression   61
  Genotype and Phenotype   61
Dominant and Recessive Genes   62
  Transmission of Multiple Variations   62
  Polygenic Transmission   64
  The Determination of Sex   64
Genetic Abnormalities   65
  Disorders Due to Abnormal Chromosomes   65
  Disorders Due to Abnormal Genes   68
Genetic Counseling and Prenatal Diagnosis   70
Relative Influence of Heredity and Environment   71
  Key Concepts of Behavior Genetics   71

v

Focusing On . . . *Technological Alternatives to Natural Conception*   72
    Adoption and Twin Studies   73

A Multicultural View: *Cultural Difference and Genetic Counseling*   74
    Cautions and Conclusions about the Influence of Heredity and Environment   76

Looking Back/Looking Forward   76

4 Prenatal Development and Birth   79

Prenatal Development and Birth   79
Stages of Prenatal Development   80
Conception   80
The Germinal Stage (First Two Weeks)   80
The Embryonic Stage (Third through Eighth Weeks)   81
The Fetal Stage (Ninth Week to Birth)   82
The Experience of Pregnancy   83

Prenatal Influences on the Child   84
Harmful Substances, Diseases, and Environmental Hazards   85
Maternal Age and Physical Characteristics   90
Prenatal Health Care   90

Birth   91
Working with *Katie Glover, OB-GYN Nurse Practitioner: Preparing for Childbirth*   92
Stages of Labor   92
Childbirth Settings and Methods   94
Problems during Labor and Delivery   98
Faulty Passenger   99
Birth and the Family   100

Looking Back/Looking Forward   100

PART 3 The First Two Years of Life   103

5 Physical Development during the First Two Years   105

PHYSICAL DEVELOPMENT   106

The Newborn   106
The First Few Hours   106
Is the Baby All Right? The Apgar Scale   107
Size and Bodily Proportions   107

Growth in Infancy   108
Physical Growth   108
Brain Growth   109

Infant States: Sleep and Arousal   111
Sleep   111
Focusing On . . . *Sudden Infant Death Syndrome*   112
Parents' Response to Infant Sleep and Arousal   113
States of Arousal   114
Sensory Acuity   115
Visual Acuity   115
Auditory Acuity   115
Tactile, Taste, and Olfactory Acuity   116

Motor Development   117
The First Motor Skills   117
Cultural and Sex Differences in Motor Development   120

Nutrition during the First Two Years   120
Breast Milk versus Formula   121
Poor Nutrition   121
Overnutrition   122

Impairments in Infant Growth   123
Low-Birth-Weight Infants   123
Failure to Thrive   124
Infant Mortality   124

6 Cognitive Development during the First Two Years   127

Studying Cognition and Memory in Infants   128
Arousal and Infants' Heart Rates   128
Recognition, Memory, and Infant Habituation   128

Infant Perception and Cognition   129
Visual Perception in Infancy   129
Auditory Perception in Infancy   132
Coordination of Sensory Information   133

Cognitive Change during Infancy: Piaget's Stage Theory   133
Stages of Sensorimotor Intelligence   134
Assessment of Piaget's Theory of Infant Cognition   137

Behavioral Learning in Infancy   139
Operant Conditioning   139
Imitation   140

Language Acquisition   141
Phonology   143
Semantics and First Words   143
Influencing Language Acquisition   144

A Multicultural View: *Cognitive Effects of Talking to Infants: A Cross-Cultural Perspective*   145

Working with *Gillian Luppiwiski, Infant Care Provider: Fostering Infants' Thinking*   147

The End of Infancy   148

7 Psychosocial Development during the First Two Years   151
[handwritten annotations: Chapter, Section, Subsec]

Early Social Relationships   152
Transition to Parenthood   153
Caregiver-Infant Synchrony   154
Social Interactions with Other Family Members   155
Interactions with Nonparental Caregivers   157
Interactions with Peers   158

Emotions and Temperament in Infancy   160
Emotions in Infancy   160
Temperament   161

Attachment Formation   163
Phases of Attachment Formation   164
Assessing Attachment: The "Strange Situation"   165

vi   Contents

Consequences of Different Attachment Patterns 167
Influences on Attachment Formation 167

A Multicultural View: *Cross-Cultural Variations in Attachment* 168

Focusing On . . . *Family-Leave Policies in the United States and Europe* 171

Working with Rachelle Turner, Infant Day-Care Coordinator: Understanding Infant Social Development 172

Long-Term and Intergenerational Effects of Attachment 174

Toddlerhood and the Emergence of Autonomy 174
Sources of Autonomy 175
Development of Self 176
Development of Competence and Self-Esteem 177

Looking Back/Looking Forward 179

PART 4 Early Childhood 181

8 Physical and Cognitive Development during Early Childhood 183

PHYSICAL DEVELOPMENT 184

Influences on Normal Physical Development 184
Genetic Background 185
Nutritional Needs during the Preschool Years 186

The Connection between Health and Poverty 186

Bladder Control 187

Focusing On . . . *Reforming Children's Health Care* 188

Motor Skill Development 189
Fundamental Motor Skills 189
Fine Motor Coordination: The Case of Drawing Skills 191
Gender Differences in Physical Development 192
Variations in Motor Skill Development 193

The Impact of Children's Growth on Adults 194
Effects of Appearance 194
Effects of Motor Skills 194
Effects of Differences in Families 195

From Preschooler to Child 197

9 Cognitive Development during Early Childhood 199

COGNITIVE DEVELOPMENT 199

Thinking among Preschoolers 200
Piaget's Preoperational Stage 200
Symbolic Thought 201
Egocentrism in Preschool Children 201
Other Aspects of Children's Conceptual Development 202
Cognition as Social Activity 203
Neostructuralist Theories of Cognitive Development 205

Language Acquisition during the Preschool Years 206
The Nature of Syntax 206
Beyond First Words: Semantic and Syntactic Relations 207
Mechanisms of Language Acquisition 209
Innate Predisposition to Acquire Language: LAD 210
Parent-Child Interactions 211

Language Variations 212
Gender Differences in Language 212
Socioeconomic Differences in Language 212
Language of Deaf and Hearing-Impaired Children 213

Working with Carolyn Eaton, Preschool Teacher: Introducing Sign Language to Young Children 214
Language Deficits or Language Differences? 215

Early Childhood Education 216
Early Education and Cognitive Theories of Development 216
Effectiveness of Early Childhood Education 216
Cultural Diversity and Best Practice in Early Education 217

A Multicultural View: *Parents' Beliefs about Intelligence: A Cross-Cultural Perspective* 218

From Preschooler to Child 219

10 Psychosocial Development during Early Childhood 223

Relationships with Family 224
Relationships with Parents 224
Patterns of Parental Authority 225

Focusing On . . . *Extended Family Supports for Child-Rearing* 226
Relationships with Siblings 229

Relationships in an Expanding Social World 231
Empathy and Prosocial Behavior 232
Conflict and Aggression 234
Responding to Aggressive Behavior 237
The Effects of Media on Preschoolers' Development 238

Play during Early Childhood 240
The Nature of Play 241
Theories of Play 241
Cognitive Levels of Play: Developmental Trends 243
Other Influences on Play and Friendship 244
Social Levels of Play 245
Play and Friendship in Early Childhood 247

Working with Javier Hernandez, Preschool Program Coordinator: Play and Friendships among Preschoolers 248

Gender Development 250
Learning Gender Schema 251
Influences on Gender Development 252
Androgyny 253

Child Abuse and Maltreatment 254
Causes 254
Consequences 255

Contents vii

A Multicultural View: *The Cultural Context of Child Abuse and Neglect* 256
    Treatment and Prevention 257
Looking Back/Looking Forward 257

PART 5 Middle Childhood 261

11 Physical Development during Middle Childhood 263
PHYSICAL DEVELOPMENT 264
Trends and Variations in Height and Weight 264
Motor Development and Athletics in Middle Childhood 266
A Multicultural View: *Dieting in Cross-Cultural Perspective* 267
    Physical Effects of Early Athletics 268
    Psychological Effects of Early Athletics 269
Health and Illness in Middle Childhood 270
    Social Influences on Illness 271
    Attention Deficit Hyperactivity Disorder 271
    Sleep 273
The Changing Child 273

12 Cognitive Development during Middle Childhood 275
COGNITIVE DEVELOPMENT 275
Piaget's Theory: Concrete Operational Skills 276
    Conservation in Middle Childhood 276
    Conservation Training 277
    Piaget's Influence on Education 278
Information-Processing Skills 279
    Memory Capacity 279
    Difficulties with Information Processing: Learning Disabilities 281
Working with *Terry Wharton, Special Education Teacher: Giving Children a Second Chance to Learn* 284
Language Development in Middle Childhood 285
    Bilingualism and Its Effects 285
Defining and Measuring Intelligence 287
    Psychometric Approaches to Intelligence 288
Information-Processing Approaches to Intelligence 289
    The Triarchic Theory of Intelligence 289
Focusing On . . . *Gifted Students: Victims or Elite?* 290
    Sociocultural Approaches to Intelligence 293
School Influences 294
    Participation Structures and Classroom Discourse 294
    Social Biases That Affect Learning 296
    The Impact of Assessment 296
The Changing Child 298

13 Psychosocial Development during Middle Childhood 301
Psychosocial Challenges of Middle Childhood 302
    The Challenge of Knowing Who You Are 302
The Sense of Self 303
    The Development of Self during Childhood 303
    Processes in Constructing a Self 305
The Age of Industry and Achievement 306
    Latency and the Crisis of Industry 306
    Achievement Motivation 307
Family Relationships 308
    The Quality of Parenting and Family Life during Middle Childhood 308
    The Changing Nature of Modern Families 309
    Divorce and Its Effects on Children 309
A Multicultural View: *Parental Expectations and Academic Achievement* 310
Focusing On . . . *The Quality of Parenting and Family Life during Middle Childhood* 312
    The Effects of Work on Families 316
    Other Sources of Social Support 318
Peer Relationships 320
    What Theorists Say about Peer Relationships 320
    The Functions of Friends 321
    The Functions of Other Peers 322
    Influences on Peer Group Membership 322
    Popularity and Rejection 325
    Conformity to Peers 328
    School Influences on Peer Relations 329
Working with *Lisa Truong, Fourth-Grade Teacher: Reducing Gender Role Stereotyping in Play* 330
Death, Loss, and Grieving during the School Years 332
    The Process of Grieving for a Childhood Loss 332
    Children's Understanding of Death 333
Looking Back/Looking Forward 334

PART 6 Adolescence 339

14 Physical Development during Adolescence 341
PHYSICAL DEVELOPMENT 343
Growth in Height and Weight 343
Puberty 345
    The Development of Primary Sex Characteristics 345
    The Development of Secondary Sex Characteristics 345
    Hormonal Changes: Physical and Social Consequences 346
    Psychological Effects of Physical Growth in Adolescence 347
Health during Adolescence 349
    Causes of Death among Adolescents 349
    Health-Compromising Behaviors 350
    Adolescent Brain Development 358
Focusing On . . . *Female Athletes and Eating Disorders* 359

15 Cognitive Development during Adolescence 363
COGNITIVE DEVELOPMENT 363

Beyond Concrete Operational Thinking 364
    Possibilities versus Realities 364
    Scientific Reasoning 365
    Logical Combination of Ideas 365
    Cognitive Development Beyond Formal Thought 365
    Implications of the Cognitive Developmental Viewpoint 366

Moral Development: Beliefs about Justice and Care 367
    Kohlberg's Six Stages of Moral Judgment 367
Working with *Jerry Acton, Math and Science Teacher: Blending the Social and Emotional with the Cognitive* 368
    Issues in the Development of Moral Beliefs about Justice 370
    Gilligan's Ethics of Care 372
    The Ethics of Care during Adolescence 373
    The Development of Social Cognition 373

Information-Processing Features of Adolescent Thought 375
    Improved Capacity to Process Information 375
    Expertise in Specific Domains of Knowledge 376

The Influence of School 377
    Cognitive Effects of Schooling 378
    Social Effects of Schooling 380
A Multicultural View: *Cross-Cultural Misunderstandings in the Classroom* 381

16 Psychosocial Development during Adolescence 385

Theories of Identity Development 386
    Ruthellen Josselson: Individuation and Identity Development 386
    Erik Erikson: The Crisis of Identity versus Role Confusion 387

Family Relationships during Adolescence 391
    Relationships with Parents 391
A Multicultural View: *Differing Cultural Views of Delinquency* 398
    Divorce, Remarriage, and Single Parenthood 398

Social Relationships during Adolescence 401
    Friendship 401
    Peer Groups 404
    Adolescents in the World of Work 407
Focusing On . . . *Can Parents Influence Their Adolescent's Choice of Peer Group?* 408

Sexuality during Adolescence 409
    Sexual Experience 409
    Sexual Orientations 412
    Sex and Everyday Life 413

Special Problems of Adolescence 413
    Adolescent Pregnancy and Parenthood 413
Working with *Janet Whallen, Nurse Practitioner: Helping Pregnant Teenagers* 416
    Teenage Depression and Suicide 418
    Juvenile Delinquency 420

Looking Back/Looking Forward 422

Glossary G-1
References R-1
Author/Name Index I-1
Subject Index I-7

Special Features

"Working with . . ." Interviews
Chapter

1. Marsha Bennington, Speech-Language Pathologist: Communication Difficulties across Development   24
2. Jeffrey Friedman, Clinical Social Worker: The Value of Developmental Theory for Helping Children, Adolescents, and Their Families   50
4. Katie Glover, OB-GYN Nurse Practitioner: Preparing for Childbirth   92
6. Gillian Luppiwiski, Infant Care Provider: Fostering Infants' Thinking   147
7. Rachelle Turner, Infant Day-Care Coordinator: Understanding Infant Social Development   172
9. Carolyn Eaton, Preschool Teacher: Introducing Sign Language to Young Children   214
10. Javier Hernandez, Preschool Program Coordinator: Play and Friendships among Preschoolers   248
12. Terry Wharton, Special Education Teacher: Giving Children a Second Chance to Learn   284
13. Lisa Truong, Fourth-Grade Teacher: Reducing Gender Role Stereotyping in Play   330
15. Jerry Acton, Math and Science Teacher: Blending the Social and Emotional with the Cognitive   368
16. Janet Whallen, Nurse Practitioner: Helping Pregnant Teenagers   416

A Multicultural View
Chapter

1. Street Children: Comparing Paraguay and North America   18
2. Street Children: Comparing Paraguay and North America   49
3. Cultural Difference and Genetic Counseling   74
6. Cognitive Effects of Talking to Infants: A Cross-Cultural Perspective   145
7. Cross-Cultural Variations in Attachment   168
9. Parents' Beliefs about Intelligence: A Cross-Cultural Perspective   218
10. The Cultural Context of Child Abuse and Neglect   256
11. Dieting in Cross-Cultural Perspective   267
13. Parental Expectations and Academic Achievement   310
15. Cross-Cultural Misunderstandings in the Classroom   381
16. Differing Cultural Views of Delinquency   398

Focusing On
Chapter

1. Wanted: A Child and Family Policy   11
2. Erik Erikson's Identity Crisis: An Autobiographical Perspective   37
3. Technological Alternatives to Natural Conception   72
5. Sudden Infant Death Syndrome   112
7. Family-Leave Policies in the United States and Europe   171
8. Reforming Children's Health Care   188
10. Extended Family Supports for Child-Rearing   226
12. Gifted Students: Victims or Elite?   290
13. The Quality of Parenting and Family Life during Middle Childhood   312
14. Female Athletes and Eating Disorders   359
16. Can Parents Influence Their Adolescent's Choice of Peer Group?   408

Preface

When we began planning this sixth edition of *Child and Adolescent Development*, our conversations kept coming back to the idea of continuity and change—for in a sense, that is what revising a text is all about. You will find many continuities between this edition and previous editions. However, there is also a great deal of new information and current research. Our major goal of this revision was to maintain and strengthen the story of continuity and change from conception to emerging adulthood, alluding to continued changes throughout adulthood when appropriate. To achieve this goal, we have organized our presentation throughout the text to emphasize four developmental themes:

- *Continuity Within Change*, which looks for continuities in the person that may be hidden by more obvious long-term changes of maturation and evolving life circumstances;
- *Lifelong Growth*, which focuses on the potential for growth at all stages of development;
- *Changing Meanings and Vantage Points*, which considers how universal experiences, such as work, play, love, and sex, take on different meanings at different stages of development; and
- *Developmental Diversity*, which notices differences created by genetic, social, and cultural circumstances within the search for general trends and patterns in human development.

In this edition, you will find these themes introduced in Chapter 1, mentioned throughout the text as we focus on specific stages of development, and highlighted at the end of each part in a special section called "Looking Back/Looking Forward." This feature revisits the four developmental themes in relation to a hinge issue that appeared in that part. The thematic orientation of this edition is designed to help students appreciate the complex combination of continuity and change from birth emerging adulthood.

We have also broadened our range of examples and applications to increase its relevance to the wide range of students who come to a developmental course from many departments and are headed for a wide range of occupational and family roles. We realize that they will be educators, health professionals such as occupational and physical therapists, and nurses, social workers, parents, and family members, all roles requiring an understanding of human development. We have revised our book with this in mind.

We believe that developmental psychology is relevant to current career and social issues that all adults face. It is especially relevant to those who will work or live with children and adolescents. We see personal involvement as positive and include a wide range of examples that will enable most readers to find themselves, and people they know, in the story of child and adolescent development.

Content and Organization

Part 1, "Studying Human Development," introduces our developmental themes and discusses the field of human development, key theories, genetics, prenatal development, and birth. Some of the changes we have made in this portion of the book include Chapter 1 reorganized to highlight the key themes of development as they are emphasized in this book. In Chapter 2, "Applications throughout Development" sections following each major set of developmental theories help students see how theories can be used.

Parts 2 through 6 are then organized chronologically: genetics, prenatal development and birth, the first two years, early childhood, middle childhood, and adolescence Within each age period, we focus in one chapter on physical development, one chapter on cognitive development, and a third chapter on psychosocial development. Although we frequently point out the interrelatedness of these three domains, we give each separate attention as well. Content changes in Parts 2 through 6 include a new section examining sleep in each age period and, as applicable, discussion of families with same-sex parents and gay and lesbian issues.

In addition to specific content changes, we have included multicultural coverage throughout the text as well, as in the special "Multicultural View" boxes, and increased integration of practical information, cultural information, and career ideas with research information.

We have also made the organization more parallel throughout the book. In the chapters on physical development, for example, we cover systemic change, health and health-compromising behaviors. The chapters on cognition cover moral development, school, and work in the same order in each stage's comparable chapters. Likewise, the chapters on psychosocial development move from discussions of theories of personality development to discussions of the family sphere to relationships in the wider world. For students, this parallelism reinforces continuities from stage to stage and will make it even easier for instructors who prefer to organize their courses topically rather than chronologically to use the book in their own way.

Tools to Enhance Learning

For a textbook to be effective, it must be read. With this in mind, we continued to hold ourselves to high standards for clear, good writing. This text is approachable, filled with real life examples that can engage students in the issues of human development and illustrations that reinforce key concepts.

A Critical Approach to Research We base our presentation on a firm understanding of current research in the field, balancing the inclusion of classic and recent studies. Yet the book is not so data driven as to be too technical for students new to the issues. Numerous hypothetical and real-life examples balance our research-based discussions. Because research findings do not always agree with one another, this book focuses both on what we know and on how we came to know it. We want students to understand how the data behind the conclusions were generated and to be able to raise questions about the validity, reliability, and generalizability of research findings. We introduce methodological concerns in Chapter 1. In addition, we present critiques of studies as we discuss them and periodically describe methods where they will have the most meaning (such as "Studying Cognition and Memory in Infants" in Chapter 6's discussion of cognitive development during the first two years.

Rich Illustration Program Numerous graphs, figures, and tables reinforce the text discussions by providing a visual guide to key concepts. These have been updated to reflect the latest demographic data. Captions to line art and photos emphasize critical points and provide additional pedagogical support. We carefully selected photographs to reinforce our emphasis on diversity in culture, race and ethnicity, gender, sexual orientation, and socioeconomic status.

Improved Learning Aids As in the previous editions, chapters open with outlines and focusing questions. New to this edition, we organize our end-of-chapter summaries around the focusing questions that appeared in the beginning of the chapter to highlight the conceptual connections among topics in each main section. Key terms lists again serve as pedagogical supports by reinforcing the important themes, ideas, and concepts in each chapter. We have included a margin glossary to this edition to further support student learning of key terms. In addition to assisting in the mastery of content, these aids encourage students to develop their personal perspectives about psychology and its practical applications.

Special Features

Looking Back/Looking Forward New to this edition, a greatly expanded section at the end of each part examines a hinge issue in light of the four themes of the book: Continuity Within Change, Developmental Growth, Changing Meanings and Vantage Points, and Developmental Diversity. The hinge issues are as follows: genetic inheritance after "Beginnings"; attachment after the "First Two Years"; friendship after "Early Childhood"; family after "Middle Childhood"; and parent-child relationships after "Adolescence." These sections reinforce the developmental themes by approaching key concepts from a fresh angle and linking them to earlier developmental periods and those yet to come.

What Do You Think? In this edition, we continue to have questions designed to stimulate reflection and discussion about the issues and concepts of development, located at the end of each major section throughout every chapter. "What Do You Think?" questions also appear at the end of the "Working With" and "Focusing On" boxes to reinforce the connections between the box and the main text. While addressed directly to the student, the "What Do You Think?" questions can also serve as a basis for class activities and discussion. Many encourage collaboration among classmates and can be used as group assignments.

"Working With" Interviews As in the previous editions, each chapter includes an interview with someone who works in the field discussing the practical application of developmental issues featured in that chapter. Robert Hoffnung's interview with a psychiatric social worker appears in Chapter 2 to enhance the discussion of psychoanalytic theory. Kelvin Seifert's new interview about teaching high school mathematics and its relationship to cognitive development in adolescence appears in Chapter 15. Interviews enable students to see the relationship between the theoretical and the practical. "What Do You Think?" questions follow the interviews to stress the connections with the text. The interviews also provide occupational examples for students who are considering possibilities for their futures. For a complete list of featured careers and topics, see page x.

A Multicultural View Again in this edition, a boxed insert in each chapter highlights an issue of development from a cross- or multicultural perspective. While this perspective is a consistent aspect of the text, we use the boxes to focus on issues of particular interest. Topics new to this edition include a comparison of street children in Paraguay and North America (Chapter 1) and a cross-cultural look at delinquency (Chapter 16). A complete list of these boxes appears on page x.

Focusing On Each chapter's "Focusing On" box expands the discussion in the text by highlighting a significant and timely issue and includes "What Do You Think?" questions to enhance the connections among the box, the chapter, and students' experiences. See page x for a full list.

Online and in Print

Student Options: Print and Online Versions

This Sixth edition of *Child and Adolescent Development* is available in multiple versions: online, in PDF, and in print as either a paperback or loose-leaf text. The content of each version is identical.

The most affordable version is the online book, with upgrade options including the online version bundled with a print version. What's nice about the print version is that it offers you the freedom of being unplugged—away from your computer. The people at Academic Media Solutions recognize that it's difficult to read from a screen at length and that most of us read much faster from a piece of paper. The print options are particularly useful when you have extended print passages to read.

The online edition allows you to take full advantage of embedded digital features, including search and notes. Use the search feature to locate and jump to discussions anywhere in the book. Use the notes feature to add personal comments or annotations. You can move out of the book to follow Web links. You can navigate within and between chapters using a clickable table of contents. These features allow you to work at your own pace and in your own style, as you read and surf your way through the material. (See "Harnessing the Online Version" for more tips on working with the online version.)

Harnessing the Online Version

The online version of *Child and Adolescent Development*, sixth edition, offers the following features to facilitate learning and to make using the book an easy, enjoyable experience:

- ***Easy-to-navigate/clickable table of contents***—You can surf through the book quickly by clicking on chapter headings, or first- or second-level section headings. And the Table of Contents can be accessed from anywhere in the book.
- ***Key terms search***—Type in a term, and a search engine will return every instance of that term in the book; then jump directly to the selection of your choice with one click.
- ***Notes and highlighting***—The online version includes study apps such as notes and highlighting. Each of these apps can be found in the tools icon embedded in the Academic Media Solutions/Textbook Media's online eBook reading platform (http://www.academicmediasolutions.com).
- ***Upgrades***—The online version includes the ability to purchase additional study apps and functionality that enhance the learning experience.

Instructor Supplements

In addition to its student-friendly features and pedagogy, the variety of student formats available, and the uniquely affordable pricing options that are designed to provide students with a flexibility that fits any budget and/or learning style, *Child and Adolescent Development*, sixth edition, comes with the following teaching and learning aids:

- ***Test Item File***—The Test Bank includes 100 multiple choice and three essay questions per chapter. Each multiple-choice question is keyed to a learning objective and a text page number. Emphasis is on providing a wealth of applied and conceptual questions. The essay questions include sample response guides.
- ***Instructor's Manual***—An enhanced version of the book offering assistance in preparing lectures, identifying learning objectives, developing essay exams and assignments, and constructing course syllabi.
- ***PowerPoint Presentations***—Key points in each chapter are illustrated in a set of PowerPoint files designed to assist with instruction. In addition, all of the chapter figures and tables are included for further ease with instruction.
- ***Online Video Labs***—A collection of high-quality, dynamic, and sometimes humorous video segments (contemporary and classic) that are produced by a variety of media from both academic and entertainment sources accessed via the web. Organized by chapter, each video segment illustrates key topics/issues discussed in that specific chapter. Each video segment is accompanied by a student worksheet, which consists of a series of discussion questions that help students connect the themes presented in the video segment back to a key topic discussed in that specific chapter.

Student Supplements and Upgrades (Additional Purchase Required)

- **Lecture Guide**—This printable lecture guide is designed for student use and is available as an in-class resource or study tool. Note: Instructors can request the PowerPoint version of these slides to use as developed or to customize.
- **Study Guide**—The student Study Guide contains learning objectives, a chapter overview and outline, a fill-in review of key terms and concepts, and two sets of multiple-choice practice questions—one set tests the student's factual knowledge and the other tests applied knowledge. The multiple-choice answer key explains why each option is correct or incorrect, a feature particularly appreciated by students.

Preface

A printable version of the online study guide is available via downloadable PDF chapters for easy self-printing and review.

- **Quizlet Study Set**—Quizlet is an easy-to-use online learning tool built from all of the key terms from the textbook. Students can turbo charge their studying via digital flashcards and other types of study apps, including tests and games. Students are able to listen to audio, as well as create their own flashcards. Quizlet is a cross-platform application and can be used on a desktop, tablet, or smartphone.

Acknowledgments

Our text benefits from the constructive suggestions and thoughtful reactions offered by reviewers of the various iterations of this text, and we are very appreciative of their help. In particular, we offer our continued gratitude to

Marlene Adelman, Norwalk Community College

Sheridan DeWolf, Grossmont College

Teresa Elliott, American University,

Catherine Dillespie, Drake University

Dale Grubb, Baldwin Wallace University

John R. Hranitz, Bloomsburg University of Pennsylvania

Herbert Merill II, Erie Community College

Mary Kay Reed, York College of Pennsylvania

Daniel J. Robin, Indiana University

Holly Scrivner, Shasta College

We wish to thank the individuals who participated in the "Working With" interviews. Thanks also to the staff at Academic Media Solutions (AMS) who worked with us to publish this new edition of *Child and Adolescent Development*: Daniel C. Luciano, president/founder of AMS, Victoria Putman of Putman Productions, and Kirsten Balayti for copyediting. We also thank Dr. Dale D. Grubb (Baldwin Wallace University) for his contribution in the early stages of this revision. We thank our families and friends for the support they provided as we worked on this book, as well as the many stories from their lives that serve as examples throughout the text.

About the Authors

As developmental psychologists, college professors who teach adolescents and adults of many ages, and parents who have seen our children through many stages of development (some as far as early adulthood), the authors bring to this project a shared interest in human development as well as training and interests that complement each other. Megan's teaching covers each age period of the lifespan and focuses on adolescence, emerging adulthood, and late life as well as health psychology and sleep; her research is focused on improving sleep among college students and older adults. Kelvin's teaching has focused on early childhood and learning theory; his recent research is on children's cognition, although his earlier research looked at gender issues in early childhood teacher education. Robert has taught about childhood, adolescence, and lifespan development; he has also done clinical work with children, adolescents, adults, and families.

Megan Clegg Kraynok is an Associate Professor of Psychology at Ohio Northern University in Ada, Ohio. She earned her B.A. at West Virginia Wesleyan College, her M.S. at the University of Pittsburgh, and her Ph.D. at West Virginia University. She has published articles on sleep among adolescents, emerging adults, and new parents, and has co-authored chapters on mental health and aging.

Kelvin Seifert is Professor Emeritus of Educational Psychology at the University of Manitoba. He received his B.A. at Swarthmore College and his Ph.D. at the University of Michigan. He is author of *Educational Psychology* (1991) and has published research on gender issues in early childhood education as well as on teachers' and parents' beliefs about children and their development.

Robert Hoffnung is Professor Emeritus of Psychology at the University of New Haven and Associate Clinical Professor of Psychiatry at the Yale University School of Medicine. He received his B.A. at Lafayette College, his M.A. at the University of Iowa, and his Ph.D. at the University of Cincinnati. He has published articles on educational, developmental, and mental health interventions with children, adolescents, and families.

Studying Human Development

PART 1

Chapter 1
Introduction: Studying Human Development

Chapter 2
Theories of Development

Source: Andi Berger/Shutterstock.com.

As individuals grow from infancy into childhood, and from childhood into adolescence, they change in some ways while remaining the same in others. Some changes may be small and fleeting, whereas others are profound and long lasting. The mix of change and constancy is the subject of this book and of the field known as *developmental psychology*.

The study of development offers much insight into human nature—why we are what we are and how we became that way. Because describing development is a complex task, this book begins with two chapters that orient you to what lies ahead. They explain just what development is and describe some of the most important tools of lifespan developmental psychology, namely the methods and theories that guide our understanding of child and adolescent development. As you read the chapters, though, keep in mind one of the most important sources of the theories: the children themselves.

Introduction: Studying Human Development

CHAPTER 1

Source: Milica Nistoran/Shutterstock.com.

Chapter Outline

The Nature of Human Development
Why Study Development?
The Life Course in Times Past
Lifespan Perspectives on Human Development
Methods of Studying Developmental Psychology
Ethical Constraints on Studying Development
Strengths and Limitations of Developmental Knowledge

Focusing Questions

- What in general is lifespan development?
- Why is it important to know about development?
- How has society's view of childhood changed over time?
- What general issues are important in human development?
- How do developmental psychologists go about studying development from conception to adolescence?
- What ethical considerations should guide the study of child and adolescent development?

What do you remember from your past? When thinking back, each of us remembers different details, but we all experience a paradoxical quality about personal memories; when comparing the past and the present, we feel as though we have changed, yet also stayed the same. As a preschooler, for example, one of the authors (Kelvin Seifert) had trouble tying his shoelaces. Now, as an adult, he can tie laces easily, but he has to admit that he has never enjoyed or excelled at tasks calling for delicate or precise physical skills. In this small way, Kelvin has both changed and stayed the same. You yourself may have experienced this same dual quality. As a schoolchild, perhaps you loved spelling "bees" or contests. Now, as an adult, you no longer participate in spelling contests and have lost some of your childhood ability to figure out and remember truly unusual spellings. But perhaps you note, too, that you can still spell better than many adults of your age, and you seem to have a general knack for handling verbal information of other kinds—like computer programming languages—without getting mixed up. Or imagine another example: As a teenager you may have constantly wondered whether you would ever overcome shyness and be truly liked and respected by peers. As an adult, in contrast, you finally believe you have good, special friends; but maybe you also have to admit that it took effort to become sociable enough to acquire them.

Continuity in the midst of change marks every human life. Sometimes changes seem more obvious than continuities, such as when a speechless infant becomes a talkative preschooler, or when a college student finishes school and begins her career in earnest. Other times continuities seem more obvious than changes, such as when an eighteen-year-old still feels like a little kid when his mom addresses him by his first and middle name. But close scrutiny of examples like these suggests that both factors may be operating, even when one of them is partially hidden. The eighteen-year-old feels like a child again, but at the same time feels different from that child. The twenty-four year old professional is now preoccupied with her job, but she still cares deeply about her friends from college who now live across the country. It takes both continuity and change to be fully human; I must be connected to my past somehow, but also neither locked into it nor fully determined by it.

The Nature of Human Development

This book is about continuity and change from conception through adolescence. Sometimes these processes are called human **development**, although this term is sometimes used to emphasize changes, rather than constancies, in physical growth, feelings, and ways of thinking. As we will see in later chapters, a focus on change may indeed be appropriate at certain points in a person's life. A girl undergoing her first menstrual period, for example, may experience a number of important changes at the same time, and rather suddenly: her body begins looking different, she begins thinking of herself differently, and other people begin treating her differently. But at other times, continuity dominates over change. As an eight-year-old settled into his elementary school and living in a stable home with his mother, for example, life may seem rather stable from day to day, month to month, or even year to year. Because this book explores development (from conception to adolescence), it will make the most sense to keep both factors in mind—both continuity *and* change—without emphasizing one over the other in advance. When we speak of human development in this book, therefore, we will mean the mix of continuities and changes that occur during a person's life, from conception to adolescence.

Note that both continuities and changes can take many forms. Changes can be relatively specific, such as when an infant takes her first unassisted step. Others can be rather general and unfold over a long time, such as when the areas of a teenager's brain responsible for planning ahead and thinking of consequences becomes more efficient over the course of adolescence and emerging adulthood. The same can be said of continuities. Some last for only a short time compared to the decades-long span of life: a four-year-old who enjoys watching Sesame Street will likely continue to enjoy watching Sesame Street. Other continuities seemingly last a lifetime: an extroverted child—one who seeks and enjoys social companionship—is likely to still seek and enjoy companionship as a teenager.

These examples may make the notion of human development seem very broad, but note that not every change or continuity is truly "developmental," and some human developments are easily overlooked or discounted. Think about the impact of the weather. A sudden cold snap makes us behave differently: we put on warmer clothing and select indoor activities over outdoor ones. A continuous spell of cold weather, on the other hand, creates constancy in behavior: we wear the same type of clothing for a period of time and engage in the same (indoor) set of activities repeatedly. In both cases, our behavior does

development Long-term changes in a person's growth, feelings, patterns of thinking, social relationships, and motor skills.

Development occasionally involves rapid, visible changes, such as learning to walk without assistance. Development also includes continuity over time, such as a love of reading.
Source: (*left*) Kitzero/Shutterstock.com, (*right*) multiart/Shutterstock.com.

not qualify as "development" because it is triggered by relatively simple external events and has no lasting impact on other behaviors, feelings, or thinking.

But true human development sometimes also can occur, yet be overlooked or dismissed as something other than development. Personal identity or sense of "self" is an example. A concept of who "I" am always seems to be with me, and often it seems so constant that I ignore it, making it "part of the woodwork" of my mind. This is likely true for you, too; your sense of who "you" are probably seems consistent or familiar to you. This fact is so much a part of our lives that it is easy to overlook its importance or to notice changes in our self-concepts when they occur. Yet for each of us, identity evolves and changes as we grow older, and the changes affect our actions and feelings differently when they occur.

Multiple Domains of Development

As these examples suggest, human development can take many forms. For convenience of discussion, this book distinguishes among three major types, or **domains**, of development: physical, cognitive, and psychosocial. The organization of the book reflects this division by alternating chapters about physical, cognitive, and psychosocial changes. The domain of **physical development**, or biological change, includes changes in the body itself and how a person uses his or her body. Some of these changes may be noticeable to a casual observer, such as the difference in how a person walks when she is two years old versus when she is eighteen years old. Others may be essentially invisible without extended observation or even medical investigation, such as the difference in the ability to see between a four-month-old and his seven-year-old sister. Like other forms of development, physical changes often span very long periods—literally years or even decades—though not always. For example, changes in height and weight occur rather rapidly during toddlerhood and the early teenage years but more slowly during late adolescence.

Cognitive development involves changes in methods and styles of thinking, language ability and language use, and strategies for remembering and recalling information. We tend to think of these abilities and skills as somewhat isolated within individuals; a person is said to "have" a good memory, for example, as if he or she carries that skill around all the time and can display it anywhere with equal ease, no matter what the situation. As later chapters will sometimes point out, however, thinking of cognitive development in this way may be more convenient than accurate: memory, language, and thinking are all heavily dependent on supports (and impediments) both from other people and from circumstances. A child learns to read more easily, for example, if parents and teachers give lots of personal support for her efforts. In this sense cognitive changes of reading "belong" to the helpful adults as well as to the child who acquires them, and the changes are best understood as partially physical and social in nature, and not merely cognitive.

domain A realm of psychological functioning.

physical development The area of human development concerned primarily with physical changes such as growth, motor skill development, and basic aspects of perception.

cognitive development The area of human development concerned with cognition; involves all psychological processes by which individuals learn and think about their environment.

psychosocial development
The area of human development concerned primarily with personality, social knowledge and skills, and emotions.

Psychosocial development is about changes in feelings or emotions as well as changes in relations with other people. It includes interactions with family, peers, and classmates, but also includes a person's personal identity, or sense of self. Because identity and social relationships evolve together, we often discuss them together in this book. And, as already pointed out, they also evolve in combination with physical and cognitive changes. A teenager who forms satisfying friendships is apt to feel more competent than one who has difficulty doing so, and he is even likely to stay healthier as well. Each domain—physical, cognitive, and psychosocial—influences each of the others.

Figure 1.1 shows some major landmarks of development in each of the three domains during a few selected stages of development. It also hints at some of the connections among specific developments, both between domains and within each single domain. Attachment to caregiver(s), for example, is noted as emerging during infancy; early attachment patterns set the stage for the kinds of friendships and romantic relationships that develop during childhood, adolescence and adulthood. This change in social circumstances is sometimes (but certainly not always) accompanied by physical changes and cognitive changes—though which change causes which is not always clear. In addition to these examples from Figure 1.1, numerous other relationships exist between and within domains of development. In later

FIGURE 1.1
Selected Landmarks of Development

Development is a continual unfolding and integration of changes in all domains, from birth until death. Changes in one domain often affect those in another domain, and changes that occur in earlier stages of life can influence those that occur during later stages.

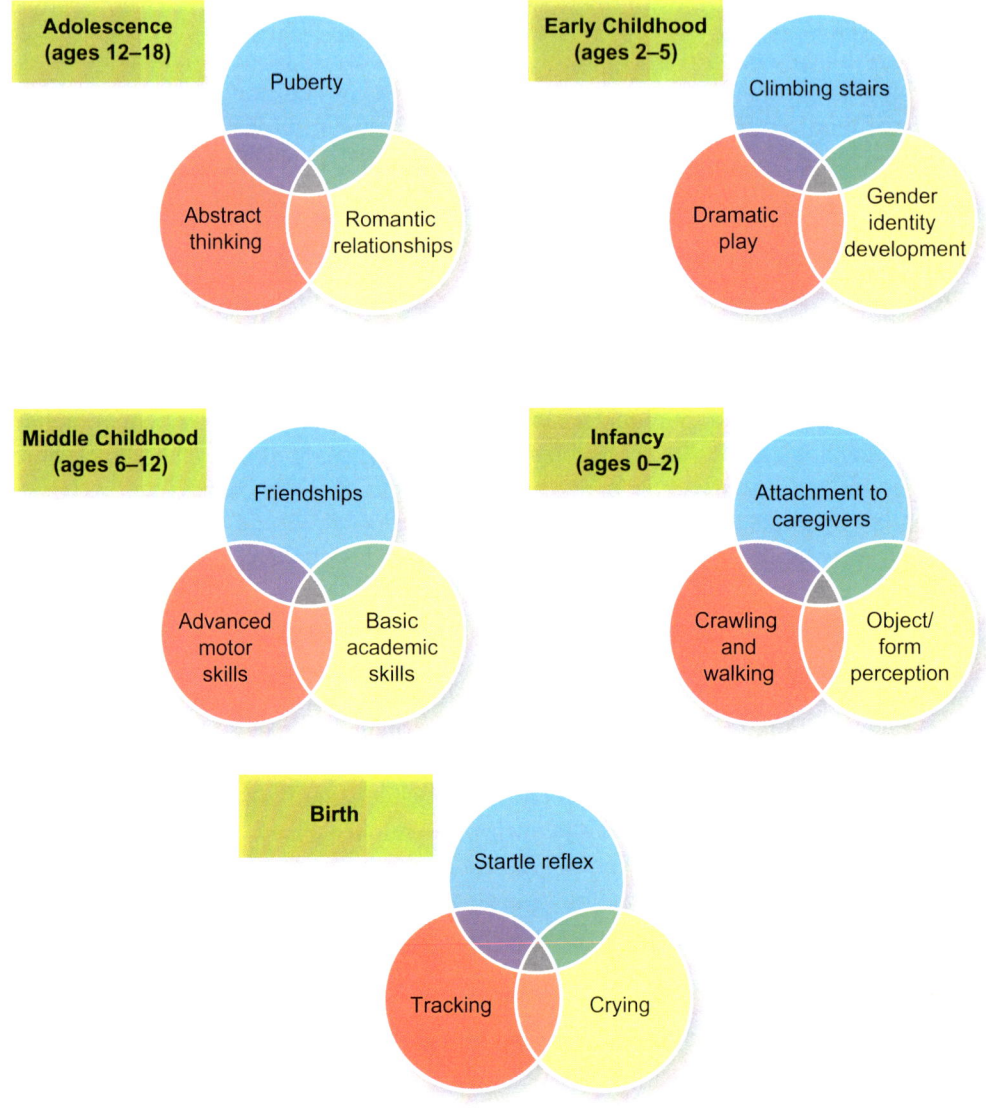

Key: For each age group, the Venn diagram represents the intersection of physical (bottom-left circle), cognitive (bottom-right), and social (top) domains of development.

Part 1 Studying Human Development

chapters we will point these out more explicitly wherever appropriate. Meanwhile, to get a better sense of what development from a developmental perspective means, consider a more extended, complete example.

Development: The Example of Jodi

So far, though we have talked about the importance of relationships among various forms of development, our examples have been a bit diverse and fragmented. How would developments tie together in the life of a real person? What relationships among them could we see then? These are not simple questions to answer fully, but you can begin to get partial answers by considering a child whom one of the authors knew personally: Jodi.

When Jodi was four, one of her brothers died. Roger had been 2-1/2 years older, a friendly kid and a decent sibling. Jodi played with him more than with her sister and other brother, who were both older than Roger. He died suddenly one winter from complications of chicken pox. The doctors said he may have reacted to the aspirin he had taken for his fever. The doctors said you weren't supposed to give aspirin to children, but Jodi didn't know that, and apparently her parents didn't know it either.

For a few years after that, they were a three-child family "with a hole in the middle," said Jodi to her best friend, where Roger was supposed to be. It was not ideal for Jodi, but it was tolerable: she didn't have the playmate she used to have, but she did have her family ("What's left of it!") and her friends from school. Life got back to normal—sort of.

When Jodi was nine, her parents adopted another child, a boy of twelve, about the same age Roger would have been had he lived. Frank had lived in numerous foster care homes, some of which had not been happy experiences for him. In two homes the discipline had been extremely strict, but it was hard for Jodi to know this because Frank did not tell her as much as he told the social workers or his new adopted parents, and her parents did not say much about Frank's past. In fact, Frank said little to Jodi about anything; he seemed distinctly cool toward all three of his new siblings—except for his periodic visits to Jodi's room at night. The first time it happened, Jodi was startled out of her sleep: Frank was standing by her bed and demanded that she take off her nightgown. That was all for that time. But he came back every few weeks, each time asking for more than the time before and threatening to hurt her badly if she revealed "our secret."

So Jodi learned not to sleep deeply. She also learned to avoid being alone in the house with Frank. In high school and college, she learned to avoid talking to boys a lot, except in a joking way and in the presence of others. In class she learned to look interested in what the instructors said even though she often was "sleeping inside," as she put it. So Jodi learned a lot from Frank, though not things she wanted to learn and not things most of her classmates were learning.

Jodi's story shows several things about human development. It shows, for example, that the domains of development all unfold together. Jodi's thoughts and feelings about Frank occurred in the context of physical changes happening to herself. Being physically older or younger may not have protected her from abuse, but it probably would have altered the experience, both in impact and in quality.

Jodi's story also suggests the importance of unique, personal experiences when exploring human development in general. Some things about Jodi may always be unique because of her encounters with Frank; she may always be a bit mistrustful of boys and men, for example. But other things about Jodi can be understood as examples of human changes that are universal or nearly universal. In experiencing abuse, for example, Jodi responds to gender role differences that pervade nearly all societies; in most societies, women enjoy less power than men do.

From the point of view of development, Jodi's story also raises questions about continuity and change across wide ranges of time. We are left wondering whether Jodi's initial responses to abuse will persist throughout her life. Assuming she will be cautious about men even as a thirty-year-old adult? After so many years go by, society itself may develop new attitudes about the significance of childhood abuse, just as society already has done in the past few decades.

FIGURE 1.2
Bronfenbrenner's Ecological Systems for Developmental Change

As shown here, Bronfenbrenner describes human development as a set of overlapping ecological systems. All of these systems operate together to influence what a person becomes as he or she grows older. In this sense, development is not exclusively "in" the person but is also "in" the person's environment. In addition to the systems pictured here, a fifth system, the *chronosystem*, refers to changes in the ecological systems over a person's lifetime and over the course of human history.

Source: Adapted from Garbarino (1992a).

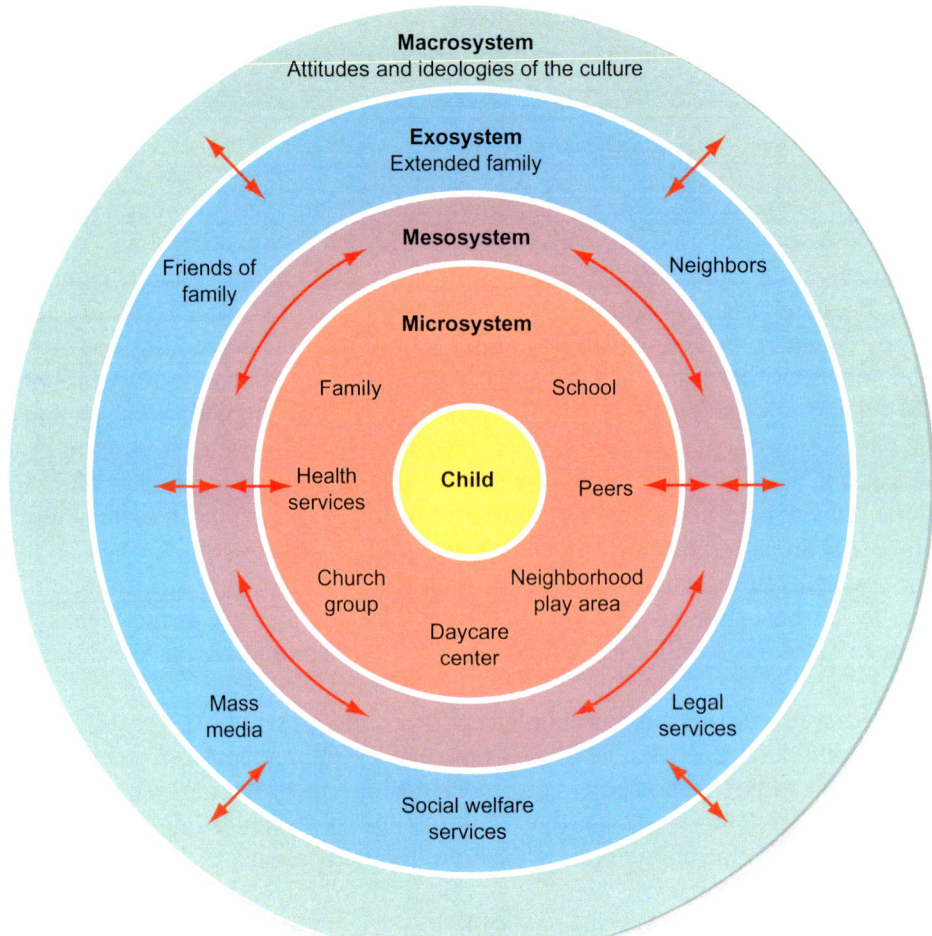

To help organize thinking about developmental questions like these, the developmental psychologist Urie Bronfenbrenner has originated a widely used framework for thinking about the multiple influences on individuals (Bronfenbrenner, 1989, 2005; Garbarino, 1992a). He describes the context of development as *ecological systems,* which are sets of people, settings, and recurring events that are related to one another, have stability, and influence the person over time. Figure 1.2 and Table 1.1 illustrate Bronfenbrenner's ecological systems.

1. The *microsystem* refers to situations in which the person has face-to-face contact with influential others. For Jodi, the microsystem consists of her immediate family (though note that the membership of this family changed over time) as well as her teachers and peers at school.

2. The *mesosystem* refers to the connections and relationships that exist between two or more microsystems and influence the person because of their relationships. An example would be the contacts between Jodi's parents and the social workers responsible for Frank's adoption: their contacts led them (perhaps wrongly) to withhold information about Frank from Jodi.

3. The *exosystem* consists of settings in which the person does not participate but still experiences decisions and events that affect him or her indirectly. An example in Jodi's case might be the medical system, which either lacked the knowledge needed to save Roger at the time of his death or had been organized in a way that interfered with communicating needed medical knowledge to Jodi's parents.

4. The *macrosystem* is the overarching institutions, practices, and patterns of belief that characterize society as a whole and take the smaller micro-, meso-, and exosystems into account. An example that affected Jodi was gender role: a widespread belief that men should dominate women may have contributed to Frank's coercive actions against Jodi, as well as to Jodi's caution with boys and men as she got older.

Part 1 Studying Human Development

TABLE 1.1 Ecological System Levels

Ecological Level	Definition	Examples	Issues Affecting the Individual
Microsystem	Situations in which the person has face-to-face contact with influential others	Family, school, peer group, church, workplace	Is the person regarded positively? Is the person accepted? Is the person reinforced for competent behavior? Is the person exposed to enough diversity in roles and relationships? Is the person given an active role in reciprocal relationships?
Mesosystem	Relationships between microsystems; the connections between situations	Home–school, workplace–family, school–neighborhood	Do settings respect each other? Do settings present basic consistency in values?
Exosystem	Settings in which the person does not participate but in which significant decisions are made affecting the individuals who do interact directly with the person	Spouse's place of employment, local school board, local government	Are decisions made with the interests of the person in mind? How well do social supports for families balance stresses for parents?
Macrosystem	"Blueprints" for defining and organizing the institutional life of the society	Ideology, social policy, shared assumptions about human nature, the "social contract"	Are some groups valued at the expense of others (e.g., sexism, racism)? Is there an individualistic or a collectivistic orientation? Is violence a norm?
Chronosystem	Changes in all of the ecological systems over the course of a person's development and over the course of human history.	The developmental impact of certain events will vary depending upon their timing during one's development, and elements of the ecological systems can change from one generation to the next.	What elements of the ecological systems are most impactful on an individual's development, given that individual's age? What factors will greatly influence the development of children born in 2015? How do those factors compare to ones that were present in 1990?

5. The *chronosystem* (not depicted in Figure 1.2) can be best thought of as a quality of all of the ecological systems: they change over time. During the course of one's lifetime, specific aspects of each person's micro-, meso-, exo-, and macrosystems will change, as will their impact on the individual's development. In Jodi's case, if Frank's actions occurred when Jodi was 19 instead of just 9 years old, the events might have played-out very differently. Additionally, over the course of human history, these same ecological systems have undergone significant changes. Today we have a heightened awareness about the developmental consequences of child maltreatment as compared to what we knew a few decades ago.

In the pages ahead we will keep in mind these multiple systems, such as those implied by Jodi's story, as well as the importance both of long-term developments during adulthood and of historical changes. Only in this way will we be able to convince you that developmental psychology has something to say about particular human lives: about how you, I, or a friend of yours changes and grows and what those changes may signify for our lives as a whole. In taking this perspective, we do not wish to imply that shorter term changes do not matter. What happened to Jodi at age nine, for example, mattered greatly to her at age ten. We do, however, want to emphasize that developmental changes often have consequences that are more than short term, and that the consequences are not necessarily identical or even similar to each other. Jodi's response to abuse one month or one year after the experience may—or may not—be the same as her response many years later. We encourage you to think of her story as a reminder of these complexities.

Why Study Development?

Knowing about human development can help you in five major ways:

1. Allow you to form realistic expectations for others;
2. Help you respond appropriately to the actions of others;
3. Enable you to distinguish between normative and non-normative behavior in others;
4. Provide insights into yourself; and
5. Inform and enhance your professional advocacy for others.

Each of these benefits is described in more detail below.

First, knowledge about development can give you realistic expectations for infants, children, and adolescents. Developmental psychology tells you, for example, when infants usually begin talking and when schoolchildren tend to begin reasoning abstractly. It also describes the issues faced by parents—and grandparents, for that matter. Admittedly, it often gives such information only as averages or generalities: when a "typical" person acquires a particular skill, behavior, or emotion. Nonetheless, the averages can help you know what to expect from specific individuals.

Second, knowledge of development can help you respond appropriately to a person's actual behavior. If a preschool boy tells his mother that he wants to marry her, should she ignore his remark or make a point of correcting his misconception? If a third-grade child seems more interested in friends than in schoolwork, should her teacher discourage contact with friends or try to figure out ways to use the friends to support the child's academic work? Developmental psychology can help answer such questions by indicating the sources and significance of many patterns of human thought, feelings, behavior, and growth.

Third, knowledge of development can help you recognize the wide range of normal behaviors, and thus when departures from normal are truly significant. If a child talks very little by age two, should her parents and doctors be concerned? What if he still does not talk much by age four? If a child becomes more argumentative when she enters adolescence, is this normal or should the parents be concerned about whether her friends are becoming a bad influence? We can answer these questions more easily if we know both what *usually* happens and what *can* happen to people as they move through life. Developmental psychology will help by placing particular behaviors in a broader context, one that (like Bronfenbrenners' framework pictured in Figure 1.2) calls attention to the many simultaneous influences on every person's life. As we will see in the chapters ahead, this perspective leads to the conclusion that the importance of any particular behavior depends not just on the age of the person doing it but on the place of the behavior in the overall life of the person.

Fourth, studying development can help you understand yourself. Developmental psychology makes explicit the process of psychological growth, processes that each of us may overlook in our personal, everyday lives. Even more important, it can help you make sense out of your own experiences, such as whether it really mattered that you reached puberty earlier (or later) than your friends did.

Finally studying development can make you a more professional advocate for the needs and rights of children and adolescents. By knowing in detail the capacities and potential of young people, you will be in a good position to persuade others of their importance and value. The "others" are diverse and include parents, professionals who work with children, and political and business leaders. All of us, including most readers of this book, have a common stake in making our society a more humane place to live. Yet, as the "Focusing On" feature indicates, we as a society can do a better job of supporting human development than we in fact have done.

> **Focusing On . . .**
>
> ### Wanted: A Child and Family Policy
>
> Parents generally do value their children, want the best for them, and make sacrifices on their behalf. In spite of this support, though, the lives of children are often difficult:
>
> - According to a recent report on child well-being from UNICEF (UNICEF Office of Research, 2013), more than 20 percent of all children in the United States under age seventeen live in families that are officially poor. This is more than twice the rate of poverty in Canada and about eight times the rate of poverty in Finland. In fact, among the world's developed countries, only Romania has a higher rate of child poverty than the United States.
>
> - While rates of immunization have increased worldwide during the past decade, a significant proportion of children have failed to receive routine immunizations against polio, measles, and other childhood diseases. The United States ranks much lower than many other developed countries, and three of the wealthiest countries in the UNICEF study—Austria, Canada, and Denmark—have the lowest rates of immunization (ranging from 81–88% of children under the age of two). Greece and Hungary reported the highest rates of childhood immunizations (both at 99% of children under age two).
>
> - About a third of all children living today will eventually experience the divorce of their parents, with all of the stress it brings (Hetherington, 1995). One of the stresses will be poverty, because the parent who usually has major custody, the mother, tends to earn much less than the father.
>
> - In the United States, on average, an infant is born into poverty every twenty-nine seconds, a child is physically punished in school every thirty seconds, and a child is killed by a firearm every three hours (Children's Defense Fund, 2012).
>
> A major reason these problems exist is that the United States lacks a comprehensive, integrated set of policies for caring for its children. Programs to remedy social problems have tended to focus on problems selectively rather than recognizing the impact of one problem on another. School programs to assist with learning difficulties, for example, tend to work with children individually, even though health, nutrition, illness, and family disruptions contribute to learning difficulties in major ways. A more effective approach is to provide a set of related and coordinated services to support families: pediatric care, combined with special help at school and a supportive social worker or nurse to visit parents at home to provide encouragement and information. When Victoria Seitz and Nancy Apfel tried this approach with some low-SES families, they found improvements in cognitive abilities not only for the children originally at risk but also for their siblings who had not even been a focus of the intervention (Seitz & Apfel, 1994)!
>
> Such combined approaches to children's welfare may look expensive and difficult when organized as special demonstration projects, but experience in other developed countries suggests that costs decrease markedly when implemented universally and that organizational problems can in fact be solved (Chafel, 1993; U.S. General Accounting Office, 1993). The real challenge, it seems, may be political: enlisting the support of leaders in government and business to develop comprehensive policies for children, and thereby ensuring the future of society.
>
> ### What Do You Think?
>
> Suppose child care were made universally available in the United States and Canada as it currently is in certain European nations. What effect would this policy have on children's development? What effect would it have on their families? Would your feelings about universal child care depend on the age of the children?

The Life Course in Times Past

Until just a few hundred years ago, children in Western society were not perceived as full-fledged members of society or even as genuine human beings (Ariès, 1962). During medieval times, infants tended to be regarded rather like talented pets: at best interesting and even able to talk, but not creatures worth caring about deeply. Children graduated to adult status early in life, around age seven or eight, by taking on major, adult-like tasks for the community. At that time, children who today would be attending second or third grade might have been caring for younger siblings, working in the fields, or apprenticed to a family to learn a trade.

Because children took on adult responsibilities so soon, the period we call *adolescence* was also unknown. Teenagers assumed adult roles. Although these roles often included marriage and childrearing, most people in their teens lived with their original families, helping with household work and with caring for other people's children until well into their twenties.

> **What Do You Think?**
>
> What do you hope to gain by studying developmental psychology (besides a college credit, of course!)? Take a minute to think about this question—maybe even jot down some notes about it. Then share your ideas with two or three classmates. How do they differ?

The concept of childhood as a distinct period in a person's life is a relatively new invention. Prior to the 19th century, children were expected to assume responsibilities and contribute to the household in important ways as soon as they were able, much like the girl in the picture who is delivering milk. From the 19th century to the present, childhood has increasingly been viewed as a time for play and the acquisition of skills and knowledge that will serve them later in life, as seen in the picture of the girl who is drawing with colored pencils while in school.
Sources: (*top*) Chippix/Shutterstock, (*bottom*) Olesya Feketa/Shutterstock.

Although this may all seem harsh by modern, middle-class standards, it was not necessarily bad in the context in which it occurred. Historians and sociologists have pointed out that children and youth did have to work, but they tended to do only tasks for which they were capable, and they earned modest respect (if not wealth) from the community because they made true economic contributions to it (Hareven, 1986; Sommerville, 1990)—an advantage modern children experience much less often. Adults at that time also showed more awareness of the profound differences among children in their formative, childhood experiences. The modern tendency to view all children as innocent and needing protection has also led, ironically, to much more uniform views about the nature of childhood and insensitivity to the impact of culture and economic class (Hendrick, 1997; Seifert, 2000).

Early Precursors to Developmental Study

Why did awareness of childhood as a special time of life eventually emerge? Society was becoming less rural and more industrialized. During the eighteenth century, factory towns began attracting large numbers of workers, who often brought their children with them. "Atrocity stories" became increasingly common: reports of young children in England becoming caught and disabled in factory machinery and of children being abandoned to the streets. Partly because of these changes, many people became more conscious of childhood and adolescence as unique periods of life, periods that influence later development. At the same time, they became concerned with arranging appropriate, helpful experiences for children.

Without a doubt, the change in attitudes eventually led to many social practices that we today consider beneficial to children and youth. One positive gain was compulsory education, instituted because children needed to be prepared for the adult world rather than simply immersed in it. Another was the passage of laws against child labor to protect children from physical hardships of factory life and make it less tempting for them to go to work instead of to school.

But these gains also had a dark side. Viewing children as innocent also contributed to increasing beliefs that children are incompetent, their activities are unimportant, and the people who care for children deserve less respect than other people. That is why, it was argued, children cannot do "real" work and why they need education (Cannella, 1997). And viewing them as innocent contributed to the idea that children are essentially passive and lacking in opinions and goals worth respecting; that is why, it was thought, adults have to supervise them in school and pass laws on their behalf (Glauser, 1997; Kitzinger, 1997). These were early signs of what later came to be called **ageism**, a prejudice against individuals based on their age, which eventually also affect social attitudes about groups of similarly aged people—especially adolescents and older adults.

The Emergence of Modern Developmental Study

During the nineteenth and twentieth centuries, the growing recognition of childhood led to new ways of studying children's behavior. One of these was the *baby biography,* a detailed diary of a particular child, usually the author's own. One of the most famous English baby biographies was written and published by Charles Darwin (1877) and contained lengthy accounts of his son Doddy's activities and accomplishments. The tradition of rich description continued in the twentieth century with Arnold Gesell, who observed children at precise ages doing specific things, such as building with blocks, jumping, and hopping (Gesell, 1926). After studying more than five hundred children, Gesell generalized standards of normal development, or **norms**—behaviors typical of children at certain ages. Although the norms applied primarily to white, middle-class children and to specific situations and abilities, they gave a wider-ranging picture of child development than was possible from baby biographies alone.

The method of descriptive observation in developmental research has persisted into the present. An influential observer in this century has been Jean Piaget, who described many details of his own three children's behavior, as well as that of adolescents (Piaget, 1963). He did not observe all of the children's possible behaviors, but rather he focused on those behaviors that illustrated their cognitive skills, or ability to think. Piaget's work has influenced modern developmental psychology quite extensively, and we will discuss his theory and the implications of his work later in this book.

ageism Prejudice or bias against an individual based on the individual's age.

norms Behaviors typical at certain ages and of certain groups; standards of normal development.

Lifespan Perspectives on Human Development

As we mentioned earlier, this book is about human development from conception through adolescence, a subset of a larger field of *lifespan development,* the study of continuity and change from birth to death. As the term implies, lifespan development is not confined to any one period of life, such as childhood, adolescence, or adulthood (sometimes psychologists call these by more specific names like *child psychology, the psychology of adolescence,* or *the psychology of adulthood*). Though this text focuses on development from conception through adolescence, the basic issues of interest in lifespan psychology are the same: a commitment to understanding how human beings think, feel, and act at different ages. It also shares a commitment to systematic study of the human condition, a commitment that we will look at more closely later in this chapter. But it also differs from other fields of developmental study in four distinct ways: (1) in dealing with the issue of human continuity and change, (2) in viewing the interplay between growth and decline, (3) in comparing how basic events of life change in meaning at different ages and when viewed by different individuals, and (4) in noting (and respecting) the wide diversity among individuals and the sources of that diversity. These themes are summarized in Table 1.2 and will come up repeatedly in the chapters ahead. To get an initial idea of what they mean, let us look briefly at each of them now.

Continuity within Change

Throughout development there are periods of stability and periods of change, and depending on the time frame being used, change sometimes seems gradual and imperceptible and sometimes seems sudden and abrupt. A cooing four-month-old infant becomes a fourteen-year-old arguing that her room is "clean enough." If we take a closer look, that four-month-old will begin cooing different sounds, then begin linking consonant sounds

TABLE 1.2 Perspectives on Human Development

Issue	Key Question
Continuity within change	How do we account for underlying continuity in qualities, behaviors, and skills in spite of apparent change?
Lifelong growth	What is the potential for growth—emotionally, cognitively, socially, and physically?
Changing meanings and vantage points	How do key life events change in meaning throughout childhood and adolescence and as a result of changing roles and experiences?
Developmental diversity	What factors create differences in individuals' development?

> **What Do You Think?**
>
> What are the merits and problems of descriptive study of human beings? One way to find out is for you and two or three classmates to make separate written observations of the "same" events. Visit a place with people in it (e.g., your student union, a store, or even your developmental psychology classroom), and separately write about what you see one particular person doing. Afterward, compare notes. How similar are your observations? How do they differ?

with vowel sounds, and will eventually begin saying words with meaning attached to those words. Some developmental transformations take years, even decades, to occur. It is the developmental perspective—the comparisons among different periods of life—that makes change seem more frequent and obvious. Such changes would be less obvious if development were studied over shorter periods of time. That four-month-old may seem like she suddenly became an argumentative teenager, but the addition of new sounds and words to her vocabulary happened gradually.

One challenge of developmental psychology is to identify the factors that underlie developmental changes that occur over the periods with which it deals. In essence, the field looks for the continuities hidden within long-term changes. Developmental psychologists asks, "Who is the person underlying long-term changes, and how does he or she direct and influence the changes?" Consider an eighteen-year-old who protested over his parents' separation at age two but now enjoys a secure relationship with his parents. Is there an underlying continuity between her behavior at two and her behavior at eighteen? Perhaps a connection exists, but is implicit: when, as a two-year-old, he cried at his mother's departure, maybe he was not just complaining about being "abandoned" but also expressing the strength of his attachment. Perhaps her tantrums over separation even showed his commitment to the relationship, both to his mother and to himself. And his protests actually may have reflected a high comfort level, rather than a low one, in his bond to his mother, showing his confidence that he would not be punished for expressing his opinion! Later, at eighteen, he is in a better position to express his strong attachment directly, particularly because he no longer feels that separations and reunions are completely out of his control. Across the two decades of his life, what was continuous was strong attachment; what was discontinuous or changeable was the way the attachment was expressed.

Lifelong Growth

Though the focus of this text is from conception through adolescence, we must keep in mind that development is lifelong. Moreover, experiences at one point in development impact future development. This theme of lifespan psychology highlights the potential for growth at all ages, including not only childhood and adolescence but also adulthood and most of old age. Growth can occur in many areas of living, although it is not inevitable. For example, the psychologist William Damon has explored the development of moral goals in a series of research studies from infancy through middle age (Damon, 1996). By "moral goals" he refers to the formation of a sense of right and wrong, as well as the disposition to act on this sense. He points out that a moral sense is never formed completely, but deepens steadily throughout the lifespan. Note in the following developmental sequence how developmental growth in one's moral sense is based upon borrowing and incorporating ideas and commitments from all of a person's previous experiences.

- During infancy and the early preschool years, moral goals depend heavily on a child's ability to *empathize* (actually feel what someone else feels) and to *sympathize* (be aware of another's feelings even though not experiencing the other's feelings directly). Empathy and sympathy direct many actions of preschoolers; a three-year-old might, for example, hand a favorite teddy bear to a crying playmate.

- During the elementary school years, children use empathy and sympathy to develop moral concepts—ideas about equity and fairness—but their opinions at this age may not necessarily translate into action consistent with their beliefs. For example, a ten-year-old will have definite personal opinions about how to distribute a reward of candy to group members when they have worked on a common project. Damon argues that elementary-aged children have not yet linked their moral goals with their self-concepts or self-identifies. So at this age it is possible to believe one thing about morality (e.g., "pay according to effort") but do another (e.g., "pay equally to all").

- In adulthood, however, moral goals gradually become reconciled with self-identity—though only a minority do so completely (Colby & Damon, 1992). Who "I" am is increasingly defined by what I believe to be right and wrong, or good and bad. Aligning my "self" with moral ideas leads to stronger commitments to actions that embody these ideals (Damon, 2008). If I believe in a certain method of payment for group work, as in the example above, I am likely to say so. At the same time, the increasing sophistication of my thinking means I may also balance self-assertion against other moral commitments, such as not offending others unnecessarily—a demonstration of empathy and sympathy. The result is less "verbal hypocrisy," as seen during childhood, but also less predictability and more diversity of both belief and action in adulthood.

From birth through late life, moral goals and moral thinking grow continuously while also changing character: from an exclusive basis in intuitions (empathy and sympathy), to distinct verbal beliefs, to beliefs and actions partially reconciled with a sense of self. The moral complexities of adulthood are based on the abilities to empathize and sympathize—the abilities developed initially in infancy and the preschool years.

Changing Meanings and Vantage Points

By nature, developmental psychology deals with key events and themes of life from a number of different lenses. Work, play, love, having friends, and the family: these and other universal experiences mean different things as a person ages and mean different things depending on a person's current roles and responsibilities. Other-sex friendships take on new forms and significance, for example, as children grow older; it means one thing to have an other-sex friend as a four-year-old but something quite different to a sixteen-year-old. Other-sex friendships also look quite different to those in the friendship than to their parents, for example.

Lifespan psychologist Jacqueline Goodnow illustrated the extent of such differences in perspective using one type of work, everyday household chores (Goodnow, 1996). Most families, whatever their size and composition, work out understandings about which family member should do which chores. Whether or not the work is divided equally, the arrangement itself is supposed to be known and agreed on by all. Goodnow points out, however, that this ideal is rarely achieved fully. An "official" division of household labor may really be understood or accepted only by the parents, or even just by one parent (most often the mother). Multiple, competing views of "who should do what" are common. Other family members (such as children) may have their own ideas about how much housework they ought to do and about which particular jobs reasonably belong to each person. Furthermore, the multiple views are also likely to change over time. One reason is that children grow and therefore acquire new housekeeping skills, engage in activities that make new housekeeping demands (like hosting friends as they get older), or leave home altogether. The other reason is that parents also grow and change their own activities and obligations; a parent may start working or get a divorce, for example, and the new conditions will alter the parent's view of what housework really needs doing and by whom. The result of these factors is twofold: in most families conflict about housework is likely at least some of the time, and any current conflict is likely to disappear eventually, to be replaced by other disagreements about housework. It is still the same housework, but people's views of it change.

Developmental Diversity

Developmental psychology searches for general trends and patterns that account for important changes during infancy, childhood, and adolescence. But developmental psychology is also likely to note *differences* in patterns of development: differences created both by individual experiences and by social and cultural circumstances (Baltes & Staudinger, 1996). The "A Multicultural View" feature, for example, describes the experience of street children in Paraguay, noting how the circumstances in Paraguay modify the impact of life on the street in that society compared to more economically developed societies such as the United States and Canada. In Paraguay, a child who lives on the street some of the time is not necessarily cut off from the support of family or other responsible adults. And not all street children live in the street full time; in fact, most do so only for limited periods. The effect of street life on children's development is therefore more variable; sometimes, in fact, street life creates a more positive context for growing up than staying in school, which costs money and often does not lead to employment later in life.

The diversity among street children in Paraguay suggests the importance of attending to diversity in development in general, and to diversity among North American children in particular. Just as in Paraguay, being a street child in the United States or Canada may be a different experience and hold different significance depending on a child's circumstances, such as the quality of prior family relationships, the resources available to the child and to the family, and the like. Understanding the developmental impact of life on the street requires taking these differences into account.

Diversity occurs not only within cultures and societies but also between cultural groups within a society. In North American society, for example, cultural differences can influence the supports for and expectations of a child in major ways. Patricia Greenfield demonstrated such influence in a research study of routine parent-teacher conferences between Anglo teachers and Latina mothers (Greenfield, 1995). Greenfield observed and analyzed the conferences in terms of differences in personal and family values expressed or implied during the conferences. During the conferences, the Anglo teachers uniformly sought to highlight the individual achievements of the child ("Carmen is doing well with her spelling"). But many of the Latina mothers preferred to direct the conversation toward how the child fit into the family and into the classroom group ("Carmen is such a help to me and so friendly"). The parents' remarks reflected differences in general cultural values—the Anglo parents valuing independence somewhat more, but the Latinx parents (sometimes) valuing *inter*dependence more. The result was frustration with the conference on the part of both teachers and parents and less effective support for the children in their efforts to succeed socially and academically.

An important issue in lifespan psychology has to do with accounting for the diversity among individuals, families, and communities. Are there principles that hold true for all people—including this Amish family and this African American family—regardless of circumstances?
Sources: (top) Ralph R. Echtinaw/Shutterstock.com, (bottom) Dragon Images/Shutterstock.com.

Yet even among these parents and teachers, there were differences: some parents and teachers adjusted to each other's conversational priorities, regardless of ethnic background. This adjustment was fortunate because chronic miscommunication among caregivers—and the subsequent less effective support—can impair a child's social and cognitive development in the long term.

Methods of Studying Developmental Psychology

scientific methods General procedures of study involving (1) formulating research questions, (2) stating questions as a hypothesis, (3) testing the hypothesis, and (4) interpreting and publicizing the results.

As a field of study, developmental psychology bases its knowledge on systematic research, study, or investigation of continuity and change in human beings. The methods used are quite diverse, but all bear some relationship to the **scientific method**, procedures to ensure objective observations and interpretations of observations. As noted in this section, the scientific method allows for considerable variety in how research studies might be conducted. In fact, it is more accurate to speak of many scientific methods rather than just one.

The Scientific Method

Due to their adherence to the scientific method, all scientific research studies have a number of qualities in common, whatever their specific topic. For various practical reasons,

> **What Do You Think?**
>
> A psychologist once said that "every parent believes in nurture until they have their *second* child." What do you think she was getting at with this comment? If you happen to be a parent of at least two children, share your opinion of the comment with a classmate who is not a parent or with one who is a first-time parent. And vice versa: if you've raised no children, or only one, compare your opinions to those of a second- or third-time parent.

the qualities cannot always be realized perfectly, but they form ideals to which to aspire (Cherry, 1995; Levine & Parkinson, 1994). The procedures are as follows:

1. *Formulating research questions.* Research begins with questions. Sometimes these questions refer to previous studies, such as when a developmental psychologist asks, "Are Professor Deepthought's studies of thinking consistent with studies of thinking from less developed countries?" Other times they refer to issues important to society, such as "Does early childhood education make kids more socially skilled later in childhood?" This part of the research process is similar to the reflection and questioning often engaged in by parents, teachers, nurses, and other professionals concerned about human growth and development.

2. *Stating questions as hypotheses.* A **hypothesis** is a statement that expresses a research question precisely. In making a hypothesis out of the earlier question regarding early childhood education, a psychologist needs to be more specific about the terms *early childhood education* and *social skills*. Is any child care center considered *early childhood education* or only those with employees with degrees in early childhood education? Does *socially skilled* mean making eye contact and smiling or does it require initiation of activities with others? After the terms of the question are clarified, the hypothesis is usually stated as an assertion that can be tested ("Children who attend preschools with early childhood education experts initiate more activities than those who did not"), rather than as a question ("Does early childhood education make children more socially skilled?").

    hypothesis A precise prediction based on a scientific theory; often capable of being tested in a scientific research study.

3. *Testing the hypothesis.* Having phrased a research question as a hypothesis, researchers can conduct an actual study about it. As the next section describes further, they can do this in a number of ways. The choice of method usually depends on the type of research question being asked, as well as convenience or efficiency, ethics, and scientific appropriateness. No research method is perfect, although some are more suited for particular research questions than others.

4. *Interpreting and publicizing the results.* After conducting the study itself, psychologists have a responsibility to report its outcomes to others by presenting them at conferences and publishing them in journal articles. Their reports should include reasonable interpretations or conclusions based on the results and enough details to all other psychologists to replicate (or repeat) a study themselves to test the conclusions. In practice, the limits of time (at a conference presentation) or space (in a journal) sometimes compromise this ideal.

There is a wide range of ways to carry out these steps, each with its own strengths and limitations. Viewed broadly, psychological studies can be organized into two groups based upon the type of research questions that the studies are designed to address: studies that attempt to answer questions about *causality*, and studies that attempt to answer questions about *association*. Researchers that ask questions about causality focus on how changes in one variable cause changes in another, while researchers who pose questions about association focus on identifying relationships (i.e., "covariations" or "correlations") between

> ### A Multicultural View
>
> #### Street Children: Comparing Paraguay and North America
>
> Like all countries of Latin America, Paraguay contains children and youths who are popularly call "street children." They are a serious concern for the authorities in this country, as indeed they are everywhere, including in North America. Who are the street children, and what do they need? The sociologist and social worker Benno Glauser investigated these questions in Paraguayan society, using interviews and case studies of street children and their families. He was surprised to find it was not at all clear what street children have in common with one another or what they therefore needed (Glauser, 1997). The ambiguities he encountered have implications for how we should think about and deal with street children in more developed societies such as the United States or Canada.
>
> In Paraguay, political leaders, social workers, and other makers of public opinion used the term "street children" to refer to youngsters in cities who lacked a home or family, spent nights on the street, and either begged or worked at various semilegal or illegal activities to get money for food. Yet Glauser found that real street children were much more diverse than this definition implies. Some still slept with their families, for example, and usually spent days on the street only to attend to a job (e.g., selling flowers). Some deliberately slept out, but only occasionally or for selected periods because of their employment (e.g., giving street directions to tourists for money could be done only in the tourist season). Some never saw their parents but slept in the home of another relative or some other responsible adult. And some (a minority) fit the definition of the authorities: they never saw family or relatives, banded together with other homeless children for mutual protection, and always slept on the street. This last group was much more vulnerable to physical abuse, more likely to become sick, and more likely to become involved in criminal and other illicit activities (e.g., drugs or child prostitution). This finding has been confirmed by other research on street children (Campos et al., 1994).
>
> Unfortunately, as Glauser discovered, the authorities tended to treat all street children as if they belonged to this last group and, therefore, were all in need of rather heavy-handed protection from abuse, disease, and poverty. Policies and actions favored (1) interrupting children's economic activities (e.g., washing car windshields at street corners), (2) moving children out of sight by having police pick them up and take them to more remote areas of the city, and (3) encouraging children to attend school and their caregivers to support children's attendance. Most of these actions proved either inappropriate or ineffective. Usually, for example, a child's job was not a "hobby" in spite of its informal status. Poor families often needed the child's income, or at least needed the child not to be an economic burden on the family. So parents and other relatives did not regret a child working. In fact, they often

variables. Different methods are then employed by researchers to seek answers to these two types of questions. These methods vary in the length of time required to complete the study, the extent of intervention and control exercised by the researcher, and the sampling strategies used to recruit participants. The methodologies often get combined in various ways, depending on the questions the studies are investigating. Table 1.3 summarizes the various possible methods and is helpful in reviewing the explanations given in the sections that follow.

Researching Questions about Causality

- What is the effect of video game violence on aggressive behavior?
- What are the effects of age on children's abilities to interpret emotions?
- What are the long-term effects of a preschool program for low-income children on academic achievement and occupational success?
- What are the effects of smartphone use at bedtime for adolescent sleep quality?

Each of the above questions addresses important cause-and-effect relationships. To clearly and convincingly answer these questions and others like them, researchers must conduct experiments.

A Multicultural View

Street Children: Comparing Paraguay and North America *continued*

believed that a job developed character and a sense of responsibility. School, on the other hand, was widely regarded as a bad investment among poor families because it led to few jobs and cost money for tuition once a child moved beyond the earliest grades (schoolchildren, in fact, often felt *more* rather than less pressure to work simply to pay the cost of education). And removing children from sight, as the police frequently did, accomplished little in the long term. Children simply walked back to their workplace or living places and began again—though often after experiencing humiliation at the hands of the police. For two reasons, in fact, Glauser suspected that Paraguayan policies and practices regarding street children were serving the interests not of the children but of well-off adults. The first was the emphasis by the police (and other leaders of society) on simply getting street children out of sight, a strategy all too common in some America communities as well (Vissing, 1996). The second was the neglect of children who might need protection and help but are "hidden" from public view, such as unpaid child servants, child prostitutes, or child soldiers in the Paraguayan army. These groups were at least as common as street children but were ignored in all public discourse.

The Paraguayan experience has two important implications about street children in more economically developed countries such as the United States. One implication is about diversity: it is likely here, as in Paraguay, that "street children" come in different types, from those who merely work the street during the day, to those who sleep there intermittently, to those who live there essentially full time. All may need protection, though not necessarily to the same extent or in the same way. As in Paraguay, street children do not necessarily lose touch totally with parents, other relatives, or other responsible adults. Alternative living arrangements (e.g., a foster home) may—or may not—be better for a child in any particular case, especially for children who already receive significant, though partial, care from their biological parents or other close relatives.

A second point is that in a developed country such as the United States, we understandably hope that school is a more productive investment than may be the case in Paraguay. Here, police and social workers may be more justified in encouraging street children to attend school than they are in less developed countries. But such reasoning may be more hope than reality even in the United States, where living conditions for poor families sometimes approach Third World conditions in spite of proximity to wealth, and where schools face tremendous educational challenges as a result (Dalglish, 1998; Kozol, 1991, 1995). Children of industrialized nations, or at least some of them, may not be so very different from children of developing nations.

TABLE 1.3 Methods of Studying Human Development

Research Question	Method	Description
Question about Causality	Experimental study	Observes persons where circumstances are carefully controlled so that just one factor varies at a time
	Cross-sectional study	Observes persons of different ages at one point in time
	Longitudinal study	Observes same group(s) of persons at different points in time
	Sequential studies	Observes persons from different cohorts at the same *and* different points in time.
Question about Association	Naturalistic study	Observes persons in naturally occurring situations or circumstances
	Correlational study	Observes tendency of two behaviors or qualities of a person to occur or vary together; measures this tendency statistically
	Survey	Brief, structured interview or questionnaire about specific beliefs or behaviors of large numbers of persons
	Interview	Face-to-face conversation used to gather complex information from individuals
	Case study	Investigation of just one individual or a small number of individuals using a variety of sources of information

Experimental Studies

If a researcher was interested in determining if playing violent video games causes an increase in aggressive behavior, the researcher could manipulate the level of violence in video games to which two groups of players are exposed—one group of participants plays a violent video game and another group plays a nonviolent video game. In order to ensure that the results from the study reflect only the effects of the level of violence in the video games, all other potential variables must be kept constant. For example, the two groups of video game players should be equivalent with respect to age, sex, level of education, familiarity with video games, etc. The conditions under which each group plays the video games should be the same as well: each group should play the games for the same amount of time and in the same kind of environment. Lastly, the researcher needs to be able to systematically, and accurately measure the level of aggression each player exhibits after playing the video games. An **experimental study** just like this was conducted by Hasan, Bègue, Scharkow, and Bushman (2013) that involved two groups of college students who played either violent or nonviolent video games twenty minutes a day for three consecutive days. After each video game session, the level of aggression of the players was assessed by measuring the duration and volume of a blast of loud noise to which the players subjected a *confederate* (someone working with the experimenter who was pretending to be a participant in the study). The results were clear: college students who played the violent video games were far more likely to subject a confederate to louder and longer blasts of noise than college students who played nonviolent video games. The significant differences between the two groups grew larger after each day's video game session. Figure 1.3 illustrates the observed pattern of aggression.

Because this study was an experiment, Hasan and his colleagues held constant all the factors that might influence aggressive behavior *except* video game content, the one they were studying. This deliberately varied factor that we believe is the cause is often called the **independent variable**. The factor that varies as a result of the independent variable, showing an effect—in this case, the level of aggression exhibited toward another person—is often called the **dependent variable**.

The experimental method also requires making decisions about the population, or group, to which the study refers. When every member of the population has an equal chance of being chosen for the study, the people selected comprise a **random sample**. If not everyone in a population has an equal chance of being chosen, the sample is said to be *biased*. Investigators can never be completely sure they have avoided systematic bias in selecting individuals to study, but they can improve their chances by defining the population they are studying as carefully as possible and then selecting participants only from that population.

experimental study A study in which circumstances are arranged so that just one or two factors or influences vary at a time.

independent variable A factor that an experimenter manipulates (varies) to determine its influence on the population being studied.

dependent variable A factor that is measured in an experiment and that *depends on*, or is controlled by, one or more independent variables.

random sample In research studies, a group of individuals from a population chosen such that each member of the population has an equal chance of being selected.

FIGURE 1.3
Effects of Violent and Nonviolent Video Games on Aggression over Time

Exposure to video games for 20 minutes during three consecutive days resulted in significantly higher rates of aggression in college students who played violent video games compared to those who played nonviolent video games.

Source: Adapted from Hasan, Bègue, Scharkow, and Bushman (2013).

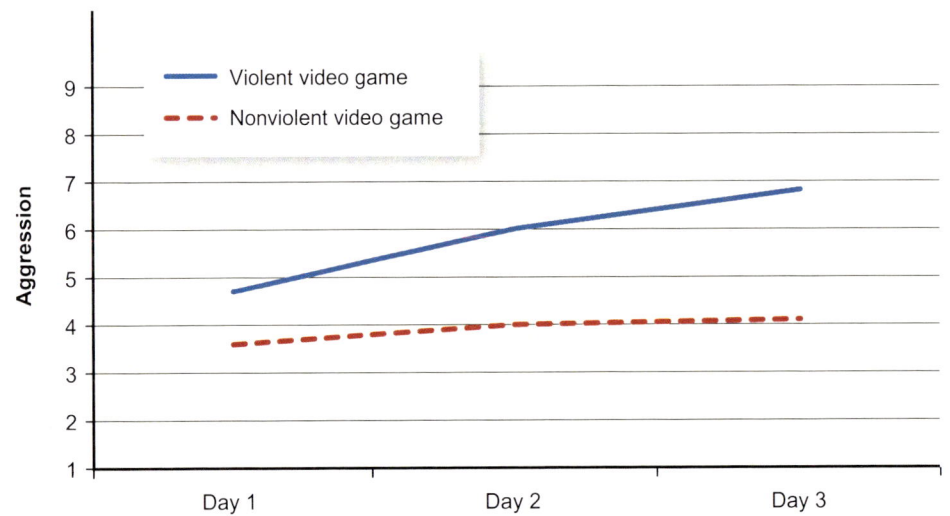

When Hasan (2013) and his research team studied the effects of violent video games on college students, for example, the population to which they limited their observations consisted only of young adults who were attending college, and sampled students from this population at random. Interpretations of their results therefore apply only to this population of young adults. In later studies, they (or other investigators) could sample other populations, such as persons of other ages or cultural backgrounds.

When assigning participants into groups, such as the violent video game group and the nonviolent videogame group, **random assignment** is used. When participants are randomly assigned to a group, each participant has an equal chance of being placed in any group so that theoretically each group is balanced. As we noted above, in the Hasan (2013) study we would want participants in each group to be similar in age, sex, education, socioeconomic status, previous violent behavior, experience playing video games, etc. Random assignment allows us to be relatively sure that any change in our dependent variable is due to differences in our independent variable and not because all of the skilled gamers are in the violent video game group.

Experimental studies incorporate a number of precautions to ensure that their findings have **validity**, meaning they measure or observe what they intend to measure. One way to improve validity is to observe not one but two sample groups, one an experimental, or treatment, group and the other a control group. The **experimental group** receives the treatment, or intervention related to the purposes of the experiment. The **control group** experiences conditions that are as similar as possible to the conditions of the experimental group, but without experiencing the crucial experimental treatment. Also, to ensure that the experimental and control groups are comparable prior to receiving any treatment or intervention, participants are usually *randomly assigned* to each group. Comparing the results of the two groups helps to explicitly establish the effects of the experimental treatment.

Because of its logical organization, the experimental method often gives clearer results than other types of studies do. But because people sometimes do not behave naturally in experimental situations, one criticism of the experimental method is that its results can be artificial.

Another limitation to the experimental method is that participants cannot always be randomly assigned to the experimental and control groups. This is frequently the case when researchers are seeking the answers to causal questions involving variables like gender, ethnicity, marital status, and age. With each of these variables, participants are already in a group (for example, male or female, single or married, child or adult, etc.); random assignment to these groups is not possible. This poses a challenge when researchers try to produce clear and compelling answers to questions like "What are the effects of age on self-esteem in elementary-aged children?" or "What are the effects of gender on the way adolescents use social media?" Because participants cannot be randomly assigned to experimental and control groups with these kinds of variables—often called "participant variables" because they describe characteristics of certain types of participants—researchers cannot be sure whether the results of their studies are caused by the variable that defines the groups (that is, the participant variable) or by some other variable. In other words, it is impossible to conduct true experiments if the independent variable is a participant variable. Instead, when researchers ask such causal questions, they must conduct **quasi-experiments**.

random assignment In research studies, each participant has an equal chance of being placed in, or assigned to, each group. This increases our confidence that differences in the dependent variable are due to the independent variable.

validity The degree to which research findings measure or observe what is intended.

experimental group In an experimental research study, the group of participants who experience the experimental treatment while in other respects experiencing conditions similar or identical to those of the control group.

control group In an experimental research study, the group of participants who experience conditions similar or identical to the experimental group, but without experiencing the experimental treatment.

quasi-experiments Experiments in which participants cannot be randomly assigned to the experimental and control groups; instead, members of pre-existing groups are selected for comparison (for example, males versus females, children versus adolescents, or private school students versus public school students).

Quasi-experimental Studies

In general, quasi-experimental studies represent a large variety of studies that share a common feature: members of pre-existing groups are selected for comparison. Of particular interest to developmental psychologists are quasi-experiments that address causal questions pertaining to changes (or continuities) in people over time. Quite often, *age* is employed as a way to quantify time or to categorize participants. Developmental psychologists can either compare people of different ages at one point in time (called a *cross-sectional study*) or compare the same people at different times as they get older (called a *longitudinal study*). A method that combines elements of both time frames is the *sequential study*. Each method has its advantages and problems.

cross-sectional study A study that compares individuals of different ages at the same point in time.

A **cross-sectional study** compares persons of different ages at a single point in time. One such study compared preschool children (age four) and early-school-age children (age six) on their ability to distinguish between real and apparent emotions (Joshi & MacLean, 1994). Half of the children lived in India, and the other half lived in Great Britain. All of the children listened to stories in which a character sometimes had to conceal his or her true feelings (such as when an uncle gives a child a toy that the child did not really want) and described both how the character really felt and how the character seemed to feel. The results shed light on how children distinguish sincerity from tactfulness. The older children were more sensitive to this distinction than the younger ones were, but the Indian children (especially girls) also were more sensitive to it than the British children were.

longitudinal study A study of the same individuals over a relatively long period, often months or years.

A **longitudinal study** observes the same participants periodically over a relatively long period, often years. An example is the twenty-three-year follow-up of the effects of a demonstration preschool program for low-income children that originally took place in 1967. The four-year-old "graduates" of the program were assessed every few years following the program until they were all twenty-seven years old (Schweinhart et al., 1993; 1999). Researchers gathered interviews, school achievement test results, and reports from teachers and (later) employers and compared them to results from an equivalent group of four-year-olds who had been identified at the time of the program but did not participate in it. The results are gratifying: the graduates have succeeded in school and employment better than the nongraduates and cost taxpayers less by needing less public aid and fewer medical and other services. Cross-sectional and longitudinal studies both have advantages and limitations. Cross-sectional studies can be completed more quickly, but they do not guarantee to show actual change *within* individuals. In the study of children's knowledge of emotions, for example, the fact that older children were more knowledgeable does not ensure that each *individual* child becomes more knowledgeable. It shows only an average trend for the group; in certain individuals, knowledge of emotions may improve little as they get older, or even decrease, whereas other individuals may experience a huge leap in knowledge! Why these differences in individual change occur remains a question—and an urgent one if you work with people as a teacher, a nurse, or a counselor. See, for example, the experiences described in the interview with Marsha Bennington, speech-language pathologist in the "Working With" feature.

cohort In developmental research, a group of subjects born at a particular time who therefore experience particular historical events or conditions.

From the perspective of lifespan psychology, however, a more serious limitation of cross-sectional studies is their inability to distinguish among **cohorts**, or groups of people born at the same time and therefore having undergone similar developmental experiences. For example, a cohort of children born in 1980 shared experiences of less pre-kindergarten education and fewer electronic devices than a cohort born in 1995. As a result of this difference, comparing their abilities and skills with electronics in the 2010s may make the older cohort (the ones born in 1980) appear less intellectually able and less skilled. A cross-sectional study may leave the impression that differences in the cohorts reflect true developmental change instead of the effects of being born earlier in the technology boom. Cross-sectional studies always contain this ambiguity, especially when they compare groups that differ widely in age, as is common in studies of adulthood.

Longitudinal studies do not eliminate the ambiguity created by historical changes in cohorts, but they at least reveal more truly "developmental" change because they show the steps by which particular individuals or groups actually change over time. But in doing so, they pose a practical problem: by definition, longitudinal studies take months or even years to complete. Over this time, some of the original participants may move away or die and stop participating, which is known as attrition. Investigators may become hopelessly bogged down with other work and fail to complete the original study, or government funding to support the work may disappear prematurely. Given these problems, psychologists have conducted cross-sectional studies much more often than longitudinal studies,

Part 1 Studying Human Development

Longitudinal studies are well-suited for studying long-term constancy and change in individuals. How are people the same after several years of maturing, and how are they different?
Source: Lyudmyla Kharlamova/Shutterstock.com.

despite the latter's special value. The dilemmas and ambiguities posed by time frames can be partially solved by **sequential studies**, which combine elements of cross-sectional and longitudinal studies. In sequential research, at least two cohorts are observed longitudinally and comparisons are made both within each cohort across time and between the cohorts at particular points in time. This approach provides information about actual developmental changes within individuals, but also about historical differences among cohorts that might create the impression of truly developmental changes.

sequential study Research in which at least two cohorts are compared both with each other and at different times.

A good example of sequential research is the work by K. Warner Schaie (1994; 2013) studying changes in cognitive abilities of adults. A variety of earlier, cross-sectional research suggested that adults' general reasoning ability *decreases* with age—for example, that older adults score lower than younger ones on tests of general academic intelligence. Schaie's sequential research, however, modified this picture substantially. By testing several successive cohorts of young adults and then testing each cohort again at a later age, Schaie found that (1) many cognitive skills do not decline with age, particularly if they are used on a daily basis; (2) earlier cohorts generally achieved lower scores than later cohorts on tests of cognitive abilities; and (3) some individuals showed more decline with age than did others. None of these findings would have resulted from either a cross-sectional or a longitudinal study alone.

Researching Questions about Association

- How is time spent at home related to the level of stress experienced by adolescents and their parents?
- How is bed-wetting related to the social stressors faced by young children?
- How are stereotypes based on race or ethnicity related to actual academic performance?
- How is bilingualism related to the reading abilities of 11-year-olds?

Notice how these questions about association differ from the earlier questions about causation. Questions about association do not imply a causal connection between two variables; they simply suggest that a relationship of some kind exists between two variables. Also, there is no implied order or sequencing of events in questions of association as there is in questions of causation. Researchers can investigate questions about association using a wide variety of research methodologies, often described as "observational methods." Researchers can either observe and note the behaviors of people directly in a variety of settings (for example, in classrooms, on playgrounds, at movie theaters, or in laboratory settings) or they can ask people to observe and report on their own behaviors by asking them to respond to a set of questions. The various methods for researching questions about association are reviewed next.

WORKING WITH Marsha Bennington, Speech-Language Pathologist

Communication Difficulties across Development

Marsha Bennington works as a speech-language pathologist for a school district and in private practice. She thus sees individuals who range widely in age, from early childhood through adulthood. She talked, among other things, about how speech and language needs change across the course of development.

Kelvin: *Speech-language pathologists used to be called "speech therapists," right? Why the name change?*

Marsha: Our clientele has changed. We see people from a greater variety of language backgrounds now. Classrooms include more kids with disabilities, and more infants with medical problems at birth survive into adulthood, thanks to modern medicine. Our work is more diverse than it used to be, and the label "speech therapy" doesn't really describe it any more.

Kelvin: *What do you mean?*

Marsha: We address more than just speech problems. People may face an underlying inability to communicate and have a lot of difficulty with syntax or word choice. They might have trouble with reading, which really grows out of problems with focusing attention or with connecting printed and spoken language. We don't just deal with young children who mispronounce specific sounds—who say /t/ for /k/, for example.

Kelvin: *Sounds like your job is as much about "cognition" as it is about speech.*

Marsha: You're right, although even "cognition" may be narrowing it down too much. Motor skills can play a role, as can people's attitudes and feeling or their parents' attitudes and support. It depends on the individuals' particular needs and on their age.

Kelvin: *Are the problems you see in young children different from those of older kids or adults you work with?*

Marsha: You can't overgeneralize, but there do seem to be differences. A "typical" referral from a kindergarten or first-grade teacher tends to be specifically speech related. A child may articulate certain sounds incorrectly—*wun* instead of *run*—or a child may have some disfluency, that is, "stutter." I do see some young children with underlying language problems—constant syntax errors and trouble with finding words—but not many at this age.

Kelvin: *Does this balance change among older students?*

Marsha: It does change. By the upper elementary grades, students are most likely initially referred to me because they're having trouble with reading. By this age, reading can become a real effort because it depends so much on fluent speech. If your spoken sound or your spoken syntax isn't "standard," it's hard to decipher written sounds or sentences.

In naturalistic research, psychologists study human behavior as it normally occurs in everyday settings. What could be learned from observing these children playing with blocks together?
Source: Dragon Images/Shutterstock.com.

Naturalistic Studies

Naturalistic studies purposely observe behavior as it normally occurs in natural settings, such as at home, at school, or in the workplace. Bei Bei and colleagues used this strategy to explore how adolescent sleep differed when in school and when on vacation (Bei et al., 2014). As you can imagine, sleeping in a sleep lab is inconvenient and uncomfortable, so the researchers in this study used an actigraph, similar to a wrist-based fitness tracker, to monitor participant sleep every day for four weeks: the last week of one term, two weeks during break, and the first week of the next term. Specifically, researchers were able to monitor when participants went to bed, how long it took them to fall asleep, how long they slept, and how much they woke up at night. During the first week of break, adolescents went to bed later and slept longer than during the school term, a pattern that stabilized during the second week of break. Older adolescents went to bed later than younger adolescents, and females in the study took longer to fall asleep and slept longer than males. Though these results might not be surprising to many, this type of information is only available to us when we can measure such behaviors where they happen and when they normally happen.

A particular strength of naturalistic research is that researchers observe naturally occurring or genuine behavior in settings that are a normal part of the participants' day. Naturalistic research does not face the criticism often levied at experimental research due to the experiment's dependence on highly controlled (and thereby, contrived) testing

> **WORKING WITH** Marsha Bennington, Speech-Language Pathologist
>
> **Communication Difficulties across the Lifespan** *continued*
>
> **Kelvin:** *What do you do in these cases?*
>
> **Marsha:** It depends! I might work on a child's oral language to build awareness of syntax or of phonological difficulties. But by the time a child is in fourth or fifth grade, strategies to compensate for reading difficulties may help more. I might encourage the child to listen carefully to the teacher's oral directions or to ask for them both orally and in writing.
>
> **Kelvin:** *Does that become more of a problem in high school and beyond?*
>
> **Marsha:** Well, adolescence can aggravate a person's self-consciousness, and any speech or language problems only add to it. The older kids I see definitely need reassurance to boost their motivation and confidence. They've started to learn to hide their problem from others, and that usually means they avoid reading and writing, avoid speaking in class, that sort of thing.
>
> **Kelvin:** *What happens after high school? The bigger world after graduation must pose challenges.*
>
> **Marsha:** It's fair to say that *every* transition poses a challenge: home to kindergarten, elementary to high school, high school and beyond. A teenager may have functioned all right in high school, thanks to some help from the speech-language pathologist, but find that her first job requires more language skills than she expected. So back she comes for more help . . . [pauses and frowns]
>
> **Kelvin:** *Except?*
>
> **Marsha:** Except that help for adults, once they're not in school, can be hard to find and too expensive for many to afford.
>
> **What Do You Think?**
>
> 1. Marsha described changes in the sorts of problems people of different ages bring to her. Do you think these should be called "developmental" changes, even though she is really talking about cross-sectional comparisons among age groups? Compare your opinion with that of a classmate.
>
> 2. Try retelling Marsha's comments form a more longitudinal (versus cross-sectional) perspective. Do they seem more or less true to life from this perspective? This question would make a good topic for an in-class debate if you and/or your instructor can organize one. In formulating your opinions, though, remember that you are talking about the development of a human *problem*, not about the normative course of development.
>
> 3. Given your ideas from questions 1 and 2, how helpful do you think the concept of "development" is for a speech-language pathologist? Would it be more or less helpful for a regular classroom teacher?

environments, but naturalistic observational research does run a greater risk of generating ambiguous results.

naturalistic study A study in which behavior is observed in its natural setting.

Correlations

Whether they are using naturalistic or more controlled research environments, most research studies look for correlations among variables. A **correlation** is a systematic relationship, or association, between two behaviors, responses, or human characteristics. When two variables tend to change in the same direction—both variables increase together or decrease together—the relationship is called a *positive correlation*; when they tend to change in opposite directions, it is called a *negative correlation*. The ages of married spouses are a positive correlation: older husbands tend to have older wives (though not strictly so). The age of a child and the frequency of bed wetting is a negative correlation: the older the child, the less frequent the bed wetting (though again, not strictly so).

correlation An association between two variables in which changes in one variable tend to occur with changes in the other. The association does not necessarily imply a causal link between the variables.

When correlated factors can be expressed numerically, psychologists use a particular statistic, the *correlation coefficient* (abbreviated *r*), to indicate the degree of relationship between two behaviors or characteristics. The correlation coefficient is calculated in such a way that its value always falls between +1.00 and –1.00. The closer to +1.00 the value, the more positive the correlation; the closer to –1.00 the value, the more negative the correlation. Correlations near 0.00 indicate no systematic relationship between behaviors or characteristics, or an essentially

Chapter 1 Introduction: Studying Human Development

random relationship. For various reasons, psychologists tend to consider correlations above +0.70 or below –0.70 as strong ones and those between +0.20 and –0.20 as weak ones.

When you read or talk about correlations, it is important to remember that correlations by themselves do not indicate whether one behavior or characteristic causes another; they indicate only that some sort of association exists between the two. The distinction is illustrated in Figure 1.4, which graphs the number of baby pictures taken versus the weight of the mother taking the photos. While the graph shows an inverse correlation—heavier mothers take fewer pictures—this does not mean that taking baby pictures is a good way to lose weight. In other words, there is no causal relation between the two. More likely, the correlation reflects the influence of a third factor that has an impact on both behaviors.

Surveys

Developmental studies vary in how many people researchers collect information about or observe. The size of the group studied is called the research **sample**. At one extreme are large-scale **surveys** in which large numbers of people are asked to respond to specific questions. Grace Kao (1995) used this method to examine patterns of school achievement among Asian American youth. She was particularly interested in a common stereotype of Asian youngsters as "model students," the belief that they excel academically. Using survey responses from about fifteen hundred Asian American students, parents, and teachers, as well as from about twenty-five thousand white counterparts, Kao compared family incomes, educational levels, and ethnic backgrounds with academic achievement. She found that the stereotype of the model student is rather misleading. Academic success varies substantially among particular Asian ethnic groups. It also depends more heavily on how much time and money particular parents invest in education for their particular children than on the educational, financial, or ethnic backgrounds of the family as such. In these ways, the Asian American students were no different from their white counterparts.

These conclusions seem especially persuasive because of the rather large sample of families on which they are based—an advantage of the survey method. But the method also has limitations. Survey questions tend to be "cut and dried" to ensure that the responses can be compared among large numbers of respondents. They tend not to explore subtleties of thinking or the reasons people have for taking certain actions or holding certain beliefs. Did some of Kao's Asian American families invest more in education because their culture encourages them to do so or because they anticipated discrimination due to their ethnic background and regarded education as insurance against the negative effects of such discrimination? To answer questions such as these, researchers need methods that invite respondents to comment more fully, such as interviews and case studies.

sample A group that is studied for research purposes.

survey A research study that samples specific knowledge or opinions of large numbers of individuals.

FIGURE 1.4
Correlation Is Not Causation

The number of pictures taken of an infant correlates with the weight of the child's mother, with heavier mothers taking fewer pictures. But this does not mean that gaining weight *causes* mothers to stop taking pictures or that taking pictures causes mothers to gain weight. More likely a third factor, such as the number of previous children to whom the mother has given birth, causes both factors separately.

Interviews

A research study that seeks complex or in-depth information may use **interviews**, or face-to-face directed conversations. Because they take time, interview studies usually focus on a smaller number of individuals than surveys do, perhaps several dozen or so. Carol Gilligan and her colleagues used interviews to learn more about how teenage girls cope with the stresses of dealing with gender role expectations as they grow up under different conditions (Brown & Gilligan, 1992; Taylor et al., 1995). Some interviews involved girls who were attending a private girls' boarding school and were from economically well-off families; others involved girls who were attending a public high school in a racially mixed, lower income community. The interview format allowed Gilligan to explore the girls' perspectives in depth and to find out when and how differences in their circumstances influenced their development as young women. As it turned out, economic and family supports did matter, but not always as Gilligan expected. A constant challenge for all girls was to find and remain true to their own perspective (or "voice," as Gilligan termed it). Doing so sometimes proved harder for well-off girls than for lower-income girls, though not necessarily.

> **interview** A face-to-face, directed conversation used in a research study to gather in-depth information.

Case Studies

When a study uses just one or a few individuals, it is called a **case study**. In general, a case study tries to pull together a wide variety of information and observations about the individual case and then present the information as a unified whole, emphasizing relationships among specific behaviors, thoughts, and attitudes in the individual. An example is a study by Robert Jimenez, Georgia Garcia, and David Pearson (1995) comparing the language skills and knowledge about reading of just three eleven-year-old children: one proficiently bilingual Latinx student, one proficiently monolingual white student, and one modestly bilingual Latinx student. Each child was interviewed at length about her perceptions of her own skills with each language. Each was also invited to "think aloud" while reading samples of text in each language (that is, the child told about her thoughts as she read along). Because of the time taken with each individual, the investigators were able to discover important subtleties about how each student read. The proficient bilingual reader, for example, thought of *each* language as an aid to understanding the other language, whereas the less fluent bilingual reader believed simply that her Spanish assisted her English.

> **case study** A research study of a single individual or small group of individuals considered as a unit.

By its nature, a case study can explore an aspect of human development, looking for new or unexpected connections among behaviors, needs, or social relationships. This is the most common use of case studies. A second use is to confirm whether connections previously found in experimental studies actually occur in everyday, nonexperimental situations, even when conditions are not carefully controlled. The second use resembles the naturalistic studies described earlier in this section.

Ethical Constraints on Studying Development

Sometimes, ethical concerns influence the methods researchers can use to study a particular question about development. Take the question of punishments administered by parents: what kinds of punishment are most effective, and for what reasons? For ethical reasons, we may be unable to experiment with certain aspects of this problem directly. Observing parents actually scolding and reprimanding their children would require delicacy at best. At worst, if the punishment became severe or physical, ethics might require our active intervention simply to protect the child from abuse.

For ethically sensitive questions, we may instead have to satisfy ourselves with less direct but more acceptable methods of study. We can interview a variety of parents about the methods of punishment they use, or we can ask experts who work directly with families what methods they think parents typically use. A few courageous families might allow us to observe their daily activities, with the understanding that we are interested in observing how they punish their children. But by being volunteers, these few families may not represent other families very well. In fact, most research studies conducted with human beings have samples that are disproportionately from western industrialized nations, highly

> **What Do You Think?**
>
> Are some methods of developmental study inherently more effective than others? Try answering this question by organizing a multisided debate. Pick a successful developmental study (you can use any of the ones described in this chapter, for example), and assign each of three or four debating teams to design and argue the merits of some *alternative* method of studying the same question. In a second round of the debate, each team can try to refute the arguments of any of the other teams. Remember: there will be more than two sides to this discussion!

educated, rich, and democratic, which can limit how we generalize our findings (Henrich, Heine, & Norenzayan, 2010).

Generally, research about human beings faces at least three ethical issues: confidentiality, full disclosure of purposes, and respect for the individual's freedom to participate (American Psychological Association, 1992; 2010). In developmental psychology, all of these issues are complicated when the subjects are naturally vulnerable—when they are young, disabled, or older adults.

1. *Confidentiality.* If researchers collect information that might damage individuals' reputations or self-esteem, they should take care to protect the identities of the participants. Observing parents' methods of managing their children might require this sort of confidentiality. Parents may not want just anyone to know how much and how often they experience conflicts with their children. Similar concerns might influence research on teachers' methods of classroom management or caregivers' styles of caring children. In such cases, investigators should not divulge the identities of participants in a study without their consent, either during the conducting of the study or afterward when the results are published.

2. *Full disclosure of purposes.* Participants in a study are entitled to know the true purposes of any research study in which they participate. Most of the time, investigators understand and follow this principle carefully. But at times it can be tempting to mislead participants. In studying teachers techniques for working with disruptive children, for example, researchers may suspect that stating this research purpose honestly will cause certain professionals, as well as the people under their care, to avoid participation. Investigators may suspect that telling the truth about the study will make the participants distort their behavior, hiding their less desirable behaviors and conflicts. In this sort of study, therefore, it might seem that intentional deception would produce more complete observations and in this sense make the research more "scientific." But investigators would purchase this benefit at the cost of their long-run reputations with participants. Purposeful deception may sometimes be permissible, but only when no other method is possible and when participants are fully informed after the study of the deception and its reasons.

3. *Respect for individuals' freedom to participate.* As much as possible, research studies should avoid pressuring individuals to participate. This may not be as simple as it first appears. Because psychologists have a relatively high status in society, some people may be reluctant to decline an invitation from them to participate in "scientific research." Investigators therefore may have to bend over backward to assure some individuals that participation is indeed voluntary. Researchers cannot simply assume that every potential participant automatically feels free to decline if approached. After all, who wants to feel like they're interfering with the progress of science?

informed consent An agreement to participate in a research study based on understanding the nature of the research, protection of human rights, and freedom to decline to participate at any time.

When all three principles are closely followed, they allow for what psychologists call **informed consent**: the people or groups being studied understand the nature of the research, believe their rights are being protected, and feel free to either volunteer or refuse to participate. Informed consent, therefore, forms a standard, or ideal, for research to aim for and one that most studies do in fact approximate.

> **What Do You Think?**
>
> Why do you think ethics has become a bigger concern for developmental research in the past three decades? Brainstorm as many ideas about this as you can: have people changed, or research projects, or the conditions of modern life, or . . . ?

As the preceding discussion indicates, however, consent that is completely informed may prove difficult to achieve in some cases. This is especially so for research on vulnerable populations, such as children, people with certain disabilities, older individuals, or members of cultural groups who do not speak the native language. These people tend to depend on the goodwill and wisdom of others, including researchers themselves, to explain the purposes of a study and keep their best interests in mind. In studying an adolescent who speaks little English, for example, investigators may well wonder whether he fully understands the purposes of a study, even when those purposes are explained. Even if the person does understand, does he feel truly free to participate or decline? Or does he, as an individual, simply assume he must cooperate with whatever investigators request?

In studying children in particular, the developmental levels of the participants should influence the way investigators resolve ethical issues (Thompson, 1990). As a rule, children understand the purposes of a research project less well than do adults. Therefore, what the child will be experiencing during the study should be described at an appropriate level, and if the child is old enough to make decisions about participation, researchers should attain assent, or their agreement to participate. Moreover, it is critical that the parents are thoroughly informed and give consent for their child's participation. Children also are more vulnerable to stressful research procedures, such as experimentation with the effects of personal criticism. Older children and adults, on the other hand, are more prone to self-consciousness and are more likely to detect—and survive—implied personal criticisms. Thus, investigators need to be more careful in studying problems that might shame a person publicly (such as by asking, "How often do you cry?" or "What problems have you had because your parents are divorced?").

Wherever possible, the right to decide about whether to participate in a research study rests with the individual, provided he or she understands the nature of the study and feels truly free to decline participation. When these conditions hold only partially, such as with a child who speaks limited English, parents or other legal guardians share the ultimate right to decide whether the child should participate. When the conditions do not hold at all, such as with infants or adults with little or no language ability, parents and guardians essentially take over the right to decide about participation.

Strengths and Limitations of Developmental Knowledge

As this chapter has demonstrated, human development has to be studied in particular ways and with certain limitations in mind. Because time is a major dimension of development, its impact must be approached thoughtfully. Yet the very nature of time poses real problems for studying at least some major questions. Especially when studied across infancy, childhood, and adolescence, people may "take too long" to develop within the time frame available to study them. Also, because lifespan psychologists deal with people, they must treat participants with respect and abide by the usual standards of decency and consideration for human needs. Finally, when dealing with especially vulnerable people, developmental psychologists must take extra care to determine the true best interests of individuals who participate in studies, even when those participants do not know what they are being asked to do or do not feel free to refuse even when they do know.

Lest these limitations sound overly discouraging, be assured that in spite of them, developmental psychologists have accumulated considerable knowledge about people of all ages in recent decades and continue to do so. The remaining chapters of this book should make that point amply clear. Developmental psychology may not have definitive answers for all important questions about human nature, but it does have the answers for a good many.

Chapter Summary

- **What in general is human development?** Human development concerns continuities and changes in a person's long-term growth, feelings, and patterns of thinking. It occurs in several domains: physical, cognitive, and psychosocial. The domains of development interact in many ways, and individuals always develop as whole persons rather than in separate parts.
- **Why is it important to know about development?** Studying development can help you develop appropriate expectations about human behavior and its changes. It can help you respond appropriately to individuals' behavior and recognize when unusual behaviors are cause for concern. Studying development can also give you self-knowledge and understanding of your past.
- **How has society's view of childhood changed over time?** Until just a few hundred years ago, childhood and adolescence were not regarded as distinct periods of life. Social changes, including the industrial revolution, led to awareness of children's unique needs and vulnerability, but also contributed to modern (and mistaken) views of children as incompetent, passive, and unimportant. In the nineteenth and twentieth centuries, the first research studies of children consisted of baby biographies and structured observations of children at specific ages.
- **What general issues are important in developmental psychology?** Developmental psychology shares much with other forms of developmental study. However, it also has a distinctive emphasis on four themes: (1) continuity within change, (2) lifelong growth, (3) changing meanings and vantage points, and (4) diversity among individuals.
- **How do developmental psychologists go about studying development?** Research about developmental psychology tries to follow the scientific method: formulating research questions, stating them as hypotheses, testing the hypotheses, and interpreting and publicizing the results. Developmental research tends to focus either on questions about causality—studied by using experimental or quasi-experimental methods—or questions about association—studied by using observational designs, including naturalistic observation, correlational designs, surveys, interviews, or case studies. Cross-sectional studies compare individuals of different ages at one point in time. Longitudinal studies observe human change directly by following the same individuals over relatively long periods of time.

  Naturalistic methods observe individuals in natural contexts as much as possible. Experimental methods try to control or hold constant extraneous conditions while varying only one or two specified variables. Surveys, interviews, and case studies each sample different numbers of people and provide different levels of context in their information.
- **What ethical considerations should guide the study of development?** Ethical considerations guide how development can be studied, sometimes ruling out certain studies altogether. Generally, studies are guided by principles of confidentiality, full disclosure of purposes, and respect for the individual's freedom to participate. Research about children and vulnerable adults should strive for informed consent from participants and their parents or guardians. The specific ethical concerns in studying development depend on the age or developmental level of the individuals studied, as well as on the content of the study itself.

Key Terms

ageism (p. 13)
case study (p. 27)
cognitive development (p. 5)
cohort (p. 22)
control group (p. 21)
correlation (p. 25)
cross-sectional study (p. 22)
dependent variable (p. 20)
development (p. 4)
domain (p. 5)
experimental group (p. 21)
experimental study (p. 20)
human development (p. 4)
hypothesis (p. 17)
independent variable (p. 20)
informed consent (p. 28)
interview (p. 27)
longitudinal study (p. 22)
naturalistic study (p. 25)
norms (p. 13)
physical development (p. 5)
psychosocial development (p. 6)
quasi-experiment (p. 21)
random assignment (p. 21)
random sample (p. 20)
sample (p. 26)
scientific method (p. 16)
sequential study (p. 23)
survey (p. 26)
validity (p. 21)

Theories of Development

CHAPTER 2

Source: Olga Enger/Shutterstock.com.

Chapter Outline

The Nature of Developmental Theories

Psychodynamic Developmental Theories

Behavioral Learning and Social Cognitive Learning Developmental Theories

Cognitive Developmental Theories

Contextual Developmental Theories

Developmental Theories Compared: Implications for the Student

Focusing Questions

- What are developmental theories, and how are they useful?
- How have psychodynamic theories influenced thinking about development?
- How have developmental theories based on learning theories contributed to our understanding of developmental change?
- How do cognitive developmental theories help us to understand changes in thinking and problem solving?
- How have contextual approaches to development broadened our view of developmental change?
- How are lifespan theories useful when examining child and adolescent development?
- How does comparing developmental theories help us to understand developmental change?

When Elizabeth, age three, began nursery school, she cried and screamed every day when her mother left her. "Home!" and "Mama!" were the only words she seemed able to produce between sobs, which continued for much of each morning. Her concerned teachers met to discuss what to do about Elizabeth.

"It's best to ignore the crying," said one teacher. "If you give her lots of special attention because of it, you will reinforce the crying, and she'll just keep going longer."

"But we can't just ignore a crying child," said another. "This is a new and strange situation, and her crying shows that she's feeling insecure and abandoned. Look at her! She needs comfort and emotional support so that she can feel safer and more secure. At least give her a hug!"

"I think she's unsure whether her mother really will come back for her," said a third teacher. "Maybe we can find ways to help her understand and remember our daily routine here."

The teachers decided to follow all of this advice. They agreed not to fuss too much over Elizabeth's tears and to give her lots of comfort and support when she was not crying. They also helped Elizabeth draw a picture chart of the daily schedule and tape it to her cubbyhole. Finally, they talked with her mother about what they had observed and the solutions they were trying.

How well did their approaches work? Elizabeth stopped crying—more quickly, in fact, than any of the teachers had expected. Although all three teachers agreed that Elizabeth clearly was happier and more at ease, no one was sure exactly how or why the change had come about.

A second question we might ask is: How might the theories we will encounter in this chapter (and throughout this text) help us understand the developmental changes we will see in Elizabeth as she moves through early childhood into the school years? What will she be like as a teenager, a young adult, and beyond? In what ways will developmental theories help us—and Elizabeth and her family—better anticipate and understand these changes? In this chapter, we explore the nature of developmental theories, with a special emphasis on their applications to the developmental changes that take place over the course of an individual's lifespan.

The Nature of Developmental Theories

Each of Elizabeth's teachers' approaches reflects a different set of ideas and beliefs about children and their development. Whether they know it or not, most people—teachers, parents, grandparents, students, and even children themselves—are guided by "informal theories" of human development. And while the preceding example focuses on early childhood, informal theories of development are used to understand older children, adolescents, and even adults.

What Is a Developmental Theory?

As we point out in Chapter 1, *human development* refers to long-term changes and continuities that occur during a person's lifetime and the patterns of those changes. Theories are useful because they help us organize and make sense of large amounts of sometimes-conflicting information about development. For example, how do we decide whether day care is good for children, and, if so, what type of day care is developmentally best? For that matter, how do we make developmental sense out of different approaches to parenting, family life, or education at various points in childhood and adolescence? In contrast to informal theories, the more formal developmental theories we will discuss in this chapter attempt to provide clear, logical, and systematic frameworks for describing and understanding the events and experiences that make up developmental change and discovering the principles and mechanisms that underlie the process of change.

What qualities should a good theory ideally have? A good theory should:

1. be *internally consistent,* meaning its different parts fit together in a logical way;
2. *provide meaningful explanations* of the actual developmental changes we are interested in, be they changes in children's thinking with age or the long-range effects of divorce on their social adjustment;

3. be *open to scientific evaluation* so that it can be revised or discarded if new or conflicting evidence appears or if a better theory is proposed;

4. *stimulate new thinking and research;* and finally,

5. *provide guidance* to parents, professionals, and other interested individuals in their day-to-day work with infants, children, and adolescents.

How Do Developmental Theories Differ?

Although all developmental theories explore the human experience at various points across the lifespan, they also differ in some important ways. In this chapter, we look at how each theory addresses basic questions about human development: To what degree is a given developmental change due to maturation (nature), and to what degree is it due to experience (nurture)? Is development a continuous process or a series of discontinuous stages? Finally, does the individual take an active or a passive role in his or her development? We can use these three questions to identify how a developmental theory is classified. Much like Elizabeth's teachers at the beginning of the chapter had different ways of explaining behaviors, developmental psychologists tend to use different worldviews to understand development. Some theories are *organismic*—focusing on the individual as the source of change. Some theories are *mechanistic*—focusing on the world as the source of change. And some theories are *interactionist*—focusing on how individuals impact their environment, which, in turn, impacts the individual. You can how these different groups of theories address the three developmental questions in Table 2.1.

Many motor skills, such as jumping rope or riding a bike, develop in predictable sequences or stages.
Source: mrfiza/Shutterstock.com.

Maturation or Experience?

Theories differ in the importance they assign to nature and nurture as causes of developmental change. *Maturation* refers to developmental changes that seem to be determined largely by biology because they occur in all individuals relatively independently of their particular experiences. Examples of maturational changes include growth in height and weight and increases in the muscle coordination involved in sitting up, walking, and running. Examples of changes due to experience, or *nurture,* include increasing skill in playing baseball, basketball, or tennis, which clearly seems to be due mostly to formal and informal learning. But for many developmental changes, the relative contributions of maturation and experience are less clear. Talking is a good example. To what degree do all children learn to talk regardless of their particular learning experiences? How much does their talking depend on their particular experiences in the family, community, and culture in which they grow up?

Continuous or Discontinuous?

Developmental theories also differ about whether developmental change is a *continuous* process, consisting of many small, incremental changes like a ramp, or *discontinuous,*

TABLE 2.1 How Developmental Theories Are Classified

Classification	Maturation or Experience?	Continuous or Discontinuous?	Active or Passive?
Organismic	Maturation	Discontinuous	Active
Mechanistic	Experience	Continuous	Passive
Interactionist	Both	Continuous	Active

Chapter 2 Theories of Development

composed of a smaller number of distinct *stages* like steps. Theorists such as Erik Erikson and Jean Piaget assume developmental change occurs in distinct, discontinuous stages. All individuals follow the same sequence, or order. Each successive stage is *qualitatively* unique from all other stages, is increasingly complex, and integrates the developmental changes and accomplishments of earlier stages. These are organismic theories.

Erikson's theory, for example, assumes an infant must first master the crisis of *trust versus mistrust;* that is, she must come to trust her caregiver's ability to meet her needs. Only then can she move on to tackle the crisis that defines the next stage, *autonomy versus shame and doubt. Autonomy* refers to a person's capacity to be independent and self-directed in his or her activities. Similarly, mastery of the crisis of *intimacy versus isolation* during early adulthood prepares an individual for the crisis of *generativity versus stagnation* that occurs during middle adulthood. These and other stages of development proposed by Erikson are discussed later in the chapter.

Learning theories, on the other hand, see development as a relatively smooth and continuous process. The development of trust and autonomy or of more sophisticated thinking and problem-solving skills is thought to occur through the numerous small changes that unfold as a child interacts with his environment. These theories focus on *quantitative* change and are mechanistic in nature.

Still other theories view developmental change as a sequence of more rounded, overlapping slopes, rather than as one continuous incline or a series of sharply defined stages, and are considered interactionist theories.

Active or Passive?

Developmental theories also differ in their view of how actively individuals contribute to their own development. For instance, behavioral learning theorists believe developmental change is caused by events in the environment that stimulate individuals to respond, resulting in the learned changes in behavior that make up development. Theorists who are interested in how thinking and problem-solving abilities develop, such as Jean Piaget, propose that such changes depend on the person's active efforts to master new intellectual problems of increasing difficulty. Likewise, Erik Erikson's theory of identity development proposes that an individual's personality and sense of identity are strongly influenced by his or her active efforts to master the psychological and social conflicts of everyday life.

These children making friends is a good example of the active role of an individual in his or her own development.
Source: Monkey Business Images/Shutterstock.com.

> **What Do You Think?**
>
> One of the three developmental questions asks whether developmental change occurs in stages or is a continuous process. How might different answers to this question affect how parents raise their children? How might they affect how teachers educate their students?

Psychodynamic Developmental Theories

Psychodynamic theorists believe development is an active, dynamic process that is influenced by both a person's inborn, biological drives and his or her conscious and unconscious social and emotional experiences. According to Sigmund Freud, a child's development is thought to occur in a series of stages. At each stage, the child experiences unconscious conflicts that he must resolve to some degree before going on to the next stage. Other influential psychodynamic approaches, such as that of Erik Erikson, place less emphasis on biological drives and unconscious conflict. Erikson focuses more on the development of a sense of identity as a result of important social, emotional, and cultural experiences.

Freudian Theory

Sigmund Freud (1856–1939) was the originator of *psychoanalysis,* the approach to understanding and treating psychological problems on which psychodynamic theory is based. Much of Freud's formal theory is outdated. However, his ideas continue to influence our understanding of personality development, including such areas as early infant-caregiver attachment, diagnosis and treatment of childhood emotional disorders, adolescent identity formation, and the long-range consequences of divorce.

The Three-Part Structure of Personality

Freud described each individual's personality as consisting of three hypothetical mental structures: the id, the ego, and the superego.

The **id**, which is present at birth, is unconscious. It impulsively tries to satisfy a person's inborn biological needs and desires by motivating behaviors that maximize pleasure and avoid discomfort with no regard for the realities involved. In this view, the newborn infant is all id, crying for food and comfort but having no idea of how to get them because she cannot distinguish between wishful fantasy and reality.

The **ego** is the largely rational, conscious, problem-solving part of the personality. It is closely related to a person's sense of self. The ego functions according to the *reality principle,* a process by which the infant learns to delay his desire for instant satisfaction and redirect it into more realistic and appropriate ways to meet his needs. This involves a shift of psychological energy from fantasy to the real parents and other caregivers who can in fact meet the infant's needs. Thus, a hungry infant shifts from imagining that the wish for food will satisfy her hunger to a more realistic focus on anticipating the appearance of her parent or other caregiver, who will feed her. An infant's developing ego, or sense of self, is based on her internalized mental images of her relationships with these caregivers.

The **superego** is the moral and ethical component of the personality. It develops at the end of early childhood. The superego includes the child's emerging sense *of conscience,* or right and wrong, as well as the *ego-ideal,* an idealized sense of how he should behave. The superego acts as an internalized, all-knowing parent. It punishes the person for unacceptable sexual or aggressive thoughts, feelings, and actions with guilt and rewards him for fulfillment of parental standards with heightened self-esteem. The superego can sometimes be overly moralistic and unreasonable, but it provides the individual with standards by which to regulate his moral conduct and take pride in his accomplishments.

id In Freud's theory, the part of an individual's personality that is present at birth, unconscious, impulsive, and unrealistic, and that attempts to satisfy a person's biological and emotional needs and desires by maximizing pleasure and avoiding pain.

ego According to Freud, the rational, realistic part of the personality; coordinates impulses from the id with demands imposed by the superego and by society.

superego In Freud's theory, the part of personality that acts as an all-knowing, internalized parent. It has two parts: the conscience, which enforces moral and social conventions by punishing violations with guilt; and the ego-ideal, which provides an idealized, internal set of standards for regulating and evaluating one's thoughts, feelings, and actions.

Stages of Psychosexual Development

Freud believed development occurs through a series of *psychosexual* stages. Each stage focuses on a different area of the body that is a source of excitation and pleasure. At each stage, developmental changes result from conflicts among the id, ego, and superego. These conflicts can threaten the person's ego, or sense of self. Pressures from the id push the person to act impulsively to achieve immediate pleasure; pressures from the ego encourage her to act more realistically by delaying satisfaction until it can be attained; and pressures from the superego push her to meet standards of moral behavior and achievement that may be overly strict or unrealistically high. Freud's psychosexual stages and the developmental processes that occur are summarized in Table 2.2.

The ego uses defense mechanisms to protect itself from such conflicts. *Defense mechanisms* are unconscious distortions of reality that keep conflicts from the ego's (self's) conscious awareness. One such defense mechanism is *repression,* in which unacceptable feelings and impulses are forced from memory and forgotten. Another is *projection,* in which a person's conflict-producing feelings, such as feelings of aggression, are mistakenly attributed to another person.

According to Freud, unresolved id-ego and superego-ego conflicts can lead to a *fixation,* or a blockage in development. Fixation can also result from parenting that is not appropriately responsive to a child's needs. For example, overindulgence during the oral stage (see Table 2.2) may result in excessive dependence on others later in life. On the other hand, infants who experience severe deprivation and frustration of their needs may later feel they have to exploit or manipulate others to meet their needs. In this view, an individual's personality traits reflect the patterns typical of the stage at which a fixation occurred.

TABLE 2.2 Freud's Psychosexual Stages and Developmental Processes

Psychosexual Stage	Approximate Age	Description
Oral	Birth–1 year	The mouth is the focus of stimulation and interaction; feeding and weaning are central.
Anal	1–3 years	The anus is the focus of stimulation and interaction; elimination and toilet training are central.
Phallic	3–6 years	The genitals (penis, clitoris, and vagina) are the focus of stimulation; gender role and moral development are central.
Latency	6–12 years	A period of suspended sexual activity; energies shift to physical and intellectual activities.
Genital	12–adulthood	The genitals are the focus of stimulation with the onset of puberty; mature sexual relationships develop.

Developmental Processes

Development occurs through a series of psychosexual stages. In each stage, the child focuses on a different area of her body, and how she invests her libido (sexual energy) in relationships with people and things reflects the concerns of her current stage. New areas of unconscious conflict among the id, ego, and superego, the three structures of personality, also occur. Conflicting pressures from the id to impulsively achieve pleasure, from the ego to act realistically by delaying gratification, and from the superego to fulfill moralistic obligations and to achieve idealistic standards all threaten the ego. The ego protects itself by means of unconscious defense mechanisms, which keep these conflicts from awareness by distorting reality.

> **Focusing On...**

Erik Erikson's Identity Crisis: An Autobiographical Perspective

How do theorists' own life experiences influence their theories of development? Here is what Erik Erikson has written about his own identity crises and how they influenced his developmental theory.

Erik Erikson was born in 1902 and died in 1994. He grew up in southern Germany with his mother, who was Danish, and her husband, a German pediatrician. Erikson recalls that "all through my earlier childhood, they kept secret from me the fact that my mother had been married previously; and that I was the son of a Dane who had abandoned her before my birth" (E. Erikson, 1975, p. 27).

As Erikson entered puberty and adolescence, identity conflicts intensified. "My stepfather was the only professional man in an intensely Jewish small bourgeois family, while I . . . was blond and blue-eyed, and grew flagrantly tall. Before long, then, I was referred to as a 'goy' [outsider] in my stepfather's temple, while to my schoolmates I was a 'Jew.' . . . Although during World War I, I tried desperately to be a good German chauvinist, [I] soon became a 'Dane' when Denmark remained neutral" (pp. 27, 28).

During this period, Erikson decided he would be an artist and a writer, rejecting his family's more middleclass values and expectations. He spent most of his time traveling, painting, writing, occasionally taking art classes, and teaching art. In looking back at these years, Erikson said that he now considered them an important part of his training (pp. 25, 26).

In fact, it was not until Erikson was almost thirty and moved to Austria that his career as a psychoanalyst and developmental theorist really began. His training in psychoanalysis was conducted by Anna Freud, who accepted him as a student after observing his work with children as a teacher in a small private school. After studying and practicing psychoanalysis in Vienna, Erikson was forced to leave Austria by the rise of Hitler. He emigrated to the United States, where he lived and worked the rest of his life.

Erikson achieved his outstanding accomplishments as a teacher, scholar, and therapist without the benefit of even a college degree, much less any other professional credentials. In the 1930s, Erikson worked as a psychoanalyst with children and debated whether to return to school for a professional degree. Instead, he accepted a research appointment at Yale Medical School and the Yale Institute of Human Relations, where he worked with an interdisciplinary team of psychologists, psychiatrists, and anthropologists and conducted field studies of the Sioux tribe of Native Americans in South Dakota.

In the 1940s, Erikson moved to California to study the life histories of children living in Berkeley and then the lives of the Yurok Indians. He joined the faculty of the University of California at Berkeley in the early 1950s but was soon fired because of his opposition to the Korean War and his refusal to sign a "loyalty oath," part of the fanatical anticommunist crusade of Senator Joe McCarthy. Erikson was reinstated as politically dependable, but resigned in support of others who were not rehired. Erikson says of this experience, "As I think back on that controversy now, it was a test of our American identity; for when the papers told us foreign-born among the nonsigners to 'go back where we came from,' we suddenly felt quite certain that our apparent disloyalty to the soldiers in Korea was, in fact, quite in line with what they were said to be fighting for. The United States Supreme Court has since confirmed our point of view" (pp. 42–43).

Erikson wrote this about that period: "It would seem almost self-evident now how the concepts of 'identity' and 'identity crisis' emerged from my personal, clinical, and anthropological observations in the thirties and forties. I do not remember when I started to use these terms; they seemed naturally grounded in the experience of emigration, immigration, and Americanization. . . . I will not describe the pathological side of my identity confusion, which included disturbances for which psychoanalysis seemed, indeed, the treatment of choice. . . . No doubt, my best friends will insist that I needed to name this crisis and to see it in everybody else in order to really come to terms with it in myself" (pp. 26, 43).

What Do You Think?

In what ways did Erikson's life experiences and the time and places in which he lived influence his developmental theory? What aspects of your own experiences and the time and places you have lived are likely to be important in shaping your own ideas about developmental continuity and change?

Erikson's Psychosocial Theory

Erik Erikson (1902–1994) grew up in Europe. He studied psychoanalysis with Freud's daughter, Anna, who strongly influenced his ideas about personality development. The "Focusing On" feature describes the relationship between Erikson's life and his theory.

In Erikson's view, personality development is a *psychosocial* process, meaning internal psychological factors and external social factors are both very important. Developmental changes occur throughout a person's lifetime and are influenced by three interrelated

For this school-age girl, learning new skills is part of mastering Erikson's developmental crisis of industry versus inferiority, while for her grandfather, sharing his lifelong love of chess is one way of mastering the crisis of ego integrity versus despair.
Source: Budimir Jevtic/Shutterstock.com.

forces: (1) the individual's biological and physical strengths and limitations; (2) the person's unique life circumstances and developmental history, including early family experiences and degree of success in resolving earlier developmental crises; and (3) the particular social, cultural, and historical forces at work during the individual's lifetime (for example, racial prejudice, poverty, rapid technological change, or war).

Psychosocial Stages of Development

Erikson proposed that development occurs in a series of eight stages, beginning with infancy and ending with old age. Each stage is named for the particular *psychosocial crisis,* or challenge, that every individual must resolve to be able to move on to the next stage. Successful mastery of the psychosocial crisis at a particular stage results in a personality strength, or *virtue,* that will help the individual meet future developmental challenges (Erikson, 1982; Miller, 2011). Table 2.3 summarizes Erikson's stages and developmental processes.

Stage 1: Trust versus Mistrust The earliest basic trust is indicated by the infant's capacity to sleep, eat, and excrete in a comfortable and relaxed way. Parents who reliably ensure daily routines and are responsive to their infant's needs provide the basis for a trusting view of the world. The proper ratio, or balance, between trust and mistrust leads to the development of hope. *Hope* is the enduring belief that one's … ure to develop such trust may seriously interfere with a child's ser… …mise her ability to master successfully the challenges of the sta…

TABLE 2.3 Erikson's Psychosocial Stages and Developm…

Psychosocial Stage	Approximate Age	Description (V…
Trust versus mistrust	Birth–1 year	Focus on oral-s… …t of trusting relati… …d of self-trust (hop…
Autonomy versus shame and doubt	1–3 years	Focus on muscu… development of … s and activities (w…
Initiative versus guilt	3–6 years	Focus on locom… limits of self-assertion and purposefulness (purpose)
Industry versus inferiority	6–12 years (latency period)	Focus on mastery, competence, and productivity (competence)
Identity versus role confusion	12–19 years (adolescence)	Focus on formation of identity and coherent self-concept (fidelity)
Intimacy versus isolation	19–25 years (early adulthood)	Focus on achievement of an intimate relationship and career direction (love)
Generativity versus stagnation	25–50 years (adulthood)	Focus on fulfillment through creative, productive activity that contributes to future generations (care)
Ego integrity versus despair	50 and older	Focus on belief in integrity of life, including successes and failures (wisdom)

Developmental Processes

Development of the ego, or sense of identity, occurs through a series of stages, each building on the preceding stages and focused on successfully resolving a new psychosocial crisis between two opposing ego qualities. No stage is fully resolved, and more favorable resolution at an earlier stage facilitates achievement of later stages.

Stage 2: Autonomy versus Shame and Doubt This stage occurs during the toddler and preschool years. *Autonomy* refers to a child's capacity to be independent and self-directed in his activities and ability to balance his own demands for self-control with demands for control from his parents and others. *Shame* involves a loss of self-respect due to a failure to meet one's own standards (Lewis, 1992). A successful outcome for this stage is the virtue *of will,* the capacity to freely make choices based on realistic knowledge of what is expected and what is possible.

Stage 3: Initiative versus Guilt This stage occurs during the preschool years. *Initiative* combines autonomy with the ability to explore new activities and ideas and to purposefully pursue and achieve tasks and goals. *Guilt* involves self-criticism due to failure to fulfill parental expectations. This crisis often involves situations in which the child takes on more than she can physically or emotionally handle, including the powerful sexual and aggressive feelings children often act out in their play. If the child is treated respectfully and helped to formulate and pursue her goals without feeling guilty, she will develop the virtue of *purpose* in her life.

Stage 4: Industry versus Inferiority As a child leaves the protection of his family and enters the world of school, he must come to believe in his ability to learn the basic intellectual and social skills required to be a full and productive member of society and to start and complete tasks successfully. The virtue of *competence* is the result. A failure to feel competent can lead to a sense of inferiority. The child who consistently fails in school is in danger of feeling alienated from society or of thoughtlessly conforming to gain acceptance from others.

Stage 5: Identity versus Role Confusion This stage coincides with the physical changes of *puberty* and the psychosocial changes of adolescence. *Identity* involves a reliable, integrated sense of who one is based on the many different roles one plays. *Role confusion* refers to a failure to achieve this integration of roles. During this stage, teenagers undergo reevaluation of who they are in many areas of identity development, including the physical, sexual, intellectual, religious, and career areas. Frequently conflicts from earlier stages resurface. A successful resolution of this crisis is the development of the virtue *of fidelity,* the ability to sustain loyalties to certain values despite inevitable conflicts and inconsistencies. Failure to resolve this crisis may lead to a premature choice of identity, a prolonged identity and role confusion, or choosing a permanently "negative" identity that may be associated with delinquent and antisocial behavior.

Erikson's final three stages focus on development during adulthood, but are described briefly below.

Stage 6: Intimacy versus Isolation Successful resolution of this stage results in the virtue of being able to experience *love.* The young adult must develop the ability to establish close, committed relationships with others and cope with the fear of losing her own identity and separate sense of self that such intense intimacy raises.

Stage 7: Generativity versus Stagnation This stage occurs during middle adulthood. Successful resolution brings the virtue of *care,* or concern for others. *Generativity* is the feeling that one's work, family life, and other activities are both personally satisfying and socially meaningful in ways that contribute to future generations. *Stagnation* results when life no longer seems purposeful.

Stage 8: Ego Integrity versus Despair This stage occurs during late adulthood. Successful resolution brings the virtue *of wisdom. Ego integrity* refers to the ability to look back on the strengths and weaknesses of one's life with a sense of dignity, optimism, and wisdom. It is in conflict with the despair resulting from health problems, economic difficulties, social isolation, and lack of meaningful work experienced by many older persons in our society.

> **What Do You Think?**
>
> Erikson proposed that cultural and social forces play a major role in developmental change. With this in mind, how might growing up as a male versus a female of your own racial and ethnic background influence how an adolescent deals with the crisis of identity versus role confusion? Compare your conclusions with those of several classmates.

According to Erikson, psychosocial conflicts are never fully resolved. Depending on his or her life experiences, each individual achieves a more or less favorable ratio of trust to mistrust, industry to inferiority, ego integrity to despair, and so on. Therefore, conflicts from earlier stages may continue to affect later development. Moreover, some stages might happen "early," based on life course. For example, a young adult diagnosed with cancer might experience issues of generativity and ego integrity versus despair at a much younger age than is typical.

Applications of Psychodynamic Developmental Theories throughout Development

attachment An intimate and enduring emotional relationship between two people, such as infant and caregiver, characterized by reciprocal affection and a periodic desire to maintain physical closeness.

As we will see in the chapters on psychosocial development throughout this text, psychodynamic theories help us understand the formation of **attachments**, the strong and enduring emotional bond that develops between an infant and his or her caregivers during the infant's first year of life (Chapter 7), the development of autonomy and self-control during infancy and toddlerhood (Chapter 7), and the development of intimate relationships during adolescence and adulthood (Chapters 16). These theories alert us to the social and emotional importance of early childhood play (Chapter 10) and help us deal with death, loss, and grieving during middle childhood (Chapter 13) and with eating disorders, depression, and delinquency during adolescence (Chapters 15 and 16). Erikson's psychosocial theory will help us see that resolving the crisis of *identity versus role confusion*, which is a major task of adolescence, has its origins in earlier experiences and continues through late adulthood, when the crisis of *ego integrity versus despair* must be negotiated.

Behavioral Learning and Social Cognitive Learning Developmental Theories

Learning is generally defined as relatively permanent changes in the capacity to perform certain behaviors that result from experience. According to the learning theories, the learning experiences that occur over a person's lifetime are the source of developmental change. Thus, changes in existing learning opportunities or the creation of new ones can modify the course of an individual's development.

Even young infants participate actively in their own development.
Source: Gelpi/Shutterstock.com.

Behavioral Learning Theories

The behavioral learning theories of Pavlov and Skinner have provided key concepts for understanding how learning experiences influence development and for helping individuals learn new, desirable behaviors and alter or eliminate problematic behaviors.

Pavlov: Classical Conditioning

classical conditioning According to Pavlov, learning in which a neutral stimulus gains the power to bring about a certain response by repeated association with another stimulus that already elicits the same response.

Ivan Pavlov (1849–1936) was a Russian scientist who first developed his behavioral theory while studying digestion in dogs. In his well-known experiments, Pavlov rang a bell just before feeding a dog. Eventually the dog salivated whenever it heard the bell, even if it received no food. Pavlov called this process **classical conditioning**. The food served as the *unconditioned stimulus*, and the salivation to the food was the *unconditioned response*. Over repeated pairings with the bell (a *neutral stimulus*) being presented before the food, those two experiences essentially became intertwined so that, eventually, the dogs began

40 Part 1 Studying Human Development

salivating when they heard the bell, even when the food was not present. When the formerly neutral stimulus—the bell—caused a response, it was then considered a *conditioned stimulus*, and the salivation to the bell was then considered the *conditioned response*.

Through the processes involved in classical conditioning, reflexes that are present at birth may help infants to learn about and participate in the world around them. For example, conditioning of the sucking reflex, which allows newborn infants to suck reflexively in response to a touch on the lips, has been reported using a tone as the conditioned stimulus (Lipsitt & Kaye, 1964). Other stimuli, such as the sight of the bottle and the mother's face, smile, and voice, may also become conditioned stimuli for sucking and may elicit sucking responses even before the bottle touches the baby's lips. Although even newborns' behavior may be classically conditioned as early as the first two days of life (Fifer et al., 2009), it cannot be reliably observed over a wide range of reflexes until about six months of age (Lipsitt, 1990). Figure 2.1 illustrates the process of classical conditioning.

Skinner: Operant Conditioning

B. F. Skinner (1904–1991) is best known for his learning theory, which is also known as **operant conditioning**. This theory is based on a simple concept called **reinforcement**, the process by which the likelihood that a particular response will occur again increases when that response is followed by a certain stimulus. *Positive reinforcement* occurs when, following a particular response (a baby saying "da-da"), a rewarding stimulus (his father smiling and saying "good boy!") is added that strengthens the response and increases the likelihood that it will recur under similar circumstances. *Negative reinforcement* also strengthens a response and increases the chance of its recurrence, but does so by removing an undesirable or unpleasant stimulus following the occurrence of that response. Consider Sarah, a four-year-old who has been crying and misbehaving at the dinner table. By quieting

operant conditioning According to Skinner, a process of learning in which a person or an animal increases the frequency of a behavior in response to repeated reinforcement of that behavior.

reinforcement According to Skinner, any stimulus that increases the likelihood that a behavior will be repeated in similar circumstances.

Illustration of Classical Conditioning

BEFORE CONDITIONING:
(A) Place a nipple in baby's mouth:

Touch of nipple (US) — — — —elicits — — — — > Sucking reflex (UR)

(B) Show baby a bottle with a nipple:

Sight of bottle — — — — —elicits — — — — > No sucking (UR)
with nipple (CS)

DURING CONDITIONING:
(C) Show baby the a bottle and place its nipples in baby's mouth.
Repeat a number of times:

Touch of nipple (US) — — — —elicits — — — — > Sucking reflex (UR)

(paired with)

Sight of bottle — — — —elicits — — — — > Sucking reflex (UR)
with nipple (CS)

AFTER CONDITIONING
(D) Show baby the bottle with nipple:

Sight of bottle — — — —elicits — — — — > Sucking reflex (UR)
with nipple (CS)

FIGURE 2.1
Illustration of Classical Conditioning

In this example, the nipple in the baby's mouth is an unconditioned stimulus (US), which with no prior conditioning brings about, or elicits, the sucking reflex, an unconditioned response (UR). (a) The nipple in the mouth elicits a sucking reflex. (b) The sight of a bottle is a neutral stimulus (NS) and has no effect. (c) Once the sight of the bottle (NS) is repeatedly paired with the nipple in the mouth (US), the sight of the bottle becomes a conditioned (learned) stimulus (CS), which now elicits sucking, the conditioned response (CR).

Chapter 2 Theories of Development

punishment According to Skinner, any stimulus that temporarily suppresses the response that it follows.

down once she gets her parents' attention, she may actually be negatively reinforcing (increasing) her parents' attention-giving responses by removing the unpleasant stimulus of crying and misbehaving. Furthermore, Sarah's parents are providing positive reinforcement in the form of attention for crying and misbehaving at the dinner table.

Punishment weakens or suppresses a behavioral response by either adding an unpleasant stimulus (a *positive punishment*) or removing a pleasurable one (a *negative punishment*) following the response's occurrence. Taking away television privileges (negative punishment) and adding an extra chore (positive punishment) following a child's misbehavior are both forms of punishment. *Extinction* refers to the disappearance of a response when a reinforcer that was maintaining a behavior is removed. Often, before the undesirable behavior reduces in the face of extinction, the person will actually increase the behavior in an attempt to elicit a response. This is known as an *extinction burst*. Frequently, the best way to extinguish an undesirable response is to ignore it, even in the face of an extinction burst, and reinforce an alternative, more desirable response. For example, at the grocery store, Bea cries for potato chips. To calm Bea down, Amal buys her chips (positively reinforcing the behavior of crying). During their next trip to the grocery store, Bea cries for chips again. Amal ignores her crying daughter, so Bea begins to scream (an extinction burst). Amal is faced with a difficult decision: If she gives in now, she has just positively reinforced a worse behavior. If Amal continues to ignore the behavior, Bea will eventually stop, at which time Amal can praise Bea for being good (positive reinforcement).

Shaping occurs when a child learns to perform new responses not already in his repertoire, or "collection." This is achieved by starting with an existing response and then modifying, or shaping, it by reinforcing small changes that bring it closer and closer to the desired behavior. Consider a dad who wishes to teach his seven-year-old daughter to hit a ball with a bat. Because she already can swing a bat, careful encouragement (a good positive reinforcer) for better and better swings and eventually for actually making contact with the ball (which is itself a good positive reinforcer) will transform, or shape, his daughter's bat swinging behavior into ball-hitting behavior, a far more enjoyable and useful one.

Social Cognitive Learning Theory

observational learning The tendency of a child to imitate or model behavior and attitudes of parents and other individuals.

Albert Bandura proposes that developmental change occurs largely through **observational learning**, or learning by observing others. Learning is *reciprocally determined,* meaning it results from interactions between the developing individual (including his behaviors, cognitive processes, and physical capacities) and his physical and social environment. Observational learning takes two forms: imitation and modeling. In *imitation,* a child is directly reinforced for repeating or copying the actions of others. In *modeling,* the child learns the behaviors and personality traits of a parent or other model through vicarious (indirect) reinforcement. A child learns to behave in ways similar to those of a parent or

Observational learning likely plays an important role as these children learn to prepare dough.
Source: Margarita Borodina/Shutterstock.com.

> **What Do You Think?**
>
> Think of some examples of developmental changes in a young child's behavior that might be accurately explained using behavioral learning theories. Then think of an example of a developmental change that does not seem to fit the behavioral model.

other model by merely observing the model receiving reinforcement for his or her actions. How influential the model will be depends on a variety of factors, including the model's relationship to the child, his or her personal characteristics, and how the child perceives the model (Bandura, 1989; Miller, 2011). Children's levels of cognitive development strongly influence their ability to observe, remember, and later perform in ways similar to the models they have watched.

The social cognitive learning approach has been useful in explaining gender development, the development of aggression, and the developmental impact of television and other media. It has also been useful to counselors and therapists who work with problems in the parent-child relationship and with children experiencing a variety of behavioral and adjustment difficulties in both outpatient and residential treatment settings.

Applications of Learning Theories throughout Development

Pavlov's and Skinner's behavioral learning theories have proved particularly useful in helping to understand development from infancy through adolescence. For example, to study the development of object perception among young infants, classical conditioning has been used to teach infants to respond to different stimuli by sucking on a pacifier. Operant conditioning and observational learning have guided the study of cognitive development during the first two years (Chapter 6) and helped to explain the development of autonomy in infancy and toddlerhood (Chapter 7). **Behavior modification**, a specific set of techniques based on operant conditioning and social cognitive learning, has been essential in helping school-age children and their families deal with *attention deficit hyperactivity disorder (ADHD)* (Chapter 1) and in helping adolescents with eating disorders and delinquent behavior (Chapters 15 and 16). Both behavioral and social cognitive learning theories can help to explain how language is acquired during the first two years (Chapter 6). Social cognitive learning theories help us to understand the role of vicarious (indirect) reinforcement and self-reinforcement in early childhood play, and the limitations of using spanking and other forms of punishment during early childhood (Chapter 10).

behavior modification Techniques based on the principles of learning theory that can be used by parents, teachers, therapists, and other professionals to help children, adolescents, and adults reduce or eliminate undesirable behaviors and learn desirable ones.

Cognitive Developmental Theories

In this section, we discuss three theoretical approaches to cognitive development: Piaget's cognitive theory, neo-Piagetian theories, and information-processing theory. All of these theories share a strong focus on how thinking and problem-solving skills develop and how such cognitive activities contribute to the overall process of development.

According to Piaget, children think in qualitatively different ways as they develop. As illustrated in the two photos, very young children usually think about objects and experiences by looking and touching, whereas many adolescents can plan and reason abstractly.
Sources: (left) Ami Parikh/Shutterstock.com; (right) Golden Pixels LLC/Shutterstock.com.

Chapter 2 Theories of Development

Piaget's Cognitive Theory

Jean Piaget (1896–1980) was one of the most influential figures in developmental psychology. Just as Freud's ideas radically changed thinking about human emotional development, Piaget's ideas have changed our understanding of the development of human thinking and problem solving, or *cognition.*

Key Principles of Piaget's Theory

Piaget believed thinking develops in a series of increasingly complex stages, or periods, each of which incorporates and revises those that precede it. Table 2.4 summarizes Piaget's cognitive stages and developmental processes. We look at his theory in greater detail in the chapters on cognitive development in childhood and adolescence.

What exactly makes a person develop from one stage of thinking and problem solving to the next? Piaget believed three processes are involved: (1) direct learning, (2) social transmission, and (3) maturation.

Direct learning results when a person actively responds to and interprets new problems and experiences based on patterns of thought and action he already knows. Piaget called these existing patterns *schemes.* A **scheme** is a systematic pattern of thoughts, actions, and problem-solving strategies that helps the individual deal with a particular intellectual challenge or situation. According to Piaget, an infant's first understanding of the world is based on a limited number of *innate schemes* made up of simple patterns of unlearned reflexes that are inherited at birth, such as sucking, grasping, and looking. These schemes rapidly change as the infant encounters new experiences through the complementary processes of *assimilation* and *accommodation.*

Assimilation is the process by which an infant interprets and responds to a new experience or situation in terms of an existing scheme. For example, a two-month-old baby who is presented with a bottle for the first time understands what is needed to suck from the bottle based on her existing sucking scheme for her mother's breast. The infant has assimilated a new situation, sucking from a bottle, into her existing scheme for sucking. As

scheme According to Piaget, a behavior or thought that represents a group of ideas and events in a person's experience.

assimilation According to Piaget, a method by which a person responds to new experiences by using existing concepts to interpret new ideas and experiences.

TABLE 2.4 Piaget's Cognitive Stages and Developmental Processes

Cognitive Stage	Approximate Age	Description
Sensorimotor	Birth–2 years	Coordination of sensory and motor activity; achievement of object permanence
Preoperational	2–7 years	Use of language and symbolic representation; egocentric view of the world
Concrete operational	7–11 years	Solution of concrete problems through logical operational operations
Formal operational	11–adulthood	Systematic solution of actual and hypothetical problems using abstract symbols

Developmental Processes

The earliest and most primitive patterns, or schemes, of thinking, problem solving, and constructing reality are inborn. As a result of both maturation and experience, thinking develops through a series of increasingly sophisticated stages, each incorporating the achievements in preceding stages. These changes occur through the processes of assimilation, in which new problems are solved using existing schemes, and accommodation, in which existing schemes are altered or adapted to meet new challenges. Together, these processes create a state of cognitive balance, or *equilibrium,* in which the person's thinking becomes increasingly stable, general, and harmoniously adjusted to the environment.

Part 1 Studying Human Development

children grow older, schemes involve increasingly complex mental processes. For example, a preschooler sees a truck but calls it a "car" because the concept of *car* is already well established in his thinking. In **accommodation**, a child changes existing schemes, or ways of thinking, when faced with new ideas or situations in which the old schemes no longer work. Instead of calling a truck by the wrong name, the preschooler searches for a new name and begins to realize that some four-wheeled objects are not cars.

According to Piaget, development results from the interplay of assimilation and accommodation, a process called *adaptation*. **Adaptation** results when schemes are deepened or broadened by assimilation and stretched or modified by accommodation.

Social transmission, Piaget's second explanation for development, is the process through which one's thinking is influenced by learning from social contact with and observation of others rather than through direct experience. *Physical maturation,* Piaget's third explanation for developmental change, refers to the biologically determined changes in physical and neurological development that occur relatively independently of specific experiences. For example, a child must reach a certain minimal level of biological development to be able to name an object.

Although research at least partially supports many of Piaget's ideas, it has found a number of shortcomings. One problem is how to explain why, in many instances, children master tasks that are logically equivalent at very different points in their development. It is also hard to explain why a child's cognitive performances on two logically similar tasks are often very different. A third problem is that Piaget's exclusive emphasis on the predetermined "logical" aspects of children's thinking often does not match the actual thought processes children appear to use and largely ignores the social, emotional, and cultural factors that influence the process (Case, 1992; Rogoff & Chavajay, 1995). Finally, Piaget's theory fails to recognize that cognitive development continues after adolescence. Some of these issues are discussed in the "A Multicultural View" feature later in the chapter.

accommodation According to Piaget, the process of modifying existing ideas or action-skills to fit new experiences.

adaptation Piaget's term for the process by which development occurs; concepts are deepened or broadened by assimilation and stretched or modified by accommodation.

Neo-Piagetian Approaches

Neo-Piagetian theories are new or revised models of Piaget's basic approach. Robbie Case, for example, proposes that cognitive development results from increases in the child's *mental space,* that is, the maximum number of schemes the child can apply simultaneously at any given time. During early childhood, most cognitive structures are rather specific and concrete, such as drawing with a pencil, throwing a ball, or counting a set of objects. As the structures guiding these actions become coordinated with one another, they form new, more efficient, higher-level cognitive structures, which in turn begin to be coordinated with other, similar structures. Thus, a child's ability to use increasingly general cognitive structures enables him to think more abstractly. Different forms of the same logical problem may require different processing skills and capacities. As a result, a child's performance on two logically similar tasks may differ significantly, and mastery of each task may occur at very different points in her development (Case, 1991b, 1991c, 1991d).

Kurt Fischer, another neo-Piagetian theorist, accepts Piaget's basic idea of stages, but uses specific *skills* instead of *schemes* to describe the cognitive structures children use in particular problem-solving tasks or sets of tasks. The breadth of a skill is determined by both the level of maturation a child's central nervous system has reached and the range of specific learning environments to which the child has been exposed (Fischer, 1994; Fischer & Pipp, 1984a, 1984b). Thus, the type of support a child receives from parents, teachers, and others in the environment plays an important role in skill acquisition. Case's "breadth of skill" idea has much in common with Lev Vygotsky's "zone of proximal development," discussed later in this chapter.

Information-Processing Theory

Another alternative to Piaget's cognitive theory is **information-processing theory**, which focuses on the precise, detailed features or steps involved in mental activities (Klahr, 1989; Seifert, 1993). Like a computer, the mind is viewed as having distinct parts that make unique contributions to thinking in a specific order.

information-processing theory Explanations of cognition that focus on the precise, detailed features or steps of mental activities. These theories often use computers as models for human thinking.

Key Principles of Information-Processing Theory

Figure 2.2 shows one information-processing model of human thinking. According to this model, when a person tries to solve a problem, she first takes in information from her environment through her senses. The information gained in this way is held briefly in the *sensory memory,* the first memory store. The sensory memory records information as it originally receives it, but the information fades or disappears within a fraction of a second unless the person processes it further.

Information to which a person pays special attention is transferred to *short-term memory (STM),* the second memory store. The short-term memory corresponds roughly to "momentary awareness," or whatever the person is thinking about at a particular instant. Short-term memory is often called "working memory" because this is the memory store where information is being acted upon. The short-term/working memory can hold only limited amounts of information—in fact, only about seven pieces of it at any one time. After about twenty seconds, information in short-term/working memory is either forgotten or processed further. At this point, it moves into *long-term memory (LTM),* the third memory store. So if you remember what you had for breakfast this morning, information about the taste and smell of your cereal entered your sensory memory for a brief moment. Some of that information was transferred to your short-term/working memory, and then some of that information was transferred to your long-term memory, where it stayed until you read the beginning of the previous sentence, which queued retrieval back into your short-term/working memory.

Information can be saved permanently in long-term memory. But doing so requires various cognitive strategies, such as rehearsing information repeatedly or organizing it into familiar categories. Unlike short-term/working memory, long-term memory probably has unlimited capacity for storage of new information, as demonstrated by a small number of individuals with highly superior autobiographical memory who can remember immense detail from their own past (LePort et al., 2012). The problem for most people comes in retrieving information, which requires that we remember how it was stored in the first place.

Developmental Changes in Information Processing

As children grow older, they experience several cognitive changes that allow them to process information more efficiently and comprehensively. The most important developmental change in information processing is the acquisition of control processes. *Control processes* direct an individual's attention toward particular input from the sensory register and guide the response to new information once it enters short-term memory. Usually control processes organize information in short-term memory. Sometimes control processes also relate information in STM to previously learned knowledge from LTM, such as when a teenager hears a song on the radio and notes its similarity to another song heard previously.

FIGURE 2.2
An Information-Processing Model of Learning

Information from the environment first enters the sensory memory. With the aid of control processes, it is then transferred to short-term/working memory, where it is either forgotten or processed further, and then to long-term memory, where it is stored for future use, at which point it is retrieved from long-term memory.

An Information-Processing Model of Learning

> **What Do You Think?**
>
> Would this theoretical approach be of any use in a health education class?

As children grow older they develop **metacognition**, an awareness and understanding of how thinking and learning work. Metacognition assists learning in a number of ways. First, it allows a person to assess how difficult a problem or learning task will be and to plan appropriate ways to approach it. More specifically, metacognition involves knowledge of self, knowledge of task variables, and knowledge of which information-processing strategies are effective in which situations (Forrest-Pressley et al., 1985).

In addition to metacognition, children acquire many other kinds of knowledge. Some children gradually become comparative experts in particular areas, such as math, sports, or getting along with peers. *Knowledge base* refers to children's current fund of knowledge and skills in various areas. A child's knowledge base in one area makes acquiring further knowledge and skills in the same area easier because the child can relate new information to prior information more meaningfully. Metacognition and an expanding knowledge base contribute to cognitive development throughout the lifespan.

According to many information-processing theorists, changes in the knowledge base are not general, stage-like transformations such as those proposed by Piaget (Chi et al., 1989). Instead, they are specialized developments of expertise based on the gradual accumulation of specific information and skills related to a field, including information and skills related to how knowledge in the field is organized and learned efficiently. A very good chess player is an expert in chess but is not necessarily advanced in other activities or areas of knowledge. Her skill probably reflects long hours spent in one major activity: playing chess games. Each hour of play enables her to build a larger knowledge base about chess; memories of board patterns, moves, and game strategies that worked in the past.

metacognition Knowledge and thinking about cognition, how learning and memory operate in everyday situations, and how one can improve cognitive performance.

Applications of Cognitive Developmental Theories throughout Development

Piaget's cognitive theory and the more recent Neo-Piagetian approaches have provided the central conceptual framework for understanding the development of thinking and problem solving throughout the lifespan. In Chapter 6, for example, Piaget's theory will help explain sensorimotor development during the first two years, and a "Working With" interview with Gillian Luppiwiski, an infant care provider, will discuss how cognitive theory can be used to foster thinking and intellectual development in infants. Cognitive theory will also help explain the development of symbolic thought and language among preschoolers (Chapter 6) and how growth in thinking and problem-solving abilities affects relationships with peers in middle childhood (Chapter 13). In Chapter 15, we will see how cognitive theory is used to design programs to foster critical thinking among adolescents; to better understand *adolescent egocentrism, imaginary audience,* and *personal fable;* and to understand moral development and the ethics of care during adolescence.

Cognitive developmental theories have been increasingly helpful in explaining intellectual functioning during early, middle, and later adulthood. In Chapter 15 we will explore the question of whether cognitive development culminates *informal operational thinking,* Piaget's fourth and final stage, or *a fifth stage of cognitive development* is needed to capture the ability to define new problems in *new and often contradictory ways* that develops during the adult years.

Contextual Developmental Theories

Contextual approaches view development as a process of reciprocal, patterned interactions between the individual and his or her physical and social environment. A leading example of this approach is the ecological systems theory of Urie Bronfenbrenner. As we saw in

Chapter 2 Theories of Development

> **What Do You Think?**
>
> How might the cognitive approach be useful to an elementary school math teacher who is preparing lesson plans?

Chapter 1, *ecological systems theory* proposes that a person's development is influenced by four interactive and overlapping contextual levels:

1. the *microsystem*—the face-to-face physical and social situations that directly affect the person (family, classroom, workplace);

2. the *mesosystem*—connections and relationships among the person's microsystems;

3. the *exosystem*—the settings or situations that indirectly influence the person (spouse's place of employment, the local school board, the local government); and

4. the *macrosystem*—the values, beliefs, and policies of society and culture that provide frameworks, or "blueprints," for organizing one's life and indirectly influence the person through their effects on the exosystem, mesosystem, and microsystem.

Another interesting example of contextual theory was developed by the Russian psychologist Lev Vygotsky (1896–1934). Vygotsky was interested in how changing historical and cultural contexts within which children's activities occur influence their cognitive development. According to Vygotsky, higher mental functions grow out of the social interactions and dialogues that take place between a child and parents, teachers, and other representatives of the culture. Through these interactions, children internalize increasingly mature and effective ways of thinking and problem solving. Some of these changes occur through discoveries that the child initiates on her own (Karpov & Haywood, 1998).

Many developmental tasks, however, occur in what Vygotsky called the *zone of proximal development*. The **zone of proximal development** refers to the range of tasks that a child cannot yet accomplish without active assistance from parents and others with greater knowledge, and the framework of support and assistance is called *scaffolding* (Blanck, 1990; Rogoff, 1990; Wertsch, 1989). See the "A Multicultural View" feature for a discussion of culture and cognitive development.

Glen Elder (1998), a pioneer in the study of development over the life course, suggests that education, work, and family create the **social trajectories**, or pathways, that guide individual development. Important life transitions, such as school entry, marriage, and the birth of a child, give these social trajectories distinctive shape and meaning for each individual. Historical changes, such as wars, economic depressions, and technological innovations, shape the social trajectories of family, education, and work, which in turn influence individual development. Though individuals are able to select the paths they follow by asserting their *human agency,* or free will, these choices are not made in a social vacuum and depend on the opportunities and constraints of social structure and culture, which themselves change over time (Elder, 1998; Hernandez, 1997; Coll et al., 1996).

Applications of Contextual Developmental Theories throughout Development

Contextual theories have become increasingly useful in understanding how individual development over the life course is influenced by and interacts with the changing life contexts in which development occurs. The discussion of Jodi and her multiple contexts of development in Chapter 1 is an excellent illustration of how Urie Bronfenbrenner's ecological systems theory helps us understand individual development. Ecological systems theory has been especially useful for understanding the multiple factors and contexts involved in divorce, teen parenthood, and juvenile delinquency and for designing programs to assist troubled adolescents and to prevent those problems from occurring (Chapter 16).

Similarly, the future developmental changes that Elizabeth, the preschooler discussed at the beginning of this chapter, is likely to experience illustrate Glen Elder's ideas about

---

zone of proximal development According to Vygotsky, the level of difficulty at which problems are too hard for children to solve alone but not too hard when given support from adults or more competent peers.

social trajectory The pathway or direction that development takes over an individual's life course, which is influenced by the school, work, family, and other important social settings in which he or she participates.

A Multicultural View

Street Children: Comparing Paraguay and North America

According to Lev Vygotsky's theory, cognitive development is largely "context specific," meaning it must be understood in terms of the particular social, cultural, and historical processes of people's everyday experiences (Vygotsky, 1978; Wertsch, 1985). Individuals growing up in different societies, cultures, and historical periods are likely to display differences in how they think and solve problems and in how cognitive development occurs. This view is very different from that of Jean Piaget, who believed cognitive development is largely "universal," meaning all individuals progress through the same developmental stages at approximately the same ages relatively independently of their particular situations and experiences.

Research based primarily on observations of children from Western industrialized societies, where formal schooling is heavily stressed, has generally supported Piaget's ideas. Studies of children growing up in other societies and cultures, however, have been more consistent with Vygotsky's views. Children growing up in cultures with little formal schooling have been found to take much longer to achieve the *concrete operational stage* of thinking and appear unable to achieve the *formal operational stage* of thinking, Piaget's final stage (Rogoff & Chavajay, 1995). Michael Cole, a pioneer in studying culture and cognitive development, concluded that the superior performance of children who had formal schooling was due to the common structure and activities of schooling and tests of cognitive development rather than to the effects of schooling on children's thinking (Cole, 1990).

Performance on tasks that require participants to classify test items into categories is one good example. Whereas individuals from Western countries typically classify test items based on their type (for example, putting animals in one group, food items in another, and tools in a third), individuals in many other nations sort the same items based on their function (for example, putting a hoe with a potato because a hoe is used to dig up a potato) (Rogoff & Chavajay, 1995).

Logical tasks that require a person to draw conclusions based on abstract, hypothetical reasoning rather than on direct personal experience are another example. Nonliterate individuals who are able to make excellent logical judgments when dealing with the immediate, practical problems of their everyday life experiences may, for cultural reasons, be unwilling to demonstrate similar reasoning abilities in situations that are not culturally familiar. The following example, taken from an interview with a nonliterate Central Asian peasant, illustrates this point:

Interviewer: In the Far North, where there is snow, all bears are white. Novaya Zemlya is in the Far North and there is always snow there. What color are the bears there?

Peasant: . . . We always speak of only what we see; we don't talk about what we haven't seen.

Interviewer: But what do my words imply?

Peasant: Well, it's like this: our tsar isn't like yours, and yours isn't like ours. Your words can be answered only by someone who was there, and if a person wasn't there, he can't say anything on the basis of your words.

Interviewer: But on the basis of my words—in the North, where there is always snow, the bears are white—can you gather what kind of bears there are in Novaya Zemlya?

Peasant: If a man was sixty or eighty and had seen a white bear and had told me about it, he could be believed, but I've never seen one, and hence, I can't say. (Luria, 1976, pp. 108–109, quoted in Rogoff & Chavajay, 1995, p. 861)

Differences in performance of common cognitive tasks may also reflect cultural differences in how a problem is defined and how it should be solved (Goodnow, 1976). European Americans, for example, believe intelligence involves technical rather than social skills. Kipsigis (Kenyan) parents include responsible participation in family and social life in their definition. For the Ifaluk of the western Pacific, intelligence means not only having knowledge of good social behavior but also performing it. Ugandan villagers associate intelligence with being slow, careful, and active, whereas westernized groups associate it with speed (Rogoff & Chavajay, 1995).

Future research will provide additional evidence regarding the social and cultural contexts of cognitive development.

---

social trajectories. For example, entry into first grade, transitions to middle school, high school, and college, entering the world of work, getting married, and having a child are all likely to be important steps in the pathways that will help give her long-term development distinctive meaning and form. At the same time, political, economic, and technological changes in society will influence Elizabeth's family, education, and work, which in turn will influence her behaviors and the particular directions her developmental choices take. Although Elizabeth will have considerable potential to assert her agency and freely choose the paths she will follow, such life choices will not be made in a social vacuum and will also depend on the opportunities and constraints that she encounters.

> **WORKING WITH** Jeffrey Friedman, Clinical Social Worker

The Value of Developmental Theory for Helping Children, Adolescents, and Their Families

Jeffrey Friedman, a clinical social worker, specializes in child development. He was interviewed in his office at a community mental health center, where he helps children, adolescents, and families with their developmental problems and consults with pediatricians about the developmental problems they encounter in their practices.

Robert: *Do you find developmental theories useful in your work?*

Jeffrey: They help a lot if you use them in a practical way and don't treat them like cookbook recipes to follow in every case. Theories also help me to avoid mistakes. They add things that I couldn't figure out from my own experience and common sense. They correct myths about people that most of us are taught to believe. Sometimes they remind me to keep the whole person in mind when I am focused on a single pressing problem, and sometimes they help me to divide a big, vague problem into small, discrete parts that are easier to work with.

Robert: *That's very interesting. How did this come about?*

Jeffrey: Before I had studied development, when I spent time with children, I assumed that they thought the same way adults do, because I couldn't remember how I thought when I was their age. Reading the work of theorists who studied children closely and working under the guidance of teachers who applied these theories has helped me to understand better the peculiar ways in which children think about and experience the world.

Robert: *Could you give an example?*

Jeffrey: Think of the way a child conceptualizes death. When a child talks about her uncle dying and being buried, you might assume that she kind of knows what death is. If you haven't read somebody's discussion about children's understanding of death, it probably wouldn't occur to ask the child what she meant so that you could help her feel better about it. Because if you *did* ask her, she might very well have told you that they're going to plant her uncle in the ground, and next spring he's going to grow up like some flower and she'll have him back again.

Robert: *Or she might think that her uncle went to sleep, but since she doesn't understand the difference between death and sleep, could be terrified that if she goes to sleep, she might also die.*

Jeffrey: Exactly.

Robert: *How do you apply theories when you're working with children and their families?*

Jeffrey: Intimate love relationships involving parents, children, other family members, and very close friends turn out to be central to a person's psychological and social well-being. Unlike more casual or superficial relationships, which we can understand intuitively pretty well, more intense love relationships are often impossible to understand based solely on what a person consciously thinks and feels about them. You find people in these family relationships all tied up in knots, doing things they don't expect or even want to do, feeling things they don't want to feel. For children, the feelings and experiences of their primary caregivers turn out to have an enormous impact on development.

Robert: *As I recall, you once worked with a group of children whose problems in their relationships with their parents were so severe that they actually stopped growing. What was this problem called?*

Jeffrey: It's called psychosocial dwarfism. I'm glad that you remembered that, because it's a very dramatic instance of how psychological theory helped to explain a very perplexing disorder!

Robert: *How so? Can you give me some details?*

Jeffrey: They were young kids, mostly six, seven, and eight years old and some as old as ten or eleven. They all were extremely small, and most were two or three years below the normal height and weight for children their age. They

Vygotsky's sociocultural approach and his concept of *zone of proximal development* help us to understand the development of problem-solving skills and intelligence during middle childhood (Chapter 12). Contextual cognitive approaches have highlighted how cognitive development is organized by external psychosocial contexts, including the demands of school and family, rather than by internal organizing structures.

WORKING WITH Jeffrey Friedman, Clinical Social Worker

The Value of Developmental Theory for Helping Children, Adolescents, and Their Families *continued*

were also intensely angry and unhappy and were doing poorly both at home and in school. People thought they were so small for their age because of malnutrition.

Robert: *Was that the problem?*

Jeffrey: Well, no. Their metabolism and growth hormones were highly abnormal, although the glands that produced the growth hormones were fine—and when the children were given growth hormones, they didn't grow. But when these children were put in the hospital and separated from their families, a surprising thing happened: their mental and physical conditions improved dramatically. They immediately started to grow, gaining on average almost a centimeter a month. When the children were returned home to their families, we were in for another surprise. Their mental states again deteriorated and the growth stopped completely.

Robert: *What were their parents like?*

Jeffrey: They weren't physically abusive, neglectful, or anything like that. In fact, they loved their children very much. Most were middle class people who lived in nice houses and had good jobs. Often they had other children who were doing just fine. As we got to know the parents better, though, we discovered that in every case at least one parent had very disturbed ways of thinking about their child—ways of thinking that they had hidden even from themselves.

Robert: *Are you talking about their "internal working models"?*

Jeffrey: Yes, the working models or mental portraits that these parents held about their dwarfed children were severely defective. Developmental theory helped me to appreciate how, in the context of intense love relationships, patterns of thoughts and feelings that parents are barely aware of can profoundly affect the psychosocial, physical, and cognitive well-being and development of their own children. Over time, I came to recognize the disturbed and irrational feelings that the parents were expressing indirectly to their children. One parent thought the child had demons in him and that God has somehow arranged things so the child was punishing the parent for things the parent had done wrong earlier in life, things the parent thought were horrible. Once the theory helped me to discover what was hidden, I could then help the parent and the child understand what was going on, so they could start to improve the situation. Although it took many months, once the quality of these parent-child relationships improved, the psychological adjustment of the children also improved. They all grew up to be individuals of normal height and weight.

Robert: *Are similar problems in the parent-child relationship found in other instances?*

Jeffrey: Yes, they are. Frequently, the physical and sexual abuse of children by parents and others who are very close to them arises from problems in the enduring patterns of thoughts and feelings that people have about their children. To understand those disturbed relationships and their impact on children's minds and bodies—and to know how best to improve things—you need developmental theories to help you understand the people involved, the factors in the situation, and the way they interact to affect a particular child and his or her family.

What Do You Think?

1. Why does Jeffrey Friedman believe that developmental theory is essential to understanding and helping individuals and their families?
2. What are your views of the differences between children's ways of thinking and those of adults? How has developmental theory influenced those views?
3. What are your thoughts about the discussion of psychosocial dwarfism? In what way were you surprised about the power of mental life to influence development? In what way were you not surprised?

Ethological Theory

Ethological theory has played an important role in studying the contribution of differences in *temperament* that are observable at birth to development through childhood and adolescence. It has also contributed to the study of the important role *attachment* plays in the development of relationships from early infancy through the life course, a topic we noted in our earlier discussion of developmental applications of psychodynamic theory.

Chapter 2 Theories of Development 51

> **What Do You Think?**
>
> Remember three-year-old Elizabeth at the beginning of this chapter? Now that you have learned more about theories of development, which theory (or theories) do you think is most useful in understanding her situation and helping her adjust to her first days of nursery school? Why?

The ethological approach attempts to apply the principles of evolutionary biology and ethology to behavioral and psychological characteristics (Ainsworth & Bowlby, 1991; Leckman & Mayes, 1998). This approach has its roots in *ethology,* the study of various animal species in their natural environments. Ethology emphasizes the ways widely shared species behaviors evolved through the process of natural selection and adaptation to different developmental contexts to ensure species survival. Developmental ethologists are interested in how certain behavioral and psychological traits or predispositions that appear to be widely shared among human beings may have developed to help ensure the evolutionary survival of the human species.

An underlying assumption is that just as human evolution has imposed certain constraints on our physical development, it may have influenced the range and nature of our behavioral development. Developmental ethologists also attempt to understand how individual differences in traits such as aggressiveness, shyness, competitiveness, and altruism reciprocally interact with the social context to mutually influence development.

One area of ethological interest has been the study of infant emotions and *temperament,* relatively enduring individual differences in infant responsiveness and self-regulation that appear to be present at birth. (See Chapter 7 for a discussion of temperament.) A second important application is the study of infant-caregiver *attachment,* the mutually reinforcing system of physical, social, and emotional stimulation and support between infant and caregiver. This pattern of attachment behaviors has also been observed in other species, and ethologists presume it has survival value for humans as well (e.g., Bowlby, 1948). (See Chapter 7 for a discussion of attachment.) Though the scope of this text is limited to childhood and adolescence, attachment has importance throughout the lifespan.

Developmental Theories Compared: Implications for the Student

We have reached the end of our review of several of the most important theories in developmental psychology. What conclusions might we draw? In what ways are these theories useful as we investigate development in the remainder of this book? As we suggested at the beginning of this chapter, theories are useful because they help us systematically organize and make sense of large amounts of sometimes inconsistent information about lifespan development. Theories also stimulate new thinking and research and guide parents, professionals, and laypersons in their day-to-day involvements with children, adolescents, and adults. In this chapter's "Working With" interview, a clinical social worker discusses this issue.

Although each theory we've explored in this chapter has significantly expanded knowledge in its particular area of focus, none should be thought to provide a complete explanation of development. Taken together, the theories are complementary and can be used in conjunction with one another to provide a comprehensive view of lifespan development. Table 2.5 summarizes the main features and key concepts for each theoretical approach discussed.

Theories help us understand and actively participate in our own development. Theories can also broaden and deepen our understanding of ourselves, the factors influencing our development, and the choices we have. They can help us better understand how our family dynamics and relationships may have influenced our current personalities and our struggles with issues such as identity, intimacy, gender role, and sexuality.

TABLE 2.5 Developmental Theories Compared

Theoretical Approach I	Main Focus	Key Concepts	Basic Assumptions
Psychodynamic			
Freud	Personality (social, emotional)	Id, ego, superego; psychosexual conflict; defense mechanisms	This broadly focused stage theory assumes a moderate role for maturation, a strong role for experience, and a moderately active developmental role for the individual.
Erikson	Personality (social, emotional, identity)	Lifespan development, psychosocial crises	This broadly focused stage theory assumes a weak to moderate role for maturation, a strong role for experience, and a highly active role for the individual.
Behavioral Learning			
Pavlov, Skinner	Learning specific, observable responses	Classical and operant conditioning, extinction, reinforcement, punishment	These narrowly focused, process-oriented theories assume a weak role for maturation, a strong role for experience, and a highly active role for the developing individual.
Social Cognitive Learning			
Bandura	Learning behavior, cognitive response patterns, social roles	Imitation, social learning, modeling, cognitive learning, reciprocal determinism, skills, capabilities	This moderately focused, process-oriented theory assumes a weak role for maturation, a strong role for experience, and a highly active role for the developing individual.
Cognitive			
Piaget	Cognitive (thinking, problem solving)	Schemes, assimilation, accommodation, equilibrium, mental space, routinization of schemes	This moderately focused stage theory assumes a strong role for maturation, a moderate role for experience, and a moderately active role for the developing individual.
Case, Fischer	Cognitive (problem-solving skills and capabilities)	Skill acquisition, optimal level of performance, higher-level skills	These moderately focused, process-oriented theories assume a moderate role for both maturation and experience and a highly active role for the developing individual.
Information processing	Cognitive (steps and processes involved in problem solving and other mental abilities)	Sensory register, short-term memory (STM), long-term memory (LTM), metacognition, knowledge base, control processes	This narrowly focused, process-oriented theory assumes a strong role for maturation, a moderate role for experience, and a highly active role for the developing individual.
Contextual			
Bronfenbrenner	Contextual (inter-active contextual influences)	Ecological contexts; microsystem, ecosystem, mesosystem, macrosystem	This broadly focused, process-oriented theory assumes a strong role for maturation, a moderate role for experience, and a highly active role for the developing individual.
Vygotsky	Contextual (cultural/historical influences)	Dialogues, zone of proximal development	This moderately focused, process-oriented theory assumes a weak role for maturation, a strong role for experience, and a highly active role for the developing individual.
Elder	Individual change within changing social and historical contexts	Education, work, and family forming social trajectories (pathways) that guide development	This broadly focused, process-oriented theory assumes a weak role for maturation, a strong role for experience, and a highly active role for the developing individual.

However, uncritical reliance on theories poses several pitfalls. Because theories guide and direct our perceptions of and thinking about people, reliance on a given theory may lead us to focus on certain aspects of development, make certain assumptions, and draw conclusions about development that are consistent with the theory but not necessarily accurate. For example, overreliance on Piaget's cognitive approach may lead a teacher to underestimate the contributions of social and emotional factors to a child's academic difficulties. Similarly, parents who interpret their child's irresponsible behavior in terms of psychological conflict may overlook the fact that the same behavior is frequently modeled and reinforced by the child's older sibling. Finally, the emphasis many developmental theories place on shared or even universal developmental trends may underestimate the role of individual differences in life conditions, events, and personal choices people face throughout their lives.

As you read the chapters that follow, notice that the theories are applied selectively based on the ages and developmental issues being discussed. We encourage you to refer back to this chapter whenever you have questions about the material and to make your own judgments about which theory (or theories) fits best. Finally, keep an eye on how your own theories of development change as you read the book and talk with your instructor and classmates. By the end of the course, if not sooner, you are likely to have a much clearer idea of your preferred theoretical orientation(s), as well as a much clearer perspective of what development is all about.

Chapter Summary

- **What are developmental theories, and how are they useful?** Theories are useful in organizing and explaining the process of development and in stimulating and guiding developmental research, theory, and practice. Theories differ in the degree to which they emphasize maturation versus experience, continuous versus stagelike development, and the individual's active versus passive participation.

- **How have psychodynamic theories influenced thinking about development?** Freud's and Erikson's theories see development as a dynamic process that occurs in a series of stages, each involving psychological conflicts that the developing person must resolve. According to Freud, personality development is energized by the conflicting functions of the id, ego, and superego. Erikson's theory outlines eight developmental stages that encompass the entire lifespan; by resolving the basic crisis of each stage—such as trust versus mistrust in infancy or intimacy versus isolation in young adulthood—the developing person attains what Erikson terms a *virtue*. Thus, for instance, the infant who resolves the trust/mistrust crisis attains the virtue of hope; the young adult who resolves the intimacy/isolation crisis attains love. Psychodynamic theories help us to understand the importance of attachment in intimate relationships throughout life and to conceptualize the process of identity formation in adolescence, to name just two lifespan applications.

- **How have developmental theories based on learning theories contributed to our understanding of developmental change?** Pavlov's theory emphasizes learning through classical conditioning as the main process through which developmental changes occur. Skinner's operant conditioning theory emphasizes the influence of reinforcement, punishment, extinction, and shaping on developmental change. Bandura's social cognitive theory emphasizes reciprocal and interactional processes involving direct, observational learning, modeling, and vicarious reinforcement. Learning theories have applications across the lifespan, particularly in helping us to understand the influence of learning on development and helping individuals modify or eliminate problematic behavior and learn new, desirable behaviors.

- **How do cognitive developmental theories help us to understand changes in thinking and problem solving throughout childhood and adolescence?** Piaget's theory explains the underlying structures and processes involved in the development of children's thinking and problem solving. Piaget suggested that thinking develops in a series of increasingly complex and sophisticated stages, each of which incorporates the achievements of those preceding it. The developing person achieves new ways of thinking and problem solving through the joint processes of assimilation (fitting a new scheme into an existing one) and accommodation (changing an existing scheme to meet the challenges of a new situation).

Neo-Piagetian theorists Robbie Case and Kurt Fischer emphasize the role of mental space, skills acquisition, and information-processing capacity in cognitive development. Information-processing theory focuses on the steps involved in thinking. Information is stored in the sensory register, then in short-term memory, and finally in long-term memory. As people grow older, they experience cognitive changes in control processes, metacognition, and their knowledge bases. Cognitive theories help us to understand and foster intellectual development, problem-solving abilities, and critical thinking skills throughout the lifespan.

- **How have contextual approaches to development broadened our view of developmental change?**
Bronfenbrenner's ecological systems theory proposes that the microsystem, microsystem, exosystem, and macrosystem form interactive and overlapping contexts for development. Vygotsky emphasizes the contribution of history and culture to development, which takes place within a child's zone of proximal development. Elder suggests that education, work, and family create the social trajectories, or pathways, that guide individual development. Etiological theory focuses on the developmental roles of behavioral dispositions and trails, such as temperament and attachment, that are thought to have evolutionary survival value for the human species. These theories are very useful in explaining how development throughout the life course interacts with and is influenced by the context in which that development occurs.

- **How does comparing developmental theories help us to understand developmental change?**
Although developmental theories differ in both focus and explanatory concepts, together they provide a comprehensive view of the process or developmental change. By systematically organizing what we already know about development and proposing explanations that can lie tested through formal and informal observations, developmental theories are so useful for experts and non-experts alike that they are well worth the effort required to understand them.

Key Terms

accommodation (p. 45)
adaptation (p. 45)
assimilation (p. 44)
attachment (p. 40)
behavior modification (p. 43)
classical conditioning (p. 40)

ego (p. 35)
id (p. 35)
information-processing theory (p. 45)
metacognition (p. 47)
observational learning (p. 42)
operant conditioning (p. 41)

punishment (p. 42)
reinforcement (p. 41)
scheme (p. 44)
social trajectory (p. 48)
superego (p. 35)
zone of proximal development (p. 48)

Beginnings

PART 2

Source: Halfpoint/Shutterstock.com.

Chapter 3
Genetics

Chapter 4
Prenatal Development and Birth

Although you may think human development starts in infancy, it actually begins at the moment of conception. We become individuals partly because of our genetic endowments, which are determined the moment sperm meets egg; partly because of events we experience will still in our mothers' wombs; and partly because of events that occur in the wider environment.

The next two chapters look at these influences, showing some of the ways heredity and environment impact who a child becomes physically, cognitively, and socially. These chapters will describe what happens during the thirty-eight weeks or so before birth, as well as the events surrounding birth itself. By childbirth the baby has already undergone many changes, and there will be many more changes throughout his or her life.

Genetics

CHAPTER 3

Source: 2TiYA/Shutterstock.com.

Chapter Outline

Mechanisms of Genetic Transmission
Individual Genetic Expression
Dominant and Recessive Genes
Genetic Abnormalities
Genetic Counseling and Prenatal Diagnosis
Relative Influence of Heredity and Environment
Looking Back/Looking Forward

Focusing Questions

- How does inheritance work?
- How are genetic differences usually transmitted from one generation to the next?
- How can experts help parents discover and respond to potential genetic problems?
- How do heredity and environment jointly influence development?

Inheritance affects a vast number of human qualities, from the color of our eyes and how tall we are to more complex characteristics, such as athletic ability, intelligence, and temperament. We begin this section by describing the basic biological processes involved in human reproduction and how genetic information from two parents is combined and conveyed to their children. Next, we discuss genetic abnormalities. Then we address an issue that psychologists have found especially important: the relationship between heredity and environment and how both contribute to individual development. Finally, we describe ways to use knowledge of these relationships to benefit parents, their children, and their children's children.

sperm Male gametes, or reproductive cells; produced in the testicles.

ovum The reproductive cell, or gamete, of the female; the egg cell.

gene A molecular structure, carried on chromosomes, containing genetic information; the basic unit of heredity.

chromosome A threadlike, rod-shaped structure containing genetic information that is transmitted from parents to children; each human sperm or egg cell contains twenty-three chromosomes, and these determine a person's inherited characteristics.

zygote The single new cell formed when a sperm cell attaches itself to the surface of an ovum (egg).

Mechanisms of Genetic Transmission

The process by which genetic information is combined and transmitted begins with *gametes*, the reproductive cells of a child's parents. In the father, the gametes are produced in the testicles, and each is called a **sperm** cell. In the mother, they develop in the ovaries, and each is called an **ovum**, or *egg cell*. The sperm and egg cells contain genetic information in molecular structures called **genes**, which form threads called **chromosomes**. Thus, the chromosomes contain the genetic material the child will inherit from the parent. Each human sperm or egg cell contains twenty-three chromosomes. All other cells of the body contain forty-six chromosomes and approximately one hundred thousand genes. A single chromosome may contain as many as twenty thousand genes. Figure 3.1 shows pictures, or *karyotypes,* of the chromosomes for a normal human male. Figure 3.2 illustrates the genetic structures involved.

The Role of DNA

The genes themselves are made of *DNA (deoxyribonucleic acid)*, the complex protein code of genetic information that directs the form and function of each body cell as it develops. DNA shares this information at conception, when a sperm from the father penetrates an egg from the mother, releasing their chromosomes, which join to form a new cell called a **zygote**. To accomplish this, reproductive cells, or gametes, divide by a process called *meiosis* and recombine into a zygote at conception. All of the other cells that make up a unique human being will develop from this original zygote through a simple division of their genes, chromosomes, and other cellular parts by means of a process called *mitosis*.

Meiosis and Mitosis

Meiosis involves the following steps. First, the twenty-three chromosomes of the egg or sperm) cell duplicate themselves. Then they break up into smaller pieces and randomly exchange segments of genetic material with one another. Next, the new chromosome pairs divide to form two separate cells. Finally, the two new cells divide again. Each of the four new cells contains a unique set of genetic material in its twenty-three chromosomes, *one-half* the usual number of chromosomes carried by all other cells. This ensures that the new, single-cell zygote that forms during conception will contain the normal forty-six chromosomes: twenty-three chromosomes from the egg and twenty-three from the sperm. Figure 3.3 illustrates the process of meiosis for sperm cells. The process for egg cells is the same.

Once the zygote forms, it and all of its descendants divide through the process of mitosis. Mitosis involves the following steps. First, the twenty-three pairs of chromosomes of a cell form a duplicate set. Next, the two sets of chromosomes move to opposite sides of the cell. Finally, a new wall forms between them, resulting in two new, identical cells, each containing the same unique set of chromosomes, genes, and DNA-based genetic code that will help guide the new organisms development. Figure 3.4 depicts the process of mitosis.

FIGURE 3.1
Chromosomes for the Normal Human Male and Female

This karyotype depicts the twenty-two pairs of chromosomes and the two sex chromosomes for the normal human male (top) and normal human female (bottom). The twenty-third pair of chromosomes determines whether the human will be male (XY) or female (XX).
Source: YKh/Shutterstock.com.

The human body contains 100 trillion cells.

There is a **nucleus** inside each human cell (except red blood cells).

Each nucleus contains 46 **chromosomes**, arranged in 23 pairs.

One **chromosome** of every pair is from each parent.

The chromosomes are filled with tightly coiled strands of **DNA**.

Genes are segments of DNA that contain instructions to make proteins—the building blocks of life.

FIGURE 3.2 Genetic Structures

Part 2 Beginnings

The Process of Meiosis for Sperm Cells

Cell with 46 chromosomes (only one pair of homologous chromosomes is shown here). Each member of the pair has begun to replicate similar to mitotic cell division.

First meiotic cell division begins, but does not proceed as in mitosis. Instead of the replicated chromosome splitting apart, one member of each homologous pair becomes a part of the first-generation daughter cell.

The second meiotic division proceeds after the first is completed; now the replicated chromosome acquired in the first-generation daughter cell splits apart.

Each of the four gametes produced by the two-step process now has acquired one member of the pair of homologous chromosomes.

FIGURE 3.3 The Process of Meiosis for Sperm Cells

As meiosis begins, DNA replicates. However, before the replicated arms split apart, one member of each pair of chromosomes moves to become part of each first-generation daughter cell. Once the first generation of daughter cells is established, the DNA copies itself and then splits as part of the second meiotic division. Thus, one copy of one member of the pair of chromosomes is contributed to each second-generation daughter cell. These two successive divisions produce four cells, each with twenty-three chromosomes.

The Process of Mitosis

Cell nucleus with a pair of chromosomes

Chromosomes split and replicate to produce two identical pairs

The pairs separate, and the cell divides

Each daughter cell now has a pair of chromosomes that is identical to the original pair

FIGURE 3.4
The Process of Mitosis

Mitotic cell division produces nearly all the cells of the body except the gametes. During mitosis, each chromosome replicates to form two chromosomes with identical genetic blueprints. As the cell divides, one member of each identical pair becomes a member of each daughter cell. In this manner, complete genetic endowment is replicated in nearly every cell of the body.

Individual Genetic Expression

How does the genetic information contained in our cells influence the development of our unique physical, intellectual, social, and emotional characteristics? In the following section, we explore this question.

Genotype and Phenotype

Genotype refers to the specific genetic information a person inherits that has the potential to influence his or her observable physical or behavioral characteristics or traits such as

genotype The set of genetic traits inherited by an individual. See also *phenotype*.

Chapter 3 Genetics 61

> **What Do You Think?**
>
> A good way to check your understanding of rather complex material is to explain it to another person. Team up with a classmate and explain the roles of meiosis and mitosis to him or her in your own words. Then ask your classmate to explain it back to you. What unanswered questions do you still have?

phenotype The set of traits an individual actually displays during development; reflects the evolving product of genotype and experience. See also *genotype*.

eye color, height, intelligence, or shyness. **Phenotype** refers to the physical and behavioral traits an individual actually exhibits, such as blue eyes; a height of five feet, ten inches; a certain intelligence test score; or a certain level of shyness. A person's phenotype is always the product of the interactions of that person's genotype with the environmental influences that occur from the formation of the first cell at conception onward.

In some cases, there is a close match between a person's original genotype and the phenotype that results. For example, inheriting genes for blue eyes generally results in actually having blue eyes. In other cases, phenotype does not coincide so closely with genotype. Two newborn infants may have inherited the identical genotype for weight at the time of conception, but one may end up heavier (or lighter) than the other because of differences in prenatal nutrition as well as diet and exercise during infancy and childhood. On the other hand, children with different genotypes for weight may end up the same weight (the same phenotype), one through dieting and the other simply by eating whatever she wanted.

Dominant and Recessive Genes

dominant gene In any paired set of genes, the gene with greater influence in determining characteristics that are physically visible or manifest.

recessive gene In any paired set of genes, the gene that influences or determines physical characteristics only when no dominant gene is present.

Genes are inherited in pairs, one from each parent. Some genes are dominant and others are recessive. A **dominant gene** will influence a child's phenotype even if it is paired with a recessive gene. A **recessive gene**, however, must be paired with another recessive gene to be able to influence the phenotype. If it is paired with a dominant gene, its influence will be controlled or blocked. More than one thousand human characteristics appear to follow the dominant-recessive pattern of inheritance (McKussick, 1988, 1995). Table 3.1 lists a number of common dominant and recessive traits.

Eye color is a good example. Suppose human eyes came in only two colors, blue and brown. Because blue eyes are a recessive trait and brown eyes are a dominant trait, a child's eyes will be blue only if he has received the appropriate blue-producing gene from both parents. If he has received it from only one parent or from neither, he will end up with brown eyes.

Transmission of Multiple Variations

allele One of several alternative forms of a gene.

The genes responsible for eye color—and, in fact, for many other traits—often take on two or more alternative forms called **alleles**. In addition to alleles for blue and brown, the gene responsible for eye color occasionally takes on a third allele, which often leads to hazel or green eyes. A person who inherits two identical alleles for a particular trait is said to be *homozygous* for that trait. A person who inherits two different alleles for the trait is said to be *heterozygous* for that trait. In the case of eye color, a heterozygous person (one brown and one blue/hazel/green allele) will therefore show the phenotype of the dominant allele and thus have brown eyes. Only a person who is homozygous will display the phenotype of one of the recessive alleles and have blue or hazel eyes. From a genetic standpoint, there are three times as many ways to have brown eyes as there are to have blue/green ones. Figure 3.5 illustrates this example.

Keep in mind, however, that although all of the patterns of inheritance for dominant and recessive traits are possible, each genotype will not necessarily occur in each family, since genes are inherited randomly. In Figure 3.5 (example 1), for instance, although it is possible that the parents will have children with the eye color genotypes of BB, Bb, bB, or bb, all of their children may in reality be BB or bb. Thus, the increased probability of a particular genotype, such as Bb, does not mean that genotype will definitely be seen. In contrast, in

62 Part 2 Beginnings

TABLE 3.1 Some Common Dominant and Recessive Traits

Dominant Trait	Recessive Trait	Dominant Trait	Recessive Trait
Brown eyes	Gray, green, hazel, or blue eyes	Short fingers	Fingers of normal length
Hazel or green eyes	Blue eyes	Double-fingers	Normally jointed fingers
Normal vision	Nearsightedness	Double-jointedness	Normal joints
Farsightedness	Normal vision	Type A blood	Type O blood
Normal color vision	Red-green color blindness	Type B blood	Type O blood
Brown or black hair	Blond hair	Rh positive blood	Rh negative blood
Nonred hair	Red hair	Normal blood clotting	Hemophilia
Curly or wavy hair	Straight hair	Normal red blood cells	Sickle-cell disease
Full head of hair	Baldheadedness	Normal protein metabolism	Phenylketonuria (PKU)
Normal hearing	Some forms of congenital deafness	Normal physiology	Tay-Sachs disease
Normally pigmented skin	Albino (completely white) skin	Huntington disease	Normal central nervous system functioning in adulthood
Facial dimples	No dimples	Immunity to poison ivy	Susceptibility to poison ivy
Thick lips	Thin lips		

Note: Many common traits show dominant or recessive patterns. Also, a pattern sometimes may be dominant with respect to one trait but recessive with respect to another.

FIGURE 3.5 Genetic Transmission of Eye Color

Example 1: Three out of four offspring will have brown eyes, and one out of four will have blue eyes. *Example 2:* Two out of four offspring will have brown eyes, and two out of four will have blue eyes.

Example 1: Both parents heterozygous

Mother: Brown Eyes (heterozygous) / Father: Brown Eyes (heterozygous)

	B	b
B	BB (homozygous)	Bb (heterozygous)
b	Bb (heterozygous)	BB (homozygous)

Example 2: One parents heterozygous and one parent homozygous

Mother: Brown Eyes (heterozygous) / Father: Blue Eyes (homozygous)

	B	b
b	Bb (heterozygous)	bb (homozygous)
b	Bb (heterozygous)	bb (homozygous)

Key: B = gene for brown eyes, which is dominant for eye color
b = gene for blue eyes, which is recessive for eye color

the genetic transmission of a sex-linked trait such as hemophilia (discussed shortly), all daughters in a given family are carriers and all sons are affected (see Figure 3.7, page 67).

Many genes have more than two alleles. As a result, the traits they govern can vary in more-complex ways. The four major human blood types, for example, are based on three

Chapter 3 Genetics 63

	Possible Alleles from Mother		
	A	B	o
A	AA	AB	Ao
B	AB	BB	Bo
o	AO	BO	oo

Possible Alleles from Father

FIGURE 3.6
Inheritance of Blood Type

In blood type inheritance, both A and B alleles are dominant, and the O allele is recessive. Therefore, the following proportions of blood types are likely to occur in the general population: Type A (AA or Ao): 3/9; Type B (BB or Bo): 3/9; Type AB: 2/9; Type O (oo): 1/9.

alleles of the same gene. Two of these alleles, type A and type B, are dominant forms, and the O allele is recessive. Figure 3.6 illustrates how these three alleles for blood type can combine in six possible ways but produce only four blood types, A, B, O, and AB. The AB blood type is an example of *codominance,* a situation in which the characteristics of both alleles are independently expressed in a new phenotype rather than one or the other being dominant, or as a mixture of the two. Because each blood type has a unique chemistry that allows it to mix only with certain other blood types, determining the compatible blood genotype is very important for people who receive blood transfusions.

Polygenic Transmission

Unlike eye color and blood type, which can vary only in a limited number of qualitatively distinct ways, the inheritance of most physical traits (including height, weight, hair and skin color, and complex personality) and behavioral traits (such as intelligence, shyness, alcoholism, and depression) do not fit the simple single-gene model just described. These traits are called *polygenic,* meaning they involve *many* genes, each with small effects, as well as environmental influences. In all of these cases, children show a marked tendency to have a phenotype that is intermediate between those of their parents, and for the most part the exact mechanisms of inheritance for such traits are still unknown (Owen & McGuffin, 1994).

Because polygenic phenotypes vary by small degrees, environment can influence them in relatively important ways. An overweight person can become more slender through a change in diet, for example, and a shy person can learn to be more outgoing. Such experiences matter less for traits that are simply transmitted by a single gene; there is no way to change eye color, even though you can cover your irises with tinted contact lenses.

The Determination of Sex

Whether a person becomes male or female depends on events at conception. All ova, or egg cells, contain a single X chromosome, whereas a sperm cell may contain either an X or a Y. If a Y-bearing sperm happens to fertilize the egg, a male (XY) zygote develops; if the sperm is X-bearing, a female (XX) zygote develops (see Figure 3.1).

During the first several weeks following conception, both male and female embryos possess a set of bisexual gonadal (sex) tissues, meaning they can develop either male or female sex structures. However, between the fourth and eighth weeks, gonadal tissue develops into testes or ovaries depending on the presence or absence of a small section of the Y chromosome, referred to as *TDF* or *testis-determining factor.* Ova fertilized by a Y-bearing sperm have TDF, and male embryos result (Page et al., 1987). More Y sperm than X sperm succeed in fertilizing the ovum, resulting in about 30 percent more male than female zygotes. By birth, however, boy babies outnumber girl babies by only about 6 percent on average, and by age thirty-five, women begin to outnumber men, suggesting that males may be more genetically vulnerable than females. Much of this vulnerability is related to *sex-linked transmission.* Unlike females, who carry XX chromosomes, males carry XY chromosome pairs. Because the Y chromosome is much shorter than its matching X chromosome - and therefore may lack many of the gene locations of the X chromosome - many genes from the mother may not be matched or counteracted with equivalent genetic material from the father. As a result, genetic abnormalities on the single, complete X chromosome are more likely to result in phenotypic abnormalities in males than in females. Table 3.2 lists a number of **sex-linked recessive traits**, abnormalities that are transmitted on the single, complete X chromosome.

sex-linked recessive traits Recessive traits resulting from genes on the X chromosome.

One such trait is *hemophilia,* an inability of the blood to clot and therefore to stop itself from flowing. Because clotting is so slow, internal bleeding can at times be life threatening (American College of Obstetricians and Gynecologists [ACOG], 1990; McKussick, 1995). Because the gene for hemophilia is located on the X chromosome, a female carrier is protected by having a normal gene on her second X chromosome. Each of her children will have a fifty-fifty chance of inheriting the abnormal gene. Daughters who get the gene will be carriers, like their mother, while sons will develop hemophilia because they lack a second X chromosome to counteract the gene's effects. Figure 3.7 illustrates this effect.

TABLE 3.2 Sex-Linked Recessive Traits

Condition	Description
Colorblindness	Inability to distinguish certain colors, usually reds and greens
Hemophilia	Deficiency in substances that allow the blood to clot; also known as bleeder's disease
Muscular dystrophy	Weakening and wasting away of muscles, beginning in childhood (Duchenne's form)
Diabetes (two forms)	Inability to metabolize sugars properly because the body does not produce enough insulin
Anhidrotic ectodermal dysplasia	Lack of sweat glands and teeth
Night blindness (certain forms)	Inability to see in dark or very dim conditions
Deafness (certain forms)	Impaired hearing or total hearing loss
Atrophy of optic nerve	Gradual deterioration of vision and eventual blindness

Note: All of the above traits are carried by the X chromosome, and all are recessive. As a result, they occur less often in females than in males.

Most human characteristics that have been studied follow the pattern of dominant-recessive and codominant inherence, and in most instances, a gene that has been inherited influences development in the same manner whether it was contributed by the biological mother or father. However, geneticists have discovered a new mode of inheritance called **genetic imprinting**, in which genes are chemically marked, or *imprinted,* such that the member of the chromosome pair contributed by either the father or the mother is activated, regardless of its genetic makeup. This imprint is most often temporary and may disappear in the next generation (Cassidy, 1995).

Genetic Abnormalities

Once in a while, genetic reproduction goes wrong. Sometimes too many or too few chromosomes transfer to a newly forming zygote. Sometimes the chromosomes transfer properly but carry particular defective genes that affect a child physically, mentally, or both. The changes almost always create significant disabilities for the child, if they do not prove fatal. Table 3.3 lists some common genetic abnormalities and the risk of their presence at birth.

Disorders Due to Abnormal Chromosomes

Most of the time, inheriting one too many or one too few chromosomes proves fatal. In a few cases, however, children with an extra or a missing chromosome survive past birth and even live fairly normal lives. It is estimated that approximately one in every 156 births in Western countries involves a chromosomal abnormality (Milunsky, 1992). One such example is Down syndrome. Persons with Down syndrome usually have three number 21 chromosomes instead of two.

Down Syndrome

Down syndrome is also called *trisomy 21* because it is generally caused by an extra twenty-first chromosome or the translocation, or transfer, of part of the twenty-first chromosome onto another chromosome. People with this disorder have almond-shaped eyes, round heads, and stubby hands and feet. Many also have abnormalities of the heart and intestinal tract, and facial deformities. They also show greater than usual vulnerability to a number of serious diseases, such as leukemia. Most children with Down syndrome live until middle

genetic imprinting A mode of inheritance in which genes are chemically marked so that the number of the chromosome pair contributed by either the father or the mother is activated, regardless of its genetic makeup.

Down syndrome A congenital condition that causes intellectual disability.

TABLE 3.3 Risk of Selected Genetic Disorders

Disorder	Description	Risk of Having a Fetus with the Disorder — Overall	With One Affected Child
Chromosomal			
Down syndrome	Extra or translocated twenty-first chromosome. Symptoms include almond-shaped eyes, round head, stubby hands and feet, abnormalities of the heart and intestinal tract, facial deformities, and vulnerability to disease. Most children with Down syndrome live until middle adulthood, but about 14 percent die by age one and 21 percent die by age ten.	1/700	1–2 percent
Klinefelter syndrome (XXY)	At least one extra chromosome, usually an X. Affected individual is phenotypically male, but has small testes and is sterile.	1/500 men	N/S[1]
Fragile X syndrome	The most common inherited form of intellectual disability. Caused by an abnormal gene on the bottom end of the X chromosome. Causes spectrum of learning difficulties ranging from mild problems to severe intellectual disability.	1/4,000 male births 1/8,000 female births	N/S[1]
Turner syndrome (XO)	Affects only females born with a single X in the sex chromosome. Are very short as adults, "webbed" necks and ears set lower than usual; fail to develop secondary sexual characteristics; problems with spatial judgment, memory, and reasoning.	1/2,500 women	N/S[1]
Dominant Gene			
Polydactyly	Extra fingers or toes. One of the most common anomalies affecting the hands or feet. Correctable by surgery.	1/300–1/100	50 percent
Achondroplasia	Rare disorder of the skeleton; most common form of dwarfism; afflicted person has shorter than normal arms and legs, large head, physical developmental delays, normal intelligence and lifespan.	1/40,000–1/15,000	50 percent
Huntington disease	Usually first affects people in their thirties and forties; gradual deterioration of the central nervous system, causing uncontrollable movements, mental deterioration, and death.	1/15,000	50 percent
Recessive Gene			
Cystic fibrosis	The most common genetic disease among white persons of Northern European descent. Abnormally thick mucus clogs the lungs, causing serious difficulties in breathing and digestion, delayed growth and sexual maturation, high vulnerability to infection, and shortened life expectancy.	1/2,500 white persons (risk of being a carrier is 1/25)	25 percent
Sickle-cell disease	Abnormal, sickle-shaped red blood cells clog blood vessels, reducing blood supply and causing pain. May cause increased bacterial infections and degeneration of brain, kidneys, liver, heart, spleen, and muscles. Shortened lifespan.	1/500 African Americans (risk of being a carrier is 1/12)	25 percent
Tay-Sachs disease	Found mostly in persons of Eastern European Jewish descent. Chemical imbalance of central nervous system. Symptoms first occur at six months of age, progressively causing severe intellectual disability, blindness, seizures, and death by third year due to lowered resistance to disease.	1/3,000 Eastern European Jews (risk of being a carrier is 1/30–1/300)	25 percent

TABLE 3.3 Risk of Selected Genetic Disorders *continued*

		\multicolumn{2}{c}{Risk of Having a Fetus with the Disorder}
Disorder	**Description**	**Overall**	**With One Affected Child**
X Linked			
Hemophilia	Lack of substance needed for blood clotting. Risk of life-threatening internal bleeding; risk of AIDS from transfusions.	1/5,000 male babies	50 percent for boy, 0 percent for girl
Multifactorial			
Congenital heart disease	Structural and/or electrical abnormalities of the heart; most common type of birth defect in the United States. May respond to medication or corrective surgery performed after birth.	1/125	2–4 percent
Neural tube defect	Serious birth defect of the spine and brain in which the tube enclosing the spine fails to close completely or normally; significant cause of infant mortality and childhood morbidity worldwide. Brain may be absent or underdeveloped (anencephaly), or spinal cord and nerve bundles may be exposed. Death or severe intellectual disability or other long-term problems for children who survive.	1–2/1,000	2–5 percent
Cleft lip/cleft palate	Gap or space in lip or hole in roof of mouth. May cause difficulties in breathing, speech, hearing, and eating. Corrective surgery at birth can repair most clefts.	1/600	2–4 percent

[1]No significant increase.

Sources: ACOG (1995); CDC, (2011b); Diamond (1989); Hagerman (1996); LPCH (2013); NICHD (2012); NHGRI (2010); Selekman (1993); Stratford (1994); USNLM (2012; 2013); Yale School of Medicine (2013).

FIGURE 3.7
Inheritance of Hemophilia, a Sex-linked Disorder

In this example of the inheritance of hemophilia, the mother is a carrier of the disease. Each daughter has a 50 percent chance of inheriting a pair of normal chromosomes and a 50 percent chance of being a carrier like her mother. However, she herself will not be affected by the disorder because her second X chromosome protects her. Each son has a 50 percent chance of being healthy and a 50 percent chance of inheriting the abnormal chromosome and acquiring hemophilia. This is because, as a male, his second sex chromosome is a Y, which does not protect him from the disorder.

Source: Alila Medical Media/Shutterstock.com.

Unaffected father: X Y
Carrier mother: X X

Unaffected daughter: X X
Carrier daughter: X X
Unaffected son: X Y
Affected son: X Y

Hemophilia B
Hemophilia A
Chromosome X

Chapter 3 Genetics 67

> **What Do You Think?**
>
> Now that you know how eye color and blood type are inherited, see if you can figure out how you inherited *your* eye color. How about your blood type?

adulthood, but about 14 percent die by age one and 21 percent die by age ten. The rate of infant mortality among children with Down syndrome is eight times higher than the infant mortality rate of children without Down syndrome (Goldman, Urbano, & Hodapp, 2011).

Although children with Down syndrome achieve many of the same developmental milestones as normal children, as they get older, they fall developmentally farther and farther behind and never "catch up" with their peers. By adulthood, most individuals with Down syndrome plateau at a level of cognitive functioning that is now described as "moderate intellectual disability." They are able to learn and follow simple routines and hold routine jobs, but because they are easily confused by change and have difficulty in making important decisions usually cannot live independently and require ongoing support from their families and community service programs (Global Down Syndrome Foundation, 2017; Sloper et al., 1990; Stratford, 1994).

Down syndrome is much more frequent in babies of mothers over age thirty-five and among older fathers. As women grow older, they experience longer exposure to environmental hazards, such as chemicals and radiation, that may affect their ovaries. In addition, because a woman's ova are formed before she is born, they are likely to undergo progressive deterioration with age (Baird & Sadovnick, 1987; Feinbloom & Forman, 1987; Halliday et al., 1995). Older fathers are at risk because their sperm cells have divided so many times that many opportunities for errors exist (Angier, 1994). Figure 3.8 summarizes the risk of having a Down syndrome baby for women of different ages.

Disorders Due to Abnormal Genes

Even when a zygote has the proper number of chromosomes, it may inherit specific genes that can create serious medical problems for the child after birth. In many cases, these problems prove lethal. In others, genetic diseases are at least manageable, if not curable.

As Table 3.3 shows, there are four main types of genetic disorders: dominant gene disorders, recessive gene disorders, X-linked disorders, and multifactorial gene disorders.

Dominant Gene Disorders

Dominant gene disorders require only one abnormal gene from either parent to affect a child. When one parent has a dominant gene disorder, each child has a 50 percent chance of

Individuals with Down syndrome, like this man, learn slowly. But with special educational help and proper support (like the labeled stove in the photo), they can lead satisfying lives.

Source: Marcel Jancovic/Shutterstock.com.

> **What Do You Think?**
>
> Woody Guthrie, the famous folk singer and father of Arlo Guthrie (also a famous folk singer), died of Huntington disease. Based on your new knowledge about this disorder, what questions might you ask Arlo about how his genetic inheritance has affected his life decisions, such as whether or not to have children?

inheriting the dominant abnormal gene for the disorder—thereby acquiring the disorder—and a 50 percent chance of inheriting a pair of recessive genes and being unaffected.

Huntington disease is a dominant gene disorder that results in a gradual deterioration of the central nervous system, causing uncontrollable movements and mental deterioration. Typically, it does not appear until affected people are in their thirties or forties, and it always proves fatal. Before that age, people usually have no way of knowing whether they will get the disease (ACOG, 1995; Halliday et al., 1995; USNLM, 2013).

Researchers have identified specific sections of the human genome that are exclusively linked to Huntington disease. The gene for the disorder appears to be located on chromosome four in the *HTT* gene, which is involved in the production of a protein called "huntingtin." A genetic blood test for Huntington disease can detect the *HTT* mutation and, therefore, can accurately diagnose the condition, but an understanding of how the gene actually causes the disease and treatments remain elusive (Horgan, 1993; USNLM, 2013).

Recessive Gene Disorders

Recessive gene disorders can occur when the fetus inherits a pair of recessive genes, one from each parent. When both parents are carriers of a recessive gene disorder, each child faces the following possibilities: (1) a 25 percent chance of inheriting the pair of recessive genes required to have the disorder; (2) a 25 percent chance of inheriting a pair of dominant genes and being unaffected; or (3) a 50 percent chance of inheriting one dominant and one recessive gene and being a carrier, like both parents.

Relationship Between Maternal Age and the Incidence of Down Syndrome

FIGURE 3.8

Relationship between Maternal Age and the Incidence of Down Syndrome

As women get older, their chances of giving birth to a baby with Down syndrome increase. At maternal age twenty-one, one in every 1,500 babies is born with Down syndrome. At maternal age thirty-four, one in every 746 babies is born with Down syndrome, increasing to 1 in 150 babies by maternal age 39. By maternal age forty-nine, one in ten babies is born with Down syndrome.

Chapter 3 Genetics

Sickle-Cell Disease

About one in 500 African Americans is affected with sickle-cell disease, and about one in twelve is a carrier of it. Sickle-cell disease is especially common in people whose families come from Africa, South or Central America (especially Panama), the Caribbean islands, Mediterranean countries (such as Turkey, Greece, and Italy), India, and Saudi Arabia (ACOG, 1995; NHLBI, 2012b). In the United States, sickle-cell disease is most prevalent among African Americans, but more than one out of every 36,000 Latinx Americans also suffer from it. In **sickle-cell disease**, the oxygen-carrying protein in the red blood cells takes on an abnormal, rigid sickle shape inside the cells, which get caught in the blood vessels, cutting off circulation, reducing oxygen supply, and causing pain. Other symptoms include increased bacterial infections and degeneration of organs that need a great deal of oxygen, including the brain, kidneys, liver, heart, spleen, and muscles. Individuals who are *heterozygous,* meaning they carry just one abnormal sickle-cell allele along with one dominant, nonsickle-cell allele, show a few signs of sickle-cell disease but also a strong immunity to malaria. Most live normal lives, but when deprived of sufficient oxygen, such as during intense physical exercise or at high altitudes, the sickling of their red blood cells can be triggered, causing pain. Individuals avoid sickle-cell disease completely by having two dominant genes or suffer badly from it because they have two recessive genes.

Although no cure exists for this disease, infants with sickle-cell disease must be given daily doses of antibiotics beginning at two months of age to reduce the chance of infection. Blood transfusions, pain medications, fluids, and hydroxyurea—a medication that stimulates the production of fetal hemoglobin, a type produced by babies that does not sickle—are also commonly used to treat sickle-cell disease. In the past, the majority of victims died before age twenty, and few lived past age forty (Diamond, 1989; Selekman, 1993). Enhanced medical care now enables people with sickle-cell disease to live to age fifty and beyond (USNLM, 2013).

sickle-cell disease A genetically transmitted condition in which a person's red blood cells intermittently acquire a curved, sickle shape. The condition sometimes can clog circulation in the small blood vessels.

Multifactorial Disorders

Multifactorial disorders result from a combination of genetic and environmental factors. The incidence of these disorders varies widely in different parts of the world, largely because of the great differences in existing environmental conditions. Table 3.3 describes a number of these disorders.

Genetic Counseling and Prenatal Diagnosis

Some genetic problems can be reduced or avoided with the help of genetic counseling. Couples likely to benefit from counseling include those who may carry genetic disorders, know of relatives with genetic disorders, or belong to an ethnic group at risk for a particular disorder, such as African Americans, who are at risk for sickle-cell disease. More immediate signs of genetic risk include the birth of an infant with some genetic disorder or the spontaneous abortion of earlier pregnancies. Table 3.4 presents guidelines for determining who should seek prenatal genetic counseling.

Genetic counselors use potential parents' medical and genetic histories and tests to help couples estimate their chances of having a healthy baby and discuss alternatives from which a couple can choose. One obvious alternative is to avoid conception completely and, perhaps, to adopt a baby. A second is to take the risk in the hope of conceiving a healthy baby. Modern methods of prenatal diagnosis can now be used to detect genetic disorders after conception but before birth, allowing the parents the choice of terminating pregnancy during the first trimester if a serious problem is detected. In addition, medical intervention early in infancy may help repair damage caused by a genetic disorder, depending on its severity. Finally, *preimplantation diagnosis,* which refers to a variety of methods to screen ova (eggs) and early embryos *before* they are implanted into the uterus, are being developed as an alternative to prenatal screening, which can be used only after a pregnancy has been established (see the "Focusing On" feature).

Most methods of preimplantation diagnosis use *in vitro* or "test tube" fertilization to identify the presence of recessive genes for hereditary and genetic conditions by selecting

TABLE 3.4 Who Should Seek Prenatal Counseling?

1. Couples who already have a child with some serious defect such as Down syndrome, spina bifida, congenital heart disease, limb malformation, or intellectual disability
2. Couples with a family history of a genetic disease or intellectual disability
3. Couples who are blood relatives (first or second cousins)
4. African Americans, Ashkenazi Jews, Italians, Greeks, and other high-risk ethnic groups
5. Women who have had a serious infection early in pregnancy (rubella or toxoplasmosis) or who have been infected with HIV
6. Women who have taken potentially harmful medications early in pregnancy or habitually use drugs or alcohol
7. Women who have had X-rays taken early in pregnancy
8. Women who have experienced two or more of the following: stillbirth, death of a newborn baby, miscarriage
9. Any woman thirty-five years or older

Source: Adapted from Feinbloom & Forman (1987, p. 129) and Simpson, Holzgreve, & Driscoll (2012).

for fertilization only those eggs that appear to be free of abnormalities. Proponents of this method believe it is a more suitable option for couples who are opposed to abortion or may have difficulty deciding to terminate a pregnancy in which the fetus may be at risk. Some critics have questioned the accuracy of the method. Others are concerned that techniques designed solely to screen embryos based on carefully considered and ethically acceptable medical reasons, will be used as a new form of *eugenics* to engineer "better babies," based on beliefs or prejudices about which human qualities are desirable and which are not, thus limiting the gene pool on which human diversity depends (Hubbard, 1993; Pappert, 1993).

Table 3.5 describes current diagnostic techniques to screen for genetic disorders. In addition, medical intervention early in infancy may help repair damage caused by a genetic disorder, depending on the severity.

Differences in cultural beliefs and expectations can affect who receives genetic counseling and the forms it takes. The "A Multicultural View" feature discusses this issue.

Relative Influence of Heredity and Environment

Untangling the effects of heredity, or nature, from those of environment, or nurture, has become the special focus of behavior genetics. *Behavior genetics* is the scientific study of how genetic inheritance *(genotype)* and environmental experience jointly influence physical and behavioral development *(phenotype).*

Key Concepts of Behavior Genetics

Every characteristic of an organism is the result of the unique interaction between the organism's genetic inheritance and the sequence of environments through which it has passed during its development. For some traits, variations in environment have minimal effect. Thus, once the genotype is known, the eventual form or phenotype of the organism is pretty well specified. For other traits, knowing the genetic makeup may be a poor predictor of the eventual phenotype. Only by specifying both the genotype and the environmental sequence can the character, or phenotype, of the organism be predicted.

Range of Reaction

Range of reaction refers to the range of possible phenotypes an individual with a particular genotype might exhibit in response to the specific sequence of environmental influences

range of reaction The range of possible phenotypes that an individual with a particular genotype might exhibit in response to the particular sequence of environmental influences he or she experiences.

Chapter 3 Genetics 71

Focusing On . . .

Technological Alternatives to Natural Conception

Earlier in this century, the only alternative for couples who were infertile was to adopt a child or to remain childless. But today's medical techniques offer a growing number of alternative options. These **assisted reproductive technologies (ARTs)** vary in practicality and popularity, but from a strictly medical standpoint, they all work fairly reliably. We will focus on two procedures that account for 97 percent of all pregnancies involving ARTs.

Artificial (donor) insemination (DI) is used in cases where infertility is caused by problems in sperm quality or production. In this procedure, fresh or previously frozen sperm from a donor are inserted into the woman's vagina and held in place for a few hours. While in most cases the donor is anonymous, he can also be a friend or a relative. Artificial insemination is safe and easy to carry out and induces pregnancy as effectively as does normal intercourse between fertile partners—a 10 to 20 percent success rate in any one month (Liebmann-Smith, 1993; van der Westerlaken, Naaktgeboren, & Helmerhorst, 1998; Silber, 1991). A controversial application of artificial insemination is *surrogate mothering*, in which sperm from the future father are inserted into the womb of a woman who agrees (usually for a fee) to give up the baby once it is born.

In vitro fertilization (IVF) is used if both eggs and sperm are normal and infertility is caused by blocked fallopian tubes that cannot be surgically repaired. With IVF, ovulation is induced with medications that cause multiple eggs to be produced. With the aid of a laparoscope and ultrasound, one or more eggs are then removed through the woman's vagina under local anesthesia. They are either mixed in a laboratory dish with sperm from the male and are allowed to fertilize in an incubator, or more commonly, a single sperm can be injected directly into the egg. Two days later, the fertilized egg or embryo is transferred back into the woman's uterus through her vagina. Additional embryos can be frozen (cryopreserved) for future use. With IVF, fertilization rates are high, although birth rates resulting from this procedure vary, depending on age: Approximately 45 percent of women under the age of thirty-five who experience IVF deliver babies, and this percentage declines steadily to under 5 percent for women over the age of forty-four (Centers for Disease Control and Prevention—Division of Reproductive Health, 2011a).

What are the experiences of families with children conceived by the new reproductive technologies? In a recent European study that compared families with a child conceived by IVF or DI with families whose children were conceived naturally or adopted, Susan Golombok and her associates found no group differences in the quality of children's emotions, behavior, or overall relationships with their parents (Golombok et al., 2006; Mac-Callum, Golombok, & Brinsden, 2007). Mothers of IVF and DI children, in fact, showed greater warmth toward and deeper emotional involvement with their children, and both mother-child and father-child interactions were more positive. At least for the families studied, genetic ties appeared to be less important for family functioning than a strong desire to become a parent.

What Do You Think?

If now (or in the future) you and your partner wished to have a child but were unable to do so by normal conception, what reservations might you have about using the new technological alternatives? Have the results of Susan Golombok's study influenced your thinking?

---

assisted reproductive technology (ART) Any infertility treatment in which fertilization of the egg occurs outside of the womb.

he or she experiences (Turkheimer & Gottesman, 1991). For example, if three infants start life with different genetic inheritances (genotypes) for intelligence—one low, one middle, and one high—the different levels of intelligence they actually develop (phenotypes), as measured by IQ tests, will depend on how well each child's intellectual development is nurtured by his or her experiences from conception onward, including the conditions created by the child's family, school, and community. Thus, in an enriched environment, the child with low genetic endowment may achieve an IQ that is actually equal to (or even higher than) that of the child with a middle-range endowment who grows up in a restricted or below-average environment. Nevertheless, the first child cannot be expected to achieve an IQ score equal to that of children with high genetic endowment, because this is beyond the upper limit of that child's range of reaction, that is, the highest level of intellectual functioning possible for that child. Figure 3.9 illustrates range of reaction for intelligence. Theorists such as Robert Sternberg (1988) and Howard Gardner (1990), however, believe intelligence consists of several different factors or dimensions, and thus range of reaction may differ according to which aspect of intelligence is being measured. We will look more closely at these theories when we examine cognitive development in middle childhood in Chapter 12.

TABLE 3.5 Conditions that Prenatal Diagnosis Can Detect

Procedure	Timing	Conditions Detected
Ultrasound	Throughout pregnancy	Pregnancy; multiple pregnancies; fetal growth and abnormalities, such as limb defects; tubal (ectopic) pregnancy; atypical fetal position
Amniocentesis	15–17 weeks	Chromosomal disorders, such as Down syndrome; neurological disorders; gender of the baby
Chorionic villus sampling (CVS)	11–12 weeks	Tests for most of the same genetic disorders as amniocentesis but is less sensitive to more subtle abnormalities
Fetoscopy	18th week	Used to confirm results from a prior prenatal test or to assess the severity of a disability already identified
Maternal serum alpha-fetoprotein (MSAFP)	15–18 weeks	Various problems, including neural tube defects and Down syndrome; positive first test is followed by additional testing, such as ultrasound and amniocentesis
Percutaneous umbilical blood sampling (PUBS)	18–36 weeks	Down syndrome, neural tube defects, Tay-Sachs disease, cystic fibrosis, sickle-cell disease; gender of the fetus; fetal infections, such as rubella, toxoplasmosis, or AIDS

Sources: ACOG (1995); D'Alton & DeCherney (1993); Feinbloom & Formtin (1987); Weiacker & Steinhard (2010).

Adoption and Twin Studies

Adoption Studies

Adoption studies compare the degree of physical or behavioral similarity between adoptive children and members of their adoptive families (with whom they have little in common genetically) with the degree of physical or behavioral similarity between these same children and members of their biological families (with whom they share half of their genes). If adoptive children share similar environments (but not genes) with their adoptive family members, differences in trait similarity to their adoptive versus biological

adoption study A research method for studying the relative contributions of heredity and environment in which genetically related children reared apart are compared with genetically unrelated children reared together.

The Concept of Range of Reaction for Intellectual Performance

FIGURE 3.9
Range of Reaction for Intellectual Performance

Range of reaction refers to the range of possible phenotypes as a result of different environments interacting with a specific genotype. As this figure shows, while intellectual performance will be impaired or facilitated for all children, depending on whether the environment is restricted, average, or enriched, the range of potential intellectual performance in reaction to different environments will be limited by the child's genetic inheritance for intelligence.

Source: Adapted from Turkheimer & Gottesman, 1991.

Chapter 3 Genetics

A Multicultural View

Cultural Difference and Genetic Counseling

The growing Asian American populations in the Western world tends to use genetic counseling infrequently (Yu, 2012). Reasons for this include lack of information, misperceptions about such services, language and cultural barriers, and cultural attitudes that strongly discourage seeking outside help for family problems.

In traditional Asian cultures, the family is the most important social unit. It is a source of material, social, and emotional support for its members and is responsible for maintaining the cultural and religious traditions that connect the present generation with past and future ones. The personal decisions and actions of an individual regarding pregnancy and genetic counseling reflect not only on herself but on her *nuclear family* (spouse and children), her *extended family* (parents, siblings, and other relatives), and *past and future generations* of her family (Chan, 1991; Wang & Marsh, 1992). John Roland, a psychologist who has studied personality development in India and Japan, believes that in addition to an *individual* and a *spiritual* sense of self, individuals growing up in such traditional societies develop a *powerful familial* self. Within this sense of self, a person experiences himself as an inseparable part of the family unit and one whose actions will be largely determined by family needs and expectations (Roland, 1988).

Three other areas of cultural difference are important for genetic counselors to understand: (1) *collective versus personal autonomy*, (2) *shame and stigma*, and (3) *directive versus nondirective authority* (Wang & Marsh, 1992).

Collective versus Personal Autonomy

A belief in *personal autonomy* is a cornerstone of Western genetic counseling, which views the patient as a self-determining individual who is largely free from the external control of family and other outside influences. The counselor's goal is to help the patient make an informed, autonomous decision about what is best by providing information in a nondirective and value-free way. This approach, however, frequently conflicts with cultural expectations of Asian patients, who hold a *collective* view of autonomy.

Collective autonomy presumes that a patient is an inseparable part of the traditional family unit and one whose actions will be largely determined by family interests. Family roles and responsibilities are rigidly and hierarchically defined based on generation, age, and gender, with the father occupying a position of unquestioned leadership and authority. This pattern serves to minimize family conflict by allowing little room for individuality and independence on the part of its members and to maintain family harmony and further the family's welfare and reputation (Roland, 1988; Wang & Marsh, 1992).

Shame and Stigma

In traditional Asian culture, which places tremendous importance on daughters being successful in finding a marriage partner, infertility is viewed as a handicapping stigma that will make a young woman unmarriageable and bring shame to herself and her family. Such problems are therefore managed within the family. To seek outside help from a genetic counselor would be a public admission of failure (Paniagua, 2005; Sue & Zane, 1987; Wang & Marsh, 1992).

Directive versus Nondirective Authority

A *nondirective approach to authority* is a second cornerstone of genetic counseling that directly conflicts with the cultural expectations of Asian patients. This approach assumes the patient is responsible for making her own decisions and should not be influenced by the counselor's own views and values. In contrast, the *directive approach* assumes that as an expert authority, the counselor should provide the patient with clear and highly structured guidance about what he should do.

The directive approach is much more consistent with the authority relations and role expectations in Asian families. It therefore is more likely to relieve high levels of anxiety, shame, and doubt by providing practical and immediate solutions to problems (Wang & Marsh, 1992). Stanley Sue, who has written extensively about these issues, suggests that families from Asian and other traditional cultures will seek help from professionals who earn credibility and trust by responding to their need for directive, immediate assistance, while also working with them to achieve more self-directed, long-term solutions (Paniagua, 2005; Sue et al., 1994; Sue, 1998; Sue, D.W., & Sue, D., 2012).

---

relatives should tell something about the influence of their genetic differences. For example, if the IQ scores of adopted children correlated more highly with the IQ scores of their biological families than with those of their adoptive families, we might conclude that heredity—nature—made a strong contribution to intelligence. However, if the IQ scores of these adoptive children were significantly higher (or lower) than those of their biological parents, this might also indicate the influence of family circumstances and other environmental factors—nurture.

> **What Do You Think?**
>
> Do modern medical techniques unwittingly perpetuate several hereditary disorders by using heroic measures to keep alive severely impaired newborns who in the past might have died? If so, does this practice pose an ethical problem?

Twin Studies

Twin studies *compare pairs of identical twins raised in the same family with pairs of fraternal twins* (50 percent shared genes) raised in the same family. Because identical twins have the exact same genetic makeup, greater similarity between identical twins than between fraternal twins on a trait such as intelligence probably would reflect the influence of heredity.

Twin Adoption Studies

Twin adoption studies compare pairs of identical twins who are raised apart since birth in different environments. Twin adoption studies provide the most effective method for understanding the gene-environment relationship in humans. If we could study identical twins who inherit exactly the same genes but are raised in truly different family environments, we would be able to separate the relative contributions of heredity and environment. The catch is to find twins who are growing up in adoptive families. An additional problem is that adoptive families are most frequently chosen with the goal of offering twins similar socioeconomic, cultural, and religious conditions and experiences, raising the question of how different their adoptive family environments really are.

Linkage and Association Studies

Linkage and association studies allow researchers to identify *polymorphisms,* certain segments of human DNA that are inherited together in a predictable pattern—as genetic markers for the genes near which they are located. *Linkage studies* seek to discover polymorphisms that are coinherited, or "linked," with a particular trait in families unusually prone to that trait. This was the case in the discovery of a genetic marker for Huntington disease, and for fragile X syndrome, which were described earlier in this chapter. *Association studies* compare the relative frequency of polymorphisms in two populations, one with the trait and one without it (Hagerman, 1996; Horgan, 1993).

twin study A research method for studying the relative contributions of heredity and environment in which the degree of similarity between genetically identical, or monozygotic, twins (developed from a single fertilized egg) is compared with the similarity between fraternal, or dyzygotic, twins (developed from two fertilized eggs).

twin adoption study Research that compares twins reared apart with unrelated persons reared together.

Shared genes or shared experiences? Studies comparing identical twins with fraternal twins raised in the same family can help to determine the influences of heredity and environment on the development of a variety of characteristics.
Source: MJTH/Shutterstock.com.

Chapter 3 Genetics

Cautions and Conclusions about the Influence of Heredity and Environment

Though substantial evidence exists that genetic inheritance plays at least a moderate role in differences in physical, intellectual, and personality traits, it is likely that such differences are influenced by *both* heredity and environmental experience. Currently, however, there is a growing trend toward minimizing environmental contributions in favor of *genetic determinism,* a belief that most, if not all, human characteristics, from intellectual functioning to gender roles and career choice, are determined primarily by genes. This tendency may in part be a reaction to *environmental determinism,* an equally simplistic view that sees experience as the central or sole cause of developmental change and dismisses the possibility that genes may also make a significant contribution. It may also reflect the explosive growth in biotechnology and the overly optimistic view it appears to have generated.

Neither biogenetic nor environmental determinism can ever lead to an adequate understanding of human development. Rather, human development is always the product of multiple levels of biological and environmental influences and human agency—the self-determining choices that each individual makes.

Looking Back/Looking Forward

Although we are just beginning our exploration of development, let's use the four main themes discussed in Chapter 1 to review where we have been and where we are going.

- **Continuity within change**—On the one hand, the physical processes involved in genetic transmission, and eventually conception, prenatal development, and birth involve enormous and rapid changes. Because the complex processes involved in conception and prenatal development are highly canalized, they tend to work very well most of the time, ensuring that physical development proceeds according to longstanding patterns and norms. In addition, significant continuity is ensured through each parent's contribution of genetic material and associated characteristics to the unique genotype of the child. The continuities and changes that occur vividly illustrate the developmental themes of experience and process or stage discussed in Chapter 2.

- **Lifelong growth**—Genetics provide the foundation for lifelong growth in the physical, cognitive, and psychosocial domains that occur from birth onward. Though physical and cognitive growth will be rapid through childhood and adolescence, important changes in this domain will continue to affect growth throughout the lifespan, and each of these changes is founded in the genetic basis provided to us at conception.

- **Changing meanings and vantage points**—Genetic differences will eventually develop into phenotypic differences over the course of an individual's life. The inheritance of an *X* or *Y* chromosome from one's father will eventually change the expectations, beliefs, and behaviors one's family and society has about them. The genes we inherit will eventually impact the genes we pass on to our own children, if we choose to do so.

- **Developmental diversity**—As we have seen in this chapter, the unique genetic inheritance of each new human being at conception provides the earliest basis for the developmental diversity that will follow. Even identical twins who share the same genotype will show subtle differences based on different prenatal experiences, such as where each is located in the womb and how easy or difficult their delivery is. As physical, cognitive, and psychosocial development progress through childhood, adolescence, and adulthood, the opportunities for diversity continue to expand, aided to a significant degree by the expanding range of experiences that become available and by the capacity all individuals have to self-determine their own development through their own choices. Differences in families, culture, ethnicity, race, gender, religion, socioeconomic status, and other life circumstances also play an important role. If two so-called "identical twins" are raised under very different life circumstances, they will still display striking phenotypical commonalities due to their shared genotypes, yet they will also be strikingly different based on their different environments, experiences, and personal choices.

Chapter Summary

- **How does inheritance work?** Genetic information is contained in a complex molecule called *deoxyribonucleic acid (DNA)*. Reproductive cells, or gametes, divide by a process called *meiosis* and recombine into a zygote at conception. Meiosis gives each gamete one-half of its normal number of chromosomes; conception brings the number of chromosomes up to normal again and gives the new zygote an equal number of chromosomes from each parent. Other body cells produce new tissue through division of their genes, chromosomes, and other cellular parts by means of a process called *mitosis*.

- **How are genetic differences usually transmitted from one generation to the next?** A person's genotype is the specific pattern of genetic information inherited in his or her chromosomes and genes at conception. A person's phenotype is the physical and behavioral traits the person actually shows during his or her life. Phenotype is the product of the interactions of genotype with environment. Although most genes exist in duplicate, some, called *dominant genes*, may actually influence the phenotype if only one member of the pair occurs. Recessive genes do not influence the phenotype unless both members of the pair occur in a particular form. Many traits are polygenic, meaning they are transmitted through the combined action of several genes. Sex is determined by one particular pair of chromosomes, called the X and Y chromosomes, and a testis-determining factor (TDF) located on a small section of the Y chromosome.

- **How can experts help parents discover and respond to potential genetic problems?** Some genetic abnormalities, such as Down syndrome (trisomy 21), occur when an individual inherits too many or too few chromosomes. Others occur because particular genes are defective or abnormal even though the chromosomes are normal. Examples include Huntington disease, sickle-cell disease, and fragile X syndrome. Genetic counseling can provide parents with information about how genetics influences the development of children and about the risks of transmitting genetic abnormalities from one generation to the next. Personal circumstances and cultural differences in beliefs and expectations must be considered in helping couples reach informed decisions about pregnancy.

- **How do heredity and environment jointly influence development?** According to behavioral geneticists, every characteristic of an organism is the result of the unique interaction between the genetic inheritance of the organism and the sequence of environments through which it has passed during its development. The concept of range of reaction describes the strength of genetic influence under different environmental conditions. Studies of identical twins and of adopted children suggest that heredity and environment operate jointly to influence developmental change. Linkage and association studies use repeated DNA segments called *polymorphisms* as genetic markers to locate abnormal genes. Neither biogenetic nor environmental determinism is likely to give us adequate understanding of human development, which is the product of genes, environment, and individual choice.

Key Terms

adoption study (p. 73)
allele (p. 62)
assisted reproductive technology (ART) (p. 72)
chromosome (p. 60)
dominant gene (p. 62)
down syndrome (p. 65)

gene (p. 60)
genetic imprinting (p. 65)
genotype (p. 61)
ovum (p. 60)
phenotype (p. 62)
range of reaction (p. 71)
recessive gene (p. 62)

sex-linked recessive traits (p. 64)
sickle-cell disease (p. 70)
sperm (p. 60)
twin adoption study (p. 75)
twin study (p. 75)
zygote (p. 60)

Prenatal Development and Birth

CHAPTER 4

Source: Leptospira/Shutterstock.com.

Chapter Outline
Prenatal Development and Birth
Prenatal Influences on the Child
Birth
Looking Back/Looking Forward

Focusing Questions

- What important developmental changes occur during prenatal development?
- What risks do a mother and baby normally face during pregnancy, and how can they be minimized?
- What happens during the birth process, what difficulties may occur, and how are they handled?

Prenatal Development and Birth

From the moment of conception, a **zygote** becomes a biological entity. How do microscopic cells become people? In the following sections, we look at the events and processes that occur from conception through birth and how they may affect later development. We also look at certain risks and problems of prenatal development and of birth and their long-term impact on the child.

zygote The single new cell formed when a sperm cell attaches itself to the surface of an ovum (egg).

Stages of Prenatal Development

Prenatal development begins with conception and continues through discrete periods, or stages. The first is the **germinal stage**, or *period of the ovum*, which occurs during the first two weeks of pregnancy; the second is the **embryonic stage**, which lasts from the third week to the eighth week; and the third is the **fetal stage**, which lasts from the eighth week until birth.

Conception

Conception normally occurs when one of the approximately 360 million sperm contained in the *semen*, which the father has ejaculated into the mother's vagina during intercourse, swims through the *cervix* (opening of the uterus) into the fallopian tube and successfully attaches itself to the surface of an ovum, or egg, released from one of the woman's ovaries (Wilcox et al, 1995). (See Figure 4.2.) As noted in the "Focusing On" in the previous chapter, some couples have difficulty conceiving through intercourse. In such cases, various technological alternatives exist to join sperm and egg. Once it becomes attached, the sperm gradually penetrates the egg. Within a few hours, the walls of the sperm cell and the *nucleus*, or center, of the egg cell both begin to disintegrate. In this process, as Figure 4.1 shows, the sperm and egg cells each release their chromosomes, which join to form a new cell called a *zygote* (Wilcox et al., 1995).

At this point, the zygote is still so small that hundreds of them could fit on the head of a pin. Yet it contains all of the necessary genetic information in its DNA molecules to develop into a unique human being.

The Germinal Stage (First Two Weeks)

The newly formed zygote now begins to divide and redivide to form a tiny sixteen-cell sphere called a morula, which between days three and four postconception begins to travel down the fallopian tube to the uterus. At five days postconception, the mass of cells, a *blastocyst,* differentiates into three layers. The *ectoderm* (upper layer) later develops into the epidermis, or outer layer of skin, nails, teeth, and hair, as well as the sensory organs and nervous system. The *endoderm* (lower layer) becomes the digestive system, liver, pancreas, salivary glands, and respiratory system. The *mesoderm* (middle layer) develops somewhat later and becomes the dermis (inner layer of skin), muscles, skeleton, and circulatory and excretory systems. In a short time the *placenta, umbilical cord,* and *amniotic sac* (discussed shortly) also will form from blastocyst cells.

---

germinal stage The stage in prenatal development that occurs during the first two weeks of pregnancy; characterized by rapid cell division. Also called the *period of the ovum*.

embryonic stage The stage in prenatal development that lasts from week 2 through week 8.

fetal stage The stage in prenatal development that lasts from the eighth week of pregnancy until birth.

conception The moment at which the male's sperm cell penetrates the female's egg cell (ovum), forming a zygote.

FIGURE 4.1
Gametes and Zygote

Each gamete, whether sperm or ovum, contains twenty-three single chromosomes. (Two chromosomes are shown in each gamete here for ease of illustration.) At fertilization, sperm and ovum combine to form a zygote with forty-six chromosomes in twenty-three pairs. (Two pairs are shown here.) In each pair, one chromosome is from the mother, and one is from the father.

Gametes and Zygote

Gametes (reproductive cells) — Fertilization — Zygote

> **What Do You Think?**
>
> Based on what you have just read, how do you view the relationship between genes and environment? To what degree do you believe most or all of human development will someday be explainable in terms of genetics? Where, in your judgment, does human agency or free will fit in?

After a few more days—about one week after conception—implantation occurs. During *implantation*, the blastocyst buries itself like a seed in the wall of the uterus. The fully implanted blastocyst is now referred to as the *embryo*. Figure 4.2 illustrates the changes that occur during the germinal stage of prenatal development.

The Embryonic Stage (Third through Eighth Weeks)

Growth during the embryonic stage (and the fetal stage that follows) occurs in two patterns: a *cephalocaudal* (head-to-tail) pattern and a *proximodistal* (near-to-far, from the center of the body outward) pattern. Thus, the head, blood vessels, and heart—the most vital body parts and organs—begin to develop earlier than the arms, legs, hands, and feet. The three-dimensional renderings shown here and also in Figure 4.3 (upper portion) later in the chapter illustrate these changes.

At *three weeks,* the head, tail, brain, and circulatory system begin to develop and the heart has begun beating. At *four weeks,* the embryo is little more than an inch long. The beginnings of a spinal cord, arms, and legs are evident, a small digestive system and a nervous system have developed, and the brain has become more differentiated (P. Harris, 1983). During *week five,* hands and lungs begin to form. During *week six,* the head grows larger, the brain becomes more fully developed, and hands, legs, and feet become more fully formed. During *week seven,* muscles form and the cerebral cortex begins to develop.

While these developments are taking place, a placenta forms between the mother and the embryo, the **placenta** is an area on the uterine wall through which the mother supplies oxygen and nutrients to the embryo and the embryo returns waste products from her bloodstream. In the placenta, thousands of tiny blood vessels from the two circulatory systems intermingle. Although only minute quantities of blood can cross the separating membranes, nutrients pass easily from one bloodstream to the other through a process called *osmosis.* Although many toxic chemicals and drugs in the mother's system do not spread easily by

placenta An organ that delivers oxygen and nutrients from the mother to the fetus and carries away the fetus's waste products, which the mother will excrete.

FIGURE 4.2
The Germinal Stage of Prenatal Development

The sperm and ovum join to form a single-celled *zygote,* which then divides and re-divides to become a multicelled *blastocyst.* The blastocyst buries, or *implants,* itself in the uterine wall. The fully-implanted blastocyst is now called an *embryo.*

Chapter 4 Prenatal Development and Birth

umbilical cord Three large blood vessels that connect the embryo to the placenta, one to provide nutrients and two to remove waste products.

amniotic sac A tough, spongy bag filled with salty fluid that surrounds the embryo, protects it from sudden jolts, and maintains a stable temperature.

osmosis, others do. As we discuss later, seemingly harmless chemicals sometimes prove devastating to the embryo.

The **umbilical cord** connects the embryo to the placenta. It consists of three large blood vessels, one to provide nutrients and two to carry waste products into the mother's body. The cord enters the embryo at a place that becomes the baby's belly button, or navel, after the cord is cut following birth.

By the end of the eighth week, an **amniotic sac** has developed. The amniotic sac is a tough, spongy bag filled with salty fluid that completely surrounds the embryo, protects it from sudden jolts, and maintains a stable temperature. The embryo floats gently in this environment until birth, protected even if its mother goes jogging, sits down suddenly, or shovels heavy snow.

The Fetal Stage (Ninth Week to Birth)

At about *eight weeks* of gestation, the embryo develops its first bone cells, which marks the end of differentiation into the major structures. At this point, the embryo acquires a new name, *the fetus,* and begins the long process of developing relatively small features, such as fingers and fingernails and eyelids and eyebrows. Their smallness, however, belies their importance. For example, the eyes undergo their greatest growth during this stage of development. The fetus's newly developing eyelids fuse shut at about ten weeks and do not reopen until the eyes themselves are essentially complete, at around sixteen to twenty weeks postconception.

Not only the eyes but most other physical features become more adult looking during this period and more truly human in proportion (P. Harris, 1983). The head becomes smaller relative to the rest of the body (even though it remains large by adult standards), partly because the fetus's long bones, the ones supporting its limbs, begin growing significantly. Thus, its arms and legs look increasingly substantial.

By *twelve weeks,* the fetus is about three inches long and able to respond reflexively to touch. By *sixteen weeks,* it has grown to about 4.5 inches in length. If its palm is touched, it exhibits a grasp reflex by closing its fist; if the sole of its foot is touched, its toes spread (Babinski reflex); and if its lips are touched, it responds with a sucking reflex. In addition, the fetal heartbeat can now be heard through the wall of the uterus.

Between the *fourth* and *fifth months* (sixteen to twenty weeks), hands and feet become fully developed, eyes can open and close, hearing is present, lungs become capable of breathing in and out, and nails, hair, and sweat glands develop. Around the sixteenth week, most pregnant women feel *quickening,* the movement of the fetus inside the womb. Fetal movements appear to grow progressively stronger and more frequent from eighteen weeks on, reaching a maximum between twenty-eight and twenty-nine weeks, after which they diminish somewhat until delivery (Primeau, 1993).

The embryonic period is characterized by remarkable differentiation and specialization as most of the body's tissues, organs, structures, and systems begin to develop, and some even become functional. The three-dimensional rendering on the left illustrates an embryo at four weeks, while the image on the right shows the embryo just one month later (at eight weeks).

Source: Sebastian Kaulitzki/Shutterstock.com.

Part 2 Beginnings

The fetal period is characterized by rapid growth. The three-dimensional renderings depict a fetus at three months *(left)*, six months *(middle)*, and nine months *(right)*. What these renderings cannot easily convey is the actual growth in length and weight during the fetal period. The fetus at three months typically weighs about 0.5 ounce and is just over two inches in length; the fetus at six months averages 1.3 pounds and is nearly twelve inches in length; the fetus at nine months averages 7.5 pounds and is about twenty inches in length.
Source: Sebastian Kaulitzki/Shutterstock.com.

By the beginning of the *seventh month,* the fetus is about sixteen inches long and weighs approximately three to five pounds. It is able to cry, breathe, swallow, digest, excrete, move about, and suck its thumb. The reflexes mentioned earlier are fully developed. Because of these capacities, the fetus is said to have attained *age of viability*, meaning it could survive if born at this point.

By the *eighth month,* the fetus weighs between five and seven pounds and has begun to develop a layer of body fat that will help it to regulate its body temperature after birth, and by *nine months* it has achieved its full birth weight. Toward the end of nine months, the average baby is about 7.5 pounds and almost twenty inches long. Growth in size stops, although fat continues to be stored, heart rate increases, and internal organ systems become more efficient in preparation for birth and independent life outside the womb.

The developing fetus is also responsive to stimuli in the external environment, such as sound and vibration (Kisilevsky et al., 1992). For example, newborn infants have been found to show preferences for stories and rhymes read aloud to them during the final six weeks of pregnancy (DeCasper et al., 1994), and intrauterine sounds, such as a mother's heartbeat, have been found to soothe newborns (Ullal-Gupta et al., 2013).

The Experience of Pregnancy

Sudah is nearing the end of her pregnancy—just eight weeks to go! She has been careful to eat a good, balanced diet and has gained about twenty-four pounds, which her doctor says is fine for her size and pre-pregnancy weight. Lately, her belly feels like a basketball, and she sometimes worries whether Dan, her husband, still finds her attractive and whether she will ever get her prepregnancy figure back. During the first two months of pregnancy, Sudah felt nauseous a lot of the time and found it hard to keep food down. She found that eating small amounts of food (especially plain crackers) throughout the day helped, as did resting more frequently—which was hard to do because she was still working full time.

Until recently, aside from getting tired more easily, Sudah has felt good. During the last few weeks, however, she has had some swelling in her legs and some back pain, and has had to go to the bathroom much more frequently because of the pressure of the baby on her bladder. Although she and Dan are anxious for the baby to arrive, they are somewhat apprehensive about whether they are grown up enough to be parents and to take on the responsibilities of parenthood.

Sudah's complaints are typical of those associated with the hormonal and physiological changes of pregnancy. More than 80 percent of pregnant women experience some degree of nausea during the first trimester, but this usually disappears by the twelfth week (Quinlan & Hill, 2003). Strategies for relieving nausea include eating small amounts of food frequently, increasing protein intake, eating dry crackers or plain yogurt, and resting more often during the day. Frequent urination is another symptom of early pregnancy and is due to hormonally induced softening of the pelvic muscles, which allows the enlarged uterus to press on the bladder. Other symptoms include fatigue, headaches, dizziness and fainting, constipation, leg cramps, heartburn, shortness of breath, swelling of legs, hands, or face, varicose veins, and backache (Davis, 1993).

In addition to the influence of hormonal changes, some of these symptoms are due to weight gain during pregnancy. Both a woman's weight before pregnancy and her weight gain during pregnancy influence the baby's birth weight. Current recommendations from the Institute of Medicine (2009) and the American College of Obstetricians and Gynecologists (ACOG, 2013) are as follows:

- Women who are underweight (body mass index [BMI] less than 18.5) before pregnancy should gain between twenty-eight and forty pounds during pregnancy,

- women of normal weight (BMI of 18.5–24.9) should gain between twenty-five and thirty-five pounds,

- women who are overweight (BMI of 25–29.9) should gain between fifteen and twenty-five pounds, and

- women who are obese (BMI of 30 and greater) prior to pregnancy should gain between eleven and twenty pounds.

More-exact recommendations for weight gain should result from consultations early in their pregnancy between pregnant women and their health care providers. Why is there so much emphasis on weight gain during pregnancy? Because the amount of weight gained during pregnancy has significant effects on the present and future health of the mother and her infant. Where does the weight gain go? The increased size of the uterus, breast tissue, blood volume, body fluid, and extra fat to prepare the woman to produce milk for breast feeding all contribute to the additional pounds (ACOG, 1995).

Pregnancy is a powerful experience that can dramatically affect how both the mother and the father feel about themselves and each other. For most prospective parents, it raises the question "Am I ready to be emotionally and economically responsible for this baby?" Couples who are experiencing pregnancy together may wonder, "How will having a baby affect our relationship with each other?" See the interview with Katie Glover for a nurse-practitioner's observations regarding pregnancy and preparation for childbirth.

Prenatal Influences on the Child

As we have noted, physical structures develop in a particular sequence and at precise times. Psychologists and biologists sometimes call such regularity *canalization*. **Canalization** refers to the tendency of genes to narrowly direct or restrict growth and development of particular physical and behavioral characteristics to a single (or very few) phenotypic outcomes and to resist environmental factors that push development in other directions (McCall, 1981).

Typically, prenatal development is a highly reliable process, so prospective parents generally worry much more than they need to about whether their baby will be "all right." In fact, 97 percent of human infants are perfect at birth, and of the 3 percent who are not, half have only minor defects such as hammertoes, extra fingers or toes, or birthmarks (CDC, 2008; Guttmacher & Kaiser, 1984).

However, certain conditions can interfere with even the highly canalized processes of fetal development. These conditions are sometimes called *risk factors*. Risk factors increase

canalization The tendency of many developmental processes to unfold in highly predictable ways under a wide range of conditions.

In addition to the visible signs of pregnancy, expectant mothers often experience a series of aches and pains associated with the changes in their bodies during pregnancy. Headaches and backaches are common, as are cramps in the legs and pain in the lower abdomen as ligaments and muscles are stretched.
Source: mathom/Shutterstock.com.

the chance that the future baby will have medical problems but do not guarantee that these problems will actually appear. Risk factors include the mothers biological characteristics, including age and physical condition, and exposure to diseases, drugs, chemicals, stress, and other environmental hazards during pregnancy.

Harmful Substances, Diseases, and Environmental Hazards

As the complex sequence of prenatal growth proceeds, the timing of the development of each new organ or body part is especially important. **Critical period** refers to a time-limited period during which certain developmental changes are highly vulnerable to disruption. This "window of opportunity" is dictated by complex genetic codes in each cell *and* by the particular set of prenatal conditions that must be in place for each change to occur. If development is disturbed or blocked during a critical period, the changes that were scheduled to occur may be disrupted or prevented from occurring at all. Figure 4.3 shows the critical periods in human development.

critical period Any period during which development is particularly susceptible to an event or influence, either negative or positive.

Especially during the early weeks of its life, development of the embryo is particularly vulnerable to disruption if it is exposed (through the mother) to certain harmful substances called *teratogens*. A **teratogen** is any substance or other environmental influence that can interfere with or permanently damage an embryo's growth. Named after an ancient Greek word meaning "monster-creating," teratogens can result in serious physical malformations and even in the death of the embryo. Teratogens are most harmful if exposure

teratogen Any substance that can harm the developing embryo or fetus.

FIGURE 4.3
Timing and Effects of Teratogens during Sensitive or Critical Periods

This figure illustrates the sensitive or critical periods in human prenatal development. The dark band indicates highly sensitive or critical periods; the light band indicates stages that are less sensitive to disruption caused by teratogens. Note that each structure has a critical period during which its development may be disrupted.

Chapter 4 Prenatal Development and Birth   85

> **What Do You Think?**
>
> For those of you who have already experienced pregnancy, what was it like? For those of you who haven't, what do you imagine the experience might be like for you? How has what you have read so far in this chapter influenced your views about pregnancy?

occurs during the critical or sensitive period for the particular physical change to occur. Teratogens include many *medicinal and nonmedicinal drugs; other chemicals; diseases* (viruses and bacteria); and certain *other harmful environmental influences*, such as radiation. Teratogens can be contracted from a variety of sources, including from other individuals who have communicable diseases, from drugs, from ingesting foods that have been contaminated, and from exposure to chemicals, X rays, and radioactivity in the workplace and in nonwork environments.

Several factors influence a teratogen's effects. The first is the *timing of exposure*. The nine months of pregnancy generally are divided into three *trimesters*, each lasting three months. Disruptions during the first trimester, when the critical periods for embryonic and fetal development occur, are most likely to result in spontaneous abortion or serious birth defects. During the third week, for example, teratogens can harm the basic structures of the heart and central nervous system that are just beginning to form. The effects of exposure in the second and third trimesters generally are less likely to be as severe.

The impact of a teratogen is also influenced by the *intensity and duration of exposure*. For example, the higher the dose (intensity) and the longer the exposure to a harmful drug such as alcohol or cocaine, the greater the chance that the baby will be harmed and that the harm will be more severe than if dose and duration are less. The *number of other harmful influences* that are also present also makes a difference. The greater the number, the greater the risk. Finally, the *biogenetic vulnerability of mother and infant* will influence a teratogen's effects. Mothers and their infants will differ in the degree to which they will be affected by exposure to a particular type and level of teratogen. For example, whereas heavy and prolonged drinking is likely to affect almost all babies, very moderate drinking may cause considerable harm for one infant but no measurable harm for another.

Medicinal Drugs

Medical science has developed countless drugs with highly beneficial effects, from curing illness to relieving pain. Yet a medication with positive effects overall may negatively affect fetal development if taken during pregnancy. A drug called *thalidomide* is a dramatic example of how such damage can occur. It also illustrates the political, economic, and social policy implications of new medical and scientific discoveries that affect human growth and development.

Thalidomide is a seemingly harmless sedative that during die late 1950s and early 1960s was widely prescribed for calming nerves, promoting sleep, and reducing morning sickness and other forms of nausea dining the early weeks of pregnancy. Although it was advertised as being completely safe, between 1958 and 1962 thousands of babies were born with birth defects that included missing, shortened, or misshapen arms and legs, deafness, severe facial deformities, seizure disorders, dwarfism, and brain damage. Not until 1961 was the drug banned in the United States, in part because the effects of teratogens were less understood then and because the federal Food and Drug Administration (FDA) was under political pressure from the drug industry to keep thalidomide on the market (Stout, 1993). It is estimated that currently there are about eight thousand thalidomide-affected adults and that twice that many babies were stillborn (dead at birth) or died shortly afterward because of defects caused by thalidomide (HHS, 2005; Stout, 1993).

Teratogenic drugs pose an even greater developmental risk in developing countries in South America, Africa, and Asia, where drugs are less strictly regulated than in the United

States. In Brazil, one of the world's largest producers of thalidomide, the drug is used to help treat the symptoms of leprosy, which afflicts almost 300,000 people in that country. This has led to a growing number of birth defects in babies born to mothers with leprosy who have taken the drug because they are not aware of its effects (Gorman, 1993; Vianna et al., 2011).

Unfortunately, the damage done by toxic drugs or chemicals does not always show itself as obviously or as soon as in the case of thalidomide. For about twenty-five years following World War II, another drug, *diethylstilbestrol (DES),* was taken by 3 million to 6 million pregnant women with histories of spontaneous abortions to prevent miscarriages. The drug was especially useful during the early months, when miscarriages occur most often. At birth, the babies of women who took DES seemed perfectly normal, and they remained so throughout childhood. As they became young adults, however, abnormal development of vaginal cells and structural abnormalities of the uterus were found in all female babies who had been exposed, and about one in one thousand eventually developed cancer of the vagina or of the cervix. The sons of DES mothers developed abnormalities in the structure of their reproductive organs and had a higher than usual rate of testicular cancer. Even the daughters who did not get cancer had significantly more problems than usual with their own pregnancies, including higher rates of spontaneous abortion and stillbirth as well as more minor problems, and they had them whether or not their families had histories of difficult births. As most of the individuals exposed to DES before birth are now reaching midlife, there is growing evidence of increased risk for autoimmune disorders such as pernicious anemia, myasthenia gravis (a nerve-muscle disorder), serious intestinal disorders, and multiple sclerosis as a result of DES damage to the immune system (Brody, 1993). DES support networks and social action groups for affected individuals and families have been formed in both Canada and the United States (Linn et al, 1988; Sato, 1993).

Nonmedicinal Drugs

Not surprisingly, drugs such as *heroin, cocaine, alcohol,* and *tobacco* also affect the fetus. Table 4.1 summarizes their effects.

Many babies born to mothers who consume alcohol during pregnancy display fetal alcohol effects (FAEs), and the most severely affected babies exhibit a cluster of defects known as *fetal alcohol syndrome (FAS).* These two effects represent two points on what is a continuum of alcohol-related teratogenic effects called *fetal alcohol spectrum disorders (FASD)* (Riley, Infante, & Warren, 2011). *Fetal alcohol effects* refer to a set of symptoms that include lower birth weight, lack of responsiveness and arousability, and increased occurrences of heart and respiratory abnormalities in infants. These infants achieve lower mental development scores at eight months and at four years and have higher rates of learning disabilities (Barr et al., 1990; Streissguth et al., 1989, 1995). Longitudinal studies show that problems with vigilance, attention, and short-term memory may be found in adolescents who experienced exposure to alcohol prenatally (Streissguth et al., 1995).

Symptoms of **fetal alcohol syndrome (FAS)** include central nervous system damage and physical abnormalities of the heart, head, face, and joints; intellectual disability and/or behavioral problems, such as hyperactivity and poor impulse control; and impaired growth and/or failure to thrive (Riley et al., 2011). Babies of heavy drinkers, particularly in the last three months of pregnancy, are at much greater risk for these problems. It is estimated that 50 to 75 percent of infants born to chronically alcoholic women may be affected (Barr et al., 1990; Blackman, 1990).

Even moderate daily drinking during pregnancy (two ounces of hard liquor, nine ounces of wine, or two beers) is associated with an increase in these disorders. The chance of fetal alcohol effects in the infant of a mother who consumes more than four drinks daily is estimated to be about 33 percent and about 10 percent for a woman who consumes between two and four drinks per day. However, drinking alcohol at lower levels (less than one drink per day) *may* be safe, as women who consumed less than one drink per day during pregnancy had

fetal alcohol syndrome (FAS) A congenital condition exhibited by babies born to mothers who consumed too much alcohol during pregnancy. They do not arouse easily and tend to behave sluggishly in general; they also have distinctive facial characteristics.

TABLE 4.1 Teratogens and Their Effects

Teratogen	Effects
Drugs	
Medicinal Drugs	
Thalidomide	Birth defects, such as missing, shortened, or misshapen arms and legs, deafness; severe facial deformities; seizure disorders; dwarfism; brain damage; fetal/infant death
Diethylstilbestrol (DES)	*Grown daughters:* Vaginal and cervical cancer; spontaneous abortions and stillbirth; autoimmune disorders, such as pernicious anemia, myasthenia gravis (a nerve-muscle disorder), intestinal disorder, multiple sclerosis
	Grown sons: Abnormalities in reproductive organs, testicular cancer
Nonmedicinal Drugs	
Heroin	Withdrawal symptoms, including vomiting, trembling, irritability, fever, disturbed sleep, an abnormally high-pitched cry; delayed social and motor development
Cocaine	Miscarriage or premature delivery, low birth weight, irritability, respiratory problems, genital and urinary tract deformities, heart defects, central nervous system problems
Marijuana	Tremors and startles among newborns; inattention, impulsivity, memory deficits, and blunted academic achievement during childhood
Alcohol	*Fetal alcohol effects (FAEs):* Lower birth weight, lack of responsiveness and arousability, heart rate and respiratory abnormalities, delayed cognitive development, learning disabilities
	Fetal alcohol syndrome (FAS): Central nervous system damage; heart defects; small head; distortions of joints; abnormal facial features; intellectual disability; behavioral disorders, such as hyperactivity and poor impulse control; impaired growth and/or failure to thrive
Tobacco	Spontaneous abortion, prematurity, fetal/infant death, reduced birth weight, poorer postnatal adjustment
Maternal Diseases	
Rubella	*First trimester:* Blindness, deafness, heart defects, damage to central nervous system, intellectual disability
	Second trimester: Problems with hearing, vision, and language
Syphilis and gonorrhea	Fetal death, jaundice, anemia, pneumonia, skin rash, bone inflammation, dental deformities, hearing difficulties, blindness
Genital herpes	Disease of skin and mucous membranes, blindness, brain damage, seizures, and developmental delay
Cytomegalovirus	Jaundice, microcephaly (very small head), deafness, eye problems, increased risk for severe illness and infant death
AIDS	Abnormally small skull; facial deformities; immune system damage; enlarged lymph glands, liver, and spleen; recurrent infections; poor growth; fever; brain disease; developmental delay; deteriorated motor skills
Toxoplasmosis	Spontaneous abortion, prematurity, low birth weight, enlarged liver and spleen, jaundice, anemia, congenital defects, intellectual disability, seizures, cerebral palsy, retinal disease, blindness

children who did not differ from abstainers on measures of attention difficulties, behavioral problems, or learning disabilities when those children were fourteen years old (O'Callaghan et al., 2007). The difficulty in determining a "safe" level of alcohol consumption for pregnant women is due to women varying significantly in the quantity of alcohol their bodies can metabolize and in the rate at which their bodies metabolize alcohol (Burd, Blair, & Dropps, 2012). The less alcohol metabolized by the mother's body, the greater the quantity of alcohol exposed to the embryo or fetus, which is why current American Academy of Pediatrics (AAP) guidelines state that no amount of alcohol consumption is safe (AAP, 2015).

Maternal Diseases

Exposure of a pregnant woman to certain viral, bacteriological, and parasitic diseases can adversely affect her baby's development. Table 4.1 summarizes the teratogenic effects of exposure to selected diseases and drugs during pregnancy. In addition, some diseases can be directly transmitted from mother to fetus, often with devastating consequences; these include syphilis and gonorrhea.

A pregnant woman with untreated syphilis can transmit the disease to her fetus. In 25 percent of cases, death of the fetus results, usually during the second trimester. An additional 25 percent of infected fetuses die soon after birth. Of those who survive, about 25 percent show symptoms such as jaundice, anemia, pneumonia, skin rash, and bone inflammation (Blackman, 1990). Fetuses that contract gonorrhea in the birth canal may later develop eye infections or become blind. It is now standard practice to put drops of silver nitrate or penicillin in newborns' eyes to protect them against these conditions, because gonorrhea may be present in the mother without obvious symptoms. HIV, which leads to pediatric AIDS, can also be directly transmitted from mother to fetus.

Pediatric AIDS

Of the approximately four million babies born in the United States each year, 100 to 200 will have HIV, the virus associated with the development of AIDS, numbers that represent a 90 percent reduction in rates of pediatric AIDS in the past twenty years (EGPAF, 2013; Lee, 1995; Task Force on Pediatric AIDS, 1989). About three-fourths of AIDS cases in children involve perinatal (at the time of birth) transmission from an infected mother to her child, either through the placenta or through contact with HIV-contaminated blood at the time of delivery (American Academy of Pediatrics, 1991; EGPAF, 2013). Children from predominantly low-socioeconomic-status families make up three-quarters of all pediatric AIDS cases in the United States, although they account for only one-fourth of all American children. Because AIDS has an incubation period of up to five years in adults, pregnant women may be unaware that they have the virus or that it can be transmitted to their offspring. Although most children infected *perinatally* show symptoms before age one, some children who are infected may live for years without symptoms. Because newborns retain the protective antibodies they receive from their mothers for several months after birth, testing a newborn for HIV antibodies can give accurate information only about the mother (Lee, 1995; Richter, 1993).

Research indicates that when antiretroviral drugs are administered to AIDS-infected women during late pregnancy, administered intravenously during labor, and given intravenously to their newborns immediately after delivery, the risk of having an HIV-infected baby can be reduced by about 4 percent (DGHA, 2013).

Pediatric AIDS is a worldwide problem, especially in sub-Saharan Africa, where 91 percent of the 3.4 million children living with HIV worldwide reside (WHO, 2013). Pregnant women in this and other impoverished regions of the world typically do not have access to the three most effective strategies to reduce mother-child transmission of HIV/AIDS: (1) administration of antiretroviral medications given to expectant mothers and then to their infants, (2) the use of cesarean deliveries or "C-sections" for AIDS-infected mothers, and (3) substitution of infant formula for breast milk (Sullivan, 2003).

Environmental Hazards

Currently the majority of women in the United States are employed outside the home, and most women who are employed when they become pregnant continue working throughout their pregnancies. Many of the environmental hazards to pregnant women and their babies are encountered in the workplace. These include (1) physical hazards such as noise, radiation, vibration, stressful physical activity, and materials handling; (2) biological hazards such as viruses, fungi, spores, and bacteria; (3) chemical hazards such as anesthetic gases, pesticides, lead, mercury, and organic solvents; and (4) radiation (Bernhardt, 1990). A mother's age and physical characteristics may also cause complications during pregnancy, as we will see in the next section.

Maternal Age and Physical Characteristics

Healthy women over age thirty-five are not at significantly greater risk for any of these complications than are younger women, although they are at greater risk for infertility and for having a child with Down syndrome (ACOG, 1995). Very young mothers, especially those in their early teens, are at significantly greater risk of having low-birth-weight infants, stillbirths, or problems during delivery. This is partly because teenage mothers have not completed their own growth, so their bodies are unable to meet the extra nutritional demands of a developing fetus. Teenage mothers are more likely to be poor and less likely to get adequate prenatal care and have the maturity of judgment to adapt their lifestyles to the demands of pregnancy (Fraser, Brockert & Ward, 1995; Coley & Chase-Lansdale, 1998). The United States has the highest rate of teenage pregnancy of all industrialized countries (Lawson & Rhode, 1993; Martin et al., 2013). Pregnant teenagers are much less likely than pregnant adults to maintain nutritious diets and get adequate prenatal care during pregnancy, and they are more likely to suffer complications and experience prolonged and difficult labor. Babies born to teenagers are more likely to be premature and suffer from low birth weight and its associated problems. They also have higher rates of neurological defects, have higher mortality rates during their first year, and are more likely to encounter developmental problems during the preschool and school years. We look more closely at the causes and consequences of teenage pregnancy in Chapter 16.

Prenatal Health Care

Adequate early prenatal care is critical to infant and maternal health, and mothers who begin prenatal care early in pregnancy have improved pregnancy and newborn outcomes, including decreased risk of low birth weight and preterm delivery. The quality of prenatal care is strongly influenced by the woman's life circumstances. Race and socioeconomic status, two factors that are closely linked in our society, play a major role. In 2008, for example, only 77 percent of white mothers and 60 percent of African American mothers began care in the first trimester. Seven percent of all mothers delayed care until the last trimester or received no care at all. These mothers were most likely to be teenagers, be unmarried, have less than twelve years of education, and already have three or more children (C. Lewis, 1993; HHS, 2011). Although the risk of problems increases the later prenatal care is begun, by far the worst outcomes occur for mothers receiving no care at all.

How can the prenatal care of high-risk mothers be improved? The *Prenatal/Early Infancy Project* conducted by David Olds and his colleagues is one promising answer to this question (Olds, 1997). Beginning in the second trimester of pregnancy, program nurses made regular home visits during which they provided education about diet and weight gain; the effects of cigarettes, alcohol, and drugs; signs of pregnancy complication; the importance of regular rest, exercise, and personal hygiene; preparation for labor and delivery and early care of the newborn; effective use of the health care system; planning for subsequent pregnancies; returning to school; and finding employment. Nurses also educated mothers about early infant temperament and how to promote infants' social, emotional, and cognitive development. Finally, nurses helped mothers expand their informal support network to include husbands, boyfriends, and other family and friends and to develop reliable, ongoing relationships with their pediatricians and other health and human service providers. Participation in the program lasted for two years, and a follow-up study was conducted when the children were four years old.

The percentage of low-birth-weight babies decreases the earlier prenatal care begins and the more years of education the mother has. Percentages of low-birth-weight infants are higher for African Americans (versus whites) among mothers who began prenatal care at the same time and had similar levels of education.

Pregnant women who participated in the program made more use of formal services, experienced greater informal social support, made more improvements in their diets, and reduced their smoking compared to similar women not in the program. Very young teenagers in the program showed a significant improvement in their babies' birth weights and a reduction in preterm deliveries. After delivery, these women displayed higher levels of infant and child care and made better use of health and social services. There was also a 75 percent reduction in verified cases of child abuse and neglect and a 42 percent decrease in subsequent pregnancies among low-socioeconomic-status unmarried women in the program (Olds, 1997).

Diet and Nutrition

For mothers with poor diets, rates of prematurity and infant mortality are higher, birth weights are lower, and the risk of congenital malformations increases (Salisbury & Robertson, 2013). Nutritionally deprived infants are less responsive to environmental stimulation and are irritable when aroused. Malnourished infants are found to have a significantly reduced number of brain cells, especially when the malnutrition occurred during the last trimester or during the first three months following birth (Lozoff, 1989). What constitutes a nutritious diet during pregnancy? As Katie Glover mentions in the "Working With" feature, pregnant women should increase consumption of fruits, vegetables, and calcium-rich and folate-rich foods and strive to eat a balanced diet overall.

Infants born to undernourished or poorly nourished mothers not only exhibit immediate effects of their nutritional deprivation, but several long-term studies reveal that they are also at risk for developing cardiovascular disease, type 2 diabetes, and metabolic and endocrine diseases later in life (Salisbury & Robertson, 2013). Evidence is accumulating that permanent adaptations are made in structure, physiology, and metabolism *in utero* in response to inadequate nutritional supply. This response, called "fetal programming" by Barker and his colleagues (Godfrey & Barker, 2001), predisposes the infant to the adult diseases previously mentioned.

Stress and Health

Stress refers to chronic feelings of worry and anxiety. Women who experience severe and prolonged anxiety just before or during pregnancy are more likely to have medical complications and give birth to infants with abnormalities than women who do not. Emotional stress has been associated with greater incidence of spontaneous abortion, difficult labor, premature birth and low birth weight, newborn respiratory difficulties, and physical deformities (Littleton, Bye, Buck, & Amacker, 2010; Norbeck & Tilden, 1983; Omer & Everly, 1988).

Birth

After thirty-eight weeks in the womb, the fetus is considered to be "full term," or ready for birth. At this point, it will weigh around 7.5 pounds, but it can weigh as little as 5.75 pounds or as much as ten pounds and still be physically normal. The fetus measures about twenty inches or so at this stage, almost one-third of its final height as an adult.

During the final weeks, the womb becomes so crowded that the fetus assumes one position more or less until birth. This orientation is sometimes called *fetal presentation*. **Fetal presentation** (or *orientation*) refers to the body part of the fetus that is closest to the mother's cervix. The most common fetal presentation, and the most desirable one medically, is head pointing downward (called a *cephalic presentation*). Two other presentations also occur: feet and rump first (*breech presentation*) or shoulders first (*transverse presentation*). These two orientations used to jeopardize an infant's survival, but modern obstetric techniques have greatly reduced their risk.

Most fetuses develop normally for the usual thirty-eight to forty weeks and face their birth relatively well prepared. When the labor process begins, it too usually proceeds normally. The uterus contracts rhythmically and automatically to force the baby downward

fetal presentation Refers to the body part of the fetus that is closest to the mother's cervix; may be head first (cephalic), feet and rump first (breech), or shoulders first (transverse).

> **WORKING WITH** Katie Glover, OB-GYN Nurse Practitioner
>
> **Preparing for Childbirth**
>
> Katie Glover was interviewed in her office at the primary health care clinic where she works. Despite her hectic schedule, Katie has a relaxed and unhurried manner. She has a three-year-old son and is currently seven months pregnant. Our interview focused on preparation for childbirth.
>
> **Rob:** *What advice do you give pregnant women about their nutrition?*
>
> **Katie:** Pregnant women need three to four glasses of milk a day and should increase consumption of fruits and vegetables, which many people don't eat regularly. As a bottom line, we recommend a balanced diet plus a few extra calories and vitamin supplements. We also recommend a twenty-five-to-thirty-pound weight gain over the course of a pregnancy, depending on the woman's size, build, and weight.
>
> **Rob:** *Why do you recommend weight gain?*
>
> **Katie:** If you figure the average baby weighs roughly 6.5 to 7.5 pounds and the average placenta weighs maybe three to five pounds, and add the extra fluid a woman retains and extra subcutaneous fat her body stores as added protection, that's about twenty to twenty-five pounds right there.
>
> **Rob:** *How do weight gain and other changes of pregnancy affect women?*
>
> **Katie:** They certainly change their body image. How a woman feels about that directly relates to how she feels about being pregnant. Someone who's thrilled about pregnancy will be happy to see her belly getting bigger. Someone who resents the pregnancy is likely to have a harder time with her body's changes. It's not just that her breasts are getting larger or her stomach is getting bigger. She can't run up and down the stairs as easily, and she can't find a comfortable position to sleep in. Pregnancy gets in the way of your life. You have to alter how you move and how you eat and how often you go to the bathroom—day and night. When all you really want is a good eight hours of sleep, you may start wondering if it's all worth it!
>
> **Rob:** *Pregnancy can be stressful, then.*
>
> **Katie:** Yes. In a way, pregnancy is a crisis. How a person copes with that crisis has a lot to do with her feelings about being pregnant as well as what her social and emotional support system is like. If her partner, parents, or friends provide good, solid support and appreciation for what she's experiencing, pregnancy is likely to be a more positive experience than if she doesn't have such support.
>
> **Rob:** *What preparation for childbirth do you offer your patients?*

through the vaginal canal (see Figure 4.4). The contractions occur in a relatively predictable sequence of stages, and as long as the baby and mother are healthy and the mother's pelvis is large enough, the baby usually is out within a matter of hours.

Stages of Labor

It is common for the mother to experience "false labor," or *Braxton-Hicks contractions,* in the last weeks of pregnancy as the uterus "practices" contracting and relaxing in preparation for actual labor. These contractions do not open the cervix as real labor contractions do.

Labor consists of three stages. The *first stage of labor,* which lasts from the first true contraction until the cervix (the opening of the uterus) is completely open, or *dilated* to 10 centimeters (4.5 inches), is the longest stage. It usually begins with relatively mild and irregular contractions of the uterus. As contractions become stronger, more regular, and more frequent, *dilation,* or widening, of the cervix increases until there is enough room for the baby's head to fit through. As it stretches and dilates, the cervix also becomes thinner, a process referred to as *effacement.* Toward the end of this first stage of labor, which may take from eight to twenty-four hours for a first-time mother, a *period of transition* begins. The cervix approaches full dilation, contractions become more rapid, and the baby's head begins to move into the birth canal. Although this period generally lasts for only a few minutes, it can be the most intense and challenging one because contractions become

WORKING WITH Katie Glover, OB-GYN Nurse Practitioner

Preparing for Childbirth *continued*

Katie: Most medical practices encourage some kind of childbirth classes. Classes typically cover the various stages of pregnancy, physiological and psychological changes a woman might experience, changes in the couple's relationship. We talk about labor and what the hospital will be like. We talk about the different kinds of pain medications that might be offered, their effects, and the risks and benefits. Most classes also teach basic relaxation and breathing techniques, which are very important. Knowing what to expect and how to deal with the anxiety and pain can really help make labor a more positive experience.

Rob: *How do you feel about birth clinics and home deliveries?*

Katie: For many people who don't want to give birth in a hospital, a birth center is ideal, whether it's freestanding or directly attached to a hospital. It offers a little more freedom of movement, a little more comfort, a different atmosphere, and reassurance that medical backup is available if needed, including quick transfer to a fully equipped hospital. Of course, parents who come to a birth center should be carefully screened beforehand for any potential medical complications.

Rob: *What about home birth?*

Katie: I think it's a good option for the very small percentage of people who are truly suited for it.

Rob: *Why is that?*

Katie: It takes a very high level of commitment to arrange a home birth. Real problems can arise if it's not something both partners agree on and believe in deeply. If both partners are always there for each other, if the home situation is a nice, clean, supportive place, and if a pediatrician and a well-trained, experienced obstetrician or midwife and good emergency medical backup are available, then go for it!

What Do You Think?

1. Katie suggests that pregnancy is a type of crisis and that how a woman copes with it will depend on her attitudes toward pregnancy and the social support she receives. How might this knowledge be used to design programs to help pregnant teenagers cope better with the "crisis" of pregnancy?
2. How might a woman's pregnancy affect the father and other family members?
3. Katie discusses alternatives to hospital birth. What additional information might you need to consider these alternatives for yourself?

---

stronger and more deeply felt, lasting from forty-five to ninety seconds each. Managing each contraction involves a great deal of concentration and energy; women typically use the period between contractions to catch their breath and prepare for the next contraction. During transition, a woman often experiences a variety of physical changes, including trembling, shaking, leg cramps, nausea, back and hip pain, burping, and perspiring, and tends to be preoccupied with feelings of pain, pressure, and hoped-for relief (McKay, 1993).

The *second stage of labor* ranges from complete dilation of the cervix to birth. Contractions continue but may be somewhat shorter, lasting forty-five to sixty seconds. Although the baby now has only a few more inches to move down the vagina to be born, the process can be slow, usually lasting between one and two hours for a first baby and less than a half-hour for women who have previously given birth. Although dilation is complete, for most women the reflexive urge to push the baby out by bearing down full strength usually develops toward the end of this stage, and often becomes irresistible. When a woman first begins to push, she may be uncoordinated and need to learn to push "with" the contraction and rest in between. How hard she pushes will depend on the strength of the contractions, which varies throughout labor. If a woman doesn't feel the urge to push, guidance from a partner can help, particularly if she had an epidural block or other local anesthetic that interferes with her bearing-down reflex.

During the *third stage of labor*, which lasts between five and twenty minutes, the afterbirth, which consists of placenta and umbilical cord, is expelled. Contractions still occur

What Do You Think?

If good prenatal diet and health care are so closely related to healthy prenatal and postnatal development, why don't all expectant mothers follow nutritious diets and receive good health care? How can adequate health care be made available to all pregnant women?

but are much weaker, and the woman may have to push several times to deliver the placenta. The medication Pitocin, a synthetic version of oxytocin, is frequently given to help the placenta to detach from the side of the uterus. Putting the baby to the mother's breast also can help because stimulation of the nipple naturally releases oxytocin (McKay, 1993).

Childbirth Settings and Methods

Until the 1800s, births in the United States generally took place in the woman's home. Usually it was attended by midwives, friends, neighbors, and family members and was viewed as a natural process rather than as a medical procedure. The **midwife** was a woman experienced in pregnancy and childbirth who traditionally served as the primary caregiver during pregnancy, childbirth, and the month or so following birth. During the 1800s, political and social factors and the emergence of medicine as a scientifically based and politically powerful profession led to the replacement of midwives by physicians as the chief birth attendants. In the 1900s, delivery moved to the hospital, where it was increasingly treated as a medical rather than a naturally occurring community event (Bogdon, 1993; Steiger, 1993).

These changes brought the benefits of modern medical technology to the birth process and resulted in decreased mortality rates for mothers and their babies, particularly in the case of high-risk pregnancies. However, they also shifted the birth process from being a natural event controlled by the pregnant woman, her family, her friends, and the community

midwife The person, usually a woman, who is the primary caregiver to a woman during pregnancy, childbirth, and the month or so following delivery.

FIGURE 4.4
The Process of Delivery

The labor and delivery process occurs in three stages, including active labor, birth, and delivery of the afterbirth. The stages vary in their duration, but the labor and delivery process for first-time mothers usually lasts between twelve and eighteen hours.

The baby in the uterus before labor

Water about to break (The baby's head now rests inside the cervix)

Transition: The baby in the birth canal

STAGE 1

The baby about to be born

The head rotates sideways after it emerges

The delivery of the placenta

STAGE 2　　　　　　　　　　　　　　　　　　　　　**STAGE 3**

Part 2 Beginnings

After all the hard work of labor, a baby! No matter how exhausted she may feel, a mother is usually glad to see her new child, especially once reassured that it is healthy.
Source: Paul Hakimata Photography/Shutterstock.com.

to a medical event controlled by physicians. As a result, all babies and their mothers were exposed to the risks associated with hospital-based medical practices, including overreliance on medication and on procedures such as episiotomies and caesarian sections (discussed a bit later).

Hospital Births

Currently 98.2 percent of all births in the United States occur in hospitals under the supervision of a physician; the remaining 1.8 percent of births occur at home or in a birth center. In recent years, the maternity wards of many hospitals have modified their environments to be more comfortable and supportive of pregnant women and their families. A growing number of hospitals now have *birthing rooms* with more comfortable furniture, muted colors and lighting, soft music, and facilities for *rooming in* that allow mother and baby to stay together until both are ready to leave the hospital. By the late 1970s, the majority of husbands were attending the birth (Simkin, 2007), and most hospitals now encourage a partner to be present during the delivery because it shortens the duration of labor somewhat and enhances the mother's satisfaction with the birth process (Hodnett et al., 2007).

Nonhospital Settings

Freestanding birth centers (FBCs) are nonhospital facilities organized to provide family-centered maternity care for women who are judged to be at low risk for obstetrical complications (Rooks et al., 1989). Equipped and staffed to handle all but the most serious medical emergencies and designed like simple but comfortable hotels, birth centers encourage the active involvement of the mother, her family, and her friends in a birth process that minimizes technical intervention deemed to be medically unnecessary and physiologically and psychologically stressful in low-risk deliveries (Eakins, 1993).

Home birth is another alternative to hospital birth available for low-risk pregnancies. In a typical home birth, normal daily activities continue through the first stage of labor. When contractions increase, the nurse-midwife or physician is called to monitor the labor. Backup arrangements with a doctor or hospital generally are in place should they be needed, and women planning on home birth are carefully screened to minimize last-minute complications requiring hospital equipment or procedures. In addition to the widely held view that hospitals are the place of choice for birth, difficulty in obtaining malpractice insurance and resistance by the medical profession are major barriers to widespread acceptance of home birth.

Prepared Childbirth

The majority of hospitals and nonhospital birth settings offer programs to help women and their partners prepare for the physical and psychological experience of birth. These include preparatory visits to the hospital or birth facility, where pregnant women and their partners can become familiar with the physical setting and procedures. Various methods

prepared childbirth A method of childbirth in which parents have rehearsed or simulated labor and delivery well before the actual delivery date.

of **prepared childbirth** have been devised to help parents rehearse, or simulate, the actual sensations of labor well before the projected delivery date. Although these methods differ from one another in certain details, all generally emphasize educational, physical, and emotional preparation for the birth process and active involvement of the mother and father (or other partner). Typically, they encourage the mother to find a coach (often her spouse or a relative) to give her personal support during labor (Lamaze, 1970; Livingston, 1993a, 1993b, 1993c).

The earliest proponent of prepared or "natural" childbirth was Grandly Dick-Read, an English physician who believed that the pain women experience during childbirth was not natural but due to a combination of fear and tension caused by cultural ignorance of the birth process and by the isolation and lack of emotional and social support women receive during labor and in hospital delivery rooms (Livingston, 1993a.). The Read method consisted of educating women about the physiology of labor and training them in progressive relaxation techniques to reduce tension, fatigue, and pain. Read also encouraged obstetricians and nurses to be more patient and to rely less heavily on medication in the birth process.

Currently the most widely used approach to prepared childbirth in the United States is the Lamaze method, which was originated in the Soviet Union; brought to France in the 1950s by Fernand Lamaze, the head of a maternity hospital; and then popularized in the United States by Marjorie Carmel, an American who had given birth to her first child at Lamaze's hospital in France and wanted to use the method for the birth of her second child in the United States. The Lamaze method differs from the Read approach in that it strongly encourages the active participation of *both* mother and father (or labor partner) during the weeks preceding delivery and during the delivery itself (Livingston, 1993b; Lothian & DeVries, 2005). The Lamaze method encourages labor either without drugs or with minimal drugs and stresses the importance of birth as a natural, shared, emotional experience (Livingston, 1993b; Lothian & DeVries, 2005).

Women who have participated in Lamaze and similar childbirth approaches report more favorable attitudes toward labor and delivery, less discomfort and stress during the birth process, less reliance on medication, and more sensitive interaction with the newborn baby (Cogan, 1980; Lindell, 1988). A father's involvement in preparing for and participating in the delivery process has been found to positively influence his experience of birth, his behavior toward mother and baby during delivery, and his relationship to his new infant (Hoffnung, 1992; Markman & Kadushin, 1986).

Another widely used method of natural childbirth was introduced by Robert Bradley, an American obstetrician who modified Read's technique. Bradley's husband-coached childbirth method stresses the importance of the father as comforter, supporter, and caregiver before and during the delivery. Bradley also emphasizes relaxation and controlled breathing in a calm, quiet, physically comfortable environment (Livingston, 1993c).

Modern Midwives and Doulas

Throughout human history and around the world, midwives have helped other women give birth. As we saw earlier, doctors largely replaced midwives in the United States in the nineteenth and early twentieth centuries, but in recent years, midwifery has been on the rise. Today, midwives in the United States are trained and licensed to give care and advice to women during pregnancy, labor, and the postpartum period, to conduct deliveries, and to care for newborn infants. Midwives also provide counseling and education not only to women giving birth but to the family and community as well, helping them with prenatal education and preparation for parenthood, family planning, and child care (Davis, 1987; Steiger, 1993).

Two kinds of midwives practice in the United States. *Direct-entry midwives* (DEMs) are self-trained or have learned midwifery skills through apprenticeship to individual practicing midwives. *Certified nurse-midwives* (CNMs) are registered nurses (RNs) with additional hospital and academic training in obstetrics. Direct-entry midwives practice mainly at home births and at privately run, freestanding birth centers, but generally are not licensed to assist in hospital deliveries. Certified nurse-midwives are licensed to practice in a wide variety of settings, including hospitals, freestanding birth centers,

Pregnant women and their partners/birth coaches attend a childbirth preparation class together. These kinds of classes reduce the stress and discomfort of childbirth, lead to less reliance on pain medication during the birth process, and have even been found to reduce the duration of labor and delivery.
Source: Monkey Business Images/Shutterstock.com.

and home births, and generally work under the supervision of a physician. Midwives historically have played an important role in poor, rural areas, particularly in the rural South, where a longstanding tradition of midwife-assisted births exists among African American women who were denied access to medical care through segregation and economic discrimination (Holmes, 1993; Steiger, 1993). In 2010, midwives assisted in about 8 percent of all births in the United States (ACNM, 2012). Today, the demographics of women choosing to have a CNM attend their birth are similar to those of national demographics, with more women in New Mexico, the Northeast, and Oregon choosing CNM-assisted birth (Declercq, 2012).

The term *doula* applies to an individual who cares for the new mother, especially when breast feeding begins after the baby is born. Like midwives, doulas have helped with the birth process around the world since the beginning of human history. Doulas do not deliver babies, but may assist a mother and midwife in the process. Depending on the culture, the role of doula may be filled by one or more relatives or friends or, at times, by a midwife. The use of doulas has increased over the last decade in the United States. Research suggests that women who receive social and emotional support from doulas have shorter labors, fewer labor and delivery complications, fewer caesareans, and less use of painkillers or artificial oxytocin; they also appear better able to cope with the demands of motherhood (Gilbert, 1998; Raphael, 1993; Scott, Klaus, & Klaus, 1999).

Medicinal Methods during Delivery

Despite adequate psychological preparation, most mothers feel some pain during labor contractions. Under good conditions, many mothers can endure this pain until the baby is delivered. But if labor takes an unusually long time or a mother finds herself less prepared than she expected, pain-reducing drugs such as narcotics or other sedatives can make the experience bearable. But such medications must be used cautiously. Most pain relievers cross the placenta and therefore can seriously depress the fetus if given at the wrong time or in improper amounts. During the final stages of delivery, two other forms of pain relief are available. Doctors may inject a sedative into the base of the woman's spine. The two most common of these procedures are an *epidural* and a *dual spinal-epidural (or "walking epidural")*. They allow the mother to remain awake and alert during the final stages of labor, but they may impede her ability to help in the delivery process by regulating her own contractions. Epidurals have also been found to lengthen the duration of labor by one and a half to three hours (Cheng, Schaffer, Nicholson, & Caughey, 2014; Shmueli et al., 2017). Nitrous oxide, which dentists commonly use, also has been used to take the edge off the pain of the peak contractions, while allowing the mother to remain conscious.

Giving a mother a general anesthetic before delivery removes all pain, of course, but both mother and child may take a long time to recover from it. Due to the heightened risk to the mother and newborn, general anesthetics are used in less than 1 percent of deliveries. In addition to the physical risks posed by general anesthetics, the bonding between mother and child may be delayed while both are recovering from the effect of the anesthesia. Table 4.2 lists

Chapter 4 Prenatal Development and Birth   **97**

TABLE 4.2 Major Medications during Childbirth and Their Effects on the Baby

Type	Administration	Positive Effects for Mother	Negative Effects for Baby
Analgesics	By injection (in controlled doses) during the first stage of labor to reduce pain	Reduces pain, causes some drowsiness and euphoria (sense of well-being and tranquility); women participate in labor and delivery	May cause drowsiness and decreased responsiveness for first few hours after birth or longer; naloxone hydrochloride (Narcon) can be used to reverse these effects
Local anesthesia—spinal	By injection into spinal canal in controlled doses when cervix is fully dilated (beginning of second stage of labor); numbs sensory and motor nerves so that mother's pelvic area and legs cannot move voluntarily	Mother can remain awake and aware during labor and delivery; can be used for either vaginal or caesarean birth; is highly effective in eliminating pain	No negative effects reported
Local anesthesia—epidural	By injection during active phase of first stage of labor to numb sensory nerves after their exit from spinal canal	Pain and sensations are generally eliminated; mother is awake; some voluntary movement is preserved, although it is less effective because a woman's sense of position and tension is blocked by the medication	No negative effects reported
General anesthesia	A mixture of nitrous oxide and oxygen is inhaled; is less commonly used than blocking agents	Easily administered, rapid onset of effect; anesthetic of choice in emergencies in which time is critical and baby must be delivered quickly	Decreased alertness and responsiveness following birth

Source: Feinbloom (2000).

the major types of medications used during labor and delivery, their administration, and their effects (Feinbloom, 2000).

Problems during Labor and Delivery

Interference with labor and delivery can occur in three ways: through *faulty power* in the uterus, a *faulty passageway* (the birth canal), or a *faulty passenger* (the baby itself). These problems actually interconnect in various ways, but it is convenient to distinguish among them (Buckley & Kulb, 1983).

Faulty Power

Sometimes the uterus does not contract strongly enough to make labor progress to a delivery. The problem can occur at the beginning of labor or develop midway through a labor that began quite normally, especially if the mother tires after hours of powerful contractions. In many cases, the doctor can strengthen the contractions by giving the mother an injection of a synthetic version of the hormone oxytocin called "Pitocin." Such *induced labor*, which occurs in about 5 percent of all deliveries, must be monitored carefully so that the artificial contractions it stimulates do not harm both baby and mother by forcing the baby through the canal before the canal is ready (WHO, 2011).

Faulty Passageway

Sometimes the placenta partially or completely covers the cervix and blocks the baby from moving down the birth canal during labor. This condition, called *placenta previa,*

Pregnant women and their partners/birth coaches attend a childbirth preparation class together. These kinds of classes reduce the stress and discomfort of childbirth, lead to less reliance on pain medication during the birth process, and have even been found to reduce the duration of labor and delivery.
Source: Monkey Business Images/Shutterstock.com.

and home births, and generally work under the supervision of a physician. Midwives historically have played an important role in poor, rural areas, particularly in the rural South, where a longstanding tradition of midwife-assisted births exists among African American women who were denied access to medical care through segregation and economic discrimination (Holmes, 1993; Steiger, 1993). In 2010, midwives assisted in about 8 percent of all births in the United States (ACNM, 2012). Today, the demographics of women choosing to have a CNM attend their birth are similar to those of national demographics, with more women in New Mexico, the Northeast, and Oregon choosing CNM-assisted birth (Declercq, 2012).

The term *doula* applies to an individual who cares for the new mother, especially when breast feeding begins after the baby is born. Like midwives, doulas have helped with the birth process around the world since the beginning of human history. Doulas do not deliver babies, but may assist a mother and midwife in the process. Depending on the culture, the role of doula may be filled by one or more relatives or friends or, at times, by a midwife. The use of doulas has increased over the last decade in the United States. Research suggests that women who receive social and emotional support from doulas have shorter labors, fewer labor and delivery complications, fewer caesareans, and less use of painkillers or artificial oxytocin; they also appear better able to cope with the demands of motherhood (Gilbert, 1998; Raphael, 1993; Scott, Klaus, & Klaus, 1999).

Medicinal Methods during Delivery

Despite adequate psychological preparation, most mothers feel some pain during labor contractions. Under good conditions, many mothers can endure this pain until the baby is delivered. But if labor takes an unusually long time or a mother finds herself less prepared than she expected, pain-reducing drugs such as narcotics or other sedatives can make the experience bearable. But such medications must be used cautiously. Most pain relievers cross the placenta and therefore can seriously depress the fetus if given at the wrong time or in improper amounts. During the final stages of delivery, two other forms of pain relief are available. Doctors may inject a sedative into the base of the woman's spine. The two most common of these procedures are an *epidural* and a *dual spinal-epidural (or "walking epidural")*. They allow the mother to remain awake and alert during the final stages of labor, but they may impede her ability to help in the delivery process by regulating her own contractions. Epidurals have also been found to lengthen the duration of labor by one and a half to three hours (Cheng, Schaffer, Nicholson, & Caughey, 2014; Shmueli et al., 2017). Nitrous oxide, which dentists commonly use, also has been used to take the edge off the pain of the peak contractions, while allowing the mother to remain conscious.

Giving a mother a general anesthetic before delivery removes all pain, of course, but both mother and child may take a long time to recover from it. Due to the heightened risk to the mother and newborn, general anesthetics are used in less than 1 percent of deliveries. In addition to the physical risks posed by general anesthetics, the bonding between mother and child may be delayed while both are recovering from the effect of the anesthesia. Table 4.2 lists

TABLE 4.2 Major Medications during Childbirth and Their Effects on the Baby

Type	Administration	Positive Effects for Mother	Negative Effects for Baby
Analgesics	By injection (in controlled doses) during the first stage of labor to reduce pain	Reduces pain, causes some drowsiness and euphoria (sense of well-being and tranquility); women participate in labor and delivery	May cause drowsiness and decreased responsiveness for first few hours after birth or longer; naloxone hydrochloride (Narcon) can be used to reverse these effects
Local anesthesia—spinal	By injection into spinal canal in controlled doses when cervix is fully dilated (beginning of second stage of labor); numbs sensory and motor nerves so that mother's pelvic area and legs cannot move voluntarily	Mother can remain awake and aware during labor and delivery; can be used for either vaginal or caesarean birth; is highly effective in eliminating pain	No negative effects reported
Local anesthesia—epidural	By injection during active phase of first stage of labor to numb sensory nerves after their exit from spinal canal	Pain and sensations are generally eliminated; mother is awake; some voluntary movement is preserved, although it is less effective because a woman's sense of position and tension is blocked by the medication	No negative effects reported
General anesthesia	A mixture of nitrous oxide and oxygen is inhaled; is less commonly used than blocking agents	Easily administered, rapid onset of effect; anesthetic of choice in emergencies in which time is critical and baby must be delivered quickly	Decreased alertness and responsiveness following birth

Source: Feinbloom (2000).

the major types of medications used during labor and delivery, their administration, and their effects (Feinbloom, 2000).

Problems during Labor and Delivery

Interference with labor and delivery can occur in three ways: through *faulty power* in the uterus, a *faulty passageway* (the birth canal), or a *faulty passenger* (the baby itself). These problems actually interconnect in various ways, but it is convenient to distinguish among them (Buckley & Kulb, 1983).

Faulty Power

Sometimes the uterus does not contract strongly enough to make labor progress to a delivery. The problem can occur at the beginning of labor or develop midway through a labor that began quite normally, especially if the mother tires after hours of powerful contractions. In many cases, the doctor can strengthen the contractions by giving the mother an injection of a synthetic version of the hormone oxytocin called "Pitocin." Such *induced labor*, which occurs in about 5 percent of all deliveries, must be monitored carefully so that the artificial contractions it stimulates do not harm both baby and mother by forcing the baby through the canal before the canal is ready (WHO, 2011).

Faulty Passageway

Sometimes the placenta partially or completely covers the cervix and blocks the baby from moving down the birth canal during labor. This condition, called *placenta previa*, which occurs in approximately one out of 200 pregnancies, is usually detected early in the third trimester of the pregnancy and causes intermittent bleeding and occasional cramping (USNLM, 2012). If left untreated, it may leave the fetus somewhat undernourished, because it prevents sufficient blood from reaching it. Sometimes it blocks a normal delivery entirely so that the baby must be delivered by caesarean section (ACOG, 1995).

Faulty Passenger

Usually a baby enters the birth canal head first, but occasionally one turns in the wrong direction during contractions. A *breech presentation*—with the bottom leading—is risky for the baby because its spine can be broken if a contraction presses it too hard against the mother's pelvis. Or the baby may not get enough oxygen because it cannot begin breathing on its own until after its nose comes out. In some cases, a skilled midwife or a doctor can deliver a breech baby with no problem, but if the baby is stuck partway out of the vagina, medical staff may use *forceps* or *ventouse* (vacuum-assisted delivery) to pull it the rest of the way out. In most cases, breech babies are either turned to the right position during delivery or delivered surgically by caesarean section.

A small but significant proportion of babies are simply too big to pass through the mother's pelvis and vaginal canal, a problem sometimes called *cephalopelvic disproportion (CPD)*—literally, a disproportion of the head and pelvis. If the mismatch is too severe and threatens the life of mother or child, the doctor may interrupt the labor and deliver the baby surgically.

Caesarean Section

Caesarean section, or *C-section,* is a procedure used in cases where the baby cannot be safely delivered through the vagina and therefore has to be removed surgically. Techniques for this surgery have improved substantially over the past decades. The operation now takes only about half an hour, most of which is devoted to sewing the mother up after getting the baby out. The number of C-sections for live births, is currently at about one in three births (Martin et al., 2013). This rate increased from 26 to 36 percent between 2003 and 2009, with the most common reason cited as "nonreassuring fetal status," a term that refers to changes in fetal heart rate, and a diagnosis that some suggest is overused, accounting for the concerning increase in C-sections (Barber et al., 2011; Morrison, 1998). Many experts and parent advocates remain concerned that the rates are too high and reflect medical practices that are not in the best interests of mothers and their babies (ACOG, 1995; Taffel, 1993).

Both supporters and critics of caesarean birth agree there are a number of good reasons to select a caesarean birth as the safest way to deliver a baby. These include the problems of placenta previa and cephalopelvic disproportion (CPD) already noted, as well as prolapsed cord, where the umbilical cord cuts off the baby's oxygen; unusual positions of the baby that make vaginal delivery impossible; severe fetal distress that cannot be corrected; and active herpes, where the baby may be infected through vaginal birth.

Nurses discussing a fetal monitoring report from the external monitor that is strapped to the expectant mother's abdomen.
Source: Tyler Olson/Shutterstock.com.

Chapter 4 Prenatal Development and Birth

Fetal Monitoring

Most hospitals and birthing centers use *electronic fetal monitoring* to record uterine contractions and the fetal heart rate. Uterine contractions are externally measured by a pressure gauge strapped to the mother's abdomen that electronically represents changes in the shape of the uterus on graph paper. Fetal heart rate can be picked up by an *external* ultrasound monitor placed on the abdomen over the uterus or *internally* by a wire, leading through the vagina and screwed into the fetus's scalp, that records more subtle electrical changes in the fetus's heart.

Although internal fetal monitoring is extremely helpful in high-risk and emergency situations, experts have questioned its routine use for low-risk deliveries. Some have suggested that the procedure may itself contribute to fetal (and maternal) distress. In addition, the mother must lie in bed for as long as the wires are attached (USNLM, 2013). Experts have also noted that by shifting the center of focus from the experience of mother and baby to readouts from the equipment, "high-tech" births may reduce certain aspects of clinical awareness that are central to good obstetric care (Davis-Floyd, 1986).

Birth and the Family

For most families, the arrival of a new baby brings many changes, and it takes some time to adjust. For first-time parents, learning to care for a new baby and rearranging family schedules to provide the almost constant attention a newborn requires are very big challenges, to say the least. The arrival of a new baby can be particularly difficult for parents who lack the economic resources, knowledge, and social and emotional support that are so important in adjusting to the complicated demands of caring for a new baby. Having a baby that is low birth weight or other problems can be particularly traumatic. Though it is unwise to generalize too broadly, adolescent parents, single parents, and parents who are educationally and economically disadvantaged are more likely to find parenthood difficult.

Nevertheless, the great majority of births in this country occur without significant problems and to families whose economic, social, and psychological resources enable them to become effective parents. For women (and their partners) who receive good preparation and training for the birth process and obtain adequate social and emotional support from family, friends, and culture, birth is likely to be a very positive and welcome event.

For parents who already have children, a newcomer to the family also creates stresses. Children naturally worry they will lose their special place in the family and the exclusive attention they enjoy once the newcomer arrives. Involving the child in the preparation for birth, for the period when the mother is in the hospital, and for the changes that will occur with the new arrival are all important ways to help a child adjust to the changes. Talking to the child about these things and listening carefully to his or her questions and concerns are particularly important. Especially with preschoolers, providing concrete information about birth, newborn babies and what they are like, and the specific changes that will occur in the family before and after the baby's birth can help allay their fears.

After the new baby arrives home, parents can do a number of things to assist the adjustment process. Giving the older child lots of verbal reassurance helps, but concrete actions often speak louder than words. One strategy is to give the child an important role in the event by providing special activities, asking friends and family members to bring a gift for the child as well as for the new baby, and including the child in daily activities with the new infant. High priority should also be placed on continuing routine activities with the older child and ensuring that each parent spends lots of special time just with him or her.

Looking Back/Looking Forward

- **Continuity within change**—In the span of 38 weeks or so, genetic material provided by the parents at conception transforms itself into a zygote, an embryo, a fetus, and finally a newborn infant. Though the changes we have discussed are primarily physical, we will see shortly that the newborn is exquisitely prepared for the

> **What Do You Think?**
>
> How might the process of birth vary depending on a family's circumstances such as age, marital status, income, race, and culture? To explore this question, have yourself and several classmates play the roles of expectant parents from different life circumstances. What did you discover?

impressive cognitive and psychosocial changes that will follow. We will also see that the physical changes exhibit a high degree of continuity with the past.

- **Lifelong growth**—Prenatal development and birth are an important part of the groundwork for lifelong growth. The amazing growth in complexity and size that occurs prenatally provides the lifelong basis for the equally amazing changes in the physical, cognitive, and psychosocial domains that occur from birth onward. During infancy, childhood, adolescence, and the adult years, elaboration and growth will occur in all three domains, although not necessarily at the same rates in each.

- **Changing meanings and vantage points**—During pregnancy and the months immediately following birth, the meanings of events are almost entirely in the minds of family members and other caregivers of the newborn. But as a combination of maturation, experience, and eventually awareness and self-determination lead the development of the infant through early, middle, and later childhood, adolescence, and adulthood, meanings and vantage points will change substantially, not only for the developing child but also for parents, siblings, and friends, who themselves are changing due to their own developmental experiences. The excitement of an infant's first steps, first words, or first friendship will give way to the excitement of the preschooler's growing athletic, verbal, and interpersonal skills.

- **Developmental diversity**—Differences imparted to us genetically at conception begin to change our developmental trajectories immediately. Moreover, exposure to stimuli, nutrients, and medications prenatally can forever change the ways our bodies and brains develop. These differences will be impacted and amplified as our environments begin to influence our physical, cognitive, and psychosocial development throughout the course of childhood and adolescence.

Chapter Summary

- **What important developmental changes occur during prenatal development?** Prenatal development begins with conception, in which a zygote is created by the union of a sperm cell from the father and an egg cell, or ovum, from the mother. It consists of discrete periods, or stages. The germinal stage occurs during the first two weeks following conception; the zygote forms a blastocyst, which differentiates into three distinct layers and then implants itself on the uterine wall to form the embryo. During the embryonic stage, weeks three through eight, the placenta and umbilical cord form and the basic organs and biological systems begin to develop. During the fetal stage, week nine until the end of pregnancy, all physical features complete their development. The experience of pregnancy includes dramatic changes in a woman's physical functioning and appearance, as well as significant psychological changes as prospective parents anticipate the birth of the baby.

- **What risks do a mother and baby normally face during pregnancy, and how can they be minimized?** Although prenatal development is highly canalized, there are critical periods—particularly during the first trimester—when embryonic development is highly vulnerable or at risk for disruptions from teratogens, substances or other environmental influences that can damage an embryo's growth. Teratogenic effects depend on the timing, intensity, and duration of exposure, the presence of other risks, and the biological vulnerability of baby and mother. Risk factors for prenatal development include both medicinal and nonmedicinal drugs, such as heroin, cocaine, alcohol, and tobacco; diseases such as syphilis, gonorrhea, and AIDS; physical and biological characteristics of the mother; and physical, biological, and chemical environmental hazards. Adequate prenatal nutrition and health care for the mother and her developing baby is associated with successful pregnancy, a normal birth, and healthy neonatal development.

- **What happens during the birth process, what difficulties may occur, and how are they handled?** Labor occurs in three distinct but overlapping stages. The first stage, during which uterine contractions increase in strength and regularity and the cervix dilates sufficiently to accommodate the child's head, takes from eight to twenty-four hours (for a first-time mother). The second stage, when the dilation of the cervix is complete and the birth itself takes place, lasts from 60 to 120 minutes. The third stage, during which the placenta is delivered, lasts only a few minutes. Nonhospital birth centers and home births are two alternatives to hospital-based births. Prepared childbirth is now widely used in both hospital and nonhospital birth settings to help women actively and comfortably meet the challenges of giving birth. Many babies are now delivered by midwives, who provide caregiving to women during pregnancy, childbirth, and the weeks following delivery. Doulas do not deliver babies, but help the mother during birth and with her newborn. Pain-reducing medications can make the experience of childbirth more comfortable, but in recent years have been used more cautiously because of their potentially adverse effects on the recovery of both infant and mother.

Problems during labor and delivery can include insufficient uterine contractions, or faulty power; a faulty passageway caused by blockage of the birth canal; and a faulty passenger, which may occur if the baby's physical position or large head prevents the completion of the journey through the birth canal. When vaginal delivery is not feasible, the physician may perform a caesarean section to deliver the baby surgically.

Learning to care for a new baby is a welcome challenge for most new parents, but it may be especially difficult for adolescent parents, single parents, and parents who are educationally and economically disadvantaged.

Key Terms

amniotic sac (p. 82)
canalization (p. 84)
conception (p. 80)
critical period (p. 85)
embryonic stage (p. 80)

fetal alcohol syndrome (FAS) (p. 87)
fetal presentation (p. 91)
fetal stage (p. 80)
germinal stage (p. 80)
midwife (p. 94)

placenta (p. 81)
prepared childbirth (p. 96)
teratogen (p. 85)
umbilical cord (p. 82)
zygote (p. 79)

The First Two Years of Life

PART 3

Source: ucchie79/Shutterstock.com.

Chapter 5
Physical Development during the First Two Years

Chapter 6
Cognitive Development during the First Two Years

Chapter 7
Psychosocial Development during the First Two Years

As parents and other proud relatives keep discovering, infants grow and change more rapidly than the rest of us. Every few weeks, or sometimes even in a matter of days, infants seem to do something new. In just months, they are able to smile, sit, and babble. In just a few more months, they begin acquiring language, show signs of make-believe play, and take their first tentative steps. They go from smiling at any human face, to preferring their parents' familiar faces, to crying and showing distress at the sight of strangers.

These changes are pivotal in many ways as they lay important foundations for all future development. The next three chapters describe these crucial changes.

Physical Development during the First Two Years

Chapter 5

Source: Bolyuk Rostyslav/Shutterstock.com.

Chapter Outline
PHYSICAL DEVELOPMENT
The Newborn
Growth during Infancy
Infant States: Sleep and Arousal
Motor Development
Nutrition During the First Two Years
Impairments in Infant Growth

Focusing Questions

- What do infants look like when they are first born? How do we know if they are healthy?
- How much do children grow during infancy?
- What changes occur in the brains of infants?
- How do infants' sleep and wakefulness patterns change as infants get older?
- What motor skills evolve during infancy?
- What do infants need nutritionally?
- What factors can impair growth during infancy?

Anne was looking at the journal she had kept about her daughter since Michelle was seven months old.

- April 9: For two weeks, she has been sleeping through the night! Maybe it helped to start nursing her just before bedtime—but it's so hard to tell. She is starting to enjoy bedtime stories, too; babbles at the book and points at the pictures.

- June 10: Michelle has been crawling all over—mostly after the dog. Gets mad, cries when Huggins walks away; struggles to crawl after him; but then forgets all about him.

- August 10: Here's Michelle's latest words: "dada" (daddy), "tigg'n" (Tigger, the cat), "buh" (book). Maybe not polished English, but she's getting there. At this rate, I'm going to lose track of her full vocabulary soon.

As Anne can attest, during the first months of life a baby's behaviors evolve rapidly. In this chapter, we trace some of these changes through the first two years of life. We begin by discussing young infants' physical growth: what they look like, how they sleep, hear, and see, and what behaviors they can already perform at birth. We also look at variations in growth and in infants' nutritional needs in the first months of life. In Chapter 6, we take a second look at infants' development, this time from a cognitive perspective. We explore infants' perceptions and representations of their surroundings and how they learn from their world even before they learn to speak. Finally, we consider one of the most universal yet remarkable of all human accomplishments: the acquisition of language.

As we will see, when compared to other parts of the childhood and adolescence, development during infancy shows more obvious growth and more discontinuity, but less diversity. Growth occurs now as at no other time of life! Babies change daily, putting on pounds and inches and acquiring new skills. "You can almost *see* them grow," said one mother. Growth—both physical and psychological—continues throughout life, but never in quite such an obvious way as in infancy. The very speed of infant growth creates important *dis*continuities: a child who cannot talk at six months, for example, is well on her way to talking at eighteen months.

As we will see, babies also show diversity. Not every infant acquires language, for example, in quite the same sequence or with the same timing. But compared to the important developments of adolescence, infant developments are among the most predictable of the lifespan, both in timing and in nature. It is possible to predict within a few months either way, for example, when most infants will take their first step or speak their first word. Such accurate predictions are rarely possible for adolescents and adults.

PHYSICAL DEVELOPMENT

The Newborn

As we saw in the last chapter, birth continues rather than initiates physical development. Most organs have already been working for weeks, or even months, prior to this event. The baby's heart has been beating regularly, muscles have been contracting sporadically, and the liver has been making its major product, bile, which is necessary for normal digestion after birth. Even some behaviors, such as sucking and arm stretching, have already developed. Two physical functions, however, do begin at birth: breathing and ingestion (the taking in of foods). These fundamental physical functions constitute the basic physical continuities that must last a lifetime. The baby's heart is the same one that will be beating eighty years and more than two billion heartbeats later; her lungs and stomach will grow larger, but they will be the same lungs and stomach taking in oxygen and food decades later when she has become elderly.

The First Few Hours

neonate A newborn infant.

When first emerging from the birth canal, the newborn infant (also called a **neonate**) definitely does not resemble most people's stereotypes of a beautiful baby. Regardless of race, skin often looks rather red. If born a bit early, the baby may also have a white, waxy substance called *vernix* on the skin, and the body may be covered with fine, downy hair called *lanugo*. If the baby was born vaginally rather then delivered surgically, its head may be somewhat elongated or have a noticeable point on it; the shape comes from the pressure of the birth canal, which squeezes the skull for several hours during labor. Within a few days or weeks, the head fills out again to a more rounded shape, leaving gaps in the bones.

The gaps are sometimes *called fontanelles,* or "soft spots," although they are actually covered by a tough membrane that can withstand normal contact and pressure. The gaps eventually grow over, but not until the infant is about eighteen months old.

Immediately after birth, many hospitals and midwives recommend Kangaroo Mother Care, which includes skin-to-skin contact between the newborn and mother for a period of time as well as breastfeeding (Boundy et al., 2016). Kangaroo Care has been linked to lower rates of infant hypothermia, hypoglycemia, and mortality as well as higher levels of oxygen in the blood (Boundy et al., 2016).

Is the Baby All Right? The Apgar Scale

The **Apgar Scale** (named after its originator, Dr. Virginia Apgar) helps doctors and nurses to decide quickly whether a newborn needs immediate medical attention. The scale consists of ratings that are simple enough for non-specialists to make, even during the distractions surrounding the moment of delivery (Apgar, 1953). To use it, someone present at the delivery calculates the baby's heart rate, breathing effort, muscle tone, skin color, and reflex irritability and assigns a score of zero to two on each of these five characteristics. Babies are rated one minute after they emerge from the womb and again at five minutes. For each rating, they can earn a maximum score of two, for a total possible score of ten, as Table 5.1 shows. Most babies earn eight, nine, or ten points, at least by five minutes after delivery. A baby who scores between five and seven points at one minute is given immediate special medical attention, which usually includes an examination by a pediatrician while oxygen is held under the baby's nose, and is then carefully observed to make sure that the Apgar scores increase to between eight and ten points at the five-minute retest. Monitoring continues during the next few hours and days for any problems that may develop (American Academy of Pediatrics, 2013a; Brazelton & Nugent, 1997).

Apgar Scale A system of rating newborns' health immediately following birth based on heart rate, strength of breathing, muscle tone, color, and reflex irritability.

Size and Bodily Proportions

A newborn baby weighs about 7.5 pounds and measures about twenty inches lying down. Her length matches her adult size more closely than her weight does: her twenty inches represent more than one-quarter of her final height, whereas her 7.5 pounds amount to only a small percentage of her adult weight.

Babies' proportions and general physical appearance may have psychological consequences by fostering *attachments*, or bonds, with the people who care for them (see Chapter 7, "Psychosocial Development in the First Two Years"). Such bonds promote feelings of security. The cuteness of infants' faces in particular seems to help. No matter what their racial or ethnic background, most babies have unusually large foreheads, features that are concentrated in the lower part of the face, eyes that are large and round, and cheeks that are high and prominent. A pattern of babyish features occurs so widely among animals, in fact, that biologists who study animal behavior suspect it has a universal and genetically based power to elicit parental or nurturing responses among adult animals (Archer, 1992;

This neonate was delivered moments before the photo was taken. Notice the vernix coating much of the newborn's body.
Source: Naypong/Shutterstock.com.

Chapter 5 Physical Development during the First Two Years 107

TABLE 5.1 The Apgar Scale Score

Characteristic	Score 0	Score 1	Score 2
Heart rate	Absent	Less than 100	More than 100 beats
Heart rate	Absent	Less than 100 beats per minute	More than 100 beats per minute
Efforts to breathe	Absent	Slow, irregular	Good; baby is crying
Muscle tone	Flaccid, limp	Weak, inactive	Strong, active motion
Skin color	Body pale or blue	Body pink, extremities blue	Body and extremities pink
Reflex irritability	No response	Frown, grimace	Vigorous crying, coughing, sneezing

Source: Apgar (1953).

Two adorable brown bear cubs.
Sources: (top) Alena Ozerova/Shutterstock.com; (bottom) Voldymyr Burdiak/Shutterstock.com.

Lorenz, 1970). Mother in some species of ducks, for example, take care of baby ducks even when the babies are not their own. Among human parents and children, attachments may start with this sort of inherent attraction of parents to infants, though, of course, it deepens as additional personal experiences accumulate across the lifespan.

Growth in Infancy

Infants experience a remarkably high rate of growth—they gain height and weight more rapidly during their first two years than at any other point during their post-birth lifetimes. And while increases in height and weight will be clearly evident and frequently measured by pediatricians (because gains in height and weight are indicative of the infant's overall health), less visible growth in the brain will also produce dramatic changes in the infant.

Physical Growth

While actual gains in height and weight can vary from infant to infant, on average, infants double their weight from 7.5 pounds at birth to about 15 pounds by the age of five months, and triple their weight to about 22 pounds by their first birthday (see Figure 5.1). Weight is gained less rapidly during the second year of life, with the average twenty-four-month-old weighing about 28 pounds, approximately four times the weight of a newborn. Young infants tend to have a plump, soft look that results from the accumulation of fat. Body fat helps the infant maintain a constant body temperature. By their first birthday, infants will have lost much of their "baby fat," a trend that continues until puberty (Fomon & Nelson, 2002).

Infants also gain height, adding approximately ten inches (twenty-five centimeters) to their newborn length of twenty inches (fifty centimeters) by their first birthday, and will continue to get taller during their second year, achieving an average height of about thirty-four inches (eighty-six centimeters) by their second birthday, which is roughly half of their adult height (see Figure 5.1). Body proportions are also changing during the first two years, revealing differences in growth for various parts of the body. At birth, the baby's head accounts for one-quarter of the newborn's total height. In other words, the head is more developed than the torso and limbs. By age two, the head accounts for one-fifth of the total height, as growth of the torso and limbs proceeds at a greater rate than the growth of the head. By adulthood, the head will account for approximately one-eighth of the total height of the average adult. As we will see in Chapter 14, adolescents also experience asymmetrical growth that makes them look gangly rather than like adorable baby ducklings.

> **What Do You Think?**
>
> What do you think attracts parents to their newborn children? Explore this question with the parents of a physically handicapped infant. How did they feel about their child (and about themselves) when the child was born?

Brain Growth

While the head may not be growing as rapidly as the rest of the body, significant development is occurring in the brain and central nervous system during the first two years of life. The **central nervous system** consists of the brain and nerve cells of the spinal cord, which together coordinate and control the perception of stimuli, as well as motor responses of all kinds. The more complex aspects of this work are accomplished by the brain, which develops rapidly from just before birth until well beyond a child's second birthday. In fact, it will be at least two decades until the brain is fully mature (Stiles & Jernigan, 2010). At seven months past conception, the baby's brain weighs about 10 percent of its final adult weight, but by birth, it has more than doubled to about 25 percent of final adult weight. By the child's second birthday, the brain has tripled to about 75 percent of its final adult weight (Freund et al., 1997).

Most of this increase results not from increasing numbers of nerve cells, or **neurons**, but from the development of a denser, or more fully packed, brain. This happens in two ways. First, the neurons generate many new dendritic fibers that connect them with one another in a process called **synaptogenesis** (see Figure 5.2). At birth, very few neuronal connections or *synapses* exist, but by age two, each neuron may be connected to hundreds or even thousands of other neurons. Growth of the dendrites is the primary reason why brain weight triples from birth to age two (Johnson, 2010). New synapses are formed in response to every experience the child has; in fact, during infancy, more synapses are formed than are necessary, a phenomenon described rather colorfully as **transient exuberance**, due to

central nervous system The brain and nerve cells of the spinal cord.

neurons Nerve cell bodies and their extensions or fibers.

synaptogenesis The forming of connections, or *synapses*, between neurons.

transient exuberance The rapid but temporary increase in the rate of synaptogenesis and, hence, the number of synapses formed between neurons during infancy.

Height and Weight Growth during the First Two Years

FIGURE 5.1

Growth Curves for the First Two Years

During infancy, rapid gains in height (left chart) and weight (right chart) are evident. On average, boys are slightly taller and heavier than girls are, but differences are minimal and are often overshadowed by increasing variability in height and weight within groups of boys and girls.

Chapter 5 Physical Development during the First Two Years

FIGURE 5.2
Anatomy of a Typical Human Neuron

This illustration shows the typical structures of a human nerve cell, including dendrites through which information typically enters the cell, the cell body, the axon covered by a myelin sheath, and the axon terminals through which nerve impulses are passed to adjacent neurons.

Source: Designua/Shutterstock.com.

synaptic pruning The process through which unused synapses and neurons are eliminated.

plasticity The degree to which a developing structure or organ (like the brain) can be influenced by the environment.

the temporarily rapid and overproductive nature of synaptogenesis at this time. Because more synapses form in response to every experience during infancy and childhood than are needed, many of these synapses are never used again. Consistent with the adage "use it or lose it," unused synapses are eliminated in a process called **synaptic pruning**. When redundant and unused synapses and neurons are eliminated, the nervous system functions more efficiently.

An important consequence of the transient exuberance that occurs during infancy is that it heightens the **plasticity** of the brain, which is the degree to which the brain reacts to experiences with the environment. Plasticity plays a central and often protective role in infant development. If an infant is raised in an enriched environment that provides lots of stimulation and nurturance, the production of synapses is amplified. However, if the infant is raised in an environment with little stimulation, the brain responds by forming and retaining fewer synapses. We can illustrate this with an explanation that is often offered for the superior verbal abilities of firstborn children when compared to their laterborn siblings. Firstborn children, at least until the second child is born, are the recipients of all of their caregivers' attention. This verbally enriched and supportive environment leads to the proliferation of synapses in the regions of the brain responsible for language—areas of the cerebral cortex in the left hemisphere of the brain. Parental attention must be divided among siblings when laterborns arrive, creating an environment for laterborns that is not as verbally-enriched as that experienced by the firstborn child (Frank, Turenshine, & Sullivan, 2010; Glass, Neulinger, & Brim, 1974), leading to lower scores on measures of verbal ability for laterborn children.

Environmental deficiencies can have long-term effects if they are severe and exposure is prolonged during infancy and early childhood. One longitudinal study in Great Britain found that "early adversity"—measured by ratings of the childhood home environment, including cleanliness, age, state of repair, and crowdedness, along with ratings of hygiene and cleanliness of the children themselves (prior to age four)—was associated with lower scores on a variety of cognitive measures through childhood and adolescence that persisted into adulthood (Richards & Wadsworth, 2004). However, plasticity serves in a protective capacity as well, as indicated in infants who suffered left-hemisphere strokes. The areas of the brain responsible for understanding and producing language are localized in the left hemisphere of the brain. However, after an intervention that included intense verbal stimulation, the right hemisphere assumed control of verbal comprehension and production, and language was able to develop normally (Rowe et al., 2009). The plasticity of the brain is greatest during infancy and early childhood, when the rates of synaptogenesis and synaptic pruning are highest.

myelination The process through which myelin, a fatty sheathing, covers the axon of some neurons.

An additional, important change in the brain during infancy that has a great impact on development is **myelination**, a process in which certain brain cells called *glia* produce fatty sheathing, or *myelin*, that gradually encases the neurons and their fibers. The myelin serves to protect and insulate the axons of neurons, allowing them to conduct neural impulses much more quickly. Myelination occurs rapidly during infancy and childhood, and then continues at a slower rate until about age thirty (Taylor, 2006).

110 Part 3 The First Two Years of Life

> **Do You Think?**
>
> Do you think that everyone grows at the rates described? Did you? What factors might lead to more or less growth during infancy? If possible, find out how tall you were on your second birthday and multiply that figure by two. How close is that number to your current height? Why might the numbers be different?

An important function of the brain is to control infants' states of sleep and wakefulness. The brain regulates the amount of stimulation infants experience, both externally and internally. Thus, periodic sleep helps infants to shut out external stimulation and thereby allows them to obtain general physical rest while strengthening and consolidating memories of what they have learned while awake. And, somewhat paradoxically, sleep may provide the opportunity for the brain to stimulate itself.

Infant States: Sleep and Arousal

Perhaps one of the biggest surprises for first-time parents is how little time they actually have to interact with their newborn babies while the babies are alert and responsive. Also, the sometimes irregular sleep patterns of newborns can prove to be both physically and emotionally challenging for parents. These challenges are compounded when new parents receive conflicting information about how to help their babies sleep better or longer when they seek advice on the subject.

Sleep

In the days immediately after birth, newborns sleep an average of sixteen hours per day, although some sleep as little as eleven hours a day and others as much as twenty-one (Michelsson et al., 1990). By age six months, babies average just thirteen or fourteen hours of sleep per day, and by twenty-four months, only eleven or twelve. But these hours still represent considerably more sleeping time than the six to eight hours typical for adults. So if infants sleep so much, why are their parents so tired?

As Figure 5.3 shows, newborns divide their sleeping time about equally between relatively active and quiet periods of sleep. The more active kind is named **REM sleep**, after the "*r*apid *e*ye *m*ovements," or twitchings, that usually accompany it. In the quieter kind of sleep, **non-REM sleep**, infants breathe regularly and more slowly, and their muscles become much limper. It takes approximately sixty minutes for an infant to cycle through REM and non-REM sleep, as compared to a ninety-minute cycle for adults. This discrepancy in the duration of infant cycling and adult cycling is thought to be one reason for new parents' exhaustion: Their sleep cycles are being continually interrupted by their infant's waking, fragmenting their sleep much like someone with a sleep disorder (Montgomery-Downs, Insana, Clegg-Kraynok, & Mancini, 2010).

Unfortunately for parents, a baby's extra sleep time does not usually include long, uninterrupted rest periods, even at night. In the first few months, it is more common for the baby to waken frequently—often every two or three hours—but somewhat unpredictably. Studies of brain development suggest that much of the unpredictability may result from the physical immaturity of the baby's nervous system: his brain may have frequent, accidental "storms" of impulses because it is not yet fully formed (Fransson et al., 2009; Sheldon et al., 1992). In most cases, the irregularities pose no problem to an infant, though as the "Focusing On" feature describes, in some children irregularities of neural activity may be related to "crib death," or sudden infant death syndrome, in a very small percentage of infants. Once a baby's sleep begins to consolidate into longer periods of wake and sleep, these periods have a tendency to "drift" so that a baby who is mostly sleeping through the night one week may be awake most of the night a few weeks later, another reason new parents are so sleepy (Kaltman & Engelmann, 1953; Par melee et al., 1964).

REM sleep A stage of sleep in which one's body is paralyzed, but one's eyes and brain are very active. REM sleep is believed to be important for memory consolidation.

non-REM sleep The stages of sleep that vary from light sleep to very deep, restorative sleep. The deeper stages of non-REM sleep play a pivotal role in helping us feel rested, growing, repairing cells, and bolstering immune function.

Chapter 5 Physical Development during the First Two Years

Focusing On...

Sudden Infant Death Syndrome

Each year, about one out of every two thousand young infants dies during sleep for no apparent reason. Doctors call this phenomenon sudden infant death syndrome (SIDS), or "crib death." The problem is most frequent among infants between ages two months and four months, although SIDS can affect babies as young as one month and as old as one year. Even though the rate of SIDS has been reduced by 50 percent since 1994, it is the leading cause of death among infants who survive the first few weeks after delivery (AAP Task Force on SIDS, 2011).

SIDS is disturbing because it is so mysterious. Typically, parents put a seemingly healthy baby down to sleep as usual, but when they come in to get her up again, they discover she is dead. Sadly, because the baby had exhibited no health problems, the parents often blame themselves for the death, suspecting that somehow they neglected their child or hurt him in some way (Kaplan, 1995). Even more unfortunately, friends and relatives often concur in blaming the parents, simply because they can think of no other way to explain SIDS. Other obvious causes simply do not happen. The baby does not choke, vomit, or suffocate; she just stops breathing.

What causes SIDS? One theory is that SIDS is an exaggerated form of normal *sleep apnea,* temporary cessations of breathing during sleep (Hunt, 1992). Another theory suggests that SIDS occurs primarily at a special transition in development, just when inborn reflexive control of breathing begins to fade in importance but before infants have firmly established voluntary control of breathing. For most infants, this transition occurs at about two to four months of age, just when SIDS strikes most often. A third theory suggests that SIDS infants suffer from heart problems: their nervous systems may fail to prompt regular, strong heartbeats and in essence cause them to suffer a heart attack. Unfortunately, no clear evidence points to any of these alternative explanations. Recent neuroscience research suggests that prenatal exposure to nicotine appears to alter receptors in the brain stem that play a role in the governance of certain autonomic functions (like heart rate and respiration). In preterm infants, prenatal exposure to nicotine impairs their recovery from *hypoxia*—low levels of oxygen in the blood—that might result from an obstruction, like a soft blanket, pillow, or stuffed animal, interfering with their supply of oxygen (AAP Task Force on SIDS, 2011).

If medical researchers could identify a basic cause, they would help future infants at risk for SIDS. Those babies could wear monitors that would indicate interruptions in breathing (if lungs are the problem) or heart rate (if that is the problem) and prompt parents or medical personnel to give the baby immediate, appropriate help. But so far, the use of monitors has not been practical on a widespread scale because they can be cumbersome, cause a lot of unnecessary alarm, and occasionally fail to function properly.

Medical research has identified several factors that make a particular family or infant more likely to experience SIDS (American Academy of Pediatrics, 2013b; Byard & Cohle, 1994). Very young mothers and fathers (younger than twenty years) stand a greater chance of having a SIDS infant, as do mothers who smoke cigarettes or have serious illnesses during pregnancy. Mothers who are poorly nourished during pregnancy also carry more

sudden infant death (SIDS) Sudden infant death syndrome (or "crib death"), an unaccountable death of an infant in its sleep.

FIGURE 5.3
Developmental Changes in Sleep Requirements

Sleep changes in nature as children grow from infancy to adulthood. Overall, they sleep less, and the proportion of REM (rapid-eye-movement) sleep decreases sharply during infancy and childhood.

Developmental Changes in Sleep Requirements

> **Focusing On . . .**
>
> ### Sudden Infant Death Syndrome *continued*
>
> risk than mothers who keep reasonably well nourished. Infants who begin daycare before four months of age also appear to be at higher risk for SIDS. Preliminary data indicate that 20 percent of SIDS deaths occur when the infants are being cared for someone other than a parent, and one-third of those deaths occurred during the first week of day care. But certain babies also are at greater risk for SIDS independent of their parents' qualities or behaviors. Boys die of SIDS more often than girls do, for example, and infants born small (less than seven pounds) die more often than larger infants do. These relationships do not mean, however, that being a boy or being small actually *causes* SIDS; they imply only that for reasons still not understood, SIDS seems to strike boys and small infants more frequently.
>
> Even taken together, these factors do not predict SIDS very accurately. The vast majority of high-risk infants do not die, whereas some infants with few risk factors die from SIDS. This circumstance creates problems in translating the studies of risk factors into concrete recommendations for medical personnel and parents because taking the risk indications too literally can arouse fears in parents unnecessarily. The most useful recommendations tend to be valid for all families, whether or not they are at risk for SIDS (Carroll & Siska, 1998). For example, the American Academy of Pediatrics (2013b) offers the following recommendations as part of their safe sleep policy for all children:
>
> - Infants should sleep on their backs until age one for every sleep; sleep positioners like foam wedges or rolled blankets designed to encourage side-sleeping should not be used.
> - Consider the use of pacifiers for naptime and nighttime sleep.
> - Infants should sleep on a firm surface that is covered by a fitted sheet.
> - Soft objects, loose bedding, bumper pads, top sheets or blankets, and stuffed animals should not be in the baby's sleep area.
> - Specifically designed sleep clothing (e.g., sleepers, snug-fitting pajamas) should be used instead of blankets.
> - The temperature in the room should be comfortable for a lightly clothed adult.
> - Never allow smoking in rooms where babies sleep.
>
> These are good pieces of advice for everyone, but unfortunately, they do not guarantee complete protection from SIDS. For parents whose babies do die, many hospitals and communities have created support groups in which couples can share their grief and come to terms with it.
>
> ### What Do You Think?
>
> If you were counseling a parent who lost a baby to SIDS, what would be your most important concern? What might you say to the parent? What might you also say to a relative of the parent who suspects that neglect may have caused the death?

Parents' Response to Infant Sleep and Arousal

The unpredictability of infants' sleep can create chronic sleep deprivation in many parents; as a group, in fact, parents of infants and toddlers—along with older teenagers—are among the most sleep-deprived people in society (Coren, 1996). Research has demonstrated that new mothers obtain about seven hours of sleep each day, which is not significantly less than the average adult gets (Mongtomery-Downs et al., 2010). So why are new parents so much more tired than the rest of us? As noted above, when babies wake up to be fed or changed, parents' sleep cycles are interrupted, causing sleep fragmentation similar to various sleep disorders (Insana & Montgomery-Downs, 2013; Montgomery-Downs et al., 2010). In fact, there is evidence that new fathers may be sleepier than new mothers are; most men do not get paternity leave and, therefore, cannot "make up" for disrupted sleep with daytime napping (Insana & Montgomery-Downs, 2013). Parents' fatigue is aggravated by living arrangements common in modem Western society. Unlike in many non-Western societies, where babies often sleep in the same bed the mother does (something that the American Academy of Pediatrics warns against), infants in our society are often "stationed" in an adjoining room, or at least in a separate bed across the room—an arrangement that makes assisting the baby more disruptive. Furthermore, many non-Western households may have a number of adults or older relatives regarded as capable of calming a baby at night. In our society, in contrast, a household commonly has only two adults, or even just one. The scarcity of "qualified" helpers places a disproportionate burden of nighttime child care on parents, and eventually contributes to fatigue.

Infants spend more time sleeping than doing anything else. Unfortunately, their sleep may not occur at night, so chronic sleep deprivation and sleep fragmentation is a real problem for most parents, particularly primary caregivers. If possible, it is helpful for the caregiver to nap at the same time as the baby. However, because of discrepancies in the time it takes infants (sixty minutes) and parents (ninety minutes) to complete a sleep cycle, even this is not optimal.
Source: Alliance/Shutterstock.com.

The "cure" for nighttime fussiness eventually depends on physical maturation, but parents can also influence their infant's sleep patterns by developing regular (though not rigid) times for and methods of waking, feeding, and sleeping that involve the infant. One study found that infants change toward more adult-like levels of wakefulness and sleep within six weeks after arriving home, provided routines are (relatively) regular (Bamford et al., 1990; Rivkees, 2003). Another found that regularity offers dividends later in childhood: comparisons of Dutch and American families found fewer sleep problems among the young children of Dutch families, whose culture encourages regularity of daily routines more strongly than North American society does (Harkness & Keefer, 1995).

The advice to strive for (relatively) regular routines is widely supported among parent advice experts, but note that it makes assumptions about families that are not always true. In some families, routines cannot be made regular because of competing pressures from other children, because of exhaustion from work or from earlier ill-timed wakings or feedings, or because the family has only one parent. Under these conditions, parents need additional support from friends, extended family, or social service workers. They cannot do it all themselves.

States of Arousal

As Table 5.2 shows, infants exhibit various states of arousal, from sleep to full wakefulness. As they get older, their patterns of arousal begin to resemble those of older children (Ferber & Kryger, 1995). The largest share of time, even among older infants, goes to the most completely relaxed and deepest form of sleep.

Obviously, a fully alert state is a time when babies can learn from their surroundings, but it may not be the only time. During REM sleep, infants' heart rates speed up in reaction to sounds, suggesting that infants may process stimulation even while asleep. But the meaning of a faster heart rate is ambiguous: changes in it may also show neural *dis*organization or an inability to shut out the world. Babies who are born prematurely confirm this possibility because they show more variability in heart rate than full-term babies when they hear sounds in their sleep (Spassov et al., 1994).

In addition to responding to external stimulation during REM sleep, the brains of infants also appear to be engaging in self-stimulation (Roffwarg, Muzio, & Dement, 1966) in this sleep phase. For quite some time, researchers have been wondering what is occurring in the minds of infants during REM sleep—are they dreaming? While this question has not been answered definitively, the brain-wave patterns of young infants in REM sleep differ

TABLE 5.2 States of Arousal in Infants

State	Behavior of Infants
Non-REM sleep	Complete rest; muscles relaxed; eyes closed and still; breathing regular and relatively slow
REM sleep	Occasional twitches, jerks, facial grimaces; irregular and intermittent eye movements; breathing irregular and relatively rapid
Drowsiness	Occasional movements, but fewer than in REM sleep; eyes open and close; glazed look; breathing regular, but faster than in non-REM sleep
Alert inactivity	Eyes open and scanning; body relatively still; rate of breathing similar to drowsiness, but more irregular
Alert activity	Eyes open, but not attending or scanning; frequent, diffuse bodily movements; vocalizations; irregular breathing; skin flushed
Distress	Whimpering or crying; vigorous or agitated movements; facial grimaces pronounced; skin very flushed

Source: Ferber and Kryger (1995).

> **What Do You Think?**
>
> How do parents deal with differences in children's sleep patterns? Ask a classmate or friend who is a parent of more than one child, or ask your own parent(s) how he or she responded to sleep differences in the children as infants. Combine your information with that of several other classmates. Do you see any trends?

from those of adults who are dreaming, suggesting that infants are not dreaming, or at least they are not dreaming in the same way that adults dream. However, at about three or four months of age, the brain-wave patterns of infants in REM sleep become similar to those of adults who are dreaming (Zampi, Fagioli, & Salzarulo, 2002).

Sensory Acuity

If you have not spent much time around infants, you may share William James' (1890) conclusion that "the baby, assailed by eyes, ears, nose, skin, and entrails at once, feels it all as one great blooming, buzzing confusion" (p. 462). William James was trained as a physician and was a professor of philosophy at Harvard University during the late nineteenth and early twentieth centuries. His writings on the intersection of physiology and philosophy helped to establish and shape the new discipline of psychology. James was pondering what parents have questioned for ages: how can infants, new to this world and with no knowledge or point of reference with which to interpret their experiences, interpret the information flooding their senses? What do they sense, and what is their understanding of it? Are they truly confused amidst the blooming buzz of sensory signals? Since James' 1890 description of infants, more than a century of research that utilized new methodologies and technologies revealed some surprising capabilities regarding the sensory acuity of infants.

Visual Acuity

Infants can see at birth, but they lack the clarity of focus or *acuity* (keenness) characteristic of adults with good vision. When looking at stationary contours and objects, newborns see more clearly at short distances, especially at about eight to ten inches—about the distance, incidentally, between a mother's breast and her face. Their vision is better when tracking moving objects, but even so their overall vision is rather poor until about one month of age (Seidel et al., 1997).

Visual acuity improves a lot during infancy, but it does not reach adult levels until the end of the preschool years. An older infant (age one to two) often has 20/30 or 20/40 vision, meaning he can see fine details at twenty feet that adults can see at thirty or forty feet. This quality of vision is quite satisfactory for everyday, familiar activities; in fact, many adults can see no better than this, without even realizing it. But this level of visual acuity does interfere with seeing distant objects.

Color vision also improves dramatically during the few months after birth. Specialized neurons called cones that are located in the retina at the back of the eye enable humans to see color, but these cones are immature at birth (Kellman & Arterberry, 2006). One-month-old infants can distinguish between black, red, and white, and their attention is drawn to bold, high-contrast color patterns. By approximately four months of age, their ability to see colors, including soft pastels and subtle differences between hues, is similar to that of adults (Franklin, Pilling, & Davies, 2005).

Auditory Acuity

Auditory acuity refers to sensitivity to sounds. Infants can hear at birth, but not as well as adults. Any sudden loud noise near an infant, such as that caused by dropping a large book on the floor, demonstrates she can hear. Such a sound produces a dramatic startle reaction, called a *Moro reflex:* The neonate extends her limbs suddenly, sometimes shakes all over, and may also cry. Not all noises produce this reaction; pure tones, such as the sound of a flute, cause relatively little response. Complex noises containing many different sounds usually produce a stronger reaction; a bag of nails spilling on the floor, for example, tends to startle infants reliably.

Regardless of the type of sound, infants tend to exhibit a preference for higher-pitched sounds than lower tones. This fact has sometimes led some experts to suggest that infants have a "natural" preference for female—that is, high-pitched—human voices. Studies of voice preferences, however, have not confirmed this possibility consistently, probably because newborns' range of special sensitivity lies well above the pitch of even female voices and because male and female voices usually are more similar in overall quality than gender stereotypes suggest. Instead, it is more accurate to say that infants prefer sounds in the middle range of pitches, which is the range most similar to human voices, male or female. Recent research on infant auditory preferences has indicated that infants exhibit a distinct preference for human speech sounds over other human and nonhuman vocalizations (Shultz & Vouloumanos, 2010), especially those that are expressed in higher pitches (Fernald & Kuhl, 1987) such as the babbling of other infants (Masapollo, Polka, & Ménard, 2016).

Tactile, Taste, and Olfactory Acuity

Newborns and infants are sensitive to touch (i.e., *tactile acuity*), as all caregivers who have comforted a crying baby by swaddling the child in a blanket or by cradling the child in their arms can attest. Also, as will be addressed in the next section, infants respond reflexively to physical contact—turning toward a touch on the cheek or closing their hands around objects that touch their palms—abilities that are present at birth (Futagi, Toribe, & Suzuki, 2009).

Can infants feel pain? This question has been the focus of much debate during the past few decades, but an increasing body of behavioral and neurological evidence seems to indicate that they can (Warnock & Sandrin, 2004; Williams et al., 2009). The degree to which infants experience pain is still being researched and is complicated by the subjective nature of the perception of pain. For example, in one study involving a control group of newborns whose heels were pricked, the newborns cried loudly in response to the pain-inducing prick. However, an experimental group of newborns who were first given a drop of sucrose before receiving the heel prick exhibited little response to the prick (Harrison et al., 2010).

As for taste and smell (technically called "olfaction"), infants reveal well-developed acuity, even prior to birth. Preferences for sweet tastes have been demonstrated by fetuses who swallow more frequently after an artificial sweetener has been added to their amniotic fluid (Booth et al., 2010). Infants smile and lick their lips when presented with sweet substances (Steiner et al., 2001), and they pucker and grimace when presented with sour or bitter substances (Kaijura, Cowart, & Beauchamp, 1992). Researchers have argued that infant preferences for sweet tastes may have evolutionary survival advantages, as breast milk tends to be sweet (Liem & Mennella, 2002). Infants also respond with facial expressions that suggest pleasure or disgust when presented with pleasant and unpleasant smells, and by four days after birth, they can discriminate between their own mother's breast smell and that of another lactating mother, keeping their heads turned toward pads with their own mother's scent (Porter & Reiser, 2005).

Can infants feel pain? Any parent who has taken a baby to the doctor for a vaccination can attest that their baby feels pain.
Source: Darren Brode/Shutterstock.com.

> **What Do You Think?**
>
> Do parenting books agree with our comments that young infants have the use of vision and hearing? That babies can feel pain and have very well-developed senses of taste and smell? Check the comments made in two or three books about the capabilities of newborn babies. Do they seem consistent, or at least not *in*consistent?

Given the remarkable sensory acuity of infants, parents may be partly right when they claim their newborn child recognizes them even from birth. What parents may be noticing is their newborn's immediate responsiveness to sights, sounds, smells, taste, and touch. They are right to exclaim over it: by taking an interest in the environment, infants create conditions where they can begin organizing (or *perceiving*) stimuli and attaching meanings to them. As we will see in the next section of this chapter, certain kinds of lines, shapes, and contours are especially interesting to a young infant. So are certain kinds of sounds. Fortunately for the development of family ties, parents are able to provide many of the most interesting sights and sounds with their own faces and voices; and partly in this way, attachments between parents and children are born.

Motor Development

Infants begin life with more than two dozen inborn **reflexes**, or automatic responses to specific stimuli. Table 5.3 summarizes the most important ones. A few reflexes, such as sucking, clearly help the baby to adapt to the new life outside the womb. Others look more like evolutionary vestiges of behaviors that may have helped earlier versions of *Homo sapiens* to cope, for example, by clinging to their mothers at the sound of danger. A few reflexes, such as blinking, breathing, and swallowing, persist throughout a person's life, but most reflexes disappear from the infant's repertoire during the first few months. Their disappearance, in fact, helps doctors to judge whether a baby is developing normally. Newborn reflexes that persist over many months may suggest damage to the nervous system or generally impaired development (El-Dib et al., 2012; Menkes, 1994).

reflex An involuntary, automatic response to a stimulus. The very first movements or motions of an infant are reflexes.

The First Motor Skills

Motor skills are voluntary movements of the body or parts of the body. They can be grouped conveniently according to the size of the muscles and body parts involved. *Gross motor skills* involve the large muscles of the arms, legs, and torso. *Fine motor skills* involve the small muscles located throughout the body. Walking and jumping are examples of gross motor skills, and reaching and grasping are examples of fine motor skills.

motor skills Physical skills using the body or limbs, such as walking and drawing.

Viewed broadly, the sequence in which skills develop follows two general trends. The **cephalocaudal principle** ("head to tail") refers to the fact that upper parts of the body become usable and skillful before lower parts do. Babies learn to turn their heads before learning to move their feet intentionally, and they learn to move their arms before they learn to move their legs. The **proximodistal principle** ("near to far") refers to the fact that central parts of the body become skillful before peripheral, or outlying, parts do. Babies learn to wave their entire arms before learning to wiggle their wrists and fingers. The former movement occurs at the shoulder joint, near the center of the body, and the latter occurs at the periphery.

cephalocaudal principle The tendency for organs, reflexes, and skills to develop sooner at the top (or head) of the body and later in areas farther down the body.

proximodistal principle Growth that exhibits a near-to-far pattern of development, from the center of the body outward.

Gross Motor Development in the First Year

Almost from birth, and before reflex behaviors disappear, babies begin doing some things on purpose. By age four weeks or so, most babies can lift their heads up when lying on their stomachs. At six or seven months, many babies have become quite adept at using their limbs; they can stick their feet up in the air and "bicycle" with them while a parent struggles valiantly to fit a diaper on the moving target. At ten months, the average baby can stand erect, but only if an adult helps. By their first birthday, one-half of all babies

TABLE 5.3 Major Reflexes in Newborn Infants

Reflex	Description	Development	Significance
Survival Reflexes			
Breathing reflex	Repetitive inhalation and expiration	Permanent, although becomes partly voluntary	Provides oxygen and expels carbon dioxide
Breathing reflex	Repetitive inhalation and expiration	Permanent, although becomes partly voluntary	Provides oxygen and expels carbon dioxide
Rooting reflex	Turning of cheek in direction of touch	Weakens and disappears by six months	Orients child to breast or bottle
Sucking reflex	Strong sucking motions with throat, mouth, and tongue	Gradually comes under voluntary control	Allows child to drink
Swallowing reflex	Swallowing motions in throat	Permanent, although becomes partly voluntary	Allows child to take in food and to avoid choking
Eyeblink reflex	Closing eyes for an instant ("blinking")	Permanent, although gradually becomes voluntary	Protects eyes from objects and bright light
Pupillary reflex	Changing size of pupils smaller in bright light and bigger in dim light	Permanent	Protects against bright light and allows better vision in dim light
Primitive Reflexes			
Moro reflex	In response to a loud noise, child throws arms outward arches back, then brings arms together as if to hold something	Arm movements and arching disappear by six months, but startle reaction persists for life	Indicates normal development of nervous system
Grasping reflex	Curling fingers around any small object put in the child's palm	Disappears by three months; voluntary grasping appears by about six months	Indicates normal development of nervous system
Tonic neck reflex	When laid on back, head turns to side, arm and leg extend to same side, limbs on opposite side flex	Disappears by two or three months	Indicates normal development of nervous system
Babinski reflex	When bottom of foot stroked, toes fan and then curl	Disappears by eight to twelve months	Indicates normal development of nervous system
Stepping reflex	If held upright, infant lifts leg as if to step	Disappears by eight weeks, but later if practiced	Indicates normal development of nervous system
Swimming	If put in water, infant moves arms and legs and holds breath	Disappears by four to six months	Indicates normal development of nervous system

can dispense with this assistance and stand by themselves without toppling over immediately (Savelsbergh, 1993). By age seven months, on the average, babies become able to locomote, or move around, on their own. At first, their methods are crude and slow; a baby might simply pivot on her stomach, for example, to get a better view of something interesting. Consistent movement in one direction develops soon after this time, although the movement does not always occur in the direction the baby intends!

Reaching and Grasping

Even newborn infants will reach for and grasp objects they can see immediately in front of them. They often fail to grasp objects successfully; they may make contact with an object but fail to enclose it in their fingers. This early, crude reaching disappears fairly soon after birth, only to reappear at about four or five months of age as two separate skills, reaching

The toddler on the left is watching his older, preschool-aged sister use a pincer grasp to perform a more precise operation using the toy tools on the workbench.
Source: Glenda/Shutterstock.com.

and grasping (Pownall & Kingerlee, 1993). During their second year, infants gain increased control over the movements of their fingers, producing a *pincer grasp* in which the thumb and forefinger are brought together to pick up small objects. These skills soon serve infants in many ways. For example, by their second birthday most babies can turn the pages in large picture books one at a time, at least if the paper is relatively indestructible. But they can also point at the pages without grasping for them. The pincer grasp also allows for improved self-feeding with their hands, fingers, and ultimately, utensils (Ho, 2010).

Walking

A reasonably predictable series of events leads to true walking in most children; Figure 5.4 describes some of these milestones. While the development of walking, overall, tends to follow a progression of "stages," on any given day, infants will exhibit creativity and resourcefulness when it comes to their mobility, so caregivers should not be alarmed if their own infant moves around a room in a manner that is unconventional (Adolph, 2008).

FIGURE 5.4 Milestones of Motor Development

Walking alone is one of the major physical achievements of the first year of life. Quite a few other physical skills usually develop prior to walking, as the figure shows. Note, though, that skills appear at different times for different individuals. Some skills may even appear "out of sequence" in some children.

Chapter 5 Physical Development during the First Two Years

> **What Do You Think?**
>
> If motor skills develop partly through learning, why not just deliberately teach infants to walk? What do you think would be the result of doing so? Do similar considerations apply for certain other important developments in infancy?

By about twelve to thirteen months, most children take their first independent steps. Well before two years, they often can walk not only forward but backward or even sideways. Some two-year-olds can even walk upstairs on two feet instead of on all fours. Usually, they use the wall or a railing to do so. Usually, too, coming downstairs proves more difficult than going up; one solution is to creep down backward, using all four limbs.

Cultural and Sex Differences in Motor Development

Differences in motor development exist among cultures and between the sexes, though they are not always large or dramatic. Certain African cultures, for example, give their infants unusually frequent chances to sit upright and to practice their "walking" reflex when held at a standing position by adults and older children (LeVine, 1994; Munroe et al., 1981). These opportunities seem to stimulate toddlers in these societies to learn to walk earlier and better than North American toddlers do. Early walking, in turn, may prove especially valuable in these societies, which do not rely heavily on cars, bicycles, or other vehicles that make walking less important. Yet, early walking may also be a genetic trait (at least partially) for these groups; without comparable training in reflex walking for North American infants, there is no way to be sure.

Yet differences in motor skills do not always appear where we might expect. Take the Navaho and Hopi tribes, whose infants spend nearly all of their first year bound and swaddled tightly to a flat board, with their arms and legs extending straight down along their bodies (J. Whiting, 1981; van Sleuwen, 2007). Apparently as a result, Navaho and Hopi toddlers do tend to acquire walking a little later than Anglo-American children do. But they do not show delays in other skills inhibited by swaddling—notably, reaching and grasping—and the deficit in walking disappears by the end of the preschool years in most cases (Connelly & Forssberg, 1997).

Culture aside, do boys and girls differ, on average, in motor development? The answer depends on distinguishing what infants *can* do from what they typically *actually* do. What they can do—their competence—has relatively little relationship to their sex. Girl and boy babies sit upright at about the same age, for example, and stand and walk at about the same time. Similar equality exists for all of the motor milestones of infancy.

How infants use their time is another matter. Almost as soon as they can move, boys show more activity than do girls. The trend begins even before birth, when male fetuses move about in their mothers' wombs more than do female fetuses (Moore & Persaud, 1998). After birth, the trend continues: girls spend more time using their emerging fine motor skills. Of course, the differences in use of time may stem partly from parents' encouragement (praise) for "gender-appropriate" behaviors. Given the young age of the children, though, and the fact that activity actually precedes birth, part of the difference must come from genetic endowment: an inborn tendency to be more (or less) active.

It is important to note that whatever their source, sex differences in infants' motor development are only averages and, in any case, rather slight. As groups, boys and girls are more alike than different, and numerous individual boys are less active than numerous individual girls, despite "average" behavior. As a practical matter, it is therefore more important for parents and teachers to respond to the qualities of the individual children for whom they are responsible than to stereotypical "gender" averages.

Nutrition during the First Two Years

As obvious as it sounds, the physical developments in infancy depend on good nutrition throughout the first two years. Like adults, babies need diets with appropriate amounts of protein, calories, and specific vitamins and minerals. For various reasons, however, infants

Swaddling infants, as has been done with this Asian baby girl, is practiced in many cultures. Swaddling tends to slow motor development at first, but not permanently. It may also allow caregivers to carry infants with them during daily activities—a circumstance that could make the skills of vocalizing less urgent to develop.
Source: szefei/Shutterstock.com.

do not always get all the nutrients they need. Often poverty accounts for malnutrition: parents with good intentions may be unable to afford the right foods. In other cases, conventional eating practices interfere: despite relatively expensive eating habits, such as going to fast-food restaurants, some families may fail to provide their children with a balanced diet.

Compared with older children, infants eat less in overall or absolute amounts. A well-nourished young baby in North America might drink somewhat less than one liter (about .95 quarts) of liquid nourishment per day. This amount definitely would not keep an older child or a young adult well nourished, although it might prevent starving. In proportion to their body weight, however, infants need to consume much more than older children or adults do. For example, every day a three-month-old baby ideally should take in more than two ounces of liquid per pound of body weight, whereas an eighteen-year-old needs only about one-third of this amount (Queen & Lang, 1993). If adolescents or young adults drank in the same proportion to their body)' weights, they would have to consume six quarts of liquid per day. That is equivalent to twenty-five cups per day, or about one cup every forty-five minutes during waking hours!

Breast Milk versus Formula

Someone (usually parents) must provide for an infant's comparatively large appetite. Whenever breastfeeding is possible, health experts generally recommend human milk, usually in conjunction with a Vitamin D supplement, as the sole source of nutrition for at least the first six months or so of most infants' lives and as a major source for at least the next six months. In some cases, of course, this recommendation proves difficult or impractical to follow. Babies who need intensive medical care immediately after birth cannot be breast-fed without special arrangements. Some women have difficulty producing milk. Also, for one reason or another, some women may choose not to breast-feed, for example, if they are taking medications that might be passed on to the baby, Also, for one reason or another some women choose not to breast-feed. For example, if a woman is taking medications that might be passed on to the baby or if job situations make breastfeeding difficult she may choose to not breast-feed. For these infants, formulas can be either safer or more convenient.

Why do pediatricians recommend breastfeeding? First, human milk seems to give young infants more protection from diseases and other ailments. Second, human milk matches the nutritional needs of human infants more closely than formula preparations do, and the makeup of human milk changes over time to meet infant nutritional needs; in particular, it contains more iron, an important nutrient for infants. Third, breastfeeding better develops the infant's jaw and mouth muscles because it requires stronger sucking motions than bottle feeding does and because it tends to satisfy infants' intrinsic needs for sucking better than a bottle does. Fourth, breastfeeding may encourage a healthy emotional relationship between mother and infant, simply because it involves a lot of close physical snuggling (La Leche League International, 1991). Breastfeeding also provides benefits to mothers: it is less expensive than formula, and it aids in postpartum weight loss, helps reduce risk for postpartum hemorrhaging, and has been linked to a reduced risk for breast, ovarian, and uterine cancer later in life (Dermer, 2001). After about six months, infants can be introduced gradually to solid foods such as strained cereals mixed with breastmilk and strained fruits. As babies become tolerant of these new foods, parents can introduce others that sometimes require a more mature digestive system, such as strained meats and cooked eggs. Overall, the shift to solid foods often takes many months to complete (see Table 5.4 for guidelines about how to do this). As it occurs, parents must begin paying more attention to their baby's overall nutritional needs because many solid foods lack the broad range of nutrients that breastmilk and formula provide.

Poor Nutrition

Often, North American diets fail to provide enough of three specific nutrients: vitamin A, vitamin C, and iron. Prolonged deficiencies of vitamins A and C seem to create deficits in motor ability and deficiency of iron appears to lead to deficits in cognitive performance (Black

In recent decades, increasing numbers of mothers have chosen to breast-feed their babies, as recommended by most pediatricians. For a significant number of parents and infants, however, partial or complete bottle-feeding remains a valuable option—for example, if fathers wish to be involved in feeding or if the mother's work schedule makes breastfeeding difficult.
Source: Ery Azmeer/Shutterstock.com.

Chapter 5 Physical Development during the First Two Years

TABLE 5.4 Changing Nutritional Needs during Infancy

Age	Parents May Begin
Birth–4 months	Complete diet of breast milk or baby formula, Vitamin D supplement as directed
4–6 months	Puréed single-grain cereal, preferably iron-fortified; begin with one to two teaspoons and work up to one-half cup, twice per day
6–8 months	Puréed vegetables or fruit, one at a time; begin with one to two teaspoons and work up to one-fourth to one-half cup per serving, twice per day
10–12 months	"Finger" foods (e.g., chopped banana, bits of dry cereal)
	Puréed meats or poultry, beginning with one to two teaspoons and working up to one-fourth to one-half cup per serving, three to four times per day.
	Soft but chopped foods (e.g., lumpy potatoes)
	Whole milk, one-half cup per serving, four to five times per day.
24 months	Milk, one-half cup per serving, four to five times per day.

Source: Adapted from the International Food Information Council, 1993, and the USNLM, 2011.

et al., 2011; Pollitt, 1995). For about 4 to 5 percent of infants, these nutritional deficiencies are serious and require immediate remedy. For another group of about the same size, the nutritional deficiencies are less severe but are still a cause for concern. In developing countries worldwide, approximately one in three children suffers from severe malnutrition (UNICEF, 2009). If undernourishment is prolonged, it may produce a condition called **stunting**, which, as the term implies, results in stunted growth—specifically, falling below the fifth percentile in height for one's age when compared to typical growth norms (Abukabar et al., 2010).

stunting Being excessively short in stature—falling under the fifth percentile for height for one's age—caused by chronic undernourishment.

Even when undernourished infants appear healthy and "bright," they may be at risk for later developmental problems because poorly nourished families often experience other serious deprivations, such as poor sanitation, inadequate health care, and lack of educational opportunities. Under these conditions, it may not take much to turn mild under nourishment into severe malnutrition and thus reduce cognitive and motor performance to below satisfactory levels.

Overnutrition

In affluent, calorie-loving societies such as our own, the problem often is not lack of food but getting too much of calorie-rich, nutrient-poor foods. Social circumstances make it difficult for parents to keep convenience food and "junk" food from their children (or to avoid it themselves!). Food manufacturers and fast-food restaurants have discovered that foods sell better if they contain high amounts of fat, sugar, and salt, and low amounts of fiber—all of which are violations of well-established nutritional guidelines (Wootan & Liebman, 1998). The short-term result during infancy can be **overnutrition**: too many calories, too much of the wrong nutrients, and not enough of other nutrients. The longer-term result can be to establish food preferences that may create health risks when the infant becomes a child and later an adult. A toddler who eats too much ice cream and chips may be "cute"; an adult who does so experiences greater risk for heart problems, diabetes, and certain forms of cancer (Bronner, 1997).

overnutrition Diet that contains too many calories and is therefore unbalanced.

Note that although overnutrition can increase an infant's weight, weight itself is not a cause for *medical* concern in infancy as long as the baby is only moderately above (or below) the average. Infants born bigger or heavier than usual tend to have diets relatively higher in calories. They also tend to drink more milk (via either breast or bottle) and other liquids than usual, and to shift earlier to solid foods. Some parents fear that heavier infants are prone to becoming overweight or obese as children or adolescents, but the evidence for

> **What Do You Think?**
>
> If you (or a partner) were expecting a child, would you prefer that the baby be breast-fed or bottle-fed? Discuss this question with a classmate of the *same* sex; then compare your responses with those of a classmate of the *opposite* sex. Do your responses differ?

this is inconclusive; some researchers have found that weight in infancy correlated little with weight in childhood and even less with weight in adulthood (Williams & Kimm, 1993). However, other researchers have found significant correlations between weight statuses during infancy (e.g., "overweight" or "obese") with weight statuses during childhood or adolescence (Gunnarsdottir & Thorsdottir, 2003; Harrington et al., 2010; Zhang et al., 2013). Parents sometimes feel concerned about a heavy infant for essentially social and psychological reasons: the paradox of a society that makes overnutrition too easy is that it also values thinness in physical appearance too much. As an infant grows into a child and then an adolescent, he or she will inevitably be affected by the social value placed on thinness. We discuss the results of this development in Chapter 11, in conjunction with discussing extremely overweight (or *obese*) children. In the meantime, though, it will be the child's parents who worry about weight on the child's behalf.

Impairments in Infant Growth

Within broad limits, healthy infants grow at various rates and become various sizes, and most of the time the differences are no cause for concern. But a small percentage do not grow as large as they should, beginning either at birth or a bit later during infancy. When a baby's size or growth is well below normal, it *is* a major cause for concern, both for the infant and for the infant's parents. At the extreme, it can contribute to infant mortality.

Low-Birth-Weight Infants

A small percentage of newborns are considered **low-birth-weight** infants if they are born weighing less than 2,500 grams, or about 5.5 pounds. The condition can result from several factors. One of the most common causes is malnourishment of the mother during pregnancy. But other harmful practices, such as smoking cigarettes, drinking alcohol, or taking drugs, also can depress birth weight. Mothers from certain segments of the population, such as teenagers and those from very low-SES backgrounds, are especially likely to give birth to low-birth-weight babies, most likely because of their own poor nourishment or their lack of access to good prenatal care. But even mothers who are well nourished and well cared for sometimes have infants who are smaller than is medically desirable. Multiple births (e.g., twins, triplets) usually result in small babies; so do some illnesses or mishaps, such as a serious traffic accident that causes damage to the placenta.

Consequences for the Infant

When birth weight is very low (less than 2,500 grams), infants' reflexes tend to be a bit sluggish, weak, and poorly organized (Brooten, 1992). Such infants do not startle as reliably or grasp as automatically and strongly at objects. Their muscles often seem flabby or overly relaxed. After delivery, the infants must cope with many tasks for which they are inadequately prepared physically, including breathing and digesting food. They also have trouble regulating their own sleep to keep it peaceful, sustained, and smooth.

Neurological limitations often can persist for the first two or three years of life, causing the baby to develop specific motor skills a bit later than other infants. A four-month-old baby who is small due to being born two months preterm, for example, in many ways resembles a two-month-old born at full term; both infants have lived eleven months from conception. Some of the delay may reflect stresses associated with early birth (such as parents' overprotectiveness) rather than the physical effects of early birth as such. Unless they are extremely small,

low birth weight A birth weight of less than 2,500 grams (about 5.5 pounds).

Chapter 5 Physical Development during the First Two Years

though, most low-birth-weight infants eventually develop into relatively normal preschoolers (Goldson, 1992). This conclusion was supported by a sophisticated study of monozygotic and dizygotic twins in addition to single births that allowed the researchers to control for maternal, environmental, and genetic factors (Datar & Jacknowitz, 2009). The results revealed very small consequences of low birth weight on cognitive and motor development at age two for most of the children in the study, but negative effects on growth were still evident at age two.

Consequences for the Parents

Although low birth weight can worry parents, the condition does not impair relationships with a child in the long term unless the parents are also under additional stresses elsewhere in their lives (Gross et al., 1997). In the short-term, though, low-birth-weight infants lack responsiveness, and initially need intensive care. These circumstances can create distance between parents and child at a time when parents want very much to reach out (literally and figuratively) and connect with their newborn. As the more mature members of the relationship, most parents are capable of understanding the reasons for the distance and of delaying their expectations for response from their child. The reflexive "social smile" normally shown at around two months, for example, may not come until age three or four months. If other stresses of life get in the way, though, waiting for the infant to finally "act normally" may be difficult or even impossible. Poverty, preexisting family conflicts, medical problems of parents, and the like put parents of low-birth-weight infants somewhat more at risk and in need of additional support from professionals, family members, and friends.

Failure to Thrive

failure to thrive A condition in which an infant seems seriously delayed in physical growth and is noticeably apathetic in behavior.

An infant or a preschool child who fails to grow at normal rates for no apparent medical reason suffers from a condition called **failure to thrive**. About 6 percent of North American children exhibit this condition at one time or another, although not necessarily continuously (Cole & Lanham, 2011; Woolston, 1993). In some ways, the condition resembles malnutrition, especially when it occurs in developing nations. Failure-to-thrive and malnourished children both develop motor and cognitive skills more slowly than usual; both experience higher rates of school failure and learning disabilities; and both are more likely to live in disadvantaged circumstances and to have parents who are enduring physical or emotional stress.

At one time, professionals tended to attribute failure to thrive to lack of nurturing and love between parent and child. A more complex picture may be closer to the truth: failure to thrive may have many sources, both physical and psychological, and depend on both the child and the environment. Consider this pattern: An infant has a genetically quiet, slow-to-respond temperament, making it more difficult for her mother to establish emotional contact. If the mother also is experiencing a number of other stresses (low income, illness, or disapproval of the new baby from others), the relationship between mother and infant is put at risk. A vicious cycle may develop of poorly timed feedings and ineffective efforts to nurture the infant, who persistently resists the mother's love and even her food. Parents in this situation often can benefit from professional help and support in learning new patterns of interacting with their babies.

Infant Mortality

infant mortality rate The frequency with which infants die compared to the frequency with which they live.

In the past several decades, health care systems in North America and around the world have substantially improved their ability to keep infants alive. The **infant mortality rate**, the proportion of babies who die during the first year of life, has declined steadily during this century. In 1950 in the United States, about twenty-nine out of every one thousand infants died; six decades later, this number was fewer than six out of every one thousand infants (CDC, 2012a). The averages conceal wide differences within society, some of which are listed in Table 5.5. In fact, there is also variability within the United States: infant mortality rates are higher in poorer states, like Mississippi, with a rate of nine out of every one thousand births, than in Massachusetts, with a rate of four out of every one thousand (United Health Foundation, 2016). Families with very low incomes are about twice as likely to

TABLE 5.5 Infant Mortality in Selected Nations

Nation	Infant Mortality (per 1,000 live births)	Nation	Infant Mortality (per 1,000 live births)
Japan	2.0	United Kingdom	4.3
Singapore	2.4	New Zealand	4.3
Finland	2.5	Poland	4.4
Norway	2.5	Canada	4.5
Sweden	2.6	Greece	4.6
Hong Kong	2.7	Hungary	4.9
South Korea	3.0	**United States, whites**	**5.1**
France	3.2	Latvia	5.2
Italy	3.3	**United States, average**	**5.8**
Spain	3.3	Chile	6.6
Belgium	3.4	Russia	6.8
Germany	3.4	**United States, nonwhites**	**11.1**
Israel	3.4	Mexico	11.6
Austria	3.4	China	12.0
Ireland	3.6	Saudi Arabia	13.2
Netherlands	3.6	Rwanda	29.7
Switzerland	3.6	South Africa	31.0
Denmark	4.0	India	39.1
Australia	4.3	Afghanistan	110.6

Sources: CDC (2012a); Central Intelligence Agency (2017).

lose an infant as families with middle-level incomes. Likewise, African-American families are twice as likely as white families to lose an infant, perhaps because of the historical correlation of race with income level and access to health care in American society. The strongest correlate with mortality is not race, however, but level of family income. As a rule of thumb, infants born to families with lower incomes are much more likely to die than infants born to families with higher incomes. Though this trend may be easy to believe when comparing poor with middle-income families, it actually holds for the full range of income in society (Finch, 2003; Pritchett, 1993). That is, infants born to middle-income families are *also* more likely to die than infants born to extremely wealthy families. The pattern holds no matter what the race or ethnic background of the child.

On average, infant mortality rates in the United States and Canada are two or three times lower than those in many less developed countries. Even so, infant mortality in the United States actually is *higher* than in numerous other developed nations, including Canada, Japan, Sweden, France, and Great Britain (Central Intelligence Agency, 2017). Cross-cultural investigations of infant mortality rates in European countries have given further clues about the reasons for the relatively high U.S. rate and have suggested ways to improve it. The research overwhelmingly indicates that parents need social supports as much as they need access to basic medical services and knowledge. Most European countries provide pregnant mothers with free prenatal care, for example, and also protect women's right to work during and after pregnancy. Pregnant women get special, generous sick leave, get at least four months of maternity leave *with pay*, and are protected from doing dangerous or exhausting work (such as night shifts). Policies such as these communicate support for pregnant mothers and their spouses in ways not currently available in the United States.

Chapter Summary

- **What do infants look like when they are first born? How do we know if they are healthy?** The average newborn has rather red-looking skin, is often covered with a waxy substance, and has a skull somewhat compressed on the top. The health of newborns born in hospitals is assessed quickly after delivery with the Apgar Scale. The average newborn at full term weighs about 7½ pounds. Regardless of cultural background, the newborn's bodily proportions make the infant look appealing to adults and may foster the formation of attachments with adults.
- **How much do children grow during infancy?** Infants grow very rapidly during the first two years of life, tripling their weight by their first birthday and adding approximately 50 percent to their length by this same time. The torso and limbs of infants grow more rapidly than their heads, enabling their bodies slowly "catch up" to the advanced development of their heads.
- **What changes occur in the brains of infants?** The brains of infants gain mass rapidly during infancy due to important changes in the neurons and to infants' experiences with their environments. Neurons become myelinated, which improves their efficiency, and they form many new synapses as infants have new experiences and acquire new skills. The efficiency of the nervous system is enhanced by the synaptic pruning process that eliminates redundant or unused synapses.
- **How do infants' sleep and wakefulness patterns change as infants get older?** Infants sleep almost twice as much as adults do, but the amount of sleep gradually decreases as they get older. The interruptions in their sleep contribute to fatigue in their parents.

- **What motor skills evolve during infancy?** Infants are born with a number of innate reflexes, but quickly develop certain motor skills during the first year, including reaching, grasping, and walking. Motor skills develop differently depending on cultural background, biological sex, and social gender roles.
- **What do infants need nutritionally?** Infants need more protein and calories per pound of body weight than older children do. Compared to formula and bottle feeding, breastfeeding has a number of practical and psychological advantages. After weaning from breast or bottle, infants need a diet rich in protein and calories. Most North American families can provide these requirements, but many cannot. A common problem in North American diets is overnutrition, which can create health risks in the long term.
- **What factors can impair growth during infancy?** One of the most important impairments to early growth is low birth weight, because the condition leads to difficulties with breathing, digestion, and sleep, and impairs normal reflexes. The problems low-birth-weight infants experience can sometimes put stress on their relationships with parents, but not necessarily. For a variety of reasons, infants sometimes fail to thrive normally. Infant mortality has decreased in the recent past, but in the United States, it is still higher than it should be.
- **How do infants' senses operate at birth?** At birth, infants already can see and hear, but with less accuracy or acuity than adults do. They have well-developed senses of taste, smell, and touch, and infants demonstrate the ability to combine information from multiple senses to better allow them to function in their environments.

Key Terms

Apgar Scale (p. 107)
central nervous system (p. 109)
cephalocaudal principle (p. 117)
failure to thrive (p. 124)
infant mortality rate (p. 124)
low birth weight (p. 123)
motor skills (p. 117)
myelination (p. 110)

neonate (p. 106)
neurons (p. 109)
non-REM sleep (p. 111)
overnutrition (p. 122)
proximodistal principle (p. 117)
plasticity (p. 110)
reflex (p. 117)
REM sleep (p. 111)

stunting (p. 122)
sudden infant death syndrome (SIDS) (p. 112)
synaptic pruning (p. 110)
synaptogenesis (p. 109)
transient exuberance (p. 109)

Cognitive Development during the First Two Years

CHAPTER 6

Source: Vitalinka/Shutterstock.com.

Chapter Outline

Studying Cognition and Memory in Infants

Infant Perception and Cognition

Cognitive Change during Infancy: Piaget's Stage Theory

Behavioral Learning in Infancy

Language Acquisition

The End of Infancy

Focusing Questions

- How do infants' senses operate at birth?
- How can infant cognition be studied?
- Do infants see and hear in the same way adults do?
- How do thinking and learning change during infancy?
- What phases do infants go through in acquiring language?

From birth, infants begin acquiring knowledge about their environments. Consider Latisha, a seven-month-old, who mimics adults who wave bye-bye at her by moving her entire arm back and forth. When Latisha is fifteen months old, she initiates waving bye-bye when her mother leaves for work, indicating that she has some understanding of what that motion means.

While infants are growing physically, they are also thinking: noticing the world around them, organizing their impressions, and even remembering their

perception The neural activity of combining sensations into meaningful patterns.

cognition All processes by which humans acquire knowledge; methods for thinking or gaming knowledge about the world.

experiences. Although these activities are often called "cognitive development," "cognition," or simply "thinking," psychologists frequently classify them according to their mental complexity. **Perception** is the less complex process and refers to the brain's immediate or direct organization and interpretation of sensations. Perceptual processes occur when an infant notices that a toy car is the same car no matter which way she orients it. **Cognition** is the more complex process and refers to thinking and other mental activities. It includes reasoning, attention, memory, problem solving, and the ability to represent objects and experiences. Infants engage in both cognition and perception, even as newborns. As we will see, the distinction between them often is blurred, with each process often supporting the other. What infants see and hear depends on what they think and vice versa—just as for adults.

Studying Cognition and Memory in Infants

How can we know whether an infant, who cannot even talk, is actually noticing sights and sounds, organizing information about them, and remembering them? Psychologists have developed two main strategies: studying changes in infants' heart rates and studying infants' tendency to *habituate* to, or get used to, novel stimuli.

Arousal and Infants' Heart Rates

One way to understand an infant's cognition is to measure heart rate (HR) with an electronic heart rate monitor attached to the chest. The changes in HR are taken to signify variations in the baby's arousal, alertness, and general contentment.

Psychologists who study infants make this assumption because among adults, HR varies reliably with attention and arousal. Typically, HR slows down, or decelerates, when adults notice or attend to something interesting but not overly exciting, such as reading the newspaper. If adults attend to something *very* stimulating, their HRs speed up, or accelerate. Watching a lab technician draw blood from your own arm, for example, often causes your HR to speed up. On the whole, novel or attractive stimuli produce curiosity and a slower HR, whereas potentially dangerous or aversive stimuli produce defensiveness, discomfort, and a faster HR, at least among adults.

Very young infants, from one day to a few months old, show similar changes, but we need to take several precautions when we study their HRs. For one thing, observations of infants' attention should be made when infants are awake and alert, and, as we already pointed out, newborn babies often spend a lot of time being drowsy or asleep. Many stimuli that lead to deceleration in adults or older children lead to acceleration in infants. Many one-month-olds show a faster HR at familiar sights, such as their mothers, even though the infants may look as though they are just staring calmly into space. Despite these problems, however, studies of HR have provided a useful way to measure infants' attention, perception, and memory.

Recognition, Memory, and Infant Habituation

Although infants cannot describe what they remember, they often indicate recognition of particular objects, people, and activities. Familiar people, such as mothers, bring forth a special response in one-year-olds, who may coo suddenly at the sight of them, stretch out their arms to them, and even crawl or walk to them if they know how. Less familiar people, such as neighbors or the family doctor, tend not to produce responses such as these and may even produce active distress, depending on the age of the infant.

Babies' responses to the familiar and the unfamiliar offer infant psychologists a second way to understand infant perception and conceptual thought. Psychologists study infants' tendency to get used to and therefore ignore stimuli as they experience them repeatedly; the tendency is often called **habituation** by psychologists (Mazur, 1994). One habituation

habituation The tendency to attend to novel stimuli and ignore familiar ones.

Part 3 The First Two Years of Life

> **What Do You Think?**
>
> Talk to a parent (preferably of an infant) about when he or she felt sure of being recognized. Do the parent's experiences suggest that infants do remember their parents? Do infants' signs of recognition apply only to their primary caregiver, or do they extend to other relatives?

strategy repeatedly offers a baby a standard, or "study," stimulus—a simple picture to look at or a simple melody to hear. Like most adults, the baby attends to the study stimulus carefully at first, but on subsequent occasions, gradually pays less attention to it. In fact, you have likely habituated to the room where you are reading this: You "tune out" the hum of your refrigerator or the sound of your air conditioner or heater until it is mentioned. As this happens, the baby is said to be *habituating* to the stimulus. After the baby has become habituated, the investigators present the original study stimulus along with a few other stimuli. If the baby really recognizes the original, she probably will attend to the others *more* because they are comparatively novel. Her HR will slow down as well.

This method has shown that young babies recognize quite a lot of past experiences. One classic habituation study found that four-month-old girls recognized a familiar visual pattern among three others that differed from the original (McCall & Kagan, 1967). Another found habituation even in newborns: they "noticed" when a light brush on their cheeks changed location, as revealed by changes in their HRs (Kisilevsky & Mnir, 1984). Sometimes, too, recognition persists for very long periods. Three-month-olds, it seems, can still recognize a picture or a toy two weeks after they first see it, as long as the objects are presented in a familiar context the second time—a performance that matches adults' recognition memory (Hayne et al., 1991).

Habituation is important not only because it provides a way to study infants' learning and development but also because it suggests that infants have memories well before they acquire language. And habituation has interesting, though speculative, implications for parent-child relationships: it suggests that young babies may begin recognizing their parents quite quickly—perhaps as quickly as the habituation psychologists have observed in laboratory experiments. Parents may not simply be imagining it, that is, when they become convinced that their baby responds differently or more fully to them than to other adults; the child may really be doing so even at just a few weeks of age.

Infant Perception and Cognition

It might seem as if infants should be better at *perception* than at *cognition* because perception involves more direct, automatic organization of sensations and requires less cognitive maturity. This hypothesis may indeed be true, but the evidence for it is surprisingly ambiguous. What *is* clear is that whatever "thinking" (or cognition) infants do does not involve language to the extent that it does in children and adults, simply because infants are only beginning to acquire language skills. If we are to see signs of infant thinking, furthermore, we should look at those behaviors infants already show, such as directing their eyes (and ears) or changing their heart rates. If we broaden our notion of cognition to include these nonverbal signs of thinking, infants show not only perception of their world but cognition about it as well. This is true even during their first year, before they understand or speak even a single word. In some situations, even six-month-olds seem to "reason" and solve problems. To see what we mean, let us look at the two most important senses—vision and hearing—and at how infants make use of both to perceive and to conceive of the world.

Visual Perception in Infancy

Given that children can see almost from birth, what do they notice? What, that is, do they perceive? Some of the earliest research on this question stirred up a lot of interest because

Young infants concentrate longer on certain shapes and contours, even when these are not part of a human face. Newborns are especially attracted to contours and to patches of light and dark. A few months later, they prefer complex patterns over simpler ones and curved lines over straight ones. Such changes are one reason (among many) why a baby's interest in crib toys changes over time.

Source: Nolte Lourens/Shutterstock.com.

it seemed to show that infants, even those just two days old, could discriminate between human faces and abstract patterns and that they looked at faces longer than at either patterned disks or plain, unpatterned disks (Fantz, 1963). The researchers presented infants with various combinations of these stimuli side by side and carefully observed which object the babies spent the most time looking at. At all ages studied (birth to six months), the infants showed a clear preference: they stared at a picture of a human face almost twice as long as at any other stimulus picture. Young infants, it seemed, were inherently interested in people.

More recent studies of visual preferences, however, have qualified this conclusion substantially (Yonas, 1988). It is not the humanness of faces that infants enjoy looking at but their interesting contours, complexity, and curvature. Newborns are particularly attracted to contours, or the edges of areas of light and dark. But such edges can be provided either by the hairline of a parent's head or by a properly constructed abstract drawing. When infants reach age two or three months, their perceptual interest shifts to complexity and curvature. At this age, infants look longer at a pattern of many small squares than at one containing just a few large squares. They also look longer at curved lines than at straight ones. Interestingly, research with young infants has also found that infants prefer to look at attractive, rather than unattractive faces (Slater et al., 2000). Attractive faces tend to possess greater symmetry to the contours of their features and are, to infants (and we suspect, adults) more visually-engaging. This same preference for attractive faces has even been demonstrated when three- and four-month-old infants were presented with attractive and unattractive cat faces (Quinn et al., 2005). The complexity, curvature, symmetry, and contours of *any* attractive face seem to draw our attention during infancy, but our attention is captured by other stimuli in our visual field as well.

Object Perception

A more complex form of perception—one that is a step closer to cognition—is *object constancy,* the perception (or is it a "belief"?) that an object remains the same despite constant changes in the sensations it sends to the eye. A baby's favorite toy duck never casts exactly the same image on the retina from one second to the next. The image continually varies depending on its distance and its orientation, or angle of viewing. Somehow, the baby must learn that this kaleidoscope of images really refers to only one constant duck—that the duck always *is* the same but keeps *looking* different.

In general, research on infant perception suggests that infants begin perceiving objects as constant very early indeed (Granrud, 1993, 2006). Consider the development of *size constancy,* the perception that an object stays the same size even when viewed from different distances. In a typical study, newborn babies are conditioned to suck on pacifiers at the sight of a cube of some specified size and placed at some precise distance. During conditioning training, sucking at the sight of cubes of other sizes or distances is deliberately *not* reinforced so that the sucking provides an indicator of the baby's recognition of an object of a particular size and at a given distance.

Later the conditioned infants are shown several cubes of different sizes and placed at different distances. The test cubes include one that casts an image exactly the size of the original but is in fact *larger and farther away.* Typically, the babies are not fooled by this apparent identity of retinal images. They prefer to look at the original cube regardless of its distance; that is, they suck on their pacifiers more vigorously while looking at the original cube than while looking at any substitute. Apparently, they know when an object really is the same size and when it only looks the same size.

Depth Perception

Depth perception refers to a sense of how far away objects are or appear to be. Infants begin acquiring this kind of perceptual skill about as soon as they can focus on objects at different distances, at around two or three months of age. This conclusion is suggested by research that has developed out of the now classic experiment with the visual cliff (Gibson & Walk, 1960). In its basic form, the **visual cliff** consists of a table covered with strong glass under which is a textured surface with colored squares. Part of the textured surface contacts the glass directly, and another part is separated from it by several feet. Visually, then, the setup resembles the edge of a table, but the glass provides ample support for an infant, even in the dropped-off area. A baby who is placed onto it will seem to float in midair.

On this apparatus, even babies just two months old discriminate between the two sides of the visual cliff. They find the deep side more interesting, as suggested by the extra time they take to study it. Young babies show little fear of the deep side, judging either by their overt behavior or by their heart rates, which tend to decrease during their investigations of the cliff. This finding implies they are primarily curious about the cliff rather than fearful of it.

Babies old enough to crawl, however, show significant fear of the visual cliff. Their heart rates increase markedly, and they will not crawl onto the deep side despite coaxing from a parent and the solid support they feel from the glass. Why the change? Perhaps infants' crawling skills allow them to perceive distances more accurately than before, because the motion of crawling causes faraway objects (including the deep side of the cliff) to move less than nearby objects (such as the shallow side). Perhaps, too, infants old enough to crawl are also old enough to focus their eyes more accurately on each side of the cliff, a physical skill that provides further perceptual information about the difference in distance of the two sides (Kermoian & Campos, 1988).

visual cliff The classic laboratory setup of a ledge covered by a sheet of glass; used to test the acquisition of depth perception. Young babies crawling on the glass discriminate between the two sides of the "cliff."

Anticipation of Visual Events

Even closer to deliberate cognition than perception of contours, objects, and depth are infants' anticipations of visual events that have not yet occurred. Signs of "looking forward" to an interesting sight are visible by observing a child's eye movements carefully. Infant psychologists have developed infrared video cameras to assist with this task, as well as a modified form of the habituation procedure, called a *visual expectation paradigm,* designed to elicit (or encourage) eye movements by the child. Typically, the infant sits in front of a large computer screen, which displays a series of interesting drawings at different locations (usually simply to the left or right) on the screen. Meanwhile, a video camera films the baby's eye movements as he directs his gaze toward the drawings. By linking the camera with the computer, it is possible to determine whether the child's eyes change direction *following* the appearance of a picture at a new location or actually *precede* or anticipate its appearance.

This procedure shows clearly that infants as young as two months do not merely follow but often anticipate the locations of pictures, and in this sense develop expectations about the environment that "foresee the future" (Canfield et al., 1997). Their anticipations, furthermore, show a variety of rule-governed qualities. By one year of age, for example, infants anticipate the location that portrays numerical sequences; they look for the spot where one more of a set will be displayed rather than a spot that will display some other number of items (Canfield & Smith, 1996). Their anticipations suggest that infants "think" in some way about what they see (engage in cognition) and do not merely register what they see automatically (engage simply in perception). In the scanning of interesting visual patterns and contours mentioned earlier, for example, they may be forming rudimentary generalizations, or rules, about what they see, such as where precisely to look to see another friendly smile.

In general, visual expectations become faster and more reliable as infants get older—most likely because they acquire more knowledge about objects and eventually learn to represent the objects mentally. Research on visual expectations also shows individual differences among infants, with some anticipating events faster, more reliably, and at earlier ages than others do (Haith et al., 1997). In at least two ways, then, infants' visual thinking resembles other forms of lifespan development: it shows continuity combined with change, and it shows diversity in developmental patterns and sequences.

Auditory Perception in Infancy

Infants respond to sounds even as newborns. But what do they perceive from sounds? What sense do they make of the sounds they hear? These questions are important, because infants' ability to discriminate among sounds makes a crucial difference in their acquisition of language, as discussed later in this chapter.

Discriminating between Sounds

In a variety of important and surprising ways, infants reveal their abilities to discriminate between different types of sounds. For example, by five months of age, infants react more to speech sounds that they hear repeated often—like their own name—than to other speech sounds. Even when similar-sounding words are used as distracters, infants can detect their own names (Mandel, Jusczyk, & Pisoni, 1995). By their first birthday, infants can separate the speech from different talkers and attend to one speaker who has mentioned the infant's name (Newman, 2005), a phenomenon that you may recognize as the "cocktail party effect," where you hear your name mentioned by someone in a room filled with people having numerous conversations. Long before they have any sense of the meanings of words, infants develop expectations regarding the rhythms, segmentation, and cadence of spoken language (Minagawa-Kawai et al., 2011), revealing remarkable perceptual abilities that prepare them for their later mastery of language.

Infants possess some impressive music perception abilities as well. Infants have a preference for melodies that are "melodic" rather than those that are dissonant (Trainor & Heinmiller, 1998), and they can distinguish between music from their own culture and music from another, showing a distinct preference for music from their own culture (Soley & Hannon, 2010). When presented with a collection of classical music excerpts, nine-month-old infants can readily distinguish between "happy" (major key, faster tempo) and "sad" (minor key, slower tempo) music, revealing a preference for happy music (Flom & Pick, 2012). And finally, two- and three-day-old infants can do what appears to mystify many adults: they can find the beat in music! When researchers played two measures of various rock-drum rhythms to newborns, the brain-wave patterns of the babies changed when the downbeat was occasionally omitted (Winkler et al., 2009). Likewise, adults who were asked to move to the music either stumbled or their movements became syncopated when the downbeat was omitted. Given that two- and three-day-old newborns have not had much time to be exposed to music, the researchers argued that humans must have some kind of innate ability to detect regular patterns of sound in music.

The infant in the photo is responding to music that, judging by her smile, she finds pleasing. The music is most likely melodic, played by instruments common in her culture, and its tempo is probably upbeat.
Source: KPG Payless/Shutterstock.com

Localization of Sounds

Infants just two months old can locate sounds, as suggested by the fact that they orient their heads toward certain noises, such as a rattle (Morrongiello, 1994). But they often take much longer to respond than do older children or adults. Instead of needing just a fraction of a second, as adults do, full-term infants require an average of two to three seconds before orienting toward ("looking at") a sound that occurs off to one side. Infants born one month preterm require even more time to respond. These delays may explain why pediatricians and others used to believe that newborn infants could not hear: the sounds

> **What Do You Think?**
>
> Do these impressive perceptual abilities mean that infants can think? And, if so, do they think in similar ways as adults? How might their thinking change as they get older? Do children simply learn "more" as they get older, or do they learn differently?

they offered to the babies, such as a single hand clap, may not have lasted long enough for the infants to respond.

Although infants can locate sounds, their skill at doing so is somewhat limited. They are better able to locate relatively high-pitched sounds, such as those made by a flute or a small bird, than low-pitched sounds, such as that made by a foghorn (Spetner & Olsho, 1990). In their first efforts to turn their heads, very young babies (one or two months old) act more as though head turning is a reflex than a search for something to see (Morrongielo, 1994). The behavior does not habituate, meaning that a young baby is just as likely to turn toward a sound after many presentations as he was after the first presentation. Also, the behavior occurs even in the dark, when there is no chance to actually see the source of a sound. Only by age five or six months do these reflexive qualities change: by that age, babies habituate quickly to repeated presentations and search only in the light, when there is something to see. In these ways, then, hearing and vision have become coordinated, but it has taken several months of learning for the change to occur.

Coordination of Sensory Information

The localization of sounds suggests that even very young babies coordinate what they see with what they hear; they seem to use sound to direct their visual gaze. But is this what really happens? Do we process different sensory signals separately and then somehow merge them to form our "perception" of an object? For example, upon entering the lobby of a movie theater, do you smell a pleasant aroma, hear popping noises, and see bags full of small, white, irregular-shaped objects and then conclude that it must be popcorn? (Just to be sure, you should probably eat some as well to confirm that it is light, crunchy-ish, buttery, and salty.) Or, do you sense all of this information concurrently and quickly arrive at a "popcorn perception"? Researchers have questioned the nature of infant perception, and several studies have suggested that infants, like adults, integrate various channels of sensory information in a process called **intermodal perception**. In addition to localizing sounds (demonstrating an integration of the visual and auditory senses), one-month-old infants are also able to recognize by sight objects that they had previously put in their mouths but had not before seen, revealing the integration of their tactile and visual senses (Schweinle & Wilcox, 2004). And by eight months of age, infants can match an unfamiliar speaker's face with the correct voice when the choices for faces and voices vary with respect to age and sex (Patterson & Werker, 2002)—and remember, these infants aren't speaking yet! Intermodal perception enables infants to efficiently learn about their physical and social environments, coordinating information from various sensory channels so that they have a fuller understanding of the world in which they are functioning.

intermodal perception The coordination and integration of multiple channels of sensory information.

Cognitive Change during Infancy: Piaget's Stage Theory

The two preceding sections highlighted continuities between infants' and adults' cognitive abilities. Infants can perceive object constancies, anticipate what they are about to see, locate sounds, and categorize certain experiences—all abilities that they share with adults. Most of the research cited is framed by some version of information-processing theory, the approach described in Chapter 2 (and elsewhere in this book) that emphasizes the importance of organizing specific input so that it becomes more meaningful, much as a computer is sometimes thought to do.

Yet infants obviously do not think "just like adults." For one thing, they use little or no language to assist in solving problems. Proud parents notwithstanding, they often also

TABLE 6.1 Some Features of Infant Cognition According to Piaget

Stage	Age	Characteristics
1: Early reflexes	Birth–1 month	Reliance on inborn reflexes to "know" the environment; assimilation of all experiences to reflexes
2: Primary circular reactions	1–4 months	Accommodation (or modification) of reflexes to fit new objects and experiences; repeated actions focusing on infant's own body
3: Secondary circular reactions	4–8 months	Repeated actions focusing on objects; actions used as means toward ends, but haphazardly; early signs of object permanence
4: Combined secondary circular reactions	8–12 months	Deliberate combinations of previously acquired actions (or schemes); A-not-B error; early signs of sense of time
5: Tertiary circular reactions	12–18 months	Systematic application of previously acquired actions (or schemes); well-organized investigation of novel objects, but always overt
6: The first symbols	18–24 months	First symbolic representations of objects; true object permanence; deferred imitation

Source: Piaget (1963).

seem slow and error prone in figuring things out. Their skills are still limited and seem worlds away from the cognitive behaviors of older children or adults. How do they transform their budding infant skills into the comparatively smooth expertise of an adult? And during infancy, in particular, how does the transformation begin?

Stages of Sensorimotor Intelligence

Jean Piaget, whose approach was described in Chapter 2, offers one of the most complete descriptions and explanations of cognitive development available (Piaget, 1963). According to Piaget, infants begin life thinking in terms of *sensory* perceptions and *motor* actions, by doing things to and with the objects around them. Piaget called this activity **sensorimotor intelligence**. He identified stages during infancy that mark significant developments in sensorimotor intelligence, as summarized in Table 6.1.

In general, the stages of infant cognition show two trends. First, infants show a trend toward symbolic thinking. Instead of needing to handle a toy car to understand it, an infant becomes increasingly able to visualize, or think about, a car without actually touching or seeing one. This ability becomes very strong by the end of the first two years of life; to Piaget, it helps mark the end of infancy. Changes in infants' toys reflect this developmental trend, as indicated in Table 6.2.

Second, infants form cognitive structures that Piaget called *schemes*. In relation to infants, **schemes** are organized patterns of actions or concepts that help the baby to make sense out of and adapt to the environment. Schemes develop well before infants can represent objects or events through language or motor skills. A newborn baby's initial grasping motions constitute an early scheme, as do her earliest sucking motions. Eventually, as described shortly, internal, or mental, concepts and ideas develop out of such patterns of behavior. These too are sometimes called *schemes* (or sometimes *schemas* or *schemata*);

sensorimotor intelligence According to Piaget, thinking that occurs by way of sensory perceptions and motor actions; characteristic of infants.

scheme According to Piaget, a behavior or thought that represents a group of ideas and events in a person's experience.

TABLE 6.2 Toys That Support Cognitive Development during Infancy

As infants get older, their toys tend to involve more complex motor skills, as well as language and make-believe. Can you see how these trends are reflected in these lists?

Birth-2 Months	6–12 Months	12–24 Months
Mobile in crib	Squeeze toys	Dolls, especially large ones
Rattle	Nested plastic cups	Toy telephone
	Boxes with lids	Puzzles (5–10 pieces)
	Soft ball	Vehicles (cars, boats, train)
	Stuffed animals	Sandbox, shovel, and pail
	Pots and pans	Water toys (cups, funnel, etc.)
	Picture books (especially cloth or cardboard)	Picture books with simple words

but Piaget himself more often called cognitive structures and patterns that develop later by names such as *operations* or *systems,* depending on their exact nature (Miller, 2011).

As we discuss more fully in Chapter 2, Piaget argued that sensorimotor intelligence develops by means of two complementary processes—assimilation and accommodation. **Assimilation** consists of interpreting new experiences in terms of existing schemes. A baby who is used to sucking on a breast or bottle may use the same action on whatever new, unfamiliar objects he encounters, such as a rubber ball or his own fist. **Accommodation** consists of modifying existing schemes to fit new experiences. After sucking on a number of new objects, an infant may modify this action to fit the nature of each new object; she may chew on some new objects (her sweater) but not on others (a plastic cup).

The interplay of assimilation and accommodation leads to new schemes and eventually to the infant's ability to symbolize objects and activities. Let us see how Piaget believed this transition occurs.

assimilation According to Piaget, a method by which a person responds to new experiences by using existing concepts to interpret new ideas and experiences.

accommodation According to Piaget, the process of modifying existing ideas or action-skills to fit new experiences.

Stage 1: Early Reflexes—Using What You Are Born with (Birth to One Month)

According to Piaget, cognitive development begins with reflexes, those simple, inborn behaviors that all normal babies can produce at birth. As it happens, the majority of such reflexes remain just that—reflexes—for the individual's entire life; sneezing patterns and blinking responses, for example, look nearly the same in adults as they do in infants. But a few are notable for their flexibility, chiefly sucking, grasping, and looking. These behaviors resemble reflexes at birth, but they quickly begin to be modified in response to experiences such as sucking on the mother's breast, on toys, and on the child's own hand. They give infants a repertoire from which to develop more complex skills, and their susceptibility to influence makes them especially important to cognitive development during infancy.

Stage 2: Primary Circular Reactions—Modifying What You Are Born with (One to Four Months)

Soon after the baby begins modifying his early reflexes, he begins to build and differentiate action schemes quite rapidly. In fact, within a month or so he sometimes repeats them endlessly for no apparent reason. Because of its repetitive quality, Piaget calls this behavior a **circular reaction**. The baby seems to be stimulated by the outcome of his own behavior, so he responds for the mere joy of feeling himself act. At this point, the circular reactions are called *primary circular reactions,* because they still focus on the baby's own body and movements. Waving an arm repeatedly constitutes a primary circular reaction; so does kicking again and again.

circular reaction Piaget's term for an action often repeated, apparently because it is self-reinforcing.

Chapter 6 Cognitive Development during the First Two Years

During this period, the young infant practices his developing schemes widely, and the behaviors rapidly become less reflexive. The baby may shape his mouth differently for sucking his fist and for sucking his blanket. In this sense, he begins to recognize the objects all around him, and implicitly, he also begins to remember previous experiences with each type of object. But this memory has an automatic or object-focused quality, unlike the large variety of more conscious memories children have later in life.

Stage 3: Secondary Circular Reactions—Making Interesting Sights Last (Four to Eight Months)

As they practice their first schemes, young infants broaden their interests to include objects and events immediately around them. Shaking her arm, for example, no longer captivates a baby's attention for its own sake; she has become too skilled at arm shaking for it to do so. Now a behavior such as this becomes useful rather than interesting. A baby at this stage may accidentally discover that shaking her arm will make a mobile spin over her head in her crib, or create an interesting noise in a toy she happens to be holding, or make parents smile with joy. In all these cases, shaking an arm becomes a means to other ends. Once primitive means are discovered, a baby at this stage will repeat a useful procedure endlessly to sustain and study the interesting results.

To differentiate this new orientation from the earlier one, Piaget called such repetitions *secondary circular reactions:* repetitions motivated by external objects and events. Secondary circular reactions create two parallel changes in the child's motor schemes. On the one hand, the infant uses existing schemes even more widely than before. She tries to suck on more and more of the toys that come her way. On the other hand, she begins to discover that schemes can be combined to produce interesting results. She may happen to reach toward an object (one scheme) and discover that doing so makes it possible to grasp the object (another scheme). At first, the combination occurs accidentally; but once it does occur, the baby at this stage can produce the new combination of schemes deliberately on future occasions.

Secondary circular reactions also implicitly show that the infant is now acquiring at least a hazy notion of **object permanence**, a belief that objects exist separately from her own actions and continue to exist even when she cannot see them. By stage 3, she will look for an object briefly even after it disappears. Naturally, her searching skills leave something to be desired, so it helps if the hidden object is actually partly visible and within easy reach; a toy duck's tail should stick out from under a blanket if that is where the toy is hidden. But the first signs of symbolic thought are there, because the infant must have some *idea* of the toy duck if she is going to bother searching for it.

object permanence
According to Piaget, the belief that people and things continue to exist even when one cannot experience them directly; emerges around age two.

Stage 4: Combined Secondary Circular Reactions—Deliberate Combinations of Means and Ends (Eight to Twelve Months)

At this stage, instead of just happening on connections among schemes by accident, the infant intentionally chooses to use a scheme as a means toward an end. In stages 1 and 2, he may have developed separate schemes for opening his mouth and for chewing food. In stage 3, he may have accidentally discovered that the first scheme is a means toward the other: mouth opening is a means toward eating. Now, in stage 4, the baby starts using this means-end connection purposefully. Like a young bird in a nest, he opens his mouth to "produce" food to chew. Of course, he may eventually discover that the connection does not always work: sitting with his mouth wide open may sometimes produce no food at all or occasionally produce bad-tasting medicine instead of good-tasting food.

At this stage, too, the infant still lacks alternatives to the single-purpose, fragmented schemes he has developed so far. As he encounters the limitations of these schemes, he gradually modifies and expands (or accommodates, as Piaget would say) his initial schemes that connected means with ends. He may learn to open his mouth at the sight of some foods but not others. He may also add other behaviors to the mouth-opening scheme, such as pointing to favorite foods, thereby turning the original scheme into a more general food-requesting scheme. As these accommodations occur, the infant moves into the next stage of cognition.

Stage 5: Tertiary Circular Reactions—Active Experimentation with Objects (Twelve to Eighteen Months)

At stage 5, the infant deliberately varies the schemes for producing interesting results, or ends. Previously, at stage 4, she could intentionally combine schemes, but only one pair at a time and only if an appropriate situation for using the combination happened to occur. Now, in dealing with a new object, the baby can run through a repertoire of schemes in a trial-and-error effort to learn about the object's properties. Piaget called the variations *tertiary circular reactions,* meaning third-level circular reactions, to distinguish them from the simpler forms of repetition that dominate the earlier stages.

These variations in behavior, however, are still organized largely by trial and error rather than by systematic plans. Given a rubber ball, for example, some babies may try dropping it from different heights and onto different objects. But no matter how delighted these infants are with the results of these variations, they will not think to vary the dropping conditions carefully or experimentally. Such actions require planning and consequently also require considerably more ability to represent objects and situations than the infant has yet developed.

Stage 6: The First Symbols—Representing Objects and Actions (Eighteen to Twenty-Four Months)

At this stage, the motor schemes the child previously explored and practiced overtly begin to occur symbolically. For the first time, the infant can begin to envision, or imagine, actions and their results without actually having to try them out beforehand.

Consider a stage 6 child who wants a favorite toy that is just barely out of reach on a high shelf. Near the shelf sits a small stool that she has played with numerous times. How to get the toy? Earlier in infancy, the baby might simply have stared and fussed and eventually either given up or cried. At this later stage, things are quite different. The baby surveys the situation, observes the stool, and pauses briefly. Then, with a purposeful air, she places the stool under the toy, climbs up, and retrieves the toy. What is important here is the lack of false starts or, conversely, the presence of only a single, correct attempt. The infant may succeed even though she never before used the stool to reach high-up objects. According to Piaget, trial and error is no longer the method of choice; now the infant tries out solutions mentally to envision their results.

Skill with mental representations makes true object permanence possible. A child at the end of infancy will search for a toy even after it has been fully hidden and even if it was hidden without her witnessing the act of hiding. If a ball disappears behind a bookcase, she will go around to the other side to look for it. She will search appropriately, even though she cannot know in advance exactly where behind the bookcase the ball will turn up. In the ball-and-blanket situation described earlier, the child can now play more complex games of hide-and-seek. She usually looks first under the blanket where the toy disappeared; if she fails to find it there, she will search under any and all other blankets and sometimes even under the table and in the experimenter's pockets. Relatively extensive search is made possible in part by the child's new conviction that toys and other objects have a permanent existence independent of her own activities with them. In other words, they do not just disappear.

All of these behaviors depend on the child's ability to form and maintain representations (thoughts or memories) of the relevant experiences, which later become available for expression again. As we will see, representational skill proves crucial in early childhood. It contributes to children's play, because much play involves re-enactment of previous experiences and roles. It makes possible much language development, because the child must learn to use words and expressions when they are appropriate and not just at the time she hears them uttered. And it makes possible the first real self-concept, because sooner or later the child realizes that he too has a (relatively) permanent existence akin to the permanence of all the things and people in his life, whether toys, pet dogs, or parents.

Assessment of Piaget's Theory of Infant Cognition

Piaget's theory stimulated considerable study of infant cognition from the 1960s through the 1980s. A lot of the research has confirmed the main features of the theory, whereas

Playing peek-a-boo becomes popular with babies as they approach their first birthday. Even though the mother disappears for a moment, the baby seems to believe that she still exists behind the tree, as shown by the baby's delight when she reappears.
Source: Serg Salivon/Shutterstock.com.

other research has called attention to additional aspects of infancy that at least complicate Piaget's original presentation, if they do not contradict it outright. Here, for example, are two of the main criticisms of the theory and a sample of the research they have inspired.

Motor versus Cognitive Limitations

Some infant psychologists question Piaget's account because they believe his stages confuse a child's motor abilities with cognitive or thinking abilities (Meltzoff et al., 1991). Object permanence, for example, implicitly depends on a child's capacity to conduct a manual search: to walk around the room, lift and inspect objects, and the like. Perhaps younger infants "lack" classic object permanence, this argument goes, simply because they lack motor skills or at best use them only clumsily.

To test this possibility, psychologists have designed new tests of object permanence that require only visual search rather than motor coordination (Baillargeon, 1993; Hespos & Baillargeon, 2001). In one experiment, infants were habituated to (repeatedly shown) the sight of a toy car sliding down an inclined track from the left and then rolling off to the right. In the middle of this track was a small screen concealing the middle portion of the track and obstructing a view of the car for part of its trip along the track. During habituation, the babies watched the car slide down the ramp, behind the screen, and out the other side. Between car trips, the screen was lifted temporarily to show that there was nothing behind it that might affect the car's movements.

After the infants had gotten used to seeing this setup and watching the car disappear and reappear predictably, they were shown one of two test events. In the first event, the screen was lifted and a toy mouse was placed directly behind the tracks. Then the screen was lowered, and the car made its usual run down the ramp and out the right side of the screen. This was called the "possible test event." The second test event was the same, except that the toy mouse was placed directly *on* the tracks. Then the screen was lowered, the car was released, it disappeared behind the screen, and—surprise!—it reappeared out the right side of the screen anyway, even though the mouse had been placed on the tracks. This was called the "impossible test event." In reality, the experimenters secretly removed the toy mouse before the car could hit it, using a hole concealed in the back of the test apparatus.

Under these conditions, infants as young as three-and-a-half months looked significantly longer at the *im*possible test event than at the possible test event. The most plausible interpretation is that the impossible event violated assumptions the infants made about the permanence of objects: they seemed to assume the toy mouse should cause a collision, presumably because they believed it continued to exist behind the screen even when they could not see it. They also seemed to assume objects retain their usual physical properties even when invisible—that the car could not simply pass through the mouse, for example, just because it was hidden.

This evidence of early object permanence, though, does not mean young infants are now ready to reason about hidden objects in the ways older children or adults do. If a preschool child experienced the experiment just described, he or she would very likely suspect a trick of some sort and consciously puzzle over what the trick might be. The three- or four-month-old infant still has much developing to do before being able to do this kind of thinking. By requiring manual search skills, though, Piaget's tasks may have delayed children from displaying their pre-existing object permanence until rudimentary reasoning skills had become established. Hence, Piaget's assertion that full object permanence (the stage 6 described earlier) involves conscious problem solving: a deliberate search for the object.

The Effects of Memory

Considerable evidence suggests that memory affects infants' performance on many cognitive tasks more than Piaget thought. Imposing slight delays—just a few seconds—when an infant searches for an object lowers success rates much more for younger infants than for older ones (Baillargeon, 1993). Much of the change may reflect younger infants' difficulties in attending to and retaining relevant cues about the object to be searched for. Younger babies seem to remember less of what they are looking for.

These trends imply that infants may have a notion of object permanence, but find it demanding to remember the relevant facts needed to search: where they last saw the object and when and whether the object was in fact moved. Perhaps infants use memory when they can but supplement it with Piagetian motor schemes whenever necessary (Case, 1992). If an infant cannot recall where a toy is hidden, at least she can reenact the means she used to find it in the past. This multiple strategy actually resembles the way adults sometimes search for a lost object: if you cannot recall where you left it, you may retrace your steps up to the time you remember seeing it last—in essence, using an action scheme.

Motor skill and memory limitations can affect the appearance of competence not only in infants but in adults as well. By showing that the limitations happen to infants, the research once again strengthens the idea of continuity in development (that infants resemble adults) and weakens the idea of change (that infants are somehow different from adults). It also suggests that the "belief in object permanence" that Piaget identified may mean something different to a young infant than to an older one. For a three- or four-month-old, an "object" is anything that remains visible when tracked with the eyes and whose movements meet reasonable expectations when tracked. For an eighteen-month-old, an "object" is whatever becomes visible when sought with the hands or feet, and meets expectations to reappear after a reasonable physical search. We will see that still later in life, the concept of "object" changes meaning again, sometimes even referring to thoughts rather than things. But that is a story for later, when we discuss adolescent thought in Chapter 10.

Behavioral Learning in Infancy

In addition to the cognitively oriented research described in the preceding sections, other research on infant learning has attempted to identify specific behaviors of infants and the relationship of the behaviors to their causes and consequences. In essence, this is the point of view of *behaviorism,* described in Chapter 2 as well as earlier in this chapter when we looked at heart rate and habituation studies. Framing infants' behaviors as examples of conditioning and of imitation often has been helpful for understanding how they learn, because infants seem to do a lot of both.

Operant Conditioning

When an infant participates in psychological research using operant conditioning, she gets a reward, or positive reinforcement, if she performs some simple action or set of actions. By turning her head, for example, she may get to see an interesting toy or picture. In this case, the reinforcement is viewing the interesting toy, and head turning becomes the learned, or conditioned, behavior. Such actions tend to be performed more often than actions that are not reinforced.

As the examples of research in this chapter show, including Figure 6.1, infants are quite capable of learning through operant conditioning. Newborns will learn to suck on their

FIGURE 6.1
Evidence of Operant Learning among Infants

When infants are rewarded for looking at a certain feature of an image, they will look at that image more frequently. Moreover, when the "rules" for the reward change, infants quickly adapt to look more frequently at the images that fit the new rules, as shown here.

Phase 1: Here, the infant must discriminate the dimension of color. Red shapes are rewarded but blue are not—provided that the child looks at the red ones.
R = Rewarded

Phase 2 Reversal Shift: In phase 2 with a reversal shift, the infant must still discriminate the *same* dimension, but a different value of the dimension. Color is still rewarded, but now it is the color blue instead of red.

Phase 2 Non-Reversal Shift: In phase 2 with a *non-reversal* shift, the infant must discriminate a *new* dimension in order to be rewarded in this case the dimension of shape. Triangles are now rewarded, regardless of color.

> **What Do You Think?**
>
> Between about eight and twelve months of age, many babies show distress at separations from their primary caregiver (usually the mother). Some psychologists suggest that the distress is a partial result of their budding belief in object permanence. Do you think this might be true? How you might explain your position to a new parent who is concerned about her baby's distress?

hands longer if doing so yields a tiny amount of sugar water delivered through a tube in the corners of their mouths. Or they will learn to blink their eyes more often if doing so causes a pleasant voice to speak or a melody to play. One reason infants seem to learn to breast-feed so easily is the strong reinforcement the behavior brings in the form of mother's milk and being touched and held closely.

Infants are predisposed to learn these particular behaviors. All examples of operant conditioning in infants rely on those few behaviors that young babies already exhibit, which are mainly their inborn reflexes. By nature, reflexes occur easily—in fact, almost *too* easily. As parents often discover, any slight provocation, such as a touch on the baby's cheek, can stimulate sucking movements in young babies. Such readiness to respond creates confusion about when infant responses really constitute learning rather than general excitement. For example, when do sucking movements show true operant learning: a specific behavior performed more often because a particular reinforcement results from it? And when do sucking movements simply amount to a reflex that is itching to occur, so to speak, and would occur in response to almost any stimulus?

The confusion between learning and excitement diminishes as babies grow older because they acquire behaviors that are more truly voluntary. Even as babies get older, however, they acquire many behaviors, both desirable and regrettable, through what appears to be operant conditioning. A six- or nine-month-old will babble longer and more frequently if parents smile and express praise when he does so. A twelve-month-old will learn to wave good-bye sooner and more frequently if reinforced with praise or encouragement. And a two-year-old may learn to scream at her older sibling when she wants a toy the older child has because her screaming has been inadvertently reinforced: it causes the older child to simply abandon the toy, or it summons a parent who assumes (not always accurately) the older child somehow caused the screaming.

Of course, these are primarily immediate, short-term effects, and they sometimes differ from long-term effects of reinforcement. An example often important to parents is crying: will picking up the baby to quiet his crying actually reinforce him for crying in the long term? Conditioning theory would predict that it would, but most research on the impact of crying has found that fast, sensitive responses to crying actually lead to *less* crying (St. James-Roberts et al., 1993; St. James-Roberts, 2007). The quieting, though, is not reliable in the short term, but may take many months to become a definite, obvious response to being picked up. This delay suggests that decreases in crying may be a product of an interaction between sensitive caregiving and neurological maturation (St. James-Roberts, 2007). Nevertheless, this long delay between increased comforting and decreased rates of crying may cause parents a lot of worry about whether they are "spoiling" their child by responding to her crying.

Imitation

A second key aspect of infant learning is imitation. As make-believe play demonstrates, children obviously learn to imitate at some point in development. But exactly how early, and by what processes? Early research on these questions generally suggested that infants can engage in different kinds of imitation at different points during infancy (Piaget, 1962). It found that infants imitated actions they could literally see themselves perform (for example, in a mirror) sooner than those they could observe only in a model. Much research over the past two decades confirms this hypothesis. Imitating a hand gesture such

Should parents comfort a crying baby, or will this reinforce the baby for crying, resulting in more frequent crying? Research indicates that, over time, fast and sensitive parental responses to crying reduce the frequency and duration of crying.
Source: vystekimages/Shutterstock.com

as waving, for example, proves easier than imitating an unusual face made by an adult (Meltzoff & Kuhl, 1994). Also, deferred imitation may not appear until close to a child's second birthday; by that time, the child can imitate a gesture an entire day after seeing a model perform it.

Despite their preference for visible actions, infants sometimes imitate actions that are relatively invisible to themselves. One-week-old babies tend to stick out their tongues in imitation of adults and wiggle their fingers after seeing adults model this behavior. Distinguishing voluntary imitation from general, automatic excitement, however, remains a problem, as it does with other studies of very young babies. One research study highlighted this ambiguity especially well. It showed babies pictures of human faces depicting various emotions (Kaitz et al., 1988). Although the babies responded with emotional facial expressions of their own, their expressions did not match those in the pictures. In fact, the emotions on the babies' faces were hard to classify at all; they just looked "wrought up" at the sight of expressive human faces. However, recent neuroscience research utilizing more sensitive measures of brain-wave activity in various regions—and, in some cases, in specific neurons—of the brain has revealed the presence of what are being called "mirror neurons," neurons that fire either when an action is being performed *or* being observed. For example, when infants see an adult who is waving, the motor cortex in the infants' brains becomes active—the same area of the motor cortex that is active when the infants are actually waiving. This same neurological response occurs with facial expressions—whether infants are watching an adult smile or are smiling themselves, the same areas of their brains are active (Del Guidice, Manera, & Keysers, 2009). Even though young infants may not be able to accurately imitate the facial expression of others, the activity of mirror neurons and the feedback they receive through their interactions with others play important roles in their development of social relationships and their understanding of the emotional states in others (Lepage & Théoret, 2007).

Language Acquisition

When Michael, the son of one of the authors, was an infant, he went through several phases in using language. At twelve weeks, Michael made open-mouthed, cooing noises when he was feeling content. Sometimes these sounds were vaguely similar to ordinary vowel sounds, but they seemed to vary unpredictably. Michael cooed a lot in the morning when he first woke up, which pleased his parents.

By six months, Michael had added consonant sounds to his vocalizations to produce complicated babbling noises. His most productive time for this activity continued to be the morning, although he "said" quite a lot whenever he was feeling generally content. Certain sounds seemed to be favorites: *da* and *gn*. Sometimes Michael repeated these and

> **What Do You Think?**
>
> Shift your focus from infants to mothers for a moment. How do you suppose *mothers* might become conditioned to breastfeeding, either positively or negatively? Think about "what's in it" for them, as well as what hassles breast-feeding can create. If possible, talk to a breast-feeding mother about her experiences.

other sounds—*da, da, da, da*. His father thought Michael repeated sounds when he was feeling especially happy.

At fifteen months, Michael could produce about six words, but he did not pronounce them as adults would. The family cat was *dat;* his favorite food, yogurt, sounded like *yugun;* and airplanes were simply *der!* (as in "Look there!"). He seemed to understand dozens of words and sentences, although it was hard to be sure because he probably picked up clues about meaning from the behavior of his parents. When Michael was tired one day, he came immediately when his mother said, "Come sit here" in a sympathetic tone of voice. But when she said the same thing in a cross tone of voice the next day, he looked at her with an impish smile and went the other way.

One day close to his second birthday, Michael sat "reading" a children's book to himself. Occasionally, real phrases could be heard ("bug ate leaf), but mostly Michael sounded as though he were mumbling or talking in the next room. When he finished, he walked to the kitchen and phrased a three-word question: "What's for lunch?"

As these examples show, language is a fundamental feature of development throughout the lifespan. It adds greatly to a person's ability to learn about new people, objects, and events. It provides a way to express feelings more precisely. And it allows a person to participate, through verbal dialogue, more fully in his or her family and community. These benefits begin appearing during infancy as soon as language begins to develop, which is usually around a child's first birthday. They increase as the child gets older and develops more skill with language. Some aspects of language, in fact, continue to improve well into adulthood; vocabulary, for example, increases in size into middle age and beyond. So do some of the more subtle uses of language, such as when to say what, and to whom. We often think of these skills simply as "tact" or diplomacy.

But the major challenge, and one that takes considerable attention and energy from an infant, is acquiring language in the first place. Language acquisition partly involves mastering its structures—its sounds and organization, for example—but partly also involves learning how language is used—its purposes and conversational conventions. Infants begin on both projects immediately. Stated more precisely, infants begin doing all of the following simultaneously:

- They learn the sounds of the language (its *phonology*).
- They learn its words (its *lexicon*).

As this trio of photos indicates, learning through imitation progresses from repeating an infant's own actions observed in a mirror *(left)* to repeating actions initiated by others *(middle)*. Toddlers can even imitate more complicated sequences of behaviors, as the boy who is pretending to do work with mom on her laptop is demonstrating *(right)*.

Sources: *(left)* Dmitry Kalinovsky/Shutterstock.com ; *(middle)* Yanik Shauvin/Shutterstock.com; *(right)* iofoto/Shutterstock.com.

- They learn the meanings of words *(semantics)*.
- They learn the purposes and ways in which words and sentences normally get used in conversation *(pragmatics)*.
- They piece together the organization of words into sentences and connected discourse *(syntax)*.

Even though infants make progress in all of these areas, we focus on phonology, lexicon, and semantics in this chapter because these are the key "tasks" of language acquisition in infancy. We will discuss pragmatics and syntax in Chapter 6 in connection with cognitive development during early childhood.

Phonology

Every language uses a finite number of **phonemes**, or sounds that speakers of the language consider distinctive and that combine to make the words of the language. English has about forty-one phonemes; other languages have more or fewer than this number. In acquiring language, infants must be sensitive to phonemes and ignore any meaningless variations. Although the task may seem demanding, it actually proves surprisingly easy, even for a baby—so easy, in fact, that some language specialists suspect human beings are genetically and physiologically predisposed toward noticing phonemic differences (Archibald, 1995; Telkemeyer et al., 2009).

Although skill at producing phonemes takes longer to develop, it too seems to be biologically influenced. Sometime between four and eight months of age, infants begin **babbling** in increasingly complex ways. They apparently do so for the sole reward of hearing themselves vocalize, a form of play with sound and an example of a Piagetian primary circular reaction.

What suggests that babbling is motivated intrinsically? The most important evidence is the fact that all physically normal infants begin babbling at approximately the same age (about six months), regardless of the culture or language to which they are exposed. Furthermore, an observational study of deaf infants found the babies "babbling" with their hands. These infants could not babble orally, but they had been exposed to American Sign Language and were observed to make repetitive hand gestures analogous to the oral babbling of hearing infants (Pettito & Marentette, 1991).

Despite this finding, most research suggests a significant influence on babbling by parents and other members of an infant's language community. Although the study on deaf infants observed a type of babbling in these babies, the fact that the babbling was gestural rather than oral suggests that the infants' language environment influenced the form their babbling took (Takei, 2001). Other research on deaf infants has confirmed this conclusion. Contrary to a long-held belief, deaf infants may *not* babble orally in the same way that hearing infants do; rather, they typically begin oral babbling some months later. In some cases, deaf infants babble only if they hear sound that is amplified, such as through a hearing aid (Marschark, 1993). Interestingly, the patterns of sounds that hearing and hearing-impaired infants produce are quite similar at first (Iyer & Oiler, 2008), diverging when hearing infants begin to narrow their speech sounds to those that occur in their native language, a change that occurs a month or so prior to the production of their first words.

phonemes Sounds that combine with other sounds to form words.

babbling Infant vocalizations produced prior to acquiring language and without verbally meaningful intent.

Semantics and First Words

The **semantics** (or meanings) of a language, and of words in particular, are never mastered fully, even by adults. To test this idea on yourself, scan any page of a large, unabridged dictionary and see how far you go before you encounter an unfamiliar word. Most people, it seems, never learn even a majority of the words or terms in their native language. This is because words get much of their meanings from the real world rather than from other words. Most of us simply do not live long enough to encounter all of these relationships with the real world.

What words do children use first? On the whole, they prefer nominals—labels for objects, people, and events—much more than other kinds of words, such as verbs or modifiers

semantics The purposes and meanings of a language.

(Hart, 1991). Among nominals, they are most likely to name things that are used frequently or that stand out in some way. The child's own mother or father therefore may be named early, but not always as early as the parents expect. *Dog* may appear as an early word more often than *sun* or *diaper* does, even though children probably experience the latter two objects more frequently than they do dogs.

Other research has found that children vary in how much they emphasize different language functions in their first utterances (Bloom, 1993). Most children have a *referential style,* meaning their first words refer to objects and objective events—*car, book,* and so on. Others have an *expressive style,* using words to express feelings and relationships—*hello* and *goody!* During the second year of life, infants with a referential style tend to make more rapid advances in vocabulary and to develop more elaborate and precise use of syntax (or grammar). The differences seem to be influenced by infants' families, though not in a direct way. Research has found that infants who develop secure attachments to their primary caregivers (in the sense developed by Mary Ainsworth (1979) and discussed in Chapter 5) tend to acquire a referential style of communicating compared to infants with less secure attachments (Meins, 1997). Why might this link occur? Infancy researchers are not sure, but have suggested that it has something to do with the secure child's being more prepared to explore the environment—and confident enough to leave the proximity of parents and familiar surroundings to do so. As a result, the child encounters more new objects and experiences, as well as more people who are somewhat *un*familiar with his language. Therefore, compared to a less adventurous child, he has a greater need to acquire a large vocabulary and more varied means of expression. However, one must be cautious when making generalizations about this finding because cultural differences can influence the kinds of words that infants learn and use (Tardiff et al., 2008),

Influencing Language Acquisition

Just how do parents and other adults actually affect infants' language development? This question has important implications for parents and other caregivers of young children, and research has begun to provide at least some of the answers.

Parental Influences

Even when infants are very young, parents often talk to them as though they were full-fledged adult partners in a conversation (though not equally in all cultures; see the "A Multicultural View" feature). Consider this mother speaking to her three-month-old child:

> **Mother:** How is Kelsey today? *(pause)* How are you? *(pause)* Good, you say? *(pause)* Are you feeling good? *(pause)* I'm glad for that. *(pause)* Yes, I am. *(pause)* What would you like now? *(pause)* Your pacifier? *(pause)* Um? *(pause)* Is that what you want? *(pause)* Okay, here it is.

By asking questions in this "conversation," the mother implies that Kelsey is capable of responding, even though her infant is much too young to do so. Furthermore, the mother leaves pauses for her baby's hypothetical responses. Observations of these kinds of pauses show that they last just about as long as in conversations between adults (Haslett, 1997); it is as though the mother is giving her baby a turn to speak before taking another turn herself. When her child remains silent, the mother even replies on her behalf. In all these behaviors, the mother teaches something about turn talking in conversations, and she expresses her faith that the infant eventually will learn these conventions herself.

When infants finally begin speaking, parents continue this strategy. At the same time, however, they also simplify their language significantly. They speak in shorter sentences, although not as short as the child's, and use simpler vocabulary, although less restricted than the child's (Bryant & Barrett, 2007; Gallaway & Richards, 1994). These extra strategies help to teach a new lesson, namely that words and sentences do in fact communicate and that language is more than interesting noises and babbling. By keeping just ahead of the infant's own linguistic skills, parents can stimulate the further development of language.

A Multicultural View

Cognitive Effects of Talking to Infants: A Cross-Cultural Perspective

Although the text implies strong support for mothers' talking with their infants, a different impression of this practice occurs if you view it in a cross-cultural context. Then the frequent one-way "conversations" and direct gazing between mother and baby seem a bit less natural or inevitable and even a bit strange.

In North America, the practice is widely regarded as a positive experience: talking with and gazing at a nonverbal infant increases in frequency until the child begins producing her own language, around the first birthday, and cuddling and holding close decrease at the same time. Parents are even given professional assistance when these changes in interaction do not occur (Yoder & Warren, 1993)! Mothers themselves believe that talking with and gazing at infants stimulates infants' intellectual competence.

Research evidence seems to support the mothers' belief. Children who have verbally interactive mothers during infancy do show better language comprehension as four-year olds and do show higher competence at solving simple problems involving both verbal and nonverbal reasoning (Samter & Haslett, 1997). But there is contrary evidence as well. In, China, for example, mothers talk to infants relatively little but cuddle and hold them relatively a lot (Ho, 1994). Yet Chinese culture values education success and Chinese children perform well in school.

The fact is that the effects of maternal talk on infants are not clear. But it is probably not a matter of stimulating thinking and language development, as many mothers themselves might believe. Maternal talk probably is much too complex for a two- or three-month-old infant to learn by hearing it directly. Instead of providing a language model directly, therefore, early verbal interaction may serve other purposes in infants' development: maybe it simply reflects the mother's general interest in and responsiveness to her child. Parents who enjoy talking to their babies as newborns are likely to still enjoy talking to them several years later, when the babies have become capable of learning and using language more effectively. If so, the relationship between early talk and later competence is a good example of a *correlation* (an association) that is not also a *cause*. In that case, too, North American mothers could (in theory) talk with their newborns a good deal less in the earliest months and still expect the babies to end up with good language skills eventually! This would be true, though, only if a mother were responsive and caring throughout the child's infancy and only if the mother did begin interacting verbally as soon as the infant showed signs of actually understanding and using language. This development pattern in fact describes mother-infant relationship in China to a certain extent (though not perfectly).

These ideas remain speculation, though, because mothers' language practices cannot, and probably should not, be manipulated simply to explore their effects on children. In any society, parents need to interact with their babies in ways they consider natural. But comparing cultural beliefs can nonetheless give clues about the deeper, less obvious effects of particular culture practices (Greenfield, 1994). Mother-infant "conversations" are a good example of a culture-bound practice virtually all parent advice books urge parents to talk with their babies. Yet in doing so, the books join parents in assuming a particular cultural value: that skillful oral expression is desirable and should be encouraged as much as possible.

Constant close contact between caregiver and infant, as between this mother and her child, may encourage more nonverbal communication and result in infants who fuss relatively little. Crying and fussing, which we associate with infancy in our society, may actually be a precursor to verbal communication, which parents encourage in North American society.
Source: wong sze yuen/Shutterstock.com.

This style is called **infant-directed speech**, or *caregiver speech,* meaning a dialect or a version of language characteristic of parents talking with young children. In addition to shorter sentences and simpler vocabulary, caregiver speech has several unique features. It tends to unfold more slowly than speech between adults and to use a higher and more variable, or singsong, pitch; it generally contains unusually strong emphasis on keywords ("Give me your *cup*"). Parents speaking to infants also tend to repeat or paraphrase themselves more than usual ("Give me the cup. The cup. Find the cup, and give it.").

infant-directed speech
The style or register of speech used by adults and older children when talking with a one- or two-year-old infant.

Chapter 6 Cognitive Development during the First Two Years

Research shows clearly that parents' conversations with babies are extremely important to the infants' development. The Harvard Preschool Project, a longitudinal study conducted at Harvard University, observed the contacts between parents and their infants that occurred naturally in the families' own homes (White, 1993). At various intervals, the infants were assessed for both intelligence and social skills. When the assessments were correlated with the results of the home observations, one result stood out clearly: the most intellectually and socially competent infants had parents who directed large amounts of language at them. The most competent babies received about twice as much language as the least competent infants in this study did. But the most competent infants also stimulated interactions with their parents, primarily by procuring various simple kinds of help, such as in pouring a glass of juice or placing the final block on a tower. These "services" probably benefited the infants by offering many opportunities for parents to talk with them ("Shall I put the block on top?").

Influences of Professional Caregivers

Language acquisition can also be supported by other adults who interact with infants extensively—notably, professional caregivers in family childcare or infant-care centers. Their forms of influence parallel those of parents (Chorale et al., 1993). *Contingent dialogue* (extending the child's verbal initiatives), for example, can easily take place at an infant care center: a toddler may name objects in the room ("Book!") or pictures displayed on the wall ("Cat!"), and the caregiver can extend those early initiatives into longer dialogues ("Yes, it's a pretty cat. Do you like cats?"). Gillian Luppiwiski's conversation with Jocelyn about Play-Doh, described in the "Working With" feature, is another example. *Contextual dialogue* (familiar language routines or rituals) can also occur: a caregiver and child may engage in predictable exchanges in preparing to go home each day ("Have you found your coat?" "Now zip it up"). To succeed, these dialogues must be simplified; that is, they should rely on infant-directed or "caregiver" speech that takes the infant's early stage of language into account. Table 6.3 lists some additional ways caregivers can assist in language development.

But important differences also exist between professional caregiver influences and parent influences. One concerns intensity and frequency: caregivers usually do not see a particular infant or toddler for as many hours as a parent does, nor do they develop relationships as emotionally intense as those of parents. Another difference concerns cultural

TABLE 6.3 Interactions That Support Language Development

Interaction	Purpose
Sitting on the floor with infant and reading books, telling stories, or singing songs	Builds trust; models interesting activities using language
Holding infant close, looking into infant's face, smiling, and talking to infant	Builds trust; models dialogue or conversation
Responding to infant's first words and gestures using caregiver's own words and gestures	Encourages dialogue and conversation; shows respect for infant's language initiatives
Offering simple choices to infant verbally ("Do you want to paint or to play outside?")	Stimulates infant to attend to language; calls attention to relationship between language and actions
Encouraging infant (especially if a toddler) to express desires and resolve differences using words ("What do you want to do?")	Encourages child to practice language; demonstrates power of verbal expression
Distress	Whimpering or crying; vigorous or agitated movements; facial grimaces pronounced; skin very flushed

> **WORKING WITH** Gillian Luppiwiski, Infant Care Provider

Fostering Infants' Thinking

Gillian Luppiwiski worked as a caregiver in an infant daycare center for ten years prior to this interview. She made numerous comments about her work: the changes she sees in the babies as they grow, the responses of mothers and fathers, the interest that even infants and toddlers show in one another. When I asked her to comment on infants' thinking abilities, she began talking about their language and problem solving behaviors and about how she and other caregivers support it.

Kelvin: *What do you notice most about these children when you're working here?*

Gillian: They change so much! Like day and night. Last fall Jocelyn could hardly move; she got so frustrated watching the older children walk around! But now she's all over the place, into *everything*—and happy as a lark.

Kelvin: *Can you figure out what she thinks about? Does it even make sense to ask about her "thoughts"?*

Gillian: Oh, yes. Like when we get out the Play-Doh, and she starts using it—poking it with her fingers, talking about it. She just started naming it, you know; she says "doh" and looks at you with a smile. And "wed" when it's red. That's her favorite color.

Kelvin: *So her language is developing.*

Gillian: Yes, and the Play-Doh helps with that. It gives her something to talk about. We support her comments, saying things like "That's right! We've got red Play-Doh today."

Kelvin: *What about other times? Even when she's not talking, does it seem like Jocelyn's "thinking"?*

Gillian: Definitely! Take the climber: she loves to climb up there and sit with Joel. That teaches her about space and depth, but she learns more by *doing* it than by talking about it. Shelley (another caregiver) might talk about it, comment on it verbally when she sees Jocelyn climbing. But Jocelyn mainly learns it by doing it.

Kelvin: *Do you ever "teach" them anything directly?*

Gillian: We don't so much teach them as make it possible for them to learn. That's how I'd put it. Shelley or I might put out a few puzzles one day, and talk with a child when she chooses to work on one—encourage her to persist in putting it together, maybe give a hint or two, but not do it for her.

Or the other day, Danny started getting out *all* the trucks! He lined them all up with the big ones at one end and the smaller ones at the other end. Sorted them! It was great to see. He needed help, though, in finding enough room to do this without tripping over Jocelyn and the others. He commented on the lineup: "All the trucks!" And so did I, by challenging him gently: "Are you sure have them *all*?"

Kelvin: *So he was grouping? Classifying things?*

Gillian: Yes. In his own way, his own two-year-old way. "Developmentally appropriate practice"—that's what educators are always talking about. That's what makes us a real *infant* center, and different from a preschool center. We try to provide developmentally appropriate things and support the children for using them.

What Do You Think?

1. Considering what Gillian said, how important is an infant care center for fostering a child's thinking ability? How does it compare to experiences that an infant or toddler might have at home?

2. Gillian says, "We don't so much teach them as make it possible for them to learn." How comfortable are you with this idea? Can it apply to working with older children (preschoolers, school-age adolescents) or only to infants and toddlers? Consult with a few classmates about this question; what do they think about it?

3. At times, Gillian seems to equate language development with cognitive development. Is there some way to distinguish these two processes in an infant center? Brainstorm an example or two of how you might do this if you were a caregiver.

---

expectations: it is common for caregivers (but rare for parents) to come from a cultural or language background that differs from the children's background. The gap can create confusion and misunderstanding between caregiver and child or between caregiver and parent. If a caregiver and a child speak different primary languages, one may lack facility with some of the words and expressions needed to communicate with the other.

> **What Do You Think?**
>
> Find out, if you can, the words you produced first as an infant and the setting in which you produced them. Pool your results with a few classmates. Are there any features common to either the words or the settings?

Overall, parents and other caregivers constitute a much more positive than negative influence on language development. Given their importance to the process, it should not be surprising that nearly all children acquire high verbal competence in just a few years. Language acquisition is "over determined": society supports language learning in so many ways that if a child fails to experience that support in one way, she or he is likely to experience it in some other way. So most of us do learn to talk!

The End of Infancy

During the first two years of life, infants become much more like individuals than they are on the day they are born. By their second birthday, they walk about, grasp at objects, and direct their attention toward particular people and activities. These physical skills facilitate certain cognitive activities, such as searching for objects that an infant "knows" exist even though he cannot see them.

The language skills that develop at the same time, in turn, contribute to the formation of social skills and relationships, as we will see in the next chapter. By age two, a child knows, and can say, who her parents and siblings are. She can also begin expressing her feelings about these people verbally: whether she is happy or sad, angry or fearful, likes someone or not. In the next chapter, we take a closer look at these social changes, which have a basis in the physical and cognitive developments of infancy.

Chapter Summary

- **How do infants' senses operate at birth?** At birth, infants already can see and hear, but with less accuracy or acuity than adults do. They have well-developed senses of taste, smell, and touch, and infants demonstrate the ability to combine information from multiple senses to better allow them to function in their environments.
- **How can infant cognition be studied?** Infants' arousal and attention can be studied by noting changes in their heart rates. Infants' recognition and memory of familiar things can be studied by observing their habituation to stimuli, or tendency to attend to novel stimuli and ignore familiar ones.
- **Do infants see and hear in the way adults do?** *Perception* refers to the immediate organization of sensations. *Cognition* refers to the processes by which perceptions are organized, and it often happens deliberately. Studies of visual perception suggest that infants under six months of age perceive a variety of patterns, including those usually found on a human face. Young infants, including newborns, show object constancy in visual perception, as well as visual anticipation of events. Infants also show sensitivity to depth, as indicated in the visual cliff experiments. Infants can localize sounds to some extent at birth, but do not do so accurately until about six months of age. Categorical thought can be demonstrated during infancy by using the reversal shift procedure.
- **How do thinking and learning change during infancy?** Piaget has proposed six stages of infant cognitive development during which infants' schemes become less egocentric and increasingly symbolic and organized. Research on Piaget's six stages generally confirms his original observations, but it also raises questions about the effects of motor skills and memory on infants' cognitive performance. Like older children and adults, infants can learn through behavioral conditioning and imitation. Behavioral learning tends to be ambiguous in infants less than three months old because it is difficult to distinguish true learning from general, automatic excitement.
- **What phases do infants go through in acquiring language?** Babbling begins around six months of age and becomes increasingly complex until it disappears sometime before the infant's second birthday. Infants

show important individual differences in their selection of first words, but generally they use words for objects in their environment that are distinctive in some way. Adults influence language acquisition mainly through modeling simplified utterances, recasting their infants' own utterances, and directing considerable language at the child as she or he grows. Professional caregivers influence language acquisition in ways similar to parents, but they must also recognize the potential effects of cultural gaps between caregiver and child.

Key Terms

accommodation (p. 135)
assimilation (p. 135)
babbling (p. 143)
circular reaction (p. 135)
cognition (p. 128)
habituation (p. 128)
infant-directed speech (p. 145)
intermodal perception (p. 133)
object permanence (p. 136)
perception (p. 128)
phonemes (p. 143)
scheme (p. 134)
semantics (p. 143)
sensorimotor intelligence (p. 134)
visual cliff (p. 131)

Psychosocial Development during the First Two Years

CHAPTER 7

Source: wavebreakmedia/Shutterstock.com

Chapter Outline

Early Social Relationships

Emotions and Temperament in Infancy

Attachment Formation

Toddlerhood and the Emergence of Autonomy

Looking Back/Looking Forward

Focusing Questions

- What emotional capabilities does an infant have? How do differences in infants' temperaments affect their social development?
- In what ways is a newborn infant capable of participating in the social world? How does caregiver-infant synchrony expand an infant's social capabilities?
- What experiences enable infants to develop secure emotional attachments with their caregivers? What are the consequences of different attachment patterns?
- Why is autonomy so central to development during toddlerhood? What parenting qualities contribute to its successful development?

Even as a newborn, Alberto was an easy baby to feed and comfort. He was also very active and responsive to the sights and sounds in his environment. Even when tired or overstimulated by the people around him, he seemed able to calm himself with just a little help from his caregiver. When he was five weeks old, Alberto just loved attention. His smiles and excitement were irresistible, and he responded to anyone who paid attention to him—from his parents to his older brother and sisters to Luisa, the family dog. However, a special mutual responsiveness seemed to be present whenever Alberto interacted with his mother, Maria, or his father, José. With either of them, Alberto's smiles, sounds, and movements seemed so highly in tune with theirs that they appeared to be having a real conversation.

By the time Alberto was four months old, he began to show a preference for his mother and his oldest sister, Lydia, who helped care for him. When he saw or heard either of them, he became especially happy, active, and noisy, which caused some jealousy among other family members.

Between ages nine and eleven months, Alberto's preferences for specific people became much stronger and more obvious. He clearly preferred his mother to any other adult and responded to his sister Lydia more than to any of the other children. Now able to crawl, he tried to follow his mother wherever she went, and he cried when she left the room. During this period, he also began to do something he had never done before: he sometimes became upset when unfamiliar people visited, even if they were friendly to him.

By the time he was almost two, Alberto was walking and talking well, had begun toilet training, and could do many things himself. He continued to be an active and happy child, but sometimes he became frustrated and upset if he did not succeed at a task. Fortunately, talking to him and giving him just the right amount of helpful guidance usually worked. Although he still demanded a good deal of attention from his mother and still preferred to play with Lydia, he rarely got upset when other family members cared for him. He also seemed quite happy to socialize with almost all friendly visitors, even those he had never met before.

These changes in Alberto are typical of some of the important psychosocial changes that occur during infancy. From the moment of birth, infants differ in their temperament—their characteristic activity levels and stylistic patterns of responding to the people and events in their new environment. As we will see in this chapter, temperamental differences in infants and how well they fit with the temperaments and expectations of their parents, other family members, and society may influence development not only in infancy but through childhood, adolescence, and adulthood as well. And although infants highly depend on their caregivers to meet their needs, they are anything but passive. Infants become active, sophisticated observers and participants in their own psychosocial development.

As an infant grows older, she comes to form close and enduring emotional attachments with the important people in her life and sometimes shows her concerns about them very dramatically. She wails when a strange nurse approaches her in the doctor's office, and she greets her mother or father warmly when one of them "rescues" her from the nurse. Secure attachment relationships, such as those developing between Alberto and his mother and other caregivers, are likely to provide an important basis for successful psychosocial development throughout life. As we will see shortly, the security of an individual's attachment relationships in infancy is an important predictor of relationships as an older child and adolescent, in romantic relationships, and in relationships with the person's own children and grandchildren. A baby may participate in relationships in more subtle ways, such as attending closely to older brothers and sisters while they play—more closely than her siblings attend to her. At times, she may express her needs or feelings in ways that confound the people around her; for example, she may refuse particular foods when a parent offers them but take them happily from a baby sitter.

These behaviors convey two major tasks of psychosocial development in infancy: the development of *trust* and *autonomy*. Infants learn what to expect from the important people in their lives. They develop strong feelings about whom they do (and do not) like to be with and what foods they prefer. The conflicts of trust versus mistrust and autonomy versus shame and doubt, which we examined in Chapter 2, intertwine closely during their first two years, although many observers of children believe trust develops earlier than autonomy does (Erikson, 1963; Maccoby, 1980; Stern, 1985a).

In this chapter, we first discuss the importance of emotions and temperament in infancy. Next, we explore the essential role of early social interactions and attachments in the development of a sense of basic trust (versus mistrust) and in the achievement of autonomy (versus shame and doubt). We examine the ways in which attachments form. Finally, we look at the emergence of self-knowledge and self-awareness during later infancy and toddlerhood.

Early Social Relationships

Infants seem to have a natural tendency to be social participants. Not only do newborns show preferences for their mothers' voices shortly after birth (Purhonen et al., 2004);

Every member of a family has unique ways of interacting with a new child.
Source: AmiParikh/Shutterstock.com.

some evidence also suggests that their perception of speech can be influenced by prenatal exposure to their mothers' speech (DeCasper & Spence, 1986; DeCasper et al., 1994; Granier-Deferre et al., 2011). Immediately after birth, infants are capable of many social responses. For example, a newborn will turn his head toward the sound of a human voice and actively search for its source and will pause regularly in his sucking pattern for human voices but not for similar, nonhuman tones.

Transition to Parenthood

Parent-child relationships begin even before a child is born. Almost as soon as pregnancy is confirmed, parents form *images* of what their child will be like and of how they as parents will respond and cope with this new human presence (Galinsky, 1987). Expecting parents often experience both excitement and fear, the precise mix depending on how much support they have for becoming parents as well as the history of support, or lack thereof, that they had for being children themselves years ago. Even after the baby is born, these images can influence the parents' internal experiences and expectations regarding a child, although this "mental portrait" is now subject to continual revision based on the parents' ongoing interactions and experiences with their baby (Anderson, 1996; Ferholt, 1991; Innamorati et al., 2010; Stern, 1995, 2004).

Having a child, particularly if it is the first, represents a major life transition that is accompanied by personal, familial, social, and, for many people, professional changes. For most parents, having a child leads them to become less concerned about themselves and more concerned with the well-being of others and about the future as embodied in their child. This shift away from self-centeredness usually comes at some emotional cost, however. During the first two years of rearing an infant, many mothers find themselves removed from much of their normal contact with other adults to devote themselves to infant care, and fathers report working harder at their jobs (Bronstein, 1988; Cowan et al., 1991; Hyman, 1995).

To accommodate the additional family tasks involved in caring for a new infant, the division of roles between husband and wife tends to become more traditional, regardless of the wife's employment, educational level, pre-existing arrangements, or beliefs about gender roles. Social and emotional patterns between parents also appear to change, as reflected in significant decreases in shared leisure and sexual activities, in fewer positive interactions with each other, and in decreased marital satisfaction and greater marital conflict (Levy-Shiff, 1994; Monk et al., 1996; Shapiro et al., 2000; Vandell et al., 1997). There is evidence that when same-sex couples become parents, the division of household labor is more equal, resulting in higher relationship satisfaction (Tornello, Kruczkowski, & Patterson, 2015; Tornello, Sonnenberg, & Patterson, 2015).

To better understand these changes, Rachel Levy-Shiff (1994) studied marital adjustment in 102 heterosexual couples from diverse sociocultural backgrounds from pregnancy through the first eight months following the birth of their first child. She found that higher levels of *paternal involvement* with the baby, especially to caregiving, was the most important factor in maintaining marital satisfaction for *both* spouses at a time when opportunities to spend time together in leisure and sexual activities are greatly reduced due to the demands of infant care. Levy-Shiff suggests that during the transition to parenthood, men and women must first solve the internal and interpersonal dilemmas of reorganizing their lives to adjust to the new demands and responsibilities of child-rearing. In most families, the birth of a first child results in gender roles becoming more differentiated and traditional, with women assuming both the main responsibilities for childcare and most of the housework. The physical and emotional drain new mothers experience may lead them to feel resentment toward their husbands because of "overload" and because of unfulfilled prenatal expectations that caring for the new baby would be more fully shared.

Similarly, in a recent longitudinal study, mothers' expectations regarding the role of the father played a significant role in not only the satisfaction that husbands and wives felt in their roles as parents but also in the effectiveness of the child-rearing each provided (Schoppe-Sullivan & Mangelsdorf, 2013). What has become very apparent is that the quality of the parenting partnership established between mothers and fathers—optimally resulting in **coparenting**—has significant developmental implications for both the parents and their children. Coparenting is comprised of four main elements (Feinberg, 2003):

coparenting A parenting partnership in which child-rearing goals, strategies, and responsibilities are shared.

- *Type of behavior exhibited between parents*—Warm and cooperative ("supportive") behavior is clearly preferable to hostile, critical, and competitive ("undermining") behavior.

- *Division of labor regarding child-rearing*—Childcare responsibilities should be shared in a manner that is satisfactory to both parents.

- *Family management*—Decisions about how the family relates to others outside of the family and how family members relate to each other should be made jointly.

- *Parenting practices*—Parents should be in agreement regarding the adoption and development of moral values, the behavioral expectations they have for their children, and the means by which they shape and enforce those behaviors (e.g., discipline techniques).

Fathers who are more involved in coparenting and sharing housework demonstrate that they are not just husbands but also good friends who are committed to meeting their partners' needs in ways that are caring and fair. It is also likely that such shared involvement increases a husband's empathy and appreciation for his wife's experience. Such participation reduces the guilt he would feel if he failed to actively share these new responsibilities. Interestingly, by freeing up their wives' time and conveying a spirit of cooperativeness, husbands create opportunities for more high-quality time with their wives, the lack of which is a major cause of dissatisfaction for many new fathers (Belsky et al., 1995; Levy-Shiff, 1994; Shapiro et al., 2000; Vandell et al., 1997). And to be clear, mothers did not necessarily expect an equal sharing of parenting responsibilities with their husbands. What was important was for the mothers and fathers to communicate effectively and to fulfill each other's expectations in their roles as parents. Under these circumstances, parenting satisfaction and the effectiveness of coparenting were heightened for both parents (Feinberg, 2003.) The transition to parenthood is the start of a lifelong process that we will discuss throughout this book. Similarly, same-sex couples' relationships fared better when the actual division of household labor matched the individuals' ideal expectations of how workload would be divided (Tornello, Sonnenberg, & Patterson, 2015).

Caregiver-Infant Synchrony

Frequently the social interactions between parent (or other caregiver) and infant involve a pattern of close coordination and teamwork in which each waits for the other to finish before beginning to respond. This pattern of closely coordinated interaction is called

caregiver-infant synchrony. Recall the description of Alberto at the beginning of this chapter. Even infants only a few weeks old are able to maintain and break eye contact with their mothers at regular intervals and to take turns with them in making sounds and body movements. Furthermore, videotape studies reveal that mother and baby have "conversations" that resemble adult dialogue in many ways, except for the child's lack of words (De Wolff & van IJzendoorn, 1997; Fish et al., 1993; Stern, 1992).

Until an infant is several months old, responsibility for coordinating this activity rests with the caregiver. But after a few months, the baby becomes capable of initiating social interchanges and influencing the content and style of her caregiver's behavior. Some of this continuity is created by the baby rather than the mother. The smiles, gazes, and vocalizing of a friendly infant prove hard for her mother to resist, and after several months of experience with such a baby, the mother becomes especially responsive to her infant's communications, further reinforcing the baby's sociable tendencies. During the infant's second year, parent and baby use gestures such as pointing, vocalizing, and alternating their gaze between objects and their partner to coordinate and sustain periods of joint attention and maintain each other's interest. High levels of joint attention and reciprocal turn taking in parent-infant interaction, sometimes referred to as *coregulation*, reflect sensitive parenting and help children to become socially competent in relationships with family members and peers (Aureli & Presaghi, 2010; Moore & Denham, 1995; Raver, 1996).

As we will see shortly, a good caregiver-infant temperament "fit" and a well-developed capacity for caregiver-infant synchrony both contribute in important ways to the establishment of the high-quality caregiver-infant relationships that serve as the basis for healthy development (Evans & Porter, 2009). Caregiver-infant relationships that lack the mutual awareness and responsiveness that make synchrony possible may reflect child-rearing difficulties and can place an infant at risk for developmental problems. Studies of interactions between depressed mothers and their infants, for example, have found that mothers' negative moods influence their babies' moods and can affect their longer-term relationships and vulnerability to depression later in life (Letourneau et al., 2011; Moore & Dunham, 1995; Nolen-Hoeksema et al., 1995; Radke-Yarrow et al., 1993).

caregiver-infant synchrony
Patterns of closely coordinated social and emotional interaction between caregiver and infant.

Social Interactions with Other Family Members

Although infants may interact more with their mothers than with anyone else, they actually live in a network of daily social relationships in which a number of other people make at least minor—and sometimes major—contributions to their social lives. Fathers often belong to this network, and so do siblings and grandparents. How do a baby's contacts with these people compare to those with his or her mother?

Father-Infant Interactions

Fathers have become increasingly involved in the care of infants and young children, spending around two or three hours per day compared to nine hours for mothers

Sharing childcare and household tasks helps all parents with the transition to parenthood.
Source: zeljkodan/Shutterstock.com.

Chapter 7 Psychosocial Development during the First Two Years

(Yeung et al., 2001). In some cases, fathers assume the role of primary caregiver, reversing the traditional expectations that fathers should set personal and professional goals over investing time and care in their children and the paternal role (Garbarino, 1993; Geiger, 1996; Hyman, 1995). As with mothers, fathers' success at maintaining high levels of caregiver-infant synchrony is related to the goodness of fit between their stress levels, personality characteristics, attitudes, and expectations, and the characteristics and needs of their babies (Bridges et al., 1997; Lundy, 2002; Noppe et al., 1991). In an interesting naturalistic study of fathers' interactions with their infants, Anju Jain, Jay Belsky, and Keith Crnic (1996) observed four groups of fathers: caregivers, playmates-teachers, disciplinarians, and disengaged fathers. Caregivers and playmate-teacher fathers were more educated, had more prestigious occupations, were better adjusted emotionally, more able to rely on others, and experienced fewer daily hassles than the disciplinarian and disengaged fathers.

Although mothers and fathers engage in similar forms of play with their infants, their styles differ. Play episodes with fathers tend to have sharper peaks and valleys: higher states of excitement and more sudden and complete withdrawals by the baby. Fathers tend to jostle more and talk less than mothers do, and they roughhouse more and play ritual games such as peek-a-boo less. These differences in style also appear in middle childhood, and such playful interactions may help prepare infants for future play with peers of both genders (Lamb & Lewis, 2003; Parke et al., 1988).

How do we explain these differences? Past experience with infants, the amount of time routinely spent with young children, demanding work schedules, and fathers' expectations about the stresses and responsibilities of parenting may all play a role. When researchers compared fathers who served as primary, full-time caregivers with fathers who took the more traditional secondary-caregiver role, they found differences in how the two groups played with their infants. Primary-caregiver fathers acted very much like mothers, smiling more and imitating their babies' facial expressions and vocalizations more than secondary-caregiver fathers did. However, almost all of the fathers were quite physical when interacting with their infants (Field, 1987; Geiger, 1996; Noppe et al., 1991; Paquette et al., 2003). These findings suggest that "cohort" effects may be at work here. (*Cohort effects* refer to developmental changes shared by individuals growing up in a particular place or under a specific set of historical circumstances.) As successive generations of fathers assume greater involvement in the care of infants due to changing societal and cultural conditions and expectations, differences in how fathers and mothers interact with their babies will likely decrease, although the rough-and-tumble aspect of the father-child relationship appears to be an enduring one (Paquette, 2004).

Interactions with Siblings

Approximately 80 percent of children in the United States and Europe grow up with siblings (Krieder & Ellis, 2011). The time they spend together in their early years frequently is greater than the time spent with their mothers or fathers (Noller, 2005). In many cultures, children are cared for by siblings. From age one or two they are fed, comforted, disciplined, and played with by a sister or brother who may be only three or four years older (Cicirelli, 1994; Dunn, 1985; Teti, 1992; Updegraff et al., 2011). Firstborn children are likely to monitor the interactions of their mother and the new baby very closely and try to become directly involved themselves. Children as young as eighteen months attempt to help in the bathing, feeding, and dressing of their sibling. At times, they also try to tip over the baby's bath, spill things, and turn the kitchen upside down when they feel jealous of their mother's attention to the new baby. Conflict between siblings is most likely to occur when parents are seen as giving preferential treatment to one child (Dunn et al., 1994; Stewart et al., 1987) or when children feel jealous when their siblings are interacting with their parents (Kolak & Volling, 2010).

In talking to their younger siblings, children make many of the same adjustments their parents do, using much shorter sentences, repeating comments, and using lots of action-getting techniques (baby talk, or "parentese"). In turn, infants tend to respond to their siblings in much the same way they do to their parents. But they also quickly learn the ways siblings differ from parents, particularly young siblings. Because younger children lack their parents' maturity and experience, they are less able to focus consistently on meeting the baby's needs rather than their own. For example, a four-year-old who is playing with his eight-month-old sister may not notice that she is becoming overstimulated and tired and needs to stop. On another occasion, he may become jealous of the attention she is getting and "accidentally" fall on her while giving her a hug. If parents (and other caregivers) keep in mind the needs and capabilities of each of their children and provide appropriate supervision, interactions with siblings are likely to benefit the development of both their new infant and his or her brothers and sisters. Secure infant-mother attachment and warmth toward each child is associated with positive relationships between siblings, while parental coldness is associated with sibling conflicts, possibly because children use their models of attachment with parents in other relationships (Volling & Belsky, 1992). It is important to note that parent attachment may be different with different siblings, and sibling attachment is also highly dependent on sibling responsiveness over time (Whiteman, McHale, & Soli, 2011).

Grandparents

For the majority of well-functioning families, and in most cultural groups in North America, grandparents become welcome companions for the new child (Nicholson & Zeese, 2008; Werner, 1991), as well as secondary sources of practical advice and childcare. This is especially true when the grandparents live geographically close to the parents, they are relatively young and in good health, and the family itself belongs to a cultural group (such as Mexican Americans) that values the participation of the extended family in raising children (Ramirez, 1989; Slomin, 1991). In some circumstances, grandparents become the primary caregivers for their child's infant (Strom et al., 1995).

Interactions with Nonparental Caregivers

In recent decades, caregiving has become increasingly important in the lives of preschool children because more mothers have returned to working outside the home, even before their children have begun public school. In 2010, just over 64 percent of all mothers with children less than six years of age worked outside the home, a number that increased to approximately 77 percent for mothers of school-aged children (HHS, 2013). (We will take a closer look at changes in the nature of families and family life when we discuss psychosocial development in early adulthood in Chapter 13.) All of these parents require suitable, high-quality care for their children for either all or part of the day. The arrangements they actually make depend on the age of the child, on their own preferences (usually family-like settings), and on the kinds of services available in the community. Among all parents who work at least part time or more, about 42 percent arrange for a relative to come into the home or take the child to

For many families, grandparents play an important role in dealing with the transition to parenthood.
Source: Rawpixel/Shutterstock.com

Chapter 7 Psychosocial Development during the First Two Years

the relative's home (Laughlin, 2013). Another 11 percent arrange for a nonrelative to care for the child in the child's home or, more commonly, in the caregiver's home.

Approximately 24 percent of infants, toddlers, and preschoolers are cared for in licensed infant and toddler childcare centers and in family day-care homes. (If you have been adding the percentages of children being cared for by relatives, nonrelatives, and day-care center staff, you have probably noticed that the numbers do not sum to 100 percent. This is because a sizable proportion of infants, toddlers, and preschoolers whose parents work have no single or consistent caregiving arrangement.) Figure 7.1 summarizes current childcare arrangements for children under two years of age. In addition to good physical facilities and developmentally appropriate programs, high-quality care for infants is best ensured by employing caregivers who are well trained and supervised and responsive to the physical, cognitive, social, and emotional needs of infants and their families (Scarr, 1998). For parents who are considering day care for their infant, knowing what to look for in a center is extremely important. Table 7.1 presents guidelines for choosing infant day care. Additional discussion of early childhood education and developmentally appropriate practices with preschoolers is found in Chapter 9.

Interactions with Peers

Young babies show considerable interest in other infants, and in much the same ways, they show interest in their parents: by gazing, smiling, and cooing. Sociability of this kind develops with peers at the same time and at the same rate that it does with parents. When given the choice, infants often prefer playing with their peers to playing with their mothers. In play situations, infants more frequently look at and follow their peers, and toddlers are more likely to talk with, imitate, and exchange toys with their peers than with their mothers. Peers also support the autonomy of the toddler from the mother and offer the toddler an alternative source of stimulation and comfort (Chadwick et al., 2004; Hartup, 1989; Rubenstein & Howes, 1983).

Parents, teachers, and other adults play a major role in the development of relationships with peers during toddlerhood, through their relationships with their toddlers, through direct instruction about social interactions, and by providing their toddlers with appropriate opportunities to be with peers in extended family, play-group, and day-care situations (Fagot, 1997; Howes et al., 1994; Parke et al., 1994). Not surprisingly, the quality of infant-parent attachment appears to be related to young children's behavior with peers. For example, securely attached children have been found to receive more positive contact from unfamiliar peers, to be better liked by peers, and to have more positive friendships with peers, compared to insecurely attached children (Belsky & Cassidy, 1994; Cassidy et al., 1996).

Toddlers in day care spend about 25 percent of their time interacting positively with other toddlers. They are more likely to express positive feelings and play competently with peers than with adults or when by themselves. Repeated contact with a peer in a familiar setting with a familiar caregiver and minimal adult interference appears to facilitate

Infants show considerable interest in interacting with other infants. When given the opportunity, they may prefer playing with their peers more than their parents.
Source: Pavel L Photo and Video/Shutterstock.com.

FIGURE 7.1

Current Childcare Arrangements for Working Mothers with Children under One Year and with Children Between One and Two Years

The majority of infants and toddlers whose mothers work are cared for in their own or another home. Somewhat more toddlers than infants go to childcare facilities. Infants are more likely than toddlers are to be cared for in "other" situations, such as accompanying their parents to work.

Under 1 Year: Own home 31.2; Other home 38.4; Childcare facility 14.1; Other 16.4

1–2 Years: Own home 32.7; Other home 41.3; Childcare facility 18.1; Other 7.8

the development of peer friendship. Peer relationships during toddlerhood in turn may promote the development of positive friendships later in childhood (Engle et al., 2011). A longitudinal study of the quality of children's relationships between infancy and nine years of age found that children's formation of close friendships as toddlers predicted their positive ratings of their friendship quality as nine-year-olds (Howes et al., 1998).

In conclusion, although infants' social interactions with their parents generally are their most important early social experiences, interactions with other family members, nonfamily caregivers, and peers also contribute to their social development. The quality and

TABLE 7.1 Guidelines for Choosing a Good Infant Day-Care Program

- Children are most likely to thrive intellectually and emotionally in programs that offer a balance between structured educational activities and an open, free environment.
- The caregiving environment should provide ample physical space (at least twenty-five square feet per child) and a variety of materials and activities to foster sensorimotor, social, and cognitive development.
- If the facility includes a playground, the equipment should be safe, clean, age-appropriate and inspected regularly. The playground should also be built on an impact-cushioning surface, be enclosed by a fence, and be monitored at all times when children are using it.
- Cleanliness and safety standards should be high: The day-care facility should be clean, diaper-changing practices should be sanitary, immunization records for all enrolled children should be current, harmful and toxic substances should be stored securely, first-aid kits should be available and staff should be trained to provide first aid.
- Class size should be small (fewer than ten children) and should include children within a two-year age range. Small centers (fewer than thirty children) usually have better staff-child ratios than centers with more children.
- The interaction style of the caregiver is a key aspect of quality care. The caregiver should be actively involved but not restrictive with the children. The caregiver should also be responsive and offer positive encouragement.
- Caregivers who have training in child development and continuing opportunities for education are most likely to provide high-quality care.
- The individual characteristics of the child should be taken into account. Some children will probably do well in a program that balances structure and openness; others may profit from either more structure or a more flexible and relaxed program.
- High staff-child ratio and low staff turnover is important. Research shows, for example, that when the staff-child ratio is at least one to three for infants, one to four for toddlers, and one to nine for preschoolers, the quality of caregiving and of children's activities within the center are both good.

Sources: Adapted from Clarke-Stewart et al. (1994); Clarke-Stewart & Allhusen (2002); National Resource Center for Health and Safety in Child Care (2013).

Chapter 7 Psychosocial Development during the First Two Years

developmental impact of experiences with siblings and peers will reflect, to some extent, the degree to which parental supervision of such contacts considers the needs of both the baby and the other children.

Emotions and Temperament in Infancy

The healthy cries of a newborn infant make it clear that infants are capable of feeling and expressing their emotions even at birth. During the first three months, infants spend about two hours crying during a typical day. And while most developmental experts recommend that caregivers respond quickly and consistently to the cries of infants (Cong et al., 2002), the ability to successfully console crying babies is often dependent upon correctly interpreting the reasons for their distress. Healthy babies produce four types of cries—the basic hunger cry, the angry cry, the pain cry, and the fussy irregular cry—all of which provide their caregivers with useful information about their physiological states of discomfort (Soltis, 2004; St. James-Roberts & Halil, 1991). Over time, as infants gain better control over their crying, it serves to convey a wider range of messages to their caregivers (Barr, 1995; Green et al., 1998). In the following sections, we discuss the role of early emotions and *temperament*—the infant's characteristic way of feeling and responding.

Emotions in Infancy

Though researchers have long recognized changes in infants' crying, smiling, frustrations, and fear of strangers and novel stimuli, there is now a growing appreciation of the range and complexity of infant emotions (Barrett, 2005; Messinger, 2002). For example, videotape studies reveal that an infant only a few weeks old is able to produce facial expressions corresponding to the range of adult emotional states, even though the infant's expressions of emotion, particularly negative emotions, do not always result from the same events that typically produce them in adults. Similarly, while physiological aspects of emotion, such as changes in heart rate, can be reliably measured, their relationships to specific emotions are not always clear (Camras et al., 1993; Oster et al., 1992). One reason for this lack of specificity is that babies' expectations and understandings appear to play an important role in their emotional reactions. For example, an incongruous stimulus, such as a mother's face covered with a mask, will produce a fear response in some situations but smiling and laughter in others.

While researchers still disagree about the earliest age at which particular emotions are present, they generally agree that most babies can reliably express basic joy and laughter by three or four months, fear by five to eight months, and more complex emotions such as shame, embarrassment, guilt, envy, and pride during toddlerhood (Barrett, 2005; Izard, 1994; Izard & Malatesta, 1987; Kochanska et al., 1998; Lewis, 1992; Weinberg & Tronick, 1994). Table 7.2 shows the approximate ages at which certain infant emotions appear.

Expressions of emotion play an important role in development by providing vital information to infants and their caregivers about ongoing experiences and interactions. Caregivers "read" these messages and use them to guide their actions in helping the infant to fulfill his needs. Very young infants also appear to be sensitive to the positive and negative emotions of their caregivers; they are quite capable of responding to adult fears and anxieties. Recent research indicates that they react in kind to those emotions expressed by their peers and siblings as well (Brownell et al., 2010). These responses are likely based on cues similar to those adults use, such as slight variations in voice quality and touch, as well as variations in facial expression and body language (Grossman, 2010). As they get older, infants display these feelings with increasing frequency and predictability (Eisenberg et al., 1995; Tronick, 1989).

Another important change in an infant's emotional life during the first year is the baby's growing ability to regulate her own expressive behaviors and associated emotional states, especially negative ones. These *self-directed regulatory behaviors* include looking away, self-comforting, and self-stimulation. These behaviors allow the infant to control her

> **What Do You Think?**
>
> What advice would you give to prospective parents about maternal employment and childcare arrangements for infants? How will (or do) your own childcare arrangements differ from those of your parents?

negative feelings by shifting her attention away from a disturbing event or by substituting positive for negative stimuli. This helps the infant adjust her emotional state to a comfortable level at which she can successfully maintain interaction with her surroundings (Buss & Goldsmith, 1998; Gianino & Tronick, 1988; Grolinck et al., 1996). During the second year, increases in the capacity for emotional self-regulation also reflect her growing ability to respond to the feelings and needs of others through helping, sharing, and providing comfort (Zahn-Waxler et al., 1992). Claire Kopp (1982, 1989) has proposed that the modulation, or self-regulation, of behavior develops over a series of five successive phases. Table 7.3 describes these phases. As we will see in later chapters, emotional regulation continues to play an important developmental role in childhood and adolescence (Berger, 2011; Caspi et al., 1995; Eisenberg et al., 1997).

Temperament

Temperament refers to an individual's consistent pattern or style of reacting to a broad range of environmental events and situations. Most researchers agree that differences in primary reaction tendencies such as sensitivity to visual or verbal stimulation, emotional responsiveness, and sociability appear to be present at birth, prior to any significant interaction with the external environment. However, researchers disagree on how much such differences are due solely to genetic inheritance and how much they reflect prenatal influences and more subtle environmental experiences during and shortly after birth (Kagan & Snidman, 1991; Kagan et al., 1995; Rothbart, 1989). Parents certainly report differences in their newborn infants' temperaments. The parents of baby Alberto and his sister Lydia, for example, clearly remember that unlike Lydia, who was a fussy and somewhat difficult baby to care for and comfort during her first few months, Alberto was a very easy baby.

In a now classic study of temperament, Alexander Thomas and Stella Chess used parents' reports of differences in their babies on the following nine dimensions: (1) activity level (2) rhythmicity (regularity of eating, sleeping, and elimination), (3) approach-withdrawal to or from novel stimuli and situations, (4) adaptability to new people and situations,

temperament Individual differences in quality and intensity of emotional responding and self-regulation that are present at birth, are relatively stable and enduring over time and across situations, and are influenced by the interaction of heredity, maturation, and experience.

TABLE 7.2 Development of Infant Emotions

Approximate Age (in months)	Emotion
0–1	Social smile
3	Pleasure smile
3–4	Wariness
4–7	Joy, anger
4	Surprise
5–9	Fear
17	Guilt, embarrassment
18	Shame

Sources: Barrett (2005); Izard (1994); Lewis (1992).

Chapter 7 Psychosocial Development during the First Two Years

TABLE 7.3 Development of Behavioral Self-Regulation (modulation) during Infancy: Phases of Self-Regulation

Approximate Ages	Phases	Features	Cognitive Requisites
Birth to 2–3 months	1. Neurophysiological modulation	Modulation of arousal, activation of organized patterns of behavior	
3–9 months+	2. Sensorimotor modulation	Change ongoing behavior in response to events and stimuli in environment	
12–18 months+	3. Control	Awareness of social demands of a situation and initiate, maintain, cease physical acts, communication, etc. accordingly; compliance, self-initiated monitoring	Intentionality, goal-directed behavior, conscious awareness of action, memory of existential self
24 months+	4. Self-control	As above; delay upon request; behave according to social expectations in the absence of external monitors	Representational thinking and recall memory, symbolic thinking, continuing sense of identity
36 months+	5. Self-regulation	As above; flexibility of control processes that meet changing situational demands	Strategy production, conscious introspection, etc.

Source: Kopp (1982), p. 202, Table 2.

(5) emotional reactivity, (6) responsiveness to stimulation, (7) quality of mood (positive or negative), (8) distractibility, and (9) attention span (Thomas & Chess, 1977, 1981). They found three general patterns of temperament.

Easy babies (40 percent of the sample) showed mostly positive moods, regular bodily functions, and good adaptation to new situations. *Difficult babies* (10 percent) displayed negative moods, irregular bodily functions, and high stress in new situations. *Slow-to-warm-up babies* (15 percent) resembled the difficult ones but were less extreme; they were moody and relatively unadaptable, but did not react vigorously to new stimuli. Finally, *mixed-pattern babies* (35 percent) did not fall neatly into any of the first three groups.

Because the original classification of temperaments was based solely on parents' reports, which sometimes can be unreliable, other studies have used two additional measures of temperament: multiple behavior ratings (by pediatricians, nurses, teachers, and other individuals familiar with the child) and direct observation of the child. These studies have confirmed earlier findings of temperamental differences at birth (Huang & Rothbart, 2002; Plomin, 1989; Seifer et al., 1994).

Classifying babies by temperamental pattern has been helpful in predicting problems for children who are difficult or slow to warm up, but not for the majority of children whose temperaments are less extreme. For example, newborn infants whose biological rhythms are irregular, who experience discomfort during feeding and elimination, and who do not communicate their needs clearly often are difficult for their parents and are more likely to experience problems in developing close relationships with them. This is particularly true when mothers have little or no help and emotional support from relatives and friends in caring for their difficult babies, although parenting can improve when such emotional support is made available (Crockenberg & McCluskey, 1986; Kerr et al., 1994; van den Boom & Hoeksma, 1994).

How stable are early differences in temperament? Predictions of later temperament based on temperamental differences among newborns are not very reliable, although predictions based on differences observed toward the end of the first year are somewhat better

> **What Do You Think?**
>
> What advice would you give to parents about how to respond to differences in their children's temperaments? What have you noticed about temperamental differences among members of your own family?

(Carlson et al., 1995; Gunnar et al., 1995; Kagan & Snidman, 1991; Little et al., 2006; Rothbart & Ahadi, 1994). This may in part reflect the influence of experience and context on temperament. In most cases, the degree to which an infant's early temperamental style contributes to personality development is likely to be influenced by how good *a fit* exists between her temperamental style and the attitudes, expectations, and responses of her parents and other caregivers. For example, an infant who is very active and demanding is more likely to maintain that temperament if these qualities are consistent with his parents' expectations and responses than would be the case if his parents expected him to be more passive and less demanding (Rickman & Davidson, 1995).

In the last two decades, researchers have begun to think of temperamental differences in infancy more broadly, as early-appearing behavioral styles that may influence social and personality development and psychological adjustment in childhood, adolescence, and adulthood (Caspi & Silva, 1995; Hartup & van Lieshout, 1995; Lengua et al., 1998; Little et al., 2006; Newman et al., 1997; Rothbart & Ahadi, 1994). For example, Denise Newman and her colleagues found that temperamental differences observed in children at age three were linked to interpersonal functioning in four important social contexts as young adults: at work, at home, with a special romantic partner, and in the wider social network. Based on behavioral observations of each child in an individual testing session, children were divided into five temperamental groups. Children who were judged to be temperamentally well adjusted, reserved, or confident at age three displayed a normal range of adjustment in all four social contexts as young adults. Children who were temperamentally inhibited as three-year-olds had lower levels of social support but normal adjustment in romantic relationships and at work as adults. Children who had been temperamentally undercontrolled (who had difficulty regulating their emotional states) at age three, reported lower levels of adjustment and greater interpersonal conflict in all four social contexts as young adults (Newman et al., 1997).

The long-term developmental effects of temperamental traits such as shyness appear to be influenced by many factors, including culture, gender, and historical period. Margaret Kerr and her colleagues compared the results of a study of how childhood shyness among Swedish eight- to ten-year-olds influenced the timing of marriage, parenthood, and career success at age thirty-five with the results of a similar longitudinal study of American children conducted in Berkeley, California, a generation earlier (Caspi et al., 1988; Kerr et al., 1996). Both American and Swedish men who were shy as children married and became fathers later than men who had no history of childhood shyness. American men who had been shy as boys began stable careers later, resulting in lower career achievement and less career stability by middle adulthood than those who were not shy as children. For Swedish men, however, childhood shyness had no effect on educational attainment, occupational stability, or income during adulthood. Both American and Swedish women who had been shy as young children married and became mothers at the same age as girls with no history of shyness. Childhood shyness was associated with lower levels of educational achievement than nonshy peers for Swedish women but not for American women. Further research is needed to determine to what degree these differences were due to culture, gender, and the different historical periods in which the two studies were conducted.

Attachment Formation

Attachment refers to the strong and enduring emotional bond that develops between infant and caregiver during the infants first year of life. This relationship is characterized by reciprocal affection and a shared desire to maintain physical closeness (Ainsworth & Bowlby, 1991; Main, 1995).

Infants vary in temperament, as can be seen by the difficult and more easygoing babies pictured here. These variations may impact long-term development.
Source: (top) szefei/Shutterstock.com; *(bottom)* Flashon Studio/Shutterstock.com.

attachment An intimate and enduring emotional relationship between two people, such as infant and caregiver, characterized by reciprocal affection and a periodic desire to maintain physical closeness.

The concept of attachment has been most strongly influenced by the etiological perspective (see Chapter 2) and, to a lesser extent, by the psychoanalytic approach. In the etiological view, the ties between infant and caregiver develop from the activation of a biologically based motivational system that is an inherited adaptation of human evolution. This system helped ensure survival by protecting infants from environmental dangers. Because the nature of the child-caregiver relationship is widely viewed as being central to successful child development, studies of attachment have come to play an important role in developmental theory. Although attachment cannot be observed directly, it can be inferred from a number of commonly observed infant behaviors that help establish and maintain physical closeness with caregivers. Three of these behaviors—crying, cooing, and babbling—are *signaling behaviors;* four others—smiling, clinging, nonnutritional sucking, and following—are *approach behaviors.* Although researchers do not agree as to whether these *specific* attachment behaviors are biologically inherited, many believe that the tendency to seek and maintain physical closeness with caregivers is biologically determined and essential to infant survival in much the same way food is.

working models Internalized perceptions, feelings, and expectations regarding social and emotional relationships with significant caregivers based on experiences with those caregivers.

Another influence has been the work of theorists who emphasize the importance of **working models**, or internalized perceptions, feelings, and expectations regarding social and emotional relationships with significant caregivers (Biringen, 1994; Mahler, et al., 1994). For example, Margaret Mahler proposes that during the first three years of life, children go through four phases in developing a psychological sense of self. A newborn infant begins life in an *autistic phase,* meaning that she is self-absorbed and has little psychological awareness of the world around her. Next, during the *symbiotic phase,* the infant experiences herself as being completely connected with and dependent on her primary caregiver, rather than as a psychologically separate person. During the *separation-individuation phase,* she begins to develop a separate sense of self. Finally, during the *object constancy phase,* the infant achieves a more stable sense of self based on her increasing ability to form reliable mental representations of her primary caregivers (called *objects*) and their responses to her (Mahler et al., 1975).

Currently most developmental psychologists believe attachment relationships develop over time as a cumulative product of the infant's repeated experiences in interaction with her main caregivers during the first two years. They also believe attachment involves a highly mutual and interactive partnership between caregiver and child, both of whom have strong, although unequal, needs to achieve physical and emotional closeness with each other. This view is influenced by discoveries about the interactive nature of social relations between infants and their caregivers (Belsky, 1996; Insabella, 1993).

According to attachment theory, once attachment with the mother (or other primary caregiver) is established, the infant uses her as a *secure base* from which to explore the environment. As the infant gradually increases his distance from the mother, the *attachment behavioral system* and accompanying feelings of fear and anxiety are more likely to be activated, and the infant begins to seek proximity (closeness) to the caregiver once again. This pattern is also activated when the infant encounters dangers such as strangers, darkness, or animals approaching. The balance between activation of the attachment system and activation of exploratory behaviors varies with the particular context and developmental level of the child (Biringen, 1994).

Phases of Attachment Formation

John Bowlby believes that attachments develop in a series of phases determined partly by cognitive changes (described in the previous chapter) and partly by interactions that appear to develop quite naturally between infants and their caregivers (Ainsworth & Bowlby, 1991; Bowlby, 1969). Table 7.4 presents these four phases. Note that *separation anxiety,* an infant's disturbance at being separated from her caregiver, and *stranger anxiety,* a wariness and avoidance of strangers, appear near the beginning of phase 3. The achievement of object permanence (see Chapter 2) is thought to be an important basis for separation anxiety and attachment development. *Stranger anxiety* is exhibited by many infants between six and nine months of age and often continues through the first year. It is thought

Attachment—the tendency of young infants and their caregivers to seek physical and emotional closeness—provides an important basis for achieving secure and trusting relationships during childhood and throughout life.
Source: michaeljung/Shutterstock.com.

TABLE 7.4 Four Stages of Attachment Formation

Phase 1: Indiscriminate Sociability (birth–2 months)

Responds actively with cries, smiles, coos, and gazes to promote contact and affection from other people; uses limited attachment behaviors less selectively than when older.

Phase 2: Attachments in the Making (2–7 months)

Increasing preference for individuals most familiar and responsive to needs; preferences reinforce parents' affection; accepts certain forms of attention and care from comparative strangers; tolerates temporary separations from parents.

Phase 3: Specific, Clear-cut Attachments (7–24 months)

Preferences for specific people become much stronger due to ability to represent persons mentally (Piaget's fourth stage of sensorimotor development; see Chapter 6); ability to crawl and walk enables toddler to seek proximity to and use caregiver as a safe base for exploration; increasing verbal skills allow greater involvement with parents and others; both *separation anxiety*—an infant's disturbance at being separated from the caregiver—and *stranger anxiety*—a wariness and avoidance of strangers—appear near the beginning of this phase.

Phase 4: Goal-coordinated Partnerships (24 months onward)

By age two, increasing representational and memory skills for objects and events; growing ability to understand parental feelings and points of view and to adjust his or her own accordingly; growing capacity to tolerate short parental absences and delays and interruptions in parents' undivided attention makes possible cooperation with others to meet needs; changing abilities are related to secure attachment relationships grounded in a sense of basic trust.

Source: Bowlby (1969).

---

to be tied to an infant's increasing ability to recognize and distinguish between familiar and unfamiliar people and to actively make sense of his interpersonal world. Whether or not a particular infant becomes wary of strangers and the strength of the reaction may vary with his temperament, the familiarity of the setting, the friendliness of the stranger, the caregiver's reaction, and how accustomed the child is to meeting strangers (Dickstein & Parke, 1988; Mangelsdorf et al., 1995).

Separation anxiety, which generally appears between nine and twelve months, involves displays of fear, clinging, crying, and related distress when an infant's parent or other caregiver leaves her (recall Elizabeth's protest when left at nursery school by her mother in Chapter 2). Separation anxiety appears to be related to how well the infant is prepared for the parents' departure and to her past experiences with separation. However, the responsiveness of the caregiver she is left with may be most important, especially for infants who *are temperamentally reactive to separation* (Gunnar et al., 1992).

Assessing Attachment: The "Strange Situation"

The most widely used method for evaluating the quality of attachment to a caregiver is called the **Strange Situation (SS)**. Originally developed by Mary Ainsworth for infants who are old enough to crawl or walk, the procedure consists of eight brief social episodes with different combinations of the infant, the mother, and an unfamiliar adult (Ainsworth et al., 1978). It presents the infant with a cumulative series of stressful experiences: being in an unfamiliar place, meeting a stranger, and being separated from the caregiver (see Table 7.5).

Based on the infants' patterns of behavior in the Strange Situation, Ainsworth and her colleagues identified three main groups. Most of the infants studied (approximately 65 to 70 percent) displayed a **secure attachment** pattern. When first alone with their

Strange Situation (SS) A widely used method for studying attachment; confronts the infant with a series of controlled separations and reunions with a parent and a stranger.

secure attachment A healthy bond between infant and caregiver. The child is happy when the caregiver is present, somewhat upset during the caregiver's absence, and easily comforted upon the caregiver's return.

Chapter 7 Psychosocial Development during the First Two Years

TABLE 7.5 Episodes in the Strange Situation (SS)

Episode	Duration	Events	Observed Attachment Behaviors
1	30 seconds	Parent and infant enter the room with the experimenter.	
2	3 minutes	Parent is seated; baby plays with toys and explores the room.	Parent as a secure base
3	3 minutes	A stranger enters room, sits down, talks with parent.	Reaction to unfamiliar adult
4	3 minutes	Parent leaves infant alone with stranger, who responds to the baby and offers comfort if baby is upset.	Separation anxiety
5	3 minutes	Parent returns, greets (comforts) baby; stranger leaves room.	Reaction to reunion
6	3 minutes	Parent leaves baby alone in room.	Separation anxiety
7	3 minutes	Stranger again enters the room and offers comfort to the baby.	Reaction to being comforted by a stranger
8	3 minutes	Parent returns; stranger leaves; parent greets/comforts baby and tries to interest her in toys.	Reaction to reunion

Source: Ainsworth et al., (1978).

anxious-resistant attachment An insecure bond between infant and caregiver in which the child shows signs of anxiety preceding separation, is intensely upset by separation, and seeks close contact when reunited while at the same time resisting the caregiver's efforts to comfort, sometimes physically pushing the caregiver away while being held.

anxious-avoidant attachment An insecure bond between infant and caregiver in which the child rarely cries when separated from the caregiver and tends to avoid or ignore the caregiver when reunited.

disorganized-disoriented attachment This pattern indicates the greatest degree of insecurity between infant and parent. When reunited with the parent, the infant exhibits confused and contradictory behavior, including unresponsiveness, turning away when held, frozen postures, and unexpected cries after being comforted.

mothers, they typically played happily. When the stranger entered, they were somewhat wary but continued to play without becoming upset. But when they were left alone with the stranger, they typically stopped playing and searched for or crawled after their mothers; in some cases, they cried. When the mothers returned, the babies were clearly pleased to see them and actively sought contact and interaction, staying closer to them and cuddling more than before. When left alone with the stranger again, the infants were easily comforted; although they showed stronger signs of distress, they quickly recovered from the upset by actively seeking contact with their mothers on their return.

The second group of infants (about 10 percent) were classified as displaying an **anxious-resistant attachment** or *ambivalent* pattern. They showed some signs of anxiety and, even in the periods preceding separation, stuck close to their mothers, and explored only minimally. They were intensely upset by separation. When reunited with their mothers, they actively sought close contact with them but at the same time angrily resisted the mothers' efforts to comfort them by hitting them and pushing them away. They refused to be comforted by the stranger as well.

The third group of infants (about 20 percent) displayed an **anxious-avoidant attachment** pattern. They initially showed little involvement with their mothers, treating them and the stranger in much the same way. They rarely cried when separated and, when reunited, showed a mixed response of low-level engagement with their mothers and a tendency to avoid them.

A fourth category, **disorganized-disoriented attachment**, has also been investigated. This pattern, which was not included in earlier studies because coding procedures were not available, indicates the greatest degree of insecurity. When reunited with their parent, these infants exhibit confused and contradictory behaviors. They may be unresponsive and turn away when held, display "frozen" postures, and cry out unexpectedly after being comforted (Lyons-Ruth & Block, 1996; Lyons-Ruth et al., 1997; Main & Solomon, 1990).

All four attachment patterns have been studied in many other countries. In all cases, around 65 to 70 percent of the children are reported to be securely attached, whereas rates of insecure attachment are much more variable (van IJzendoorn & Kroonenberg, 1988). The "A Multicultural View" feature discusses cross-cultural variations in attachment.

Consequences of Different Attachment Patterns

Secure attachment early in infancy benefits babies in several ways during their second year of life. Securely attached toddlers tend to cooperate better with their parents than other babies do (Londerville & Main, 1981). They comply better with rules such as "Don't run in the living room!" and they are also more willing to learn new skills and try new activities their parents show them (such as when a parent says, "Sit with me for a minute and see how I do this"). When faced with problems that are too difficult for them to solve, toddlers who are securely attached are more likely than others to seek and accept help from their parents. At age five, these children tend to adapt better than other children to changes in preschool situations (Arend et al., 1979; Matas et al., 1978; Slade, 1987), and college students who demonstrate secure attachments tend to be more adaptable, manage stress better, and have better interpersonal skills than their nonsecurely attached peers (Hamarta, Deniz, & Saltali, 2009).

Less securely attached infants may not learn as well from their parents. Anxious-resistant infants often respond with anger and resistance to their parents' attempts to help or teach them. Such babies may at times invest so much time and energy in conflicts that they are unable to benefit from their parents' experience and to explore their environment. Given a roomful of toys and a mother who has recently returned from an absence, for example, a child may use up a lot of time alternating between being angry at and snuggling with his mother instead of getting on with his play. Anxious-avoidant infants do not have this particular problem, but because of their tendency to avoid interaction with their parents, they also miss out on parental efforts to teach or help them and ultimately may discourage parents from even trying to help (Behrens, Hesse, & Main, 2007; Matas et al., 1978; Stevenson-Hinde & Verschueren, 2002).

The disorganized-disoriented attachment pattern generally is found in seriously disturbed caregiving situations where interactions between mothers and their infants are inconsistent, and out of tune with or inappropriately responsive to the infant's physical, social, and emotional needs. Parents who display disorganized-disoriented attachment behaviors may think of and interact with their infants in inappropriate ways. For instance, they may display role reversal, where the parent inappropriately expects to be cared for by her infant, or they may respond to their infants in overly intrusive, withdrawing, or rejecting ways. An infant's attempts to communicate or modify this behavior are often ignored or overridden, leading to the disorganized-disoriented infant attachment behaviors noted earlier. Disorganized-disoriented infant attachment behavior increases with the severity of family risk factors and places infants at risk for future problems, such as aggression, conduct disorder, anxiety, difficulty interacting with peers, and other developmental difficulties (Kerns & Brumariu, 2014; Lyons-Ruth & Block, 1996; Lyons-Ruth et al., 1997; Main & Solomon, 1990).

Differences in attachment appear to persist even into the preschool years. One study found that children rated as securely attached at age one seemed more likely to seek attention in positive ways in nursery school at age four (Sroufe et al., 1983). When they needed help because of sickness or injury, or just wanted to be friendly, they found it easy to secure attention by approaching their teachers fairly directly, and they seemed to enjoy the attention when they received it. Anxious-avoidant or anxious-resistant infants tended to grow into relatively dependent preschool children. They sought help more frequently but seemed less satisfied with what they got. However, methods of seeking attention differed between these two groups. Anxious-resistant children showed signs of chronic complaining or whining, whereas anxious-avoidant children tended to approach their teachers very indirectly, literally taking a zigzagging path to reach them. Having done so, they typically waited passively for the teachers to notice them. As noted earlier, disorganized-disoriented infants are often at risk for developmental difficulties.

Attachment is not limited to the periods of infancy and early childhood. We will discuss the long-term and intergenerational effects of attachment later in this chapter.

Influences on Attachment Formation

So far, we have emphasized the general aspects of attachment. In this section, we discuss some of the factors that appear to influence the quality of attachment between infants and their mothers, as well as other important caregivers.

A Multicultural View

Cross-Cultural Variations in Attachment

Almost all infants become attached to their parents in some way. However, the patterns by which they do so vary around the world. Studies on the Strange Situation report that whereas 65 to 70 percent of children studied appear to be securely attached, rates of insecure attachment are much more variable (Super & Harkness, 2010; van IJzendoorn & Krooneuherg, 1988). Among infants from northern Germany, for example, anxious-avoidant attachment patterns occur twice as often as they do among North American infants. Among infants from Japan, on the other hand, anxious-resistant responses occur approximately three times as often as they do in the United States, while anxious-avoidant attachment is virtually nonexistent (Bretherton & Waters, 1985; Takahashi, 1990). Similar patterns were found among Korean children (Jin et al., 2010).

These variations result partly from differences in cultural values around the world and partly from the child-rearing practices these values foster. In northern Germany, people value personal independence especially strongly (Grossmann et al., 1985; Super & Harkness, 2010) and believe children should obey parents more consistently than is usually expected in North America. As a result, infants need to learn not to make excessive demands on parents; they must minimize crying and fussing and do without extra bodily contact. During early infancy, mothers entourage these qualities by remaining relatively unresponsive to their infants' moment-by-moment behavior. Thus, in northern Germany, unresponsiveness may not signify personal rejection of the child as much as a desire to raise a good citizen. The results show up in the Strange Situation as anxious-avoidant attachment: a larger than usual number of young children seem indifferent when reunited with their mothers.

Child-rearing practices probably also influence the attachment responses of Japanese children. Separations between Japanese infants and their mothers are quite rare by North American standards. Most Japanese infants have very little experience with strangers. Typically they are left alone or with another adult only two or three times per month on average, usually someone already intimate with the child, such as the father or a grandparent (Mikaye et al., 1985). Their extreme protests to the Strange Situation resemble the anxious-resistant pattern of crying, anger, fear, and clinging when the mother returns. Korean mothers were more likely to stay near their children after the reunion period even after the children had calmed (Jin et al., 2012). As with the German infants, however, it is more likely that these behaviors represent the fulfillment of typical cultural practices rather than failures in child-rearing.

Some researchers have also noted that distribution of attachment types may vary within as well as across cultures. In a study of infants from southern Germany, the distribution of attachment types did not differ significantly from those reported for infants in the United States (Grossmann & Grossmann, 1990; van IJzendoorn & Kroonenberg, 1988). Studies of attachment among Israeli infants raised in kibbutz communities provide further evidence of cultural differences in attachment within a particular society. Kibbutz children were raised in communal peer groups by *metapelot* (nurse/educators), spending regular time with their families during evenings, weekends, and holidays. Kibbutz infants successfully formed attachments to both their parents and their communal caregivers, but a larger proportion displayed insecure attachment patterns compared to Israeli infants raised in the city or infants raised in the United States.

This difference appears to be related to kibbutz sleeping arrangements, which differ among kibbutz communities. When Abraham Sagi and his colleagues compared infants from kibbutz infants' houses with home-based sleeping arrangements with infants who slept in their infants' houses (communal sleeping arrangements), they found that although the two groups did not differ in temperament or life events, only 48 percent of the infants with communal sleeping arrangements were rated as securely attached to their mothers compared to 80 percent of the infants who slept at home. These researchers conclude that although group care and multiple caregiving of high quality did not necessary interfere with the formation of close relationships between parents and children or with the development of social skills, it appears that the sleeping arrangements in the kibbutz communities did (Aviezer et al., 1994; Sagi et al., 1995, 1997).

Cultural values and practices, however, cannot explain all the differences. Even in northern Germany, for example, many babies become securely attached even though their mothers follow culturally approved practices of aloofness. In Japan, some infants become anxious-resistant even though their mothers follow essentially Western child-rearing styles, which include considerable experience with baby sitters and other nonparental caregivers. Observations of these babies in their homes suggest that they were born with somewhat irritable or fussy temperaments, which may predispose them to becoming anxious-resistant despite their mothers' practices.

On balance, attachment seems to result from the combination of several influences, including cultural values, inborn temperament, and the child-rearing practices of the particular family. The developmental meaning of attachment may vary too. What looks like an attachment failure for one child may be a success for another, depending on the circumstances.

The Role of the Mother

A major determinant of individual differences in attachment is the quality of the infant-mother relationship during the child's first year. A mother's capacity to respond sensitively and appropriately to her infant and to feel positively about the child as well as the child's strengths and limitations appears to be more important than the amount of contact or caregiving. Mothers of securely attached infants are more responsive to their babies' crying, more careful and tender in holding them, and more responsive to their particular needs and feelings during both feeding and nonfeeding interactions than are mothers of less securely attached infants (Ainsworth, 1994; DeWolff & van IJzendoorn, 1997; Posada & Kaloustian, 2010).

Differences in infant temperament are likely to affect the mother-infant relationship and the quality of attachment. Infants with irritable temperaments tend to receive less maternal involvement, which in turn may negatively influence the quality of attachment. With appropriate interventions, however, such negative cycles may be interrupted.

In one study of the influence of temperament and mothering on attachment, Dymphna van den Boom (1994) helped mothers to respond to their temperamentally difficult six-month-old infants in more sensitive and developmentally appropriate ways by adjusting their behaviors to the infants' unique cues. Mothers gained practice in imitating their infants' behaviors and repeating their own verbal expressions. They also learned to notice when their infants were gazing at them versus when they were not and to coordinate the pace and rhythm of their own behavior with those of their infants. Mothers who received such help were found to be significantly more responsive, stimulating, visually attentive, and able to regulate their infants' behavior than a similar group of mothers who did not get assistance. Infants of these mothers had higher scores on sociability, self-soothing, and exploration, cried less often, and at twelve months of age were much more likely to be securely attached.

Being securely attached herself makes the mother more likely to have a child who is securely attached. The quality of the mother-child relationship is influenced by the mother's *working models*—her perceptions, expectations, and assumptions about her infant, herself, and their relationship. Past mother-infant interactions, the mother's memories of her own childhood, and similar factors also may play a significant role in mother-child attachment relationships (Bretherton, 1997; Mahler et al., 1975; Posada & Kaloustian, 2010; Stern, 1985b; van IJzendoorn & Bakermans-Kranenberg, 1997). A mother's capacity to establish and maintain a secure attachment relationship with her infant is also influenced by her socioeconomic status (SES), which affects her ability to focus on her infant rather than on finding housing, food, work, and other necessities.

The Role of the Father

Although children are most likely to form strong attachment relationships with their mothers, who most often are their primary caregivers, they may form equally strong attachments with their fathers. Studies of father-infant attachment in the United States and other countries suggest that the processes involved are similar and that fathers display the same range of attachment relationships mothers do, and most studies have found no differences in most babies' preferred attachment figures during their first two years (Lamb, 1997; van IJzendoorn & De Wolff, 1997). It is worth noting that when fathers utilize poor parenting practices, their children are more likely to demonstrate insecure attachment, though no significant impact was found on attachment for fathers engaging in good parenting, suggesting that the quality of father-child interactions are particularly important (Brown et al., 2007).

As we pointed out earlier in the chapter, however, fathers and mothers interact with their infants somewhat differently. Fathers generally are more vigorous and physical in their interactions, and mothers are quieter and more verbal. Such differences in the quality of mother-infant versus father-infant attachment relationships are likely to reflect gender-related differences in caregiving opportunities, experiences, and expectations, as well as gender-related differences in the current division of childcare and other household responsibilities within the family (Akande, 1994; Brown, Mangelsdorf, & Neff, 2012; Ferketich & Mercer, 1995; Owen & Cox, 1997; Volling & Belsky, 1992).

Day care, even for infants and toddlers, has few negative effects on children as long as the care is of high quality and parents feel satisfied.

Source: Dmitri Maruta/Shutterstock.com.

For example, Geoffrey Brown and his colleagues (2012) found that the security of father-infant attachment at three years can be predicted from attachment at thirteen months—specifically, the quality of their interactions, the father's attitudes and sensitivity toward the infant, and the amount of time spent with the infant. In addition, research by Nathan Fox and his colleagues (1991) found that the security of attachment to one parent also appears to be closely related to the security of attachment to the other parent. Thus, an infant with a secure (or insecure) attachment to her mother is likely to have the same quality of attachment to her father.

Overall, the better the psychological and social adjustment and life circumstances of the infant and his parents, the greater the probability of a secure attachment. For example, fathers of secure infants tend to be more extroverted and agreeable than fathers of insecure infants, to have more successful marriages, and to experience more positive emotional spillover between work and family (Belsky, 1996). Chronic marital conflict before and after the birth of a child can interfere with sensitive, involved parenting and thereby predict insecurity in attachment relationships, particularly for fathers. An infant's ongoing exposure to parents who are upset and angry and the distress that such exposure causes may contribute to disorganized infant-caregiver attachment behavior (Belsky, 1996; Owen & Cox, 1997).

The Effects of Maternal Employment

As we noted earlier, in 2010 approximately 64 percent of mothers with children six years old or less and around 77 percent of mothers of school-aged children were in the work force (HHS, 2013). Length of maternity leave may influence the quality of mother-infant interactions. Roseanne Clark and her colleagues interviewed and videotaped employed mothers of four-month-old infants in their homes during feeding time. They found that shorter maternity leaves were associated with lower quality of mother-infant interactions. This was especially true for mothers who reported more depressive symptoms or who perceived their infants as having more difficult temperaments. These mothers expressed less positive effect, sensitivity and responsiveness in interactions with their infants compared to mothers who had longer leaves (Clark et al., 1997). Family-leave policies in the United States and Europe are discussed in the "Focusing On" feature.

Most infants of mothers who are employed either full or part time are securely attached, although full-time employed mothers are somewhat more likely than part-time employed and mothers who are not employed outside the home to have insecurely attached infants (Belsky, 1988b; Clarke-Stewart, 1989; L. Hoffman, 1989). However, these results must be viewed with caution because the effects of maternal employment on the infant or young child are rarely direct. They are almost always based on a variety of family factors, including SES and cultural differences, the mother's "morale," the father's attitude toward his wife's employment, the type of work and number of hours it demands, the husband-wife relationship, the father's role in the family, the availability and quality of nonmaternal care, and the mother's and father's feelings about separation from their child (Scan, 1998; Silverstein, 1991).

Cynthia Stifter and her colleagues compared mother-child interactions and attachment patterns in families in which mothers returned to full- or part-time employment outside the

> **Focusing On...**
>
> ### Family-Leave Policies in the United States and Europe
>
> In 1993, the United States enacted its first national Family and Medical Leave Act, guaranteeing up to twelve weeks of *unpaid* leave per year to any worker who is employed for at least twenty-five hours per week at a company with more than fifty employees. Family leaves are allowed after the birth of a child or an adoption to care for a child, spouse, or parent with a serious health condition, as well as for a health condition that makes it impossible for the worker to perform a job. After the leave, the worker is assured of his or her old job or an equivalent position (Hyde et al., 1996).
>
> How does U.S. family-leave policy compare with that in other countries? Most industrialized countries have much more generous policies than those in the United States, providing not only more extended leaves of absence so that working parents can take care of their young children but also financial support for part or all of the leave period (Frank & Zigler, 1996; Kamerman, 1991). In almost every country in the world, one parent can take a paid infant care leave supported by the employer or a social insurance fund. If both parents choose to continue to work, they are guaranteed access to high-quality day care for their child. In Sweden, the mother and the father split up to sixteen-month paid leave to stay home with a new infant, and both parents are required to take off a minimum of three months.
>
> In France, working mothers are entitled to 100 percent reimbursement for four months through the social security system and then up to two more years of unpaid leave with a job guarantee. In Germany, a parent taking a leave of absence from work is entitled to 2/3 of their salary for up to fourteen months. German women may also take off the last 6 weeks of their pregnancy, and there are limits on the types of work, hours of work, and timing of work expecting and nursing mothers are permitted to do.
>
> It seems evident that while the twelve weeks of unpaid leave provided by the U.S. family-leave policy was a step in the right direction, policies in Europe go much farther in helping parents to directly meet the needs of their babies without undue economic hardship and risk to their jobs.
>
> In a review of research on the impact of the Family and Medical Leave Act, Christopher Ruhm (1997, 2000) found that because the leaves are short and unpaid and only half of the workforce is eligible under the law, it has had little impact. Women are more likely than men to work for smaller companies that are exempt from the law, and women who have less education and make less money are the least likely to take full advantage of leave time (American Institutes for Research, 2013). Ruhm suggests that coverage of more workers, extension of the number of weeks of leave allowed, and payment during all or part of the leave would greatly increase the benefit to families and children (Ruhm, 2000). When considering financial and health costs and benefits to employers, families, and society at large, having a longer, *paid* leave would easily outweigh the temporary financial burden to companies or the government (Bartick & Reinhold, 2010; Galtry & Callister, 2005).
>
> ### What Do You Think?
> What arguments would you make to support raising family-leave policies in the United States to the level of many European countries? What other examples of family support policies (e.g., health care) that fall short of what is needed for children's healthy development can you think of? Would you make the same arguments for these that you did for family leave?

home before their infants were five months old with those in families in which mothers remained at home full time, and found that employment did not directly affect attachment. However, when employed mothers were experiencing high levels of separation anxiety because of the severe time constraints imposed by work schedules, they were more likely to have infants who developed anxious-avoidant attachments. Although they were equally sensitive and responsive to their infants as working mothers who were not anxious, highly anxious mothers were much more likely to be "out of synch" and overcontrolling when interacting with their infants (Stifter et al., 1993).

The Effects of Day Care and Multiple Caregivers

The growing number of dual-wage and single-parent families and changing views about child-rearing and family life have led to increased interest in nonmaternal childcare to supplement the care given within families. The effects of day care and other forms of nonmaternal care on attachment in infants and toddlers are difficult to evaluate for many of the same reasons cited in the discussion of maternal employment. The gender of the child, the child's temperament, the mother's (and father's) feelings about both day care and maternal employment, and the

> **WORKING WITH** Rachelle Turner, Infant Day-Care Coordinator
>
> ### Understanding Infant Social Development
>
> Rachelle is the infant coordinator in a day-care center, where she has taught for the past four years. She began working as a day-care teacher during her college years and plans to eventually work as a therapist in a program serving young children and their families.
>
> **Rob:** *What do you like most about working with infants?*
>
> **Rachelle:** I find working with infants fascinating because so much is packed into the first year of life. It's amazing to see how rapid the changes are. Because you're with the children eight hours a day, five days a week, you can observe the very small changes in development that happen, even on a week-to-week basis.
>
> **Rob:** *What differences in early infant temperament do you find?*
>
> **Rachelle:** There are differences in napping patterns, for example. If, as an infant, a child needs you to rub his back or rock him gently to go to sleep, often he will want the same kind of thing as a three-year-old when he is going down for a nap on a cot. Or you might see him rocking himself to go to sleep. On the other hand, there's the child you can just put in his crib, and he'll just grab his blanket and go to sleep. When he's older, you can say, "OK, it's nap time," and he'll get on his cot and go to sleep. It often seems like children are their own person from day one.
>
> **Rob:** *Do you have another example?*
>
> **Rachelle:** Some infants aren't happy until they can crawl and go get what they want, while others seem perfectly content with just sitting up and having you plop toys in front of them. Infants can really differ in how active or passive they are in learning to crawl or walk and in their style of exploring their physical and social world. They also differ in their moods and in whether they are irritable or not.
>
> **Rob:** *What about their social relationships?*
>
> **Rachelle:** Their changing interactions with other children are interesting. A five-month-old infant will be attracted to another child, but will not, of course, play with the child. She'll pull the other infant's hair and touch its face and clothes. She'll want to explore it and see what it is, just like a doll. Toward the end of the first year, infants recognize their friends, and smile and laugh when they see them. They now want to go on the climber or play blocks together.
>
> **Rob:** *So their social skills change during the first year from exploring each other as objects to interacting with each other as unique individuals. What changes do you see during the second year?*
>
> **Rachelle:** Once they can actually say the child's name, they'll call him to come play. Games like

mother's reasons for working all play a role. Other factors include the type of childcare arrangement (day-care center, in-home day care, relative), the stability of the arrangement, the child's age of entry, the quality of day care, and the quality of the child-caregiver relationship (Belsky & Rovine, 1988; Scarr, 1998). See the interview with Rachelle Turner in the "Working With" feature for a look at social interactions in an infant day-care center.

While some infant care researchers have found evidence that one-year-olds who attend centers more than twenty hours per week tend to form less secure attachments to their parents (Belsky & Nezworski, 1988; Belsky & Rovine, 1988) and to fathers in particular (Quan et al., 2013), others have reported that negative attachment outcomes tend to be associated with little or part-time rather than full-time infant care. Babies in infant care centers show *more* social confidence than do infants reared at home (Anderson, 1989; Roggman et al., 1994). Moreover, children of mothers who work outside the home exhibit fewer internalizing behaviors, such as anxiety and depression, as well as higher levels of achievement overall (Lucas-Thompson, Goldbert, & Prause, 2010).

A large-scale study of more than one thousand infants and their mothers at ten different sites supports the finding that an infant's childcare experience alone is neither a risk nor a benefit for the infant-mother attachment relationship as measured by the Strange Situation. Childcare that is of poor quality or unstable may increase the developmental risks to an infant whose caregiving already lacks sensitivity and responsiveness, but high-quality childcare and preschool programs might serve to buffer the negative impacts of less-than-optimal

> ### WORKING WITH Rachelle Turner, Infant Day-Care Coordinator
>
> **Understanding Infant Social Development** *continued*
>
> hide-and-seek, chasing each other, or knocking blocks over together. They interact because the child makes it fun. It's not the imagination that three-year-old friends have, but it's definitely play and excitement when they see each other. They'll run up to each other, and they'll hug and kiss and be affectionate, and they know the other child isn't a doll. And if one gets hurt, they'll say, "Oh, Anne has a boo-boo," because she's a person in their life.
>
> **Rob:** *What have you observed about infants' ability to form attachment relationships with nonparental adult caregivers?*
>
> **Rachelle:** If you are affectionate and responsive to an infant's unique habits and needs around feeding, changing and sleeping, and comforting and stimulation, she'll quickly come to know you and form an attachment to you. Particularly if a child is in day care full time, if an unfamiliar parent or delivery person comes into the center, or if a child is upset for some other reason, she will crawl or run to a caregiver or want to be held or to sit in your lap.
>
> **Rob:** *How does it feel from the caregiver's perspective?*
>
> **Rachelle:** Very strong feelings of attachment develop. Remember, unlike a typical household where laundry, cooking, and other tasks compete with childcare, we spend almost all of our time observing and interacting with the children. I get very attached. When children leave, it's very hard to have children coming in and out of your life. You think about them constantly.
>
> **Rob:** *Are parents sometimes jealous of your relationship with their baby?*
>
> **Rachelle:** Yes. A parent might give the child excessive gifts, or become critical of the teacher, or make a point of telling the teacher something she didn't know about the child. I try to reassure parents by asking them for information about their child and by being interested in changes they have observed rather than just focusing on changes I have noticed.
>
> #### What Do You Think?
>
> 1. What qualities do you think make a good day-care teacher?
> 2. As a current or prospective parent, how comfortable would you feel putting your child in Rachelle's care? Why?
> 3. How closely do Rachelle's examples of temperamental differences and attachment fit your own understandings based on reading the chapter?

home environments (Love et al., 2005) or of children without a secure maternal attachment (Buyse, Verschueren, & Doumen, 2009). Thus, the effects of childcare on attachment and the attachment relationship itself depend primarily on the nature of ongoing interactions between mother and child and on the family, neighborhood, and other contexts that either support or undermine the quality and reliability of the mother-infant relationship (Belsky, 1996; Cowan, 1997; NICHD, 1997; Owen & Cox, 1997; Posada & Kaloustian, 2010).

What about attachments to multiple caregivers? Though expectations based on infant-mother attachment relationships may help guide an infant in forming new attachments, infants and nonmaternal caregivers are capable of establishing unique and independent relationships based more on their reciprocal exchanges and individual qualities than on a "model" developed from mother-child interactions (Zimmerman & McDonald, 1995). The attachments infants form with their center caregivers, for example, appear to be no less secure than their attachments to their parents, and the two sets of attachments are relatively independent of each other. Thus, even an infant who exhibited an insecure pattern of attachment relationships with his or her family might still form secure attachments with other caregivers (Buyse, Verschueren, & Doumen, 2009; Goosens & van IJzendoorn, 1990).

There is also evidence that in a variety of other contexts, including extended families and communal child-rearing settings such as the Israeli kibbutz and the Efe people of Zaire, secure relationships with multiple professional and nonprofessional caregivers are not only possible but may even contribute to the child's well-being by either adding to a network

> **What Do You Think?**
>
> What advice would you give new parents about the roles of fathers, maternal employment, and infant day care in supporting secure attachment and optimal social/emotional development for their infants? What recommendations would you give to your elected representatives regarding infant and toddler day-care programs for families with working and nonworking mothers?

of secure attachments or compensating for their absence (Sagi et al., 1997; Tronick et al., 1992). On the Israeli kibbutz, infants and toddlers are raised in same-age peer groups by community childcare providers. Among the Efe, infants and toddlers experience a pattern of multiple relationships—with mother, father, other adults, and children. In such cases, the extended family or community child-rearing network may be more predictive of attachment relationships than the mother-child relationship alone.

Long-Term and Intergenerational Effects of Attachment

The long-term and intergenerational effects of attachment have been of growing interest to developmental researchers. Attachment patterns in infancy are predictive of attachment in childhood, adolescence, and adulthood, and the attachment relationships parents experienced in their own childhoods are related to the attachment relationships they develop in romantic relationships (Simpson et al., 2007) and with their own children (Main, 1995; Mickelson et al., 1997; Pesonen et al., 2003; Trinke & Bartholomew, 1997; van IJzendoorn & Bakermans-Kranenburg, 1997).

The Adult Attachment Interview (AAI) has been used to evaluate the childhood attachment relationships adults had with their own parents and other caregivers (George et al., 1985). Based on their responses, adults are classified into four main attachment patterns that parallel the infant attachment patterns identified by the Strange Situation (SS). Marinus van IJzendoorn (1995) analyzed eighteen studies of how well parents' AAI attachment classifications predicted their own infants' attachment classifications in the Strange Situation. He found that in approximately 75 percent of the cases, the security of the parents own attachment classification predicted the security of the infants attachment.

In one longitudinal study, AAI classifications of expectant mothers and fathers predicted the attachment classifications of their infants at twelve and eighteen months in the SS. Mothers and fathers with a dismissing attachment pattern were more likely to have an insecure-avoidant pattern of infant-parent attachment in the Strange Situation. An autonomous-secure pattern for both parents predicted secure infant-parent patterns of attachment. Mothers whose adult attachment patterns were classified as unresolved were likely to show a disorganized pattern of attachment to their infants in the SS (Steele et al., 1996). Attachment patterns appear to be transmitted across the lifespan as well. Diane Benoit and Kevin Parker (1994) studied the transmission of attachment across three generations: infants, mothers, and grandmothers. They found that mothers' AAI classifications during pregnancy predicted infants' SS classifications in approximately 68 percent of the cases and grandmothers' AAI classifications did so in 49 percent of the cases.

What accounts for the long-term, intergenerational transmission of attachment? One important factor is the caregiver's sensitivity in reliably and appropriately responding to the baby's signals (Barlow & Durand, 1995; Posada & Kaloustian, 2010). Another is living in families and communities that provide the economic, social, and emotional conditions that support and promote the working models and interactions that are the basis for secure attachment and adequate parent-child relationships. In fact, parents with a history of insecure attachment are more likely have children with a secure attachment when those parents obtain sufficient social support (Raby et al., 2015)

Toddlerhood and the Emergence of Autonomy

By the second year of life, infants who have experienced sufficient caregiver-infant synchrony and achieved relatively secure attachment relationships with their parents and other caregivers have developed a sense of *basic trust* (versus *mistrust*) about the world. According to Erik Erikson (1963), by resolving this crisis in the first stage of psychosocial development, an infant's trusting view of the world leads to the development of *hope,* the enduring belief that one's wishes are attainable (see Chapter 2's overview of the eight stages in Erikson's theory of psychosocial development across the lifespan).

Despite lingering anxieties about separations, the achievement of a basic sense of trust in their relationships with their caregivers enables toddlers to become increasingly interested in new people, places, and experiences. For example, an eighteen-month-old may no longer bother to smile at his mother while he plays near her, and he does not need to return to her for reassurance as often as he used to. Parents may welcome these changes as a move toward greater independence and at the same time experience a loss of intimacy for which they may not be quite ready. This shift is both inevitable and developmentally important. For one thing, an older infant can move about rather easily and therefore find much to explore without help from others. The newfound abilities to crawl, climb, and walk make her more interesting as a playmate for other children and thus less dependent on her parents for her social life. For another, her rapidly developing thinking and communication skills contribute to her increasing autonomy.

These competencies create new challenges for both toddlers and their families as a new developmental crisis emerges: the psychosocial crisis *of autonomy versus shame and doubt.* **Autonomy** refers to a child's capacity to be independent and self-directed in his activities and his ability to balance his own demands for self-control with demands for control from his parents and others. *Shame* involves both a loss of approval by people important to the child and a loss of self-respect due to a failure to meet one's own standards (Lewis, 1992). Toddlers must somehow practice making choices—an essential feature of autonomy—in ways that cause no serious harm to themselves or others.

Parents must learn to support their child's efforts to be autonomous, but must do so without overestimating or underestimating the child's capabilities or the external dangers and internal fears she faces. If they are unable to provide such support and instead show their disapproval of failures by shaming their child, a pattern of self-blame and doubt may develop. In such a case, the child is more likely to be either painfully shy and unsure of herself or overly demanding, self-critical, and relatively unable to undertake new activities and experiences freely. Cross-cultural research demonstrates that maternal use of shaming is linked to higher levels of anxiety throughout childhood (Gershoff et al., 2010).

Parents also must help their infant master this crisis of autonomy by continually devising situations in which their relatively mature baby can play independently and without undue fear of interference—by putting the pots and pans within reach but hiding the knives, for instance. Children also need social as well as physical safety. Chewing on a sister's drawing or dumping the dirt out of the flowerpots may not have dangerous physical consequences, but it can have negative social effects. Thus, parents must help their infant learn how to avoid social perils by being selective about the child's activities.

autonomy An individual's ability to govern and regulate her or his own thoughts, feelings, and actions freely and responsibly while at the same time overcoming feelings of shame and doubt.

Sources of Autonomy

Why should infants and toddlers voluntarily begin to exert self-control over their own behavior? Developmental psychologists have suggested several possible answers to this question based on the various theories outlined in Chapter 2. Each has some plausibility, although none is complete in itself.

Operant Conditioning

Operant conditioning stresses the importance of reinforcement for desirable behaviors. According to this view, adults will tend to reinforce a child for more grown-up behaviors, such as independent exploration ("What did you find?") and self-restraint ("I'm glad you didn't wet your pants"). Operant conditioning resembles identification in assuming parents can motivate children, but it also assumes their influence occurs in piecemeal ways; that is, the child acquires specific behaviors rather than whole personality patterns.

After their first birthday, infants begin to show increasing autonomy in their play and other activities, which sometimes leads them to unsafe situations such as this little girl climbing out of her crib. This autonomy is fostered by their improving motor skills and cognitive development.
Source: Michael Pettigrew/Shutterstock.com.

Observational Learning

According to the theory of *observational learning,* the key to acquiring autonomy and self-control lies in the child's inherent tendency to observe and imitate parents and other caregivers. If parents act gently with the child's baby sister, for example, the child will come to do so too (although his interpretation of *gently* may occasionally be influenced by feelings of sibling rivalry). Similarly, if a young child observes her mother taking pots and pans from the kitchen cabinet, it is a fair bet that she will attempt to do the same. In fact, much home "childproofing" is necessitated by a young child's skill at observational learning. The process of observational learning implies that autonomy and self-control are acquired in units, or behavioral chunks, that are bigger than those described by operant conditioning but smaller than those acquired in identification.

Social Referencing: A Common Denominator

All three explanations of the development of autonomy have something in common: they involve **social referencing**, the child's sensitivity to the feelings of his parents and other adults and his ability to use these emotional cues to guide his own emotional responses and actions (Baldwin & Moses, 1996; Bretherton, 1992; Pelaez et al., 2012; Witherington et al., 2010). For example, infants and toddlers exhibit social referencing when they visit a strange place. Should they be afraid of the new objects and people or not? How safe is it to be friendly and to explore? In the absence of past experiences of their own, they evaluate such situations based on their parents' responses: if their parents are relaxed and happy, they are likely to feel that way too; if their parents are made tense or anxious by the situation, the children probably will feel that way also. Even very young infants use their caregivers and even strangers to guide their responses, for example, approaching and playing with unfamiliar toys if a nearby stranger is smiling and avoiding them if the person looks fearful (Klinnert et al., 1986; Walden & Kim, 2005; Witherington et al., 2010).

social referencing The child's sensitive awareness of how parents and other adults are feeling and ability to use these emotional cues as a basis for guiding his or her own emotional responses and actions. Social referencing is important for the development of autonomy.

Development of Self

The sense of self that develops late in infancy shows up in everyday situations as well as in situations involving self-control. Its development appears to follow a sequence that begins with *physical self-recognition and self-awareness,* followed by *self-description and self-evaluation,* and then by *knowledge of standards and emotional response to wrongdoing* (Kochanska et al., 1995; Stipek et al., 1990).

Self-Recognition and Self-Awareness

One interesting series of studies explored this phenomenon in infants nine to twenty-four months old by testing their ability to recognize images of themselves in mirrors, on television, and in still photographs (Asendorpf et al., 1996; Lewis et al., 1985; Rochat, 2003). Because most of the infants could not verbally indicate whether or not they recognized themselves, the researchers secretly marked each infant's nose with a red mark. When placed in front of a mirror, infants from fifteen to twenty-four months of age touched their bodies or faces more frequently than they did before they were marked. Infants around fifteen to eighteen months also began to imitate their marked images by making faces, sticking out their tongues, or watching themselves disappear and reappear at the side of a mirror. These self-recognition behaviors never occurred in infants younger than fifteen months and increased from 75 percent at eighteen months to 100 percent at twenty-four months. When presented with videotaped images of themselves in which a stranger sneaked up on them, infants as young as nine months displayed self-recognition based on *contingent cues,* that is, connections between their own movements and the movements of the image they were viewing. By approximately fifteen months, infants were increasingly able to distinguish themselves from other infants by using *noncontingent cues* such as facial and other physical features (Lewis & Brooks-Gunn, 1979a; Lewis et al., 1985). Many children do not refer to the child on the video as "me" reliably until they are nearly four years old (Rochat, 2003).

Self-Description, Self-Evaluation, and Emotional Response to Wrongdoing

Between nineteen and thirty months of age, children develop the cognitive competence and vocabulary to describe and represent themselves in terms of physical characteristics such as size *(little, big)*, type of hair *(curly, red)*, and eye color. By the end of their second year, most children show an increasing appreciation of the standards and expectations of others regarding their behavior toward both people and things. For example, a broken toy can trouble a child even if she did not break it; she may show it to an adult and verbally express concern and a need for help ("Broken!" or "Daddy fix?"). A crack in the kitchen linoleum may now receive close scrutiny, even though several months earlier, it went unnoticed, and several months later, it may go unnoticed again. Language that implies *knowledge of standards*—evaluative vocabulary such as *bad, good, dirty, nice*—appears as well (Bretherton, 1995). Such knowledge combines with other behaviors to suggest that the child is beginning to sense an identity for himself. There is also reason to believe that verbal and nonverbal reactions of toddlers to flawed objects are associated with the early development of a sense of morality. When faced with situations in which they believe they have been responsible for a "mishap" such as breaking a toy, toddlers' responses include acceptance of responsibility, apologies, a focus on reparations (repairing the wrong), and distress (Kochanska et al., 1995).

By age two, children show satisfaction in *initiating challenging activities* or behaviors for themselves, and they often smile at the results. A child builds a tower of blocks higher than usual and smiles broadly the moment she completes it. Another makes a strange noise—say, a cat meowing—and then smiles with pride. In each case, the child confronts a task that is somewhat difficult by her current standards, but attempts it anyway. Her behavior suggests an awareness of what competent performance amounts to and of her own ability to succeed. This knowledge reflects part of her sense of self and contributes to its further development.

Development of Competence and Self-Esteem

From the beginning of infancy through the end of toddlerhood, children achieve a growing sense of basic trust, autonomy, competence, and ultimately self-esteem. In fact, these developments go hand in hand. Autonomy, as we discussed earlier, is made possible by a child's secure and basically trustworthy relationships with his primary caregivers. **Competence**—skill and capability—develops as a result of the child's natural curiosity and desire to explore the world and the pleasure he experiences in successfully mastering and controlling that world (White, 1993). Much like the infants need for proximity and attachment to caregivers, his motivation to explore and master the world is thought to be relatively autonomous and independent of basic physiological needs for food, water, sleep, and freedom from pain.

competence An individual's increased skill and capability in successfully exploring, mastering, and controlling the world around them.

Based on many years of observational study, Burton White (1993) suggests that a socially competent toddler is likely to display capabilities in the following areas:

1. Getting and holding the attention of adults in socially acceptable ways
2. Using adults as resources after first determining that a task is too difficult
3. Expressing affection and mild annoyance to adults
4. Leading and following peers
5. Expressing affection and mild annoyance to peers
6. Competing with peers
7. Showing pride in personal accomplishments
8. Engaging in role play or make-believe activities

What everyday rules for behavior guide parents' efforts to socialize their toddlers and preschool-age children? To answer this question, Heidi Gralinski and Claire Kopp (1993)

> **What Do You Think?**
>
> How do you think seeing your toddler develop competence and self-esteem would affect your feelings and self-evaluation as a parent and caregiver? How might these feelings affect your child in turn?

observed and interviewed mothers and their children in these age groups. They found that for fifteen-month-olds, mothers' rules and requests centered on ensuring the children's safety and, to a lesser extent, protecting the families' possessions from harm; respecting basic social niceties ("Don't bite"; "No kicking"); and learning to delay getting what they wanted (versus getting it immediately). As children's ages and cognitive sophistication increased, the numbers and kinds of prohibitions and requests expanded from the original focus on child protection and interpersonal issues to family routines, self-care, and other concerns regarding the child's independence. By the time children were three, a new quality of rule emerged: "Do not scream in a restaurant, run around naked in front of company, kick your sister, take the tablet when someone is using it, fight with children in school, or pick your nose."

Not surprisingly, a toddler's social competence is influenced by the nature of the parent-toddler relationship. Even though they do not spend more time interacting with their children than mothers of less competent children, mothers of highly competent children support and encourage their toddlers' curiosity and desire to explore the world around them by providing a rich variety of interesting toys and experiences that are both safe and appropriate to the children's level of competence. They also play with their toddlers in ways that are responsive to the children's interests and needs and use language their toddlers can clearly understand.

Observations of mothers and their two-year-olds found that toddlers' capacity for both compliance with parental directions and self-assertion was associated with *authoritative parenting* relationships (see Chapter 10) consisting of a combination of control and guidance and an appropriate sharing of power with warmth, sensitivity, responsiveness, and child-centered family management techniques (Farrant et al., 2012). High levels of defiance and parent-toddler conflict were most likely to be associated with more authoritarian, power-assertive control strategies. In situations where the toddler had said "no" to the mother, maternal negative control was most likely to elicit defiance (Crockenberg & Litman, 1990; White, 1993).

Mothers of competent toddlers are also more likely to encourage their children to accomplish the tasks they had initiated themselves by actively guiding them and praising them for achievements rather than actually performing the tasks for them (White, 1993). As you might expect, this approach requires considerable patience, the ability to tolerate the child's frustration when things do not work out the first few times, and a firm belief in the child's need and potential to be an autonomous and competent person. Perhaps the most important quality of these mothers is their ability to interact sensitively and appropriately with their children and to experience pleasure and delight in these interactions (at least most of the time). The same quality appears to be most important in the development of secure attachment relationships and continues to be important throughout childhood.

Toddlers who grow up in supportive environments are likely to be better adjusted in their development than children whose environments are less supportive. A natural outcome of such parenting is the early emergence of a strong sense of **self-esteem**: a child's feeling that she is an important, competent, powerful, and worthwhile person whose efforts to be autonomous and take initiative are respected and valued by those around her (Erikson, 1963; Harter, 1983; Robins & Trzesniewski, 2005). The development of self-esteem during infancy and toddlerhood is closely tied to the achievement of a positive ratio of autonomy versus shame and doubt and initiative versus guilt during the developmental crises that, according to Erikson, occur during this period (Erikson, 1963). Young children generally have very high self-esteem, likely due to the encouragement

self-esteem An individual's belief that he or she is an important, competent, powerful, and worthwhile person who is valued and appreciated.

they receive when learning new tasks (Robins & Trzesniewski, 2005) As we will see, the childhood experiences that follow infancy continue to make major contributions to this important aspect of identity.

Looking Back/Looking Forward

Let us now look at how the developmental lifespan themes outlined in Chapter 1 apply to our discussion of infancy. We will focus on attachment, which plays a central role in infancy and influences development throughout the life cycle.

- **Continuity within change**—Attachment relationships begin in early infancy and are an important aspect of the parent-child relationships that are the foundation of psychosocial development. Although the ways in which parent-child attachment is expressed change as a child moves from infancy through childhood and adolescence, and into adulthood, there is considerable continuity within these changes as reflected in the finding that a child who is classified as being securely (or insecurely) attached in infancy and early childhood will very likely continue to display that pattern as an adolescent, as a parent, and as a grandparent. One important reason is that the internal mental working models of both parent and child that are thought to organize and guide early infant-caregiver interactions continue to do so even though the particular forms of the interactions undergo developmental change.

- **Lifelong growth**—The physical, cognitive, and psychosocial growth that occurs from infancy through adulthood affects how attachment is expressed in important ways. How secure (or insecure) attachment is displayed during adolescence, for example, is markedly different than the way it was displayed in early childhood or the ways in which it will be manifested in romantic relationships during adulthood. These changes are also a product of the striking growth in cognitive abilities achieved in adolescence and early adulthood. Thus, a youngster who attends college in Colorado maintains a psychological sense of attachment with his parents in Connecticut, even though most of their interactions are by e-mail, Facebook interactions, phone calls, Snapchat, FaceTime, holiday visits and, on rare occasions, "snail-mail."

- **Changing meanings and vantage points**—The meaning of attachment to children and their parents changes significantly as they move through the life cycle. The meaning of attachment for a mother and her preteen daughter, for example, will differ significantly from that experienced during the daughter's early childhood years, and will likely have changed for each of them when the pre-teen is a parent herself and her mother is both a parent of an adult child and a grandmother. Remember, however, that despite the changes in vantage points and meanings, it is also highly likely that all three generations—grandmother, mother, and child—will share the same attachment classification, reflecting the theme of continuity within change mentioned earlier.

- **Developmental diversity**—The lifespan theme of diversity is reflected in the development of attachment in two ways. The first and more obvious way is in the four attachment classifications that appear to describe the great majority of children and parents who have been studied. As we have seen in this chapter, a secure pattern of attachment for both infant and parent during the first two years is generally associated with much more positive long-term developmental outcomes than is a disorganized pattern for the child and parent. The second major source of developmental diversity in attachment relationships is the many factors in addition to a parent's sensitivity and responsiveness that affect the quality of attachment and of the overall parent-child relationship. One example is differences in the frequency with which the various attachment patterns are observed in different cultures and in different contexts within a particular culture.

Chapter Summary

- **What emotional capabilities does an infant have? How do differences in infants' temperament affect their social development?** Newborn infants have a natural tendency to actively participate in their social world. *Caregiver-infant synchrony* refers to the closely orchestrated social and emotional interactions between an infant and his or her caregiver and provides an important basis for the development of attachment relationships. The similarities in the type and quality of an infant's interactions with mother and father are much greater than the differences. The effects of nonmaternal care and maternal employment on infant and toddler development depend on the specific circumstances, but in general do not appear to be negative. When given the opportunity to do so, infants engage in active social interactions with their siblings and peers and often prefer them to their parents as playmates.

- **In what ways is a newborn infant capable of participating in the social world? How does caregiver-infant synchrony expand an infant's social capabilities?** Infants appear to be capable of a complex range of emotional responses and are quite sensitive to the feelings of their caregivers. They probably use cues similar to those adults use, such as variations in voice quality, smell, touch, facial expression, and body language. Even at birth, infants exhibit differences in temperament, patterns of physical and emotional responsiveness, and activity levels. These differences both influence and are influenced by the feelings and responses of their caregivers.

- **What experiences enable infants to develop secure emotional attachments with their caregivers? What are the consequences of different attachment patterns?** Attachment, the tendency of young infants and their caregivers to seek and maintain physical and emotional closeness with each other, is thought to provide an important basis for achieving secure and trusting relationships during early infancy. Attachment develops in a series of phases from indiscriminate sociability at birth to goal-coordinated partnerships at two years. The Strange Situation, in which the infant is confronted with the stress of being in an unfamiliar place, meeting a stranger, and being separated from his or her parent, has been used to study the development of attachment. Secure attachment is most likely to develop when the caregiver responds sensitively and appropriately to the infant and the infant can use the caregiver as a safe base for exploration. Insecurely attached infants tend to be less able than securely attached infants are to get help from parents and teachers when they need it or to accept it when it is offered. Infants are equally capable of forming secure attachments to their mothers and to their fathers, and to other caregivers as well, even though in the majority of families the mother is the primary caregiver. The effects of both maternal employment and day care on attachment depend largely on how the mother feels about herself and her role as a parent and how the situation helps or hinders her ability to care for and enjoy her baby. The quality of her experience and the quality and consistency of the day care are also important. Attachment patterns can be long-term, often affecting three generations of parents and their children.

- **Why is autonomy so central to development during toddlerhood? What parenting qualities contribute to its successful development?** Sources of the growing autonomy that characterizes the second year of infancy include identification, operant conditioning, observational learning, and social referencing. Toddlerhood also brings significant increases in self-knowledge and self-awareness. These changes are reflected in the toddler's increasing awareness of adult standards, distress at behaviors modeled by unknown adults, and pride in her or his accomplishments. Toddlers are strongly motivated to achieve greater competence through successfully mastering and controlling the physical and social worlds around them. Competence is fostered by parents who encourage their infant's curiosity by providing opportunities that are challenging, safe, and appropriate to the child's capabilities. Increased self-esteem in the infant is the natural outcome of supportive parenting.

Key Terms

anxious-avoidant attachment (p. 166)
anxious-resistant attachment (p. 166)
attachment (p. 163)
autonomy (p. 175)
caregiver-infant synchrony (p. 155)
competence (p. 177)
coparenting (p. 154)
disorganized-disoriented attachment (p. 166)
secure attachment (p. 165)
self-esteem (p. 178)
social referencing (p. 176)
Strange Situation (p. 165)
temperament (p. 161)
working models (p. 164)

Early Childhood

PART 4

Source: Samuel Borges Photography/Shutterstock.com.

Chapter 8
Physical and Cognitive Development during Early Childhood

Chapter 9
Cognitive Development during Early Childhood

Chapter 10
Psychosocial Development during Early Childhood

Although most of us remember relatively little from our preschool years, parents often believe those years are among the most gratifying for their children. Perhaps, this is because children become more equal participants in their families during this time than during infancy; yet, they have not begun the process of creating lives for themselves outside the family. Parents therefore have much to do during these years, and they may still believe they can shape or influence their children fully. Later, it will become harder to hold to this idea.

Preschoolers become more social during this period, partly because of the more complex motor skills they acquire—skills such as riding a tricycle or climbing a jungle gym—which can impress parents as well as friends. In addition, new cognitive skills allow preschool children to express themselves more precisely than they could as infants, as well as try out new social roles in play. Their world expands rapidly during these years—a process that is both exhausting and exhilarating for children, as well as for their parents.

Physical and Cognitive Development during Early Childhood

CHAPTER 8

Source: Gserban/Shutterstock.com.

Chapter Outline

PHYSICAL DEVELOPMENT

Influences on Normal Physical Development

The Connection between Health and Poverty

Bladder Control

Motor Skill Development

The Impact of Children's Growth on Adults

From Preschooler to Child

Focusing Questions

- What pathway does physical growth normally take during early childhood?
- How is poverty related to children's health?
- When do children achieve bladder control?
- What motor skills do children acquire during the preschool years?
- How does children's growth affect parents and other adults?
- What are the special features and strengths of preschoolers' thinking?
- How does the language of preschool children differ from that of older children?
- What social and cultural factors account for variations in preschoolers' language and speech?
- What constitutes good early childhood education?

"Kitty run!" says Zöe, age three. She is pointing to the neighborhood cat.

"Yes," replies her father. "She's chasing a bird."

Zöe nods and says, "Bird gone now. Bad kitty?" and looks to her father for confirmation.

"It's OK this time," says her father. "The bird flew away soon enough."

At this, Zöe walks off to find the cat, curious to learn what else it might do.

Two features of this incident are especially noteworthy: Zöe's language and her mobility. Little more than a year ago, neither could have occurred. As a preschooler, however, she is developing the ability to deal with her world in symbols, in this case through oral language. She is also developing new physical skills that serve her interests and abilities; for example, she can walk up to the cat simply to learn more about it.

In the next two chapters, we look in detail at physical and cognitive development during early childhood. Many of the examples will suggest relationships between the two domains, as well as their impact on the third domain of psychosocial development. The fact that preschoolers sleep less than they did as infants, for example, is the beginning of a lifelong trend that will affect both child and parents, creating new options for each. For the child, staying awake longer facilitates attending school; for parents, the child's attending school makes adult-focused activities, such as a job or a hobby, easier to arrange than before their children began school. Parents who are ready for the growth and changes in their preschoolers but do not feel pressured to hurry those changes will likely influence their children's development in many positive ways. The changes will also set the stage for even more indirect forms of parenting typical of later phases of childhood and adolescence, discussed in Chapters 13 and 16.

PHYSICAL DEVELOPMENT

Influences on Normal Physical Development

Physical growth during the preschool years is relatively easy to measure and gives a clear idea of how children normally develop during this period. Table 8.1 and Figure 8.1 show the two most familiar measurements of growth, standing height and weight. At age two, an average child in North America measures about thirty-three or thirty-four inches tall, or about two feet, ten inches. Three years later, at age five, he or she measures approximately forty-three inches, or about one-third more than before. The typical child weighs twenty-seven to twenty-eight pounds by age two but about forty-one pounds by age five. Meanwhile, other measurements change in less obvious ways. The child's head grows about one inch in circumference during these years, and body fat decreases as a proportion of total bodily tissue.

For a preschool child who is reasonably healthy and happy, physical growth is remarkably smooth and predictable, especially compared to many cognitive and social developments. Overall, physical growth contains no discrete stages, plateaus, or qualitative changes such as those Piaget proposed for cognitive development. At the same time, however, important differences develop among individual children and among groups of children. Often the

TABLE 8.1 Average Height and Weight during Early Childhood

	Girls		Boys	
Age (Years)	Height (inches)	Weight (pounds)	Height (inches)	Weight (pounds)
2	33.5	26.5	34.1	28.6
3	37.0	30.9	37.4	31.7
4	39.8	35.0	40.2	35.3
5	42.3	39.7	42.9	40.8

Source: Centers for Disease Control and Prevention (2000).

FIGURE 8.1

Growth in Height and Weight from Two to Eighteen Years

differences simply create interesting physical variety among children, but sometimes they do more than affect appearance. Being larger (or smaller) than usual, for example, can make a child stronger (or less strong) than others of the same age, and therefore more (or less) able to master certain sports or other physical activities. Size can also affect how parents and other adults respond to the child; larger children may seem older and be treated as such, whether or not they are psychologically ready. For both reasons, a child might gain (or lose) self-confidence, and even gain (or lose) popularity among peers.

The overall smoothness of growth means that childhood height and weight can predict adult height and weight to a significant extent, although not perfectly. A four-year-old who is above average in height tends to end up above average as an adult. Nevertheless, correlation between childhood height and adult height is imperfect because of individual differences in nutrition and health and, most of all, in the timing of puberty. In particular, children who experience puberty later than average tend to grow taller than children who experience it early (Sanfilippo et al., 1994; Yousefi et al., 2013)—a source of diversity that we will say more about in Chapter 13 in connection with adolescence and its impact.

Genetic Background

Most dimensions of growth are influenced substantially by heredity. Tall parents tend to have tall children, and short parents usually have short children. Weight shows similar patterns, although it can be influenced strongly by habits of exercise and diet.

Races and ethnic groups around the world also differ slightly in average growth patterns (Eveleth & Tanner, 1990), and general trends demonstrate that children born in countries with low to middle income are more likely to be low birth weight (5.5 pounds or less) and to exhibit slower growth throughout childhood (Adair et al., 2013). Children from Asian groups, such as Chinese and Japanese, tend to be shorter than European and North American children are. The latter, in turn, tend to be shorter than children from African societies are. Shape differs among these groups as well, although the differences do not always become obvious until adolescence. Asian children tend to develop short legs and arms relative to their torsos, and relatively broad hips. African children do just the opposite: they tend to develop relatively long limbs and narrow hips. Keep in mind, though, that these differences are only average tendencies. Racial and ethnic groups tend to overlap in size and shape more than they differ (that is what makes us all human!). From the point of view of parents, teachers, and other professionals, the most important physical differences among children are individual ones: there are large and small children in every racial and ethnic group, among both boys and girls, and in every community (Doherty, 1996). If you are responsible for children as individuals, recognizing their individual differences is likely to be your priority.

As a result of improvements in nutrition and health care, children in industrialized nations are often taller than in earlier times. But there are important variations among societies—even among industrialized ones—that apparently are influenced genetically.

Source: wckiw/Shutterstock.com.

Chapter 8 Physical and Cognitive Development during Early Childhood

Nutritional Needs during the Preschool Years

For a time, a young preschooler (such as a three-year-old) may eat less than he or she did as a toddler and become much more selective about foods as well. Michael, the son of one of the authors, ate every meal voraciously as a two-year-old; a year later, he rarely finished a meal, even though he was significantly taller and heavier by then. Elizabeth, his sister, followed a similar but more pronounced pattern. As a toddler, she ate most foods except ice cream ("Too sweet," she said!), but as a young preschooler, she sometimes hardly ate—though she did decide then that she liked ice cream. Later, their appetites returned. As a nineteen-year-old, Michael routinely ate about twice as much as other members of the family did. Elizabeth, at sixteen, was no longer a picky eater—and became especially enthusiastic about ice cream.

Parents may worry about such changes, but in fact, they are normal and result from the slowing down of growth after infancy. Preschool children simply do not need as many calories per unit of their body weight as they did immediately after birth. They do need variety in their foods, however, just as adults do, to ensure adequate overall nutrition. Given preschoolers' newfound selectiveness about eating, providing the variety needed for good nutrition sometimes can be a challenge to parents and other caregivers.

How can one ensure healthy variety in a preschool child's diet? Experts generally discourage coercion ("Eat your vegetables because I say so!") because it teaches children to associate undesired foods with unpleasant social experiences (Endres & Rockwell, 1993; Ventura & Worobey, 2013). They also discourage using sweet foods and drinks as a reward for eating undesired foods ("If you eat your vegetables, then you can have your ice cream") because it implicitly overvalues the sweets and undervalues the undesired food still further. For children who are particularly picky and who do not like to try new foods, sticker rewards for trying new foods have been successful (Corsini et al., 2013). In addition, providing many opportunities for children to try foods, even vegetables the children "don't like," in conjunction with nonfood reinforcement like a sticker increases liking for those vegetables (Fildes, van Jaarsveld, Wardle, & Cooke, 2014). The best strategy seems to be casual, repeated exposure to the food without insisting that the child eat it (Andrien, 1994). Getting children involved in age-appropriate food preparation, such as tearing and washing lettuce, cleaning and breaking apart cauliflower or broccoli, and weighing pasta, was linked to children eating more overall, including vegetables (van der Horst, Ferrage, & Rytz, 2014). Observations of children's eating habits confirm what parents often suspect as well: children's food preferences are influenced by the adult models around them. In the long term, preschoolers tend to like the same foods as their parents and other important adults. More generally, they practice many of their parents' other health behaviors (such as exercise) as well.

The Connection between Health and Poverty

In settings of middle and high socioeconomic status, preschool children as a group are among the healthiest human beings alive, though not as healthy as they will become in childhood, adolescence, and young adulthood. They experience comparatively few major illnesses as long as they get enough of the right things to eat and as long as their parents have reasonable access to modern medical care. As parents often note, preschoolers do experience frequent minor illnesses: various respiratory infections, ear infections, and stomach flus. These typically strike a young child several times per year, which is three or four times as often as for adults and about twice as often as for school-age children (Engels, 1993). For well-fed children whose families have access to medical care, however, these illnesses rarely prove serious or life threatening. Colds and flu do cause worry, as well as create challenges for working parents in arranging childcare.

But this optimistic picture of preschoolers' health may be misleading. Since 1997, when the Children's Health Insurance Program (CHIP), which provides low- or no-cost insurance to children whose families make too much to qualify for Medicaid but cannot afford insurance, passed, rates of uninsured children have decreased significantly. This trend has stabilized with the passage of the Affordable Care Act (ACA), so that currently,

> **What Do You Think?**
>
> How do you suppose parents evaluate their child's height and weight? Explore this problem by asking two or three parents how satisfied they are with their child's height and weight. Do you think parents' feelings have any relationship to the actual size of their child?

only 5 percent of children lack health insurance coverage (Artiga & Ubri, 2017). However, most states that did not accept the Medicaid expansion of the ACA have uninsured child rates of 10 percent or higher (Kenney et al., 2014). Moreover, temporary funding of CHIP and possible repeals of ACA make many children vulnerable to losing access to medical care. Young children from these families are substantially less healthy than are those from middle- and high-SES families. Low-SES preschoolers contract 25 to 50 percent more minor illnesses than do preschoolers as a whole, and they are more often malnourished and face food insecurity, meaning that they chronically lack the quantity and quality of food to thrive, as well as essential vitamins, iron, and protein (American Academy of Pediatrics, 1993; McCurdy, Gorman, Kisler, & Metallinos-Katsaras, 2012; Wilkinson, 1996). Children growing up at or near the poverty level are also substantially more likely to be overweight or obese (McCurdy et al., 2012).

Whether in North America or around the world, minor illnesses combined with malnourishment put children's health at risk for additional illnesses, both minor and major. Malnourishment also contributes to delays in social, language, and cognitive development, possibly because it leads to lack of energy and lack of interest in new experiences. In one study based in Kenya (Africa), even a temporary food shortage (due to a few months of local drought) impaired children's health and school performance two years later (McDonald et al., 1994).

How can we counteract these problems? In general, strategies can focus either on individuals and their particular communities or on systematic reorganization of the health care system and food security systems as a whole. Among individually oriented strategies, an important one is to educate children and families about health and nutrition. For example, pamphlets can be distributed in schools or medical clinics, and public health professionals can make presentations in classrooms, community clubs, or churches. However, these efforts work best when they are multifaceted, including education in combination with improving access to high-quality food and health care. The "Focusing On" feature proposes additional alternatives.

Educational activities can be effective if they build on the knowledge of health and nutrition low-SES parents and their children already have and avoid assuming the public is completely ignorant about these matters. Good programs also improve individuals' self-efficacy about engaging in health-promoting behaviors, and as noted earlier, work best when public policy (like changes to the health care system or expanding programs such as the Supplemental Nutrition Assistance Program) makes engaging in health-promoting behaviors easier. In this sort of situation, it is helpful to organize intervention programs aimed at providing parents and children with the knowledge they need. However, such programs must respect the culture and economic situations of the families, which usually influence food preferences in major ways. Put simply, certain foods acquire symbolic meanings (such as turkey for American Thanksgiving), regardless of their precise nutritional value. Other foods may never be tried, no matter how worthwhile they are nutritionally, because they cost too much or seem too strange or foreign to a particular family or cultural group.

Bladder Control

Sometime during the preschool years, to parents' great relief, most children acquire control of their bladder. The process includes many false starts and accidents. Most commonly, daytime control comes before nighttime control, generally beginning between the ages of

Focusing On...

Reforming Children's Health Care

In all societies, the health care system provides less help to poor families than to well-off ones. Low-SES mothers receive less medical attention during pregnancy, causing health problems in themselves or their fetuses to be overlooked, and are more likely to give birth to a low birth-weight infant (Krans & Davis, 2014). Infants of low-income mothers are less likely to receive checkups from a doctor and less likely to be seen by a doctor if they get sick (Bury, 1997; Wilkinson, 1996). However, children who have access to Medicaid and CHIP, described next, are much more likely to get checkups and to see health professionals early in an illness (Rudowitz, Artiga, & Arguello, 2014).

Why does access to health care depend so heavily on personal income? In the United States, medical services for the poor are paid through Medicaid, a federally sponsored insurance program created in the 1960s. It pays for some basic health services, such as taking a child with an ear ache to a general practitioner, but it reimburses the doctor only up to a certain point. Doctors who charge more price themselves out of the market for low-SES families, which have significantly fewer doctors and clinics to choose from but children who experience more illnesses than do children from higher-SES families (Fitzgerald et al., 1994). In 1997, the Children's Health Insurance Program (CHIP) was created, which assists states in providing insurance to children whose families cannot afford insurance but make too much money for Medicaid eligibility. As of 2017, nearly nine million children in the United States were enrolled in CHIP (Medicaid, 2018).

Though there have been significant strides in improving access to health care for children and adults alike, many children still lack access to health care. In some states, uninsured rates for children are over 15 percent, due in part to lack of parents' awareness of eligibility (Rudowitz, Artiga, & Arguello, 2014).

How can society and concerned individuals reduce these economically based inequalities in health care? Numerous reforms have been proposed centering on one of three ideas: community involvement, prevention, and reorganization of services. Reforms that focus on community involvement seek to reduce the psychological and geographical distance between medical staff and the people they serve. Some hospitals and cities have established small community health clinics in areas of greatest need (the inner city). They hire medical staff who establish rapport with the parents and children who seek help, recruit local community members to serve on their governing and advisory boards, and charge low fees based on families' ability to pay.

Reforms that focus on primary prevention seek to keep disease from striking in the first place. These actions often deal with relatively healthy children (who have not gotten sick yet) and the conditions that make illness likely rather than illness itself. Lead poisoning is a good example: community health experts often cite lead as one of the most hazardous health threats to preschool children (Tesman & Hills, 1994). Lead accumulates in the body and eventually damages the nervous system and can cause death. People pick it up accidentally from many sources, but the most prominent culprit is the interior wall paint used in about 75 percent of all homes and apartments built before 1980. Because there is no cure for lead poisoning, prevention strategies have dominated the response of the health care profession: educating parents to the dangers, pressing for legislation outlawing lead-based paints (and lead-based gasoline), removing leaded paint in some homes, and checking/remediating local water systems when tap water tests high for lead content.

Reforms that focus on reorganization generally involve more self-conscious planning of medical services. Immunization and health-screening programs based in schools, for example, allow programs to reach a higher percentage of children than programs in community health clinics (Behrman, 1993; Behr-man & Stacey, 1997; Jacob et al., 2016). "Front-line" professionals often can improve access dramatically without compromising quality of care: most childhood illnesses, for example, can be treated effectively by a nurse as long as the nurse knows when a particular illness deserves referral to the doctor and appropriate specialized services are indeed available.

What Do You Think?

1. Look back on your own elementary school hearing or eye tests from the point of view of the teachers and nurses. Can you see any limitations to "mass screening," as well as advantages to it?
2. Is there a case to be made for *limiting* health care to the poor? What would it be? And what might be the long-term implications of limiting health care?

> **What Do You Think?**
>
> Suppose you are a teacher or caregiver at a childcare center, and one of your children often seems hungry throughout the day. How could you tell whether the child is undernourished or simply has a big appetite? Compare your strategies for answering this question with those of a classmate.

two and three (Bloom, Seeley, Ritchey, & McGuire, 1993) and becoming reliable for most children by the age of four (Jansson, Hanson, Sillén, & Hellström, 2005), although individual children vary widely and somewhat unpredictably. Typically, too, daytime control of the bladder occurs at very nearly the same time. Some pediatricians believe this fact implies that children decide when they wish to begin exercising control, perhaps to begin feeling more grown up. In the early stages of toilet training, therefore, reminders and parent-led visits to the toilet may make little difference to most toddlers. Nonetheless, they may help in the long term as a form of behavioral conditioning: a child comes to associate seeing and sitting on the toilet with the relief of emptying a full bladder, as well as with the praise parents confer on the child for successes.

Nighttime bladder control often takes much longer to achieve than daytime control. About one-half of all three-year-olds still wet their beds at least some of the time, and as many as one in five six-year-olds do the same (American Psychiatric Association, 1994). The timing of nighttime control depends on several factors, such as how deeply children sleep and how large their bladders are. It also depends on anxiety level; worried children tend to wet their beds more often than relaxed children do. Unfortunately, parents sometimes contribute to young children's anxieties by becoming overly frustrated about changing wet sheets night after night.

Achieving bladder control reflects the large advances children make during the preschool years in controlling their bodies in general. It also reflects parents' accumulated efforts to encourage physical self-control for their children. The combined result is that children of this age can begin focusing on what they actually want to do with their bodies.

In the long run, successful bladder control depends on both physical growth and the child's own motivation. Forcing children prematurely to control themselves may produce results, but only in the immediate future.
Source: Maurizio Milanesio/Shutterstock.com.

Motor Skill Development

As young children grow, they become more skilled at performing basic physical actions. Often a two-year-old can walk only with considerable effort; hence the term *toddler*. But a five-year-old can walk comfortably in a variety of ways: forward and backward, quickly and slowly, skipping and galloping. A five-year-old also can do other vigorous things that were impossible a few years earlier. Running, jumping, and climbing all occur with increasing smoothness and variety. Children can carry out certain actions that require accuracy, such as balancing on one foot, catching a ball reliably, or drawing a picture.

In this section, we examine in more detail how children reach milestones such as these. Because family conditions vary a great deal, we will make certain assumptions. In particular, we will assume children have no significant fears of being active—that they have a reasonably (but not excessively) daring attitude toward trying out new motor skills, they are in good health, and their physical growth has evolved more or less optimally. These assumptions do not hold for all children or families, as we note later in this section, but they make a good starting point for understanding motor development.

Fundamental Motor Skills

Healthy preschool children obviously have moved well beyond the confines of reflex action, which constituted the first motor skills of infancy. From ages two to about five, they experiment with the simple voluntary actions that adults use extensively for their normal activities, such as walking, running, and jumping (Kalverboer et al., 1993). For older children, these actions usually are the means to other ends. For very young children, they lie very much in the foreground and frequently are goals in themselves. Table 8.2 summarizes some of these activities.

> **What Do You Think?**
>
> Imagine how you would talk to a parent who was concerned about the child's bed-wetting at night. What would you say? If you or your instructor can arrange it, try acting out a meeting to discuss bed-wetting between a concerned parent and a childcare center worker or director.

Walking and Running

From a child's point of view, walking may seem absurd at first: it requires purposely losing balance, then regaining balance rapidly enough to keep from falling (Rose & Gamble, 1993). As older infants, children still must pay attention to these facts, even after a full year or so of practice. Each step is an effort in itself. Children watch each foot in turn as it launches (or lurches) forward; they may pause after each step before attempting the next. By their second or third birthday, however, their steps become more regular and their feet get closer together (Adolph et al., 2012). Stride, the distance between feet in a typical step, remains considerably shorter than that of a typical adult. This makes short distances easy to walk but long distances hard to navigate for a few more years.

Jumping

At first, a jump is more like a fast stretch: the child reaches for the sky rapidly, but her feet fail to leave the ground. Sometime around her second birthday, one foot, or even both feet, may finally leave the ground. Such early successes may be delayed, however, because the child may thrust her arms backward to help herself take off, as though trying to push herself off the floor. Later, perhaps around age three, she shifts to a more efficient arm movement—reaching forward and upward as she jumps—which creates a useful upward momentum.

Success in these actions depends partly on the type of jump the child is attempting. Jumping down a step is easier than jumping across a flat distance, and a flat or broad jump is easier than a jump up a step. By age five or so, most children can broad-jump across a few feet, although variations among individuals are substantial.

TABLE 8.2 Milestones in Preschool Motor Development

Approximate Age	Gross Motor Skill	Fine Motor Skill
2.5–3.5 years	Walks well; runs in straight line; jumps in air with both feet	Copies a circle; scribbles; can use eating utensils; stacks a few small blocks
3.5–4.5 years	Has a walking stride 80 percent that of adult; runs at one-third adult speed; throws and catches large ball, but is stiff-armed	Buttons with large buttons; copies simple shapes; makes simple representational drawings
4.5–5.5 years	Balances on one foot; runs far without falling; can "swim" in water for short distance	Uses scissors; draws people; copies simple letters and numbers; builds complex structures with blocks

Note: The ages given above are approximate, and skills vary with the life experiences available to individual children and with the situations in which the skills are displayed.

Source: Kalverboer et al. (1993).

Throwing and Catching

For infants and toddlers, first throws may consist of simply waving an object, releasing it suddenly, and watching it take off. Once intentional throwing begins, however, children actually adopt more stereotyped methods initially, using a general forward lurch, regardless of the ball's size or weight. As skill develops, children vary their movements according to the size of the ball. Catching proceeds through analogous phases, from stereotyped, passive extension of arms to flexible movement of hands in a last-minute response to the oncoming ball.

Fine Motor Coordination: The Case of Drawing Skills

Not all motor activities of young children involve the strength, agility, and balance of their whole bodies. Many require the coordination of small movements but not strength. Tying shoelaces calls for such **fine motor coordination**; so do washing hands, buttoning and zipping clothing, eating with a spoon, and turning a doorknob.

One especially widespread fine motor skill among young children is drawing. In North American culture, at least, virtually every young child tries using pens or pencils at some time and often tries other artistic media as well. The scribbles or drawings that result probably serve a number of purposes. At times, they may be used mainly for sensory exploration; a child may want to get the feel of paintbrushes or felt-tip pens. At other times, drawings may express thoughts or feelings; a child may suggest this possibility by commenting, "It's a horse, and it's angry." Children's drawings also probably reflect their knowledge of the world, even though they may not yet have the fine motor skills they need to convey their knowledge fully. In other words, children's drawings reveal not only fine motor coordination but also their self-concepts, emotional and social attitudes, and cognitive development.

Drawing shows two overlapping phases of development during early childhood. From about two and a half to four years of age, children focus on developing nonrepresentational skills, such as scribbling and purposeful drawing of simple shapes and designs. Sometime around age four, they begin attempting to represent objects (Coles, 1992). Yet, although representational drawings usually follow nonrepresentational ones, the two types stimulate each other simultaneously. Children often describe their early scribbles as though they referred to real things, and their practice at portraying real objects helps them to further develop their nonrepresentational skills (Coates & Coates, 2006).

Prerepresentational Drawing

Around the end of infancy, children begin to scribble. A two-year-old experiments with whatever pen, crayon, or pencil is available, almost regardless of its color or type, behaving like an infant and like a child. As with an infant, efforts focus primarily on the activity

fine motor coordination Ability to smoothly carry out small movements that involve precise timing but not strength.

Skills that require fine motor coordination—like creating this drawing—develop through identifiable steps or stages. At first, children tend to make random marks or scribbles; later, they coordinate these into patterns; still later, they coordinate patterns into representations of objects that become increasingly recognizable by parents and teachers.
Source: borisow/Shutterstock.com.

Chapter 8 Physical and Cognitive Development during Early Childhood itself: on the motions and sensations of handling a pen or pencil. But like an older child, the two-year-old often cares about the outcome of these activities: "That's a Mommy," he says of his drawing, whether it looks much like one or not. Contrary to a popular view of children's art, even very young children are concerned not only with the process of drawing but with the product as well (Broughton et al., 1996).

A child's interest in the results of her drawing shows up in the patterns she imposes on even her earliest scribbles. Sometimes, she fills up particular parts of the page quite intentionally—the whole left side, say, or the complete middle third. And she often emphasizes particular categories of strokes: lots of straight diagonals or many counter-clockwise loops. Different children select different types of motions for emphasis, so the motions are less like universal stages than like elements of a personal style.

Representational Drawing

While preschool children improve their scribbling skills, they also develop an interest in representing people, objects, and events in their drawings. This interest often far precedes their ability to do so. A three-year-old may assign meanings to scribbles or blobs in his drawing; one blob may be "Mama," and another may be "our house." Events may happen to these blobs, too: Mama may be "going to the store" or "looking for me." During the early childhood years, and for a long time thereafter, the child's visual representations are limited by comparatively rudimentary fine motor skills. Apparently, children know more, visually speaking, than their hands can portray with pens or brushes. Only as children reach school age do their drawings of people become relatively realistic.

What happens to drawing skills beyond the preschool years depends on a child's experiences and on the encouragement (or lack thereof) received from others. Drawings in later years become even more realistic—more "photographic" or draftsmanlike in style. But not all children stay with art in the long term, due to the combined influence of competing academic interests, the priorities of friends, or even dislike of a teacher. We will discuss these types of influence again in Chapter 13 in connection with social and motivational changes during middle childhood.

Gender Differences in Physical Development

As is true during infancy, preschool boys and girls develop at almost exactly the same average rates. This applies to practically any motor skill of which young children are capable, and it applies to both gross and fine motor skills. Any nursery classroom, therefore, is likely to contain children of both sexes who can run very well and children of both sexes who can paint well or tie their shoelaces without help. This is especially true among younger preschool children (age three or four).

By the time children begin kindergarten (usually at age five), slight gender differences in physical development and motor skills appear, with boys tending to be (slightly) bigger, stronger, and faster (Kalverboer et al., 1993) and with better ball skills, while girls demonstrate better manual dexterity (Junaid & Fellowes, 2006). Yet these differences are noticeable only as averages and only by basing the averages on very large numbers of children. Despite the slight differences, therefore, more than 95 percent of children are more skillful and bigger than some members of *both* sexes, and less skillful and smaller than certain others of both sexes.

By the time children start school, a few children in any community are bigger, stronger, and faster than *any* other children, and most of them are boys. Furthermore, these few individuals may get much more than their share of attention because of their superior physical skills. This contributes to the (mistaken) impression that boys are larger and more skillful than girls *in general.* In this way (among many others) are stereotypes born.

The differences in motor skills might be more accurately called *gender* differences than *sex* differences because they probably derive partly from the social roles boys and girls begin learning early in the preschool years. Part of the role differences includes how preschool children spend their time. Preschool boys do spend more time than girls in active and rough-and-tumble play, and girls spend more time doing quiet activities such as drawing or playing with stuffed animals. Children of both sexes, furthermore, reinforce or support one another more for engaging in gender-typed activities, behavioral shaping that is often less flexible for boys than for girls (Davies, 1991; Kite, Deaux, & Haines, 2008). These differences may create the twin impressions that boys are less capable of fine motor skills and that girls are physically weaker, or at least are less inclined toward gross motor activity.

Variations in Motor Skill Development

Although the preceding sections may have implied that young children acquire motor skills at highly similar rates, in reality they show considerable variability in both fundamental and fine motor skill development. At age three, some children already can walk fast and catch a ball skillfully, but others are still having trouble with both tasks. At age five, some children can use scissors skillfully to cut out shapes for kindergarten art projects, but others still find scissors difficult or even mystifying. Whatever the motor skill, individual children will vary at it.

Like other human differences, these probably result from variations in experience, motivation, and biological endowment. Because of family background or preschool educational experiences, some children may be encouraged more than usual toward active play. Not surprisingly, they develop the skills for active play—like running, jumping, or throwing—sooner than children who experience less encouragement for active play. Weight also plays a role. Children who are overweight or obese lag behind their normal-weight peers in gross motor skills—a gap that grows over time (D'Hondt et al., 2013). Research has demonstrated that children with parents who engage in more physical activity, particularly if that activity is with their children, are more active, skilled, and healthy (Hinkley et al., 2008; Loprinzi & Trost, 2010; Spurrier et al., 2008).

Experience also plays a large role in drawing or other fine-motor activities. Some children receive more encouragement and opportunity than others. Early successes breed satisfaction with the emerging skills and encourage the development of motivation to refine the initial skills further. Before long, as we saw earlier in the case of gender differences in motor skill development, small initial differences in opportunity and skill become larger differences in skill and motivation.

Biological and genetic background probably also plays a role in motor skill development, although for most children it is hard to sort out how strong these influences are. The most obvious evidence for biological influence—as well as for the questionability of its importance—is the experiences of children with physical disabilities. A child born with cerebral palsy (a disorder of the nervous system that impairs motor coordination) may not

On the average, boys and girls develop motor skills at almost the same rate during the preschool years, but marked differences emerge among individuals within each sex, even at this age.
Source: ESB Professional/Shutterstock.com.

Chapter 8 Physical and Cognitive Development during Early Childhood

> **What Do You Think?**
>
> Suppose you are a childcare center worker, and one of your four-year-olds seems to be especially clumsy at throwing and catching a ball. Should you do something about this, and if so, what should you do? Consult with a classmate for a second opinion. Would you feel the same way if the child seemed clumsy or "uninspired" at drawing?

learn to walk, jump, throw, or draw at the same times or to the same extent as a child who never experiences this condition. Yet contrary to common stereotypes of children with disorders, the motor development of a child with cerebral palsy is *not* determined solely by the disorder; it is also determined by the child's opportunities and encouragement to learn new motor skills. The final motor achievements of children with this disorder will show diversity just as will the achievements of peers without disorders, and some of the diversity will be the result of education, not biology (Smith, 1998).

The Impact of Children's Growth on Adults

Even though physical growth unfolds largely independently of other forms of development in infancy, growth interacts indirectly in a number of ways with a child's social relationships. A child's physical appearance and particular motor skills can affect how adults and older children respond to the child. A family's attitudes, as well as their economic and social circumstances, can affect opportunities for children to acquire physical skills, and constrain opportunities as well.

Effects of Appearance

From birth—and despite the biases from their own parents—children vary in how attractive their faces seem to adults and other children. As a rule, some individuals look younger than others of the same age. In general, having a young-looking face depends on having large features and a large forehead; that is, facial features should be wide-set and located relatively low on the front of the skull. Even slight changes in these proportions—just a fraction of an inch—can make an adult seem many years older or younger, an infant seem six months older or younger, or a preschooler seem one or two years older or younger.

In general, younger-looking children are also rated as more attractive than older-looking children by both adults and peers, and adults tend to expect more mature behaviors from older-looking children (Parsons, Young, Kumari, Stein, & Kringelbach, 2011). This coincidence of stereotypes—of youthfulness and attractiveness—may contribute to differences in how parents and other adults respond to preschoolers as individuals. Parents and other caregivers need to be made aware of these possibilities, even if differences in response stem partly from innate human reactions to infantile (or babylike) appearance.

Effects of Motor Skills

Consider the changes in size that preschool children experience. A two-year-old often is still small enough to be handled. When necessary, parents can pick up and move a child from one place to another, physically removing the child from danger, and carrying the child (at least partway) if a distance is too far. By age five, a child often has outgrown these physical interactions, not only figuratively but literally. Parents or other adults may still lift and cuddle the child sometimes in play or in an emergency, but they probably are beginning to avoid doing so on a regular basis. To a significant extent, the child may now simply be too bulky and tall. More and more rarely can parents save the child from danger by picking the child up or by speeding the child along a long hallway by carrying the child piggyback. Parents must somehow get children to do these things for themselves.

Usually, of course, parents succeed at this task. By age five, a child can think and talk about her own actions much more than before, and these improvements help guide her own actions.

The handling that used to be literal now becomes mostly figurative. Now *handling* means negotiating and discussing with the child rather than lifting her up or carting her around.

Improvements in motor skills also change the agenda for a child's daily activities. A two-year-old may spend a good part of his day experimenting with fundamental skills: walking from one room to another, tearing toilet paper to shreds, or taking pots and pans out of a cupboard. These activities often are embedded in an active social and cognitive life: the child may smile (or frown) at his parents while he works and may "talk" about what he is doing as well. But the motor aspects of his activities absorb a significant part of his attention throughout the day. The child may return repeatedly to a staircase, for instance, as though compelled to get the hang of climbing it; no reward needs to lie at the top step except the satisfaction of a job well done.

A two-year-old's parents therefore must spend a lot of time ensuring that the child comes to no physical harm during motor explorations. They must make sure the child does not fall down the stairs, tumble into the toilet bowl, or discover a sharp knife among the pots. Their role as safety experts can dominate their contacts with the child, particularly if the child is active. Table 8.3 lists common accidents, remedies, and preventions.

By the end of early childhood, minute-to-minute physical surveillance recedes in importance, even though, of course, a concern about safety remains. Rules about dangers make their appearance ("Don't climb on that fence; it's rickety"), along with the hope that a five-year-old can remember and follow the rules at least some of the time. The shift toward rules also results from increasing confidence in the child's motor skills. Now parents are apt to believe their child can go up and down stairs without stumbling very often—and they are usually right.

During the preschool period, many parents discover a special need for patience in their dealings with their children. Simple actions such as tying shoelaces or putting on socks may take longer than before, simply because children now insist on doing many of these things themselves. For similar reasons, walking to the store may now take longer; a three- or four-year-old may prefer to push the stroller rather than ride in it, thus slowing everyone down. And preschoolers may have their own agenda on a walk, such as noticing little rocks on the sidewalk or airplanes in the sky, which differ from parents' goals. On good days, these behaviors offer some of the joys of raising children, but on bad days, they often irritate even the most patient of parents.

Effects of Differences in Families

A child's growth has a different impact on adults depending on the priorities of parents and on the circumstances of the family and community to which the child belongs. What

The new motor skills that preschoolers develop bring new risks and create new safety concerns for parents and other caregivers. What hazards may be waiting for this boy? And how should adults deal with them?
Source: Viacheslav Nikolaenko/Shutterstock.com.

TABLE 8.3 Common Accidents, Remedies, and Preventions among Preschoolers

Accidents	What to Do	How to Prevent
Drowning	Unless you are trained in water safety, extend a stick or other device. Use heart massage and mouth-to-mouth breathing when and as long as needed.	Teach children to swim as early in life as possible. Supervise children's swim sessions closely. Have children stay in shallow water.
Choking on small objects	If a child is still breathing, do not attempt to remove object; see a doctor instead. If breathing stops, firmly strike child twice on small of back. If this does not help, grab child from behind, put your fist just under his or her ribs, and pull upward sharply several times.	Do not allow children to put small objects in their mouths. Teach them to eat slowly, taking small bites. Forbid vigorous play with objects or food in mouth.
Cuts with serious bleeding	Raise cut above level of heart; apply pressure with cloth or bandage. If necessary, apply pressure to main arteries of limbs.	Remove sharp objects from play areas. Insist on shoes wherever ground or floor may contain sharp objects. Supervise children's use of knives.
Fractures	Keep injured limb immobile; see a doctor.	Discourage climbing and exploring in dangerous places, such as trees and construction sites. Allow bicycles only in safe areas.
Burns	Pour cold water over burned area; keep it clean; then cover with *sterile* bandage. See a doctor if burn is extensive.	Keep matches out of reach of children. Keep children well away from fires and hot stoves.
Poisons	On skin or eye, flush with plenty of water. If in stomach, phone poison control center doctor for instructions. Induce vomiting only for selected substances.	Keep dangerous substances out of reach of children. Throw away poisons when no longer needed. Keep syrup of ipecac in home to induce vomiting, but use *only* if advised by doctor.
Animal bites	Clean and cover with bandage; see a doctor.	Train children when and how to approach family pets. Teach them caution in approaching unfamiliar animals.
Insect bites	Remove stinger, if possible. Cover with paste of bicarbonate of soda (for bees) or a few drops of vinegar (for wasps and hornets).	Encourage children to recognize and avoid insects that sting, as well as their nests. Encourage children to remain calm in the presence of stinging insects.
Poisonous plants (e.g., poison ivy)	Remove affected clothing. Wash affected skin with strong alkali soap as soon as possible.	Teach children to recognize toxic plants. Avoid areas where poisonous plants grow.

Source: Adapted from O'Keefe (1998).

seems like a risky behavior to one parent (e.g., climbing up on a large boulder) may seem like constructive skill building to another, with consequent differences in encouragement or prohibitions for the child. What seems like a healthy amount of weight for a child to one parent may seem skinny (or plump) to another, with consequent differences in parents' unconscious appraisals of the child's attractiveness.

But settings and circumstances matter as well. In families with many children and few adults, child minding may become the responsibility of older siblings as much as (or more than) of adults. In extended families—those with nonparental relatives living at home or nearby—child minding may become partly the responsibility of other adult relatives. If parents work (or if a single parent works), relatives or other "caregivers for hire" take on much of the responsibility. All of these circumstances alter the settings in which preschoolers grow and the relationships that become prominent during early childhood. Some settings may provide the child with safer places for physical exploration than do other settings, resulting in fewer worries about safety expressed by caregivers. Some families may include so many children that differences in a particular child's physical

> **What Do You Think?**
>
> How did your own parents' work schedules, the number of children in your family, and family finances influence the joy or irritation they experienced? Did the *number* of parents raising you (one or more than one) make a difference?

appearance make little difference simply because caregivers are distributing their attention widely among many children or activities. Individual parents may or may not be aware that alternatives to their particular childcare arrangements exist, and because they often have not participated in the alternatives, they may find them hard to appreciate. But the range of childcare arrangements is very real, as is the range of opportunities they offer to young children (Cannella, 1997).

From Preschooler to Child

The physical changes we have talked about in this chapter create new relationships with parents and other caregivers, who in turn stimulate further changes. Preschoolers' new motor skills may stimulate adults to encourage various talents actively and with more focus than before. Once catching and throwing make their appearance, playing ball becomes a possibility; once scribbling stabilizes, skillful and interesting drawing seems just around the corner. And so parents and other interested adults encourage children toward these new skills, among others. Sometimes, the teaching and learning seem easier now, too, because adults no longer have to monitor a child's every move and can concentrate increasingly on the goals of movements. Just a few years before, "one false step" might have meant a child would literally fall. But now, this term has become only a metaphor for mistakes in general, not for physical mishaps specifically.

The cognitive developments of early childhood are equally influential on relationships, and we will investigate these changes in the next chapter.

Chapter Summary

- **What pathway does physical growth normally take during early childhood?** Between the ages of two and five, growth slows down and children take on more adultlike bodily proportions. Usually growth is rather smooth during the preschool period, though genetic, social, and nutritional differences can affect growth to some extent. Children's appetites often are smaller in the preschool years than in infancy, and children become more selective about what they eat.
- **How is poverty related to children's health?** The general health of a child is associated with the economic resources of the child's family, with higher-SES preschoolers tending to be healthier than lower-SES preschoolers. A number of possible causes for the association exist, including greater access to health care among well-off families.
- **When do children achieve bladder control?** Children tend to achieve daytime bladder control early in the preschool period. Nighttime bladder control tends to come later in the period.
- **What motor skills do children acquire during the preschool years?** Preschoolers acquire and refine many fundamental motor skills, including walking, jumping, throwing, and catching. Fine motor skills such as drawing also emerge during this period, progressing from prerepresentational to representational drawings. Children vary in motor skill development because of both their biological endowment and their experiences.
- **How does children's growth affect parents and other adults?** Preschoolers' changing facial features, size, and motor skills influence parents' responses and methods of childrearing to some extent. Because of differences in circumstances, families respond uniquely to differences in children's growth.

Key Terms

fine motor coordination (p. 191)

Cognitive Development during Early Childhood

CHAPTER 9

Source: Monkey Business Images/Shutterstock.com.

Chapter Outline

COGNITIVE DEVELOPMENT
Thinking among Preschoolers
Language Acquisition during the Preschool Years
Language Variations
Early Childhood Education
From Preschooler to Child

Focusing Questions

- What are the special features and strengths of preschoolers' thinking?
- How does the language of preschool children differ from that of older children?
- What social and cultural factors account for variations in preschoolers' language and speech?
- What constitutes good early childhood education?

COGNITIVE DEVELOPMENT

In addition to their physical changes, preschool children develop new abilities to represent objects and experiences. They begin to notice, for example, that their particular way of viewing the objects across a room differs from the perspective of a family member already sitting on the other side. They begin to distinguish between appearances and reality; that is, when you cover a doll with a costume, it still is "really" the same doll. And they become able to communicate new understandings such as these to others. The changes are in thinking, or *cognition,* and are called *cognitive development*.

Thinking among Preschoolers

Much of the research on cognitive development owes its intellectual roots to the observations and theorizing of Jean Piaget. During the 1960s and 1970s, considerable effort went toward testing his ideas about cognitive development. Overall, the research led first to modifications of, and in some cases, challenges to, Piaget's major proposals, such as the existence of comprehensive cognitive stages that unfold in a predictable order or the idea that thinking is really an individual activity rather than a social one. To put these later findings in proper context, however, we must first keep in mind Piaget's key ideas about the changes young children experience during the preschool years.

Piaget's Preoperational Stage

At about age two, according to Piaget, children enter a new stage in their cognitive development (Piaget, 1963; Wadsworth, 1996). Infancy has left them with several important accomplishments, such as the belief that objects have a permanent existence and the capacity to set and follow simple goals, such as emptying all the clothes from every drawer in the house. Infancy has also left them with the knowledge that all of their senses register the same world; now a child knows that hearing his mother in the next room means that he will probably see her soon and that seeing her probably also means he will hear from her.

preoperational stage In Piaget's theory, the stage of cognition characterized by increasing use of symbolic thinking but not yet by logical groupings of concepts.

The **preoperational stage**, roughly ages two through seven, extends and transforms these skills. During this stage, children become increasingly proficient at using *symbols*—words or actions that stand for other things. During this period, they also extend their belief in object permanence to include *identities,* or constancies, of many types: a candle remains the same even as it grows shorter from burning, and a plant growing on the windowsill remains the same plant, even though its growth changes its appearance from day to day.

Preoperational children also sense many *functional relationships,* or variations in their environments that normally occur together. Preschool children usually know that the hungrier they are, the more they will want to eat; the bigger they are, the stronger they tend to be; and the faster they walk, the sooner they will arrive somewhere. Of course, they still do not know the precise functions or relationships in these examples—exactly how *much* faster they will arrive if they walk a particular distance more quickly—but they do know that a relationship exists.

These are all cognitive strengths of preschool children, and they mark cognitive advances over infancy. But as the *pre-* in the term *preoperational* implies, Piaget's original theorizing actually focused on the limitations of young children's thinking relative to that of school-age children. The term *operations* referred to mental actions that allow a child to reason about events he or she experiences. Piaget's observations suggested that from age two to seven,

The play of preschoolers often relies on their growing abilities to represent objects and events symbolically. A cardboard box becomes a car, and the porch becomes a racetrack.
Source: Orange-studio/Shutterstock.com.

children often confuse their own points of view with those of other people, cannot classify objects and events logically, and often are misled by single features of their experiences. As later sections of this chapter point out, however, more recent research has substantially qualified this perspective; in essence, it has found that children often are more cognitively astute than Piaget realized. Their specific cognitive skills are all based on a key ability that Piaget *did* recognize: the ability to represent experiences symbolically.

Symbolic Thought

As we just noted, *symbols* are words, objects, or behaviors that stand for something else. They take this role not because of their intrinsic properties but because of the intentions of the people who use them. A drinking straw is just a hollow tube and does not become a symbol until a preschooler places it in the middle of a mound of sand and declares it to be a birthday candle. Likewise, the sound /bahks/ lacks symbolic meaning unless we all agree that it refers to a hollow object with corners: *box*.

Probably the most significant cognitive achievement of the preoperational period is the emergence and elaboration of **symbolic thought**, the ability to think by making one object or action stand for another. Throughout their day, two-year-olds use language symbolically, such as when they say "Milk!" to procure a white, drinkable substance from the refrigerator. They also use symbolic thought in make-believe play by pretending to be people or creatures other than themselves. By about age four, children's symbolic play often combines complex actions (getting down on all fours), objects (using a table napkin for a saddle), language (shouting "Neigh!"), and coordination with others (getting a friend to be a rider).

Symbolic thinking helps preschool children organize and process what they know (Carlson & Beck, 2009; Goldman, 1998; Nelson, 1996). Objects and experiences can be recalled more easily if they have names and compared more easily if the child has concepts that can describe their features. Symbols also help children communicate what they know to others, even in situations quite different from the experience itself. Having gone to the store, they can convey this experience to others either in words ("I went shopping") or through pretend play ("Let's play school, and I'll be the teacher."). By its nature, communication fosters social relationships among children, but it also fosters cognitive development by allowing individual children to learn from the experiences of others. More precisely, communication allows individuals to learn from the symbolic representations of others' experiences.

symbolic thought Mentally using one thing to represent something else.

Egocentrism in Preschool Children

Egocentrism refers to the tendency of a person to confuse his or her own point of view and that of another person. The term does not necessarily imply selfishness at the expense of others, but a centering on the self in thinking. Young children often show egocentrism in this sense, but not always. Piaget illustrated their egocentrism by showing children a table on which models of three mountains had been constructed and asking them how a doll would see the three mountains if it sat at various positions around the table. Three-year-olds (the ones in Piaget's preoperational stage) commonly believed the doll saw the layout no differently than they did (Piaget & Inhelder, 1967).

On the other hand, when the task concerns more familiar materials and settings, even preschool children adopt others' spatial perspectives (Steiner, 1987). For example, instead of using Piaget's three-mountain model, suppose we use a "police officer" doll that is searching for a "child" doll and place them among miniature barriers that sometimes obscure the dolls' "view" of each other and sometimes do not. When these procedures are followed, four-year-olds have relatively little difficulty knowing when the two dolls can "see" each other and when the barriers truly are "in the way."

In oral communication, preschoolers also show distinct but incomplete egocentrism. A variety of studies have documented that preschoolers often explain tasks rather poorly to others, even though their language and understanding are otherwise skillful enough to explain them better (Nelson, 1996). Copying a simple diagram according to instructions from a preschooler can prove next to impossible, no matter how sensitive the listener is. On the other hand, preschool children do show awareness of the needs of a listener. They

egocentrism Inability to distinguish between one's own point of view and that of another person.

Chapter 9 Cognitive Development during Early Childhood

explain a drawing more clearly, for example, to a listener who is blindfolded, apparently because the blindfold emphasizes the listener's need for more complete information.

In these studies, young children show both similarity to and difference from the adults they will become. All of us, young or old, show egocentrism at times; indeed, our own thinking is often the only framework on which we can base our actions and conversations with others, at least initially. As we mature, though, we learn more about others' thoughts, views, and feelings, as well as more about how to express ourselves more precisely. In these ways, we (hopefully!) differ from four-year-olds.

Other Aspects of Children's Conceptual Development

Along with their symbolic skills, preschool children develop specific cognitive skills. They become able to classify objects, and by the end of the early childhood period, some can even attend to changes in objects involving more than one feature at a time. They move beyond rote counting to a meaningful understanding of the concept of *number*. They also acquire an intuitive sense of the differences among fundamentally different types of concepts, such as the difference between a living dog and a toy robot made to act like a dog.

Classification Skills

classification Grouping of objects according to standards or criteria.

Classification refers to the placement of objects in groups or categories according to some specific standards or criteria. Young preschool children, even those just three years old, can reliably classify objects that differ in just one dimension, or feature, especially if that dimension presents fairly obvious contrasts. Given a collection of pennies and nickels, a preschooler usually can sort them by color, which is their most obvious dimension of difference. Given a boxful of silverware, a young child might sort the items by type: knives, forks, and spoons. Or she might group dishes by how they are used in real life, putting each cup with one saucer rather than separating all the cups from all the saucers. These simple groupings represent cognitive advances over infancy.

Reversibility and Conservation

reversibility Ability to return mentally to earlier steps in a problem.

conservation A belief that certain properties (such as quantity) remain constant, despite changes in perceived features, such as dimensions, position, and shape.

Some classification problems require **reversibility** in thinking, or the ability to undo a problem mentally and go back to its beginning. If you accidentally drop a pile of papers on the floor, you may be annoyed, but you know that in principle the papers are all there: you believe (correctly) that the papers that have scattered can be "unscattered" if you pick them up and sort them into their correct order again. Reversibility, it turns out, contributes to a major cognitive achievement of middle childhood: **conservation**, or the ability to perceive that certain properties of an object remain the same or constant despite changes in the object's appearance. On average, children do not achieve conservation until about age six.

To understand reversibility and conservation, consider the task shown in Figure 9.1. First, you show a preschool child two tall glasses with exactly the same amount of water in each. Then the child watches you pour the water from one of the glasses into a third, wide glass. Naturally, the water line in the wide glass will be lower than it was in the tall one. Finally, you ask the child, "Is there more water in the wide glass than in the [remaining] tall glass, or less, or just as much?"

Children less than five years old typically say that the tall glass has either less or more water than the wide glass, but not that the two glasses are the same. According to Piaget, this happens because the child forgets the identity of the water levels seen only a moment earlier; in this sense, the child is a nonreversible thinker and cannot imagine pouring the water back again to prove the glasses' equality. Instead, the child is limited to current appearances. More often than not, a big difference in appearance leads a child to say that the amount of water changes as a result of its being poured. In Piagetian terms, the child fails to conserve, or to believe in the constancy of the amount of liquid, despite its visible changes (Inhelder & Piaget, 1958). Not until the early school years do conservation and reversibility become firmly established.

First, you show a preschool child two tall glasses with exactly the same amount of water in each.

Then the child watches you pour water from one of the glasses into a third, wide glass.

Finally, you ask the child, "Is there more water in the wide glass than in the (remaining) tall glass, or less, or just as much?"

A child who lacks reversibility (is nonconserving) in thinking about liquids says either, "The tall glass has more," or "The wide glass has more." The child is fooled by its appearance.

FIGURE 9.1
Conservation of Liquid Quantity

Does a child believe that liquid quantity remains constant (is "conserved"), despite changes in its shape? The method illustrated here, or some variation of it, is often used to answer this question.

In the meantime, tasks that require conservation are affected significantly by how they are presented or described to the child. When given a series of conservation tasks, for example, a child tends to alternate conserving with nonconserving responses (Elbers et al., 1991). Why? Perhaps repeating the question makes some children believe that the experimenter wants them to change their response; after all, why else would she repeat herself? Because most children begin the conservation task by agreeing that the glasses hold equal amounts of water, obliging children may feel compelled to give nonconserving responses against their own better judgment. It seems, therefore, that children may take Piagetian tasks as social events, as well as cognitive ones.

The Concept of Number

Like many parents, Piaget correctly noted that children do not fully grasp how the conventional number system works during the first few years of life (Piaget, 1952). Preschoolers may, of course, count, such as when a three-year-old says, "One, two, three, blast off!" before tossing a ball high into the air. But such counting, Piaget argued, lacks understanding; it essentially is a rote activity, though children as young as two or three understand the *magnitude* of numbers, which is demonstrated when a child asks for "more" or "a lot more" when a parent is doling out a treat (Ginsburg, Cannon, Eisenband, & Pappas, 2008). To fully understand the concept of number, a child must comprehend three ideas. The first is that a one-to-one correspondence exists between items in a set and number names. The second is *cardinality,* the idea that the total number of a set corresponds to the last number named when the items are counted. And the third is *ordinality,* the concept that numbers always occur in a particular order (the second item to be counted is always called the "second," for example).

Research stimulated by these ideas about number generally has concluded that Piaget underestimated preschoolers' knowledge of number. Many four-year-olds, and even some three-year-olds, can reliably say the numbers in sequence, at least up to some modest limit such as *five* or *six.* They also know that different sets of items should be counted with the same sequence of numbers, that each item should be counted only once, and that any set can be counted in more than one order. For this and other reasons, some psychologists have argued that children may have an innate conception of number, or at least that they can learn underlying notions of number from appropriate experiences during infancy (Case, 1998; Ginsburg et al., 2008; Kirschner, 1997).

Cognition as Social Activity

Variations in cognitive performance occur partly because young children depend on the social context or circumstances to develop new thinking skills. In spite of our stereotypes of thinking as a solitary, independent activity, children learn not only from interacting with objects and the physical environment but also from interacting with adults or others with more

situated cognition Thinking that occurs jointly with others and is embedded in a particular context or activity setting.

social constructivism A theory that views learning as resulting from active dialogue and interaction between an individual and his or her community.

activity settings Group situations in which a shared focus of attention and shared goals facilitates an individual's learning from others in the group.

zone of proximal development According to Vygotsky, the level of difficulty at which problems are too hard for children to solve alone but not too hard when given support from adults or more competent peers.

Much cognitive change occurs because of the mutual development of meaning that happens in the "zone of proximal development," where two people focus on a common activity. In this case, the mother stimulates her daughter to learn about cooking, and the daughter stimulates the mother to learn about the daughter's growing knowledge and abilities.
Source: Dragon Images/Shutterstock.com.

experience. Psychologists who study this sort of thinking often call it **situated cognition** and call their perspective **social constructivism** (Kirschner & Whitson, 1997; Rogoff et al., 1993). A parent who is cooking dinner, for example, may invite a four-year-old to help with preparations, during which the child observes and works on a number of cognitive tasks: measuring amounts for ingredients, sequencing the steps in the preparations, attending to the time needed for each task. Interactions about the tasks being pursued in common form a context, or **activity setting**, for learning (Lave, 1997). In an activity setting, the older or less experienced individuals provide problems and activities, as well as tasks that allow a younger, less experienced person to become a legitimate—though perhaps marginal or peripheral—participant in the situation. When cooking, for example, the parent determines the menu and in other ways sets the agenda for the activity: "We will make X instead of Y tonight." The parent also provides tasks for the apprentice-cook (in this case, the child) to do. The tasks ensure that the child belongs or participates successfully, although they also provide only a marginal role for the child at first, in keeping with his or her immaturity and lack of experience with the challenges of cooking.

Viewed this way, thinking seems far less solitary than Piaget pictured it, and far more social. Children figure things out not by manipulating objects and observing the results of the manipulations but by interacting (in activity settings) with a community of people, including parents, teachers, and peers. In doing so, the young, inexperienced preschooler is able to work on problems or tasks that might prove too difficult to attempt alone; yet the support and guidance of others allow considerable success! The interactions that allow the child to succeed are sometimes called the **zone of proximal development** (or **ZPD**). The concept of the ZPD originated with the Russian psychologist Lev Vygotsky (Newman & Holzman, 1993; Vygotsky, 1978) and has created a lot of interest among developmental psychologists because it suggests ways in which knowledge and thinking skills may originate and evolve. Consider this conversation between a six-year-old girl and her grandfather, while the two sort some scrap lumber piled behind the grandfather's hardware business:

Grandfather: We have to put the spruce here and the pine over there.

Girl: Spruce here? (Tosses one piece, but to the wrong pile)

Grandfather: No, there. (Moves her piece to the correct pile)

Girl: What's this? (Notices letter S scribbled in pencil on a piece)

Grandfather: That's for *spruce*. Put it with the spruce.

Girl: (Pondering the letter S). Spruce. OK. (Tosses piece correctly) So this is pine? (Looks at a piece with a *P* written on it)

Grandfather: Yep. Put it over there. (The two continue sorting for a while. Girl examines each piece for letters. Eventually she finds one with no letter written on it.)

Girl: Someone should write the name on this one. (Notices a knothole in the piece) I think it's pine.

Grandfather: You're right about that. Here's a pencil. (Tosses her a pencil)

Girl: (Writes *P* on the piece of scrap pine.) Know what? I can write *pine*! (Smiles) I bet I can write *spruce*, too.

Grandfather: (Looks at the letter *P* she has written.) Yeah, says *pine* all right. You might say it says *pine*.

In this example, the grandfather (and his pile of scrap wood) provided an activity setting in which the girl learned about differences between two woods, spruce and pine, as well as a way to represent the differences with letters. Without his presence and comments, considered *scaffolding* by Vygotsky, she might not have succeeded as well in this task. On the other hand, the grandfather did not simply "teach" the girl how to sort wood or to read the letters *S* and *P,* as a teacher might conventionally do in a classroom. Instead, he provided a task needed in his world (sorting the scrap wood is part of his business) and a way to involve the girl in the task. The interactions create a zone of proximal development for the girl. When she makes a mistake, the grandfather either simply corrects it matter-of-factly (such as when she tosses a piece in the wrong pile) or revises his own goals temporarily to fit hers (such as when she claims, mistakenly, that she has spelled the whole word *pine* using only its first letter). At the beginning of the task, the girl needs more assistance, or scaffolding. However, as the girl comes to understand and, eventually, become an expert at the task, she needs less scaffolding, or assistance.

As you might suppose, the nature of the ZPD depends on the experiences and circumstances of the child. Parents with "bookish" interests, for example, and the resources and time to provide book-related activity settings will more often provide ZPDs that encourage bookish and school-oriented skills in their children. Those with an outgoing, social disposition will provide ZPDs that encourage interpersonal interest and sensitivity in their children. Yet, reproduction of parents' priorities is not inevitable. Much also depends on how a child interprets an activity setting. An opportunity to learn to play the piano, for example, can be experienced as either attractive or boring, or as either an invitation or burdensome drudgery. What is provided is not necessarily what the child takes up or appropriates (Cobb et al., 1997; Guralnick, 2008).

Neostructuralist Theories of Cognitive Development

As the studies described so far suggest, preschoolers show considerable new strengths in using symbolic thought. They can take others' perspectives to some extent, develop a usable theory of how the human mind works, and distinguish between appearances and reality at least some of the time. Many of Piaget's classic observations on Swiss children have proven true: preschool children do have trouble focusing on two dimensions of an object at once and therefore have difficulty with conservation tasks throughout most of the preschool period. Other Piagetian observations have underestimated children's ability and stimulated research that has led to new ways of thinking about children's capacities. For example, unlike Piaget's claims, preschool children have a partial understanding of number.

Research has complicated our picture of children's cognitive development. Many psychologists have sought to keep Piaget's commitment to stagelike progressions in development and at the same time revise the content or details of those progressions (Case, 1998). Instead of proposing comprehensive, "grand" stages of thinking, as Piaget did, they argue that stages may be much more focused in content. Research based on this premise has, in fact, identified stages of spatial representation, of shapes, of mathematical ability, of patterns, and of interpersonal awareness, among others (Case, 1992; Ginsburg et al., 2008). Each of these skills seems to develop through predictable stages, but do so independently of the other domains. As individuals, children therefore show unique patterns and timing of development across many areas of thinking and skills (Wozniak & Fischer, 1993).

This newer view of cognitive stages is sometimes called **neostructuralist theory**, or *neo-Piagetian theory* because of its roots in the ideas of Piaget. As a result of focusing attention on more specific cognitive achievements, it has also paid more attention to *how*, or by what processes, children acquire new cognitive skills. One neostructuralist line of research explored the process of learning to draw by noting how it consists of the successive coordination of simpler skills (Dennis, 1992). Natalia begins her second year of life able to visually track objects as well as reach for objects. With practice, by the time she reaches age three, Natalia has learned to coordinate these two schemes into a single cognitive skill that enables scribbling. As she continues to practice with this newly consolidated scheme, she begins coordinating it with other, more advanced schemes, such as *comparing* scribbles with the orientation and edges of the paper. When tracking edges of a paper and tracking scribbles eventually become coordinated, Natalia can finally begin controlling lines and curves. Now the stage is set for her first representational drawings, such as stick-figure people.

From the neostructuralist perspective, then, cognitive development during early childhood is not all of one piece when it unfolds but has many components—many forms of

neostructuralist theory Relates to recent theories of cognition that emphasize the structure or organization of thinking.

> **What Do You Think?**
>
> What do you think parents of young children *believe* about preschoolers' cognitive abilities? What if you asked parents (1) how much their *children* know when *parents* are happy or upset and (2) would their children think that a clay ball was the same "amount" if it were squashed into a pancake shape? Would parents' expectations about these questions coincide with the research described in this section? If possible, interview a real-life parent or two to test your prediction.

thinking, as well as perceptual and language developments. As a result, it is important to understand each piece separately from the others and to combine them to get a well-rounded picture of young children. Therefore, in the next section we look at another major piece of the puzzle of children's thinking: language acquisition.

Language Acquisition during the Preschool Years

For most children, language expands rapidly after infancy. They learn words, form ever-longer sentences, and engage in more-complex dialogue. Fairly early in the preschool years, most children have mastered the basic sounds, or *phonology,* that make their first language meaningful and distinctive. They have also made a good beginning at acquiring a vocabulary of single words. We described both of these achievements in Chapter 6 in connection with infants' cognitive development. Now, during early childhood, children's most striking achievements involve *syntax,* or the way the child organizes utterances, and *pragmatics,* or knowledge about how to adjust utterances to the needs and expectations of different situations and speakers. As it turns out, these twin achievements show both diversity and uniformity across children, and therefore, they raise important questions about language acquisition and how parents and other caregivers can influence it. In this section, we look at these questions, beginning with preschoolers' achievements in the area of syntax.

The Nature of Syntax

syntax Rules for ordering and relating the elements of a language.

The **syntax** of a language is a group of rules for ordering and relating its elements. Linguists call the elements of language *morphemes. Morphemes* are the smallest meaningful units of language; they include words as well as a number of prefixes and suffixes that carry meaning (the /s/ in *houses* or the /re/ in *redo*) and verb-tense modifiers (the /ing/ in *going*).

Syntactic rules operate on morphemes in several ways. Sometimes, they mark important relationships between large classes or groups of words. Consider these two pairs of sentences:

1a. Roberto helped Barbara.	1b. Barbara helped Roberto.
2a. Frank helps Ruije.	2b. Frank helped Ruije.

These sentences differ in meaning because of syntactic rules. In the first pair, a rule about the order, or sequence, of words tells us who is giving the help and who is receiving it: the name preceding the verb is the agent (the helper), and the name following the verb is the recipient (the "helpee"). In the second pair, the morphemes /es/ and /ed/ tell something about when the event occurred; adding /es/ to the end of the word signifies that it is happening now, but adding /ed/ means it happened in the past. These rules, and many similar ones, are understood and used by all competent speakers of the language. Unlike textbook authors, however, the speakers may never state them and may be only barely aware of them.

Unfortunately, for a child learning to talk, some syntactic rules have only a small range of application, and still others have irregular exceptions. Most words, for example, signal pluralization (the existence of more than one) by having an /s/ or /es/ added at the end; *book* means one volume, and *books* means more than one. But a few words use other methods to signal the plural. *Foot* means one, and *feet,* not *foots,* means more than one; *child* means one and *children* more than one; and *deer* can mean either one animal or several.

Thus, in acquiring syntax, a young child confronts a mixed system of rules. Some apply widely and regularly, and others apply narrowly and exceptionally. Added to these complexities is the fact that the child often hears utterances that are grammatically incomplete or even incorrect. Somehow, he or she must sort these out from the grammatically acceptable utterances while at the same time trying to sort out the various syntactic rules and the contexts for using them.

Beyond First Words: Semantic and Syntactic Relations

Before age two, children begin linking words when they speak. Initially the words seem to be connected by their *semantic relations,* or the meanings intended for them, rather than by *syntactic relations,* the relations among grammatical classes of words such as nouns, verbs, and adjectives. This is particularly true when the child is still speaking primarily in two-word utterances (sometimes called *duos).* As the mean length of a child's utterances increases to three words and more, syntactic relations become much more noticeable.

Duos and Telegraphic Speech

These ideas were documented in a classic set of three case studies of early language acquisition by Roger Brown (1973). When the children Brown observed were still speaking primarily in two-word utterances, their utterances were organized around eight possible semantic relationships; these are listed in Table 9.1, along with examples. The meanings of the utterances were determined by the intended relationships among the words, and the intentions of the preschool speakers often were discernible only by observing the context in which the utterances were made. "Mommy sandwich" could mean "the type of sandwich Mommy usually eats," or "Mommy is eating the sandwich," or "Mommy, give me a sandwich," all depending on the conversational context.

The reason for the ambiguity is that two-word utterances leave out indicators of syntactic relationships. One syntactic indicator is word order: due to word order, "the boy chased the girl" means something different than "the girl chased the boy." Children who still speak in duos do not use word order randomly, but they do tend to be less predictable about it than more linguistically mature children, whose utterances can be several words long. Another indicator of syntactic relationships is inflections, prepositions, and conjunctions. An older child will add *'s* to indicate possession (as in "Mommy's sandwich") and use words such as *in* and *on* to indicate location (as in "jump on the stair"). Leaving these indicators out makes

TABLE 9.1 Semantic Relations in Two-Word Utterances
A child's earliest utterances are organized not according to adultlike grammar but according to particular semantic or meaning-oriented relationships such as those listed in this table. Often the intended, underlying relationships are ambiguous and can be discerned only by an attentive, observant adult at the time of the utterance.

Relationship	Example
Agent + action	Baby cry
Action + object	Eat cookie
Agent + object	Bobby cookie
Action + locative (location)	Jump stair
Object + locative	Teddy bed
Possessor + possessed	Mommy sandwich
Attribute + object	Big dog
Demonstrative + object	There Daddy

holographic speech When a single word is used to communicate a thought, such as when a child says "up" instead of "pick me up."

the speech sound stilted and ambiguous; therefore, it is also called **holographic speech** or *telegraphic speech*—presumably because it sounds like a telegram. Telegraphic speech is characteristic of children's first efforts to combine words (around eighteen months to two years), but it can persist well after children begin using longer, more syntactic utterances some of the time.

Regularities and Overgeneralizations

After highly individual beginnings, certain aspects of syntax develop in universal and predictable patterns. English-speaking children have a tendency to know more nouns than verbs, a bias that is not as marked among children learning languages such as Korean or Mandarin. In many Asian languages, verbs end sentences, likely making them "stick out" to the children (Hoff, 2008). The present progressive form *-ing* occurs quite early in most children's language, the regular plural morphemes *-s* and *-es* somewhat later, and articles such as *the* and *a* still later (Hoff, 2008; Marcus et al., 1992).

At a slightly older age, most English-speaking children begin using auxiliary verbs to form questions, but they do so without inverting word order, as adults normally do. At first, a child will say, "Why you are cooking?" and only later "Why are you cooking?" This suggests that language acquisition involves more than just copying adult language; after all, adults rarely model incorrect forms. To a certain extent, children's language seems to compromise between the new forms children hear and the old forms they already can produce easily.

Sometimes, in fact, early syntax becomes *too* regular, and children make **overgeneralizations**. Around age three, preschool children often make errors, such as always adding *–ed* to indicate past tense, even when it is not appropriate as in the sentence: "I runned faster than Maddie." The child uses the wrong but more regular form as opposed to the correct but irregular forms of an earlier age. Usually by early school age, they shift back again, although not necessarily because anyone teaches or forces them to do so. Apparently, their overgeneralizations represent efforts to try out new rules of syntax that they have finally noticed.

overgeneralizations When children use common rules of speaking in all situations, even when inappropriate, such as adding *–s* to indicate a plural form such as, "Do you see all the deers?"

The Predisposition to Infer Grammar

As these examples suggest, and as research confirms (Marcus et al., 1992), young children seem to infer grammatical relationships, rather than simply copy others' speech. The tendency was first documented about sixty years ago in a research study by Hilda Berko (1958), but it is still used in many current tests of children's language development (Brindle, 2015; McDaniel et al., 1996). Instead of asking children about real words, the experimenter in Berko's classic study showed them pictures of imaginary creatures and actions that had nonsense words as names. With one picture, a child was told, "Here is a wug." Then he was shown two pictures and told, "Here are two of them. Here are two_____." Most children, even those as young as two and a half, completed the sentences with the grammatically correct word, *wugs*. Because they could not possibly have heard the term before, they must have applied a general rule for forming plurals, one that did not depend on copying any language experiences specifically but came from inferring the underlying structure of many experiences taken together. The rule most likely operated unconsciously because these children were very young indeed.

The Limits of Learning Rules

Preschoolers' skill at acquiring syntactic rules, however, obscures a seemingly contradictory fact about the acquisition of syntax: much syntax must be learned by rote. As we have pointed out, most children use irregular forms (such as *foot/feet*) correctly before they shift to incorrect but more regular forms. The most reasonable explanation for the change is that they pick up the very first sentence forms simply by copying, word for word, the sentences they hear spoken. Presumably, they copy many regular forms by rote, too, but the very regularity of these forms hides the haphazard, unthinking way in which children acquire them.

Although children eventually rely on rule-governed syntax, they probably still learn a lot of language by rote. Many expressions in a language are *idiomatic,* meaning they bear no logical relation to normal meanings or syntax. The sentence "How do you do?", for example, usually is not a literal inquiry as to how a person performs a certain action; and the sentence "How goes it?", meaning "How is it going?", does not even follow the usual rules of grammar. Because words and phrases such as these violate the rules of syntax and meaning, children must learn them one at a time.

Mechanisms of Language Acquisition

Exactly how do children learn to speak? For most children, several factors may operate at once. In general, current evidence can best be summarized as follows: language seems to grow through the interaction of an active, thinking child with certain key people and linguistic experiences. The preceding sections describe in part this active, thinking child; the upcoming sections describe some possible key interaction experiences.

Reinforcement

A commonsense view, one based essentially on behaviorist principles, is that children learn to speak through reinforcement. According to this idea, a child's caregivers reinforce vocal noises whenever they approximate a genuine word or utterance, and this reinforcement causes the child to vocalize in increasingly correct (or at least adultlike) ways (Skinner, 1957). In the course of babbling, an infant may happen to say "Ma-ma-ma-ma," to which his proud parent smiles and replies cheerfully, "How nice! You said 'Mama'!" The praise reinforces the behavior, so the infant says "Ma-ma-ma-ma" more often after that. After many such experiences, parents begin to reinforce only closer approximations to *mama,* leading finally to a true version of this word. The process would be an example of *shaping,* discussed in Chapter 2 in connection with behavioral/learning theory.

Among preschool children, the same process could occur if parents reinforced correct grammatical forms and ignored or criticized errors or relatively immature utterances. Parents might respond more positively to the sentence "I have three feet" than to the sentence "I have two foots." According to the principles of reinforcement (see Chapter 2), the child would tend not only to use the correct version more often but also to generalize the correct elements of this sentence to other, similar utterances.

Analysis of conversations between parents and children confirms this possibility, at least in indirect form and for the early stages of language acquisition. One study compared parents' responses to simple but grammatical sentences made by their two- and three-year-old children to their responses to ungrammatical utterances (Penner, 1987). Parents did not correct their children's grammar directly, but they were more likely to elaborate on the child's topic if the utterance was a grammatical one.

Imitation and Practice

In some sense, children obviously must imitate their native language to acquire it. This is an idea borrowed from the social learning variety of behaviorism. In daily life, though, the process of imitation is subtle and often indirect. Children do not imitate everything they hear, but most copy certain selected utterances, often immediately after hearing them. Sometimes the utterances chosen for imitation involve familiar sentence forms that contain new, untried terms, and sometimes they contain familiar terms cast into new, untried forms. The imitated terms and forms return later in the child's spontaneous speech. At first, these utterances resemble the rote learning mentioned earlier, and they seem to help the child by emphasizing or calling attention to new morphemes and syntax.

Imitation may also help children acquire language by initiating playful practice with new expressions. The child in essence plays around with the new forms she learns and in doing so consolidates her recently acquired knowledge, just as she does in other forms of play, such as those discussed in Chapter 10. Because quite a bit of language play remains unobserved by adults, its extent is hard to judge, but a lot obviously does go on even in children as young as two years (Messer, 1994). Children ages eighteen to thirty months who had older siblings diagnosed with autism demonstrated delays in communication, language, gesturing, and social skills, suggesting that such imitation may be maladaptive as well (Toth, Dawson, Meltzoff, Greenson, & Fein, 2007).

Much learning happens through imitation and practice. These boys see both reading and social skills demonstrated by their grandmother and then practice the same skills themselves.
Source: rSnapshotPhotos/Shutterstock.com.

Innate Predisposition to Acquire Language: LAD

The ease and speed children show in acquiring language have caused some linguists and psychologists to conclude that children have an innate predisposition, or built-in tendency, to learn language (Chomsky, 1994). For convenience, the innate tendency is sometimes called the *language acquisition device,* or *LAD.* According to this viewpoint, LAD functions as a kind of inborn road map to language. It guides the child to choose appropriate syntactic categories as he tries to figure out the comparatively confusing examples of real speech that he ordinarily hears. It helps him find his way through the mazelike structure of language with relatively few major errors instead of having to explore and construct his own language map, as the Piagetian viewpoint implies.

The most persuasive reason for postulating the LAD is the *poverty of content* in the speech to which most infants and preschoolers are exposed. According to this argument, the language children encounter is too incomplete and full of everyday grammatical errors (too "impoverished") to serve as a satisfactory guide in learning the grammatical structure of the language (Baker, 1995). Parents sometimes speak in incomplete sentences, sometimes make grammatical errors, and sometimes do not speak at all when speaking might prove helpful to a child learning the language.

However, children who hear a wider variety of words have larger vocabularies that grow more quickly than children who hear fewer, more simple vocabularies (Hoff, 2008). But even in spite of any poverty of content children seem remarkably resilient in acquiring language. Children isolated from language through parental neglect, for example, have learned some language later in life, but their language usually is limited in amount and complexity. In a less tragic example, identical twins often create a private language that they speak only with each other. In many cases, their private language seems to delay normal language development, though the delay rarely causes serious lasting damage to their development (Mogford, 1993).

A final piece of evidence that a LAD exists is that preschool children do not simply copy their parents' language directly, yet they seem to figure out and use many of its basic syntactic relationships remarkably well. Berko's "wug" experiment discussed earlier illustrates this ability dramatically. In forming plurals they have never heard spoken before, children seem to demonstrate a grammatical skill that is more innate than learned.

The Limits of LAD

Although this evidence suggests that children have a built-in ability to acquire language, it does not show that experience plays no role at all. The evidence from twins and neglected children emphasizes just the opposite: that certain experiences with language may be crucial, especially early in life. Ordinarily, almost every preschooler encounters these experiences. They may consist of hearing others talk and of being invited to respond to others verbally. But the fact that they happen to everyone does not mean that children do not learn from them; it means only that what children learn is universal.

Furthermore, experiences affect the version of language children acquire, even when they supposedly grow up in the same language community. As pointed out earlier, children vary in the vocabulary they learn and in the grammar they use; even by age three or four, children often do not define grammatical categories as abstractly as adults do or necessarily in the same way other children do. Most preschoolers eventually revise their grammatical categories to coincide with conventional adult grammar, thus obscuring their individuality. But as we will see in Chapter 8, large differences persist in older children's styles of communicating, even after they have mastered the basic structure of language.

All things considered, the fairest conclusion we can draw is a moderate one: that children are both predisposed to acquire language and in need of particular experiences with it. Skill with language is neither given at birth nor divorced entirely from other cognitive development. A special talent for language may be given to all normal children, however, and many crucial experiences for developing that talent may happen to occur rather frequently among infants as they grow up.

Parent-Child Interactions

Certain kinds of verbal interactions apparently help children acquire language sooner and better. Parents can help by speaking in relatively short sentences to their preschoolers and using more concrete nouns than pronouns, though this also depends on whether the task or topic at hand calls for concrete or abstract ideas (Hoff-Ginsberg, 1997). For children under the age of eighteen months, parents can make sure that they respond to children's speech with information that relates to what the child is doing or experiencing (Hoff, 2008). In the following pair of comments, the first helps a child learn language more than the second does:

Parent 1: Take your shoes off. Then put your shoes in the closet. Then come kiss Mama goodnight.

Parent 2: After you take off your shoes and put them in the closet, come kiss me goodnight.

As we noted in Chapter 6, the simplified style of the first set of comments is one aspect of a version of language called **infant-directed speech**, or sometimes "motherese." Another aspect of this version is the use of a high-pitched voice. Infant-directed speech is used intuitively by adults with young children and even by older children with younger children (Messer, 1994).

One of the most helpful kinds of verbal interactions is *recasting* a child's utterances: repeating or reflecting back what the child says, but in slightly altered form. For instance:

infant-directed speech The style or register of speech used by adults and older children when talking with a one- or two-year-old infant.

Child: More milk.

Parent: You want more milk, do you?

Recasting helps because it highlights slight differences among ways of expressing an idea. In doing so, it may make the child more aware of how she expresses her idea—its form or organization—as well as call attention to the idea itself.

Most of the techniques for stimulating language development provide young preschoolers with a framework of language that simultaneously invites them to try new, unfamiliar language forms and simplifies and clarifies other aspects of language. Some psychologists call this framework *scaffolding* (Bruner, 1996; Reeder, 1996): like real scaffolds used in building construction, parents' language scaffolds provide a temporary structure within which young children can build their own language structures. As such, it functions much like Vygotsky's zone of proximal development mentioned earlier: helpful scaffolding changes and grows in response to the child's continuing development, always building a bit beyond the child's current independent abilities but never very far beyond.

Chapter 9 Cognitive Development during Early Childhood

> **What Do You Think?**
>
> Suppose that you were asked to speak to a parent group, and a parent complained about her four-year-old's use of poor grammar. What advice could you give to this parent? Rehearse your comments with a classmate to determine how appropriate they are.

These and similar findings have been translated into curricula for education of young children, particularly for those learning English as a second or third language (Proctor, Dalton, & Grisham, 2007) and even of infants (Spodek & Saracho, 1993). Fortunately, the most useful methods of interaction often are those that parents and teachers use intuitively anyway; training for them therefore really consists of emphasizing and refining their use.

Language Variations

Not surprisingly, parents vary in how they talk to their children, and these differences may influence the version of language children acquire as they grow up. It is unclear, however, how language variations affect other aspects of children's development, such as thinking ability. Let's consider three other sources of language variation: gender, socioeconomic status (SES), and hearing ability.

Gender Differences in Language

Within any one community, girls learn nearly the same syntax boys do, but they acquire very different pragmatics, or discourse patterns. Overall, the differences reflect society's gender stereotypes. For example, girls phrase requests indirectly more often than boys do; girls more often say, "Could you give that to me?" instead of "Give me that." Also, they more frequently expand on comments made by others, rather than initiating their own. These differences appear especially in mixed-gender groups and are noticeable not only among adults but also among children as soon as they are old enough to engage in conversation (Coates, 1993; Coates, 2015).

The sexes reinforce their language differences with certain nonverbal gestures and mannerisms. Girls and women tend to maintain more eye contact than boys and men do; they blink their eyelids at more irregular intervals and tend to nod their heads as they listen (Arliss, 1991). Boys and men use eye contact less in ordinary conversation, blink at regular intervals, and rarely nod their heads when listening.

Gender differences in discourse patterns may contribute to gender segregation: members of each gender may feel that members of the other gender do not really understand them, that they do not "speak the same language." Boys and girls therefore begin drifting apart during the preschool years, almost as soon as they begin using language (Ramsey, 1995), possibly due in part to acquiring language. The emerging segregation, in turn, reinforces gender differences in language patterns (Fagot, 1994). Boys reinforce one another for their assertive discourse style, and girls and their (mostly female) teachers reinforce one another for their "considerate" style. In the end, then, cognitive development supports social development, and social development supports cognitive development.

Socioeconomic Differences in Language

Most research has found low-SES children to be less skilled in using formal, school-like language than middle- or high-SES children (Heath et al., 1991). Research also shows that low-SES children are up to a year behind their higher-SES peers by the age of four, due in part to the infrequency with which they hear adults with large vocabularies speak (Hoff, 2008). In practice, this means low-SES children perform less well in verbal test situations, but outside of those situations, their language differences are less clear-cut. These facts have created controversy about the importance of socioeconomic differences in language development.

What is the significance of socioeconomic differences in tests of language development? Some psychologists point out that most tests of language skills favor middle-SES versions of English in both vocabulary and style of *discourse,* or conversational patterns (Gopaul-McNicol & Thomas-Presswood, 1998; Miramontes et al., 1997), and that several popular verbal intelligence scales confound actual verbal ability with socioeconomic status (Chapman, Fiscella, Duberstein, Kawachi, & Muennig, 2014). This bias is due to the content selected for individual test questions and to the ways tests are normally conducted. A question on one of these tests might ask children to describe a dishwasher, but few low-SES families own this appliance. Other questions might draw on experiences that only middle-SES children usually enjoy, such as trips on airplanes or visits to museums.

Perhaps most important, middle-SES families use styles of discourse that include many "test" questions or questions to which parents already know the answers. At the dinner table, parents may ask their preschooler, "What letter does your name begin with?" even though they already know the answer and their child knows that they know. Exchanges such as these probably prepare young children for similar exchanges on genuine tests by making testing situations seem more natural and homelike.

In contrast, low-SES children more often lack prior experience with "test" question exchanges. They can give relatively elaborate answers to true questions such as "What did you do yesterday morning?" when the adult really does not know the answer. But they tend to fall silent when they suspect the adult already can answer the question (for example, "What are the names of the days of the week?"). Their silence is unfortunate because rhetorical, or "test," questions become especially common when preschoolers enter school and because active participation in questioning and answering helps preschoolers' learning substantially.

Language of Deaf and Hearing-Impaired Children

Children with hearing impairments often do not develop oral language skills as fully as other children do, but they are quite capable of acquiring a language of gestures called **American Sign Language (ASL)**. In fact, language development in ASL children provides much of the reason for considering ASL a true language, one as useful for communication as any verbal language, such as English.

How can this be so? Signing consists of subtle gestures of the fingers and hands made near the face. In general, each gesture functions like a morpheme. For example, holding the fingers together gently (which signers call a "tapered *O*") can mean either *home* or *flower,* depending on whether it is placed near the cheek or under the nose. Other sign-morphemes affect the syntax of expressions: gestural equivalents of *-ing* and *-ed.* Individual signs are linked according to syntactic rules, just as in English. After some practice, signers can "speak" (or gesture) as quickly and effortlessly as people who use English can.

American Sign Language (ASL) System of nonverbal gesturing that is used by many people who are deaf or hearing impaired and that functions as a language.

Sign language has the qualities of oral language, including grammar, subtlety, and expressiveness. This mother and child are communicating about the child's day at school. Unfortunately, in hearing communities (such as classrooms), it can be hard to appreciate the capacities of sign language.
Source: adriaticfoto/Shutterstock.com.

Chapter 9 Cognitive Development during Early Childhood

> **WORKING WITH** Carolyn Eaton, Preschool Teacher
>
> ### Introducing Sign Language to Young Children
>
> Carolyn Eaton teaches in a nursery school that serves only children who are deaf or who have moderate or severe hearing impairment. Everyone in the school communicates in American Sign Language (ASL): teachers, the children themselves, and (as much as possible) the parents. When they start the program, the children and parents often know very little ASL.
>
> **Kelvin:** *How do they acquire this new language? Carolyn talked about some of the ways.*
>
> **Carolyn:** In a lot of ways, the program really looks like any other nursery program, though maybe one with a lot of language emphasis. We always have a theme for the week. That's how we organize the vocabulary, the signs.
>
> **Kelvin:** *Can you give an example of a theme?*
>
> **Carolyn:** Last week's theme was "The Three Little Pigs." I told the story in ASL and read a picture book—one of the children had to hold it because I needed two hands to sign with. I emphasized key signs, like the ones for pig and three and the signs for brick, and straw, and house. I invited the children to make those signs with me when I came to them in the story.
>
> **Kelvin:** *Do you do other things related to the week's theme?*
>
> **Carolyn:** We'd have other conversations—in ASL, of course—about pigs and animals. And about trusting strangers, for that matter—that's in that story too! We might act out the story at some point, with signs instead of words. It depends partly on the vocabulary and fluency of the children.
>
> **Kelvin:** *Is it harder to understand preschoolers' signing than adults'?*
>
> **Carolyn:** It varies with the child, just like oral language. Most three- and four-year-olds tend to use less complex sign vocabulary and simpler expressions than adults. I found it hard at first to simplify my signing appropriately, the way you simplify oral language for young hearing children. There's a signing equivalent of "motherese" that you have to learn, or you won't be understood.
>
> **Kelvin:** *I noticed a parent today in the class signing to the kids. Does that happen a lot?*
>
> **Carolyn:** We have a parent volunteer just about every day. Because not all parents can volunteer, we have the kids take home a page each day that describes what's going on in the class and shows drawings of the signs we're currently emphasizing. We encourage the parents to learn them and use them at home. We also run two signing

What happens to infants and young children with hearing impairments who grow up learning ASL from their parents as their first language? Studies show they experience the same steps in signing development that speaking children do in language development. At about the age when infants babble, signing children begin "babbling" with their hands, making gestures that strongly resemble genuine ASL signs but that signers recognize as gestural "nonsense" (Marschark, 1993). As with verbal babbling, signing infants apparently engage in gestural babbles playfully when waking up in the morning or going to sleep at night.

When signing infants reach ages two and three, they experience a phase of one-word signing similar to the holophrases often observed among speaking children. They also experience two-word, telegraphic signing. As with speech, their signs at this point often omit important syntactic gestures and do not follow the usual conventions of word order (or, in this case, signing order) (Bellugi et al., 1993; Goldin-Meadow, 2008). Signing vocabulary increases rapidly during the early preschool period, in amounts comparable to the increases speaking children experience. Even the kinds of words acquired parallel those speaking children acquire; signing preschoolers tend to learn signs for dynamic, moving objects first, as is true for speaking children. The "Working With" interview with preschool teacher Carolyn Eaton describes some of these developments.

Still another reason to consider ASL a true language comes from observations of hearing preschoolers whose parents purposely used both English and ASL during the period when the children normally acquired language (Prinz & Prinz, 1979). During their preschool years, these children became thoroughly bilingual, using ASL and English interchangeably. Especially significant, however, were their patterns of language development, which essentially paralleled those shown by conventionally bilingual children. A clear example concerned

> **WORKING WITH** Carolyn Eaton, Preschool Teacher
>
> **Introducing Sign Language to Young Children** *continued*
>
> classes for the families of the preschoolers to help them communicate with their signing child.
>
> **Kelvin:** *Is it hard for them to learn?*
>
> **Carolyn:** Like everything else, people vary a lot. Some start learning immediately as soon as they learn that their child will always be deaf, and they're fluent by the time the child is a toddler. Others still haven't learned by the time the child is in grade school.
>
> Personally, I think it has a lot to do with how accepting the parents are of the child's hearing impairment. If they're still grieving over the child's loss, they make less progress at ASL.
>
> **Kelvin:** *Your program does seem language oriented—ASL oriented, that is.*
>
> **Carolyn:** It really is, though we also deal with all the other stuff that happens to children—friendships among peers, for example. Did you see that argument between two kids that was going on just as you were arriving today?
>
> **Kelvin:** *It looked fierce, judging by the children's faces. What was it about?*
>
> **Carolyn:** Well, Billy wrecked a roadway that two other kids had made in the sand table. They were upset, signed Billy to get lost, and that got Billy upset. That's when I stepped in.
>
> **Kelvin:** *I noticed how intently you were looking at Billy when you gave him a "talking to."*
>
> **Carolyn:** I sure was—but in all ASL conversations, not just scoldings, you have to look to see the signs. You get good at reading people's moods that way too, especially if you learn signing as early as these children did.
>
> **What Do You Think?**
>
> 1. Judging by Carolyn's comments, how does the acquisition of ASL resemble the acquisition of oral language? How does it differ?
>
> 2. Among speech-language pathologists and deaf people generally, there has been heated debate about whether to emphasize ASL experiences, even if they sometimes segregate children from the hearing community, or to emphasize oral language experiences, even if hearing-impaired children have trouble acquiring them. How might you decide between these alternatives? Compare your thoughts on this issue with one or two classmates' thoughts.

vocabulary. Like verbal bilinguals, these children first acquired a single vocabulary that intermingled elements from both ASL and English but included few direct translations. If children understood and used the sign for "tree," they would be unlikely to understand and use the spoken word *tree*. The children eventually acquired translations and thus finally possessed duplicate vocabularies. But acquiring duplicate terms took several years, just as it does with verbally bilingual children.

Language Deficits or Language Differences?

Although we have presented gender differences, socioeconomic differences, and American Sign Language as variations on language development that are equally worthy, society as a whole does not always agree with this assessment. In certain situations, each variation tends to be considered unsatisfactory, and the speaker (or, for ASL, the signer) may be considered deficient in linguistic or cognitive ability. The discourse patterns associated with females are often considered less satisfactory for learning and discussing mathematics, for example, than the discourse patterns associated with males (Walkerdine, 1997). In school, therefore, some girls are more likely to be judged less competent in math than they really are. Students with a language background other than English, whether it is Spanish, ASL, or something else, are at risk for being considered "unintelligent" simply because they cannot communicate fluently in the particular land of language—middle-class oral and written English—that historically has dominated schooling at all levels. Language biases pose a challenge for anyone who works with children professionally (Gopaul-McNicol & Thomas-Presswood, 1998). However, as we will see in Chapter 8, where we look further at bilingualism and its effects, there are ways to overcome language biases and to honor the diversity and talents of all children.

Chapter 9 Cognitive Development during Early Childhood

> **What Do You Think?**
>
> How do you think early childhood teachers should respond to language variety in preschoolers? Should they encourage it, discourage it, or simply accept it? This is an important issue in education and would make for a lively debate in class!

Early Childhood Education

Developing cognitive skills influence an important experience for many preschool children: early childhood education. Programs for three- and four-year-olds take many forms. Look at these experiences:

- Juan goes to *family day care* for three full days each week. His care occurs in his caregiver's home, with only four other children.

- Denzel goes to a *childcare center* full time, five days a week. The center consists of two rooms modified from a church basement. About twenty children attend the center and are cared for by four adults.

- Cary goes to a part-time *nursery school* four mornings per week. There are twelve children and two adults.

Early Education and Cognitive Theories of Development

As with the diversity of these childcare arrangements, there is diversity in the developmental perspectives guiding the arrangements. Some programs draw heavily on Piaget's ideas about cognitive development, especially the notion that children construct knowledge by interacting with the environment actively (Marlowe, 1998). They provide sensorimotor activities, such as sand and water play, as a basis for fostering preoperational activities such as make-believe play. Other programs organize cognitive activities around structured materials, which teachers guide children to use in particular ways. Nurseries and centers inspired by Maria Montessori (Cuffaro, 1991; Montessori, 1964; Lillard, 2012) may give children sets of cylinders graded by size and designed to fit snugly into a set of size-graded holes in a board. A child experiments with the cylinders and holes to discover the best way to fit them.

Still other early education programs borrow from Vygotsky's views of cognition as originating in social and cultural activities. These programs emphasize cooperative problem-solving activities and *emergent literacy,* a way of introducing reading and writing by situating it in everyday, valued experiences (Morrow, 1996). For example, instead of teaching children to recognize letters or familiar words at a special time each day, the early childhood teacher might simply provide a classroom rich in print materials and encourage children to come to him with words or letters that they themselves want to learn.

Effectiveness of Early Childhood Education

Evaluations of early childhood programs suggest that a wide range of approaches, including those just mentioned, are about equally effective in promoting overall cognitive growth, although the choice of curriculum does seem to influence *the pattern* of skills children acquire (Lillard, 2012; Schweinhart et al., 1993).

Three factors seem to underlie successful early childhood programs, whatever their format and curriculum. First, the staff members of successful programs regard themselves as competent observers of children's educational needs and as being capable of making important decisions in tailoring a curriculum to particular children. Second, the vast majority of successful programs and teachers view an early childhood curriculum as an integrated whole, rather than as consisting of independent subject areas or skills. Singing a song, for example, is not just "music"; it also fosters language development, motor skills (if the children dance along), arithmetic (through counting and rhythm), and social studies (if the words are about people and life in the community).

Third, successful early childhood programs involve parents, either directly as volunteers in the classroom or indirectly as advisers on governing boards, in certain school activities, or in additional services that support families. The federally sponsored program of early education called *Head Start,* for example, owes much of its effectiveness to parent involvement (Ames, 1997; Love, Banks Tarullo, Raikes, & Chazan-Cohen, 2008). To get federal funding, local centers are required to create parent advisory boards to guide policy and practice at the centers. They are also encouraged to provide other family support services, such as parent support groups and dental screening for children.

Cultural Diversity and Best Practice in Early Education

A careful look at successful programs for young children raises an important question: are there "best" ways to support children's learning despite the cultural and individual diversity among children? A major professional association for early childhood education, the National Association for the Education of Young Children (NAEYC), argues that there are and has described its recommendations in detail in an influential book called *Developmentally Appropriate Practice: Birth to Age Eight* (Bredekamp & Copple, 1997; Copple & Bredekamp, 2009; Gestwicki, 1995). **Developmentally appropriate practices** are ways of assisting children's learning that are consistent with children's developmental needs and abilities. Table 9.2 lists a few of the practices recommended by the NAEYC as they relate to the preschool years.

developmentally appropriate practice Methods and goals of teaching considered optimal for young children, given current knowledge of child development.

The NAEYC recommendations seem reasonable in many ways. Who can object, for example, to providing children with choices for their preschool play or to supporting their dialogues and initiatives with comments from the teacher or caregiver? Yet cross-cultural comparisons of early childhood programs complicate the picture somewhat by revealing that some practices in early education in North America are really culture bound rather than universally beneficial to children.

In Japan, for example, early childhood programs are more likely to value large-group activities (such as singing or putting on a skit) in the belief that such activities develop commitment to the child's community—in this case, the community of the classroom

TABLE 9.2 Developmentally Appropriate Practices with Preschoolers

Principle	Examples
Caregivers provide ample space for active play.	Program has access to outdoor space or gymnasium with climbing apparatus, tricycles, etc.
Caregivers allow children choices in activities.	Classroom has several learning centers: dramatic play (dress-up), block building, books and reading area, art area, etc.
Caregivers provide long periods of uninterrupted time.	Group transitions (e.g., from indoor to outdoor activities) are kept to a minimum. Activities tend to begin and end individually.
Activities and materials are relevant to children's experiences.	Books are gender fair and culture fair. Relevant cultural holidays are noted and celebrated through appropriate activities in class.
Caregivers ensure that the environment is safe and free of hazards.	Climbing apparatus has soft mats underneath (if indoors) or soft sand (if outdoors). Furniture is sturdy. Sharp objects (knives, scissors) are supervised carefully when used.

Source: Adapted from Bredekamp & Copple (1997).

A Multicultural View

Parents' Beliefs about Intelligence: A Cross-Cultural Perspective

In our society, parents mean particular things when they refer to children's *intelligence:* they are usually talking about a child's verbal skills and reasoning abilities, especially as they occur in school or school-like tasks. This view of intelligence is so deeply grounded in our culture that an entire psychological field has developed to measure it, complete with standardized "intelligence" tests and experts to help teachers and parents interpret the tests.

But not all societies think of intelligence in this way. The Kipsigis in East Africa frame the idea of intelligence rather differently, placing it more explicitly in its social context (Harkrtess & Super, 1992). They speak of a child being *ng'om,* meaning not only verbally skilled and sociable but also responsible to others. A child who is *ng'om* is quick to learn household tasks, for example, but also reliable about doing them without being reminded. The Kipsigis recognize, in principle, that a child can have verbal skill in the abstract. In practice, however, they regard such an isolated or abstract skill as a unique ability that requires a special term to describe it: *ng'om en sukul,* or "smart in school." Furthermore, *ng'om* is a quality shown only by preschoolers; neither an infant nor an adult can be *ng'om* because she or he is not expected to be responsible to others in the same way preschoolers are.

Such a socially embedded notion of intelligence differs radically from the usual North American idea. In our society, parents are likely to distinguish clearly between a child's sense of responsibility to others and his or her intelligence (Goodnow, 1996). They may consider the former desirable but not an intrinsic part of intelligence as such. When interviewed about the qualities shown by preschoolers, parents of preschoolers tend to name relatively "cognitive" features: an intelligent child is inquisitive, curious, imaginative, self-reliant, and able to play independently (Harkness & Super, 1992). These features of intelligence take individual autonomy for granted rather than social harmony: being intelligent is something you do by or on behalf of yourself, not with or on behalf of others.

These cultural differences begin to make sense if we consider the settings in which Kipsigis and North American parents and preschoolers live. A Kipsigis preschooler typically is part of an extended family. There are likely to be children of all ages close at hand, related to one another in largely complex ways; older children typically care for younger children from an early age; and children's chores are likely to take on "real" economic importance as children get older. Such a setting seems sure to reward children for showing responsibility to others.

In our own society, a preschooler is likely to live with a small family; relatively few or even no immediate relatives may be close at hand; parents expect that school will figure prominently in the preschooler's future; and parents themselves are likely to be working for a living. This sort of setting favors children who can "teach themselves" to a certain extent, that is, play with and learn from materials on their own. It also favors children who orient themselves toward school-like activities—toward number and memory games, for example, and books and letters. An "intelligent" child is one who can do these things, which have much less to do with responsibility to others than is the case for a Kipsigis child. Cultural differences such as these can pose problems for many preschoolers in our own society when they finally enter school. Historically, modern schooling has encouraged the culturally conventional definitions of intelligence as individual activity and those of cognitive activity as separate from the daily needs of the community. Students generally "do their own work" and focus on tasks (such as a set of math problems) that are created specifically for school settings.

When these assumptions do not fit the cultural expectations of particular children or their families, however, teachers are challenged to modify them. Teachers must then find other ways for children to "be intelligent"—ways that involve greater responsibility to others, for example, and greater concern for the real needs of the child's community (Gopaul-McNicol & Thomas-Presswood, 1998). Though it takes effort, there are ways to accomplish these changes in teaching philosophy; some of these changes are discussed in Chapter 8 in connection with bilingualism and the influence of school in the middle years.

(Kotloff, 1993). The time given to large-group activities, however, probably would seem excessive to some preschool educators in North America, where the development of individual initiative is more highly valued.

In Italy, early childhood programs emphasize involvement of parents much more heavily than do most North American programs (Edwards & Kutaka, 2015). They also place children in permanent groups from their entrance at age three until they leave the program for public school at age six. Over recent decades, societal changes, such as higher divorce rates, increasing numbers of women working outside the home, and economic difficulties, have challenged the early childhood care systems, but Italian culture persists in supporting these programs (Edwards & Kutaka, 2015).

> **What Do You Think?**
>
> Is early childhood education a "social" or a "cognitive" activity? Decide what you think about this question. Then, if you can, talk about it with one or two experienced teachers of young children. How does your opinion compare to theirs?

These comparisons suggest that the best practices in early education may need to take account of cultural differences and values regarding children's development (Mallory & New, 1994). For programs in ethnically diverse societies such as the United States, this means more than including songs and brief mentions of the holidays of various cultural groups. The central values and attitudes of cultural groups served by a particular center or nursery school must find their way into the daily activities of the program. Particular centers, therefore, will experience cultural diversity in different ways.

As the "A Multicultural View" feature shows, in these culturally diverse programs, cognition, or thinking, itself can take on diverse meanings. Educators who work with young children therefore need to do more than understand preschool cognition: they also need to explore how it might be understood and used by particular children and communities with specific social relationships and values. The next chapter turns to these important topics.

From Preschooler to Child

The physical and cognitive changes we have talked about in this chapter create new relationships with parents and other caregivers, who in turn stimulate further changes. Preschoolers' new motor skills may stimulate adults to encourage various talents actively and with more focus than before. Once catching and throwing make their appearance, playing ball becomes a possibility; once scribbling stabilizes, skillful and interesting drawing seems just around the corner. And so parents and other interested adults encourage children toward these new skills, among others. Sometimes, the teaching and learning seem easier now, too, because adults no longer have to monitor a child's every move and can concentrate increasingly on the goals of movements. Just a few years before, "one false step" might have meant a child would literally fall. But now, this term has become only a metaphor for mistakes in general, not for physical mishaps specifically.

The cognitive developments of early childhood are equally influential on relationships. New cognitive abilities create new individuality in children. In spite of differences in temperament among infants, it is not they but preschoolers who have more identifiable personalities. By age four or five, conversations become possible; moods can be expressed not only through gestures and body language but also through words; and a child's lasting interests become more obvious to those who know the child. All of these changes create new meanings for the idea of parenting. Attending to physical needs begins to recede in importance (though not completely), and attending to psychological needs comes more to the fore. As parents shift their relationship to accommodate these changes, they are more likely to remember their own childhoods once again, and with renewed vividness. The memories can be good, bad, traumatic, or mixed; but whatever they are like, they force reassessment of parents' *own* personal histories and identities, and their relationships with their *own* parents, the preschooler's grandparents. We saw aspects of these changes in Chapter 5's discussion of attachment formation, and we will explore them further. We come to them first in Chapter 8, which describes where preschoolers' new physical growth and cognitive skills lead them during middle childhood. We come to them again in Chapter 13, which discusses the impact of parenting on parents in more detail. First, though, we must complete the portrait of young children by discussing the development of their social relationships and their emotional growth in the next chapter.

Chapter Summary

- **What pathway does physical growth normally take during early childhood?** Between the ages of two and five, growth slows down and children take on more adultlike bodily proportions. Usually growth is rather smooth during the preschool period, though genetic, social, and nutritional differences can affect growth to some extent. Children's appetites often are smaller in the preschool years than in infancy, and children become more selective about what they eat.
- **How is poverty related to children's health?** The general health of a child is associated with the economic resources of the child's family, with higher-SES preschoolers tending to be healthier than lower-SES preschoolers. A number of possible causes for the association exist, including greater access to health care among well-off families.
- **When do children achieve bladder control?** Children tend to achieve daytime bladder control early in the preschool period. Nighttime bladder control tends to come later in the period.
- **What motor skills do children acquire during the preschool years?** Preschoolers acquire and refine many fundamental motor skills, including walking, jumping, throwing, and catching. Fine motor skills such as drawing also emerge during this period, progressing from prerepresentational to representational drawings. Children vary in motor skill development because of both their biological endowment and their experiences.
- **How does children's growth affect parents and other adults?** Preschoolers' changing facial features, size, and motor skills influence parents' responses and methods of childrearing to some extent. Because of differences in circumstances, families respond uniquely to differences in children's growth.
- **What are the special features and strengths of preschoolers' thinking?** Several explanations of preschoolers' thinking exist. According to Piaget, preschoolers' thinking is preoperational, or characterized by emerging skills with symbolic representation. Preoperational thinking is also characterized by egocentrism, the assumption that your own point of view is shared by others, and by rudimentary skill with classification, reversibility, conservation, and number. A more recent but prominent explanation for preschoolers' cognitive development is social constructivism, the idea that thinking develops through shared, interactive activities. When activity settings are shared with more skilled or knowledgeable others, a zone of proximal development occurs that allows and encourages a child to learn and perform beyond what he or she could do alone. A third recent explanation is offered by neostructuralist theories of cognitive development, which use Piaget's belief in stages but focus on changes in relatively specific cognitive skills.
- **How does the language of preschool children differ from that of older children?** During the preschool years, children make major strides in acquiring the syntax, or grammar, of their native language. Young children's first word combinations are related by semantics and omit syntactic relationships. When syntax does appear, it is sometimes marked by errors of overgeneralization. Infants and preschoolers are reinforced, though only indirectly, for using correct syntax in their early utterances. Children probably acquire some syntax through imitation and practice of language models. The ease of language acquisition despite the poverty of the content of speech that children hear may mean that children possess an innate language acquisition device, or LAD. Parents assist children's language acquisition by recasting the children's utterances, providing expansions or scaffolding that support children's speech, and using a special style of talk called *infant-directed speech.*
- **What social and cultural factors account for variations in preschoolers' language and speech?** Language varies between girls and boys in ways that support gender stereotypes. It also varies according to socioeconomic class in ways that prepare middle-SES children better than low-SES children for school settings. The variations raise issues about when and whether particular children's language is deficient or merely different from the norm.
- **What constitutes good early childhood education?** Early childhood education programs take a variety of forms, many of which have been influenced by theories of cognitive development. Three factors characterize successful programs: a staff oriented toward observing the children, an integrated view of the curriculum, and significant involvement of parents in the program. Cultural diversity challenges early childhood educators to identify teaching practices that are not only developmentally appropriate but also culturally appropriate.

Key Terms

activity settings (p. 204)
American Sign Language (ASL) (p. 213)
classification (p. 202)
conservation (p. 202)
developmentally appropriate
    practice (p. 217)
egocentrism (p. 201)
holographic speech (p. 208)
infant-directed speech (p. 211)
neostructuralist theory (p. 205)
overgeneralizations (p. 208)
preoperational stage (p. 200)
reversibility (p. 202)
situated cognition (p. 204)
social constructivism (p. 204)
symbolic thought (p. 201)
syntax (p. 206)
zone of proximal development
    (ZPD) (p. 204)

Psychosocial Development during Early Childhood

CHAPTER 10

Chapter Outline

Relationships with Family

Relationships in an Expanding Social World

Play during Early Childhood

Gender Development

Child Abuse and Maltreatment

Looking Back/Looking Forward

Source: bikeriderlondon/Shutterstock.com.

Focusing Questions

- How do different styles of parenting influence preschoolers' relationships with peers?
- How do preschoolers handle conflicts with peers?
- Why is play so important in preschoolers' development, and how does play change as they approach school age?
- How does a child's understanding of gender differences change during the preschool years? What factors influence a child's flexibility about gender-role stereotypes?
- What factors appear to contribute to child abuse and neglect? What are the consequences of maltreatment, and how might child maltreatment be prevented?

When Selena was two, she would crouch down on the floor with her rear end sticking out in imitation of the prominent haunches of Tigger, the family cat. From time to time, she made a noise sort of like a cat's meow. Keeping her head low, she looked around carefully for acknowledgment from her parents. Occasionally she walked like a cat, although her walk looked more like a rabbit's hopping. Tigger himself was not impressed by all of this.

Selena's skills as a performer and her active awareness of her audience illustrate an important milestone during the early childhood years: the development of psychological and social skills. During early childhood, many activities and events that occupy a child's waking hours involve social interaction with other people. These others include parents, grandparents, and siblings, as well as friends and acquaintances in the neighborhood and community. Many of these interactions also involve play. The nature of our play and its role in our lives changes with age and experience, but the capacity to engage in playful activity and the social skills that make this possible continue to develop throughout our lives. The social skills and unique personality a preschool child develops are largely a result of social interactions within and outside his or her family.

In this chapter, we explore the process through which preschoolers develop the capacity to relate to others in empathic and prosocial ways and to successfully deal with conflict and aggression. As with play, psychosocial development is a lifelong process. We will examine the conditions that foster or undermine such development and their consequences for lifespan development. We will also explore an aspect of early childhood development with profound and lifelong impact: the development of gender. Finally, we will discuss the serious problem of child maltreatment, including its causes, long-term consequences, treatment, and prevention.

Relationships with Family

Are your earliest memories of yourself alone, or do they include other people? Chances are that it's the latter, for young children spend a good deal of their time relating to others. In this section, we discuss children's relationships with their parents and siblings—relationships that in many ways set the stage for social interactions beyond the family sphere.

Relationships with Parents

During the preschool years, the attachment relationships between children and their parents and other caregivers discussed in Chapter 7 continue to play a central role in children's social and emotional development. However, young children's expanding ability to initiate verbal and physical activity and their exploding powers of imagination can at times be a challenge to their parents. These changes require parents to support their preschoolers' efforts to take on the world while also appreciating young children's limitations and need for restraints that ensure their physical and emotional safety and protect their self-esteem. Preschoolers often test the limits their parents impose and are frequently inconsistent in their ability to understand and conform to parental wishes. At times they express their strong desire to control their environment by refusing to eat certain foods or wear certain clothing, or by insisting on playing the same game or having the same story read to them over and over again.

Understanding the need for family rules poses a challenge to preschoolers, but making those rules also creates a challenge for parents, at least those living in the individualistic culture of North America. In this society, unlike most others, parents are expected to devise their own standards for rearing children, largely independently of other families' standards or expectations—a kind of "private enterprise" system of child-rearing. For instance, it is up to parents as individuals to decide how much anger their child should be allowed to express, how early and well she should learn manners, or how much candy she can eat. Parents' independence in deciding on these standards increases their power to shape their child's behavior in the short run. But it also increases their dilemma over which standards to choose because they observe that other parents often make choices different from their own (Piotrowski, 1997). These factors may help explain why community members are often reluctant to say something to someone else's child who misbehaves or to offer advice or assistance to a parent who might find it useful. And the lack of clear standards for good parenting is precisely the kind of ambiguous role that creates stress during early adulthood.

Enforcing family rules may be less of a problem in cultures and societies that encourage less individualism and stronger, more prolonged interdependence among kin, community, or both. In Chinese American and Japanese American families, for example, grandparents and other relatives retain considerable prestige and influence in child-rearing matters, even after

All parents discipline their children sometimes. Their methods make a difference. Being respectful of a child's thoughts and feelings and calling attention to the consequences of misbehaving is more effective than spanking, at least in the long run.

Source: Iakov Filimonov/Shutterstock.com.

a couple has married and given birth to children (Chao, 1994; Huang & Ying, 1989; Nagata, Cheng, & Tsai-Chae, 2010). Even as preschoolers, children are taught ways to show respect for their elders, such as caution in asking questions and readiness to obey orders. In such a situation, parents lose some decision-making authority to grandparents, in-laws, or "the community." But parents also gain family and community backing for their position: it is not just an adult or two, Mom and Dad, who decide whether talking in a loud voice is rude but an extended array of relatives and friends (Skolnick & Skolnick, 1989). And for individuals who expect to have the support of extended family and friends, not having that social support can be quite difficult (Leidy, Guerra, & Toro, 2012). The "Focusing On" feature discusses extended family members' participation in child-rearing.

In general, parent-child relationships during early childhood that are warm, respectful, empathic, and mutually responsive generally work best for children and their families. This is revealed both by how children and their parents interact and by the perceptions they have about each other. When mothers shared a mutually responsive orientation with their young children, children developed a secure attachment and better internalized maternal rules and values, and mothers relied less often on power to influence their children (Heikamp, Trommsdorff, Druey, Hübner, & von Suchodoletz, 2013; Kochanska, 1997). Preschoolers who have more positive mental representations of the mothering they receive, as revealed in the stories they make up about a mother and her child, have fewer behavior problems and less psychological distress than children whose mental representations are more negative (Oppenheim et al., 1997; Stocker, 1994). In the section that follows, we discuss the main patterns of parental authority observed among North American families and their developmental impact.

Patterns of Parental Authority

One of the most important aspects of a parent-child relationship is the parent's style of authority. Observations of North American families of preschoolers suggest that child-rearing styles can be classified into four groups: *authoritative, authoritarian, permissive,* and *indifferent* (Darling & Steinberg, 1993; Grusec et al., 1997; Lamb et al., 1992; Maccoby & Martin, 1983; Sorkhabi & Mandara, 2013). In most families, however, none of these styles exists in a "pure" form and parenting styles can change as children grow older and as other family changes occur.

Authoritative Parenting

Authoritative parents exert a high degree of control, demand a lot of their children, and monitor their children's behavior, but also are responsive, child centered, and respectful of their children's thoughts, feelings, and participation in decision making. For example,

authoritative parenting
A style of child-rearing characterized by a high degree of control, clarity of communication, maturity demands, and nurturance.

> ### Focusing On...
>
> **Extended Family Supports for Child-Rearing**
>
> In American society in particular, parents are held, and hold themselves, responsible for the physical care of their children. Whether parents are rich or poor, Caucasian or African American, divorced or married, society expects them to provide food for their children, as well as clothing and a place to sleep. In reality, many families share these responsibilities with relatives, friends, and professionals of various kinds. In a typical week, a child may spend significant time not only with his biological parents but also with a grandparent, a neighbor, and (depending on the child's age) a teacher or day-care center worker. The mixture of responsibility depends partly on the local circumstances of the particular family. It also reflects cultural and economic differences. Mexican American families, for example, value the participation of grandparents and other relatives in child-rearing. Many nonwhite families report the participation in family life of *fictive kin*—neighbors or friends who develop a relationship with the family that closely resembles that of a blood relative (Leidy et al., 2012; Ramirez, 1989, 1998). Though fictive kin are more common among ethnic and racial minorities, they are also an important part of the white experience.
>
> These additional adults supplement what parents provide, often literally by providing alternative persons to cook meals and arrange other daily routines and by bolstering the psychological goals and emotional supports provided by the biological parents. A study of African American families confirmed this conclusion by investigating the emotional climate in two- and three-generational families (Tolson & Wilson, 1990). Interviews with all members of the families, including the children, found that three-generational families (those with a resident grandparent) saw themselves as organized more informally and spontaneously than two-generational (two-parent) families, which in turn saw themselves as organized more informally and spontaneously than one-parent families. In other words, the greater the number of parents (including a grandparent), the *fewer* the rules for children to follow and the *more* flexible the daily scheduling of activities, even though larger families had to coordinate the activities of more individuals. While this trend may seem contradictory, the family members themselves suggested the reason when interviewed: more adults in the house meant individual parents had more backup support in carrying out their functions as parents and therefore needed to rely on preset procedures less heavily.
>
> The benefits of backup support are psychological as well as physical. Children who report higher levels of kinship support also note that they are more likely to feel connected with their teachers and schools and to value hard work (Pallock & Lamborn, 2006). The interviews described earlier also found that African American families with more than one parent placed significantly greater emphasis on moral and ethical issues and on determining how best to deal with both individual members and people outside the family (Tolson & Wilson, 1990; Wilson et al., 1995). To achieve this benefit, however, it did not matter whether the second "parent" was a father; it occurred just as frequently when a mother and a grandmother were the resident parents. Other research, in fact, suggests that it may not even matter whether the additional parents live at home, as long as they participate actively in the life of the family. In another interview study, successful minority single parents reported developing and depending on networks of family and personal relationships (Lindblad-Goldberg, 1989). What mattered was not the form or pattern of the networks but their existence and importance in helping the parent carry out the roles of child-rearing.
>
> **What Do You Think?**
> What types of extended family supports did you experience during your childhood and adolescence? In what ways did you find them beneficial, and in what ways were they not?

although it may be easier for a parent to respond to a child's request for help in building something or getting dressed by doing it for the child, an authoritative parent is likely to provide only the amount of help that will enable that child to accomplish the task independently. Such parents tend to be democratic and rational in their decision making and to respond to their children with warmth and empathy.

When it comes to discipline, authoritative parents assume that their preschoolers should be treated with respect, even when they have misbehaved severely. They believe that discipline should be a positive learning experience, focused on helping children to understand what the rules are. They try to determine why children break the rules, and they expect age-appropriate responsibility for children's misbehavior. They want children to internalize parental standards and to develop competence so that children can make better decisions about how to behave in the future. For example, when faced with a preschooler whose water-play at the sink has resulted in a flood, an authoritative parent is likely to ask the child how it happened, what he was thinking, and what he remembered about the rules about using the sink for water-play. The parent's response would focus on helping the child understand why the parent was upset (the flood could damage the floor and downstairs ceiling and be costly to repair), helping him assume age-appropriate responsibility for his actions (perhaps by having him help mop up the floor), and having him explain how such "catastrophes" could be avoided in the future. The consequences would also be designed to increase the child's understanding of the misbehavior (for example, requiring him to help clean up the mess and not allowing water-play privileges for the rest of the week).

Preschoolers of authoritative parents tend to be self-reliant, self-controlled, and able to get along well with their adult caregivers and peers (Hart et al., 1992; Hoeve et al., 2009; Kuczynski & Kochanska, 1995). For example, Leon Kuczynski and Grazyna Kochanska (1995) found that children who experienced authoritative child-rearing as toddlers were more responsive to parental guidance and had fewer behavior problems at age five. In particular, the demands of these authoritative mothers emphasized competence, prosocial behavior, and positive actions ("Ask him to share"; "Pour the milk carefully"; "Put away your toys") rather than demands to inhibit behavior ("Don't hit"; "Don't spill the milk"; "Don't leave a mess").

Authoritative parenting is also associated with high self-esteem, internalized moral standards, psychosocial maturity, autonomy, and academic success. In addition, it appears to foster relationships with peers and family that display the same qualities of warmth and respect for others during middle childhood, adolescence, and beyond (Baumrind, 1991a, 1991b; Darling & Steinberg, 1993; Hoeve et al., 2009; Pettit et al., 1997). We will look at the relationship between authoritative parenting and prosocial behavior later in this chapter.

Authoritarian Parenting

Like authoritative parents, **authoritarian** parents are demanding of their children and exert high control over them. However, they tend to be less warm and responsive than authoritative parents, and more arbitrary and undemocratic in decision making. They frequently impose their rules or views on their children based on their own greater power and authority, with little sensitivity to their children's thoughts and feelings. They rarely explain the purpose behind the rules, making it less likely that children will internalize those guidelines. Parent-child relationships that depend on arbitrary, "power-assertive" control and that ignore children's feelings and need for independence often have a negative effect on children. Children of authoritarian parents tend to be relatively distrustful of others, unhappy with themselves, and to have lower self-esteem. They also tend to have poorer peer relations, poorer school adjustment, less life satisfaction, and lower school achievement than do children with authoritative parents (Hart et al., 1990; Lamb et al., 1992; Milevsky, Schlecter, Netter, & Keehn, 2006). We discuss the impact of authoritarian parenting on older children in Chapters 9 (middle childhood) and 11 (adolescence).

The disciplinary techniques authoritarian parents use differ from those of authoritative parents, in part because they do not see the development of responsibility in young children as a collaborative process and place less emphasis on mutual respect. When faced with misbehavior, they are more likely to focus on the arbitrary assertion of parental power and authority than on understanding the child's thoughts and feelings about the misbehavior or on helping the child understand and take responsibility for it. In the extreme, the combination of rigid and arbitrary power assertion and insensitivity to a child's thoughts and feelings can increase the likelihood of child maltreatment, which we discuss a little later in the chapter. By modeling disrespectful and insensitive behavior, such parenting can elicit and reinforce similar behavior in children and lead to escalating cycles of negative reinforcement and coercion (Patterson, 1982).

Authoritarian parenting is more frequent in large families, in minority families, and in working-class families (Greenberger et al., 1994), and fathers are more likely to be

authoritarian parenting A style of child-rearing characterized by a high degree of control and demands on children's maturity and a low degree of clarity of communication and nurturance.

authoritarian than mothers. Parenting styles and beliefs about how children should be raised differ across societies and cultures (Bornstein et al., 1998; Rudy & Grusec, 2006; Stevenson-Hinde, 1998). For example, authoritarian parenting is more common in cultures in which family relations are hierarchically structured based on age, family role, and gender. Ruth Chao (1994) has questioned the validity of Western European concepts of authoritative and authoritarian parenting for Chinese families. Chinese child-rearing is based on Confucian principles that require children to show loyalty to and respect for their elders and require elders to responsibly train, discipline, and otherwise "govern" young children. High degrees of parental authority and control are viewed as positive and essential aspects of the *chiao shun,* or "training," needed to set a standard of acceptable family and community conduct. Chao suggests that cultural differences such as these may explain why authoritarian parenting, which is associated with poor school achievement among European American children, is linked to high levels of school achievement among Chinese children. Authoritarian parenting is more common among mothers in collectivistic societies than individualistic societies, and authoritarian parents in collectivistic cultures were not as likely as authoritarian parents in individualistic cultures to view their children negatively (Rudy & Grusec, 2006). Central to such cultural differences are differences in values and assumptions about what kind of people parents want their children to be and what kinds of parenting and other developmental influences will best help them get there. It is also important to consider the context in which families live. In poor neighborhoods with high rates of violence and risky behavior, the use of punitive authoritarian parenting does not seem to have the same negative outcomes among African American boys as with other demographic groups, perhaps demonstrating a better "match" for these boys (Roche, Ensminger, & Cherlin, 2007).

Permissive Parenting

permissive parenting A style of parenting in which parents make relatively few demands on their children but clearly communicate their warmth and interest and provide considerable care and nurturance.

Permissive parents appear to show two patterns. **Permissive** parents are warm, sensitive, caring, and generally responsive to their children's thoughts and feelings. However, they exert low levels of control and make relatively few demands, permitting their children to make almost all of their own decisions. Also, while they clearly communicate their warmth, love, and caring, their communication tends to be less clear in situations requiring them to set limits on their children's behavior.

Permissive parents rarely assert their disciplinary control directly. They tend to rely on their children to learn and conform to what is expected and to internalize parental values on their own, based on observing their parents and reacting to their parents' expressions of upset and satisfaction regarding their children's behavior. Therefore, children with permissive parents tend to lack self-reliance and self-control and to have lower self-esteem and slightly higher rates of depression as they enter their adolescent years (Milevsky et al., 2007). This is also true of children with indifferent parents, described next, who seem to be emotionally detached and not to care what their children do (Loeb et al., 1980). Permissive and indifferent parenting might be particularly problematic when children are raised in more dangerous, high-risk neighborhoods (Roche et al., 2007). However, cross-cultural research linked both authoritative and permissive parenting with positive outcomes, such as high self-esteem, low numbers of problem behaviors, and personal competence among Spanish families (Garcia & Gracia, 2009).

Indifferent Parenting

indifferent parenting A style of parenting in which parents' permissiveness reflects an avoidance of child-rearing responsibilities, sometimes with detrimental results.

Indifferent parents are detached and emotionally uninvolved. They are inconsistent in setting and maintaining age-appropriate standards and expectations for their children and in fulfilling their parental responsibilities (Lamb et al., 1992; Maccoby & Martin, 1983). Discipline by indifferent parents tends to be inconsistent, erratic, and out of step with the developmental needs of their children.

Children with indifferent parents may turn to peers or others for help in setting limits and learning morality, which puts them at increased risk of peer pressure. These children tend to have various degrees of developmental difficulties, including a low ability to tolerate frustration and control their impulsive and aggressive behavior. They also tend to have difficulty in making life choices and setting long-term goals. These factors likely play a role in the higher rates of delinquency found among these children (Hoeve et al., 2009). Additionally, they experience the highest rates of depression and the lowest rates of self-esteem and life satisfaction, compared to children reared with any of the other three parenting styles (Milevsky et al., 2007). At the extreme, indifferent parents may neglect their children's physical and emotional needs in ways that place them at risk for serious developmental and emotional problems. Child neglect and abuse are discussed later in this chapter.

Table 10.1 summarizes the main patterns of parental authority. While most parents are fairly consistent in their parenting styles, under certain circumstances, they may exhibit other styles. For example, a parent with an authoritative style may respond, on occasion, to an overtired child in an impatient and authoritarian manner after explaining to her for the tenth time why it is time to go to bed.

Changes Over Time

Patterns of child-rearing tend to change over time. Authoritarian parents, for instance, often ease up and shift to a more permissive or authoritative style as their children grow older. Changes in the family situation, such as the birth of another child, also can make a difference. The experience gained from rearing their first child frequently enables parents to be more comfortable and flexible in rearing the children who follow. Help from older children in caring for younger siblings can also reduce the stresses of parenting. On the other hand, additional children increase the family's overall childcare and economic burdens, so more relaxed parenting is not always the outcome. Other changes within a family, such as separation, divorce, and remarriage, as well as changes in employment, standard of living, and health, also may influence child-rearing. Families that are under stress tend to be more rigid, arbitrary, and authoritarian in rearing their children than families that are not.

Although parenting styles influence early childhood development, it should not be assumed that they alone determine a child's developmental course. First, these styles reflect average patterns and do not describe the unique pattern of interactions and experiences that characterizes the relationship between any particular parent and child. The quality and developmental impact of a particular parent-child relationship will be influenced by the unique qualities of the parent, the child, and their interactions and experiences in the relationship. Second, although parents are certainly important, other individuals both within and outside of the family may contribute in vital ways to psychosocial development during early childhood.

Relationships with Siblings

Brothers and sisters are major participants in the social activities of many preschoolers. Though adjustment to the birth of a sibling often leads to increased behavior problems in older siblings, these increases tend to be temporary (Baydar et al., 1997). Studies have shown that most young children are very interested in babies and speak to their baby

TABLE 10.1 Patterns of Parental Authority

Parenting Style	Control	Responsiveness
Authoritative	High	High
Authoritarian	High	Low
Permissive	Low	High
Indifferent	Low	Low

brothers and sisters in ways very similar to those of adult caregivers. Preschoolers also listen carefully to conversations between their parents and older brothers and sisters, as reflected in their efforts to join in family conversations. Their awareness of caregiving interactions between their parents and younger siblings helps them to respond to their younger siblings' distress with appropriate caregiving behaviors (Dunn & Shatz, 1989; Garner et al., 1994) and to initiate prosocial, helping behaviors (Howe, Ross, & Recchia, 2011).

Older siblings show similar behavior when they simplify their language while explaining a task to a younger sibling (Hoff-Ginsberg & Krueger, 1991). Among bilingual families, children who communicate with their siblings using the second language tend to be more proficient in that language (Duursma et al., 2007). Siblings also provide important role models for their preschool brothers and sisters, helping them learn social skills and parental expectations. Both the friendly and aggressive interactions of siblings contribute to the development of preschoolers' understandings of the feelings, intentions, and needs of people other than themselves (Brown & Dunn, 1992; Dunn, 1985; Howe et al., 2011).

Influences on Sibling Relationships

Sibling relationships do not occur in a vacuum. For example, they are influenced by the quality of the relationships their parents have with their children and with each other. Negative behaviors of both older and younger siblings, such as aggression (East, 2009), were linked to negative aspects of the mother-child relationship and, for older siblings, to negative aspects of the parents' marital relationship (Erel et al., 1998). When parents have good relationships with their children, siblings are more likely to get along (East, 2009). The quality of young children's social relationships with siblings is also predictive of the quality of their relationships with friends, not only in early childhood but in middle childhood, adolescence, and adulthood as well (Bank et al., 1996; East, 2009; Volling et al., 1997). In a seven-year longitudinal study of the relationships between thirty-nine sibling pairs from mixed-SES families, Judy Dunn, Cheryl Slomkowski, and Lynn Beardsall (1994) followed the children from preschool through middle childhood and early adolescence. Sibling pairs included older male—younger female, older female—younger male, boy-boy and girl-girl dyads. The average ages of the sibling pairs were three years and six and a half years at the beginning of the study and ten years and thirteen and a half years when the study was completed. Sibling pairs were studied at four points in time: when the younger sibling was three years old, six years old, eight years old, and ten years old.

Sibling relationships are important to social development. The warm and relaxed relationship between this preschooler and his school-age brother is likely to contribute positively to the quality of their other social relationships.
Source: Blend Images/Shutterstock.com.

> **What Do You Think?**
>
> What style of parental authority best describes what you experienced as a child? Did it change during middle childhood and adolescence? If you now have children or expect to in the future, which pattern of parenting do (will) you use? Why?

Dunn and her colleagues found considerable continuity in siblings' positive feelings and behaviors (affection, warmth, intimacy, cooperation) and negative feelings and behaviors (competition, jealousy, fighting) toward one another from early childhood and through early adolescence. Their detailed interviews with the children and their mothers revealed that the majority of children provided support for each other when faced with such problems as difficulties with other children at school, maternal illness, or accidents and illnesses that they themselves had suffered. Good relationships among siblings also helped protect children who were experiencing the stress of parental conflict (Waite, Shanahan, Calkins, Keane, & O'Brien, 2011). Finally, both siblings and their mothers attributed negative changes in sibling relationships to new friendships the children formed outside the family during middle childhood.

Given the social opportunities that siblings offer, one might expect children growing up with brothers and sisters to develop social skills earlier and more rapidly, and perhaps to end up with better skills than children who lack siblings. But having siblings can have its down side as well. For instance, caring for a younger sibling is likely to enhance the younger child's social competence, but being burdened with the younger child's care may also limit the older child's opportunities to spend time with peers. How siblings will affect a particular child's social development is likely to depend on the degree to which parents recognize and respond appropriately to the social needs of all of their children. Siblings continue to play an important role in childhood and adolescence.

Only Children

Of course, not every child has a sibling. What impact does growing up as an "only child" have on development? Two widely held but conflicting views exist regarding this question. One view suggests that being an only child is a negative experience because it deprives only children of the advantages of having siblings and "spoils" them because they are the sole focus of their parents' attention. The second view sees only childhood as an advantage, allowing parents to be more responsive and attentive than they would be if they had to share their time and resources with other children (Rosenberg & Hyde, 1993). Research suggests that only children perform as well or somewhat better on various measures—including self-esteem, achievement motivation, and academic success—than those from two-child families who must share their parents with siblings, and that the greatest problem only children and their families face may be the prejudicial views about them (Eckstein et al., 2010; Falbo, 1992; Falbo 2012; Laybourn, 1990). There is some evidence that only children have slightly less social contact with family members as they grow up, but these differences between only children and those with siblings are quite small (Trent & Spitze, 2011).

Relationships in an Expanding Social World

As we have just seen, parents and siblings have a profound and long-lasting impact on the child's developing social skills. In early childhood, the child's social world expands and changes, providing new opportunities for testing out these skills, and new challenges as well. Children learn from many sources that they can influence their social relationships through their own helpful or aggressive behavior, as we now explore.

Empathy and Prosocial Behavior

empathy A sensitive awareness of the thoughts and feelings of another person.

Empathy, the ability to experience vicariously the emotions of another person, is thought to play an important role in the successful development of friendships and other close emotional relationships (Eisenberg et al., 1989). *Prosocial behavior* refers to positive social actions that benefit others, such as sharing, helping, and cooperating. Some prosocial behaviors are *altruistic,* meaning they are voluntarily aimed at helping others with no expectation of rewards for oneself. The development of both empathy and prosocial behavior is related to sound parent-child relationships and secure attachment during infancy and toddlerhood, which we discussed in Chapter 5.

Preschool children will respond helpfully to another person's distress in a variety of situations. For example, mothers' observational reports of the prosocial behavior of their four- and seven-year-olds at home indicate that spontaneous helping occurred in both age groups more frequently than did sharing and giving, affection and praise, or reassuring and protecting (Grusec, 1991). Young children are able to empathize in other settings as well. One study of children at a day-care center playground found that more than 90 percent of the time, a crying child generated concerned and mostly helpful responses from the other children (Sawin, 1979). About half of the children who were near the distressed child looked as though they would cry themselves. Almost 20 percent of the nearby children tried to console the child directly (and their actions did, in fact, help reduce the crying); other children sought out an adult on the playground; still others threatened revenge on the child who caused the upset. Children as young as fourteen months will reliably help another person retrieve an object that they cannot reach, and as they get older, children engage in more complex prosocial tasks (Hamann, Warneken, & Tomasello, 2012; Warneken & Tomasello, 2007).

Development of Prosocial Behavior

Prosocial behavior, or helpfulness, is well established by the time a child reaches the preschool years. An early, classic study found that all of the following helping behaviors occurred with significant frequency among four-year-olds (Murphy, 1937): assisting another child, comforting another child, protecting another child, warning another child of danger, giving things to another child, and inquiring of a child in trouble. Today, we find these behaviors not only among preschool children but even among children younger than two (Eisenberg & Mussen, 1989; Radke-Yarrow & Zahn-Waxler, 1987; Warneken & Tomasello, 2007).

Between the ages of two and six, children give increasingly complex reasons for helping and are more strongly influenced by nonaltruistic as well as altruistic motives and concerns (Eisenberg et al., 1989; Yarrow & Waxler, 1978). An older child may justify helpfulness

This girl is comforting her sister, who is upset. Important gains in children's capacity for empathy and emotional support develop during the preschool years.

Source: szefei/Shutterstock.com.

in terms of gaining approval from peers in general, rather than in terms of concern for the well-being of the child in distress. Or a child may justify withholding help because of fear of disapproval from adults—for example, if the child has been instructed to let the day-care or nursery school teachers handle children in trouble.

Sources of Prosocial Behavior

Potential sources of individual differences in prosocial responses include age, gender, temperament, childcare experience, social competence with peers, and friendship status (Farver & Branstetter, 1994). Prosocial behaviors increase with age due to gains in cognitive functioning, social skills, and moral reasoning and to more socialization experiences that enhance prosocial responsiveness (Eisenberg & Mussen, 1989; Warneken & Tomasello, 2007). No consistent gender differences in prosocial responses have been found, although some studies have found girls to be more prosocial than boys.

There is some evidence that differences in temperament affect children's prosocial behavior. Young children who display high levels of prosocial behavior tend to be active, outgoing, and emotionally expressive. This pattern is similar to the temperamentally *easy child,* whose high levels of adaptiveness, positive mood, and approachfulness (tendency to approach) may help him initiate and sustain more peer interaction than *difficult* or *slow-to-warm-up children,* who are more likely to avoid peer contact (Buss & Plomin, 1984; Farver & Branstetter, 1994; Kim & Jang, 2010).

Early exposure to prosocial experiences with peers, parents, and other important individuals may be the best predictor of later prosocial behavior. Jo Ann Farver and Wendy Branstetter (1994) studied prosocial behavior among preschoolers ages three to four and a half in three childcare programs. They found that the type and quality of peer contact children experienced more than the length of time children spent in their prior or current preschool programs influenced their prosocial tendencies. Early peer relationships are most likely to foster prosocial responsiveness when teachers, parents, and other adults create an environment that supports it and provides models for children to observe and imitate.

Prosocial competence among preschoolers may also depend on how often parents initiate informal play activities. Gary Ladd and Craig Hart (1992) found that children whose parents frequently arranged for them to play with peers and actively involved them in arranging play activities displayed higher levels of prosocial behavior. Children who more frequently initiated informal peer contacts were better liked by their classmates.

Overall differences in parenting styles also appear to influence preschoolers' prosocial behavior. Children whose parents are authoritative in their disciplinary styles engage in more prosocial, empathic, and compassionate behavior and less antisocial behavior in day-care, playground, and school settings later in life (Carlo et al., 2007) than do children whose parents have authoritarian discipline styles (Hart et al., 1992; Main & George, 1985; Zahn-Waxler et al., 1979). There is also evidence that fostering sympathy among children increases their prosocial behaviors (Carlo, McGinley, Hayes, Batenhorst, & Wilkinson, 2007; Carlo, Mestre, Samper, Tur, & Armenta, 2011).

Cross-cultural studies have provided some additional insights into the significance of parental support and encouragement (Carlo et al., 2011; Trommsdorff, Friedlmeier, & Mayer, 2007). In mainly rural societies where mothers worked in the fields and children assumed major childcare and household responsibilities, children had more opportunities to experience prosocial roles and to behave prosocially. Firstborn children, who had the most helping experience, tended to be more prosocial than lastborn or only children. Children raised in close-knit, communal Israeli kibbutz communities, which place high value on cooperation and prosocial behavior, exhibited higher levels of cooperation and prosocial behavior than did children from rural or big-city areas (Eisenberg et al., 1990; Whiting & Edwards, 1988).

What practical steps can parents and teachers take to increase altruism and prosocial behavior in the children they care for? Two techniques that have proven successful in increasing such behavior among preschoolers are (1) verbal approval and encouragement for being empathic, sympathetic, respectful, and helpful to others and (2) arranging regular play opportunities that support and encourage sharing, cooperation, and helping.

Conflict and Aggression

So far, our discussion of social relationships has focused on the ability of preschoolers to get along reasonably well with one another. However, preschoolers also get very angry and express their feelings in aggressive ways: grabbing one another's toys, pushing, hitting, scratching, and calling names. What types of interpersonal conflicts make preschoolers angry, and how do they cope with their angry feelings? Richard Fabes and Nancy Eisenberg (1992) observed the causes of anger and reactions to provocations among preschool children between ages 3 and 6½ while the children were at play. Conflict over possessions was the most common cause of anger, and physical assault was the second most frequent cause. In most types of anger conflicts, the majority of children responded by expressing angry feelings (particularly boys) or by actively attempting to defend themselves in non-aggressive ways (particularly girls). Active resistance was most likely in conflicts over material things such as toys and least likely in conflicts involving compliance with teachers and other adults. In contrast, venting of angry feelings was least likely in material conflicts and most likely in compliance conflicts with adults, suggesting that the particular coping strategy chosen depends, in part, on how controllable the child sees the situation to be. Children's use of aggressive revenge (hitting or threatening) and tattling was most frequent when their anger was caused by physical assault.

Aggression refers to actions that are intended to harm another person or an object. Aggressive actions frequently are divided into two types. **Overt aggression** harms others through physical damage or the threat of physical damage such as pushing, hitting, kicking, or threatening to "beat up" a peer. In contrast, **relational aggression** harms others through damage or threat of damage to their peer relationships, for example, by threatening to withdraw friendship to get one's way or by using social exclusion or rumor spreading as a form of retaliation. Children tend to express their aggression in ways that are most likely to interfere with or damage the social goals of their target and in ways that are socially acceptable for their gender. Consequently, boys are more likely to use overt, physical forms of aggression that hinder the dominance goals of boys, whereas girls are more likely to use more verbal, relational forms of aggression that effectively hinder the social intimacy goals that are more typical of girls' peer relationships (Card, Stucky, Sawalani, & Little, 2008; Crick et al., 1997). Although the harmful effects of overt aggression have long been obvious, recent studies indicate that relationally aggressive behaviors are also highly aversive and damaging to both victims and aggressors. The majority of children view these behaviors as mean, hostile acts that cause harm and are often carried out in anger, and children who are frequently the target of relationally aggressive acts experience more psychological distress, such as depression and anxiety, than do their

aggression A bold, assertive action that is intended to hurt another person or to procure an object.

overt aggression Actions that harm others through physical damage or the threat of such damage, such as pushing, hitting, kicking, or threatening to "beat up" a peer.

relational aggression Actions that harm others through damage or threat of damage to their peer relationships.

Hostile aggression among preschoolers is frequently associated with frustrations at being unable to solve a conflict over wants and desires, as well as with angry and jealous feelings that may result when they cannot get what they want.
Source: SpeedKingz/Shutterstock.com.

nontargeted peers (Card et al., 2008). Relationally aggressive boys and girls have poorer social and emotional adjustment and report higher levels of loneliness, depression, and negative self-perceptions than do their nonrelationally aggressive peers. Children who frequently engage in relational aggression are also far more likely to experience peer rejection, currently and in the future (Card et al., 2008; Crick, 1996; Crick & Grotpeter, 1995; Grotpeter & Crick, 1996).

When expressed in acceptable ways, aggression may be not only tolerable but even desirable. Aggressive actions allow a child to communicate and fulfill legitimate needs, such as when he takes back a toy that is rightfully his or stands up for his integrity against unfair insults. Often, however, hostile motivations complicate matters and create additional distress. The anger and rage children sometimes experience can be quite upsetting to them as well as to their parents and others. For example, a mother who observes her four-year-old attack a playmate, perhaps biting her or pulling her hair, is likely to be upset for multiple reasons, including her own child's unhappiness, the pain and distress of the other child, her belief that biting is "dirty fighting," and concerns about how all of this reflects on her as a parent.

Temperamental Differences in Aggression

Temperamental differences that are present at birth may make aggressive behavior and parent-child conflict more likely during early childhood. For example, babies who are low in their ability to regulate their physical and emotional states and high in emotional intensity may be especially prone to overt expressions of anger, frustration, and aggressive behavior, whereas those with a high ability to regulate these states are more likely to cope more constructively with their anger and frustration. Children who have difficulty regulating emotions are particularly prone to be aggressive when reacting to some type of perceived offense, such as someone bumping into them (Vitaro, Barker, Boivin, Brendgen, & Tremblay, 2006).

Consistent with this view, Nancy Eisenberg and her colleagues found that babies with especially "difficult" temperaments at six months of age experienced significantly more conflict with their mothers at age three than did babies with less difficult temperaments (Eisenberg & Fabes, 1992; Eisenberg et al., 1994; Rothbart, 2007). As three-year-olds, these children were more likely to be uncooperative, ignore their parents' disciplinary efforts, and respond in insulting and unpleasant ways. Their frustrated parents used a wide variety of methods to attempt to control them, including forbidding certain activities, threatening punishment, and using physical restraint. Thus, the ongoing interactions between these difficult children and their parents seemed likely to be escalating a cycle of aggression (Eisenberg et al., 1994). Of course, many active or difficult babies do not become aggressive three-year-olds, perhaps because the expression of temperament is largely a product of child-caregiver interactions. For example, when parents engage in authoritarian-type parenting, their children were more likely to be reactively aggressive, as described earlier, and proactively aggressive, such as intimidating others to get what they want (Vitaro et al., 2006).

A fifteen-year longitudinal study conducted by Avshalom Caspi and his colleagues found a relationship between early childhood temperament, including emotional instability, restlessness, impulsiveness, negativism, and teacher and parent reports of problems with aggression in middle childhood and adolescence (Caspi et al., 1995). Temperamental and family characteristics at age three have also been found to predict convictions for violent criminal activities at age eighteen (DeLisi & Vaughn, 2014; Henry et al., 1996).

Child-Rearing Styles and Aggression

As in the case of prosocial behavior discussed earlier, styles of child-rearing and the overall quality of the parent-child relationship are likely to significantly influence children's use of aggression in coping with interpersonal anger. There is some evidence that both indifferent and extremely authoritarian parenting styles are likely to be associated with higher levels of aggression and lower levels of prosocial behavior (DeKlyen et al., 1998; Herrenkohl et al., 1997; Hoeve et al., 2009). Longitudinal research by Kenneth Dodge and his colleagues found that children who experienced family violence, harsh, punitive (and potentially abusive) parenting styles, and parental rejection or hostility in their preschool years were much more likely to be both aggressive and victims of bullying in middle childhood than peers who received more supportive parenting (Deater-Deckhard et al., 1996; Schwartz et al., 1997; Vitaro et al., 2006).

All of the following child-rearing characteristics have been found to contribute to aggressiveness in preschoolers, especially when they are part of an ongoing pattern (Hart et al., 1990; Martin, 1975; Vitaro et al., 2006):

1. Lack of acceptance of the child, dislike of the child, and criticism of the child for being the sort of person she or he currently is or is becoming

2. Excessive permissiveness, particularly if it includes indifference to the child's true needs for reasonable but consistent limits and emotional support

3. Discipline that does not respect the child's ability and need to understand the reasons for the punishment and its meaning to the parent

4. Inconsistent discipline, which fails to provide the child with a reasonable and predictable basis for learning to regulate his or her behavior

5. A "spare the rod and spoil the child" belief that *too little* physical discipline would be harmful, which often results in impulsive and overly harsh use of discipline

6. Unclear rules and expectations for the child, particularly those regarding interactions with other family members

Children whose parents are able to accept their hostile-aggressive impulses and actions and respectfully guide their efforts to discover nonhostile methods for resolving conflicts and asserting their needs are most likely to learn to manage their aggression. The child-rearing orientation of such parents closely corresponds to the authoritative parenting style, which is strongly associated with the development of prosocial behavior.

Peer Influences on Aggression

Peers can also contribute to aggression by acting in ways that provoke aggressive retaliation. A child surrounded by provocative peers is likely to acquire a similar style herself and, in doing so, stimulate further aggressive behavior in her peers.

Some preschool children are continually involved in conflicts. They constantly either lose battles and arguments or lose potential friends by depending too much on hostile, aggressive actions to get what they need. Kenneth Dodge and his colleagues (Dodge & Coie, 1987; Schwartz et al., 1997) believe that a combination of low peer status and lack of social competence in the preschool period may contribute to a child's tendency to behave aggressively. When entering a new group, for example, aggressive children have difficulty in accurately processing and evaluating information about what is expected and in generating appropriate responses when faced with threats or provocation. Such children may have a biased pattern of thinking that leads them to overestimate the harmful intentions of their peers and to respond aggressively in situations that do not warrant it. The labeling of others' behavior that may actually be neutral and innocuous as aggression is called **hostile attribution bias**. Children are more likely to engage in hostile attribution bias and to react aggressively with those perceived as enemies (Peets, Hodges, Kikas, & Salmivalli, 2007). The aggressive, hostile behavior of an unpopular preschooler may also be his way of externalizing anger and distress he is experiencing due to similar problems at home.

hostile attribution bias
The tendency to view others' behavior as aggressive, even when those behaviors are innocuous, which often leads to a hostile, reactive response.

Media Influences on Aggression

As many concerned parents realize, television, films, video games, and other media exert a strong influence on children, and much of that influence centers on physical violence. Researchers estimate that three-to-four-year-olds watch two or more hours of television each day and that viewing TV violence increases children's aggressive behavior, at least in the short run. Numerous studies indicate that watching violence *disinhibits,* or releases, violent behavior in children who are already prone to anger and aggression, and also sets up scripts that guide behavior (Bushman & Huesmann, 2006; Clarke & Kutz-Costes, 1997; Huston et al., 1989). Viewing violent media may also increase the likelihood that a child engages in hostile attribution bias, which subsequently increases aggression (Gentile, Coyne, & Walsh, 2011). Longitudinal studies have linked the amount of TV violence viewed between the ages of two and five to antisocial behavior five years later for boys, even when accounting for preexisting behavioral problems and parenting factors such as education, depression, and responsiveness (Christakis & Zimmerman, 2007). Media are so pervasive in many preschoolers' lives that we consider their impact separately in the next section.

Responding to Aggressive Behavior

Children who have difficulty controlling their aggression experience considerable problems. Often they become aggressive at inappropriate times and in self-defeating ways, getting into fights with children and adults who are stronger than they are. Peers and parents alike find it difficult not to attribute malicious motives to children who seem out of control and appear unresponsive to generally agreed-on standards of behavior (Kutner, 1989). Children who are overly aggressive can stimulate strong feelings of inadequacy, guilt, anger, and loss of control in their parents, leading to an increased risk that parents will respond in angry, punitive, ways.

Spanking and Other Forms of Punishment

In general, preschoolers conform to parental expectations, especially if those expectations are communicated in a clear, understandable way that conveys warmth and respect for the child. Even when a child resists, patient explanation and responsiveness to his feelings and perceptions generally resolve the problem. In instances when a preschooler "loses it" and throws a tantrum or refuses to comply with a parent's reasonable and necessary demands, firm but respectful physical restraint and guidance may also be needed until the child has regained self-control. In dangerous situations requiring immediate action, such as when a child runs into the street or is about to touch something hot, parents may use strong reprimands or spanking to stop the risky behavior and prevent it from happening again. However, using spanking as a punishment is not only ineffective, it can teach children to fear their parents and that physical violence is an appropriate means to control others.

Some parents rely on spanking and punishment as a regular part of their child-rearing discipline. James Comer and Alvin Poussaint (1992), two prominent child psychiatrists, point out that children who were spanked by thoughtful, loving parents rarely have problems as a result of the spanking. Nevertheless, Comer and Poussaint caution that punishment is not the best way to provide discipline, especially in cases where parents are having difficulty with their preschoolers. A better alternative is to physically remove the child from the dangerous situation and to talk about why the parent is upset, why the child's behavior is unacceptable, and expectations of how to behave in the future.

What problems are associated with spanking and punishment in general? Although verbal or physical punishment can suppress misbehavior in the short run, it is not an effective or desirable long-run strategy, particularly if it is harsh or frequent. One obvious problem is that preschoolers are very likely to imitate the behavior of the adult models who punish them (Bandura, 1991; Emery, 1989; Taylor, Manganello, Lee, & Rice, 2010). Using aggressive behavior such as verbal threats or spanking to reduce a child's unacceptable behavior is likely to increase the very behavior it seeks to control. A child who is hit by an angry parent learns to act on his own anger in similar ways, which is surely not the lesson his parents intend. Even moderate use of spanking appears to contribute to child aggression. One large-scale study conducted by Robert Larzelere (1986) using a nationally representative sample of parents with at least one child age three to seventeen living at home found that the use of physical punishment was positively associated with child aggression. In situations where spanking was frequent and reasons were rarely provided, the association between spanking and child aggression dramatically increased. Excessive reliance on spanking and other forms of punishment is strongly linked to child maltreatment, a topic we discuss later in this chapter.

A second problem with spanking and other forms of punishment is that a child quickly learns to fear and avoid the punishing adult, thus reducing opportunities for adult supervision and constructive adult-child interactions. Third, because punishment quickly suppresses the child's undesirable behavior in the short run, it serves to reinforce adult reliance on punishment and reduce the likelihood of exploring other ways to respond to the child's unacceptable behavior. Fourth, to the extent that punishment reduces the guilt a child feels for misbehaving, it reinforces the child's reliance on external (parental) control rather than internal, self-control of his behavior (Comer & Poussaint, 1992).

Helping Aggressive Children and Their Parents

Several principles have emerged from work with aggressive children and their families aimed at helping them learn more constructive ways of interacting. The most successful approaches frequently involve working with the entire family. The first step is to carefully observe the child's interactions with peers and adults to discover consistent patterns in what triggers the aggression and how each family member may unintentionally reinforce the patterns of problem behavior (Kutner, 1989; Patterson et al., 1989).

Structure, predictability, and consistency of routine are important for all preschoolers, especially for children who have difficulty controlling their aggressive behavior. For such children, aggressive outbursts are most likely to occur in unstructured and ambiguous situations. Such circumstances aggravate their tendency to distort information about potential harm and to perceive themselves as being at risk. Thus, neutral behavior, such as the approach of another child, is misinterpreted as an aggressive act (Dodge et al., 1994; Peets et al., 2007).

Once the patterns of aggression are discovered, parents can learn to recognize the early signs and intervene by either changing the situation or removing their preschooler before things escalate. The most successful methods involve reinforcement of positive behaviors through warmth, affection, and parental approval; reasoning with children and talking to them calmly about the situation (Sheehan & Watson, 2008); assertiveness training to help children meet their needs for attention in less self-destructive ways; and increasing predictability and consistency in children's everyday lives (Kutner, 1989; Patterson, 1989).

Another successful approach to modifying destructive family processes and problems with childhood aggression uses social learning theory methods such as coaching, modeling, and reinforcing alternative patterns of parent-child interaction. After carefully observing the parent-child interaction, the therapist describes and then demonstrates alternative ways to deal with the child's hostile, aggressive, or disobedient behaviors. As parents gain more confidence in their competence, they become more effective parents; as children learn to resolve conflicts in more appropriate ways, their problematic behavior decreases (Patterson, 1982, 1985).

The Effects of Media on Preschoolers' Development

As influential as parents and family are in the lives of preschoolers, media have become another potent force in teaching preschoolers about the wider world. More than 99 percent of American homes have at least one television set (Siebens, 2013). Eighty-four percent of homes have a computer, and 75 percent of households have Internet access (File & Ryan, 2014). When all media consumption is combined, the average American consumes about 15.5 hours of media per day (Short, 2015). Most children are exposed to media on television and computers from the time they are born, and American children spend as much or more time, on average, watching TV than in any other waking activity, including play (Calvert, 2008; Condry, 1993). Differences in family circumstances significantly affect young children's TV viewing. Living in neighborhoods that parents thought of as unsafe was linked to increased media use, and children whose parents engage in limit setting consumed less media than those with parents who did not set limits (Lee, Bartolic, & Vandewater, 2009).

As Figure 10.1 shows, a typical three-year-old is in front of a TV set approximately two hours per day. Viewing time increases during the preschool years and peaks at about 2.5 hours per day (Ofcom, 2014; Vandewater, 2007). Boys and girls appear to watch equal

FIGURE 10.1

Media Use among Children

Hours of media consumption per week for children of different ages.
Source: Ofcom, 2014.

amounts of television. The same basic developmental pattern has been found in a number of European countries, Canada, and Australia, and the amount of time using any kind of media other than print has increased significantly since 1999, mostly due to increased time using multiple types of media at one time (Rideout, Foehr, & Roberts, 2010).

Not surprisingly, the types of programs children prefer to watch also change with age. Until they are age three or four, children prefer programs such as "Bubble Guppies," "Sesame Street," and "Caillou," which are designed for children and feature language, characters, and events at a level children can readily understand. Children ages three to five tend to watch more cartoons, and children ages five to seven increasingly watch comedies, action shows, and special-interest programs that are more cognitively demanding and aimed at general audiences (Huston et al., 1990).

What Do Kids See on TV?

Television viewing has been found to influence children's social development in a number of areas, including aggression, prosocial behavior, consumer behavior, executive functioning, eating behaviors, and gender stereotypes (Anderson & Anderson, 2010; Christakis & Zimmerman, 2007; Coyne, Linder, Rasmussen, Nelson, & Collier, 2014; Huston & Wright, 1996; Lillard & Peterson, 2011). The relationships between viewing aggression on TV and children's aggressive behavior are notable.

Preschoolers have a special problem in coping with violence on TV: their lack of skill in figuring out the motives of characters portrayed and the subtleties of plots. A heinous murder on television may look the same to a preschooler as one committed in self-defense or to protect innocent people. Also, some of the most violent TV programs are those produced for children; Saturday morning cartoons, which are now available any time on cartoon-based channels and streaming content services like Netflix, average more than twenty violent acts per hour (Gerbner et al., 1986; Kirsh, 2006). Programs such as "Spider Man," "Iron Man," "Teen Titans," and "Adventure Time" and many films that young children view also contain substantial amounts of violent content. Violent video and computer games pose similar problems for young children and their parents (Adachi & Willoughby, 2011; Emes, 1997). Adult supervision and help in understanding television programs therefore are especially important for very young children. Unfortunately, one of television's main attractions for some parents is that it makes adult supervision unnecessary by keeping children passively occupied.

Recent widespread concern about children's exposure to television violence has led to a new U.S. communications law stipulating that all new TV sets be equipped with a "violence chip," or V-chip. The V-chip "reads" TV programming and allows parents to tune out shows that they consider too violent for their children based on a rating system. Though technologies exist to control children's media consumption and limit exposure to violent programming, most parents do not actually use them (Calvert, 2008).

In addition, television programs designed for children (and for adults) often convey a highly stereotyped and distorted social world that values being male, youthful, handsome, and white over being female, old, handicapped, dark-skinned, or foreign born. Despite efforts to broaden the portrayals of gender roles, women continue to be cast in strongly sex-typed roles such as teacher, secretary, nurse, or homemaker. On television, women solve problems less frequently, need help more often, listen better, and talk less than men do and behave in other gender-stereotypical ways. These patterns also prevail for children's television despite widespread concern about the ways gender stereotypes limit girls' expectations. One reason for this may be that boys, who are reinforced largely by their peers, show much greater interest in shows with action heroes than in programs that present less stereotypic male activities. The significance of these patterns is not lost on advertisers, who are interested in buying time on programs that most effectively sell their products (Calvert, 2008; Wright et al., 1995).

However, television is also a very useful educational tool for supporting children's intellectual and social development. Studies have found, for example, that programs modeling cooperative, prosocial behavior are likely to increase children's prosocial behavior and that children who are exposed to nongender and nonracially stereotyped programs are more likely than other children to behave in less stereotypic ways (Calvert, 2008; Liebert & Sprafkin, 1988).

How Do Parents Affect Viewing Patterns?

The types of programs TV networks and streaming services provide and the choices parents make about what their children view strongly affect young children's viewing patterns (Calvert, 2008; Huston et al., 1992). Families vary considerably in their attitudes toward television and the amount and type of guidance they provide for their children. While nearly 40 percent of the parents of preschoolers sometimes use TV to keep their children occupied, between 40 and 60 percent state that they regularly limit the number of hours their children can watch, and 50 to 60 percent have consistent rules regarding which types or which specific programs their children are allowed to view (Calvert, 2008; Comstock, 1991; Gentile, Nathanson, Rasmussen, Reimer, & Walsh, 2012). It is important to note that when surveying children and their parents, parents' estimates of these monitoring behaviors are significantly higher than their children's estimates of the same monitoring behaviors (Gentile et al., 2012).

Current recommendations for media use during early childhood are that children age two and under should not watch TV or use other types of entertainment, and that after age two, media should be limited, that parents should use media along with their children, and that families should set up times and places that are "screen-free" to encourage physical activity, reading, and traditional game playing (American Academy of Pediatrics, 2016; Connell, Lauricella, & Wartella, 2015). Though increasing numbers of children have their own television (33 percent of children age six or under have their own television—Vandewater et al., 2007), the amount of time that parents spend watching television is the strongest predictor of child viewing time, even when accounting for bedroom TV access (Bleakley, Jordan, & Hennessy, 2013). When considering other types of media, co-use rates shift. Parents are most likely to use books and TV along with their children, but much less likely to use computers or video games along with their children, even though this type of media sharing has been linked to more prosocial behaviors, higher levels of cohesiveness within a family, higher child self-efficacy, and more use of educational websites (Connell, Lauricella, & Wartella, 2015).

Play during Early Childhood

In our society and many others, play dominates the preschool years. What are the play activities of a preschooler like, and what important contributions does play make to a child's development? Before we tackle these questions, we must first agree on what we mean by *play*.

> **What Do You Think?**
>
> When you were a child, how did your family deal with the issues of prosocial behavior, aggression, and television? If you become a parent (or are now a parent), what might you change and what might you keep the same? Why?

The Nature of Play

One useful approach to defining *play* focuses on the attitudes and dispositions of children themselves (Saracho & Spodek, 1998). First, play is *intrinsically* (rather than *extrinsically*) motivated. Children engage in play mainly because it is enjoyable and reinforcing for its own sake rather than because it is useful in achieving external goals.

Second, play is *process* oriented rather than *product* oriented. At the local playground, for instance, children may care very little about the goal of using the slide, to get from top to bottom, but likely care a lot about their style of sliding—whether they go head first or feet first, or how fast they go.

Third, play is *creative* and *nonliteral.* Although it resembles real-life activities, it differs from them in that it is not bound by reality. For example, a child who is "play fighting" looks different than one who really is fighting, and a child playing Mommy typically acts differently than one who is actually caring for a baby brother or sister. The features that reveal an activity as play rather than the real thing vary with the particular type of play and the situation; a play fight may include smiles and laughter, and a make-believe mother may be exaggeratedly bossy. Whatever the signs, they communicate the message that "this behavior is *not* what it first may appear to be." Even so, it is common for a preschooler to become so caught up in a round of dramatic play that he forgets for a moment that it is not real and becomes truly frightened when his make-believe mother tells him he has been bad and must sit in the corner.

Fourth, play tends to be governed by *implicit rules*—that is, rules that can be discovered by observing the activity, rather than rules that are formally stated and that exist independently of the activity. For example, although no rule book exists for playing house, children implicitly understand that there can be two parents and that these actors must live up to certain expectations. If one player deviates too widely from the expected role, the other children are likely to correct her for it ("Hey, babies don't drive cars; only big people do that!").

Fifth, play is *spontaneous* and *self-initiated,* meaning it is engaged in only under a child's own free will and is not evoked or controlled by others. Finally, play is *free from major emotional distress.* Play does not normally occur when a child is in a state of fear, uncertainty, or other kind of significant stress. It might be interesting to think about play in your own childhood, adolescence, and adulthood and see to what degree it has involved these six qualities.

Theories of Play

There are four main theoretical approaches to play: psychoanalytic, learning, ethological, and cognitive. Although each theory emphasizes a somewhat different aspect of play, all hold that play activities make a major contribution to the development of important social and emotional skills and understandings during the preschool years. Moreover, play during early childhood has important implications for the development and refinement of social information processing, empathy, emotional regulation, conflict management, perspective taking, and skilled social interaction over the lifespan (Creasey et al., 1998; Power, 2011).

Psychoanalytic Theory

Psychoanalytic theories emphasize the social and emotional importance of play in early childhood. Play gives a child an opportunity to *gain mastery* over problems by rearranging objects and social situations in ways that allow her to imagine she is in control. Following an especially painful and upsetting experience, such as being suddenly separated from a parent who is hospitalized for a serious illness, a child may display *repetition compulsion,* repeating the experience over and over in symbolic play with dolls or other toys to gain greater control, or resolution, of the distress.

Play also allows a child to use fantasy to *gain satisfaction for wishes and desires* that are not possible to fulfill in reality due to limitations in the child's abilities and life situation. Play also provides an opportunity for *catharsis,* the release of upsetting feelings that cannot be expressed otherwise. Finally, play allows children to *gain increased power* over the environment by rearranging it to suit their own needs and abilities (Lewis, 1993). These facets of play are particularly useful in helping young children in therapeutic sessions (James & Countryman, 2012; Kool & Lawver, 2010).

Learning Theory

Learning theorists view play as a major means by which children progressively learn adult skills and social roles. A child learns in three ways: through her own experience of being praised or encouraged for her own actions (direct reinforcement), through observations of adults and other children being reinforced for their activities (vicarious reinforcement), and through the experience of setting a goal and achieving it (cognitive or self-reinforcement).

For example, what might a three-year-old who is playing with wooden blocks be learning about the adult world? For one thing, building with blocks gives the child an opportunity to learn about the nature and design of physical structures and space. The child also learns about how hard blocks are, how high they can be piled, and how many small ones equal a larger one. She might also learn about her own capabilities and limitations as a builder: how high she can reach, how many blocks he can carry at once, and so forth. Playing with blocks also exposes the child to adult expectations and practices, such as when and where blocks can be used, picked up, and stored and how to share blocks, take turns, and cooperate with others.

Ethological Theory

Theorists such as A. D. Pellegrini and Peter Smith (1998) believe that children's **physical activity play**—vigorous physical activity that occur in a playful context—has a basis in human evolution and serves several adaptive developmental functions. Examples include running, climbing, chasing, and play fighting. Physical activity play begins in early infancy, peaks during childhood, declines during adolescence, and all but disappears

physical activity play
Vigorous physical activity that occurs in a playful context, has a basis in human evolution, and serves several adaptive developmental functions.

In early childhood, the process of doing things often matters more than the outcome. Even doing the dishes can seem like play.
Source: Pressmaster/Shutterstock.com.

by adulthood. It appears to take three forms. The first is *rhythmic stereo types.* These repetitive movements, such as body rocking and foot kicking displayed by infants and the repetitive play interactions between parents and older infants, such as bouncing the baby on one's knee or tossing and catching the infant, are thought to help infants improve their sensorimotor skills. A second form of physical activity play, *exercise play,* emerges at the end of the first year. Exercise play includes chasing, jumping, pushing and pulling, lifting, and climbing. It appears to peak in the preschool and early primary grades, and is thought to contribute to the development of physical strength, endurance, and coordination. The third form, *rough-and-tumble play,* includes vigorous behaviors such as wrestling, grappling, kicking, tumbling, and chasing in a playfully aggressive way. Rough-and-tumble play increases through the preschool years and peaks at around eight to ten years, just prior to early adolescence. It is thought to provide a way for children to assess their own physical strength compared to the strength of others, establish dominance status in peer groups, assist in emotion-regulation development, and gain skill at recognizing and responding appropriately to the emotional states of others (Power, 2011). Fathers are more likely than mothers to engage in rough-and-tumble play with their children, which can lead to higher rates of aggression later in childhood if those fathers do not take a dominant role in that play (Flanders, Leo, Paquette, Pihl, & Séguin, 2009).

Cognitive Theory

Cognitive theorists, discussed in Chapter 2, have identified four major kinds of play that they believe develop sequentially in parallel with the major stages of cognitive development (Piaget, 1962; Smilansky, 1968). Table 10.2 describes the different types of cognitive play.

Cognitive Levels of Play: Developmental Trends

Functional Play

Functional play, which involves simple, repeated movements such as splashing water or digging in a sandbox, is most common during the sensorimotor period. Because it requires no symbolic activity, functional play makes up more than one-half of the play activity of older infants and toddlers. By the time a child reaches kindergarten or first grade, however, functional play has decreased to less than one-quarter of his total play time. This shift occurs partly because some of the physical activities typical of functional play become incorporated into more symbolic forms of play (Hetherington et al., 1979; Sponseller & Jaworski, 1979).

functional play A cognitive level of play that involves simple, repeated movements and a focus on one's own body.

TABLE 10.2 Types of Cognitive Play

Type	Description and Examples
Functional play	Simple, repetitive movements—sometimes, with objects or own body
	Example: Shoveling sand, pushing a toy
Constructive play	Manipulation of physical objects to build or construct something
	Example: Building with blocks
Pretend play	Substituting make-believe, imaginary, and dramatic situations for real ones
	Example: Playing house or Superman
Games with rules	Play that is more formal and governed by fixed rules
	Example: Jumping rope, hide-and-seek

Constructive play, such as block building, is probably the most common form of play in early childhood.
Source: Ami Parikh/Shutterstock.com.

constructive play A type of play that involves manipulation of physical objects to build or construct something.

pretend play Play that substitutes imaginary situations for real ones. Also called *fantasy* or *dramatic play.*

games with rules A cognitive level of play involving relatively formal activities with fixed rules.

Constructive Play

Constructive play involves manipulation of physical objects, such as using blocks to build something. This form of play is evident in older infants and preschoolers, although it is not always clear where functional play ends and constructive play begins. For example, a child who at first appears to be building a mountain out of sand may forget about her goal and end up just shoveling the sand for the fun of it. As the child grows older, however, the constructive elements of play become quite clear. Not only does she build a mountain; she builds it in a certain shape and adds a road leading to it and perhaps a car or two to make the trip.

Pretend Play

Pretend play (also called *fantasy* or *dramatic play*) substitutes imaginary situations for real ones, such as in playing house or Superman, and dominates the preoperational period. Pretend play occurs even among toddlers and probably begins as soon as a child can symbolize, or mentally represent, objects. Family roles (including mother, father, brother, sister, baby, and even family pet) and *character roles* based on fictionalized heroes, such as Batman, Disney princesses, Iron Man, and Kung Fu Panda, are most likely to be dramatized by preschool children. Pretend play grows in frequency and complexity during the preschool years and eventually decreases again later in childhood, when social pressures to act more "grown up" reduce it in public settings (Dunn, 1985; Howes & Matheson, 1992; Kavanaugh & Engel, 1998; Russ & Dillon, 2011). The complexity, flexibility, and elaborateness of preschoolers' fantasy play also appear to be positively related to the quality of their family relationships, to the support and the nurturance preschoolers receive from their parents, and to the specific reinforcement parents give them for such play (Howe et al., 1998; Ladd & Hart, 1992). Though children have less unstructured time for play than they did in the past, they display just as much emotional expression and more imagination in their play (Russ & Dillon, 2011).

Pretend play is a good example of how new forms of experience are assimilated into existing schemes of cognitive understanding. In addition to allowing the child to practice and expand schemes already acquired, such play contributes to the consolidation and expansion of cognitive skills during early childhood (Piaget, 1962; Vygotsky, 1967). Early pretend play, when suitably nurtured by family members and other individuals or settings in which a child participates, plays an important role in the development of fantasy and make-believe in middle childhood and of daydreaming and overt pretend play in adulthood (Power, 2011; Singer, 1995).

Games with Rules

Games with rules, such as Simon Says and hide-and-seek, first appear during the concrete operational period, when children are five or six years old, and peak in frequency toward the end of elementary school (Rubin & Krasnor, 1980). Piaget (1964), in fact, did his original studies of moral development by interviewing and observing children playing rule-based games. The rules for many such games apparently develop out of the more flexible, "made-up" rules of pretend play. Instead of continuing to negotiate roles and behaviors as they go along, young children gradually learn to agree on them beforehand and to stand by their agreements throughout a play episode. Due to their greater formality, games with rules can become traditions handed down from one sibling to another, from older to younger playmates, and from generation to generation. Hopscotch, for example, has been around in some form for many generations.

Other Influences on Play and Friendship

The composition of a particular child's play is likely to be influenced by the range of play opportunities caregivers provide and the types of play they encourage. For example, a parent or caregiver who insists that the child always be learning something or trying something new may make play a stressful rather than a rewarding experience for the child. Outside

In dramatic play, children take on pretend roles, like the "doctor" and "patient" here. Realistic props such as the white coat and stethoscope in the photograph encourage dramatic play, although they are not always necessary.
Source: XiXinXing/Shutterstock.com.

the home, children who attend childcare centers with qualified staffs, developmentally appropriate programs, and safe, well-designed, and well-equipped play areas have been found to develop more complex forms of pretend play at earlier ages, to engage in much less unoccupied and solitary play, to have less screen time, and to interact more positively with adults than children in less adequate centers (Howes & Matheson, 1992; Susa & Benedict, 1994; Tandon, Zhou, Lozano, & Christakis, 2011; Trawick-Smith & Dziurgot, 2011). Some centers help teach pretend play to children with autism spectrum disorder to help them glean the benefits of pretend play with their peers, such as language development (Barton & Pavilanis, 2012).

Having adequate time for play is also important. Large amounts of television viewing can reduce the amount of time available for play, and watching programs with high levels of violence has been associated with decreased levels of fantasy play (Tandon et al., 2011; van-der-Voort & Valkenburg, 1994).

Although play is a universal activity and occurs in all cultures, its frequency, forms, and functions also vary with cultural and socioeconomic contexts (Farver & Shin, 1997; Milteer et al., 2012; Roopnarine et al., 1994). For example, in countries such as Kenya, India, Ecuador, and Brazil, where many children spend a large part of the day doing household chores and assisting their families in getting food or money, time and opportunity for play are far more limited than for children in Mexico, the Philippines, or the United States (Campos et al., 1994; Hoffnung, 1992; Whiting & Whiting, 1975).

Even when free time, space, and toys are limited, however, most children find a way to play. They use common household objects such as pots, pans, and furniture, as well as outdoor items such as trees, sticks, rocks, sand, empty cans, and discarded equipment, as props for their make-believe and sociodramatic play. However, the range and developmental appropriateness of play activities under such circumstances are likely to be more restricted than in the case of children who play in more supportive settings. Table 10.3 summarizes age-appropriate recommendations for preschool play materials for children growing up in the United States.

Social Levels of Play

Play also varies according to how social it is—that is, how much and in what ways children involve others in their play activities. Mildred Parten studied social participation among children ages two to five and proposed that children's play develops in six stages, or levels, of sociability (Parten, 1932). Although subsequent researchers have questioned whether Parten's categories

TABLE 10.3 General Characteristics and Appropriate Play Materials for the Preschool Child

Age	General Characteristics	Appropriate Play Materials
2	Uses language effectively. Large-muscle skills developing, but limited in the use of small muscle skills. Energetic, vigorous, and enthusiastic, with a strong need to demonstrate independence and self-control.	Large-muscle play materials: Swing sets, outdoor blocks, toys to ride on, pull toys, push toys. Sensory play materials: Clay, finger paints, materials for water play, blocks, books, dolls and stuffed animals.
3	Expanded fantasy life, with unrealistic fears. Fascination with adult roles. Still stubborn, negative, but better able to adapt to peers than at age two. Early signs of product orientation in play.	Props for imaginative play (e.g., old clothes). Miniature life toys. Puzzles, simple board games, art materials that allow for a sense of accomplishment (e.g., paintbrushes, easels, marker pens, crayons).
4	Secure, self-confident. Need for adult attention and approval—showing off, clowning around, taking risks. Plan more than threes, but products often accidental. Sophisticated small-muscle control allows for cutting, pasting, sewing, imaginative block building with smaller blocks.	Vehicles (e.g., tricycles, Big Wheels). Materials for painting, coloring, drawing, woodworking, sewing, stringing beads. Books with themes that extend well beyond the child's real world.
5	Early signs of logical thinking. Stable, predictable, reliable. Less self-centered than at four. Relaxed, friendly, willing to share and cooperate with peers. Realistic, practical, responsible.	Cut-and-paste and artistic activities with models to work from. Simple card games (e.g., Go Fish), table games (e.g., Bingo), and board games (e.g., Chutes and Ladders), in which there are few rules and the outcomes are based more on chance than on strategy. Elaborate props for dramatic play.

Source: Hughes (1991), p. 70.

actually form a developmental sequence, her distinctions continue to be useful to people who study young children. Table 10.4 describes the six types of play Parten identified.

How Play Changes with Age

As we saw in the Chapter 7 discussion of psychosocial development during infancy, even very young infants actively interact with the objects and people in their environment, and by twelve months of age, their play interactions with peers become more frequent, particularly those that involve toys. Access to peers through play groups or day care and parental support tend to increase the likelihood of peer play.

Mildred Parten (1932) found that parallel play accounted for almost half of early childhood play activity, whereas solitary' play occupied about one-fourth, associative play one-fifth, and cooperative and unoccupied play less than one-tenth of the total. Parallel and solitary play appeared to decline throughout the preschool years, whereas associative play and cooperative play, which involve greater social participation, increased with age.

As preschoolers get older, play involving coordinated interactions increases. These interactions include imitation; complementary exchanges in which playmates take different roles, such as driver or passenger in pretend play; and more complex combinations of imitation and complementary exchanges (Eckerman et al., 1989; Power, 2011). Preschool children's highest level of peer social play also increases with age, progressing through a sequence of parallel play, simple social play, complementary and reciprocal play, cooperative social pretend play, and finally complex social pretend play. Children who spend more of their play time in complex forms of play appear to have greater overall social competence with their peers. The nature and number of available playmates are

TABLE 10.4 Parten's Social Levels of Play

Type	Description and Examples
Unoccupied play	The child wanders about, watching whatever is of momentary interest, but does not become involved in any activity.
Solitary play	The child plays alone with different toys or other objects and with no direct or indirect awareness of or involvement with other children, even if nearby.
Onlooker play	The child watches others play without actually entering into the activities; is clearly involved with what is happening and usually is within speaking distance of the participants.
Parallel play	Two or more children play with the same toys in a similar way, in close proximity, and with an awareness of each other's presence; they do not share toys, talk, or interact except in very minimal ways.
Associative play	Children engage in a common activity and talk about it with each other, but they do not assign tasks or roles to particular individuals and are not very clear about their goals.
Cooperative play	Children consciously form groups to make something, attain a goal, or dramatize a situation; one or two members organize and direct the activity, with children assuming different roles and responsibilities.

Source: Parten (1932).

also important (Benenson et al., 1997; Howes & Matheson, 1992; Power, 2011). See the "Working With" interview with Javier Hernandez for a discussion of play and friendship during early childhood.

Play and Friendship in Early Childhood

Preschool children are simultaneously pulled in two directions. On the one hand, they seek the security and intimacy that come from playing continually with a familiar friend; on the other, they want to participate in the variety of activities that many different children make possible.

The Evolution of Friendship

John Gottman and Jennifer Parkhurst (1980) made extensive home observations of preschoolers between ages three and six as the children played with friends and new acquaintances. They found that play between younger children and their friends included frequent and extensive fantasy role playing, whereas older children's friendships focused more on the actual activities they were doing than on make-believe roles. Younger children communicated more clearly with their friends than did older children and were more responsive to their friends' requests for information or explanation. They also worked harder to create a "climate of agreement" by avoiding disagreements. They did this by immediately discussing the reasons for a disagreement or explaining them away and by using positive social comparisons with their friends to create a sense of common ground and solidarity. Older children were better able to tolerate differences and disagreements and had less need to use positive social comparisons to manage conflict in their friendships.

Due to the "management" problems just noted and the emphasis on overt, concrete, shared activities—such as whether to build a sand castle, how to draw a dog, how to cook a pretend dinner—early friendships tend to be somewhat unstable and may change on a weekly or even daily basis. A preschool child will drop a friend relatively easily and later

> **WORKING WITH** Javier Hernandez, Preschool Program Coordinator
>
> **Play and Friendships among Preschoolers**
>
> Javier Hernandez coordinates a privately run preschool program that serves a middle- and working-class community. A parent himself, he has a degree in early childhood education and has worked in preschool and day-care programs for almost six years. Javier was interviewed during nap time in the day-care center office and talked about ways in which children's playing styles evolve over time.
>
> **Rob:** *Your program serves a pretty wide age range. Do you see the kids' play change as they grow older?*
>
> **Javier:** Yes, I do. Most of the two-year-olds' play involves sharing toys and turn taking—"it's my turn, it's your turn." They might share building blocks or share crayons when they draw. They can follow simple directions, like for circle time at the beginning and end of the day and for various other activities.
>
> **Rob:** *How do three-year-olds play differently?*
>
> **Javier:** Between three and three and a half, you see an amazing increase in dramatic and fantasy play. The games become more complex and are rarely what they appear to be. The two-year-olds see the climber, as just a climber, but the three-year-olds see it as a car, a spaceship, a house, or anything else they decide. The kids all make up different names and are deeply into imaginative role playing. They're always trying to involve you in their fantasy play.
>
> **Rob:** *What about rules?*
>
> **Javier:** They're very interested in rules—setting them and following them. They'll tell each other, "Oh, we can't do that now" or "We can't go that way" or "That's not the way we do it," or "You have to sit down." They're really into structure and delight in pointing out the right and wrong way to do things. There's a lot of tattling; I'll frequently overhear "You're going to get in trouble if you do that" or "You can't walk up the slide."
>
> **Rob:** *This is quite different behavior than the two-year-olds.*
>
> **Javier:** Yes. The two-year-olds are more apt to hit or push another kid, who will cry until the teacher comes over. With three-year-olds, the one who gets hit or pushed cries, but goes and then tells the teacher, "He hit me" and watches to see what you're going to do about it.
>
> **Rob:** *So this also reflects the superior verbal and cognitive abilities of three-year-olds?*
>
> **Javier:** Yes. The two-year-olds do a lot of copy-catting. What one wants, the other one wants, and they want everything to be the same. Their attention spans are much shorter, and they change their minds quickly. They often forget

make up to her just as easily. Sometimes she will even exchange goods for friendship: "If you give me a piece of candy, I'll be your best friend!"

Preschoolers are also capable of sustaining relationships with playmates that last for a year or more (Howes, 1988; Howes et al., 1998; Poulin & Chan, 2010). These preferences are an important step in forming more lasting friendships later in childhood, as well as a basis for learning to get along with others. By age three to four, friendships become more involved and durable. Certain pairs of children develop a liking for each other and purposely try to spend time together. In fact, approximately 80 percent of three-to-four-year-olds spend a substantial amount of time with at least one special "associate," or playmate. Children in nursery school spend at least 30 percent of their time with one other peer. Typically, the pairings develop in situations that encourage physical proximity, such as the children's neighborhood play group, day-care center, or preschool classroom. Pairs of preschool friends exhibit greater reciprocity and interdependence with each other in their parallel play, requesting, and following/imitating activities than they do with mere acquaintances (Goldstein et al., 1989; Power, 2011).

About 75 percent of nursery school children are involved in reciprocated friendships, as reflected in time spent in one another's company, nursery school teachers' reports, and interviews with their mothers. This number increases through adolescence, with 80 to 90 percent of teenagers reporting having mutual friends and several "close" or "good" friends. Friendship networks are small among preschool children, consisting of one or

WORKING WITH Javier Hernandez, Preschool Program Coordinator

Play and Friendships among Preschoolers *continued*

what they want, and you can never be sure just what they're after.

Rob: *And the three-year-olds?*

Javier: They have much longer attention spans. They'll get so involved in a story that they won't move a muscle. And you have to point out and explain every detail of every picture in the book.

Rob: *You have to satisfy their desire to fully understand exactly what is going on?*

Javier: Exactly. Two-year-olds will keep on saying *why* just for the sake of it. Three- and four-year-olds really want a solid answer and are generally satisfied once they hear one they like. They're really listening to what you're saying, whereas the two-year-olds are mainly practicing their verbal skills.

Rob: *What about friendships and prosocial behavior among preschoolers?*

Javier: If one two-year-old is aggressive toward another and you say, "That wasn't very nice, you hurt his feelings and I think you need to say you are sorry," she may go over to the child and say, "sorry," but five minutes later might do the same thing again. Three-and four-year-olds tend to be more aware of other children's feelings and of their own. They base their friendships on who is nice to them and are better able to appreciate how it feels to be hurt. If you say, "Well, would you like it if she did that to you?" they are likely to say, "No, I wouldn't like it."

Rob: *Are they better able to take care of each other?*

Javier: Yes. We have two children who started in the infant room and went all the way up to kindergarten together. By the last few months they were here, if Larry said anything to Jenelle that she was sensitive about, she would just fall apart because "He's my best friend." She would get very sad and look to us to help them make up and mend their friendship. Then Larry would apologize, and they would hug. Older preschoolers seem to know a lot about each other's personalities. They know what to expect of each other and are very aware of what other children are doing.

What Do You Think?

1. In what ways do Javier's examples of preschool play and peer interactions demonstrate the interplay of cognitive and social development?
2. In what ways do Javier's descriptions of preschool friendships parallel the discussion of preschool friendship and its management in the chapter?

---

two best friends. School-age children, in contrast, average three to five best friends, a figure than remains fairly constant during adolescence and early adulthood (Hartup & Stevens , 1997; Poulin & Chan, 2010).

These children are involved in parallel play. They are probably aware of each other's presence, but they are using separate toys and are preoccupied primarily with their own activities.
Source: otnaydur/Shutterstock.com.

Chapter 10 Psychosocial Development during Early Childhood

The development of social competence and the ability to understand others' emotions and mental states during early childhood depend in part on the frequency with which playmates, parents, and other children initiate informal play activities. During the preschool years, children begin to initiate their own peer contacts and receive play invitations from peers, a trend that increases through the early childhood years (Bhavnagri & Parke, 1991; Maguire & Dunn, 1997; Power, 2011).

Conceptions of Friendship

Young children form internal representations of peer and friendship relations in much the same way they form internal representations of adult caregivers and attachments, a working model for friendships they will utilize into adulthood (Howes, 1996; Welch & Houser, 2010). In the minds of younger preschoolers, a friend is someone who does certain things with you; a friend is someone (anyone, in fact) whom you like to play with, share toys with, or talk with a lot, rather than someone with whom they share a compassionate relationship (Ahn, 2011; Field et al., 1994). "A friend," as one preschooler put it, "lets you hold his doll or truck or something."

As children near school age, more permanent, personal qualities enter into their conceptions (Howes, 1996). Now the crucial features of a friend are more often dispositional, that is, related to how the friend is likely to behave in the future. A friend is still very much "someone you like," but she is also someone whom you trust, whom you can depend on, and who likes and admires you. To be friends in this sense, two children must know each other's likes and preferences better than before, and they must also be increasingly aware of thoughts and feelings that the friend may keep hidden. Nevertheless, each child is still likely to focus primarily on his own needs to the exclusion of his friend's. As one child said, "A friend is someone who does what you want"; and as another said, "A friend doesn't get you in trouble." Neither of these children understands that sometimes he or she should return these favors; later, during the school years, they will likely think of this.

Making and keeping friends requires good social skills and is an important indication of good social adjustment. Kindergarten children who already have maintained earlier established friendships with children who now attend the same school have more positive attitudes toward school than children without such friendships. Having friends predicts increases in self-esteem among preadolescents, and adolescents who have good friends are less likely to experience psychosocial disturbances during school transitions than those without good friends (Hartup & Stevens, 1997; Poulin & Chan, 2010). In fact, when children experienced a stressful event—for example, being excluded from an activity—those children with friends had less of a stress response than those without friends (Peters, Riksen-Walraven, Cillessen, & de Weerth, 2011). Finally, a twelve-year longitudinal study found that having friends during preadolescence predicted successful social adaptation in early adulthood, including positive attitudes toward family members and general feelings of self-esteem (Bagwell et al., 1996). As we will discover in the chapters that follow, having friends, the identities of one's friends, and the quality of the friendships one has play an important developmental role throughout life (Hartup & Stevens, 1997; Poulin & Chan, 2010).

Now that we have concluded our discussion of play in early childhood, we turn to discussing gender development, which profoundly affects almost all other developmental changes in early childhood and in the years that follow.

Gender Development

Gender influences important aspects of social development in early childhood. As used here, the term **gender** refers to learned or socially constructed categories (feminine and masculine) in contrast to *sex,* which refers to biological categories (male and female). Most children go through at least three steps in gender development (Shepherd-Look, 1982). First, they develop beliefs about *gender identity,* that is, which sex *they* are. Second, they develop *gender preferences,* attitudes about which sex they wish to be; gender preference does not always coincide with gender identity. Third, they acquire *gender constancy,* a

gender The thoughts, feelings, and behaviors associated with being male or female by one's culture.

> **What Do You Think?**
>
> Many political leaders (and a significant number of parents who have voted for them) have criticized spending money on preschool programs in which children spend their time "playing" rather than learning important preschool skills. How would you respond to such critics regarding the importance of play for preschool children?

belief that the sex of a person is biologically determined, permanent, and unchanging no matter what else about the person changes. All three aspects of gender contribute to a child's general knowledge of **gender-role stereotypes** (also called *sex roles*), the very powerful (but not necessarily welcome or accurate), culturally sanctioned messages regarding which gender-related behaviors are and are not acceptable. Different cultures have different stereotypes and therefore send different messages to parents and children.

gender-role stereotypes The culturally "appropriate" patterns of gender-related behaviors expected by society. Also called sex roles.

Learning Gender Schema

From age two onward, preschoolers use gender-role stereotypes to guide their behaviors. Children's gender preferences and knowledge of stereotypes regarding toys and activities increase significantly with age: whereas twenty-four-month-olds typically do not show consistent gender preferences in toys and activities, thirty-month-olds consistently prefer "same-gender" to "opposite-gender" objects and activities. Gender-role stereotypes about personal qualities develop more slowly. Only by age five or so do children begin to know which gender is "supposed" to be aggressive, loud, and strong and which is "supposed" to be gentle, quiet, and weak. Knowledge of gender stereotypes regarding personal qualities continues to develop throughout childhood and adolescence (Bailey & Zucker, 1995; Halim & Ruble, 2010; Huston & Alvarez, 1990).

Most children acquire *gender identity,* the ability to label themselves correctly as boys or girls, between ages two and three and are able to correctly label other children and adults as well. Some children develop gender identity early, before age twenty-eight months, and others not until later. Early identifiers exhibit significantly more gender-stereotyped play, such as car play for boys and doll play for girls, than later identifiers do (Fagot & Leinbach, 1989; Fagot et al., 1992; Halim & Ruble, 2010).

Gender constancy, the understanding that one's gender is permanent and will never change, first appears by age four or five. A young preschool child may say she can switch gender just by wanting to or say that even though she is a girl now, she was a boy as an infant or may grow up to become a man as an adult. And a two-year-old may have only a hazy notion of what defines gender, believing perhaps that certain hairstyles, clothing, and toys make the crucial difference. Most children, however, achieve a reliable sense of gender constancy between ages seven and nine (Bem, 1989; Emmerich & Sheppard, 1982; Halim & Ruble, 2010).

A *gender schema* is a pattern of beliefs and stereotypes about gender that children use to organize information about gender-related characteristics, experiences, and expectations. A child's gender schema is thought to develop through a series of stages. First, a child learns through social experiences what kinds of things are directly associated with each sex, such as "boys play with cars" and "girls play with dolls." Next, around ages four to six, the child moves to the second stage and begins to develop more indirect and complex associations for information relevant to his or her own sex but not for the opposite sex. For example, a child who knows that boys like trucks and boys like cars should now be able to infer that someone who likes trucks will also like cars. Finally, by age eight or so, the child moves to the third stage, where he has also learned the associations relevant to the opposite sex and has mastered the gender concepts of masculinity and femininity that link information within and among various content areas. Thus, a child will know the pattern of interests that are stereotypically associated with being masculine (cars, action toys, football) or feminine (dolls, "dress-up," princesses) (Bem, 1987; Halim & Ruble, 2010; Martin et al., 1990; Ruble, 1988).

Chapter 10 Psychosocial Development during Early Childhood

Though not pertinent in this chapter, the previous terms regarding gender are independent of the discussion of sexual orientation—whether an individual is homosexual, heterosexual, or bisexual. We will discuss sexual orientation in Chapter 16.

Influences on Gender Development

If gender development is largely a process of learning socially constructed definitions of "boy" and "girl," we would expect the child's social circle of parents and peers to influence that process. In the following section, we explore how this occurs.

Parents

Many theorists hold parents responsible for the development of gender differences, either blaming or congratulating them depending on the theorist's point of view. When asked about their child-rearing philosophies, parents tend to express belief in gender equality, but their actions often differ from their statements (Fagot, 1982). Observations of parents playing with their preschool children reveal that parents support their children for gender-stereotyped activities more than for cross-gender activities. Boys get praised more for playing with blocks than for playing with dolls, and parents generally support physical activity in boys more than in girls. Boys who engage in cross-gender behaviors are viewed more negatively than girls who engage in cross-gender behaviors (Sandnabba & Ahlberg, 1999), and parents who reinforce children for playing with same gender and punish cross-gender play have children who seem to develop gender schemas earlier (Halim & Ruble, 2010). As children approach school age, parents begin assigning household chores according to gender: girls more often fold the laundry, and boys more often take out the trash. Parents are also more likely to reward sons for being assertive, independent, active, and emotionally unexpressive and to reward daughters for being accommodating, dependent, more passive, and emotionally expressive (Fagot & Hagan, 1991; Halim & Ruble, 2010; Lytton & Romney, 1991).

The socialization of females appears to emphasize interpersonal relatedness and emotional expressivity, whereas socialization of males emphasizes autonomy and agency. These orientations have been associated with sex-typed differences in the way parents talk to and interact with their children. In emphasizing causes and consequences of emotions with boys, mothers might orient them toward seeing emotions as problems to be solved and controlled rather than experienced and understood. Mothers' conversations with girls focus on the emotional states themselves, perhaps encouraging girls to focus directly on their own feelings and reactions and orienting them toward an interpersonal approach involving emotional sensitivity, and parents are more likely to talk to their daughters about physical appearance than their sons (Cervantes & Callanan, 1998; Halim & Ruble, 2010; Leaper et al., 1998).

Peers

In some ways, peers may shape gender differences more strongly than parents do. Early in the preschool years, even before age three, children prefer to play in same-sex groups and respond differently to partners of the opposite sex than to those of the same sex (Maccoby, 1990; Martin & Ruble, 2010; Power, 2011). In play situations, girls tend to withdraw from a boy partner more often than from a girl partner, and boys heed prohibitions made by another boy more often than they do those that come from a girl. Even when preschoolers are not playing actively, they watch peers of the same sex more often than they do peers of the opposite sex.

Children of this age also respond to reinforcement more reliably if it comes from a child of their own sex. If a boy compliments another boy's block building, the second boy is much more likely to continue building than he is if a girl compliments it. Conversely, if a boy criticizes the building, the other boy is more likely to stop than if a girl criticizes it. Parallel patterns occur for girls, who tend to persist in whatever other girls compliment or praise and stop whatever they criticize or ignore. For both sexes, teachers' reinforcements have less influence than peers' in determining children's persistence at activities (Fagot, 1982). What makes these patterns

The ease with which these children adopt both stereotyped and nonstereotyped roles in playing "tea party" illustrates the flexible qualities associated with androgyny.
Source: Monkey Business Images/Shutterstock.com.

important is that children tend to reinforce play activities that are considered appropriate for their own sex. Children who deviate from expected gender-stereotyped activities, such as boys playing with dolls, often find themselves largely ignored and unpopular, even after they return to expected activities (Martin & Ruble, 2010; Lamb & Roopnarine, 1979). As we saw earlier, the content of many children's TV shows—and the toys they promote—also sends powerful messages about gender stereotypes (Coyne et al., 2014). Thus, peer pressures to practice conventional gender roles are both strong and continuous, and they occur even if teachers and other adults try to minimize gender-typed play.

Androgyny

How we choose to define *gender* also can affect our understanding of what it means to be male or female. On the one hand, definitions that tend to exaggerate positive gender differences run the risk of perpetuating gender-role stereotyping and inequality; on the other hand, definitions that minimize real differences may be used to deny boys and girls the physical, cognitive, and social developmental opportunities appropriate to their different gender-related needs. One positive consequence of focusing on differences associated with gender is that doing so increases our awareness and appreciation of feminine (and masculine) qualities. A positive consequence of efforts to minimize gender differences is to help equalize treatment under the law and access to equal opportunity for males and females (Hare-Mustin & Marecek, 1988).

Androgyny refers to a situation in which gender roles are flexible, allowing all individuals, male and female, to behave in ways that freely integrate behaviors traditionally thought to belong exclusively to one or the other sex. Many people think of "masculine" and "feminine" as opposite ends of a single scale. Rather, "masculinity" and "femininity" are separate scales, and androgyny is a state of being high in both. In this view, both girls and boys can be assertive *and* yielding, independent *and* dependent, instrumental (task oriented) *and* expressive (feelings oriented). Sandra Bem (1981, 1987) and others (e.g., Lamke, 1982a, 1982b) have found that adolescent and young adult males and females use both masculine and feminine characteristics to describe their own personalities. Bem believes androgynous individuals are less concerned about which activities are appropriate or inappropriate and therefore are more flexible in their responses to various situations. For example, we find that girls who are less strict in their gender roles are also less likely to experience stereotypically feminine psychological disorders, such as eating disorders (McHale, Corneal, Crouter, & Birch, 2001).

androgyny A tendency to integrate both masculine and feminine behaviors into the personality.

> **What Do You Think?**
>
> A hockey coach's five-year-old son enjoys playing with dolls with his female peers. Because of this, his dad has encouraged him to play with GI Joe dolls and play football more often because he is worried that his son may become homosexual. What gender influence is this hockey coach having on his son's gender development? What advice would you give this parent based on your reading of this chapter?

What are the implications of androgyny? Because the notion of androgyny challenges certain fundamental beliefs that individuals have about gender, it holds the potential to reduce gender-role stereotyping and its detrimental developmental effects in early childhood and beyond (Stake, 1997). Because society holds stricter sex-role expectations for males, androgyny might be more beneficial for women than it is for men.

Child Abuse and Maltreatment

Child abuse and maltreatment by parents and other caregivers is a serious social problem, with approximately 2.1 million new cases reported each year, nearly 20 percent of which are substantiated (U.S. Department of Health and Human Services, 2015). A significant number of these cases involve infants, toddlers, and preschool-aged children, who are particularly vulnerable because of their immaturity and dependence. In 2013, children less than one year of age had the highest victimization rate (U.S. Department of Health and Human Services, 2015). Maltreatment may consist of physical, sexual, or emotional *abuse*, or of physical or emotional *neglect*, and nearly 80 percent of the cases of maltreatment in 2013 were due to neglect (Finkelhor, 1995; Wolock, 1998; U.S. Department of Health and Human Services, 2015). Parents—in particular, mothers—are the most likely perpetrators of abuse. The opioid epidemic is causing an ever-increasing number of children to be removed from unsafe home environments and into an already overloaded and underfunded foster-care system (Wiltz, 2016).

Causes

The causes of physical child abuse and neglect are best understood within the developmental-ecological contexts within which they occur. These include parent and child characteristics, parenting and parent-child interactions, and the broader context of family, community, and culture.

Parent and Child Characteristics

One explanation for maltreatment is that the aggressive and antisocial behavior involved in abuse was previously learned by the parent during her or his own childhood, through modeling and direct reinforcement. The risk of maltreatment is much higher when parenting is extremely authoritarian (overly harsh and lacking in empathy) or when it is indifferent and neglectful of a child's needs. This explanation, however, fails to explain why two-thirds of parents who were abused themselves do not abuse their own children.

A second, more promising explanation of the causes of abuse is based on the idea of *internal working models*, the mental representations that organize and guide a parent's experiences, relationship, and interactions with the child (Bowlby 1988; Farrangy et al., 1991; Stern, 1985b). The internal working models of an abusive parent are based on past experiences with the child, the parent's own childhood experiences, and the beliefs and expectations held by his or her own abusive parents. These models are often characterized by a distorted, unbalanced view of the child (overly negative or overly positive) and are associated with pervasive failures in parental empathy, parent-infant synchrony, and attachment (Belsky, 1993; Ferholt, 1991; Main & Goldwyn, 1989; Wolock, 1998).

Mothers who were abused as children are much less likely to abuse their own children if they experienced one nonabusive, supportive, and close relationship while growing up (Jaffee et al., 2013). It may be that these close relationships help reduce the trauma of having been abused because research has demonstrated that victims of child abuse who continue to experience trauma from that abuse as an adult are more likely to become abusers themselves (Milner et al., 2010). These mothers are also likely to display greater self-awareness regarding their own abuse, be involved in a more satisfying social relationship, and have more extensive social supports than mothers who do abuse (Belsky, 1993; Caliso & Milner, 1992).

Personality characteristics that significantly compromise a parent's ability to provide good parenting may also increase the risk of abuse, particularly if they interfere with getting social and emotional support from others. Difficulty with impulse control, emotional instability, high levels of depression, anxiety, or hostility, and abuse of alcohol or drugs can all impair a parent's capacity to respond to a child in empathic and responsible ways.

Parenting and Parent-Child Interactions

Parenting and parent-child interactions also play a role. Abusive parents are more likely than nonabusive parents to rely on physical punishment and negative control strategies such as hitting, grabbing, and pushing, or threats and disapproval, rather than on reasoning to guide or discipline their children. They are also less likely to adjust their disciplinary techniques appropriately to different kinds of misbehavior (Belsky, 1993; Herrenkohl et al., 1997). During an abusive episode, the overtly aggressive behavior (physical punishment) on which an abusive parent relies is transformed into an act of interpersonal violence. A parent with a strong predisposition toward anxiety, depression, and hostility may become so irritated with the child that she or he loses control and physical or verbal punishment escalates into abuse.

Family, Community, and Cultural Factors

Poverty, unemployment, marital conflict, social isolation, and family dysfunction can increase the risk of abuse; so can shorter-term stressors, such as emotional distress, economic or legal problems, or the birth of a new baby (Belsky, 1988b; Cicchetti & Olson, 1990; Garbarino, 1992b). Economic conditions, child and family social welfare policies, and cultural values and expectations regarding the care and protection of children can indirectly contribute to the risk of abuse and neglect (Black & Krishnakumar, 1998). In fact, the home and family environment is the single most important factor in determining whether a child is likely to be abused or not (Jaffee et al., 2004). For example, societies that condone the use of violence against women (who are the primary caregivers of children) are likely to have higher rates of child abuse than societies that treat women with respect. The role of differing cultural values and expectations regarding child maltreatment is discussed in the "A Multicultural View" feature.

Consequences

Neglected infants, toddlers, and preschoolers often are deprived of sufficient food, clothing, shelter, sanitation, and medical care, which may interfere with their physical, intellectual, social, and emotional development and place them at risk for serious illness or even death (Egeland, 1988; U.S. Department of Health and Human Services, 2015). Abused or neglected preschoolers often develop emotional problems that include insecure attachment relationships, lack of empathy, and emotional detachment. They are also more likely to exhibit behavioral problems, such as aggressiveness and withdrawal, toward peers than other children are (Cicchetti & Olson, 1990; Dodge et al., 1990; Klimes-Dougan & Kistner, 1990; Pianta et al., 1989; Sousa et al., 2011). Physical abuse during early childhood is linked to aggressive and violent behaviors in adolescents and adults, including violence toward nonfamily members, children, dating partners, and spouses; higher rates of mental-health problems; higher rates of risky sexual behavior; and higher rates of drug abuse (Kendall-Tackett et al., 1993; Malinosky-Rummell & Hansen, 1993; Norman et al., 2012). Victims of child abuse have lower earning potential

A Multicultural View

The Cultural Context of Child Abuse and Neglect

Can the ideas one culture holds about child abuse and neglect be validly applied to others? According to Jill Korbin, who has extensively studied child abuse and neglect in many different cultural and societal contexts, culturally appropriate definitions of child abuse and neglect require an awareness of both the viewpoint of an "insider" to a particular culture, termed the *emic* perspective, and the viewpoint of an "outsider" to that culture, or the *etic* perspective (Korbin, 1991, 1987, 1981). Such definitions must include three dimensions: (1) cultural differences in child-rearing practices, (2) treatment of children that deviates from cultural norms, and (3) societal abuse and neglect.

Cultural differences in child-rearing include practices considered acceptable in the culture in which they occur but abusive or neglectful by outsiders. For example, most middle-class American parents believe it is developmentally important for young children to sleep separately from their parents, but traditional Japanese and Hawaiian-Polynesian cultures, which highly value interdependence among family members, view isolating children at night as potentially dangerous to healthy child development. Another example concerns a woman in London who cut the faces of her two young sons with a razor blade and rubbed charcoal into the cuts. She was arrested for child abuse, but officials soon learned that she and her children belonged to an East African tribal group that traditionally practiced facial scarification. When viewed from within her culture, her actions were an attempt to protect her children's cultural identity, for without such markings they would be unable to participate as adults in the culture of their birth (Korbin, 1987).

Many cultures have practiced such initiation rites as a normal part of child-rearing before and during adolescence. Where, for example, is the line drawn between male circumcision during adolescence and circumcision at birth? How would a European or an American convince traditional people in highland New Guinea that circumcision is more painful for an adolescent than for an infant? How would traditional highland New Guinea people convince Europeans or Americans that (1) circumcision has no meaning for an infant, who cannot understand its deep cultural significance, and (2) infancy is a time when the child should be spared all discomfort? How is the line drawn between facial scarification and orthodontia (braces), both of which cause pain and discomfort but are intended to enhance the child's attractiveness?

Idiosyncratic child abuse and neglect involves treatment of children that deviates from established standards of acceptable treatment within a particular culture. Although they may differ, all societies have such standards. For example, in one Polynesian culture known for its indulgence of children, a child can be pinched lightly on the mouth for misbehavior, but more severe punishments are prohibited. When one man left a scratch on the lip of his grandchild, he was severely criticized by his cultural group. By their *emic* standards, his behavior was abusive, although from the *etic* perspective of American parents, it is unlikely that such behavior would be of great concern.

Societal abuse and neglect refers to harm caused to children by societal conditions, such as poverty and inadequate housing, health care, and nutrition, all of which either contribute significantly to abuse or neglect or are considered abusive or neglectful in themselves. For example, the widespread famine in Ethiopia and Somalia and the inadequate nutrition in India and Chile have had devastating effects on the physical, cognitive, and socioemotional development of millions of children. In many countries, physical, sexual, and emotional exploitation and abuse of children are very common. Even in affluent countries such as our own, social policy regarding aid to parents with dependent children, early childhood health care and nutrition, childcare, and employment can significantly harm (or help) the development of young children. Where does responsibility lie, and what should be done about this?

It seems likely that neither a single, universal standard nor a completely relativistic, "anything goes" standard for determining abuse and neglect is acceptable. The challenge, then, is to develop an approach that incorporates developmental values and standards for "good enough" care and treatment of children that should be universal and values standards that afford more room for cultural and societal diversity.

---

as adults and lower educational attainment (Currie & Widom, 2010). Abuse and neglect have also been lined to higher risk of serious chronic health problems, such as diabetes, lung disease, and malnutrition, as an adult (Widom, Czaja, Bentley, & Johnson, 2012).

The most common symptoms reported for preschoolers who have been sexually abused include nightmares, posttraumatic stress disorder, depression and emotional withdrawal, regressive and immature behavior, anxiety disorders, and problems with aggression and inappropriate sexual behavior (Hornor, 2010; Kendall-Tackett et al., 1993). The developmental stage at which sexual abuse occurs is particularly significant in determining longer-term outcomes. For example, incest (sexual abuse by a parent or other family member) disrupts

> **What Do You Think?**
>
> If you were a preschool teacher, what behaviors in a child might lead you to suspect child maltreatment? What help is available to parents who may be at risk for abusing or neglecting their children?

the development of social functioning and self-esteem and increases risk for personality disorders, eating disorders, and substance abuse during adolescence and early adulthood (Finkelhor, 1995; Spaccarelli, 1994), as we will see in Chapter 14.

Treatment and Prevention

Dealing with child maltreatment involves working directly with the abused infant, toddler, or preschooler, the parents, and the family after abuse (or the threat of abuse) has been discovered. One goal is to protect the child from further mistreatment and help her recover from the physical and psychological consequences. Another is to assist the abusing parent(s) in establishing a parent-child relationship and family environment that adequately ensures the preschooler's safety and supports his developmental needs.

Intensive professional help, including family counseling and psychotherapy, often can help parents and child understand the causes, consequences, and personal meanings of their destructive feelings and behaviors so they will be able to live together in less destructive ways. A key aspect of treatment is to help parents improve their parenting skills. Self-help groups such as Parents Anonymous, parent aides who assist abusive and neglectful families in their homes, crisis nurseries, foster care or respite care for the abused child, and short-term residential treatment for family members or the entire family unit are among the treatment alternatives that have met with some success (Willis et al., 1992; Wolfe et al., 1997). Unfortunately, those who would benefit from these programs and services often lack availability and access to them (Burns et al., 2004).

Early intervention programs that target "high-risk" families, including those headed by low-SES mothers and teenage mothers, have focused on helping parents improve their parenting skills, the family climate, and their ability to better cope with the stressful life events and conditions. Programs that teach parents how to evaluate why problems occur and then make those problems less likely to occur in the future have reduced the rate of abuse among high-risk families (Bugental et al., 2010). Programs that include early and extended contact between parents and their newborn infants to improve the early parent-child relationship, parent education about child development and everyday childcare problems, and home visitors and parent aides who assist parents with young children tend to be effective. They also offer training and support in home safety, money management, job finding, health maintenance and nutrition, leisure time counseling, and help in developing stronger social support networks (Rosenberg & Reppucci, 1985; Willis et al., 1992).

Other prevention efforts attempt to reduce or eliminate the causes of abuse by changing more general conditions that affect *all* children and families. These *social policy* efforts include education for parenthood programs, elimination of corporal punishment, the development of a bill of rights for children, and various social policy supports for parents and their children, including more and better jobs, funding for preschools and day-care centers, affordable health care, and so forth.

Looking Back/Looking Forward

Let us explore how the lifespan themes outlined in Chapter 1 apply to early childhood. Our focus here will be on friendship and its developmental importance throughout the life cycle.

- **Continuity within change**—Friendships emerge in toddlerhood and early childhood and continue to play an important developmental role throughout middle childhood, adolescence, and adulthood. An individual's capacity to make friends, the types of friends one chooses, and the quality of one's friendships over the lifespan show considerable continuity, and having (or not having) enough good friends is predictive of better (or worse) adjustment and developmental well-being at every age. Some of this continuity may be due to temperamental characteristics, such as shyness or outgoingness, as well as to relationships and developmental opportunities within and outside the family that stay fairly constant. On the other hand, changes in one's family, school, and neighborhood environments and the major physical and cognitive changes that occur through middle childhood, adolescence, and adulthood facilitate significant changes in opportunities to make friends, whom one chooses as friends, and the nature of one's friendships. For example, moving to a new school or spending a month at summer camp creates new possibilities for friendship experiences, the friends one chooses, and the quality of one's friendships. The physical, cognitive, and psychosocial changes that occur from early childhood through adolescence and adulthood also expand and alter the nature and meaning of friendship.

- **Lifelong growth**—The ability to establish and maintain friendships, sophistication in thinking about qualities of friendship, and the breadth and complexity of friendship activities grow as physical, cognitive, and psychosocial skills expand. Although preschoolers do participate in initiating and maintaining new friendships, they still largely depend on adults to arrange opportunities to be with the peers with whom friendships eventually develop. These capacities undergo major growth as an individual progresses through middle childhood, adolescence, and young adulthood, growth that for many continues throughout middle and later adulthood, when increases in wisdom and good judgment based on past experience replace gains in physical and cognitive skills and capacities as the main source of growth.

- **Changing meanings and vantage points**—How one thinks about friendship and the role and meaning of friendship in one's life changes as one moves through the life cycle. Whereas a preschooler may think of friendship largely in terms of a partner with whom to share enjoyable play activities, older children, adolescents, and adults attribute progressively deeper meanings to their friendships, which include intimacy, trust, and mutual understanding. Similarly, as individuals move through the life cycle, they become increasingly reliant on the friendships they establish outside of their immediate families for intimacy and social and material support.

- **Developmental diversity**—The diversity of friendships is a product of differences in the opportunities and expectations associated with gender, culture, SES, and family background, as well as individual differences in personality, life experiences, and personal choices. In European American culture, for example, friendships among females tend to place greater emphasis on relationship and emotional intimacy, whereas friendships among men tend to emphasize shared activities. However, differences in relationships with parents and siblings during early and middle childhood, in school and neighborhood settings during middle childhood and adolescence, or in work and family settings during early and middle adulthood can all contribute to developmental diversity in the friendships of a given individual.

Chapter Summary

- **How do different styles of parenting influence preschoolers' relationships with peers?** In early childhood, a child's relationships with parents and other family members are a central source of psychosocial development. Parenting styles differ in their demands for maturity, need for control, and responsiveness to their children's feelings and needs. Such differences are associated with differences in parent-child relationships and developmental outcomes. Authoritative parents display high levels of control, demands for maturity, and responsiveness to their children's feelings and needs. Their children tend to show greater self-reliance, self-control, and achievement. Authoritarian parents display high levels of control and maturity demands but low levels of responsiveness to their children's feelings and needs. Their children tend to be more distrustful and unhappy with themselves, and show lower school achievement than children of authoritative parents. Permissive parents display high levels of responsiveness but very low levels of control and maturity demands. Their children tend to lack self-reliance and self-control. Indifferent parents are detached, uninvolved, and inconsistent. They display low levels of control, maturity demands, and responsiveness. Their children tend to lack self-reliance and self-control and may be at risk for more severe social and emotional problems. Parents often use mixtures of parenting styles, and the preferred parenting style may change as children grow older.

Both siblings and friends also make an important contribution to social development during the preschool years. The quality of children's social relationships with their siblings is predictive of the quality of their relationships with their friends. Ultimately, however, it is the parent's responsibility to help children establish and maintain positive social relationships.

- **How do preschoolers handle conflicts with peers?** As children grow older, the support and judgments of parents and other adults contribute increasingly to children's feelings of empathy and prosocial activities. Preschoolers commonly exhibit both overt and relational aggression to assert their needs and resolve conflicts. As they grow older, verbal methods replace physical ones and overall aggression declines. Children who cannot control their aggression can be helped to do so with methods such as assertiveness training and social learning theory strategies. Parents can learn to spot the triggers of their children's aggression and respond effectively. Television viewing and video and computer game playing significantly influence preschoolers' social development in such areas as aggression, prosocial behavior, and gender stereotyping.

- **Why is play so important in preschoolers' development, and how does play change as they approach school age?** Play for its own sake is the major waking activity of preschoolers. Psychoanalytic theory emphasizes the mastery and wish fulfillment functions of play, whereas learning theory stresses the acquisition of social skills through imitation and observation. Ethological theory emphasizes the evolutionary roots and adaptive developmental functions of physical play. Cognitive theory emphasizes that play develops in a sequence that generally parallels the major stages of cognitive development. It includes functional play, constructive play, pretend play, and play involving games with rules. Mildred Parten has identified six social levels of play: unoccupied, solitary, onlooker, parallel, associative, and cooperative play. The type of setting is important to the development of social play.

Whereas early friendships are unstable and depend on specific shared play activities, friendships along older preschoolers involve expectations about future behavior. Preschoolers' friendships become more durable and involve a greater degree of shared activity with age. As they near school age, the more permanent and personal qualities of friendship become increasingly important.

- **How does a child's understanding of gender differences change during the preschool years? What factors influence a child's flexibility about gender-role stereotypes?** During early childhood, children acquire an understanding of gender-typed behaviors and gender identity. A sense of gender constancy—the belief that being male or female is biologically determined and permanent—typically is not achieved until ages seven to nine. Because the development of stereotypes about personal qualities appears to depend on the ability to think abstractly, children do not gain a clear and stable concept of gender until the school years. Influences on gender development include differential expectations and treatment of boys and girls by parents, peers, and the media. A more flexible approach to gender roles enables children to adopt more androgynous behaviors and attitudes.

- **What factors appear to contribute to child abuse and neglect? What are the consequences of maltreatment, and how might child maltreatment be prevented?** More than two million cases of child abuse are reported annually. Types of abuse include physical, psychological, and sexual. Neglect can be physical or emotional. Causes of maltreatment occur at the levels of the individual parent, the family, the community, and the culture. Consequences of abuse and neglect include a range of developmental, adjustment, and emotional problems. Responses to abuse and neglect frequently focus on treating the victims and their families. Prevention efforts include early intervention programs targeting "high-risk" families and attempts to change more general conditions that affect all children and families.

Key Terms

aggression (p. 234)
androgyny (p. 253)
authoritarian parenting (p. 227)
authoritative parenting (p. 225)
constructive play (p. 244)
empathy (p. 232)

functional play (p. 243)
games with rules (p. 244)
gender (p. 250)
gender-role stereotypes (p. 251)
hostile attribution bias (p. 236)
indifferent parenting (p. 228)

overt aggression (p. 234)
permissive parenting (p. 228)
physical activity play (p. 242)
pretend play (p. 244)
relational aggression (p. 234)

Middle Childhood

PART 5

Chapter 11
Physical Development during Middle Childhood

Chapter 12
Cognitive Development during Middle Childhood

Chapter 13
Psychosocial Development during Middle Childhood

Source: iofoto/Shutterstock.

Because growth slows after the preschool years, children in middle childhood have more time and energy to develop skills of all sorts, from riding a skateboard to making friends. An accumulation of language practice and symbolic, make-believe play pay off: school-age children can think more logically than ever before, at least if they choose to and usually only when thinking relates to concrete matters. These new competencies, combined with children's experience of attending school, make peers more important than ever before.

Adults often remember middle childhood as the best years of their youth, though it is not clear that children themselves would agree with this assessment. For high-SES families, the world now likely seems secure, children's health is excellent, and children's skills and abilities improve steadily and visibly year by year. For families with fewer resources, though, the middle childhood years can be just as challenging as the periods before and after.

Physical Development during Middle Childhood

CHAPTER 11

Source: Rawpixel.com/Shutterstock.

Chapter Outline

PHYSICAL DEVELOPMENT

Trends and Variations in Height and Weight

Motor Development and Athletics in Middle Childhood

Health and Illness in Middle Childhood

The Changing Child

Focusing Questions

- What trends in height and weight occur among school-age children?
- What improvements in motor skills do children usually experience during the school years, and how do these improvements affect children's involvement in athletic activity?
- What kinds of illnesses occur among schoolchildren? How does children's socioeconomic status affect their health?

Carmen and Mercedes were sisters. When Carmen was six and Mercedes nine, they both decided they wanted to buy skates. The problem was to find the money. They sold lemonade at the curbside: "DRINX, 25 SENTS" said a sign made by Carmen. In three days they had sold ten drinks. "That's $2.50," noted Mercedes. "Not nearly enough." Carmen puzzled over how long it would take them to earn enough; she thought maybe about a year, but she wasn't sure.

After a few more days—and increasing discouragement—their mother brought home one pair of used skates. "It's to share," she said, "because it's all I can afford. And besides, the two of you are nearly the same size!" This arrangement was not ideal. At first the girls did try to take turns with the skates, but trouble soon developed. Carmen had a way of taking rather long turns, and tended not only to use the skates herself but to share them

263

with her friends. When it was Mercedes' turn, Mercedes took the skates to school to use at practices with the recently formed skating team. Soon Mercedes became the student-manager for the team, and spent a lot of her practice time arranging tournaments and other activities rather than actually skating herself. Eventually differences emerged between the sisters. Carmen became more skilled at actually skating, but Mercedes came to know more about the sport itself and could say more about it when asked. Carmen complained about sharing the skates because Mercedes "didn't really use them" at school. Mercedes complained that Carmen was selfish and unfair, and "ought to learn to share better," but eventually she gave up her turns altogether, despite continued encouragement from her mother.

The events between Carmen and Mercedes hint at features of development that we will discuss in the next three chapters. One feature is the diversity of children's development: children grow and change at different rates, just as Carmen and Mercedes in terms of both their skating skills and their knowledge of skating. Children can also show profound differences in the meaning they give to the "same" activity, differences that result from diversity in the ways the domains of development work together in the lives of individuals. For one child (such as Carmen), success at a physical skill can be a source of self-esteem and peer approval. For another (such as Mercedes), success provides a stimulus for cognitive growth: it becomes something about which to talk and think, and perhaps to win friends as an indirect result. For still another person (their mother), success at skating becomes a challenge in providing for others fairly rather than gaining personal recognition.

These features of middle childhood are variations on two of our lifespan development themes: developmental diversity and changing meanings and vantage points, which have come up throughout this book and we will revisit in this chapter as well. As Carmen's and Mercedes' experiences also show, developments in all three domains—physical, cognitive, and psychosocial—occur simultaneously and influence one another intimately. We explore them separately only for convenience of discussion.

PHYSICAL DEVELOPMENT

In general, children's physical growth slows during middle childhood (ages six to twelve) even more than it does during early childhood. Specific physical skills are easier to teach than they used to be because children now find them easier to learn. For a school-age child, instruction and practice in baseball make a more obvious difference in skill development than they did when she was still a preschooler. This means the child can now acquire physical and athletic skills that may give a lifetime of satisfaction. But children *can* get hurt during physical activity, and athletic games can emphasize competition that is unrealistic or discouraging.

Children are relatively healthy during the school years, but they do sometimes have accidents or get sick. A few children also develop problems that have ambiguous physical causes; such children may show excessive motor activity even in quiet situations or difficulties in learning specific academic skills. Such problems may originate from subtle differences in how the nervous system operates in these children, although this is far from certain.

In the sections that follow, we review these ideas in more detail. We begin by looking at normal trends and variations in overall growth during middle childhood. Then we examine specific motor skill and athletic development and their psychological effects on children. Finally, we discuss health in the school years, with special reference to children who are overly active and on normative sleep and common sleep disorders among children.

Trends and Variations in Height and Weight

As Figure 11.1 shows, children grow steadily during middle childhood, from about forty-six inches and forty-five pounds at age six to almost sixty inches and eight pounds at age

FIGURE 11.1

Growth in Height and Weight from Two to Eighteen Years

During the early school years, children continue to grow at a smooth rate, though more slowly than in early childhood and infancy. By the middle and later parts of this period, however, weight and height begin to accelerate as children move into puberty. The growth spurts usually begin sooner for weight than for height and sooner for girls than for boys.

twelve (Center for Disease Control, 2000; Engels, 1993). At the same time, variations among children are often significant. For example, that the average height of eight-year-old girls varies from forty-five inches in South Korea to almost fifty-one inches in Russia. And at any age within any one society, individual variations are even more dramatic. The shortest and tallest six-year-olds in North America differ by only two or three inches, but the shortest and tallest twelve-year-olds differ by more than one foot. The changes are a source of both pride and dismay to individual children.

Toward the end of elementary school, girls tend to become significantly taller than boys of the same age. The difference results partly from girls' earlier puberty and partly from the timing of the growth spurt associated with puberty for each sex. For boys, a spurt in height tends to *follow* the other physical changes of adolescence, such as the growth of pubic hair and the deepening of the voice. For girls, a spurt in height usually *precedes* the growth of breasts and pubic hair. We look again at these and other physical changes of puberty in Chapter 14. For some children, the gap in timing creates problems with self-esteem and relating to the opposite sex. As we will see, though, the impact is far from uniform. Boys react differently than girls, as do their families and communities, and some young adolescents mind very little if they look young for their age—or old.

A more lasting problem than early or late puberty is **obesity**, a condition of being significantly overweight. Medically, obesity is defined by the ratio of a person's height and weight, a statistic called the *body mass index,* or BMI. Individuals with an excessive BMI tend to be about 30 to 50 percent overweight compared to their peers of the same height and age (St. Jean, 1997). By this definition, a child who is obese and is fifty-four inches tall will weigh more than eighty-five pounds instead of the normal sixty-five pounds. In our society, about one-third of children are overweight and 18 percent of children are obese (Centers for Disease Control and Prevention, 2015). The condition can be especially difficult for girls because current cultural norms emphasize physical thinness for females and fashion models in the media typically are thin to a degree that would be considered medically underweight and unhealthy for most girls and women. Most people (including most medical professionals) assume that the problems associated with obesity are caused by excess weight as such, and therefore assume a primary goal for obese people is to lose weight (Dalton, 1997). A careful look at medical research about obesity and weight control, however, suggests that the link between weight and health is not so simple (Gaesser, 1996). Sometimes excess weight may be the result rather than the cause of an ailment (as in the case of diabetes). Other times it may be the result not of eating too much but of insufficient physical activity. Inactivity, in turn, may

obesity The state of being extremely overweight, specifically to a body mass index of 30 or over.

Chapter 11 Physical Development during Middle Childhood

be caused not by "laziness" buy by social prejudices. An overweight person may feel self-conscious about exercising in public due to our society's bias against the "wrong" type of body, yet also be unmotivated to exercise in private, where no social support is available. Moreover, issues like not having access to affordable, nutritious, less-processed food (Swinburn et al., 2011), parents not having cooking skills or the time to cook (Davis et al., 2011; Fulkerson et al., 2011), increasing portion sizes (Fisher, Liu, Birch, & Rolls, 2007; Wanink, Painter, & North, 2005), and even insufficient sleep (Cappuciio et al., 2008; Chen, Beydoun, & Wang, 2008) all contribute to the explosion of obesity rates in the past few decades. These attitudes and factors are essentially social problems, not personal ones; and as the "A Multicultural View" feature (see page 261) indicates, the attitudes are *not* shared by all societies.

Unfortunately, for either a child or an adult, losing weight permanently is difficult to do. For a child, dieting or exercise must have the full support of parents and siblings, because these people have such substantial influence on meal preparation and on a child's daily activities (Ebbeling, Pawlak, & Ludwig, 2002; Pittman & Kaufman, 1994). Yet family members may find support is difficult to sustain over the long periods of time most weight control programs require. The collective willpower may simply be lacking, especially because overweight children tend to have siblings and parents who are overweight themselves. Table 11.1 lists some additional guidelines for addressing weight issues in children.

Motor Development and Athletics in Middle Childhood

Fundamental motor skills continue to improve during the school years and gradually become specialized in response to each child's particular interests, physical aptitudes, life experiences, and the expectations of others. Unlike a preschooler, older children are no longer content simply to run, jump, and throw things; now they put these skills to use in complex, active play. Sometimes this consists of informal, child-organized games, such as hide-and-seek, in which children use motor skills. At other times, active play involves formal sports such as gymnastics, swimming, or hockey.

During the school years, children develop the ability to play games with rules. Some of these games are informal, such as after-school hopscotch, and some are formal and adult

Late in childhood, girls often grow taller and faster than boys of the same age. The disparity can create awkward moments for members of both sexes, though many children do not seem to be concerned about it at all. When these children become older adolescents or young adults, they may not even remember that a disparity occurred.
Source: Franck Boston/Shutterstock.

TABLE 11.1 Guidelines for Responding to a Child's Weight Problem

1. *Make sure the child really needs to lose weight.* Weighing only a little (10 percent) more than average poses no medical risk and may cause a child few social problems in the long term. If a child is teased for his or her weight, learning ways to cope with the teasing may be more effective than trying to lose weight.

2. *Consult with a doctor or a trained nutritionist before starting the child on a diet program.* A diet should aim at stabilizing weight or causing a loss of only about one pound per week at most. It should be balanced nutritionally and include snacks. Crash diets or food fads should be avoided at all costs; they are not effective and can seriously jeopardize a child's health.

3. *Develop a program of exercise appropriate for the child.* Start slowly and build up gradually. Try to incorporate activities that the child enjoys and that can fit into his or her daily routines conveniently.

4. *Seek support from the child's whole family, as well as from teachers or others whom the child sees regularly.* These people must show respect for the child's efforts, offer encouragement, and avoid tempting the child to break a diet or give up on exercise. Most of all, participate *with* the child in programs of activity or programs to control eating. Modeling appropriate eating and physical activity is one of the most important factors in child and whole-family health.

A Multicultural View

Dieting in Cross-Cultural Perspective

In our society, self-administered dieting and exercise has become a major industry. Countless books have been published to help individuals lose weight and gain muscle, and many of them are intended for children. A quick search of Amazon.com produces thousands of hits for children's diet books. Attaining a culturally valued bodily "look" can become a major personal project, one that for many children begins in middle to late childhood and continues well into adulthood.

At the heart of North Americans' preoccupation with body image is not only a concern with nutrition and health but also a commitment to crucial cultural values. One of these values is *individualism,* a belief that people are fundamentally autonomous and responsible for themselves. From this notion comes the belief that your body indeed belongs to you and that you personally are responsible for how it looks. How it compares to social ideals of physical beauty therefore indicates your success as a member of society as well as your ongoing commitment to participation in society. A lean, thin body (supposedly) shows self-discipline and restraint, two socially admired qualities, because it implies that you have been eating and exercising responsibly. To achieve these things, numerous individuals embark on exercise and diet programs for varying periods of time. Girls and women are especially likely to do so because they are almost certain to be judged by their physical appearance repeatedly, even during childhood, and children who perceive themselves as being overweight are more likely to "diet" by means of skipping meals, reducing food intake, or exercising at a younger age (Balantekin, Savage, Marini, & Birch, 2014; Chung, Perrin, & Skinner, 2103). Children are at particular risk for early dieting if their parents encourage them to diet or lose weight (Balantekin et al., 2014), which is linked to higher risk of adult obesity and with risky dieting, such as fasting, using laxatives, or using diet pills (Enriquez, Duncan, & Schur, 2013).

Yet a preoccupation with diet and exercise is not universal. The Fiji islanders in the South Pacific, for example, seemed generally indifferent to the size or weight as recently as the mid-1990s (Becker, 1994). Fijians had definite ideals about physical appearance: a person should have sturdy calf muscles, for example, and generally look "well fed" (a bit plump by our standards), and Fijians would frequently comment on one another's physical looks constantly and directly: everyday greetings often included teasing about whether a person looks fatter (or thinner) than in the past.

The paradox of personal indifference combined with public frankness was accounted for by the Fijians' fundamental orientation to their *community* rather than to themselves as individuals. What was important to an individual Fijian was not personal achievement or standing out from the average but showing a nurturing and caring attitude toward friends, family, and children. A primary vehicle for attaining these goals was food: serving food was and is a major way to show interest and attention to others' needs, both physical and emotional. According to custom, Fijians open their windows and doors during mealtimes so that the event becomes more truly public, and anyone passing by is cordially (and sincerely) invited in to share the food. Extra food is routinely prepared for each meal to allow for this possibility, because it is considered a social disgrace to be unable to share food generously with whoever happens to come by.

The Fiji islanders, therefore, considered dieting to be self-centered and irresponsible because it prevented a person from either giving or receiving nurturance from the community. In a sense, a person's body "belongs" to the community rather than to the individual. Secret eating was a serious social mistake, as was secret noneating (dieting). Parents observed their children carefully for changes in appetite, as well as for changes in weight (either up or down) that might imply fluctuations in appetite not because they wanted their children to achieve a certain size but because they wanted them to participate fully in both the giving and receiving of community care, and an important way of participating is through food.

However, between the 1990s and 2010, Fiji experienced great economic development, leading to more exposure to Western values, ideals, and media (Gerbasi et al., 2014). This influx of Western influence changed both perception of the ideal body and peer attitudes toward ideal body types, which led to a significant increase in the number of girls dieting and engaging in disordered eating (Becker, 2004; Gerbasi et al., 2014).

In pre-1990s Fiji, it was not the cultivation of a certain body image that conferred prestige, as was and is true in North American society. Instead, it was the cultivation of social relationships, particularly those that made nurturance possible. Which orientation toward body image and food do you think is preferable? The focus on caregiving spared most Fijian children from worries about their physical appearance, as well as from discouragement caused by unsuccessful dieting or exercise programs to improve physical looks (Gerbasi et al., 2014; Sault, 1994). But a negative effect also is possible: the focus on community can create problems for children who *must* limit their eating for health reasons, such as diabetes or intestinal flu. In a strongly communal society, these situations can prove especially worrisome to both child and family because they require deliberately limiting participation in a central social practice: the daily abundant sharing of food.

Chapter 11 Physical Development during Middle Childhood

> **What Do You Think?**
>
> Is concern about height and weight really a gender issue? Why or why not? Check your perceptions by polling ten male and ten female acquaintances (it's easier if you collaborate in doing this task) about whether they think they weigh more than, less than, or close to the ideal. Then ask them how they think members of the opposite sex would answer the same question, on average.

sponsored, such as Little League softball. In any case, traditional team sports now begin to have meaning for children because they can understand and abide by a game's rules. At the same time, children's improvements in coordination and timing enhance their performance in all kinds of sports, whether individual or group.

What lasting physical and psychological effects do early athletics have on children? This question has not been studied as thoroughly for children as it has for adolescents and adults, but a few tentative answers are possible. On balance, athletic activity probably helps children much more than it hurts them. However, it does carry a few significant risks. Table 11.2 summarizes the benefits and the risks.

Physical Effects of Early Athletics

The most obvious risks in athletics are sports-related injuries: bruises of various kinds and severity, damage to muscles (sprains), concussions, and broken or dislocated bones (Backx, 1996; Caine, Maffulli, & Caine, 2008). Do such injuries actually pose a problem for child development? Some researchers express concern about the frequency of athletic injuries, especially in childhood. The injuries usually receive only short-term medical attention: once bones or muscles appear to be healed, they are promptly ignored, and the athlete is encouraged to return to play. Given the special stresses of athletic activity, this short-run approach may allow minor but long-term disabilities to develop (Caine et al., 2008; Smith, 1996).

Other researchers point out that most children who are injured during sports have relatively minor injuries, and the benefits of participation therefore considerably outweigh the risks. They cite the physical benefits of athletics. For example, children involved in regular athletics may develop better physical endurance than nonathletic children; this means their hearts and large muscles may function more efficiently (Rowland, 1993), and more fit children are less likely to get injured (Caine et al., 2008). As a result, they may be better able to undertake ordinary daily activities with less effort.

TABLE 11.2 Physical and Psychological Effects of Childhood Athletics

	Physical Effects	Psychological Effects
Positive Effects	Better physical fitness Improved motor coordination	Training in achievement motivation (e.g., bettering previous running times) Support for teamwork (e.g., basketball)
Negative Effects	Sports-related injuries, such as knee injuries (football), back problems (gymnastics), shoulder pain (baseball), concussions (football, rugby)	Competition engendering more concern with winning than with performance as such Excessive pressure from adults to practice, perform well, and win

In addition to obvious physical benefits, athletics can also encourage achievement motivation, discipline, and a sense of self-esteem. Critics worry, though, that some sport activities may also cause injuries and destructive competition.
Source: Fotokostic/Shutterstock.

Psychological Effects of Early Athletics

The immense popularity of early athletics probably stems at least in part from the psychological benefits attributed to participation. Participation in athletics has been linked to having fewer mental health problems during adolescence (Steiner et al., 2000). Sports, it is hoped, develop achievement motivation, teamwork, and a tolerance for or even enjoyment of competition. How well do early athletics in fact realize these goals?

Training in Achievement Motivation

Most sports provide standards against which children can assess their performances. Goals can be scored, distances measured, and times clocked. Children's performances can then be compared with the youngsters' own previous scores, with those of their peers, or with those of top-scoring individuals or teams.

Whether this information really encourages higher athletic achievement depends on how a child uses it. Kindergarten children tend to remember their sports history poorly. Therefore, they approach each performance as a unique event. For example, Dalia may find each swim meet enjoyable in its own right, but she thinks little about bettering a past performance or correcting previous mistakes. During the school years, however, comparing oneself to standards becomes a prominent concern (Weiss, 1993). This concern does motivate some children to better their performances, but it also undermines motivation for children who believe athletic standards are arbitrary, externally imposed, or unreasonably difficult to meet.

Teamwork and Competition

Many sports promote teamwork, that is, cooperation with a select group of individuals. This goal certainly is a positive one, but it comes only if a child's team wins. What happens to losers? Among schoolchildren, even the most gracious loser shows significant stress. Research has found that losers become less sociable, refuse to talk about the game, and miss game practices more often than winners do (Petlichkoff, 1996). Losing teams also show a marked tendency to pinpoint blame by scapegoating individual members or events during a sporting season. If one "big play" seemingly lost a crucial basketball game, the players may dwell on that event more than it deserves, and they may stew about one or

> **What Do You Think?**
>
> Do childhood athletics by nature foster a competitive spirit among players? Or does competitiveness develop from stimulation by coaches and parents? This issue can spark a lively in-class discussion, especially if you can include a person who has been successful at competitive athletics as well as someone who has not!

two players who seemed most responsible for that play. These negative effects of losing are exacerbated and likely, in part, caused by parent behavior. When parents model bad sportsmanship—yelling at coaches, referees, their own children, or other children—children also engage in negative behaviors, but when coaches and spectators display positive behaviors like encouragement, the players will model those positive behaviors (Arthur-Banning, Wells, Baker, & Hegreness, 2009).

For some children, the path away from being a loser consists of training harder to win. For substantial numbers of others, however, it consists of learning not to take a sport too seriously—to treat it as "just a game" played for social and fitness reasons rather than for competitive success. Unfortunately the historical association of athletics with competition, glory, and "manliness" (for boys) can make this transition difficult for certain sports in some communities (Messner & Sabo, 1994). When a truly recreational approach to sports proves impossible, some children may adopt new interests and activities (such as watching television) that have fewer health benefits than sports do.

Health and Illness in Middle Childhood

Whether they are physically active or not, children usually are relatively healthy in the school years in the sense that they experience illnesses or accidents with serious medical consequences only rarely. School-age children also have colds and minor viral illnesses less often than preschool children and infants do. But illnesses and accidents can still disrupt the lives of individual children, which partly accounts for why medical professionals and parents may disagree about whether or not schoolchildren are "really" healthy in general.

mortality The proportion of persons who die at a given age; the rate of death.

One sign of good health is very low **mortality**, or the proportion of persons dying at a given age. In recent years, only about three or four children in every ten thousand die between ages six and thirteen, compared to twice this number among preschoolers and four times this figure among adolescents (U.S. Department of Commerce, 1998). The low rate of mortality is part of a historical trend extending back over the past century in which death rates have declined for all age groups, but especially for children.

On the average, schoolchildren get sick only about one-half as often as preschoolers do, though still about twice as often as do their parents. From parents' point of view, therefore, illnesses probably still seem rather frequent; nearly one-quarter of the parents in one survey reported that during the preceding two weeks their children were "too sick to carry on as normal" (Coiro, 1994), meaning the children stayed home from school for at least one day. As parents often point out, a sick child has a substantial impact on the work and leisure schedules of the rest of the family, especially parents. This is particularly true for families living at or near the poverty line, discussed later.

Most common childhood diseases are *acute illnesses,* meaning they have a definite beginning, middle, and end. Most childhood acute illnesses, such as colds, gastrointestinal flu, chicken pox, and measles, develop from *viruses,* complex protein molecules that come alive only when they infect a host tissue (such as a child's nose). Despite popular belief, no drugs can combat viral infections. (This is not the case with bacteria that invade the body; they can be effectively fought off with antibiotic drugs.) Instead, viral illnesses must run their course, and the child's natural immunities must work the real cure.

By the school years, about 5 to 10 percent of children develop *chronic illnesses,* or conditions that persist for many months without significant improvement. In the United States and other developed countries, the most common chronic conditions occur in the lungs and affect breathing (United Nations International Children's Emergency Fund, 1998). Some children develop *asthma,* or persistent congestion in the lungs; others develop chronic coughs or allergies. Other chronic complaints concern specific sensory organs. About one child in one hundred, for example, experiences problems in hearing or seeing. These and other chronic health problems become more frequent with age.

Social Influences on Illness

The seriousness of illnesses varies according to children's social and socioeconomic status, but not the frequency. In general, parents in higher-SES families report that their school-age children get sick just about as often as those from lower-SES families, but higher-SES parents report keeping their children at home for shorter periods of time (Fitzgerald et al., 1994). Moreover, families near or below the poverty line are less likely to note that their children are in very good or excellent health (about 75 percent), compared to families with incomes of $75,000 or more reporting very good or excellent health (90 percent; CDC, 2014).

What accounts for the difference? Low-SES families probably lack money for doctors' visits, access to special child care when a child is sick, and permission to take time off from work to tend to a sick child. Therefore, to merit staying home from school or visiting a doctor, a child must have a relatively major illness, such as a seriously high fever or severe diarrhea. The result of these circumstances shows up in the longer average stay at home when illness finally receives special attention.

Race and sex appear to matter too. African American families report *fewer* illnesses per child than do white families of similar SES, and all families of both races report *more* illnesses for girls than for boys of the same age (CDC, 2014; Johnson, 1995). In fact, school-age girls appear to get sick almost as often as preschool children of both sexes do; boys, however, get sick less frequently as they get older. Each of these differences probably reflects cultural influences. Medical care and an "on-call," stay-at-home parent may be less available to African American children than to white children, for example, necessitating that they continue to attend school even with minor illnesses. Furthermore, gender expectations may encourage girls to seek care for minor ailments and encourage boys to ignore such ailments, trends that continue into adulthood. In these ways, "illness" is not simply an objective reality but a perception by the child—or, more precisely, a perception combined with a response by the community.

Attention Deficit Hyperactivity Disorder

A small number of school-age children, especially boys, seem to be extremely active and have considerable trouble concentrating on any one activity for long (American Psychiatric Association, 2013). Their problem is called **hyperactivity**, or **attention deficit/hyperactivity disorder (ADHD)**. A second-grade teacher described one student with ADHD like this:

> Joey was friendly when you greeted him; "Hi!" he would say brightly, and smile. But he would never settle down. First he dumped the class's main supply of pencils out on a table; he sort of lunged at one of the pencils, but before he began writing, he left the table, looking for something new. During a reading lesson, I asked Joey to read silently until I finished helping another child; but Joey found this hard to do. He glanced in my direction; tapped a neighboring child on the shoulder; giggled; and kept scanning the room for "more." A child happened to drop a book; Joey laughed at this harder than the others, and jumped up quickly to pick the book up. He was probably trying to help, but in doing so he knocked his own papers all over the floor. Instead of picking up the papers, he only picked up his pencil, and headed off to sharpen it. And the morning was still only half over!

hyperactivity Excessive levels of activity and an inability to concentrate for normal periods of time.

attention deficit/hyperactivity disorder (ADHD) Excessive levels of activity and an inability to concentrate for normal periods of time.

Note that *most* children show excessive activity—behavior such as Joey's—*some* of the time. Only a few children really exhibit extremely high activity levels consistently enough to warrant professional attention, and there is evidence that ADHD is overdiagnosed, particularly among boys (Bruchmüller, Margraf, & Schneider, 2012). In fact, other problems, such as insufficient or disturbed sleep, have symptoms similar to ADHD among children (Chervin et al., 1997).

Chapter 11 Physical Development during Middle Childhood

Current guidelines require a minimum of six symptoms (a partial list follows) be present for a minimum of six months and in at least two domains (school, home, social) before the age of twelve, and the symptoms must interfere with daily functioning and not be explained by other disorders to be diagnosed as ADHD (American Psychiatric Association, 2013; CDC, 2016):

- Has trouble maintaining attention on tasks, work, or play
- Makes careless mistakes
- Does not follow through on tasks
- Is easily distracted or forgetful
- Has difficulty organizing activities
- Loses things
- Is fidgety or squirms
- Talks excessively and interrupts
- Acts as if "driven by a motor"
- Cannot stay in seat or moves about when inappropriate

Because no one is sure what makes some children overactive, and because ADHD usually persists throughout an individual's childhood and beyond, no single strategy for treating or dealing with the condition exists (Rutter, 1995). However, a group of strategies, usually involving stimulant medications in conjunction with other therapies, have proven helpful for the majority of children with this problem.

To reduce immediate symptoms, the most effective treatment is a stimulant medication. Some commonly used and effective stimulants have been *Ritalin* and *Focalin* (also called *methylphenidate*), *Adderall* (also called *mixed-salts amphetamine*), and *Strattera* (also called *atomoxetine*) which, paradoxically, quiet the child's behavior by "waking up" the central nervous system, that is, making it more alert (Heal, Smith, & Findling, 2011). When used properly, these medications have few short-term or long-term negative side effects; contrary to popular belief, they do not blunt growth, make the child lethargic, depressed, drowsy, or lacking in spontaneity (Barbaresi et al., 2006; Cherkes-Julkowski et al., 1997; Spencer et al., 2006). Instead, these medications make the child less bossy, argumentative, and noisy and better able to focus on tasks. In fact, long-term use of the stimulant medications used to treat ADHD might actually normalize activity in certain parts of the brain responsible for attention (Hart, Radua, Nakao, Mataix-Cols, & Rubia, 2013).

In addition to medication, behavior modification often helps to alter some of the most undesirable or counterproductive behaviors of an ADHD child. As the term implies, **behavior modification** is a psychotherapeutic technique that identifies specific behaviors that need changing, as well as straightforward techniques for eliminating or reducing them (Kazdin, 1994). In classrooms, several behavioral techniques are commonly used either alone or in conjunction, such as reviewing classroom rules regularly and having children earn points for following the rules or receiving a "time-out" for breaking rules (Fabiano et al., 2007). Praise, stickers, and special privileges also might be earned for following rules, and daily "report cards" of behaviors are often sent home to parents. Sometimes high-status peers are used to model or demonstrate appropriate behaviors. The active child simply watches a classmate complete an assignment slowly instead of at lightning speed; then the child tries to copy the same slow style in doing the assignment himself. The teacher, of course, reinforces (usually with praise) the modulated behavior when it occurs. One study found that medications, behavior modification, and the combination of the two positively impacted children's classroom behavior, and that low-intensity behavior modification in combination with low-dose stimulants had the same effect as high dosages of stimulants (Fabiano et al., 2007).

One key quality of behavior modification is its consistency and predictability, and parents and teachers can help significantly by striving to provide these qualities in the child's everyday environment. At home this means meals, play times, and bedtimes should come

---

behavior modification Techniques based on the principles of learning theory that can be used by parents, teachers, therapists, and other professionals to help children, adolescents, and adults reduce or eliminate undesirable behaviors and learn desirable ones.

> **What Do You Think?**
>
> Some experts argue that children with ADHD are not so much "disturbed" as "disturbing." What do you suppose they mean by this comment? Speculate about ways that home and school could be made less "disturbing" for a hyperactive child. Offer your ideas to a teacher or some other person who has experience with children's behavior problems. What does this person think?

at about the same times every day and follow roughly the same pattern. At school, lessons should have a regular, predictable format. In either setting, rules of acceptable and unacceptable behavior should be clear, simple, and relatively consistent. All of these strategies help the child with ADHD by temporarily reducing the demands on her attention-directing capacities and allowing these abilities to develop at her own pace.

When these strategies are followed, between 25 and 50 percent of all children eventually outgrow the problem, although they often report continuing to feel restless and distractible as adults (Fischer & Barkley, 2007; Karam et al., 2015; Weiss & Hechtman, 1993). The remaining children show some greater risk as adults for antisocial behaviors, such as failure to pay parking tickets, some inattention and impulsivity (Karam et al., 2015), and more fidgety behavior than those never diagnosed with ADHD (Halperin et al., 2008).

Sleep

As noted previously, some children with sleep disorders, which limit or disrupt sleep, seem as though they suffer from ADHD (Chervin et al., 1997). During middle childhood, children should be awake and alert during the day, sleep between nine and eleven hours each night, and rarely nap, a shift that occurs when children begin formal schooling (National Sleep Foundation, 2015). As with other areas of wellness during middle childhood, most children during this period of life get adequate, good-quality sleep, though it is important for parents to maintain a relaxing bedtime routine in a dark, cool, quiet room with a regular bedtime and wake-time for children. Prepubescent children are often lark-like—that is, their natural preference is to go to sleep early and wake early in the morning—a trend that, as we will see, changes with puberty. As with earlier childhood, refusal to go to sleep is a common problem during middle childhood as is difficulty going to sleep due to anxiety (Meltzer & Mindell, 2006). Practicing good sleep hygiene (noted previously) may help with these problems. If a child is sleepy or distracted during the day or does not wake up feeling refreshed, it is best to discuss the specific problems with a pediatrician, as these issues may be indicative of a serious sleep disorder, such as obstructive sleep apnea or an anxiety disorder.

The Changing Child

One point of child development that should be becoming clear is that all development is impacted by context. Even a child's height and weight influence acceptance by peers and personal self-esteem. A child needs sufficient nutrition and sleep in order to experience some of the advances in cognitive skills, such as memory and language, that we will explore in the next chapter.

Chapter Summary

- **What trends in height and weight occur among school-age children?** Although growth slows during middle childhood, children still develop significant differences in height and weight by the end of this period. Toward the end of the elementary school years, girls tend to grow taller than boys, and the difference can create embarrassment for some children. Weight can become a significant issue for some children in the school years because of both fears of social rejection and (in extreme cases) risks of medical problems.

- **What improvements in motor skills do children usually experience during the school years, and how do they affect children's involvement in athletic activity?** Motor skill development during middle childhood emphasizes coordination and timing rather than strength and fundamental skill. Athletics during middle childhood involve physical risks, as well as experience in achievement motivation, teamwork, and competition—with both good and bad effects.
- **What kinds of illnesses occur among schoolchildren? How does children's socioeconomic status affect their health?** Overall, schoolchildren are among the healthiest people in society, as shown by their low mortality. Compared to preschoolers, school-age children catch fewer minor acute illnesses, but a small percentage do suffer from significant chronic medical problems. Family SES and parents' beliefs about illness affect how much children actually stay at home as a result of getting sick. Attention deficit hyperactivity disorder (ADHD) affects a small percentage of school-age children and may result from a combination of genetic, physical, and social causes. Treatment of ADHD sometimes includes medications and behavior modification techniques.

Key Terms

attention deficit/hyperactivity disorder (ADHD) (p. 271)

behavior modification (p. 272)
hyperactivity (p. 271)

mortality (p. 270)
obesity (p. 265)

Cognitive Development during Middle Childhood

CHAPTER 12

Source: GagliardiImages/Shutterstock.

Chapter Outline

COGNITIVE DEVELOPMENT

Piaget's Theory: Concrete Operational Skills

Information-Processing Skills

Language Development in Middle Childhood

Defining and Measuring Intelligence

Information-Processing Approaches to Intelligence

School Influences

The Changing Child

Focusing Questions

- What new cognitive skills do children acquire during the middle childhood? What are the psychological and practical effects of these new skills?
- How does memory change during middle childhood? How do these changes affect thinking and learning?
- What new changes in language emerge during middle childhood?
- What is general intelligence, and how can it be measured?
- How does school affect children's cognitive development?

COGNITIVE DEVELOPMENT

The ADHD example at the end of the previous chapter is a good illustration of how a particular human change or condition can affect all domains of development simultaneously: it is partly physical (due to differences in the brain and brain functioning) as well as social (expectations about what is normative and what is expected), but influences the child's ability to think, as well as his feelings and relationships with others. It is also a relatively unusual condition, the kind we called *nonnormative* in Chapter 1. Therefore, it does not directly represent the most common or even universal changes in thinking or social life in middle childhood, the ones we have been calling *normative*. In this section, we describe the normative changes with respect to children's cognition (or thinking). As you will see, though, understanding the "usual" changes in thinking is not straightforward. Even when a cognitive development occurs widely in the school years, it usually varies in timing, intensity, and context. This caution applies to all four of the topics that follow: the development of concrete operational thinking, of information-processing skills, of language, and of general intelligence. In each of these areas there are "typical" developments in middle childhood, but also diversity.

Piaget's Theory: Concrete Operational Skills

As we discussed in Chapter 2, Jean Piaget developed a comprehensive theory of cognitive development from birth through adolescence. During middle childhood, according to this theory, children become skilled at **concrete operations**, mental activities focused on real, tangible objects and events. Concrete operations have three interrelated qualities, none of which is reliably present among preschool children: decentration, sensitivity to transformations, and reversibility (Piaget, 1965; Wadsworth, 1996). *Decentration* means attending to more than one feature of a problem at a time. For example, in estimating the number of pennies spread out on a table, a school-age child probably will take into account not only how large the array is but also how far apart individual pennies seem to be. *Sensitivity to transformations* means having different perceptions of the same object and combining them in logical ways. For example, when judging whether two clay balls have the same volume after one ball is squeezed into a pancake, a school-age child concentrates on the actual process of change in appearance—the transformation—rather than on how the clay looks either beforehand or afterwards. *Reversibility* of thought means understanding that certain logical operations (for example, addition) can be reversed by others (subtraction). All in all, the concrete operational child constructs a view of the world that emphasizes quantitative relationships for the first time. Now many facts seem logically necessary that earlier appeared arbitrary or even incomprehensible. In judging whether the amount of clay stays the same after being squashed flat, the child now reasons that the amount *must* be the same if nothing was added or taken away when the clay was squashed.

Concrete operations cause important transformations in the cognitive skills children develop in the preoperational period. In classifying objects, children can group things in more than one way at a time by about age seven. They know that a person can be *both* a parent and a teacher at the same time, for example, rather than just one or the other. They also understand that some classifications are inclusive of others, for example, that a particular animal can be both a dog and a pet. As a result, they usually can answer correctly a question such as "Are there more boys in your class or more children?" Preschool children, in contrast, often fail to answer such a question correctly unless it is further simplified or clarified.

Conservation in Middle Childhood

Some cognitive skills make their first real appearance during middle childhood. Probably the best known of these skills is **conservation**, a realization that certain properties of an object necessarily remain constant despite changes in the object's appearance. An example of conservation of quantity is the one described in Chapter 9 in which two tall, narrow glasses contain exactly the same amount of water. If you empty one glass into a wide, low tray, you create a substantial perceptual change in the water; it looks quite different than before and quite different than the water in the remaining tall glass, as Figure 12.1 shows. Will a child know that the wide tray has the same amount of water the tall glass does? If he does, he conserves, meaning he shows a belief in the water's underlying constancy despite a perceptual change.

Piaget (1965) found that after about age seven, most children did indeed conserve quantity in the water glass experiment. In fact, he found that by a year or two later, children conserved on a lot of other tasks as well, including the ones illustrated in Figure 12.1. Each task depicted requires believing in some form of invariance despite perceptual change.

---

concrete operations Logical thinking about concrete or tangible objects and processes; especially characteristic of middle childhood.

conservation A belief that certain properties (such as quantity) remain constant despite changes in perceived features such as dimensions, position, and shape.

	Original Setup	Alter as Shown	Ask Child	Usual Answer
Conservation of liquid			Which has more liquid?	Has more
Conservation of mass			Do they both weigh the same, or does one weigh more than the other?	Weighs more
Conservation of number			Are there still as many pennies as nickels, or more of one than the other?	More
Conservation of length			Are they the same length, or is one longer?	Is longer
Conservation of length			Is one pencil as long as the other, or is one longer?	Is longer

The clay balls, like the water glasses, require believing that mass remains constant; the bent wires and the pencils, that distance or length remains constant; and the coins, that number remains constant.

Conservation Training

Specialists agree that children do not begin life conserving but instead acquire this skill somehow. How do they do it? Piaget argued that biological maturation and countless experiences with physical objects that show conservation properties enable children to mentally construct conservation. These experiences are numerous and diverse, and although they can be taught explicitly, Piaget believed they have a fuller, more general influence on development if allowed to emerge naturally.

But many psychologists have tried to teach conservation anyway. In recent studies, investigators tried to prevent children from being distracted by coaching them to talk about what was happening ("Nothing is being added or taken away") or to compare the important dimensions closely ("Watch the height *and* the width"). Such efforts do produce greater conserving in a large number of children, though not in all (Wadsworth, 1996). Conservation has even been taught successfully to children with developmental delays and intellectual disabilities (Hendler & Weisberg, 1992).

However, trained children often do not maintain conservation concepts the same way "natural" conservers tend to do; they are more likely to give up their belief when even slightly challenged. "Natural" conservers are more steadfast in their commitment to conservation (although even they can be led to give it up if an experimenter shows strong skepticism about it). All in all, it seems that conservation may not develop during childhood as inevitably as Piaget first believed.

FIGURE 12.1
Conservation Experiments

As Piaget demonstrated, conservation (or the perception of invariance) emerges on a wide scale in middle childhood. In some cases, the child realizes that amounts of liquid or of solid mass remains constant; in other cases, he or she realizes that length or number remains constant. Early in middle childhood, however, the child often holds one of these beliefs without necessarily holding another, or holds one belief only on some occasions and not on others.

Chapter 12 Cognitive Development during Middle Childhood

The same can be said about other forms of logical thinking that emerge during middle childhood (Piaget, 1983). Piaget noted, for example, that children become able to *seriate,* or arrange objects in sequence according to some dimension such as length or size. They understand *temporal relations,* or the nature of time, better than they did as preschoolers; an eight-year-old knows that time unfolds in a single, constant flow marked by calendars, clocks, and landmark events. And children at this age can represent the *spatial relations* of their surroundings. They can make maps and models of familiar places, such as their homes, their classrooms, or the local shopping mall.

Piaget's Influence on Education

Although Piaget commented on educational issues (Piaget, 1970), he never intended his research to serve as a theory of education. At no time, in particular, did he offer advice about problems that normally concern teachers, such as how to teach reading or other conventional school subjects, how to motivate students, or how to evaluate students' learning. Nonetheless, his ideas and approach have significantly influenced educators, particularly those in early childhood education (Elkind, 1994a). At the heart of this influence is Piaget's *constructivist philosophy:* the assumption that children develop their own concepts through active engagement with the environment. Also at the heart is Piaget's emphasis on stages of cognition. These two ideas have jointly influenced teaching methods, curriculum content, and methods for assessing student progress.

Teaching Methods

Educators have borrowed Piaget's idea that true knowledge originates from active manipulation of materials (Samuelsson & Carlsson, 2008; Seifert, 1993). Children learn about weights, for instance, by actually weighing various objects on a scale rather than by reading about weights in a book or hearing their teacher talk about them. A commitment to active learning, in turn, encourages teachers and curriculum planners to put more tangible activities into educational programs wherever possible, as well as to sequence activities from the tangible to the abstract. Reading about insects still has a place in learning about those creatures, but collecting (and handling) some real bugs probably should come first. Moreover, virtual or computerized "hands-on" learning serves similar purposes and has similar benefits (Klahr, Triona, & Williams, 2007).

Curriculum Content

Piagetian theory has influenced specific curriculum content by providing many particular ideas about what cognitive competencies to expect from children of particular ages or levels of development (Kamii, 1994; Waite-Stupiansky, 1997). The conservation skills

Piaget's idea that thinking begins with manipulation and activity has been interpreted to support many elementary education programs that emphasize active learning. Here, a child discovers the properties of conservation of mass by shaping bowls from clay.
Source: file404/Shutterstock.

Part 5 Middle Childhood

> **What Do You Think?**
>
> Given Piaget's ideas about how thinking develops in middle childhood, what would be a good way to evaluate students' academic work in elementary school? Work with a classmate or two to devise an evaluation plan for a favorite grade level and subject. Then see how your plan compares to plans devised by classmates and (if possible) to those composed by an experienced teacher.

described earlier imply that elementary school children should develop a greater ability to solve problems no matter *how* the problems are presented. Compared to preschoolers, older children should be less distracted by seemingly small changes in drawings in their books or seemingly insignificant changes in how a teacher phrases assignments. In Piagetian terms, the children have become more "decentered."

Likewise, acquisition of concrete operations should help school-age children in a number of other ways. For instance, many academic tasks require multiple classification, which preschoolers often do not understand reliably. A written assignment may ask children to "list all the machines you can think of that begin with *c.*" This task requires classifying objects in two ways at once: first, by whether or not something is in fact a machine, and second, by whether or not it begins with the letter *c.*

Piaget's cognitive theory has guided many curriculum planners and teachers to select and evaluate academic tasks such as these. The theory itself does not, of course, lead to accurate selections for all children, because not all children move through Piagetian stages at the same rate. In addition, most children are capable of abstract thinking to a certain extent, even if they are not as skilled as adolescents or adults are (Keating, 2011; Metz, 1995). Despite these limitations, though, Piagetian theory gives us valuable guidance about how children gradually adapt and reorganize their thinking as they grow older.

Assessment of Students' Progress

Throughout his work, Piaget emphasized the importance of children's actual thought processes and what those processes actually allow children to accomplish. This approach is evident in Piaget's heavy use of partially structured interviews and problem-solving tasks. Many educators believe such dialogues and tasks offer a much better way to assess students' progress than do traditional classroom tests and assignments, which tend to emphasize knowledge that is rote and taken out of context (Hill & Ruptic, 1994; Ruiz-Primo, 2011). Recent revisions to Piaget's approach, sometimes called "neo-Piagetian" theory, have made the approach even more attractive to educators by focusing more closely on *how* children learn and proposing cognitive stages that are more specific, and therefore more accurate, than Piaget's original proposals (Case & Edelstein, 1994).

Information-Processing Skills

A major alternative to Piaget's way of understanding the cognitive changes of middle childhood is in terms *of information-processing theory* (described in Chapter 2), which focuses on how children organize and remember information. By school age, children's short-term memories already are well developed—though not perfectly, as we indicate shortly. Their long-term memories, however, have significant limitations at the beginning of this period. For most children the limitations diminish as they get older, but for a few information processing remains a problem serious enough to interfere with school performance throughout elementary school and beyond. As with the development of concrete operational thinking, then, children simultaneously show both common trends and individual diversity in developing this form of thinking.

Memory Capacity

According to popular wisdom, children remember better as they get older. But how true and universal is this idea really? In everyday life, children obviously do not perform as well as adults do on some tasks, such as remembering to put away their clothes at the end of the day. But in other ways they seem to perform equally well; for example, they will remember their grandparents when they see them again after months or even years of absence.

Working Memory

Some of these differences in memory may depend on which parts of the information-processing model the children happen to be using. Some tasks rely primarily on *working memory,* a feature of thinking that holds information only for a short period, perhaps up to twenty seconds, and allows mental manipulation of that information (see Chapter 2). On tasks that emphasize working recognition memory, school-age children perform less well than adults do. This tendency can be demonstrated by showing individuals a set of digits briefly and then immediately asking them whether the set included a particular digit (Cowan, 1997). Under these conditions, recognition of a test digit improved steadily, with eight-year-olds remembering only about three digits and adults remembering about seven. Not surprisingly, too, the time it took a participant to recognize a test digit *did* depend on how many digits were shown in the original set, regardless of the person's age. Showing six digits made the task take longer than showing just three, no doubt because the person evaluated the test digit against a larger number of alternatives.

This study assessed a variation of **recognition memory**, in which a person merely compares an external stimulus or cue with preexisting experiences or knowledge. Recognition memory is involved when children look at snapshots of a holiday celebration months in the past: their faces light up, and they may describe aspects of the celebration they had apparently forgotten. **Recall memory**, in contrast, involves remembering information in the absence of external cues, such as when trying to remember a friend's telephone number without looking it up. In research, recall is often studied by providing a list of numbers and asking participants to provide that list in the order it was provided or in backward order. Children also get better at recall tasks such as this over the course of childhood and adolescence (Conklin, Luciana, Hooper, & Yarger, 2007). Recall generally is more difficult than recognition, but it shows the same developmental trend recognition does: school-age children can recall better than preschoolers, but not as well as adults. Figure 12.2 illustrates this trend.

Another factor that plays a role in working memory is that of attention. To succeed at any of the tasks noted earlier, one must actually pay attention to what is being presented even if there is some distraction. Our ability to focus on a single thing and ignore any other stimuli, much like you are doing now by focusing on this sentence even though there is ambient noise in the room, is known as **selective attention**. Over the course of childhood and adolescence, selective attention improves in part because we get better at inhibiting responses as the frontal cortex of the brain matures (Booth et al., 2003). Thus, ten-year-old Da'Sean is much better at focusing on his prealgebra homework than when he was seven even though his sister is watching cartoons in the same room.

Long-Term Memory

Long-term memory (LTM) is the feature of thinking that holds information for very long periods, perhaps even indefinitely. It is not clear how much long-term memory changes during childhood, or even whether it changes at all, because LTM relies increasingly on complex strategies of information storage and retrieval. Younger children may remember less because they have experienced fewer memorable events or because they use fewer methods of deliberately remembering information and experiences.

To understand how LTM changes during childhood, consider how children and adults recall short stories they have heard (Wolf, 1993). By age six, children already understand the basic narrative structure of stories—that such stories contain characters, situations, and plots with a beginning, a middle, and an end. Not surprisingly, therefore, children show many similarities to adults in recalling stories. Like adults, they recall important features of a story ("Goldilocks was not supposed to enter the bears' house") and ignore or forget trivial details ("Goldilocks was wearing brown shoes"). They also recall the essences of sentences rather than their exact wording.

---

recognition memory Retrieval of information by comparing an external stimulus or cue with preexisting experiences or knowledge.

recall memory Retrieval of information by using relatively few external cues.

selective attention The ability to maintain focus on one thing even in the presence of distractions.

FIGURE 12.2

Developmental Changes in Recall Memory

In the study represented here, children were asked to recall a series of digits shortly after hearing them. The points on the graph represent the average number of digits subjects were able to recall, and the bars represent the ranges of typical performance at each age. Recall of digits improves during middle childhood and almost reaches adult levels by age twelve, though not quite.

But compared to adults, the recollections of school-age children include fewer inferences based on the sentences they actually hear (McNamara et al., 1991). As children get older, they begin to "read between the lines" more frequently, at least when recalling stories, and making inferences about characters' goals within a story may improve recall for a story (Lynch & van den Broek, 2007). This tendency lends color and detail to their retellings as they get older, although they sometimes risk misstating the facts of a story.

Implications for Elementary Education

The structure, or "architecture," of memory may affect how children can learn during the school years. A younger student who can remember only three bits of information needs to have information organized in smaller chunks than an older student who can remember six bits at a time. The younger child may have trouble remembering a phone number long enough to dial it, for example, unless the teacher can offer some learning strategies for doing this task. More significant for learning, research shows that elementary school students' ability to solve arithmetic problems is correlated with the extent of their working memories; in one study, "larger" working memory meant greater accuracy in solving problems (Swanson et al., 1993). Children's limitations in terms of long-term memory, on the other hand, pose a different challenge: school-age children *can* remember ideas and facts for long periods, but their teachers may need to help them see connections among the stories, ideas, and other material they learn in school.

Difficulties with Information Processing: Learning Disabilities

However, improvements in information processing do not occur uniformly for all children. During middle childhood, between 5 and 12 percent of children are diagnosed with neurodevelopmental disorders, or specific learning disabilities, disorders in basic information processing that interfere with understanding or using language, either written or spoken (Geary, 2004; Lerner, 1993; Olulade, Napoliello, & Eden, 2013). Usually a **learning disability** causes poor academic achievement, although low achievement is not in and of itself evidence of a learning disability. Learning disabilities have no obvious physical cause, as blindness or hearing impairment do, and do not result from a general slowness of thinking, as intellectual disability does.

Learning disabilities take many forms. One of the more common forms is called *dyslexia,* literally an inability to read. The diversity of symptoms among children with dyslexia reflects the diversity among learning disabilities in general. For some children, dyslexia consists of "word blindness": they can read letters singly (such as *c, a,* or *t*) but not in combinations that make words, such as *cat.* In other forms of dyslexia, children can read words but fail to comprehend them. They can copy words accurately or transcribe them from oral dictation, but

learning disability Difficulty in learning a specific academic skill such as reading or arithmetic.

they cannot explain what they have written afterward, no matter how simple the vocabulary. Some children with dyslexia can read combinations of digits that make large numbers; for example, they can read *123* as "one hundred and twenty-three" but not as "one, two, three," even when they try. Most children with dyslexia have these problems in combination. Yet they seem normal in every other respect; their everyday conversations seem perfectly intelligent and their motor skills just as developed as other children's verbal and motor skills.

Such problems in processing information are likely caused by learning disabilities (Olulade, et al., 2013). Some children with dyslexia may find visual recognition especially difficult or time-consuming. Several researchers have reached this conclusion after studying a phenomenon called *perceptual masking,* in which some letters are hard to read because of the presence of other letters nearby. To understand this problem, consider the following arrangement of letters:

```
w e k
q w e k l
a q w e k l m
s a q w e k l m n
d s a q w e k l m n p
g f d s a q w e k l m n p y b
c v g f d s a q w e k l m n p y b h t
```

If you look at the *e* in the top line, you probably will still be able to see the letters *w* and *k* clearly using your peripheral vision (the corner of your eye). If you look at the *e* in a line farther down, you can still see the end letters relatively clearly, but the middle letters become almost impossible to pick out clearly. Trying to notice the middle letters does help you to perceive them, but when you make this effort, the end letters become hard to discern. Perceiving one set of features in this display masks others—hence the term *perceptual masking.* Without a lot of practice, few people, adults or children, can see very many letters at once.

Some (though not all) children with dyslexia show especially strong perceptual masking (Snowling & Stackhouse, 1996). Compared to same-aged normal readers, they must stare at words for rather long periods, consciously shifting attention from one subset of letters to another in a way similar to the staring required to "see" the letters displayed on this page, similar to "normal" readers who are younger. Once they figure out the letters in a word, however, they can connect meanings with them fairly quickly and accurately.

The gap in speed between perceiving and associating may account for many errors made by children with dyslexia. A ten-year-old may look at the word *conceal* and say something like "concol," or look at *alternate* and say "alfoonite." In making these mistakes, children may literally be reading what they see and guessing about the rest. Unfortunately, they may see fewer letters than normal same-aged readers usually discern.

Causes of Learning Disabilities

What causes some children to have a learning disability such as dyslexia? The symptoms sometimes resemble what happens to individuals who suffer injuries to their brains (Rourke & Del Dotto, 1994). For this reason, some professionals have suggested that many learning disabilities, including dyslexia, may reflect undetected minimal brain damage that occurred during the birth process or even before birth which discourages some parents and professionals from helping children with learning disabilities on the grounds (probably mistaken) that organically based problems are beyond control. However, relatively high rates of learning disabilities among children with a close family member, such as a parent or twin, with learning disabilities suggest some kind of genetic basis (Geary, 2004). Current thought suggests that a combination of genetics and environment likely plays a causal role in the development of learning disabilities (Peterson & Pennington, 2012).

A more helpful explanation for learning disabilities focuses on cognitive functions rather than on brain anatomy. In this view, disabilities may result from subtle differences in how the mind of a child normally organizes, focuses on, and processes information. To see what this idea means, consider what children must do to read an ordinary page of print. First, they must perceive the letters and words as visual patterns. Then they must combine those patterns into larger strings that constitute phrases and sentences resulting in phonological coding, which can be thought of as "words in their head." Finally, they must connect those strings with meanings to form ideas. While all of these steps are going on, they must also scan ahead to recognize the upcoming visual patterns on the page. If any of these steps fails to occur or occurs in the wrong sequence or at the wrong speed, a child may appear to have dyslexia. Current research suggests that difficulty in visual recognition might be caused by dyslexia rather than being a cause of dyslexia, suggesting that the breakdown occurs with the phonological coding (Olulade et al., 2013; Peterson & Pennington, 2012).

Helping Children with Specific Learning Disabilities

Because learning disabilities become a problem primarily in school settings, school professionals have taken increasing responsibility in recent years for helping children who develop these problems. Most commonly, help consists of careful diagnosis of which steps of thinking cause difficulty for a child, followed by individual educational plans to strengthen those particular steps (Alexander & Slinger-Constant, 2004; Lyon, 1993). For instance, children with problems in perceptual masking can be given exercises in which they purposely work to improve this skill. Often such special work can be done in a regular class during a normal school day, but at least some of it requires individual tutoring so that the professional can monitor and give precise assistance to the child's thinking as it actually occurs. Depending on the child's needs and the school's circumstances, regular classroom teachers, parents, or trained special educators can act as tutors as well as additional sources of encouragement and support for the child. The Working With interview with Terry Wharton discusses issues of special education in more detail.

Children with learning disabilities usually are old enough to have feelings and opinions about their problems. Eventually, in fact, a major problem in some learning disabilities may become *self-consciousness* about failing to learn, in addition to any cognitive or perceptual problems as such. A child who cannot read well usually becomes painfully aware of this fact sooner or later and worries about what teachers, parents, and peers may think of her as a result. Parents can help with this problem by being optimistic about the child's eventual capacity to learn academic skills, in spite of current difficulties, and being supportive rather

There are numerous ways of helping children with learning disabilities; no single way is guaranteed to be always effective. This teacher, for example, is helping a girl with her reading by using a computer that provides extra assistance and responds to her particular learning needs.
Source: Rob Marmion/Shutterstock.

Chapter 12 Cognitive Development during Middle Childhood

WORKING WITH Terry Wharton, Special Education Teacher

Giving Children a Second Chance to Learn

Terry Wharton has a wide range of experience in classroom teaching and special education. He currently teaches a class of second to fourth graders who have shown significant behavioral and emotional problems in regular classrooms. There are only eight students in his class, all of them boys, and two teacher assistants—definitely not the typical teacher-to-student ratio. Terry spoke about the philosophy guiding his program and about how he and his assistants reconcile it with conventional academic expectations for the primary grades.

Terry: We emphasize making the class nonpunitive and nonaversive. For these kids, school has been a disaster socially—lots of fights with classmates, conflicts with teachers and other adults. We have to provide successes and confidence to counteract the downward spiral of their self-esteem.

Kelvin: *How do you do that without leading to further fights and conflicts? Eight of these kids in one room could be explosive!*

Terry: Well, we do have to plan activities carefully and guide their choices more than usual. At the start of the year, the children only come for half a day, and I plan a series of activities they are sure to enjoy and to be able to do, like setting up a personal datebook or calendar to use later in the year. By the end of that first day, they really feel successful.

Kelvin: *Given your students, how much is it like ordinary school?*

Terry: Oh lots, actually! Academics are a priority. We have a "news" time where everyone relates some interesting personal experience. Then I read to them for a few minutes. Then they write in journals, either about the story or about something else that concerns them.

Kelvin: *Do the kids like the journals?*

Terry: I must admit, at first they resisted. They seemed very self-conscious about their writing skills and about revealing their thoughts and feelings. But lately it's been amazing; you should read them! Their growth with the journals is impressive. They talk about the story, or about their fears and hopes for their family.

Kelvin: *What about math?*

Terry: They don't seem as uncomfortable about math as they do about writing and reading; I'm not sure why. We work on basic arithmetic skills using some of the latest manipulatives.

Kelvin: *Manipulatives?*

Terry: Like sets of unit blocks that you can combine to illustrate addition problems. They seem to like that. But you know what surprised me the most? Workbooks! When I taught a regular primary-grade class, I tried to avoid those because I felt they were too structured, but these students love them; they even ask to do them! I think it gives them a feeling of clear progress and a sense of control over their own efforts. They can see clearly that they are getting work done.

Kelvin: *So your program is indeed academic? You do work on cognitive skills?*

Terry: Absolutely. The cognitive skills develop only because we're also supporting these students socially, though. The two go hand in hand. I think that's true for all children, but working with these kids with behavior problems has really brought that idea home to me.

Kelvin: *Where else do you see academic and social connections?*

Terry: With the parents, certainly. We make a big effort to involve the parents in our program. Several times a year we have "family celebrations," lunches where the child's whole family is invited. The parents have responded enthusiastically. Some parents work as volunteers in the school. They've been a real help, and even if they are not in the same classroom, it's reassuring to be in the same building as their child.

Kelvin: *These sound like good ideas for all classrooms and parents. Do you agree?*

Terry: Yes, I do. But they're especially valuable for these particular parents because they've had so many bad experiences with schools, either because of their child's problems or when they were students themselves. It builds their confidence as parents.

What Do You Think?

1. Do you think Terry would define the word *cognitive* the same way this chapter does?
2. Terry did not comment on the fact that his class is all boys. Do you think gender is important to consider in teaching a class like this? Why or why not?
3. Terry mentions that his students enjoy workbooks for mathematics, even though he personally does not consider them a good idea initially. How do you feel about this issue? What do you suppose Piaget or an information-processing theorist would say about using workbooks?

> **What Do You Think?**
>
> Think about the methods you yourself have used to remember new information. What are they, and how are they consistent with the discussion in this chapter about how memory develops during middle childhood? Compare your own memory strategies with those of classmates. How are they similar? How are they different?

than critical of the child's efforts to do so. Teachers can help in these same ways, and in addition can encourage a positive, supportive climate in the child's classroom and school. In fact, children and adolescents with high levels of determination and self-efficacy, which can be fostered by parents and teachers, do better in school and are more likely to go on to college than those with low levels of these qualities (Field, Sarver, & Shaw, 2003).

Another major problem among children diagnosed with learning disabilities is the social stigma associated with the diagnosis. This stigma may serve as a self-fulfilling prophesy, leading some to feel hopeless about their abilities. The label of having a learning disability also puts many children at increased risk for bullying (Mishna, 2003). The social impact of school is so important, in fact, that we discuss it again later in this chapter. First, though, let us look at another major cognitive change of middle childhood: the development of language. As we will see, this development also has both cognitive and social effects.

Language Development in Middle Childhood

As we saw in Chapters 6 and 9, language development is a gradual process, one that continues to unfold during middle childhood. Vocabulary keeps growing, of course, and the ways children use words and sentences become more subtle, more complex, and more like adults' (Anglin, 1993). Contrary to the impressions young school-age children sometimes give, though, they have not necessarily mastered syntax. They often are confused by a number of common sentence forms until well into the elementary school years. To six-year-olds, for example, the sentence *The baby is not easy to see* means "The baby cannot see very well"; the sentence *I don't think it will rain tomorrow* is likely to mean "I know for a fact that it won't rain."

Mistakes like these may hardly be noticeable to parents and teachers if a child otherwise has normal language ability and has been acquiring only one language since birth. A school-age child can make himself understood for most everyday purposes and can express basic feelings. What is primarily still missing at this age is an extended vocabulary and skill in the more subtle or specialized uses of language—needs that therefore become the focus of many elementary school programs. The fact that language is actually changing or "developing" during middle childhood, in fact, may seem obvious only if a child is acquiring *two* languages during this period. In that case, the basic issues of language acquisition all come to the fore: problems in phonology (the sounds of a new language), lexicon (vocabulary), syntax (grammar), and pragmatics (language use). Next, we investigate the cognitive and social effects of bilingualism.

Bilingualism and Its Effects

Although most monolinguals may not realize it, a majority of children around the world are able to speak two languages and therefore are bilingual (Romaine, 1995). Bilingualism is common in the United States even though most American households primarily use English at home; somewhere between 60 million and 65 million individuals regularly use a language other than English (U.S. Bureau of the Census, 2015a). This represents about 26 percent of the population, but the proportion is actually much higher in some cities and regions such as Los Angeles where more than 50 percent of the population speaks a language other than English at home (U.S. Bureau of the Census, 2015a).

Does bilingualism benefit children's cognitive development? Research suggests that it does, but primarily when children acquire both languages equally well and when both

Fully bilingual children have cognitive advantages over monolinguals, but only as long as both languages and their related cultures are treated with respect by teachers and society. These Latino children are well on their way to becoming bilingual. What attitudes will they encounter about their language and heritage?

Source: wkstock/Shutterstock.

balanced bilingual A person who is equally fluent in two languages rather than more fluent in one language than in the other.

metalinguistic awareness The ability to attend to language as an object of thought rather than attending only to the content or ideas of a language.

languages are treated with respect by teachers and other representatives of the community (Bialystok & Hakuta, 1994). Language specialists call such children **balanced bilinguals**.

Cognitive Effects of Bilingualism

For one thing, balanced bilingual children show greater cognitive flexibility—skill at detecting multiple meanings of words and alternative orientations of objects—than monolingual children do. Bilingual children can substitute arbitrary words for normally occurring words relatively easily without changing any other features of the sentence. If asked to substitute *spaghetti* for *I* in the sentence "I am cold," bilingual children more often produce the exact substitution, "Spaghetti am cold," and resist the temptation to correct the grammar ("Spaghetti is cold") as monolinguals more often do. Such flexibility shows **metalinguistic awareness**, the knowledge that language, and in this case individual words, can be an object of thought. Metalinguistic awareness develops because bilingual experiences often challenge children to think consciously about what to say and how to say it (Jimenez et al., 1995). A question such as "What if a dog were called a cat?" therefore poses fewer conceptual problems for bilinguals. So do follow-up questions such as "Would this 'cat' meow?" or "Would it purr?" Those who are bilingual are also better at aspects of cognitive control. That is, when speaking, they must inhibit one language to speak in another language, demonstrating superior executive control compared to monolingual individuals (Costa, Hernández, & Sebastián-Gallés, 2008).

However, all of these cognitive advantages apply primarily to balanced bilingual children, those with equal skill in both languages. What about the unbalanced bilinguals, those with more skill in one language than in the other? Does knowledge of a second language help, even if it is limited? Some research suggests that even those children without balanced language skill demonstrate improved attentional performance on tasks (Yang, Yang, & Lust, 2011). Though many cognitive benefits have been associated with bilingualism, overall impact may be more mixed largely because of the interplay of social attitudes surrounding language differences in society (Pease-Alvarez, 1993; Yang et al., 2011).

Social Effects of Bilingualism

When children acquire two languages, one language usually has more prestige than the other. In the United States, the "preferred," or most important, language almost always is English. Its prestige results not only from its widespread use but also from its association

> **What Do You Think?**
>
> Think about a language you wish you could speak fluently. Why would you like to be able to use this language? In forming your opinion, what assumptions are you making about the culture or people who use this language?

with success and power: all the important people in American society, it seems, speak English fluently. These circumstances create negative attitudes or stereotypes about people who speak other languages and challenge educators to overcome social prejudices at the same time they facilitate learning new grammar, vocabulary, and usage (Soto, 1997). Negative stereotypes also apply to those who can speak English but do so with a "foreign" accent (Gluszek & Dovidio, 2010).

The influence of language on attitudes can be documented through experiments using the *matched guise technique.* In this procedure, perfectly balanced and fluent bilinguals tape record standard messages in each of their two languages, and the messages are interspersed among other tape-recorded messages to disguise the identities of the bilingual speakers. Then listeners evaluate the competence and social attractiveness of each speaker. Time after time, two consistent trends occur in studies of this type. First, speakers of English are rated more highly than speakers of other languages. Second, listeners from non-English-speaking cultural groups rate the English speakers more highly than they do speakers of their own language. The prestige of English, in other words, comes from sources in addition to English speakers themselves.

Negative attitudes toward non-English languages reduce children's school performance by making them less willing to use their primary, or first, language in public and reducing their self-confidence about linguistic skills in general. Fortunately, however, educational programs exist that can counteract these effects by treating children's first language as an educational resource rather than a liability. Overall, research favors *additive bilingual education,* programs that develop language skills in *both,* of a child's languages rather than attempting to replace a first language with English (Hernandez, 1997). As a practical matter, such programs usually are conducted partly in each language, depending on children's current language skills, but they do not confine either language to isolated "lessons" lasting only short periods each day. The challenge is a double one: to foster new language skills while promoting respect for a child's original language and culture. In countries where language is less strongly associated with economic or social status (for example, Canada, where about 25 percent of the population speaks French as a first language), bilingual education often does not include this double agenda (Johnson & Swain, 1997). Therefore, successful bilingual programs more often emphasize simple immersion in a second language and tend to ignore a child's first language without negative educational effects.

Defining and Measuring Intelligence

All of the cognitive changes discussed so far—concrete operational thinking, memory development, and language—constitute aspects of **intelligence**, a term that refers to adaptability or a general ability to learn from experience. Often *intelligence* also refers to the ability to reason abstractly especially by using language, as well as an ability to integrate old and new knowledge. In recent years, some psychologists have broadened the term *intelligence* to refer to social skills, talents of various kinds (such as a talent for music), or bodily skills. The traditional orientation toward reasoning and problem solving, however, still dominates discussions of intelligence, and partly as a result many standardized tests have been developed to measure these forms of intelligence.

The multitude of definitions of intelligence can create confusion for parents and professionals who have responsibility for helping children to develop their fullest potentials. Some of the complexity can be sorted out by noting that views of intelligence can be organized around three major theoretical approaches. The oldest and therefore best developed view is the **psychometric approach**, which is based on standardized, quantitative

intelligence A general ability to learn from experience; also refers to ability to reason abstractly.

psychometric approach to intelligence A view of intelligence based on identifying individual differences in ability through standardized test scores.

measurement of abilities and achievement. More recently, researchers oriented toward *information processing* and toward *sociocultural* issues also have developed theories of intelligence, although these approaches have not been tied to standardized testing to any significant extent.

Psychometric Approaches to Intelligence

Psychometric definitions of intelligence have developed out of *standardized tests,* all of which share three important features. First, they always contain clearly stated questions that have relatively specific answers. The questions usually draw on logical reasoning and verbal skills, which schools typically require. Second, standardized tests always include clear, standard procedures for administration and scoring. Often they provide a script for the person giving the test, as well as specific printed guidelines about when and how to credit particular answers. Third, such tests present information about how large groups of comparable individuals perform to allow evaluation of the performances of particular groups or individuals (Aiken, 1996).

Kinds of Standardized Tests

Standardized tests serve many purposes, but for convenience we can classify them into two major groups: achievement tests and aptitude, or ability, tests. **Achievement tests** measure individuals' existing skills or knowledge; they try to assess current attainment in a particular realm of human behavior. Children often encounter such tests in the form of scholastic achievement tests, such as tests of reading achievement or arithmetic achievement. By nature, such tests usually draw heavily on the typical curriculum content of the subject area being tested.

Aptitude tests measure ability or try to estimate future performance in some realm of behavior. A test of scholastic aptitude, for instance, tries to estimate a child's potential for success in school. Because of their goal, aptitude tests contain a broader range of questions than achievement tests do. A scholastic aptitude test probably would include questions from several major school subjects and draw on basic academic skills such as reading and mathematical reasoning.

In practice, aptitude and achievement tests are less distinct than these definitions make them sound. Often achievement tests are very effective predictors of future performance; children's current skills in arithmetic, for instance, predict their future mathematical performance about as well as any aptitude test can do. Also, aptitude tests can successfully predict future progress only by sampling skills and knowledge children have already attained. Nonetheless, the distinction remains useful for those who develop and use tests. In general, measuring aptitude means looking to the future, whereas measuring achievement means assessing the past.

Once norms have been calculated, standardized tests, and especially achievement tests, can serve two purposes. On the one hand, they can help educators know how well particular schools or classrooms are functioning in general. For example, all classrooms using a particular curriculum can be compared with classrooms using another curriculum, or all classrooms in one school can be compared with all classrooms in the city or even with a national cross-section.

On the other hand, standardized tests sometimes can aid individual children. The most common approach involves screening students who need special educational help. If teachers find that a certain student is learning the curriculum very slowly, they may ask a school psychologist to test the child's general scholastic ability in the hope of diagnosing or clarifying his or her learning problems. Although the results of such a test cannot stand alone, they often contribute to the complex process of assessing the learning needs of a particular child. Standardized tests can also help to identify students with superior abilities in specific areas; the Focusing On feature looks at educational issues pertaining to these gifted students.

As you may suspect, standardized tests serve neither of these purposes perfectly. Factors other than ability, such as a child's health or motivation to succeed, affect performance. So do physical disabilities, such as visual impairment. More indirectly, cultural and language

achievement test A test designed to evaluate a person's current state of knowledge.

aptitude test A measurement of ability that estimates future performance in some realm of behavior.

differences among children affect performance on standardized tests. These additional influences deserve special discussion because they affect all children throughout society.

Biases of Intelligence and General Ability Tests

Although they attempt to measure general qualities, tests of ability and intelligence contain various biases. For example, many intelligence tests rely heavily on language in all of its forms— listening, speaking, and reading. Many also emphasize problems that have specific answers and that play down divergent or creative thinking. Also, although they do not focus on speed, intelligence tests tend to favor children who answer fairly rapidly and take little time to mull over their solutions.

Because schools also emphasize all of these features, intelligence tests measure academic ability better than they do any other skill. Some psychologists, in fact, have suggested calling them measures of *academic intelligence,* or school ability, to make this limitation clear (Anastasi & Urbina, 1997).

The biggest problem with intelligence tests, however, comes from their cultural assumptions, which have originated entirely from white, middle-SES experiences in Western Europe and North America. The tests show their assumptions or biases in at least two ways. First, individual questions often demand knowledge that children can gain only by thorough immersion in white, middle-SES society. One question might ask children to describe the purpose of a garden hose, thereby assuming previous contact with a garden in their backyards. Another question might ask children to define the word *drama* or *concerto,* thereby assuming the sort of education that provides this information.

Even when tests avoid this type of bias, they suffer from other, more subtle cultural assumptions. Some ethnic groups and cultures do not value conversations that emphasize abstract or general propositions, as is common in classrooms or intellectual discussions; using this style may seem rude or at least boring (Heath, 1993). Children from these groups therefore cannot be expected to take tests that rely heavily on this form of dialogue. Also, in some cultural groups contact with strange adults is extremely rare, so children from such groups may find sitting alone in a room with an unfamiliar test administrator rather perplexing or even frightening. For such children, any questions the administrator asks may seem much less important than figuring out this adult's real motives.

Information-Processing Approaches to Intelligence

Some psychologists have responded to the limitations of psychometric views by developing other definitions and theories of intelligence. One way or another, all of the newer approaches broaden the nature and sources of intelligence. From these perspectives, more children seem to qualify as "intelligent" than is the case when children are assessed psychometrically.

The Triarchic Theory of Intelligence

An approach that draws explicitly on principles of information-processing theory is the **triarchic theory of intelligence** proposed by Robert Sternberg (Sternberg, 1994, 1997, 2006). This theory broadens the psychometric approach by incorporating recent ideas from research on *how* thinking occurs. To do this, Sternberg proposed three realms of cognition or, in his words, "subtheories" (hence the name *triarchic),* each of which contributes to general intelligence.

The triarchic theory of intelligence, developed by Robert Sternberg, identifies three different realms of thinking: componential, experiential, and contextual. Philosophically, the theory is rooted in information-processing theory.

The first realm of intelligence concerns the *components* of thinking. These resemble the basic elements of the information-processing model described in Chapter 2. Components include skills at coding, representing, and combining information, as well as higher-order skills such as planning and evaluating one's own success in solving a problem or performing a cognitive task.

triarchic theory of intelligence A view of intelligence as consisting of three components: (1) adaptability, (2) information-processing skills, and (3) the ability to deal with novelty.

Focusing On...

Gifted Students: Victims or Elite?

For years some educators have worried that *gifted students* (those capable of high performance in some or all academic areas, social leadership, or the performing arts) (see Table 12.1) become bored with the normal curriculum, isolated from their peers socially, and sometimes unproductive in school and career (Ross, 1993). Their "problem" was too much talent, but gifted students were believed to be potential victims of conventional schooling in the way students with learning or physical disabilities are and, similarly, often face the stigma of labeling (Berline, 2009).

In response to these concerns, some schools have created programs of gifted education. Typically these include a "pull-out" program: for an hour or two each week, students designated as gifted work in a separate classroom on activities designed to meet their needs or more commonly in high schools a school-within-a-school model that provides a special curriculum to students (Matthews & Kitchen, 2007). Often students work independently on projects of their own choosing, such as learning about local butterflies, designing a computer program, or creating a portfolio of paintings. Sometimes they are also linked with community experts (called *mentors*) who help them develop these interests. Regular classroom teachers are encouraged to recognize their interests and abilities by-allowing time to pursue the projects and periodically grouping gifted children together for tasks related to the regular curriculum (Gallagher & Gallagher, 1994).

This portrait of gifted education is attractive but highly controversial. A number of educators, parents, and political leaders argue that gifted education creates an overprivileged group of students (Margolin, 1994). In the pull-out programs, students receive much more time and attention from teachers than in a typical classroom and enjoy more freedom in using their time. Ironically, it is argued, the curriculum for gifted students is much *less* rigorous than that for regular students; gifted children do not necessarily read more books, write more essays, or learn more mathematics than others

TABLE 12.1 Some Characteristics of Gifted Students Renzudlli (1994)

Characteristic	Examples
Well-above-average ability	Can think abstractly; skilled at verbal and numerical reasoning; adapts well to novel situations; rapid and accurate memory
Task commitment	Shows high level of interest, enthusiasm, perseverance, and self-confidence; sets high standards for success
Creativity	Shows original thoughts; open to new experiences and information; curious, speculative, sensitive to detail and to aesthetic characteristics of ideas and things

---

The second realm of intelligence concerns how individuals cope with their *experiences*. How effectively do they respond to novelty in solving new problems? For example, a person may follow a dinner recipe accurately when it is written in imperial measurements (ounces, teaspoons) but fail miserably when the same recipe is presented in metric units (milliliters, grams). How quickly can that person adjust to the new form of the task and solve it as automatically as was possible with the old form?

The third realm of intelligence concerns the *context* of thinking. People show this form of intelligence to the extent to which they can adapt to, alter, or select environments relevant to and supportive of their abilities (Sternberg & Wagner, 1994). In taking a university course, for example, a student may try diligently to complete the course assignments as given, in essence adapting himself to the environment of the course. If this strategy does not work satisfactorily, the student may complain about the assignments to the professor in an effort to alter them. If the altered assignments do not work for him, the student may drop the course and select another. All of these behaviors show contextual intelligence (though not necessarily of a kind that may please professors!).

Table 12.2 summarizes the three realms of thinking, or cognition. These realms describe the processes of intelligence in more detail than classic psychometric approaches to intelligence have done. They also suggest an explanation for why

> **Focusing On . . .**
>
> ### Gifted Students: Victims or Elite? *continued*
>
> do. There has been a call to improve the curriculum of gifted programs by incorporating more critical thinking, problem solving, social studies, and foreign languages (VanTassel-Baska, 2006).
>
> Furthermore, the gifted programs tend to treat students as if they were broadly talented in all areas, even though research and professional teachers' experiences suggest that many students have selected talents— math but not English, for example, or music but not athletics (Gardner, 1997). This makes gifted programs more compatible with the preexisting strengths of high-SES families and white, English-speaking families, which may constitute a subtle form of racism. In fact, African American students are significantly less likely to be part of gifted programs and are disproportionally placed in special education programs that provide unequal education (Blanchett, 2006; Darlin-Hammond, 1997).
>
> Gifted education responded to these criticisms by making entrance into gifted programs more flexible: relying less on standardized test scores and more on students' own interest in volunteering for the program. Another is to arrange more activities for gifted students in the regular classroom and fewer in pull-out situations (Maker, 1993). A third is to redefine gifted education as *enrichment:* activities that tie conventional curriculum goals (reading, arithmetic) to students' own prior interests and talents. All students may be invited to pull-out activities, and activities focus on particular areas of the normal curriculum.
>
> Integrating gifted and regular education in these ways is more equitable but does not eliminate the basic educational controversy underlying gifted education: fostering excellence and fostering equality of education. Some researchers argue, for example, that having highly talented students work with less talented ones may accentuate rather than reduce elitism. Differences between higher and lower performers become obvious to all students, day in and day out, and create tensions within the classroom that can be reduced when the gifted program is integrated into classrooms and schools (Berlin, 2009; Gallagher, 1993). Students may still prefer classmates with similar levels of academic motivation, both to work with and to be friends with; so informal social segregation may develop even in a room that is officially integrated. Enrichment activities also are harder to schedule if they invite volunteers and focus on specific school subjects; they cannot overlap with regular class times because some students are ahead and motivated in the enrichment subject but may need extra help in the "regular" subject that they miss. That leaves lunch periods and before and after school for enrichment periods, times that teachers may need for class preparations and "refueling." Despite problems, many excellent enrichment programs exist in schools and have succeeded reasonably well in creating flexible yet challenging learning opportunities.
>
> ### What Do You Think?
>
> Some educators argue that the idea of a "bored gifted student" is a contradiction in terms. Why do you think they believe this? What do *you* think of this possibility?

individuals sometimes seem intelligent in different ways: perhaps one person has an advantage at internal processing of information, another adjusts to new experiences especially well, and a third has a knack for adapting, altering, or selecting appropriate environments in which to work. Given these possibilities, it would not be surprising

TABLE 12.2 The Triarchic Theory of Intelligence

Realm of Intelligence	Examples
Componential	Coding and representing information; planning and executing solutions to problems
Experiential	Skill with novel problems and familiar problems in novel settings; skill at solving problems automatically as they become familiar
Contextual	Deliberate adaptation, alteration, and selection of learning environments to facilitate problem solving

if psychometric tests favored certain children and cultural groups more than others, because the environments of some families and cultures foster the learning of testlike behaviors more than others do.

Gardner's Theory of Multiple Intelligences

Like Sternberg, Howard Gardner (1993a) has proposed that general ability consists of several elements or factors. However, Gardner has defined these factors in ways that reflect the influence of culture and society even more explicitly than the triarchic theory does. He argues that not one but **multiple intelligences** exist and take the following forms (Davis, Christodoulou, Seider, & Gardner, 2011):

multiple intelligences According to Howard Gardner's theory of intelligence, alternative forms of intelligence or adaptability to the environment.

- *Language skill* A child with this talent speaks comfortably and fluently and learns new words and expressions easily. She also memorizes verbal materials, such as poems, much more easily than other children do.

- *Musical skill* This child not only plays one or more musical instruments but also sings and discerns subtle musical effects. Usually musical talent also includes a good sense of timing, or rhythm.

- *Logical skill* A child with this skill organizes objects and concepts well. Using a microcomputer, for example, comes easily, as does mathematics.

- *Spatial skill* This child literally can find his way around. He knows the streets of the neighborhood better than most children his age do; if he lives in the country, he can find his way across large stretches of terrain without getting lost.

- *Kinesthetic, or body balance, skill* This child is sensitive to the internal sensations created by body movement. As a result, she finds dancing, gymnastics, and other activities requiring balance easy to learn.

- *Interpersonal skill* A child with interpersonal skill shows excellent understanding of others' feelings, thoughts, and motives.

- *Intrapersonal skill* A child with intrapersonal skill has a good understanding of his own. For children with either interpersonal, intrapersonal, or both of these skills, handling social encounters comes relatively easily.

- *Naturalist* This child has the ability to identify and categorize different things in the natural world such as plants and animals.

This boy's skill playing the piano, keeping time, and playing accompaniment for himself demonstrates an important part of intelligence: musical ability.
Source: Arvind Balaraman/Shutterstock.

Part 5 Middle Childhood

Gardner argues that these intelligences are distinct, for several reasons. First, some of them can be physically located within the brain. Certain language functions occur within particular, identifiable parts of the brain, as do kinesthetic or balance functions. Second, the intelligences sometimes occur in pure form; some individuals with intellectual disabilities play a musical instrument extremely well, even though their language ability may be limited and they cannot reason abstractly. Third, each intelligence involves particular, core skills that clearly set it off from the others. Being musical requires a good sense of pitch, but this skill contributes little to the other intelligences.

Like Sternberg's ideas, the theory of multiple intelligences implies criticisms of psychometric definitions of intelligence and of the standardized intelligence testing associated with psychometric definitions. Strictly speaking, however, the notion of multiple intelligences may really criticize the *use* of conventional tests beyond their intended purposes.

Sociocultural Approaches to Intelligence

Sociocultural definitions of intelligence give even more importance than information-processing theories do to the social setting. In the **sociocultural perspective**, intelligence is not actually "in" individual persons but instead resides in the interactions and activities that occur *among* individuals (Wertsch et al., 1995). In this view, it is not the individual who adapts to, learns, and modifies knowledge but the person and his or her environment in combination. For example, a child may make many mistakes on a test of arithmetic computation but be able to locate the most economical items at the local candy store almost infallibly, even if the items come in odd sizes (1⅞ versus 2¼ ounces) or odd prices (34 cents versus 49 cents) (Chaiklin & Lave, 1993). That is because the knowledge needed for comparison shopping is contained not only in the shopper's mind but also in the overall structure of shopping in the candy store's environment. With practice, a child learns how to sort out pricing clues that depend very little on the computational procedures learned in grade school. Some of the clues involve rough estimations, such as when the prices of two items differ widely but their sizes differ only a little. Others involve nonarithmetic knowledge, such as recommendations from other shoppers or memories of where the store kept the bargains on previous visits. The intelligence needed for comparison shopping thus is only partly "in" the child; the rest is more accurately said to be distributed among the store shelves, the conversations with other shoppers, and the history of events at the store.

A key concept in understanding the sociocultural view of intelligence is the *zone of proximal development (ZPD)*, originated by the Russian psychologist Lev Vygotsky and discussed in Chapter 6 (Vygotsky, 1978, 1997). The ZPD refers to the level of problem solving at which a child cannot solve a problem alone but can do so when assisted by an adult or a more competent peer. For example, a six-year-old may find the telephone directory too difficult to use alone but may be quite able to look up a phone number when given a bit of help from a parent. Implicit in the ZPD is the idea of shared knowledge, or shared cognition. Knowledge of how to use the phone directory exists at first in the interaction or relationship between two people—parent and child—and only gradually becomes located fully within the developing child. Likewise, knowledge of academic skills such as reading and mathematics also begins in the interactions between adults and children and only later becomes internalized by individual children. In fact, as the internalization progresses, children tend to perform better on tests of reasoning and language and therefore seem more "intelligent" in the psychometric sense.

Note that in emphasizing the social context of intellectual development, the sociocultural approach turns the issue of cultural bias on psychometric tests into an outcome to be expected and explored rather than a problem to be overcome or minimized. This changes the key question about intelligence from one about individuals to one about groups and communities. Instead of asking why some individuals seem more intelligent than others, the sociocultural view points out that some social *settings* may nurture and encourage individuals who show extra measures of talent, skill, and knowledge more than individuals from other settings. In this sense, some families, classrooms, and workplaces may be more "intelligent" than others.

sociocultural perspective on intelligence A view of intelligence that emphasizes the social and cultural influences on ability rather than the influence of inherent or learned individual differences.

Good balance, as shown by this girl, is not a prominent goal of the academic curriculum, but it may be an expression of a fundamental form of human intelligence: kinesthetic ability.
Source: Nataliya Turpitko/Shutterstock.

Even though building a model boat may be too difficult for these children to do alone, they are able to successfully turn some scrap wood into a seaworthy vessel when assisted by a more experienced adult. Change in performance because of such assistance is part of what Vygotsky meant by the zone of proximal development.

Source: Brendan Delany/Shutterstock.

The differences are well known by all psychologists interested in intelligence, including those who do not approach the topic from a sociocultural perspective. What is unique about the sociocultural perspective is the priority it gives to the impact of the community on individuals' cognitive development (Salomon & Perkins, 1998).

School Influences

Next to the family, school probably is the single most important influence during middle childhood. Each year children spend about eleven hundred hours at school and often many additional hours in school-related activities. Experiences at school give children opportunities to develop cognitive skills, language, and various talents and abilities. School also provides an arena for social development: for developing a self-image and self-esteem, cultivating peer relationships, and learning to deal with the diversity and conflicts that are an inevitable part of most people's lives. In the next chapter we look at social developments like these more fully, not only as they unfold in school but also in the lives of children more broadly. First, though, we will look at how school affects children's learning and therefore their cognitive development as well. Schools—and classrooms in particular—affect learning in three main ways: through fostering particular patterns of discourse, through the social biases of students and teachers, and through assessment (or evaluation) of student's learning. These factors also influence students' social development, but for now we will focus on how they affect learning and cognition.

Participation Structures and Classroom Discourse

discourse Extended verbal interaction.

participation structures Regular patterns of discourse or interaction in classrooms with unstated rules about how, when, and to whom to speak.

Classrooms provide particular patterns and styles of **discourse**, or language interaction, that influence how, when, and with whom children can speak (Gee & Green, 1998). Recurring patterns of classroom interaction are sometimes called **participation structures** and probably seem familiar if you have attended school for many years. They correspond roughly to common teaching strategies, except that participation structures include not only the teacher's behavior but students' behavior as well. Table 12.3 lists several of the most common participation structures.

As you may have noted from your own experience as a student, however, participation structures do not always work as intended, nor do they usually have the same effect on

> **What Do You Think?**
>
> Should standardized tests of ability be used in schools? If so, when and with whom, and for what purpose? Consult with several classmates about this issue. Then, if possible, compare the opinions of several professionals, such as a special education teacher and an occupational therapist. How do you think their work affects their opinions?

TABLE 12.3 Common Participation Structures in Classrooms

Structure	Teacher's Behavior	Students' Behavior	Assumptions
Lecture	Talk; tell ideas; answer questions	Listen; take notes; ask questions	Students think about what teacher says; do not daydream
Discussion	Set topic or broad question	Say something relevant; take others' comments into account	Know something about the topic before beginning class
Group work	Set general task; select group members	Work out details of solution to task	Do a fair share of the work; cooperate; compromise as needed

all students. One reason is that students bring to a classroom different expectations about discourse language and about work relationships: what seems like an invitation to work on a group project to one student may seem like an invitation to relax to another, in spite of a teacher's explicit efforts to focus students on work per se. This can be a problem if the discourse a student experienced at home has differed significantly in style from the discourse typically used at school.

Another reason is that teachers' discourse is always heavily laced with **control talk,** patterns of speech that collectively remind students that the teacher has power over their behavior and verbal comments. Even during "indirect" participation structures such as discussion or group work, teachers regularly do all of the following, among other things, to remind students of the teacher's influence:

- *Designate speakers* by calling on one student rather than another
- *Declare when a comment is valuable or irrelevant* by saying, for example, "That's a good idea" or "How can you relate [your comment] to what we were just talking about?"
- *Changing the topic or activity* by saying "Now let's do X [instead of Y]."

Hopefully teachers' control talk empowers rather than silences students by providing fair opportunities for individual children to express ideas, ask questions, and engage in higher-order thinking (O'Connor & Michaels, 1996; Orland-Barak & Yinon, 2007). There is a constant danger, however, that teachers' talk will empower only certain students at the expense of others. The inequity can occur when certain students get called on more than others or the ideas of certain students are declared to be irrelevant or inappropriate more often than the ideas of other students. One way to combat control talk and bias is to have teachers critically evaluate their own performance in the classroom (Orland-Barak & Yinon, 2007). As we note in the next section, such inequities sometimes do occur in practice as a result of social biases on the part of both teachers and other students. But they are not inevitable.

control talk A style or register of speech used by teachers to indicate their power over activities, discussion, and behavior of students.

Chapter 12 Cognitive Development during Middle Childhood   **295**

Social Biases That Affect Learning

Observations of classroom teaching show that both teachers and other students sometimes respond differently to a student on the basis of gender, race, or ethnic background in ways that parallel gender, racial, and ethnic biases in society at large. On the average, for example, teachers are more likely to speak to boys from a physical distance, such as from across the room, and to speak to girls at close range, such as at arm's length (Delamont, 1996; Wilkinson & Marrett, 1985). During discussions and question-and-answer sessions, furthermore, teachers tend to call on boys 10 to 30 percent more often than on girls, depending on the subject and grade level (Measor & Sykes, 1992). Both behaviors create an impression in the minds of students that boys are somehow more important than girls—more worthy of public notice. However, other studies have demonstrated that children, particularly boys, perceive that teachers treat boys more harshly than girls (Myhill & Jones, 2006).

Classmates, too, show biases like these. During group work, for example, teammates sometimes reproduce society's gender and racial biases: speaking and listening to boys more than to girls, for example, and to white children more than to nonwhite children (Cohen, 1994). However, when similar bias was investigated examining not just race but proportion of African American and Caucasian children in a classroom, an interesting pattern appeared: When the number of African American children in a classroom increased, measures of bias decreased (Jackson, Barth, Powell, & Lochman, 2006).

This suggests that, as we saw in Chapter 10's discussion of gender development, children tend to reinforce one another for gender-appropriate behavior—including being assertive if, and only if, you are a boy and cooperative (or nonassertive) if, and only if, you are a girl (Maccoby 1995). But the biases are not inevitable. Some teachers and classmates do not express them at all, and educational interventions have successfully trained teachers and even classmates to include all students equitably, regardless of gender, race, or ethnic background (Cohen & Latan, 1997; Denson, 2009; Leaper, 1994).

The Impact of Assessment

assessment The diagnosis of an individual's strengths, needs, and qualities.

For most children, school becomes a primary setting for **assessment**, teachers' diagnosis and evaluation of students' strengths, weaknesses, and progress at learning. Assessment has a profound impact on students' perceptions of themselves and of one another (Wigfield et al., 1998), either positive, negative, or both at once. The nature of the influence depends on the structure of goals the child experiences. Most schools and teachers use some combination of individualized, competitive, and cooperative goals, and educational research has found that each has distinct effects both on students' learning and on their social relationships.

Individualized Goals

With individualized goals, each student is judged on his or her own performance, regardless of the performance of others. In principle, therefore, every student could achieve top evaluations, failing evaluations, or any mixture in between. Sometimes this kind of assessment is called "grading on an absolute standard," because performance of each individual is compared to a standard rather than to other students. It is common in the teaching of relatively structured subjects, such as elementary arithmetic, where standards can be defined clearly. Research on individualized goal structures generally has found that this arrangement heightens students' attention to mastering content and skills, and makes them relatively indifferent to judging their overall abilities or those of other students (Johnson & Johnson, 1994). Unfortunately individualized goals also make students less interested in what they can teach one another and less appreciative of (because less focused on) one another's diverse knowledge and skills. Individualized goals also do not lend themselves equally well to all content or topics; performing in a school play or on a sports team, for example, depends as much on good coordination among individuals as it does on skills possessed by individuals themselves.

Competitive Goals

With competitive goals, students are assessed in comparison to one another, and some individuals therefore are judged to be better than others; there are "winners" and "losers." Competitive goals are common in school sports competitions (only one person or team can take first place), but also in many nonathletic tournaments and contests of all kinds (e.g., a schoolwide spelling bee). They are also implied, though not stated, when teachers post marks or scores in rank order for students' inspection. Competitive goals make students concerned with how they expect to perform relative to others, regardless of how well they perform in any absolute sense. Competitive goals also tend to make students think of their own abilities as fixed entities ("You either have it or you don't") rather than as the result of effort and hard work on their own part. For both these reasons, competitive goals can interfere with sustained motivation to learn, and eventually therefore reduce engagement with activities that develop thinking skills such as those described earlier in this chapter. They can also reduce the self-esteem of "losers" as well as lower the status of losers among peers. Every year, for example, about 35 percent of children drop out of competitive athletics, and the most common reason is a feeling of discouragement about losing (Gould & Eklund, 1996; Petlichkoff, 1996; Salguero, Gonzalez-Boto, Tuero, & Marquez, 2003).

Cooperative Goals

With cooperative goals, individuals share in rewards or punishments, and a group's overall performance is the key to success. Cooperative goals are commonly used, for example, for major group projects or presentations in elementary school (e.g., a term project about "castles and dragons"). They focus attention on helping other group members and on attending to and being accepting of diversity among fellow students, and away from judging differences along some single scale of performance. They also promote a belief that learning or knowledge is intrinsically a shared or group phenomenon rather than something that exists only inside the heads of individuals (Salomon & Perkins, 1998).

Cooperative goals have become increasingly common in elementary schools partly because research strongly suggests that they benefit students' learning, motivation, and social relationships more than either individualistic or competitive goals, particularly in classrooms that are multicultural or otherwise diverse (Slavin, 1996). But cooperative learning does have

Educational research has found important benefits when students have cooperative, rather than competitive goals. Individuals learn from each other, both slower and faster students feel more motivated, and students become more tolerant of the differences among them.

Source: Monkey Business Images/Shutterstock.

> **What Do You Think?**
>
> What participation structures worked best for you in elementary school? Is there a single answer to this question either for you or for others? If you were a teacher, which structure would you try to emphasize, and why?

problems. If cooperative groups of students are not supervised enough, they can reproduce the gender and racial biases of the larger society, as described earlier in this section. This problem can be alleviated if the teacher chooses tasks that truly need diverse talents for completion (e.g., a project that needs an artist, a good writer, and a good oral presenter) and highlights this fact to students. Another problem is that some individuals in a cooperative work group may "overspecialize," that is, focus only on their own tasks and ignore helping and learning from others. Other individuals "social loaf," meaning they can take advantage of others' hard work without contributing their own fair share of effort. Teachers report that students get off-topic and socialize during work time and that preparation for these types of activities can be cumbersome (Gillies & Boyle, 2010). Some of these problems can be alleviated by combining individualized and cooperative assessments; some part of students' final grade depends on their own efforts, and another part on the group's combined performance as well as monitoring students' time management.

The Changing Child

As noted in the previous chapter, the cognitive advances we see during childhood (and throughout life) occur in conjunction with, and are impacted by, physical and social changes. Thinking skills such as conservation or long-term memory are influenced not only by a child's own efforts to make sense of her world but also by learning experiences often provided by others. And language turns out to be more than an automatic acquisition of grammatical rules; it also involves learning how a child's community prefers to communicate. Evidently a child's social surroundings—the people around him, both young and old—make quite a difference in development during these years. In the next chapter, we look at these surroundings in more detail.

Chapter Summary

- **What new cognitive skills do children acquire during the middle childhood? What are the psychological and practical effects of these new skills?** School-age children develop concrete operational thinking, that is, reasoning focused on real, tangible objects. A very important new skill is conservation, the belief that certain properties, such as size or length, remain constant in spite of perceptual changes. Efforts to train children in conservation have had moderate success, although when applied in a variety of circumstances, training does not persist as strongly as naturally developed conservation. Concrete operational children also acquire new skills in seriation, temporal relations, and spatial relations. Piaget's ideas about cognitive development have influenced educators' styles of teaching and the content of early childhood curricula.

- **How does memory change during middle childhood? How do these changes affect thinking and learning?** Both short-term and long-term memory improve with age, partly as a result of other cognitive developments such as growing skills in using learning strategies. Improvements in logical reasoning sometimes assist the development of long-term memory, as does increasing richness or familiarity of knowledge as schoolchildren grow older. Learning disabilities can be understood in part as the result of problems in information processing. Providing learning assistance that focuses on specific aspects of information processing can sometimes benefit students.

- **What new changes in language emerge during middle childhood?** Although school-age children already are quite skillful with language, they continue to

- have difficulties with certain subtle features of syntax. Bilingual children develop certain cognitive advantages over monolingual children, at least if their bilingualism is relatively balanced; the advantages include cognitive flexibility and metalinguistic awareness. Often, however, bilingual individuals must cope with prejudices against their native language and the culture of that language.
- **What is general intelligence, and how can it be measured?** Intelligence is a general ability to learn from or adapt to experience. Traditionally, intelligence has been studied from the perspective of psychometric testing, but newer perspectives based on information-processing theory and on sociocultural principles have challenged this perspective. A view of intelligence based on information-processing theory is the triarchic theory of Robert Sternberg, which divides intelligence into components, experiences, and the context of thinking. Howard Gardner's theory of multiple intelligences identifies six distinct cognitive capacities: language skill, musical skill, logical skill, spatial skill, kinesthetic skill, and interpersonal/ intrapersonal skills. The sociocultural view of intelligence regards thinking as being distributed among individuals who interact and communicate, and it locates cognitive development in the zone of proximal development.
- **How does school affect children's cognitive development?** School provides experience in particular patterns of language interaction called participation structures. The teacher's language is marked by large amounts of control talk, comments or other linguistic markers that remind students of the power difference between students and teachers. Classroom interaction is also marked by a gender bias in which teachers and students both favor boys' comments over girls'. School is also a primary arena of assessment for children, as well as a setting that provides experience with individual, competitive, and cooperative goals.

Key Terms

achievement test (p. 288)
aptitude test (p. 288)
assessment (p. 296)
balanced bilingual (p. 286)
concrete operations (p. 276)
conservation (p. 276)
control talk (p. 295)
discourse (p. 294)

intelligence (p. 287)
learning disability (p. 281)
metalinguistic awareness (p. 286)
multiple intelligences (p. 292)
participation structures (p. 294)
psychometric approach
    to intelligence (p. 287)
recall memory (p. 280)

recognition memory (p. 280)
selective attention (p. 280)
sociocultural perspective
    on intelligence (p. 293)
triarchic theory of intelligence (p. 289)

Psychosocial Development during Middle Childhood

CHAPTER 13

Source: bikeriderlondon/Shutterstock.

Chapter Outline

Psychosocial Challenges of Middle Childhood

The Sense of Self

The Age of Industry and Achievement

Family Relationships

Peer Relationships

Death, Loss, and Grieving during the School Years

Looking Back/Looking Forward

Focusing Questions

- What major psychosocial challenges do children face during middle childhood?
- What important changes occur in a child's sense of self during middle childhood?
- What is *achievement motivation*, and what forms does it take?
- How have changes in the nature of the family, such as increases in the proportion of single parent and dual-wage-earner families, affected children's psychosocial development?
- How do peers contribute to development during middle childhood?
- How do children deal with death, loss, and grieving during the school years?

Nickie is nine years old and in second grade. Between practicing soccer, baseball, and basketball and playing with his friends, playing video games, or watching TV with his older brother Alex, doing his homework, walking the dog, and carving a model race car for his Cub Scout den with his father, he is always on the go. Until recently, if asked about his popularity or how he was doing at school or sports, Nickie would answer with a noncommittal "OK" or "I don't know." Lately, however, he has begun to talk more about himself: who he is and how well he is (or is not) doing as a ballplayer, a friend, a student, a brother, and a son.

Middle childhood, approximately ages six through twelve, is a time when the developmental changes of early childhood are rapidly consolidated and children ready themselves for adolescence and the movement to full adulthood. By the time they start school, most children have learned something about human nature and are beginning to learn the psychological and social skills needed to successfully deal with an increasingly complex world. Children's increasing involvements outside the family and their growing capacity for independence and self-direction contribute to changes in their relationships with parents and other family members.

Middle childhood also brings about an increased focus on peer relationships, and school offers the primary arena for contacts with **peers**, children of about the same age and development level who share common attitudes and interests. Peers offer certain benefits, such as freedom from the watchful eyes of parents and teachers. But they also demand loyalty and conformity. "Be nice to everyone except Rachel" may be a rule in one circle of friends; "Homework is for geeks" may be a rule in another. School-age children must learn to coordinate these expectations with those of parents, who sometimes disagree with peers.

To meet all of these demands simultaneously, children must learn to regulate their behavior from within. Somehow they must find ways to control their expressions of aggression, impatience, grief, and other strong impulses and emotions. Doing so becomes easier as they develop concepts of themselves as individuals, knowledge of their own needs and values, and a sense of how these needs and values compare with those of other people. In this chapter, we will explore how the changes that occur during middle childhood build on the achievements of early childhood and provide the groundwork for the major changes that accompany adolescence, which will soon follow.

peers Individuals who are of approximately the same age and developmental level and share common attitudes and interests.

Psychosocial Challenges of Middle Childhood

During the school years, children's psychosocial development includes five major challenges: the challenge of knowing who you are, the challenge to achieve, the challenge of family relationships, the challenge of peers, and the challenge of school. We summarize the nature of those challenges and then discuss the first four in greater detail in the sections that follow (see Chapter 8 for school influences).

The Challenge of Knowing Who You Are

Throughout middle childhood, children develop a deeper understanding of the kinds of people they are and what makes them unique. They also acquire a more fully developed sense of self as a framework for organizing and understanding their experiences. These notions do not yet constitute the type of stable identity that develops throughout adolescence and adulthood and continues to form throughout life, but they do lay the groundwork for later development. During middle childhood, a child at least can ask, "Am I a popular sort of person?" or "Am I a good athlete?" The answers may still be rather simplistic, but they are beginning to take on meaning nonetheless.

The Challenge to Achieve

Some psychologists consider the major crisis of this age period to be the development of competence, self-confidence, and willingness to achieve to the best of one's ability. Of course, children care about their competence even in infancy. But during middle childhood, this motive is complicated by children's growing awareness of others opinions about their efforts.

The Challenge of Family Relationships

We discuss several important aspects of family life in this chapter, including recent changes in family roles and family membership due to changing employment patterns and divorce rates. These changes in the traditional family structure have raised the questions of who is responsible for doing what within a family and what constitutes a family in the first place.

Furthermore, all too often school-age children must share the challenge of holding the family together. While family relationships remain an important part of schoolchildren's lives, peers become increasingly important.

The Challenge of Peers

The fourth major challenge of middle childhood is relationships with other children, or peers. As we point out later in this chapter, peers serve even more important purposes for schoolchildren than they do for preschoolers, and most school-age children choose to spend a great deal of their time in peer-related activities.

The Challenge of School

During middle childhood, school is second only to the family in influence on children's social and emotional development. Observing and interacting with a large number of diverse children and adults other than their parents give children an opportunity to learn new social skills, values, and beliefs and to develop a fuller sense of identity. As we saw in Chapter 12, participation structures, gender and racial bias, and assessment goals can all influence cognitive development, as well as the child's sense of self.

The Sense of Self

Throughout infancy, childhood, and adolescence, children actively construct a **sense of self**, a structured way of thinking about themselves that helps them to organize and understand who they are based on the views of others, on their own experiences, and on cultural categories such as gender and race. This structure rapidly evolves during middle childhood and becomes increasingly organized and complex. In fact, although a sense of self often is called a *self-concept,* it functions more as a theory that organizes a pattern of related ideas than as a single concept. A child actively constructs and continually revises his or her sense of self based on increasing age and experience (Damon & Hart, 1992), and throughout life we form and shift our identity as a means to maintain self-esteem, find meaning in our lives, and obtain feelings of belongingness (Vignoles, Regalia, Manzi, Golledge, & Scabini, 2006).

sense of self A structured way in which individuals think about themselves that helps them to organize and understand who they are based on the views of others, their own experiences, and cultural categories such as gender and race.

For example, at age six, Mina loved playing with dolls and also loved holding and caring for babies. She noticed that her parents and others commented on this preference, so nurturance became part of Mina's idea of herself: "I'm someone who likes babies," she sometimes thought. But later experiences modified this idea. Toward the end of elementary school, Mina discovered that she often preferred playing softball to playing house. Somehow, at age ten or eleven, she had to incorporate this reality into her sense of self: "I'm a good ballplayer," she realized. By the start of adolescence, she still was not sure how to reconcile these two concepts of herself: her interest in child care and her interest in sports. Someday she may succeed in doing so, but not at age twelve.

To a large extent, a child's notion of self grows out of social experiences with other selves or, put more plainly, out of contacts with other children and adults. Learning what it means to be female in their cultural context, for example, occurs as girls meet other individuals who also are female. Learning what it means to be happy occurs as children see other people express happiness. As personal and individual as a sense of self is, then, it reflects generalizations about others, and it cannot develop without considerable social contact (Lewis & Brooks-Gunn, 1979b).

The Development of Self during Childhood

How do children acquire a sense of self? Once children recognize themselves in a mirror, at about eighteen months of age, the next step involves basic social labels or categories. By the end of the second year of life, most children label their gender ("I'm a boy" or "I'm a girl"), their age ("I'm two"), and their species ("I'm a person"). Labels such as these pave the way for later, more complete knowledge of self.

At first, however, most such labels lack permanence. At age two or three, a boy may claim he can become a girl under certain circumstances—"when I grow up" or "if I grow my hair long" (Marcus & Overton, 1978). Or a very young child may say she can become

During middle childhood, children develop preliminary notions of their personal qualities and psychological identity. What do you suppose this girl's sense of herself might be?

Source: Zurijeta/Shutterstock.

self-constancy The belief that one's identity remains permanently fixed; established sometime after age six.

a different individual "if I change my name" (Guardo & Bohan, 1971). **Self-constancy**, a belief that identity remains permanently fixed, does not become firm until the early school years, sometime after age six. At this time, a child becomes convinced he will stay the same person indefinitely into the future, will remain human in all circumstances, and will keep his gender forever. Beliefs such as these are what a sense of self means.

Younger children, up to age five or six, tend to define themselves in terms of observable features and behaviors such as hairstyles or how fast they can run (Rosenberg, 1979). Around age eight, some children form a more stable sense of self by including psychological traits in their self-descriptions. At first, the traits are feelings and qualities that have no apparent reference to other human beings: "I am brave," says the child, or "I am cheerful." By implication these traits describe her as an entire personality and in all possible situations, with little recognition of people's usual variations in moods. At first, too, the child describes the traits in bold, global terms that ignore the possibility that opposing feelings or qualities sometimes exist within the same person. The child may vacillate in describing her own qualities without realizing it. Sometimes she will say, "I am dumb," meaning *completely* dumb, and other times she will say, "I am smart," meaning *completely* smart (Harter, 1977). Neither statement suggests the child recognizes that both descriptions contain an element of truth.

By the end of middle childhood, fuller integration of contradictory traits occurs. Around age ten or twelve, children begin to recognize that they can feel more than one way about any particular situation or person; they can both like and hate their teachers or enjoy and dislike school more or less at the same time (Selman, 1980). With this recognition comes the ability to use trait labels in less global ways and to express qualities in particular situations. When an older child says, "I am smart," he no longer means "I am always smart in every possible way and in every activity." Now he more likely means "I am smart in a number of significant situations, but not in all." During middle childhood, children become increasingly able to interrelate the different categories of traits and develop more patterned and integrated self-descriptions (Damon & Hart, 1988; Fischer et al., 1990). They develop a more coherent sense of self, as demonstrated in their ability to write long, interlinked stories of their lives, a skill with which younger children struggle (Bohn & Bernsten, 2008).

These changes contribute to the development of a more flexible sense of self, in which the same individual can be characterized in a variety of ways depending on the circumstances. The situation-bound qualities school-age children express usually describe them more accurately than the global traits and observable features on which younger children rely. But a school-age child's consciousness of inner traits still lacks the subtlety and flexibility found in adolescents and adults, who recognize that the stability of self involves multiple dimensions and ongoing change.

> **What Do You Think?**
>
> What do you remember about changes in your sense of self during your school years? What conflicting traits do you recall, and how did you integrate them?

However, significant cultural differences exist in how the concept of self is constructed, and the idea of self probably is not a discrete psychological entity in all cultures (Hoare, 1994). In Asian countries such as India, Japan, and Nepal, for example, three distinct senses of self appear to exist simultaneously even in adulthood: a family self, in which one's sense of self is defined almost exclusively in relationship to one's family; a spiritual self, which is defined and organized in terms of religious beliefs; and an individualized self, which is closer to the European-American sense of self just described (Roland, 1988).

Processes in Constructing a Self

To a large degree, the process of developing an identity and a sense of self during middle childhood reflects a growing awareness of relationships with other people (Damon & Hart, 1988). Children construct their identities by distinguishing their thoughts and feelings from those expressed by others. When children of various ages are asked how they would feel if their parents expressed certain emotions, such as sadness, anger, or happiness, preschoolers are likely to say they would feel the same emotions: they would be angry if their parents were angry, sad if they were sad, and so on. Older children, however, are more likely to name complementary rather than identical emotions; if their parents felt angry, for example, they would feel fearful (Harter & Barnes, 1983).

Additional evidence comes from studies of how children gradually acquire a fuller understanding of shame and pride. By the early school years (age six or seven), children begin to explicitly mention an external audience in defining these two terms (Seidner et al., 1988). For example, one seven-year-olds definition was "My teacher was proud when I earned 100 percent on the test"; another's was "My mother was ashamed when I lost my temper at the neighbor." Such attention to others implies awareness that others sometimes observe the child's self and suggests that school-age children distinguish between their own emotions and those of others—something they must do to develop a mature sense of self. Additionally, the shame and guilt children perceive from the adults around them impact their own experience of shame and guilt throughout childhood and adolescence (Rosemary, Arbeau, Lall, & De Jaeger, 2010; Walter & Burnaford, 2006).

School-age children often devote themselves to the long, slow mastery of complicated skills, such as learning to play the violin.
Source: wavebreakmedia/Shutterstock.

A child's emerging sense of self during middle childhood is part of a broader process of personality development. In the following section, we briefly discuss how two major developmental theorists, Sigmund Freud and Erik Erikson, view this process.

The Age of Industry and Achievement

When viewed as part of the overall lifespan, the years from six to twelve seem especially important to the achievement of competence. Children spend countless hours in school acquiring skills in reading, writing, and mathematics. Many of these hours also contribute to learning the unofficial curriculum of school: how to get along with teachers and with other children. Outside of school, children often devote themselves to the long, slow mastery of particular skills. One child may spend years learning to play baseball; another may devote the same amount of time to learning how to care for a zoo of pet hamsters, dogs, and birds.

Latency and the Crisis of Industry

Psychodynamic theories such as those proposed by Freud and Erikson explain such behavior in terms of the emotional relationships that precede it in early childhood. Preschool children feel envy, awe, and competitiveness with respect to their parents. At first, these feelings have a magical quality: children simply want to be like their parents. Inevitably they are disappointed to learn that merely wanting such things does not make them come true.

In this regard, Freud emphasized the emotional hardship of preschoolers' disappointment and their consequent repression of their magical wishes regarding their parents (Freud, 1983). A five-year-old, he argued, cannot continue indefinitely to wish for intimacy with his opposite-sex parent and for success in competition with his same-sex parent. These feelings (which Freud termed the *Oedipus* and *Electra conflicts*) disrupt life if they persist too long. The child eventually represses the feelings, meaning he pushes them completely out of awareness. As it happens, this repression occurs at about the time most children begin school—around age six or seven—and continues until adolescence. Freud called this the **latency** period, meaning a child's earlier unresolved feelings have gone underground and are waiting to resurface in the future (at the beginning of adolescence). During this period, the schoolchild focuses on building competencies and skills as a defense—an unconscious, self-protective behavior—against his earlier romantic feelings toward his parent. Developing talents, whether in sports, art, academics, or whatever, also helps to keep the child's mind off his earlier disappointment, which lingers on unconsciously.

Erikson went beyond Freud's ideas to stress not only the defensive, negative functions of skill building but its positive functions as well (Erikson, 1963, 1968). According to Erikson, children try consciously to become more like their parents and more like adults in general. Becoming competent helps children reach this goal in two ways. First, it helps them through *identification*, a process by which they experience themselves as being like their parents and thus capable of becoming genuine adults; second, it helps them to gain similar recognition from others.

Erikson called this process the crisis of **industry versus inferiority**, meaning children of this age concern themselves with their capacity for *industry*, or the ability to do good, productive work. Children who convince themselves and others of this capacity develop relatively confident, positive concepts of themselves. Those who do not tend to suffer from feelings of poor self-esteem and *inferiority*, a sense of inadequacy or general lack of competence. According to Erikson, most children end up with a mixture of self-confidence and fear of inferiority, but self-confidence predominates in most cases (we hope). (See Chapter 2.)

In addition, the crisis of industry versus inferiority gives healthy school-age children a more or less permanent motivation to achieve particular, definable standards of excellence. Children's continuing sense that they can achieve and that their industry will pay off is shaped by their earlier successes and failures in school. No longer are children happy just to draw pictures, for example; now they want to draw *well*. With persistence and support, children often do reach higher standards of excellence in many activities than they did as preschoolers, and most of the time they are happy about doing so.

Partly because of the connection between industry and increasing competence, psychologists have devoted a lot of attention to the development of achievement motivation among school-age children. In the next section, we look at some of this work.

---

latency According to Freud, the stage of development between the phallic and genital stages. Sexual feelings and activities are on hold as the child struggles to resolve the oedipal conflict.

industry versus inferiority Erikson's fourth crisis, during which children concern themselves with their capacity to do good work and thereby develop confident, positive self-concepts or else face feelings of inferiority.

Achievement Motivation

Achievement motivation is the tendency to show initiative and persistence in attaining certain goals and increasing competence by successfully meeting standards of excellence. What matters most is the approach to a task rather than the importance of the task itself. An individual can reveal achievement motivation as either a student or a college professor, for example, and as either an amateur chess player or a world-class chess grand master. As long as the individual strives toward a standard of excellence that is reasonable, he or she possesses achievement motivation. Usually, too, this motivation leads to increased competence compared to one's previous level.

achievement motivation Behavior that enhances competence or enhances judgments of competence.

Differences in Achievement Motivation

There appear to be two distinct kinds of achievement motivation. The first, **learning orientation**, relies on *intrinsic motivation,* that is, motivation that comes from within the learner and relates directly to the task and its accomplishment. A learning orientation leads children to concentrate on learning as an end in itself; they will practice jumping rope just to see whether they can do it. The second type of motivation, **performance orientation**, involves *extrinsic motivation,* meaning motivation comes not from the learner but from other individuals who see and evaluate her. In this instance, the person the child is trying to please or satisfy is not herself but others (Dweck & Leggett, 1988; Elliot & Dweck, 2013; Erdley et al., 1997; Ginsburg & Bronstein, 1993; Hayenga & Corpus, 2010).

learning orientation Achievement motivation that comes from the learner and the task.

performance orientation Achievement motivation stimulated by other individuals who may see and evaluate the learner rather than by the intrinsic nature of the task itself.

Motivational orientations play an important role in children's development. For example, higher levels of intrinsic motivation have been associated with an internal sense of control, feelings of enjoyment, and various mastery-related characteristics such as curiosity, creativity, exploration, persistence in completing tasks, and a preference for taking on challenges. They are also linked to higher academic performance and learning, feelings of academic competence, and perceptions of what contributes to academic success or failure (Cain & Dweck, 1995; Ginsburg & Bronstein, 1993; Hayenga & Corpus, 2010; Masten & Coatsworth, 1998; Vansteenkiste, Lens, & Deci, 2006).

Achievement Motivation in Middle Childhood

During middle childhood, children become more performance oriented than they were at earlier ages. At the beginning of this period, children express considerable optimism about their abilities. Kindergartners tend to rank themselves at the top of their class in scholastic ability, even though they rank other children relatively accurately (Stipek & Hoffman, 1980). This implies a learning orientation; for young children, achievement is something they do without either the involvement or the evaluations of others (Frieze et al., 1981).

During the next several years, however, children begin to believe that having an ability depends partly on whether other people give them credit for having it. This belief lies at the core of the performance orientation. It does not replace a learning orientation; rather, it takes a place alongside it. Now being "smart" means partly that a child's teachers, parents, and friends *say* she is smart and partly that she possesses certain skills in reading, mathematics, and the like regardless of what others say (Feld et al., 1979).

Successful achievement becomes more complicated in middle childhood. Consider swimming. Late in infancy and during the preschool years, a child may be motivated to learn to swim simply by being given chances to experiment in the water. During the school years, however, that child may ask herself or himself what other people, especially parents and friends, will think about learning to swim. Most people will value swimming to some extent, of course. But even very respectable progress in swimming may not look like much of an achievement if the child's family and friends hold very high athletic standards or place little value on athletics in the first place.

As we saw in Chapter 12, academic achievement is one of the principal types of achievement children focus on during middle childhood. Also, because schools tend to group children homogeneously by age and ability, children of similar age and ability form the principal peer group for many developing children. The main exception to this pattern is siblings, who often are an important peer system influence as well. We will take a closer look at sibling influences later in this chapter.

Environmental factors also can influence motivational orientation. Environments that provide optimal challenge, offer feedback that promotes competence, and support children's autonomous and independent behaviors are likely to facilitate the development of intrinsic motivation, whereas environments that strongly emphasize extrinsic rewards, deadlines, and adult control tend to undermine intrinsic motivation and foster an extrinsic motivational orientation (Deci & Ryan, 1987; Masten & Coatsworth, 1998; Reynolds & Temple, 1998; Vansteenkiste et al., 2006).

Cultural background also can influence children's achievement orientations. For example, Chinese and Japanese mothers believe more strongly than American mothers do that academic success depends on one's own efforts rather than on factors beyond one's control, such as inborn ability or external conditions. This intrinsically motivated, achievement-oriented view is likely shared by their children and may help account for the higher academic achievement of Asian students over American students (Jose & Bellamy, 2011; Stevenson & Lee, 1990). The Multicultural View feature discusses ethnic differences in parental expectations for academic achievement.

As children grow older, they shift toward a performance orientation and become more similar to adults in their achievement motivation. This in part reflects the increasing importance of peers and children's changing perceptions of social comparisons (Pomerantz et al., 1995). At this stage, children take others' opinions more and more seriously and often seek out those opinions on a variety of matters.

Family factors are also important. Several studies have examined how parental monitoring of homework, parental reactions to grades, and general family style influenced achievement motivation orientation among children. When parents heavily supervised homework (by helping, checking, reminding, or insisting), reacted to grades with punishment, criticism, uninvolvement, or extrinsic rewards, and displayed overcontrolling (authoritarian) or undercontrolling (permissive) styles of parenting, children were more likely to have extrinsic (performance) motivational orientations and lower academic performance. On the other hand, children whose parents responded to grades with encouragement and were supportive of their children's autonomy (authoritative parenting style) were more likely to have intrinsic motivational orientation and higher academic performance (Ginsburg & Brostein, 1995; Gonzalez & Wolters, 2006). This academic benefit of authoritarian parenting persists throughout a child's education, including college (Turner, Chandler, & Heffer, 2009). Paradoxically, Asian parents are more likely to utilize authoritarian parenting with their children without the negative impact noted previously (Kordi & Baharudin, 2010). As we will see in the section that follows, the opinions of family members are quite important in this regard.

Family Relationships

Families continue to influence children's development strongly during middle childhood, although, as we will soon see, the influence of peers grows dramatically in this period as well. However, parental influence differs from that of peers due both to parents' greater experience and psychological maturity and to the greater material resources and power they possess. In this section, we discuss how the particular circumstances and characteristics of families affect family relationships and psychosocial development during middle childhood.

The Quality of Parenting and Family Life during Middle Childhood

During middle childhood, as children gradually learn more about their parents' attitudes and motivations and the reasons for family rules, they become better able to control their own behavior. This change has a major impact on the quality of relations between school-age children and their parents. Parents find themselves monitoring the moment-to-moment behavior of their children less closely than in earlier years. They need not always watch carefully as their child pours a glass of milk, and they do not always have to remind him

> **What Do You Think?**
>
> Survey several classmates about their current learning orientations and the extent to which those orientations grew out of middle childhood experiences. What advantages and disadvantages do you see in each of these orientations?

to use the toilet before getting in the car. Parenting style affects the ways in which such monitoring is expressed, and as discussed in the Focusing On feature, also impacts the quality of parent-child interactions.

Nevertheless, parents do continue to monitor children's efforts to take care of themselves, but in less direct ways. Instead of simply arranging for a child's friend to visit, parents increasingly use comments such as "If you want to have Lin sleep over next week, you'd better call by tomorrow." Instead of helping their child put on each item of clothing in the morning, they will more likely confine themselves to some simple reminder ("It's time to get dressed") on the assumption that the child can take care of the details of dressing.

The Changing Nature of Modern Families

The stereotypical family—a father who works, a mother who cares for the family full time—shows little similarity to families of today. In 1955, 60 percent of families in North America fit this popular stereotype. By 2012, only 20 percent of North American families conformed to this model, and unlike the stereotype of a well-educated, affluent woman staying at home to care for her child or children, nearly half of stay-at-home mothers have a high school diploma or less, with 34 percent living in poverty (Cohn, Livingston, & Wang, 2014). Additionally, fathers make up 16 percent of all stay-at-home parents, a number that has been steadily increasing over the last three decades (Livingston, 2014).

Today an increasing number of mothers work outside the home. Eighty percent of married women and 91 percent of single women with children under eighteen are employed (see Figure 13.1). This is more than double the rates in 1960 and is a trend that is expected to remain relatively stable, with most fluctuations being due to economic changes over time (Cohn, Livingston, & Wang, 2014).

Divorce also has become much more common, as Figure 13.1 shows. Between 1950 and 2015, the U.S. divorce rate quadrupled, with about 10 percent of those age fifteen and up reporting that they are currently divorced (U.S. Bureau of the Census, 2015b). Approximately 70 percent of first marriages will last at least ten years, with that number dropping to about 55 percent after twenty years (Copen, Daniels, Vespa, & Mosher, 2012). Approximately 27 percent of children younger than eighteen live in single-parent households, 86 percent with their mothers and 14 percent with their fathers (U.S. Bureau of the Census, 2015c). Because approximately two-thirds of divorced parents remarry, most children of divorce will live in a *reconstituted family* consisting of parent, stepparent, siblings, and stepsiblings.

Divorce and Its Effects on Children

Most parents who divorce must make major adjustments in their lives, and these adjustments often affect their children deeply. First, many divorcing parents face sudden economic pressures. Some find themselves financially responsible for two households, that of their former spouse and children and that of the new spouse and children. Many divorced mothers must take on new or additional employment to meet their household responsibilities, and even so their standard of living frequently declines (Dewilde & Uunk, 2008; Hetherington et al., 1989). For many of these women, a reduction of economic resources often is accompanied by dependence on welfare; poorer-quality housing, neighborhoods, schools, and child care; and the need to move to a neighborhood they can afford, which often leads to loss of social support for the child from familiar friends, neighbors, and teachers. In contrast, both noncustodial and custodial fathers are more likely to maintain or improve their standard of living following divorce.

A Multicultural View

Parental Expectations and Academic Achievement

Differences in academic achievement among African American, Latino, and Caucasian children appear early during the elementary school years and continue throughout elementary, junior, and senior high school. One study found that at second grade, about 5 percent of white children and more than 15 percent of African American and Latino children were performing below grade level in mathematics, and by sixth grade 20 percent of white children, more than 40 percent of Latino children, and 50 percent of African American children were performing below grade level (Norman, 1988).

One popular explanation is that lower achievement of minority children is due to low levels of achievement motivation resulting from poverty, family disruption, inadequate academic support, low parental education, and low parental expectations for children's academic success (De Civita, Pagani, Vitaro, & Tremblay, 2004; Häkkinen, Kirjavainen & Uusitalo, 2003; Lee & Bowen, 2006). This view has been challenged by a large-scale study of African American, Latino, and white urban elementary school children and their mothers (Stevenson et al., 1990). In one study, Harold Stevenson and his colleagues examined the role parents played in their children's education and parents' and children's beliefs about children's current school performance and their educational future. Mothers and teachers were also asked how the children's performances might be improved.

What did the researchers find? First, when only families from similar economic and educational backgrounds were compared, the achievement levels of the African American and Latino children were *not* substantially lower than those of the white children. Second, beliefs about the children's educational achievement held by both the Latino and African American children and their mothers were very similar to those typically associated with higher rather than lower levels of achievement.

When the entire sample was examined, the following findings emerged. All mothers agreed that parents should work closely with their children on schoolwork. African American mothers expressed the

Active encouragement and support from parents plays an important role in fostering academic achievement during middle childhood.
Source: zulufoto/Shutterstock.

FIGURE 13.1
Percentage of Stay-at-Home Mothers, 1967–2012

The long-term trends for stay-at-home mothers with children age 18 and under.
Source: Cohn, Livingston, & Wang (2014).

Divorce involves many psychological pressures as well. The parent who takes primary custody of the children must learn to manage a household alone, which is a major physical and psychological burden. Some parents may feel deeply isolated from relatives or friends to whom they used to feel close. If relatives do live nearby, divorcing parents often must rely on them for the first time, simply to procure help with child care and household work.

> ### A Multicultural View
>
> #### Parental Expectations and Academic Achievement *continued*
>
> greatest interest in helping their children, followed by Latino and then white mothers. Latino mothers were less confident about their knowledge of English and of the American school system, but were still eager to help their children with schoolwork, stressed the importance of school, and had high regard for their children's intellectual abilities and academic achievement. They also shared with the African American mothers (and their children's teachers) a strong belief in the importance of homework and competency examinations, and the potential value of a longer school day. They held high expectations for their children's futures, though not as high as those of the African American and white mothers.
>
> Most of the African American mothers were familiar with what teachers expected of their children. They reported spending more time teaching their children academic skills than the other parents and evaluated their children's skills, abilities, and academic achievement in reading and math very highly. Their children rated their own performances very highly as well and believed they were working hard. Surprisingly, though, African American students' evaluations of their school performances were unrelated to their actual levels of achievement in reading and math, which suggests they had not received or internalized realistic feedback about their academic performances from either their parents, their teachers, or both (Alexander & Entwisle, 1988; Bock & Moore, 1986).
>
> These findings challenge the view that the below expected performances of African American and Latino elementary school children are due to low levels of achievement motivation, parental expectations, or parental support, though there is evidence that particularly among poorer children lower academic achievement may be due to lower maternal educational expectations for their children (De Civita et al., 2004; Häkkinen et al., 2003). What else, then, accounts for the decreasing academic achievement of minority elementary school children and increasing rates of academic failure and dropping out in junior and senior high school? One possibility is that teachers and staff may have lower academic expectations for minorities, who are overrepresented in the low academic tracks compared with other student groups, leaving these students with both inadequate preparation and unrealistic expectations about the academic demands of junior and senior high school (Reed, 1988). Additionally, less parental involvement among African American and Latino parents, perhaps due to schedule constraints, lower educational attainment, or subtle racism has been linked to lower achievement (Lee & Bowen, 2006). As these children approach adolescence, the schools they attend and the families in which they live fail to adequately meet their emerging needs for intellectual challenge and academic support, for adult supervision and independence, and for relationships with teachers and parents that enable them to believe a relationship exists between their academic efforts and the rewards available to them in American society (De Civita et al., 2004; Eccles, 1993; Lee & Bowen, 2006; Stevenson et al., 1990).

FIGURE 13.2

Percentage of U.S. Citizens Reporting That They Are Currently Married or Divorced Each Year

This chart outlines the percentage of people in the United States age fifteen and up reporting each year that they are either married or divorced. Though approximately 45 percent of all first marriages end in divorce within twenty years, only about 10 percent of the population reports that they are currently divorced.

Source: U.S. Bureau of the Census (2015b).

Even before actual separation and divorce, many such families go through long periods of distress, tension, and discord. For most, these pressures continue to create stress for two or three years following separation (Coley, 1998; Hetherington et al, 1998). However, when there is a great deal of strife in a marriage, many adults feel happier after a divorce, particularly if they were the one to initiate it, and children fare better when their parents

Chapter 13 Psychosocial Development during Middle Childhood

Focusing On...

The Quality of Parenting and Family Life during Middle Childhood

As in the early childhood years that precede and the adolescent years that follow, the quality of the parent-child relationship and overall family life play an important developmental role in middle childhood. A seven-year longitudinal study conducted by Gregory Pettit, John Bates, and Kenneth Dodge (1997) found that supportive, authoritative-style parenting involving high levels of mother-to-child warmth, active teaching of social skills, positive interest and involvement in their children's peer relationships, and use of discipline based on reasoning rather than power assertion observed when children were five years old predicted higher levels of adjustment at age 12.

High levels of supportive parenting also helped reduce the negative developmental effects of low SES, family stress, and single parenthood. Studies of school-age African American children living in both two-parent and single-parent families have demonstrated that children's academic and psychosocial competence was positively related to harmonious family interactions, emotional caregiving and support, low levels of overt conflict between parents (in two-parent households), family involvement with children's school activities, parental optimism and religious involvement, and adequacy of family financial resources (Bean, Barber, & Crane, 2006; Brody & Flor, 1997, 1998; Brody et al., 1994). For single-parent, mother-headed households, *no-nonsense* parenting, which included high levels of physical and emotional control and displays of warmth and affection, helped to protect children from dangerous neighborhood surroundings and involvement in antisocial activity and promoted the development of self-regulation. This type of parenting falls between the authoritative and authoritarian parent styles, employing

TABLE 13.1 Immediacy and Focus of Parental Concerns and Parenting Goals

Focus of Parental Concern	Immediacy of Parental Concern	
	Short Term	**Long Term**
Focus on relationship	Wanting to reach fair and equitable resolutions to an interaction; wanting to promote everyone's happiness.	Wanting to build or maintain love, trust, and close family connections.
	Example: I want us to be able to enjoy doing this together.	*Example:* I hope she realizes that I'll always be here to help her through hard times.
Focus on child	Wanting to understand the child's point of view in a given situation; wanting to promote the child's happiness.	Wanting to teach the child values, social rules or important lessons for the child's future benefit.
	Example: I want to find out what's making him so upset.	*Example:* She needs to understand that she can't give up on things so easily.
Focus on parent	Wanting to control, change, or end a child's current behavior; wanting to meet the parent's wishes or agenda.	Wanting to have an obedient or respectful child; wanting to ensure a given behavior isn't repeated in the future.
	Example: I need to have peace and quiet.	*Example:* I'll make sure he listens next time.

Source: Adapted from Hastings & Grusec (1998), p. 470.

do not experience psychological distress following a divorce (Amato, 2010). Divorce is especially hard for children during the school years. Having outgrown the self-centeredness of the preschool years, school-age children increasingly identify with and rely on their parents as role models to help them establish their own sense of who they are and how they should behave. At a time when children are just learning to be independent from home life, divorce threatens the safe base they have come to rely on to help make increasing independence possible. The adjustment to divorce is easier for some children than for others, and the process is more difficult for children whose parents use less effective

> **Focusing On...**
>
> ### The Quality of Parenting and Family Life during Middle Childhood *continued*
>
> a higher level of control than authoritative parenting style and greater warmth and nurturance than authoritarian parenting style (Brody & Flor, 1998), and it seems that higher levels of psychological control might not carry the same risk for depression and anxiety when displayed by African American parents as compared to European American parents (Bean et al., 2006).
>
> The goals that parents hope to achieve also play an important role in determining how they interact with their children, especially when faced with parent-child disagreements. Paul Hastings and Joan Grusec (1998) studied a sample of 78 fathers and 110 mothers to explore how their parenting goals influenced interactions during disagreements with their young children. Parenting goals reflected three main areas of parental concern: *relationship-centered* goals, focused on maintaining and improving the parent-child relationship; *child-centered* goals, focused on concern with understanding the child's viewpoint and promoting the child's happiness and well being; and *parent-centered* goals focused on controlling or changing the child to meet the parent's wishes or agenda. The interventions parents reported using also depended on whether their focus was on the short-term or long-term consequences. Table 13.1 shows descriptions and examples of these three parenting goals, both short-term and long-term.
>
> Hastings and Grusec found that women were more likely than men to focus on relationship-centered goals. Short-term, parent-centered goals were more likely when parent-child disagreements occurred in public situations (e.g., while grocery shopping, visiting friends, playing in the park). Long-term, child- and relationship-centered goals were associated with higher levels of parental empathy. Parent-centered goals were associated with power assertion, child-centered goals with reasoning, and relationship-centered goals with warm, negotiating, and cooperative parenting behavior. Parents who focused on solving parent-child disagreements that fulfilled their own needs (parent-centered goals) were most likely to be punitive and controlling and least likely to resolve conflicts by talking with their children, working out a compromise, or being warm and accepting. When parents' concerns were centered on children's needs, however, open communication and providing explanations were the strategies most preferred, and coercion, punishment, and negative criticism were avoided. Strong power assertion was even less likely when parents were highly invested in promoting the quality of family relationship. Instead, negotiation, compromise, shared control, and affection were the strategies of choice.
>
> Parenting goals were related not only to what the child had done but to the parents' judgments about their child's motivations and to parents' feelings about the situation. Parents who were focused on parent-centered, long-term goals were more likely to believe that their children's misbehaviors were deliberate, to experience annoyance, upset, and concern, and to have decreased sympathy for their child's wishes compared to parents who focused on child-centered, short-term goals. Although changes occur in parental goals and in the context of parent-child disagreements as children move through adolescence and adulthood, parenting goals continue to play an important role in how parents and their children interact with and experience each other.
>
> #### What Do You Think?
> 1. What is your view of the "no-nonsense" parenting described earlier? How successfully do you think it joins the advantages of authoritative and authoritarian parenting styles? Why do you think psychological control is related to higher rates of depression and anxiety among European American children but not African American children?
> 2. Thinking back to conflicts with your parents in your own middle childhood, what long-term and short-term goals best describe the parenting you experienced?
>
> Two dimensions on which parenting goals may vary are the immediacy of a parent's concern (short term versus long term) and the focus of concern (parent, child, or relationship). This table presents the six types of parenting goals that result when two dimensions are combined and examples of the goals a parent might have when dealing with a child's tantrum during the shared activity.

parenting styles following divorce, whose parents argue and do not make an attempt to get along following a divorce, if a parent is suffering from mental health problems, or when children lose contact with one of their parents (Amato, 2010). Though previous research has found differential impact of divorce for boys versus girls, more recent research has not demonstrated sex differences among children whose parents divorce (Amato, 2010; Amato & Dorius, 2010). However, the loyalty conflicts frequently created by parents who are competing for their children's allegiance can make children fearful that they will lose one of their parents in the process.

Moreover, couples who divorce are more likely to demonstrate maladaptive behaviors when they argue, such as criticizing one another, displaying contempt, being defensive, and stonewalling one another (Fowler & Dillow, 2011; Gottman & Levenson, 2000). These types of behavior, which may present as hostility or becoming distant, are related to higher rates of anxiety and antisocial behaviors among children (Katz & Gottman, 1993). It may be that preexisting factors that increase risk for divorce also increase risk for problem behaviors among the children living in these homes.

Perhaps the most important factor in reducing the negative effects of divorce during the school years is parents' efforts to reduce their own conflicts and cooperate in providing the best parenting possible for their children. Also important is the appropriate use of professional help to successfully work out postdivorce arrangements, resolve emotional conflicts more effectively, and develop the skills needed to sustain strong and supportive parent-child relationships (Amato, 2010; Amato et al., 1995; Stolberg & Walsh, 1988). Close relationships with authoritative parents who are warm and supportive, but still provide firm, consistent control and supervision, particularly in the period immediately following divorce, are associated with positive adjustment in children and adolescents (Hetherington et al., 1998; Simons & Johnson, 1996). Table 13.2 presents suggestions for parenting during or following divorce.

Custody Arrangements

The parent with physical custody of the children (usually the mother) finds herself dealing not only with her children but also with major new roles and likely the financial stress of being a single parent.

Parents without physical custody of the children (usually fathers) do not face these daily hassles, but they do report feeling rootless, dissatisfied, and unjustly cut off from their children. Seeing his children every other week or on school vacations may prevent a father from knowing them intimately and being part of their everyday lives, and lead him to become increasingly reliant on special events (such as going to Disney World) when contacts do occur. Noncustodial parents may also believe their financial and emotional support for their children goes unappreciated. As a result, some fathers decrease contact with their children.

For noncustodial fathers and mothers alike, both the quantity and quality of parent-child relationships differ compared to parents who have custody. Noncustodial mothers are, on the average, less competent than custodial mothers in controlling and monitoring their children's behavior, although they are more effective at this than noncustodial fathers. Noncustodial mothers are also more interested in and better informed about their children's activities, more supportive, sensitive, and responsive to their children's needs, and better able to communicate with their children than noncustodial fathers are (Hetherington et al., 1998). Compared to noncustodial mothers, the postdivorce parenting of fathers is less predictable. Some fathers who were previously attached to and involved with their children find their new role too limited and painful and drift away from their children, whereas others become more involved with their children. The quality of the noncustodial father's relationship with his children and the circumstances in which contacts with them occur are much more important than frequency of visits. When noncustodial fathers remain actively involved in their children's activities and emotional lives, positive developmental outcomes are supported. Even limited contact with noncustodial fathers can enhance children's adjustment when it occurs under supportive, low-conflict conditions (Clarke-Stewart & Hayward, 1996; Simons & Beaman, 1996). In recent years we have seen a trend among fathers being quite involved in their children's lives, which is linked to fewer behavioral problems and better psychological and academic outcomes for their children (Amato & Dorius, 2010).

Sometimes parents are able to *establish joint custody,* a legal arrangement in which parental rights and responsibilities continue to be shared in a relatively equal manner. The mechanics of the arrangement vary with the child's age and the family's circumstances. The children may live with each parent during alternate weeks, parts of weeks, or even parts of the year. Or, when the children are older, one or more children may live with one parent and the rest with the other parent. Joint custody tends to promote greater contact with both parents after divorce, facilitate fathers' involvement, and make mothers' parenting

TABLE 13.2 Suggestions for Divorcing Parents with School-Age Children

1. Don't pretend that the divorce is "good," and don't expect your child to appreciate your reasons for the divorce.
2. Avoid assigning blame for the divorce or criticizing the other party in your child's presence.
3. Reassure your child that she or he did not cause the divorce and will continue to be loved and cared for by both parents.
4. Don't put your child on the spot by involving him or her in divorce-related decisions.
5. Keep your child informed about divorce-related events and decisions in a timely and frank manner.
6. Avoid making changes in your child's normal routines as much as possible.
7. Allow your child full freedom to express his or her feelings both to you and to other trusted adults.

Here are some suggestions for helping children handle parental dating and remarriage:

1. Wait until you know your new romantic interest fairly well before arranging for your friend and your child to spend time together.
2. Allow your child to get used to this person gradually, at the child's own pace.
3. Keep your child informed about your relationship, but don't force your child to make decisions about it.
4. Involve your child in plans regarding living arrangements, marriage, and other important changes in an appropriate manner.
5. Seek agreement with your new partner or spouse on childrearing philosophy and practices.

Source: Adapted from Philadelphia Child Guidance Center (1994), pp. 85–90.

responsibilities less burdensome. Its success, however, depends on parents' willingness and ability to rearrange their lives and maintain the levels of mutual respect and cooperation required to make this arrangement work (Arditti, 1992). The cooperation and negotiation necessary for joint custody might be easier for families who obtain divorce education and/or have someone to help mediate points of contention (Amato, 2010).

Remarriage and Blended Families

Most divorced parents remarry within a few years, creating blended families consisting of the remarried parents and their children. The most common type of **blended family** results when a mother marries a man who does not have custody of his children by a previous marriage, but families with stepmothers occur as well. In both situations, the stepparent and stepchildren must somehow acknowledge the previous attachments they bring to the new family. Children may need to recognize and accept the fact that their new stepparent has other children, about whom he or she cares a great deal, living somewhere else. Also, the new stepparent must accept the fact that the stepchildren have another, "real" father or mother somewhere and strong attachments to that parent.

Younger children are able to eventually form an attachment with a competent stepparent who utilizes authoritative parenting (Hetherington et al., 1999). This is particularly true when children maintain a good relationship with their biological father and stepfather (King, 2006). Stepfathers who establish parent-child relationships based on warmth, friendly involvement, and mutual respect rather than on assertion of parental authority are more likely to be accepted by both boys and girls, although daughters, especially those approaching adolescence, appear to have a more intense and sustained negative reaction to their mothers' remarriage and more difficulty accepting and interacting with their new stepfathers (Hetherington et al., 1998; Vuchinich et al., 1991).

blended family A family created from a combination of stepchildren, stepparents, and stepsiblings.

Stepmothers generally are more emotionally involved and take a more active role in discipline than stepfathers do, but gaining acceptance from the stepchildren is not easy for them either (Hetherington et al., 1998). In one study of parent-child relationships in stepmother families, John Santrock and Karen Sitterle (1987) found that despite their active involvement in parental and childrearing activities and ongoing efforts to establish good relationships with their stepchildren, stepmothers tended to be viewed as somewhat detached, unsupportive, and uninvolved, a feeling the stepmothers themselves shared. One explanation for these negative views is that the stepmother may be a target for her stepchildren's displaced anger, hurt, and disappointment toward their noncustodial mother. It might also be the case that stepmothers and children compete for the fathers' attention (Pasley & Moorefield, 2004). Child attachment and closeness to their biological father are related to lower rates of depression, anxiety, and externalizing problems among children living with a biological father and a stepmother, with no impact, positive or negative, for the relationship with a stepmother (King, 2007). However, other studies have demonstrated that children feel closer to their stepmothers than their fathers (Berg, 2003). Though research sometimes conflicts on the exact impact of stepparents, the overall story is that children fare best when they have good relationships with biological parents and stepparents who utilize authoritative parenting.

Because divorce is a social reality that affects development throughout the lifespan, we return to this issue when we discuss psychosocial development in adolescence (Chapter 11) and early adulthood (Chapter 16). In the next section, we look at the developmental effects of work on families during the school years.

The Effects of Work on Families

Regardless of family structure, work affects family life profoundly, although not always in simple or straightforward ways. Jobs determine daily schedules, of course, which in turn affect how much time parents have for their children. Job schedules also influence which parent or child does particular household chores. Men and women who have more flexible work schedules and autonomy within their work tend to negotiate work/life balance more easily (Grzywacz & Butler, 2005; Hegewisch & Gornick, 2011). Moreover, in countries with policies supporting families, including time off to care for sick children and affordable childcare, women, in particular, are more likely to work and have better jobs than those in countries without such generous policies (Gupta, Smith, & Verner, 2008; Hegewisch & Gornick, 2011). However, it is important to note that such policies may limit women's career advancement (Gupta et al., 2008; Hegewisch & Gornick, 2011).

Work also impacts parents' self-esteem and thus their happiness as human beings and as parents. People with jobs that they find challenging and rewarding report they tend to experience a positive spillover effect that makes their family lives easier and more rewarding (Grzywacz & Butler, 2005). However, it is also true that people might experience a negative spillover effect when they work jobs that are stressful and cause conflict at home (Cinamon, Weisel, & Tzuk, 2007). Jobs also contribute to SES and therefore affect many aspects of family life (Greenberger et al., 1994; Kohn et al., 1986). All of these effects are magnified by the fact that an increasing number of families are headed by two working parents or by a single parent who works.

Effects of Maternal Employment

Despite the once popular view that mothers should stay at home to care for their children, research suggests that maternal employment as such usually does children no developmental harm (Gottfried et al., 1994; Hoffman, 1984a, 1984b), and it might actually improve the woman's home life and interactions with her children and spouse (Greenhaus & Powell, 2006; Grzywacz & Butler, 2005; Patel, Govender, Paruk, & Ramgoon, 2006). What does matter is whether a woman chooses to work or not to work and the family and systems-based support that is given—or not—to families (Hegewisch & Gornick, 2011). Mothers who can make this choice and who live in relatively supportive families suffer no setbacks in their relations with their children. Mothers who feel forced either to work or not to work are less fortunate; they report more stressful relations with their children.

However, maternal employment often does influence children's development in some ways. For example, families with working mothers divide housework and child care more evenly than do families without employed mothers (Hoffman, 1983). In dual-worker families, fathers do some household chores relatively more often and spend more time alone with their children. Even so, parents tend to take on gender-stereotypic tasks with working mothers still doing the majority of housework and child care equaling thirty-four hours per week compared to husbands doing about twenty hours of housework per week (Bartley, Blanton, & Gilliard, 2005). This can lead to discord and feelings of inequality within the home, particularly when either parent is doing the majority of stereotypically female work, such as cooking and cleaning (Bartley et al., 2005). Additionally, in families with working mothers, children often are expected to help with household chores and caring for younger brothers and sisters.

The blend of housework and breadwinning seems to create less stereotyped attitudes in the children of working mothers regarding the "proper" roles of mothers and fathers. Both sons and daughters witness nurturant behavior in their fathers and occupational competence in their mothers. Especially as they approach adolescence, children are likely to support women's employment in general, and daughters usually expect to work outside the home when they get older. Studies of school-age children of employed women indicate they are as well or better adjusted and hold less rigid views of gender roles than do children of women who do not work outside the home (Hoffman, 1984a, 1984b, 1989; Kawaguchi & Miyazaki, 2009; Moorehouse, 1991).

Many working mothers compensate for possible negative effects of their employment through more frequent shared activities or "quality time" with their children. A high level of shared mother-child activities serves as a buffer against the long hours and other disruptive demands of full-time jobs. Children are likely to match or exceed their peers in school achievement and adjustment when shared mother-child activities are more frequent (Gottfried et al., 1994; Moorehouse, 1991).

Effects of Parental Unemployment

When a parent loses a job, significant economic, social, and psychological disruption for children and their families can result. Loss of income can require parents and their children to make major sacrifices in their lifestyles. In many cases, the search for a new job or for affordable housing may cause a family to uproot itself, forcing children and parents to leave their friends and social support network behind. Leaving their existing school and

In most families with two working parents, all family members share household responsibilities.
Source: J2R/Shutterstock.

neighborhood peers and gaining acceptance in a new neighborhood and school is particularly difficult during middle childhood (Cooksey et al., 1997; Liem & Liem, 1988; Price, 1992). Parental job loss also has a negative impact on child academics, specifically when a father becomes unemployed (Rege, Telle, & Votruba, 2011).

Children who experience family economic hardship are vulnerable to a broad range of difficulties, including problems with peer relations, academic performance, and psychological adjustment. The impact of such hardships is significantly influenced by how severe they are, how long they last, and how well parents can mobilize their material and psychological resources to deal with adversity while continuing to provide good parenting for their children (Bolger et al., 1995; Yoshikawa, Aber, & Beardslee, 2012).

After-School Care

One common challenge working parents face is finding after-school supervision for their children. In cases where after-school programs do not exist and siblings, friends, and other relatives are not available, older (and sometimes younger) elementary school-age children are left at home by themselves. Many parents in this situation carefully work out after-school procedures, including strict limits on what a self-care child may do and a checkup phone call from work to ensure that everything is okay; others leave their children to their own resources.

Comparisons of formal after-school programs with three other arrangements (mother care, informal adult supervision, and self-care) for a sample of low-SES third-graders from nine urban schools showed that attending after-school programs was associated with better grades and conduct in school as well as with better peer relations and emotional adjustment (Posner & Vandell, 1994). Children who attended such programs were exposed to more learning opportunities, spent more time in enrichment lessons (such as music and dance), and spent less time watching TV and in unstructured neighborhood activities than children in other forms of care. They also demonstrate better social competence and have more motivation in school when they attend engaging after-school programs (Mahoney, Parente, & Lord, 2007).

Formal after-school programs may be less important for children who live in communities that provide safe and constructive after-school opportunities. Nevertheless, even for these children, close parental monitoring of their after-school plans and activities and authoritative parenting (respectful acceptance and firm control) tend to promote good academic performance and social adjustment as well as keep them out of trouble. Lower levels of such parental involvement and stressful, unsupportive family circumstances are associated with poorer academic and social adjustment and more problem behaviors (Bean, Barber & Crane, 2006; Galambos & Maggs, 1991; Roelofs et al., 2006; Steinberg, 1986; Vandell & Ramanan, 1991).

Other Sources of Social Support

Most school-age children establish sources of social support other than parents, including siblings and other adults. When interviewed about people, places, and activities that they found satisfying and helpful in conducting their lives, children revealed a large number of social supports from pets and make-believe friends to family members, peers, and sponsored activities such as church or the local library (Bryant, 1985).

Sibling Support

Perhaps most noteworthy is the high frequency with which siblings (as well as peers) were named as sources of support. During middle childhood, brothers and sisters provide one another with companionship, friendship, social support, and mentoring. Because of their greater maturity, older children frequently serve as role models and mentors to younger siblings, helping to transmit customs and family expectations and providing challenges that (hopefully) lead the younger children to new learning (Azmitia & Hesser, 1993; Howe, Ross, & Recchia, 2011). When siblings have caring, trusting relationships with one another, they have better relationships with their peers, and among girls, there are fewer symptoms of depression (Kim, McHale, Crouter, & Osgood, 2007). As we will see, siblings continue to serve as an important source of social support through adolescence as well.

Many studies have examined how siblings transmit knowledge by teaching one sibling a new task and then having that child teach their siblings. When older siblings are put into the "teacher" role, they tend to use scaffolding (discussed in Chapter 12), especially when their sibling is significantly younger (Howe et al., 2011). Much younger siblings are also less likely to ask questions of their older sibling. In more structured "teaching" situations, older siblings provided more explanations and positive feedback and gave learners more control over the task than did older peers; young children more often prompted their older siblings' explanations, pressured them into giving them more control over tasks, and performed at higher levels than when taught by their peers (Azmitia & Hesser, 1993). When younger siblings are assigned the "teacher" role, they tended to focus on learner-centered strategies, collaborating with their older siblings to teach the new task (Howe et al., 2011). During unstructured learning tasks, younger siblings tended to observe, imitate, and consult with their older siblings, who in turn were more likely to spontaneously provide them with guidance than were older peers (Azmitia & Hesser, 1993).

It is not surprising that older brothers and sisters tend to develop relationships with younger siblings that combine dominance and nurturance, the two major elements of mentoring relationships. However, as children moved toward the end of middle childhood, relationships between siblings became less domineering and more egalitarian, and reported levels of intensity and conflict also decreased (Buhrmeister & Furman, 1990).

Siblings tend to be less domineering and more nurturant in families in which children feel secure and parents get along well together (Brody et al., 1992; Dunn et al., 1994). Gene Brody and his colleagues (1992) found that school-age siblings whose fathers treat them with equality and impartiality during problem-solving discussions, whose families are generally harmonious even when discussing problems, and whose parents perceive family relationships to be close are less likely to experience sibling conflict than children in families that function less effectively. However, when there is conflict between parents and children, there is also likely to be conflict between siblings (Pike, Coldwell, & Dunn, 2005), and sibling conflict has been linked to higher rates of depression symptoms (Kim et al., 2007).

Beyond Siblings

As noted previously, many children report seeking out adults other than their parents, especially grandparents, with whom to talk and confide. Family pets and sometimes even neighbors' pets also served as confidants. Children also reported using hobbies to unwind and feel better about themselves (although some of the hobbies, such as collecting stamps

During the school years, grandparents and other adults and other children within and outside the immediate and extended family provide invaluable sources of social support for children.
Source: Monkey Business Images/Shutterstock.

> **What Do You Think?**
>
> What are your views about the impact of maternal employment on child development? In what ways do your views reflect your own experiences as a child?

or playing a musical instrument, were relatively nonsocial). Other children reported having special hideaways where they went to be alone for awhile. Many children sought out peers for activities when they needed an emotional lift or felt confused; but this was not the case on every occasion, and not all of the children did so (Bryant, 1985, 1994).

In general, as children move through middle childhood, their sources of support increasingly broaden. This makes them better able to manage particular stresses, whether inside or outside their families. At all ages during the elementary school years, children seemed happiest when they reported the widest range of social supports and when that range emphasized informal rather than formal supports.

As the preceding discussions imply, family members offer significant support in middle childhood. Another important source of support during middle childhood is one's peers, as we explore in the next section.

Peer Relationships

The peer group is second only to the family as a context within which developmental changes occur (Hartup, 1989). Throughout childhood, some of children's most important relationships involve peers. As early as age two, children enjoy playing with or next to one another, and by age three or four they often prefer the company of peers, even when adults are available. Time spent with peers increases steadily during middle childhood. By the late elementary school years, about one-half of children's social interactions are with peers (Ellis et al., 1981). Peer relationships acquire a special intensity during late childhood and the transition to adolescence that typically occurs between fifth and seventh grades. During this period, children have increased unsupervised contact with peers and begin to place greater importance on peers' approval, views, and advice. At the same time, they spend less time with their parents and display greater emotional distance and psychological independence from them (B. Brown, 1990; Grundy, Gondoli, & Salafia, 2010; Larson et al., 1996).

What Theorists Say about Peer Relationships

Piaget

According to Jean Piaget, one important function of peers is to help school-age children overcome their *egocentrism*, or their tendency to assume everyone views the world in the same way they do (Piaget, 1963). Playing together, children inevitably run into conflicts over toys and priorities, arguing over who should use a new set of felt pens or what and where they should draw. In settling such disagreements, children gradually come to understand and value different points of view, a capacity that is central to living successfully in a pluralistic, democratic society.

Sullivan

The most comprehensive theory about peers was proposed by Harry Stack Sullivan. Like Piaget, Sullivan argued that relationships with peers have fundamentally different qualities than those with adults (Sullivan, 1953; Youniss, 1980). In particular, peers foster skills in compromise, cooperation, and competition. But unlike Piaget, Sullivan emphasized the value of peers in promoting emotional health. Peers create a life for children outside their families, and in doing so they help correct the emotional biases families inevitably give their children, biases that Sullivan called emotional *warps*. For instance, an eight-year-old with shy, reserved parents may learn from peers that not all people are shy and reserved. Or a ten-year-old whose parents care little about competitive athletics may discover from peers that athletic competition matters quite a lot to some people.

According to Sullivan, this form of learning occurs during the **juvenile period**, which begins around age five and continues until nine or ten. In this period, children show increasing interest in playmates of similar age and status. As they near the end of the elementary school years, they supposedly focus this interest on just a few select friends of the same gender, whom Sullivan called *chums*. These relationships provide children with models for later intimate relationships.

juvenile period Proposed by Sullivan, a period between ages five and ten when children show increasing interest in developing intense friendships or "chum relationships" with peers of the same gender.

The Functions of Friends

Children's relationships with peers consist of multiple levels of interpersonal experiences. At one level, a child interacts with a group of peers in the classroom or neighborhood and occupies a social position among those peers. This level, which is referred to as *social status, group acceptance,* or *popularity,* is group oriented and reflects social acceptance or popularity of the individual from the peer group's perspective. Another level of peer relationship involves *friendship,* a subjectively defined, voluntary, and reciprocal relationship between two individuals. Peer popularity and friendship are distinct but interrelated, and success or failure in one does not necessarily dictate success or failure in the other (Bukowski & Hoza, 1989; George & Hartman, 1996; Rodkin, Ryan, Jamison, & Wilson, 2013).

During the early school years, friendships provide an arena for "activity and opportunity": children base friendships on shared interests and activities, exchanges of possessions, and concrete supportive behaviors. By second or third grade, children become better able to live with differing perspectives within their friendships and feel less pressure to choose between one or the other, which, in part, contributes to more stable friendships as children move toward adolescence (Hartup, 1997; Hartup & Stevens, 1997; Poulin & Chan, 2010; Rawlins, 1992; Selman, 1981).

As children move into later childhood and preadolescence, *equality* and *reciprocity* become key elements of friendship interactions. Exchanging favors and sharing activities continue to matter as children get older, but by the time they enter fifth and sixth grades they place greater emphasis on psychological qualities such as intimacy, trust, mutual support, and loyalty. This is particularly true for girls. Friendship begins to involve a concept of a relationship based on a reciprocity between equals, each with distinct but compatible personalities. Sharing between friends shifts from an unreflective, *symmetrical reciprocity* based on "tit-for-tat" to a *cooperative reciprocity* based on mutual and deliberate sharing of assistance and resources that are intended to serve as tokens of friendship. Actually doing the same things or sharing the same objects becomes correspondingly less important. (Hartup & Stevens, 1997; Keller & Wood, 1989; Pasterski, Golombok, & Hines, 2011; Rawlins, 1992).

By fifth or sixth grade, children can even adopt an independent, or third-party perspective, comparing their own points of view with those of their friends (Berndt, 1988; Choudhury, Blakemore, & Charman, 2006; Furman & Bierman, 1984; Selman, 1980). As one eleven-year-old put it about a good friend, "He thinks that I don't study enough, and that he studies just about the right amount for schoolwork. But you know what *I* think? I think that I'm just trying to keep schoolwork from bothering me too much, and that *he* works too hard. I wonder what the teachers think." Judging by statements such as this, friendship at this stage appears to be an intimate collaboration between two people who are mutually committed to building the relationship, which has acquired an importance beyond the particular needs of either friend.

In a review of literature on friendships and their developmental significance, Willard Hartup (1997) argues that the developmental implications of friendships cannot be specified without distinguishing among *having friends,* the *identity of one's friends,* and *friendship quality.* Friends provide one another with cognitive, emotional, and social *scaffolding* that differs from what nonfriends provide and that having friends supports favorable developmental outcomes across *normative transitions,* predictable changes that almost all children experience, such as entering school, starting middle school, and puberty (Denham et al., 2011; Hartup, 1997). However, predicting developmental outcomes also requires knowledge of the attitudes and behavioral characteristics of children's friends as well as the qualitative features of those relationships. Cognitive and social scaffolding are similar to Vygotsky's zone of proximal development, and normative transitions are similar to the *normative crisis model* of adult development, both of which we discussed in Chapter 2.

The Functions of Other Peers

Like friendships, peer activities appear to serve several important functions. First, they provide a context for sociability, enhancement of relationships, social status, and a sense of belonging. Second, they promote concern for achievements and a reliable and integrated sense of who one is. Finally, they provide opportunities for instruction and learning (Rodkin, et al., 2013; Rubin, Fredstrom, Bowker, 2008; Zarbatany et al., 1990).

Children's reliance on peers versus parents for help appears to increase with age. According to fourth-graders, friends provide support less frequently than do mothers and fathers, the most frequent providers. Seventh-graders, however believe same-sex friends and parents are equally supportive, whereas tenth-graders view same-sex friends as the most frequent source of support even though parents remain important throughout childhood and adolescence (De Goede, Branje, Delsing & Meeus, 2009; Furman & Buhrmester, 1992). Although the functions of children's peer relationships show considerable similarity to those with adults, several features are unique to peer relationships. Attachments with parents and other adults or older children are "vertical and complementary," meaning they involve individuals who have greater knowledge, competence, and social power. Peer relationships, in contrast, are "horizontal and symmetrical" in that they involve individuals of approximately equal knowledge, competence, and social power (Hartup, 1989). They are by nature voluntary and reciprocal relationships among comparative equals. This means that a child must act in a way that explicitly supports the relationship—be friendly, that is—if he expects the relationship to survive. Children apparently understand these differences intuitively, because they typically attribute an obedience orientation to relationships between adults and children but attribute play and recreation orientations to relationships among children (Berndt, 1988; Youniss, 1980).

Influences on Peer Group Membership

Most of children's peer interactions occur in groups. In defining a peer group, elementary school children emphasize the importance of shared activities such as walking to school, talking on the telephone, listening to music, playing games, and just hanging out; however, sharing attitudes becomes most important as children approach adolescence (O'Brien & Bierman, 1988; Pasterski et al., 2011; Zarbatany et al., 1990). Living in the same neighborhood, attending the same school, and participating in the same community organizations all contribute to the likelihood that peer groups will form.

Children's peer groups are not simply random assortments of individuals but are influenced by many factors. Three of the most important factors are age, gender, and racial or ethnic background.

Age

Children play mostly with others of approximately the same age and, when asked, say they prefer to be friends with their agemates. But contrary to a common impression, schoolchildren may spend anywhere from one-quarter to one-half of their time with companions who are more than two years older or younger and say they prefer to seek help and comfort from older children (Ellis et al., 1981; French, 1984). School imposes an upper limit on these cross-age contacts, however, because classrooms usually group children according to age, and there is relatively little research examining benefits and drawbacks to mixed-age peer groups (Poulin & Chan, 2010; Rubin et al., 2008).

Groups with mixed ages have certain special qualities. Older children show more nurturant behavior, such as tying the shoelaces of a younger child or buttoning the child's sweater. Younger children show greater dependence by asking for help with schoolwork or agreeing to older peers' preferences for play activities, and it is likely that older children help scaffold skills for the younger children (Poulin & Chan, 2010; Rubin et al., 2008; Vygotsky, 1978). However, mixed-age groups also tend to be less "sociable" than same-age groups; they chat or have friendly conversations less often, for example. Same-age groups encourage the opposites of all of these qualities: children give and receive less practical help, show more friendliness to one another, and get into conflicts more often (Brody et al., 1983; Furman & Buhrmester, 1992).

Gender

Although mixed-gender play occurs during the elementary school years, first-graders generally name children of their own gender as best friends. Observations of younger schoolchildren during free play show that during cooperative play periods, they interact about four times as often with children of their own gender as they do with those of the opposite gender (Golombok & Fivush, 1994; Maccoby & Jacklin, 1987; Pasterski et al., 2011). This ratio actually increases as children approach adolescence; by third grade most peer groups contain only one gender, and by fifth grade virtually all do. As children move into middle school and adolescence, however, the trend reverses (Poulin & Chan, 2011; Shrum et al., 1988).

How do we interpret this tendency toward gender-based separation during middle childhood? Eleanor Maccoby argues that gender differences emerge primarily in social situations and vary with the gender composition of the dyads (two-person relationships) and groups involved, and that children spontaneously choose same-gender playmates even in situations where they are not under pressure from adults to do so because they find same-gender play partners more compatible (Maccoby, 1990; Pasterski et al., 2011). During the later preschool years, two factors seem to be important. First, the rough-and-tumble style and emphasis on competition and dominance that is characteristic of boys appear to be unappealing to most girls, who in general prefer play that is more cooperative and less aggressive (Pasterski et al., 2011). Second, girls discover that their growing reliance on polite suggestion to influence others is increasingly ineffective with boys and therefore avoid choosing boys as playmates (Maccoby, 1990).

Further support for the idea that playmate selection may be more heavily influenced by sharing gender-based play activities than by merely being of the same gender comes from a laboratory study of playmate choice among six-to-eight-year-olds conducted by Gerianne Alexander and Melissa Hines. When given the choice of selecting a playmate based on gender versus preferred style of play, style of play appeared to be more important for both boys and girls. Boys chose female playmates who had masculine play styles (including toys, rough-and-tumble play, and activity level), whereas girls chose male playmates with more feminine play styles (Alexander & Hines, 1994).

Over time, children find same-gender play partners more compatible and segregate themselves into same-gender groups. As children enter adolescence, childhood patterns carry into cross-gender interactions in which girls' styles may put them at a disadvantage. Though patterns of mutual influence may be more symmetrical in intimate, young adult male-female couples, these gender-related differences in style are still present and subsequently manifest themselves in the roles and relationships of parenthood (Maccoby, 1990). However, because girls tend to have smaller friend groups with higher levels of disclosure and intimacy, boys, too, might be at a disadvantage when they begin having other-sex friendships or romantic partnerships if they lack these skills (Pasterski et al., 2011; Poulin & Chen, 2010).

Despite the pervasiveness of gender segregation in peer relationships, a small but stable subgroup of children maintain cross-gender relations beyond the age when such relationships are the norm. Donna Kovacs, Jeffrey Parker, and Lois Hoffman (1996) studied cross-sex friendships among more than seven hundred third- and fourth-grade boys and girls from diverse SES backgrounds. They found that 14 percent of the children had one or more reciprocal opposite-sex friendships. Children with primarily opposite-sex friendships had poorer social skills than other children with friends, but held fewer stereotypes about gender roles than other children and were better adjusted than children with no friends. Children involved in opposite-sex friendships that were secondary to their same-sex friendships were as well adjusted as children with only same-sex friendships. African American children, who comprised about one-third of the children studied, were more likely than European American children to have opposite-sex friends. African American children from single-parent homes had more opposite-sex friends than those from two-parent homes, perhaps because they were likely to live in extended, multigenerational family settings in which they interacted with many female family members and few adult males.

Adult norms and expectations regarding gender stereotyping also can have an impact. Children growing up in families that downplay gender typing in their child-rearing values and practices are less stereotyped in their activities, interests, and gender-typed beliefs. However, gender flexibility in children's play behavior or friendship preferences is more likely to be evident in situations where it is supported, or at least not actively discouraged, by parents, teachers, and other adults (Halim & Ruble, 2010; Hoffman, 1989; Maccoby, 1990; Moorehouse, 1991; Weisner & Wilson-Mitchell, 1990).

Even when parents work hard to encourage friendships that are not gender stereotyped, peers often exert considerable pressure toward conformity with same-gender friendship patterns. On his ninth birthday, Alex, a fourth-grader, solved this problem by having an all-boy "public" birthday party and later having a special "private" one with his lifelong best friend, Katie. For interesting firsthand observations of the role of gender in peer group play, see the interview with Lisa Truong.

Racial and Ethnic Background

Patterns of segregation and preferences based on racial and ethnic differences are a fact of life in much of our society (Havekes, Bader, & Krysan, 2016; Quintana, 2011; Shrum et al., 1988). Racial and ethnic awareness are especially important during middle childhood, because children of this age are in the process of committing themselves to society and to the values and standards of the majority culture. They are also developing their own self-concepts.

Racial segregation and preference often reflect certain types of prejudice. *Prejudice* is a positive or negative attitude toward an individual based solely on the person's membership in a particular group. Prejudices are frequently based on *stereotypes,* patterns of rigid, overly simplified, and generally inaccurate ideas about the characteristics of another group of people. Stereotypes often involve negative ideas associated with race, ethnic or cultural background, religion, SES, age, gender, and sexual orientation. Although prejudices based on stereotypes do not necessarily determine a person's overt behavior, they often do. Frequently prejudice is associated with *discrimination*—actions toward members of the targeted group, such as exclusion or mistreatment, that reflect prejudicial attitudes toward that group.

Studies that asked children to name their friends have found that children are more likely to name peers of their own race, particularly if that race is the majority one. This trend begins in the preschool years and increases throughout middle childhood until children reach high school (Asher et al., 1982; Poulin & Chan, 2010; Rubin et al., 2008; Shrum et al., 1988). The degree to which family, neighborhood, and school settings are supportive (or unsupportive) of cross-race friendships is also likely to influence a child's peer preferences. Among children and adolescents, social contact both inside and outside of school may influence intergroup attitudes. Maureen Hallinan, Roy Teixeira, and Richard Williams studied black-white interracial friendships among fourth- through seventh-graders in integrated classrooms. They found that the more African American students a classroom contained, the more likely European American students were to choose a black peer as a best friend. One study found that for African American students to be "liked" on average, as much or more than European American students in a class, the class needed to be at least 66 percent African American (Jackson, Barth, Powell, & Lochman, 2006). However, having a higher proportion of white students in a classroom did not increase the likelihood of a black student choosing a white friend, nor does having a low proportion of white children reduce how much they are "liked" on average (Hallinan & Teixeira, 1987; Hallinan & Williams, 1989; Jackson et al., 2006). Similar findings were found in studies examining Latino children. Latino children had higher ratings of liking in classrooms that were at least half Latino and where there was bilingual instruction (Tropp & Prenovost, 2008). Yet though cross-race friendships are more likely to develop in integrated schools, they are difficult to maintain outside of school unless the children live in interracial neighborhoods or participate in team sports or other integrated activities (DuBois & Hirsch, 1990; Howes & Wu, 1990).

Can racial and ethnic prejudice be reduced? Middle to late childhood seems to be an age period in which people display high levels of prejudice and are more susceptible to programs designed to reduce prejudice (Raabe & Beelmann, 2011). Elementary school programs that emphasize multicultural competence and awareness by integrating multicultural activities

A school or neighborhood setting that is ethnically diverse may foster peer interactions and friendships among schoolchildren from different ethnic groups. The playground of their school provides an excellent place for these girls to "hang out" and take selfies.
Source: Mat Hayward/Shutterstock.

in both academic and extracurricular activities and actively involve children's families and other community members in school activities can successfully foster friendship and peer acceptance among students from different racial, ethnic, and cultural backgrounds (Bojko, 1995; Raabe & Beelmann, 2011). *Magnet schools* that use specialized programs in science, language, or the arts to attract students from school districts representing a variety of ethnic and cultural backgrounds have also successfully increased diversity on a long-term basis, though their implementation often requires several school districts to work together, which can be difficult and cumbersome (Ayscue & Orfield, 2016; Rossell, 1988).

Cooperative learning experiences that allow mixed groups of children to work as a team to achieve common academic goals also have had some success in fostering cross-race acceptance and enhancing children's self-esteem. In one program based on this "jigsaw" technique, children from different racial and ethnic backgrounds were assigned to different parts of a single project. They quickly learned to work together to complete the task and developed more positive feelings about both themselves and one another (Johnson et al., 1984; Slavin, 1996). Other programs have successfully reduced prejudice and stereotyping while increasing liking long term by having children from different ethnic backgrounds spend several sessions playing games, exploring their similarities and differences, and practicing perspective taking and empathy skills (Berger, Benatov, Abu-Raiya, & Tadmor, 2016).

Popularity and Rejection

When peers are asked to evaluate one another's popularity, or likability, by "nominating" whom they like most or would choose to play with, children generally are classified as "popular" or as occupying one of three unpopular statuses: "rejected," "controversial," or "neglected." Popular children receive many positive and very few negative votes from their peers; rejected children receive many negative and few positive peer nominations; controversial children receive many positive and negative peer nominations; and neglected children receive few positive or negative nominations (Coie et al., 1982).

The Popular Child

Easily noticed characteristics, such as having the "right" hairstyle or the "right" body build, being athletic, or having an attractive-sounding name, are quite important to acceptance and popularity in the early grades. As children get older, they increasingly choose their friends on the basis of personal qualities such as honesty, empathy, kindness, trust, humor, and creativity (Furman & Bierman, 1983; Hymel, Closson, Caravita, & Villancourt, 2011; Poulin & Chan, 2010; Reaves & Roberts, 1983).

sociometric popularity
A type of popularity based on social status and prestige.

perceived popularity
A type of popularity based on how well liked someone is.

Some popular children are well liked, are able to easily initiate and maintain social interactions, and understand social situations. They possess a high degree of interpersonal skills and tend to behave in ways that are prosocial, cooperative, and in tune with group norms (Hymel et al., 2011; Masten & Coatsworth, 1998). These children have **sociometric popularity**, which is based on being well liked by peers due to having good social skills (Hymel et al., 2011).

Some children are popular based on status and prestige—a type of popularity known as **perceived popularity**. They excel in athletics, wear stylish clothing and special material possessions, such as an expensive pair of athletic shoes, and influence status with peers (Dodge, 1986; Hartup, 1983; Hymel et al., 2011). These children might actually not be well liked among their peers, but still maintain social status (Hymel et al., 2011). In fact, children who try to build their social status might actually be aggressive and still see increases in their perceived popularity (Neal, 2009; Rodkin et al., 2013).

Some of the assets just noted, such as peer competence and athletic ability, remain valuable to children as they move into adolescence, and others (such as the athletic shoes) may not. But during childhood, such advantages create prestige for individual children within particular peer groups and also make membership in the "best," or highest-status, groups possible. Because of the importance of peer relationships during the school years, the interpersonal competencies associated with peer acceptance and popularity are likely to have a positive impact not only on a child's current adjustment but also on her or his longer-term psychological well-being (Bukowski et al., 1996; Hymel et al., 2011; Masten & Coatsworth, 1998).

The Unpopular Child

Peers describe unpopular children, particularly those classified as "rejected," as unpleasant, disruptive, selfish, and having few positive characteristics. Such children are likely to exhibit socially inappropriate aggression, overactivity, inattention or immaturity, and, not surprisingly, behavioral and academic problems in school (Bier-man et al., 1993; Cillessen & Bellmore, 2011). Because they lack the social skills needed to successfully join and participate in peer groups, they are blamed by peers for their own deviance and are often actively disliked and excluded from activities (Cillessen & Bellmore, 2011; Coie et al., 1991; Masten & Coatsworth, 1998).

Some children are considered unpopular because they are shy, which is often due to social anxiety or being overly self-conscious (Buss, 1986). Very withdrawn children carry many of the burdens of lacking a friendship network, such as rejection and being victimized, as well as increased symptoms of anxiety and depression and academic problems (Rubin, Coplan, & Bowker, 2009).

Thomas George and Donald Hartman (1996) studied the friendship networks of popular, average, and unpopular fifth- and sixth-graders. They found that all children reported having at least one *unilateral friend,* a person whom they consider to be a friend but who does not feel the same way about them. Unpopular children were less likely than popular children to have at least one *reciprocal friend,* someone who shares their view that a mutual friendship exists. The unilateral friendship networks of unpopular children contained more younger school-age friends and fewer same-age friends than the friendship networks of popular children. Moreover, in unilateral friendships, there is a pattern of one child being disliked (this child usually does not have good social skills) and one child who dislikes but remains "friends" (this child usually has good social skills; Olsen et al, 2012). The reciprocal friendship networks of unpopular children were smaller, more evenly distributed within and outside of the classroom, and contained fewer average and popular friends of the opposite sex than those of popular children.

In a twelve-year longitudinal study that followed fifth-graders to young adulthood, Catherine Bagwell, Andrew Newcomb, and William Bukowski (1998) found that peer-rejected children were at risk for later difficulties. Children who were rejected by their peers and had no good friend at age ten had lower levels of aspiration, participated in fewer organizations and activities, had a less active social life and experienced more psychological problems, including depression and anxiety in adolescence and early adulthood, compared to children who were not rejected and who had a friend.

Unpopular children may behave aggressively or selfishly without realizing it. Ironically, because they tend to be excluded from groups, they find few chances to learn social skills and problem solving skills that would help them relate better to other children.
Source: karnavalfoto/Shutterstock.

Aggression

Among both boys and girls, the highest levels of aggression are displayed by children who are classified as unpopular-rejected. However, girls and boys appear to differ in the form their aggressive behavior most typically takes. Boys are more likely to attack peers through *overt aggression* (such as hitting, pushing, or verbally threatening to hurt others), whereas girls are more likely to display *relational aggression* involving harming others through purposeful manipulation and damage of their peer relationships (Card, Stucky, Sawalani, & Little, 2008; Crick & Grotpeter, 1995; Crick, 1997).

Jennifer Grotpeter and Nicki Crick (1996) conducted a study to discover whether the social problems that relationally aggressive and overtly aggressive children typically experience in peer group situations also occur in their one-to-one friendships. Children who were relationally aggressive in their peer group did exhibit high levels of relational aggression, intimacy, exclusivity, and jealousy within their friendships. In contrast, children who were overtly aggressive with their peers exhibited low levels of intimacy but greatly valued companionship and spending time with their friends, and placed great importance on having friends who joined them in using aggression to harm children outside the friendship. Thus, children who are not themselves aggressive but develop friendships with overtly aggressive peers may nevertheless be pulled into aggressive encounters against other children. Children who possess high levels of emotional expressiveness, emotional insight, and empathy are better able to manage their own anger in social interactions and to display higher levels of empathy and prosocial behavior with friends than children who lack such qualities (Roberts & Strayer, 1996).

Family, culture, and neighborhood contexts also are important when understanding aggressive behavior. In families where parents are hostile, coercive, disrespectful, or engage in corporal punishment, children are much more likely to be more aggressive and less socially competent with their peers (Coyne, Nelson, & Underwood, 2011; MacKinnon-Lewis et al., 1994, 1997). In a large-scale study of second- through fifth-graders, Janis Kupersmidt and her colleagues found that living in middle-SES neighborhoods had a strong protective effect on aggressive behavior and peer rejection, particularly among African American children from low-SES, single-parent families who lived in such neighborhoods (Kupersmidt et al., 1995). Similar patterns of disadvantaged boys utilizing increasing rates of physical aggression have been found in another large-scale longitudinal study conducted in Canada (Côté et al., 2006).

For children living in war zones or in other dangerous environments such as communities where gang and drug activity and the wounding and killing of friends and relatives are everyday occurrences, the developmental toll on children and their parents is immense (Wandersman & Nation, 1998). Youngsters who are exposed to ongoing violence suffer from chronic emotional distress, learning problems, sleep disturbances, and preoccupation with their own safety and the safety of those they depend on and care about. They are also more likely to have problems with aggression, impulse control, and conflict resolution in both school and nonschool settings. Children may cope with chronic danger by adopting a world view that may be dysfunctional in any "normal" situations in which they are expected to participate. For example, although being hyperaggressive may help ensure survival in a dangerous neighborhood, it is likely to be dysfunctional and stimulate peer and teacher rejection if used to cope with disappointments and disputes in most school situations (Garbarino & Kostelny, 1996; Kozol, 1995; Marsella, 1998; Masten & Coatsworth, 1998; McCloyd, 1998; Sagi-Schwartz, 2008). In addition, some adaptations to chronic danger, such as emotional withdrawal, may cause problems for the next generation when those individuals themselves become parents.

The same links between danger and trauma observed in children may operate directly among parents. Parental adaptations to dangerous environments may produce childrearing strategies that interfere with normal development. A parent who forbids her child to play on the floor to keep him away from the poison put there to kill rats that infest the apartment may deprive her child of opportunities for exploratory play. A parent who forbids his child to play outside for fear of shooting incidents may limit the child's opportunities for athletic and social interaction with other children and adults outside the immediate family (Garbarino et al., 1991).

How successfully such children cope with their circumstances also depends on the support and guidance they get from family members and school personnel, social services, and the community at large. Considerable success in reducing aggression and fostering prosocial behavior has been reported for school-based intervention programs designed to teach older elementary and junior high school children assertiveness and interpersonal cognitive problem-solving skills as well as home-based programs focused on training parents how to avoid behaviors that increase child aggression (Coyne et al., 2011; Hudley & Graham, 1993; O'Donnell et al., 1995; Shure & Spivak, 1988). Despite such efforts, however, it is unlikely that these problems will be resolved without social and economic changes that significantly reduce or eliminate the dangerous conditions under which many children and their families currently live.

Aggression over the Life Course

Based on a review of studies of the development of aggression over the life course, Rolf Loeber and Magda Stouthamer-Loeber (1998) propose three developmental types of violent individuals: (1) a life-course type, (2) a limited-duration type, and (3) a late-onset type. Individuals with a life-course type of aggression display aggressiveness in childhood and become increasingly aggressive as they move through adolescence and into adulthood (Pakiz et al., 1997). This group accounts for the largest proportion of violent adults. Individuals who display a limited-duration pattern of aggression outgrow aggression either during the preschool-elementary school period or in late adolescence-early adulthood. Finally, a small minority of individuals display a late-onset pattern of aggression, showing no signs of aggression earlier in their lives and first displaying violent behavior during adulthood.

Gender differences in aggression, as expressed by frustration and rage, are not found in infancy, but do emerge in the preschool period, when boys are more likely than girls to display both overt (physical) aggression and relational (emotional) aggression. During the school years, girls display significantly more relational aggression, whereas boys exhibit substantially more overt aggression, including, in the extreme, group and gang fighting, aggravated assault, sexual violence, and homicide (Loeber & Stouthamer-Loeber, 1998).

Conformity to Peers

Because peer groups involve social equals, they give children unique opportunities to develop their own beliefs without having parents or older siblings dominate or dismiss them. But in doing so, peer groups also present challenges. Acceptance and support by groups matter intensely to children, who are still learning what kind of people they are and acquiring the skills they need to interact with others. As a result, peer groups often influence their members very strongly indeed: they demand conformity to group expectations in return for continued acceptance and prestige.

Pressures to conform sometimes lead children to violate personal values or needs or those of parents and other adult authorities. One child might feel pressured into paying dues she cannot afford, joining fights she does not want to participate in, or shunning children who do not belong to her own group. Another might feel pressured to wear clothes that his parents consider outrageous or to perform poorly at school. In return for these behaviors and attitudes, the children remain in good standing with their peers. Despite these differences, however, there tends to be high agreement between children, their peer group, and parents on important issues such as moral and ethical standards, standards of appropriate behavior, schooling, and future goals (Damon, 1988; Fine, 1982; Knafo & Schwartz, 2003).

Peer groups can exert positive pressures as well. For example, they can encourage athletic and academic achievement and create commitments to fairness and reciprocity, at least within an immediate circle of peers: "When someone buys a candy bar at the drugstore, she shares it with the rest of us. Then we do the same thing the next time if *we* get something nice." Peer conformity can also support "good" behavior such as avoiding smoking, drinking, or other drugs or abstaining from risky sexual activity. Whether the pressures are positive or negative, however, peer groups offer a key setting for acquiring social skills, evaluating and managing personal relationships, and handling competition and cooperation.

A study of the natural, self-selected peer groups of fourth- and fifth-graders conducted by Thomas Kindermann (1993) found that children tend to associate with peers who share similar norms regarding involvement in school. Children who were academically oriented and highly engaged in school tended to affiliate with classmates who had similar motivational orientations; the same was true for children who were disengaged from school and lacked academic motivation. Although their memberships changed somewhat during the year, peer groups remained quite stable in terms of their norms regarding academic orientation.

School Influences on Peer Relations

According to Erik Erikson, school is one of the main arenas in which children resolve the crisis of industry versus inferiority. Interactions with teachers and other children provide important opportunities to develop cognitive and social skills, gain knowledge about the world, and cultivate peer relationships that are central to the development of self-concept during middle childhood.

School Culture

Each school has its own culture, which includes the values, beliefs, traditions, and customary ways of thinking and behaving that make it unique and distinguish it from other schools and institutions. One school may especially value its innovative academic programs and the high achievement levels of its students, whereas another school may prioritize the degree of student involvement in school-sponsored activities, and a third the active involvement of parents in providing special resources. The closer the fit between the school culture and the values and expectations of the children (and families) it serves, the more likely will the school's developmental impact be positive. Students both learn and function better in classrooms in which the instructional approach, pattern and rhythm of verbal interaction and student participation, and strategies for motivating students are in tune with their family and cultural expectations and when teachers utilize strategies similar to authoritative parenting (Vygotsky, 1997; Walker, 2008; Wigfield et al., 1998).

Clearly, teachers strongly influence a school's culture—and its children. In fact, with the exception of their parents, most elementary school children spend more time with their teachers than with any other adults. Teachers therefore play a very significant role in the lives of school-age children. Observational studies of daily classroom life reveal

> **WORKING WITH** Lisa Truong, Fourth-Grade Teacher
>
> ### Reducing Gender Role Stereotyping in Play
>
> Lisa Truong is a fourth-grade teacher at a "follow-through" elementary school that serves students from citywide head-start preschool and kindergarten programs as well as children from the local neighborhood. Her classroom is a well-organized, friendly, cheerful place filled with children's drawings and other projects. Lisa provides richly detailed observations of gender differences in peer group and play activities among fourth-graders.
>
> **Rob:** *How would you describe peer relations among fourth-graders?*
>
> **Lisa:** Often children's academic ability sets the tone and pace for their friendships. Children who do well academically tend to be friends with other kids who are bright.
>
> **Rob:** *Why do you think this is so?*
>
> **Lisa:** In part because of parent pressure. Parents are interested in their children having good friends. Another reason may be that much of the teaching here occurs in small skill groups. These group children with the same academic needs together. They also focus on group dynamics, teaching the children to work with other people. When we go outside for recess, the children do tend to stay in those same groups.
>
> **Rob:** *What other factors seem to influence peer groups?*
>
> **Lisa:** Boy-girl differences are very important. As much as I've tried to encourage girls to play football or soccer and boys to do things like four-square and jump-rope, it really does break down by gender as to how they play outside. Girls tend to play jump-rope, and boys tend to play soccer on the field—it's almost automatic. Girls also tend to go to the swings and slide much more than the boys.
>
> **Rob:** *Why do you think this happens?*
>
> **Lisa:** At this age, girls are getting more social and interactive. Often I see girls walking slowly and talking. Even their jump-rope is more consistently interactive and coordinated—with turn taking and things like that—than the boys' play. You should see the girls play foursquare! It involves a lot of verbal interaction and social coordination.
>
> **Rob:** *How so?*
>
> **Lisa:** Four people stand in a 10-foot-by-10-foot square drawn in chalk and divided into four smaller squares. The person in the fourth square is in control of whatever the category will be. So, for example, that person will say "Colors" and then bounce the ball into any of the other players' squares. They will have to name a color and catch the ball, or they're out.
>
> **Rob:** *There's a rhythm to it?*
>
> **Lisa:** You have to keep the rhythm, and you can't name the same color twice— or animal, country, movie star, or whatever the category is. The

that the elementary school teacher engages in as many as one thousand interpersonal exchanges with pupils each day (Cazden, 1988). As we saw in Chapter 12, teachers' styles of classroom management vary considerably. However, all effective teachers establish learning environments that are calm, predictable, and engaging and provide smooth transitions from one activity to the next. They also stay on top of the classroom situation by keeping in tune with their students, in both their communication of academic content and their responses to the constantly changing social and emotional needs of thirty or more children (Linney & Seidman, 1989). In other words, they create an environment with clear rules and expectations, effective controls, open communication, high nurturance, and respectful relationships that encourage students to participate as fully as possible in school and classroom life. Not surprisingly, effective teacher-student relationships tend to be authoritative in that their qualities parallel those of the authoritative parenting style discussed in Chapter 10 (Walker, 2008).

The Student's Experience

What do students experience in the classroom? According to Philip Jackson, particularly in traditional, teacher-centered classrooms, students spend a great deal of time waiting for the

> **WORKING WITH** Lisa Truong, Fourth-Grade Teacher
>
> **Reducing Gender Role Stereotyping in Play** *continued*
>
> categories get more complex as the year goes on. The kids almost always start the year with colors, and by the end of the year it will be something much more specific, like Spice Girls songs or names of rock stars. This group of girls also made up a great hand-clapping game about music groups; the way they thought it through and the rules they made up were fascinating.
>
> **Rob:** *What are the boys doing?*
>
> **Lisa:** They're playing soccer and kick-ball, building forts, or skateboards, if they can. Or they'll collect things and investigate the environment. At the beginning of the year, we studied insects and their natural habitats in science. Once the boys got outside, they tried to find every single little bug they could, and they would come in and show it.
>
> **Rob:** *It seems fourth-grade boys are less interested in make-up games than girls.*
>
> **Lisa:** Yes, that's true. Boys tend to play games that emphasize physical rather than social interaction and where they follow rules that are already made up for them.
>
> **Rob:** *How permanent are these peer group patterns?*
>
> **Lisa:** They seem long-lasting. The group I described was made up of five girls who are very, very close. They're all good students, and all happen to be white. I've been trying to encourage them to be less of a clique and interact with other people more.
>
> **Rob:** *How else might teachers encourage greater interaction?*
>
> **Lisa:** Our school is committed to helping children interact in a way that doesn't break down along sex role or racial lines. I talk to them about it very upfront, and I say I think there should be more interaction between boys and girls and blacks and whites. When we have social studies activities, the rule is that groups will be mixed. The children understand this and help make it work.
>
> **What Do You Think?**
> 1. Lisa's observations of her students illustrate how closely play and social development are interrelated. What examples in the interview demonstrate this?
> 2. How has Lisa attempted to reduce gender-role stereotyping in her fourth-graders' peer group and play activities? Based on this chapter, what additional things might she consider trying?
> 3. Discuss how Lisa's observations demonstrate the interaction of physical, cognitive, and social domains in her fourth-graders' development. How are the three domains reflected in gender differences in peer groups and play activities?

teacher or other students, delaying fulfillment of their needs until given permission to do so by the teacher, and contending with distractions and social disruption. Students must wait to ask a question, wait to get permission to leave their seats, wait to have a question answered, wait for the next assignment, or wait to use the computer (Jackson, 1986).

Although these observations are cause for concern, many classrooms are conscientiously organized to minimize such difficulties and provide a learning environment that is academically stimulating and supportive of children's developmental needs. Though the teaching styles may vary, the experiences of the great majority of students in well-run classrooms are largely positive. Students in such classrooms feel like respected members of their classroom and school communities. They are eager to learn and are active participants in classroom activities, both academic and nonacademic. Effective school environments also provide children with opportunities to freely interact with and form developmentally beneficial relationships both with peers and with children of different ages, developmental levels, and backgrounds. The Working With interview with fourth-grade teacher Lisa Truong (pages 330–331) is a good example of how a teacher uses her authoritative relationships with her students and her awareness of school and classroom culture to reduce gender-role stereotyping in peer group activities.

> **What Do You Think?**
>
> Children's growing exposure to peer group influences during middle childhood is a source of concern for both parents and teachers. What advice might you give to parents and teachers regarding the best ways to deal with this challenge?

Death, Loss, and Grieving during the School Years

While for obvious reasons interest in death and dying has been greatest for those interested in the adult years, experiences with death have a developmental impact throughout the lifespan. For example, approximately 1.5 million children in the United States live in single-parent families because the other parent has died (Owens, 2008). One study of death, loss, and grieving among middle school children found that 41 percent had been personally involved with death within the previous year; death of a grandparent or great-grandparent was most frequently mentioned (Glass, 1991). However, deaths of parents, siblings, other relatives, family friends, other children, and pets were also noted. Though the loss of a parent may be the most difficult for children, the death of a sibling due to an illness such as sudden infant death syndrome (SIDS), AIDS, cystic fibrosis, or cancer, or to accidents or suicide, also can have a profound effect on children at various ages (Birenbaum et al., 1991; Davies, 1995; Dyregorov & Dyregrov, 2005; Fangos & Nickerson, 1991; Packman, Horsley, Davies, & Kramer, 2006; Powell, 1991).

The Process of Grieving for a Childhood Loss

Loss or bereavement refers to being separated from someone to whom one was emotionally attached; *grieving* refers to the complex emotional, cognitive, and perceptual reactions and experiences that accompany the loss (Mullan et al., 1995). John Baker and his colleagues propose that for bereaved children the grieving process includes three phases, each involving certain psychological tasks (Baker et al., 1992).

Early-phase tasks include understanding the fact that someone has died, the implications of the death, and protecting oneself and one's family from both physical harm and the full emotional impact of the loss. Children need information at an age-appropriate level about death in general and about the nature of the particular death. Euphemistic explanations (e.g., "Mother has gone to sleep") should be avoided because they tend to interfere with children's

Approximately 1.5 million children in the United States live in single-parent families because the other parent has died, and experiences with death have developmental impact throughout the lifespan.
Source: Twin Design/Shutterstock.

need to understand what really happened. Bereaved children listen intently and watch others' reactions, ask questions, and reenact elements of the events in their play; if there are gaps in their understanding, they tend to fill in the missing pieces with fantasy. Children also need to feel they are safe and in a secure environment. Because of fears that they too will die or that their families will disintegrate, children and their families may engage in a variety of self-protective mechanisms such as denial, distortion, emotional numbing, and even physical isolation from people.

Middle-phase tasks of grieving include accepting and emotionally acknowledging the reality of the loss, exploring and reevaluating one's relationship to the person who died, and bearing the intense psychological pain involved. *Late-phase tasks* require that the child consolidate a new sense of personal identity that includes both the experience of the loss and identifications with the deceased person; safely develop new emotional relationships without excessive fear of loss or guilt; construct his or her own inner representation of the deceased, based on past and current experiences, thoughts, and feelings, that enable the child to maintain an ongoing emotional connection (attachment) with the deceased; wholeheartedly resume the age-appropriate developmental tasks and activities that were interrupted by the loss; and successfully cope with the painful memories associated with the loss that are likely to resurface at points of developmental transition or on specific anniversaries, such as the date of the person's death.

Just as the adopted child faces the question "How could they give me up?" and the child of divorce the question "Why did my father (or mother) leave me?", the child who has lost a parent to death must deal with how and why the parent died and what the parent's presence may have been like had it continued over time. Children's efforts to remain connected to the deceased parent include locating the deceased (for example, "in heaven"), experiencing the deceased (such as believing the parent is watching them), reaching out to the deceased (visiting the cemetery and "speaking" to the person), having waking memories of the deceased, and cherishing physical objects linked to the deceased (Silverman et al., 1992).

Children's Understanding of Death

Between ages five and seven, when the transition from preoperational to concrete operational modes of thinking occurs (see Chapters 9 and 12), most children come to understand that death is an irreversible, nonfunctional, and universal state: that once a living thing dies, it cannot be made alive again; that all life-defining functions cease at death; and that all living things eventually die. In contrast, younger children think death is reversible under some circumstances, attribute various life-defining functions to dead things, and think that certain individuals (often including themselves) will not die (Slaughter, 2005; Speece & Brent, 1984). For example, several months after losing his beloved dog, Millie, 4-year-old Bryson visited Millie's grave with his mother. After several minutes, Bryson asked his mother if they were going to unbury Millie so they could play, even though his parents had discussed the finality of death with him several times.

Developmental Impact

The developmental impact of death experienced during childhood depends on a number of factors, including the significance of the person to the child, the nature of the death and the conditions surrounding it, the child's strengths and vulnerabilities at the time of the loss, the amount of support available to the child to successfully grieve the loss, the amount of material and psychological disruption in the child's family as a result of the loss, and the quality of the child's relationships with other survivors. When children understand the biological basis of death, they have less fear and anxiety about death (Slaughter & Griffiths, 2007). Studies of college students and older adults who experienced the death of a parent during childhood have found that being able to talk freely with the surviving parent about the circumstances of the death, express sorrow about the death, or ask questions about the deceased parent helped to protect them from the onslaught of depression in adulthood. Greater involvement in activities such as attending funeral-related events, keeping mementos of

> **What Do You Think?**
>
> Based on your own experiences with death during your middle childhood, how well does the description of the mourning process fit with what you remember? How are the challenges of dealing with loss due to death similar to the challenges of dealing with the losses due to divorce discussed earlier in this chapter?

the dead parent, openly expressing anger about the death to someone else, hearing stories about the deceased parent, seeing pictures in the home of the dead parent, and visiting the grave decreased the risk of subsequent depression (Saler & Skolnick, 1992).

Helping Children with Bereavement

The work of Kelly Lohnes and Neil Kalter (1994) is an excellent example of preventive intervention with groups of parentally bereaved elementary school-age children. Groups of five to seven children met for twelve weeks of one-hour sessions designed to achieve the following: (1) normalize children's reactions to and experiences of the death of a parent, (2) clarify confusing and frightening death-related issues, (3) provide a safe place for children to experience and rework emotionally painful aspects of the death and the stresses of living in a single-parent household, (4) help children develop coping strategies for particularly troubling feelings and family and peer dynamics, (5) help children maintain an emotional connection (attachment) to the deceased parent, and (6) share the children's concerns about parental death and its aftermath with surviving parents (and stepparents) through newsletters.

Group activities included bereavement stories, drawings, role playing, and discussion to help children express and understand their feelings and experiences related to loss and bereavement. Some of the thoughts, feelings, and experiences of these children, which in other contexts might have raised concerns about severe disturbance, were in fact common for parentally bereaved children who were otherwise developmentally normal. For example, children typically reported hallucinations of their dead parent, believed the parent would return, and wished to be "dead" to be reunited with their parent. If ignored or misunderstood by adults, such fantasies, distortions, and symptoms may contribute to psychological disorder. Knowledge that such behaviors are normal for such children, however, can enable mental health professionals, surviving parents, school personnel, pediatricians, and other concerned individuals to more effectively help these children mourn their loss and minimize negative developmental effects such as health problems, decline in school performance, and emotional problems (Lohnes & Kalter, 1994).

A similar program, the Family Bereavement Program (FBP), has been associated with reduced risk for problematic grief—having intrusive negative thoughts about a loved one's death or having impaired ability to function normally. This program focuses on improving the relationship between the child and caregiver by helping the parent (cognitive behavioral techniques are taught to caregivers to help with their own bereavement), the child (providing coping techniques and more realistic perceptions of their experiences, providing opportunities to discuss feelings), and the relationship between the two (teaching positive parenting skills, communication skills, and strategies to reduce child stress) (Ayers et al., 2013). In a study comparing those who went through the FBP to a control group, the FBP group showed significantly fewer markers of problematic grief up to six years later (Sandler et al., 2010).

Looking Back/Looking Forward

In a variety of ways, middle childhood is the time when a child becomes a person in a more adult sense than ever before. Although relationships with peers, teachers, and others outside the family play an increasingly important role, the family and the relationships it provides are still central to a child's development. Let us now briefly review how the changing contributions of family to development illustrate our four lifespan developmental themes.

- **Continuity Within Change**—In many ways, the family of middle childhood is a continuation of the family a child experienced during early childhood and infancy. For the majority of children, the cast of characters is much the same, although additional siblings may have been added, and the basic relationships, assumptions, and expectations that constitute the family's culture are still recognizable. The parent-child relationships of middle childhood are fairly continuous with those of early childhood, and are predictive of adolescence and early adulthood. On the other hand, significant changes in the family and its developmental role also come about. In middle childhood, families must change to adapt to the expanding worlds of school, neighborhood, and peers in their children's lives. The micro-management that characterized the toddler and preschool years gives way to more arm's-length oversight and more active collaboration between parent and child in maintaining and monitoring activities. For some families, relocation, divorce, or remarriage may alter established patterns that significantly influence developmental trajectories in the short and longer run.

- **Lifelong Growth**—The developmental changes and growth experienced by the individuals who constitute a family contribute to and are influenced by developmental changes in the family unit itself. The physical, cognitive, and psychosocial growth that school-age children experience is not independent of the developmental changes taking place in the young and later middle-aged adults who are their parents and in younger and/or older siblings. The family and its culture, values, and material and emotional support will continue to be a presence through preadolescence, adolescence, early adulthood, and beyond.

- **Changing Meanings and Vantage Points**—Talk with a kindergartner, a third-grader, and a fifth-grader about their families and the changing meanings that come with their changing vantage points will most likely be obvious. By fifth grade, the self-knowledge, intellectual and physical mastery, and skills at forming and maintaining relationships with peers and adults contribute to more complex and sophisticated views of family. The greatly expanded knowledge of one's own family and of the families of friends and neighbors that accompanies middle childhood and early adolescence allows children to more fully assess and understand their parents, siblings, aunts, uncles, and cousins in new ways. The profound physical, cognitive, and psychosocial changes that occur in adolescence contribute to identity consolidation and to an accelerated process of separation and individuation that significantly alters relationships between a teenager and his or her family and the meaning of *family* to each member. This process continues during early adulthood, when most individuals leave home and eventually create new families, developments that lead once again to altered vantage points and changing meanings, During the adult years that follow, the developmental meanings of *family* and the vantage points from which it is viewed continue to change as we parent our own children, our aging parents, and our grandchildren.

- **Developmental Diversity**—Although we can discern many similarities in families and their developmental functions, families are quite diverse, varying with SES, religious and cultural traditions, and—most important—the unique personalities and developmental trajectories of the members that comprise them. Families differ in the challenges and adversities they face; the kind of work family members do; how they work together; and how they resolve disputes, celebrate joys, cope with misfortune, raise children, view the world, and so on. Thus, a family that has recently emigrated in search of better opportunities will likely face the challenges and adversities of newcomers with few economic resources, limited social support, and the need to learn a new language, cultural skills, and traditions while maintaining the integrity of their own. They may also experience discrimination if their culture is one that faces prejudice or if they have arrived at a time when newcomers in general are viewed as threatening. The many different cultural groups that have immigrated to this country have contributed greatly to the diversity of families and the developmental opportunities they provide.

Another important source of developmental diversity lies in the uniqueness of each family. Because no two family members can have exactly the same vantage point or experience their family in exactly the same way, considerable diversity exists in the relationships between children and their families and in how a given family affects a given child. The richness and variety of developmental opportunities a particular family provides for a particular school-age child will depend in part on where that family and immediate and extended family members are in their own individual and collective developmental trajectories.

Chapter Summary

- **What major psychosocial challenges do children face during middle childhood?** During the school years, children face challenges concerning the development of an identity or a sense of self, achievement, family relationships, peer relationships, and school.
- **What important changes occur in a child's sense of self during middle childhood?** During middle childhood, children develop a sense of self, acquire a belief in self-constancy and in relatively permanent psychological traits, and learn to distinguish their thoughts and feelings from those of others.
- **What is *achievement motivation*, and what forms does it take?** According to some psychodynamic theorists, schoolchildren repress their earlier romantic attachments to their parents and focus instead on developing a sense of industry and achievement. During middle childhood, children shift their achievement orientation from an exclusive focus on learning, or a task orientation, to a performance orientation that includes others' responses to their achievements.
- **How have changes in the nature of the family, such as increases in the proportion of single-parent and dual-wage-earner families, affected children's psychosocial development?** Most mothers now work at least part time, and their employment generally seems to have no negative effects on their children. Nevertheless, maternal employment influences the division of household labor and children's attitudes about gender roles. When parents are unemployed, both they and their families experience significant stress. Providing good after-school supervision is a challenge for working parents. For children in unsupportive environments, formal after-school programs offer considerable benefits. Schoolchildren often find emotional support from adults other than parents, as well as from siblings, friends, pets, and hobbies.
Divorce has become more common in North American families and usually creates stress for all family members, although girls and boys react differently to divorce. Blended families, which result from remarriage, pose considerable challenges; however, younger children form attachments with stepparents more easily than adolescents do.
- **How do peers contribute to development during middle childhood?** Piaget believes that peers help children to overcome their egocentrism by challenging them to deal with perspectives other than their own. According to Sullivan, peers help children to develop democratic ways of interacting and also offer the first opportunities to form close or intimate relationships with others outside the family. Early in the school years, a friend is someone with whom a child shares activities and toys, but later in this period, a friend becomes someone whom the child can count on and with whom she or he can share intimacies.

In general, peers seem to serve unique functions by creating voluntary relationships of equality among children. Groups of peers vary in membership and behavior in terms of age, gender, and racial or ethnic group. Peer groups tend to segregate themselves by both gender and race. Popular children possess a number of socially desirable qualities, including well-developed social skills and confidence in themselves, Unpopular children exhibit less desirable qualities, such as aggression, selfishness, and bossiness. Peers exert pressure to conform on individual children, and this pressure can have either positive or negative effects. Children are influenced by their school's culture. This influence is more likely to be positive if the school's culture and the child's familial culture are compatible. The environment a teacher creates and his or her expectations of students shape children's school experiences and can contribute to greater student learning and positive peer involvement.
- **How do children deal with death, loss, and grieving during the school years?** Between ages five and seven, most children come to understand that death is an irreversible, nonfunctional, and universal state:

that once a living thing dies, it cannot be made alive again; that all life-defining functions cease at death; and that all living things eventually die. Prevention groups help parentally bereaved children normalize their reactions to and experiences of the death, clarify confusing and frightening death-related issues, safely deal with emotionally painful aspects of the death and stresses of living in a single-parent household, cope with troubling feelings and family and peer dynamics, maintain an emotional connection (attachment) to the deceased parent, and help make surviving parents (and grandparents) aware of their children's concerns.

Key Terms

achievement motivation (p. 307)
blended family (p. 315)
industry versus inferiority (p. 306)
juvenile period (p. 321)
latency (p. 306)
learning orientation (p. 307)
peers (p. 302)
perceived popularity (p. 326)
performance orientation (p. 307)
self-constancy (p. 304)
sense of self (p. 303)
sociometric popularity (p. 326)

PART 6
Adolescence

Source: Monkey Business Images/Shutterstock.com.

Chapter 14
Physical Development during Adolescence

Chapter 15
Cognitive Development during Adolescence

Chapter 16
Psychosocial Development during Adolescence

The adolescent years are a time of change, challenge, conflict, and confusion for everyone. We must come to terms with changes in our bodies as they suddenly grow taller and mature sexually. We must learn to negotiate the conflicts that arise when establishing a more equitable relationship with parents. And we are faced with the natural challenges that follow when thinking about leaving home someday, even if not immediately. Achieving independence becomes a driving issue during this developmental period, though one that will take years to resolve.

How difficult these challenges turn out to be depends on a variety of circumstances. For some teens, the timing of puberty can make adolescence especially hard—or easy. For others, newly forming abilities to think about life's larger issues can make life seem suddenly confusing, though at the same time full of exciting future possibilities. For many young people, dating or even just talking to those of the other sex becomes both intriguing and frustrating as they overcome childhood habits of relating only to members of their own sex. Despite these unique experiences and the myths about the troubling teen years, for most individuals, on average, adolescence is no more or less stressful than other periods of development across the lifespan.

Physical Development during Adolescence

CHAPTER **14**

Source: Rawpixel.com/Shutterstock.com.

Chapter Outline

PHYSICAL DEVELOPMENT
Growth in Height and Weight
Puberty
Health during Adolescence

Focusing Questions

- What is meant by *adolescence,* and what changes in society contributed to its gaining recognition as a developmental stage?
- What changes in height, weight, and appearance can be expected during adolescence, and how do they differ for girls and boys?
- What are the effects of early, "on-time," and late development during puberty, and how do the effects differ for girls and boys?
- What major health problems do adolescents face, and in what ways are adolescents more at risk than other age groups?
- What has recent research in neuroscience discovered about brain development during adolescence?

Dillon is fourteen. Beginning last summer, he has started looking and acting different than before. He has grown nearly two inches in the last six months, a fact that his mother comments on with pride, but also with a note of dismay when his clothing no longer fits. Sometimes, Dillon would prefer that no one notice the changes. Just a year or two ago, he appeared well coordinated and athletic in school sports. Now he feels clumsy, trips over himself, and bumps into things. Even his "normal" voice has abandoned him. Sometimes it has that familiar sound; then suddenly, it will have the deep resonance of his

341

father's voice. Worst of all for Dillion is when, unexpectedly and at the most embarrassing moments, his voice cracks and breaks into awkward high-pitched expressions.

Yet physically, Dillon feels very optimistic. So far, he has experienced no major illnesses, accidents, or violence; in fact, he secretly feels invulnerable to these mishaps, as if they could happen only to others, not to him. Feeling physically invulnerable allows him to be careless about his body in small but significant ways. He sometimes eats more "junk food" than he should, fails to brush his teeth, or goes a few days without enough sleep. Sometimes, especially when his parents aren't aware of it, he performs reckless stunts on his bike or considers joining his friends in their casual experimentation with smoking or drinking. At times, he consciously rides in a car without wearing a seat belt, not realizing that driving is statistically the most dangerous current activity in his life. Eventually, he may pay a price for these behaviors, but for now, he has other things on his mind.

adolescence The stage of development between childhood and adulthood, around ages ten to twenty-two.

Dillon is experiencing one version of **adolescence**, the period of development from about age twelve to age twenty that leads from childhood to emerging adulthood. As you might imagine, Dillon's is not the only possible experience of adolescence; in the next three chapters, we will catch glimpses of other, very different experiences, as well as look at key programs of research meant to describe adolescence in general terms. As we will see, adolescence is a paradoxical time when young girls and boys sometimes resemble children, while at other times, they resemble young women and men. For any teenager, the particular mix of qualities and behaviors depends on the teenager's age and on the unique roles and responsibilities that he or she encounters along the way.

Compared to adolescent roles and responsibilities in many traditional cultures around the world, those in modern industrial societies are relatively unpredictable, and young people often feel ill-prepared to meet them as a result. Most male teenage Australian aborigines, for example, go on a yearlong walkabout through the desert, carrying only a few simple weapons for protection; their chances of survival, however, are high due in large part to much of their childhood being spent developing the skills that will help them meet the challenges in this rite of passage. Most adolescent girls in the hunting-and-gathering society of the Inuit of Alaska and northern Canada have a good idea of what it takes to be an adult woman: they have already witnessed and perhaps assisted in the bearing of and caring for children, as well as gathering and preparing food. But because of technology, urbanization, and other social changes, teenagers in many developed countries often have little idea of what kind of work they will do as adults, what kind of family they will live in, or even where they will live.

In fact, some psychologists have proposed that adolescence be defined primarily as a time of transitions (Blakemore & Mills, 2014). Friendships for teenagers, for example, share qualities with friendships in childhood (friends are not yet a primary source of advice and support on the most important questions of life), but also some qualities with friendships in adulthood (friends *are* a source of support about many matters, such as clothing styles and assessments of mutual acquaintances). Thinking skills are in some ways childlike (the limits of thinking and reasoning are not yet noticed) and in other ways adultlike (much thinking can now be abstract). Physically, adolescents can sometimes look like children and sometimes like adults, and sometimes like a cross between the two; for confirmation, simply attend a social event at any junior high school.

Because viewing adolescence as a transition highlights the place of this period in the human lifespan as a whole, we will often use it to frame the discussion in this chapter. But sometimes we will also use two other widely held views of adolescence. One, as described by G. Stanley Hall, sees adolescence as a time of "storm and stress," a period when major physical, intellectual, and emotional changes create tremendous distress and crisis within the individual and conflict between the person and society. As you may recall, Sigmund Freud believed development is full of conflict, especially in adolescence. Erik Erikson and others have suggested that a lack of stable and predictable role expectations due to rapid changes in society may make the transition from childhood to adulthood more difficult (Elkind, 1994; Erikson, 1963, 1968).

Current research, however, suggests that adolescence is not intrinsically a time of severe "storm and stress" in personality development or in relationships with parents. Most adolescents in the United States adapt to the changes in themselves quite well and adjust to the changing demands and expectations of parents and society in a relatively smooth and peaceful way (Arnett, 1999). The same appears to be generally true in a number of other cultures, both Western and non-Western, where the majority of teenagers have been found to have positive self-images and good emotional adjustment (Hurrelmann, 1994; Seiffge-Krenke et al., 2012).

Though adolescence is not an unusually problematic period for most youngsters, in the United States and Great Britain the onset of adolescence is associated with more frequent negative feelings among many adolescents and increased rates of behavioral and psychological problems for some (Brooks-Gunn & Warren, 1989; Hamburg, 1994; Larson & Ham, 1993; Oldehinkel, Verhulst, & Ormel, 2011). In certain ethnic groups, for example, between 15 and 20 percent of adolescents in the United States drop out of school before completing high school; adolescents have the highest arrest rate of any age group; and a large number of adolescents use alcohol and drugs on a regular basis (Eccles et al., 1993; Johnston et al., 2012). How negative or positive the changes associated with adolescence are likely to be will depend on the degree of fit between adolescents' developing needs and the opportunities offered them by their social environments, school and home being two of the most important. Furthermore, the increased stress some adolescents experience may be due not simply to the external environment but also to developmental changes in adolescents' subjective construction of their environments (Larson & Ham, 1993).

We discuss these and other social aspects of adolescence in detail in this chapter and the next. First, though, let's look more closely at the physical changes of adolescence and their effects on development.

PHYSICAL DEVELOPMENT

Growth in Height and Weight

Although nearly everyone—including Dillon at the start of this chapter—experiences a rapid **growth spurt** during adolescence, there is much irregularity in the pattern and pace of growth, and significant variability in its timing. Generally speaking, growth during adolescence starts from the extremities inward, so that hands and feet get larger, then arms and legs, and finally the torso grows. This pattern of growth is one reason young adolescents feel and look awkward. The change in height is particularly striking, as Figure 14.1 shows. The maximum rate of growth occurs around age eleven or twelve for girls and about two years later for boys. In those years, many girls grow three inches in a single year, and many boys grow more than four inches, ultimately achieving average heights of approximately sixty-four inches for females and sixty-nine inches for males (Merenstein et al., 1997). The reason for males' greater average height is that boys start their growth spurt two years later than girls do and thus undergo two additional years of childhood growing. The average girl is around fifty-four or fifty-five inches tall when she begins her growth spurt, whereas the average boy is fifty-nine or sixty inches tall when he begins his. Because both boys and girls add around nine or ten inches during adolescence and grow relatively little afterward, women end up being shorter than men on average.

Weight also increases during adolescence, as a result of both overall growth and the adolescent growth spurt in particular. But weight is more strongly influenced than height by diet, exercise, and general lifestyle, and therefore changes in weight are less predictable from past size and growth patterns. What *is* relatively predictable, however, is the impact of diet, exercise, and lifestyle on a young person's future: more calories and less exercise contribute to heavier weight as an adult. Unfortunately, teenagers' social habits often contribute to the problem because "junk food" and sedentary activities (like playing

growth spurt A rapid change in height and weight that occurs in puberty and is preceded and followed by years of comparatively little increase.

> **What Do You Think?**
>
> In what ways has the "discovery" of adolescence as a developmental stage been helpful for teenagers and their families? In what ways has it been a problem? How would you describe your personal experience with adolescence?

video games or surfing social media) are both inexpensive and easily available, not to mention socially preferred, or "in."

These changes in weight tend to affect girls more than boys because of society's gender-role expectations. In general, girls are expected to look slender, while at the same time a bit curvaceous. Yet girls, not boys, are the ones who experience the greatest gains in body fat as a part of the adolescent growth spurt. During this period, total body fat for boys declines from an average of 18 or 19 percent to 11 percent of body weight, whereas for girls it increases from about 21 percent to around 26 or 27 percent (Sinclair, 1990). The average weight gain during the growth spurt is about thirty-eight pounds for girls and forty-two pounds for boys. These pounds are distributed differently among individuals, of course, but in general, girls end up with more fat tissue than boys at the end of adolescence, a sex difference that continues into adulthood.

Whether male or female, most teenagers (and adults!) do not end up with the height, weight, or other physical characteristics that match either society's ideals or their own. Teenage boys may worry about not looking muscular or tall enough. But because of social pressures to "look good," girls will worry even more: at some time or other, most may feel they are too heavy, and many may worry about being too tall as well. The "Focusing On" feature later in the chapter describes how such concerns contribute to eating disorders in some young athletes; later in this chapter, we will discuss how chronic worries about physical appearance affect many adolescent girls and adult women.

FIGURE 14.1
Physical Development During Adolescence

Puberty involves a number of age specific changes in both boys and girls, as this graph shows. One of the most obvious changes—the "growth spurt" or rate of increase in height—occurs significantly sooner in girls than in boys. But as with trends in final adult stature, many individual exceptions exist.

344 Part 6 Adolescence

> **What Do You Think?**
>
> What pattern (timing, rate) did changes in your own height and weight follow during adolescence? What do you remember thinking and feeling about those changes?

Puberty

Puberty is a set of physical changes that marks the completion of sexual development, or reproductive maturity. The changes that contribute directly to making sexual reproduction possible are called **primary sex characteristics**. Other changes, which are simply correlated or associated with the primary changes, are called **secondary sex characteristics**.

The Development of Primary Sex Characteristics

For boys, the most basic sign of sexual maturation is rapid growth of the penis and scrotum (the sack of skin underneath the penis that contains the testicles), which begins at around age twelve and continues for about five years for the penis and seven years for the scrotum (Kagan, 1998). During this time, the penis typically doubles or triples in length, prompting the almost inevitable locker room comparisons as boys become increasingly aware of the physical changes in themselves and their friends. Although penis size has almost nothing to do with eventual success at overall sexual functioning, for adolescent boys it sometimes seems to be an all-important sign of their new status as men (Malina, 1990; Merenstein et al., 1997).

During adolescence, enough live sperm are produced in the testes to make reproduction a real possibility for the first time. Sometime around age twelve, boys are likely to experience their first ejaculation of *semen,* a sticky fluid produced by the prostate gland, which is located near the penis just inside the body cavity. Semen carries the sperm to the penis and provides it with a medium in which to live after ejaculation. Most boys have their first ejaculation during masturbation; as *nocturnal emissions,* or "wet dreams," during sleep; or, less frequently, as emissions that occur spontaneously upon waking. Most males report experiencing nocturnal emissions about one or two years before puberty and the accompanying dreams are frequently, but not always, erotic in nature. The sexual changes just discussed and the unexpected erections and uncomfortable sexual fantasies and sensations that boys sometimes experience are common sources of embarrassment. Less frequently, they are a source of more serious discomfort and conflict.

For girls, the appearance of the first menstrual period, called **menarche**, signals sexual maturity. In most societies, menarche also symbolizes the shift from girlhood to womanhood, and typically occurs after the peak of the girls' growth spurt. Even though the girls may be experiencing their first periods, it does not necessarily mean that they are fertile. From the occurrence of the girls' first periods, their menstrual cycles may take between twelve and eighteen months to achieve regularity in terms of predictable timing and consistency with respect to the release of ova from the ovaries (Christensen et al., 2010). Menarche occurs rather late in a girl's sexual maturation and is preceded by a number of other changes, including enlargement of the breasts, the appearance of pubic hair, and broadening of the hips and shoulders. As the growth spurt peaks, the uterus, vagina, labia, and clitoris continue to develop, as do the ovaries.

The Development of Secondary Sex Characteristics

Both boys and girls experience a number of physical changes that create secondary sex characteristics, notably in their breasts, body hair, and voices. These changes do not directly contribute to their physical ability to reproduce, but they do make the two sexes look more adultlike and more stereotypically masculine or feminine.

Breasts

Girls first develop breast "buds," or slightly raised nipples, at the beginning of puberty. During the following several years, the nipples grow darker, the areolas (the pigmented

---

puberty The period of early adolescence characterized by the development of full physical and sexual maturity.

primary sex characteristics Characteristics that make sexual reproduction possible. For females, consist of the vagina, uterus, fallopian tubes, and ovaries; for males, consist of the penis, scrotum, testes, prostate gland, and seminal vesicles.

secondary sex characteristics Sex characteristics other than the sex organs, such as extra layers of fat and pubic hair.

menarche The first menstrual period.

Chapter 14 Physical Development during Adolescence   345

areas surrounding the nipples) increase in size, and the breasts continue to grow until they reach their full size. Given the attention our culture devotes to breasts, it is not surprising that breast development is a potential source of concern for many adolescent girls. Breasts that are "too big," "too small," different sizes, or the "wrong" shape may cause embarrassment, lower self-esteem, and depressive symptoms (Yuan, 2012), and in many cases, girls experience outright harassment due to these physical developments.

Boys, too, undergo a small amount of breast development, and their areolas become larger and darker much as they do in girls. A few boys experience enough tissue growth to cause them some embarrassment, but these "breasts" usually return to typical male size in a year or two.

Body Hair

When their genital development is relatively advanced, both boys and girls acquire more body hair, although boys generally grow more of it than girls do. The first growth is simply a fine fuzz around the genitals called *pubic hair,* which then darkens and becomes coarser. At the same time, underarm or *axillary hair* begins to appear which eventually becomes dark and coarse as well (Archibald, Graber, & Brooks-Gunn, 2006).

Voice

In both sexes, the voice deepens near the end of puberty and becomes richer in overtones so that it sounds less like a flute or whistle and more like a violin or clarinet. These changes make the adolescent's voice sound more truly adult, but the fluctuations in voice qualities that some adolescents experience can be a cause of considerable (although usually temporary) embarrassment.

Hormonal Changes: Physical and Social Consequences

testosterone A sex hormone, sometimes called the *male sex hormone* because its high concentration in boys stimulates growth of the penis and related male reproductive organs.

estrogen A sex hormone, sometimes called the *female sex hormone* because its high concentration in girls stimulates the growth of the ovaries and vagina during puberty.

For both boys and girls, the onset of puberty brings increases in the levels of all sex hormones in the blood, but the pattern by which it does so differs for each sex. **Testosterone** (also called *male sex hormone),* a particular type of androgen, and **estrogen** *(or female sex hormone)* are two of the most important sex hormones. Although both hormones are present in males and females, the high concentration of testosterone in boys stimulates the growth of the penis and related male reproductive organs, and the high concentration of estrogen in girls stimulates the growth of the ovaries and vagina. Androgens are thought to influence the strength of the sex drive in both sexes.

Hormones affect more than just sexual characteristics. For example, they are responsible for the typical differences between girls' and boys' overall body builds. In general, the sex that has shorter bones and more rounded curves (female) also has higher estrogen levels, and the sex that has longer bones and larger muscles (male) also has higher levels of testosterone (Cheek, 1974; Tanner, 1990).

Testosterone stimulates muscle and bone growth in both sexes. Throughout most of childhood, boys and girls are about equally muscular. Prior to adolescence boys and girls have roughly the same number and sizes of muscle fibers, and they can exert about the same amount of strength with their muscles. Although individual children vary around the averages, as groups, the two sexes differ very little until the onset of puberty (Lundren et al., 2011; Malina, 1990).

Puberty changes this gender equality to some extent. On average, boys become more muscular than the average girl does, even though postpubescent girls are more muscular than their childhood selves. From early childhood to adolescence, boys experience close to a fourteen-fold increase in the size of the largest muscles in their bodies (for example, in their thighs), but girls experience only a ten-fold increase (Froberg & Lammert, 1996; Malina, 1990). Because these changes are only averages, it is not unusual for many adolescent girls in middle school and high school to actually be stronger than some of their male classmates.

Individual differences in physical development result in part from differences in life experiences that either promote or interfere with muscular growth. And some of the differences in experiences are linked to society's gender-role expectations. Teenage boys more often receive encouragement or feel pressure to participate in sports and to take on jobs and responsibilities that involve physical work (Coakley, 1996). The higher level of activity and physical exertion leads to greater bone and muscle mass as boys mature and become adults. In the decades since the passage of Title IX—an act that eliminated sex discrimination in publicly funded educational and co-curricular activities—young girls have also received greater encouragement and support for being physically active and for participating in organized sports, resulting in stronger muscle development than had been seen in prior generations of adolescent girls. The emphasis on muscle development for girls as a whole is less intense than what is felt by their male peers.

In spite of these social effects, many of the physical differences between the sexes result from genetically programmed development. Genetically triggered changes in estrogen levels during adolescence, for example, lead to increases in the fat deposited under the skin, as well as to final maturation of bones. The higher concentration of estrogen in girls, combined with the higher concentration of testosterone in boys mentioned earlier, means that girls end up with more fat tissue than boys do as a proportion of their body weight, and boys end up with more muscle tissue than girls do. Hence, the tendency toward conventional sex differences in physical appearance: boys look more muscular and girls have more curves (Kagan, 1998)—though only as average trends.

Psychological Effects of Physical Growth in Adolescence

Given how rapid the physical changes of puberty are, it is not surprising that adolescents often are preoccupied—and dissatisfied—with how they look. When dissatisfaction occurs, it is most noticeable early in the adolescent years, but it is also common during the later teen years and well into adulthood (Blashill & Wilhelm, 2013; Connolly et al., 1996; Fox, 1997; Yuan, 2012). It would seem, then, that a milestone as important as puberty should affect individuals deeply, perhaps leading to long-term effects that last even into adulthood. Psychologists therefore have searched for predictable psychological effects of physical growth, both short term and long term; however, the results of this research have not been fully conclusive.

Timing of Puberty

Research exploring the social-emotional consequences related to when an adolescent begins and ends puberty accelerated in the 1980s. A series of longitudinal studies explored the impact of the timing of puberty on individuals' well-being (Livson & Peskin, 1981a, 1981b; Tobin-Richards et al., 1983). The studies tried to answer some very important questions: Was it better to experience puberty earlier than usual, or later, or "on time"? And did these timings have a different effect depending on whether you were a boy or a girl?—Teenage participants were followed for several years, and eventually even for several decades—they were especially helpful in determining the effects of timing. This research suggested intriguing trends in the effects of timing and gender, as summarized in Table 14.1. The trends themselves, however, also masked important individual differences in responses to puberty, which more recent research has highlighted.

Even among adolescents who are the same age, differences in physical maturity are common and can contribute to social advantages, challenges, or anxieties. And while there is great variability in the timing of puberty, there is an increased interest in physical appearance experienced by most adolescents, as revealed through the recent trend—explosion?—in taking, sending, and posting "selfies."
Source: karelnoppe/Shutterstock.com.

TABLE 14.1 Trends in Adolescents' Reactions to the Onset of Puberty

For adolescents who begin puberty early, initial reactions among males tend to be positive and later reactions are negative, while the reverse is true for females. Late-maturing males first react negatively and later react positively. Late-maturing females first react positively, and later reactions are mixed. These trends, however, conceal variability among individuals.

Time of Onset	Time of Reaction	Typical Reactions of Males	Typical Reactions of Females
Early maturation	Initial/short term	Positive	Negative
	Later/long term	Mixed	Positive
Late maturation	Initial/short term	Negative	Positive
	Later/long term	Positive	Mixed

What did the original longitudinal research find? First, it suggested that *early-maturing boys* seemed to experience initial advantages as teenagers. They enjoyed a head start on muscle growth compared to their peers, a change that apparently stimulated peers, teachers, and others to treat them like adults sooner. The boys responded positively to this treatment and, through a sort of self-fulfilling prophecy, actually became more confident and mature in their behavior. By the same token, though, they were more conforming to adult standards than usual for adolescents and less open to the minor risk-taking characteristic of adolescents as a whole (Lightfoot, 1997). These differences continued into early adulthood: a decade after puberty, early-maturing men were still more responsible and self-controlled, but also more rigid in relating to peers. Most important, though, was a lowering of their self-esteem; as later-maturing boys caught up with them physically, the early-maturing boys received less attention and respect from others, and experienced a loss of self-esteem.

Late-maturing boys, on the other hand, face some very specific and paradoxical outcomes. Many still resembled children as late as age sixteen, and unfortunately, tended to be judged as children as a result. Teachers and parents rated these individuals as impulsive, immature, and lacking self-confidence. Their ratings may have been partly stereotypical based on how the boys looked, but also partly based on accurate observations. The late-maturing boys generally participated less in key social activities, such as sports and sports-focused social activities, and therefore had fewer opportunities to learn social skills in the same way as their early maturing peers. The good news, however, was that these boys tended to feel less pressure to become socially or sexually active. Perhaps as a result, they felt better about themselves as young adults than did the early maturers.

What about girls? *Early-maturing girls* did not experience early timing as an advantage as boys did. Their earlier physical development put them out of step with gender-role expectations for girls of the same age. Because they now looked older and more sexually mature, parents and teachers worried about their behavior, especially because they often received attention from older students at their school. In addition, because they were relatively short when they acquired normal female fat tissue and "curves," they tended to look plumper than average. Both changes tended to create stress for early-maturing girls. Yet the effect did not last into adulthood: at age thirty, the early maturers reported feeling *more* poised and self-directed than usual, perhaps *because* of experiencing and surviving social disapproval as teenagers.

Late-maturing girls experienced a complementary trend. As teenagers, they were rated by parents and teachers as more attractive and as better social leaders. In fact, the girls actually did become school leaders more often than usual. By age thirty, though, they reported feeling *less* poised than early maturers, and less sure of where their lives were heading.

Part 6 Adolescence

become adults. In the decades since the passage of Title IX—an act that eliminated sex discrimination in publicly funded educational and co-curricular activities—young girls have also received greater encouragement and support for being physically active and for participating in organized sports, resulting in stronger muscle development than had been seen in prior generations of adolescent girls. The emphasis on muscle development for girls as a whole is less intense than what is felt by their male peers.

In spite of these social effects, many of the physical differences between the sexes result from genetically programmed development. Genetically triggered changes in estrogen levels during adolescence, for example, lead to increases in the fat deposited under the skin, as well as to final maturation of bones. The higher concentration of estrogen in girls, combined with the higher concentration of testosterone in boys mentioned earlier, means that girls end up with more fat tissue than boys do as a proportion of their body weight, and boys end up with more muscle tissue than girls do. Hence, the tendency toward conventional sex differences in physical appearance: boys look more muscular and girls have more curves (Kagan, 1998)—though only as average trends.

Psychological Effects of Physical Growth in Adolescence

Given how rapid the physical changes of puberty are, it is not surprising that adolescents often are preoccupied—and dissatisfied—with how they look. When dissatisfaction occurs, it is most noticeable early in the adolescent years, but it is also common during the later teen years and well into adulthood (Blashill & Wilhelm, 2013; Connolly et al., 1996; Fox, 1997; Yuan, 2012). It would seem, then, that a milestone as important as puberty should affect individuals deeply, perhaps leading to long-term effects that last even into adulthood. Psychologists therefore have searched for predictable psychological effects of physical growth, both short term and long term; however, the results of this research have not been fully conclusive.

Timing of Puberty

Research exploring the social-emotional consequences related to when an adolescent begins and ends puberty accelerated in the 1980s. A series of longitudinal studies explored the impact of the timing of puberty on individuals' well-being (Livson & Peskin, 1981a, 1981b; Tobin-Richards et al., 1983). The studies tried to answer some very important questions: Was it better to experience puberty earlier than usual, or later, or "on time"? And did these timings have a different effect depending on whether you were a boy or a girl?—Teenage participants were followed for several years, and eventually even for several decades—they were especially helpful in determining the effects of timing. This research suggested intriguing trends in the effects of timing and gender, as summarized in Table 14.1. The trends themselves, however, also masked important individual differences in responses to puberty, which more recent research has highlighted.

Even among adolescents who are the same age, differences in physical maturity are common and can contribute to social advantages, challenges, or anxieties. And while there is great variability in the timing of puberty, there is an increased interest in physical appearance experienced by most adolescents, as revealed through the recent trend—explosion?—in taking, sending, and posting "selfies."
Source: karelnoppe/Shutterstock.com.

TABLE 14.1 Trends in Adolescents' Reactions to the Onset of Puberty

For adolescents who begin puberty early, initial reactions among males tend to be positive and later reactions are negative, while the reverse is true for females. Late-maturing males first react negatively and later react positively. Late-maturing females first react positively, and later reactions are mixed. These trends, however, conceal variability among individuals.

Time of Onset	Time of Reaction	Typical Reactions of Males	Typical Reactions of Females
Early maturation	Initial/short term	Positive	Negative
	Later/long term	Mixed	Positive
Late maturation	Initial/short term	Negative	Positive
	Later/long term	Positive	Mixed

What did the original longitudinal research find? First, it suggested that *early-maturing boys* seemed to experience initial advantages as teenagers. They enjoyed a head start on muscle growth compared to their peers, a change that apparently stimulated peers, teachers, and others to treat them like adults sooner. The boys responded positively to this treatment and, through a sort of self-fulfilling prophecy, actually became more confident and mature in their behavior. By the same token, though, they were more conforming to adult standards than usual for adolescents and less open to the minor risk-taking characteristic of adolescents as a whole (Lightfoot, 1997). These differences continued into early adulthood: a decade after puberty, early-maturing men were still more responsible and self-controlled, but also more rigid in relating to peers. Most important, though, was a lowering of their self-esteem; as later-maturing boys caught up with them physically, the early-maturing boys received less attention and respect from others, and experienced a loss of self-esteem.

Late-maturing boys, on the other hand, face some very specific and paradoxical outcomes. Many still resembled children as late as age sixteen, and unfortunately, tended to be judged as children as a result. Teachers and parents rated these individuals as impulsive, immature, and lacking self-confidence. Their ratings may have been partly stereotypical based on how the boys looked, but also partly based on accurate observations. The late-maturing boys generally participated less in key social activities, such as sports and sports-focused social activities, and therefore had fewer opportunities to learn social skills in the same way as their early maturing peers. The good news, however, was that these boys tended to feel less pressure to become socially or sexually active. Perhaps as a result, they felt better about themselves as young adults than did the early maturers.

What about girls? *Early-maturing girls* did not experience early timing as an advantage as boys did. Their earlier physical development put them out of step with gender-role expectations for girls of the same age. Because they now looked older and more sexually mature, parents and teachers worried about their behavior, especially because they often received attention from older students at their school. In addition, because they were relatively short when they acquired normal female fat tissue and "curves," they tended to look plumper than average. Both changes tended to create stress for early-maturing girls. Yet the effect did not last into adulthood: at age thirty, the early maturers reported feeling *more* poised and self-directed than usual, perhaps *because* of experiencing and surviving social disapproval as teenagers.

Late-maturing girls experienced a complementary trend. As teenagers, they were rated by parents and teachers as more attractive and as better social leaders. In fact, the girls actually did become school leaders more often than usual. By age thirty, though, they reported feeling *less* poised than early maturers, and less sure of where their lives were heading.

> **What Do You Think?**
>
> Talk with one or two classmates about how the timing of their own maturation affected their adolescence. Did it fit any of the patterns described here? Or were they one of the people who created the variability also described here? On balance, what implications do you see for teachers and parents, given that puberty creates both pattern and diversity at the same time?

Nonnormative Effects of Puberty

Although the trends regarding the timing of puberty are intriguing, they also mask variability in teenagers' experiences. Research about the psychological impact of puberty has highlighted this fact, and has been more cautious in generalizing about both the short- and long-term effects of timing. In reviewing studies about this question, the psychologist Sucheta Connolly and her colleagues concluded that puberty has little lasting impact on adolescents, immediately or during emerging adulthood (Connolly et al., 1996). In the short term, physical changes are co-occurring with stresses in the family. As a result, parents and the young adolescent are conflicted about how to respond to the changes—as a welcome transition or as a source of ongoing worry. Yet, in the long run, during later adolescence or early adulthood, family relationships return to a quality characteristic of the prepubescent family dynamic, good or bad. Other social and emotional effects, such as changes in self-esteem or in peer relationships, are much more variable than similar, both in the short term and in the long term. As older adolescents move into adulthood, furthermore, the effects of puberty become even more obscure and harder to generalize about. For example, in a longitudinal study based on interviews of women from college age through midlife, the psychologist Ruthellen Josselson found that self-esteem and attitudes about self commonly changed markedly—either for good or for ill—regardless of what they were initially (Josselson, 1996).

Health during Adolescence

During adolescence, health concerns for both teens and their parents represent a "good news/bad news" paradox. In some ways, adolescents are among the healthiest of all people. They tend to have fewer colds and ear infections than young children or adults do (Fry, 1974). Compared to adults, they suffer fewer of the illnesses and physical damage associated with prolonged exposure to physical and emotional stress and with aging.

Nevertheless, there are a few select experiences that occur during adolescence where the health risks are greater than those for younger children and adults. Compared to either age group, teens are much more likely to be injured in motor vehicle accidents, misuse alcohol and other substances, experience unwanted pregnancy, as well as problems associated with inadequacies in their diet and health and mental health care (Balk & Corr, 1996).

These statistical realities have a number of effects. During adolescence, teenagers assume a sense of personal invulnerability. As a result, they often dismiss or discount risky behaviors in themselves or in the situations in which they find themselves. In a similar fashion, their view of death or potential disability is one of a distant phenomenon, not something that can happen to them. This contributes to a sense of insulation from danger, a manner of thinking that we will discuss in Chapter 15. Ironically, many teens then consider the possibility of an accident, drug abuse, or pregnancy as less risky than they really are. As adolescents grow into adulthood, furthermore, they discover that these same risk factors have created diversity among young adults: those young adults who have experienced them face very different lives than those who have not.

Causes of Death among Adolescents

Although adolescents are less affected by some of the health problems that lead to death in younger children and adults, the death rate during adolescence is one of the highest

School-based health care programs that are responsive to the special needs and vulnerabilities of adolescents can make an important contribution to helping teenagers to take responsibility for their own health care. As teenagers get older, it may be less and less realistic to rely on parents to ensure that they get the medical attention that they need.
Source: Rob Marmion/Shutterstock.com.

for all age groups. Both the risky environments in which many teenagers live and the risk-taking behavior associated with adolescence undoubtedly contribute to this statistic (Lightfoot, 1996; Nappe & Nappe, 1996). Most causes of death among adolescents are preventable. The leading causes are motor vehicle accidents (more than fifteen thousand per year), homicide and other forms of intentional violence (more than six thousand per year), and self-inflicted harm or suicide (more than five thousand yearly; Balk & Corr, 1996). More recently, the overall percentage of teen deaths has dropped to below 1 percent of all deaths that occur in the United States each year, to an average of 16,375 deaths per year from 1996 to 2006 (Minino, 2010). Nevertheless, the top-five causes remain constant, with unintentional accidents causing 48 percent of all deaths, over 70 percent of which are traffic accidents, followed by homicide (13 percent) and suicide (11 percent), and then deaths due to physical causes like cancer (6 percent) and heart disease (3 percent; Minino, 2010).

Race, gender, and social-economic status (SES) also play a significant role in mortality rates for teens. For all adolescents, regardless of gender, non-Hispanic black teenagers are 37 percent more likely to die during adolescence than their Hispanic and non-Hispanic white peers (Minino, 2010). The mortality rate for males is consistently greater than it is for adolescent females at all ages but significantly so as teenagers transition into emerging adulthood.

Male mortality rates are in large measure due to certain lifestyle choices and/or conditions in their communities that make them significantly more at risk than their female peers. Middle-SES males are likely to believe that risk taking and experimentation with cars and motorcycles, alcohol consumption, and drug use are signs of masculinity. Males from low-SES families and those from minority groups fare even worse. They are at still greater risk for accidental death and homicide because of dangers inherent when they live in inner-city environments. Survival in these neighborhoods can often lead to the use and sale of drugs, participation in gangs, and exposure to various forms of physical violence, including the use of lethal weapons (Takanishi, 1993). The figures for young black men are alarmingly high due to disproportionately high rate of death by homicide in this group. A non-Hispanic black teen is two times more likely to die by a homicide than a Hispanic male, and fifteen times more likely than a non-Hispanic white male (Minino, 2010).

Health-Compromising Behaviors

Although adolescents are not prone to the infectious diseases of childhood, they often adopt habits that are damaging to their health. Poor diet, lack of sleep, use of alcohol or drugs, and unsafe sexual practices can all lead to a number of serious diseases. Infectious mononucleosis, hepatitis, and a variety of *sexually transmitted infections (STIs)* constitute major health risks during adolescence.

Sexually Transmitted Infections

Teenagers and young adults under twenty-five account for more than 50 percent of the 20 million STI cases reported annually. It is estimated that 25 percent of adolescents will become infected with an STI before graduating from high school (CDC—Division of STD Prevention, 2013; Moore et al., 1996). Adolescent females have the highest rates of gonorrhea, cytomegalovirus, chlamydia, and pelvic inflammatory disease of any age group. STIs can cause pelvic inflammatory disease, which places young women at risk for subsequent development of ectopic pregnancy and infertility (Shafer & Moscicki, 1991).

Risk factors for STIs include the increased acceptability of early sexual activity throughout our culture and inadequate use of contraceptives. The acceptability of early sexual activity in the United States is apparent when fifteen-year-old American adolescents are compared to their counterparts in other developed countries (including France, England, Russia, Canada, and Israel): The percentage of fifteen-year-olds in the United States who are sexually active is far higher (41 percent) than any of the other countries (whose rates range from 14 percent in Israel to 33 percent in Russia) (Gabhainn et al., 2009). Another specific, significant risk factor is the age of first sexual intercourse. Later initiation of sexual intercourse is correlated with lower rates of STIs among adolescents (Kaestle et al., 2005). Early adolescents often lack the cognitive maturity to plan ahead, accurately appraise their risks, and make effective decisions—especially in emotionally charged situations. These characteristics result in inconsistent or ineffective contraceptive practices (Nelson & Neinstein, 2008). Additional data from the cross-cultural study of fifteen-year-olds just mentioned also revealed that rates of condom use among those same fifteen-year-olds was lowest among the American adolescents; just 68 percent of sexually active American fifteen-year-olds reported using a condom during their last intercourse, compared with 84 percent of the teen respondents from France (Gabhainn et al., 2009).

The most common form of contraception used by adolescents in the United States is condoms; condoms are the contraceptive method of choice for approximately two-thirds of sexually active adolescents (American Academy of Pediatrics, 2007). While the pill may be more effective in reducing the chances for an unwanted pregnancy, condoms provide significant protection against STIs and HIV, whereas the pill provides none. However, as noted earlier, adolescents frequently do not make use of any form of contraception, putting them at risk for STIs and pregnancy. Inadequate health and sex education at home and in the schools must be held accountable. Comprehensive sex education, ideally provided *before* adolescents begin having sex, provides information about sex, data on effectiveness and how to use different forms of contraception, and how to talk about and refuse unwanted sexual activity. There is no evidence that comprehensive sex education encourages adolescents to engage in sex, a worry for many parents and educators (Kirby & Laris, 2009). Moreover, comprehensive sex education increases use of contraception, reduces unwanted pregnancies, and may delay adolescents' initiation of sex (Kohler, Manhart, & Lafferty, 2008; Stanger-Hall & Hall, 2011; Tortolero et al., 2010). Abstinence-only sex education, which is still quite common in many school districts, has been found to be ineffective: it does not delay initiation of sex, it actually decreases the likelihood that an adolescent will have safe sex, and it has been linked to higher rates of teen pregnancy (Stanger-Hall & Hall, 2011).

Drug Use

High rates of experimentation with drugs, alcohol, and tobacco are typical of adolescents. Since 1975, thousands of high school seniors across the United States have completed annual surveys about their drug use as part of a large, ongoing research program at the University of Michigan called "Monitoring the Future." (Eighth- and tenth-graders were included in this national survey starting in 1991.) These data have revealed several interesting trends in drug use over the past several decades, as depicted in Figure 14.2:

- Overall, rates of drug use among high school seniors has declined for almost all types of drugs;
- Alcohol—by far—remains the most frequently used drug;
- Rates of marijuana use have fluctuated over the years as a direct result of changing perceptions of its harm—as public concern about the harmful effects of marijuana use decrease, marijuana use increases;
- Unlike the trends for all other drugs in the survey, rates of marijuana use among high school seniors are currently rising (Johnston et al., 2014).

Drug use continues to be a problem for youth and young adults, and by extension, society at large. As shown in Figure 14.3, despite exposure to D.A.R.E. ("Drug Abuse Resistance Education") or other drug and alcohol education programs, as adolescents mature, they become increasingly likely to use alcohol and other drugs. Despite what appear to be disappointing results regarding educators' attempts to reduce the risks to adolescents that are posed by the use of drugs and alcohol, the overall decline in drug use and significant decreases in the use of specific drugs should offer some sense of optimism. When societal attitudes toward specific drugs change, so too do use of those drugs among adolescents. For example, the consumption of synthetic marijuana and the use of bath salts, both sold over-the-counter, showed steep drops in the 2013 Monitoring the Future survey data after news stories and drug resistance curricula highlighted the risks posed by their use (Johnston et al., 2014). Significant declines for use of synthetic marijuana and bath salts were seen at all three grade levels: down 3.5 percent for seniors, 1.3 percent for tenth-graders, and 0.4 percent among eighth-graders (Johnston et al., 2014). Rates for bath salts have shown a similar decline, even though their usage rates are low to begin with. Johnston (2014) and his team found that more teens are accurately perceiving the serious risks with synthetic drugs and are more disapproving of the drugs and even of their peers who use these substances.

Marijuana use seems to ebb and flow with the times for teens. But recent legislation to legalize marijuana in nine states and to make medical marijuana available in twenty-nine

FIGURE 14.2

Trends in Drug Use among American High School Seniors

According to an annual survey, rates of drug use among high school seniors in the United States have been declining since the 1990s. However, marijuana use appears to be increasing among today's high school seniors.

Source: Johnston et al., 2014.

FIGURE 14.3

Rates of Selected Drug Use Among Eighth-, Tenth-, and Twelfth-Graders in the United States

Each of these graphs reveals a similar pattern of drug use among students in the eighth, tenth, and twelfth grades: the percentage of users increases as the grade level increases. Rates of (a) alcohol consumption, (b) marijuana use, and (c) the use of all other illicit drugs are highest among high school seniors, who report having greater access to drugs and alcohol and the financial resources to be able to buy them.

Source: Johnston et al., 2014.

(a) Alcohol use

(b) Marijuana use

(c) All other illicit drug use

other states has had a significant effect on the perceived risk and level of disapproval associated with using this substance. Legal marijuana appears to have reduced the perceived risks of using the drug and lowered one's disapproval of its use, while conversely increasing the availability of the drug to teens. In fact, Johnston et al. (2014) noted that just over a third of teens reported that in states where marijuana was legal, their source for the drug was a person who had a prescription for medical marijuana.

Chapter 14 Physical Development during Adolescence

When the use of drugs turns to abuse, the effects on personal development are extremely destructive, particularly if the use is prolonged or chronic. Even short-term use of illicit drugs such as heroin, cocaine, and inhalants exposes the user to considerable physical risk of injury or death due to overdose, contamination of the drug, or both. Moderate use of certain drugs may also have destructive physical and psychological effects by disrupting normal patterns of eating, sleeping, and physical activity and masking psychological problems that require attention. Prescription drugs may also pose a threat for adolescents. A proper medicinal dose of the drug taken as prescribed is not usually physically dangerous, but the physical, social, and psychological risks involved in abusing these drugs are enormous. Finally, a number of these drugs cause physical addiction and psychological dependence. Physical addiction involves a biological dependence on the drug; withdrawal can be painful and sometimes life threatening. In most cases, tolerance to the drug increases with prolonged use, requiring higher doses to maintain the same level of effect and thus increasing the user's exposure to the drug's negative effects.

Alcohol and Tobacco

Perhaps the most troubling information to come out of the Monitoring the Future study was the continued prominence of alcohol use among teens. Despite dramatic drops in the use of alcohol by teens over the past two decades, nearly 70 percent of teens will have had at least one alcoholic drink by their senior year, and binge-drinking (five or more drinks in a row, at least once in the past two weeks) rates are still a concern with 5.1 percent of eighth-graders, 13.7 percent of sophomores, and 22.1 percent of seniors engaging in this behavior (Johnston et al., 2014).

What is the impact of the drugs most commonly used by teenagers—alcohol and tobacco? In many ways, their effects are more serious than the effects of more exotic drugs simply because they are used so widely and therefore affect a wider range of users, abusers, and non-users. For example, the use of alcohol was once associated with nearly half of all deaths from motor vehicle crashes involving adolescents (Tillman, 1992). It now accounts for less than a third of these deaths. In a recent estimate by the FBI, the National Traffic Safety Administration, and the CDC, 68 percent of fatalities connected to underage drinking were for reasons other than motor vehicle accidents. Alcohol was directly implicated in 30 percent of teen homicides, 14 percent of suicides, 9 percent of alcohol poisonings, and 15 percent by other means (Copeland, 2013). Because alcohol is heavily advertised and socially valued as a sign of adulthood and independence, is readily available at low cost, and is a potent short-term reducer of anxiety, it continues to be very popular among adolescents, even as the lifetime use rates decline. For the same reasons, it continues to be popular among young adults as well.

Cigarette smoking makes some teenagers feel more grown up and more sociable and accepted by their friends. As a result, many teenagers smoke cigarettes in spite of the health risks.
Source: Elena Rostunova/Shutterstock.com.

The use of tobacco products were at one time widely advertised as a sign of adulthood. Early adolescents were particularly susceptible to this "ready-made" symbol of maturity. Beginning in the 1970s, warning labels were required on every pack of cigarettes, and ads for cigarettes were banned from television and radio. Anti-smoking campaigns replaced the pro-smoking ads that permeated the airways. As a consequence, the use of smoking tobacco (in the past 30 days) has declined, especially over the past two decades. After peaking in the mid-1990s, use of cigarettes has fallen by 79 percent for eighth-graders and 70 percent for tenth-graders, and a less dramatic but significant drop of over 50 percent for high school seniors (Johnston et al., 2014). The rates for lifetime use, having smoked a cigarette at any time through high school, has also declined to 15, 26, and 38 percent, respectively, for eighth-, tenth-, and twelfth-graders in the same Monitoring The Future Study.

Three factors have contributed to these dramatic declines in the use of cigarettes. First, fewer and fewer young adolescents are even experimenting with smoking. Second, the strong anti-smoking campaigns have been successful in heightening the perceived risks inherent in smoking, and finally, teens are increasingly more likely to view smoking in a disapproving manner today than at any time in the past (Johnston et al., 2014). For more adolescents, the idea of smoking appears to no longer be "cool," and eight out of ten eighth-graders responded on the Monitoring the Future Study for 2013 that they would rather date someone who did not smoke! Peer pressure appears to be having a positive effect on teens turning away from smoking. The results were not as dramatic for the use of smokeless tobacco. Additionally, between 4 and 14 percent of adolescents report having used e-cigarettes, which is an emerging concern, especially as many perceive e-cigarettes as less harmful than traditional cigarettes—a belief not necessarily backed by scientific evidence (Hildick-Smith et al., 2015; Raloff, 2015; Russell & Ludwig, 2015).

Patterns of both drinking and smoking are strongly influenced by the lifestyles of family members and peers and by the environments in which they live. Among family members, minimal, moderate, and heavy levels of drinking, smoking, and drug use, including legally prescribed medications, are strongly associated with very similar patterns of use among adolescents. Peer pressure is also thought to significantly influence which drugs a teenager uses, in what circumstances, and how much and how often, although some findings indicate that its contribution may be overestimated (Bauman & Ennett, 1994; O'Connell, Boat, & Warner, 2009).

Because most initial experiences with cigarettes, alcohol, and illicit drugs occur during the early teenage years, prevention efforts are now being directed at this age group. These efforts have focused on reducing exposure to drugs, altering the social environment, and changing the attitudes and behaviors of the drug user (or potential user). In general, however, drug prevention programs have not proven very effective. Those that show promise are peer programs and school-based prevention efforts involving life skills training designed to increase knowledge and build confidence and overall social competence in areas such as risk assessment, decision making, self-directed behavior change, capacity to cope with anxiety, and conflict resolution (Hamburg, 1997; Lynch & Bonnie, 1994). Another area showing promise are recent studies looking at parenting practices that encourage greater self-disclosure between parents and teens and increased levels of parental warmth. Improved communication within the family has a positive effect on delaying substance use by adolescents and in improving outcomes for adolescents already involved in substance abuse treatment (Bertrand et al., 2013).

Sleep

When Caia's parents go to bed at 10:00 p.m. each weekday, she goes into her room and finishes her homework for the day. She knows she should go to sleep because she has to be up at 6:00 a.m. to get ready for school, but she first wants to see the pictures that her friends have posted on Instagram and if anyone has favored any of her tweets. Before she knows it, it is 12:00 a.m., so Caia turns off the lights, but she's not very tired. She lays in bed for nearly forty-five minutes before she finally dozes off to sleep.

The average adolescent needs between 9 and 9.5 hours of sleep per night to feel well rested and function during the daytime hours (Mercer, Merrit, & Cowell, 1998). As you might suspect, most adolescents do not obtain nearly that much sleep—the average American teenager gets 7 to 7.5 hours of sleep per night (Mercer et al., 1998). So why such a wide discrepancy in the amount of sleep adolescents *need* and what they *get*?

Our sleep drive works like a gas tank—at night we fill up our sleep reserves, and we use those sleep reserves during the day. Part of the job of our circadian rhythm is to keep us awake at the end of the day when our sleep reserves are running low and to keep us asleep at night to completely fill up those reserves. During childhood, these two processes—sleep drive and circadian rhythm—work so that children feel sleepy relatively early in the evening. There is a curious change in the circadian rhythm that coincides with the beginning of puberty such that melatonin onset shifts to a later time, as does sleep onset (Carskadon, 1990; Carskadon, Acebo, & Jenni, 2004; Carskadon et al., 1998). Therefore, a child like Caia who, before puberty, was tired at 8:00 and would fall asleep at 8:30, now does not feel sleepy until much later in the night. In fact, if Caia went to bed when her parents did, she would likely just lay in bed for hours unable to fall asleep. To compound the problem of this biological shift, Caia is also exposing herself to light when looking at her computer and cell phone late in the evening which, as we have already learned, further delays melatonin release and subsequent sleep time (Burke et al., 2015; Chang et al., 2015; Orzech et al., 2016).

Changes in adolescent sleep are especially problematic because, though onset of sleep has a biological shift toward a later time, adolescents must still wake up early for school, which effectively truncates adolescents' sleep (Carskadon, 1990; Wolfson & Carskadon, 1998). Sleep deprived adolescents do not perform as well as well-rested peers in school, have a more difficult time paying attention, and are more likely to get into car accidents (Carskadon, 1990; Danner & Phillips, 2008). When adolescents do not obtain enough sleep, they are more likely to engage in a host of risky behaviors such as smoking, not getting enough exercise, using drugs and alcohol, as well as reporting sadness, hopelessness, and thoughts about suicide (McNight-Eily et al., 2011).

To combat this very serious, widespread problem, some school districts have changed their school start times to allow adolescents to obtain more sleep. Not surprisingly, students in these districts got more sleep, reported feeling more awake and alert in class, were absent and late less often, reported better mental and physical health, were more motivated in school, and had fewer car accidents (Boergers, Gable, & Owens, 2014; Danner & Phillips, 2008; Owens, Belon, & Moss, 2010; Wahlstrom, 2002).

Nutritional Problems

Consider these two students:

- Miguel, age sixteen, leaves school at 4:00. On his way home, he stops by a convenience store with his friends and buys himself a large soft drink (300 calories) and a bag of French fries (400 calories). As a result, he is not hungry when dinner is served at 6:00; in fact, he doesn't finish his dinner. By the next morning, he is hungry again because he has not eaten for more than fourteen hours. He is too rushed to have breakfast, but on his way to school, he buys a candy bar at the same convenience store he visited yesterday.

- Susan, also age sixteen, leaves school at 4:00. On her way home, she stops by a convenience store with her friends, where they buy themselves various snacks. Susan buys herself nothing, though, because she believes she is slightly overweight. Later, for the same reason, she eats almost none of her dinner, causing mild worry for her parents. Still later, she sneaks out of the house without telling anyone, goes to the convenience store, and buys herself several candy bars, which she consumes on the spot. She feels sick, but doesn't throw up—this time.

Miguel and Susan are not unusual in their eating habits. Of all age groups in society, adolescents have some of the most unsatisfactory nutritional behaviors (Barness, 1993). Many of their eating habits—a tendency to skip meals, to snack (especially on "junk" foods), to consume fast foods, and (especially for girls) to diet—place them at dietary risk. Inadequate nutrition can interfere with a teenager's ability to concentrate at school or work, and it can interfere with activities with peers. The negative effects may not seem serious to many teenagers because their youth gives them comparative resilience to bounce back after a period of poor nutrition, preventing them from feeling ill as a consequence. In the short term, furthermore, many (but not all) teenagers neither gain weight from eating too many calories nor lose it from too much dieting. Yet poor nutritional habits definitely contribute to serious health problems in adulthood if they persist on a long-term basis.

Like dependence on drugs, dependence on "empty calories" and the obesity that sometimes results are problems that affect a significant portion of the teenage population. Adolescents and young adults who are overweight suffer increased health risks, including hypertension, respiratory disease, orthopedic disorders, and diabetes. In a bi-annual survey of American high school students, an estimated 13 percent of today's teenagers are considered obese, while another 15 percent were identified as overweight (Center for Disease Control, 2012). Major causes of obesity include a biologically inherited tendency to be overweight, childhood diet, family attitudes and habits regarding food, and lack of exercise (Mela & Roberts, 1998). Parental concerns about weight, especially with daughters, are strong indicators for young girls to begin internalizing about their weight and perhaps inhibiting their ability to self-regulate their eating patterns (Nickerson & Nagle, 2005).

Obesity is particularly difficult for adolescents who already are struggling to develop a comfortable and realistic view of their changing bodies. It can significantly impair teenagers' sense of themselves as physically attractive people and their overall identity development. In some cases, obesity can severely limit social opportunities due to both exclusion by peers and self-isolation. Because overweight adolescents do not conform to the social ideal of thinness, they also suffer from discrimination that limits their access to education, employment, marriage, housing, and health care (DeJong, 1993; Gortmaker et al., 1993; Puhl & King, 2013).

An obsession with excessive thinness is also a problem, especially for girls. Despite a growing appreciation of physical strength and fitness in women, thanks in part to women like Serena Williams and Abby Wambach, a lean body is still the dominant cultural standard for feminine beauty. Many adolescent girls try to lose weight to achieve a degree of slenderness that may not be possible for them. Eaton's study (CDC, 2012) of youth risk behaviors revealed the pervasiveness of a teen's concern with weight. Almost a third (29.2 percent) of all high school students described themselves as overweight, with 35 percent of females using this description, compared to 24 percent of their male peers. In addition, students reported going to significant lengths to either lose weight or simply not gain weight. Almost half (46 percent) of high school students reported wanting to lose weight, including 12.2 percent who fasted for twenty-four hours; 5.1 percent who took diet pills, powders, or liquids; and 4.3 percent who used laxatives or vomited within the past thirty days prior to the survey (CDC, 2012). These risky behaviors, paired with inadequate knowledge about dietary requirements and poor eating habits, often lead to inadequate nutrition for many teenage girls and serious eating disorders for a vulnerable few.

Eating Disorders

In its extreme form, the quest for thinness can become an eating disorder. **Anorexia nervosa**, **bulimia nervosa**, and **binge eating disorder** are three types of eating disorders that include extreme emotions, beliefs and attitudes, and behaviors regarding food and weight issues (Swanson, Crow, LeGrange, Swendsen, & Merikanagas, 2011). Recent prevalence rates have remained steady nationwide, affecting 0.3 percent of teens diagnosed with anorexia, 0.9 percent who are bulimic, and 1.6 percent with binge eating disorders (Swanson et al., 2011). Also, it is estimated that about 20 percent of adolescent girls (2.5 million) exhibit less extreme bulimic behaviors and an additional 20 percent engage in less extreme but still unhealthy dieting behaviors (Graber et al., 1996).

The *Diagnostic and Statistical Manual of Mental Disorders* (DSM-5; American Psychological Association, 2013) made some changes to the definition and criteria for eating disorders in the *DSM-5*. The major symptom of anorexia is extreme weight loss, or in adolescents, failure to maintain normal weight gain for age and gender through self-starvation that is tied to an obsessive fear of becoming fat. Anorexic youngsters experience severe disturbances in three areas of psychological functioning. The first is in persistent energy intake restriction, resulting in significant weight loss, or an unhealthy lack of weight gain for teens and children.

anorexia nervosa A physical and psychological disturbance that causes a person to refuse to eat sufficient food and to develop an increasingly unrealistic view of his or her body; most individuals with anorexia are teenage girls.

bulimia nervosa Disorder in which a person, usually a teenage girl, eats huge amounts of food and then vomits it to avoid gaining weight.

binge eating disorder A disorder in which a person feels out of control of his or her eating and consumes much more than most people would eat in a short period of time, sometimes even when he or she is not hungry.

A girl (call her Jill) is five feet, six inches tall and weighs eighty-seven pounds. Jill looks like a walking skeleton. Her weight is twenty-seven pounds less than what is expected for her, using the measure of 85 percent of expected weight for age. Jill's current weight is consistent with anorexia. But when she views herself in a mirror, she sees someone who is too fat and needs to continue dieting, the second disturbance of functioning. Her distorted perceptions activate behaviors that interfere with weight gain and lead to the third disturbance, a dangerous and unrealistic view of her own body image. Jill does not recognize the danger in her severe weight loss, believing that her thinness is what defines her (APA, 2013). A common physiological side effect of anorexia is amenorrhea, the cessation of menstruation in women. This is no longer considered a criterion in the new *DSM-5* diagnosis for anorexia nervosa.

Bulimia is a related eating disorder that frequently involves a recurrent "binge-purge" syndrome in which as many as 4,800 calories are eaten at a time, mostly in the form of sweets and other "forbidden" and fattening food, and then immediately purged by forced vomiting, laxatives, excessive exercise, and/or other cathartics. About half of all people suffering from anorexia also have bulimic eating patterns (Fairburn & Wilson, 1993). Women at greatest risk for bulimia are those who have most deeply accepted and internalized the social and cultural norms that equate fat with the bad and ugly, and thinness with the good and beautiful (Hesse-Biber, 1996).

Binge eating disorder (BED) is a new addition to specific types of eating disorders identified in the *DSM-5*. This separate disorder was included to address the risky eating patterns of large numbers of adolescents and college-age samples whose loss-of-control eating or recurring episodes of binge eating are becoming more common (APA, 2013). Like the other eating disorders, BED is more prevalent among adolescent girls than among their male peers, where roughly 10 percent of those seeking treatment for eating disorders are male. One commonality with all eating disorders, regardless of gender, is the high degree of comorbidity with other psychological conditions like anxiety disorders, depression, bi-polar disorders, and stressors within the family (APA, 2013; Rieck, Jackson, Martin, Petrie, & Greenleaf, 2013).

Anorexia, bulimia, and binge eating are frequently associated with various influences from family members, friends, and the media. For adolescent females and males, their body image and self-esteem are closely aligned with messages they receive from parents, peers, and images in the media, where thinness (for girls) and upper body strength (for boys) is highly valued (Ata, Ludden, & Lally, 2007).

Successful treatment of anorexia generally requires a multiple focus and an effective team of physicians, therapists, and family members. First, it must deal with the medical concerns and risks associated with severe weight loss, and then it must be supported by family counseling with the adolescent and her parents. Second, antidepressant medications have proven helpful in reducing the depression and risk of suicide that are present in many cases, and may require a psychiatric consult or monitoring of medications by the family practice physician. Family therapy has also proven effective for treating teens with anorexia nervosa, while intensive cognitive behavior therapy (CBT) is recommended for bulimia nervosa and binge eating disorders (Hay, 2013). The treatment must address the underlying family problems and the self-defeating interactions among family members that are invariably related to anorexia. Finally, individual therapy with the anorexic adolescent must focus on helping her to uncover her own abilities and resources for independent thinking, judging, and feeling. It must help her, or him, to achieve autonomy and self-directed identity by helping the adolescent become aware of, express, and act on his or her own impulses, feelings, and needs. The "Focusing On" feature looks at how these issues and solutions express themselves in the lives of competitive athletes.

Adolescent Brain Development

The recent emergence of interest among neuroscientists in the developing adolescent brain is providing new ways of understanding both the cognitive and social-emotional changes that have an impact on how teens function. In the not too distant past, it was assumed that brain development reached maturity by midadolescence. The significant gains in adolescent

Focusing On...

Female Athletes and Eating Disorders

Statistics show that athletic activities requiring a lean physical body predispose serious, competitive female participants to eating disorders. In figure skating, gymnastics, and ballet, more than half of competitive females report some form of pathological dieting, and as many as 25 percent are dangerously underweight or undernourished (Graber et al., 1996; Zerbe, 1993). This figure is more than double that for other women athletes (e.g., softball or basketball) and many times higher than for women in general. Eating disorders among skaters, gymnasts, and ballet dancers usually take the form of either *anorexia nervosa* or *bulimia*.

Several factors contribute to the prevalence of eating disorders among individuals in the "lean" sports. Competitive skating and ballet require much practice and pencil-like proportions to make turns and lifts, setting the stage for excessive exercise and a compulsion to prove one's worth through competitions. Most winners of Olympic competitions in these sports are teenagers, and the females are five to ten years younger than their male counterparts (Ryan, 1995). It is important to note that eating disorders also impact males: Adam Rippon spoke out about his disordered eating during the 2018 Winter Olympics. Youth makes them likely to be slender, both because some have not yet fully experienced puberty and because exercising so intensely tends to delay the onset of puberty. Their immaturity makes them less likely to question the intense exercise needed to succeed at skating or gymnastics.

Some young females may seem not obviously troubled because their activities support society's gender-role expectations. Both their talent and appearance are what the public often wants to see: a childlike body combined with a cooperative spirit, one that performs on demand and does not mind being looked at intently or even erotically (Guttmann, 1996; Hesse-Biber, 1996). Under these conditions, it becomes easy to hide an eating disorder. The public at large is eager *not* to hear about the downside to its image of perfection. And coaches, parents, and the girl herself find it easier to interpret symptoms as normal signs of stress or as normal self-discipline associated with training. At the beginning of a girl's sports career, in fact, they may be right: self-disciplined practice only later deteriorates into an addiction to public acclaim.

The experience of these athletes suggests ways to prevent and treat individuals with eating disorders. For example, both girls and their families need to understand the pervasiveness of gender-role expectations and social conventions that value thinness, docility, and youth for females (Hesse-Biber, 1996). This goal usually takes two strategies. One is to control and simplify a girl's environment to eliminate behaviors and stimuli that contribute to weight loss—by counseling family members about appropriate behavior or arranging for the girl or woman to live away from her family for a time. Unsolicited compliments on thinness should be reduced. So should criticisms for *not* eating, which can be interpreted as personal attacks and contribute to feeling helpless. The second strategy is to encourage a sense of autonomy and self-direction so that the girl feels less at the mercy of others' expectations and admiring (and sometimes envious) gazes. Accomplishing this goal usually requires counseling or therapy for the girl herself (Zerbe, 1993). To the extent that a girl can understand the link between an action as personal as eating and broad social issues about gender equity and about respect for the young, she can begin to see that eating problems are widespread and that her growing insights about her experiences, if shared appropriately, can sometimes help others with similar experiences.

What Do You Think?

1. Not everyone with an eating disorder is a young female. How would the experiences of others with this problem differ from those presented here?
2. If you knew someone who you suspected had an eating disorder, how might you deal with it? Compare your answer with that of a classmate.
3. When boys participate in sports that fit traditional male gender stereotypes for looks and behavior, what risks are they exposed to that may be analogous to the experience of some girls with eating disorders?

---

problem-solving abilities—described in the next section—and the relative absence of further obvious cognitive changes during adulthood led to the belief that the brain achieved full physiological maturity during the teen years. Research conducted at the National Institute of Mental Health (Giedd, 2004), the Institute for Cognitive Neuroscience in London (Blakemore, 2012), and elsewhere has demonstrated that the human brain continues to develop, with some exuberance, during adolescence and into emerging adulthood.

Research using fMRI (functional magnetic resonance imaging) technology has revealed that during adolescence the human brain experiences a period of rapid growth that continues into early adulthood (Luna et al., 2013). An increase in the production of gray matter is

> **What Do You Think?**
>
> Why do you think adolescents are at such high risk for injury, death, and health problems? What recommendations for preventing such serious outcomes might you make to a group of high school students and their parents?

also accompanied by increases in myelination, resulting in faster and more efficient neural pathways. Also contributing to the efficiency in neural processing is a resurgence of synaptic pruning (see the coverage of brain development during infancy in Chapter 5), a process that "weeds out" unused neural connections and allows more space for new pathways to form for information processing and storage (Giedd, 2004). It is now understood that brain development during adolescence occurs in a process guided by two principles. One is the "use it or lose it principle" seen in increased synaptic pruning, and the second is a "back-to-front" maturing process that is reexperienced during the teenage years (Gogtay et al., 2004).

"Use It or Lose It"

The process of pruning eliminates redundant or rarely used synapses and neurons, producing a brain that not only processes information more efficiently, but also a brain that is more specialized and differentiated than the brains of children (Casey et al., 2008). Abilities and knowledge acquired during childhood but not practiced or accessed during adolescence may be lost during adolescence as the synapses and neurons in inactive neural pathways are pruned. This is not to say that specific memories from one's past, knowledge acquired years ago, or actions that have not been performed in a long time (when was the last time you folded a paper airplane or a paper fortune teller?) will be lost forever as a result of pruning. Accessing the memories or knowledge may take longer or require some mental reconstruction, or you may have to relearn some skills that have gotten "rusty" over the years. There are some serious implications to the "use it or lose it" principle, however. During the rapid period of brain development occurring during adolescence, how the adolescents choose to stimulate their brains will significantly shape the physiological development of their brains (Casey et al., 2008). The adolescent who sits at a computer and spends hours playing video games online every day will likely have a brain that develops in different ways than the adolescent who spends hours after school with basketball teammates, volunteers in the community every month, and works for the family business on weekends.

"Back to Front"

This second principle suggests that the prefrontal cortex, home to much of the executive functioning of the brain, matures later during adolescence than regions further back in the brain, like the limbic system (Gogtay et al., 2004). The limbic system is associated with the processing of emotions and attaching meanings to memories, whereas the executive functions of the prefrontal cortex are used for logical reasoning, impulse control, and planning. Because the limbic system is maturing faster than the prefrontal cortex in teens, their impulses may be driving their development in ways that impact their social functioning (Blakemore, 2012) and risk-taking behaviors (Winters & Arria, 2011) that we will examine more closely in Chapter 16. Also, as a result of their limbic system maturing earlier than their prefrontal cortex, the decision making and behavior of adolescents are more likely than that of children or adults to be highly influenced by affective information and emotional cues. Specifically, when adolescents are in situations where they are trying to control their behavior, emotions will likely win out over logic (Casey et al., 2008). This physiological "back-to-front" maturational sequence helps to explain why sex education and drug awareness programs so often fail to impact the actual behavior of many adolescents. As Laurence Steinberg (2004) eloquently observed:

> It is easier to put on a hypothetical condom during an act of hypothetical sex than it is to put on a real one when one is in the throes of passion. It is easier to just say no to a hypothetical beer than it is to a cold frosty one on a summer night. (p. 53)

> **What Do You Think?**
>
> Try to remember a situation during your early adolescence where you acted in a way that, looking back, causes you to ask, "What was I thinking?!" Why do you think you acted that way? Could your behavior be, in part, explained by the "back-to-front" principle? What roles did emotion or logic play in your decision-making at the time?

The changes in the adolescent brain described earlier may also shed insights on the underlying causes for increasing sophistication in the reasoning abilities of adolescents. The proliferation of neuronal synapses and the process of myelination, complemented by the pruning process, enable adolescents to confront the many challenges of adolescence—numerous changes in family and peer relationships, expectations to assume increased responsibility inside and outside of the home, greater challenges being presented in their schoolwork, and growing pressure to clarify what kind of an adult they want to become in the future, just to name a few. We'll take a look into the mind of the adolescent in the next chapter.

Chapter Summary

- **What is meant by *adolescence*, and what changes in society contributed to its gaining recognition as a developmental stage?** Adolescence, which begins around age ten and lasts until about age twenty-two, is a developmental transition between childhood and adulthood. Some theories of adolescence emphasize the "storm and stress" of the period, whereas others portray it as a continuation of developmental trends begun in childhood.
- **What changes in height, weight, and appearance can be expected during adolescence, and how do they differ for girls and boys?** Adolescents experience significant increases in height and weight, but variations in the timing of the "growth spurt" among teenagers are even more striking. On average, boys start their growth spurt later than girls. Individual variations create worries about personal appearance for some adolescents.
- **What are the effects of early, "on-time," and late development during puberty, and how do the effects differ for girls and boys?** In addition to increases in height and weight, a larger pattern of changes occurs called *puberty*, which leads to full physical and sexual maturity. Primary sexual maturation among boys includes rapid growth of the penis and scrotum and production of fertile semen; among girls, it is marked by menarche, or the beginning of menstrual cycles. Maturation of secondary sex characteristics includes enlargement and development of the breasts, growth of body hair, deepening of the voice, and increased production of sex-related hormones.

  Although girls and boys are equally muscular prior to adolescence, during puberty boys experience significantly greater increases in muscle tissue than girls do. Girls experience a somewhat greater increase in body fat than boys do. The physical sex differences of puberty are accentuated by differences in life experiences related to gender-role expectations.

  For boys, the effects of early maturation tend to be positive in the short run but negative in the long run. Late maturation tends to have the reverse effects. For girls, early maturation tends to be more stressful in the short term but positive in the long term. Late maturers tend to experience immediate benefits during adolescence and no serious long-term negative effects. The timing of puberty affects only average response to puberty; individuals with identical timing vary widely in their responses, depending on their circumstances.
- **What major health problems do adolescents face, and in what ways are adolescents more at risk than other age groups?** Adolescent patterns of illness and health care are influenced by individual and family attitudes and resources. Adolescents are a high-risk group for injury and death due to risky lifestyles and their myth of invulnerability. Major health-compromising behaviors of adolescence include exposure to sexually transmitted diseases; alcohol, tobacco, and drug abuse; inadequate diet; insufficient sleep; and eating disorders.
- **What has recent research in neuroscience discovered about brain development during adolescence?** The brains of adolescents experience a period of rapid development, including the formation of new synapses, myelination, and the pruning of excess or unused

Chapter 14 Physical Development during Adolescence

neural pathways. Consistent with the "use it or lose it" principle, these changes have long-term implications for the cognitive functioning of the adolescent. Also, different parts of the brain mature at different points during adolescence, resulting in the increased influence of emotion over logic when it comes to adolescent decision making.

Key Terms

adolescence (p. 342)
anorexia nervosa (p. 357)
binge eating disorder (p. 357)
bulimia nervosa (p. 357)
estrogen (p. 346)
growth spurt (p. 343)
menarche (p. 345)
primary sex characteristics (p. 345)
puberty (p. 345)
secondary sex characteristics (p. 345)
testosterone (p. 346)

Cognitive Development during Adolescence

CHAPTER 15

Source: Monkey Business Images/Shutterstock.com.

Chapter Outline

COGNITIVE DEVELOPMENT

Beyond Concrete Operational Thinking

Moral Development: Beliefs about Justice and Care

Information-Processing Features of Adolescent Thought

The Influence of School

Focusing Questions

- To what extent are adolescents capable of abstract reasoning?
- How does cognitive development affect adolescents' knowledge and beliefs about their identities and about morality?
- How do adolescents show improved information processing in everyday activities?
- What cognitive and social effects do school and work have on adolescent development?

COGNITIVE DEVELOPMENT

Teenagers' growing cognitive competencies broaden the horizons of their world substantially. For example, the question "What if the United States went to war again when I'm older?" is more meaningful to an adolescent than to a child, even though both are equally inexperienced with the realities of war. So is the question "What if I had been born really poor or fabulously rich?" Adolescents can imagine what these situations might be like even though they have not experienced them in a concrete way. In general, thinking about the possible creates a new skill for speculating about important events and guessing about daily experiences (Keating & Sasse, 1996). It also stimulates adolescents to daydream or fantasize about their actions and feelings. And it helps them to make more astute inferences about human motivations ("Perhaps she did that because . . .") and to critique their own and others' actions.

Psychologists have explained and interpreted these new talents from two major points of view. The first is the *cognitive developmental viewpoint,* often associated with the work of Piaget. The second is the more recent approach of *information-processing theory,* which analyzes human thinking as a complex storage, retrieval, and organizing system for information, much like a computer. Both theories have been discussed elsewhere in this book (see especially Chapter 2); here we focus on how they relate to adolescence in particular.

Beyond Concrete Operational Thinking

formal operational thought Thinking based on previously acquired concrete mental operations and involving hypothetical reasoning and attention to the structure or form of ideas.

During adolescence, many teenagers go beyond the *concrete operational thought* described in Chapters 6 and 8 and begin developing a more abstract way of thinking called **formal operational thought**. Piaget (1983) saw this new operational thinking emerging around age eleven in many though not all adolescents. This new form of thinking frees individuals from reasoning only about the here-and-now, and allows them to be more fully logical and systematic in analyzing ideas. When using formal operational thought, individuals show some combination of three skills: they can imagine the possible rather than being limited to the real, they use scientific reasoning, and they combine ideas skillfully. Although these skills represent cognitive advances over the concrete thinking of childhood, it is important to note that they are not necessarily the "final," most mature forms of cognitive development. Later research indicates that there is a wide range of variance with how, when, and how often adolescents and young adults use formal operation thinking (Keating, 2004; Kuhn, 2008). Some teenagers and young adults never develop formal operational thought at all, and as we will see in later discussions of adult thinking (Chapters 12, 14, and 16), other kinds of thinking develop later in life that might best be called "wisdom." Before we get to those chapters, though, let us look in more detail at the main features of formal operational drought.

Possibilities versus Realities

Formal thought involves attention to possibilities rather than merely to actual realities. A parent discovers this when presenting a problem to be solved by her two children, ages nine and fifteen. When asked how to get the cable television signal working again, the nine-year-old said call the cable company, while the fifteen-year-old offered three possible fixes (like checking the cable hook-up, rebooting the system, checking the input device on the TV) that could be tried before calling cable company help line. All offerings were

Many teenagers become able to solve problems scientifically. But like these students in a biology laboratory class—and like most adults—they still need ample concrete experiences to support their abstract thinking. It is also common for them to have trouble using scientific thought outside a structured school situation.
Source: Miles Studio/Shutterstock.com.

possible solutions; the difference was that the younger child, using concrete operational thought, saw one option, while the teenager, using formal operational thought, imagined multiple solutions and their outcomes when reasoning through the problem. Even though the teenager is not a "cable repair-person," she is knowledgeable about electronics from personal experience, and more importantly, understands that there is more than one solution to any problem. In fact, this young adolescent is approaching the problem more scientifically than her younger brother, utilizing the second new skill developed at this stage.

Scientific Reasoning

Formal thought also involves scientific reasoning, the same kind psychologists use in designing many of their studies of human development. This quality reveals itself when adolescent students must solve some problem systematically. Piaget called this newly developed ability *hypothetical-deductive reasoning*, thinking that involves forming a hypothesis, testing possible solutions, and making judgments about the outcomes (Inhelder & Piaget, 1958). For example, how do youngsters in an art class figure out methods for mixing basic colors of paint to produce various intermediate shades and other colors? Those capable of formal operations in effect design an experiment to test all the available combinations of colors. They form hypotheses, or hunches, about how certain colors affect each other when mixed. Then they try out their hypotheses by mixing each basic color with every other basic color, being careful to try every possibility. By carefully observing the results of this procedure, they can draw logical conclusions about how to mix colors. This procedure in effect uses the scientific method.

The major difference with using this skill compared to a concrete operational child is the systematic way the older teen works toward a solution. A younger child would play around with the paint, mixing colors as well, but doing so in a more random and haphazard manner, most likely taking little formal notice of the results of her random actions. A precocious ten-year-old, familiar with painting, may solve the problem, but it is more likely this solution is a blend of experience and memory, rather than hypothetical-deductive reasoning. Even very bright kids in middle childhood do not use combinatorial thinking with the skill and persistence of a teen who is capable of formal operational thought.

Logical Combination of Ideas

The third feature of formal operational thought involves combining ideas logically. Unlike less cognitively mature children, formal thinkers can hold several ideas in mind at once and combine or integrate them in logical ways. When asked to explain why some students perform better in school than others do, concrete operational thinkers are likely to latch on to one reason or another: "Some kids are smarter" or "Some kids work harder." In contrast, formal operational thinkers often give combinations of reasons, as this first-year college student did:

> Well, I think it depends. Sometimes it pays just to be smart. But it also helps to work hard—except when the teacher doesn't notice. Some kids do better because they have taken courses before in the same area. Your first class in literature is likely to be harder than your fifth class in that subject.

As this example shows, the ability to combine ideas sometimes makes formal operational thinkers qualify their opinions more than preformal operational thinkers do. The world is no longer black and white. It has many more shades of gray for the adolescent than it does for a concrete operational thinker.

Cognitive Development Beyond Formal Thought

Piaget and other psychologists have identified formal, or abstract, thought as a major achievement of the adolescent years. But for most human beings, it may not be the final or highest cognitive achievement. One clue to this possibility comes from adolescents themselves: some teenagers overuse logical thinking when they first achieve facility with it (Leadbetter, 1991). They may believe all problems, including ambiguous ones such as achieving world peace, can be solved by the proper application of rational principles and careful reasoning. Teenagers may fail to notice that some problems by nature resist the application of general logic and may inherently have multiple, partial solutions. Later, as adults, they will take a more ad hoc, pragmatic approach to most problem solving (Sinnott, 1998). Additionally, the use of formal operational skills may not prove helpful when applied to problems or situations that are more emotional than logical or rational.

Consider Ana, a twelfth-grader who recently has begun a sexual relationship with her boyfriend. Ana gets along well with her parents, and respects their values. She knows they will worry and feel hurt if they learn of her sexual intimacy. She further believes that, generally, friends and family should have no secrets. By continuing her sexual activities, she seems to be violating this principle. On the other hand, she and her boyfriend regard their behavior as a personal and private matter, and she worries that telling her parents would violate this privacy, which she also considers her right. Telling her parents might also create a lot of bad feelings among Ana, her boyfriend, and her parents. In this case, her principles do not seem to point her toward a good solution: Ana believes that no matter what she does, somebody will get hurt, some ethical principle will be violated, or both.

Ana's situation suggests the importance of nonrational choices or judgments in solving real-life problems. Like Ana, many people may wish to be reasonable; that is, they may wish to rely on formal logic and may even believe they use it a lot. But in practice, most people use formal logic consistently only when solving academic problems posed by teachers, especially when the problems are deliberately scientific in nature (Bartsch, 1993). Less systematic reasoning serves as well or better for solving daily problems.

For older adolescents, the cognitive challenge consists of converting formal reasoning from a goal in itself to a *tool* used for broader purposes and tailored to the problems at hand (Myers, 1993). Ana cannot reach a sound decision about informing her parents of her sexual activities if she focuses on formal principles about truthfulness and privacy to the exclusion of more personal facts, which in this case include her knowledge of her boyfriend's and her own parents' probable responses and feelings. Taking these circumstances into account leads to the "best," or most mature, solution, but it may not lead to a solution that is fully logical in Piaget's sense. As adolescents grow into young adults, this sort of postformal thought becomes more common.

Implications of the Cognitive Developmental Viewpoint

As indicated earlier, formal operations begin developing early in adolescence and are fully formed by the end of the high school years (Piaget, 1983). All teenagers supposedly develop wide-ranging thinking abilities that have a formal, abstract nature and apply to many specific experiences and daily problems. In reality, however, the actual cognitive performances of adolescents fail to conform to this picture in several ways. First, a majority of adolescents (and even adults) use formal thinking inconsistently or even fail to use it at all (Lakoff, 1994). In explaining why a car is not working properly, for example, many adolescents and adults merely describe the car's symptoms: "The brakes are making a weird noise" or "It won't shift into third gear." An adolescent must have both an *experience base* and a *skill base* to mechanically resolve the problem using a structured and logical approach to the problem (Flavell et al., 1993). Yet, the inconsistency remains when this skilled teenage mechanic has difficulty applying the same logic and reason in his English classroom when trying to write a persuasive essay on gun control or on the soccer field when trying to devise strategies to neutralize an exceptionally skilled midfielder.

It seems, then, that formal operational thought does describe adolescents' thinking, but only partially or intermittently. Formal thought helps teenagers to argue with their parents more skillfully than they could as children, thereby contributing to the stereotype

> **What Do You Think?**
>
> Outside of school- or job-related tasks, most people actually use formal operational thinking rather little in their everyday lives. How much do *you* actually use it? Think of a situation other than school (shopping, visiting a friend, cooking) in which you need to use abstract thinking to function effectively. What does your answer imply about the place of formal thought in adolescents' overall development?

of teenagers as being relatively "rebellious." Formal thought also makes teenagers more skillful at cultivating friendships, potential dates, and social contacts; now they can imagine and anticipate the consequences of various friendly (and unfriendly) strategies. And formal thought means teenagers are more ready than children are to grapple with philosophical and abstract topics at school; literary analysis can now begin to make sense, for example, and so can at least some theoretical concepts in science. The "Working With" interview describes how these changes look from the point of view of one high school mathematics teacher, Jerry Acton.

Moral Development: Beliefs about Justice and Care

As adolescents move into adulthood and gradually develop formal thought, allowing them to reason with concepts of greater complexity and abstract thinking, they also develop a personal **morality**, or sensitivity to and knowledge of what is right and wrong. Moral thinking develops in two ways: in the form of increasingly logical and abstract principles related to fairness and justice and in the form of increasingly sophisticated ways of caring about the welfare of friends, family, and self (Noam & Wren, 1993). Each of these trends is somewhat related to gender: boys tend to emphasize ethical thinking about justice rather abstractly, and girls typically emphasize an ethics of care. But the gender difference is not large; most individuals develop both kinds of ethical thinking to a significant extent. Lawrence Kohlberg (1963; Kohlberg et al., 1983) developed a major theory of moral development constructed around the issues of fairness and justice, while Carol Gilligan (1982) looked at the ethics of care as the basis for moral development in women. Both are stage theories in the cognitive developmental tradition, reminiscent of Piaget's approach to cognitive development.

morality Sensitivity to and knowledge about what is right and wrong.

Kohlberg's Six Stages of Moral Judgment

Lawrence Kohlberg proposed six stages of moral judgment that develop slowly across three levels, well into middle adulthood (Kohlberg & Hersh, 1977; Schrader, 1990). The stages were derived initially from interviews of boys aged ten, thirteen, and sixteen, but later research included adolescent females. The interviews were conducted in much the same style as Piaget's classic interviews about cognitive development: Children and adults of various ages responded individually to hypothetical stories that contained moral dilemmas. Kohlberg, like Piaget, believed that moral development occurred in a stagelike fashion and was based on an individual's level of cognitive development; over time, as cognitive abilities change, one's moral reasoning will also change.

Kohlberg identified three distinct levels of moral reasoning. Level 1 was *preconventional reasoning*, based on one's automatic acceptance of cultural rules of right and wrong, and the perception of the consequences (rewards or punishments) that may result from one's actions. Good behaviors are those that are rewarded, while a behavior is reasoned to be bad if punishment follows that action. Level 2 was defined as involving *conventional reasoning*. At this level, reasoning is less egocentric and embraces the expectations of others important to the individual, including family, school, and community. What is considered right is whatever conforms to the rules or values established by society at the macro level and the family at the micro level. Level 3 of moral development identified by Kohlberg was *postconventional reasoning*. Moral values, or

Chapter 15 Cognitive Development during Adolescence

WORKING WITH Jerry Acton, Math and Science Teacher

Blending the Social and Emotional with the Cognitive

Jerry Acton teaches math, chemistry, and physics in high school. I wanted to interview him to learn more about how students think about these traditionally "cognitive" subjects. What I learned, though, was that success in these subjects depended heavily on social and emotional factors—on students' attitudes and motivations, and not just on their thinking abilities as such. The blending of the domains of development was especially evident in Jerry's tenth-grade math class, the one we spent most time discussing.

Kelvin: *I've heard a lot of generalizations about math—stereotypes about learning it, so to speak. I've heard that math is inherently abstract, for example, and that it's very sequentially organized, and that you have to be willing to work independently if you want to do well in math. What do you think about these ideas? Do they explain why some students do better in math than others? Tell me about your own classes.*

Jerry: For my classes, I would say that *maturity* makes the biggest difference. Maybe it's because these are tenth-graders—people who have just arrived at senior high school and are still getting used to it. The more successful students in math classes are the ones who are the most mature.

Kelvin: *What do you mean by "mature"?*

Jerry: I mean the ones who are prepared to come to class to work, to listen, to ask questions, and to do work in class, as opposed to coming to class because it is a convenient place to socialize with friends. The mature ones already seem to see value and usefulness to math, without my having to persuade them of that idea.

Kelvin: *That makes it sound like there's not much need for you as the teacher—like students either choose to work or they don't, and there's not much you can do about it. Surely that's not what you mean?*

Jerry: Oh no, there's still lots to do! One thing I do to motivate the less self-motivated students is give them a structured environment: one where our tasks are predictable, where there's routine. With a good routine, they know what to expect and the tasks are organized into steps that they understand and can do. We always do mental math first, then review the day's homework, then start a new lesson, and so on. I find that variations from the format inevitably throw some students "off their stride," and less gets done.

Kelvin: *That reminds me of the sequencing idea. People sometimes say that you have to learn math concepts in a certain sequence or else you risk getting hopelessly lost in the long term. Is that true?*

Jerry: Yes, in a sense it *is* true. But teachers can do things to keep students from getting lost as a result. In our new curriculum, for example, we use "spiral sequencing," where we revisit topics periodically and give daily review in between visits. If you're sick for a whole week, you don't miss out altogether on a particular math topic. And all the teachers in my school now use cumulative testing, which gives students incentives for consolidating

---

what is right, are now considered independent of what an authority says is right. What is right is based on an individual's perception of universal moral principles apart from the group's rules or laws (Kohlberg & Hersh, 1977). Each of Kohlberg's three levels of moral development was subdivided into two stages, resulting in a model of moral reasoning that comprised six stages.

Table 15.1 summarizes the six proposed stages. The stages form a progression in two ways. First, earlier stages represent more egocentric thinking than later stages do. Second, earlier stages by their nature require more specific or concrete thinking than later stages do. For instance, in Stage 1 (called *heteronomous morality,* which focuses on punishment and obedience), a child makes no distinction between what he believes is right and what the world tells him is right; he simply accepts the perspectives of the authorities as his own, primarily to avoid punishment for doing wrong, or "being bad." By Stage 4 (social system orientation), when the child is an adolescent, he realizes that individuals vary in their points of view, but he still takes for granted the existing overall conventions of society as a whole. This stage is often referred to as the "law-and-order" stage because laws are needed to maintain the social order. He cannot yet imagine a society in which those

> **WORKING WITH** Jerry Acton, Math and Science Teacher
>
> **Blending the Social and Emotional with the Cognitive** *continued*
>
> what they know so that there are no "holes" in their math knowledge at the end of the course.
>
> **Kelvin:** *Still, by its nature, math must be pretty abstract, even in tenth grade.*
>
> **Jerry:** You're right about that. Especially in the course called "precalculus," which actually says in its advertising that it *is* abstract and is intended for students who already enjoy math. How do you offer concrete, hands-on activities related to factoring? What are the everyday uses for factoring? [*Smiles.*] Most students *do* learn better if you can make the material more down to earth and relate it to familiar activities.
>
> But I have found ways to move in that direction. This year we used graphing calculators, for example, which the students really enjoy. The calculators make it a lot easier to create graphs—much faster and less laborious. With the calculators, you can actually play around with graphing different functions instead of taking fifteen minutes just to draw one by hand. When we get tire computer lab set up properly, we'll be able to do even more.
>
> **Kelvin:** *Sounds like with the calculators, students could even work together. They could do problems and projects cooperatively.*
>
> **Jerry:** That's indeed the case. Students can do problems independently, for example, and then compare their results. We'll be able to do more joint work, in fact, when we get the computer lab set up.
>
> **Kelvin:** *I often think of math as being an especially "solitary" activity, not one that lends itself to working with others. Would you agree?*
>
> **Jerry:** I've found that there are ways for students in math to work together, like with the graphing calculators. Sometimes, in fact, I've actually had trouble with students cooperating *too* much; it seems like they're always wanting to consult with each other about how to do certain problems or about what the answers are. Then I wish they would function more independently of each other. A mix is best: cooperation combined and independence combined.
>
> **What Do You Think?**
>
> 1. Given Jerry Acton's comments, would you describe mathematical success as a "cognitive" skill, a "social" skill, or as some combination? Explain your reasoning.
> 2. Do you believe there is indeed truth in the stereotypes or expectations about mathematics that Kelvin expressed at the beginning of the interview? How would you qualify these ideas, taking into account both Jerry's comments and your own knowledge and beliefs?
> 3. Sometimes mathematics is traditionally thought of as a "boy's" subject more than a "girl's." Judging by Jerry's comments, do you think this is true for his class? Do you still think it could be true for mathematics students in general?

conventions might be purposely modified, for example, by passing laws or agreeing on new rules. Only by Stage 5 (the stage of social contract) and Stage 6 (the stage of universal principles) can he do so fully. At Stage 5, one understands that laws and authority can be questioned and that changes can be made for increased fairness and justice for the greater good of society. Stage 6—a level that few individuals exhibit—describes a person who has developed an independent moral code based on universal ethical principles, which may justify violating established laws to honor these principles.

In the school years, children most commonly show ethical reasoning at Stage 2, the instrumental-relativist orientation, but some may begin showing Stage 3 or 4 reasoning toward the end of this period (Colby & Kohlberg, 1987). For the majority of youth and adults, Stage 3 (interpersonal-conformity orientation) and Stage 4 (social system orientation) characterize their most advanced moral thinking. In Stage 3, a person's chief concern is with the opinions of her peers: an action is morally right if her immediate circle of friends says it is right. Often, this way of thinking leads to helpful actions, such as taking turns and sharing possessions. But often it does not, such as when friends decide to shoplift from a store or bully a kid at school who is perceived as weaker and more

TABLE 15.1 Kohlberg's Stages of Moral Judgment

Stage	Nature of Stage
Preconventional Level *(emphasis on avoiding punishments and getting awards)*	
Stage 1 Heteronomous morality; punishment and obedience orientation	Good is what follows externally imposed rules and rewards and is whatever avoids punishment
Stage 2 Instrumental-relativist orientation purpose; ethics of market exchange as it benefits the individual. "The "I'll scratch your back, if you scratch my back" orientation.	Good is whatever is agreeable to the individual and to anyone who gives or receives favors; no long-term loyalty
Conventional Level *(emphasis on social rules)*	
Stage 3 Interpersonal conformity; ethics of peer opinion, the "good boy" or "good girl" orientation	Good is whatever brings approval from friends as a peer group
Stage 4 Social system orientation: conformity to social system; ethics of law and order	Good is whatever conforms to existing laws, customs, and authorities
Postconventional Level *(emphasis on moral principles)*	
Stage 5 Social contract, legalistic orientation; ethics of social contract and individual rights	Good is whatever conforms to existing procedures for settling disagreements in society; the actual outcome is neither good nor bad
Stage 6 Universal-ethical principles orientation. Ethics of self-chosen universal principles	Good is whatever is consistent with personal, general moral principles

vulnerable. The desire to be a "good boy" or "good girl" is often defined by what the peer group determines is the right thing to do.

In Stage 4, the person shifts from concern with peers to concern with the opinions of community or society in the abstract: now something is right if the institutions approve. This broader source of moral judgment spares Stage 4 children from the occasional tyranny of friends' opinions; now they may refuse to sneak a smoke or to experiment with alcohol or drugs just because their friends urge them to do so. This change makes teenagers less *opportunistic* than children and less inclined to judge based on immediate rewards or punishments they experience personally. Instead, they evaluate actions on the basis of principles of some sort. For the time being, the principles are rather conventional; they are borrowed either from ideas expressed by immediate peers and their parents, or from socially accepted rules and principles, whatever they may be. If friends agree that premarital sex is permissible, many teenagers are likely to adopt this idea as their own, at least as a general principle. But if friends or family believe premarital sex is morally wrong, teenagers may adopt this alternative belief as a principle. (Note, however, that whether a teenager actually acts according to these principles is another matter. Moral action does not always follow from moral belief.)

postconventional moral judgment In Kohlberg's theory, an orientation to moral justice that develops beyond conventional rules and beliefs.

A few young adults develop **postconventional moral judgment**, meaning that for the first time ethical reasoning goes beyond the judgments society conventionally makes about right and wrong. Adolescents' growing ability to use abstract formal thought stimulates this development, though it does not guarantee it. Unlike schoolchildren, they can evaluate ethical ideas that *might* be right or wrong given certain circumstances that can only be imagined.

Issues in the Development of Moral Beliefs about Justice

As Figure 15.1 indicates, Kohlberg's six stages of moral judgment have held up well when tested on a wide variety of children, adolescents, and adults. The stages of moral thinking shown in Table 15.1 do seem to describe how moral judgment develops, at least when individuals focus on hypothetical dilemmas posed in stories. When presented with

FIGURE 15.1

Longitudinal Development of Moral Reasoning

In a longitudinal follow-up study of Kohlberg's original sample, Colby and her colleagues showed that participants showed consistent upward advances in moral reasoning with age. The graph shows the extent to which participants gave responses characteristic of each of Kohlberg's six stages from age ten through adulthood. With development, responses associated with the preconventional level (Stages 1 and 2) declined, whereas responses associated with the conventional level (Stages 3 and 4) increased. Few young adults moved to the postconventional level (Stages 5 and 6) of moral reasoning.

Source: Adapted from Colby et al., 1983.

stories about risky but fictional sexual behaviors, adolescents of both sexes evaluated the actions of the stories' characters in line with Kohlberg's stages (Jadack et al., 1995).

Even so, Kohlberg's theory of moral judgment leaves a number of important questions unanswered. One is whether the theory really recognizes the impact of prior knowledge on beliefs; another is whether the theory distinguishes clearly enough between conventions and morality. One especially important question has to do with gender differences: does Kohlberg's theory really describe the moral development of girls as well as that of boys?

Issue 1: Form versus Content of Moral Beliefs

Despite the theory's plausibility, a number of developmental psychologists have questioned important aspects of it. Can the form of ethical thinking really be separated from content to the degree Kohlberg proposes? Perhaps not. Some studies have found that when people reason about familiar situations, they tend to have more mature (that is, higher-stage) ethical responses (Lickona, 1991). For instance, children have a better sense of fairness about playing four-square on the playground than about whether to steal a drug for a spouse who is dying (one of Kohlberg's fictional dilemmas). In addition, young women think in more mature (more "developed") ways about ethical problems of special concern and familiarity to women, such as whether to engage in premarital sex or whether to have an abortion (Bollerud et al., 1990). To some extent, therefore, what someone thinks about affects the ethics she or he applies.

Issue 2: Conventions versus Morality

According to some psychologists, some inconsistencies in moral beliefs may arise because the theory does not fully distinguish between social conventions and morality (Nucci & Turiel, 1993). **Social conventions** refer to the arbitrary customs and agreements about behavior that members of society use, such as table manners and forms of greeting and dressing. *Morality,* as we already pointed out, refers to the weightier matters of justice and right and wrong. By nature, social conventions inevitably generate widespread agreement throughout society, whereas morality does not necessarily do so. Yet Kohlberg's six-stage theory glosses over these differences by defining some of its stages in terms of social conventions and others in terms of morality. Stage 4 (social system orientation), for example, seems to refer to social conventions as well as to moral matters, but Stage 5 (social contract orientation) refers only to moral judgment. It is also important to keep in mind that Kohlberg's focus was not delineating between social conventions and morality per se, but in viewing the moral reasoning used in commenting on the actions of people facing the fictional moral dilemmas.

social conventions Arbitrary customs and agreements about behavior that members of a society use.

Chapter 15 Cognitive Development during Adolescence

Issue 3: Gender Differences in Morality?

One especially important criticism of Kohlberg's theory of moral justice has to do with possible gender bias. Do Kohlberg's stages describe both genders equally well? And does his theory undervalue ethical attitudes that may develop more fully in girls and women than in boys and men? The best-known investigations of these questions have been pursued by one of Kohlberg's colleagues at Harvard, Carol Gilligan, and her associates.

Gilligan's Ethics of Care

According to Gilligan and others, boys and girls tend to view moral problems differently (Taylor, Gilligan, & Sullivan, 1995; Gordon, Benner, & Noddings, 1996). As they grow up, boys learn to think more often in terms of general ethical principles that they can apply to specific moral situations. They might learn that deception is bad in principle and thus evaluate a specific instance of deception of a friend against this generalization. The principles boys learn also tend to emphasize independence, autonomy, and the rights of others. This orientation biases boys to ignore or minimize others' possible needs. Perhaps reasoning that if a friend is at home sick with a cold, it may seem better to leave him alone until he gets better, rather than check on how well he is recovering.

Girls tend to develop a different sort of morality as they grow up. Instead of seeing moral judgment as a set of abstract principles to apply to specific situations, girls tend to develop an ethics of care, a view that integrates principles with the contexts in which judgments must be made. A girl therefore may have learned that deception is usually bad, but she may also reason that deception is ethical in certain circumstances, such as when a friend needs reassurance about the quality of a term paper that is actually mediocre but took a lot of time and effort to write. Viewing ethics in context grows out of a general concern for the needs of others more than for one's independence. A friend who is depressed therefore deserves a visit or a phone call; leaving her alone seems more like neglect than like respect for her autonomy. Table 15.2 summarizes Gilligan's stages of moral development.

These differences are only tendencies, not dramatic or sharply drawn gender differences. But they are enough, argues Gilligan, to make Kohlberg's theory seem to underestimate the moral development of girls and women. Concern with context and with others' needs causes girls to score closer to the middling, conventional levels of moral judgment, where peers' opinions matter most. When asked if a child should inform authorities about a friend who often shoplifts small items from a local department store, a girl is likely to give priority to one part of the problem in particular: that of balancing each person's views and needs in the particular situation. Doing so means wondering, among other things, whether informing will alienate peers not only from the shoplifter but also from the informer. On the other hand, it also means wondering whether keeping silent will make her risk losing the trust and respect of important adults, such as parents and teachers.

TABLE 15.2 Gilligan's Stages of Moral Development

Stage	Features
Stage 1 *Survival orientation*	Egocentric concern for self, lack of awareness of others' needs; "right" action is what promotes emotional or physical survival
Stage 2 *Conventional care*	Lack of distinction between what others want and what is right; "right" action is whatever pleases others best
Stage 3 *Integrated care*	Coordination or integration of needs of self and of others; "right" action takes account of self as well as others

Source: Gilligan (1982).

It also means considering the amount of emotional pain that will befall the shoplifting friend at the hands of either angry parents or the police. Taking all of these considerations into account can make the final decision seem hesitant, tentative, and apparently lacking in principle, whichever way the decision goes.

Reviews of moral judgment have qualified Gilligan's ideas somewhat but have also lent them support. When faced with hypothetical dilemmas, females show as much capacity as males to reason in terms of abstract ethical principles (Gilligan & Wiggins, 1987). When faced with real-life dilemmas, however, girls make different choices (Taylor et al., 1995). For example, adolescent girls who personally confront the decision of whether to engage in premarital intercourse often show more concern than do boys for the context in which they make their decisions and for the impact of their decisions on relationships with others. Gilligan's claims of gender bias in Kohlberg's stages have also proven to be unfounded; studies have shown females exhibiting higher levels of ethical reasoning than males using Kohlberg's stages (White, 1999). What appears consistent across both theories is that justice-oriented moral reasoning and needs/care-oriented moral reasoning takes time—years, in fact—to develop.

The Ethics of Care during Adolescence

As with the morality of justice, young people develop an ethics of care during adolescence, but like ethical justice, it remains somewhat conventional during the teenage years. During the school years, children develop significant concern about others' needs and welfare and begin viewing actions as good if the actions take others' needs and welfare into account (Larrabee, 1993). However, egocentrism persists in that teenagers often fail to distinguish between actions that merely *please* others and actions that are "right" in a deeper, ethical sense. For example, if parents will be pleased if their adolescent enrolls in complex science and mathematics courses in high school, doing so may seem "right" to the youngster, even if he has little interest or aptitude in those areas.

As with the ethics of justice, a few individuals move beyond conventional pleasing of others toward *integrated care,* in which the young person realizes that pleasing everyone is not always possible but it is important to balance everyone's needs, including her own (Larrabee, 1993). Deciding whether or not to take a part-time job, for example, now becomes a matter of reconciling the impact of the job on family, friends, and self. Some individuals may gain (the teenager herself may earn more money and make new friends), but others may lose (parents and friends may see less of her). The gains and losses must be balanced, rather than viewed completely as gains.

Overall, then, the moralities of justice and care begin taking into account a broader array of both interpersonal circumstances and general principles than was true during the school years. Teenagers more often refer to principles in evaluating actions, although they still do not always act on their principles. Often they also regard pleasing others as ethically good or right, even though they are learning to deal with the impossibility of pleasing everyone perfectly. Like many other cognitive developments, these changes result from adolescents' growing capacities to reason abstractly.

The Development of Social Cognition

Most developmental psychologists agree that the new cognitive skills of adolescents have important effects on their **social cognition**, or their knowledge and beliefs about interpersonal and social matters. Moral beliefs are one example of social cognition; in this section we look at three others: egocentrism and its expression as beliefs in an imaginary audience and a personal fable.

social cognition Knowledge and beliefs about interpersonal and social matters.

Adolescent Egocentrism

When adolescents first begin to reason abstractly, they often become overly impressed with this skill; it seems to them that anything can be solved "if only people would be reasonable" (that is, logical). This attitude can make teenagers idealistic and keep them from appreciating the practical limits of logic (Bowers, 1995). They may wonder why no one has ever "realized" that world war might be abolished simply by explaining to all the world powers the obvious dangers of war. Or they may wonder why their parents have not noticed the many "errors" they have made in raising children.

The development of formal thought also leads to a new kind of confusion between an adolescent's own thoughts and those of others. This confusion of viewpoints amounts to a form of egocentrism. Unlike the egocentrism of preschoolers, which is based on concrete problems, **adolescent egocentrism** concerns more abstract thoughts and problems.

adolescent egocentrism The tendency of adolescents to perceive the world (and themselves) from their own perspective.

The Imaginary Audience

Adolescent egocentrism sometimes shows itself in teenagers' preoccupation with the reactions of others. Thirteen-year-olds often fail to differentiate between how they feel about themselves and how others feel about them. Instead, they act as though they are performing for an **imaginary audience**, one that is as concerned with their appearance and behavior as they themselves are (Elkind, 1985).

Teenagers also reveal concern with an imaginary audience through *strategic interactions* with their peers, encounters that aim to either reveal or conceal personal information indirectly. The almost universal use of the Internet and social media by adolescents today serves as a means of interacting with real people who make up an imaginary audience. Teens use Facebook, Instagram, and Twitter posts to solicit "likes" or "followers" that create the perception of popularity to the individual and to others. In day-to-day encounters with peers, the imaginary audience can make life miserable for a self-conscious teen. Can you recall going to school the day after you got your hair cut, or the day a pimple appeared on your nose or forehead? If you were like most teenagers, you were certain that everyone would notice and that they would tease and make fun of you. Throughout the day, you likely focused on wanting to go home or hide in the restroom.

imaginary audience A characteristic of young adolescents in which they act as though they are performing for an audience and believe that others are as concerned with their appearance and behavior as they themselves are.

We all have experienced embarrassing moments. It is just that, during adolescence, they seem so much worse due to the natural changes inherent with the age, but also due to the existence of the imaginary audience. Alberts, Elkind, and Ginsburg (2007) acknowledge that the imaginary audience does not disappear after adolescence—adults are also egocentric. It is just that during the teenage years, it is harder to differentiate between our own perspective and the view that others have of us and of their own world.

The Personal Fable

As a result of their egocentrism, teenagers often believe in a **personal fable**, the notion that their own lives embody a special story that is heroic and completely unique. For example, one high school student may be convinced that no love affair has ever reached

personal fable Adolescents' belief that their own lives embody a special story that is heroic and completely unique.

Adolescent egocentrism is often expressed as a preoccupation with how others respond and as a belief in personal invulnerability. This girl (left photo) may be spending a lot of time choosing clothes because she is concerned about what others will think of how she looks. The boy (right photo) may be willing to risk a broken limb in skateboarding because he does not really believe that he can be injured.
Sources: (left) dean bertoncelj/Shutterstock.com; (right) bikeriderlondon/Shutterstock.com.

the romantic heights of his involvement with a classmate. Another may believe she is destined for great fame and fortune by virtue of (what she considers to be) her unparalleled combination of charm and academic talent.

In experiencing these feelings and ideas, adolescents fail to realize how other individuals feel about them as well (Alberts et al., 2007). Early in adolescence, they still have only limited empathy, or the ability to understand reliably the abstract thoughts and feelings of others and compare those thoughts and feelings with their own. In fact, much of adolescence consists of developing these social skills. So does most of adulthood, for that matter; we never really finish learning how to understand others or comparing our own experiences with those of others. But adolescence is the time when most people begin learning to consider other viewpoints in relation to their own and developing complex ideas about moral, political, and religious questions, among others, in response.

However, not all teenagers seem equally egocentric, and even those who do show this quality only when compared to adults, not to younger children. Investigations of adolescents' belief in an imaginary audience show that teenagers are just as likely to develop greater empathy or interpersonal sensitivity during this developmental period as they are to develop greater self-centeredness (Lapsley, 1991). Accurate awareness of others' opinions about oneself apparently develops alongside, and sometimes even instead of, self-conscious preoccupation with others' opinions. The relative balance between these two developments depends, among other things, on the quality of relationships between parents and the adolescent: closer and more supportive relationships lead to greater realism and less self-consciousness.

Information-Processing Features of Adolescent Thought

As we saw in Chapter 2, information-processing theory sees human cognition as a complex storage and retrieval system, governed largely by an "executive" control system that transfers information between working and long-term memory and organizes information for more efficient and meaningful handling and retrieval. When cognition is viewed this way, development consists largely of overcoming the bottlenecks in processing information, especially those caused by the limited capacities of the executive and short-term memory. As children mature into adolescents, they develop strategies for taking in, organizing, and remembering larger amounts of information more quickly and with less effort. The most important of these strategies are included in Figure 15.2 and explained more fully next.

Improved Capacity to Process Information

Typically, an adolescent can deal with, or process, more information than a child can (Gathercole et al., 2004). A first-grader may remember three or four random digits (3 9 5 1), but a teenager usually can remember six or seven. And when a first-grader asks an adult how

FIGURE 15.2

Developmental Changes in Information Processing

Although the basic nature of information processing remains the same from childhood to adolescence, important changes occur in several features, as the figure indicates. Working memory may increase in capacity, control processes become more efficient, and long-term memory contains more specific knowledge about problem solving, or "how to think."

> **What Do You Think?**
>
> Suppose you are starting your first job in a helping profession, such as nursing or teaching. How much would you want your work to be guided by an ethics of justice and how much by an ethics of care? Exchange your feelings about this question with a classmate or a friend.

to spell a word, he can hold only two or three letters in his mind at a time; the adult has to dole them out singly or in very small groups *(LO . . . CO . . . MO . . . TI. . . VE)*. A teenager, however, can more often encounter much longer groupings of letters and still reconstruct the word accurately.

Several developmental changes allow for this increase in processing capacity during adolescence. As mentioned earlier in this chapter, changes in the physiology of the brain contribute to more efficient processing of information. The streamlined neural networks that result from pruning and the myelination process are especially important changes when it comes to processing information in working memory. Because the capacity of working memory is limited with respect to quantity of information it can hold and length of time that it can be accessed, *speed of processing* is a significant determinant of how much information can be handled at one time and, therefore, the degree of complexity of the problems or situations that can be addressed at any given time (Demetriou et al., 2002).

Metacognition (awareness and regulation of one's own thought processes) also improves during adolescence, enabling teenagers to select increasingly more effective strategies for handling whatever cognitive challenges they face (Kuhn, 2009). For example, if an adolescent has an exam in one of his classes next week, he will choose a strategy that will help him best prepare for that exam based upon his knowledge about the exam structure (Will it be a multiple-choice or an essay exam?), the teacher (Does the teacher usually expect lots of details, or does the teacher focus on larger, key constructs?), his desired grade (How much time and effort will it take to get an "A" on this test?), and his current level of mastery of the content (Does the material make sense to some extent, or do I need to invest considerably more effort to comprehend the content?). And then, while studying, the adolescent's metacognitive abilities will allow him to assess his level of mastery and to change tactics if his approach to studying is not producing the desired results. Metacognition impacts processing capacity in that the adolescent does not allocate limited cognitive resources to information he already understands, and he can invoke strategies that will reduce the volume of information he needs to process at one time (e.g., mnemonics or other strategies for organizing or clustering information reduce the cognitive "load" posed by the information being processed).

Increases in *attention* also enhance information-processing capacity during adolescence. Compared to children, adolescents are able to stay on task longer, select more relevant information to the task at hand, and inhibit intrusive or distracting thoughts as they tackle challenging problems (Luna et al., 2013). Looking back at Figure 15.2, you can see how many elements of the model of information processing undergo significant changes during adolescence that result in their achievement of almost adult-like sophistication in their problem-solving abilities. What limits the information-processing capabilities of adolescents, when compared to adults, is their relative lack of expertise and experience.

Expertise in Specific Domains of Knowledge

- *Jerry can play the piano well, but his math skills are so-so.*

- *Marni cannot carry a tune, much less play one on the piano. But her math skills are excellent.*

- *Jamal has a real talent for drawing cartoon figures. But he has learned not to make or display drawings in class, because a few of his teachers regard them as "doodling."*

Like Jerry, Marni, and Jamal, many adolescents have begun to be comparative experts in specific domains of knowledge or skill. The domains may or may not have much to do with school learning, and therefore may sometimes go unnoticed by friends or teachers. Typically, the expertise results from years of interest in and practice with a skill or area of knowledge. In some cases, the area of expertise continues to develop during adulthood. Any further development that may occur will depend on whether key people continue to support the development and what alternative demands are made on the individual's time and attention.

The emergence of expertise reframes the issues about general intelligence discussed in Chapter 12, with regard to middle childhood. During adolescence, the issue is now about the nature and breadth of specialized knowledge. Instead of representing an all-purpose competence, **expertise** refers to the long, slow acquisition of specific knowledge, along with improvements in how the knowledge is organized. In the long term, highly developed expertise resembles what we often think of as a general "ability" (Sternberg, 1998). The difference between expertise and "ability" is a focus on completion versus ongoing development: *expertise* tends to refer to knowledge and skills that are still growing, whereas *ability* implies knowledge and skills that have already been formed.

expertise Specialized experience in specific domains of knowledge that enables efficient and effective performance and is not hampered by age.

A place where ability and expertise merge may be viewed in the area of problem solving. Experts in a chosen area of interest or ability, even in adolescence, show identifiable differences in how they solve problems, compared to their peers with less expertise. Teens who are considered effective problem solvers are better at (1) focusing their attention on what is important, (2) holding more information in both working and long-term memory by chunking information into procedural knowledge that is easily retrieved, (3) taking more time to analyze a problem initially, and (4) monitoring their own performance and progress (Woolfolk, 2013). Here we see that, even during adolescence, the executive functions in the prefrontal cortex of the brain can show the maturity to balance the influences of the limbic system, especially in areas where the teen is highly interested and personally motivated. Referring again to Figure 15.2, notice how much the components of "expertise" focus on the relationship between working memory and long-term memory. A fast and fluid relationship between these two memory stores, governed by enhanced executive functioning (i.e., "control processes"), is central to the thought processes of experts.

In areas outside of one's zone of expertise, an adolescent's performance may be no better than average. Studies of expertise in adulthood show the nature of this sort of competence especially clearly (Gregg & Leinhardt, 1995). A highly trained physicist knows many more concepts about physics than a beginner does, but not necessarily more about geography, English grammar, or other areas of knowledge. A mathematician knows countless formulas and solution methods, thanks to years of experience in learning them, but her talent is no guarantee that she can solve problems about business management, classroom teaching, or nursing. This is also true in athletics: an outstanding baseball player may not be as proficient in golf, or a talented figure skater may be no better at skiing than a person first taking up the sport. The sort of "earned" competence such individuals show becomes increasingly prominent in adulthood.

The Influence of School

In modern industrialized countries, school plays a formal role in developing certain forms of expertise, while at the same time introducing young people to new social relationships. From the point of view of adolescents, school is *both* a cognitive and social experience, and activities often serve both purposes at once. Participating in the school's chess club may improve your cognitive functioning and problem-solving abilities, but it may also facilitate making new friends. Listening attentively to a math teacher may help clarify some part of the math curriculum and result in a good grade, but it also may result in the teacher becoming your advocate due to your work ethic. Participating on a school sport team may enhance your athletic abilities, but it may also improve your self-discipline and group functioning skills. Unfortunately, the converse can occur: an activity may fail either to teach, to provide desirable social contact, or both. To clarify the connections between the cognitive and social effects of

> **What Do You Think?**
>
> Think of an activity or area of knowledge in which you consider yourself a relative expert. How much of your expertise has resulted from knowing a lot of specific facts about the area? How much has resulted from organizing your knowledge better than other people do? Compare your opinions with a classmate's or a friend's, especially if she or he is an expert in areas other than yours.

schooling, we look at each area separately in this section. As you will see, each area influences the other significantly, though not always in ways teachers and parents desire.

Cognitive Effects of Schooling

School influences adolescents' thinking through both a formal curriculum and an informal curriculum. The *formal curriculum* refers to a school's official program: the courses offered, the books required for reading, and the assignments expected for completion. The *informal curriculum* includes the unplanned activities and relationships that influence students' academic knowledge and motivation to learn—their relationships with teachers, for example, or the "gossip" and other tips related to schoolwork picked up from classmates. Both the formal and the informal curriculum are extremely diverse. One emphasizes the cognitive skills that may influence or impede success, while the other is based on how a student performs using noncognitive skills like optimism, resilience, and grit (Tough, 2012). What one student learns can be quite unlike what another learns because of differences in students' experiences in school as well as differences in their personal backgrounds.

In spite of the diversity that normally exists among teachers, students, and classroom experiences, most schools *seek* to develop students' broad ability at **critical thinking**, the ability to solve problems and to think reflectively and creatively about ideas and issues, usually for purposes of making decisions or taking actions (Keating & Sasse, 1996). Schools are also recognizing that critical-thinking skills can be encouraged when understanding how students use preferences for learning that Howard Gardner (1993b) identified as multiple intelligence or seem to excel in the noncognitive skills mentioned earlier. Whether they actually succeed is another question, which we will return to soon. First, though, let's look at what critical thinking involves and what, therefore, may be required to encourage it among students.

critical thinking Reflection or thinking about complex issues, usually to make decisions or take actions.

The Nature of Critical Thinking

Critical thinking is a broad, practical skill: it can help a person figure out why an unfamiliar appliance broke down, how to compose a term paper, how to resolve a conflict with a friend, how to decide what kind of career path to pursue, or how to evaluate the quality and the source of information provided. As these examples suggest, not all critical thinking occurs in school settings, and this fact poses a challenge to teachers and curriculum experts whose access to students generally is limited to classrooms and related environments.

What does critical thinking involve? Educators and psychologists have analyzed it in various ways, but usually point out the following elements (King & Kitchener, 1994):

1. *Basic operations of reasoning* To think critically, a person must be able to classify, generalize, deduce conclusions, and perform other logical steps mentally.

2. *Domain-specific knowledge* To deal with a problem, a person must know something about its topic or content. To evaluate a proposal for a new, fairer tax system, a person must know something about the existing tax system. To resolve a personal conflict, a person has to know something about the person with whom he is having the conflict.

3. *Metacognitive knowledge* (knowledge about how human thinking works, including one's own) Effective critical thinking requires a person to monitor when she really understands an idea, know when she needs new information, and predict how easily

she can gather and learn that information. In other words, she has to be able think about her own thinking!

4. *Values, beliefs, and dispositions* Thinking critically means valuing fairness and objectivity. It means having confidence that thinking does in fact lead to solutions. It also means having a persistent and reflective disposition when thinking.

Interestingly, research has found that students themselves understand these elements of critical thinking (Nichols et al., 1995). Furthermore, compared to grade-school children, adolescents regard critical thinking as a fairer and more appropriate purpose of schooling.

Programs to Foster Critical Thinking

Educators have devised a number of programs intended to foster the qualities needed for critical thinking (French & Rhodes, 1992), many of which serve adolescents. The programs differ in their particulars: they last for various lengths of time, emphasize different thinking skills, and draw on content from different areas of the standard school curriculum. Some programs are integrated into the curriculum, meaning they replace a traditional course in some subject area; others are taught separately and draw content from several areas at once.

But experts do agree on several general principles that enhance the quality of programs that teach critical thinking. First, critical thinking is best taught directly and explicitly. Critical thinking does not develop on its own by unconscious osmosis, so to speak (Keefe & Walberg, 1992). Watching the teacher or a classmate think critically does not guarantee that a student will become a better thinker. Neither does giving a student a lot of practice in simple mental operations, such as basic addition or simple logical puzzles.

Second, good programs for teaching thinking offer lots of practice at solving actual problems. Merely describing the elements of critical thinking (as this text is doing) does not turn students into skillful thinkers. To accommodate the need for practice, the most successful educational programs last at least a full academic year and sometimes also weave the thinking skills into other, related courses to extend the effects of the program still further.

Third, successful programs try to create an environment explicitly conducive to critical thinking. Typically, they expect teachers to model important critical-thinking skills themselves, such as thinking out loud while they explain a solution to a problem. The programs also expect teachers to convey confidence in students' ability to think while providing constructive, explicit criticism of ideas, whether their own or those of the students. For example, one technique is to invite individual students to temporarily act as teacher or constructive critic (Slavin, 1995). Teaching critical-thinking skills is not a passive enterprise. It requires active learning, timely feedback, and increasingly more challenging experiences to keep the students and teachers engaged.

No Child Left Behind Act

A fairly recent and controversial national reform effort to enhance the cognitive impact of schooling on children and adolescents likely had an impact on your school experiences if you are a traditional-aged college student. In 2002, the U.S. Congress passed the *No Child Left Behind Act (NCLB)*. This act was designed to improve school performance overall and to increase the level of academic proficiency in high school graduates. The law specified detailed educational benchmarks for many grades and mandated standardized testing to assess the learning of every child (however, many children, school districts, and even entire states have been exempted from these standards). The law has faced much criticism on several fronts. Mandating that students pass tests simply forces teachers to "teach to the tests" (Koretz, 2008); anxiety levels in students are greatly increased (Samuels, 2005); some students—especially those in low-income districts or those with learning disabilities—are greatly disadvantaged under the structure of the standardized tests (Yeh, 2008).

The long-term impact of the No Child Left Behind Act is still not clear, and the debate about its merits continues, yet educators and the public support the increases in funding that the law brought to many districts, the attempt to gather objective measures of school and student success, the emphasis on teacher training, the adoption of more effective pedagogies, and the heightened national interest in improving K–12 education in the United States (Sunderman, 2008). In December 2015, NCLB was replaced with the Every Student Succeeds Act (ESSA), which maintains the funding increases of NCLB while providing more local control over educations systems and reducing some of the testing burden placed on schools and educators by NCLB (U.S. Department of Education, 2015).

Whatever differences may exist in programs designed to improve the educational experiences of adolescents, programs that teach critical thinking develop greater expertise in academic disciplines draw on the spirit, if not the literal, research findings, of several strands of cognitive theory concerning the adolescent years. One strand is Piagetian, with its concern for how logic and reasoning gradually develop. Another is information-processing theory, with its focus on specific ways of organizing ideas and coordinating new ideas with preexisting ones. A third strand is the concern with the social and cultural context of cognitive development in adolescence: how people and settings affect a young person's thinking. As the "A Multicultural View" feature indicates, cultural differences and misunderstandings can complicate teachers' efforts to encourage critical-thinking skills and content mastery in the classroom. Social influences are so important, in fact, that we discuss them more fully in the next section.

Social Effects of Schooling

For early adolescents, the period following graduation from elementary school can be one of increased social and emotional stress: their new school is usually larger, teachers are more numerous, new friendships must be formed, and students must adjust to being the youngest, least knowledgeable members of the school community. In the United States, schools have tried to address these concerns with transitions and school buildings that are more developmentally appropriate. The older model of a K–6 elementary school, followed by junior high school for grades 7–9, and ending with a grades 10–12 high school, while still used in some areas, is no longer the norm. Research in the 1990s on the junior high school model indicated a need for change. Some of the studies found that in the course of their first year of junior high, students report less positive attitudes about school, poorer achievement, and lower levels of participation in extracurricular activities (Eccles et al., 1996; Finders, 1997; Otis et al., 2005). New students (especially girls) report feeling less positive about themselves (Benner & Graham, 2009), and instances of both bullying and being bullied—often with sexual overtones—are widespread (Lee et al., 1996). A new structural model—including less disruptive school transitions—needed to be instituted, one that was both developmentally sound and safe for young adolescents.

middle school School designed to meet the needs of young adolescents, and usually spanning approximately fifth- through eighth-grade and enrolling students of about age ten through thirteen.

A major response to these stresses has been to create **middle schools**, which are deliberately organized to take students' developmental needs into account. Middle schools typically span fifth through eighth grades. They share features both of elementary schools, such as smaller size and fewer class changes per day, and of high school, such as specialization in class subjects. A primary feature of middle schools is the assignment of students to a "home-base" or homeroom class that students visit every day and where the teacher acts as an adviser to help them to navigate the new challenges of postelementary education (Galassi et al., 1997). Studies of the impact of middle schools suggest that these changes can indeed help young adolescents adjust—but only if the teachers actually understand the students' developmental needs and adjust their ways of relating to students accordingly. In general, adjustment is more likely to succeed if teachers work together collegially supporting one another's efforts to innovate in classroom practices (Louis et al., 1996; Peterson et al., 1996).

Dropping Out of High School

Despite the efforts of schools and parents to help students make the transition to high school, some adolescents may not make the adjustment. Approximately 7 percent of all students drop out of high school (U.S. Department of Education, 2014), although for several reasons the significance of this percentage is somewhat hard to interpret (Ianni & Orr, 1996). First, school jurisdictions vary in how they define "dropping out" (some leave

A Multicultural View

Cross-Cultural Misunderstandings in the Classroom

Consider these classroom situations and their impact:

- Student 1 is quiet when his teacher speaks to him, but he generally looks down at the floor or away from her when she speaks. Even when the teacher encourages him to express his own ideas, Student 1 pauses and looks away for what feels like an eternity to the teacher.

- Student 2 writes an essay for a social studies class entitled "Jobs in the Global Economy." To the teacher, the essay seems to meander all over the place and does not state its theme until the final paragraph. "It's as if you were telling me what you were thinking," the teacher wrote on the essay afterward, "instead of stating and then justifying a position."

- Student 3 rarely answers questions completely when the teacher calls on her in class; she just mumbles an answer or remains silent. But when collaborating with a small group on a project or an activity, she is lively, talkative, and focused on the task.

There are many possible reasons for these situations. One common explanation is *cross-cultural miscommunication,* culturally based differences in how individuals interpret comments and behaviors. Observations of conversations show that cultures vary in communication styles and that children acquire the styles in the course of learning their native language (Scollon & Scollon, 1994).

Cultural communication styles can vary in the following ways, among others:

1. *Timing:* speakers expect different lengths of pauses between conversational turns, from many seconds to only a fraction of a second or even to a "negative" pause (overlapping comments).

2. *Deductiveness/inductiveness:* in some cultures, speakers are expected to state their point immediately (use a "topic sentence") and then justify their position; in others, speakers more often lead up to the main point indirectly, describing their thought processes along the way.

3. *Politeness indicators:* in some cultures, it is especially important to indicate respect for those in authority, chiefly by listening quietly, head bowed, averting the speaker's eyes, and expecting the authority (teacher) to determine the topic and length of a conversation.

These cultural differences can pose problems whenever members of more than one culture come together to interact. For children and adolescents, therefore, cultural mismatch is especially likely in classrooms in large urban areas or large culturally diverse suburbs, particularly in contacts between teachers and students. If the teacher "speaks the culture" of white, mainstream English, she or he will tend to use and expect relatively short pauses between conversational turns in classroom discussions. The teacher will also tend to use and expect a deductive style of turn taking, with the topic stated immediately by whoever initiates a conversational exchange. And although the teacher may expect moderate indications of respect for his or her right to initiate topics of conversation, she or he may also expect students to initiate ideas and concerns of their own.

When a student's culture supports other communication styles, the teacher can easily misinterpret the cultural underpinnings of the behavior and view student as either unintelligent, lacking in confidence, or deliberately resistant to learning (Lustig & Koester, 1993). Yet these sorts of mismatches are precisely what occur, and always to the disadvantage of the student. What the teacher sees and hears are pauses that are too long, eye contact that is poor, comments that stray from the topic, and silence in response to invitations to speak. What the student experiences, though, may be quite different: he or she may see and hear a teacher who is too talkative, stares at individuals too much, and seems insincere in issuing invitations to ask questions.

But such misunderstandings can be overcome. Training in intercultural communication exists and is effective when focused on the key cultural misunderstandings of particular conversational partners. In the teaching profession, some of the most elaborate training occurs for teachers of English as a Second Language (Paulston, 1992), but programs are also developing in many business communities (Brislin & Yoshida, 1994; O'Hara-Devereaux & Johansen, 1994), where economic activity increasingly spans more than one country, language, and cultural community. The programs vary in detail, of course, but share a common assumption: that awkwardness between culturally different speakers is likely the result of legitimate differences in communication styles rather than of inferiority of one style or the other.

---

students out of their records if they are more than eighteen). Second, some dropouts—possibly as many as one-third—return to complete school in any one year; they might better be called temporary school leavers rather than permanent dropouts. Third, students drop out for a variety of reasons, ranging from general alienation from schooling, to family crises, to difficulties in fitting in with peers and teachers. Some of the reasons are more serious and long lasting than others and contribute to variations in students' tendency to return to school to complete a diploma.

Although the dropout rate is not evenly distributed among schools and communities, the significance of concentrations of dropouts is surprisingly ambiguous. A few large, inner-city high schools have high dropout rates, for example; as many as 50 percent of each entering ninth-grade class may not graduate. Dropping out is more frequent among nonwhite students (8 to 13 percent) than among white students (4 percent); yet this trend obscures the fact that half of all dropouts are white. Furthermore, dropping out is more frequent among low-income families than among middle- and high-income families; yet this trend can distract attention from the fact that nationwide, half of all dropouts are from middle-income families. These somewhat paradoxical statistics suggest an especially important point for teachers and other people who work with youth professionally: that although social categories (race, SES, urban residence) *correlate* with dropping out, they do not *cause* it. (See Chapter 1 for a discussion of the difference between correlation and causation.) Most adolescents *do* graduate from high school, even in urban communities, as do most youth who are nonwhite or poor.

resilience Ability to withstand and even profit from stressful experiences.

Educational research therefore has looked for factors contributing to **resilience** in youth, to the factors that allow individual adolescents to cope with and overcome difficult circumstances. In general, the studies point to the importance of adults seeing and responding to the potential of individual teenagers, whether the adults be parents, school personnel, members of the community, or some combination of the three (Altenbaugh, 1995; Caterall, 1998). This is supported by research showing that adolescents, particularly those at risk for dropping out, who are engaged in extracurricular pursuits are less likely to drop out (Mahoney & Cairns, 1997; Wang & Fredricks, 2014). The research also suggests that teenagers do not necessarily get discouraged, nor necessarily drop out, because they become aware of belonging to social categories that have high dropout rates. One study of urban African American youth found that those with the most conscious, articulate knowledge of racial discrimination were precisely the individuals most likely to *stay* in school and perform well (O'Connor, 1997)!

Even though the existence of dropouts implies that high schools may be limiting the potential of some students, it is important to recognize that many high schools are quite successful at providing both academic and social opportunities to which many students might not have access otherwise. Many educational observers and researchers have identified the qualities that lead to school effectiveness and success (Gallagher, 1996; Sizer, 1996; Slavin, 1998). For one thing, both teachers and students must be able to work in their own ways, even when those ways may be unconventional. Only by doing so can they honor the developmental diversity in

A supportive relationship between a teacher and student—like the one pictured here—is especially important to the academic success of the student. These students are more likely to achieve greater academic proficiency and are less likely to drop out because of this caring relationship. Of course, it is also helpful if the school district is well funded, as this one appears to be, equipped with current technology and the training to use it effectively in the classroom.
Source: Goodluz/Shutterstock.com.

Part 6 Adolescence

> **What Do You Think?**
>
> Some educators argue that you cannot teach thinking skills in *general,* because a person always thinks about something in *particular.* Why do you think they take this position? This issue makes for a useful debate in class, especially if you adopt the position contrary to the one you truly embrace!

most high school communities. For another, schools need to focus the attention of everyone—teachers, students, and parents—on their primary purpose: to promote learning. Given the diversity among students, teachers, and communities, it can be challenging to reconcile this second purpose with the first. Yet most high schools manage to do so, even if not perfectly.

Employment

School is not the only arena in which adolescents test their growing cognitive skills. Many also join the work force, either in addition to or in place of attending school. The majority of teenagers report participating in "formal" paid work outside the home, and many others engage in "informal" paid work such as babysitting and yardwork within their own homes (Mortimer & Finch, 1996). Informal work is likely to be a first paid job. Because it is fairly continuous with the chores and responsibilities of childhood, it provides a more gradual transition to the demands of adult work. Formal adult work typically takes place in commercial or other organizational settings. It represents a greater departure from childhood work and involves more relationships with adults, closer supervision, and more systematic monitoring of job performance.

The types of jobs frequently reported by teenagers include supermarket, restaurant, or retail store worker; office worker; and semiskilled worker. Most of these jobs are on the margins of the economy, and as such tend to offer low wages and little future as a career. For teenagers from economically well-off families, these facts may be just as well, because they create little temptation to pursue the job to the exclusion of schoolwork. For a large percentage of teenagers from low-SES families, the dead-end quality of first jobs poses a serious problem: these young people often depend on employment to pay their daily living expenses as well as those of their families (Newman, 1996).

Ideally, work during adolescence serves three important functions. First, it facilitates the transition from school to work. Second, it provides structure for involvement in family- and school-related activities. Finally, it provides an arena outside of home and school for gaining social experience and the material rewards needed to have an independent life with peers. How work influences adolescent mental health and adjustment depends on the type and level of workplace stress, the relevance of job-related skills to future careers, and the compatibility between the demands and experiences of work and school (Bell et al., 1996).

The intensity of formal work as measured by the number of hours worked per month is also important. Students who work more than ten hours per week do more poorly academically, report more psychological problems (depression, anxiety fatigue, sleeping difficulty), and physical problems (headaches, stomachaches, colds) than other students. They are also more likely to use drugs, smoke cigarettes, and engage in delinquent activities, regardless of ethnicity, SES, or age. In contrast, working fewer than ten hours per week generally appears to have no negative effects (Mortimer et al., 1994). It is also possible, of course, that students with intensive work involvements had more preexisting problems.

For teenagers whose families can afford it, working more than a moderate number of hours per week may be developmentally unwise because it interferes with academic activities, exposes them to negative environments and role models, and limits the amount of monitoring and supervision they receive from parents, teachers, and other positive role models. Moreover, becoming accustomed to having a paycheck that may be

Chapter 15 Cognitive Development during Adolescence

used entirely for leisure pursuits might be a financial hindrance when these adolescents become adults and the majority of their income goes to food, rent, insurance, and the like (Bachman, 1983). Many students, particularly those receiving appropriate levels of adult monitoring and support, make sensible decisions about the role of work in their lives, adjusting their choice of work and number of hours to meet their other important academic and social needs. We will look in the next chapter at the importance of interactions with adults and peers during adolescence.

Chapter Summary

- **To what extent are adolescents capable of abstract reasoning?** During adolescence, some teenagers (though not all) develop formal operational thought, or the ability to reason about ideas regardless of their content. Formal thought is characterized by an ability to think about possibilities, by scientific reasoning, and by an ability to combine ideas logically. Research on adult thinking suggests that formal operations are not the final point of cognitive development, or necessarily a step toward mature thinking.

- **How does cognitive development affect adolescents' knowledge and beliefs about their identities and about morality?** Adolescents develop two forms of morality—one oriented toward justice and one oriented toward caring for self and others. Lawrence Kohlberg proposed six stages in the development of moral judgments oriented toward justice. A number of issues regarding Kohlberg's theory have yet to be resolved, including the significance of the content (versus the form) of moral beliefs, differences between conventions and morality, and the possibility of gender differences in moral development. Carol Gilligan proposed forms of moral development oriented toward interpersonal caring; on average, these forms may be slightly more characteristic of females than males, though many exceptions exist.

  Despite their improved cognitive skills, adolescents still sometimes show egocentrism by believing in an "imaginary audience" and in a "personal fable," or biography of their lives.

- **How do adolescents show improved information processing in everyday activities?** During adolescence, information-processing skills continue to improve. Teenagers acquire greater expertise in particular areas of knowledge or skill, a trend that continues into adulthood.

- **What cognitive and social effects do school and work have on adolescent development?** School has significant effects on adolescents' lives, both cognitively and socially. Cognitively, school encourages the development of critical thinking, the ability to reflect about complex issues to make decisions or take actions. Educational programs to foster critical thinking usually do so explicitly, offer practice in solving problems, and create an environment conducive to critical thinking. Socially, school can be stressful for youngsters, especially early in adolescence. Many teenagers drop out of high school each year, though their reasons vary; the majority, however, complete school with a reasonable degree of success. Many students work part time while attending school, and the experience has diverse effects, depending on the particular job and circumstances of the student.

Key Terms

adolescent egocentrism (p. 374)
critical thinking (p. 378)
expertise (p. 377)
formal operational thought (p. 364)
imaginary audience (p. 374)

middle school (p. 380)
morality (p. 367)
personal fable (p. 374)
postconventional moral judgment (p. 370)

resilience (p. 382)
social cognition (p. 373)
social conventions (p. 371)

Psychosocial Development during Adolescence

CHAPTER 16

Chapter Outline

Theories of Identity Development

Family Relationships during Adolescence

Social Relationships during Adolescence

Sexuality during Adolescence

Special Problems of Adolescence

Looking Back/Looking Forward

Source: melis/Shutterstock.com.

Focusing Questions

- What conflicts do adolescents typically experience in their search for identity? What factors support or hinder successful identity development?
- What special challenges does adolescence pose for parents? How do differences in parenting style affect parent-teenager relationships?
- In what ways do adolescent friendships and peer groups play a constructive role, and how are concerns about their negative influence justified?
- What changes in sexual activities and attitudes occur among teenagers? How are they related to other aspects of adolescent development?
- Why are adolescents at risk for problems such as pregnancy, depression, and delinquency?

As we have discovered, adolescence is a time of dramatic physical and cognitive changes. Although the rate at which these changes occur varies greatly, by the end of this period, most adolescents look like adults and are physically and intellectually capable of most adult activities. But as important as these changes are, the changes that occur in the social-emotional domain may be even more significant. Perhaps the most important change is the progress adolescents make in achieving a full-fledged and integrated psychological identity that is mature, adult, unique, and separate from those of parents, friends, and other important childhood figures. A stable identity gives teenagers a more integrated sense of who they really are, what they believe in, and their realistic limitations and capabilities. Zoe, who has just begun her senior year of high school, put it this way:

> It's not just that I'm all grown up now—physically, I mean. It's that I have grown up inside, too. I feel different, more like a grownup than a child. Although there are still many things I'm unsure of, I finally have a much clearer sense of who I am and what is important to me and what I believe in. And this may sound strange, but the sense of independence and separateness that I now feel means I can often be close to my parents and friends without losing a sense of who I am and my confidence in my ability to succeed at achieving the things I really want. In a way, it feels like I'm at the end of a long journey and ready to start off on a new one.

As Zoe's thoughts reveal, she has embraced an enhanced capacity for psychological autonomy, intimacy, and relatedness to her parents, family, and friends, and she has made significant strides in achievement and self-esteem. All are very important accomplishments of adolescence (Allen et al., 1994).

In this chapter, we initially look at the process of adolescent identity development, as well as the related processes by which adolescents develop a healthy sense of autonomy, achievement, intimacy, and sexuality. We explore several important aspects of the teenager's changing social world, including relationships with parents and peers, the development of friendships, and the impact of school and work. We also look at adolescent sexuality and how it is influenced by current social trends and personal beliefs. Finally, we explore the special problems adolescents face today and some strategies for preventing them.

Theories of Identity Development

Parents often are surprised at how much care and reflection an eighteen- or nineteen-year-old has given to who he is and how strong his sense of personal direction can be. Just a few short years ago, this same child was irritable and uncertain at home and with his peers. A clear path forward was uncharted and navigated with frustrating fits and starts. Now, this emerging adult reveals a sense of purpose, welcomes opportunities for demonstrating his maturing skills, and transitions from someone who was only interested in the moment to someone with an eye on attainable goals and aspirations in the near future. How is this possible? What are the contributing factors that lead to the development of a strong sense of personal identity? Several theorists have explored this process.

Ruthellen Josselson: Individuation and Identity Development

individuation The process by which an adolescent develops a unique and separate personal identity. Consists of four subphases: differentiation, practice and experimentation, rapprochement, and consolidation.

Individuation is the process by which an adolescent develops a unique personal identity or sense of self, one distinct and separate from all others. Ruthellen Josselson (1980) has proposed that the individuation process consists of four separate but overlapping subphases: differentiation, practice and experimentation, rapprochement, and consolidation of self.

During the *differentiation* subphase early in adolescence, the teenager recognizes that she is psychologically different from her parents. The dual discovery that she is no longer an extension of her parents and that they are not as wise, powerful, and all-knowing as she thought earlier sometimes leads her to often question and reject her parents' values and advice, even if they are reasonable.

In the *practice and experimentation* subphase, the fourteen- or fifteen-year-old may believe he knows it all and can do no wrong. He may deny any need for caution or advice and actively challenge his parents at every opportunity. A sense of youthful invincibility clouds his judgment. He now turns to like-minded friends, who provide the support and approval he previously sought from adults. In a discussion of plans to go to a multiband rock concert with his friends, for example, Alonzo will completely dismiss his parents' concerns about the risks and dangers in attending. Instead, he will convincingly plead to his parents (and himself) that his friends, who went to last year's concert, have assured him that it was perfectly safe. After all, they know what they are talking about!

During the *rapprochement* subphase, teens begin to make a healthy course correction. Toward the middle of adolescence, a teenager has achieved enough separateness from her parents that she is now able to *conditionally* reaccept their authority. Often, she will alternate between experimentation and rapprochement—on some occasions, challenging her parents, and at other times, being conciliatory and cooperative. Maria is a good case in point. Having just turned fifteen, she goes to great lengths to accept responsibility around the house, but often becomes highly indignant and argumentative when her parents still insist on a curfew and on knowing where she is going and who she is going with when she leaves the house in the evening.

It is during the final *consolidation-of-self* subphase, which lasts through adolescence and into early adulthood, that an individual develops a sense of personal identity. This milestone development provides the basis for understanding self and others, and for maintaining a sense of autonomy, independence, and individuality. Shannon, a high school junior who will soon be applying to colleges, is a good example. Viewed by herself and her family as somewhat disorganized and lacking maturity and a clear life direction, Shannon in fact surprised them during the college application process. On her own initiative, Shannon met with the school counselor and accessed college websites to take virtual tours of the schools she was interested in for starters. She then created her own "self-evaluation plan," in which she listed the academic and social qualities she wanted in a school, along with her personal strengths and weaknesses as a student. Added to her plan were the cost, location, admission criteria, and application deadlines for the top seven schools she thought would be a good fit for her. Shannon then invited her parents into the decision-making process by viewing the schools online and planning college visits with them. Her parents were amazed by the initiative and industriousness Shannon displayed in the search process. But they were also very proud of her maturity and independence in taking on this important task.

The process of individuation continues throughout the teenage years and into early adulthood. As we will see shortly, Josselson's ideas about individuation dovetail with Erikson's theory, which holds that the major task of adolescence is to resolve the crisis of identity successfully.

For these adolescent girls, it is likely that their willingness to engage in what has traditionally been a male sport reflects a strong sense of individual identity and self-direction, as well as changing cultural expectations regarding female participation in sports.
Source: Shawn Pecor/Shutterstock.com.

Erik Erikson: The Crisis of Identity versus Role Confusion

According to Erik Erikson (see Chapter 2), the key developmental challenge of adolescence is to resolve the crisis of **identity versus role confusion** (Erikson, 1963). In forming an identity, an adolescent selectively accepts or rejects the many different aspects of herself that she acquired as a child and forms a more coherent and integrated sense of unique identity (Damon & Hart, 1988; Harter, 1989; Harter & Monsour, 1992). During middle childhood, she may have formed separate views of herself based on her school success or athletic abilities, and most significantly, on how her friends viewed her. In adolescence, however, she mulls over the significance of all of these impressions taken together and integrates them into a single identity encompassing all of her strengths and weaknesses and an awareness of what this all means. An adolescent's increasing capacity for abstract thought and self-understanding (see Chapter 15) plays a central role in this process.

identity versus role confusion The fifth of Erikson's psychosocial crises, in which one must integrate one's many childhood skills and beliefs and gain recognition for them from society.

As adolescents experiment with different roles in their search to create a coherent sense of identity, many experience a sense of *false self*—that is, a sense that one is acting in ways that do not reflect one's true self as a person, or the "real me." Each of the many different role-related selves that adolescents experience, such as self with parents, self with friends, self as a classmate, and self with a girlfriend or boyfriend, contains qualities that seem to contradict one another. For example, an adolescent may be outgoing with friends but shy with a romantic partner, or cheerful with friends and depressed with parents (Harter et al., 1996).

Susan Harter and her colleagues (Harter et al., 1996) asked middle school and high school students to describe their true and their false selves. Descriptions of their true selves included "the real me inside," "my true feelings," "what I really think and feel," and "behaving the way I want to behave and not how someone else wants me to be." False selves were described as "being phony," "putting on an act," "expressing things you don't really believe or feel," or "changing yourself to be something that someone else wants you to be." False-self beliefs and behaviors could have both a positive role in identity formation and a negative one. The path taken by a teen is often influenced by parental support and one's perception of exploring their false self. Adolescents who reported high levels of positive support from parents and peers engaged in fewer false-self behaviors than those who experienced lower levels and poorer quality of support. Teens who engaged in false-self behavior as a healthy way to experiment with new roles reported more positive feelings about themselves, higher self-worth, greater hopefulness about the future, and more knowledge of their true selves than teens who engaged in false-self behavior to please, impress, or win the approval of parents and peers or because they were experiencing depression or other problems.

Psychosocial Moratorium

psychosocial moratorium According to Erikson, the latency period that precedes puberty and provides a temporary suspension of psychosexual development.

According to Erikson (1968), adolescence provides a **psychosocial moratorium**, a period during which the youth is free to suspend or delay taking on adult commitments and to explore new social roles. The goal of role experimentation is to find a place, or niche, that is clearly defined and yet seems uniquely made for him. The adolescent may devote this time to study, work, travel, or even rebellious and/or delinquent behaviors, depending on prevailing social, cultural, and economic conditions, as well as on his individual capacities and needs.

The type of psychosocial moratorium an adolescent encounters (or whether she encounters one at all) will largely depend on the opportunities for identity exploration provided by her family, culture, society, and the global pathways available in a changing world (Jensen & Arnett, 2012). For example, children growing up under conditions of poverty and deprivation, gender inequality, or during periods of war and social upheaval are likely to experience more limited and less supportive moratorium opportunities than are children living under more optimal circumstances.

Identity Diffusion

identity diffusion A failure to achieve a relatively coherent, integrated, and stable identity.

Identity diffusion is one of the four identity statuses researched by Marcia (1966) that we will explore in detail. However, in a broader context, identity diffusion is the failure to achieve a relatively coherent, integrated, and stable identity, and it may take a number of forms. The first is *avoidance of closeness* with others. A second form—*diffusion of time perspective*—involves the belief that one is out of sync with others, fearing that important opportunities may be lost forever. Time diffusion is sometimes followed by feelings of depression and despair over the length of time it takes for a comfortable sense of identity to finally be achieved. The third form—*diffusion of industry*—may involve an inability to concentrate on school- or work-related tasks or an excessive preoccupation with a single activity that interferes with accomplishing other things. A final and more extreme form of identity diffusion is the choice of a negative identity. A **negative identity** involves the rejection of positive roles and valued opportunities made available by one's family or community resources, and the acceptance of socially undesirable roles, leading to delinquent and/or antisocial behaviors that we will discuss later in the chapter.

negative identity A form of identity diffusion involving rejection of the roles preferred by one's family or community in favor of socially undesirable roles.

The Relationship Between Identity and Intimacy

According to Erikson, successful resolution of the crisis of identity versus role confusion prepares the adolescent for the crisis of intimacy versus isolation, which occurs in early adulthood. A clear and coherent sense of identity provides a basis for achieving intimacy in friendships and love relationships and for tolerating the fear of losing one's sense of self when intimacy becomes very intense and of experiencing loneliness and isolation if a relationship ends. However, the establishment of an intimate relationship with a partner frequently occurs prior to, or simultaneously with, the resolution of identity issues. The lifelong challenges of successfully forming and maintaining intimate long-term relationships with friends, co-workers, lovers, marriage partners, and eventually our own children all require that we develop an increasingly reliable sense of who we are and where we are going.

Identity Status

Guided by Erikson's ideas, researchers such as James Marcia (1966, 1980) and Jane Kroger (2007; Kroger et al., 2010) have empirically studied identity development during adolescence. Marcia interviewed students ages eighteen to twenty-two about their occupational choices and religious and political beliefs and values, all central aspects of identity (Marcia, 1980, 1993; Marcia et al., 1993). He classified students into four categories of **identity status**, based on varying combinations of (1) *exploration* (whether or not they had gone through an "identity crisis" as described by Erikson) and (2) *commitment* (the degree to which they were now committed to an occupational choice and to a set of personal, religious, and political values and beliefs). Table 16.1 describes these categories.

Marcia's findings were as follows:

identity status Marcia's four categories of identity development: identity achievement, identity diffusion, moratorium, and foreclosure.

1. *Identity-achieved* individuals have experienced and successfully resolved a period of crisis by either reevaluating past choices and beliefs and accepting those of value or by adopting new beliefs based on their own terms and exploration, not solely those of their parents or another authority figure.

2. *Identity-diffused* individuals may or may not have experienced a crisis but are defined by the absence of exploration and commitment regarding their values and beliefs. These individuals lack a meaningful sense of direction in general and display little concern about personal identity formation (Dunkle & Anthis, 2001).

3. *Moratorium* individuals are presently *in* crisis, actively struggling to make commitments based on their own beliefs and goals. They remain preoccupied with exploring, and hopefully achieving, successful compromises among their parents' wishes, the demands of society, and their own capabilities.

4. *Foreclosed* individuals have "prematurely" committed themselves to important aspects of identity without having experienced any significant exploration through conflict or crisis. Consequently, the commitments formed are mostly through identification with their parents' beliefs and goals, or the influence of another external authority.

Most adolescents seem to progress toward a status of identity achieved. For both males and females, identity achievement is rarest among early adolescents and most frequent among older high school students, college students, and young adults. During junior and senior high school, identity diffusion and identity foreclosure are the most common identity statuses. Although diffused and foreclosed statuses significantly decrease during the later high school and college years, only about one-third of college juniors and seniors and one-quarter of adults studied have been found to be identity achieved (Archer & Waterman, 1988; Meilman, 1979).

Dunkle and Anthis (2001) conducted a short-term longitudinal study testing the relationship of identity exploration and commitment to the creation of possible selves. As young

TABLE 16.1 Crisis and Commitment in Marcia's Theory of Identity Status

According to James Marcia, adolescents can be classified into four categories of identity status based on the presence or absence of an identity crisis or exploration and whether or not they are committed to an occupational choice and a set of religious values and beliefs.

Identity Status	Crisis (Exploration)	Commitment
Achieved	Present	Present
Diffused	Present/absent	Absent
Moratorium	In process	In process
Foreclosed	Absent	Present

Source: Marcia (1980).

Chapter 16 Psychosocial Development during Adolescence

adolescents begin to imagine possible selves, both ideal and feared, identity exploration was more active as the number of possible selves generated grew. The researchers also discovered that as teens entered later adolescence and established more consistent possible selves, the commitment to setting and working toward these goals also increased. By exploring many possible selves in early adolescence, young teens begin to prune and shape the real self they present to the world as they transition from later adolescence into emerging adulthood.

Differences in social class, culture, and ethnicity may also affect identity development, depending on the context specific to an individual's life circumstances. Just as adolescents growing up during the Depression were much less likely to have the opportunity to experience a moratorium, minority youths living in poverty today are also likely to be much more limited in opportunities for identity status exploration than middle-class suburban teens attending college. Youngsters who live in poor neighborhoods where gangs, drugs, and violence are common and rates of school dropout and unemployment are high, and who lack positive adult and peer role models, are more likely to encounter difficulties in forming positive identities than adolescents growing up in a more supportive environment (Bat-Chava et al., 1997; McCloyd, 1998).

The proportion of individuals at each identity status appears to vary with the specific identity area involved. Identity achievement was the most frequent status in the area of *religious beliefs;* identity achievement and moratorium were the most frequent statuses where *vocational choice* was concerned; identity foreclosure was the most common status in the area of *gender-role preferences;* and identity diffusion was the most frequent status in the area of *political philosophies* (Archer, 1982; Krager, 1995; Marcia et al., 1993; Waterman, 1982, 1985). For example, when Jean Phinney and her colleagues conducted in-depth interviews with Asian American, Latinx, and white American-born male and female high school students to assess stage of ethnic identity development, they found no significant differences based on either ethnic group or gender in the percentages of youngsters who were in the diffusion/foreclosure stage, moratorium stage, or achievement stage of ethnic identity development (Phinney et al., 1997). Groups did differ, however, in which issues were of most concern in resolving their identity crises. Nearly one-third of all adolescents in the United States are from non-European American backgrounds, and they, in turn, are from a variety of life circumstances (see Figure 16.1).

Few differences between males and females have been found on measures of identity. Both genders are equally represented among the four identity statuses and seem to develop in similar ways. Although early studies suggested that the identity statuses might have different psychological meanings and consequences for males and females, more recent research indicates that the meanings and implications appear to be quite similar for both genders (Archer & Waterman, 1988; Gilligan, 1987; Marcia, 1993).

FIGURE 16.1
Ethnic Makeup of Youth in the United States, 2014

Adolescents with Latinx origins make up the largest percentage of ethnic minority youth in the United States, followed by adolescents from African origins, Asian multiethnic, Native American/Alaskan Native, and Native Hawaiian/Pacific Islander backgrounds.

Source: Adapted from Colby & Ortman (2015), p. 10.

- White: 52%
- Latinx: 24.40%
- Black: 13.80%
- Asian: 4.70%
- Multiethnic: 4.10%
- Native American/Alaskan Native: 0.90%
- Native Hawaiian/Pacific Islander: 0.20%

> **What Do You Think?**
>
> To what degree have you experienced the developmental crisis of identity versus role confusion proposed by Erikson? Which of Marcia's four identity statuses best describes you at this point in your development?

Although making progress in mastering Erikson's crisis of identity versus role confusion is a central task of adolescence, the process of developing an identity continues throughout the entire lifespan.

Family Relationships during Adolescence

The search for identity and the achievement of a mature psychological sense of autonomy and relatedness affect all of an adolescent's relationships. Ties with parents must make room for an increasing interest in peers and a new commitment to the life among comparative equals that peers provide. A young teenager's efforts to become more physically and emotionally independent from his parents and closer to his friends may be stressful, but more often than not, the problems and conflicts of this period are relatively minor. Full-blown upheavals and more serious problems of adolescence are most likely to occur in families and communities in which a poor fit exists between the developmental needs of adolescents and the opportunities and supports that are available (Eccles et al., 1993; Offer & Schonert-Reichl, 1992). We first explore relationships within the family, and then look at social relationships in the wider world.

Relationships with Parents

Even though the majority of teens get along well with their parents on a daily basis, parent-teenager relationships are likely to feel slightly "unstable" or "out of joint" some of the time. This is in part a result of the increasingly stressful pace of modern family life and the different ways adolescents and their parents choose to spend their time. Both adolescents and their parents tend to agree that differences in the activities, expectations, and interests of each family member make it difficult for them to find times to do things together and find activities that are of mutual interest (Larson & Richards, 1994).

The disconnectedness that parents and teenagers sometimes feel may also reflect teenagers' sensitivity to the discrepancies between their own and their parents' views of how their families function—whether individuals really get along with one another, for example, and who really makes decisions around the house (Carlson et al., 1991). Parents may think they listen to their teenager's opinions about what household chores she should do, but she herself may regard the "listening" as shallow or meaningless because parents evidently decide who does what chores anyway. When discrepancies such as these come into the open, conflicts usually arise ("You always say X, but you really mean Y!"). That is the bad news. The good news is that the conflicts frequently serve as catalysts for further growth in teenagers' social maturity and to reconcile gaps between parents and their nearly grown children (Holmbeck & O'Donnell, 1991; Robin et al., 1990). An important task of adolescence is to achieve adequate psychological separation, or independence, from one's parents, complimenting a parental goal of parent-adolescent relationships evolving to a more egalitarian and horizontal dimension by the later teenage years (Collins & Steinberg, 2006; Van Doon et al., 2011).

Achieving psychological separation from one's parents entails four important accomplishments: *functional independence*—the ability to manage one's own personal and practical affairs with minimal help from one's parents; *attitudinal independence*—a view of oneself as unique and separate from one's parents and having a personal set of values and beliefs; *emotional independence*—freedom from being overly dependent on parents for approval, intimacy, and emotional support; and *conflictual independence*—freedom from excessive anxiety, guilt, resentment, anger, or responsibility toward one's parents

(Moore, 1984, 1987; Sullivan & Sullivan, 1980). From the perspectives of adolescents themselves, the most significant indicators of successful separation from parents are gaining economic independence, living on their own, graduating from school, and being free to make their own life choices without being overly concerned about what their parents may think (Moore, 1987). These indicators may continue to need more time to fully develop before feeling fully independent. This further exploration occurs during emerging adulthood, a new period of development that Jeffery Arnett (2004) described as the winding road from the late teens through the mid-twenties.

The lifespan perspective reminds us that the process of separating from parents to achieve emotional independence during adolescence continues during early adulthood. During early adulthood the safe-base function parents continue to provide for adolescents generally shifts to a significant other, a spouse, or a friend (Hazen & Shaver, 1990). With the development of intimacy within a relationship, and the decision to start a family, the emerging adult now enters the stage of young adulthood envisioned by Erikson (1963), but starting much later in the lives of those in the millennial generation (Arnett, 2004; Arnett, 2012; Arnett, Ramos, & Jensen, 2001).

Although the majority of college students expect to live briefly with their parents after graduation, in our culture leaving home is still a powerful metaphor for achieving psychological separation, and differences in how parents and adolescents understand and react to this experience are common. Many of the everyday conflicts between adolescents and their parents over chores, curfews, school, and social activities reflect different perspectives about the approaching separation. Adolescents' tendency to view themselves as increasingly emancipated from their parents' conventional perspectives and control may create conflict between a parent's need to maintain the usual family norms while allowing the child increasing independence (Smetana, 1995). We will examine the varying dynamics behind parent-adolescent conflicts, but first, let's explore the changes that occur in the amount of time, the interests, and the activities that teenagers share with their family from early through later adolescence.

In studies by Reed Larson and his colleagues, fifth- through twelfth-graders from white working- and middle-class backgrounds carried electronic beepers and provided reports on their experiences when contacted at random times over the course of a week (Larson, 1997; Larson et al., 1996). Figure 16.2 shows the amount of time adolescents spent with family decreased from 35 percent of waking hours in fifth grade to just 14 percent in twelfth grade. By the end of senior high school, these teenagers were spending

Although leaving home is often accompanied by mixed feelings, the overall quality of adolescent-parent relationships often improves after teenagers have left.
Source: XiXinXing/Shutterstock.com.

significantly less time in leisure and daily maintenance activities with family, and this decline was greatest for time spent with the entire family and time spent with siblings. Despite these changes, however, the connection between these adolescents and their parents remained stable over time, as reflected in the amount of time they spent talking with and being alone with their parents. In many cases, stable parent-teen relationships encourage more time for exploration—first in the home and then outside the home. Early adolescents replaced family time with time spent alone at home, whereas for older adolescents, access to friends, having a car, having a job, and receiving permission from parents to stay out later all affected time spent away from home. Table 16.2 presents the changes in percentage of different activities with family by grade.

These changes, even in healthy families, often lead to conflicts between the teen seeking more independence and the parents who want to hold on a little longer to the child they miss and the adolescent they encounter. The changes and conflicts often stimulate unresolved feelings in parents. As one parent put it, "Sometimes I'm not sure which is more upsetting to me, my teenage daughter's pain and confusion about who she is or similar feelings that are stirred up from my own difficult adolescence." Whether designed to protect their child, or to remain in control, arguments will erupt between parents and adolescents. As many psychologists and parents alike have discovered, arguments during the teenage years are a "ubiquitous phenomenon" during this developmental stage (Montemayor, 1983; Robin et al., 1990; Robin & Foster, 1989). Higher levels of parent-adolescent conflict are more likely to occur in families experiencing divorce, economic hardship, or other serious stressors, including mental health disorders (Flanagan, 1990; Hetherington et al., 1998; McLoyd, 1990; Robin & Foster, 1989; Smetana et al., 1991). Keep in mind, too, that high overall levels of adolescent-parent conflict are frequently a continuation of a pattern that existed during middle childhood.

Where adolescents and parents do differ is in the emphasis, or strength, of those attitudes and values. Most disagreements between teens and parents are about relatively mundane matters affecting the teenager's current social life and behavior, such as styles of dress, hair length, choices of friends, dating, curfews, telephone use, participation in household chores and family activities, and choice of music. For preferences such as these, teenagers agree more with their peers than with their parents, thus leading to arguments about differing points of view and who should decide the outcome. Resolving these conflicts has been the focus of a good deal of research. As teens move from early to later adolescence, they seek more of an equal say in their daily activities, and parents are not opposed to join them in this. In a perfect world, the ideal transition from vertical,

FIGURE 16.2

Age Differences in Time Spent by Adolescents with Family Members

Between fifth and twelfth grades, the amount of time spent with various family members decreases. The greater decrease is in time spent with the entire family.

Source: Adapted from Larson et al. (1996) p. 748.

TABLE 16.2 Percentage of Experience Sampling Method Reports in Different Activities with Family, by Grade Level

All activities with family decrease with increasing grade level, except talking and transportation.

Activity	5	6	7	8	9	10	11	12
Homework	3.1	1.4	1.5	2.2	1.7	0.9	0.3	0.4
Chores	1.5	1.8	1.7	1.4	2.0	1.2	0.9	1.1
Eating	3.9	2.6	1.8	2.6	2.2	1.6	1.4	1.8
Transportation	1.5	1.5	0.9	1.1	1.6	1.4	0.9	0.8
Personal maintenance	3.5	2.1	1.7	2.0	2.1	1.6	1.1	1.7
Watching TV	9.9	7.6	6.0	6.7	6.9	4.5	2.9	3.4
Active leisure	5.4	3.4	3.5	2.0	2.4	1.2	0.5	1.2
Talking	2.3	3.1	2.8	2.7	3.0	2.2	2.1	2.3
Idling	2.1	1.3	1.3	0.8	1.6	1.1	0.5	0.4
Totals	33.2	24.8	21.2	21.5	23.5	15.7	10.6	13.1

Note: ESM = Experience sampling method. *Source:* Larson et al. (1996).

asymmetrical parent-child relationships to ones that are more horizontal and even (Collins & Steinberg, 2006; VanDoon et al., 2011) would happen without conflict. Yet, in reality, this change takes place by successfully navigating and negotiating the minefields of parent-adolescent conflict. Despite the many changes taking place, the majority of adolescents and parents continue to get along rather well together. They also tend to share similar attitudes and values about important issues and decisions, such as ideas of right and wrong, what makes a marriage good, and the long-run value of education. (Collins, 1991; Larson, 1997; Larson & Richards, 1994). More importantly, despite the increasing time that teens spend with peers and the increasing influence of peers, when it comes to the basic attitudes and values that guide long-term life choices, adolescents have consistently rated their parents' advice more highly than their friends' (Carlson et al., 1991; Grusec et al., 1996).

Parenting Styles

During adolescence, a fine line exists between sensitive, respectful parental involvement and intrusive over involvement that fails to adequately appreciate adolescents' need for separateness and independence. As in early and middle childhood, a parent-adolescent relationship that establishes a secure emotional base is most likely to result in a mutually satisfactory exploration of autonomy and relatedness (Allen et al., 1994).

Not surprisingly, the parenting styles discussed in Chapter 7 are related to various aspects of adolescent development, including personality, academic achievement, and social and emotional adjustment (Ge et al., 1996; Glasgow et al., 1997; Steinberg et al., 1994; Weiss & Schwarz, 1996). Recall that *authoritative* parents exercise high degrees of demandingness in setting appropriate behavioral boundaries and establishing high levels of responsiveness to their children's needs and moods. *Authoritarian* parents also exercise high degrees of demandingness and control, but provide low levels of emotional responsiveness, warmth, and nurturance. *Permissive* parents are low in demanding behavioral controls, mixed in their clarity of communication, and very high in warmth and nurturance, whereas *indifferent* parents do little to monitor their children's behavior and exhibit low levels of control, clarity of communication, maturity demands, and nurturance (Baumrind, 1991; Lamborn et al., 1996; Steinberg et al., 1994). Adolescents whose families display an authoritative parenting style have been found to experience better relationships at home and better performance and social adjustment at school (Smetana, 1995; Steinberg et al., 1992). Adolescents with indifferent (neglectful) parents experience the lowest level of adjustment. Parenting styles were found to have significant effects on a wide range of adolescent behaviors. For example, in a one-year longitudinal study of 2,300 fourteen- to eighteen-year-olds from different ethnic and SES backgrounds, Laurence Steinberg and his colleagues discovered that differences in parenting styles were related to differences in psychosocial development, school achievement, internalized distress, and behavior problems (Steinberg et al., 1994).

These developmental differences continued or increased over time. Generally, teenagers raised in authoritative homes maintained or improved in all areas. Adolescents from authoritarian homes maintained good adjustments in all areas except internalized distress, which increased during the year studied. Adolescents from permissive homes were psychosocially well adjusted in interactions with peers and family, but showed declines in school adjustment and increases in school misconduct over the year. Finally, teens raised in indifferent homes showed the poorest adjustment in all areas at the beginning of the year, with sharp drops in work and school adjustment and increases in delinquency and drug and alcohol abuse one year later.

Parenting style and the quality of the parent-child relationship can exert influence far beyond the boundaries of the family. Contact among parents in a community and between adolescents and nonfamilial adults can benefit (or harm) children by creating and supporting shared community expectations regarding adolescent behavior (Coleman, 1988). For example, adolescents whose friends described their parents as authoritative earned higher grades in school, spent more time on homework, felt more academically competent, and reported lower levels of delinquency and substance abuse (Fletcher et al., 1995).

How children perceive their relationships with their parents may also influence their relationships with peers, particularly during early adolescence (Fuligni & Eccles, 1993). Early adolescents strongly desire relationships with parents that are less restrictive and provide increased opportunities to participate in decisions that affect their own lives. Children who fail to perceive these opportunities may lose hope that their parents will ever acknowledge that they are maturing and deserve to be treated more like adults. These teenagers may sacrifice developmentally important experiences with adults for the sake of peer relationships that appear to offer greater opportunity for respect and support. They are less likely to seek advice from their parents and more likely to consult with friends about important issues. In some cases, they may orient toward peers so strongly that they are willing to forgo their parents' rules, their schoolwork, and even their own talents to ensure peer acceptance (Fuligni & Eccles, 1993).

Craig Mason and his colleagues found that the style of parental control that African American mothers employed depended on who their children's peers were (Craig et al., 1996). For teenagers whose peers engaged in a relatively low level of problem behaviors—such as gang activity, drug use, stealing, truancy, and fighting, with or without a weapon—the optimal level of parental control required to influence their problem behaviors was relatively low, and remained relatively low, even if parents increased or decreased their control. But for adolescents who associated with peers involved in higher levels of problem behavior, the optimal level of parental control was higher, and deviations from this level led to significant increases in their own problem behavior.

In summary, parents and adolescents get along best when decision making is consistent and collaborative, decisions are perceived as being fair and reasonable rather than arbitrary, and the developmental needs and sensitivities of all family members, both parents and children, are respected. Self-reliance and self-control and the successful academic and social achievement associated with authoritative parenting during childhood are also fostered by these qualities during adolescence (Baumrind, 1989, 1991a; Hart et al., 1990). An authoritative style of parenting continues to be positively associated with the quality of parent-child relationships throughout the lifespan.

The closeness of this mother, daughter, grandmother, and great grandmother illustrates that good parenting styles affect the quality of relationships throughout the lifespan.
Source: Blend Images/Shutterstock.com.

SES The socioeconomic status of an individual or family that is determined by level of education, income, and type of work, as well as by lifestyle and social values. Also called *social class.*

SES and Ethnic Differences in Families

As noted earlier, the type of family in which they grow up significantly influences adolescents. One useful way to describe families is by **SES** *(socioeconomic status,* or *social class),* which is determined by parents' levels of education, incomes, and type of work, as well as by their lifestyles and cultural values. Studies of families in the United States, Great Britain, and Italy have found that differences between the values, child-rearing practices, and expectations of middle-class parents and those of working- and lower-class parents closely parallel differences in the amount of autonomy, independence, and satisfaction enjoyed in their day-to-day work experiences (Greenberger et al., 1994; Kohn et al., 1986).

These studies found that adolescents in middle-class families were encouraged to be independent and to regulate or control their own behavior rather than rely on the rewards or punishments of others to determine how they would act. The parents' child-rearing styles tended to be democratic or authoritative rather than authoritarian. Working-class parents were much more authoritarian than middle-class parents in their child-rearing patterns and were less likely to support their children's attempts to be independent and participate in family decision making until their children were ready to leave home.

Recent research supports these findings (Glasgow et al., 1997; Greenberger et al., 1994; Steinberg et al., 1994). For example, Laurence Steinberg and his colleagues found similar relationships among parenting styles and SES in a sample often thousand ninth through twelfth-grade students from different ethnic backgrounds and family structures (biological parents or other parenting arrangement). Authoritative parenting (based on student reports) generally was more common in middle-class than in working-class families, although ethnic differences and differences in family structure were also important. Table 16.3 gives the percentages of authoritative families for each level of SES and ethnic group. In addition, for all ethnic groups and family types, adolescents from authoritative families had better school grades, were more self-reliant, and exhibited less delinquent behavior than those from nonauthoritative families (Steinberg et al., 1991).

There is, however, some reason for caution in drawing conclusions. For one thing, it is unlikely that the categories the researchers used to classify family structure, SES, culture, and parenting style adequately capture the range of relationships and contexts that are at work. For another, these categories do not adequately take into account changes in family structure and parenting style and differences in parenting styles when more than one parent is involved. (In thinking about your own adolescence, how accurately is the parenting

TABLE 16.3 Percentages of Families with Authoritative Parenting Styles in Different SES Levels, Ethnic Groups, and Parenting Situations

| | Working-Class Family Structure || Middle-Class Family Structure ||
Ethnic Group	Biological Parents	Other*	Biological Parents	Other
White	17.2	11.5	15.0	17.6
African American	13.4	12.2	14.0	16.0
Latinx	10.7	9.8	15.8	12.9
Asian	7.5	6.1	15.6	10.8

SES differences: Middle-class parents were more likely to be authoritative than working-class parents in all ethnic groups, with the exception of white biological parents.

Ethnic differences: The highest percentage of authoritative parenting occurred for whites, followed by African Americans, Latinx, and Asians.

Differences in family structure: In both working-class and middle-class Latinx and Asian families and for working-class white and African American families, authoritative parenting occurred more frequently with biological parents than with other parenting arrangements. For both middle-class white and African American families, however, authoritative parenting was less frequent with biological parents than with other parenting arrangements.

*Includes single-parent households, stepfamilies, and other family arrangements.
Source: Adapted from Steinberg et al. (1991), Table 1, p. 25.

style in your family, including the family structure, cultural, SES, and community contexts in which you were raised, captured by the categories just mentioned?)

The Role of Ethnicity and Community in Family Decision Making

Susie Lamborn, Sanford Dornbusch, and Laurence Steinberg (1996) conducted a two-year longitudinal study of the relationship among ethnicity, community context, and styles of family decision making and adolescent adjustment among European American, Latinx, African American, and Asian American high school students. Three types of family decision making were studied: *unilateral teen* (decisions made by the teenager alone), *unilateral parent* (decisions made by the parent alone), *and joint parent-teen* (decisions made jointly be parent and teenager). For all four ethnic groups, unilateral teen decisions were associated with poorer adolescent adjustment one year later, whereas joint parent-teen decision making was associated with improved adjustment. Teens whose parents allowed them a great deal of decision-making autonomy over a wide range of issues reported higher rates of deviant behavior, lower academic competence, and poorer psychosocial functioning, whereas those whose parents engaged in joint decision making with them reported higher academic competence and more positive psychosocial functioning.

Community context interacted with ethnic background in three distinct patterns of influence. For Latinx living in ethnically mixed neighborhoods, the impact of joint decision making on adjustment was more positive and the impact of unilateral teen decision making more negative. Among African American youth, however, the negative impact of unilateral teen decision making was greater for those living in predominantly white communities, compared to those in ethnically mixed communities. Finally, for European and Asian Americans, living in an ethnically mixed versus an all-white or Asian American neighborhood did not appear to affect the impact of type of decision making on adolescent adjustment (Lamborn et al., 1996). The "A Multicultural View" feature describes adaptive strategies that families of minority youths use to cope with the challenges they often face.

> ### A Multicultural View
>
> #### Differing Cultural Views of Delinquency
>
> Cultures differ widely in how they judge the appropriateness of adolescents' delinquent behavior and how they respond when it occurs. Jeffrey Arnett (1992) suggests that this is largely due to important forces outside of the microsystem of family and peer group that strongly influence adolescent socialization. As we saw in Chapter 1's discussion of ecological systems of development, mesosystem, exosystem, and macrosystem influences include the school community, legal system, cultural beliefs, and the media. In Arnett's view, some cultures value independence and free self-expression more highly than they value conformity. These *broad socialization* cultures have no commonly accepted belief systems by which to judge right and wrong behavior. Such cultures tolerate a wide range of deviations from cultural expectations without severe upset or punishment. In contrast, *narrow socialization* cultures subscribe to ideologies that strictly set forth what constitutes right and wrong behavior. Such cultures value conformity and adherence to standards of the community over individual autonomy, and are more likely to severely punish deviations from community standards or norms. This helps explain why behaviors considered delinquent in one society are tolerated in others.
>
> A study by Jeffrey Arnett and Lene Jensen (1997) which compared socialization and risk behavior among middle class adolescents in Denmark and the United States lends support to this view. Overall, socialization was narrower among the Danish youth, who had more household obligations, greater community stability, and more adults beyond their immediate families involved in their socialization. Rates of risk-taking and delinquent behavior were higher for American teens, who were raised in a more broadly socialized culture. American teens had higher rates of high-speed and drunk driving and of minor criminal behavior such as shoplifting and vandalism, whereas Danish youth had higher rates of riding a bicycle or moped while intoxicated. Danish adolescents also had higher rates of sexual intercourse than American adolescents, but because Americans were less likely to use contraception, overall rates of unprotected sex (without contraception) were almost identical.
>
> Another good example of cultural difference with regard to delinquent behavior is the use of alcohol. While adolescent drinking of alcoholic beverages is a cause of great concern in the United States, in Jamaica, adolescent drinking is not a sign of delinquent behavior and there are few legal restrictions against it (Smith & Blinn Pike, 1994). In European countries, attitudes about teenage drinking and the amount of weekly drinking that occurs vary widely. Adolescents in Greece and Italy, for example, drink almost twice as much alcohol per week than teenagers in Ireland, and adolescents in Spain are able to consume considerably more alcohol per week than are adolescents in the United States before they are categorized as "drinkers" (Recio Adrados, 1995; van Reek et al., 1994). Studies of juvenile delinquency in England, France, Germany, Japan, South Africa, and the United States also find that differences in cultural tradition and national character play an important role in how delinquency is defined, how prevalent it is, and how it is treated (Corley & Smitherman, 1994; McCall, 1995).
>
> Whether or not adolescent social behavior is viewed as deviant is also affected by the status of the particular adolescent subculture within the majority culture and by how adolescents view that culture. For example, Mexican American teenagers may decide to join a gang as

Divorce, Remarriage, and Single Parenthood

Over the past half century, divorce has become a common event in American domestic experience. Almost half of all first marriages in the United States end in divorce, with about one million children experiencing their parents' divorce each year (CDC, 2009). Divorce affects children of every race, religion, ethnic background, and socioeconomic level. Adolescents feel the impact of a change in family structure, whether that change occurs in their childhood or during their teenage years. In addition, one-third of American children will experience the remarriage of a parent because roughly one-half of divorced adults will remarry within four years of their first divorce (Hetherington, 2005). Creating new family structures from intact, single-parent, blended family, and stepfamily configurations, each with their own set of challenges, tests adolescents who are in the process of establishing their own separate identity (Hetherington, 2005; Kleinsorge and Covitz, 2012). Adjusting to a parent's divorce is truly a transactional process, especially for adolescents, and a number of factors influence whether the outcomes associated with parental divorce are positive, negative, or a combination of the two.

> ### A Multicultural View
>
> #### Differing Cultural Views of Delinquency *continued*
>
> a way of retaining their own culture of origin and rejecting the majority values found in American public schools (Calabrese & Noboa, 1995). A large-scale international survey of youth-related offenses among fourteen- to twenty-one-year-old boys and girls from thirteen countries found that youth from low educational and low-SES circumstances reported more violent and property-related-offenses than did those from more mainstream social and economic circumstances, but that drug offenses and more minor youth-related offenses were equally distributed across all SES backgrounds (McQuoid, 1996).
>
> Most of the research discussed earlier focuses on Western industrialized countries. To what extent is adolescent antisocial behavior an expected occurrence in nonindustrial societies? To answer this question, cultural anthropologists Alice Schlegel and Herbert Barry (1991) analyzed cross-cultural differences regarding such expectations in a sample of 186 nonindustrial societies from around the world. The antisocial behaviors studied included hostile speech, fighting, crimes against persons, theft, sexual misbehavior, destruction of property, and drunkenness or misuse of other drugs. Direct information about antisocial behavior among adolescent boys was available for fifty-four societies, twenty-four of which expected antisocial behavior to occur and thirty of which did not. Similar information was available for adolescent girls in thirty-four societies, six of which expected it to be present and twenty-eight of which did not. In general, antisocial behavior was less likely in societies in which adolescent boys spent a significant amount of time with adults, and was more likely in societies in which adolescents spent much of their time in organized peer groups, particularly when peer activities were highly competitive.
>
> Schlegel and Barry also found that some societal organizations appear to promote adolescent misbehavior, either because the conditions that contribute to it are not recognized or because preventing such conditions would be too costly or disrupt other arrangements. For example, when it is economically advantageous to have groups of adolescent boys working apart from adults and adult supervision, risk of aggressive and other antisocial activities is likely to increase. They cite the case of the African Masai, who live in the highlands of Kenya and Tanzania. Masai adolescent boys are responsible for herding cattle and are sometimes suspected of stealing cattle to add to their own herds. Among Abkhaz adolescent boys, who live in the Georgian Republic (formerly part of the Soviet Union) and spend much of their time with peers, theft is a central feature of economic and political life and boys are trained to steal. However, if this thievery is turned against community members and even other peers, it is then punished. Antisocial behavior, while publicly deplored, may also be tolerated or even condoned if it serves individual family interests, such as fighting with an enemy's child or stealing from a disliked or envied neighbor.
>
> Antisocial behavior, particularly among adolescent boys, is more likely in cultures that define adolescence as a new stage that involves a sharp break from childhood and includes a rapid transition to adult character, the development of new roles in the family and in the community, and increased opportunities to own property and to choose a spouse. Adolescent antisocial behaviors are also more likely when such behavior is prevalent among adult men.

Based on their extensive review of the literature on the impact of divorce and remarriage on children and adolescents, Mavis Hetherington and her colleagues proposed a transactional model similar to the ecological model used by Uri Bronfenbrenner (see Chapter 1) to understand how the many complex factors work together to influence children's adjustment (Hetherington et al., 1998). Figure 16.3 diagrams how these factors interact. The main factors to consider include (1) the individual characteristics of the parents, including their personality, education, and psychological problems; (2) the nature of the marital transition (marriage and remarriage); (3) stressful life experiences and economic changes associated with divorce (and remarriage); (4) the composition of the family following divorce or remarriage; (5) the types and amount of social support available to family members; (6) the amount of parental distress; (7) the family process, including the nature and quality of the relationships among family members; (8) the individual characteristics of the children, including age, gender, temperament, and intelligence, as well as strengths and vulnerabilities; and (9) the adjustment of the child or adolescent. This "transactional model" helps us to understand the risks associated with divorce and remarriage to the adjustment of children, adolescents, and adults. Chapter 9 includes additional discussion of the impact of divorce on school-age children.

FIGURE 16.3

A Transactional Model of the Predictors of Children's Adjustment Following Divorce and Remarriage

The arrows connecting the boxes indicate their influence on one another in together contributing to children's and teens' adjustment to marital transitions.

Source: Hetherington et al. (1998).

(a) Individual characteristics of parents (e.g., personality, education, psychological problems)
(b) Marital transitions; divorce and remarriage
(c) Stressful life experiences/economic change
(d) Family composition
(e) Social support
(f) Parental distress
(g) Family process
(h) Individual characteristics of child (e.g., age, gender, temperament, intelligence)
(i) Child/adolescent adjustment

Marital Conflict

Marital conflict is a well-known source of distress for both parents and children, and particularly for adolescents, whose struggles to separate from their families to establish an independent and autonomous identity often involve an increased need for a safe "home base" from which to separate and a heightened awareness of hostility and conflict between their parents (Harold & Conger, 1997; Hetherington et al., 1998). Some conflict is normal in marriages; in fact, children learn the strategies and skills needed to deal with conflict in their own lives by observing their parents' successful strategies for coping with marital discord. However, in families where levels of conflict and disagreement are too high because parents are unable to resolve them, children and adolescents are negatively affected (Cummings & Cummings, 1988). Recent research has shown both behavioral adjustment problems as well as a physiologic reaction in children living in a family where the parents are experiencing a high degree of conflict (Kleinsorge and Covitz, 2012; Nunes-Costa et al., 2009). Life in high-stress families can produce higher levels of cortisol in the brain, increasing anxiety, sleep disturbances, weight management, and greater irritability for both children and adolescents (Nunes-Costa et al., 2009). A majority of divorces involve a failure of parents to successfully resolve their conflicts, a problem that often intensifies during the process of separation and divorce, and may persist even after the marriage has ended, when the need to share parenting responsibilities may continue.

The Impact of Divorce and Remarriage

Between one-quarter and one-third of adolescents in divorced and remarried families become disengaged from their families, minimizing the time they spend at home and avoiding interactions, activities, and communication with family members. When this disengagement is associated with lack of adult support and supervision and with involvement with a delinquent peer group, antisocial behavior and school problems are more likely. However, if the adolescent has a relationship with a caring adult outside the home, such as the parent of a friend, a teacher, a neighbor, or a coach, disengagement may be a positive solution to a disrupted family situation (Hetherington et al., 1998).

Children in divorced families tend to "grow up" faster due in part to early assignment of responsibilities, more autonomy in making decisions, and less adult supervision. Whether this is a positive or negative developmental consequence depends on whether or not the demands are within the adolescent's capabilities. If adolescents perceive themselves as being unfairly burdened with responsibilities that interfere with their other activities, resentment, rebellion, and noncompliance may result (Hetherington et al., 1998).

Adolescents who grow up in troubled families that remain together but have high levels of unresolved marital conflict and hostility are likely to experience negative developmental consequences as well. For families in which destructive and unresolved conflicts between parents cannot be resolved, divorce may provide the best solution and result in improved developmental outcomes for the teenagers and other children involved (Harold & Conger, 1997; Hetherington et al., 1998).

Lifespan Effects

The effects of divorce and remarriage are experienced throughout the lifespan. Compared to children from two-parent, nondivorced families, children, adolescents, and adults from divorced and remarried families are at increased risk for developing difficulties in adjustment, including academic problems, psychological disorders, lower self-esteem, and problems in their relationships with parents, siblings, and peers. The normative developmental tasks of adolescence and early adulthood—developing intimate relationships and autonomy—are especially hard. In addition to experiencing some of the same behavior problems found in childhood, adolescents are more likely to drop out of school, be unemployed, become sexually active at an earlier age, have children out of wedlock, associate with antisocial peers, and be involved in delinquent activities and substance abuse. Both male and female adolescents whose parents have divorced are more likely to become teenage parents, and single parenthood most adversely affects the lives of adolescents who experience declining SES and who drop out of school (Conger & Chao, 1996; Demo & Acock, 1996; Hetherington et al., 1998; Simons & Chao, 1996; Whitbeck et al., 1996).

Adult children of divorced and remarried families have more adjustment problems, less satisfaction with their lives, lower socioeconomic achievement, higher marital instability, and more problems in their marital interactions than adults from families that remained intact (Hetherington et al., 1998). Many young adults who are children of divorce have witnessed their separated, divorced, or widowed mothers become **displaced homemakers** due to loss of their conventional roles of wife and mother and lack of preparation for employment and single parenthood. They tend to hold more negative views of marriage as a result. Many divorced fathers lack the *kinkeeping skills* needed to keep in touch with their children and other family members, such as phoning, sending birthday cards, or visiting, skills that traditionally have been in the province of women.

displaced homemaker A woman who committed herself to the conventional roles of wife and mother, lost these roles due to separation, divorce, or widowhood, and was unprepared for employment and single parenthood.

Social Relationships during Adolescence

We already touched on the interplay among peer group, ethnic and community context, parenting styles, and family decision making, and their impact on development. Now we will consider the direct influence of friends, peers, and work on adolescent development in more detail.

Friendship

Friends matter a lot during adolescence. Peer relationships temporarily supplant the parent's role as the source of greatest influence for the adolescent. As teens become more mobile, and spend more time away from home, they seek the company of others who look, think, feel, and act like themselves. Friends offer reassurance, understanding and advice, and emotional and social support in stressful situations. The opportunity to share inner feelings of disappointment as well as happiness with close friends enables the adolescent to better deal with her emotional ups and downs. Furthermore, a capacity to form close, intimate friendships during adolescence is related to overall social and emotional adjustment and competence (Buhrmester, 1990; Reid et al., 1989).

> **What Do You Think?**
>
> Think about your own separation and individuation with regard to your parents. How similar were your concerns to those described in the text?

Especially during early and middle adolescence, friendships help teens to become more independent of parents and other authority figures and to resist the seemingly arbitrary demands of family living. Friends provide one another with cognitive and social scaffolding that differs from what acquaintances provide. Having good friends supports positive developmental outcomes during periods of developmental change (Hartup, 1996). Friends also promote independence simply by providing knowledge of a world beyond the family. Teenagers learn that not every young person is required to be home by the same hour every night, that some parents expect their children to do more household chores than other parents do, and that other families hold different religious or political views. The processes of sharing feelings and beliefs and exploring new ideas and opinions with friends play an important role in helping adolescents define their sense of self (Rawlins, 1992).

Qualities of Adolescent Friendships

Friends strongly influence adolescent development by virtue of their positive and negative characteristics, attitudes, values, and behaviors and through the quality of the friendship. A friendship based on mutual respect and trust, intimacy, and prosocial behavior is likely to help the adolescent cope with stressful situations in the family and in school. Friendships that lack these qualities are likely to be less helpful or even destructive (Dusek, 1991; Hartup, 1996).

During the teenage years, the basis of what makes a close friendship changes. When asked to define close friendships and how they are initiated, maintained, and ended, adolescents report that *mutual understanding* and *intimacy* are most important, whereas school-age children emphasize shared activities. Unlike cooperation between younger children, adolescent mutuality depends on the understanding that other people share some of one's own abilities, interests, and inner experiences and on an appreciation of each person's uniqueness. In fact, early adolescents share a fascination with the particular interests, life histories, and personalities of their friends; young teenagers want to understand friends as unique individuals and be understood by them in the same way. The ability of adolescents to recognize the advantages of complementary relationships—relationships in which two people with different strengths and abilities cooperate for mutual benefit—makes possible friendships that involve greater commitment, permanence, and loyalty. Intimacy in adolescent friendships includes self-revelation, confidence (in keeping secrets), and a sense of exclusivity (Damon, 1983; Youniss, 1980).

The quality of friendships during early adolescence appears to have long-term effects on development. Catherine Bagwell, Andrew Newcomb, and William Bukowski (1998) conducted a twelve-year longitudinal study of thirty young adults who had a stable, reciprocal best friend or "chum" in fifth grade and thirty young adults who had been without a chum. Adults who had close friends as early adolescents experienced better adjustment in school and family relationships and had less difficulty with authority figures than those who did not. Adults who had been rejected by peers in their early adolescence did more poorly in school, had greater difficulty with authorities, had lower levels of aspiration, and participated in fewer organizations and social activities in later adolescence and early adulthood. Finally, lower levels of peer rejection during early adolescence predicted more successful overall life adjustment and feelings of self-worth in adulthood.

Gender and Friendships

How do friendships between girls and boys differ? Friendships formed by boys generally involve lower levels of emotional intimacy than those of girls, who are better able to express feelings and more comfortable with giving emotional support to one another. During the junior high and early high school years, girls appear to develop greater intimacy with the opposite sex than boys do. They also tend to have one or two close friends, whereas adolescent boys often have many friends with whom they are less intimate. Adolescent boys may be more likely to equate intense intimacy exclusively with heterosexual friendships, whereas girls at this age can be comfortably close with both male and female friends.

To better understand developmental changes in the patterns and gender differences in the activities, thoughts, and feelings associated with friendship during adolescence, Maryse Richards and her colleagues had 218 adolescents in fifth through eighth grade carry electronic pagers for one week and complete self-report forms in response to signals received at random times during their waking hours (Richards et al., 1998). When paged, the teens responded to questions about with whom they were talking, about whom they were thinking, and what their subjective experiences were, including body image, mood, motivation, self-esteem, and excitement, at the moment they were contacted. These same adolescents underwent the same procedure four years later, when they were in grades nine through twelve.

The researchers found that both the amount of time adolescents spent with and thought about same-sex friends and the positive feelings they experienced did not decline across adolescence and into high school. Compared to fifth- and sixth-graders, adolescents in high school spent more time with opposite-sex friends and more time thinking about them. Fifth- and sixth-grade girls spent approximately an hour a week in the presence of a boy and less than two hours thinking about an individual of the opposite sex, while fifth- and sixth-grade boys spent less than an hour in the presence of a girl and less than an hour thinking about girls. By eleventh and twelfth grades, however, girls were spending almost ten hours a week with a male companion, whereas boys were spending approximately five hours a week with a female companion.

Compared to boys, girls' opposite-sex companionship and frequency of thoughts about boys had increased dramatically from eighth to twelfth grade. The oldest girls spent roughly eight hours each week thinking about a boy, while the oldest boys spent approximately five to six hours per week thinking about a girl. During early adolescence, seventh- and eighth-graders spent more time thinking about the opposite sex (four to six hours) than actually being with the opposite sex (thirty to eighty minutes). By eleventh and twelfth grades, this trend had shifted, and more time was spent in the actual presence of the other sex. In general, girls spent more time interacting with and thinking about boys and girls, whereas boys, when not with their peers, spent very little time thinking about either.

According to Richards and her colleagues, it is developmentally normative for pre- and young adolescents to be more romantically involved in fantasy than in reality. The adolescents in their study reported that time spent with opposite-sex peers was more exciting and that they felt more attractive and important, enjoyed more positive feelings, and felt much more "in love" than when they were with same-sex peers. However, when alone and thinking about the opposite sex, subjective experiences were less positive. Older adolescents felt especially negative and unmotivated, perhaps because they missed the company of their girlfriend or boyfriend. We take a closer look at these and related issues later in this chapter.

Interethnic Friendships

Friendships between adolescents from different ethnic groups tend to be relatively rare. Among adults in the United States, anywhere from 40% (Dunsmuir, 2013) to 90% (Cox, Navarro-Rivera, & Jones, 2016) of white adults report that all of their friends are also white. A similar trend is present among adolescents (Pica-Smith & Poynton, 2014). As we saw in Chapter 13's discussion of psychosocial development in middle childhood, however, the social contexts in which potential friendship interactions occur seem to make an important difference. In one study of school and neighborhood friendship patterns among African American and white students attending integrated junior high schools, most students reported having a close other-race school friend, but only about one-quarter saw such a friend frequently outside school. (Giordano et al., 1993). A study of diverse schools with no racial group exceeding 50% demonstrated that having cross-ethnic interactions were related to higher GPA and higher expectations of teachers

Sharing interests with friends is important to teenagers, as it is to children. At the same time, though, less tangible qualities, such as loyalty, mutual respect, and intimacy, become increasingly important in friends, especially among older adolescents.

Source: oneinchpunch/Shutterstock.com.

on those students (Lewis, Nishina, Hall, Cain, Bellmore, & Witkow, 2018). Moreover, having a diverse group of friends during these formative years is linked with less prejudice and racial bias throughout life, better social skills, and higher academic attainment (Pica-Smith & Poynton, 2014).

Living in a neighborhood with children from other ethnic groups appears to increase the likelihood of having close other-race friends outside of school. Having a higher proportion of neighborhood friends attending one's school also affects other-race friendship. Living in a racially mixed neighborhood may help to create more positive attitudes toward members of other ethnic groups and provide a meeting ground on which cross-race friendships can develop outside of school. The informal peer activities that occur in neighborhood settings are more likely to promote close friendships across groups than the more formal, teacher-directed activities in school. Interethnic friendships are strongly influenced by the attitudes adolescents hold about their own and other ethnic groups (DuBois & Hirsch, 1993; Giordano et al., 1993; Phinney et al., 1997).

Peer Groups

Peer groups play an even greater role in the everyday lives of adolescents than they do for younger children. They also tend to be more structured and organized, frequently include individuals from a relatively wide age range, and are much less likely to be all male or all female. Peer groups are an important component of an adolescent's *social convoy,* the network of social relationships that follow a person over his or her lifetime, changing in structure but providing continuity in the exchange of support, as we will see in Chapter 17 on psychosocial development in late adulthood. Who is included in this social convoy of support is determined by the adolescent's emotional attachment to the person and by the person's role in the adolescent's life (Levitt et al., 1993). Peers provide a teenager with critical information about who he is, how they are, how they should act, what they are like, and so forth. They offer an environment for making social comparisons between one's own actions, attitudes, and feelings and those of others. These are important ingredients in an adolescent's development of self-concept and identity (Connolly et al., 1987). Most important, peer groups provide a support base outside of the family from which the teenager can more freely try on the different identity roles that ultimately will contribute to her adult personality: popular, brain, normal, druggie, outcast, partyer, punk, grind, clown, banger, nerd, lover, and so forth (B. Brown et al., 1993; Stone & Brown, 1998; Durbin et al., 1993).

Peer groups can also exert powerful pressures to conform. Especially when the family fails to serve as a constructive corrective force, such pressures may contribute to a prolonged period of identity diffusion or to premature identity foreclosure, for example, as a teenage parent, drug addict, or gang member (Dishion et al., 1988; Patterson & Dishion, 1985). Conformity to peer pressure can be particularly disruptive during early adolescence. Frank Vitaro and his colleagues examined how the characteristics of their friends affected delinquency among eleven- and twelve-year-old boys who were judged by their teachers to be either highly disruptive, moderately disruptive, moderately conforming, or highly conforming (Vitaro et al., 1997). They found that only moderately disruptive boys appeared to be negatively influenced by hostile-aggressive friends and exhibited more delinquent behavior at age thirteen. Highly disruptive boys were the most delinquent at age thirteen, regardless of their friends' characteristics, and boys who were judged to be moderately or highly conforming appeared to be unaffected by their friends' characteristics. We will explore the contribution of peers to negative developmental outcomes more fully when we discuss juvenile delinquency later in this chapter.

Peer Group Structure

Adolescent peer groups generally are of two types—the clique and the crowd. The **clique** is a small, close-knit group of two or more members (with an average of six members) who are intimately involved in a number of shared purposes and activities and exclude those who are not. The **crowd** is a larger, less cohesive group of between fifteen and thirty members (with an average of twenty members) generally consists of from two to four cliques, and is usually based on stereotyping (geeks, jocks, druggies, etc.).

Clique membership allows teenagers to have a few select friends they know well and who share important interests and activities, whereas membership in a crowd provides contact with a much broader group of peers on a more casual basis. The small size and intimacy of a clique make it like a family in which the adolescent can feel comfortable and secure. The major clique activity seems to be talking, and cliques generally meet during the school week. Advantages of clique membership include security, a feeling of importance, and acquisition of socially acceptable behaviors (such as academic, social, or athletic competence) that are part of conforming to the clique's norms. However, conformity can also suppress individuality and may promote "in-group" snobbishness, intolerance, and other negative values and behaviors. Involvement with a clique of antisocial peers is associated with various adolescent adjustment problems, including substance abuse, school dropout, delinquency, and gang membership, although which is cause and which is effect is uncertain (Dishion et al., 1988; Patterson & Dishion, 1985).

Crowds usually gather at parties and other organized social functions, which typically take place on weekends. They tend to include both males and females, thereby providing opportunities for mixed-sex interactions and promoting transition from same-sex to mixed-sex cliques. Crowd membership also provides opportunities to interact with individuals from a broad range of backgrounds and experiences, but can also promote snobbishness and can pose real or imagined threats to parental and teacher authority. Cliques and crowd affiliations were often limited by geography, at least until teens became more mobile after receiving their driver's license. Access to new peer groups and crowds is now available worldwide with adolescent use of the Internet and the new technological advances in social media.

clique A small, close-knit peer group of two or more members (average of six members) who are intimately involved in a number of shared purposes and activities and exclude those who are not.

crowd A large, loosely knit peer group of between fifteen and thirty members (average of twenty members) that generally consists of from two to four cliques and is usually based on stereotypes.

Social Media and Peer Influence: Teens and Social Media

Adolescents born between the early 1980s and 2000 are collectively known as the Millennials, or Generation Y. Following on the heels of the preceding generations identified as the Baby Boomers (born between 1946 and 1964) and Generation X (born between 1965 and 1982). This generation has grown up in an ever-expanding world of technological advances and the rise of the global community. Nowhere is this more evident than in the Millennials' involvement in and interactions with social media.

Teens in the second decade of the twenty-first century are as connected to the Internet for social development as earlier generations were to the schoolyard or their community neighborhood. In fact, most adolescents spend as much time, if not more, in their "virtual neighborhoods" as they do interacting with peers in the hallways of their schools or the streets of their hometown. The use of social media and accessing social media sites on the Web is, according to O'Keeffe and Clark-Pearson (2011), one of the most common activities engaged in by children and teens today. In a recent survey conducted by the Pew Research Center (Madden et al., 2013), 95 percent of teens reported that they use the Internet. Every day, and multiple times each week, young teens and transitional teens go online to share "what's happening" with others in their school, in neighboring towns, and across the globe. They do so on sites like Facebook, Snapchat, and Instagram. About 79 percent of all teens use Snapchat, followed closely by the 76 and 73 percent who use Facebook and Instagram, respectively. Forty percent of all adolescents use Twitter to follow and inform their friends about their daily activities (Statista, 2017). Roughly 93 percent of all teenagers have smartphones with Internet access, and they spend almost 200 minutes each day utilizing them (Statista, 2017). Smartphones allow teens to connect at all times to their virtual neighborhood via tweets, posts, and instant updates on important events in their busy lives.

When "hanging out" on these social media sites, many adolescents wrestle with a classic adolescent paradox. In striving for identity formation, all teens crave the dual constructs of privacy from their parents and greater personal and social independence (Dunkle & Anthis, 2001; Erikson, 1968; Jensen & Arnett, 2012). In their virtual neighborhoods, where their online reputations are formed, many teens are vulnerable to sharing too much private information, especially to strangers. Madden et al. (2013) found that while on various social media sites, 92 percent of teens use their real names and post pictures of themselves and their friends and family. In addition, 85 percent will share their actual birthdays online, 53 percent will post their e-mail addresses, 25 percent will include "selfie" videos of various activities, while 20 percent of all teens will give out their cell phone numbers. In keeping with the advances in technology, roughly 16 percent of all teens will activate the location app on their social media sites, so anyone who is following them knows exactly where they are at that moment. The privacy paradox emerges when the latest survey data indicate that only 60 percent of all adolescents using social media set their profiles to private! What may be private to mothers and fathers, who do not access their teens' websites, is common knowledge to friends, acquaintances, and total strangers.

The other half of the paradoxical problem with teens and social media is in their desire for independence in establishing their own separate identity. The identity they form online may not be congruent with their persona in the "real" world of day-to-day interactions with people at home and at school. Opportunities or pressure to participate in cyberbullying or being coerced to engage in innocent flirting that may evolve into hard-core sexting are often hard to resist (Patchin & Hinduja, 2006). In much the same way as face-to-face peer pressure is difficult to resist for the developing adolescent, giving in to "virtual" social pressures can define an adolescent's online reputation in ways that can be hurtful and damaging (Geddes, 2014; Hinduja & Patchin, 2007).

By nature, adolescents struggle with the self-regulation of their behaviors and emotions, and thus are very susceptible to peer pressure as they navigate through their vast social media networks. But not all peer pressure is negative. Proper use of social media often benefits adolescents by enhancing their technological skills, developing their communication skills, and providing opportunities for social connections with peers who share similar interests (O'Keeffe & Clark-Pearson, 2011). For teens who are socially awkward in face-to-face interactions, social media allow them to engage in conversations that may reinforce their social confidence. Like any new phenomenon that gains enormous popularity with adolescents, more research is needed to assess both the benefits and the cost of social media for teens, their parents, and the community.

Parental Influence

Parents of adolescents frequently are concerned that their children will be excessively influenced by peer pressure and that peer influence will replace their own guidance. Laurence Steinberg and Anne Levine (1990) suggest that parents can help their adolescents with their

TABLE 16.4 Guidelines for Parents Concerning Their Adolescents' Friends

Helping Adolescents to Deal with Peer Pressure
- Build self-esteem by helping your adolescent discover her or his strengths and special talents.
- Encourage independence and decision making within the family.
- Talk about situations in which people have to choose among competing pressures and demands.
- Encourage your adolescent to anticipate difficult situations and plan ahead.
- Encourage your adolescent to form alliances with peers who share his or her values and your family's values.
- Know your adolescent's friends.
- Don't jump to hasty conclusions based on peers' appearance, dress, language, or interests.
- Allow time for peer activities.
- Remain close to your adolescent.

When to Be Concerned
- If your adolescent has no friends at all
- If your adolescent is secretive about her or his social life
- If your adolescent suddenly loses all interest in friends
- If all of your adolescent's friends are much older than him or her

Source: Adapted from Steinberg & Levine (1990), pp. 183–187.

friendships and relationships with peers in a number of ways. Table 16.4 lists these guidelines. The "Focusing On" feature discusses recent research findings on parental influence.

Adolescents in the World of Work

Adolescents balance many roles: son or daughter, friend, peer, student. Many also add "employee" to the mix. As we saw in Chapter 15, work has an impact on cognitive development and on identity formation as well. Participation in work within and outside the family provides a major base for the development of competence and sense of identity and self, especially during adolescence. Working with others can produce a broad range of benefits, from sound work habits to the development of helpfulness toward others, responsibility for the welfare of others, a sense of agency or personal efficacy, and an appreciation of the needs and feelings of others (Grusec et al., 1996).

For both male and female adolescents, participation in household work and the consequences of such involvement depend on the helper's motivations, the meaning of the work activity, and the social context in which it occurs. In a two-year longitudinal study of one thousand ninth-graders and their parents, Kathleen Call, Jeylan Mortimer, and Michael Shanahan (1995) found that adolescents from large families with fewer financial resources and mothers who were employed responded to the needs of their families by taking on more household responsibilities than adolescents from smaller families with more resources. Girls who were more competent to begin with chose work that allowed them to be helpful to others, and the opportunity to be helpful to others at work strengthened their sense of competency. Doing household chores increased a sense of competency for African American and Hispanic American boys, but decreased such feelings for European American boys, perhaps because the former group saw helping out as being

Focusing On . . .

Can Parents Influence Their Adolescent's Choice of Peer Group?

It has long been accepted that parental influence declines sharply during adolescence due to the increasing counterinfluence of peer groups over which parents have little control. However, recent large-scale studies of high school students challenge this view.

Bradford Brown and his colleagues studied parenting practices and peer affiliation in a sample of more than 3,700 high school students drawn from a variety of socioeconomic, ethnic, and family backgrounds (e.g., first-time two-parent, divorced, remarried) and types of communities (urban, suburban, rural) (Brown et al., 1993; Brown & Huang, 1996). To determine peer group affiliation, school administrators identified a set of boys and girls in each grade and within each ethnic group who represented a cross-section of the student body. Researchers interviewed students in small groups composed of individuals of the same sex, grade level, and ethnic background. Each group listed the school's major crowds and identified two boys and two girls in the same grade who were the leaders or most prominent members of each crowd.

Identified leaders then individually placed each student in the same grade level in one of the crowds that had been named. In addition, all students in the sample were surveyed about family characteristics, parenting practices, and adolescent behaviors related to academics, drug use, and self-reliance.

Brown and his colleagues found that levels of authoritative parenting (as reflected by parental monitoring, encouragement of achievement, and support for joint decision making) were significantly associated with teenagers' levels of academic achievement, drug use, and self-reliance. These factors, in turn, were closely related to the type of crowd an adolescent belonged to (popular, jock, brain, normal, druggie, and outcast).

The authors concluded that parents can indirectly influence the behaviors by which teenagers become associated with a particular crowd and that peer group norms serve to reinforce behaviors and predispositions that parenting strategies and/or family background characteristics influence. Although parenting practices and family background cannot *determine* a teenager's crowd affiliation, their influence should be taken seriously.

How might this parental influence work? Anne Fletcher and her colleagues (Fletcher et al., 1995) asked students about parenting practices in their families and about their academic achievement, psychosocial competence, behavior problems, and personal distress. Each student's friends independently evaluated the degree to which authoritative parenting was present in the peer network, as indicated by parental acceptance and involvement, behavioral supervision and strictness, and granting of psychological autonomy.

What did they find? Adolescents whose friends described their parents as authoritative earned higher grades in school, spent more time on homework, had more positive perceptions of their academic competence, and reported lower levels of delinquency and substance abuse. Fletcher and her colleagues suggest that authoritative parenting is associated with adolescent competence; competent, well-adjusted adolescents with authoritative parents select (and are selected by) peers similar in competence and background; and within-peer-group experiences maintain and strengthen a higher level of adjustment. Less competent adolescents with nonauthoritative parents are more likely to select peers who are similar to themselves, thus maintaining and amplifying their limitations. Adolescent delinquent activities may be unlikely due to the higher level of shared social control provided by a network of authoritative parents.

What Do You Think?

What role did your parents play in your peer relationships? What role did the parents of your friends play? If you were the parent of a teenager, how would you help your child make wise choices about peers?

This small, close-knit clique of high school students hangs out during lunch on a fairly regular basis to relax, talk, and hang out.
Source: Rawpixel.com/Shutterstock.com.

---

important to their families' functioning, whereas the latter saw them as burdensome and lacking in value.

Family dynamics also affected the relationship between helping with household work and feelings of competency and concern for others. For girls living in families where the father-daughter relationship was not supportive and the mother's manner of assigning

> **What Do You Think?**
>
> In what ways are your own experiences similar to the text's description of friendship, peer groups, and work during adolescence? In what ways do they differ?

household tasks diminished the girl's sense of autonomy and independence, participating in household chores undermined rather than enhanced feelings of competency (Call et al., 1995). Teenagers who were expected to do household work that benefited members of the family and expected to do it on a routine or self-regulated basis were more likely to show spontaneous concern for the welfare of others. Work that focused on what is one's "own," such as cleaning one's own room, or was based on frequent requests for assistance (i.e., nagging) was not associated with increased concern for others (Grusec et al., 1996).

How work outside the family influences adolescent development depends on how well it fits the developmental needs of the individual and his or her family, including the type and level of workplace stress, the relevance of job-related skills to future careers, and the compatibility between the demands and experiences of work and those of school. Further discussion of the relationship between work and school activities appears in Chapter 15.

Sexuality during Adolescence

The popular idea that adolescence is a highly sexual period of life is accurate, but for reasons beyond the physical. Sexual identity and sexual activity are not solely focused on sexual intercourse and the risks of pregnancy. During adolescence, the expression of sexual urges interacts closely with the need to establish a secure sexual identity that is reasonably free from anxiety, shame, or despair—an identity that is capable of fulfilling the need for healthy, intimate relationships with others (Zimmer-Gembeck & Helfand, 2008).

Sexual Experience

Trends in adolescent sexual activity in the United States peaked in the 1980s and 1990s, showing earlier initiation of intercourse, increased premarital intercourse, a greater number of partners, and ineffective and inconsistent use of contraceptives. Recent studies have attempted to add clarity to the prevailing data that the median age of first intercourse was 15.5 years for girls and 14.75 years for boys (Guttmacher Institute, 2013; CDC-YRBS, 2012). The national Youth Risk Behavior Survey (YRBS) reviewed the trends in adolescent sexual behaviors from 1991 to 2011. The trends in prevalence data showed a steady decrease from a high in 1991 of 54.1 percent of teens reporting they had had sexual intercourse, to a low of 45.6 percent a decade later in 2001. Over the next ten years, the prevalence rates remained statistically unchanged (CDC-YRBS, 2012). Table 16.5 lists the trends from 1991 to 2011. A fact sheet by the Guttmacher Institute (2013) broke this down further by age. Fewer than 2 percent of twelve-year-olds have had sex by their twelfth birthday, but within the next three years, by age fifteen, the figure rises to 16 percent, reaching close to half of all teens (48 percent) by age seventeen, and 61 and 71 percent by ages eighteen and nineteen, respectively (Guttmacher Institute, 2013).

These trends, as alarming as they were to parents, were about the same in the United States as in Western European nations (Coley & Chase-Lansdale, 1998; Seidman & Rieder, 1994). A close review of this most recent data from the Center for Disease Control's (CDC) biennial Youth Risk Behavior Surveillance survey (2012) is important in other ways. While showing a slight decline in adolescent sexual behaviors from previous decades, one area that has remained constant is the timing of a teen's first sexual activity and its impact on later development. In a sequential longitudinal study of the timing of first intercourse and psychosocial adjustment, Raymond Bingham and Lisa Crockett (1996) surveyed seventh-, eighth-, and ninth-grade adolescents annually through their graduation from twelfth grade. They found that for both boys and girls, earlier timing of first sexual intercourse was associated with longitudinal patterns of

TABLE 16.5 Rates of Adolescent Sexual Activity by Gender, Ethnic Group, and Grade

Gender	Ethnic Group			Grade			
	White	African American	Latinx	9	10	11	12
Male	44.0%	66.9%	53.0%	37.8%	44.5%	54.5%	62.6%
Female	44.5	53.6	43.9	27.8	43.0	51.9	63.6
Total	44.3	60.0	48.6	32.9	43.8	53.2	63.1

Note: Percentages are of high school students who report ever having sexual intercourse.
Source: Centers for Disease Control (2012).

greater difficulty with the transition to adolescence and with poorer psychosocial adjustment. Similarly, Armour and Haynie's (2007) longitudinal study also found that an early debut of sexual experience increased the risks of engaging in delinquent behaviors within the following year for both genders. Later developmental difficulties were found to last well beyond that first year and were more disruptive if teens were sexually active much earlier than members of their peers (Armour & Haynie, 2007).

Longitudinal patterns of development differed for early (before the median age), middle (after the median age), and late (still virgins) initiators of intercourse. Adolescents who had first sexual intercourse early demonstrated the poorest psychosocial adjustment in ninth grade, and the same negative pattern persisted through twelfth grade. Adolescents who postponed first sexual intercourse the longest (were still virgins) had the most positive ninth-grade adjustment and the most positive developmental trajectory through twelfth grade. They reported more positive psychosocial development, more positive family relationships, more frequent church attendance, greater commitment to education, and lower involvement with problem behaviors than those who initiated intercourse earlier. These longitudinal outcomes were not associated with the timing of first intercourse; rather, they appeared to be a continuation of enduring developmental paths based on childhood differences in temperament, personality, and family and life circumstances that were already well established before ninth grade (Bingham & Crockett, 1996; Dorius et al., 1993).

Sexual Attitudes and Behaviors

In 1992 Robert Michael, John Gagnon, and Edward Laumann conducted the National Health and Social Life Survey (NHSLS). They interviewed more than three thousand U.S. residents ages eighteen to fifty-nine about their sex lives, histories, and attitudes (Gagnon et al., 1994; Michael et al., 1994). They report that people's attitudes about sex fell into three broad categories: traditional, relational, or recreational. *Traditional* people said that "their religious beliefs always guide their sexual behavior." *Relational* people said that "sex should be part of a loving relationship." *Recreational* people said that "sex need not have anything to do with love." Not surprisingly, older married people had more traditional views of sex, whereas younger unmarried people held more recreational views.

Table 16.5 presents sexual activity rates by gender, ethnic group, and grade based on data collected by the U.S. Centers for Disease Control (2012). As the table indicates, rates of intercourse increase from ninth through twelfth grade for both males and females, with a higher percentage of males reporting intercourse at each grade level and overall. African American high school students report the highest overall rate of sexual intercourse (60.0 percent), followed by Latinx teens (48.6 percent) and white teens (44.3 percent). For each ethnic group, in past surveys, a higher percentage of males than females reported having had sexual intercourse. The exception was this latest YRBS survey (CDC, 2012), which showed white males and white females with almost identical percentages for the category of ever having had sexual intercourse.

By and large, girls tend to be more conservative than boys in their sexual attitudes, values, and actions, whereas boys tend to be more sexually active and to have more sexual encounters. This may be due to the fact that although boys' and girls' interest in sex is driven, in part, by testosterone, girls tend to be influenced more by environment and social expectations than are boys (Crockett, Raffaelli, & Moilanen, 2006; James et al., 2012). Girls are more likely to emphasize intimacy and love as a necessary part of sexual activity and less likely to engage in sex merely as a physically pleasurable activity (Leigh, 1989; White & DeBlassie, 1992; Zimmer-Gembeck & Helfand, 2008).

Dating

Since the beginning of this century, dating has tended to begin earlier, thus increasing the time span over which teenage dating takes place. Currently many adolescent girls begin dating at age twelve and boys at age thirteen, with almost one-half of boys and more than one-half of girls reporting dating at least once a week and approximately one-third dating two or three times per week. Only 10 percent of male and female high school seniors report never having dated (Savin-Williams & Berndt, 1990).

Dating is a major avenue for exploring sexual activity in both consensual (Zani, 1993) and nonconsensual (Small & Kerns, 1993) experiences. Because dating is occurring at younger ages and can also lead to violence and victimization, where and how young people learn about dating can be an important asset to establishing healthy boundaries in relationships. Regarding sources of information on dating and relationships, young girls tend to use a wider range of sources than their male peers. Not only do girls seek out friends, parents, and traditional and social media, as well as sexual education teachers in school, but they also trust these sources of information more than young boys (Wood et al., 2002). Boys, according to Wood et al. (2002), tend to explore fewer sources of information and appear to trust and value what they learn from the girls they date.

In recent years, with the advent of social media, dating has taken on a different aura than what was considered traditional dating just a few years ago. Group dating has become more common, which is less formal than one-to-one dating, and terms like "hooking-up" are often used synonymously with having a date. Smart phones and Internet access have led to an increase in teen cyberdating, making teens more vulnerable to cyberbullying and incidents of dating violence. Teen dating violence has become more frequent, leading to efforts to educate and protect young women and men as they embark on more intimate relationships. Whether dating in a group, or in a special dyad, there has been a growing awareness that dating situations may lead to sexual activity that is coerced. In a nationally representative survey, 42 percent of rape victims were first raped before age eighteen, and 30 percent of female rape victims were first raped between the ages of eleven and seventeen (Black et al., 2011). Among those who had first experienced rape, physical violence, or stalking from an intimate partner, over 22 percent of females and 15 percent of males also report this occurring in adolescence, between the ages of eleven and seventeen (Breiding, Chen, & Black, 2014). Teen dating violence also mirrors incidents of stalking, coercion, and intimidation that occur in emerging adult and adult relationships, often leading to serious, and at times tragic, outcomes for the developing adolescent (Zweig et al., 2013).

When there is a confluence of sexual intimacy, social media, and adolescent disinhibition, a perfect storm of tragic proportions is a very real potential outcome. The suicidal death of Jessica Logan is such an occurrence. Jessica, a high school senior in Ohio, sent nude pictures of herself to her boyfriend, at his urging. When they broke up, the pictures appeared on social media sites of Jessica's classmates, and the cyberbullying went viral at her school. Jessica even appeared on a local TV station in her hometown to share her story in hopes that no one else would have to go through what she had to endure. After that show, and after her graduation, having attended a friend's funeral, Jessica returned home and hung herself. Jessica's story made national news, and in 2012, the state of Ohio passed the Jessica Logan Act to help schools enforce cyberbullying in their school districts.

Sexual Orientations

Our discussion so far has centered on issues related to heterosexual orientation. But as in the population at large, not all adolescents are heterosexual. Reliable statistics on sexual orientation are difficult to obtain. Kaufman (2008) reports on a large-scale Canadian study in which 1.5 percent of adolescent males and 3 percent of females identified themselves as either bisexual, mostly homosexual, or 100 percent homosexual. In one large-scale study in the United States of thirty-eight thousand adolescents in grades seven through twelve, 88.2 percent described themselves as predominantly heterosexual (exclusively interested in the other sex), 1.1 percent as predominantly homosexual (exclusively interested in the same sex) or bisexual (interested in members of both sexes), and 10.7 percent as uncertain about their sexual orientation (Remafedi et al., 1992, 2007). Other studies have found that between 3 and 6 percent of teenagers report that they are lesbian or gay (Patterson, 1995).

Due largely to the political and educational efforts of the "equal rights" and "gay rights" movements, public acceptance of gay, lesbian, and bisexual orientations has increased significantly during the past several decades. This acceptance acknowledges the right of individuals to freely practice their own sexual orientations and lifestyles and to receive protection from discrimination. However, other researchers have found that **homophobia** (dislike, fear, and discrimination against homosexuals) remains strong among adolescents (Stokes, 1985; Williams & Jacoby, 1989). Negative attitudes toward gay, lesbian, bisexual, and transgendered individuals put LGBT youth at risk for greater mistreatment and victimization than other students. Violence against students in the LGBT community can include bullying and cyberbullying, harassment, and physical assault. In one large study of middle school and high school students, 80 percent of the students had been harassed verbally at school, while 40 percent were physically harassed, and one in five had been physically assaulted, all because of their sexual orientation (Kosciw et al., 2009). Unsurprisingly, in this same study, roughly 60 percent of the LGBT youth indicated they did not feel safe at school.

Because of persisting widespread homophobia, gay, lesbian, and bisexual adolescents are likely to experience feelings of attraction for members of the same sex for several years before actually *coming out,* or publicly acknowledging their sexual orientation (Patterson, 1995). A study by Ritch Savin-Williams (1995) found that for gay males initiation of sexual behavior with same-sex partners was closely associated with biological changes of puberty (early maturers initiated same-sex encounters earlier than did late maturers), whereas sexual behavior with opposite-sex partners began according to a youngster's age and level of social and emotional development.

Current understanding of the development of sexual-minority orientations is that the trajectory of development—same-sex interest, recognizing one's sexual orientation, and dating—is quite different for different individuals, depending on where they live, ethnicity, gender, socioeconomic status, etc. (Diamond & Savin-Williams, 2006). Though cross-gender behavior in childhood appears to be strongly associated with sexual-minority orientations in adolescence and adulthood for both males and females, a substantial proportion of gay and lesbian adults report no or few cross-gender behaviors in childhood (Bailey & Zucker, 1995; Golombok & Tasker, 1996; Green, 1987). In a unique longitudinal study, Susan Golombok and Fiona Tasker (1996) compared the sexual orientations of twenty-five adults who had been raised as children by lesbian mothers with a group of twenty-one adults who had been raised by heterosexual single mothers. Although children from lesbian families were more likely to explore same-sex relationships, all but two children raised by lesbian mothers (and all children raised by heterosexual mothers) identified themselves as heterosexual in adulthood, a difference that was not statistically significant.

A number of researchers are also exploring the contributions of biological and genetic predispositions to the development of sexual-minority orientations (Balter, 2015; Byne, 1994; Diamond & Savin-Williams, 2006; LeVay & Hamer, 1994; Patterson, 1995). One approach has sought to discover physical differences between the brains of male and female animals and humans; the second has explored the role of genes by using family and twin

homophobia Fear, dread, hostility, or prejudice directed toward gay and lesbian persons and the resulting mistreatment and discrimination.

> **What Do You Think?**
>
> When you were an adolescent, what were your attitudes toward premarital sex, dating, and sexual orientations? In what ways, if any, have your attitudes changed since then?

adoption studies to analyze the frequencies with which homosexuality occurs in families and by directly examining DNA. There is evidence that activity among certain genes, without differences in DNA, is linked to homosexuality among men (Balter, 2015), and there have also been links to prenatal development in that men with more older brothers are more likely to identify as gay (Ashley, 2013). However, as with most aspects of development, who we become is due to an interplay of nature and nurture that is different for each of us, and sexual orientation is likely due to a complex interaction between environment and genetics (Diamond & Savin-Williams, 2006).

The challenging task of achieving a secure sexual identity is considerably more difficult for nonheterosexual adolescents, who have the added burdens of grappling with their difference and the anxieties and dangers involved. Homosexual and bisexual teenagers frequently experience rejection by their families, peer groups, schools, places of worship, and other community institutions—the very groups adolescents depend on for support. The verbal abuse, the AIDS-related stigmatization, the threat of physical attack, and other forms of victimization they encounter put them at greater risk for mental health problems. However, strong support from family, friends, school and community, and antidiscrimination legislation and education about nonheterosexuality can all serve as buffers against these negative outcomes by creating an environment that allows these adolescents to successfully master the challenges of identity formation (Diamond & Savin-Williams, 2006; Hershberger & D'Augelli, 1995).

Sex and Everyday Life

Although sexuality plays an important role in adolescents' feelings, fantasies, and social relationships, it does not necessarily dominate their lives. As noted earlier, changes in sexuality during adolescence involve not only physical maturation and the development of new social skills; they also play a major role in the development of intimacy and personal identity. Reasons for engaging in sexual activity or for not having sex during adolescence vary, based on social, emotional, and moral attitudes and beliefs of the teenager. For those who abstain from having sex, religious reasons tend to predominate for males and females, followed by the desire to not get pregnant or to get someone pregnant, followed by not having found the right person yet (Martinez, Copen, & Abma, 2011). Keep in mind, however, that the nature and role of sexual activity in the lives of adolescents vary considerably depending on culture, SES, and overall life circumstances (Seidman & Rieder, 1994).

Sometimes, identity development is complicated by sexual issues. It can also be affected by social problems specific to teenagers, as we will see in the next section.

Special Problems of Adolescence

In Chapter 14, we looked at the special physical and health risks adolescents face as a group. Their lack of experience, their need to experiment with new and sometimes risky social roles, and the lack of educational and economic opportunities and social support they frequently encounter can place adolescents at high risk for developing certain psychosocial problems. In this section, we discuss three special problems of adolescence: teenage pregnancy and parenthood, adolescent depression and suicide, and juvenile delinquency.

Adolescent Pregnancy and Parenthood

Despite the declining rates in teen pregnancy over the past decades, nearly one million adolescent girls get pregnant each year. In the United States, nearly four out of every ten teen girls will get pregnant at least once before they turn twenty, according to the National Campaign to Prevent Teen Pregnancy (Kirby, 2007). In 1990, 1,040,000 adolescents under age twenty became pregnant, and approximately 530,000 (51 percent) of them gave birth (Alan Guttmacher Institute, 1994). By the end of the decade, the teen pregnancy rate declined by almost 20 percent, from 117 pregnancies per 1,000 women ages fifteen to nineteen, to 94 per 1,000 (Guttmacher Institute, 2002). Birth rates for nineteen-year-olds were double those for fifteen- to seventeen-year-olds, and rates for those under fifteen years were extremely low. In 1995, birth rates for white fifteen- to nineteen-year-olds were 39.3 per 1,000, compared to 106.7 per 1,000 for Hispanics and 99.3 per 1,000 for African Americans (Ventura et al., 1997). Like pregnancy rates, teen birth rates have also declined to their lowest rates ever recorded: 39.1 births per 1,000 women ages fifteen to nineteen—a decline of 37 percent since the all-time highs were recorded in 1991 (Ventura & Hamilton, 2011). However, it is important to note that current teen pregnancy rates in the United States are still significantly higher than in any other industrialized nation (Sedgh et al., 2015).

Causes of Teen Pregnancy

Causes of teen pregnancy include individual, family, neighborhood, and societal characteristics, suggesting that a contextual or ecological approach similar to that used in our discussion of the impact of divorce earlier in this chapter will be useful here. Female adolescents who live in communities with high rates of poverty and who themselves are raised in poverty by single parents with low levels of education are at higher risk of becoming pregnant. In fact, in 1988, 60 percent of adolescent mothers lived in poverty at the time of their babies' birth (Alan Guttmacher Institute, 1994; Coley & Chase-Lansdale, 1998). The majority of teen pregnancies are thought to involve experiences of poverty and perceptions of limited life opportunities and choices. Life experiences associated with poverty, such as alienation at school, being surrounded by role models of unmarried parenthood and unemployment, and lack of educational opportunities and stable career prospects, tend to lower the perceived costs of early motherhood (Coley & Chase-Lansdale, 1998). In addition, the loss of most low-skill, high-paying manufacturing jobs due to changes in the U.S. economy has increased unemployment and poverty in our inner cities and strikingly changed the context and course of development during the teenage years and the early twenties. Although median ages of completing school, marriage, and childbearing have significantly increased for middle-class adolescents, lower-SES populations have not adapted to these changes by delaying starting their families. Adolescent childbearing, which in the past occurred mostly in the context of marriage with an employed husband, is now occurring among unmarried teenagers with few prospects for economic security (Coley & Chase-Lansdale, 1998; Rosenheim & Testa, 1992; Wilson, 1996).

Decisions about Contraception

Although American teenagers do not exhibit different patterns of sexual activity than adolescents in many industrial countries, they use contraception less consistently and effectively. In 1990 the rate of teenage births in the United States was almost twice that of Great Britain, the country with the next highest rate; more than four times greater than those of Sweden and Spain; seven times greater than those of Denmark and the Netherlands; and fifteen times greater than that of Japan (Coley & Chase-Lansdale, 1998). Recent data show very little change in the United States compared to other developed countries. According to data from the United Nations Statistical Division (2008), the adolescent birth rate in Canada was one-third the rate in the United States (fourteen versus thirty-nine births per one thousand fifteen- to nineteen-year olds). The rates per one thousand teen women in Germany and Italy were ten and seven, respectively—less than 25 percent the U.S. rate.

The great majority of teenage pregnancies are the result of inadequate or no contraception. Despite the steady decline in teen pregnancy over the past twenty years, many teenagers remain startlingly uninformed about the basics of reproduction or feel emboldened by their own personal fable, believing they are "immune" to pregnancy or at least at very low risk. Roughly 20 to 25 percent of all teenagers do not use contraceptives the first time they have sex, and many—particularly, younger adolescents—delay using contraception for a year or more after the first intercourse (Coley & Chase-Lansdale, 1998; Martinez, Copen, & Abma, 2011).

Although birth control pills are popular, they are not reliable during the first month of use. Birth control implants take about a week to be effective. Only intrauterine devices, condoms, or a diaphragm and contraceptive jelly are really effective for first intercourse. But adolescents do not like to use these contraceptives because they imply a preparedness for sex, are expensive or unavailable when needed, can be messy, reduce pleasure, and increase anxiety due to inexperience in their use. Irregular use of contraception is associated with lack of knowledge about contraceptives, low SES, poor communication with parents, having teenage friends who became parents, low educational achievement and aspirations, high levels of anxiety, low self-esteem, and feelings of fatalism, powerlessness, and alienation (Coley & Chase-Lansdale, 1998). Because lack of knowledge and lack of planning are major barriers in adolescent use of contraception, other more long-acting forms of birth-control, such as implants and intrauterine devices (IUDs), might be most beneficial for many teens and have been linked to lower birth rates and lower abortion rates (Peipert et al., 2012). In fact, after the passage of the Affordable Care Act, which made contraception free to those with insurance, several states recorded lower teen pregnancy rates and lower abortion rates (Rickettes, Klinger, & Schwalberg, 2014). In the "Working With" interview, Janet Whallen, a nurse practitioner, discusses her experiences with pregnant teens.

Parent-Teen Communication about Sexual Behavior

The helplessness that many parents feel about influencing their teens' sexual behavior may in part reflect a failure to communicate effectively about such matters. This is illustrated in a recent study by James Jaccard and his colleagues of African American adolescents ages fourteen to seventeen, which found little agreement between the mothers' perceptions and reports of their teenagers' sexual behavior and the teenagers self-reports (Jaccard et al., 1998). Adolescent perceptions and reports were more predictive of actual sexual behavior than maternal reports. Mothers significantly underestimated the sexual activity of their teens, and teens tended to underestimate their mothers' level of disapproval of their sexual activity. While 58 percent of the teens in the study had engaged in sexual intercourse, only 34 percent of the mothers thought that was the case. This was particularly true for older mothers who were satisfied with their parent-teen relationship but did not talk with their teens about sex and strongly disapproved of premarital sex. Teens were more likely to underestimate their mothers' opposition to premarital sex if the mothers were not religious, if the teens' friends viewed it favorably, if they reported little communication about sex with their mothers, and if they were male.

Parent-teen communication is a complex process, especially when adolescent sexual behavior is the topic. It takes good communication, which allows both parties to share their needs and expectations and to negotiate differences, for parents to successfully influence their teens. Efforts to improve parent-teen communication must address five important aspects: (1) the *extent* of the communication, as indicated by the frequency and depth; (2) the *style* or manner in which the information is communicated; (3) the *content* of the communication; (4) the *timing* of the communication; and (5) the *general family environment* in which the communication takes place, as reflected in the overall quality of the parent-teen relationship (Jaccard et al., 1998).

Consequences of Teenage Parenthood

Many teenage mothers may see having a baby as a way to prematurely crystallize their identities because motherhood and marriage promise to establish them in a secure adult role and help them to escape role confusion. Such fantasies generally are not realized, however. Teenage mothers are less likely to finish high school, find a stable paying job, enter secure marriages, or achieve equal job status or income in their lifetimes. They are also more likely to get pregnant again within two years (Richio, Phipps, & Raker, 2010; Rigsby et al., 1998). Teenage fathers are less negatively affected, largely because they generally do not assume responsibility for raising their children (Coley & Chase-Lansdale, 1998; Furstenberg et al., 1989).

> **WORKING WITH** Janet Whallen, Nurse Practitioner
>
> ### Helping Pregnant Teenagers
>
> Janet Whallen was interviewed in her office, which is located in a neighborhood health care center serving disadvantaged Hispanic and African American individuals and families. Janet's warm, low-key style made it easy to see why teenagers would find her easy to talk with. Our interview focused on the experiences of pregnant teens.
>
> **Rob:** *What special problems do pregnant teenagers face?*
>
> **Janet:** Most of the sexual relationships these teenagers are involved in are fairly short-lived. A young woman or man might have three or four partners in a year. When a young woman becomes pregnant, the chances that she'll still be with the same boyfriend when she delivers nine months later are fairly slim.
>
> **Rob:** *Nine months would be a long relationship?*
>
> **Janet:** For someone who is only fourteen or fifteen, it is. Very few of these girls have the baby's father with them in any way, shape, or form at the time of delivery.
>
> **Rob:** *Why is this so?*
>
> **Janet:** Sometimes, the guy gets scared or loses interest because the girl is starting to get fat. Or the girl or guy was already losing interest even before the pregnancy occurred. Whatever the reason, I think shorter relationships are fairly typical of early adolescent behavior.
>
> **Rob:** *In what other ways are the experiences of pregnant teenagers typical of adolescents in general?*
>
> **Janet:** They have very little sense of the implications of the decisions they make. They make most choices based on short-term consequences, and those choices are tightly connected to peer approval. There are also lots of rebellion issues against important adults, whether parents or teachers.
>
> **Rob:** *How does this rebelliousness affect pregnancy?*
>
> **Janet:** Teenagers are very sensitive about many things, from small issues to big ones: being told to eat certain things or to wear certain clothes—you know, "you're going to look fat if you wear that"—about smoking or not smoking, getting home on time after school or staying out late on Friday night, about how their parent will feel about their being sexually active or getting pregnant. I have to be very careful to give advice in a way that they don't find threatening.
>
> **Rob:** *Sounds like typical adolescent behavior.*
>
> **Janet:** I have kids who will come in for an appointment with four or five giggling teenage friends, who'll sit outside the office and heckle and laugh. They'll all be talking about who is going out with whom, who passed notes to whom in class, who cut class for what reasons, where they bought their clothes. You would never know you were in the middle of an inner-city clinic for pregnant teenagers.
>
> **Rob:** *Are these pregnant teenagers in danger of losing connection with their peer culture?*

Teenage mothers are more likely than older women to experience complications such as anemia and toxemia during pregnancy, as well as prolonged labor. Their babies are more likely to be premature, have low birth weight, and have neurological defects, and are also more likely to die during their first year. For some children of teenage mothers, delays in cognitive development begin to emerge during the preschool years and continue into the school years. Many children show behavioral problems, including aggression and lack of impulse control. In adolescence, they have higher rates of grade failure, delinquency, incarceration (for males), and early sexual activity and pregnancy than their peers born to older mothers (Coley & Chase-Lansdale, 1998). As Rebekah Coley and Lindsey Chase-Lansdale point out, however, both teenage mothers and their children display a wide range of diversity in their development and functioning, due in large part to the resources available to the mother and child (Pittard, Laditka, & Laditka, 2008). Although children of teenage mothers are at risk of becoming teenage parents, it is estimated that only between one-quarter and one-third of the daughters and one-tenth of the sons of teen parents become teen parents themselves. These researchers also note that the lower SES experienced by the majority of teen parents appear to be more important predictors of children's and adolescents' functioning than is maternal age at birth.

> **WORKING WITH** Janet Whallen, Nurse Practitioner
>
> ### Helping Pregnant Teenagers *continued*
>
> **Janet:** Not as much as you might think. Unlike in middle-class communities, where teenagers are expected to complete high school and go to college, there is relatively little stigma attached to becoming pregnant during high school—although there may be a little bit more if pregnancy occurs in junior high.
>
> **Rob:** *Why do teenagers become pregnant in the first place?*
>
> **Janet:** I wish I knew the answer to that one! Failure to use effective birth control is, of course, the immediate factor. And some teenagers want to have a little baby to care for and be close to and to feel important and needed, or they see pregnancy as a way to gain adult status. Another reason is that sex is a big deal and getting pregnant isn't.
>
> **Rob:** *What do you mean?*
>
> **Janet:** Many of these kids become sexually active at age twelve or thirteen, and some even before they start having their periods. Most of them have little extra money, so they don't go shopping, or buy CDs, or collect this or that. A lot of them are involved in Pentecostal or Baptist churches, so they don't do drugs and they don't drink. But they do sex.
>
> **Rob:** *It's an enjoyable activity, and it's inexpensive.*
>
> **Janet:** Well . . . intimacy is involved too, but for many young teens, sex is mainly a way to have immediate fun. Getting pregnant simply happens, with little thought about its deeper social, emotional, or philosophical significance.
>
> **Rob:** *What social supports are available to these youngsters?*
>
> **Janet:** Family or extended family members often will babysit and share other childcare responsibilities. Sometimes the boyfriend's family will also become involved, even when he's out of the picture. Many teen moms are back to being teenagers fairly soon after having their babies. Some graduate from high school and get a job, and a few go on to college. A significant number do not finish school. Unfortunately, we are finding that an increasing number get pregnant again soon after the first baby.
>
> ### What Do You Think?
>
> 1. If Janet Whallen were working with pregnant teens in the community in which you spent your adolescence, in what ways might her observations be different? In what ways might they be the same? Why?
> 2. What are your views about the causes of teenage pregnancy?
> 3. What strategies might you recommend for preventing teen pregnancy among low-SES, inner-city youth?

Involvement of Grandmothers

An understanding of teenage parenthood truly requires a lifespan perspective. The transition to parenthood is a challenging one, even for married young adults who are well educated and enjoy economically and socially supportive circumstances. For single teenage mothers, the transition often is much more difficult. Many teenage mothers end up living with their own mothers. The quality of child-rearing practices for teenage parents living in three-generation families appears to be positively related to the quality of their relationships with their own mothers (the baby's grandmother). Adolescent mothers whose own mothers provided authoritative parenting, helped them care for their new babies, and modeled appropriate parenting behaviors in a way that respected their daughters' autonomy became better parents themselves than teen mothers without such support. However, although living in the same household as their mothers resulted in positive mother-grandmother relationships for younger teen mothers, mother-grandmother relationships were better for older teenage mothers when the adolescent daughter and her mother lived in separate households (Apfel & Switz, 1991; Chase-Lansdale et al., 1994; Wakschlag et al., 1996).

Prevention and Support Programs

Programs to prevent teen pregnancy must be responsive to adolescents' developmental needs and life contexts. Comprehensive sex education is most effective at getting adolescents to delay initiation of intercourse and to use contraception. For teens who are at high risk because of their life circumstances, programs that include comprehensive, developmentally oriented services—medical care and contraceptive services, social services, family and educational support, and school-linked parenting education—appear to be maximize efficacy. One such program conducted at Johns Hopkins University was successful in delaying the age at which sexual activity was initiated, increased contraceptive use, reduced the frequency of sexual relations, and reduced the pregnancy rate by 30 percent, while comparison school rates increased by 58 percent (Hardy & Zabin, 1991).

Effective support programs for pregnant teenagers and teenage parents generally focus on providing pre- and postnatal health care, economic support, childcare and parenting support, education, and job training. The Prenatal/Early Infancy Project (Olds, 1988) still stands as a model for assisting teenage parents and their children and for reducing the likelihood of unplanned pregnancies in the future. It clearly demonstrates close connections between issues in adolescent development and themes associated with prenatal development, infancy, and early childhood development. It also highlights the interconnectedness of the three main developmental domains of physical, cognitive, and psychosocial development discussed in Chapter 1.

This five-year longitudinal study focused on single, first-time-pregnant adolescents from low-SES circumstances. The program (1) provided prenatal parent education; (2) helped to involve family members and friends in the pregnancy, birth, early care of the child, and support of the mother; and (3) helped to link family members with formal health and human services. Prenatal and pediatric care was available through a local team of private obstetricians and pediatricians. A central feature of the program was an ongoing caregiving relationship with an experienced nurse who made regular home visits during and for two years following the pregnancy. During the pregnancy, the nurse provided parenting education focused on helping the pregnant teen improve her diet and monitor her weight gain, identify signs of pregnancy complication, adopt a healthy lifestyle (e.g., eliminate use of cigarettes), prepare for labor and delivery, prepare for the early care of the newborn, make appropriate use of the health care system, and make plans regarding subsequent pregnancies, returning to school, and finding employment. After the baby was born, the nurse provided home-based infancy education designed to improve the young mother's understanding of her infant's temperament and to promote the infant's physical, cognitive, and psychosocial development.

To evaluate the long-term impact of the program, the teen mothers and their children were followed from early pregnancy until their children were four years old. Adolescent mothers who received postnatal nurse home care made better use of formal health and social services, experienced greater informal social support, improved their diets more, and reduced the number of cigarettes smoked compared to a similar group of women who had not received such nursing care. High-risk teen mothers benefited the most. For very young teenagers, there was a 335-gram improvement in their babies' birth weight and for women who smoked, a 75 percent reduction in preterm delivery. Among poor, unmarried, high-risk teens who received postnatal nurse home care, there was a 75 percent reduction in reported cases of child abuse and neglect (from 19 to 4 percent). These at-risk mothers found their children easier to care for, used less punishment and restriction and a greater number of growth-promoting playthings, needed to use the emergency room fewer times for their babies' health care, and, during the children's second year, used the emergency room 56 percent fewer times for children's accidents than did similar mothers who did not receive nurse home care (Olds, 1988).

Teenage Depression and Suicide

Depressive disorders involve disturbances of emotion that affect individuals' entire mental lives. Two key subtypes of depressive disorder exist: major depressive disorder (MDD), which involves a single episode or recurrent episodes of depression, and dysthymia, which involves chronic depressive symptoms. Individuals with either type of depressive disorder experience a pervasive mood disturbance that involves feelings of sadness and loss of interest or pleasure in most activities; feelings of fear, anger, self-criticism, and hopelessness; and disturbances in sleep, appetite, ability to concentrate, sexual interest, and energy level. Depression is frequently accompanied by other problems such as anxiety, social withdrawal, disruptive disorder, and substance abuse (Cicchetti & Toth, 1998; American Psychiatric Association, 2013; Peterson et al., 1993).

It is estimated that at any point in time, between 0.4 and 2.5 percent of children and from 0.4 and 8.3 percent of adolescents suffer from MDD, and between 15 and 20 percent of adolescents suffer from MDD over their lifetimes. Approximately 0.6 to 1.7 percent of children and 1.6 to 8.0 percent of adolescents suffer from dysthymia at any point in time. Depression during childhood and adolescence are nonnormative experiences that interfere with children's development. The average length of an episode of MDD in children and adolescents is from seven to nine months. Approximately 90 percent of MDD episodes end within two years following their onset, and the remaining 10 percent last longer. MDD frequently recurs in children and adolescents. Dysthymia episodes last much longer than MDD episodes, with the average length being four years. Because the development of dysthymia often leads to a recurrent depressive disorder, early diagnosis and treatment are important. There is some evidence that a significant increase in the prevalence of depression during early to middle adolescence occurs among both males and females and that rates are higher for girls, who may be more likely to deal with their upsets by internalizing them rather than externalizing them in a more aggressive manner (Cicchetti & Toth, 1998).

Causes of Depression in Adolescence

Dante Cicchetti and Sheree Toth (1998) suggest that the causes of depression are best understood from an ecological systems perspective similar to that of Uri Bronfenbrenner (see Chapter 1). In this view, the development of depression is related to the multiple, dynamic interactions among environmental forces, caregiver characteristics, and the characteristics of the developing child and adolescent. At each ecological level of influence, certain risk and preventive factors may influence the development of depressive problems. At the individual level, some infants may be born with a biological vulnerability to depression due to genetic or nongenetic factors. Family influences include the unique family circumstances, both biological and psychosocial, in which the child and adolescent develops. Although genetic factors account for some within-family depression, genetics alone cannot fully explain the development of depression. For one thing, many depressed children display rapid recovery when hospitalized, even without additional interventions. For another, a number of family characteristics have been associated with the development and maintenance of depression, including parental depression, anxiety, substance abuse, and maltreatment. Family transitions, low SES, and acute and chronic negative life events involving significant losses through parental death, divorce, or separation or involving child maltreatment have been associated with the occurrence of depression during childhood and adolescence (Bronfenbrenner, 1989; Cicchetti & Toth, 1998; Downey & Coyne, 1990).

Children and adolescents who live in a family in which one or more parents are depressed, have other serious emotional problems, or experience a serious and pervasive disturbance in the parent-child relationship, including physical or emotional abuse, are at much greater risk for depression as well as other forms of psychopathology. In addition, the environments provided by the schools and neighborhoods in which a child grows up can play an important role in the development of depression. Neighborhoods that are unsafe and unsupportive may create levels of stress that are developmentally disruptive, particularly during early and middle adolescence. Especially during the early adolescent transition to middle school, school environments that respond inappropriately to adolescents' academic and psychosocial needs can alienate them from academic activities and from prosocial activities with peers, and contribute to school failure, antisocial behavior, drug abuse, and depression (Cicchetti & Toth, 1998; Downey & Coyne, 1990; Eccles, 1993; Garbarino, 1992b; Jacobvitz & Bush, 1996). Depression is often a factor in adolescent suicide.

Chapter 16 Psychosocial Development during Adolescence

Suicide during Adolescence

Among adolescents and young adults, suicide is the third leading cause of death among individuals ages fifteen to twenty-four (CDC, 2005). Between 6 and 13 percent of adolescents have reported attempting suicide at least once in their lives, and the ratio of attempted to successful suicides is estimated to be as high as fifty to one (CDC-MMWR, 2012; Garland & Zigler, 1993; Meehan et al., 1992; Rubenstein et al., 1998). Suicide attempts are estimated to be three to nine times more common among girls, but boys succeed three times as often, in part because they use more effective methods, such as knives and guns (Holden, 1986).

More adolescents seriously consider suicide (15.8 percent) and make a suicide plan (12.8 percent) than actually take the step to attempt suicide (7.8 percent), according to the most recent data on youth risk behaviors by the Center for Disease control (2012). Native Americans maintain the highest prevalence rates for attempted suicides, compared to other racial/ethnic groups, with African Americans reporting the lowest rates for all age groups (CDC, 2005; Prinstein, 2008). When considering prevalence rates among youth in grades nine through twelve, however, black teens show a higher incidence of attempting suicide (8.3 percent) than white or Hispanic teens, even though both black males and females are less likely to consider suicide attempts or make a suicide plan (CDC-MMWR, 2012). Nonfatal suicide attempts are also a major concern for adolescents, given that this form of self-injurious behavior occurs much more frequently, There are twenty-five incidents of nonfatal self-harm for every single completed suicide, according to recent estimates (Evans et al., 2005; Prinstein, 2008).

For teens, the reasons for attempting suicide or self-injury are complex and occur within a context of various psychological disorders but may also present in the absence of any prevailing psychopathology. Students who are depressed or suffer other mental or physical disabilities are at risk for suicide ideation and attempts, but the desire to self-harm may also stem from unresolved family conflicts, social rejection, sexual orientation issues, or an impulsive act occurring at a moment of deep despair or impaired functioning (Bradley, 2002; Duncan & Hatzenbuehler, 2014; Institute of Medicine, 2002; Prinstein, 2008). Whatever the individual reason, suicide attempts almost always represent cries for help with the personal turmoil and feelings of intense loneliness, isolation, and hopelessness that depressed or troubled youngsters experience (Rubenstein et al., 1998). Although most teenagers who are not depressed still experience moments of unhappiness, and most who are depressed do not attempt suicide, signs of unhappiness and depression should not be dismissed, particularly if they persist. Also, because a large percentage of those who attempt suicide have threatened or attempted it before, such threats should be taken very seriously. Adolescent egocentrism, the exaggerated feeling that one's uniqueness makes it impossible for anyone else to truly understand one's problems, may intensify a teenager's feelings of loneliness and isolation and contribute to a tendency not to seek help and to reject help that is available.

Attempts to prevent suicide include early detection and intervention in family and personal crises, school-based education about depression and suicide risk factors, training in problem solving and coping skills, crisis counseling, and emergency hot lines. Treatment for teens who attempt suicide generally involves therapy with both the adolescent and his or her family (Garland & Zigler, 1993; Rubenstein et al., 1989).

Juvenile Delinquency

juvenile delinquency A pattern of destructive or antisocial activities and lawbreaking offenses committed by adolescents.

Juvenile delinquency refers to a pattern of destructive or antisocial activities and lawbreaking offenses committed by adolescents. In 2012, more than half a million juveniles were arrested in the United States for less serious *status offenses*, or offenses that are illegal based on age, such as joy riding, drinking alcohol, or running away (Federal Bureau of Investigation, 2013). For more serious crimes, such as larceny or theft, robbery, or forcible rape, arrests for violent offenses by juveniles decreased by approximately 40 percent between 2006 and 2012 (Federal Bureau of Investigation, 2013). Arrests and imprisonment for status offenses may serve as an introduction to the criminal world for some adolescents, especially those who already feel very weak ties to the rest of the majority society.

There is some evidence that the main route to chronic delinquency follows a predictable developmental sequence of experiences. The first step involves ineffective parenting and problematic family interaction processes, both of which frequently contribute to childhood conduct disorders. In the second step, the conduct-disordered behaviors lead to academic failure and peer rejection. During later childhood and early adolescence, continuing failure at school and peer rejection lead to a third step: increased risk for depressed mood and involvement in a deviant peer group. Children who follow this developmental sequence are assumed to be at high risk for engaging in chronic delinquent behavior (Patterson et al., 1989).

Factors associated with delinquency include a caregiver-child relationship characterized by hostility, lack of affection, underinvolvement, and lack of supervision; overly harsh and authoritarian methods of discipline; a high degree of family conflict and disorganization; a parent with a personality disturbance and a delinquent history of her or his own; impoverished living conditions; lack of attachment to any prosocial institution such as school, job, or religious organization; lack of positive adult role models; and exposure to neighborhood environments in which violence, crime, and delinquent behavior are prevalent (Dishion et al., 1995; Romig et al., 1989; Sarafino & Armstrong, 1986). As discussed in the "A Multicultural View" feature, these factors vary from culture to culture, as do the delinquent behaviors in which teens engage.

Longitudinal studies of delinquency and antisocial behavior have found that aggression during the preschool period is predictive only of serious forms of antisocial behavior in adolescence and adulthood. For these children, who are mostly boys, the onset of minor aggression (annoying others and bullying) tends to precede the onset of physical fighting (including gang fighting), which in turn precedes the onset of more extreme violence (aggravated assault, robbery, and rape). The majority of violent male adults exhibited a life course pattern initially characterized by both aggressive behavior and symptoms of attention deficit hyperactivity disorder (ADHD) during their preschool years, followed by more serious forms of conduct disorder and antisocial behavior during adolescence and adulthood. A second, limited-duration pattern is shown by individuals who outgrow aggression either during the preschool-elementary school age period or in late adolescence-early adulthood. A third, late-onset pattern accounts for individuals who become violent during adulthood but do not have a history of aggression earlier in their lives (Loeber & Stouthamer-Loeber, 1998).

Gangs

Many delinquent youngsters belong to gangs. A gang is a relatively permanent group of individuals with a clearly identified leadership and organizational structure and clear role expectations for its members. Gangs identify with or claim control over "territory" in the community and engage in violence and other forms of illegal activities, such as fighting, vandalism, theft, and drug dealing, on an individual or group basis. A gang is likely to have a group name, an initiation rite, nicknames for members, and gang symbols such as colors, tattoos, hand signs, or jewelry (Miller, 1990; Winfree et al., 1994).

The incidence of gang-related homicides, drive-by shootings, home invasions, and related violent and illegal activities in schools and communities is an ongoing national concern (Pryor & McGarell, 1993; Takata & Zevitz, 1990). Typically gangs are formed by individuals from low-SES and racial or ethnic minority and immigrant backgrounds. Traditionally gang members have mainly been adolescent males, but the growth of gangs in prisons and increased gang involvement in the drug trade have expanded the age range to include children as young as nine as well as adults, and also increased female involvement to some degree (Goldstein & Soriano, 1994; Lasley, 1992).

Gangs are thought to provide alternative economic opportunities and social supports for disadvantaged and alienated youths who face high levels of uncertainty, instability, and danger in their families and neighborhoods. For such adolescents, gang membership offers a surrogate "family," a sense of identity and belonging, and status, power, and protection, as well as the material benefits of criminal activity (Curry & Spergel, 1988; Knox, 1991).

A gang typically reinforces its members for associating exclusively with other members, conforming to pro-gang attitudes and behaviors, and rejecting the values of parents, teachers, and mainstream peers (Winfree et al., 1994). Many of the individual, family, and social factors associated with gang membership, gang activity, and its prevention are similar to those linked to juvenile delinquency.

Reducing and Preventing Delinquency

Most adolescents, of course, do not become delinquents or join gangs. Adolescents who are at risk for delinquency sometimes can be helped by programs that make available the support and opportunities that will allow successful experimentation with other roles and identities. These include community houses, YMCAs, police athletic leagues, summer camps, crisis drop-in centers, and telephone hot lines, as well as outpatient and residential treatment programs to assist more disturbed teenagers and their families. Unfortunately, such interventions have been found to produce mostly short-term effects and lose their impact unless continued on a long-term basis (Patterson et al., 1989).

Intensive early childhood intervention programs for at-risk preschool children and their families have achieved significant success in reducing delinquency and related problems later in life (Zigler et al., 1992). The High/Scope Perry Preschool Program, for example, provided a high-quality preschool, weekly home visits by teachers, and extensive parent involvement for three- and four-year-olds from low-SES families. Long-term longitudinal follow-up studies of these children at age nineteen and again at age twenty-seven found significantly lower rates of school dropout, illiteracy, unemployment, welfare dependence, and arrest for delinquent or criminal behavior than for a comparable group of children who did not participate in the program. They reveal how early childhood intervention can help generate and support ongoing family processes that foster positive development into the adulthood years (Hamburg, 1994; Luster & McAdoo, 1996; Schweinhart & Weikart, 1992).

Looking Back/Looking Forward

We have reached the end of our discussion of adolescence. How do the developmental issues of adolescence reflect the four lifespan themes discussed in Chapter 1? Changing relationships with parents are an important aspect of adolescent development. Let's look at the four lifespan themes with this issue in mind.

- **Continuity within change**—The theme of continuity and change is very much in evidence during adolescence. Though the attachment relationships with parents that have developed during childhood continue to grow and develop, the separation from parents and the emergence of a more integrated and adult identity and sense of self strongly indicate that adolescence is indeed a transition to adulthood that heavily involves change. And though the striking changes in physical and cognitive capabilities that emerge in adolescence most certainly affect the quality of parent-teen relationships, lifelong consistencies in temperament, cognitive style, and beliefs about parenting ensure a certain degree of continuity as well. The various styles of parenting that we first discussed in Chapter 7 continue to be associated with better or worse developmental outcomes during the teen years, and there is good reason to believe that an authoritative parenting style will continue to benefit midlife parents as their children become young adults and their parents age. Patterns of parenting and the nature of a particular parent-child relationship can also change in response to the changing experiences, needs, and expectations of both parent and child. For example,

> **What Do You Think?**
>
> What advice might you give to concerned parents regarding how they can protect their children from teenage pregnancy and delinquency? What advice might you give to the governor of your state regarding programs to prevent these problems?

family changes such as the birth of additional children, divorce, and remarriage may have a significant impact on children, parents, and their relationships.

- **Lifelong growth**—The quality of parent-teen relationships significantly reflects a process of lifelong growth in physical, cognitive, moral, and psychosocial complexity, competence, and maturity rooted in the earlier developmental experiences of both adolescents and their parents. Effective parenting during infancy and childhood reflects parents' growing ability to respectfully and appropriately respond to their children's unique temperament and attachment needs, and to provide parental caregiving with the appropriate amount of control, clarity of communication, demand for maturity, and nurturance for their children at each period of development. Likewise, the capacity of children to participate in a relationship with their parents grows with age and experience, continuing through adolescence into early adulthood, when many adolescents will become parents themselves, and into middle adulthood, when they may provide care for their own parents as well.

- **Changing meanings and changing vantage points**—The meaning of the parent-child relationship undergoes significant changes as children and their parents move through the developmental life cycle. During infancy and toddlerhood, the child's experience of herself is largely tied to her attachments to and dependence on her caregivers, who in turn experience strong attachment to the child and an intense sense of responsibility for all aspects of her well-being. Meanings of their relationship and vantage points of both child and parent undergo major developmental changes as the physical, cognitive, and psychosocial capabilities of the child unfold and as the parents, who are experiencing their own developmental changes of adulthood, respond to and are responded to by their developing child. As a first- or second-grader, a child may see his parent(s) as all-knowledgeable and all-powerful. He has limited capability to understand the dynamics of the parent-child relationship, and expects his parent(s) to meet all of his needs and solve all of his problems. By the time he is in fifth or sixth grade, the child's capabilities, needs, and expectations will have changed significantly, as will his understanding of the parent-child relationship and his own contributions to it.

- **Developmental diversity**—Parents all over the world share the goal of caring for their children in a way that fosters their physical, cognitive, and psychosocial development and well-being. However, the ways in which parents from different societies, cultures, and ethnic groups and from different cultural, ethnic, racial, religious, gender, and SES backgrounds and circumstances within a particular society or culture actually raise their children show great diversity. This diversity is influenced by the beliefs, values, expectations, and life circumstances of parents, their children, and others around them, all of which may change over time. Relationships between teenagers and their parents today differ significantly from those of their parents' or grandparents' generation. The information revolution we are now experiencing may further influence the diversity of parent-child relationships in ways we can only imagine. And while all parent-child relationships have much in common, even within a given set of life circumstances, each follows a diverse developmental course because every individual family and the parents and children within it experience and interact with one another and the world around them in ways that are unique.

Chapter Summary

- **What conflicts do adolescents typically experience in their search for identity? What factors support or hinder successful identity development?** The process of individuation, or becoming a separate and independent person, appears to follow a predictable pattern: differentiation, practice, and experimentation; rapprochement; and consolidation of self. A key task of adolescence is successful resolution of the psychosocial crisis of identity versus role confusion. Erik Erikson calls the period of experimentation and uncertainty that precedes the achievement of a stable adult identity the *psychosocial moratorium*. Identity formation involves selectively keeping and integrating certain aspects of one's earlier childhood identity and discarding others. Successful resolution of the identity conflicts typical of adolescence depends in part on having adequate opportunities to experiment with different identities and roles. Differences in life circumstances due to social class, culture, and historical period may increase or decrease such opportunities. James Marcia has identified four identity statuses among older adolescents: identity achievement, identity diffusion, moratorium, and foreclosure. Though ethnic groups do not appear to differ in the percentages of youngsters who are in each stage, groups may differ in which issues are of most concern in resolving their identity crises.

- **What special challenges does adolescence pose for parents? How do differences in parenting style affect parent-teenager relationships?** Although not conflict free, relationships between adolescents and their parents are for the most part mutually rewarding. Teenagers appear to feel most positive about authoritative parenting styles and more negative about parents who are authoritarian. Authoritative, authoritarian, permissive-indulgent, and permissive-indifferent parenting styles are related to various aspects of adolescent development, including personality, academic achievement, social and emotional adjustment, delinquency, and substance abuse. Although adolescents and their parents may differ on some details of everyday life, they generally agree on the more important questions involving basic values. Approaching parent-adolescent conflicts in ways that are mutually respectful and that are performed with an understanding of active listening skills reduces complications brought about through these natural conflicts. Social class differences influence the educational and career expectations parents have for their adolescent children and adolescents have for themselves, and ethnicity, community context, and styles of family decision making also may influence adolescent adjustment. Finally, in recent years, an increasing number of adolescents have encountered the stresses of growing up in a family that has experienced marital conflict, divorce, remarriage, or single parenthood.

- **In what ways do adolescent friendships and peer groups play a constructive role, and how are concerns about their negative influence justified?** During adolescence, friendships become increasingly stable, intimate, and mutual. They also become the primary source of influence in a teen's life. Both small, cohesive cliques and larger, less intimate crowds appear to be important aspects of peer group participation. Teenagers participate in peer groups to please parents and teachers, gain peer acceptance and popularity, and conform. The meteoric rise in the use of social media, (smartphones and the Internet) has altered adolescents' social world and their communication skills. Parents and teens are traveling this new road together. Adolescents need a supportive hand in helping them navigate their "virtual neighborhood" in the same way parents guided them through the trials and tribulations of their real neighborhood in the past.

    Participation in work within and outside the family provides a major base for the development of competence and sense of identity and self during adolescence. Participation in household work and its consequences depend on the helper's motivations, the meaning of the work activity, and the social context in which it occurs. How work outside the family affects adolescent development depends upon how well it fits the developmental needs of the individual and his or her family.

- **What changes in sexual activities and attitudes occur among teenagers? How are they related to other aspects of adolescent development?** Adolescents' sexual needs are closely tied to their need to establish a secure identity and to achieve both intimacy and independence. Girls and boys differ in their reasons for their first experience of sexual intercourse and in their attitudes toward sexual activities. In the United States, dating is the major pathway to adolescent sexual activity. Unfortunately, sexual aggression and date rape continue to be serious problems, with long-term consequences for both the victims of teen dating violence and also for those who do the intimidation, harassment, or physical assaults. Acceptance of youngsters with nonheterosexual orientations has increased significantly in the first decades of the twenty-first century. Yet, the prejudice and discrimination that persist can make accepting their true identity more difficult for gay, lesbian, and bisexual adolescents as they transition into the emerging adulthood years of college or the world of work.

- **Why are adolescents at risk for problems such as pregnancy, depression, and delinquency?** Although a great deal is known about the causes, pregnancy and parenthood continue to be a major problem faced by a growing number of adolescents. The majority of teen pregnancies involve experiences of poverty and perceptions of limited life opportunities and choices. American teenagers do not exhibit different patterns of sexual activity than adolescents in many industrial countries, but they use contraception less consistently and effectively. Effective parent-teen communication is essential if parents are to positively influence their teens' sexual behavior, as is comprehensive sex education. Two other problems common during adolescence are depression and juvenile delinquency. Causes of depression include environmental influences, family and caregiver characteristics, and the characteristics of the developing child and adolescent. Longitudinal studies have found that aggression during early childhood is predictive of more serious forms of delinquent behavior in adolescence and adulthood.

Key Terms

clique (p. 405)
crowd (p. 405)
displaced homemaker (p. 401)
homophobia (p. 412)
identity diffusion (p. 388)
identity status (p. 389)
identity versus role confusion (p. 387)
individuation (p. 386)
juvenile delinquency (p. 420)
negative identity (p. 388)
psychosocial moratorium (p. 388)
SES (p. 396)

Glossary

A

accommodation According to Piaget, the process of modifying existing ideas or action-skills to fit new experiences.

achievement motivation Behavior that enhances competence or enhances judgments of competence.

achievement test A test designed to evaluate a person's current state of knowledge.

activity settings Group situations in which a shared focus of attention and shared goals facilitate an individual's learning from others in the group.

adaptation Piaget's term for the process by which development occurs; concepts are deepened or broadened by assimilation and stretched or modified by accommodation.

adolescence The stage of development between childhood and adulthood, around ages ten to twenty-two.

adolescent egocentrism The tendency of adolescents to perceive the world (and themselves) from their own perspective.

adoption study A research method for studying the relative contributions of heredity and environment in which genetically related children reared apart are compared with genetically unrelated children reared together.

ageism Prejudice or bias against an individual based on the individual's age.

aggression A bold, assertive action that is intended to hurt another person or to procure an object.

allele One of several alternative forms of a gene.

American Sign Language (ASL) System of nonverbal gesturing that is used by many people who are deaf or hearing impaired and that functions as a language.

amniotic sac A tough, spongy bag filled with salty fluid that surrounds the embryo, protects it from sudden jolts, and helps to maintain a fairly stable temperature.

androgyny A tendency to integrate both masculine and feminine behaviors into the personality.

anorexia nervosa A physical and psychological disturbance that causes a person to refuse to eat sufficient food and to develop an increasingly unrealistic view of his or her body; most individuals with anorexia are teenage girls.

anxious-avoidant attachment An insecure bond between infant and caregiver in which the child rarely cries when separated from the caregiver and tends to avoid or ignore the caregiver when reunited.

anxious-resistant attachment An insecure bond between infant and caregiver in which the child shows signs of anxiety preceding separation, is intensely upset by separation, and seeks close contact when reunited while at the same time resisting the caregiver's efforts to comfort.

Apgar Scale A system of rating newborns' health immediately following birth based on heart rate, strength of breathing, muscle tone, color, and reflex irritability.

aptitude test A measurement of ability that estimates future performance in some realm of behavior.

assessment The diagnosis of an individual's strengths, needs, and qualities.

assimilation According to Piaget, a method by which a person responds to new experiences by using existing concepts to interpret new ideas and experiences.

assisted reproductive technology (ART) Any infertility treatment in which fertilization of the egg occurs outside the womb.

attachment An intimate and enduring emotional relationship between two people, such as infant and caregiver, characterized by reciprocal affection and a periodic desire to maintain physical closeness.

attention deficit/hyperactivity disorder (ADHD) See *hyperactivity*.

authoritarian parenting A style of childrearing characterized by a high degree of control and demands on children's maturity and a low degree of clarity of communication and nurturance.

authoritative parenting A style of childrearing characterized by a high degree of control, clarity of communication, maturity demands, and nurturance.

autonomy An individual's ability to govern and regulate her or his own thoughts, feelings, and actions freely and responsibly while at the same time overcoming feelings of shame and doubt.

autonomy versus shame and doubt The second of Erikson's psychosocial crises of children ages one to three during which they struggle to control their own thoughts, feelings, and actions.

B

babbling Infant vocalizations produced prior to acquiring language and without verbally meaningful intent.

balanced bilingual A person who is equally fluent in two languages rather than more fluent in one language than in the other.

basic dualism William Perry's term for a perspective toward intellectual and ethical problems from which students view truth in terms of right or wrong, good or bad, and we or they.

behavior modification Techniques based on the principles of learning theory that can be used by parents, teachers, therapists, and other professionals to help children, adolescents, and adults reduce or eliminate undesirable behaviors and learn desirable ones.

binge eating disorder A disorder in which a person feels out of control of his or her eating and consumes much more than most people would eat in a short period of time, sometimes even when he or she is not hungry.

bulimia nervosa A disorder in which a person, usually a teenage girl, eats huge amounts of food and then vomits it to avoid gaining weight.

C

canalization The tendency of many developmental processes to unfold in highly predictable ways under a wide range of conditions.

caregiver-infant synchrony Patterns of closely coordinated social and emotional interaction between caregiver and infant.

case study A research study of a single individual or small group of individuals considered as a unit.

cellular theories Theories of aging that focus on the processes that take place within and between the cells, leading to the breakdown of cells, tissue, and organs. Sometimes referred to as *wear and tear theories*.

central nervous system The brain and nerve cells of the spinal cord.

cephalocaudal principle The tendency for organs, reflexes, and skills to develop sooner at the top (or head) of the body and later in areas farther down the body.

chromosome A threadlike, rod-shaped structure containing genetic information that is transmitted from parents to children; each human sperm or egg cell contains twenty-three chromosomes, and these determine a person's inherited characteristics.

circular reaction Piaget's term for an action often repeated, apparently because it is self-reinforcing.

classical conditioning According to Pavlov, learning in which a neutral stimulus gains the power to bring about a certain response by repeated association with another stimulus that already elicits the same response.

classification Grouping of objects according to standards or criteria.

clique A small, closely knit peer group of two or more members (average of six members) who are intimately involved in a number of shared purposes and activities and exclude those who are not.

cognition All processes by which humans acquire knowledge; methods for thinking or gaming knowledge about the world.

cognitive development The area of human development concerned with cognition; involves all psychological processes by which individuals learn and think about their environment.

cognitive mechanics Basic memory processes, such as sensory information input, visual and motor memory, and the processes of discrimination, categorization, and coordination, that are likely to decline in late adulthood.

cohort In developmental research, a group of subjects born at a particular time who therefore experience particular historical events or conditions.

competence An individual's increased skill and capability in successfully exploring, mastering, and controlling the world around them.

conception The moment at which the male's sperm cell penetrates the female's egg cell (ovum), forming a zygote.

concrete operations Logical thinking about concrete or tangible objects and processes; especially characteristic of middle childhood.

conservation A belief that certain properties (such as quantity) remain constant despite changes in perceived features such as dimensions, position, and shape.

constructive play A type of play that involves manipulation of physical objects to build or construct something.

control group In an experimental research study, the group of participants who experience conditions similar or identical to the experimental group, but without experiencing the experimental treatment.

control talk A style or register of speech used by teachers to indicate their power over activities, discussion, and behavior of students.

coparenting A parenting partnership in which child-rearing goals, strategies, and responsibilities are shared.

correlation An association between two variables in which changes in one variable tend to occur with changes in the other. The association does not necessarily imply a causal link between the variables.

critical period Any period during which development is particularly susceptible to an event or influence, either negative or positive.

critical thinking Reflection or thinking about complex issues, usually to make decisions or take actions.

cross-sectional study A study that compares individuals of different ages at the same point in time.

crowd A large, loosely knit peer group of between fifteen and thirty members (average of twenty members) that generally consists of from two to four cliques and is usually based on stereotype.

D

dependent variable A factor that is measured in an experiment and that *depends on,* or is controlled by, one or more independent variables.

development Long-term changes in a person's growth, feelings, patterns of thinking, social relationships, and motor skills.

developmentally appropriate practice Methods and goals of teaching considered optimal for young children given current knowledge of child development.

disorganized-disoriented attachment This pattern indicates the greatest degree of insecurity between infant and parent. When reunited with the parent, the infant exhibits confused and contradictory behavior, including unresponsiveness, turning away when held, frozen postures, and unexpected cries after being comforted.

displaced homemaker A woman who committed herself to the conventional roles of wife and mother, lost these roles due to separation, divorce, or widowhood, and was unprepared for employment and single parenthood.

domain A realm of psychological functioning.

dominant gene In any paired set of genes, the gene with greater influence in determining characteristics that are physically visible or manifest.

Down syndrome A congenital condition that causes intellectual disability.

E

ego According to Freud, the rational, realistic part of the personality; coordinates impulses from the id with demands imposed by the superego and by society.

egocentrism Inability to distinguish between one's own point of view and that of another person.

embryonic stage The stage in prenatal development that lasts from week 2 through week 8.

empathy A sensitive awareness of the thoughts and feelings of another person.

estrogen A sex hormone, sometimes called the *female sex hormone* because its high concentration in girls stimulates the growth of the ovaries and vagina during puberty.

experimental group In an experimental research study, the group of participants who experience the experimental treatment while in other respects experiencing conditions similar or identical to those of the control group.

experimental study A study in which circumstances are arranged so that just one or two factors or influences vary at a time.

expertise Specialized experience in specific domains of knowledge that enables efficient and effective performance and is not hampered by age.

F

failure to thrive A condition in which an infant seems seriously delayed in physical growth and is noticeably apathetic in behavior.

expertise Specialized experience in specific domains of knowledge that enables efficient and effective performance and is not hampered by age.

fetal alcohol syndrome (FAS) A congenital condition exhibited by babies born to mothers who consumed too much alcohol during pregnancy. They do not arouse easily and tend to behave sluggishly in general; they also have distinctive facial characteristics.

fetal presentation Refers to the body part of the fetus that is closest to the mother's cervix; may be head first (cephalic), feet and rump first (breech), or shoulders first (transverse).

fetal stage The stage in prenatal development that lasts from the eighth week of pregnancy until birth.

fine motor coordination Ability to smoothly carry out small movements that involve precise timing but not strength.

formal operational thought Thinking based on previously acquired concrete mental operations and involving hypothetical reasoning and attention to the structure or form of ideas.

functional play A cognitive level of play that involves simple, repeated movements and a focus on one's own body.

G

games with rules A cognitive level of play involving relatively formal activities with fixed rules.

gender The thoughts, feelings, and behaviors associated with being male or female by one's culture.

gender-role stereotypes The culturally "appropriate" patterns of gender-related behaviors expected by society. Also called *sex roles*.

gene A molecular structure, carried on chromosomes, containing genetic information; the basic unit of heredity.

general adaptation syndrome The pattern of physical response to stress identified by Hans Seyle, which has three stages: alarm, resistance, and exhaustion. Confrontation with a stressor sets the stress response in motion. The syndrome appears to be irreversible and accumulates to constitute the signs of aging.

genetic imprinting A mode of inheritance in which genes are chemically marked so that the number of the chromosome pair contributed by either the father or the mother is activated, regardless of its genetic makeup.

genotype The set of genetic traits inherited by an individual. See also *phenotype*.

germinal stage The stage in prenatal development that occurs during the first two weeks of pregnancy; characterized by rapid cell division. Also called the *period of the ovum*.

growth spurt A rapid change in height and weight that occurs in puberty and is preceded and followed by years of comparatively little increase.

H

habituation The tendency to attend to novel stimuli and ignore familiar ones.

holographic speech A single word used to communicate a thought, such as when a child says "up" instead of "pick me up."

homophobia Fear, dread, hostility, or prejudice directed toward gay, lesbian, and bisexual persons and the resulting mistreatment and discrimination.

hostile attribution bias The tendency to view others' behavior as aggressive, even when those behaviors are innocuous, which often leads to a hostile reactive response.

hyperactivity Excessive levels of activity and an inability to concentrate for normal periods of time. See *attention deficit hyperactivity disorder*.

hypothesis A precise prediction based on a scientific theory; often capable of being tested in a scientific research study.

I

id In Freud's theory, the part of an individual's personality that is present at birth, unconscious, impulsive, and unrealistic, and that attempts to satisfy a person's biological and emotional needs and desires by maximizing pleasure and avoiding pain.

identity diffusion A failure to achieve a relatively coherent, integrated, and stable identity.

identity status Marcia's four categories of identity development: identity achievement, identity diffusion, moratorium, and foreclosure.

identity versus role confusion The fifth of Erikson's psychosocial crises, in which one must integrate one's many childhood skills and beliefs and gain recognition for them from society.

imaginary audience A characteristic of young adolescents in which they act as though they are performing for an audience and believe that others are as concerned with their appearance and behavior as they themselves are.

independent variable A factor that an experimenter manipulates (varies) to determine its influence on the population being studied.

indifferent parenting A style of parenting in which parents' permissiveness reflects an avoidance of child-rearing responsibilities, sometimes with detrimental results; these parents are detached and emotionally uninvolved.

individuation The process by which an adolescent develops a unique and separate personal identity. Consists of four subphases: differentiation, practice and experimentation, rapprochement, and consolidation.

industry versus inferiority Erikson's fourth crisis, during which children concern themselves with their capacity to do good work and thereby develop confident, positive self concepts or else face feelings of inferiority.

infant-directed speech The style or register of speech used by adults and older children when talking with a one- or two-year-old infant.

infant mortality rate The frequency with which infants die compared to the frequency with which they live.

information processing theory Explanations of cognition that focus on the precise, detailed features or steps of mental activities. These theories often use computers as models for human thinking.

informed consent An agreement to participate in a research study based on understanding the nature of the research, protection of human rights, and freedom to decline to participate at any time.

initiative versus guilt Erikson's third psychosocial crisis, during which a child's increasing ability to initiate verbal and physical activity and expanding imaginative powers lead to fantasies of large and sometimes frightening proportions.

intelligence A general ability to learn from experience; also refers to ability to reason abstractly.

intermodal perception The coordination and integration of multiple channels of sensory information.

J

juvenile delinquency A pattern of destructive or antisocial activities and lawbreaking offenses committed by adolescents.

juvenile period Proposed by Sullivan, a period between ages five and ten when children show increasing interest in developing intense friendships or "chum relationships" with peers of the same gender.

L

latency According to Freud, the stage of development between the phallic and genital stages. Sexual feelings and activities are on hold as the child struggles to resolve the oedipal conflict.

learning disability Difficulty in learning a specific academic skill such as reading or arithmetic.

learning orientation Achievement motivation that comes from the learner and the task.

lifespan development The broad changes and continuities that constitute a person's identity and growth from birth to death.

longitudinal study A study of the same individuals over a relatively long period, often months or years.

low birth weight A birth weight of less than 2,500 grams (about 5.5 pounds).

M

menarche The first menstrual period.

metacognition Knowledge and thinking about cognition, how learning and memory operate in everyday situations, and how one can improve cognitive performance.

metalinguistic awareness The ability to attend to language as an object of thought rather than attending only to the content or ideas of a language.

middle school School designed to meet the needs of young adolescents, and usually spanning approximately fifth- through eighth-grade and enrolling students of about age ten through thirteen.

midwife The person, usually a woman, who is the primary caregiver to a woman during pregnancy, childbirth, and the month or so following delivery.

morality Sensitivity to and knowledge about what is right and wrong.

mortality The proportion of persons who die at a given age; the rate of death.

motor skills Physical skills using the body or limbs, such as walking and drawing.

multiple intelligences According to Howard Gardner's theory of intelligence, alternative forms of intelligence or adaptability to the environment.

myelination The process through which myelin, a fatty sheathing, covers the axon of some neurons.

N

naturalistic study A study in which behavior is observed in its natural setting.

negative identity A form of identity diffusion involving rejection of the roles preferred by one's family or community in favor of socially undesirable roles.

neonate A newborn infant.

neostructuralist Relates to recent theories of cognition that emphasize the structure or organization of thinking.

neurons Nerve cell bodies and their extensions or fibers.

non-REM sleep The stages of sleep that vary from light sleep to very deep, restorative sleep. The deeper stages of non-REM sleep play a pivotal role in helping us feel rested, growing, repairing cells, and bolstering immune function.

norms Behaviors typical at certain ages and of certain groups; standards of normal development.

O

obesity The state of being extremely overweight, specifically to a body mass index of 30 or over.

object permanence According to Piaget, the belief that people and things continue to exist even when one cannot experience them directly; emerges around age two.

observational learning The tendency of a child to imitate or model behavior and attitudes of parents and other nurturant individuals.

operant conditioning According to Skinner, a process of learning in which a person or an animal increases the frequency of a behavior in response to repeated reinforcement of that behavior.

overnutrition Diet that contains too many calories and is therefore unbalanced.

overt aggression Actions that harm others through physical damage or the threat of such damage, such as pushing, hitting, kicking, or threatening to "beat up" a peer.

ovum The reproductive cell, or gamete, of the female; the egg cell.

P

participation structures Regular patterns of discourse or interaction in classrooms with unstated rules about how, when, and to whom to speak.

peers Individuals who are of approximately the same age and developmental level and share common attitudes and interests.

perceived popularity A type of popularity based on social status and prestige.

perception The neural activity of combining sensations into meaningful patterns.

performance orientation Achievement motivation stimulated by other individuals who may see and evaluate the learner rather than by the intrinsic nature of the task itself.

permissive parenting A style of parenting in which parents make relatively few demands on their children but clearly communicate their warmth and interest and provide considerable care and nurturance.

personal fable Adolescents' belief that their own lives embody a special story that is heroic and completely unique.

phenotype The set of traits an individual actually displays during development; reflects the evolving product of genotype and experience. See also *genotype*.

phonemes Sounds that combine with other sounds to form words.

physical activity play Vigorous physical activity that occurs in a playful context, has a basis in human evolution, and serves several adaptive developmental functions.

physical development The area of human development concerned primarily with physical changes such as growth, motor skill development, and basic aspects of perception.

placenta An organ that delivers oxygen and nutrients from the mother to the fetus and carries away the fetus's waste products, which the mother will excrete.

plasticity The degree to which a developing structure or organ (like the brain) can be influenced by the environment.

postconventional moral judgment In Kohlberg's theory, an orientation to moral justice that develops beyond conventional rules and beliefs.

postformal cognitive development An adult stage of cognitive development that follows formal operations, the last of Piaget's four stages. Although different theorists use different terms, postformal thought is characterized by relative and non-absolute thinking that accepts and synthesizes contradiction and helps adults deal with the ambiguities of real life problems.

preoperational stage In Piaget's theory, the stage of cognition characterized by increasing use of symbolic thinking but not yet by logical groupings of concepts.

pretend play Play that substitutes imaginary situations for real ones. Also called *fantasy* or *dramatic play*.

primary sex characteristics Characteristics that make sexual reproduction possible. For females, consist of the vagina, uterus, fallopian tubes, and ovaries; for males, consist of the penis, scrotum, testes, prostate gland, and seminal vesicles.

proximodistal principle Growth that exhibits a near-to-far pattern of development, from the center of the body outward.

psychometric approach to intelligence A view of intelligence based on identifying individual differences in ability through standardized test scores.

psychosocial development The area of human development concerned primarily with personality, social knowledge and skills, and emotions.

psychosocial moratorium According to Erikson, the latency period that precedes puberty and provides a temporary suspension of psychosexual development.

puberty The period of early adolescence characterized by the development of full physical and sexual maturity.

punishment According to Skinner, any stimulus that temporarily suppresses the response that it follows.

Q

quasi-experiments Experiments in which participants cannot be randomly assigned to the experimental and control groups; instead, members of pre-existing groups are selected for comparison (for example, males versus females, young adults versus older adults, or private school students versus public school students).

R

random assignment In research studies, each participant has an equal chance of being placed in, or assigned to, each group. This increases our confidence that differences in the dependent variable are due to the independent variable.

random sample In research studies, a group of individuals from a population chosen such that each member of the population has an equal chance of being selected.

range of reaction The range of possible phenotypes that an individual with a particular genotype might exhibit in response to the particular sequence of environmental influences he or she experiences.

recall memory Retrieval of information by using relatively few external cues.

recessive gene In any paired set of genes, the gene that influences or determines physical characteristics only when no dominant gene is present.

recognition memory Retrieval of information by comparing an external stimulus or cue with pre-existing experiences or knowledge.

reflex An involuntary, automatic response to a stimulus. The very first movements or motions of an infant are reflexes.

reinforcement According to Skinner, any stimulus that increases the likelihood that a behavior will be repeated in similar circumstances.

relational aggression Actions that harm others through damage or threat of damage to their peer relationships.

REM sleep A stage of sleep in which one's body is paralyzed, but one's eyes and brain are very active. REM sleep is believed to be important for memory consolidation.

resilience Ability to withstand and even profit from stressful experiences.

reversibility Ability to return mentally to earlier steps in a problem.

S

sample A group that is studied for research purposes.

scheme According to Piaget, a behavior or thought that represents a group of ideas and events in a person's experience.

scientific methods General procedures of study involving (1) formulating research questions, (2) stating questions as a hypothesis, (3) testing the hypothesis, and (4) interpreting and publicizing the results.

secondary sex characteristics Sex characteristics other than the sex organs, such as extra layers of fat and pubic hair.

secure attachment A healthy bond between infant and caregiver. The child is happy when the caregiver is present, somewhat upset during the caregiver's absence, and easily comforted upon the caregiver's return.

selective attention The ability to maintain focus on one thing even in the presence of distractions.

self-constancy The belief that one's identity remains permanently fixed; established sometime after age six.

self-esteem An individual's belief that he or she is an important, competent, powerful, and worthwhile person who is valued and appreciated.

semantics The purposes and meanings of a language.

sense of self A structured way in which individuals think about themselves that helps them to organize and understand who they are based on the views of others, their own experiences, and cultural categories such as gender and race.

sensorimotor intelligence According to Piaget, thinking that occurs by way of sensory perceptions and motor actions; characteristic of infants.

sequential study Research in which at least two cohorts are compared both with each other and at different times.

SES The socioeconomic status of an individual or family that is determined by level of education, income, and type of work, as well as by lifestyle and social values. Also called *social class.*

sex-linked recessive traits Recessive traits resulting from genes on the X chromosome.

sickle-cell disease A genetically transmitted condition in which a person's red blood cells intermittently acquire a curved, sickle shape. The condition sometimes can clog circulation in the small blood vessels.

SIDS Sudden infant death syndrome (or "crib death"), an unaccountable death of an infant in its sleep.

situated cognition Thinking that occurs jointly with others and is embedded in a particular context or activity setting.

social cognition Knowledge and beliefs about interpersonal and social matters.

social constructivism A theory that views learning as resulting from active dialogue and interaction between an individual and his or her community.

social conventions Arbitrary customs and agreements about behavior that members of a society use.

social referencing The child's sensitive awareness of how parents and other adults are feeling and ability to use these emotional cues as a basis for guiding his or her own emotional responses and actions. Social referencing is important for the development of autonomy.

social trajectory The pathway or direction that development takes over an individual's life course, which is influenced by the school, work, family, and other important social settings in which he or she participates.

sociocultural perspective on intelligence A view of intelligence that emphasizes the social and cultural influences on ability rather than the influence of inherent or learned individual differences.

sociometric popularity A type of popularity based on how well liked someone is.

sperm Male gametes, or reproductive cells; produced in the testicles.

Strange Situation (SS) A widely used method for studying attachment; confronts the infant with a series of controlled separations and reunions with a parent and a stranger.

stress The arousal of the mind and body in response to demands made on them by unsettling conditions or experiences (stressors).

stunting Being excessively short in stature—falling under the fifth percentile for height for one's age—caused by chronic undernourishment.

superego In Freud's theory, the part of personality that acts as an all-knowing, internalized parent. It has two parts: the conscience, which enforces moral and social conventions by punishing violations with guilt, and the ego-ideal, which provides an idealized, internal set of standards for regulating and evaluating one's thoughts, feelings, and actions.

survey A research study that samples specific knowledge or opinions of large numbers of individuals.

synaptic pruning The process through which unused synapses and neurons are eliminated.

synaptogenesis The forming of connections, or synapses, between neurons.

syntax Rules for ordering and relating the elements of a language.

T

temperament Individual differences in quality and intensity of emotional responding and self-regulation that are present at birth, are relatively stable and enduring over time and across situations, and are influenced by the interaction of heredity, maturation, and experience.

teratogen Any substance that can harm the developing embryo or fetus.

testosterone A sex hormone, sometimes called the *male sex hormone* because its high concentration in boys stimulates growth of the penis and related male reproductive organs.

transient exuberance The rapid but temporary increase in the rate of synaptogenesis and, hence, the number of synapses formed between neurons during infancy.

trait A relatively enduring disposition of an individual; a characteristic way of thinking, feeling, and acting.

triarchic theory of intelligence A view of intelligence as consisting of three components: (1) adaptability, (2) information-processing skills, and (3) the ability to deal with novelty.

trust versus mistrust In Erikson's theory, the psychosocial crisis of children from birth to one year involving whether they can rely on their parents to reliably meet their physical and emotional needs.

twin adoption study Research that compares twins reared apart with unrelated persons reared together.

twin study A research method for studying the relative contributions of heredity and environment in which the degree of similarity between genetically identical, or monozygotic, twins (developed from a single fertilized egg) is compared with the similarity between fraternal, or dizygotic, twins (developed from two fertilized eggs).

U

umbilical cord Three large blood vessels that connect the embryo to the placenta, one to provide nutrients and two to remove waste products.

V

validity The degree to which research findings measure or observe what is intended.

visual cliff The classic laboratory setup of a ledge covered by a sheet of glass; used to test the acquisition of depth perception. Young babies crawling on the glass discriminate between the two sides of the "cliff."

W

working models Internalized perceptions, feelings, and expectations regarding social and emotional relationships with significant caregivers based on experiences with those caregivers.

Z

zone of proximal development According to Vygotsky, the level of difficulty at which problems are too hard for children to solve alone but not too hard when given support from adults or more competent peers.

zygote The single new cell formed when a sperm cell attaches itself to the surface of an ovum (egg).

References

A

Abukabar, A., Holding, P., Vijver, F. J. R., Newton, C., & Baar, A. V. (2010). Children at risk for developmental delay can be recognized by stunting, being underweight, ill health, little maternal schooling or high gravity. *Journal of Child Psychology and Psychiatry, 51,* 652–659.

Adachi, P. J., & Willoughby, T. (2011). The effect of violent video games on aggression: Is it more than just the violence? *Aggression and Violent Behavior, 16*(1), 55–62.

Adair, L., Fall, C., Osmond, C., Stein, A., Martorell, R., Ramirez-Zea, . . . & Victoria, C. (2013). Associations of linear growth and relative weight gain during early life with adult health and human capital in countries of low and middle income: Findings from five birth cohort studies. *Lancet, 382,* 525–534.

Adolph, K. E. (2008). Learning to move. *Current Directions in Psychological Science, 17,* 213–218.

Adolph, K. E., Cole, W. G., Komati, M., Garciaguirre, J. S., Badaly, D., Lingeman, J. M., . . . & Sotsky, R. B. (2012). How do you learn to walk? Thousands of steps and dozens of falls per day. *Psychological Science, 23*(11), 1387–1394.

Agras, W. S., Kraemer, H. C., Berkowitz, R. I., Korner, A. F., & Hammer, L. D. (1987). Does a vigorous feeding style influence early development? *Journal of Pediatrics, 110,* 799–804.

Ahn, J. (2011). "You're my friend today, but not tomorrow": Learning to be friends among young US middle-class children. *American Ethnologist, 38*(2), 294–306.

Aiken, L. (1996). *Assessment of intellectual functioning* (2nd ed.). New York, NY: Plenum Press.

Ainsworth, M. (1973). The development of infant mother attachment. In B. M. Caldwell, & H. N. Ricciuti (Eds.), *Review of child development research: Vol. 3.* Chicago: University of Chicago Press.

Ainsworth, M. (1979). Infant-mother attachment. *American Psychologist, 34,* 932–937.

Ainsworth, M. S., & Bowlby, J. (1991). An etiological approach to personality development. *American Psychologist, 46,* 333–341.

Ainsworth, M., Blehar, M., Waters, E., & Wall, S. (1978). *Strange-situation behavior of one-year-olds. Its relation to mother-infant interaction in the first year and to qualitative differences in the infant-mother attachment relationship.* Hillsdale, NJ: Erlbaum.

Akande, A. (1994). What meaning and effects does fatherhood have in child development? *Early Child Development and Care, 101,* 51–58.

Åkerstedt, T. (2006). Psychosocial stress and impaired sleep. *Scandinavian Journal of Work, Environment & Health, 32*(6), 493–501.

Alan Guttmacher Institute. (1994). *Sex and America's teenagers.* New York, NY: Author.

Alberts, A., Elkind, D., & Ginsberg, S. (2007). The personal fable and risk-taking in early adolescence. *Journal of Youth and Adolescence, 36,* 71–76.

Aldous, M. B., & Edmonson, M. B. (1993). Maternal age at first childbirth and risk of low birth weight and preterm delivery in Washington State. *Journal of the American Medical Association, 270,* 2574–2577.

Alegria, M., Woo, M., Cao, Z., Torres, M., Meng, X. L., & Striege-Moore, R. (2007). Prevalence and correlates of eating disorders in Latinos in the United States. *International Journal of Eating Disorders, 40*(S3), S15–S21.

Alexander, A. W., & Slinger-Constant, A. M. (2004). Current status of treatments for dyslexia: Critical review. *Journal of Child Neurology, 19*(10), 744–758.

Alexander, G. M., & Hines, M. (1994). Gender labels and play styles: Their relative contribution to children's selection of playmates. *Child Development, 65,* 869–879.

Alexander, K. L., & Entwisle, D. R. (1988). Achievement in the first 2 years of school: Patterns and processes. *Monographs of the Society for Research in Child Development, 53*(2, Serial No. 218).

Alexander, L. L., & LaRosa, J. H. (1994). *New directions in women's health.* Boston: Jones and Bartlett.

Alfonso, M. (2006). The impact of community college attendance on baccalaureate attainment. *Research in Higher Education, 47*(8), 873–903.

Allen, J. P., Hauser, S. T., Bell, K. L., & O'Conner, T. G. (1994). Longitudinal assessment of autonomy and relatedness in adolescent-family interactions as predictors of adolescent ego development and self esteem. *Child Development, 65,* 179–194.

Altenbaugh, R. (1995). *Caring for kids: Critical studies of urban school leavers.* Washington, DC: Falmer Press.

Altman, L. K. (1998, June 30). U. N. plans to treat 30,000 HIV-infected pregnant women. *New York Times,* p. A–15.

Amato, P. R. (2010). Research on divorce: Continuing trends and new developments. *Journal of Marriage and Family, 72*(3), 650–666.

Amato, P. R., & Dorius, C. (2010). Fathers, children, and divorce. In M. E. Lamb (Ed.), *The role of the father in child development, 5,* 177–200.

Amato, P. R., & Hohmann-Marriott, B. (2007). A comparison of high and low-distress marriages that end in divorce. *Journal of Marriage and Family, 69,* 621–638.

Amato, P. R., Loomis, L. S., & Booth, A. (1995). Parental divorce, marital conflict, and offspring well-being during early adulthood. *Social Forces, 73,* 895–915.

Ambry, M. K. (1992). Childless chances. *American Demographics, 14*(4), 55.

American Academy of Pediatrics. (1991). *Facts about children with AIDS.* Elk Grove Village, IL: Author.

American Academy of Pediatrics. (1993). *Pediatric nutrition handbook.* Elk Grove Village, IL: Author.

American Academy of Pediatrics. (2007). Contraception and adolescents. *Pediatrics, 120,* 1135–1148.

American Academy of Pediatrics. (2013a). *Apgar scores.* Retrieved from http://www.healthychildren.org/English/ages-stages/prenatal/delivery-beyond/pages/Apgar-Scores

American Academy of Pediatrics. (2013b). *A child care provider's guide to safe sleep.* Retrieved from http://www.healthychildren.org/English/familylife/work-play/Pages/A-Child-Care-Provider%27s-Guide-to-Safe-Sleep

American Academy of Pediatrics. (2015). *Fetal alcohol spectrum disorders.* Retrieved from http://pediatrics.aappublications.org/content/early/2015/10/13/peds.2015–3113

American Academy of Pediatrics. (2016). *Media and children.* Retrieved from https://www.aap.org/en-us/advocacy-and-policy/aap-health-initiatives/pages/media-and-children.aspx

American Academy of Pediatrics Task Force on Sudden Infant Death Syndrome (AAP Task Force on SIDS). (2011). SIDS and other sleeprelated deaths: Expansion of recommendations for a safe infant sleeping environment. *Pediatrics, 128,* 1341–1367.

American Civil Liberties Union (ACLU). (2014). Employment non-discrimination act. Retrieved from https://www.aclu.org/hiv-aids_lgbt-rights/employment-non-discrimination-act

American Civil Liberties Union. (n.d.). Nondiscrimination laws: State by state. Retrieved August 7, 2016 from https://www.aclu.org/map/non-discrimination-laws-state-state-informationmap

American College of Nurse-Midwives (ACNM). (2012). *CNM/CM-attended birth statistics.* Retrieved from http://www.midwife.org/CNM/CM-attended-Birth-Statistics

American College of Obstetricians and Gynecologists (ACOG). (1995). *Planning for pregnancy, birth, and beyond* (2nd ed.). New York, NY: Penguin.

American College of Obstetricians and Gynecologists (ACOG). (2013). Weight gain during pregnancy: Committee opinion number 548. *Obstetrics & Gynecology, 121,* 210–212.

American Institutes for Research. (2013). Parental leave that might pay for itself. Retrieved from http://www.air.org/resource/parental-leave-mightpay-itself

American Psychiatric Association. (2013). *Diagnostic and statistical manual of mental disorders* (5th ed.). Arlington, VA: American Psychiatric Publishing.

American Psychological Association. (1992). Ethical principles of psychologists and code of conduct *American Psychologist, 47*(12), 1060–1073.

American Psychological Association. (1996). *Body image, eating disorders, and obesity: Integrative guide for assessment and treatment.* Washington, DC: Author.

American Psychological Association. (2005). *Lesbian and gay parenting.* Washington, DC: Author. Retrieved from http://www.apa.org/pi/lgbt/resources/parenting-full.pdf

American Psychological Association. (2010). 2010 amendments to the 2002 "ethical principles of psychologists and code of conduct." *American Psychologist, 65,* 493.

Ames, L. (1997). *Women reformed, women empowered: Poor mothers and the endangered promise of Head Start.* Philadelphia: Temple University Press.

Ames, L. B. (1983). *Your one-year-old.* New York, NY: Dell.

Anastasi, A., & Urbina, S. (1997). *Psychological testing* (7th ed.). Upper Saddle River, NJ: Prentice-Hall.

Anderson, A. M. (1996). The father-infant relationship: Becoming connected. *Journal of the Society of Pediatric Nurses, 1,* 83–92.

Anderson, B. (1989). Effects of public day care: A longitudinal study. *Child Development, 60,* 857–866.

Anderson, L. M., & Anderson, J. (2010). Barney and breakfast: Messages about food and eating in preschool television shows and how they may impact the development of eating behaviours in children. *Early Child Development and Care, 180*(10), 1323–1336.

Anderson, S. A., Russell, C. S., & Schumm, W. A. (1983). Perceived marital quality and family lifecycle categories: A further analysis. *Journal of Marriage and the Family, 45,* 127–139.

Anderson, S., & Winefield, A. H. (2011). The impact of underemployment on psychological health, physical health, and work attitudes. In D. C. Maynard, & D. C. Feldman (Eds.) *Underemployment: Psychological, Economic, and Social Challenges* (pp. 165–185). New York, NY: Springer.

Andrien, M. (1994). *Social communication in nutrition: A methodology for intervention.* Rome: Food and Agricultural Organization of the United Nations.

Angier, N. (1994, May 17). Genetic mutations tied to father in most cases. *New York Times,* p. C12.

Anglin, J. (1993). Vocabulary development: A morphological analysis. *Monographs of the Society for Research on Child Development,* 58(10, Serial No. 238). Chicago: University of Chicago Press.

Apfel, N. H., & Seitz, V. (1991). Four models of adolescent mother-grandmother relationships in Black inner-city families, *Family Relations, 40,* 421–429.

Apgar, V. (1953). A proposal for a new method of evaluation in the newborn infant. *Current Research in Anesthesia and Analgesia, 32,* 260.

Aquilino, W. S. (1990). The likelihood of parent-adult child coresidence: Effects of family structure and parental characteristics. *Journal of Marriage and the Family, 52,* 405–419.

Aquilino, W. S., & Supple, K. R. (1991). Parent-child relations and parent's satisfaction with living arrangements when adult children live at home *Journal of Marriage and the Family, 53,* 13–27.

Archer, S. L. (1982). The lower age boundaries of identity development. *Child Development, 53,* 1551–1556.

Archer, S. L., & Waterman, A. S. (1988). Psychological individualism: Gender differences or gender identity? *Human Development, 31,* 65–81.

Archibald, A. B., Graber, J. A., & Brooks-Gunn, J. (2006). Pubertal processes and physiological growth in adolescence. In G. R. Adams, & M. D. Berzonsky (Eds.), *Blackwell handbook of adolescence.* Malden, MA: Blackwell.

Archibald, J. (Ed.). (1995). *Phonological acquisition and phonological theory.* Hillsdale, NJ: Erlbaum.

Arditti, J. A. (1992). Differences between fathers with joint custody and noncustodial fathers. *American Journal of Orthopsychiatry, 62,* 186–195.

Arend, R., Gove, F., & Sroufe, L. (1979). Continuity of individual adaptation from infancy to kindergarten: A predictive study of ego-resiliency and curiosity in preschoolers. *Child Development, 50,* 950–959.

Ariès, P. (1962). *Centuries of childhood: A social history of family life* (R. Baldick, trans.). New York, NY: Vintage.

Arliss, L. (1991). *Gender communication.* Englewood Cliffs, NJ: Prentice-Hall.

Armour, S., & Haynie, D. (2007). Adolescent sexual debut and later delinquency. *Journal of Youth and Adolescence, 36*(2), 141–153.

Armstead, C. A., Lawler, K. A., Gordon, G., Cross, J., & Gibbons, J. (1989). Relationship of racial stressors to blood pressure responses and anger expression in black college students. *Health Psychology, 8,* 541–557.

Arnett, J. J. (1992). Reckless behavior in adolescence: A developmental perspective. *Developmental Review, 12,* 339–373.

Arnett, J. J. (1999). Adolescent storm and stress, reconsidered. *American Psychologist, 54,* 317–326.

Arnett, J. J. (2000). Emerging adulthood: A theory of development from the late teens through the twenties. *American Psychologist, 55*(5), 469–480.

Arnett, J. J. (2004). *Emerging adulthood: The widening road from the late teens through the twenties.* New York, NY: Oxford University Press.

Arnett, J. J. (2016). Introduction: Emerging adulthood theory and research: Where we are and where we should go. In J. J. Arnett (Ed.), *The Oxford handbook of emerging adulthood* (pp. 1–7). New York, NY: Oxford University Press.

Arnett, J. J., & Jensen, L. A. (1997). Socialization and risk behavior in two countries: Denmark and the United States, *Youth & Society, 26,* 1994, 3–22.

Arnett, J. J., Ramos, K. D., & Jensen, L. A. (2001). Ideological views in emerging adulthood: Balancing autonomy and community. *Journal of Adult Development, 8*(2), 69–80.

Arthur-Banning, S., Wells, M. S., Baker, B. L., & Hegreness, R. (2009). Parents behaving badly? The relationship between the sportsmanship behaviors of adults and athletes in youth basketball games. *Journal of Sport Behavior, 32*(1), 3–18.

Asendorpf, J. B., Warkentin, V., & Baudonniere, P. M. (1996). Self-awareness and other-awareness II: Mirror self-recognition, social contingency awareness, and synchronic imitation. *Developmental Psychology, 32,* 313–321.

Asber, S., Renshaw, P., & Hymel, S. (1982). Peer relations and the development of social skills. In S. Moore, & C. Cooper (Eds.), *The young child: Reviews of research: Vol. 3.* Washington, DC: National Association for the Education of Young Children.

Ashley, K. B. (2013). The science on sexual orientation: A review of the recent literature. *Journal of Gay & Lesbian Mental Health, 17*(2), 175–182.

Ata, R. N., Ludden, A. B., & Lally, M. M. (2007). The effects of gender and family, friend, and media influences on eating behaviors and body image during adolescence. *Journal of Youth and Adolescence, 36*(8), 1024–1037.

Aureli, T., & Presaghi, F. (2010). Developmental trajectories for mother-infant coregulation in the second year of life. *Infancy, 15,* 557–585.

Aviezer, O., van IJzendoom, M. H., Sagi, A., & Schuengel, C. (1994). "Children of the Dream" revisited: 70 years of collective early child care in Israeli kibbutzim. *Psychological Bulletin, 116,* 99–116.

Avioli, P. S. (1989). The social support functions of siblings in later life. *American Behavioral Scientist, 33*(1), 45–57.

Ayers, T. S., Wolchik, S. A., Sandler, I. N., Twohey, J. L., Weyer, J. L., Padgett-Jones, S., . . . & Kriege, G. (2013). The Family Bereavement Program: Description of a theory-based prevention program for parentally-bereaved children and adolescents. *Omega: Journal of Death and Dying, 68*(4), 293–314.

Ayscue, J. B., & Orfield, G. (2016). Perpetuating separate and unequal worlds of educational opportunity through district lines: School segregation by race and poverty. In *Race, Equity, and Education* (pp. 45–74). Springer International Publishing.

Azmitia, M., & Hesser, J. (1993). Why siblings are important agents of cognitive development: A comparison of siblings and peers. *Child Development, 64,* 430–444.

B

Bachman, J. G. (1983). Premature affluence: Do high school students earn too much. *Economic Outlook USA, 10*(3), 64–67.

Backx, F. (1996). Epidemiology of pediatric sports related injuries. In O. Bar-Or (Ed.), *The child and adolescent athlete* (pp. 163–172). Oxford, UK: Blackwells.

Badgett, M. V. L., Lau, H., Sears, B., & Ho, D. (2007). Bias in the workplace: Consistent evidence of sexual orientation and gender identity discrimination. *The Williams Institute.*

Badgett, M. V. L., & Mallory, C. (2014, December). Patterns of relationship recognition for same-sex couples: Divorce and terminations. *The Williams Institute.* Retrieved from http://williamsinstitute.law.ucla.edu/wp-content/uploads/Badgett-Mallory-Divorce-Terminations-Dec-2014.pdf

Bagwell, C. L., Newcomb, A. F., & Bukowski, W. M. (1996). *Preadolescent friendships and peer rejection as predictors of adult adjustment.* Unpublished manuscript, University of Richmond, Department of Psychology, Richmond, VA.

Bagwell, C. L., Newcomb, A. F., & Bukowski, W. M. (1998). Preadolescent friendship and peer rejection as predictors of adult adjustment. *Child Development, 69,* 140–153.

Bailey, J. M., & Zucker, K. J. (1995). Childhood sex-typed behavior and sexual orientation: A conceptual analysis and quantitative review *Developmental Psychology, 31,* 43–55.

Baillargeon, R. (1991). Object permanence in infants: Further evidence. *Child Development. 62,* 1227–1246.

Baillargeon, R. (1993). The object concept revisited: New directions in the investigation of infants' physical knowledge. In C. Granrud (Ed.), *Visual perception and cognition in infants,* pp. 265–316. Hillsdale, NJ: Erlbaum.

Bain, L. (1993). *Parents' guide to childhood emergencies.* New York, NY: Delta.

Baird, P., & Sadovnick, A. D. (1987). Life expectancy in Down syndrome. *Journal of Pediatrics, 110,* 849–854.

Baker, C. (1995). *English syntax* (2nd ed.). Cambridge, MA: MIT press.

Baker, J. E., Sedney, M. A., & Gross, E. (1992). Psychological tasks for bereaved children. *American Journal of Orthopsychiatry, 62,* 105–116.

Balantekin, K. N., Savage, J. S., Marini, M. E., & Birch, L. L. (2014). Parental encouragement of dieting promotes daughters' early dieting. *Appetite, 80,* 190–196.

Baldwin, D. A., & Moses, L. J. (1996). The ontogeny of social information gathering. *Child Development, 67,* 1915–1939.

Balk, D., & Corr, C. A. (1996). Adolescents, developmental tasks, and encounters with death and bereavement. In C. A. Corr, & D. E. Balk (Eds.), *Handbook of adolescent death and bereavement* (pp. 3–24). New York, NY: Springer.

Balter, M. (2015). Can epigenetics explain homosexuality puzzle? *Science, 350*(6257), 148.

Bamford, F., Bannister, R., Benjamin, C., Hillier, V., Ward, B., & Moore, W. (1990). Sleep in the first year of life. *Developmental Medicine and Child Neurology, 32,* 718–724.

Bandura, A. (1989). Social cognitive theory. In R. Vasta (Ed.), *Annals of Child Development. Theories of child development: Revised formulations and current issues.* Greenwich, CT: JAI Press.

Bandura, A. (1991). Social cognitive theory of moral thought and action. In W. Kurtines, & J. Gewirtz (Eds.), *Handbook of moral behavior and development: Vol. 1* (pp. 45–104). Hillsdale, NJ: Erlbaum.

Bandura, A., Cioffi, D., Taylor, C. B., & Brouillard, M. E. (1988). Perceived self-efficacy in coping with cognitive stressors and opioid activation. *Journal of Personality and Social Psychology, 55,* 479–488.

Bank, L., Patterson, G. R., & Reid, J. B. (1996). Negative sibling interaction patterns as predictors of later adjustment problems in adolescent and young adult males. In G. H. Brody et al. (Ed.), *Sibling relationships: Their causes and consequences* (pp. 197–229). Norwood, NJ: Ablex.

Barber, E., Lundsberg, L., Belanger, K., Pettker, C., Funai, E., & Illuzzi, J. (2011). Contributing indications to the rising cesarean delivery rate. *Journal of Obstetrics & Gynecology,* 118, 29–38.

Barbaresi, W. J., Katusic, S. K., Colligan, R. C., Weaver, A. L., Leibson, C. L., & Jacobsen, S. J. (2006). Long-term stimulant medication treatment of attention-deficit/hyperactivity disorder: Results from a population-based study. *Journal of Developmental & Behavioral Pediatrics, 27*(1), 1–10.

Barlow, D. H., & Durand, V. M. (1995). *Abnormal psychology: An integrative approach.* Pacific Grove, Cal: Brooks/Cole.

Barnes, G. M., Welte, J. W., & Dintcheff, B. (1992). Alcohol misuse among college students and other young adults: Findings from a general population study in New York State. *The International Journal of the Addictions, 27,* 917–934.

Barness, L. (Ed.). (1993). *Pediatric nutrition handbook* (3rd ed.). Elk Grove Village, IL: American Academy of pediatrics.

Barr, H. M., Streissguth, A. P., Darby, B. L., & Sampson, P. D. (1990). Prenatal exposure to alcohol, caffeine, tobacco, and aspirin: Effects on fine and gross motor performance in 4-year-old children. *Developmental Psychology, 26,* 339–348.

Barr, R. G. (1995). The enigma of infant crying: The emergence of defining dimensions. *Early Development and Parenting, 4,* 225–232.

Barrett, K. C. (2005). The origins of social emotions and self-regulation in toddlerhood: New evidence. *Cognition and Emotion, 19,* 953–979.

Barry, C. M., Madsen, S. D., & DeGrace, A. (2016). Growing up with a little help from their friends in emerging adulthood. In J. J. Arnett (Ed.), *The Oxford handbook of emerging adulthood* (pp. 215–229). New York, NY: Oxford University Press.

Bartholomew, J. B., Morrison, D., & Ciccolo, J. T. (2005). Effects of acute exercise on mood and well-being in patients with major depressive disorder. *Medicine and Science in Sports and Exercise, 37*(12), 2032–2037.

Bartick, M., & Reinhold, A. (2010). The burden of suboptimal breastfeeding in the United States: A pediatric cost analysis. *Pediatrics, 125*(5), e1048–e1056.

Barton, E. E., & Pavilanis, R. (2012). Teaching pretend play to young children with autism. *Young Exceptional Children, 15*(1), 5–17.

Bartsch, K. (1993). Adolescents' theoretical thinking. In R. Lerner (Ed.), *Early adolescence: Perspectives on research, policy, and intervention,* pp. 143–159. Hillsdale, NJ: Erlbaum.

Baruch, G., Barnett, R., & Rivers, C. (1983). *Lifeprints: New patterns of love and work for today's woman.* New York, NY: McGraw Hill.

Bat-Chava, Y., Allen, L., Aber, J. L., & Seidman, E. (1997, April). *Racial and ethnic identity and the contexts of development.* Paper presented at the annual meeting of the Society for Research in Child Development, Washington, DC.

Bauman, K. E., & Ennett, S. T. (1994). Peer influence on adolescent drug use. *American Psychologist, 49,* 820–822.

Baumrind, D. (1968). Authoritative vs. authoritarian parental control. *Adolescence, 3,* 255–272

Baumrind, D. (1971). Current patterns of parental authority. *Developmental Psychology Monographs, 4* (No. 1, Pt. 2).

Baumrind, D. (1989). Raising competent children. In W. Damon (Ed.), *Child development today and tomorrow* (pp. 349–378). San Francisco: Jossey Bass.

Baumrind, D. (1991). The influence of parenting style on adolescent competence and substance abuse. *Early Adolescence, 11,* 56–95.

Baumrind, D. (1991a). Effective parenting during the early adolescent transition. In P. Cowan, & M. Hetherington (Eds.), *Family transitions.* Hillsdale, NJ: Erlbaum.

Baumrind, D. (1991b). Parenting styles and adolescent development. In R. M. Lerner, A. C. Petersen, & J. Brooks-Gunn (Ed.), *The encyclopedia of adolescence.* New York, NY: Garland.

Baydar, N., Hyle, P., & Brooks-Gunn, J. (1997). A longitudinal study of the effects of the birth of a sibling during preschool and early grade school years. *Journal of Marriage and the Family, 59,* 957–965.

Bayley, N. (1955). On the growth of intelligence. *American Psychologist, 10,* 805–823.

Beale, E. A., Baile, W. F., & Aaron, J. (2005). Silence is not golden: Communicating with children dying from cancer. *Journal of Clinical Oncology, 23*(15), 3629–3631.

Bean, R. A., Barber, B. K., & Crane, D. R. (2006). Parental support, behavioral control, and psychological control among African American youth: The relationships to academic grades, delinquency, and depression. *Journal of Family Issues, 27*(10), 1335–1355.

Bechara, A. (2005). Decision making, impulse control and loss of willpower to resist drugs: A neurocognitive perspective. *Nature Neuroscience, 8,* 1458–1463.

Becker, A. (1994). Nurturing and negligence: Working on others' bodies in Fiji. In T. Csordas (Ed.), *Embodiment and experience: The existential ground of culture and self* (pp. 100–115). New York, NY: Cambridge University Press.

Becker, A. E. (2004). Television, disordered eating, and young women in Fiji: Negotiating body image and identity during rapid social change. *Culture, Medicine and Psychiatry, 28*(4), 533–559.

Becker, G. (1996). *Accounting for tastes.* Cambridge, MA: Harvard University Press.

Behrens, K. Y., Hesse, E., & Main, M. (2007). Mothers' attachment status as determined by the Adult Attachment Interview predicts their 6-year-olds' reunion responses: A study conducted in Japan. *Developmental Psychology, 43*(6), 1553.

Behrman, J., & Stacey, N. (Eds.) (1997). *The social benefits of education.* Ann Arbor, Mich. University of Michigan Press.

Behrman, R. (Ed.) (1993). *The future of children: School-linked services.* Los Altos, CA: Center for the Future of Children. The David and Lucille Packard Foundation.

Bei, B., Allen, N. B., Nicholas, C. L., Dudgeon, P., Murray, G., & Trinder, J. (2014). Actigraphy-assessed sleep during school and vacation periods: A naturalistic study of restricted and extended sleep opportunities in adolescents. *Journal of Sleep Research, 23*(1), 107–117.

Bell, K., Allen, J., Hauser, S., & O'Connor, T. (1996). Family factors and young adult transitions: Educational attainment and occupational prestige. In J. Graber, J. Brooks-Gunn, & A. Petersen (Eds.), *Transitions through adolescence* (pp. 345–366). Mahwah, NJ: Erlbaum.

Bellugi, U., Van Hoek, K., Lillo-Martin, D., & O'Grady, L. (1993). The acquisition of syntax and space in young deaf signers. In D. Bishop, & K. Mogford (Eds.), *Language development in exceptional circumstances* (pp. 132–149). Hillsdale, NJ: Erlbaum.

Belsky, J., & Cassidy, J. (1994). Attachment and close relationships: An individual-difference perspective. *Psychological Inquiry, 5,* 27–30.

Belsky, J. (1988a). The "effects" of infant day care reconsidered. *Early Childhood Research Quarterly, 3,* 235–272.

Belsky, J. (1988b). Child maltreatment and the emergent family system. In K. Browne, C. Davies, & P. Strattan (Eds.), *Early prediction and prevention of child abuse* (pp. 291–302). New York, NY: Wiley.

Belsky, J. (1993). Etiology of child maltreatment: A developmental-ecological analysis. *Psychological Bulletin, 114,* 413–434.

Belsky, J. (1996). Parent, infant and social-contextual antecedents of father-son attachment security. *Developmental Psychology, 32,* 905–913.

Belsky, J., & Nezworski, T. (Eds.) (1988). *Clinical implications of attachment.* Hillsdale, NJ: Erlbaum.

Belsky, J., & Rovine, M. (1988). Nonmaternal care in the first year of life and the security of infant-parent attachment. *Child Development, 59,* 157–176.

Belsky, J., & Rovine, M. (1990). Patterns of marital change across the transition to parenthood: Pregnancy to three years postpartum. *Journal of Marriage and the Family, 52,* 5–19.

Belsky, J., & Cassidy, J. (1994). Attachment and close relationships: An individual-difference perspective. *Psychological Inquiry, 5,* 27–30.

Belsky, J., Crnic, K., & Gable, S. (1995). The determinants of coparenting in families with toddler boys: Spousal differences and daily hassles. *Child Development, 66,* 629–642.

Bem, S. L. (1981). Gender schema theory: A cognitive account of sex typing. *Psychological Review, 88,* 354–364.

Bem, S. L. (1987). Gender schema theory and its implications for child development: Raising gender-aschematic children in a gender-schematic society. In M. R. Walsh, et al. (Eds.), *The psychology of women: Ongoing debates* (pp. 226–245). New Haven, CT: Yale University Press.

Bem, S. L. (1989). Genital knowledge and gender constancy in preschool children *Child Development, 60,* 649–662.

Benenson, J. F., Apostololeris, N. H., & Parnass, J. (1997). Age and sex differences in dyadic and group interaction. *Developmental Psychology, 33,* 538–543.

Benner, A. D., & Graham, S. (2009). The transition to high school as a developmental process among multiethnic urban youth. *Child Development, 80,* 356–376.

Benoit, D., & Parker, K. C. H. (1994). Stability and transmission of attachment across three generations. *Child Development, 65,* 1444–1456.

Benson, P., & Elkin, C. (1990). *Effective Christian education: A national study of Protestant denominations.* Minneapolis: Search Institute.

Beresford, T. (1993). Abortion counseling. In B. K. Rothman (Ed.), *The encyclopedia of childbearing.* New York, NY: Henry Holt.

Berg, E. C. (2004). The effects of perceived closeness to custodial parents, stepparents and nonresident parents on adolescent self-esteem. *Journal of Divorce & Remarriage, 40*(1–2), 69–86.

Berger, A. (2011). *Self-regulation: Brain, cognition and development.* Washington, DC: American Psychological Association.

Berger, R., Benatov, J., Abu-Raiya, H., & Tadmor, C. T. (2016). Reducing prejudice and promoting positive intergroup attitudes among elementary-school children in the context of the Israeli–Palestinian conflict. *Journal of School Psychology, 57,* 53–72. doi:10.1016/j.jsp.2016.04.003

Berko, J. (1958). The child's learning of English morphology, *Word, 14,* 150–177.

Berlin, J. E. (2009). It's all a matter of perspective: Student perceptions on the impact of being labeled gifted and talented. *Roeper Review, 31*(4), 217–223.

Berndt, T. J. (1988). The nature and significance of children's friendships. In R Vasta (Ed.), *Annals of child development: Vol. 5* (pp. 155–186). Greenwich, CT: JAI Press.

Bernhardt, J. S. (1990). Potential workplace hazards to reproductive health. *Journal of Obstetrical and Gynecological Nursing, 19,* 53–62.

Bertrand, K., Richer, I., Brunelle, N., Beaudoin, I., Lemmieux, A., & Menard, J-M. (2013). Substance abuse treatment for adolescents: How are family factors related to substance use change. *Journal of Psychoactive Drugs, 45*(1), 28–38

Bertrand, M., & Mullainathan, S. (2004). Are Emily and Greg more employable than Lakisha and Jamal? A field experiment on labor market discrimination. *American Economic Review, 94,* 991–1013.

Besedovsky, L., Lange, T., & Born, J. (2012). Sleep and immune function. *Pflügers Archiv-European Journal of Physiology, 463*(1), 121–137.

Beveridge, D. (1993). Violence against pregnant women. In B. K. Rothman (Ed.), *The encyclopedia of childbearing.* New York, NY: Henry Holt.

Bhavnagri, N., & Parke, R. D. (1991). Parents as direct facilitators of children's peer relationships: Effects of age of child and sex of parent. *Journal of Social and Personal Relationships, 8,* 423–40.

Bialystok, E., & Hakuta, K. (1994). *The science and psychology of second language acquisition.* New York, NY: Basic Books.

Bianchi, S. M. (2014). A demographic perspective on family change. *Journal of Family Theory & Review, 6,* 35–44.

Bianchi, S. M., Robinson, J. P., & Milke, M. A. (2006). *The changing rhythms of American family life.* Russell Sage Foundation.

Bierman, K. L., Smoot, D. L., & Aumiller, K. (1993). Characteristics of aggressive-rejected, aggressive (nonrejected), and rejected (nonaggressive) boys. *Child Development, 64,* 139–151.

Bingham, C. R., & Crockett, L. J. (1996). Longitudinal adjustment patterns of boys and girls experiencing early, middle and late sexual intercourse. *Developmental Psychology, 32,* 647–658.

Bird, G., & Melville, K. (1994). *Families and intimate relationships.* New York, NY: McGraw-Hill.

Black, M., & Krishnakumar, A. (1998). Children in low-income, urban settings. *American Psychologist, 53,* 635–646.

Black, M. C., Basile, K. C., Breiding, M. J., Smith, S. G., Walters, M. L., Merrick, M. T., Chen, J., Stevens, M. R. (2011). *The national intimate partner and sexual violence survey (NISVS): 2010 summary report.* Atlanta, GA: National Center for Injury Prevention and Control, Centers for Disease Control and Prevention.

Black, M. M., Quigg, A. M., Hurley, K. M., & Pepper, M. R. (2011). Iron deficiency and iron-deficiency anemia in the first two years of life: Strategies to prevent loss of developmental potential. *Nutrition Reviews, 69,* S64–S70.

Blackman, J. A. (1990). *Medical aspects of developmental disabilities in children birth to three* (2nd ed.). Rockville, MD: Aspen Publishers, Inc.

Blakemore, S. J. (2012). Development of the social brain in adolescence. *Journal of the Royal Society of Medicine, 105,* 111–116.

Blanchett, W. J. (2006). Disproportionate representation of African American students in special education: Acknowledging the role of white privilege and racism. *Educational Researcher, 35*(6), 24–28.

Blanck, G. (1990). The man and his cause. In L. C. Moll (Ed.), *Vygotsky and education: Instructional implications and applications of sociohistorical psychology.* Cambridge, UK: Cambridge University Press.

Blashill, A. J., & Wilhelm, S. (2013). Body image distortions, weight, and depression in adolescent boys: Longitudinal trajectories into adulthood. *Psychology of Men & Masculinity.* Advance online publication. doi: 10.1037/a0034618

Bleakley, A., Jordan, A. B., & Hennessy, M. (2013). The relationship between parents' and children's television viewing. *Pediatrics, 132*(2), e364–e371.

Blier, M. J., & Blier-Wilson, L. A. (1989). Gender differences in self-rated emotional expressiveness. *Sex Roles, 21*(3–4), 287–295.

Bloom, D. A., Seeley, W. W., Ritchey, M. L., & McGuire, E. J. (1993). Toilet habits and continence in children: An opportunity sampling in search of normal parameters. *Journal of Urology, 149*(5), 1087–1090.

Bloom, L. (1993). *The transition from infancy to language: Acquiring the power of expression.* New York, NY: Cambridge University Press.

Blumberg, M. L., & Lester, D. (1991). High school and college students' attitudes toward rape. *Adolescence, 26,* 727–729.

Bock, R. D., & Moore, E. G. J. (1986). *Advantage and disadvantage: A profile of American youth.* Hillsdale, NJ: Erlbaum.

Boergers, J., Gable, C. J., & Owens, J. A. (2014). Later school start time is associated with improved sleep and daytime functioning in adolescents. *Journal of Developmental & Behavioral Pediatrics, 35*(1), 11–17.

Bogdon, J. C. (1993). Childbirth practices in American history. In B. K. Rothman (Ed.), *The encyclopedia of childbearing.* New York, NY: Henry Holt, 1993.

Bohn, A., & Berntsen, D. (2008). Life story development in childhood: The development of life story abilities and the acquisition of cultural life scripts from late middle childhood to adolescence. *Developmental Psychology, 44*(4), 1135.

Bojko, M. (1995). The multi-cultural program at O'Brien Elementary School, Personal communication.

Bolger, K. E., Patterson, C. J., Thompson, W. W., & Kupersmidt, J. B. (1995). Psychosocial adjustment among children experiencing persistent and intermittent family economic hardship; *Child Development, 66,* 1107–1129.

Bollerud, K., Christopherson, S., & Frank, E. (1990). Girls' sexual choices: Looking for what is right: The intersection of sexual and moral development. In C. Gilligan, N. Lyons, & T. Hanmer (Eds.), *Making connections: The relational worlds of adolescent girls at Emma Willard School* (pp. 274–285). Cambridge. MA: Harvard University Press.

Bonoti, F., Leondari, A., & Mastora, A. (2013). Exploring children's understanding of death: Through drawings and the death concept questionnaire. *Death Studies, 37*(1), 47–60.

Booth, A., & Amato, P. R. (1994). Parental marital quality, parental divorce, and relations with parents. *Journal of Marriage and the Family, 56,* 21–34.

Booth, A., & Johnson, E. (1988). Premarital cohabitation and marital success. *Journal of Family Issues, 9,* 387–394.

Booth, D. A., Higgs, S., Schneider, J., & Klinkenberg, I. (2010). Learned liking versus inborn delight: Can sweetness give sensual pleasure or is it just motivating? *Psychological Science, 21,* 1656–1663.

Booth, J. R., Burman, D. D., Meyer, J. R., Lei, Z., Trommer, B. L., Davenport, N. D., . . . & Mesulam, M. M. (2003). Neural development of selective attention and response inhibition. *Neuroimage, 20*(2), 737–751.

Borchardt, K., & Noble, M. (Ed.). (1997). *Sexually transmitted diseases: Epidemiology, pathology, diagnosis, and treatment.* Boca Raton, FL: CRC Press.

Bordo, S. (1993). *Unbearable weight: Feminism, Western culture, and the body.* Berkeley, CA: University of California Press.

Bornstein, M. H., Haynes, O. M., Azuma, H., Galperin, C., Maital, S., Ogino, M., . . . Wright, B., et al. (1998). A cross-national study of self-evaluations and attributions in parenting: Argentina, Belgium, France, Israel, Italy, Japan, & the United States. *Developmental Psychology, 34,* 662–676.

Bouchard, C., & Shephard, R. J. (1993). Physical activity, fitness, and health: The model and key concepts. In C. Bouchard, R. J. Shephard, & T. Stephens (Eds.), *Physical activity, fitness, and health* (pp. 11–23). Champaign, IL: Human Kinetics.

Bowers, R. (1995). Early adolescent social and emotional development: A constructivist perspective. In M. Wavering (Ed.), *Educating young adolescents,* pp. 79–110. New York, NY: Garland.

Bowlby, J. (1969). *Attachment and loss: Vol. 1. Attachment.* New York, NY: Basic Books.

Bowlby, J. (1973). *Attachment and loss: Vol. 2. Separation, anxiety, and anger.* New York, NY: Basic Books.

Bowlby, J. (1979). *The making and breaking of affectional bonds.* London: Tavistock Publications.

Bowlby, J. (1980). *Attachment and loss: Vol. 3. Loss, sadness, and depression.* New York, NY: Basic Books.

Bowlby, J. (1988). *A secure base: Clinical applications of attachment theory.* London: Routledge.

Bowlby, J. (1988). Developmental psychology comes of age. *American Journal of Psychiatry, 145,* 1–10.

Boyd, M., & Pryor, E. T. (1989). The cluttered nest: The living arrangements of young Canadian adults. *Canadian Journal of Sociology, 14,* 461–477.

Bradley, M. (2002). *Yes your teen is crazy! Loving your kid without losing your mind.* Gig Harbor, WA: Harbor Press.

Brazelton, T. B. (1976). Early mother-infant reciprocity. In V. G. Vaughn III, & T. B. Brazelton (Eds.), *The family: Can it be saved?* Chicago: Yearbook Medical Publishers.

Brazelton, T. B., and Nugent, J. (1997). *Neonatal behavioral assessment scale* (4th ed.), New York, NY: Cambridge University Press.

Bredekamp, S., & Copple, C. (Eds.) (1997). *Developmentally appropriate practice in early childhood programs* (rev. ed.), Washington, DC; National Association for the Education of Young Children.

Breiding, M. J., Chen J., & Black, M.C. (2014). *Intimate partner violence in the United States—2010.* Atlanta, GA: National Center for Injury Prevention and Control, Centers for Disease Control and Prevention.

Breiding, M. J., Smith, S. G., Basile, K. C., Walters, M. L., Chen, J., & Merrick, M. T. (2014). Prevalence and characteristics of sexual violence, stalking, and intimate partner violence victimization—National Intimate Partner and Sexual Violence Survey, United States, 2011. Centers for Disease Control and Prevention, 63(SS08), 1–18. Retrieved from http://www.cdc.gov/mmwr/preview/mmwrhtml/ss6308a1.htm?s_cid=ss6308a1_e

Bretherton, I. (1995). A communication perspective on attachment relationships and internal working models. *Monographs of the Society for Research in Child Development, 60,* 310–329.

Bretherton, I., & Waters, E. (1985). Growing points in attachment theory. *Monographs of the Society for Research in Child Development, 50* (12, Serial No. 209).

Bretherton, I., McNew, S., & Beeghly-Smith, M. (1981). Early person knowledge as expressed in gestural and verbal communications. In M. Lamb, & L. Sherrod (Eds.), *Infant social cognition.* Hillsdale, NJ: Erlbaum.

Bridge, J. A., McBee-Strayer, S. M., & Cannon, E. A. (2012). Impaired decision-making in adolescent suicide attempters. *Journal of the American Academy of Child and Adolescent Psychiatry, 51*(4), 394–403.

Bridges, L. J., Grolnick, W. A., & Connell, J. P. (1997). Infant emotion regulation with mothers and fathers. *Infant Behavior and Development, 20,* 47–57.

Brindle, J. A. (2015). Waali plural formation: A preliminary study on variation in noun class realization. *Journal of African Languages and Linguistics, 36*(2), 163–192.

Briones, T. L., Klintsova, A. Y., & Greenough, W. T. (2004). Stability of synaptic plasticity in the adult rat visual cortex induced by complex environment exposure. *Brain Research, 1018,* 130–135.

Brislin, R., & Yoshida, T. (1994). *Intercultural communication training: An introduction.* Thousand Oaks, CA: Sage.

Brody, G. H., & Flor, D. L. (1997). Maternal psychological functioning, family processes, and child adjustment in rural, single-parent African American families. *Developmental Psychology, 33,* 1000–1011.

Brody, G. H., & Flor, D. L. (1998). Maternal resources, parenting practices, and child competence in rural, single-parent African American families. *Child Development, 69,* 803–816.

Brody, G. H., Graziano, W. G., & Musser, L. M. (1983). Familiarity and children's behavior in same-age and mixed-age peer groups *Developmental Psychology, 19,* 569–576.

Brody, G. H., Stoneman, Z., Flor, D. L., McCrary, C., Hastings, L., & Conyers, O. (1994). Financial resources, parent psychological functioning, parent co-caregiving, and early adolescent competence in rural two-parent African American families. *Child Development, 65,* 590–605.

Brody, G. H., Stoneman, Z., McCoy, J. K., & Forehand, R. (1992). Contemporary and longitudinal associations of sibling conflict with family relationship assessments and family discussions about sibling problems. *Child Development, 63,* 391–400.

Brondel, L., Romer, M. A., Nougues, P. M., Touyarou, P., & Davenne, D. (2010). Acute partial sleep deprivation increases food intake in healthy men. *American Journal of Clinical Nutrition, 91*(6), 1550–1559.

Bronfenbrenner, U. (1989). Ecological systems theory. In R. Vasta (Ed.), *Annals of child development: Vol. 6. Six theories of child development: Revised formulations and current issues.* Greenwich, CT: JAI Press.

Bronfenbrenner, U. (2000). Ecological theory. In A. Kazdin (Ed.), *Encyclopedia of psychology.* Washington, DC: American Psychological Association.

Bronfenbrenner, U. (Ed.) (2005). *Making human beings human: Bioecological perspectives on human development.* Thousand Oaks, CA: Sage.

Bronner, F. (Ed.) (1997). *Nutrition policy in public health.* New York, NY: Springer.

Bronstein, P. (1988). Marital and parenting roles in transition. In P. Bronstein, & C. Cowan (Eds.), *Fatherhood today: Men's changing role in the family* (pp. 3–12). New York, NY: Wiley.

Brooks-Gunn, J., & Warren, M. (1989). Biological and social contributions to negative affect in young adolescent girls. *Child Development, 60,* 40–55.

Brooten, D. (Ed.) (1992). *Low-birth-weight neonates.* Philadelphia: Lippincott.

Brophy, J. (1983). Research on the self-fulfilling prophecy and teacher expectations. *Journal of Educational Psychology, 75,* 631–666.

Broughton, D., Eisner, E., & Ligtvoet, J. (Eds.) (1996). *Evaluating and assessing the visual arts in education.* New York, NY: Teachers College Press.

Brown, B. B. (1990). Peer groups and peer cultures. In S. S. Feldman & G. R. Elliot (Eds.), *At the threshold: The developing adolescent* (pp. 171–196). Cambridge, MA: Harvard University Press.

Brown, B. B., & Huang, B. (1995). Examining parenting practices in different peer contexts: Implications for adolescent trajectories. In L. J. Crockett, A. C. Crouter, et al. (Eds.) (1995). *Pathways through adolescence: Individual development in relation to social contexts: The Penn State series on child & adolescent development* (pp. 151–174). Mahwah, NJ: Lawrence Erlbaum Associates.

Brown, B. B., Mounts, N., Lainborn, S. D., & Steinberg, L. (1993). Parenting practices and peer group affiliation in adolescence. *Child Development, 64,* 467–482.

Brown, G. L., Mangelsdorf, S. C., & Neff, C. (2012). Father involvement, paternal sensitivity, and father–child attachment security in the first 3 years. *Journal of Family Psychology, 26*(3), 421.

Brown, G. L., McBride, B. A., Shin, N., & Bost, K. K. (2007). Parenting predictors of father-child attachment security: Interactive effects of father involvement and fathering quality. *Fathering: A Journal of Theory, Research, and Practice about Men as Fathers, 5*(3).

Brown, J. R., & Dunn, J. (1992). Talk with your mother or your sibling? Developmental changes in early family conversations about feelings. *Child Development, 63,* 336–349.

Brown, L., & Gilligan, C. (1992). *Meeting at the crossroads: Women's psychology and girls' development.* Cambridge, MA: Harvard University Press.

Brown, R. (1973). *A first language: The early stages.* Cambridge, MA: Harvard University Press.

Brownell, C. A., Nichols, S. R., & Svetlova, M. (2010). Toddlers' understanding of peers' emotions. *Journal of Genetic Psychology, 171,* 35–53.

Bruchmüller, K., Margraf, J., & Schneider, S. (2012). Is ADHD diagnosed in accord with diagnostic criteria? Overdiagnosis and influence of client gender on diagnosis. *Journal of Consulting and Clinical Psychology, 80*(1), 128–138.

Bruner, J. (1996). *The culture of education.* Cambridge, MA: Harvard University Press.

Bryan, E. (1995). The death of a twin. *Palliative Medicine, 9,* 187–192.

Bryant, B. K. (1985). The neighborhood walk: Sources of support in middle childhood. *Monographs of the Society for Research on Child Development, 50* (3, No. 210).

Bryant, B. K. (1994). How does social support function in childhood? In F. Nestmann, & K. Hurrelmann (Eds.). *Social networks and social support in childhood and adolescence. Prevention and intervention in childhood and adolescence, 16* (pp. 23–35). Berlin, Germany: Walter De Gruyter.

Bryant, G. A., & Barrett, H. C. (2007). Recognizing intentions in infant-directed speech: Evidence for universals. *Psychological Science, 18,* 746–751.

Buchmann, C., & DiPrete, T. A. (2006). The growing female advantage in college completion: The role of family background and academic achievement. *American Sociological Review, 71*(4), 515–541.

Buckley, K., & Kulb, N. (Eds.). (1983), *Handbook of maternal-newborn nursing.* New York, NY: Wiley.

Bugental, D. B., Ellerson, P. C., Lin, E. K., Rainey, B., Kokotovic, A., & O'Hara, N. (2010). A cognitive approach to child abuse prevention. *Journal of Family Psychology, 16*(3), 243–258.

Buhrmester, D. (1990). Intimacy of friendship, interpersonal competence, and adjustment during preadolescence and adolescence. *Child Development, 61,* 1101–1111.

Buhrmester, D., & Furman, W. (1990). Perceptions of sibling relationships during middle childhood and adolescence. *Child Development, 61,* 1387–1398.

Bukowksi, W. M., Newcomb, A. F., & Hartup, W. W. (1996). *The company they keep: Friendship in childhood, and adolescence.* New York, NY: Cambridge University Press.

Bukowski, W. M., & Hoza, B. (1989). Popularity and friendship: Issues in theory, measurement, and outcome. In T. J. Berndt, & G. W. Ladd (Eds.), *Peer relationships in child development* (pp. 15–45). New York, NY: Wiley.

Bumpass, L. L., Sweet, J. A., & Cherlin, A. (1991). The role of cohabitation in declining rates of marriage. *Journal of Marriage and the Family, 53,* 913–927.

Burd, L., Blair, J., & Dopps, K. (2012). Prenatal alcohol exposure, blood alcohol concentrations and elimination rates for the mother, fetus and newborn. *Journal of Perinatology, 32,* 652–659.

Burdette, H. L., Whitaker, R. C., Hall, W. C., & Daniels, S. R. (2006). Maternal infant-feeding style and children's adiposity at 5 years of age. *Archives of Pediatrics & Adolescent Medicine, 160*(5), 513–520.

Bureau of Labor Statistics, U. S. Department of Labor. (2015). Time spent working by full- and part-time status, gender, and location in 2014. *The Economics Daily.* Retrieved from http://www.bls.gov/opub/ted/2015/time-spent-working-by-full-and-part-timestatus-gender-and-location-in-2014.htm

Burke, T., Marwald, R., McHill, A., Chinoy, E., Snider, J., Bessman, S., . . . & Wright, K. (2015). Effects of caffeine on the human circadian clock in vivo and in vitro. *Science Translational Medicine, 7,* 305ra146. doi: 10.1126/scitranslmed.aac5125.

Burns, B. J., Phillips, S. D., Wagner, H. R., Barth, R. P., Kolko, D. J., Campbell, Y., & Landsverk, J. (2004). Mental health need and access to mental health services by youths involved with child welfare: A national survey. *Journal of the American Academy of Child & Adolescent Psychiatry, 43*(8), 960–970.

Bury, M. (1997). *Health and illness in a changing society.* New York, NY: Routledge.

Bushman, B. J., & Huesmann, L. R. (2006). Short-term and long-term effects of violent media on aggression in children and adults. *Archives of Pediatrics & Adolescent Medicine, 160*(4), 348–352.

Buss, A. H. (1986). *Social behavior and personality.* Hillsdale, NJ: Erlbaum.

Buss, A. H., & Plomin, R. (1984). *Temperament: Early developing personality traits.* Hillsdale, NJ: Erlbaum.

Buss, K. A., & Goldsmith, H. H. (1998). Fear and anger regulation in infancy: Effects on the temporal dynamics of affective expression. *Child Development, 69,* 359–384.

Buyse, E., Verschueren, K., & Doumen, S. (2011). Preschoolers' attachment to mother and risk for adjustment problems in kindergarten: Can teachers make a difference? *Social Development, 20*(1), 33–50.

Byard, R., & Cohle, S. (1994). *Sudden death in infants, children, and adolescents.* New York, NY: Cambridge University Press.

Byne, W. (1994, May). The biological evidence challenged. *Scientific American,* pp. 50–55.

Byrne, A., & Carr, D. (2005). Caught in the cultural lag: The stigma of singlehood. *Psychological Inquiry, 16*(2–3), 84–90.

C

Cain, K. M., & Dweck, C. S. (1995). The relation between motivational patterns and achievement cognitions through the elementary school years. *Merrill-Palmer Quarterly, 41,* 35–52.

Caine, D., Maffulli, N., & Caine, C. (2008). Epidemiology of injury in child and adolescent sports: Injury rates, risk factors, and prevention. *Clinics in Sports Medicine, 27*(1), 19–50.

Calabrese, R. L., & Noboa, J. (1995). The choice for gang membership by Mexican-American adolescents. *High School Journal, 226*–235.

Caldwell, J. C., & Caldwell, P. (1990). High fertility in sub-Saharan Africa. *Scientific American, 262*(5), 118–125.

Caliso, J., & Milner, J. (1992). Childhood history of abuse and child abuse screening. *Child Abuse and Neglect, 16,* 647–659.

Call, K. T., Mortimer, J. T., & Shanahan, M. J. (1995). Helpfulness and the development of competence in adolescence. *Child Development, 66,* 129–138.

Calvert, S. L. (2008). Media and early development. In K. McCartney, & D. Phillips (Eds.), *Blackwell handbook of early childhood development* (pp. 508–529). Malden, MA: Blackwell Publishing.

Campion, M. J. (1993). Childbearing with a disability In B. K. Rotliman (Ed.), *The encyclopedia of childbearing.* New York, NY: Henry Holt.

Campos, A. P. (1990). Social work practice with Puerto Rican terminally ill clients and their families. In J. K. Parry (Ed.), *Social work practice with the terminally ill: A transcultural perspective* (pp. 129–143). Springfield, IL: Charles C. Thomas.

Campos, R., Raffaelli, M., Ude, W., Greco, M., Ruff, A., Rolf, J., Antunes, C. M., Halsey, N., Greco, D., & Street Youth Study Group. (1994). Social networks and daily activities of street youth in Belo Horizonte, Brazil *Child Development, 65,* 319–330.

Camras, L. A., Sullivan, J., & Michel, G. (1993). Do infants express discrete emotions? Adult judgments of facial, vocal, and body actions. *Journal of Nonverbal Behavior, 17,* 171–186.

Cancian, F. M. (1986). The feminization of love. *Signs: Journal of Women in Culture and Society, 11,* 692–709.

Canella, G. (1997). *Deconstructing early childhood education.* New York, NY: Peter Lang.

Canfield R., Smith, E., Brezsnyak, M., & Snow, K. (1997). Information processing through the first year of life: A longitudinal study using the visual expectation paradigm. *Monographs of the Society for Research in Child Development, 62* (2, Serial No. 250).

Canfield, R., & Smith, E. (1996). Number-based expectations and sequential enumeration by 5-month-old-infants. *Developmental Psychology, 32,* 269–279.

Cannella, G. (1997). *Deconstructing early childhood education: Social justice and revolution.* New York, NY: Peter Lang Publishers.

Cantos, A. L., Neidig, P. H., & O'Leary, K. D. (1994). Injuries of women and men in a treatment program for domestic violence. *Journal of Family Violence, 9*(2), 113–124.

Capaldi, D. M., Knoble, N. B., Shortt, J. W., & Kim, H. K. (2012). A systematic review of risk factors for intimate partner violence. *Partner Abuse, 3*(2), 231–280.

Cappuccio, F. P., D'Elia, L., Strazzullo, P., & Miller, M. A. (2010) Sleep duration and all-cause mortality: A systematic review and meta-analysis of prospective studies. *Sleep, 33,* 585–592.

Cappuccio, F. P., Taggart, F. M., Kandala, N., Currie, A., Peile, E., Stranges, S., & Miller, M. A. (2008). Meta-analysis of short sleep duration and obesity in children and adults. *Sleep, 31*(5), 619–626.

Card, N. A., Stucky, B. D., Sawalani, G. M., & Little, T. D. (2008). Direct and indirect aggression during childhood and adolescence: A meta-analytic review of gender differences, intercorrelations, and relations to maladjustment. *Child Development, 79*(5), 1185–1229.

Carlin, D. B., & Winfrey, K. L. (2009). Have you come a long way, baby? Hillary Clinton, Sarah Palin, and sexism in 2008 campaign coverage. *Communication Studies, 60,* 326–343.

Carlo, G., McGinley, M., Hayes, R., Batenhorst, C., & Wilkinson, J. (2007). Parenting styles or practices? Parenting, sympathy, and prosocial behaviors among adolescents. *Journal of Genetic Psychology, 168*(2), 147–176.

Carlo, G., Mestre, M. V., Samper, P., Tur, A., & Armenta, B. E. (2011). The longitudinal relations among dimensions of parenting styles, sympathy, prosocial moral reasoning, and prosocial behaviors. *International Journal of Behavioral Development, 35*(2), 116–124.

Carlson, C. I., Cooper, C. R., & Spradling, V. Y. (1991). Developmental implications of shared versus distinct perceptions of the family in early adolescence. *New Directions for Child Development, 51,* 13–32.

Carlson, E. A., Jacobvitz, D., & Sroufe, A. L. (1995). A developmental investigation of inattentiveness and hyperactivity. *Child Development, 66,* 37–54.

Carlson, S. M., & Beck, D. M. (2009). Symbols as tools in the development of executive function. In A. Winsler, C. Fernyhough, & I. Montero (Eds.), *Private speech, executive functioning, and the development of verbal self-regulation* (pp. 163–175). Cambridge University Press.

Carpenter, C. L., Yan, E., Chen, S., Hong, K., Arechiga, A., Kim, W. S., . . . & Heber, D. (2013). Body fat and body-mass index among a multiethnic sample of college-age men and women. *Journal of Obesity, 2013,* 1–7.

Carroll, J., & Siska, E. (1998). SIDS: Counseling parents to reduce the risk. *American Family Physician, 57*(9) [On-line]. Available: www.sids.org.

Carskadon, M. A. (1990). Patterns of sleep and sleepiness in adolescents. *Pediatrician, 17*(1), 5–12.

Carskadon, M. A., Acebo, C., & Jenni, O. G. (2004). Regulation of adolescent sleep: Implications for behavior. *Annals of the New York Academy of Sciences, 1021*(1), 276–291.

Carskadon, M. A., Wolfson, A. R., Acebo, C., Tzischinsky, O., & Seifer, R. (1998). Adolescent sleep patterns, circadian timing, and sleepiness at a transition to early school days. *Sleep, 21,* 871–881.

Case, R. (1991a). *The mind's staircase: Exploring the conceptual underpinnings of children's thought and knowledge.* Hillsdale, NJ: Erlbaum.

Case, R. (1991b). General and specific views of the mind, its structure, and its development. In R. Case (Ed.), *The mind's staircase* (pp. 3–16). Hillsdale, NJ: Erlbaum.

Case, R. (1991c). A neo-Piagetian approach to the issue of cognitive generality and specificity. In R. Case (Ed.), *The mind's staircase* (pp. 17–36). Hillsdale, NJ: Erlbaum.

Case, R. (1991d). Advantages and limitations of the neo-Piagetian position. In R. Case (Ed.), *The mind's staircase* (pp. 37–51). Hillsdale, NJ: Erlbaum.

Case, R. (1992). Neo-Piagetian theories of intellectual development. In H. Beilin, & P. Pufall (Eds.), *Piaget's theory: Prospects and possibilities.* Hillsdale, NJ: Erlbaum.

Case, R. (1998, April). *Fostering the development of number sense in the elementary and middle grades.* Paper presented at the annual meeting of the American Educational Research Association, San Diego.

Case, R., & Edelstein, W. (1993). *The new structuralism in cognitive development: Theory and research on individual pathways.* New York, NY: Karger.

Casey, B. J., Jones, R. M., & Hare, T. A. (2008). The adolescent brain. *Annals of the New York Academy of Sciences, 1124,* 111–126.

Casey, B. J., Tottenham, N., Liston, C., & Durston, S. (2005). Imaging the developing brain: What have we learned about cognitive development? *Trends in Cognitive Science, 9,* 104–110.

Caspi, A., & Silva, P. A. (1995). Temperamental qualities at age 3 predict personality traits in young adulthood: Longitudinal evidence from a birth cohort. *Child development, 66,* 486–498.

Caspi, A., Elder, G. H., Jr., & Bern, D. J. (1988). Moving away from the world: Life-course patterns of shy children. *Developmental Psychology, 24,* 824–831.

Caspi, A., Henry, B., McGee, R., Moffitt, T., & Silva, P. (1995). Temperamental origins of child and adolescent behavior problems: From age 3 to age 15. *Child Development, 66,* 55–68.

Cassell, D. (1994). *Encyclopedia of obesity and eating disorders.* New York, NY: Facts on File Press.

Cassidy, J., Kirsh, S. J., Scolton, K. L., & Parke, R. D. (1996). Attachment and representations of peer relationships. *Developmental Psychology, 32,* 892–904.

Cassidy, S. B. (1995). Uniparental disomy and genomic imprinting as causes of human genetic disease. *Environmental and Molecular Mutagenesis, 25,* 13–20.

Castañeda, D. M. (1993). The meaning of romantic love among Mexican-Americans. *Journal of Social Behavior and Personality, 8,* 257–272.

Caterall, J. (1998). Risk and resilience in student transitions to high school. *American Journal of Education, 106*(2), 302–333.

Cazden, C. (1988). *Classroom discourse.* Portsmouth, NH: Heinemann.

Cazenave, N. A., & Straus, M. A. (1990). Race, class network embeddedness, and family violence: A search for potent support systems. In M. A. Straus & R. J. Gelles, with C. Smith (Eds.), *Physical violence in American families: Risk factors and adaptations to violence in 8,145 families* (pp. 321–339). New Brunswick, NJ: Transaction.

Centers for Disease Control and Prevention. (1992, January 3). Sexual behavior among high school students—United States, 1990. *Morbidity and Mortality Weekly Report, 40,* 885–888.

Centers for Disease Control and Prevention. (1998). *National vital statistics report, 47*(4). Bethesda, MD: National Center for Health Statistics.

Centers for Disease Control and Prevention (CDC). (2000). *2 to 20 years: Boys stature-for-age and weight-for-age percentiles.* Retrieved from http://www.cdc.gov/growthcharts/data/set1clinical/cj41l021.pdf

Centers for Disease Control and Prevention (CDC). (2000). *2 to 20 years: Girls stature-for-age and weight-for-age percentiles.* Retrieved from http://www.cdc.gov/growthcharts/data/set1clinical/cj41l022.pdf.

Centers for Disease Control and Prevention (CDC). (2005). *Web-based Injury Statistics Query and Reporting System (WISQARS).* Available from www.cdc.gov/ncipc/wisqars/default.htm

Centers for Disease Control and Prevention (CDC). (2008, January 11). Update on overall prevalence of major birth defects—Atlanta, Georgia, 1978–2005. *Morbidity and Mortality Weekly Report, 57,* 1–5.

Centers for Disease Control and Prevention (CDC). (2010). *10 leading causes of death by age group, United States—2010.* Retrieved from https://www.cdc.gov/injury/wisqars/pdf/10lcid_all_deaths_by_age_group_2010-a.pdf

Centers for Disease Control and Prevention – Division of Reproductive Health. (2011a). *2009 assisted reproductive technology success rates: National summary and fertility clinic reports.* Atlanta, GA: U.S. Department of Health and Human Services.

Centers for Disease Control and Prevention (CDC). (2011b). *Facts about Down syndrome.* Retrieved from http://www.cdc.gov/ncbddd/birthdefects/downsyndrome.html.

Centers for Disease Control and Prevention (CDC). (2012a). *National vital statistics reports, 61* (No. 6). Hyattsville, MD: National Center for Health Statistics. Retrieved from http://www.cdc.gov/nchs/data/nvsr/nvsr61/nvsr61_06.pdf

Centers for Disease Control and Prevention (CDC) – Office of Surveillance, Epidemiology, and Laboratory Services (2012b). *Morbidity and mortality weekly report: Abortion surveillance—United States 2009, 61* (No. SS-8).

Centers for Disease Control and Prevention (CDC). (2012c). Youth Risk Behavior Surveillance, United States, 2011. *Morbidity and Mortality Weekly Report, 61*(4), 10–12. Retrieved from http://www.cdc.gov/HealthyYouth/yrbs/index.htm?s_cid=tw_cdc16.

Centers for Disease Control and Prevention (CDC) – Division of STD Prevention. (2013b). *Sexually transmitted disease surveillance 2012.* Atlanta, GA: U.S. Department of Health and Human Services.

Centers for Disease Control and Prevention (CDC). (2015a). *Childhood obesity facts.* Atlanta, GA. Retrieved from http://www.cdc.gov/healthyschools/obesity/facts.htm

Centers for Disease Control and Prevention (CDC). (2015b). *Infertility.* Retrieved from http://www.cdc.gov/nchs/fastats/infertility.htm

Centers for Disease Control and Prevention (CDC). (2015c). *Insufficient sleep is a public health problem.* Retrieved from http://www.cdc.gov/features/dssleep/

Centers for Disease Control and Prevention (CDC). (2016a). *Attention-deficit/hyperactivity disorder (ADHD) symptoms and diagnosis.* Retrieved from http://www.cdc.gov/ncbddd/adhd/diagnosis.html

Centers for Disease Control and Prevention (CDC). (2016b). *HIV/AIDS: HIV among youth.* Retrieved from http://www.cdc.gov/hiv/group/age/youth/

Centers for Disease Control and Prevention (CDC). (2016c). *HIV in the United States: At a glance.* Retrieved from http://www.cdc.gov/hiv/statistics/overview/ataglance.html

Centers for Disease Control and Prevention (CDC). (2016d). *Smoking & tobacco use: Current cigarette smoking among adults in the United States.* Retrieved from http://www.cdc.gov/tobacco/data_statistics/fact_sheets/adult_data/cig_smoking/

Centers for Disease Control and Prevention (CDC) – National Center for Health Statistics. (2016e). *Obesity and overweight.* Retrieved from http://www.cdc.gov/nchs/fastats/obesity-overweight.htm

Centers for Disease Control and Prevention – Division of Reproductive Health. (2016f). *Reproductive health: Infertility FAQs.* Atlanta, GA: U.S. Department of Health and Human Services. Retrieved from http://www.cdc.gov/reproductivehealth/infertility/

Centers for Disease Control and Prevention (CDC). (2016g). *Youth and tobacco use.* Retrieved from http://www.cdc.gov/tobacco/data_statistics/fact_sheets/youth_data/tobacco_use/

Central Intelligence Agency. (2017). *The world factbook.* Washington, DC: Author. Retrieved from https://www.cia.gov/library/publications/the-world-factbook/rankorder/2091rank.html

Cervantes, C. A., & Callanan, M. A. (1998). Labels and explanations in mother-child emotion talk: Age and gender differentiation *Developmental Psychology, 34,* 88–98.

Chadwick, A., Hay, D. F., & Payne, A. (2004). Peer relations in childhood. *Journal of Child Psychology and Psychiatry, 45,* 84–108.

Chafel, J. (1993). *Child poverty and public policy.* Washington, DC: The Urban Institute.

Chan, S. (1991). *Asian Americans: An interpretive history.* Boston: Twayne Publishers.

Chandra, A., Copen, C. E., & Stephen, E. H. (2013). Infertility and impaired fecundity in the United States, 1982–2010: Data from the National Survey of Family Growth. *National Health Statistics Reports, 67,* 1–19.

Chang, A., Aeschbach, D., Duffy, J., & Czeisler, C. (2015). Evening use of light-emitting eReaders negatively affects sleep, circadian timing, and next-morning alertness. *Proceedings of the National Academy of Sciences, 112,* 1232–1237.

Chao, R. K. (1994). Beyond parental control and authoritarian parenting style: Understanding Chinese parenting through the cultural notion of training. *Child Development, 65,* 1111–1119.

Chapleau, K. M., Oswald, D. L., & Russell, B. L. (2008). Male rape myths: The role of gender, violence, and sexism. *Journal of Interpersonal Violence, 23*(5), 600–615. doi: 10.1177/0886260507313529

Chase-Lansdale, P. L., Brooks-Gunn, J., & Zamsky, E. S. (1994). Young African-American multigenerational families in poverty: Quality of mothering and grandmothering. *Child Development, 65,* 373–393.

Chatters, L. M., Taylor, R. J., & Jayakody, R. (1994). Fictive kinship relations in Black extended families. *Journal of Comparative Family Studies, 25,* 297–312.

Cheatham, H. E., & Berg-Cross, L. (1992). College student development: African Americans reconsidered. Special issue: College student development. *Journal of College Student Psychotherapy, 6*(3–4), 167–191.

Cheek, D. (1974). Body composition, hormones, nutrition and growth. In M. Grumbach, G. Grave, & F. Mayer (Eds.), *Control of the onset of puberty.* New York, NY: Wiley.

Chen, P. S. D., Lambert, A. D., & Guidry, K. R. (2010). Engaging online learners: The impact of Web-based learning technology on college student engagement. *Computers & Education, 54*(4), 1222–1232.

Chen, X., Beydoun, M. A., & Wang, Y. (2008). Is sleep duration associated with childhood obesity? A systematic review and meta-analysis. *Obesity, 16*(2), 265–274.

Cheng, Y. W., Shaffer, B. L., Nicholson, J. M., & Caughey, A. B. (2014). Second stage of labor and epidural use: A larger effect than previously suggested. *Journal of Obstetrics and Gynecology, 123,* 527–535.

Cherkes-Julkowski, M., Sharp, S., & Stolzenberg, J. (1997). *Rethinking ADHD.* Cambridge, MA: Brookline Books.

Cherry, F. (1995). *"Stubborn particulars" of social psychology: Essays on the research process.* New York, NY: Routledge.

Chervin, R. D., Bassetti, C., Ganoczy, D. A., & Pituch, K. J. (1997). Pediatrics and sleep symptoms of sleep disorders, inattention, and hyperactivity in children. *Sleep, 20*(12), 1185–1192.

Chesters, J. (2012). Gender attitudes and housework: Trends over time in Australia. *Journal of Comparative Family Studies, 43,* 511–526.

Children's Defense Fund. (1992). *The state of America's children, 1992.* Washington, DC: Author.

Children's Defense Fund. (1993). *Progress and peril: Black children in America: A fact book and action primer.* Washington, DC: Author.

Children's Defense Fund. (2012). *The state of America's children handbook.* Washington, DC: Author.

Chodorow, N. (1978). *The reproduction of mothering.* Berkeley: University of California Press.

Chomsky, N. (1994). *Language and thought.* Wakefield, RI: Moyer Bell Publishers.

Chosak, R. (1998). Personal communication.

Choudhury, S., Blakemore, S. J., & Charman, T. (2006). Social cognitive development during adolescence. *Social Cognitive and Affective Neuroscience, 1*(3), 165–174.

Christakis, D. A., & Zimmerman, F. J. (2007). Violent television viewing during preschool is associated with antisocial behavior during school age. *Pediatrics, 120*(5), 993–999.

Christensen, K. Y., Maisonet, M., Rubin, C., Holmes, A., Flanders, W. D., Heron, J., . . . & Marcus, M. (2010). Progression through puberty in girls enrolled in a contemporary British cohort. *Journal of Adolescent Health, 47,* 282–289.

Chung, A. E., Perrin, E. M., & Skinner, A. C. (2013). Accuracy of child and adolescent weight perceptions and their relationships to dieting and exercise behaviors: A NHANES study. *Academic Pediatrics, 13*(4), 371–378.

Cicchetti, D., & Olson, K. (1990). The developmental psychopathology of child maltreatment. In M. Lewis, & S. Miller (Eds.), *Handbook of development psychopathology.* New York, NY: Plenum Press.

Cicchetti, D., & Toth, S. L. (1998). The development of depression in children and adolescents. *American Psychologist, 53,* 221–241.

Cicirelli, V. G. (1994). Sibling relationships in crosscultural perspective. *Journal of Marriage and the Family, 56,* 7–20.

Cicirelli, V. G. (1995). *Sibling relationships across the life span.* New York, NY: Plenum.

Cillessen, A. H. N., & Bellmore, A. D. (2011). Social skills and social competence in interactions with peers. In P. K. Smith, & C. H. Hart (Eds.), *The Wiley-Blackwell handbook of childhood social development* (2nd ed., pp. 393–412). Malden, MA: Blackwell Publishing.

Cinamon, R. G., Weisel, A., & Tzuk, K. (2007). Work–family conflict within the family crossover effects, perceived parent–child interaction quality, parental self-efficacy, and life role attributions. *Journal of Career Development, 34*(1), 79–100.

Clark, R., Hyde, J. S., Essex, M. J., & Klein, M. H. (1997). Length of maternity leave and quality of mother-infant interaction. *Child Development, 68,* 363–383.

Clarke, A. T., & Kutz-Costes, B. (1997). Television viewing, educational quality of the home environment, and school readiness. *Journal of Educational Research, 90,* 279–285.

Clarke-Stewart, K. A. (1989). Daycare: Maligned or malignant? *American Psychologist, 44,* 266–273.

Clarke-Stewart, K. A., & Allhusen, V. D. (2002). Nonparental caregiving. In M. Bornstein (Ed.), *Handbook of parenting: Vol. 3: Being and becoming a parent* (2nd ed., pp. 215–252). Mahwah, NJ: Lawrence Erlbaum Associates.

Clarke-Stewart, K. A., Gruber, C. P., & Fitzgerald, L. M. (1994). *Children at home and in day care.* Hillsdale, NJ: Lawrence Erlbaum Associates.

Clarke-Stewart, K. A., & Hayward, C. (1996). Advantages of father custody and contact for the psychological well-being of school-age children. *Journal of Applied Developmental Psychology, 17,* 239–270.

Clay, D., Vignoles, V. L., & Dittmar, H. (2005). Body image and self-esteem among adolescent girls: Testing the influence of sociocultural factors. *Journal of Research on Adolescence, 15*(4), 451–477.

Clopton, N. A., & Sorell, G. T. (1993). Gender differences in moral reasoning: Stable or situational, *Psychology of Women Quarterly, 17,* 85–101.

Clouston, S. A., Kuh, D., Herd, P., Elliott, J., Richards, M., & Hofer, S. M. (2012). Benefits of educational attainment on adult fluid cognition: International evidence from three birth cohorts. *International Journal of Epidemiology, 41,* 1729–1736. doi: 10.1093/ije/dys148

Coakley, J. (1996). Socialization through sports. In O. Bar-Or (Ed.), *The child and adolescent athlete* (pp. 353–363). London: Blackwell Science.

Coates, E., & Coates, A. (2006). Young children talking and drawing. *International Journal of Early Years Education, 14*(3), 221–241.

Coates, J. (1993). *Women, men, and communication* (2nd ed.), New York, NY: Longman.

Coates, J. (2015). *Women, men and language: A sociolinguistic account of gender differences in language.* Routledge.

Cobb, P., Gravemeijer, K., Yackel, E., McClain, K., & Whitenack, J. (1997). Mathematizing and symbolizing: The emergence of chains of signification in one first-grade classroom. In D. Kirschner, & J. Witson (Eds.), *Situated cognition: Social, semiotic, and psychological perspectives* (pp. 151–234). Mahwah, NJ: Erlbaum.

Cogan, R. (1980). Effects of childbirth preparation. *Clinical Obstetrics and Gynecology, 23,* 1–14.

Cohen E. (1994). *Designing group work: Strategies for the heterogeneous classroom* (2nd ed.), New York, NY: Teachers College Press.

Cohen, E., & Latan, R. (Eds.). (1997). *Working for equity in heterogeneous classrooms.* New York, NY: Teachers College Press.

Cohen, M. (1998). *The attention zone: Parents' guide to ADHD.* Washington, DC: Brunner/Mazel.

Cohen, N. (1997). *The development of memory in childhood.* Hove, UK: Psychology Press.

Cohen, S., Doyle, W. J., Alper, C. M., Janicki-Deverts, D., & Turner, R. B. (2009). Sleep habits and susceptibility to the common cold. *Archives of Internal Medicine, 169*(1), 62–67.

Cohn, D., Livingston, G., & Wang, W. (2014). *Pew Research Center social and demographic trends: After decades of decline, a rise in stay-at-home mothers.* Retrieved from http://www.pewsocialtrends.org/2014/04/08/after-decades-of-decline-a-rise-in-stay-at-home-mothers/

Coie, J. D., Dodge, K. A., Terry, R., & Wright, V. (1991). The role of aggression in peer relations: An analysis of aggression episodes in boys' play groups. *Child Development, 62,* 812–826.

Coiro, M. (1994). *Health of our nation's children.* Hyattsville, MD: United States Department of Health and Human Services.

Colby, A., & Damon, W. (1992). *Some do care: Contemporary lives of moral commitment.* New York, NY: Free Press.

Colby, A., & Kohlberg, L. (1987). *The measurement of moral judgment.* New York, NY: Cambridge University Press.

Colby, A., Kohlberg, L., Gibbs, J., & Lieberman, M. (1983). A longitudinal study of moral development. *Monographs of the Society for Research on Child Development, 48*(1–2), Serial No. 200.

Colby, S. L., & Ortman, J. M. (2015). Projections of the size and composition of the U.S. population: 2014 to 2060. Retrieved from https://census.gov/content/dam/Census/library/publications/2015/demo/p25-1143.pdf

Coldren, J., & Colombo, J. (1994). The nature and process of preverbal learning. *Monographs of the Society for Research in Child Development, 59*(2, Serial No. 241), 1–75.

Cole, M. (1990). Cultural psychology. In J. Berman (Ed.), *Nebraska symposium on motivation, 1989: Cross-cultural psychology* (pp. 279–336). Lincoln, NE: University of Nebraska Press.

Cole, S. Z., & Lanham, J. S. (2011). Failure to thrive: An update. *American Family Physician, 83,* 829–834.

Coleman, J. (1988). Social capital in the creation of human capital. *American Journal of Sociology, 94,* 95–120.

Coles, R. (1992). *Their eyes meeting the world: Drawings and paintings of children.* Boston: Houghton Mifflin.

Coles, R., & Stokes, G. (1985). *Sex and the American teenager.* New York, NY: Harper & Row

Coley, R. L. (1998). Children's socialization experiences and functioning in single-mother households: The importance of fathers and other men. *Child Development, 69,* 219–230.

Coley, R. L., & Chase-Lansdale, P. L. (1998). Adolescent pregnancy and parenthood: Recent evidence and future directions. *American Psychologist, 53,* 152–166.

Coll, C. G., Lamberty, G., Jenkins, R., McAdoo, H. P., Crnic, K., Wasik, B. H., & Garcia, H. V. (1996). An integrative model for the study of developmental competencies in minority children. *Child Development, 67,* 1891–1914.

College Board/National Journal. (2014). *Next America poll, spring 2014.* Retrieved from http://www.corpsnetwork.org/sites/default/images/blog%20posts/2014/2014%20April/College%20Board_next%20america%20poll_2.pdf

Collins, W. A. (1991). Shared views and parent-adolescent relationships. *New Directions for Child Development, 51,* 103–110.

Collins, W. A., & Steinberg, L. (2006). Adolescent development in interpersonal context. In W. Dammon, & N. Eisenberg (Eds.), *Handbook of child psychology: Vol. 4. Socioemotional processes* (pp. 1003–1067). New York, NY: Wiley.

Comer, J. P., & Poussaint, A. F. (1992). *Raising black children.* New York, NY: Plume.

Comstock, F. (1991). *Television and the American child.* San Diego: Academic Press.

Condry, J. (1993, Winter). Thief of time, unfaithful servant: Television and the American Child. *Daedalus, 122,* 259–278.

Cong, X., Hashemi, F., & Ludington-Hoe, S. M. (2002). Infant crying: Nature, physiologic consequences, and select interventions. *Neonatal Network: The Journal of Neonatal Nursing, 21,* 29–36.

Conger, R. D., & Chao, W. (1996). Adolescent depressed mood. In R. L. Simons et al. (Eds.), *Understanding differences between divorced and intact families: Stress, interaction, and child outcome* (pp. 81–93). Thousand Oaks, CA: Sage.

Conklin, H. M., Luciana, M., Hooper, C. J., & Yarger, R. S. (2007). Working memory performance in typically developing children and adolescents: Behavioral evidence of protracted frontal lobe development. *Developmental Neuropsychology, 31*(1), 103–128.

Connell, S. L., Lauricella, A. R., & Wartella, E. (2015). Parental co-use of media technology with their young children in the USA. *Journal of Children and Media, 9*(1), 5–21.

Connelly, K., & Forssberg, H. (Eds.) (1997). *Neurophysiology and neuropsychology of motor development.* London: MacKeith Press.

Connolly, J., White, D., Stevens, R., & Burstein, S. (1987). Adolescent self-reports of social activity: Assessment of stability and relations to social adjustment. *Journal of Adolescence, 10,* 83–95.

Connolly, S., Paikoff, R., & Buchanan, C. (1996). Puberty: The interplay of biological and psychosocial processes in adolescence. In G. Adams, R. Montemayor, & T. Gullotta (Eds.), *Psychosocial development during adolescence* (pp. 259–299). Thousand Oaks, CA: Sage.

Cook, J. (1988). Who "mothers" the chronically mentally ill? *Family Relations, 37,* 42–49.

Cooksey, E. C., Menaghan, E. G., & Jekielek, S. M. (1997). Life course effects of work and family circumstances on children. *Social Forces, 761,* 637–667.

Cooney, T. M. (1994). Young adults' relations with parents: The influence of recent parental divorce. *Journal of Marriage and the Family, 56,* 45–56.

Cooney, T. M., & Kurz, J. (1996). Mental health outcomes following recent parental divorce: The case of young adult offspring. *Journal of Family Issues, 17,* 495–213.

Cooney, T. M., & Uhlenberg, P. (1990). The role of divorce in men's relations with their adult children after mid-life. *Journal of Marriage and the Family, 52,* 677–688.

Cooper, M. H. (1994). Regulating tobacco. *CQ Researcher. 4*(36), 844–858.

Copeland, L. (2013, April, 17). Most teen-drinking deaths aren't traffic related. *USA Today.* Retrieved from http://www.usatoday.com/story/news/nation/2013/04/17/underage-drinking-maddalcohol/2070405/

Copen, C. E., Daniels, K., & Mosher, W. D. (2013). First premarital cohabitation in the United States: 2006–2010 national survey of family growth. *National Health Statistics Reports, 64,* 1–16. Retrieved from http://www.cdc.gov/nchs/data/nhsr/nhsr064.pdf

Copen, C. E., Daniels, K., Vespa, J., & Mosher, W. D. (2012). First marriages in the United States: Data from the 2006–2010 National Survey of Family Growth. *National Health Statistics Reports, 49,* 1–22. Retrieved from http://www.cdc.gov/nchs/data/nhsr/nhsr049.pdf#x2013;2010%20 National%20Survey%20of%20Family%20 Growth%20 [PDF%20-%20419%20KB%3C/a%3E

Copple, C., & Bredekamp, S. (Eds.) (1997). *Developmentally appropriate practice in early childhood programs serving children from birth through age 8* (3rd ed.), Washington, DC: National Association for the Education of Young Children.

Coren, S. (1996). *Sleep thieves.* New York, NY: Free Press.

Corley, C. J., & Smitherman, G. (1994). Juvenile justice: Multicultural issues. In J. E. Hendricks, B. Byers, et al. (Eds.), *Multicultural perspectives in criminal justice and criminology.* (pp. 259–290). Springfield, IL: Charles C. Thomas.

Corman, C. (1995). Treatments for a puzzling disease. In M. L. Ballweg & The Endometriosis Association (Eds.), *The endometriosis sourcebook* (pp. 237–247). Chicago, IL: Contemporary Books.

Corsini, N., Slater, A., Harrison, A., Cooke, L., & Cox, D. N. (2013). Rewards can be used effectively with repeated exposure to increase liking of vegetables in 4–6-year-old children. *Public Health Nutrition, 16*(05), 942–951.

Costa, A., Hernández, M., & Sebastián-Gallés, N. (2008). Bilingualism aids conflict resolution: Evidence from the ANT task. *Cognition, 106*(1), 59–86.

Côté, S., Vaillancourt, T., LeBlanc, J. C., Nagin, D. S., & Tremblay, R. E. (2006). The development of physical aggression from toddlerhood to preadolescence: A nation wide longitudinal study of Canadian children. *Journal of Abnormal Child Psychology, 34*(1), 68–82.

Cousineau, T. M., & Domar, A. D. (2007). Psychological impact of infertility. *Best Practice & Research Clinical Obstetrics & Gynaecology, 21*(2), 293–308.

Couturier, J., Kimber, M., & Szatmari, P. (2013). Efficacy of family-based treatment for adolescents with eating disorders: A systematic review and meta-analysis. *International Journal of Eating Disorders, 46*(1), 3–11.

Cowan, C., Cowan, P., Heming, G., & Miller, N. (1991). Becoming a family: Marriage, parenting, and child development. In P. Cowan, & M. Hetherington (Eds.), *Family transitions* (pp. 79–110). Hillsdale, NJ: Erlbaum.

Cowan, N. (Ed.). (1997). *Development of memory in childhood.* Hove: Psychology Press.

Cowan, P. A. (1997). Beyond meta-analysis: A plea for a family systems view of attachment. *Child Development, 68,* 571–591.

Cowan, P. A., & Cowan, C. P. (1988). Changes in marriage during the transition to parenthood: Must we blame the baby? In G. Y. Michaels, & W. A. Goldberg (Eds.), *The transition to parenthood: Current theory and research* (pp. 114–154). Cambridge, UK: Cambridge University Press.

Cox, D., Navarro-Rivera, J., & Jones, R. P. (2016). Race, religion, and political affiliation of Americans' core social networks. Retrieved from https://www.prri.org/research/poll-race-religion-politics-americans-social-networks/

Cox, M., & Harter, K. S. M. (2003). Parent-child relationships. In M. H. Bornstein, L. Davidson, C. L. M. Keyes, K. A. Moore, & The Center for Child Well-being (Eds.), *Well-being: Positive development across the life course* (pp. 191–204). Mahwah, NJ: Lawrence Erlbaum.

Cox, M. J., Owen, M. T., Henderson, V. K., & Margand, N. A. (1992). Prediction of infant-father and infant-mother attachment *Developmental Psychology, 28,* 474–483.

Coyne, S. M., Linder, J. R., Rasmussen, E. E., Nelson, D. A., & Collier, K. M. (2014). It's a bird! It's a plane! It's a gender stereotype!: Longitudinal associations between superhero viewing and gender stereotyped play. *Sex Roles, 70*(9–10), 416–430.

Coyne, S. M., Nelson, D. A., & Underwood, M. (2011). Aggression in children. In P. K. Smith, & C. H. Hart (Eds.), *The Wiley-Blackwell handbook of childhood social development* (2nd ed., pp. 491–509). Malden, MA: Blackwell Publishing.

Creasey, G. L., Jarvis, P. A., & Berk, L. E. (1998). Play and social competence. In O. N. Saracho & B. Spodek, et al. (Eds.), *Multiple perspectives on play in early childhood education.* SUNY series. *Early Childhood Education: Inquiries and Insights* (pp. 116–143). Albany, NY: State University of New York Press.

Crick, N. R. (1997). Engagement in gender normative versus nonnormative forms of aggression: Links to social-psychological adjustment. *Developmental Psychology, 33,* 610–617.

Crick, N. R. (1997). The role of overt aggression, relational aggression, and prosocial behavior in the prediction of children's future social adjustment. *Child Development, 67,* 2317–2327.

Crick, N. R., & Grotpeter, J. K. (1995a). Relational aggression, gender, and social-psychological adjustment. *Child Development, 66,* 710–722.

Crick, N. R., & Grotpeter, J. K. (1995b). Relational aggression, overt aggression, and friendship: Victims of relational and overt aggression. *Development & Psychopathology, 8,* 367–380.

Crick, N. R., Casas, J. F., & Mosher, M. (1997). Relational and overt aggression in preschool. *Developmental Psychology, 33,* 579–588.

Crockenberg, S. B., & Litman, C. (1990). Autonomy and competence in 1-year-olds: Maternal correlates of child defiance, compliance, and self-assertion. *Developmental Psychology, 26,* 961–971.

Crockenberg, S. B., & McCluskey, K. (1986). Change in maternal behavior during the baby's first year of life. *Child Development, 57,* 746–753.

Crockett, L. J., Raffaelli, M., & Moilanen, K. L. (2006). Adolescent sexuality: Behavior and meaning. In G. R. Adams, & M. D. Berzonsky (Eds.), *Blackwell handbook of adolescence* (pp. 371–392). Malden, MA: Blackwell Publishing.

Crosby, F. J. (1991). *Juggling: The unexpected advantages of balancing career and home for women and their families.* New York, NY: The Free Press.

Crowl, A. L., Ahn, S., & Baker, J. (2008). A metaanalysis of developmental outcomes for children of same-sex and heterosexual parents. *Journal of GLBT Family Sciences, 4*(3), 385–407.

Cuffaro, H. (1991). A view of materials as the texts of the early childhood curriculum. In B. Spodek, & O. Saracho (Eds.), *Issues in early childhood curriculum* (pp. 64–85). New York, NY: Teachers College Press.

Cui, M., & Donnellan, M. B. (2009). Trajectories of conflict over raising adolescent children and marital satisfaction. *Journal of Marriage and Family, 71,* 478–494.

Cummings, E. M., & Cummings, J. L. (1988). A process-oriented approach to children's coping with adults' angry behavior, *Developmental Review, 8,* 296–321.

Currie, J., & Widom, C. S. (2010). Long-term consequences of child abuse and neglect on adult economic well-being. *Child Maltreatment, 15*(2), 111–120.

Curry, G. D., & Spergel, I. (1988). Gang homicide, delinquency, and community. *Criminology, 26,* 381–05.

Curtin, S. C., Warner, M., & Hedegaard, H. (2016). *Suicide rates for females and males by race and ethnicity: United States, 1999 and 2014.* Retrieved from http://www.cdc.gov/nchs/data/hestat/suicide/rates_1999_2014.pdf

Cushman, P. (1991). Ideology obscured: Political uses of the self in Daniel Stern's infant. *American Psychologist, 46,* 206–219.

D

Dalglish, P. (1998). *The courage of children: My life with the world's poorest kids.* New York, NY: HarperCollins.

D'Alton, M. E., & DeCherney, A. H. (1993). Prenatal diagnosis. *New England Journal of Medicine, 32,* 114–120.

Dalton, S. (Ed.) (1997). *Overweight and weight management,* Gaithersburg, MD: Aspen Publishers.

Damon, W. (1983). *Social and personality development: Infancy through adolescence.* New York, NY: Norton.

Damon, W. (1988). *The moral child.* New York, NY: Cambridge University Press.

Damon, W. (1996). The lifelong transformation of moral goals through social influence. In P. Baltes, & U. Staudinger (Eds.), *Interactive minds: Lifespan perspectives on social foundations of cognition* (pp. 198–221). New York, NY: Cambridge University Press.

Damon, W. (2008). The moral north star. *Educational Leadership, 66,* 8–12.

Damon, W., & Hart, D. (1988). *Self-understanding in childhood and adolescence,* New York, NY: Cambridge University Press.

Damon, W., & Hart, D. (1992). Self-understanding and its role in social and moral development. In M. C. Bornstein, & M. E. Lamb (Eds.), *Developmental psychology: An advanced textbook* (3rd ed., pp. 421–164). Hillsdale, NJ: Erlbaum.

Danner, F., & Phillips, B. (2008). Adolescent sleep, school start times, and teen motor vehicle crashes. *Journal of Clinical Sleep Medicine: JCSM: Official Publication of the American Academy of Sleep Medicine*, 4(6), 533.

Darling, C. A., Davidson, J. K., & Passarello, L. C. (1992). The mystique of first intercourse among college youth: The role of partners, contraceptive practices, and psychological reactions. *Journal of Youth and Adolescence*, 21, 97–117.

Darling, N., & Steinberg, L. (1993). Parenting style as context: An integrative model. *Psychological Bulletin*, 113, 487–496.

Darling-Hammond, L. (1997). *The right to learn.* San Francisco: Jossey-Bass.

Darwin, C. (1877). A biographical sketch of an infant. *Mind*, 2, 286–294.

Datar, A., & Jacknowitz, A. (2009). Birth weight effects on children's mental, motor and physical development: Evidence from twins data. *Maternal and Child Health Journal*, 13, 780–794.

Davajan, V., & Israel, R. (1991). Diagnosis and medical treatment of infertility. In A. L. Stanton, & C. Dunkel-Schetter (Eds.), *Infertility.* (pp. 17–28). New York, NY: Plenum.

Davies, B. (1991). Accomplishment of genderedness in preschool children. In L. Weis, P. Altbach, G. Kelly, & H. Petrie (Eds.), *Critical perspectives in early childhood education.* Albany, NY: State University of New York Press.

Davies, B. (1995). Sibling bereavement research: State of the art. In I. B. Corless, B. B. Germino, & M. A. Pittman (Eds.), *A challenge for living: Dying, death, and bereavement,* Boston: Jones and Bartlett Publishers.

Davis, E. (1993). Common complaints of pregnancy. In B. K. Rothman (Ed.), *The encyclopedia of childbearing,* New York, NY: Henry Holt.

Davis, E. (1997). *Heart and hands: A midwife's guide to pregnancy and birth.* Berkeley, CA: Celestial Arts.

Davis, J. N., Ventura, E. E., Cook, L. T., Gyllenhammer, L. E., & Gatto, N. M. (2011). LA Sprouts: A gardening, nutrition, and cooking intervention for Latino youth improves diet and reduces obesity. *Journal of the American Dietetic Association*, 111(8), 1224–1230.

Davis, K., Christodoulou, J., Seider, S., & Gardner, H. (2011). The theory of multiple intelligences. *The Cambridge handbook of intelligence*, 485–503.

Davis-Floyd, R. E. (1986). Birth as an American rite of passage. In K. L. Michaelson (Ed.), *Childbirth in America: Anthropological perspectives,* South Hadley, MA: Bergin & Garvey.

Davis-Kean, P. E. (2005). The influence of parent education and family income on child achievement: The indirect role of parental expectations and the home environment. *Journal of Family Psychology*, 19(2), 294–304.

Deater-Deckhard, S., Dodge, K. A., Bates, J. E., & Pettit, G. S. (1996). Physical discipline among African-American and European-American mothers: Links to children's externalizing behavior. *Developmental Psychology*, 32, 1065–1072.

DeCasper, A. J., & Spence, M. J. (1986). Prenatal maternal speech influences newborns, perception of speech sounds. *Infant Behavior and Development*, 9, 133–150.

DeCasper, A. J., Lecanuet, J. P., Busnel, M. C., & Granier-Deferre, C. (1994). Fetal reactions to recurrent maternal speech. *Infant Behavior and Development*, 17, 159–164.

Deci, E. L., & Ryan, R. M. (1987). The support of autonomy and the control of behavior. *Journal of Personality and Social Psychology*, 56, 1024–1037.

De Civita, M., Pagani, L., Vitaro, F., & Tremblay, R. E. (2004). The role of maternal educational aspirations in mediating the risk of income source on academic failure in children from persistently poor families. *Children and Youth Services Review*, 26(8), 749–769.

Declercq, E. (2011). Trends in midwife-attended births in the United States, 1989–2009. *Journal of Midwifery & Women's Health*, 57, 321–326.

De Goede, I. H., Branje, S. J., Delsing, M. J., & Meeus, W. H. (2009). Linkages over time between adolescents' relationships with parents and friends. *Journal of Youth and Adolescence*, 38(10), 1304–1315.

DeJong, W. (1993). Obesity as a characterological stigma: The issue of responsibility and judgments of task performance. *Psychological Reports*, 73, 963–970.

DeKlyen, M., Biernbaum, M. A., Speltz, M. L., & Greenberg, M. T. (1998). Fathers and preschool behavior problems. *Developmental Psychology*, 34, 264–275.

Delamont, S. (1996). *Women's place in education.* Brookfield, MA: Avebury Publishers.

Del Guidice, M., Manera, V., & Keysers, C. (2009). Programmed to learn? The ontogeny of mirror neurons. *Developmental Science*, 12, 350–363.

DeLisi, M., & Vaughn, M. G. (2014). Foundation for a temperament-based theory of antisocial behavior and criminal justice system involvement. *Journal of Criminal Justice*, 42(1), 10–25.

Dembe, A. E., & Yao, X. (2016). Chronic disease risks from exposure to long-hour work schedules over a 32-year period. *Journal of Occupational & Environmental Medicine/American College of Occupational and Environmental Medicine.* doi: 10.1097/JOM.0000000000000810

Demetriou, A., Christou, C., Spanoudis, G., & Platsidou, M. (2002). The development of mental processing: Efficiency, working memory, and thinking. *Monographs for the Society of Research in Child Development*, 67(1, Serial No. 268).

Demo, D. H., & Acock, A. C. (1996). Family structure, family process, and adolescent well-being. *Journal of Research on Adolescence*, 6, 457–488.

Denham, S., Warren, H., von Salisch, M., Benga, O., Chin, J., & Geangu, E. (2011). Emotions and social development in childhood. In P. K. Smith, & C. H. Hart (Eds.), *The Wiley-Blackwell handbook of childhood social development* (2nd ed., pp. 413–433). Malden, MA: Blackwell Publishing.

Dennis, S. (1992). Stage and structure in the development of children's spatial reasoning. In R. Case (Ed.), *The mind's staircase* (pp. 229–245). Hillsdale, NJ: Erlbaum.

Denson, N. (2009). Do curricular and cocurricular diversity activities influence racial bias? A metaanalysis. *Review of Educational Research*, 79(2), 805–838.

Dermer, A. (2001). A well-kept secret: Breastfeeding's benefits to mothers. *New Beginnings*, 18(4), 124–127.

DeRosier, M. E., Cillessen, A. H. N., Coie, J. D., & Dodge, K. A. (1994). Group social context and children's aggressive behavior. *Child Development*, 65, 1068–1079.

Desiderato, L. L., & Crawford, H. J. (1995). Risky sexual behavior in college students: Relationships between number of sexual partners, disclosure of previous risky behavior, and alcohol use. *Journal of Youth & Adolescence*, 24, 55–68.

DeSilver, D. (2013). *Pew Research Center: Many states already bar workplace discrimination against gays.* Retrieved from http://www.pewresearch.org/fact-tank/2013/11/06/many-states-already-barworkplace-discrimination-against-gays/

DeVita, V., Hellman, S., & Rosenberg, S. (Eds.) (1997). *AIDS: Etiology, diagnosis, treatment, and prevention* (4th ed.), Philadelphia: Lippincott-Raven.

DeWolff, M. S., & van IJzendoorn, M. H. (1997). Sensitivity and attachment: A meta-analysis on parental antecedents of infant attachment. *Child Development*, 68, 571–591.

D'Hondt, E., Deforche, B., Gentier, I., De Bourdeaudhuij, I., Vaeyens, R., Philippaerts, R., & Lenoir, M. (2013). A longitudinal analysis of gross motor coordination in overweight and obese children versus normal-weight peers. *International Journal of Obesity*, 37(1), 61–67

Diamant, A., & Cooper, H. (1991). *Living a Jewish life,* New York, NY: HarperPerennial.

Diamond, J. (1989, February). Blood, genes, and malaria. *Natural History*, 8–18.

Diamond, L. M., & Dubé, E. M. (2002). Friendship and attachment among heterosexual and sexual minority youths: Does the gender of your friend matter? *Journal of Youth and Adolescence*, 31(2), 155–166.

Diamond, L. M., & Savin-Williams, R. C. (2006). The intimate relationships of sexual-minority youths. In G. R. Adams, & M. D. Berzonsky (Eds.), *Blackwell handbook of adolescence* (pp. 371–392). Malden, MA: Blackwell Publishing.

Diamond, M. C. (1988). *Enriching heredity: The impact of the environment on the anatomy of the brain.* New York, NY: The Free Press.

Dickinson, G. E. (1992). First childhood death experiences, *Omega*, 25, 169–182.

Dickstein, S., & Parke, R. D. (1988). Social referencing in infancy: A glance at fathers and marriage. *Child Development*, 59, 506–511.

Dietrich, J., & Salmela-Aro, K. (2016). Emerging adults and work: A model of phase-adequate engagement. In J. J. Arnett (Ed.), *The Oxford handbook of emerging adulthood* (pp. 334–345). New York, NY: Oxford University Press.

Dinsa, G. D., Goryakin, Y., Fumagalli, E., & Suhrcke, M. (2012). Obesity and socioeconomic status in developing countries: A systematic review. *Obesity Reviews*, 13(11), 1067–1079.

Dishion, T. J., Andrews, D. W., & Crosby, L. (1995). Antisocial boys and their friends in early adolescence: Relationship characteristics, quality, and interactional process. *Child Development*, 66, 139–151.

Dishion, T. J., Reid, J. R., & Patterson, G. R. (1988). Empirical guidelines for a family intervention for adolescent drug use. *Journal of Chemical Dependency Treatment*, 1, 181–216.

Divisi, D., Di Tommaso, S., Salvemini, S., Garramone, M., & Crisci, R. (2006). Diet and cancer. *Acta Biomedica-Ateneo Parmense*, 77(2), 118.

Division of Global HIV/AIDS (DGHA) – Centers for Disease Control and Prevention. (2013). *Strategy for an AIDS-free generation.* Retrieved from http://www.cdc.gov/globalaids/global-hiv-aids-atcdc/interventions.html

Dodge, K. A. (1986). A social information processing model of social competence in children. In M. Perlmutter (Ed.), *Minnesota symposia on child psychology: Vol. 18.* Hillsdale, NJ: Erlbaum.

Dodge, K. A., & Coie, J. D. (1987). Social-information processing factors in reactive and proactive aggression in children's peer groups. *Journal of Personality and Social Psychology*, 53, 1146–1158.

Dodge, K. A., Coie, J. D., Pettit, G. S., & Price, J. M. (1990). Peer status and aggression in boys' groups: Developmental and contextual analysis. *Child Development*, 61, 1289–1309.

Dodge, K. A., Pettit, G. S., & Bates, J. E. (1994). Socialization mediators of the relationship between socioeconomic status and child conduct problems. *Child Development*, 65, 649–665.

Doherty, D. (Ed.). (1996). *Measurement in pediatric exercise science.* Champaign, IL: Human Kinetics Press.

Dollinger, S. M. C., & Hoyer, W. J. (1996). Age and skill differences in the processing demands of visual inspection. *Applied Cognitive Psychology*, 10(3), 225–239.

Donati, T. (1995). Single parents and wider families in the new context of legitimacy. *Marriage & Family Review*, 20(1–2), 27–42.

Dorius, G. L., Heaton, T. B., & Steffen, P. (1993). Adolescent life events and their association with the onset of sexual intercourse. *Youth and Society*, 25, 3–23.

Doty, R. L., Shaman, P., Applehaum, S. L., Giberson, R., Sikosorski, L., & Rosenberg, L. (1984). Smell identification ability: Changes with age. *Science*, 226, 1441–1443.

Downey, G., & Coyne, J. C. (1990). Children of depressed parents: An integrative review. *Psychological Bulletin*, 108, 50–76.

Dreyer, P. H. (1982). Sexuality during adolescence. In B. B. Wolman (Ed.), *Handbook of developmental psychology.* Engle-wood Cliffs, NJ: Prentice-Hall.

Dubois, D. L., & Hirsch, B. J. (1990). School and neighborhood friendship patterns of blacks and whites in early adolescence. *Child Development, 61,* 524–536.

DuBois, D. L., & Hirsch, B. J. (1993). School/nonschool friendship patterns in early adolescence. *Journal of Early Adolescence, 13,* 102–122.

Duck, S., & Wright, P. H. (1993). Reexamining gender differences in same-gender friendships: A close look at two kinds of data. *Sex Roles, 28,* 709–727.

Dudley, J. R. (1991). Increasing our understanding of divorced fathers who have infrequent contact with their children. *Family Relations, 40,* 279–285.

Duncan, D. T., & Hatzenbuehler, M. L. (2014). Lesbian, gay, bisexual, and transgender hate crimes and suicidality among a population-based sample of sexual-minority adolescents in Boston. *American Journal of Public Health, 104*(2), 272–278.

Dunkel-Schetter, C., & Lobel, M. (1991). Psychological reactions to infertility. In A. L. Stanton, & C. Dunkel-Schetter (Eds.), *Infertility* (pp. 29–57). New York, NY: Plenum.

Dunkle, C. E., & Anthis, K. S. (2001). The role of possible selves in identity formation: A short-term longitudinal study. *Journal of Adolescence, 24,* 765–776.

Dunn, J. (1985). *Sisters and brothers,* Cambridge, MA: Harvard University Press.

Dunn, J. (1988). Connections between relationships: Implications of research on mothers and siblings. In R. A. Hinde, & J. Stevenson-Hinde (Eds.), *Relationships within families: Mutual influences.* Oxford: Clarendon Press.

Dunn, J., & Shatz, M. (1989). Becoming a conversationalist despite (or because of) having an older sibling. *Child Development, 60,* 399–10.

Dunn, J., Slomkowski, C., & Beardsall, L. (1994). Sibling Relationships from the preschool period through middle childhood and early adolescence. *Developmental Psychology, 30,* 315–324.

Dunphy, D. C. (1963). The social structure of urban adolescent peer groups. *Sociometry, 26,* 230–246.

Dunsmuir, L. (2013). Many Americans have no friends of another race: Poll. Retrieved from https://www.reuters.com/article/us-usa-poll-race/many-americans-have-no-friends-of-another-race-poll-idUSBRE97704320130808

Dupont, R. L. (1988). The counselor's dilemma: Treating chemical dependence at college. In T. M. Rivinus (Ed.), *Alcoholism/chemical dependency and the college student* (pp. 41–61). New York, NY: Haworth Press.

Durbin, D. L., Darling, N., Steinberg, L., & Brown, B. B. (1993). Parenting style and peer group membership among European-American adolescents. *Journal of Research on Adolescence, 3,* 87–100.

Dusek, J. B. (1991). *Adolescent development and behavior* (2nd ed.), Englewood Cliffs, NJ: Prentice-Hall.

Dusek, J. B. (Ed.) (1985). *Teacher expectancies,* Hillsdale, NJ: Erlbaum.

Duursma, E., Romero-Contreras, S., Szuber, A., Proctor, P., Snow, C., August, D., & Calderón, M. (2007). The role of home literacy and language environment on bilinguals' English and Spanish vocabulary development. *Applied Psycholinguistics, 28*(01), 171–190.

Dweck, C. S., & Leggett, E. L. (1988). A social-cognitive approach to motivation and personality. *Psychological Review, 95,* 256–273.

Dyregrov, K., & Dyregrov, A. (2005). Siblings after suicide—"The forgotten bereaved". *Suicide and Life-Threatening Behavior, 35*(6), 714–724.

E

Eagle, M. (1984). *Recent developments in psychoanalysis: A critical evaluation.* New York, NY: McGraw-Hill.

Eakins, P. S. (1993, September). Obstetric outcomes at the birth place in Menlo Park: The first seven years. *Birth, 16,* 123–129.

Earnshaw, V. A., Bogart, L. M., Dovidio, J. F., & Williams, D. R. (2013). Stigma and racial/ethnic HIV disparities: Moving toward resilience. *American Psychologist, 68*(4), 225.

East, P. (1998). Racial and ethnic differences in girls' sexual marital, and birth *expectations. Journal of Marriage and the Family, 60,* 150–162.

East, P. (2009). Adolescents' relationships with siblings. In R. Learner, & L. Steinberg (Eds.), *Handbook of adolescent psychology* (3rd ed., pp. 43–73). New York, NY: Wiley.

Ebbeling, C. B., Pawlak, D. B., & Ludwig, D. S. (2002). Childhood obesity: Public-health crisis, common sense cure. *Lancet, 360*(9331), 473–482.

Eccles, J., Lord, S., & Buchanan, C. (1996). School transitions in early adolescence: What are we doing to our young people? In J. Graber, J. Brooks-Gunn, & A. Petersen (Eds.), *Transitions through adolescence* (pp. 251–284). Mahwah, NJ: Erlbaum.

Eccles, J. S. (1993). Development during adolescence: The impact of stage-environment fit on young adolescents' experiences in schools and families. *American Psychologist, 48,* 90–101.

Eccles, J. S., Midgley, C., Wigfield, A., Buchanan, C. M., Reuman, D., Flanagan, C., & MacIver, D. (1993). Development during adolescence: The impact of stage-environment fit on young adolescents' experiences in schools and families. *American Psychologist, 48,* 90–101.

Eckerman, C. O., Davis, C. C., & Didow, S. M. (1989). Toddlers' emerging ways of achieving social coordinations with a peer. *Child. Development, 60,* 440–453.

Eckstein, D., Aycock, K. J., Sperber, M. A., McDonald, J., Van Wiesner, V., Watts, R. E., & Ginsburg, P. (2010). A review of 200 birth-order studies: Lifestyle characteristics. *Journal of Individual Psychology, 66*(4), 408–434.

Edenfield, T. M., & Blumenthal, J. A. (2011). Exercise and stress reduction. In R. Contrada, & A. Baum (Eds.), *The handbook of stress science: Biology, psychology, and health* (pp. 301–319). New York, NY: Springer.

Edmondson, B., Waldrop, J., Crispell, D., & Jacobsen, L. (1993). Single parents. *American Demographics, 15*(12), 36–37.

Edwards, C., Gandini, L., & Furman, G. (Eds.) (1993). *The hundred languages of children.* Norwood, NJ: Ablex.

Edwards, C. P., & Kutaka, T. S. (2015). Diverse perspectives of parents, diverse concepts of parent involvement and participation: Contrasts between Italy and the United States. Chapter prepared for S. M. Sheridan, & E. M. Kim (Eds.), *Foundational Aspects of Family-School Partnerships* (pp. 35–54).

Egeland, B. (1988). The consequences of physical and emotional neglect on the development of young children. In A. Cowan (Ed.), *Child neglect,* Washington, DC: National Center on Child Abuse and Neglect.

Eisenberg, N., & Fabes, R. A. (1992). Emotion, self-regulation, and social competence. In M. Clark (Ed.), *Review of personality and social psychology, Vol. 14: Emotion and social behavior* (pp. 119–150). Newbury Park, CA: Sage.

Eisenberg, N., & Mussey, P. H. (1989). *The roots of prosocial behavior in children.* Cambridge: Cambridge University Press.

Eisenberg, N., Fabes, R. A., Murphy, B., Maszk, P., Smith, M., & Karbon, M. (1995). The role of emotionality and regulation in children's social functioning: A longitudinal study. *Child Development, 66,* 1360–1384.

Eisenberg, N., Fabes, R. A., Nyman, M., Bernzweig, J., & Pinuelas, A. (1994). The relations of emotionality and regulation to children's anger-related reactions. *Child Development, 65,* 109–128.

Eisenberg, N., Fabes, R. A., Schaller, M., & Miller, P. (1989). Sympathy and personal distress: Development, gender differences, and interrelations of indices. In N. Eisenberg (Ed.), *Empathy and related emotional responses: New directions for child development* (pp. 107–126). San Francisco: Jossey-Bass.

Eisenberg, N., Fabes, R. A., Shepard, S. A., Murphy, B. C., Guthrie. I. K., Jones. S., Friedman, J., Poulin, R., & Maszk, P. (1997), Contemporaneous and longitudinal production of children's social functioning from regulation and emotionality. *Child Development, 68,* 642–664.

Eisenberg, N., Hertz-Lazarowitz, B., & Fuchs, I. (1990). Prosocial moral judgment in Israeli kibbutz and city children: A longitudinal study. *Merrill Palmer Quarterly, 36,* 273–285.

Elbers, E., Wiegersma, S., Brand, N., & Vroon, P. (1991), Response alternation as an artifact in conservation research. *Journal of Genetic Psychology, 152,* 47–56.

Elder, G. H., Jr. (1988). The life course as developmental theory. *Child Development, 69,* 1–12.

Elderhostel. (n.d.) Retrieved from http://www.roadscholar.org/

El-Dib, M., Massaro, A. N., Glass, P., & Aly, H. (2012). Neurobehavioral assessment as a predictor of neurodevelopmental outcome in preterm infants. *Journal of Perinatology, 32,* 299–303.

Elizabeth Glaser Pediatric AIDS Foundation (EGPAF). (2013). *HIV and AIDS in the U.S.* Retrieved from http://www.pedaids.org/What-We-re-Doing/Public-Policy-Advocacy/Domestic-Policy

Elkind, D. (1985). Egocentrism redux. *Developmental Review, 5,* 218–226.

Elkind, D. (1994a). *A sympathetic understanding of the child* (3rd ed.). Boston: Allyn & Bacon.

Elkind, D. (1994b). *Ties that stress: The new family imbalance.* Cambridge, MA: Harvard University Press.

Elliot, A. J., & Dweck, C. S. (Eds.). (2013). *Handbook of competence and motivation.* Guilford Publications.

Ellis, S., Rogoff, B., & Cromer, C. (1981). Age segregation in children's social interactions. *Developmental Psychology, 17,* 399–407.

Elzinga, C. H., & Liefbroer, A. C. (2007). Destandardization of family-life trajectories of young adults: A cross-national comparison using sequence analysis. *European Journal of Population/ Revue européenne de Démographie, 23*(3–4), 225–250.

Emery, R. E. (1989). Family violence. *American Psychologist, 44,* 321–328.

Emes, C. E. (1997). Is Mr. Pac Man eating our children? A review of the effect of video games on children. *Canadian Journal of Psychiatry, 42,* 409–114.

Emmerich, W., & Sheppard, K. (1982). Development of sex-differentiated preferences during late childhood and adolescence. *Developmental Psychology, 18,* 407–417.

Endres, J., & Rockwell, R. (1993). *Food, nutrition, and the young child* (4th ed.), Columbus, Ohio: Merrill.

Engle, J. M., Lasky, N., & McElwain, N. L. (2011). Presence and quality of kindergarten children's friendships: Concurrent and longitudinal associations with child adjustment in the early school years. *Infant and Child Development, 20,* 365–386.

Enriquez, E., Duncan, G. E., & Schur, E. A. (2013). Age at dieting onset, body mass index, and dieting practices. A twin study. *Appetite, 71,* 301–306.

Erdley, C. A., Cain, K. M., Loomis, C. C., Dumas-Hines, F., & Dweck, C. S. (1997). Relations among children's social goals, implicit personality theories, and responses to social failure. *Developmental Psychology, 33,* 263–272.

Erel, O., Margolin, G., & John, R. S. (1988). Observed sibling interaction: Links with marital and mother-infant relationship. *Developmental Psychology, 34,* 268–298.

Erikson, E. H. (1963). *Childhood and society* (2nd ed.). New York, NY: Norton.

Erikson, E. H. (1968). *Identity, youth and crisis.* New York, NY: Norton.

Erikson, E. H. (1975). "Identity Crisis" in autobiographical perspective. In E. Erikson, *Life history and the historical moment.* New York, NY: Norton.

Erikson, E. H. (1982). *The life cycle completed: A review.* New York, NY: Norton.

Ettelbrick, P. (1991). Legal protections for lesbians. In B. Sang, J. Warsbow, & A. J. Smith (Eds.), *Lesbians at midlife: A creative transition* (pp. 258–264). San Francisco: Spinsters Book Company.

Evans, C. A., & Porter, C. L. (2009). The emergence of mother-infant co-regulation during the first year: Links to infants' developmental status and attachment. *Infant Behavior & Development, 32*, 147–158.

Evans, E., Hawton, K., Rodham, K., & Deeks. J. (2005). The prevalence of suicidal phenomena in adolescents: A systematic review of population-based studies. *Suicide and Life Threatening Behavior, 35*(3), 239–252.

Eveleth, P., & Tanner, J. (1990). *Worldwide variation in human growth* (2nd ed.). New York, NY: Cambridge University Press.

Ewing, A. T., Andre, J., Blair-Broeker, C. T., Fineburg, A. C., Henderson Daniel, J., Higa, J. J., & Weaver, K. A. (2010). When and where people learn psychological science: The sun never sets. In D. F. Halpern (Ed.), *Undergraduate education in psychology: A blueprint for the future of the discipline* (pp. 81–93). Washington, DC: American Psychological Association.

F

Faber, N. B. (1991). The process of pregnancy resolution among adolescent mothers. *Adolescence, 26*, 697–716.

Fabes, R. A., & Eisenberg, N. (1992). Young children's coping with interpersonal anger. *Child Development, 63*, 116–128.

Fabes, R. A., Eisenberg, N., McCormick, S. E., & Wilson, M. S. (1988). Preschoolers' attributions of the situational determinants of others' naturally occurring emotions. *Developmental Psychology, 24*, 376–385.

Fabiano, G. A., Pelham, W. E., Gnagy, E. M., Burrows-MacLean, L., Coles, E. K., Chacko, A., . . . Robb, J. A. (2007). The single and combined effects of multiple intensities of behavior modification and methylphenidate for children with attention deficit hyperactivity disorder in a classroom setting. *School Psychology Review, 36*(2), 195–216.

Fabrikant, G. (1996). The young and restless audience. *New York Times*, C1.

Fagot, B. I. (1994). Peer relations and the development of competence in boys and girls. In C. Leaper (Ed.), *Childhood gender segregation: Causes and consequences: New directions for child development* (pp. 53–66). San Francisco: Jossey-Bass.

Fagot, B. I., & Hagan, R. (1991). Observations of parent reactions to sex-stereotyped behaviors: Age and sex effects, *Child Development, 62*, 617–628.

Fagot, B. I., & Leinbach, M. D. (1989). The young child's gender schema: Environmental input, internal organization. *Child Development, 60*, 663–672.

Fagot, B. I., Leinbach, M. D., & O'Boyle, C. (1992). Gender labeling, gender stereotyping, and parenting behaviors. *Developmental Psychology, 28*, 225–230.

Fagot, B. (1997). Attachment, parenting, and peer interactions of toddler children. *Developmental Psychology, 33*, 489–499.

Fairburn, C., & Wilson, T. (Eds.). (1993). *Binge eating*. Guilford, CT: Guilford Press.

Falbo, T. (1992) Social norms and the one-child family: Clinical and policy implications. In F. Boer, J. Dunn, et al. (Eds.), *Children's sibling relationships* (pp. 71–82). Hillsdale, NJ: Erlbaum.

Falbo, T. (2012). Only children: An updated review. *Journal of Individual Psychology, 68*(1), 38–49.

Famighetti, R. (1996). *World almanac and book of facts 1997*. Mahwah, NJ: World Almanac Book.

Fangos, J. H., & Nickerson, B. G. (1991). Long-term effects of sibling death during adolescence. *Journal of Adolescent Research, 6*, 70–82.

Fantz, R. (1963). Pattern vision in newborn infants. *Science, 140* 296–297.

Farrangy, P., Steele, H., & Steele, M. (1991). Maternal representations of attachment during pregnancy predict the organization of infant-mother attachment at one year of age. *Child Development, 62*, 891–905.

Farrant, B. M., Devine, T. A., Maybery, M. T., & Fletcher, J. (2012). Empathy, perspective taking and prosocial behaviour: The importance of parenting practices. *Infant and Child Development, 21*(2), 175–188.

Farver, J. A. M., & Shin, Y. L. (1997). Social pretend play in Korean- and Anglo-American preschoolers. *Child Development, 68*, 544–556.

Farver, J. M., & Branstetter, W. H. (1994). Preschoolers' prosocial responses to their peers' distress. *Developmental Psychology, 30*, 334–341.

Faulkner, R. A., Davey, M., & Davey, A. (2005). Gender-related predictors of change in marital satisfaction and marital conflict. *American Journal of Family Therapy, 33*, 61–83.

Fedele, N. M., Golding, E. R., Grossman, F. K., & Pollack., W. S. (1988). Psychological issues in adjustment to first parenthood. In G. Y. Michaels, & W. A. Goldberg (Eds.), *The transition to parenthood: Current theory and research* (pp. 85–113), Cambridge, UK: Cambridge University Press.

Federal Bureau of Investigation. (2013). *Easy access to FBI arrest statistics: 1994–2012*. Washington, DC: U.S. Department of Justice.

Feeney, J., & Noller, P. (1996). *Adult attachment*. Thousand Oaks, CA: Sage.

Feifel, H. (1990). Psychology and death: Meaningful rediscovery. *American Psychologist, 45*, 537–543.

Feinberg, M. E. (2003). The internal structure and ecological context of coparenting: A framework for research and intervention. *Parenting: Science and Practice, 3*, 95–131.

Feinbloom, R. I. (2000). *Pregnancy, birth and the early months (3rd ed.): The thinking woman's guide*. Cambridge, MA: Da Capo Press.

Feld, S., Ruhland, D., & Gold, M. (1979). Developmental changes in achievement motivation. *Merrill-Palmer Quarterly, 25*, 43–60.

Feldman, S. S., & Quatman, T. (1988). Factors influencing age expectations for adolescent autonomy: A study of early adolescents and parents *Journal of Early Adolescence, 8*, 325–343.

Ferber, R., & Kryger, M. (Eds.). (1995). *Principles and practice of sleep medicine in the child*. Philadelphia: Saunders.

Ferholt, J. B. (1991). Psychodynamic parent psychotherapy: Treating the parent-child relationship. In M. Lewis (Ed.), *Comprehensive textbook of child psychiatry*. New York, NY: Saunders.

Ferketich, S. L., & Mercer, R. T. (1995). Paternal infant attachment of experienced and inexperienced fathers during infancy. *Nursing Research, 44*, 31–37.

Fernald, A., & Kuhl, P. (1987). Acoustic determinants of infant preference for motherese speech. *Infant Behavior and Development, 10*, 279–293.

Fernandez, R. M., & Campero, S. (2012). Gender sorting and the glass ceiling in high tech. MIT Sloan Research Paper No 4989-12. doi: 10.2139/ssrn.2067102

Field, D. (1987). A review of preschool conservation training. *Developmental Review, 7*, 210–251.

Field, J. (1987). Development of auditory-visual localization in infants. In B. McKenzie, & R. Day (Eds.), *Perceptual development in early infancy* (pp. 175–198). Hillsdale, NJ: Erlbaum.

Field, S., Sarver, M. D., & Shaw, S. F. (2003). Self-determination a key to success in postsecondary education for students with learning disabilities. *Remedial and Special Education, 24*(6), 339–349.

Field, T., & Roopnarine, J. (1982). Infant-peer interactions. In T. Field (Ed.), *Review of human development*. New York, NY: Wiley.

Field, T., Miller, J., & Field, T. (1994). How well preschool children know their friends. *Early Child Development and Care, 100*, 101–109.

Fifer, W. P., Byrd, D. L., Kaku, M., Eigsti, I. M., Isler, J. R., Grose-Fifer, J., . . . & Balsam, P. D. (2010). Newborn infants learn during sleep. *Proceedings of the National Academy of Sciences, 107*(22), 10320–10323.

Figueredo, A. J., Sefcek, J. A., & Jones, D. N. (2006). The ideal romantic partner personality. *Personality and Individual Differences, 41*(3), 431–441.

Fildes, A., van Jaarsveld, C. H., Wardle, J., & Cooke, L. (2014). Parent-administered exposure to increase children's vegetable acceptance: A randomized controlled trial. *Journal of the Academy of Nutrition and Dietetics, 114*(6), 881–888.

File, T., & Ryan, C. (2014). *Computer and internet use in the United States: 2013*. Retrieved from https://www.census.gov/history/pdf/2013computeruse.pdf

Finch, B. K. (2003). Early origins of the gradient: The relationship between socioeconomic status and infant mortality in the United States, *Demography, 40*, 675–699.

Finders, M. (1997). *Just girls: Hidden literacies and life in junior high*. New York, NY: Teachers College Press.

Fine, G. A. (1982). Friends, impression management, and preadolescent behavior. In S. Asher, & J. Gottman (Eds.), *The development of children's friendships*. New York, NY: Cambridge University Press.

Fine, M., & Kurdek, L. A. (1992). The adjustment of adolescents in stepfather and stepmother families. *Journal of Marriage and the Family, 54*, 725–736.

Fingerhut, A. W., & Maisel, N. C. (2010). Relationship formalization and individual and relationship wellbeing among same-sex couples. *Journal of Social and Personal Relationships, 27*, 956–969.

Finkel, E. J., Eastwick, P. W., Karney, B. R., Reis, H. T., & Sprecher, S. (2012). Online dating: A critical analysis from the perspective of psychological science. *Psychological Science in the Public Interest, 13*(1), 3–66.

Finkelhor, D. (1995). The victimization of children: A developmental perspective. *American Journal of Orthopsychiatry, 65*, 177–193.

Fischer, K. (1980). A theory of cognitive development: The control and construction of hierarchies of skills. *Psychological Review, 87*, 477–531.

Fischer, K., & Pipp, S. L. (1984a). The process of stage transition: A neo-Piagetian view. In R. Sternberg (Ed.), *Mechanisms of cognitive development*. San Francisco: Freeman.

Fischer, K., & Pipp, S. L. (1984b). Processes of cognitive development: Optimal level and skill acquisition. In R. J. Sternberg (Ed.), *Mechanisms of cognitive development* (pp. 45–90). New York, NY: Freeman.

Fischer, K., Shaver, P., & Carnochan, P. (1990). How emotions develop and how they organize development. *Cognition and Emotion, 4*, 81–127.

Fish, M., Stifter, C. A., & Belsky, J. (1993). Early patterns of mother-infant dyadic integrations: Infant, mother, and family demographic antecedents. *Infant Behavior and Development, 16*, 1–18.

Fisher, C. B., & Lerner, R. M. (Eds.) (1994). *Applied developmental psychology*. New York, NY: McGraw Hill.

Fitzgerald, H., Lester, B., & Zuckerman, B. (1994). *Children of poverty: Research, health, and policy issues*. New York, NY: Garland.

Fivush, R. (1989). Exploring sex differences in emotional content of mother-child conversations about the past. *Sex Roles, 20*, 675–691.

Flaks, D. K., Ficher, I., Materpasqua, F., & Joseph, G. (1995). Lesbians choosing motherhood: A comparative study of lesbian and heterosexual parents and their children. *Developmental Psychology, 31*, 105–114.

Flanagan, C. A. (1990). Change in family work status: Effects on parent-adolescent decision making. *Child Development, 61*, 163–177.

Flanders, J. L., Leo, V., Paquette, D., Pihl, R. O., & Seguin, J. R. (2009). Rough-and-tumble play and the regulation of aggression: An observational study of father–child play dyads. *Aggressive Behavior, 35*(4), 285–295.

Flavell, J. H., Miller, P. H., & Miller, S. A. (1993). *Cognitive development* (3rd ed.). Englewood Cliffs, NJ: Prentice-Hall.

Fleming, R., Leventhal, H., Glynn, K., & Ershler, J. (1989). The role of cigarettes in the initiation and progression of early substance use. *Addictive Behaviors, 14,* 261–272.

Fletcher, A. C., Darling, N. E., Steinberg, L., & Dornbusch, S. M. (1995). The company they keep: Relation of adolescents' adjustment and behavior to their friends' perceptions of authoritative parenting in the social network. *Developmental Psychology, 31,* 300–310.

Flom, R., & Pick, A. D. (2012). Dynamics of infant habituation: Infants' discrimination of musical excerpts. *Infant Behavior and Development, 35,* 697–704.

Fomon, S. J., & Nelson, S. E. (2002). Body composition of the male and female reference infants. *Annual Review of Nutrition, 22,* 1–17.

Forrest-Pressley, D., Mackinnon, G., and Waller, T. (1985). *Metacognition, cognition and human performance.* Orlando: Academic Press.

Fowler, C., & Dillow, M. R. (2011). Attachment dimensions and the four horsemen of the apocalypse. *Communication Research Reports, 28*(1), 16–26.

Fowler, J. W. (1986). Faith and the structuring of meaning. In C. Dykstra, & S. Parks (Eds.), *Faith development and Fowler* (pp. 15–42). Birmingham, AL: Religious Education Press.

Fowler, J. W. (1991). *Stages of faith and religious development.* New York, NY: Crossroads Press.

Fox, K. (Ed.) (1997). *The physical self: From motivation to well-being.* Champaign, IL: Human Kinetics.

Fox, N. A., Kimmerly, N. L., & Schafer, W. D. (1991). Attachment to mother/attachment to father: A meta-analysis. *Child Development, 62,* 210–225.

Frank, M., & Zigler, E. F. (1996). Family leave: A developmental perspective. In E. F. Zigler, S. L. Hagan, et al. (Eds.), *Children, families and government: Preparing for the Twenty-First Century* (pp. 117–131). New York, NY: Cambridge University Press.

Frank, T., Turenshine, H., & Sullivan, S. J. (2010). *The effect of birth order on personality, intelligence and achievement.* Paper presented at the 118th Annual Convention of the American Psychological Convention, San Diego, CA.

Franklin, A., Pilling, M., & Davies, I. (2005). The nature of infant color categorization: Evidence from eye movements on a target detection task. *Journal of Experimental Child Psychology, 91,* 227–248.

Fransson, P., Skiold, B., Engstrom, M., Hallberg, B., Mosskin, M., Aden, U., . . . & Blennow, M. (2009). Spontaneous brain activity in the newborn brain during natural sleep—an fMRI study in infants born at full term. *Pediatric Research, 66,* 301–305.

Franz, W., & Reardon, D. (1992). Differential impact of abortion on adolescents and adults. *Adolescence, 27,* 161–172.

Franzini, L., Ribble, J. C., & Keddie, A. M. (2001). Understanding the Hispanic paradox. *Ethnicity & Disease, 11,* 496–518.

Fraser, A. M., Brochert, J. E., & Ward, R. H. (1995). Association of young maternal age with adverse reproductive outcomes. *New England journal of Medicine, 332,* 113.

Frech, A., & Williams, K. (2007). Depression and the psychological benefits of entering marriage. *Journal of Health and Social Behavior, 48*(2), 149–163.

French, D. C. (1984). Children's knowledge of the social functions of younger, older, and same-aged peers. *Child Development, 55,* 1429–1433.

French, J., & Rhodes, C. (1992). *Teaching thinking skills: Theory and practice* (2nd ed.), New York, NY: Garland.

Freud, S. (1983). *A general introduction to psychoanalysis* (rev. ed.), New York, NY: Washington Square Press.

Frezza, M., DiPadova, C., Pozzato, G., Terpin, M., Baraona, E., & Lieber, C. S. (1990). High blood alcohol levels in women. *New England Journal of Medicine, 322*(2), 95–99.

Frieze, I., Francis, W., & Hanusa, B. (1981). Defining success in classroom settings. In J. Levine, & M. Wang (Eds.), *Teacher and student perceptions.* Hillsdale, NJ: Erlbaum.

Frisco, M. L., & Williams, K. (2003). Perceived housework equity, marital happiness, and divorce in dual-earner households. *Journal of Family Issues, 24,* 51–73.

Froberg, K., & Lammert, O. (1996). Development of muscle strength during childhood. In O. Bar-Or (Ed.), *The child and adolescent athlete* (pp. 25–41). London: Blackwell Science.

Fry, J. (1974). *Common diseases: Their nature, incidence, and care,* Philadelphia: Lippincott.

Fry, R. (2009). *College enrollment hits all-time high, fueled by community college surge.* Pew Research Center. Retrieved from http://www.pewsocialtrends.org/files/2010/10/collegeenrollment.pdf

Fuhrman, T., & Holmbeck, G. N. (1995). A contextual moderator analysis of emotional autonomy and adjustment in adolescence. *Child Development, 66,* 793–811.

Fuligni, A. J., & Eccles, J. S. (1993). Perceived parent-child relationships and early adolescent's orientation toward peers. *Developmental Psychology, 29,* 622–632.

Fulkerson, J. A., Kubik, M. Y., Rydell, S., Boutelle, K. N., Garwick, A., Story, M., . . . & Dudovitz, B. (2011). Focus groups with working parents of school-aged children: What's needed to improve family meals? *Journal of Nutrition Education and Behavior, 43*(3), 189–193.

Fumagalli, M., Ferrucci, R., Mameli, F., Marceglia, S., Mrakic-Sposta, S., Zago, S., . . . & Cappa, S. (2010). Gender-related differences in moral judgments. *Cognitive Processing, 11*(3), 219–226.

Furman, W. (1982). Children's friendships. In T. Field (Ed.), *Review of human development.* New York, NY: Wiley.

Furman, W. (1989). The development of children's social networks. In D. Belle (Ed.), *Children's social networks and social supports.* New York, NY: Wiley.

Furman, W., & Bierman, K. L. (1983). Developmental changes in young children's conceptions of friendship. *Child Development, 54,* 549–556.

Furman, W., & Bierman, K. L. (1984). Children's conceptions of friendship: A multidimensional study of developmental changes. *Developmental Psychology, 20,* 925–931.

Furman, W., & Buhrmester, D. (1992). Age and sex differences in perceptions of networks of personal friendships. *Child-Development, 63,* 103–115.

Furstenberg, F. F., Jr., Brooks-Gunn, J., & Chase-Lansdale, L. (1989). Teenaged pregnancy and childbearing. *American Psychologist, 44,* 313–320.

Furstenberg, F. F., Jr., & Cherlin, A. J. (1991). *Divided families: What happens to children when parents part?* Cambridge, MA: Harvard University Press.

Futagi, Y., Toribe, YH., & Suzuki, Y. (2009). Neurological assessment of early infants. *Current Pediatric Reviews, 5,* 65–70.

G

Gabhainn, S. N., Baban, A., Boyce, W., & Godeau, E. (2009). How well-protected are sexually active 15-year-olds? Cross national patterns in condom and contraceptive pill use 2002–2006. *International Journal of Public Health, 54,* 209–215.

Gaesser, G. (1996). *Big fat lies.* New York, NY: Fawcett-Columbine Books.

Galambos, N. L., & Maggs, J. L. (1991). Out-of-school care of young adolescents and self-reported behavior. *Developmental Psychology, 27,* 644–655.

Galassi, J., Gulledge, S., & Cox, N. (1997). Middle school advisories: Retrospect and prospect. *Review of Educational Research, 67*(3), 301–338.

Galinsky, E. (1987). *The six stages of parenthood.* Reading, MA: Addison-Wesley.

Gallagher, J. (1993). Comments on McDaniel's "Education of the Gifted and the Excellence-Equity Debate." In J. Maker (Ed.), *Programs for the gifted in regular classrooms* (pp. 19–22). Austin, TX: Pro-Ed Publishers.

Gallagher, J., & Gallagher, S. (1994). *Teaching the gifted child* (4th ed.). Boston: Allyn & Bacon.

Gallagher, M. (1996). *Turning points in middle schools.* Thousand Oaks, CA: Corwin Press.

Gallaway, C., & Richards, B. (1994). *Input and interaction in language acquisition.* New York, NY: Cambridge University Press.

Gallup. (2016). *Marriage.* Retrieved from http://www.gallup.com/poll/117328/marriage.aspx

Galotti, K. M. (1989). Gender differences in self reported moral reasoning: A review and new evidence. *Journal of Youth and Adolescence, 18,* 475–488.

Galtry, J., & Callister, P. (2005). Assessing the optimal length of parental leave for child and parental wellbeing: How can research inform policy? *Journal of Family Issues, 26*(2), 219–246.

Galvan, A., Hare, T. A., Parra, C. E., Penn, J., Voss, K., Glover, G., & Casey, B. J. (2006). Earlier development of the accumbens relative to orbitofrontal cortex might underlie risk taking behavior in adolescents. *Journal of Neuroscience, 26,* 6885–6892.

Gándara, P., & Hopkins, M. (Eds.) (2010). *Forbidden language: English learners and restrictive language policies.* New York, NY: Teachers College Press.

Ganong, L. H., & Coleman, M. (1993a). A meta-analytic comparison of the self-esteem and behavior problems of stepchildren to children in other family structures. *Journal of Divorce & Remarriage, 19*(3–4), 143–163.

Ganong, L. H., & Coleman, M. (1993b). An exploratory study of stepsibling subsystems. *Journal of Divorce & Remarriage, 19*(3–4), 125–141.

Ganong, L. H., Coleman, M., & Maples, D. (1990). A meta-analytic review of family structure stereotypes. *Journal of Marriage and the Family, 52,* 287–297.

Garbarino, J. (1982). Sociocultural risk: Dangers to competence. In C. Kopp, & J. Krakow (Eds.), *Child development in a social context.* Reading, MA: Addison-Wesley.

Garbarino, J. (1992a). *Children and families in the social environment* (2nd ed.), New York, NY: Aldine de Gruyter.

Garbarino, J. (1992b). *Children in danger.* New York, NY: Jossey-Bass.

Garbarino, J. (1993). Reinventing fatherhood. *Families in Society, 74,* 52–54.

Garbarino, J., & Kostelny, K. (1996). The effects of political violence on Palestinian children's behavior problems: A risk accumulation model. *Child Development, 67,* 33–45.

Garbarino, J., Kostelny, K., & Dubrow, N. (1991). What children can tell us about living in danger. *American Psychologist, 46,* 376–383.

Garcia, F., & Gracia, E. (2009). Is always authoritative the optimum parenting style? Evidence from Spanish families. *Adolescence, 44*(173), 101–131.

Gardiner, H. W., Mutter, J. D., & Kosmitzki, C. (1998). *Lives across cultures: Cross-cultural human development.* Boston: Allyn & Bacon.

Gardner, H. (1993a). *Frames of mind: The theory of multiple intelligences* (2nd rev. ed.), New York, NY: Basic Books.

Gardner, H. (1993b). *Multiple intelligences: Theory in practice.* New York, NY: Basic Books.

Gardner, H. (1997). *Extraordinary minds: Portraits of exceptional individuals and an examination of our extraordinariness.* New York, NY: Basic Books.

Gardner, H. (2006). *Multiple intelligences: New horizons in theory and practice.* New York, NY: Basic Books.

Garland, A. F., & Zigler, E. (1993). Adolescent suicide prevention: Current research and social policy. *American Psychologist, 48,* 169–182.

Garner, P. W., Jones, D. C., & Palmer, D. J. (1994). Social cognitive correlates of preschool children's sibling caregiving behavior. *Developmental Psychology, 30,* 906–911.

Garrison, M. E. B., Blalock, L. B., Zarski, J. J., & Merritt, P. B. (1997). Delayed parenthood: An exploratory study of family functioning. *Family Relations, 46,* 281–290.

Gartrell, N. K., Bos, H. M., & Goldberg, N. G. (2011). Adolescents of the U.S. National Longitudinal

Lesbian Family Study: Sexual orientation, sexual behavior, and sexual risk exposure. *Archives of Sexual Behavior, 40*(6), 1199–1209.

Gates, G. J., & Newport, F. (2012, October). *Special report: 3.4% of U.S. adults identify as LGBT.* Gallup. Retrieved from http://www.gallup.com/poll/158066/special-report-adults-identify-lgbt.aspx

Gathercole, S. E., Pickering, S. J., Ambridge, B., & Wearing, H. (2004). The structure of working memory from 4 to 15 years of age. *Developmental Psychology, 40,* 177–190.

Gavin, L., & Furman, W. (1989). Age differences in adolescents' perceptions of their peer groups. *Developmental Psychology, 25,* 827–834.

Ge, X., Best, K. M., Conger, R. D., & Simons, B. L. (1996). Parenting behaviors and the occurrence and co-occurrence of adolescent depressive symptoms and conduct problems. *Developmental Psychology, 32,* 717–731.

Geary, D. C. (2004). Mathematics and learning disabilities. *Journal of Learning Disabilities, 37*(1), 4–15.

Gecas, V., & Seff, M. A. (1990). Families and adolescents: A review of the 1980s. *Journal of Marriage and the Family, 52,* 941–958.

Geddes, J. K. The secret life of kids online: What you need to know. *Parenting.* Retrieved from http://www.parenting.com/article/kids-socialnetworking

Gee, J., & Green, J. (1998). Discourse analysis, learning, and social practice: A methodological study. In D. Pearson, & A. Iran-Nejad (Eds.), *Review of research in education* (Vol. 23, pp. 119–170), Washington, DC: American Educational Research Association.

Geiger, B. (1996). Fathers as primary caregivers. Westport, CT: Greenwood Press/Greenwood Publishing Group.

Gelles, R. (1998, August). Violence and pregnancy: Are pregnant women at greater risk of abuse? *Journal of Marriage and the Family, 50,* 841–847.

Gelles, R. J., & Cornell, C. P. (1983). *International perspectives on family violence.* Lexington, MA: D. C. Heath.

Gentile, D. A., Coyne, S., & Walsh, D. A. (2011). Media violence, physical aggression, and relational aggression in school age children: A short-term longitudinal study. *Aggressive Behavior, 37*(2), 193–206.

Gentile, D. A., Nathanson, A. I., Rasmussen, E. E., Reimer, R. A., & Walsh, D. A. (2012). Do you see what I see? Parent and child reports of parental monitoring of media. *Family Relations, 61*(3), 470–487.

George, C., Kaplan, N., & Main, M. (1985). *The Adult Attachment Interview.* Unpublished manuscript, University of California at Berkeley, Department of Psychology.

George, T. P., & Hartiman, D. P. (1996). Friendship networks of unpopular, average, and popular children. *Child Development, 67,* 2310–2316.

Gerbasi, M. E., Richards, L. K., Thomas, J. J., Agnew-Blais, J. C., Thompson-Brenner, H., Gilman, S. E., & Becker, A. E. (2014). Globalization and eating disorder risk: Peer influence, perceived social norms, and adolescent disordered eating in Fiji. *International Journal of Eating Disorders, 47*(7), 727–737.

Gerbner, G., Gross, L., Signorielli, N., & Morgan, M. (1986). *Television's world: Violence profile No. 14–15.* University of Pennsylvania, Annenberg School of Communications, Philadelphia.

Gershoff, E. T., Grogan-Kaylor, A., Lansford, J. E., Chang, L., Zelli, A., Deater-Deckard, K., & Dodge, K. A. (2010). Parent discipline practices in an international sample: Associations with child behaviors and moderation by perceived normativeness. *Child Development, 81*(2), 487–502.

Gesell, A. (1926). *The mental growth of the preschool child* (2nd ed.), New York, NY: Macmillan.

Gestwicki, C. (1995). *Developmentally appropriate practice: Curriculum and development in the early years.* Albany, NY: Delmar.

Gholson, B. (1994). Cognitive processes explain learning across the life span: Infants and toddlers are people too. *Monographs of the Society for Research in Child Development, 59* (4, Serial No. 241), 76–89.

Gianino, A., & Tronick, E. Z. (1988). The mutual regulation model: The infant's self and interactive regulation coping and defense. In T. Field, P. McCabe, & N. Schneiderman (Eds.), *Stress and coping* (pp. 47–68). Hillsdale, NJ: Erlbaum.

Gibbs, J. C., Basinger, K. S., Grime, R. L., & Snarey, J. R. (2007). Moral judgment development across cultures: Revisiting Kohlberg's universality claims. *Developmental Review, 27*(4), 443–500.

Gibson, E., & Walk, R. (1960). The visual cliff. *Scientific American, 202,* 64–71.

Giedd, J. N. (2004). Structural magnetic resonance imaging of the adolescent brain. *Annals of the New York Academy of Science, 1021,* 77–85.

Gilbert, A. N., & Wysocki, C. J. (1987). The results: Smell survey. *National Geographic, 172,* 514–525.

Gilbert, S. (1998, May 19). Benefits of assistant for childbirth go far beyond the birthing room. *New York Times,* p. F-7.

Gilbert, S. P., & Weaver, C. C. (2010). Sleep quality and academic performance in university students: A wake-up call for college psychologists. *Journal of College Student Psychotherapy, 24*(4), 295–306.

Gillies, R. M., & Boyle, M. (2010). Teachers' reflections on cooperative learning: Issues of implementation. *Teaching and Teacher Education, 26*(4), 933–940.

Gilligan, C. (1982). *In a different voice: Psychological theory and women's development.* Cambridge, MA: Harvard University Press.

Gilligan, C. (1987). Adolescent development reconsidered. In C. Irwin (Ed.), *Adolescent social behavior and health.* San Francisco: Jossey-Bass.

Gilligan, C., & Attanucci, J. (1988). Two moral orientations: Gender differences and similarities. *Merrill-Palmer Quarterly, 34,* 223–237.

Gilligan, C., & Wiggins, G. (1987). The origins of morality in early childhood relationships. In J. Kagarr, & S. Lamb (Eds.), *The emergence of morality in young children* (pp. 277–305). Chicago: University of Chicago Press.

Ginsburg, H. P., Cannon, J., Eisenband, J., & Pappas, S. (2008). Mathematical thinking and learning. In K. McCartney, & D. Phillips (Eds.), *Blackwell handbook of early childhood development* (pp. 208–230). Malden, MA: Blackwell Publishing.

Ginsburg, G. S., & Bronstein, P. (1993). Family factors related to children's intrinsic/extrinsic motivational orientation in academic performance. *Child Development, 64,* 1461–1474.

Giordano, P. C., Cernkovich, S. A., & Demaris, A. (1993). The family and peer relations of black adolescents. *Journal of Marriage and the Family, 55,* 277–287.

Glasgow, K. L., Dornbusch, S. M., Troyer, L., Steinberg, L., & Ritter, P. L. (1997). Parenting styles, adolescents' attributions, and educational outcomes in nine heterogeneous high schools. *Child Development, 68,* 507–529.

Glass, D. C., Neulinger, J., & Brim, O. C. (1974). Birth order, verbal intelligence, and educational aspiration. *Child Development, 45,* 807–811.

Glass, J. C., Jr. (1990). Changing death anxiety through education in the public schools. *Death Studies, 14,* 31–52.

Glass, J. C., Jr. (1991). Death, loss, and grief among middle school children: Implications for the school counselor. *Elementary School Guidance and Counseling, 26,* 139–148.

Glauser, B. (1997). Street children: Deconstructing a construct. In A. James, & A. Prout (Eds.), *Constructing and reconstructing childhood* (2nd ed., pp. 145–164). Washington, DC: Falmer.

Glick, P. C., & Lin, S. L. (1986). More young adults are living with their parents: Who are they? *Journal of Marriage and the Family, 48,* 107–112.

Global Down Syndrome Foundation. (2017). Down Syndrome Misconceptions vs. Reality. Retrieved from https://www.globaldownsyndrome.org/about-down-syndrome/misconceptions-vs-reality/

Gluszek, A., & Dovidio, J. F. (2010). The way they speak: A social psychological perspective on the stigma of non-native accents in communication. *Personality and Social Psychology Review, 14*(2), 214–237.

Godfrey, K. M., & Barker, D. J. P. (2001). Fetal programming and adult health. *Public Health Nutrition 4,* 611–624.

Gogtay, N., Giedd, J. N., Lusk, L., Hayashi, K. M., Greenstein, D., Vaituzis, A. C., . . . & Toga, A. W. (2004). Dynamic mapping of the human cortical development during childhood through early adulthood. *Proceedings National Academy of Sciences, USA, 101(PART 21):* 8174–8179.

Gold, J. M., Bubenzer, D. L., & West, J. D. (1993). Differentiation from ex-spouses and stepfamily marital intimacy. *Journal of Divorce & Remarriage, 19*(3–4), 83–95.

Goldberg, A. E., & Allen, K. R. (2013). Same-sex relationship dissolution and LGB stepfamily formation: Perspectives of young adults with LGB parents. *Family Relations, 62*(4), 529–544.

Golden, C. (1996). Relational theories of white women's development. In J. C. Chrisler, C. Golden, & P. D. Rozee (Eds.), *Lectures on the psychology of women* (pp. 229–242). New York, NY: McGraw Hill.

Goldin-Meadow, S. (2008). How children learn language: A focus on resilience. In K. McCartney, & D. Phillips (Eds.), *Blackwell handbook of early childhood development* (pp. 252–273). Malden, MA: Blackwell Publishing.

Goldman, L. (1998). *Children's play: Mime, mimesis, and make-believe.* New York, NY: Oxford.

Goldman, S. E., Urbano, R. C., & Hodapp, R. M. (2011). Determining the amount, timing, and causes of mortality among infants with Down syndrome. *Journal of Intellectual Disability Research, 55,* 85–94.

Goldscheider, F. K. (1997). Family relationships and life course strategies for the 21st century. In S. Dreman (Ed.), *The family on the threshold of the 21st century: Trends and implications* (pp. 73–85). Mahwah, NJ: Erlbaum.

Goldscheider, F. K., & DaVanzo, J. (1986). Semiautonomy and transition to adulthood. *Social Forces, 65,* 187–201.

Goldson, E. (1992). The longitudinal study of very low birth-weight infants and its implications for interdisciplinary research and public policy. In C. Greenbaum, & J. Auerbach (Eds.), *Longitudinal studies of children at psychological risk: Cross-national perspectives* (pp. 43–64). Norwood, NJ: Ablex.

Goldsteen, K., & Ross, C. E. (1989). The perceived burden of children. *Journal of Family Issues, 10,* 504–526.

Goldstein, A. P., & Soriano, F. I. (1994). Delinquent gangs. In L. Eron, & J. Gentry (Eds.), *Violence and youth: Psychology's response: Vol II Papers of the American Psychological Association on Violence and Youth.* Washington, DC: American Psychological Association.

Goldstein, S., Field, T., & Healy, B. T. (1989). Concordance of play behavior and physiology in preschool friends. *Journal of Applied Developmental Psychology, 10,* 3337–3351.

Golombok, S., & Fivush, R. (1994). *Gender development.* New York, NY: Cambridge University Press.

Golombok, S., & Tasker, F. (1996). Do parents influence the sexual orientation of their children? Findings from a longitudinal study of lesbian females. *Developmental Psychology, 32,* 3–11.

Golombok, S., MacCallum, F., Murray, C., Lycett, E., & Jadva, V. (2006). Surrogacy families: Parental functioning, parent-child relationships and children's psychological development at age 2. *Journal of Child Psychology and Psychiatry, 47,* 213–222.

Goniewicz, M. L., Knysak, J., Gawron, M., Kosmider, L., Sobczak, A., Kurek, J., . . . & Jacob, P. (2014). Levels of selected carcinogens and toxicants in vapour from electronic cigarettes. *Tobacco Control, 23*(2), 133–139.

Gonzaga, G. C., Turner, R. A., Keltner, D., Campos, B., & Altemus, M. (2006). Romantic love and sexual desire in close relationships. *Emotion, 6*(2), 163–179.

Gonzalez, A. L., & Wolters, C. A. (2006). The relation between perceived parenting practices and achievement motivation in mathematics. *Journal of Research in Childhood Education, 21*(2), 203–217.

Goodnow, J. (1996). Collaborative rules: How are people supposed to work with one another? In P. Baltes, & U. Staudinger (Eds.), *Interactive minds: Lifespan perspectives on social foundations of cognition* (pp. 163–197). New York, NY: Cambridge University Press.

Goodnow, J. J. (1976). The nature of intelligent behavior: Questions raised by cross-cultural studies. In L. B. Resnick (Ed.), *The nature of intelligence*. Hillsdale, NJ: Erlbaum.

Goodnow, J. J. (1996). From household practices to parents' ideas about work and interpersonal relationships. In S. Harkness, & C. Super (Eds.), *Parents' cultural belief systems: Their origins, expressions, and consequences*. New York, NY: Guildford Press.

Goodnow, J. J., Miller, P. M., & Kessel, F. (Eds.) (1995). Cultural practices as contexts for development. *New directions for child development:* No. 67. San Francisco: Jossey-Bass.

Goosens, F. A., & van IJzendoorn, M. H. (1990). Quality of infants' attachments to professional caregivers: Relation to infant-parent attachment and day-care characteristics. *Child Development, 61*, 832–837.

Gopaul-McNicol, S., & Thomas-Presswood, T. (1998). *Working with linguistically and culturally different children*. Boston: Allyn and Bacon.

Gorchoff, S. M., John, O. P., & Helson, R. (2008). Contextualizing change in marital satisfaction during middle age: An 18-year longitudinal study. *Psychological Science, 19*, 1194–1200.

Gordon, S., Benner, P., & Noddings, N. (1996). *Caregiving: Readings in knowledge, practice, ethics, and politics*. Philadelphia: University of Pennsylvania Press.

Gordon, T. H., & Conger, R. D. (1997). Marital conflict and adolescent distress: The role of adolescent awareness. *Child Development, 68*, 333–350.

Gorman, C. (1993, June 13). Thalidomide's return. *Time*, June 13, p. 67.

Gortmaker, S. L., Must, A., Perrin, J. M., Sobol, A. M., & Dielz, W. H. (1993). Social and economic consequences of overweight in adolescence and young adulthood. *New England Journal of Medicine, 329*, 1008–1012.

Gottesman, I. I. (1963). Heritability of personality: A demonstration. *Psychological Monographs, 77*(Whole No. 572).

Gottfried, A. E., Bathurst, K., & Gottfried, A. W. (1994). Role of maternal and dual-earner employment status in children's development: A longitudinal study from infancy through early adolescence. In A. E. Gottfried, A. W. Gottfried, et al. (Eds.), *Redefining families: Implications for children's development* (pp. 55–97). New York, NY: Plenum Press.

Gottman, J. M. (1994). *What predicts divorce?* Hillsdale, NJ: Lawrence Erlbaum.

Gottman, J. M., Coan, J., Carrere, S., & Swanson, C. (1998). Predicting marital happiness and stability from newlywed interactions. *Journal of Marriage and the Family, 60*, 5–22.

Gottman, J. M., & Levenson, R. W. (2000). The timing of divorce: Predicting when a couple will divorce over a 14-year period. *Journal of Marriage and Family, 62*(3), 737–745.

Gottman, J. M., Levenson, R. W., Swanson, C., Swanson, K., Tyson, R., & Yoshimoto, D. (2003). Observing gay, lesbian, and heterosexual couples' relationships: Mathematical modeling of conflict interaction. *Journal of Homosexuality, 45*(1), 65–91.

Gottman, J., & Parkhurst, J. (1980). A developmental theory of friendship and acquaintanceship. In A. Collins (Ed.), *Minnesota symposia on child psychology: Vol. 13*. Hillsdale, N. J: Erlbaum.

Gould, D., & Eklund. (1996). Emotional stress and anxiety in the child and adolescent athlete. In O. Bar-Or (Ed.), *The child and adolescent athlete* (pp. 383–398). Oxford, UK: Blackwells.

Grabe, S., Ward, L. M., & Hyde, J. S. (2008). The role of the media in body image concerns among women: A meta-analysis of experimental and correlational studies. *Psychological Bulletin, 134*(3), 460.

Graber, J., Brooks-Gunn, J., & Petersen, A. (1996). *Transitions through adolescence: Interpersonal domains and context*. Mahwah, NJ: Erlbaum.

Gralinski, J. H., & Kopp, C. (1993). Everyday rules for behavior: Mothers' requests to young children. *Developmental Psychology, 29*, 573–584.

Granier-Deferre, C., Bassereau, S., Ribereiro, A., Jacquet, A., & DeCasper, A. J. (2011). A melodic contour repeatedly experienced by human near-term fetuses elicits a profound cardiac reaction one month after birth. *PLoS ONE, 6*, 1–10.

Granrud, C. (Ed.) (1993). *Visual perception and cognition in infancy*. Englewood Cliffs, NJ: Erlbaum.

Granrud, C. (2006). Size constancy in infants: 4-month-olds' responses to physical versus retinal image size. *Journal of Experimental Psychology: Human Perception and Performance, 32*, 1398–1404.

Green, J. A., Gustafson, G. E., & McGhie, A. C. (1998). Changes in infants' cries as a function of time in a cry bout. *Child Development, 69*, 271–279.

Green, M. (1994). *Sigh of relief: A first-aid handbook for childhood emergencies*. New York, NY: Bantam Books.

Green, R. (1987). *The "sissy boy" syndrome and the development of homosexuality*. New Haven, CT: Yale University Press.

Greenberg, R. A., Haley, N. J., Etzel, R. A., & Loda, F. A. (1984). Measuring the exposure of infants to tobacco smoke. *New England Journal of Medicine, 310*, 1075–1078.

Greene, B. (1994). Lesbian and gay sexual orientations: Implications for clinical training, practice, and research. In B. Greene, & G. M. Herek (Eds.), *Lesbian and gay psychology: Theory, research, and clinical applications* (pp. 1–24). Thousand Oaks, CA: Sage.

Greenfield, P. (1994). Independence and interdependence as developmental scripts: Implications for theory, research, and practice. In P. Greenfield, & R. Cocking (Eds.), *Cross-cultural roots of minority child development* (pp. 1–40). Hillsdale, NJ: Erlbaum.

Greenfield, P. (1995, March 30). *Independence and interdependence in school conferences between Anglo teachers and Hispanic parents*. Paper presented at the biennial meeting of the Society for Research on Child Development, Indianapolis.

Greenhaus, J. H. (1988). Career exploration. In M. London, & E. M. Mone (Eds.), *Career growth and human resource strategy* (pp. 17–30). New York, NY: Quorum.

Greenhaus, J. H., & Powell, G. N. (2006). When work and family are allies: A theory of work-family enrichment. *Academy of Management Reviews, 31*, 72–92.

Gregg, M., & Leinhardt, C. (1995). Mapping out geography: An example of epistemology and education. In *Review of Educational Research, 64*(2), 311–361.

Greil, A. L. (1993). Infertility: Overview. In B. K. Rothman (Ed.), *The encyclopedia of childbearing*. New York, NY: Henry Holt.

Grimes, D. A., Benson, J., Singh, S., Romero, M., Ganatra, B., Okonofua, F. E., & Shah, I. H. (2006). *Unsafe abortion: The preventable pandemic* (World Health Organization journal paper). Retrieved from http://www.who.int/reproductivehealth/topics/unsafe_abortion/article_unsafe_abortion.pdf

Grolinck, W. S., Bridges, L. J., & Connell, J. P. (1996). Emotional regulation in two-year-olds: Strategies and emotional expression in four contexts. *Child Development, 67*, 928–941.

Gross, R., Spiker, D., & Haynes, C. (1997). *Helping low-birth-weight, premature babies*. Stanford, CA: Stanford University Press.

Grossmann, K., Grossmann, K., Spangler, G., Suess, G., & Unzner, L. (1985). Maternal sensitivity and newborns' orientation responses as related to quality of attachment in northern Germany. In I. Bretherton, & E. Waters (Eds.), Growing points of attachment theory and research. *Monographs of the Society for Research on Child Development, 50*, 233–256.

Grossmann, K. E., & Grossmann, K. (1990). The wider concept of attachment in cross-cultural research. *Human Development, 33*, 31–47.

Grossmann, T. (2010). The development of emotion perception in face and voice during infancy. *Restorative Neurology and Neuroscience, 28*, 219–236.

Grotpeter, J. K., & Crick, N. R. (1996). Relational aggression. overt aggression, and friendship. *Child Development, 67*, 2328–2338.

Grotpeter, J. K., & Crick, N. R. (1996). *Second chances: Men, women and children a decade after divorce*. Boston: Houghton Mifflin.

Grubb, A., & Turner, E. (2012). Attribution of blame in rape cases: A review of the impact of rape myth acceptance, gender role conformity and substance use on victim blaming. *Aggression and Violent Behavior, 17*(5), 443–52.

Grühn, D., Gilet, A. L., Studer, J., & Labouvie-Vief, G. (2011). Age-relevance of person characteristics: Persons' beliefs about developmental change across the lifespan. *Developmental Psychology, 47*, 376–387.

Grundy, A. M., Gondoli, D. M., & Salafia, E. H. B. (2010). Hierarchical linear modeling analysis of change in maternal knowledge over the transition to adolescence. *Journal of Early Adolescence, 30*(5), 707–732.

Grusec, J. E. (1991). Socializing concern for others in the home. *Developmental Psychology, 27*, 338–342.

Grusec, J. E., Goodnow, J. J., & Cohen, L. (1996). Household work and the development of concern for others. *Developmental Psychology, 32*, 999–1007.

Grusec, J. E., Rudy, D., & Martini, T. (1997). Parenting cognition and child outcomes: An overview of implications for children's internalization of values. In J. E. Grusec, L. Kuczynski, et al. (Eds.), *Parenting and the internalization of values: A handbook of contemporary theory* (pp. 259–282). New York, NY: Wiley.

Grzywacz, J. G., & Butler, A. B. (2005). The impact of job characteristics on work-to-family facilitation: Testing a theory and distinguishing a construct. *Journal of Occupational Health Psychology, 10*(2), 97.

Guarda, A. S. (2008). Treatment of anorexia nervosa: Insights and obstacles. *Physiology & Behavior, 94*(1), 113–120.

Guardo, C., & Bohan, J. (1971). Development of a sense of self-identity in children. *Child Development, 42*, 1909–1921.

Gunnar, M. R., Proter, F. L., Wolf, C. M., Rigatuso, J., & Larson, M. C. (1995). Neonatal stress reactivity; Predictions of later emotional temperament. *Child Development, 66*, 1–13.

Gunnarsdottir, I., & Thorsdottir, I. (2003). Relationship between growth and feeding in infancy and body mass index at the age of 6 years. *International Journal of Obesity and Metabolic Disorders, 27*, 1523–1527.

Gunner, M. R., Larson, M. C., Hertsgaard, L., Harris, M. L., & Bodersen, L. (1992). The stressfulness of separation among nine-month-old infants: Effects of social context variables and infant temperament. *Child Development, 63*, 290–303.

Gupta, N. D., Smith, N., & Verner, M. (2008). The impact of Nordic countries' family friendly policies on employment, wages, and children. *Review of Economics of the Household, 6*(1), 65–89.

Guralnick, M. J. (2008). Family influences on early development: Integrating the science of normative development, risk and disability, and intervention. In K. McCartney, & D. Phillips (Eds.), *Blackwell handbook of early childhood development* (pp. 44–61). Malden, MA: Blackwell Publishing.

Guttmacher, A., & Kaiser, I. (1984). *Pregnancy, birth, and family planning.* New York, NY: Signet.

Guttmacher Institute. (2002). Teen pregnancy trends and lessons learned. *The Guttmacher Report on Public Policy, 5*(1). Retrieved from http://www.guttmacher.org/pubs/tgr/05/1/gro50107.html

Guttmacher Institute. (2012). *Facts on induced abortion worldwide.* Retrieved from http://www.who.int/reproductivehealth/publications/unsafe_abortion/induced_abortion_2012.pdf

Guttmacher Institute. (2013a). *Counseling and waiting periods for abortion.* Retrieved from http://www.guttmacher.org/statecenter/spibs/spib_MWPA.pdf

Guttmacher Institute. (2013b). *Facts on American teens sexual and reproductive health.* Retrieved from http://www.guttmacher.org/pubs/FB-ATSRH.html.

Guttman, A. (1996). *The erotic in sports.* New York, NY: Columbia University Press.

H

Hackel, L. S., & Ruble, D. N. (1992). Changes in the marital relationship after the first baby is born: Predicting the impact of expectancy disconfirmation. *Journal of Personality & Social Psychology, 62,* 944–957.

Hagerman, R. J. (1996). Biomedical advances in developmental psychology: The case of fragile-x syndrome. *Developmental Psychology, 32,* 416–424.

Haith, M., Wass, T., & Adler, S. (1997). Infant visual expectations: Advances and issues. *Monographs of the Society for Research in Child Development, 62* (2, Serial No 250).

Häkkinen, I., Kirjavainen, T., & Uusitalo, R. (2003). School resources and student achievement revisited: New evidence from panel data. *Economics of Education Review, 22*(3), 329–335.

Halim, M. L., & Ruble, D. (2010). Gender identity and stereotyping in early and middle childhood. In J. C. Chrisler, & D. R. McCreary (Eds.), *Handbook of gender research in psychology* (pp. 495–525). New York, NY: Springer.

Hall, G. C. N., & Barongan, C. (1997). Prevention of sexual aggression. Sociocultural risk and protective factors. *American Psychologist, 52,* 5–14.

Halliday, J. L., Watson, L. F., Lumley, J., Danks, D. M., & Sheffield, L. S. (1995). New estimates of Down syndrome risks of chorionic villus sampling, amniocentesis, and live birth in women of advanced maternal age from a uniquely defined population. *Prenatal Diagnosis, 15,* 455–465.

Hallinan, M. T., & Williams, R. A. (1989). Interracial friendship choices in secondary schools. *American Sociological Review, 54,* 67–78.

Hallinan, M., & Teixeira, R. (1987). The stability of students' interracial friendships. *American Sociological Review, 52,* 653–664.

Hallowell, E., & Ratey, J. (1994). *Driven to distraction: ADHD children as adults.* New York, NY: Pantheon Books.

Halperin, J. M., Trampush, J. W., Miller, C. J., Marks, D. J., & Newcorn, J. H. (2008). Neuropsychological outcome in adolescents/young adults with Childhood ADHD: Profiles of persisters, remitters and controls. *Journal of Child Psychology and Psychiatry, and Allied Disciplines, 49*(9), 958–966.

Hamann, K., Warneken, F., & Tomasello, M. (2012). Children's developing commitments to joint goals. *Child Development, 83*(1), 137–145.

Hamarta, E., Deniz, M., & Saltali, N. (2009). Attachment styles as a predictor of emotional intelligence. *Educational Sciences: Theory and Practice, 9*(1), 213–229.

Hamburg, D. (1997). Towards a strategy for healthy adolescent development. *American Journal of Psychiatry, 154*(6), 7–12.

Hamburg, D. A. (1994). *Today's children: Creating a future for a generation of crisis.* New York, NY: Times Books.

Hamilton, B. E., Martin, J. A., & Osterman, M. J. K. (2016, June). Births: Preliminary data for 2015. *National Vital Statistics Reports, 65*(3), 1–15. Retrieved from http://www.cdc.gov/nchs/data/nvsr/nvsr65/nvsr65_03.pdf

Hamilton, N. G. (1989). *Self and others: Object relations in theory and practice.* Northvale, NJ: Jason Aronson.

Hamilton, P. M. (1984). *Basic maternity nursing* (5th ed.). St. Louis: Mosby.

Hardy, J. B. (1991). Pregnancy and its outcome. In W. R. Hendee (Ed.), *The health of adolescents: Understanding and facilitating biological, behavioral, and social development* (pp. 250–281). San Francisco: Jossey-Bass.

Hare-Mustin, R. T., & Marecek, J. (1988). The meaning of difference: Gender theory, postmodernism, and psychology. *American Psychologist, 43,* 455–64.

Hareven, T. (1986). Historical changes in the family and the life course: Implications for child development. In A. Smuts, & H. Hagen (Eds.), *History and research in child development. Monographs of the Society for Research on Child Development, 50* (4–5, Serial No. 211).

Harkness, S., & Keefer, C. (1995, February). *Cultural influences on sleep patterns in infancy and early childhood.* Paper presented at the annual meeting of the American Association for the Advancement of Science, Atlanta.

Harkness, S., & Super, C. (1992). Parental ethnotheories in action. In I. Sigel, A. McGillicuddy-DeLisi, & J. Goodnow (Eds.), *Parent belief systems: The psychological consequences for children* (2nd ed., pp. 373–392). Hillsdale, NJ: Erlbaum.

Harkness, S., Super, C., & Keefer, C. (1992). Learning to be an American parent: How cultural models gain directive force. In R. D'Andrade, & C. Strauss (Eds.), *Human motives and cultural models* (pp. 163–178). New York, NY: Cambridge University-Press.

Harold, G. T., & Conger, R. D. (1997). Marital conflict and adolescent distress: The role of adolescent awareness. *Child Development, 68,* 333–350.

Harrington, J. W., Nguyen, V. Q., Paulson, J. F., Garland, R., Pasquinelli, L., & Lewis, D. (2010). Identifying the "tipping point" age for overweight pediatric patients. *Clinical Pediatrics, 49,* 638–643.

Harris, P. (1983). Infant cognition. In Paul Mussen (Ed.), *Handbook of child psychology: Vol. 4.* New York, NY: Wiley.

Harrison, A. O., Wilson, M. N., Pine, C. J., Chan, S. Q., & Buriel, R. (1990). Family ecologies of ethnic minority children. *Child Development, 61,* 347–362.

Harrison, D., Bueno, M., Yamada, J., Adams-Webber, T., & Stevens, B. (2010). Analgesic effects of sweet-tasting solutions for infants: Current state of equipoise. *Pediatrics, 126,* 894–902.

Hart, B. (1991). Input frequency and children's first words *First Language, 11,* 289–300.

Hart, C. H., DeWolf, D. M., Wozniak, P., & Burts, D. C. (1992). Maternal and paternal disciplinary styles: Relations with preschoolers' playground behavioral orientations and peer status. *Child Development, 63,* 879–892.

Hart, C. H., Ladd, G. W., & Burleson, B. R. (1990). Children's expectations of the outcomes of social strategies; Relations with socioeconomic status and maternal disciplinary styles. *Child. Development, 61,* 127–137.

Hart, C. H., Nelson, D. A., Robinson, C. C., Olsen, S. F., & McNeilly-Chocque, M. K. (1998). Overt and relational aggression in Russian nursery school-age children: Parenting style and marital linkages. *Developmental Psychology, 34,* 687–697.

Hart, H., Radua, J., Nakao, T., Mataix-Cols, D., & Rubia, K. (2013). Meta-analysis of functional magnetic resonance imaging studies of inhibition and attention in attention-deficit/hyperactivity disorder: Exploring task-specific, stimulant medication, and age effects. *JAMA Psychiatry, 70*(2), 185–198.

Harter, S. (1977). A cognitive-developmental approach to children's expression of conflicting feelings and a technique to facilitate such expression in play therapy. *Journal of Consulting and Clinical Psychology, 45,* 417–432.

Harter, S. (1983). Developmental perspectives on self system. In E. M. Hetherington (Ed.), *Handbook of child psychology: Vol. 4. Socialization, personality, and social development* (4th ed., pp. 275–285). New York, NY: Wiley.

Harter, S. (1989). Processes underlying adolescent self-concept formation. In R. Montemayor (Ed.), *Advances in adolescent development: Vol 2. Transition from childhood to adolescence.* New York, NY: Russell Sage Foundation.

Harter, S., & Barnes, R. (1983). *Children's understanding of parental emotions: A developmental study.* Unpublished paper, 1981. Cited in S. Harter, *Developmental perspectives on the self-system.* In P. Mussen (Ed.), *Handbook of child psychology: Vol. 4.* New York, NY: Wiley.

Harter, S., & Monsour, A. (1992). Developmental analysis of conflict caused by opposing attributes in the adolescent self-portrait. *Developmental Psychology, 28,* 251–260.

Harter, S., Marold, D. B., Whitesell, N. R., & Cobbs, G. (1996). A model of the effects of perceived parent and peer support on adolescent false self behavior. *Child Development, 67,* 360–374.

Hartup, W. W. (1983). Peer relations. In P. Mussen (Ed.), *Handbook of child psychology: Vol. 4.* New York, NY: Wiley.

Hartup, W. W. (1989). Social relationships and their developmental significance. *American Psychologist, 44,* 120–126.

Hartup, W. W. (1996). The company they keep: Friendships and their developmental significance. *Child Development, 67,* 1–13.

Hartup, W. W. (1997). The company they keep: Friendships and adaptation in the life course. *Psychological Bulletin, 121,* 355–370.

Hartup, W. W., & Stevens, N. (1997). Friendships and adaptation in the life course. *Psychological Bulletin, 121,* 335–370.

Hasan, Y., Bègue, L., Scharkow, M., & Bushman, B. J. (2013). The more you play, the more aggressive you become: A long-term experimental study of cumulative violent video game effects on hostile expectations and aggressive behavior. *Journal of Experimental Social Psychology, 49,* 224–227.

Haslett, B. (1997). *Children communicating: The first 5 years.* Mahwah, NJ: Erlbaum.

Hastings, P. D., & Grusec, J. E. (1998). Parenting goals as organizers of responses to parent-child disagreement. *Developmental Psychology, 34,* 465–479.

Havekes, E., Bader, M., & Krysan, M. (2016). Realizing racial and ethnic neighborhood preferences? Exploring the mismatches between what people want, where they search, and where they live. *Population Research and Policy Review, 35*(1), 101–126.

Hawkins, J. D., Graham, J. W., Maguin, E., Abbott, R., Hill, K. G., & Catalano, R. F. (1997). Exploring the effects of age of alcohol use initiation and psychosocial risk factors on subsequent alcohol misuse. *Journal of Studies on Alcohol, 58,* 280–290.

Hay, P. (2013). A systematic review of evidence for psychological treatments in eating disorders, 2005–2012. *International Journal of Eating Disorders, 46*(5), 462–469.

Hayenga, A. O., & Corpus, J. H. (2010). Profiles of intrinsic and extrinsic motivations: A person-centered approach to motivation and achievement in middle school. *Motivation and Emotion, 34*(4), 371–383.

Hayes, C. (1987). *Risking the future: Adolescent sexuality, pregnancy and childbearing.* Washington, DC: National Academy Press.

Hayne, H., Rovee-Collier, C., & Borza, M. (1991). Infant memory for place information. *Memory and Cognition, 19,* 378–386.

Hazen, C., & Shaver, P. (1987). Romantic love conceptualized as an attachment process. *Journal of Personality and Social Psychology, 53,* 511–524.

Hazen, C., & Shaver, P. (1990). Love and work: An attachment-theoretical perspective. *Journal of Personality and Social Psychology, 59,* 270–290.

Heal, D. J., Smith, S. L., & Findling, R. L. (2011). ADHD: Current and future therapeutics. In C. Stanford, & R. Tannock (Eds.), *Behavioral neuroscience of attention deficit hyperactivity disorder and its treatment* (pp. 361–390). Berlin: Springer-Verlag Berlin Heidelberg.

Heath, S. (1993). *Identity and inner-city youth: Beyond ethnicity and gender.* New York, NY: Teachers' College Press.

Heath, S., Mangolia, L., Schlecter, S., & Hull, G. (Eds.). (1991). *Children of promise: Literate activity in linguistically and culturally diverse classrooms.* Washington, DC: National Education Association.

Heckhausen, J., & Krueger, J. (1993). Developmental expectations for the self and most other people: Age-grading in three functions of social comparison. *Developmental Psychology, 29,* 539–548.

Hegewisch, A., & Gornick, J. C. (2011). The impact of work-family policies on women's employment: A review of research from OECD countries. *Community, Work & Family, 14*(2), 119–138.

Hegewisch, A., Leipmann, H., Hayes, J., & Hartmann, H. (2010). *Separate and not equal? Gender segregation in the labor market and the gender wage gap.* Institute for Women's Policy Research, Washington, DC. Retrieved from https://iwpr.org/publications/separate-and-not-equal-gender-segregation-in-the-labor-market-and-the-gender-wage-gap/

Heikamp, T., Trommsdorff, G., Druey, M. D., Hübner, R., & Suchodoletz, A. V. (2013). Kindergarten children's attachment security, inhibitory control, and the internalization of rules of conduct. *Frontiers in Psychology, 4,* 1–11.

Helfer, M. E., Kempe, R. S., & Krugman, R. D. (Eds.) (1997). *The battered child.* Chicago: University of Chicago Press.

Helfer, R. E., & Kempe, R. S. (Eds.). (1987). *The battered child* (4th ed.), Chicago: University of Chicago Press.

Helton, A., McFarlane, J., & Anderson, E. T. (1987). Battered and pregnant: A prevalence study. *American Journal of Public Health, 77,* 1337–1339.

Hendler, M., & Weisberg, P. (1992). Conservation acquisition, maintenance, and generalization by mentally retarded children using equality rule training. *Journal of Experimental Child Psychology, 53,* 258–276.

Hendrick, H. (1997). Constructions and reconstructions of British childhood: An interpretative survey, 1800 to the present. In A. James, & A. Prout (Eds.), *Constructing and reconstructing childhood* (pp. 34–62). London, UK: Falmer.

Henrich, J., Heine, S. J., & Norenzayan, A. (2010). The weirdest people in the world? *Behavioral and Brain Sciences, 33*(2–3), 61–83.

Henry, B., Caspi, A., Moffitt, T. E., & Silva, P. A. (1996). Temperamental and familial predictors of violent and nonviolent criminal convictions: Age 3 to age 18. *Developmental Psychology, 32,* 614–623.

Herbenick, D., Reece, M., Schick, V., Sanders, S. A., Dodge, B., & Fortenberry, J. D. (2010). Sexual behavior in the United States: Results from a national probability sample of men and women ages 14–94. *Journal of Sexual Medicine, 7*(s5), 255–265.

Hergenrather, J. R., & Rabinowitz, M. (1991). Age related differences in the organization of children's knowledge of illness, *Developmental Psychology, 27,* 952–959.

Herman, J. (1992). *Trauma and recovery: The aftermath of violence: From domestic abuse to political terror.* New York, NY: Basic Books.

Hernandez, D. J. (1997). Child development and the social demography of childhood. *Child Development, 68,* 149–169.

Hernandez, H. (1997). *Teaching in multilingual classrooms.* Upper Saddle River, NJ: Merrill.

Herrenkohl, R. C., Egolf, B. P., & Herrenkohl, E. C. (1997). Preschool antecedents of adolescent assaultive behavior. A longitudinal study. *American Journal of Orthopsychiatry, 67,* 422–32.

Hershberger, S. L., & D'Augelli, A. R. (1995). The impact of victimization on the mental health and suicidality of lesbian, gay, and bisexual youths. *Developmental Psychology, 31,* 65–74.

Hespos, S. J., & Baillargeon, R. (2001). Infants' knowledge about occlusion and containment events: A surprising discrepancy. *Psychological Science, 12,* 141–147.

Hesse-Biber, S. (1996). *Am I thin enough yet? The cult of thinness and commercialization of identity.* New York, NY: Oxford University Press.

Hetherington, E. M. (2005). Divorce and the adjustment of children. *Pediatrics In Review, 26*(5), 163–169.

Hetherington, E. M., Bridges, M., & Insabella, G. M. (1998). What matters? What does not? Five perspectives on the association between marital transitions and children's adjustment. *American Psychologist, 53,* 167–184.

Hetherington, E. M., Henderson, S. H., Reiss, D., Anderson, E. R., Bridges, M., Chan, R. W., . . . & O'Connor, T. G. (1999). Adolescent siblings in stepfamilies: Family functioning and adolescent adjustment. *Monographs of the Society for Research in Child Development, 64,* Serial No. 259.

Hildick-Smith, G. J., Pesko, M. F., Shearer, L., Hughes, J. M., Chang, J., Loughlin, G. M., & Ipp, L. S. (2015). A practitioner's guide to electronic cigarettes in the adolescent population. *Journal of Adolescent Health, 57*(6), 574–579.

Hill, R., & Ruptic, C. (1994). *Practical aspects of authentic assessment.* Norwood, MA: Christopher-Gordon Publishers.

Hills, A. P., King, N. A., & Armstrong, T. P. (2007). The contribution of physical activity and sedentary behaviours to the growth and development of children and adolescents. *Sports Medicine, 37*(6), 533–545.

Hinde, R. A. (1989). Ethological relationships and approaches. In R. Vasta (Ed.), *Anna's of Child Development: Six theories of child development–Revised formulations and current issues.* Greenwich, CT: JAI Press.

Hinkley, T., Crawford, D., Salmon, J., Okely, A. D., & Hesketh, K. (2008). Preschool children and physical activity: A review of correlates. *American Journal of Preventive Medicine, 34*(5), 435–441.

Ho, D. (1994). Cognitive socialization in Confucian heritage cultures. In P. Greenfield, & R. Cocking (Eds.), *Cross-cultural roots of minority child development* (pp. 285–314). Hillsdale, NJ: Erlbaum.

Ho, E. S. (2010). Measuring hand function in the young child. *Journal of Hand Therapy, 23,* 323–328.

Hoare, C. H. (1994). Psychosocial identity development in United States society: Its role in fostering exclusion of cultural others. In E. P. Salett, & D. R. Koslow (Eds.), *Race, ethnicity and self: Identity in multicultural perspective.* Washington, DC: National Multicultural Institute.

Hochschild, A. (1989). *The second shift: Working parents and the revolution at home.* New York, NY: Viking.

Hodnett, E. D., Gates, S., Hofneyr, G. J., & Sakala, C. (2007). Continuous support for women during childbirth. *Cochrane Database of Systematic Reviews, 3.*

Hoeve, M., Dubas, J. S., Eichelsheim, V. I., Van der Laan, P. H., Smeenk, W., & Gerris, J. R. (2009). The relationship between parenting and delinquency: A meta-analysis. *Journal of Abnormal Child Psychology, 37*(6), 749–775.

Hoff, E. (2008). Language experience and language milestones during early childhood. In K. McCartney, & D. Phillips (Eds.), *Blackwell handbook of early childhood development* (pp. 233–251). Malden, MA: Blackwell Publishing.

Hoff-Ginsberg, E. (1997). *Language development.* Pacific Grove, CA: Brooks/Cole.

Hoff-Ginsberg, E., & Krueger, W. (1991). Older siblings as conversational partners. *Merrill-Palmer Quarterly, 37,* 465–482.

Hoffman, L. W. (1983). Increased fathering: Effects on the mother. In M. Lamb, & A. Sagi (Eds.), *Fatherhood and family policy.* Hillsdale, NJ: Erlbaum.

Hoffman, L. W. (1984a). Maternal employment and the young child. In M. Perlmutter (Ed.), *The Minnesota symposium on child psychology: Vol. 17.* Hillsdale, NJ: Erlbaum.

Hoffman, L. W. (1984b). Work, family, and the socialization of the child. In R. Parke (Ed.), *Review of child development research: Vol. 7.* Chicago: University of Chicago Press.

Hoffman, L. W. (1989). Effects of maternal employment in the two-parent family. *American Psychologist, 44,* 283–292.

Hoffnung, A. (1992). *Shoeshine boys of Cuenca, Ecuador.* Unpublished paper, Reed College, Portland.

Hoffnung, M. (1992). *What is a mother to do? Conversations on work and family.* Pasadena, CA: Trilogy Books.

Hoffnung, M. (1995). Motherhood: Contemporary conflict for women. In J. Freeman (Ed.)., *Women: A feminist perspective* (5th ed., pp. 162–181). Palo Alto, CA: Mayfield.

Hoffnung, M. (1998, November). Women's changing attitudes toward work and family. Paper presented at the Conference on Work and Family: Today's Realities and Tomorrow's Visions, Boston, MA.

Hofland, B. F. (1994). When capacity fades and autonomy is constricted: A client-centered approach to residential care. *Generations, 18*(4), 31–35.

Hogan, N. S., & DeSantis, L. (1992). Adolescent sibling bereavement: An ongoing attachment. *Qualitative Health Research. 2,* 159–177.

Hoge, D., Johnson, B., & Luidens, D. A. (1993). Determinants of church involvement of young adults who grew up in Presbyterian churches. *Journal for the Scientific Study of Religion, 32,* 242–255.

Hogenkamp, P. S., Nilsson, E., Nilsson, V. C., Chapman, C. D., Vogel, H., Lundberg, L. S., . . . & Dickson, S. L. (2013). Acute sleep deprivation increases portion size and affects food choice in young men. *Psychoneuroendocrinology, 38*(9), 1668–1674.

Holden, C. (1986). Youth suicide: New research focuses on growing social problem. *Science, 233,* 839–841.

Holmbeck, G., & O'Donnell, K. (1991). Discrepancies between perceptions of decision making and behavioral autonomy. In R. Paikoff (Ed.), *Shared views of the family during adolescence* (pp. 51–70). San Francisco: Jossey-Bass.

Holmes, B. M., & Johnson, K. R. (2009). Adult attachment and romantic partner preference: A review. *Journal of Social and Personal Relationships, 26*(6–7), 833–852.

Holmes, L. J. (1993). Midwives, southern black. In B. K. Rothman (Ed.), *The encyclopedia of childbearing.* New York, NY: Henry Holt.

Hong, J. S., & Garbarino, J. (2012). Risk and protective factors for homophobic bullying in schools: An application of the socio-ecological framework. *Educational Psychology Review, 24*(2), 271–285.

Horgan, J. (1993, June). Eugenics revisited. *Scientific American,* 120–128.

Horn, J. L. (1970). Organization of data on life-span development of human abilities. In L. R. Goulet, & P. B. Baltes (Eds.), *Life-span developmental psychology: Research and theory* (pp. 424–466). New York, NY: Academic Press.

Hornor, G. (2010). Child sexual abuse: Consequences and implications. *Journal of Pediatric Health Care, 24*(6), 358–364.

Horwitz, A. V., & White, H. R. (1998). The relationship of cohabitation and mental health: A study of a young adult cohort. *Journal of Marriage and the Family, 60,* 505–514.

House, S. J., Landis, K. R., & Umberson, D. (1988). Social relationships and health. *Science, 241,* 540–544.

Howe, N., Petrakos, H., & Rinaldi, C. M. (1998). "All the sheeps are dead. He murdered them": Sibling pretense, negotiation, internal state language, and relationship quality. *Child Development, 69,* 182–191.

Howe, N., Ross, H. S., & Recchia, H. (2011). Sibling relations in early and middle childhood. In P. K. Smith, & C. H. Hart (Eds.), *The Wiley-Blackwell handbook of childhood social development* (2nd ed., pp. 356–372). Malden, MA: Blackwell Publishing.

Howes, C. (1988). Peer interaction of young children. *Monographs of the Society for Research in Child Development, 53*(Serial No. 2170), 1–78.

Howes, C. (1996). The earliest friendships. In W. M. Bukowski, A. F. Newcomb, et al. (Eds.), *The company they keep: Friendship in childhood and adolescence. Cambridge Studies in Social and Emotional Development* (pp. 66–86). New York, NY: Cambridge University Press.

Howes, C., & Matheson, C. C. (1992). Sequences in the development of competent play with peers: Social and social pretend play. *Developmental Psychology, 28*, 961–972.

Howes, C., & Wu, F. (1990). Peer interactions and friendships in an ethnically diverse school setting. *Child Development, 61*, 537–541.

Howes, C., Hamilton, C. E., & Matheson, C. C. (1994). Children's relationships with peers: Differential associations with aspects of the teacher-child relationship. *Child Development, 65*, 253–263.

Howes, C., Hamilton, C. E., & Philipsen, L. C. (1998). Stability and continuity of child-caregiver and child-peer relationships. *Child Development, 69*, 418–426.

Hu, J. M., Wechter, M. E., Geller, E. J., Nguyen, T. V., & Visco, A. G. (2007). Hysterectomy rates in the United States, 2003. *Obstetrics and Gynecology, 110*, 1091–1095.

Huang, L., & Ying, Y. (1989). Chinese-American children and adolescents. In J. Gibbs, & L. Huang (Eds.), *Children of color* (pp. 30–66). San Francisco: Jossey-Bass.

Hubbard, R. (1993). Genetics. In B. K. Rothman (Ed.), *The encyclopedia of childbearing*. New York, NY: Henry Holt.

Hudley, C., & Graham, S. (1993). An attributional intervention to reduce peer-directed aggression among African-American boys. *Child Development, 64*, 124–138.

Hughes, F. P. (1991). *Children, play and development*. Boston: Allyn & Bacon.

Hughes, M. S. (1987). Black students' participation in higher education. Special issue: Blacks in U.S. higher education. *Journal of College Student Personnel, 28*(6), 532–545.

Hunt, C. (Ed.). (1992). *Apnea and SIDS*. Philadelphia: Saunders.

Hunt, W., & Zakhari, S. (1995). *Stress, gender, and alcohol-seeking behavior*. Bethesda, MD: National Institutes of Health/National Institute of Alcohol Abuse and Alcoholism.

Hurrelmann, K. (1994). *International handbook of adolescence*. Westport, CT: Greenwood Press.

Huston, A. C. (1994). *Children in poverty: Designing research to affect policy*. Social policy report, vol. 8(2). Ann Arbor, MI: Society for Research on Child Development.

Huston, A. C., & Wright, J. C. (1996). Television and socialization of young children. In T. M. MacBeth et al. (Eds.), *Tuning in to young viewers: Social science perspectives on television* (pp. 37–60). Thousand Oaks, CA: Sage.

Huston, A. C., Watkins, B., & Kunkel, D. (1989). Public policy and children's television. *American Psychologist, 44*, 424–433.

Huston, A. C., Wright, J. C., Rice, M. L., Kerkman, D., & St. Peters, M. (1990). Development of television viewing patterns in early childhood: A longitudinal investigation. *Developmental Psychology, 26*, 409–420.

Hwang, J., & Rothbart, M. K. (2002). Measuring infant temperament. *Infant Behavior & Development, 25*, 113–116.

Hyde, J. S., Essex, M. J., Clark, R., Klein, M. H., & Byrd, J. E. (1996). Parental leave: Policy and research. *Journal of Social Issues 56*, 91–109.

Hyman, J. P. (1995). Shifting patterns of fathering in the first year of life: On intimacy between fathers and their babies. In J. L. Shapiro, M. J. Diamond, & M. Greenberg (Eds.), *Becoming a father: Contemporary, social, developmental, and clinical perspectives*. (pp. 256–267). New York, NY: Springer.

Hymel, S., Closson, L. M., Caravita, S. C. S., & Vaillancourt, T. (2011). Social status among peers: From sociometric attraction to peer acceptance to perceived popularity. In P. K. Smith, & C. H. Hart (Eds.), *The Wiley-Blackwell handbook of childhood social development* (2nd ed., pp. 375–322). Malden, MA: Blackwell Publishing.

I

Ianni, F., & Orr, M. (1996). Dropping out. In J. Graber, J. Brooks-Gunn, & A. Petersen (Eds.), *Transitions through adolescence* (pp. 285–322). Mahwah, NJ: Erlbaum.

Ingersoll, B. (1998). *Daredevils and daydreamers: New perspectives on ADHD*. New York, NY: Doubleday.

Inhelder, B., & Piaget, J. (1958). *The growth of logical thinking from birth to adolescence*. New York, NY: Basic Books.

Innamorati, M., Sarracino, D., & Dazzi, N. (2010). Motherhood constellation and representational change in pregnancy. *Infant Mental Health Journal, 31*, 379–396.

Insana, S. P., & Montgomery-Downs, H. E. (2013). Sleep and sleepiness among first-time postpartum parents: A field-and laboratory-based multimethod assessment. *Developmental Psychobiology, 55*(4), 361–372.

Institute of Medicine. (2002). *Reducing suicide: A national imperative*. Washington, DC: National Academies Press.

Institute of Medicine. (2009). *Weight gain during pregnancy: Reexamining the guidelines*. Washington, DC: National Academies Press.

Isabella, R. A., & Belsky, J. (1991). Interactional synchrony and the origins of infant-mother attachment: A replication study. *Child Development, 62*, 373–384.

Iyer, S. N., & Oiler, D. K. (2008). Prelinguistic vocal development in infants with typical hearing and infants with severe-to-profound hearing loss. *Volta Review, 108*, 115–138.

Izard, C. E. (1982). *Measuring emotions in infants and children*. New York, NY: Cambridge University Press.

Izard, C. E. (1994). Innate and universal facial expressions: Evidence from developmental and cross-cultural research. *Psychological Bulletin, 115*, 288–299.

Izard, C. E., & Malatesta, C. (1987). Perspectives on emotional development: I. Differential emotions theory of early emotional development. In J. Osofsky (Ed.), *Handbook of infant development* (2nd ed., pp. 494–554). New York, NY: Wiley.

J

Jaccard, J., Dittus, P. J., & Gordon, V. V. (1998). Parent-adolescent congruency in reports of adolescent sexual behavior and in communications about sexual behavior. *Child Development, 69*, 247–261.

Jacket, L. S., & Ruble, D. N. (1992). Changes in the marital relationship after the first baby is born: Predicting the impact of expectancy disconfirmation. *Journal of Personality & Social Psychology, 62*, 944–957.

Jackson, D. D. (1996). People say, you poor thing, and I'm thinking, I have four healthy kids. *Smithsonian, 27*(6), 30–39.

Jackson, P. (1986). *The practice of teaching*. Chicago: University of Chicago Press.

Jackson, M. F., Barth, J. M., Powell, N., & Lochman, J. E. (2006). Classroom contextual effects of race on children's peer nominations. *Child Development, 77*(5), 1325–1337.

Jacob, B. A. (2002). Where the boys aren't: Noncognitive skills, returns to school and the gender gap in higher education. *Economics of Education Review, 21*, 589–598.

Jacob, V., Chattopadhyay, S. K., Hopkins, D. P., Morgan, J. M., Pitan, A. A., Clymer, J. M., & Community Preventive Services Task Force. (2016). Increasing coverage of appropriate vaccinations: A community guide systematic economic review. *American Journal of Preventive Medicine, 50*(6), 797–808.

Jacobvitz, D. B., & Bush, N. F. (1996). Reconstructions of family relationships: Parent-child alliances, personal distress, and self-esteem. *Developmental Psychology, 32*, 732–743.

Jadack, R., Hyde, J., Moore, C., & Keller, M. (1995). Moral reasoning about sexually transmitted diseases. *Child Development, 66*, 167–177.

Jaffee, S. R., Bowes, L., Ouellet-Morin, I., Fisher, H. L., Moffitt, T. E., Merrick, M. T., & Arseneault, L. (2013). Safe, stable, nurturing relationships break the intergenerational cycle of abuse: A prospective nationally representative cohort of children in the United Kingdom. *Journal of Adolescent Health, 53*(4), S4–S10.

Jaffee, S. R., Caspi, A., Moffitt, T. E., Polo-Tomas, M., Price, T. S., & Taylor, A. (2004). The limits of child effects: Evidence for genetically mediated child effects on corporal punishment but not on physical maltreatment. *Developmental Psychology, 40*(6), 1047.

Jaggars, S. S., & Bailey, T. (2010). Effectiveness of fully online courses for college students: Response to a Department of Education meta-analysis. Community College Research Center, Columbia University.

Jain, A., Belsky, J., & Crnic, K. (1996). Beyond fathering behaviors: Types of dads. *Journal of Family Psychology, 10*, 431–442.

James, J., Ellis, B. J., Schlomer, G. L., & Garber, J. (2012). Sex-specific pathways to early puberty, sexual debut, and sexual risk taking: Tests of an integrated evolutionary–developmental model. *Developmental Psychology, 48*(3), 687–02.

James, T., & Countryman, J. (2012). Psychiatric effects of military deployment on children and families: The use of play therapy for assessment and treatment. *Innovations in Clinical Neuroscience, 9*(2), 16.

James, W. (1890). *The principles of psychology*. Boston: Henry Holt.

Jansson, U. B., Hanson, M., Sillén, U., & Hellström, A. L. (2005). Voiding pattern and acquisition of bladder control from birth to age 6 years—A longitudinal study. *Journal of Urology, 174*(1), 289–293.

Jensen, L. A., & Arnett, J. J. (2012). Going global: New pathways for adolescents and emerging adults in a changing world. *Journal of Social Issues, 68*(3), 473–492.

Jetter, K. M., & Cassady, D. L. (2006). The availability and cost of healthier food alternatives. *American Journal of Preventive Medicine, 30*(1), 38–44.

Jimenez, R., Garcia, G., & Pearson, D. (1995). Three children, two languages, and strategic reading: Case studies in bilingual/monolingual reading. *American Educational Research Journal, 32*(1), 67–97.

Jin, M. K., Jacobvitz, D., Hazen, N., & Jung, S. H. (2012). Maternal sensitivity and infant attachment security in Korea: Cross-cultural validation of the Strange Situation. *Attachment & Human Development, 14*(1), 33–44.

Johnson, D., & Johnson, P. (1994). *Learning together and alone* (4th ed.). Boston: Allyn and Bacon.

Johnson, D. W., Johnson, R. T., & Maruyama, G. (1984). Goal interdependence and interpersonal attraction in heterogeneous classrooms: A meta-analysis. In N. Miller, & M. B. Brewer (Eds.), *Groups in contact: The psychology of desegregation*. New York, NY: Academic Press.

Johnson, M. (1995). Patriarchal terrorism and common couple violence: Two forms of violence against women. *Journal of Marriage and the Family, 57*, 283–295.

Johnson, R. (Ed.). (1995). *African-American voices: African-American health educators speak out*. New York, NY: National League for Nursing.

Johnson, R., & Swain, M. (Eds.). (1997). *Immersion education: International perspectives*. New York, NY: Cambridge University Press.

Johnson, W. (2010). Understanding the genetics of intelligence: Can height help? Can corn oil? *Current Directions in Psychological Science, 19,* 177–182.

Johnston, L., O'Malley, P., & Bachman, J. (1992). *Drug use among American high school students, college students and other young adults: National trends through 1991.* Rockville, MD: National Institute on Drug Abuse.

Johnston, L. D., O'Malley, P. M., Bachman, J. G., Schulenberg, J. E., & Miech, R. A. (2014). *Monitoring the future—National survey results on drug use, 1975–2013: Volume I, Secondary school students.* Ann Arbor, MI: Institute for Social Research, The University of Michigan.

Johnston, L. D., O'Malley, P. M., Bachman, J. G., & Schulenberg, J. E. (2012). *Monitoring the future—National results on adolescent drug use: Overview of key findings, 2011.* Ann Arbor, MI: Institute for Social Research, The University of Michigan.

Jose, P. E., & Bellamy, M. A. (2011). Relationships of parents' theories of intelligence with children's persistence/learned helplessness: A cross-cultural comparison. *Journal of Cross-Cultural Psychology,* 1–19

Joseph, K. S., Allen, A. C., Dodds, L., Turner, L. A., Scott, H., & Liston, R. (2005). The perinatal effects of delayed childbearing. *Obstetrics & Gynecology, 105,* 1410–1418.

Joshi, M., & MacLean, M. (1994). Indian and English children's understanding of the distinction between real and apparent emotion. *Child Development, 65,* 1372–1384.

Josselson, R. (1977). Adolescence in the life cycle. *Journal of Youth and Adolescence, 6*(1), 103–105.

Josselson, R. (1980). Ego development in adolescence. In J. Adelson (Ed.), *Handbook of adolescent psychology.* New York, NY: Wiley.

Joung, I. M. A., Stronks, K., van de Mheen, H., van Poppel, F. W. A., van der Meer, J. B. W., & Mackenbach, J. P. (1997). The contribution of intermediary factors to marital status differences in self-reported health. *Journal of Marriage and the Family, 59,* 476–490.

Julian, T. W., & McKenry, P. C. (1993). Mediators of male violence toward female intimates. *Journal of Family Violence, 8*(1), 39–56.

Junaid, K. A., & Fellowes, S. (2006). Gender differences in the attainment of motor skills on the movement assessment battery for children. *Physical & Occupational Therapy in Pediatrics, 26*(1–2), 5–11.

Jung, C. G. (1933). *Modern man in search of a soul* (W. S. Dell & C. F. Baynes, Trans.). New York, NY: Harcourt Brace Jovanovich.

K

Kaestle, C. E., & Halpern, C. T. (2005). Sexual activity among adolescents in romantic relationships with friends, acquaintances, or strangers. *Archives of Pediatrics & Adolescent Medicine. 159*(9), 849–853.

Kagan, J. (1998). *The Gale encyclopedia of childhood and adolescence: Puberty* (pp. 521–523). Detroit: Gale Research.

Kagan, J., Arcus, D., Snidman, N., Feng, W. Y., Handler, J., & Greene, S. (1995). Reactivity in infants: A cross-national comparison. *Developmental Psychology, 30,* 342–345.

Kagan, J., & Snidman, N. (1991). Temperamental factors in human development. *American Psychologist, 46,* 856–862.

Kagan, S. (1983). Children, families, and government: Preparing for the 21st century. In E. Zigler, S. Kagan, & E. Klugman (Eds.), *Children, families, and government* (p. 117–131). New York, NY: Cambridge University Press.

Kaijura, H., Cowart, B. J., & Beauchamp, G. K. (1992). Early developmental change in bitter taste responses in human infants. *Developmental Psychobiology, 25,* 375–386.

Kaitz, M., Meschulach-Sarfaty, O., Auerbach, J., & Eidelman, A. (1988). A re-examination of newborns' ability to imitate facial expressions. *Developmental Psychology, 24,* 3–7.

Kalverboer, A., Hopkins, B., & Geuze, R. (1993). *Motor development in early infancy and late childhood.* New York, NY: Cambridge University Press.

Kamii, C. (1994). *Young children continue to reinvent arithmetic* (3rd ed.), New York, NY: Teachers College Press.

Kantor, G. K., & Straus, M. A. (1990). The "drunken bum" theory of wife beating. In M. A. Straus & R. J. Gelles, with C. Smith (Eds.), *Physical violence in American families: Risk factors and adaptations to violence in 8,145 families* (pp. 203–224). New Brunswick, NJ: Transaction.

Kao, G. (1995). Asian-Americans as model minorities? A look at their academic performance. *American Journal of Education, 103,* 121–159.

Kaplan, H. (1979). *Disorders of sexual desire.* New York, NY: Brunner/Mazel.

Kaplan, K., & Wadden, T. (1986). Childhood obesity and self-esteem. *Journal of Pediatrics, 109,* 367–370.

Kaplan, L. (1995). *No voice is ever wholly lost.* New York, NY: Simon & Schuster.

Karam, R. G., Breda, V., Picon, F. A., Rovaris, D. L., Victor, M. M., Salgado, C. A. I., . . . & Caye, A. (2015). Persistence and remission of ADHD during adulthood: A 7-year clinical follow-up study. *Psychological Medicine, 45*(10), 2045–2056.

Karoly, L. A. (2009). The future at work: Labor-market realities and the transition to adulthood. In I. Schoon, & R. K. Silbersen (Eds.), *Transitions from school to work: Globalization, individualization, and patterns of diversity* (pp. 352–384). Cambridge, UK: Cambridge Books Online.

Karpov, Y. V., & Haywood, H. C. (1998). Two ways to elaborate Vygotsky's concept of mediation: Implications for instruction. *American Psychologist, 53,* 27–36.

Kashani, I. A., Langer, R. D., Criqui, M. H., Nader, P. R., Rupp, J., Sallis, J. F., & Houghton, R. (1991). Effects of parental behavior modification on children's cardiovascular risks. *Annals of the New York, NY: Academy of Sciences, 623,* 447–449.

Kates, E. (1995). Escaping poverty: The promise of higher education. *Social Policy Report 9*(1). Ann Arbor, MI: Society for Research on Child Development.

Katz-Wise, S. L., Priess, H. A., & Hyde, J. S. (2010). Gender-role attitudes and behavior across the transition to parenthood. *Developmental Psychology, 46*(1), 18–28.

Kaufman, M. (2008). Adolescent sexual orientation. *Paediatrics & Child Health, 13*(7), 619–623.

Kavanaugh, R. D., & Engel, S. (1998). The development of pretense and narrative in early childhood. In O. Saracho, B. Spodek, et al. (Eds.), *Multiple perspectives on play in early childhood education.* SUNY series, *Early Childhood Education: Inquiries and Insights* (pp. 80–99). Albany, NY: State University of New York Press.

Kawaguchi, D., & Miyazaki, J. (2009). Working mothers and sons' preferences regarding female labor supply: Direct evidence from stated preferences. *Journal of Population Economics, 22*(1), 115–130.

Kazdin, A. E. (1994). *Behavior modification in applied settings* (5th ed.), Pacific Grove, CA Brooks/Cole.

Keating, D. (2011). Cognitive and brain development. In R. Learner, & L. Steinberg (Eds.), *Handbook of adolescent psychology* (2nd ed.). New York, NY: Wiley.

Keating, D., & Sasse, D. (1996). Cognitive socialization in adolescence: Critical period for a critical habit of mind. In G. Adams, R. Montemayor, & T. Gullotta (Eds.), *Psychosocial development during adolescence* (pp. 232–258). Thousand Oaks, CA: Sage.

Keefe, J., & Walberg, H. (Eds.) (1992). *Teaching for thinking.* Reston, VA: National Association of Secondary School Principals.

Keller, M., & Wood, P. (1989). Development of friendship reasoning: A study of interindividual differences and intraindividual change. *Developmental Psychology, 25,* 820–826.

Kellman, P. J., & Arterberry, M. E. (2006). Infant visual perception. In W. Damon, & R. M. Lerner (Eds.), *Handbook of child psychology: Vol. 2. Cognition,*

perception, and language (6th ed.). Hoboken, NJ: Wiley.

Kelly, M. (2009). Women's voluntary childlessness: A radical rejection of motherhood? *WSQ: Women's Studies Quarterly, 37*(2), 157–172.

Kelly, M. P., Strassberg, D. S., & Kircher, J. R. (1990). Attitudinal and experiential correlates of anorgasmia. *Archives of Sexual Behavior, 19,* 165–177.

Kendall-Tackett, K. A., Williams, L. M., & Finkelhor, D. (1993). Impact of sexual abuse on children: A review and synthesis of recent empirical studies. *Psychological Bulletin, 113,* 164–180.

Kendler, H., & Kendler, T. (1962). Vertical and horizontal processes in problem solving. *Psychological Review, 69,* 1–16.

Kenkel, W. F., & Gage, B. A. (1983). The restricted and gender-typed occupational aspirations of young women: Can they be modified? *Family Relations: Journal of Applied Family & Child Studies, 32*(1) 129–138.

Kenney, G., Alker, J., Anderson, N., McMorrow, S., Long, S., Wissoker, D., . . . & Brooks, T. (2014). *A first look at children's health insurance coverage under the ACA in 2014.* Health Reform Monitoring Survey. Retrieved from http://hrms.urban.org/briefs/Childrens-Health-Insurance-Coverage-under-the-ACA-in-2014.html

Kermoian, R., & Campos, J. (1988). Locomotor experience: A facilitator of spatial cognitive development. *Child Development, 59,* 908–917.

Kerns, K. A., & Brumariu, L. E. (2014). Is insecure parent–child attachment a risk factor for the development of anxiety in childhood or adolescence? *Child development perspectives, 8*(1), 12–17.

Kerpelman, J. L., Pittman, J. F., Saint-Eloi Cadely, H., Tuggle, F. J., Marinda Harrell-Levy, M. K., & Adler-Baeder, F. M. (2012). Identity and intimacy during adolescence: Connections among identity styles, romantic attachment and identity commitment. *Journal of Adolescence, 35,* 1427–1439.

Kerr, M., Lambert, W. W., & Bern, D. J. (1996). Life course sequel of childhood shyness in Sweden: Comparison with the United States. *Developmental Psychology, 32,* 1100–1105.

Kerr, M., Lambert, W. W., Stattin, H., & Klackenberg-Larsson, I. (1994). Stability of inhibition in a Swedish longitudinal sample. *Child Development, 65,* 138–146.

Kim, J. Y., McHale, S. M., Crouter, A. C., & Osgood, D. W. (2007). Longitudinal linkages between sibling relationships and adjustment from middle childhood through adolescence. *Developmental Psychology, 43*(4), 960.

Kim, S. K., & Jang, Y. (2010). The effect of children's temperament, parenting behavior and parenting stress on preschool children's prosocial behavior. *Korean Journal of Community Living Science, 21*(4), 605–618.

Kindermann, T. (1993). Natural peer groups as contexts for individual development: The case of children's motivation in school. *Developmental Psychology, 29,* 979–977.

King, P., & Kitchener, K. (1994). *Developing reflective judgment.* San Francisco: Jossey-Bass.

King, P. M., & Kitchener, K. S. (2004). Reflective judgment: Theory and research on the development of epistemic assumptions through adulthood. *Educational Psychologist, 39*(1), 5–18.

King, P. M., & Kitchener, K. S. (2016). Cognitive development in the emerging adult: The emergence of complex cognitive skills. In J. J. Arnett (Ed.), *The Oxford handbook of emerging adulthood* (pp. 105–125). New York, NY: Oxford University Press.

King, V. (2006). The antecedents and consequences of adolescents' relationships with stepfathers and nonresident fathers. *Journal of Marriage and Family, 68*(4), 910–928.

King, V. (2007). When children have two mothers: Relationships with nonresident mothers, stepmothers, and fathers. *Journal of Marriage and Family, 69*(5), 1178–1193.

Kinsey, A. C., Pomeroy, W. B., & Martin, C. E. (1948). *Sexual behavior in the human male.* Philadelphia: Saunders.

Kirby, D. (2007). *A matrix of risk and protective factors affecting teen sexual behavior, pregnancy, childbearing, and sexually transmitted diseases.* Retrieved from http://thenationalcampaign.org/resource/matrix-risk-and-protective-factors

Kirby, D., & Laris, B. A. (2009). Effective curriculum-based sex and STD/HIV education programs for adolescents. *Child Development Perspectives, 3*(1), 21–29.

Kirschner, D. (1997). The situated development of logic in infancy: A case study. In D. Kirschner, & J. Whitson (Eds.). *Situated cognition: Social, semiotic, and psychological perspectives* (pp. 83–96). Mahwah, NJ: Erlbaum.

Kirschner, D., & Whitson, J. (Eds.) (1997). *Situated cognition: Social, semiotic, and psychological perspectives.* Mahwah, NJ: Erlbaum.

Kirsh, S. J. (2006). Cartoon violence and aggression in youth. *Aggression and Violent Behavior, 11*(6), 547–557.

Kisilevsky, B. S., & Muir, D. W. (1984). Neonatal habituation and dishabituation to tactile stimulation during sleep. *Developmental Psychology, 20*, 367–373.

Kisilevsky, B. S., Muir, D. W., & Low, J. A. (1992). Maturation of human fetal responses to vibroacoustic stimulation. *Child Development, 63*, 1497–1508.

Kitchener, K. S., & King, P. M. (1990). The reflective judgment model: Ten years of research. In M. Common, C. Armon, L. Kohlberg, F. Richards, T. Grotzer, & J. Sinnott (Eds.), *Adult development: Models and methods in the study of adolescent and adult thought.* New York, NY: Praeger.

Kite, M. E., Deaux, K., & Haines, E. L. (2008). Gender stereotypes. In F. Denmark, & M. A. Pauldi (Eds.), *Psychology of women: A handbook of issues and theories* (pp. 205–236). Westport, CT: Greenwood Publishing Group.

Kitzinger, J. (1997). Who are you kidding? Children, power and the struggle against sexual abuse. In A. James, & A. Prout (Eds.), *Constructing and reconstructing childhood* (pp. 165–189). London, UK: Falmer.

Klahr, D. (1989). Information processing approaches. In R. Vasta (Ed.), *Annals of child development: Vol. 6. Six theories of child development* (pp. 133–187). Greenwich, CT: JAI Press.

Klahr, D., Triona, L. M., & Williams, C. (2007). Hands on what? The relative effectiveness of physical versus virtual materials in an engineering design project by middle school children. *Journal of Research in Science Teaching, 44*(1), 183–203.

Klein, H. (1995). Urban Appalachian children in northern schools: A study in diversity. *Young Children, 50*(3), 10–16.

Kleinsorge, C., & Covitz, L. M. (2012). Impact of divorce on children: Developmental considerations. *Pediatrics in Review, 33*(4), 147–155.

Kleitman, N., & Engelmann, T. G. (1953). Sleep characteristics of infants. *Journal of Applied Physiology, 6*(5), 269–282.

Klimes-Dougan, B., & Kistner, J. (1990). Physically abused preschoolers' responses to peers' distress. *Developmental Psychology, 26*, 599–602.

Klinnert, M. D., Emde, R. N., Butterfield, P., & Campos, J. J. (1986). Social referencing: The infant's use of emotional signals from a friendly adult with mother present. *Developmental Psychology, 22*, 427–432.

Knafo, A., & Schwartz, S. H. (2003). Parenting and adolescents' accuracy in perceiving parental values. *Child Development, 74*(2), 595–611.

Knox, G. W. (1991). *An introduction to gangs.* Berrien Springs, MI: Vande Vere.

Koch, P. B. (1988). The relationship of first intercourse to later sexual functioning concerns of adolescents. *Journal of Adolescent Research, 3*, 345–362.

Kochanska, C., Casey, R. J., & Fukumoto, A. (1995). Toddlers' sensitivity to standard violations. *Child Development, 66*, 643–656.

Kochanska, G. (1992). Children's interpersonal influence with mothers and peers. *Developmental Psychology, 28*, 491–499.

Kochanska G. (1997). Mutually responsive orientation between mothers and their young children: Implications for early socialization. *Child Development, 68*, 94–112.

Kochanska, G., Coy, K. C., Tjebkes, T. L., & Husarek, S. J. (1998). Individual differences in emotionality in infancy. *Child Development, 64*, 375–390.

Kohlberg, L. (1958). *The development of modes of thinking and choices in years 10 to 16.* (Doctoral Dissertation), University of Chicago, Chicago, IL.

Kohlberg, L. (1963). The development of children's orientations toward a moral order: I. Sequence in the development of moral thought. *Vita Humana, 6*, 11–33.

Kohlberg, L., & Hersh, R. H. (1977). Moral development: A review of the theory. *Theory Into Practice, 16*, 53–61.

Kohlberg, L., Levine, C., & Hewer, A. (1983). *Moral stages: A current formulation and a response to critics.* New York, NY: Karger.

Kohler, P. K., Manhart, L. E., & Lafferty, W. E. (2008). Abstinence-only and comprehensive sex education and the initiation of sexual activity and teen pregnancy. *Journal of Adolescent Health, 42*(4), 344–351.

Kohn, M. L. (1969). *Class and conformity: A study in values,* Homewood, IL: Dorsey Press.

Kohn, M. L., Slomczynski, K. M., & Schoenbach, C. (1986). Social stratification and the transmission of values in the family: A cross-national assessment. *Sociological Forum, 1*, 73–102.

Kokko, K., Pulkkinen, L., & Mesiäinen, P. (2009). Timing of parenthood in relation to other life transitions and adult social functioning. *International Journal of Behavioral Development*, 1–10.

Kolak, A. M., & Volling, B. L. (2010). Sibling jealousy in early childhood: Longitudinal links to sibling relationship quality. *Infant and Child Development, 20*, 213–226.

Kool, R., & Lawver, T. (2010). Play therapy: Considerations and applications for the practitioner. *Psychiatry, 7*(10), 19–24.

Kopp, C. (1982). Antecedents of self-regulation: A developmental perspective. *Developmental Psychology, 18*, 199–214.

Kopp, C. (1989). Regulation of distress and negative emotions: A developmental view. *Developmental Psychology, 25*, 343–354.

Koralek, D., Colker, L., & Dodge, D. (1993). *The what, why, and how of high-quality early childhood education: A guide for on-site supervision.* Washington, DC: National Association for the Education of Young Children.

Korbin, J. E. (Ed.). (1981). *Child abuse and neglect: Cross-cultural perspectives.* Berkeley, CA: University of California Press.

Korbin, J. E. (1987). Child abuse and neglect: The cultural context. In R. E. Heifer & R. S. Kemp (Eds.), *The battered child* (4th ed.). Chicago: University of Chicago Press.

Korbin, J. E. (1991). Cross-cultural perspectives and research dilutions for the 21st century. *Child Abuse and Neglect, 15*, 67–77.

Kordi, A., & Baharudin, R. (2010). Parenting attitude and style and its effect on children's school achievements. *International Journal of Psychological Studies, 2*(2), 217.

Koretz, D. (2008). The pending reauthorization of NCLB: An opportunity to rethink the basic strategy. In G. L. Sunderman (Ed.), *Holding NCLB accountable: Achieving accountability, equity, and school reform.* Thousand Oaks, CA: Corwin Press.

Kosciw, J. G., Greytak, E. A., Diaz, E. M., & Bartkiewicz, M. J. (2010). *The 2009 National School Climate Survey: The experiences of lesbian, gay, bisexual and transgender youth in our nation's schools.* New York, NY: Gay, Lesbian Straight Education Network.

Koss, M. P., Heise, L., & Russo, N. F. (1994). The global health burden of rape. *Psychology of Women Quarterly, 18*, 509–537.

Kotelchuck, M. (1976). The infant's relationship to the father: Experimental evidence. In M. E. Lamb (Ed.), *The role of the father in child development,* New York, NY: Wiley.

Kotloff, L. (1993). Fostering cooperative group spirit and individuality: Examples from a Japanese preschool. *Young Children, 48*(3), 17–24.

Kovacs, D. M., Parker, J. G., & Hoffman, L. W. (1996). Behavioral, affective and social correlates of involvement in cross-sex friendships in elementary school. *Child Development, 67*, 2269–2286.

Kozlowski, L. T., Wilkinson, D. A., Skinner, W., Kent, C., Franklin, T., & Pope, M. (1989). Comparing tobacco cigarette dependence with other drug dependencies: Greater or equal "difficulty quitting" and "urges to use," but less "pleasure" from cigarettes. *Journal of the American Medical Association, 261*, 898–901.

Kozol, J. (1991). *Savage inequalities: Children in America's schools,* New York, NY: Crown.

Kozol, J. (1995). *Amazing grace: The lives of children and the conscience of the nation,* New York, NY: Crown.

Kramer, D. A. (1989). Development of an awareness of contradiction across the life span and the question of post formal operations. In M. L. Commons, J. D. Sinnott, F. A. Richards, & C. Armon (Eds.), *Adult development: Vol. 1. Comparisons and applications of developmental models* (pp. 133–159). New York, NY: Praeger.

Krans, E. E., & Davis, M. M. (2014). Strong start for mothers and newborns: Implications for prenatal care delivery. *Current Opinion in Obstetrics & Gynecology, 26*(6), 511–515.

Kreider, R. M., & Ellis, R. (2001). *Number, timing, and duration of marriages and divorces: 2009.* US Census Bureau. Retrieved from http://www.census.gov/prod/2011pubs/p70-125.pdf

Kreider, R. M., & Ellis, R. (2011). Living arrangements of children: 2009. *Current population reports* (pp. 70–126). Washington, DC: U.S. Census Bureau.

Krieger, N., Waterman, P. D., Hartman, C., Bates, L. M., Stoddard, A. M., Quinn, M. M., . . . & Barbeau, E. M. (2006). Social hazards on the job: Workplace abuse, sexual harassment, and racial discrimination—A study of black, Latino, and white low-income women and men workers in the United States. *International Journal of Health Services, 36*(1), 51–85.

Kroeger, R. A., & Smock, P. J. (2014). Cohabitation: Recent research and implications. In J. Treas, J. Scott, & M. Richards (Eds.), *The Wiley-Blackwell companion to the sociology of families* (pp. 217–235). Hoboken, NJ: Wiley.

Kroger, J. (1995). The differentiation of "firm" and "developmental" foreclosure identity statuses: A longitudinal study. *Journal of Adolescent Research, 10*, 317–337.

Kroger, J. (2007). *Identity development: Adolescence through adulthood.* Thousand Oaks: Sage Publications.

Kroger, J., & Green, K. E. (1996). Events associated with identity status change. *Journal of Adolescence, 19*(5), 477–491.

Kroger, J., & Marcia, J. E. (2011). The identity statuses: Origins, meanings, and interpretations. In S. J., Schwartz, K., Luyczk, & V. L. Vignoles (Eds.), *Handbook of identity theory and research.* New York, NY: Springer.

Kuczynski, L., & Kochanska, G. (1995). Function and content of maternal demands: Developmental significance of early demands for competent action. *Child Development, 66*, 616–628.

Kuhn, D. (2008). Formal operations from a twenty-first century perspective. *Human Development, 51* (Special Issue: Celebrating a Legacy of Theory with New Directions for Research on Human Development), 48–55.

Kuhn, D. (2009). Adolescent thinking. In R. M. Lerner & L. Steinberg (Eds.), *Handbook of adolescent psychology, Vol. 1: Individual bases of adolescent development* (3rd ed., pp. 152–186). Hoboken, NJ: Wiley.

Kulkarni, A. D., Jamieson, D. J., Jones Jr, H. W., Kissin, D. M., Gallo, M. F., Macaluso, M., & Adashi, E. Y. (2013). Fertility treatments and multiple births in the United States. *New England Journal of Medicine, 369*(23), 2218–2225

Kunitz, S. J., & Levy, J. E. (1994). *Drinking careers: A twenty-five year study of three Navajo populations,* New Haven, CT: Yale University Press.

Kurdek, L. A. (1991). The relations between reported well-being and divorce history, availability of a proximate adult, and gender. *Journal of Marriage and the Family, 53,* 71–78.

Kurdek, L. A. (1994). The nature and correlates of relationship quality in gay, lesbian, and heterosexual cohabiting couples: A test of the individual difference, interdependence, and discrepancy models. In B. Greene & G. M. Herek (Eds.), *Lesbian and gay psychology: Theory, research, and clinical applications* (pp. 133–155). Thousand Oaks, CA: Sage.

Kurdek, L. A. (2005). What do we know about gay and lesbian couples? *Current Direction in Psychological Science, 14,* 251–254. doi: 10.1111/j.0963-7214.2005.00375.x

Kutner, L. (1989, March 16). Parent and child: Responding to aggressive behavior. *New York Times,* p. C–1.

L

Labouvie-Vief, G. (1985). Intelligence and cognition. In J. E. Birren & K. W. Schaie (Eds.), *Handbook of the psychology of aging* (2nd ed., pp. 500–539). New York, NY: Van Nostrand Reinhold.

Labouvie-Vief, G. (1992). A neo-Piagetian perspective on adult cognitive development. In R. J. Sternberg & C. A. Berg (Eds.), *Intellectual development,* New York, NY: Cambridge University Press.

Lackey, C., & Williams, K. R. (1995). Social bonding and the cessation of partner violence across generations. *Journal of Marriage and the Family, 57,* 295–305.

LaCroix, A. Z., & Haynes, S. G. (1987). Gender differences in health effects of workplace. In R. C. Barnett, L. Biener, & G. K. Baruch (Eds.), *Gender and stress* (pp. 96–121). New York, NY: The Free Press.

Ladd, G. W., & Hart, C. H. (1992). Creating informal play opportunities: Are parents' and preschoolers' initiations related to children's competence with peers? *Developmental Psychology, 28,* 1179–1187.

Lakoff, G. (1994). What is a conceptual system? In W. Overton & D. Palermo (Eds.), *The nature and ontogenesis of meaning* (pp. 41–90). Hillsdale, NJ: Erlbaum.

La Leche League International. (1991). *The womanly art of breastfeeding* (5th ed.), New York, NY: Plume Books.

Lamaze, F. (1970). *Painless childbirth: Psychoprophylactic method.* Chicago: Henry Regnery.

Lamb, M. (1977a). The development of mother-infant and father-infant attachments in the second year of life. *Developmental Psychology, 13,* 637–648.

Lamb, M. (1977b). Father-infant and mother-infant interactions in the first year of life. *Child Development, 48,* 167–181.

Lamb, M., & Roopnarine, J. (1979). Peer influences on sex-role development in preschoolers. *Child Development, 50,* 1219–1222.

Lamb, M. E. (1997). The development of father-infant relationships. In Michael E. Lamb (Ed.), *The role of the father in child development* (3rd ed., pp. 104–120). New York, NY: Wiley.

Lamb, M. E., Keterlinus, R. D., & Fracasso, M. P. (1992). Parent-child relationships. In M. H. Bornstein & M. E. Lamb (Eds.), *Developmental psychology: An advanced textbook* (pp. 465–518). Hillsdale, NJ: Erlbaum.

Lamb, M. E., & Lewis, C. (2003). Fathers' influences on children's development: The evidence from two-parent families. *European Journal of Psychology of Education, 18,* 211–228.

Lamborn, S. D., Dornbusch, S. M., & Steinberg, L. (1996). Ethnicity and community context as moderators of the relations between family decision making and adolescent adjustment. *Child Development, 67,* 383–301.

Lamke, L. K. (1982a). Adjustment and sex-role orientation. *Journal of Youth and Adolescence, 11,* 247–259.

Lamke, L. K. (1982b). The impact of sex-role orientation on self-esteem in early adolescence. *Child Development, 53,* 1530–1535.

Lamport, M. A. (1993). Student-faculty informal interaction and the effect on college student outcomes: A review of the literature. *Adolescence, 28*(112), 971–990.

Lansford, J. E. (2009). Parental Divorce and Children's Adjustment. *Perspectives on Psychological Science, 4*(2), 140–152.

Lanz, M., & Tagliabue, S. (2007). Do I really need someone in order to become an adult? Romantic relationships during emerging adulthood in Italy. *Journal of Adolescent Research, 22*(5), 531–549.

Lapsley, D. (1991). Egocentrism theory and the "new look" at the imaginary audience and personal fable. In R. Lerner, A. Petersen, & J. Brooks-Gunn (Eds.), *Encyclopedia of adolescence: Vol 1* (pp. 281–286). New York, NY: Garland.

LaRossa, R. (1992). Fatherhood and social change. In M. S. Kimmel & M. A. Messner (Eds.), *Men's lives* (2nd ed., pp. 521–535). New York, NY: Macmillan.

Larrabee, M. (1993). *An ethic of care: Feminist and Interdisciplinary perspectives.* New York, NY: Routledge.

Larson, R. W., & Ham, M. (1993). Stress and "storm and stress" in early adolescence: The relationship of negative events with dysphoric affect. *Developmental Psychology, 29,* 130–140.

Larson, R. W., & Richards, M. H. (1994). *Divergent realities: The emotional lives of mothers, fathers and adolescents.* New York, NY: Basic Books.

Larson, R. W. (1997). The emergence of solitude as a constructive domain of experience in early adolescence. *Child Development, 68,* 80–93.

Larson, R. W., & Richards, M. H. (1994). *Emergent Realities.* New York, NY: Basic Books.

Larson, R. W., Richards, M. H., Moneta, G., Holmbeck, G., & Duckett, E. (1996). Changes in adolescents' daily interaction with their families from ages 10–18: Disengagement and transformation. *Developmental Psychology, 32,* 744–54.

Larzelere, R. E. (1986). Moderate spanking: Model or deterrent of children's aggression in the family? *Journal of Family Violence, 1,* 27–37.

Lasley, J. R. (1992). Age, social context, and street gang membership. *Youth and Society, 23,* 434–451.

Laughlin, L. (2013). Who's minding the kids? Child care arrangements: Spring 2011. *Current population reports* (pp. 70–135). Washington, DC: U.S. Census Bureau.

Lave, J. (1997). The culture of acquisition and the practice of understanding. In D. Kirschner & J. Whitson (Eds.), *Situated cognition: Social, semiotic, and psychological perspectives* (pp. 17–36). Mahwah, NJ: Erlbaum.

Lavner, J. A., & Bradbury, T. N. (2010). Patterns of change in marital satisfaction over the newlywed years. *Journal of Marriage and Family, 72*(5), 1171–1187.

Lawrence, E., Jeglic, E. L., Matthews, L. T., & Pepper, C. M. (2006). Gender differences in grief reactions following the death of a parent. *OMEGA—Journal of Death and Dying, 52,* 323–337.

Lawrence, E., Rothman, A. D., Cobb, R. J., Rothman, M. T., & Bradbury, T. N. (2008). Marital satisfaction across the transition to parenthood. *Journal of Family Psychology, 22*(1), 41.

Lawson, A., & Rhode, D. L. (1993). *The Politics of Pregnancy: Adolescent Sexuality and Public Policy,* New Haven, CT: Yale University Press.

Lawson A. E., & Wollman, W. T. (2003). Encouraging the transition from concrete to formal operations. An experiment. *Journal of Research in Science Teaching, 40*(Supplemental), S33–S50.

Laybourn, A. (1990). Only children in Britain: Popular stereotype and research evidence. *Children and Society, 4,* 386–400.

Lazarus, R. S. (1993). From psychological stress to the emotions: A history of changing outlooks. *Annual Review of Psychology, 44,* 1–21.

Leadbetter, B. (1991). Relativistic thinking in adolescence. In R. Lerner, A. Petersen, & J. Brooks-Gunn (Eds.), *Encyclopedia of adolescence: Vol. 1* (pp. 921–925). New York, NY: Garland.

Leaper, C. (Ed.). (1994). *Childhood gender segregation: Causes and consequences* (pp. 7–18). San Francisco: Jossey-Bass.

Leaper, C., Anderson, K. J., & Sanders, P. (1998). Moderators of gender effects on parents' talk to their children: A meta-analysis. *Developmental Psychology, 34,* 3–27.

Leary, W. E. (1995, January 31). Sickle cell trial called success, halted early. *The New York Times,* p. C–1.

Leckman, J., & Mayes, L. C. (1998). Understanding developmental psychopathology: How useful are evolutionary concepts? *Journal of the American Academy of Child and Adolescent Psychiatry, 37,* 1011–1021.

Lee, C. Y. S., & Doherty, W. J. (2007). Marital satisfaction and father involvement during the transition to parenthood. *Fathering, 5*(2), 75.

Lee, F. R. (1995, May 9). For women with AIDS, anguish of having babies. *The New York Times,* pp. A1–B6.

Lee, J. S., & Bowen, N. K. (2006). Parent involvement, cultural capital, and the achievement gap among elementary school children. *American Educational Research Journal, 43*(2), 193–218.

Lee, S. J., Bartolic, S., & Vandewater, E. A. (2009). Predicting children's media use in the USA: Differences in cross-sectional and longitudinal analysis. *British Journal of Developmental Psychology, 27*(1), 123–143.

Lee, V. E., Mackie-Lewis, C., & Marks, H. M. (1993). Persistence to the baccalaureate degree for students who transfer from community college. *American Journal of Education, 102*(1), 80–14.

Lee, V., Croninger, R., Linn, E., & Chen, X. (1996). The culture of sexual harassment in secondary schools. *American Educational Research Journal, 33*(2), 383–418.

Lee, Y. J., & Aytac, I. A. (1998). Intergenerational financial support among whites, African Americans, and Latinos. *Journal of Marriage and the Family, 60,* 426–441.

Leeies, M., Pagura, J., Sareen, J., & Bolton, J. M. (2010). The use of alcohol and drugs to self-medicate symptoms of posttraumatic stress disorder. *Depression and Anxiety, 27*(8), 731–736.

Lehman, D. R., & Nisbett, R. E. (1990). A longitudinal study of the effects of undergraduate training on reasoning. *Developmental Psychology, 26,* 952–960.

Leidy, M. S., Guerra, N. G., & Toro, R. I. (2012). Positive parenting, family cohesion, and child social competence among immigrant Latino families. *Journal of Latina/o Psychology, 1,* 3–13.

Leigh, B. C. (1989). Reasons for having sex: Gender, sexual orientation, and relationship to sexual behavior. *Journal of Sex Research, 26,* 199–209.

Leigh, B. C., & Stall, R. (1993). Substance use and risky sexual behavior for exposure to HIV: Issues of methodology, interpretation, and prevention. *American Psychologist, 10,* 1035–1045.

Leming, M. R., & Dickinson, G. E. (1994). *Dying, death, and bereavement* (3rd ed.). New York, NY: Holt, Rinehart & Winston.

Leon, A. S., & Fox, S. M., III. (1981). Physical fitness. In E. L. Wynder (Ed.), *The book of health* (pp. 283–341). New York, NY: Franklin Watts.

Leonard, L. G., & Denton, J. (2006). Preparation for parenting multiple birth children. *Early Human Development, 82*(6), 371–378.

Lepage, J. F., & Théoret, H. (2007). The mirror neuron system: Grasping others' actions from birth? *Developmental Science, 10,* 513–524.

LePort, A. K., Mattfeld, A. T., Dickinson-Anson, H., Fallon, J. H., Stark, C. E., Kruggel, F., . . . & McGaugh, J. L. (2012). Behavioral and neuroanatomical investigation of highly superior autobiographical memory (HSAM). *Neurobiology of Learning and Memory, 98*(1), 78–92.

Lerner, J. (1993). *Learning disabilities* (6th ed.). Boston: Houghton Mifflin.

Lerner, R. M. (1996). Relative plasticity, integration, temporality, and diversity in human development: A developmental contextual perspective about theory, process, and method. *Developmental Psychology, 32,* 781–786.

Letourneau, N., Watson, B., Duffett-Leger, L., Hegadoren, K., & Tryphonopoulos, P. (2011). Cortisol patterns of depressed mothers and their infants are related to maternal-infant interactive behaviours. *Journal of Reproductive and Infant Psychology, 29,* 439–459.

LeVay, S., & Hamer, D. H. (1994, May). Evidence for a biological influence in male homosexuality. *Scientific American,* 44–49.

Levine, G., & Parkinson, S. (1994). *Experimental methods in psychology.* Hillsdale, NJ: Erlbaum.

LeVine, R. (1994). *Child care and culture: Lessons from Africa,* New York, NY: Cambridge University Press.

Levitt, M. J., Guacci-Franco, N., & Levitt, J. L. (1993). Convoys of social support in childhood and early adolescence: Structure and function. *Developmental Psychology, 29,* 811–818.

Levitt, M. J., Weber, R. A., & Guacci, N. (1993). Convoys of social support: An intergenerational analysis. *Psychology & Aging, 8*(3), 323–326.

Levy-Shiff, R. (1994). Individual and contextual correlates of marital change across the transition to parenthood. *Developmental Psychology, 30,* 591–601.

Lewis, C. T. (1993). Prenatal care in the United States. In B. K. Rothman (Ed.), *The encyclopedia of childbearing,* New York, NY: Henry Holt.

Lewis, J. A., Nishina, A., Hall, A. R., Cain, S., Bellmore, A., & Witkow, M. R. (2018). Early adolescents' peer experiences with ethnic diversity in middle school: Implications for academic outcomes. *Journal of Youth and Adolescence, 47*(1), 194–206.

Lewis, J. M. (1993). Childhood play in normality, pathology and therapy. *American Journal of Orthopsychiatry, 63,* 6–15.

Lewis, M. (1992). *Shame: The exposed self,* New York, NY: The Free Press.

Lewis, M., & Brooks-Gunn, J. (1979a). *Social cognition and the acquisition of self,* New York, NY: Plenum Press.

Lewis, M., & Brooks-Gunn, J. (1979b). Toward a theory of social cognition: The development of the self. In I. Uzgiris (Ed.), *Social interaction and communication during infancy.* San Francisco: Jossey-Bass.

Lewis, M., Brooks-Gunn, J., & Jaskir, J. (1985). Individual differences in visual self-recognition as a function of mother-infant attachment relationship. *Developmental Psychology, 21,* 1181–1187.

Lichten, E. (2003). Children and the death of a parent. In C. D. Bryant (Ed.), *Handbook of death and dying* (Vol. 2, pp. 871–879). Thousand Oaks, CA: Sage Publications.

Liebmann-Smith, J. (1993). Infertility: Overview. In B. K Rothman (Ed.), *The encyclopedia of childbearing,* New York, NY: Henry Holt.

Lickona, T. (1991). Moral development in the elementary school classroom. In W. Kurtines & J. Gewirtz (Eds.), *Handbook of moral behavior and development: Vol. 3* (pp. 143–162). Hillsdale. NJ: Erlbaum.

Liem, D. G., & Mennella, J. A. (2002). Sweet and sour preferences during childhood: Role of early experiences. *Developmental Psychology, 41,* 388–395.

Liem, R., & Liem, J. H. (1988). Psychological effects of unemployment on workers and their families. *Journal of Social Issues, 44,* 87–105.

Lightfoot, C. (1997). *The culture of adolescent risk-taking.* New York, NY: Guilford Press.

Lightfoot, S. L. (1983). *The good high school: Portraits of character and culture.* New York, NY: Basic Books.

Lillard, A. S. (2012). Preschool children's development in classic Montessori, supplemented Montessori, and conventional programs. *Journal of School Psychology, 50*(3), 379–401.

Lillard, A. S., & Peterson, J. (2011). The immediate impact of different types of television on young children's executive function. *Pediatrics, 128*(4), 644–649.

Lin, I. F. (2008). Consequences of parental divorce for adult children's support of their frail parents. *Journal of Marriage and Family, 70,* 113–28.

Lindblad-Goldberg, M. (1989). Successful minority single-parent families. In L. Combrinck-Graham (Ed.), *Children in family contexts* (pp. 116–134). New York, NY: Guilford.

Lindell, S. G. (1988). Education for childbirth: A time for change. *Journal of Obstetrics, Gynecology, and Neonatal Nursing,* 17, 108–112.

Linn, S., Lieverman, E., Schoenbaum, S. C., Monson, R. R., Stubblefield, P. G., & Ryan, K. (1988). Adverse outcomes of pregnancy in women exposed to diethylstilbestrol in utero. *Journal of Reproductive Medicine, 33,* 3–7.

Linney, J. A., & Seidman, E. (1989). The future of schooling. *American Psychologist, 44,* 336–340.

Lips, H. M. (1993). *Sex & gender* (2nd ed.). Mountain View, CA: Mayfield.

Lipsitt, L. (1990). Learning and memory in infants. *Merrill-Palmer Quarterly, 35,* 53–66.

Lipsitt, L., & Kaye, H. (1964). Conditioned sucking in the newborn. *Psychonomic Science, 1,* 29–30.

Lisitsa, E. (2013). *The four horsemen: The antidotes.* The Gottman Institute. Retrieved from https://www.gottman.com/blog/the-four-horsemen-the-antidotes/

Little, T. D., Mroczek, D. K., & Shiner, R. L. (2006). *Handbook of personality development.* Mahwah, NJ: Lawrence Erlbaum Associates.

Littleton, H. L., Bye, K., Buck, K., & Amacker, A. (2010). Psychosocial stress during pregnancy and perinatal outcomes: A meta-analytic review. *Journal of Psychosomatic Obstetrics & Gynecology, 31,* 219–228.

Liu, H., Bravata, D. M., Olkin, I., Nayak, S., Roberts, B., Garber, A. M., & Hoffman, A. R. (2007). Systematic review: The safety and efficacy of growth hormone in the healthy elderly. *Annals of Internal Medicine, 146,* 104–115.

Liu, H., & Umberson, D. J. (2008). The times they are a changin': Marital status and health differentials from 1972 to 2003. *Journal of Health and Social Behavior, 49*(3), 239–253.

Liu, R. T., & Mustanski, B. (2012). Suicidal ideation and self-harm in lesbian, gay, bisexual, and transgender youth. *American Journal of Preventive Medicine, 42*(3), 221–228.

Livingston, G. (2014a). *Pew Research Center social and demographic trends: Growing number of dads home with the kids.* Retrieved from http://www.pewsocialtrends.org/2014/06/05/growing-number-of-dads-home-with-the-kids/

Livingston, G. (2014b, December). *Fewer than half of U.S. kids today live in a 'traditional' family.* Pew Research Center. Retrieved from http://www.pewresearch.org/fact-tank/2014/12/22/less-than-half-of-u-s-kids-today-live-in-a-traditional-family/

Livingston, G., & Cohn, D. (2010). *Childlessness up among all women; down among women with advanced degrees.* Pew Research Center. Retrieved from http://www.pewsocialtrends.org/2010/06/25/childlessness-up-among-all-women-down-among-women-with-advanced-degrees/

Livingston, G., Parker, K., & Rohal, M. (2014). *Four-in-ten couples are saying "I do" again: Growing number of adults have remarried.* Pew Research Center. Retrieved from http://www.pewsocialtrends.org/2010/06/25/childlessness-up-among-all-women-down-among-women-with-advanced-degrees/

Livingston, M. (1993a). Read method: Natural childbirth In B. K. Rothman (Ed.), *The encyclopedia of childbearing.* New York, NY: Henry Holt.

Livingston, M. (1993b). Psychoprophylactic method (Lamaze). In B. K. Rothman (Ed.), *The encyclopedia of childbearing.* New York, NY: Henry Holt.

Livingston, M. (1993e). Bradley method: Husband coached childbirth. In B. K. Rothman (Ed.), *The encyclopedia of childbearing* New York, NY: Henry Holt.

Livson, N., & Peskin, H. (1981a). Perspectives on adolescence from longitudinal research. In J. Adelson (Ed.), *Handbook of adolescent psychology.* New York, NY: Wiley.

Lock, M. (1996). Death in technological time: Locating the end of meaningful life. *Medical Anthropology Quarterly, 10,* 575–600.

Lockery, S. A. (1991). Family and social supports: Caregiving among racial and ethnic minority elders. *Generations, 15*(4), 58–62.

Loeb, R. C., Horst, L., & Horton, P. J. (1980). Family interaction patterns associated with self-esteem in preadolescent girls and boys. *Merrill-Palmer Quarterly, 26,* 203–217.

Loeber, R., Menting, B., Lyman, D. R., Moffitt, T. E., Southamer-Loeber, M., Stallings, R., Farrington, D. P., & Pardini, D. (2012). Findings from the Pittsburgh Youth Study: Cognitive impulsivity and intelligence as predictors of the age-crime curve. *Journal of the American Academy of Child and Adolescent Psychiatry, 51*(11), 1136–1149.

Loeber, R., & Stouthamer-Loeber, M. (1998). Development of juvenile aggression and violence: Some common misconceptions and controversies. *American Psychologist, 53,* 242–259.

Lohnes, K. L., & Kalter, N. (1994). Preventative intervention groups for parentally bereaved children. *American Journal of Orthopsychiatry, 64,* 594–603.

Londerville, S., & Main, M. (1981). Security of attachment, compliance, and maternal training methods. *Developmental Psychology, 17,* 289–299.

Lopez, M. H., & Gonzalez-Barrera, A. (2014). *Women's college enrollment gains leave men behind.* Pew Research Center. Retrieved from http://www.pewresearch.org/fact-tank/2014/03/06/womens-college-enrollment-gains-leave-men-behind/

Loprinzi, P. D., & Trost, S. G. (2010). Parental influences on physical activity behavior in preschool children. *Preventive Medicine, 50*(3), 129–133.

Lothian, J., & DeVries, C. (2005). *The official Lamaze guide: Giving birth with confidence.* Minnetonka, MN: Meadowbrook Press.

Louis, K., Marks, H., & Kruse, S. (1996). Teachers' professional community in restructuring schools. *American Educational Research Journal, 33*(4), 757–800.

Love, J. M., Banks Tarullo, L., Raikes, H., & Chazan-Cohen, R. (2008). Head Start: What do we know about its effectiveness? What do we need to know? In K. McCartney & D. Phillips (Eds.), *Blackwell handbook of early childhood development* (pp. 549–575). Malden, MA: Blackwell Publishing.

Love, J. M., Kisker, E. E., Ross, C., Raikes, H., Constantine, J., Boller, K., . . . & Fuligni, A. S. (2005). The effectiveness of early head start for 3-year-old children and their parents: Lessons for policy and programs. *Developmental Psychology, 41*(6), 885.

Lozoff, B. (1989). Nutrition and behavior. *American Psychologist, 44,* 231–236.

Lucas-Thompson, R. G., Goldberg, W. A., & Prause, J. (2010). Maternal work early in the lives of children and its distal associations with achievement and behavior problems: A meta-analysis. *Psychological Bulletin, 136*(6), 915.

Lucile Packard Children's Hospital at Stanford (LPCH). (2013). *Down syndrome (trisomy 21).* Retrieved from http://www.lpch.org/DiseaseHealthInfo/HealthLibrary/genetics/downs.html

Luna, B., Paulson, D. J., Padmanabhan, A., & Geier, C. (2013). The teenage brain: Cognitive control and motivation. *Current Directions in Psychological Science, 22,* 94–100.

Lundy, B. L. (2002). Paternal socio-psychological factors and infant attachment: The mediating role of synchrony in father-infant interactions. *Infant Behavior & Development, 25,* 221–236.

Luo, S., & Zhang, G. (2009). What leads to romantic attraction: Similarity, reciprocity, security, or beauty? Evidence from a speed-dating study. *Journal of Personality, 77*(4), 933–964.

Luria, A. R. (1976). *Cognitive development: Its cultural and social foundations.* Cambridge, MA: Harvard University Press.

Luster, T., & McAdoo, H. (1996). Family and child influences on educational attachment: A secondary analysis of the High/Scope Perry Preschool data. *Developmental Psychology, 32,* 26–35.

Lustig, M., & Koester, J. (1993). *Intercultural competence: Interpersonal communication across cultures.* New York, NY: Harper-Collins.

Lynch, B., & Bonnie, R. (Eds.). (1994). *Growing up tobacco free.* Washington, DC: National Academy Press.

Lynch, J. S., & van den Broek, P. (2007). Understanding the glue of narrative structure: Children's on-and off-line inferences about characters' goals. *Cognitive Development, 22*(3), 323–340.

Lyon, G. (1993). *Better understanding learning disabilities: New views for research and. their implications for education and public policy.* Baltimore: Paul Brookes.

Lyons-Ruth, K., & Block, D. (1996). The disturbed caregiving system: Conceptualizing the impact of childhood trauma on maternal caregiving behavior during infancy. *Infant Mental Health Journal, 17,* 257–275.

Lyons-Ruth, K., Easterbrooks, M. A., & Cibelli, C. D. (1996). Infant attachment strategies, infant mental lag, and maternal depressive symptoms: Predictors of internalizing and externalizing problems at age 7. *Developmental Psychology, 33,* 681–692.

Lytton, H., & Romney, D. M. (1991). Parents' sex-related differential socialization of boys and girls: A meta-analysis *Psychological Bulletin, 109,* 267–296.

M

MacCallum, F., Golombok, S., & Brinsden, P. (2007). Parenting and child development in families with a child conceived through embryo donation. *Journal of Family Psychology, 21,* 278–287.

Maccoby, E. E. (1995). The two sexes and their social systems. In P. Moen, G. Elder, & K. Luscher (Eds.), *Examining lives in context: Perspectives on the ecology of human development* (pp. 347–364). Washington, DC: American Psychological Association.

Maccoby, E. E. (1980). *Social development, psychological growth, and parent-child relations.* New York, NY: Harcourt Brace Jovanovich.

Maccoby, E. E. (1990). Gender and relationships: A developmental account. *American Psychologist, 45,* 513–520.

Maccoby, E. E., & Jacklin, C. (1980). Sex differences in aggression: A rejoinder and reprise. *Child Development, 48,* 964–980.

Maccoby, E. E., & Martin, J. A. (1983). Socialization in the context of the family: Parent-child interaction In E. M. Hetherington (Ed.), *Handbook of child psychology: Vol. 4. Socialization, personality, and social development* (4th ed., pp. 1–101). New York, NY: Wiley.

MacDorman, M. F., Anderson, R. N., & Strobino D. M. (1997). Annual summary of vital statistics–1996. *Pediatrics, 100*(6), 905–918.

Mackenbach, J. P. (2012). The persistence of health inequalities in modern welfare states: The explanation of a paradox. *Social Science & Medicine, 75,* 761–769. doi: 10.1016/j.socscimed.2012.02.031

MacKinnon-Lewis, C., Starnes, R., Volling, B., & Johnson, S. (1997). Perceptions of parenting as predictors of boys' sibling and peer relations. *Developmental Psychology 33,* 1024–1031.

MacKinnon-Lewis, C., Volling, B. L., Lamb, M. E., Dechman, K., Rabiner, D., & Curtner, M. E. (1994). A cross-contextual analysis of boys' social competence: From family to school. *Developmental Psychology, 30,* 325–33.

MacNeil, S., & Byers, E. S. (1997). The relationships between sexual problems, communication, and sexual satisfaction. *Canadian Journal of Human Sexuality, 6,* 277–283.

Macrae, C., Stangar, C., & Hawthorne, M. (1996). *Stereotypes and stereotyping* Guilford. CT: Guilford Press.

Madden, M., Lenhart, A., Cortesi, S., Gasser, U., Duggan, M., Smith, A., & Beaton, M. (2013). *Teens, social media and privacy.* Pew Research Internet Privacy. Retrieved from http://www.pewinternet.org/2013/05/21/teens-social-mediaand-privacy.

Maguire, M. D., & Dunn, J. (1997). Friendships in early childhood and social understanding. *International Journal of Behavioral Development, 21,* 669–686.

Mahler, M., Pine, F., & Bergman, A. (1975). *The psychological birth of the human infant: Symbiosis and individuation.* New York, NY: Basic Books.

Mahoney, J. L., & Cairns, R. B. (1997). Do extracurricular activities protect against early school dropout? *Developmental Psychology, 33*(2), 241.

Mahoney, J. L., Parente, M. E., & Lord, H. (2007). After-school program engagement: Links to child competence and program quality and content. *Elementary School Journal, 107*(4), 385–04.

Main, M. (1995). Recent studies in attachment: Overview, with selected implications for clinical work. In S. Goldberg, R. Muir, & J. Kerr (Eds.), *Attachment theory: Social, developmental, and clinical perspectives* (pp. 407–470). Hillsdale, NJ: Analytic Press.

Main, M., & George, C. (1985). Responses of abused and disadvantaged toddlers to distress in agemates: A study in the day care setting. *Developmental Psychology, 21,* 407–412.

Main, M., & Goldwyn, R. (1989). Predicting rejection of her infant from mother's representation of her own experience: Implications for the abused-abusing intergenerational cycle. *Child Abuse and Neglect, 8,* 203–217.

Main, M., & Solomon, J. (1990). Procedures for identifying infants as disorganized/disoriented during the Ainsworth Strange Situation. In M. Greenberg, D. Cicchetti, & E. M. Cummings (Eds.), *Attachment in the preschool years: Theory, research and intervention* (pp. 121–160). Chicago: University of Chicago Press.

Main, M., Kaplan, N., & Cassidy, J. (1985). Security in infancy, childhood and adulthood: A move to the level of representation. In I. Bretherton & E. Waters (Eds.), *Growing points in attachment. Monographs of the Society for Research in Child Development, 50*(1–2), 66–104.

Maker, J. (Ed.) (1993). *Programs for the gifted in regular classrooms.* Austin, TX: Pro-Ed Publishers.

Malina, R. M. (1990). Physical growth and performance during the transition years (9–16). In R. Montemayor, G. R. Adams, & T. P. Gullotta (Eds.), *From childhood to adolescence: A transitional period?* (pp. 41–62). Newbury Park, CA: Sage.

Malinosky-Rummell, R., & Hansen, D. J. (1993). Long-term consequences of childhood physical abuse. *Psychological Bulletin, 114,* 68–79.

Mallory, G., & New, R. (Eds.). (1994). *Diversity and develop-mentally appropriate practice. Challenges for early childhood education.* New York, NY: Teachers' College Press.

Mandel, D. R., Jusczyk, P. W., & Pisoni, D. B. (1995). Infants' recognition of the sound patterns of their own names. *Psychological Science, 6,* 314–317.

Mangelsdorf, S. C., Shapiro, J. R., & Marxolf, D. (1995). Developmental and temperamental differences in emotion regulation in infancy. *Child Development, 66,* 1817–1828.

Marcia, J. (1980). Identity in adolescence. In J. Adelson (Ed.), *Handbook of adolescent psychology.* New York, NY: Wiley.

Marcia, J. E. (1966). Development and validation of ego identity status. *Journal of Personality and Social Psychology, 3,* 551–558.

Marcia, J. E. (1993). The relational roots of identity. In J. Kroger (Ed.), *Discussions on ego identity* (pp. 101–120), Hillsdale, NJ: Erlbaum.

Marcia, J. E., Waterman, A. S., Matteson, D. R., Archer, S. L., & Osofsky, J. L. (1993). *Ego Identity: A handbook for psychosocial research.* New York, NY: Springer-Verlag.

Marcus, D., & Overton, W. (1978). The development of cognitive gender constancy and sex role preferences. *Child Development, 49,* 434–444.

Marcus, G., Pinker, S., Ullman, M., Hollander, M., Rosen, T., & Xu, F. (1992). Overregularization in language acquisition. *Monographs of the Society for Research on Child Development, 57*(4, Serial No. 228).

Margolin, L. (1994). *Goodness personified: The emergence of gifted children.* New York, NY: Aldine de Gruyter.

Markiewicz, D., Lawford, H., Doyle, A. B., & Haggart, N. (2006). Developmental differences in adolescents' and young adults' use of mothers, fathers, best friends, and romantic partners to fulfill attachment needs. *Journal of Youth and Adolescence, 35*(1), 121–134.

Markman, H. J., & Kadushin, F. S. (1986). Preventive effects of Lamaze training for first-time parents: A short-term longitudinal study. *Journal of Consulting and Clinical Psychology, 54,* 872–874.

Marlowe, B. (1998). *Creating and sustaining the constructivist classroom* Thousand Oaks, CA: Corwin Press.

Marschark, M. (1993). *Psychological development of deaf children.* New York, NY: Oxford.

Marsella, A. J. (1998). Urbanization, mental health, and social deviancy: A review of issues and research. *American Psychologist, 53,* 624–634.

Marshall, E. A., & Butler, K. (2016). School-to-work transitions in emerging adulthood. In J. J. Arnett (Ed.), *The Oxford handbook of emerging adulthood* (pp. 316–333). New York, NY: Oxford University Press.

Martin, B. (1975). Parent-child relations. In F. Horowitz (Ed.), *Review of child development research: Vol. 4.* Chicago: University of Chicago Press.

Martin, C. L., & Ruble, D. N. (2010). Patterns of gender development. *Annual Review of Psychology, 61,* 353.

Martin, C. L., Wood, C. H., & Little, J. K. (1990). The development of gender stereotype components. *Child Development, 61,* 1891–1904.

Martin, J. A., Hamilton, B. E., Ventura, S. J., Osterman, M. J. K., & Matthews, T. J. (2013). Births: Final data for 2011. *National Vital Statistics Reports, 62.* Retrieved from http://www.cdc.gov/nchs/data/nvsr/nvsr62/nvsr62_01.pdf

Martin, J. A., Hamilton, B. E., Ventura, S. J., Oserman, M. J. K., Wilson, E. C., & Mathews, T. J. (2012). Births: Final data for 2010. *National Vital Statistics Reports, 61*(1), 1–72. Retrieved from http://www.cdc.gov/nchs/data/nvsr/nvsr61/nvsr61_01.pdf

Martinez, G., Copen, C. E., & Abma, J.C. (2011). Teenagers in the United States: Sexual activity, contraceptive use, and childbearing, 2006–2010 National Survey of Family Growth. *National Center for Health Statistics. Vital Health Statistics, 23*(31).

Masapollo, M., Polka, L., & Ménard, L. (2016). When infants talk, infants listen: Pre-babbling infants prefer listening to speech with infant vocal properties. *Developmental Science, 19*(2), 318–328.

Mason, A. W., Hitch, J. E., Kosterman, R., McCarty, C. A., Herrenkohl, T. I., & Hawkins, J. D. (2010). Growth in adolescent delinquency and alcohol use in relation to young adult crime, alcohol use disorders, and risky sex: A comparison of youth from low-versus middle income backgrounds. *Journal of Child Psychology and Psychiatry, 51*(12), 1377–1385.

Mason, C. A., Cauce, A. M., Gonzales, N., & Hiraga, Y. (1996). Neither too sweet nor too sour: Problem peers, maternal control, and problem behavior in African American adolescents. *Child Development, 67*, 2115–2130.

Masten, A. S., & Coatsworth, J. D. (1998). The development of competence in favorable and unfavorable environments. *American Psychologist, 53*, 205–220.

Masters, W. H., & Johnson, V. E. (1966). *Human sexual response*. Boston: Little, Brown.

Masters, W. H., Johnson, V. E., & Kolodny, R. C. (1992). *Human sexuality* (4th ed.). Boston: Little, Brown.

Masters, W. H., Johnson, V. E., & Kolodny, R. C. (1994). *Heterosexuality*. New York, NY: HarperCollins.

Matas, L., Arend, R. A., & Sroufe, L. A. (1978). Continuity of adaptation in the second year. The relationship between quality of attachment and later competence. *Child Development, 49*, 547–555.

Mathews, T. J., & Hamilton, B. E. (2016). *Mean age of mothers is on the rise: United States, 2000–2014. NCHS data brief, no 232*. Hyattsville, MD: National Center for Health Statistics. Retrieved from http://www.cdc.gov/nchs/products/databriefs/db232.htm

Matos, K. (2015). *Modern families: Same-and different-sex couples negotiating at home*. Retrieved from http://www.familiesandwork.org/downloads/modern-families.pdf

Matthews, D., & Kitchen, J. (2007). School-within-a-school gifted programs perceptions of students and teachers in public secondary schools. *Gifted Child Quarterly, 51*(3), 256–271.

Matthews, S. H., & Rosner, T. T. (1988). Shared filial responsibility: The family as the primary caregiver. *Journal of Marriage and the Family, 50*, 185–195.

Mazur, J. (1994). *Learning and behavior* (3rd ed.), Englewood Cliffs, NJ: Erlbaum.

McCall, G. J. (1995). Juvenile delinquency in Germany, South Africa, and America: Explorations in national character. In J. Braun, et al. (Eds.). *Social pathology in comparative perspective: The nature and psychology of civil society.* (pp. 117–132). Westport, CT: Praeger Publishers/Greenwood Publishing Group.

McCall, R. (1981). Nature-nurture and the two realms of development: A proposed integration with respect to mental development. *Child Development, 52*, 1–12.

McCall, R., & Kagan, J. (1967). Stimulus schema discrepancy and attention in the infant. *Journal of Experimental Child Psychology, 5*, 381–390.

McCloyd, V. C. (1998). Socioeconomic disadvantage and child development. *American Psychologist, 53*, 185–204.

McCrae, R. R. (Ed.). (1992). The five-factor model: Issues and applications [Special issue]. *Journal of Personality, 60*(2).

McCrea, R. R., & John, O. P. (1992). An introduction to the five-factor model and its applications. *Journal of Personality, 60*, 175–216.

McCurdy, K., Gorman, K. S., Kisler, T. S., & Metallinos-Katsaras, E. (2012). Maternal mental health and child health and nutrition. In V. Maholmes & R. B. King (Eds.), *The Oxford handbook of poverty and child development* (pp.124–144). New York, NY: Oxford University Press.

McDaniel, D., McKee, C., & Smith, H. (1996). *Methods of assessing children's syntax* Cambridge, MA: MIT Press.

McDonald, M., Sigman, M., Espinosa, M., & Neumann, C. (1994). Impact of a temporary food shortage on children and their mothers. *Child Development, 65*, 404–415.

McGinnis, M., Richmond, J. B., Brandt, E. N., Windom, R. E., & Mason, J. O. (1992). Health progress in the United States: Results of the 1990 objectives for the nation. *Journal of the American Medical Association, 268*, 2545–2552.

McGoldrick, M., Pearce, J. K., & Giordano, J. (Eds.). (1982). *Ethnicity and family therapy*. New York, NY: Guilford.

McHale, S. M., Corneal, D., Crouter, A., & Birch, L. (2001). Gender and weight concerns in early and middle adolescence: Links with well-being and family characteristics. *Journal of Clinical Child Psychology, 30*, 338–348.

McHale, S. M., Crouter, A. C., & Tucker, C. J. (2001). Free-time activities in middle childhood: Links with adjustment in early adolescence. *Child Development, 72*(6), 1764–1778.

McIntosh, J. L., & Drapeau, C. W. (for the American Association of Suicidology). (2014, June 19). *U.S.A. suicide 2011: Official final data*. Washington, DC: American Association of Suicidology. Retrieved from http://www.suicidology.org

McKay, M. M. (1994). The link between domestic violence and child abuse: Assessment and treatment considerations. *Child Welfare, 73*, 29–39.

McKay, S. (1993). Labor: Overview. In B. K. Rothman (Ed.), *The encyclopedia of childbearing*. New York, NY: Henry Holt.

McKnight-Eily, L. R., Eaton, D. K., Lowry, R., Croft, J. B., Presley-Cantrell, L., & Perry, G. S. (2011). Relationships between hours of sleep and health-risk behaviors in US adolescent students. *Preventive Medicine, 53*(4), 271–273.

McKussick, V. A. (1995). *Mendelian inheritance in man: Catalogues of autosomal dominant, autosomal recessive, and X-linked phenotypes* (10th ed.). Baltimore: Johns Hopkins University Press.

McLoyd, V. C. (1990). The impact of economic hardship on Black families and children: Psychological distress, parenting and socioemotional development. *Child Development, 61*, 311–346.

McLoyd, V. C. (1998). Socioeconomic disadvantage and child development. *American Psychologist. 53*, 185–204.

McNamara, T., Miller, D., & Bransford, J. (1991). Mental models and the construction of meaning. In P. Pearson (Ed.), *Handbook of reading research: Vol. 2* (pp. 490–511). New York, NY: Longman.

McQuoid, Joan. (1996). The ISRD Study: Self-report findings from N. Ireland. *Journal of Adolescence, 19*, 95–98.

Measor, L., & Sykes, P. (1992). *Gender and schools* New York, NY: Cassell.

Meehan, P. J., Lamb, J. A., Saltzman, L. E., & O'Carroll, P. W. (1992). Attempted suicide among young adults: Progress toward a meaningful estimate of prevalence. *American Journal of Psychiatry, 149*, 41–44.

Meilman, P. (1979). Cross-sectional age changes in ego identity status during adolescence. *Developmental Psychology, 15*, 230–231.

Meins, E. (1997). *Security of attachment and the social development of cognition*. Hove: Psychology Press.

Mela, D., & Roberts, P. (1998). *Food, eating, and obesity: Psychobiological basis of appetite and weight control* New York, NY: Chapman and Hall.

Meltzer, L. J., & Mindell, J. A. (2006). Sleep and sleep disorders in children and adolescents. *Psychiatric Clinics of North America, 29*(4), 1059–1076.

Meltzoff, A., & Kuhl, P. (1994). Faces and speech: Intermodel processing of biologically relevant signals in infants and adults. In D. Lewkowicz & R. Lickliter (Eds.), *The development of intersensory perception* (pp. 335–370). Hillsdale, NJ: Erlbaum.

Meltzoff, A., Kuhl, P., & Moore, M. K. (1991). Perception, representation, and control of action in newborns and young infants. In M. Weiss & P. Zelazo (Eds.), *Newborn attention: Biological constraints and the influence of experience* (pp. 377–411). Norwood, NJ: Ablex.

Mendelson, B., & White, D. (1995). Children's global self-esteem predicted by body-esteem but not by weight. *Perceptual & Motor Skills, 80*, 97–98.

Mendoza, J. A., Zimmerman, F. J., & Christakis, D. A. (2007). Television viewing, computer use, obesity, and adiposity in US preschool children. *International Journal of Behavioral Nutrition and Physical Activity, 4*(1), 1.

Menkes, J. (1994). *Textbook of child neurology* (5th ed.). Philadelphia: Williams and Wilkins.

Mennuti, R. B., & Creamer, D. G. (1991). Role of orientation, gender, and dilemma content in moral reasoning. *Journal of College Student Development, 32*, 241–248.

Mercer, C. H., Fenton, K. A., Johnson, A. M., Wellings, K., Macdowall, W., McManus, S., . . . & Erens, B. (2003). Sexual function problems and help seeking behaviour in Britain: National probability sample survey. *British Medical Journal, 327*, 426–427.

Mercer, P. W., Merritt, S. L., & Cowell, J. M. (1998). Differences in reported sleep need among adolescents. *Journal of Adolescent Health, 23*(5), 259–263.

Meredith, H. (1981). Body size and form among ethnic groups of infants, children, youth, and adults. In R. Munroe, R. Munroe, and B. Whiting (Eds.), *Handbook of cross-cultural human development*. New York, NY: Garland Press.

Merenstein, G., Kaplan, D., & Rosenberg, A. (1997). *Handbook of pediatrics* (18th ed.). Norwalk, CT: Appleton and Lange.

Mersky, J. P., Topitzes, J., & Reynolds, A. J. & Arthur, J. (2012). Unsafe at any age: Linking childhood and adolescent maltreatment to delinquency and crime. *Journal of Research in Crime and Delinquency, 49*(2), 295–318.

Messer, D. (1994). *The development of communication: From social interaction to language*. New York, NY: Wiley.

Messinger, D. S. (2002). Positive and negative: Infant facial expressions and emotions. *Current Directions in Psychological Science, 11*, 1–6.

Messner, M., and Sabo, D. (1994). *Sex, violence, and power in sports* Freedom, CA: Crossing Press.

Metz, K. (1995). Reassessment of developmental constraints on children's science instruction. *Review of Educational Research, 65*(2), 93–128.

Michelsson, K., Rinne, A., & Paajanen, S. (1990). Crying, feeding and sleeping patterns in 1 to 12-month-old infants. *Child: Care, health and. development, 116*, 99–111.

Mickelson, K. D., Kessler, R. C., & Shaver, P. R. (1997). Adult attachment in a nationally representative sample. *Journal of Personality and Social Psychology, 73*, 1092–1106.

Mikaye, K., Chen, S., & Campos, J. (1985). Infant temperament, mother's mode of interaction, and attachment in Japan. In I. Bretherton & E. Waters (Eds.), Growing points of attachment theory and research. *Monographs of the Society for Research on Child Development. 50*(209).

Milevsky, A., Schlechter, M., Netter, S., & Keehn, D. (2007). Maternal and paternal parenting styles in adolescents: Associations with self-esteem, depression and life-satisfaction. *Journal of Child and Family Studies, 16*(1), 39–47.

Miller, B. (1987). Gender and control among spouses of the cognitively impaired: A research note. *The Gerontologist, 27*, 447–453.

Miller, B. (1990). Gender differences in spouse caregiver strain: Socialization and role explanations. *Journal of Marriage and the Family, 52*, 311–321.

Miller, P. (2011). *Theories of developmental psychology* (5th ed.). New York, NY: W. H. Freeman.

Miller, P., & Simon, W. (1980). The development of sexuality in adolescence. In J. Adelson (Ed.), *Handbook of adolescent psychology*. New York, NY: Wiley.

Miller, T., & Winston, R. (1990). Assessing development from a psychosocial perspective. In D. Creamer & associates (Eds.), *College student development: Theory and practice for the 1990s* (Media Publication No. 49). Alexandria, VA: American College Personnel Association.

Miller, W. B. (1990). Why the United States has failed to solve its youth gang problem. In C. R. Huff (Ed.), *Gangs in America* (pp. 263–287). Newbury Park, CA: Sage.

Millstein, S. G. (1989). Adolescent health: Challenges for behavioral scientists. *American Psychologist, 44*, 837–842.

Milner, J. S., Thomsen, C. J., Crouch, J. L., Rabenhorst, M. M., Martens, P. M., Dyslin, C. W., . . . & Merrill, L. L. (2010). Do trauma symptoms mediate the relationship between childhood physical abuse and adult child abuse risk? *Child Abuse & Neglect, 34*(5), 332–344.

Milteer, R. M., Ginsburg, K. R., Mulligan, D. A., Ameenuddin, N., Brown, A., Christakis, D. A., . . . & Levine, A. E. (2012). The importance of play in promoting healthy child development and maintaining strong parent-child bond: Focus on children in poverty. *Pediatrics, 129*(1), e204–e213.

Milunsky, A. (1992). *Heredity and your family's health.* Baltimore: Johns Hopkins University Press.

Minagawa-Kawai, Y., van der Lely, H., Ramus, F., Sato, Y., Mazuka, R., & Dupoux, E. (2011). Optical brain imaging reveals general auditory and language-specific processing in early infant development. *Cerebral Cortex, 21,* 254–261.

Minino, A. M. (2010). Mortality among teenagers aged 12–19 years: United States, 1999–2006. *NCHS Data Brief, 37.* Retrieved from http://www.cdc.gov/nchs/data/databriefs/db37.

Minnotte, K. L., Minnotte, M. C., Pedersen, D. E., Mannon, S. E., & Kiger, G. (2010). His and her perspectives: Gender ideology, work-to-family conflict, and marital satisfaction. *Sex Roles, 63,* 425–438.

Miramontes, O., Nadeau, A., & Commins, N. (1997). *Restructuring schools for linguistic diversity.* New York, NY: Teachers College Press.

Mirecki, R. M., Chou, J. L., Elliott, M., & Schneider, C. M. (2013). What factors influence marital satisfaction? Differences between first and second marriages. *Journal of Divorce & Remarriage, 54*(1), 78–93.

Mishna, F. (2003). Learning disabilities and bullying double jeopardy. *Journal of Learning Disabilities, 36*(4), 336–347.

Mogford, K. (1993). Language development in twins. In D. Bishop & K. Mogford (Eds.), *Language development in exceptional circumstances* (pp. 80–95). Hillsdale, NJ: Erlbaum.

Monk, T. H., Essex, M. J., Smider, N. A., Klein, M. H. (1996). The impact of the birth of a baby on the time structure and social mixture of a couple's daily life and its consequences for well-being. *Journal of Applied Social Psychology, 26,* 1237–1258.

Montemayor, R. (1983). Parents and adolescents in conflict: All families some of the time and some families most of the time. *Journal of Early Adolescence, 9,* 417–428.

Montessori, M. (1964). *The Montessori method.* New York, NY: Schocken Books.

Montgomery, M. J., & Côté, J. E. (2003). College as a transition to adulthood. In G. R. Adams & M. D. Berzonsky (Eds.), *Blackwell handbook of adolescence.* Malden, MA: Blackwell.

Montgomery, M. J., & Sorell, G. T. (1997). Differences in love attitudes across family life stages. *Family Relations, 46,* 55–61.

Montgomery, R. J. (1992). Gender differences in patterns of child-parent caregiving relationships. In J. W. Dwyer & R. T. Coward (Eds.), *Gender, families, and elder care* (pp. 65–83). Newbury Park, CA: Sage.

Montgomery-Downs, H. E., Insana, S. P., Clegg-Kraynok, M. M., & Mancini, L. M. (2010). Normative longitudinal maternal sleep: The first 4 postpartum months. *American Journal of Obstetrics and Gynecology, 203*(5), 465-e1.

Moore, C., & Dunham, P. (1995). *Joint attention: Its origins and role in development.* Hillsdale, NJ: Erlbaum.

Moore, D. (1984). Parent-adolescent separation: Intrafamilial perceptions and difficulty separating from parents. *Personality and Social Psychology Bulletin, 10,* 611–619.

Moore, D. (1987). Parent-adolescent separation: The construction of adulthood by late adolescents. *Developmental Psychology, 23,* 298–307.

Moore, K., & Persaud, T. (1998). *The developing human: Clinically oriented embryology* (6th ed.). Philadelphia: Saunders.

Moore, S., Rosenthal, D., & Mitchell, A. (1996). *Youth, AIDS, and sexually transmitted diseases,* London: Routledge.

Moorehouse, M. J. (1991). Linking maternal employment patterns to mother-child activities and children's school competence. *Developmental Psychology, 27,* 295–303.

Moran, E. G. (1993). Domestic violence and pregnancy. In B. K. Rothman (Ed.), *The encyclopedia of childbearing.* New York, NY: Henry Holt.

Morell, V. (1995). Attacking the causes of "silent" infertility. *Science 269*(5225), 775–777.

Morgan, J. P., & Roberts, J. E. (2010). Helping bereaved children and adolescents: Strategies and implications for counselors. *Journal of Mental Health Counseling, 32*(3), 206.

Morin, R. (2013). *Study: Opposition to same sex marriage is likely to be understated in public opinion polls.* Pew Research Center. Retrieved from http://pewresearch.org/fact-tank/2013/09/30/opposition-to-same-sex-marriage-may-be-understated-in-public-opinion-polls

Morrison, E. H. (1998). Common peripartum emergencies. *American Family Physician, 58,* 1593–1604.

Morrongiello, B. (1994). Effects of colocation on auditory-visual interactions and cross-modality perception in infants. In D. Lewkowicz & R. Lickliter (Eds.), *The development of intersensory perception* (pp. 235–264). Hillsdale, NJ: Erlbaum.

Morrow, L. (1996). *Motivating reading and writing in diverse classrooms: Social and physical contexts in a literature-based program.* Urbana, IL: National Council of Teachers of English.

Mortimer, J., & Finch, M. (Eds.). (1996). *Adolescents, work, and family.* Thousand Oaks, CA: Sage.

Mortimer, J., Shanahan, M., & Ryu, S. (1994). The effects of adolescent employment on school-related orientation and behavior. In R. Silbereisen & E. Todt (Eds.), *Adolescence in context: The interplay of family, school, peers, and work in adjustment* (pp. 304–326). New York, NY: Springer-Verlag.

Muehlenhard, C., & Linton, M. (1987). Date rape. *Journal of Counseling Psychology, 34,* 186–196.

Munroe, R., Munroe, R., & Whiting, J. (1981). Male sex-role resolutions. In *Handbook of cross-cultural human development,* New York, NY: Garland.

Muraco, A. (2006). Intentional families: Fictive kin ties between cross-gender, different sexual orientation friends. *Journal of Marriage and Family, 68*(5), 1313–1325.

Murphy, J. M., & Gilligan, C. (1980). Moral development in late adolescence and adulthood: A critique and reconstruction of Kohlberg's theory. *Human Development, 23,* 77–104.

Murphy, L. (1937). *Social behavior and child personality.* New York, NY: Columbia University Press.

Murry, V. M., Bynum, M. S., Brody, G. H., Willert, A., & Stephens, D. (2001). African American single mothers and children in context: A review of studies on risk and resilience. *Clinical Child and Family Psychology Review, 4*(2), 133–155.

Murstein, B. I. (1988). A taxonomy of love. In R. J. Stemberg & M. L. Brown (Eds.), *The psychology of love.* New Haven, CT: Yale University Press.

Museus, S. D., & Quaye, S. J. (2009). Toward an intercultural perspective of racial and ethnic minority college student persistence. *Review of Higher Education, 33*(1), 67–94.

Myers, J. (1993). Curricular designs that resonate with adolescents' ways of knowing. In R. Lerner (Ed.), *Early adolescence: Perspectives on research, policy, and intervention* (pp. 191–206). Hillsdale, NJ: Erlbaum.

Myhill, D., & Jones, S. (2006). "She doesn't shout at no girls": Pupils' perceptions of gender equity in the classroom. *Cambridge Journal of Education, 36*(1), 99–113.

N

National Center for Education Statistics (NCES). (1997). *Digest of education statistics, 1997.* Washington, DC: U.S. Department of Education, Office of Educational Research and Improvement.

National Center for Education Statistics (NCES). (2010). *Digest of education statistics.* Retrieved from http://nces.ed.gov/programs/digest/d12/tables/dt12_486.asp

National Center for Health Statistics. (2013). *Health, United States, 2012: With special feature on emergency care.* Hyattsville, MD: Public Health Service.

National Heart, Lung, and Blood Institute (NHLBI). (2012b). *Sickle cell anemia.* Retrieved from http://www.nhlbi.nih.gov/health/health-topics/topics/sca/

National Human Genome Research Institute (NHGRI). (2010). *Learning about fragile X syndrome.* Retrieved from http://www.genome.gov/19518828

National Institute of Child Health and Human Development (NICHD). (2012). *Klinefelter syndrome: Condition information.* Retrieved from https://www.nichd.nih.gov/health/topics/klinefelter/conditioninfo/

National Institute of Mental Health (NIMH). (2007). Suicide in the U.S.: Statistic and prevention. Retrieved from http://www.nimh.nih.gov/health/publications/suicide-in-the-us-statistics-and-prevention/index.shtml#CDC-Web-Tool

National Institute on Alcohol Abuse and Alcoholism. (1997, July). Youth drinking: Risk factors and consequences. *Alcohol Alert, 37.*

National Institute on Alcohol Abuse and Alcoholism. (2006). *Alcohol alert: Young adult drinking.* Retrieved from http://pubs.niaaa.nih.gov/publications/aa68/aa68.htm

National Institute on Alcohol Abuse and Alcoholism. (2016). *Alcohol facts and statistics.* Retrieved from https://www.niaaa.nih.gov/alcohol-health/overviewalcohol-consumption/alcohol-facts-and-statistics

National Resource Center for Health and Safety in Child Care. (2013). *Choosing child care.* Retrieved from http://childcareaware.org/families/choosing-quality-child-care/

National Science Foundation. (n.d.) *Chore wars: Men, women, and housework.* Retrieved August 12, 2016, from https://www.nsf.gov/discoveries/disc_images.jsp?cntn_id=111458

National Sleep Foundation. (2015). *National Sleep Foundation recommends new sleep durations.* Washington, DC. Retrieved from https://sleepfoundation.org/press-release/national-sleep-foundation-recommends-new-sleep-times

National Sleep Foundation. (n.d.) *Healthy sleep habits.* Retrieved from https://sleepfoundation.org/press-release/national-sleep-foundation-recommends-new-sleep-times

Neal, J. W. (2009). Social aggression and social position in middle childhood and early adolescence: Burning bridges or building them? *Journal of Early Adolescence,* 1–16.

Nelson, A. I., & Neinstein, L. S. (2008). Contraception. In L. S. Neinstein, C. M. Gordon, D. K. Katzman, & D. S. Rosen (Eds.), *Handbook of adolescent health care.* Philadelphia, PA: Lippincott, Williams & Wilkins.

Nelson, K. (1996). *Language in cognitive development: Emergence of the mediated mind.* New York, NY: Cambridge University Press.

Newman, F., & Holzman, L. (1993). *Lev Vygotsky: Revolutionary scientist.* New York, NY: Routledge.

Newman, K. (1996). Working poor: Low-wage employment in the lives of Harlem youth. In J. Graber, J. Brooks-Gunn, & A. Petersen (Eds.), *Transitions through adolescence* (pp. 323–344), Mahwah, NJ: Erlbaum.

Newman, R. S. (2005). The cocktail party effect in infants revisited: Listening to one's own name in noise. *Developmental Psychology, 41,* 352–362.

NICHD Early Child Care Research Network. (1997). The effects of infant child care on infant-mother attachment security: Results of the NICHD study of early child care. *Child Development. 68,* 860–879.

Nichojs, J., Nelson, J., & Gleaves, K. (1995). Learning "facts" versus learning that most questions have many answers: Student evaluations of contrasting curricula. *Journal of Educational Psychology, 87*(2), 253–260.

Nickerson, A. B., & Nagle, R. J. (2005). Parent and peer attachment in late childhood and early adolescence. *Journal of Early Adolescence, 25*, 223–249.

Noam, G., & Wren, T. (1993). *The moral self.* Cambridge, MA: MIT Press.

Noble, V. (1992). *Shakti woman.* San Francisco: Harper.

Noble, K. D., & Drummond, J. E. (1992). But what about the prom? Students' perceptions of early college entrance. Special issue: Challenging the gifted: Grouping and acceleration. *Gifted Child Quarterly, 36*(2), 106–111.

Nock, M. K., & Mendes, W. B. (2008). Physiological arousal, distress tolerance, and social problem-solving deficits among adolescent self-injurers. *Journal of Consulting Clinical Psychology, 76*, 28–38.

Noh, S., Dumas, J. E., Wolf, L. C., & Fisman, S. (1989). Delineating sources of stress in parents of exceptional children. *Family Relations, 38*, 456–461.

Nolen-Hoeksema, S., Wolfson, A., Mumme, D., & Guskin, K. (1995). Helplessness in children of depressed and nondepressed mothers. *Developmental Psychology, 31*, 377–387.

Noller, P. (2005). Sibling relationships in adolescence: Learning and growing together. *Personal Relationships, 12*, 1–22.

Noppe, I. C., Noppe, L. D., & Hughes, F. P. (1991). Stress as a predictor of the quality of parent-infant interactions. *Journal of Genetic Psychology, 152*, 17–28.

Noppe, L., & Noppe, I. (1996). Ambiguity in adolescent understandings of death. In C. Corr & D. Balk (Eds.), *Handbook of adolescent death and bereavement* (pp. 25–41). New York, NY: Springer Publishing.

Norbeck, J. S., & Tilden, V. P. (1983). Life stress, social support, and emotional disequilibrium in complications of pregnancy: A prospective, multivariate study. *Journal of Health and Social Behavior, 24*, 30–46.

Norman, C. (1988). Math education: A mixed picture. *Science, 241*, 408–409.

Norman, R. E., Byambaa, M., De, R., Butchart, A., Scott, J., & Vos, T. (2012). The long-term health consequences of child physical abuse, emotional abuse, and neglect: A systematic review and metaanalysis. *PLoS Med, 9*(11), e1001349.

Northrup, C. (1994). *Women's bodies, women's wisdom.* New York, NY: Bantam.

Nucci, L., & Turiel, E. (1993). God's word, religious rules, and their relation to Christian and Jewish children's concepts of morality. *Child Development, 64*, 1475–1491.

Nunes-Costa, R. A., Lamela, D. J., & Figueiredo, B. F. (2009). Psychosocial adjustment and physical health in children of divorce. *Journal of Pediatrics, 85*(5), 385–396.

O

Oberg, M., Jaakkola, M. S., Woodward, A., Peruga, A., & Prüss-Ustün, A. (2011). Worldwide burden of disease from exposure to second-hand smoke: A retrospective analysis of data from 192 countries. *Lancet, 377*(9760), 139–146.

O'Brien, R. W., Smith, S. A., Bush, P. J., & Peleg, E. (1990). Obesity, self-esteem, and health locus of control in black youths during transition to adolescence. *American Journal of Health Promotion, 5*(2), 133–139.

O'Brien, S. F., & Bierman, K. L. (1988). Conceptions and perceived influence of peer groups: Interviews with preadolescents and adolescents. *Child Development, 59*, 1360–1365.

O'Callaghan, F. V., O'Callaghan, M., Najman, J. M., Williams, G. M., & Bor, W. (2007). Prenatal alcohol exposure and attention, learning and intellectual ability at 14 years: A prospective longitudinal study. *Early Human Development, 83*, 115–123.

O'Connell, E., Boat, T., & Warner K. E. (Eds.). (2009). *Preventing mental, emotional, and behavioral disorders among young people.* Washington, DC: National Academies Press.

O'Connor, C. (1997). Dispositions toward (collective) struggle and educational resilience in the inner city: A case analysis of six African-American high school students. *American Educational Research Journal, 34*(4), 593–629.

O'Connor, M., & Michaels, S. (1996). Shifting participant frameworks: Orchestrating thinking practices in group discussions. In D. Hicks (Eds.), *Discourse, learning, and schooling* (pp. 63–103). New York, NY: Cambridge University Press.

O'Connor, P. (1992). *Friendships between women.* New York, NY: Harvester Wheatshaft.

O'Donnell, J., Hawkins, J. D., Catalano, R. F., Abbott, R. D., & Day, L. E. (1995). Preventing school failure, drug use bind delinquency among low-income children: Long-term intervention in elementary schools. *American Journal of Orthopsychiatry, 65*, 87–100.

OECD. (2013, January). *Cohabitation rate and prevalence of other forms of partnership.* Retrieved from http://www.oecd.org/els/soc/SF3_3_Cohabitation_rate_and_prevalence_of_other_forms_of_partnership_Jan2013.pdf

OECD. (2015). *Education at a glance 2015: OECD indicators.* OECD Publishing. Retrieved from http://dx.doi.org/10.1787/eag-2015-en

Ofcom. (2014). *Children and parents: Media use and attitudes report.* Retrieved from http://stakeholders.ofcom.org.uk/binaries/research/media-literacy/media-use-attitudes-14/Childrens_2014_Report.pdf

Offer, D., & Schonert-Reichl, K. A. (1992). Debunking the myths of adolescence: Findings from recent research. *Journal of the American Academy of Child and Adolescent Psychiatry, 31*, 1003–1014.

Office for National Statistics. (2012). *Statistical bulletin: Divorces in England and Wales: 2012.* Retrieved from http://www.ons.gov.uk/peoplepopulationandcommunity/birthsdeathsandmarriages/divorce/bulletins/divorcesinenglandandwales/2014-02-06#age-atdivorce

O'Hara-Devereaux, M., & Johansen, R. (1994). *Globalwork: Bridging distance, culture, and time.* San Francisco: Jossey-Bass.

Ohayon, M. M., Carskadon, M. A., Guilleminault, C., & Vitiello, M. V. (2004). Meta-analysis of quantitative sleep parameters from childhood to old age in healthy individuals: Developing normative sleep values across the human lifespan. *Sleep, 27*, 1255–1273.

O'Keeffe, G. S., & Clark-Pearson, K. (2011). The impact of social media on children, adolescents, and families. *Pediatrics 127*(4), 800–805.

O'Keefe, M. (Ed.). (1998). *Brady emergency care* (8th ed.). Upper Saddle River, NJ: Prentice-Hall.

Oldehinkel, A. J., Verhulst, F. C., & Ormel, J. (2011). Mental health problems during puberty: Tanner stage-related differences in specific symptoms. The TRAILS study. *Journal of Adolescence, 34*, 73–85.

Olds, D. L. (1997). The prenatal/early infancy project: Fifteen years later. In G. Albee, & T. Gullotta (Eds.), *Issues in children's and families' lives: Primary prevention works* (pp. 41–68). Thousand Oaks, CA: Sage Publications.

Olsen, J. P., Parra, G. R., Cohen, R., Schoffstall, C. L., & Egli, C. J. (2012). Beyond relationship reciprocity: A consideration of varied forms of children's relationships. *Personal Relationships, 19*(1), 72–8.

Olson, M. R., & Haynes, J. A. (1993). Successful single parents. *Families in Society: The Journal of Contemporary Human Services, 74*(5), 259–267.

Oppenheim, D., Emde, R. N., & Warren, S. (1997). Preschoolers face moral dilemmas: A longitudinal study of acknowledging and resolving internal conflict. *International Journal of Psychoanalysis, 78*, 943–957.

Orathinkel, J., & Vansteenwegen, A. (2007). Do demographics affect marital satisfaction? *Journal of Sex & Marital Therapy, 33*, 73–85.

Orland-Barak, L., & Yinon, H. (2007). When theory meets practice: What student teachers learn from guided reflection on their own classroom discourse. *Teaching and Teacher Education, 23*(6), 957–969.

Orzech, K., Grandner, M., Roane, B., & Carskadon, M. (2016). Digital media use in the 2 h before bedtime is associated with sleep variables in university students. *Computers in Human Behavior, 55*, 43–50.

Oshio, T., Nozaki, K., & Kobayashi, M. (2013). Division of household labor and marital satisfaction in China, Japan, and Korea. *Journal of Family and Economic Issues, 34*(2), 211–223.

Oster, H., Hegley, D., & Nagel, L. (1992). Adult judgments and fine-grained analysis of infant facial expressions: Testing the validity of a priori coding formulas. *Developmental Psychology, 28*, 1115–1131.

Oswald, R. F., & Masciadrelli, B. P. (2008). Generative ritual among nonmetropolitan lesbians and gay men: Promoting social inclusion. *Journal of Marriage and Family, 70*, 1060–1073.

Otis, N., Grouzet, F. M. E., & Pelletier, L. G. (2005). Latent motivational change in an academic setting: A three-year longitudinal study. *Journal of Educational Psychology, 97*, 170–183.

Overman, J. J., & Carmichael, S. T. (2014). Plasticity in the injured brain: More than molecules matter. *Neuroscientist, 20*, 15–28.

Owen, M. T., & Cox, M. J. (1997). Marital conflict and the development of infant-parent attachment relationships. *Journal of Family Psychology, 11*, 152–164.

Owens, D. (2008). Recognizing the needs of bereaved children in palliative care. *Journal of Hospice and Palliative Nursing, 10*, 14–16.

Owens, J. A., Belon, K., & Moss, P. (2010). Impact of delaying school start time on adolescent sleep, mood, and behavior. *Archives of Pediatrics & Adolescent Medicine, 164*(7), 608–614.

P

Padilla-Walker, L. M. (2016). Moral development during emerging adulthood. In J. J. Arnett (Ed.), *The Oxford handbook of emerging adulthood* (pp. 449–463). New York, NY: Oxford University Press.

Page, D. C. Mosher, R., Simpson, E. M., Fisher, E. M., Mardon, G., Pillack, J., McGillivray, B., de la Chapelle, A., & Brown, L. G. (1987). The sex-determining region of the human Y chromosome encodes a finer protein. *Cell, 51*, 1091–1104.

Page, H. (1989). Estimation of the prevalence and incidence of infertility in a population: A pilot study. *Fertility and Sterility, 51*, 571–577.

Pagliaro, A., & Pagliaro, L. (1996) *Substance abuse among children and adolescents: Nature, extent, and effects from conception to adulthood.* New York, NY: Wiley.

Pakiz, B., Reinherz, H. Z., & Giaconia, R. M. (1997). Early risk factors for serious antisocial behavior at age 21: A longitudinal community study. *American Journal of Orthopsychiatry, 67*, 92–101.

Pallock, L. L., & Lamborn, S. D. (2006). Beyond parenting practices: Extended kinship support and the academic adjustment of African-American and European-American teens. *Journal of Adolescence, 29*(5), 813–828.

Paniagua, F. A. (2005). *Assessing and treating culturally diverse clients: A practical guide.* Thousand Oaks, CA: Sage.

Pappert, A. (1993). Preimplantation diagnosis. In B. K. Rothman (Ed.), *The encyclopedia of childbearing.* New York, NY: Henry Holt.

Paquette, D. (2004). Theorizing the father-child relationship: Mechanisms and developmental outcomes. *Human Development, 47*, 193–219.

Paquette, D., Carbonneau, R., Dubeau, D., Bigras, M., & Tremblay, R. E. (2003). Prevalence of father-child rough-and-tumble play and physical aggression in preschool children. *European Journal of Psychology of Education, 18*, 171–189.

Parke, R. D., Burks, V. M., Carson, J. L., Neville, B., & Boyum, L. A. (1994). Family-peer relationships. A tripartite model. In R. D. Parke & S. G. Kellam

(Eds.), *Exploring family relationships with other social constructs* (pp. 115–146). Hillsdale, NJ: Erlbaum.

Parke, R. D., MacDonald, K. B., Beitel, A., & Bhavnagri, N. (1988). The role of the family in the development of peer relationships. In R. Peters & R. J. McMahan (Eds.), *Marriages and families: Behavioral treatment and processes.* New York, NY: Brunner/Mazel.

Parker, R. G. (1995). Reminiscence: A community theory framework. *Gerontologist, 35,* 515–525.

Parker, S. E., Mai, C. T., Canfield, M. A., et al. (2010). Updated national birth prevalence estimates for selected birth defects in the United States, 2004–2006. *Birth Defects Research: A Clinical Molecular Teratology, 88,* 1008–1016.

Parmelee, A. H., Wenner, W. H., & Schulz, H. R. (1964). Infant sleep patterns: From birth to 16 weeks of age. *Journal of Pediatrics, 65*(4), 576–582.

Parsons, C. E., Young, K. S., Kumari, N., Stein, A., & Kringelbach, M. L. (2011). The motivational salience of infant faces is similar for men and women. *PloS ONE, 6*(5), e20632.

Parten, M. (1932). Social play among preschool children. *Journal of Abnormal and Social Psychology, 27,* 243–269.

Pascarella, E. T., & Terenzini, P. T. (1991). *How college affects students: Findings and insights from twenty years of research.* San Francisco: Jossey-Bass.

Pasley, K., & Moorefield, B. S. (2004). Stepfamilies: Changes and challenges. In M. Coleman & L. H. Ganong (Eds.), *Handbook of contemporary families* (pp. 317–330). Thousand Oaks, CA: Sage.

Pasterski, V., Golombok, S., & Hines, M. (2011). Sex differences in social behavior. In P. K. Smith, & C. H. Hart (Eds.), *The Wiley-Blackwell handbook of childhood social development* (2nd ed., pp. 281–298). Malden, MA: Blackwell Publishing

Patchin, J. W., & Hinduja, S. (2006). Bullies move beyond the schoolyard: A preliminary look at cyberbullying. *Youth Violence and Juvenile Justice, 4*(2), 148–169.

Patterson, C. J. (1995). Sexual orientation and human development: An overview. *Developmental Psychology, 31,* 3–11.

Patterson, C. J. (1997). Children of lesbian and gay parents. In T. H. Ollendick & R. J. Prinz (Eds.), *Advances in clinical child psychology* (Vol. 19, pp. 235–282). New York, NY: Plenum.

Patterson, C. J. (2006). Children of lesbian and gay parents. *Current Directions in Psychological Science, 15*(5), 241–44.

Patterson, G. R. (1982). *Coercive family processes.* Eugene, OR: Castilia Press.

Patterson, G. R. (1985). *A social learning approach to family intervention: Vol. 1. Families with aggressive children.* Eugene, OR: Castilia Press.

Patterson, G. R., & Dishion, T. J. (1985). Contributions of families and peers to delinquency. *Criminology, 23,* 63–79.

Patterson, M. L., & Werker, J. F. (2002). Infants' ability to match dynamic phonetic and gender information in the face and voice. *Journal of Experimental Child Psychology, 81,* 93–115.

Paulston, C. (1992). *Linguistic and communicative competence: Topics in ESL.* Philadelphia, PA: Multilingual Matters Ltd.

Paus, T. (2009). Brain development. In R. Lerner & L. Steinberg (Eds.), *Handbook of adolescent psychology* (3rd ed., Vol. 1, pp. 95–115). New York, NY: Wiley.

Pease-Alvarez, L. (1993). *Moving in and out of bilingualism: Investigating native language maintenance and shift in Mexican-descent children.* Santa Cruz, CA: National Center for Research on Cultural Diversity, University of California.

Peets, K., Hodges, E. V., Kikas, E., & Salmivalli, C. (2007). Hostile attributions and behavioral strategies in children: Does relationship type matter? *Developmental Psychology, 43*(4), 889.

Peipert, J. F., Madden, T., Allsworth, J. E., & Secura, G. M. (2012). Preventing unintended pregnancies by providing no-cost contraception. *Obstetrics and Gynecology, 120*(6), 1291–1297.

Pelaez, M., Virues-Ortega, J., & Gewirtz, J. L. (2012). Acquisition of social referencing via discrimination training in infants. *Journal of Applied Behavior Analysis, 45*(1), 23–36.

Pelligrini, A. D., & Smith, P. K. (1998). Physical activity play: The nature and function of a neglected aspect of play. *Child Development, 69,* 577–598.

Penner, S. (1987). Parental responses to grammatical and un-grammatical child utterances. *Child Development, 58,* 376–384.

Peplau, L. A., & Cochran, S. D. (1990). A relationship perspective on homosexuality. In D. P. McWhirter, S. A. Sanders, & J. M. Reinisch (Eds.), *Homosexuality/heterosexuality: Concepts of sexual orientation* (pp. 321–349). New York, NY: Oxford University Press.

Peplau, L. A., & Fingerhut, A. W. (2007). The close relationships of lesbians and gay men. *Annual Review of Psychology, 58,* 405–424.

Perrin, A. J., Cohen, P. N., & Caren, N. (2013). Are children of parents who had same-sex relationships disadvantaged? A scientific evaluation of the no-differences hypothesis. *Journal of Gay & Lesbian Mental Health, 17*(3), 327–336.

Perry, W. G. (1970). *Forms of intellectual and ethical development in the college years.* New York, NY: Holt.

Pesonen, A. K., Räikkönen, K., Keltikangas-Järvinen, L., Strandberg, T., & Järvenpää, A. L. (2003). Parental perception of infant temperament: Does parents' joint attachment matter? *Infant Behavior and Development, 26*(2), 167–182.

Peters, E., Riksen-Walraven, J. M., Cillessen, A. H., & de Weerth, C. (2011). Peer rejection and HPA activity in middle childhood: Friendship makes a difference. *Child Development, 82*(6), 1906–1920.

Petersen, A. C., Compas, B. E., Brooks-Gunn, J., Stemmler, M. E., & Grant, K. E. (1993). Depression in adolescence. *American Psychologist, 48,* 155–168.

Peterson, P., McCarthey, S., & Elmore, R. (1996). Learning from school restructuring. *American Educational Research Journal, 33*(1), 119–153.

Peterson, R. L., & Pennington, B. F. (2012). Developmental dyslexia. *Lancet, 379*(9830), 1997–2007.

Petlichkoff, L. (1996). The drop-out dilemma in youth sports. In O. Bar-Or (Ed.), *The child and adolescent athlete* (pp. 418–432). Oxford, UK: Blackwell.

Pettit, G. S., Bates, J. E., & Dodge, K. A. (1997). Supportive parenting, ecological context, and children's adjustment: A seven-year longitudinal study. *Child Development, 68,* 908–923.

Pettit, G., Dodge, K., & Brown, N. (1988). Early family experience, social problem solving patterns, and children's social competence. *Child Development, 59,* 107–120.

Pettito, L., & Marentette, P. (1991). Babbling in the manual code: Evidence for the ontogeny of language. *Science, 251,* 1493–1496.

Philadelphia Child Guidance Center. (1994). *Your child's emotional health: The middle years.* New York, NY: Macmillan.

Philippe, F. L., & Vallerand, R. J. (2008). Actual environments do affect motivation and psychological adjustment: A test of self-determination theory in a natural setting. *Motivation and Emotion, 32,* 81–89.

Phinney, J. S. (1989). Stages of ethnic identity development in minority group adolescents. *Journal of Early Adolescence, 9,* 34–49.

Phinney, J. S., Dennis, J., & Osorio, S. (2006). Reasons to attend college among ethnically diverse college students. *Cultural Diversity and Ethnic Minority Psychology, 12*(2), 347–366.

Phinney, J. S., Ferguson, D. L., & Tate, J. D. (1997). Intergroup attitudes among ethnic minority adolescents: A causal model. *Child Development, 68,* 955–969.

Piaget, J. (1952). *The child's conception of number.* New York, NY: Norton.

Piaget, J. (1962). *Play, dreams, and imitation in childhood.* New York, NY: Norton.

Piaget, J. (1963). *The origins of intelligence in children.* New York, NY: Norton.

Piaget, J. (1964). *The moral development of the child* New York, NY: Free Press.

Piaget, J. (1965). *The child's conception of the world.* Totowa, NJ: Littlefield, Adams.

Piaget, J. (1983). Piaget's theory. In P. Mussen (Ed.), *Handbook of child psychology: Vol. 1,* New York, NY: Wiley.

Piaget, J., & Inhelder, B. (1967). *The child's conception of space.* New York, NY: Norton.

Pianta, R., Egeland, B., & Erikson, M. (1989). The effects of maltreatment on the development of young children. In D. Cicchetti & V. Carlson (Eds.), *Child Maltreatment.* New York, NY: Cambridge University Press.

Pica-Smith, C., & Poynton, T. A. (2014). Supporting interethnic and interracial friendships among youth to reduce prejudice and racism in schools: The role of the school counselor. *Professional School Counseling, 18*(1), 82–89.

Pike, A., Coldwell, J., & Dunn, J. F. (2005). Sibling relationships in early/middle childhood: Links with individual adjustment. *Journal of Family Psychology, 19*(4), 523–532.

Pillemer, K., & Suitor, J. J. (1991). "Will I ever escape my child's problems?" Effects of adult children's problems on elderly parents. *Journal of Marriage and the Family, 53,* 585–594.

Piotrowski, C. (1997). Rules of everyday family life: The development of social rules in mother-child and sibling relationships. *International Journal of Behavioral Development, 21,* 571–598.

Piran, N. (1997). Prevention of eating disorders; Directions for future research. *Psychopharmacology Bulletin, 33,* 419–423.

Pittard, W. B., Laditka, J. N., & Laditka, S. B. (2008). Associations between maternal age and infant health outcomes among Medicaid-insured infants in South Carolina: Mediating effects of socioeconomic factors. *Pediatrics, 122*(1), e100–e106.

Pittman, T., & Kaufman, M. (1994). *All shapes and sizes: Promoting fitness and self-esteem in your overweight child.* Toronto: Harper Perennial Books.

Pitts, D. G. (1982). Visual acuity as a function of age. *Journal of the American Optometric Association, 53,* 117–124.

Plante, T. G., & Rodin, J. (1990). Physical fitness and enhanced psychological health. *Current Psychology: Research and Reviews, 9,* 3–24.

Plomin, R. (1989). Environment and genes: Determinants of behavior. *American Psychologist, 44,* 105–111.

Plomin, R. (1990). *Nature and nurture: An introduction to human behavioral genetics.* Pacific Grove, CA: Brooks/Cole.

Plomin, R., Owen, M. J., & McGuffin, P. (1994). The genetic basis of behavior. *Science, 264,* 1733–1739.

Pollitt, E. (Ed.). (1995). *The relationships between undernutrition and behavioral development in children.* Washington, DC: American Institute of Nutrition.

Pollock, M. L., Foster, C., Knapp, D., Rod, J. L., & Schmidt, D. H. (1987). Effect of age and training on aerobic capacity and body composition of master athletes. *Journal of Applied Physiology, 62,* 725–731.

Pomerantz, E. M., Ruble, D. N., Frey, K. S., & Greulich, F. (1995). Meeting goals and confronting conflict: Children's changing perceptions of social comparison. *Child Development, 66,* 723–738.

Porter, R. H., & Reiser, J. J. (2005). Retention of olfactory memories by newborn infants. In R. T. Mason, P. M. LeMaster, & D. Müller-Schwarze (Eds.), *Chemical Signals in Vertebrates.* New York, NY: Springer.

Portrie, T., & Hill, N. R. (2005). Blended families: A critical review of the current research. *Family Journal, 13*(4), 445–451.

Posada, G., & Kaloustian, G. (2010). Attachment in infancy. In J. G. Bremner, & T. D. Wachs (Eds.), *The Wiley-Blackwell handbook of infant development* (pp. 483–509). Malden, MA: Wiley-Blackwell Publishing.

Posner, J. K., & Vandell, D. L. (1994). Low-income children's after-school care: Are there beneficial effects of after-school programs? *Child Development, 65,* 440–456.

Potter, D. (2012). Same-sex parent families and children's academic achievement. *Journal of Marriage and Family, 74*(3), 556–571.

Poulin, F., & Chan, A. (2010). Friendship stability and change in childhood and adolescence. *Developmental Review, 30*(3), 257–272.

Powell, M. (1991). The psychosocial impact of sudden infant death syndrome on siblings. *Irish Journal of Psychology, 12,* 235–247.

Power, H., & Everly, G. S. (1988). Psychological factors in preterm labor: Critical review and theoretical synthesis. *American Journal of Psychiatry, 145,* 1507–1513.

Power, T. G. (2011). Social play. In P. K. Smith, & C. H. Hart (Eds.), *The Wiley-Blackwell handbook of childhood social development* (2nd ed., pp. 455–471). Malden, MA: Blackwell Publishing.

Pownall, T., & Kingerlee, S. (1993). *Seeing, reaching, and touching: Relationships between vision and touching in infants.* New York, NY: Harvester and Wheatsheaf.

Price, R. H. (1992). Psychosocial impact of joblessness on individuals and families. *Current Directions in Psychological Science, 1,* 9–11.

Primeau, M. R. (1993). Fetal movement. In B. K. Rothman (Ed.), *The encyclopedia of childbearing.* New York, NY: Henry Holt.

Prinstein, M. J. (2008). Introduction to the special section on suicide and non-suicidal self-injury: A review of the unique challenges and important directions for self-injury science. *Journal of Consulting and Clinical Psychology, 76*(1), 1–8.

Prinz, P., & Prinz, E. (1979). Simultaneous acquisition of ASL and spoken English. *Sign Language Studies, 25,* 283–296.

Pritchett, L. (1993). *Wealthier is healthier.* Washington, DC: The World Bank.

Proctor, C. P., Dalton, B., & Grisham, D. L. (2007). Scaffolding English language learners and struggling readers in a universal literacy environment with embedded strategy instruction and vocabulary support. *Journal of Literacy Research, 39*(1), 71–93.

Pryor, D. W., & McGarell, E. F. (1993). Public perceptions of youth gang crime: An exploratory analysis. *Youth and Society, 24,* 399–418.

Puhl, R. M., & King, K. M. (2013). Weight discrimination and bullying. *Best Practice & Research Clinical Endocrinology & Metabolism, 27*(2), 117–127.

Pulakos, J. (1989). Young adult relationships: Siblings and friends. *Journal of Psychology, 123*(3), 237–244.

Purhonen, M., Kilpeläinen-Lees, R., Valkonen-Korhonen, M., Karhu, J., & Lehtonen, J. (2004). Cerebral processing of mother's voice compared to unfamiliar voice in 4-month old infants. *International Journal of Psychophysiology, 52,* 257–266.

Q

Quadrel, M. J., Fischoff, B., & Davis, W. (1993). Adolescent (in) vulnerability. *American Psychologist, 48,* 102–116.

Quan, J., Bureau, J. F., Yurkowski, K., Moss, E., & Pallanca, D. (2013). The association between time spent in daycare and preschool attachment to fathers and mothers: An exploration of disorganization. *International Journal of Arts and Sciences, 6*(2), 415–422.

Queen, P., & Lang, C. (1993). *Handbook of pediatric nutrition.* Gaithersburg, MD: Aspen Publishers.

Quinlan, J. D., & Hill, D. A. (2003). Nausea and vomiting of pregnancy. *American Family Physician, 68,* 121–128.

Quinn, P. C., Kelly, D. J., Kang, L., Pascalis, O., & Slater, A. M. (2008). Preference for attractive faces in human infants extends beyond conspecifics. *Developmental Science, 11,* 76–83.

Quintana, S. M. (2011). Ethnicity, race, and social development. In P. K. Smith, & C. H. Hart (Eds.), *The Wiley-Blackwell handbook of childhood social development* (2nd ed., pp. 299–318). Malden, MA: Blackwell Publishing.

R

Raabe, T., & Beelmann, A. (2011). Development of ethnic, racial, and national prejudice in childhood and adolescence: A multinational meta-analysis of age differences. *Child Development, 82,* 1715–1737.

Raby, K. L., Steele, R. D., Carlson, E. A., & Sroufe, L. A. (2015). Continuities and changes in infant attachment patterns across two generations. *Attachment & Human Development, 17*(4), 414–428.

Radke-Yarrow, M., Nottelmann, E., Belmont, B., & Welsh, J. D. (1993). *Journal of Abnormal Child Psychology, 21,* 683–695.

Radke-Yarrow, M., & Zahn-Waxler, C. (1987). Roots, motives, and patterns in children's prosocial behavior. In J. Reykowski, J. Karylowski, D. Bar-Tal, & E. Staub (Eds.), *Origins and maintenance of prosocial behaviors.* New York, NY: Plenum Press.

Radmacher, K., & Azmitia, M. (2006). Are there gendered pathways to intimacy in early adolescents' and emerging adults' friendships? *Journal of Adolescent Research, 21*(4), 415–448.

Raloff, J. (2015). The dangers of vaping: Teens are falling for flavored e-cigs, but the vapors they inhale may be toxic. *Science News, 188*(1), 18–21.

Ramirez, O. (1998). Mexican-American children and adolescents. In J. Gibbs & L. Huang (Eds.), *Children of color: Psychological interventions with culturally diverse youth* (2nd ed.) (pp. 215–239). San Francisco: Jossey-Bass.

Ramsey, P. (1995). Changing social dynamics in early childhood classrooms. *Child Development, 66,* 764–773.

Ramu, G. N. (1991). Changing family structure and fertility patterns: An Indian case. *Journal of Asian and African Studies, 26*(3–4), 189–206.

Raphael, D. (1993). Doula. In B. K. Rothman (Ed.), *The encyclopedia of childbearing.* New York, NY: Henry Holt.

Raver, C. C. (1996). Relations between social contingency in mother-child interaction and two-year-old's social competence. *Developmental Psychology, 32,* 850–859.

Rawlins, W. K. (1992). *Friendship matters: Communication, dialectics, and the life course.* New York, NY: Aldine DeGruyter.

Rawson, N. (2003). Age-related changes in perception of flavor and aroma. *Generations, 27,* 20–26.

Reaves, J., & Roberts, A. (1983). The effect of type of information on children's attraction to peers. *Child Development, 54,* 1024–1031.

Reccio Adrados, J. L. (1995). The influence of family, school, and peers on adolescent drug misuse. *International Journal of the Addictions, 30,* 1407–1423.

Recker, R. R., Davies, K. M., Hinders, S. M., Heaney, R. P., Stegman, M. R., & Kimmel, D. B. (1992). Bone gain in young adult women. *Journal of the American Medical Association, 268,* 2403–2408.

Reeder, K. (Ed.). (1996). *Literate apprenticeships: The emergence of language and literacy in the preschool years.* Norwood, NJ: Ablex.

Rege, M., Telle, K., & Votruba, M. (2011). Parental job loss and children's school performance. *Review of Economic Studies, 78,* 1462–1489.

Reid, M., Landesman, S., Treider, R., & Jaccard, J. (1989). "My family and friends": Six- to twelve-year-old perceptions of social support. *Child Development, 60,* 896–910.

Reilly, R. R., Brown, B., Blood, M. R., & Malatesta, C. Z. (1981). The effects of realistic previews: A study and discussion of the literature. *Personnel Psychology, 34,* 832–834.

Remafedi, G. (2007). Adolescent homosexuality. In R. M. Kliegman, R. E. Behrman, J. B. Jenson, & B. F. Stanton (Eds.), *Nelson textbook of pediatrics* (pp. 67–68). Philadelphia, PA: WB Saunders Company.

Remafedi, G., Resnick, M., Blum, R., & Harris, L. (1992). Demography of sexual orientation in adolescents. *Pediatrics, 89,* 714–721.

Renzulli, J. (1994). *Schools for talent improvement.* Mansfield Center, CT: Creative Learning Press.

Reuter, M. A., & Conger, R. D. (1995). Antecedents of parent-adolescent disagreements. *Journal of Marriage and the Family, 57,* 435–448.

Rey-Lopez, J. P., Vicente-Rodríguez, G., Biosca, M., & Moreno, L. A. (2008). Sedentary behaviour and obesity development in children and adolescents. *Nutrition, Metabolism and Cardiovascular Diseases, 18*(3), 242–251.

Reynolds, A. J., & Temple, J. A. (1998). Extended early childhood intervention and school achievement: Age thirteen findings from the Chicago Longitudinal Study. *Child Development, 69,* 231–246.

Richards, M., & Wadsworth, M. E. J. (2004). Long term effects of early adversity on cognitive function. *Archives of Disease in Childhood, 89,* 922–927.

Richards, M. H., Crowe, P. A., Larson, R., & Swarr, A. (1998). Developmental patterns and gender differences in the experience of peer companionship during adolescence. *Child Development, 69,* 154–163.

Richio, L. J., Phipps, M. G., & Raker, C. A. (2010). Repeat teen birth: Does delivery mode make a difference? *American Journal of Obstetrics and Gynecology, 203,* 453–458.

Richter, P. (1993). HIV and pregnancy. In B. K. Rothman (Ed.), *The encyclopedia of childbearing.* New York, NY: Henry Holt.

Ricketts, S., Klingler, G., & Schwalberg, R. (2014). Game change in Colorado: Widespread use of long-acting reversible contraceptives and rapid decline in births among young, low-income women. *Perspectives on Sexual and Reproductive Health, 46*(3), 125–132.

Rickman, M. D., & Davidson, R. J. (1995). Personality and behavior in parents of temperamentally inhibited and uninhibited children. *Developmental Psychology, 30,* 346–354.

Rideout, V. J., Foehr, U. G., & Roberts, D. F. (2010). Generation M2: Media in the lives of 8- to 18-year-olds. Henry J. Kaiser Family Foundation. Retrieved from http://files.eric.ed.gov/fulltext/ED527859.pdf

Rieck, T., Jackson, A. W., Martin, S. B., Petrie, T. A., & Greenleaf, C. A. (2013). Relation between depression and physical fitness of middle school students. *Medicine & Science in Sport & Exercise, 45*(6), 1083–1088.

Riggle, E. D., Rotosky, S. S., & Riggle, S. G. (2010). Psychological distress, well-being, and legal recognition in same-sex couple relationships. *Journal of Family Psychology, 24*(1), 82–86.

Rigsby, D. C., Macones, G. A., & Driscoll, D. A. (1998). Risk factors for rapid repeat pregnancy among adolescent mothers: A review of the literature. *Journal of Pediatric and Adolescent Gynecology, 11*(3), 115–126.

Riley, E. P., Infante, M. A., & Warren, K. R. (2011). Fetal alcohol spectrum disorders: An overview. *Neuropsychology Review, 21,* 73–80.

Rivkees, S. A. (2003). Developing circadian rhythmicity in infants. *Pediatrics, 112,* 373–381.

Roberts, W., & Strayer, J. (1996). Empathy, emotional expressiveness, and prosocial behavior. *Child Development, 67,* 449–470.

Robertson, M. (1992). *Starving in the silences.* New York, NY: New York University Press.

Robin, A. L., & Foster, S. L. (1989). *Negotiating parent-adolescent conflict: A behavioral family systems approach.* New York, NY: Guilford Press.

Robin, A. L., Koepke, T., & Moye, A. (1990). Multidimensional assessment of parent-adolescent relations. *Psychological Assessment: A Journal of Consulting and Clinical Psychology, 2*(4), 451–459.

Robins, R. W., & Trzesniewski, K. H. (2005). Self-esteem development across the lifespan. *Current Directions in Psychological Science, 14*(3), 158–162.

Rochat, P. (2003). Five levels of self-awareness as they unfold early in life. *Consciousness and Cognition, 12*(4), 717–731.

Roche, K. M., Ensminger, M. E., & Cherlin, A. J. (2007). Variations in parenting and adolescent outcomes among African American and Latino families living in low-income, urban areas. *Journal of Family Issues, 28*(7), 882–909.

Rodgers, J. L., & Rowe, D. C. (1993). Social contagion and adolescent sexual behavior: A developmental EMOSA model. *Psychological Review, 100,* 479–510.

Rodkin, P. C., Ryan, A. M., Jamison, R., & Wilson, T. (2013). Social goals, social behavior, and social status in middle childhood. *Developmental Psychology, 49*(6), 1139.

Roelofs, J., Meesters, C., ter Huurne, M., Bamelis, L., & Muris, P. (2006). On the links between attachment style, parental rearing behaviors, and internalizing and externalizing problems in non-clinical children. *Journal of Child and Family Studies, 15*(3), 319–332.

Roggman, L. A., Langlois, J. H., Hubbs-Tait, L., & Rieser-Danner, L. A. (1994). Infant day-care, attachment, and the "file drawer problem." *Child Development, 65,* 1429–1443.

Rogoff, B. (1990). *Apprenticeship in thinking.* New York, NY: Oxford University Press.

Rogoff, B., & Chavajay, P. (1995). What's become of research on the cultural basis of cognitive development? *American Psychologist, 50,* 859–877.

Rogoff, B., Mistry, J., Goncu, A., & Mosler, C. (1993). Guided participation in cultural activity by toddlers and caregivers. *Monographs of the Society for Research in Child Development, 58*(8, Serial No. 236).

Roland, A. (1988). *In search of self in India and Japan: Toward a cross-cultural psychology.* Princeton, NJ: Princeton University Press.

Romaine, S. (1995). *Bilingualism* (2nd ed.). Oxford, UK: Black-wells.

Romig, D. A., Cleland, C., & Romig, J. (1989). *Juvenile delinquency: Visionary approaches.* Columbus, Ohio: Merrill.

Rooks, J. P., Weatherby, N. L., Ernst, E. K., Stapleton, S., Rosen, D., & Rosenfield, A. (1989). Outcomes of care in birth centers. *New England Journal of Medicine, 321*(26), 1804–1811.

Room, R. (2004). Smoking and drinking as complementary behaviors. *Biomedicine and Pharmacotherapy, 58,* 111–115. doi: 10.1016/j.biopha.2003.12.003

Roopnarine, J. L., Johnson, J. E., & Hooper, F. H. (Eds,). (1994). *Children's play in diverse cultures.* Albany, NY: State University of New York Press.

Rose, J., & Gamble, J. (1993). *Human walking* (2nd ed.). Baltimore: Williams and Williams.

Rosemary, S. L., Arbeau, K. A., Lall, D. I., & De Jaeger, A. E. (2010). Parenting and child characteristics in the prediction of shame in early and middle childhood. *Merrill-Palmer Quarterly, 56*(4), 500–528.

Rosenberg, B. G., & Hyde, J. S. (1993). The only child: Is there only one kind of only? *Journal of Genetic Psychology, 154,* 269–282.

Rosenberg, M. S. (1979). *Conceiving the self.* New York, NY: Basic Books.

Rosenberg, M. S., & Repucci, N. D. (1985). Primary prevention of child abuse. *Journal of Consulting and Clinical Psychology, 53,* 576–585.

Rosenfeld, M. J., & Thomas, R. J. (2012). Searching for a mate: The rise of the internet as a social intermediary. *American Sociological Review, 77*(4), 523–547.

Rosenheim, M. K., & Testa, M. F. (Eds.). (1992). *Early parenthood and coming of age in the 1990's.* New Brunswick, NJ: Rutgers University Press.

Ross, H., Tesla, C., Kenyon, B., & Lollis, S. (1990). Maternal intervention in toddler peer conflict: The socialization of principles of justice. *Development Psychology, 26,* 994–1003.

Ross, J., & Kahan, J. P. (1983). Children by choice or by chance: The perceived effects of parity. *Sex Roles, 9,* 69–77.

Ross, P. (1993). *National excellence: The case for developing America's talent.* Washington, DC: United States Department of Education.

Rossell, C. H. (1988). How effective are voluntary plans with magnet schools? *Educational Evaluation and Policy Analysis, 10,* 325–342.

Rossi, A. S. (1982). Transition to parenthood. In L. R. Allman & D. T. Jaffe (Eds), *Readings in adult psychology: Contemporary perspectives* (2nd ed., pp. 263–275). New York, NY: Harper & Row.

Rossi, A. S., & Rossi, P. H. (1990). *Of human bonding: Parent child relations across the life course.* New York, NY: Aldine de Gruyter.

Rothbart, M. (1989). Temperament in childhood: A framework. In G. Kohnstamm, J. Bates, & M. Rothbart (Eds), *Temperament in childhood* (pp. 59–73) New York, NY: Wiley.

Rothbart, M. K. (2007). Temperament, development, and personality. *Current Directions in Psychological Science, 16*(4), 207–212.

Rothbart, M. K., & Ahadi, S. (1994). Temperament and the development of personality *Journal of Abnormal Psychology, 103,* 55–66.

Rothbart, M. K., Hanley, D., & Albert, M. (1986). Gender differences in moral reasoning. *Sex Roles, 15,* 645–653.

Rothman, K. J. (2008). BMI-related errors in the measurement of obesity. *International Journal of Obesity, 32,* S56–S59.

Rourke, B., & Del Dotto, J. (1994). *Learning disabilities: Neuropsychological perspectives.* Thousand Oaks, CA: Sage.

Rowe, M. L., Levine, S. C., Fisher, J. A., & Goldin-Meadow, S. (2009). Does linguistic input play the same role in language learning for children with and without early brain injury? *Developmental Psychology, 45,* 90–102.

Rowland, T. (1993). The physiological impact of intensive training on the prepubertal athlete. In B. Cahill and A. Pearl (Eds.), *Intensive participation in children's sports* (pp. 167–194). Champaign, IL: Human Kinetics Press.

Rubenstein, J. L., & Howes, C. (1976). The effects of peers on toddler interaction with mother and toys. *Child Development, 47,* 597–605.

Rubenstein, J. L., & Howes, C. (1983). Social-emotional development of toddlers in day care: The role of peers and of individual differences. *Advances in Early Education and Day Care, 3,* 13–45.

Rubenstein, J. L., Halton, A., Kasten, M. A., Rubin, C., & Stechler, G. (1998). Suicidal behavior in adolescents: Stress and protection in different family contexts. *American Journal of Orthopsychiatry, 68,* 274–284.

Rubenstein, J. L., Heeren, T., Housman, D., Rubin, C., & Stechler, G. (1989). Suicidal behavior in "normal" adolescents: Risk and protective factor's. *American Journal of Orthopsychiatry, 59,* 59–71.

Rubin, K., Fredstrom, B., & Bowker, J. (2008). Future directions in . . . Friendship in childhood and early adolescence. *Social Development, 17*(4), 1085–1096.

Rubin, K. H., Coplan, R. J., & Bowker, J. C. (2009). Social withdrawal in childhood. *Annual Review of Psychology, 60,* 141.

Rubin, K. H., & Krasnor, L. (1980). Changes in the play behaviors of preschoolers: A short-term longitudinal investigation. *Canadian Journal of Behavioral Science, 12,* 278–282.

Ruble, D. N. (1988). Sex-role development. In M. H. Bornstein & M. E. Lamb (Eds.), *Developmental psychology: An advanced textbook* (2nd ed., pp. 411–460). Hillsdale, NJ: Erlbaum.

Ruble, D. N., Martin, C. L., & Berenbaum, S. (2006). Gender development. In W. Damon, & R. M. Lerner (Series Eds.), & N. Eisenberg (Vol. Ed.), *Handbook of child psychology: Vol. 3. Social, emotional and personality development* (6th ed.). Hoboken, NJ: Wiley.

Rudowitz, R., Artiga, S., & Arguello, R. (2014). *Children's health coverage: Medicaid, CHIP, and the ACA.* Retrieved from http://kff.org/healthreform/issue-brief/childrens-health-coveragemedicaid-chip-and-the-aca/

Rudy, D., & Grusec, J. E. (2006). Authoritarian parenting in individualist and collectivist groups: Associations with maternal emotion and cognition and children's self-esteem. *Journal of Family Psychology, 20*(1), 68–78.

Rueter, M. A., & Conger, R. D. (1995). Interaction style, problem solving behavior, and family problem-solving effectiveness. *Child Development, 66,* 98–115.

Ruhm, C. J. (1997). The Family and Medical Leave Act. *Journal of Economic Perspectives, 11,* 175–186.

Ruhm, C. J. (2000). Parental leave and child health. *Journal of Health Economics, 19*(6), 931–960.

Ruiz-Primo, M. A. (2011). Informal formative assessment: The role of instructional dialogues in assessing students' learning. *Studies in Educational Evaluation, 37*(1), 15–24.

Russ, S. W., & Dillon, J. A. (2011). Changes in children's pretend play over two decades. *Creativity Research Journal, 23*(4), 330–338.

Russell, K., & Ludwig, B. (2015). *Smoking is out; vaping is in. The rise of e-cigarettes among US youth.* Retrieved from http://jdc.jefferson.edu/cgi/iewcontent.cgi?article=1952&context=hpn

Russell, R. M. (1992). Nutrient requirements. In J. B. Wyngaarden, L. H. Smith, & J. C Bennett (Eds.), *Cecil textbook of medicine, Vol. 2* (19th ed., pp. 1147–1151). Philadelphia: Saunders.

Rutter, M. (1995). *Psychosocial disturbances in young people.* New York, NY: Cambridge University Press.

Ryan, J. (1995). *Little girls in pretty boxes: The making and breaking of elite gymnasts and figure skaters.* New York, NY: Double-Day.

S

Saad, L. (2013). Gallup politics: Majority of Americans still support Roe v. Wade decision. Retrieved from http://www.gallup.com/poll/160058/majorityamericans-support-roe-wade-decision.aspx

Safety-belt use and motor-vehicle-related injuries– Navajo Nation, 1988–1991. (1992, September 25). *Morbidity and Mortality Weekly Report, 41*(38), 705.

Sagi, A., van Ijzendoorn, M. H., Aviezer, O., Donnell, F., & Mayseless, O. (1994). Sleeping out of home in a kibbutz communal arrangement: It makes a difference for infant-mother attachment. *Child Development, 65,* 992–1004.

Sagi-Schwartz, A. (2008). The well being of children living in chronic war zones: The Palestinian—Israeli case. *International Journal of Behavioral Development, 32*(4), 322–336.

Saler, L., & Skolnick, N. (1992). Childhood parental death and depression in adulthood: Roles of surviving parent and family environment. *American Journal of Orthopsychiatry, 62,* 504–516.

Salguero, A., Gonzalez-Boto, R., Tuero, C., & Marquez, S. (2003). Identification of dropout reasons in young competitive swimmers. *Journal of Sports Medicine and Physical Fitness, 43*(4), 530.

Salisbury, C., & Robertson, C. (2013). Maternal nutrition: Building foundations of long-term good health. *Nutrition Bulletin, 38,* 249–253.

Salomon, G., & Perkins, D. (1998). Individual and social aspects of learning. In P. D. Pearson & A. Iran-Nejad (Eds.), *Review of research in education* (Vol. 23, pp. 1–24). Washington, DC: American Educational Research Association.

Samter, W., & Haslett, B. (1997). Family influences on communicative and social development. In B. Haslett & W. Samter (Eds.), *Children communicating: The first five years* (pp. 160–191). Mahwah, NJ: Erlbaum.

Samuels, C. A. (2005). Special educators discuss NCLB effect at national meeting. *Education Week, 24,* 12.

Samuelsson, I. P., & Carlsson, M. A. (2008). The playing learning child: Towards a pedagogy of early childhood. *Scandinavian Journal of Educational Research, 52*(6), 623–641.

Sanders, S. A., Graham, C. A., & Milhausen, R. R. (2008). Predicting sexual problems in women: The relevance of sexual excitation and sexual inhibition. *Archives of Sexual Behavior, 37*(2), 241–251.

Sandler, I. N., Ma, Y., Tein, J. Y., Ayers, T. S., Wolchik, S., Kennedy, C., & Millsap, R. (2010). Long-term effects of the family bereavement program on multiple indicators of grief in parentally bereaved children and adolescents. *Journal of Consulting and Clinical Psychology, 78*(2), 131–143.

Sandnabba, N. K., & Ahlberg, C. (1999). Parents' attitudes and expectations about children's crossgender behavior. *Sex Roles, 40*(3–4), 249–263.

Sanfilippo, J., Finkelstein, J., & Styne, D. (Eds.) (1994). *Medical and gynecological endocrinology* Philadelphia: Hanley and Belfus.

Santrock, J., & Sitterle, K. (1987). Parent-child relationships in stepmother families. In K. Pasley & M. Ihinger-Tallman (Eds.), *Remarriage and stepparenting: Current research and theory,* New York, NY: Guilford Press.

Saracho, O. N., & Spodek, B. O. (1998). A historical overview of theories of play. In O. N. Saracho & B. Spodek, et al. (Eds.), *Multiple perspectives on play to early childhood education.* SUNY series, *Early Childhood Education: Inquiries and Insights* (pp. 1–10). Albany, NY: State University of New York Press.

Sarafino, E., & Armstrong, J. (1986). *Child and adolescent development.* New York, NY: West.

Sato, D. (1993). DES: Diethylstilbestrol. In B. K. Rothman (Ed.), *The encyclopedia of childbearing.* New York, NY: Henry Holt.

Saucier, M. G. (2004). Midlife and beyond: Issues for aging women. *Journal of Counseling and Development, 82,* 420–425.

Sault, N. (Ed.). (1994). *Many mirrors: Body image and social relations.* New Brunswick, NJ: Rutgers University Press.

Savelsbergh, G. (1993). *Development of coordination in infancy.* New York, NY: North-Holland.

Savin-Williams, R. C. (1995). An exploratory study of pubertal maturation timing and self-esteem among gay and bisexual male youths. *Developmental Psychology, 31,* 56–64.

Savin-Williams, R. C., & Berndt, T. (1990). Peer relations during adolescence. In S. Feldman & G. Elliot (Eds.), *At the threshold: The developing adolescent.* Cambridge, MA: Harvard University Press.

Sawin, D. (1979). *Assessing empathy in children: A search for an elusive construct.* Paper presented at the meeting of the Society for Research on Child Development, San Francisco.

Scanzoni, J., Polonko, K., Teachman, J., & Thompson, L. (1989). *The sexual bond: Rethinking families and close relationships.* Newbury Park, CA: Sage.

Scarr, S. (1998). American child care today. *American Psychologist, 53,* 95–108.

Schiller, B. (2004). *The economics of poverty and discrimination* (9th ed.). Upper Saddle River, NJ: Pearson Prentice Hall.

Schlegel, A., & Barry, H. (1991). *Adolescence: An anthropological inquiry* (pp. 133–156). New York, NY: Free Press.

Schmid, S. M., Hallschmid, M., Jauch-Chara, K., Born, J., & Schultes, B. (2008). A single night of sleep deprivation increases ghrelin levels and feelings of hunger in normal-weight healthy men. *Journal of Sleep Research, 17*(3), 331–334.

Schoppe-Sullivan, S. J., & Mangelsdorf, S. C. (2013). Parent characteristics and early coparenting behavior at the transition to parenthood. *Social Development, 22,* 363–383.

Schrader, D. (Ed.). (1990). *The legacy of Lawrence Kohlberg (New Directions in Child Development,* No. 47). San Francisco: Jossey-Bass.

Schulenberg, J., Maggs, J., and Hurrelmann, K. (Eds.). (1997). *Health risks and developmental transitions during adolescence.* New York, NY: Cambridge University Press.

Schulman, E. P., Steinberg, L., & Piquero, A. R. (2013). The age-crime curve in adolescence and early adulthood is not due to age differences in economic status. *Journal of Youth and Adolescence, 42,* 848–860.

Schwartz, D., Dodge, K. A., Pettit, G. S., & Bates, J. (1997). The early socialization of aggression and bullying *Child Development, 68,* 665–675.

Schweinhart, L., Barnes, H., & Weikart, D. (1993). Significant benefits: The High/Scope Perry Preschool Study through age 27. (*Monographs of the High/Scope Educational Research Foundation,* No. 10). Ypsilanti, MI: High/Scope Press.

Schweinhart, L., & Weikart, D. (1992). The High/Scope Perry Preschool Study, similar studies, and their implications for public policy in the United States. In D. Slegelin (Ed.), *Early childhood education: Policy issues for the 1990's* (pp. 67–88). Norwood, NJ: Ablex.

Schweinhart, L., & Weikart, D. (1999). The advantages of High/Scope: Helping children lead successful lives. *Educational Leadership, 57,* 76–77.

Schweinle, A., & Wilcox, T. (2004). Intermodal perception and physical reasoning in young infants. *Infant Behavior and Development, 27,* 246–265.

Scollon, R., & Scollon, S. (1994). *Intercultural communication: A discourse approach.* Oxford, UK: Blackwell.

Scott, K. D., Klaus, P. H., & Klaus, M. H. (1999). A comparison of intermittent and continuous support during labor: A meta-analysis. *Journal of Women's Health & Gender-Based Medicine, 8,* 1257–1264.

Scraton, S. (1992). *Shaping up to womanhood: Gender and girls' physical education.* Philadelphia: Open University Press.

Sedgh, G., Finer, L. B., Bankole, A., Eilers, M. A., & Singh, S. (2015). Adolescent pregnancy, birth, and abortion rates across countries: Levels and recent trends. *Journal of Adolescent Health, 56*(2), 223–230.

Seidel, H., Rosenstein, B., & Pathak, A. (Eds.). (1997). *Primary care of the newborn* (2nd ed.). St. Louis: Mosby.

Seidman, S. N., & Rieder, R. O. (1994). A review of sexual behavior in the United States. *American Journal of Psychiatry, 151,* 330–341.

Seidner, L. B., Stipek, D. J., & Feshbach, N. D. (1988). A developmental analysis of elementary school-aged children's concepts of pride and embarrassment. *Child Development, 59,* 367–377.

Seifer, R., Sameroff, A. J., Barrett, L. C., & Krafechuk, E. (1994). Infant temperament measured by multiple observations and mother reports. *Child Development, 65,* 1478–1490.

Seifert, K. (1993). Cognitive development in early childhood. In B. Spodek (Ed.), *Handbook of research on the education of young children* (3rd ed., pp. 7–40). New York, NY: Macmillan.

Seifert, K. (2000). Uniformity and diversity in everyday views of "the" child. In S. Harkness (Ed.), *New directions in child development: Parental belief systems in cultural context.* San Francisco: Jossey-Bass.

Seiffge-Krenke, I. (2010). Predicting the timing of leaving home and related developmental tasks: Parents' and children's perspectives. *Journal of Social and Personal Relationships, 27*(4), 495–518.

Seiffge-Krenke, I. (2016). Leaving home: Antecedents, consequences, and cultural patterns. In J. J. Arnett (Ed.), *The Oxford handbook of emerging adulthood* (pp. 177–189). New York, NY: Oxford University Press.

Seitz, V., & Apfel, N. (1994). Parent-focused intervention: Diffusion effects on siblings. *Child Development, 65*(2), 677–683.

Selekman, J. (1993). Update: New guidelines for the treatment of infants with sickle cell disease. *Pediatric Nursing,* 19, 800–809.

Selman, R. (1980). *The growth of interpersonal understanding,* New York, NY: Academic Press.

Selman, R. (1981). The child as friendship philosopher. In S. Asher & J. Gottman (Eds.), *The development of children's friendships.* New York, NY: Cambridge University Press.

Seltzer, M. M., Greenberg, J. S., Floyd, F. J., Pettee, Y., & Hong, J. (2001). Life course impacts of parenting a child with a disability. *American Journal on Mental Retardation, 106,* 265–286.

Selye, H. (1985). History and present status of the stress concept. In A. Monat and R. Lazarus (Eds.), *Stress and coping.* New York, NY: Columbia University Press.

Shafer, M. B., & Moscicki, A. (1991). Sexually transmitted diseases. In W. R. Hendee (Ed.), *The health of adolescents: Understanding and facilitating biological, behavioral, and social development* (pp. 211–249). San Francisco: Jossey-Bass.

Shapiro, A. F., Gottman, J. M., & Carrere, S. (2000). The baby and the marriage: Identifying factors that buffer against decline in marital satisfaction after the first baby arrives. *Journal of Family Psychology, 14,* 59–70.

Shapiro, J. P. (1993). *No pity: People with disabilities forging a new civil rights movement.* New York, NY: Random House.

Shaughnessy, L., Doshi, S. R., & Everett Jones. (2004). Attempted suicide and associated health risk behaviors among Native American high school students. *Journal of School Health, 74,* 177–182.

Sheehan, M. J., & Watson, M. W. (2008). Reciprocal influences between maternal discipline techniques and aggression in children and adolescents. *Aggressive Behavior, 34*(3), 245–255.

Sheldon, S., Spire, J., & Levy, H. (1992). *Pediatric sleep medicine.* Philadelphia: Saunders.

Shepherd-Look, D. (1982). Sex differentiation and the development of sex roles. In B. Wolman (Ed.), *Handbook of developmental psychology.* Englewood Cliffs, NJ: Prentice-Hall.

Shmueli, A., Salman, L., Chen, R., & Hiersch, L., Gabbay-Benziv, R., & Wiznitzer, A. (2017). The duration of the second stage of labor – Do we underestimate the impact of epidural analgesia? *American Journal of Obstetrics and Gynecology, 216,* S429.

Short, J. E. (2015). *How much media? 2015 report on American consumers.* Retrieved from http://www.marshall.usc.edu/faculty/centers/ctm/research/how-much-media

Shrum, W., Cheek, N. H., & Hunter, S. M. (1988). Friendship in school: Gender and racial homophily. *Sociology of Education, 61,* 227–239.

Shulman, S., & Connolly, J. (2016). The challenge of romantic relationships in emerging adulthood. In J. J. Arnett (Ed.), *The Oxford handbook of emerging adulthood* (pp. 230–244). New York, NY: Oxford University Press.

Shultz, S., & Vouloumanos, A. (2010). Three-month olds prefer speech to other naturally occurring signals. *Language Learning and Development, 6,* 241–257.

Shure, M. B., & Spivak, G. (1988). Interpersonal cognitive problem solving. In R. II. Price, W. L. Cowen, R. P. Lorion, & J. Ramos-McKay (Eds.), *14 ounces of prevention: A casebook for practitioners* (pp. 69–82). Washington, DC: American Psychological Association.

Silber, S. J. (1991). *How to get pregnant with the new technology.* New York, NY: Warner Books.

Silverman, P. R., Nickman, S., & Worden, J. W. (1992). Detachment revisited: The child's reconstruction of a dead patent. *American Journal of Orthopsychiatry, 62,* 494–505.

Silverman, P., & Worden, J. (1993). Children's reactions to the death of a parent. In M. Stroebe, W. Stroebe, & R. Hansson (Eds.), *Handbook of bereavement: Theory, research, and intervention* (pp. 300–315). Cambridge: Cambridge University Press.

Silverstein, L. B. (1991). Transforming the debate about child care and maternal employment. *American Psychologist, 46,* 1025–1032.

Simkin, P. (2007). *The birth partner, third edition: A complete guide to childbirth for dads, doulas, and all other labor companions.* Boston, MA: Harvard Common Press.

Simonds, W. (1993). Politics of abortion. In B. K. Rothman (Ed.), *The encyclopedia of childbearing.* New York, NY: Henry Holt.

Simons, R. L., & Beaman, J. (1996). Fathers' parenting. In R. L. Simons et al. (Eds.), *Understanding differences between divorced and intact families:*

Simons, R. L., & Chao, W. (1996). Conduct problems. In R. L. Simons et al. (Eds.), *Understanding differences between divorced and intact families: Stress, interaction, and child outcome* (pp. 81–93). Thousand Oaks, CA: Sage.

Simons, R. L., & Johnson, C. (1996). Mothers' parenting. In R. L. Simons et al. (Eds.), *Understanding differences between divorced and intact families: Stress, interaction and child outcome* (pp. 81–93). Thousand Oaks, CA: Sage.

Simpson, J. A., Collins, W. A., Tran, S., & Haydon, K. C. (2007). Attachment and the experience and expression of emotions in romantic relationships: A developmental perspective. *Journal of Personality and Social Psychology, 92*(2), 355–367.

Simpson, J. L., Holzgreve, W., & Driscoll, D. A. (2012). Genetic counseling and genetic screening. In S. G. Gabbe, J. R. Niebyl, & J. L. Simpson (Eds.), *Obstetrics: Normal and problem pregnancies* (6th ed.). Philadelphia, PA: Elsevier Churchill Livingstone.

Sinclair, D. (1990). *Human growth after birth* (5th ed.). New York, NY: Oxford University Press.

Singer, J. L. (1995). Imaginative play in childhood: Precursor of subjunctive thought, daydreaming, and adult pretending games, In A. D. Pellegrini (Ed.), *The future of play theory: A multidisciplinary inquiry into the contributions of Brian Sutton-Smith.* SUNY series, *Children's Play in Society* (pp. 187–219). Albany, NY: State University of New York Press.

Sizer, T. (1996). *Horace's hope* Boston: Houghton Mifflin.

Skinner, B. F. (1957). *Verbal behavior.* New York, NY: Appleton-Century-Crofts.

Skolnick, A., & Skolnick, J. (1989). *Families in transition: Rethinking marriage, sexuality, childrearing and family organization* (6th ed.). New York, NY: Scott Foresman.

Slade, A. (1987). Quality of attachment and early symbolic play. *Developmental Psychology, 23,* 78–85.

Slater, A., Bremner, G., Johnson, S. P., Sherwood, P., Hayes, R., & Brown, E. (2000). Newborn infants' preference for attractive faces: The role of internal and external facial features. *Infancy, 1,* 265–274.

Slater, A., & Morrison, V. (1991). Visual attention and memory at birth. In M. Weiss & P. Zelazo (Eds.), *Newborn attention: Biological constraints and the influence of experience* (pp. 256–277). Norwood, NJ: Ablex.

Slavin, R. (1996). Research on cooperative learning and achievement: What we know, and what we need to know. *Contemporary Educational Psychology, 21,* 43–69.

Slavin, R. (Ed.). (1998). *Show me the evidence: Promising programs for American schools.* Thousand Oaks, CA: Corwin Press.

Slavin, R. E. (1995). *Cooperative learning* (2nd ed.) Boston: Allyn & Bacon.

Slaughter, V. (2005). Young children's understanding of death. *Australian Psychologist, 40*(3), 179–186.

Slaughter, V., & Griffiths, M. (2007). Death understanding and fear of death in young children. *Clinical Child Psychology and Psychiatry, 12*(4), 525–535.

Slomin, M. (1991). *Children, culture, and ethnicity: Evaluating and understanding the impact.* New York, NY: Garland.

Sloper, P., Turner, S., Knussen, C., & Cunningham, C. C. (1990). Social life of school children with Down's syndrome. *Child Care, Health, and Development, 16,* 235–251.

Small, S. A., & Kearns, D. (1993). Unwanted sexual activity among peers during early and middle adolescence: Incidence and risk factors. *Journal of Marriage and the Family, 55,* 941–952.

Smetana, J. G. (1995). Parenting styles and conceptions of parental authority during adolescence. *Child Development, 66,* 299–316.

Smetana, J. G., Killen, M., & Turiel, E. (1991). Children's reasoning about interpersonal and moral conflicts. *Child Development, 62,* 629–644.

Smilansky, S. (1968). *The effects of sociodramatic play on disadvantaged preschool children.* New York, NY: Wiley.

Smith, A. (1996). Rehabilitation of children following sport- and activity-related injuries. In O. Bar-Or (Ed.), *The child and adolescent athlete* (pp. 224–244). Oxford, UK: Blackwells.

Smith, D. (1998). *Inclusion: Schools for all students.* Belmont. CA: Wadsworth.

Smith, D. E., & Blinn Pike, L. (1994). Relationship between Jamaican adolescent's drinking patterns and self-image: A cross-cultural perspective. *Adolescence, 29,* 429–437.

Smith, J. F., Eisenberg, M. L., Glidden, D., Millstein, S. G., Cedars, M., Walsh, T. J., . . . & Katz, P. P. (2011). Socioeconomic disparities in the use and success of fertility treatments: Analysis of data from a prospective cohort in the United States. *Fertility and Sterility, 96*(1), 95–101.

Snarey, J. R. (1985). Cross-cultural universality of social-moral development: A critical review of Kohlbergian research. *Psychological Bulletin, 97,* 202–232.

Snowling, M., & Stackhouse, J. (1996). *Dyslexia, speech, and language: A practitioner's handbook.* San Diego: Singular Publishers Group.

Soldier, L. (1993). Working with Native-American children, *Young Children, 47*(6), 15–21.

Soley, G., & Hannon, E. E. (2010). Infants prefer the musical meter of their own culture: A cross-cultural comparison. *Developmental Psychology, 46,* 286–292.

Soltis, J. (2004). The signal functions of early infant crying. *Behavioral and Brain Sciences, 27,* 443–490.

Sommerville, J. (1990). *The rise and fall of childhood* (2nd ed.). New York, NY: Vintage Books.

Sood, A. B., Razdan, A., Weller, E. B., & Weller, R. A. (2006). Children's reactions to parental and sibling death. *Current Psychiatry Reports, 8*(2), 115–120.

Sorenson, S., & Bowie, P. (1994). Vulnerable populations: Girls and young women. In L. Eron & J. Gentry (Eds.), *Violence and youth: Psychology's response: Vol. II. Papers of the American Psychological Association on Violence and Youth.* Washington, DC: American Psychological Association.

Sorkhabi, N., & Mandara, J. (2013). Are the effects of Baumrind's parenting styles culturally specific or culturally equivalent? In R. E. Larzelere, A. S. Morris, & A. W. Harrist (Eds.) *Authoritative parenting: Synthesizing nurturance and discipline for optimal child development* (pp. 113–135). Washington, DC: American Psychological Association.

Soto, L. (1997). *Language, culture, and power: Bilingual families and the struggle for quality education.* Albany, NY: State University of New York Press.

Sousa, C., Herrenkohl, T. I., Moylan, C. A., Tajima, E. A., Klika, J. B., Herrenkohl, R. C., & Russo, M. J. (2011). Longitudinal study on the effects of child abuse and children's exposure to domestic violence, parent-child attachments, and antisocial behavior in adolescence. *Journal of Interpersonal Violence, 26*(1), 111–136.

Spaccarelli, S. (1994). Stress, appraisal, and coping in child sexual abuse: A theoretical and empirical review. *Psychological Bulletin, 116,* 340–362.

Spassov, L., Curzi-Dscalovi, L., Clairambualt, J., Kauffman, F., Eiselt, M., Medigue, C., & Peirano, P. (1994). Heart rate and heart-rate variability during sleep in small-for-gestational-age newborns. *Pediatric Research, 35,* 500–505.

Speece, M. W., & Brent, S. B. (1984). Children's understanding of death: A review of three components of the death concept. *Child Development, 55,* 1671–1686.

Spencer, S. M., & Patrick, J. H. (2009). Social support and personal mastery as protective resources during emerging adulthood. *Journal of Adult Development, 16*(4), 191–198.

Spencer, T. J., Faraone, S. V., Biederman, J., Lerner, M., Cooper, K. M., Zimmerman, B., & Concerta Study Group. (2006). Does prolonged therapy with a long-acting stimulant suppress growth in children with ADHD? *Journal of the American Academy of Child & Adolescent Psychiatry, 45*(5), 527–537.

Spetner, N., & Olsho, L. (1990). Auditory frequency resolution in human infants. *Child Development, 61,* 632–652.

Spirito, A., Stark, L., Fristad, M., Hart, K., & Owens-Stively, J. (1989). Adolescent suicide attempters hospitalized on a pediatric unit. In S. Chess, A. Thomas, & M. E. Hertzig (Eds.), *Annual progress in child psychiatry and child development.* New York, NY: Brunner/Mazel.

Spodek, B., & Saracho, O. (Eds.). (1993). *Language and literacy in early childhood education.* New York, NY: Teachers' College Press.

Sponseller, D., & Jaworski, A. (1979). *Social and cognitive complexity in young children's play.* Paper presented at the annual meeting of the American Educational Research Association, San Francisco.

Spurrier, N. J., Magarey, A. A., Golley, R., Curnow, F., & Sawyer, M. G. (2008). Relationships between the home environment and physical activity and dietary patterns of preschool children: A cross-sectional study. *International Journal of Behavioral Nutrition and Physical Activity, 5*(1), 31.

Sroufe, L. A. (1979). The coherence of individual development: Early care, attachment, and subsequent developmental issues. *American Psychologist, 34,* 834–841.

Sroufe, L. A., Fox, N., & Pancake, V. (1983). Attachment and dependency in developmental perspective. *Child Development, 54,* 1615–1627.

St. James-Roberts, I. (2007). Helping parents to manage infant crying and sleeping: A review of the evidence and implications for services. *Child Abuse Review, 16,* 47–69.

St. James-Roberts, I., & Halil, T. (1991). Infant crying patterns in the first year: Normal community and clinical findings. *Journal of Child Psychology and Psychiatry, 32,* 951–968.

St. James-Roberts, I., Harris, G., & Messer, D. (Eds.). (1993). *Infant crying, feeding, and sleeping: Development, problems, and treatments.* New York, NY: Harvester Wheatsheaf.

St. Jeor, S. (Ed.). (1997). *Obesity assessment: Tools, methods, interpretations.* New York, NY: Chapman & Hall.

St. Peters, M., Fitch, M., Huston, A. C., Wright, J.C., & Eakins, D. J. (1991). Television and families: What do young children watch with their parents? *Child Development, 62,* 1409–1423.

Stack, C. B. (1981). Sex roles and survival strategies in an urban black community. In F. C. Steady (Ed.), *The black woman cross-culturally* (pp. 349–367). Cambridge, MA: Shinkman.

Stack, C. B. (1993). The culture of gender: Women and men of color. In M. J. Larrabee (Ed.), An *ethic of care: Feminist and interdisciplinary perspectives* (pp. 108–111). New York, NY: Routledge.

Stake, J. E. (1997). Integrating expressiveness and instrumentality in real-life settings: A new perspective on the benefits of androgyny. *Sex Roles, 37,* 541–564.

Stander, V., & Jensen, L. (1993). The relationship of value orientation to moral cognition: Gender and cultural differences in the United States and China explored. *Journal of Cross-Cultural Psychology, 24,* 42–52.

Stanger-Hall, K. F., & Hall, D. W. (2011). Abstinence-only education and teen pregnancy rates: Why we need comprehensive sex education in the US. *PLoS ONE, 6*(10), e24658.

Stathopoulou, G., Powers, M. B., Berry, A. C., Smits, J. A., & Otto, M. W. (2006). Exercise interventions for mental health: A quantitative and qualitative review. *Clinical Psychology: Science and Practice, 13*(2), 179–193.

Statista. (2017). Reach of leading social media and networking sites used by teenagers and young adults in the United States as of February 2017. Retrieved from https://www.statista.com/statistics/199242/social-media-and-networking-sites-used-by-us-teenagers/

Steele, H., Steele, M., & Fonagy, P. (1996). Associations among attachment classifications of mothers, fathers, and their infants. *Child Development, 67,* 541–555.

Steiger, C. (1993). Midwifery: Overview. In B. K. Rothman (Ed.), *The encyclopedia of childbearing.* New York, NY: Henry Holt.

Steinberg, L., Lamborn, S. D., Darling, N., Mounts, N. S., & Dornbusch, S. M. (1994). Over-time changes in adjustment and competence among adolescents from authoritative, authoritarian, indulgent, and neglectful families. *Child Development, 65,* 754–770.

Steinberg, L. D. (1986). Latchkey children and susceptibility to peer pressure: An ecological analysis. *Developmental Psychology, 22,* 433–439.

Steinberg, L. D. (2004). Risk taking in adolescence: What changes, and why? In R. E. Dahl & L. P. Spear (Eds.), *Adolescent brain development: Vulnerabilities and opportunities* (Vol. 1021, pp. 51–58), New York, NY: New York Academy of Sciences.

Steinberg, L. D., Lamborn, S. D., Dornbusch, S. M., & Darling, N. (1992). Impact of parenting practices on adolescent achievement: Authoritative parenting, school involvement, and encouragement to succeed. *Child Development, 63,* 1266–1281.

Steinberg, L. D., & Levine, A. D. (1990). *You and your adolescent: A parent's guide to development from 10 to 20.* New York, NY: Harper & Row.

Steinberg, L. D., Mounts, N. S., Lamborn, S. D., & Dornbusch, S. M. (1991). Authoritative parenting and adolescent adjustment across varied ecological niches. *Journal of Research in Adolescence, 1,* 19–36.

Steiner, G. (1987). Spatial reasoning in small-size and large-size environments; In search of early prefigurations of spatial cognition in small-size environments. In B. Inhelder, D. de Caprona, & A. Wells (Eds.). *Piaget today.* Hillsdale, NJ: Erlbaum.

Steiner, H., McQuivey, R. W., Pavelski, R., Pitts, T., & Kraemer, H. (2000). Adolescents and sports: Risk or benefit? *Clinical Pediatrics, 39*(3), 161–166.

Steiner, J. E., Glasser, D., Hawilo, M. E., & Berridge, I. C. (2001). Comparative expression of hedonic impact: Affective reactions to taste by human infants and other primates. *Neuroscience & Biobehavioral Reviews, 25,* 53–74.

Steptoe, A., Peacey, V., & Wardle, J. (2006). Sleep duration and health in young adults. *Archives of Internal Medicine, 166*(16), 1689–1692.

Stern, D. N. (1992). *Diary of a baby.* New York, NY: Basic Books.

Stern, D. N. (1995). *The motherhood constellation: A unified view of parent-infant psychotherapy* New York, NY: Basic Books.

Stern, D. N. (2004). The motherhood constellation: Therapeutic approaches to early relational problems. In A. J. Sameroff, S. C. McDonough, & K. L. Rosenblum (Eds.), *Treating parent-infant relationship problems: Strategies for intervention* (pp. 29–42). New York, NY: Guilford Press.

Sternberg, R. J. (1987). *The triangle of love: Intimacy, passion, commitment.* New York, NY: Basic Books.

Sternberg, R. J. (1988). *The triarchic mind: A new theory of human intelligence.* New York, NY: Penguin Books.

Sternberg, R. J. (1992). Intellectual development: A satiric fairy tale. In R. J. Sternberg & C. A. Berg (Eds.), *Intellectual development* (pp. 381–394). New York, NY: Cambridge University Press.

Sternberg, R. J. (1994). *Thinking and problem solving.* San Diego: Academic Press.

Sternberg, R. J. (1997). *Thinking styles.* New York, NY: Cambridge University Press.

Sternberg, R. J. (1998). Abilities are forms of developing expertise. *Educational Researcher, 27*(3), 11–21.

Sternberg, R. J. (2006). The nature of creativity. *Creativity Research Journal, 18*(1), 87–98.

Sternberg, R. J., & Wagner, R. (Eds.). (1994). *Mind in context: Interactionist perspectives on human intelligence.* New York, NY: Cambridge University Press.

Stets, J. E. (1990). Verbal and physical aggression in marriage. *Journal of Marriage and the Family, 52,* 501–514.

Stevenson, H. W., & Lee, S. Y. (1990). Contexts of achievement: A study of American, Chinese, and Japanese children. *Monographs of the Society for Research in Child Development, 55.*

Stevenson, H. W., Chen, C., & Uttal, D. H. (1990). Beliefs and achievement: A study of black, white and Hispanic children, *Child Development, 61,* 508–523.

Stevenson-Hinde, J. (1998). Parenting in different cultures: Time to focus, *Developmental Psychology, 34,* 698–700.

Stevenson-Hinde, J., & Verschueren, K. (2002). Attachment in childhood. In P. K. Smith, & C. H. Hart (Eds.), *Blackwell handbook of childhood social development* (pp. 182–204). Oxford: Blackwell.

Stewart, R. B., Mobley, L. A., Van Tuyl, S. S., & Salvador, M. A. (1987). The firstborn's adjustment to the birth of a sibling: A longitudinal assessment. *Child Development, 58,* 341–355.

Stickgold, R. (2005). Sleep-dependent memory consolidation. *Nature, 437*(7063), 1272–1278.

Stifter, C. A., Coulehan, C. M., & Fish, M. (1993). Linking employment to attachment: The mediating effects of maternal separation anxiety and interactive behavior. *Child Development, 64,* 1451–1460.

Stiles, J., & Jernigan, T. L. (2010). The basics of brain development. *Neuropsychology Review, 20,* 327–348.

Stipek, D. J., Gralinski, H., & Kopp, C. B. (1990). Self-concept development in the toddler years. *Developmental Psychology, 26,* 972–977.

Stocker, C. (1994). Children's perceptions of relationship with siblings, friends and mothers: Compensatory processes and links with adjustment. *Journal of Child Psychology and Psychiatry, 35,* 1447–1459.

Stokes, G. (1985). The social profile. In R. Coles & G. Stokes (Eds.), *Sex and the American teenager* (pp. 31–144). New York, NY: Harper & Row.

Stolberg, A. L., & Walsh, P. (1988). A review of treatment methods for children of divorce. In S. A. Wolchik & P. Karoly (Eds.), *Children of divorce* (pp. 299–321). New York, NY: Gardner Press.

Stone, M. R., & Brown, B. B. (1998). In the eye of the beholder: Adolescents' perceptions of peer crowd stereotypes. In R. E. Muuss, H. D. Porton, et al. (Eds.), *Adolescent behavior and society; A book of readings* (5th ed.). (pp. 158–169). New York, NY: McGraw Hill.

Stoppa, T. M., & Lefkowitz, E. S. (2010). Longitudinal changes in religiosity among emerging adult college students. *Journal of Research on Adolescence, 20*(1), 23–38.

Stout, B. C. (1993). Thalidomide. In B. K. Rothman (Ed.), *The encyclopedia of childbearing.* New York, NY: Henry Holt.

Stratford, B. (1994). Down syndrome is for life. *International Journal of Disability, Development and Education, 41,* 3–13.

Straub, R. O. (2014). *Health Psychology* (4th ed.). New York, NY: Worth.

Straus, M. A., & Smith, C. (1990). Violence in Hispanic families in the United States: Incidence rates and structural interpretations. In M. A. Straus & R. J. Gelles, with C. Smith (Eds.), *Physical violence in American families: Risk factors and adaptations to violence in 8,145 families* (pp. 341–367). New Brunswick, NJ: Transaction.

Straus, M. A., Gelles, R. J., & Steinmetz, S. (1980). *Behind closed doors: Violence in the American family.* Garden City, NY: Anchor.

Streissguth, A. P., Barr, H. M., Sampson, P. D., Darby, B. L., & Martin, D. C. (1989). IQ at age 4 in relation to maternal alcohol use and smoking during pregnancy. *Developmental Psychology, 25,* 3–11.

Streissguth, A. P., Bookstein, F. L., Sampson, P., & Barr, H. (1995). Attention: Prenatal alcohol and continuities of vigilance and attentional problems from 4 through 14 years. *Development and Psychopathology, 7,* 419–446.

Striegel-Moore, R. H. (1997). Risk factors for eating disorders. In M. S. Jacobson, J. M. Rees, N. H. Golden, & C. E. Irwin (Eds.), Adolescent nutritional disorders: Prevention and treatment. *Annals of the New York Academy of Sciences, 817,* pp. 98–109.

Striegel-Moore, R. H., & Bulik, C. M. (2007). Risk factors for eating disorders. *American Psychologist, 62*(3), 181–198.

Striegel-Moore, R., & Smolak, L. (1996). The role of race in the development of eating disorders. In L. Smolak, M. P. Levine, & R. Striegel-Moore (Eds.), *The developmental psychopathology of eating disorders: Implications for research, prevention, and treatment* (pp. 259–284). Mahwah, NJ: Erlbaum.

Sue, D. W., & Sue, D. (2012). *Counseling the culturally diverse: Theory and practice* (6th ed.). Hoboken, NJ: John Wiley & Sons.

Sue, S. (1998). In search of cultural competence in psychotherapy and counseling. *American Psychologist, 53,* 440–448.

Sue, S., & Zane, N. (1987). The role of culture and cultural techniques in psychotherapy: A critique and reformulation. *American Psychologist, 42,* 37–45.

Sue, S., Zane, N., & Young, W. (1994). Research on psychotherapy with culturally diverse populations. In A. E. Bergin & S. L. Garfield (Eds.), *Handbook of psychotherapy and behavior change* (4th ed., pp. 783–820). New York, NY: Wiley.

Sullivan, H. (1953). *The interpersonal theory of psychiatry.* New York, NY: Norton.

Sullivan, J. L. (2003). Prevention of mother-to-child transmission of HIV—What next? *Journal of Acquired Immune Deficiency Syndrome, 34,* S67–S72.

Sullivan, K., & Sullivan, A. (1980). Adolescent-parent separation. *Developmental Psychology, 16,* 93–99.

Sunderman, G. L. (Ed.) (2008). *Holding NCLB accountable: Achieving accountability, equity, and school reform.* Thousand Oaks, CA: Corwin Press.

Super, C. M., & Harkness, S. (2010). Culture and infancy. In J. G. Bremner, & T. D. Wachs (Eds.), *The Wiley-Blackwell handbook of infant development* (pp. 623–649). Malden, MA: Wiley-Blackwell Publishing.

Susa, A. M., & Benedict, J. O. (1994). The effects of playground design on pretend play and divergent thinking. *Environment and Behavior, 26,* 560–579.

Swanson, H., Cooney, J., & Brock, S. (1993). The influence of working memory and classification ability on children's word problem solution. *Journal of Experimental Child Psychology, 55,* 374–395.

Swanson, S. A., Crow, S. J., Le Grange, D., Swendsen, J., & Merikangas, K. R. (2011). Prevalence and correlates of eating disorders in adolescents. Results from the national comorbidity survey replication adolescent supplement. *Archive of General Psychiatry, 68*(7), 714–723.

Swinburn, B. A., Sacks, G., Hall, K. D., McPherson, K., Finegood, D. T., Moodie, M. L., & Gortmaker, S. L. (2011). The global obesity pandemic: Shaped by global drivers and local environments. *Lancet, 378*(9793), 804–814.

Syed, M. (2016). Emerging adulthood: Developmental stage theory, or nonsense? In J. J. Arnett (Ed.), *The Oxford handbook of emerging adulthood* (pp. 11–25). New York, NY: Oxford University Press.

T

Taber-Thomas, B., & Perez-Edgar, K. (2016). Emerging adulthood brain development. In J. J. Arnett (Ed.), *The Oxford handbook of emerging adulthood* (pp. 126–141). New York, NY: Oxford University Press.

Taffel, S. M. (1993). Cesarean birth: Social and political aspects, In B. K. Rothman (Ed.), *The encyclopedia of childbearing.* New York, NY: Henry Holt.

Takahashi, K. (1990). Are the key assumptions of the "Strange Situation" procedure universal? A view from Japanese research. *Human Development, 33,* 23–30.

Takanishi, R. (1993). The opportunities of adolescence–Research, interventions, and policy: Introduction to the special issue *American Psychologist, 48,* 85–88.

Takanishi, R., & Hamburg, D. (Eds.). (1997). *Preparing adolescents for the 21st century.* New York, NY: Cambridge University Press.

Takata, S., & Zevitz, R. (1990). Divergent perceptions of group delinquency in a midwestern community: Racine's gang problem. *Youth and Society, 21,* 282–305.

Takei, W. (2001). How do deaf infants attain first signs? *Developmental Science, 4,* 71–78.

Tandon, P. S., Zhou, C., Lozano, P., & Christakis, D. A. (2011). Preschoolers' total daily screen time at home and by type of child care. *Journal of Pediatrics, 158*(2), 297–300.

Tannen, D. (1990). *You just don't understand.* New York, NY: Morrow.

Tanner, J. L. (2006). Recentering during emerging adulthood: A critical turning point in life span human development. In J. J. Arnett & J. L. Tanner (Eds.), *Emerging adults in America: Coming of age in the 21st century* (pp. 21–55). Washington, DC: American Psychological Association.

Tanner, J. L. (2016). Mental health in emerging adulthood. In J. J. Arnett (Ed.), *The Oxford handbook of emerging adulthood* (pp. 499–520). New York, NY: Oxford University Press.

Tanner, J. M. (1981). Growth and maturation during adolescence. *Nutrition Review, 39,* 43–55.

Tanner, J. M. (1990). *Fetus into man. Physical growth from conception to maturity* (rev. ed.). Cambridge, MA: Harvard University Press.

Tardiff, T., Fletcher, P., Liang, W., Zhang, Z., Kaciroti, N., & Marchman, V. (2008). Baby's first 10 words. *Developmental Psychology, 44,* 929–938.

Task Force on Pediatric AIDS. (1989). Pediatric AIDS and human immunodeficiency virus infection: Psychological issues. *American Psychologist, 44,* 258–264.

Tasker, F. L., & Golombok, S. (1997). *Growing up in a lesbian family.* New York, NY: Guilford.

Taylor, C. A., Manganello, J. A., Lee, S. J., & Rice, J. C. (2010). Mothers' spanking of 3-year-old children and subsequent risk of children's aggressive behavior. *Pediatrics, 125*(5), e1057–e1065.

Taylor, J., Gilligan, C., & Sullivan, A. (1995). *Between voice and silence: Women and. girls, race and relationship.* Cambridge, MA: Harvard University Press.

Taylor, M. J. (2006). Neural bases of cognitive development. In E. Bialystok & F. I. M. Craik (Eds.), *Lifespan cognition: Mechanisms of change.* New York, NY: Oxford University Press.

Taylor, P., Cohn, D., Livingston, G., Wang, W., & Dockterman, D. (2010). *The new demography of American motherhood.* Pew Research Center. Retrieved from http://www.pewsocialtrends.org/files/2010/10/754-new-demography-of-motherhood. pdf

Taylor, S. E. (1998). *Health psychology.* New York, NY: McGraw Hill.

Telama, R., Yang, X., Viikari, J., Välimäki, I., Wanne, O., & Raitakari, O. (2005). Physical activity from childhood to adulthood: A 21-year tracking study. *American Journal of Preventive Medicine, 28*(3), 267–273.

Telkemeyer, S., Rossi, S., Kock, S. P., Nierhaus, T., Steinbrink, J., Poeppel, D., Obrig, H., & Wartenburger, I. (2010). Sensitivity of newborn auditory cortex to the temporal structure of sounds. *Journal of Neuroscience, 29,* 14726–14733.

Terenzini, P. T., Pascarella, E., & Blinding, G. S. (1996). Students' out-of-class experiences and their influence on learning and cognitive development: A literature review. *Journal of College Student Development, 37,* 149–162.

Tesman, J., & Hills, A. (1994). Developmental effects of lead exposure in children. *Social Policy Report: Society for Research on Child Development, 8*(3).

Teti, D. M. (1992). *Sibling interaction.* New York, NY: Plenum Press.

Thomas, A., & Chess, S. (1977). *Temperament and development.* New York, NY: Bruner/Mazel.

Thomas, A., & Chess, S. (1981). The role of temperament in the contributions of individuals to their development. In R. Lerner & N. Busch-Rossnagle (Eds.), *Individuals as producers of their development: A life-span perspective.* New York, NY: Academic Press.

Thompson, R. A. (1990). On emotion and self-regulation. In R. A. Thompson (Ed.), *Nebraska symposium on motivation: Vol. 36* (pp. 383–483). Lincoln, NE: University of Nebraska Press.

Thornton, W. L., Paterson, T. S., & Yeung, S. E. (2013). Age differences in everyday problem solving: The role of problem context. *International Journal of Behavioral Development, 37,* 13–20.

Tidwell, N. D., Eastwick, P. W., & Finkel, E. J. (2013). Perceived, not actual, similarity predicts initial attraction in a live romantic context: Evidence from the speed-dating paradigm. *Personal Relationships, 20*(2), 199–215.

Tillman, P. (1992). *Adolescent alcoholism.* Bethesda, MD: U.S. Department of Health and Human Services.

Tobin-Richards, M. H., Boxer, A. M., & Petersen, A. C. (1983). The psychological significance of pubertal change: Sex differences in perceptions of self during early adolescence. In J. Brooks-Gunn & A. C. Petersen (Eds.), *Girls at puberty: Biological and psychological perspectives* (pp. 127–154). New York, NY: Plenum.

Topa, G., Moriano, J. A., Depolo, M., Alcover, C. M., & Morales, J. (2009). Antecedents and consequences of retirement planning and decisionmaking: A meta-analysis and model. *Journal of Vocational Behavior, 75,* 38–55.

Tortolero, S. R., Markham, C. M., Peskin, M. F., Shegog, R., Addy, R. C., Escobar-Chaves, S. L., & Baumler, E. R. (2010). It's your game: Keep it real: Delaying sexual behavior with an effective middle school program. *Journal of Adolescent Health, 46*(2), 169–179.

Toth, K., Dawson, G., Meltzoff, A. N., Greenson, J., & Fein, D. (2007). Early social, imitation, play, and language abilities of young non-autistic siblings of children with autism. *Journal of Autism and Developmental Disorders, 37*(1), 145–157.

Tough, P. (2012). *How children succeed: Grit, curiosity, and the hidden power of character.* Boston: Houghton Mifflin Harcourt.

Townshend, J. M., Kambouropoulos, N., Griffin, A., Hunt, F. J., & Milani, R. M. (2014). Binge drinking, reflection impulsivity, and unplanned sexual behavior: Impaired decision-making in young social drinkers. *Alcoholism: Clinical and Experimental Research, 38*(4), 1143–1150.

Trainor, L. J., & Heinmiller, B. M. (1998). The development of evaluative responses to music: Infants prefer to listen to consonance over dissonance. *Infant Behavior & Development, 21,* 77–88.

Trautman, P. D., & Shaffer, D. (1989). Pediatric management of suicidal behavior. *Pediatric Annals, 18,* 134–143.

Trawick-Smith, J., & Dziurgot, T. (2011). 'Good-fit' teacher–child play interactions and the subsequent autonomous play of preschool children. *Early Childhood Research Quarterly, 26*(1), 110–123.

Trent, K., & Spitze, G. D. (2011). Growing up without siblings and adult sociability behaviors. *Journal of Family Issues, 32*(9), 1178–1204.

Trinke, S., & Bartholomew, K. (1997). Hierarchies of attachment relationships in young adulthood. *Journal of Social and. Personal Relationships, 14,* 603–625.

Trommsdorff, G., Friedlmeier, W., & Mayer, B. (2007). Sympathy, distress, and prosocial behavior of preschool children in four cultures. *International Journal of Behavioral Development, 31*(3), 284–293.

Tronick, E. Z. (1989). Emotions and emotional communication in infants. *American Psychologist, 44,* 112–119.

Tronick, E. Z., Morelli, G. A., & Ivey, P. K. (1992). The Efe forager infant and toddler's pattern of social relationships: Multiple and simultaneous. *Developmental Psychology, 28,* 568–577.

Tropp, L. R., & Prenovost, M. A. (2008). The role of intergroup contact in predicting children's interethnic attitudes: Evidence from meta-analytic and field studies. In S. R. Levy & M. Killen (Eds.), *Intergroup attitudes and relations in childhood through adulthood* (pp. 236–248). New York, NY: Oxford University Press.

Turkheimer, E., & Gottesman, I. I. (1991). Individual differences and the canalization of human behavior. *Developmental Psychology, 27,* 18–22.

Turner, E. A., Chandler, M., & Heffer, R. W. (2009). The influence of parenting styles, achievement motivation, and self-efficacy on academic performance in college students. *Journal of College Student Development, 50*(3), 337–346.

U

Uddin, M., Sipahi, L., Li, J., & Koenen, K. C. (2013). Sex differences in DNA methylation may contribute to risk of PTSD and depression: A review of existing evidence. *Depression and Anxiety, 30*(12), 1151–160.

Ullal-Gupta, S., Vanden Bosch der Nederlanden, C., Tichko, P., Lahav, A., & Hannon, E. (2013). Linking prenatal experience to the emerging musical mind. *Frontiers in Systems Neuroscience, 7,* 1–7.

Umberson, D. (1987). Family status and health behaviors: Social control as a dimension of social integration. *Journal of Health and Social Behavior, 38,* 306–319.

Umberson, D. (1989). Relationships with children: Explaining patents' psychological well-being. *Journal of Marriage and the Family, 51,* 999–1012.

UNICEF Office of Research. (2013). Child well-being in rich countries: A comparative overview, *Innocenti Report Card 11,* UNICEF Office of Research. Florence, IT: Author.

United Health Foundation. (2016). *America's health rankings: Infant mortality rates.* Retrieved from http://www.americashealthrankings.org/MS/IMR

United Nations International Children's Emergency Fund (UNICEF). (1993). *The state of the world's children, 1992.* New -York: Oxford University Press.

United Nations International Children's Emergency Fund (UNICEF). (1995). *The slate of the world's children, 1995.* New York, NY: Oxford University Press.

United Nations International Children's Emergency Fund (UNICEF). (1998). *State of the world's children, 1997.* New York, NY: Oxford University Press.

United Nations International Children's Emergency Fund (UNICEF). (2009). *The state of the world's children: Maternal and newborn health, 2009.* Retrieved from http://www.unicef.org/sowc09/index.php

United Nations Statistics Division. (2008). *Demographics yearbook.* Retrieved from http://unstats.un.org/unsd/demographic/products/dyb/dyb2008htm

Updegraff, K. A., McHale, S. M., Killoren, S. E., & Rodriguez, S. A. (2011). Cultural variations in sibling relationships. In J. Caspi (Ed.), *Sibling development: Implications for mental health practitioners.* New York, NY: Springer.

U.S. Bureau of the Census. (1990a). *Statistical abstract of the United States* (110th ed.). Washington, DC: U.S. Government Printing Office.

U.S. Bureau of the Census. (1990b). *Who's minding the kids? Current population reports* (Series P-70, No. 20.). Washington, DC: U.S. Government Printing Office.

U.S. Bureau of the Census. (1991). *Statistical abstract of the United States* (111th ed.). Washington, DC: U.S. Government Printing Office.

U.S. Bureau of the Census. (1992). Marital status and living arrangements: March 1991. *Current Population Reports,* Series P-20, No. 461. Washington, DC: U.S. Government Printing Office.

U.S. Bureau of the Census. (1992a). *Statistical abstract of the United States, 1992* (112th ed.). Washington, DC: U.S. Government Printing Office.

U.S. Bureau of the Census. (1992b). *Poverty in the United States, 1991.* Washington, DC: U.S. Government Printing Office.

U.S. Bureau of the Census. (1994). *Statistical abstract of the United States: 1993* (113th ed.). Washington, DC: U.S. Government Printing Office.

U.S. Bureau of the Census. (1994). *Statistical abstract of the United States: 1994* (114th ed.) Washington, DC: U.S. Government Printing Office.

U.S. Bureau of the Census. (1995a). Live births, deaths, marriages, and divorces: 1900–1994. *Statistical abstract of the United States* (115th ed.). Washington, DC: U.S. Government Printing Office.

U.S. Bureau of the Census. (1995b). Employment status of and presence and age of children: 1960–1994. *Statistical abstract of the United States* (115th ed.). Washington, DC: U.S. Government Printing Office.

U.S. Bureau of the Census. (2008). *Nearly half of preschoolers receive child care from relatives.* Retrieved from http://www.census.gov/newsroom/releases/archives/children/cb08-31.html

U.S. Bureau of the Census. (2010). *America's families and living arrangements: 2010.* Retrieved from https://www.census.gov/population/www/socdemo/hh-fam/cps2010.html

U.S. Bureau of the Census. (2012a). Births, deaths, marriages, and divorces. *Statistical abstract of the United States: 2012.* Retrieved from https://www.census.gov/prod/2011pubs/12statab/vitstat.pdf

U.S. Bureau of the Census. (2012d). *Statistical abstract of the United States: 2012.* Retrieved from https://www.census.gov/compendia/statab/2012/tables/12s0010.pdf

U.S. Bureau of the Census. (2015a). *Current population survey, March and annual social and economic supplements, 2015 and earlier.* Retrieved from http://www.census.gov/hhes/families/files/ms2.csv

U.S. Bureau of the Census. (2015b). *Detailed languages spoken at home and ability to speak English for population 5 years and over: 2009–2013.* Retrieved from http://www.census.gov/data/tables/2013/demo/2009-2013-lang-tables.html

U.S. Bureau of the Census. (2015c). *Families and living arrangements.* Retrieved from http://www.census.gov/hhes/families/data/marital.html

U.S. Bureau of the Census. (2015d). *Families and living arrangements: Children.* Retrieved from http://www.census.gov/hhes/families/data/cps2015C.html

U.S. Bureau of Labor Statistics. (1995). Bulletin 2307.

U.S. Bureau of Labor Statistics and the Census Bureau. (2013). *Current population survey, 2013 annual social and economic supplement.* Retrieved from http://www.census.gov/hhes/www/cpstables/032013/pov/pov01_100.htm.

U.S. Congress, Office of Technology Assessment. (1988). *Infertility: Medical and social choices* (OTA-BA-358). Washington, DC: U.S. Government Printing Office.

U.S. Congressional Budget Office. (1993). *Trends in health spending.* Washington, DC: Author:

U.S. Department of Commerce. (1995). *Statistical abstract of the United States, 1994.* Washington, DC: U.S. Government Printing Office.

U.S. Department of Commerce. (1998). *Statistical abstract, of the United States, 1997.* Washington, DC: U.S. Government Printing Office.

U.S. Department of Education. (1997). *Digest of education statistics, 1997.* Washington, DC: National Center for Education Statistics.

U.S. Department of Education. (2014). *The condition of education, 2014.* Washington, DC: National Center for Education Statistics.

U.S. Department of Education. (2015). *Every Student Succeeds Act (ESSA), 2015.* Retrieved from http://www.ed.gov/essa

U.S. Department of Education, National Center for Education Statistics. (2016a). Undergraduate retention and graduation rates. *The condition of education 2016.* Retrieved from https://nces.ed.gov/programs/coe/indicator_ctr.asp

U.S. Department of Education, National Center for Education Statistics. (2016b). *Digest of education statistics.* Retrieved from https://nces.ed.gov/programs/digest/d14/tables/dt14_311.15.asp?current=yes

U.S. Department of Health and Human Services. (1993). *Health United States, 1992.* (DHHS Pub. No. (PHS) 93-1232). Washington, DC: U.S. Government Printing Office.

U.S. Department of Health and Human Services. (1994). *Preventing tobacco use among young people* Washington, DC: Author.

U.S. Department of Health and Human Services. (1993). *Talking to children about death.* Washington, DC: U.S. Government Printing Office.

U.S. Department of Health and Human Services (HHS; National Toxicology Program). (2005). *Thalidomide.* Retrieved from http://ntp.niehs.nih.gov/

U.S. Department of Health and Human Services (HHS; Maternal and Child Health Bureau). (2009). *Child health USA 2008–2009.* Rockville MD: U.S. Department of Health and Human Services.

U.S. Department of Health and Human Services (HHS; Maternal and Child Health Bureau). (2011). *Child health USA 2011.* Rockville, MD: U.S. Department of Health and Human Services.

U.S. Department of Health and Human Services. (2015). *Child maltreatment 2013: Summary of key findings.* Retrieved from https://www.childwelfare.gov/pubPDFs/canstats.pdf

U.S. Department of Labor. (2014). *Earnings.* Washington, DC: Women's Bureau. Retrieved from https://www.dol.gov/wb/stats/earnings_2014.htm#Ratios

U.S. Department of Labor. (2015). *Women of working age.* Washington, DC: Women's Bureau. Retrieved from https://www.dol.gov/wb/stats/latest_annual_data.htm#labor

U.S. Department of Labor (Bureau of Labor Statistics). (2013, October). *Marriage and divorce: Patterns by gender, race, and educational attainment.* Retrieved from https://www.bls.gov/opub/mlr/2013/article/marriage-and-divorce-patterns-by-gender-race-and-educational-attainment.htm

U.S. Department of Labor (Bureau of Labor Statistics). (2016, July). *Labor force statistics from the current population survey.* Retrieved from http://www.bls.gov/web/empsit/cpsee_e16.htm

U.S. Equal Employment Opportunity Commission. (2013). *Charge statistics FY 1997 through FY 2013.* Retrieved http://eeoc.gov/eeoc/statistics/enforcement/charges.cfm

U.S. General Accounting Office. (1993). *Preventive home care for children: Experience from select foreign countries.* Washington, DC: Author.

U.S. National Center for Health Statistics. (1991). *Vital statistics of the United States.* Washington, DC: U.S. Government Printing Office.

U.S. National Library of Medicine (USNLM). (2011). *Age-appropriate diet for children.* Retrieved from http://www.nlm.nih.gov/medlineplus/ency/article/002455.htm

U.S. National Library of Medicine (USNLM). (2012). *Genetics home reference: Cystic fibrosis.* Retrieved from http://ghr.nlm.nih.gov/condition/cystic-fibrosis

U.S. National Library of Medicine (USNLM). (2012). *Placenta previa.* Retrieved from http://www.ncbi.nlm.nih.gov/pubmedhealth/PMH0001902/

U.S. National Library of Medicine (USNLM). (2013). *Fetal electrocardiogram (ECG) for fetal monitoring during labor.* Retrieved from http://www.ncbi.nlm.nih.gov/pubmedhealth/PMH0010486/

U.S. National Library of Medicine (USNLM). (2013). *Genetics home reference: Huntington disease.* Retrieved from http://ghr.nlm.nih.gov/condition/huntington-disease

U.S. Select Committee on Children, Youth, and Families. (1992). *Health care reform: How do women, children, and teens fare?* Washington, DC: U.S. Government Printing Office.

V

Vaillant, G. E. (1977). *Adaptation to life.* Boston: Little, Brown.

van den Boom, D. C., & Hoeksma, J. B. (1994). The effect of infant irritability on mother-infant interaction: A growth-curve analysis. *Developmental Psychology, 30,* 581–590.

van der Horst, K., Ferrage, A., & Rytz, A. (2014). Involving children in meal preparation. Effects on food intake. *Appetite, 79,* 18–24.

van der Voort, T. H. A., & Valkenburg, P. M. (1994). Television's impact on fantasy play: A review of research. *Developmental Review, 14,* 227–251.

van der Westerlaken, L. A., Naaktgeboren, N., & Helmerhorst, F. M. (1998). Evaluation of pregnancy rates after intrauterine insemination according to indication, age, and sperm parameters. *Journal of Assisted Reproduction and Genetics, 15,* 359–364.

Van Doorn, M. D., Branje, S. J. T., & Meeus, W. H. J. (2011). Developmental changes in conflict resolution styles in parent-adolescent relationships: A four-wave longitudinal study. *Journal of Youth and Adolescence, 40,* 97–107.

van Hasselt, M., Kruger, J., Han, B., Caraballo, R. S., Penne, M. A., Loomis, B., & Gfroerer, J. C. (2015). The relation between tobacco taxes and youth and young adult smoking: What happened following the 2009 US federal tax increase on cigarettes? *Addictive Behaviors, 45,* 104–109.

Van Houtven, C. H., Coe, N. B., & Skira, M. M. (2013). The effect of informal care on work and wages. *Journal of Health Economics, 32,* 240–252.

van IJzendoorn, M. H. (1992). Review. Intergenerational transmission of parenting: A review of studies in nonclinical populations. *Developmental Review, 12,* 76–99.

van IJzendoorn, M. H. (1995). Adult attachment representations, parental responsiveness, and infant attachment: A meta-analysis on the predictive validity of the adult attachment interview. *Psychological Bulletin, 117,* 387–403.

van IJzendoorn, M. H., & Bakermans-Kranenburg, M. J. (1997). Intergenerational transmission of attachment: A move to the contextual level. New York, NY: Guilford Press.

van IJzendoorn, M. H., & de Wolff, M. S. (1997). In search of the absent father–meta-analysis of infant-father attachment: A rejoinder to our discussants. *Child Development, 68,* 604–609.

van IJzendoorn, M. H., & Kroonenberg, P. M. (1988). Cross-cultural patterns of attachment: A meta-analysis of the Strange Situation. *Child Development, 59,* 147–156.

van Reek, J., Adrizaanze, H., & Knibbe, R. (1994). Alcohol consumption and correlates among children in the European Community. *International Journal of Addictions, 29,* 15–21.

van Sleuwen, B. E., Engelberts, A. C., Boore-Boonekamp, M. M., Wietse, K., Schulpen, T. W. J., & L'Hoir, M. P. (2007). Swaddling: A systematic review. *Pediatrics, 120,* 1097–1106. Vandell, D. L. (1980). Sociability with peers and mothers in the first year. *Developmental Psychology, 16,* 355–361.

Vandell, D. L., & Ramanan, J. (1991). Children of the national longitudinal survey of youth: Choices in after-school care and child development. *Developmental Psychology, 27,* 637–643.

Vandell, D. L., Hyde, J. S., Plant, E. A., & Essex, M. J. (1997). Fathers and "others" as infant-care providers: Predictors of parents' emotional well-being and marital satisfaction. *Merrill-Palmer Quarterly, 43,* 361–385.

Vanderlinden, J. (1997). *Trauma, dissociation, and impulse dyscontrol in eating disorders.* Bristol, PA: Brunner/Mazel.

Vandewater, E. A., Rideout, V. J., Wartella, E. A., Huang, X., Lee, J. H., & Shim, M. S. (2007). Digital childhood: Electronic media and technology use among infants, toddlers, and preschoolers. *Pediatrics, 119*(5), e1006–e1015.

Vansteenkiste, M., Lens, W., & Deci, E. L. (2006). Intrinsic versus extrinsic goal contents in self-determination theory: Another look at the quality of academic motivation. *Educational Psychologist, 41*(1), 19–1.

VanTassel-Baska, J. (2006). A content analysis of evaluation findings across 20 gifted programs: A clarion call for enhanced gifted program development. *Gifted Child Quarterly, 50*(3), 199–215.

Varni, J. W., Setoguchi, Y., Rappaport, L. R., & Talbot, D. (1992). Psychological adjustment and perceived social support in children with congenital/acquired limb deficiencies. *Journal of Behavioral Medicine, 15,* 31–44.

Ventura, A. K., & Worobey, J. (2013). Early influences on the development of food preferences. *Current Biology, 23*(9), R401–R408.

Ventura, S. J., & Hamilton, B. E. (2011). U.S. teenage birthrate resumes decline. *NCHS Data Brief,* No. 58. Hyattsville, MD: National Center for Health Statistics.

Ventura, S. J., Martin, J. A., Curtin, S. C., & Mathews, T. J. (1997). Report of final natality statistics, 1995. *Monthly Vital Statistics Report, 45*(11, Suppl. 2). Hyattsville, MD: National Center for Health Statistics.

Vianna, F. S. L., Lopex-Camelo, J. S., Leite, J. C. L., Sanseverina, M. T., V., Dutra, M. G. D., Castilla, E. E., & Schuler-Faccini, L. (2011). Epidemiological surveillance of birth defects compatible with thalidomide embryopathy in Brazil. *PLos ONE, 6.* Retrieved from http://www.ncbi.nlm.nih.gov/pmc/articles/PMC3130769/

Victor, S. B., & Fish, M. C. (1995). Lesbian mothers and their children: A review for school psychologists. *School Psychology Review, 24,* 456–479.

Vigilant, L. G., & Williamson, J. B. (2003). To die, by mistake: Accidental deaths. In C. D. Bryant (Ed.), *Handbook of death and dying* (Vol. 1, pp. 211–222). Thousand Oaks, CA: Sage Publications.

Vignoles, V. L., Regalia, C., Manzi, C., Golledge, J., & Scabini, E. (2006). Beyond self-esteem: Influence of multiple motives on identity construction. *Journal of Personality and Social Psychology, 90*(2), 308.

Vissing, Y. (1996). *Out of sight, out of mind: Homeless children and families in small-town America.* Lexington, KY: University Press of Kentucky.

Vitaro, F., Barker, E. D., Boivin, M., Brendgen, M., & Tremblay, R. E. (2006). Do early difficult temperament and harsh parenting differentially predict reactive and proactive aggression? *Journal of Abnormal Child Psychology, 34*(5), 681–691.

Vitaro, F., Tremblay, R. E., Kerr, M., Pagani, L., & Bukowski, W. M. (1997). Disruptiveness, friends' characteristics, and delinquency in early adolescence: A test of two competing models of development. *Child Development, 68,* 676–689.

Volling, B. L., & Belsky, J. (1992). Contribution of mother-child and father-child relationships to the quality of sibling interaction: A longitudinal study. *Child Development, 63,* 1209–1222.

Volling, B. L., & Belsky, J. (1992). Infant, father, and marital antecedents of infant-father attachment security in dual-earner and single earner families. *Journal of Behavioral Development, 15,* 83–100.

Volling, B. L., Youngblade, L. M., & Belsky, J. (1997). Young children's social relationships with siblings and friends. *American Journal of Orthopsychiatry, 67,* 102–111.

Vosler, N. R., & Proctor, E. K. (1991). Family structure and stressors in a child guidance clinic population. *Families in Society: The Journal of Contemporary Human Services, 72*(3), 164–174.

Vygotsky, L. (1997). *Educational psychology.* Boca Raton, FL: St. Lucie Press.

Vygotsky, L. S. (1967). Play and its role in the mental development of the child. *Soviet Psychology, 12,* 62–76.

Vygotsky, L. S. (1978). *Mind in society: The development of higher psychological processes.* Cambridge, MA: Harvard University Press.

W

Wadden, T. A., & Stunkard, A. J. (1985). Social and psychological consequences of obesity. *Annals of Internal Medicine, 106,* 1062–1067.

Wadden, T. A., Brown, G., Foster, G. D., & Linowitz, J. R. (1991). Salience of weight-related worries in adolescent males and females. *International Journal of Eating Disorders, 10,* 407–414.

Wadsworth, B. (1996). *Piaget's theory of cognitive and affective development: Foundations of constructivism.* 5th ed. White Plains, NY: Longman.

Wadsworth, M. (1986). Serious illness in childhood and its association with later-life achievement. In R. Wilkinson (Ed.). *Class and health: Research and longitudinal data.* London: Tavistock.

Wahistrom, K. (2002). Changing times: Findings from the first longitudinal study of later high school start times. *NASSP Bulletin, 86*(633), 3–21.

Wainright, J. L., & Patterson, C. J. (2006). Delinquency, victimization, and substance use among adolescents with female same-sex parents. *Journal of Family Psychology, 20*(3), 526–530.

Waite, E. B., Shanahan, L., Calkins, S. D., Keane, S. P., & O'Brien, M. (2011). Life events, sibling warmth, and youths' adjustment. *Journal of Marriage and Family, 73,* 902–912.

Waite-Stupiansky, S. (1997). *Building understanding together: A constructivist approach to early childhood education.* Albany, NY: Delmar.

Wakschlag, L. S., Chase-Landsdale, P. L., & Brooks-Gunn, J. (1996). Not just "ghosts in the nursery": Contemporaneous intergenerational relationships and parenting in young African-American families. *Child Development, 67,* 2131–2147.

Walden, T. A., & Kim, G. (2005). Infants' social looking toward mothers and strangers. *International Journal of Behavioral Development, 29*(5), 356–360.

Waldman, S. (1993). Contraception: Defining terms, In B. K. Rothman (Ed.), *The encyclopedia of childbearing.* New York, NY: Henry Holt.

Walker, J. M. (2008). Looking at teacher practices through the lens of parenting style. *Journal of Experimental Education, 76*(2), 218–240.

Walkerdine, V. (1997). Redefining the subject in situated cognition theory. In D. Kirshner & J. Whitson (Eds.), *Situated cognition: Social, semiotic, and psychological perspectives* (pp. 57–70). Mahwah, NJ: Erlbaum.

Walter, J. L., & Burnaford, S. M. (2006). Developmental changes in adolescents' guilt and shame: The role of family climate and gender. *North American Journal of Psychology, 8*(2).

Walton, G. M., & Cohen, G. L. (2011). A brief social-belonging intervention improves academic and health outcomes of minority students. *Science, 331*(6023), 1447–1451.

Wandersman, A., & Nation, M. (1998). Urban neighborhoods and mental health: Psychological contributions to understanding toxicity, resilience, and interventions. *American Psychologist, 53,* 647–656.

Wang, M. T., & Fredricks, J. A. (2014). The reciprocal links between school engagement, youth problem behaviors, and school dropout during adolescence. *Child Development, 85*(2), 722–737.

Wang, Y., & Zhang, Q. (2006). Are American children and adolescents of low socioeconomic status at increased risk of obesity? Changes in the association between overweight and family income between 1971 and 2002. *American Journal of Clinical Nutrition, 84*(4), 707–716.

Wansink, B., Painter, J. E., & North, J. (2005). Bottomless bowls: Why visual cues of portion size may influence intake. *Obesity Research, 13*(1), 93–101.

Wardle, F. (1995). Alternatives . . . Bruderhof education: Outdoor school. *Young Children, 50*(3), 68–74.

Warneken, F., & Tomasello, M. (2007). Helping and cooperation at 14 months of age. *Infancy, 11*(3), 271–294.

Warnock, F., & Sandrin, D. (2004). Comprehensive description of newborn distress behavior in response to acute pain (newborn male circumcision). *Pain, 107,* 242–255.

Waterman, A. S. (1982). Identity development from adolescence to adulthood: An extension of theory and a review of research. *Developmental Psychology, 18,* 341–358.

Waterman, A. S. (1985). Identity in the context of adolescent psychology. *New Directions for Child Development, 39,* 5–24.

Webb, N. (Ed.) (1993). *Helping bereaved children: A handbook for practitioners.* New York, NY: Guilford Press.

Wechsler, H., Davenport, A., Dowdall, G., Moeykens, B., & Castillo, S. (1994). Health and behavioral consequences of binge drinking in college: A national survey of students on 140 campuses. *Journal of the American Medical Association, 272,* 1672–1677.

Wechsler, H., Rigotti, N. A., Gledhill-Hoyt, J., & Lee, H. (1998). Increased levels of cigarette use among college students: A cause for national concern. *Journal of the American Medical Association, 280,* 1673–1678.

Weinberg, M. K., & Tronick, E. Z. (1994). Beyond the face: The empirical study of infant affective configurations of facial, vocal, gestural, and regulatory behaviors. *Child Development, 65,* 1503–1515.

Weisner, T. S., & Wilson-Mitchell, J. E. (1990). Nonconventional family life-styles and sex typing in six-year-olds. *Child Development, 61,* 1915–1933.

Weiss, G., & Hechtman, L. (1993). *Hyperactive children grown up* (2nd ed.). New York, NY: Guilford Press.

Weiss, L. H., & Schwarz, C. (1996). The relationship between parenting types and older adolescents' personality, academic achievement, adjustment, and substance abuse. *Child Development, 67,* 2101–2114.

Wellman, H., & Hickling, A. (1994). The mind's "I": Children's conception of the mind as an active agent. *Child Development, 65*(6), 1564–1581.

Wertsch, J. V. (1985). *Vygotsky and the social formation of mind.* Cambridge, MA: Harvard University Press.

Wertsch, J. V. (1989). A socio-cultural approach to mind. In W. Damon (Ed.), *Child development today and tomorrow* (pp. 14–33). San Francisco: Jossey-Bass.

Wertsch, J. V., del Rio, P., & Alvarey, A. (1995). *Sociocultural studies of mind.* New York, NY: Cambridge University Press.

White, B. (1975). Critical influences in the origins of competence. *Merrill-Palmer Quarterly, 21,* 243–266.

White, B. (1993). *The first three years of life* (Rev. ed.). New York, NY: Simon & Schuster.

White, R. D. (1999). Are women more ethical? Recent findings on the effects of gender on moral development. *Journal of Public Administration Research and Theory, 3,* 459–471.

White, S. D., & DeBlassie, R. R. (1992). Adolescent sexual behavior. *Adolescence, 27,* 183–191.

Whitehurst, G., Epstein, J., Angell, A., Payne, A., Crone, D., & Fischel, J. (1994). Outcomes of an emergent literacy intervention in Head Start. *Journal of Educational Psychology, 86*(4), 542–555.

Whiteman, S. D., McHale, S. M., & Soli, A. (2011). Theoretical perspectives on sibling relationships. *Journal of Family Theory & Review, 3*(2), 124–139.

Whiting, B. B., & Edwards, C. P. (1988). *Children of different worlds.* Cambridge, MA: Harvard University Press.

Whiting, B. B., & Whiting, J. (1975). *Children of six cultures: A psychocultural analysis.* Cambridge, MA: Harvard University Press.

Whiting, J. W. M. (1981). Environmental constraints on infant care practices. In R. Munroe, R. H. Monroe, & B. B. Whiting (Eds.), *Handbook of cross-cultural development.* New York, NY: Garland Press.

Widom, C. S., Czaja, S. J., Bently, T., & Johnson, M. S. (2012). A prospective investigation of physical health outcomes in abused and neglected children: New findings from a 30-year followup. *American Journal of Public Health, 102,* 1135–1144.

Wieacker, P., & Steinhard, J. (2010). The prenatal diagnosis of genetic diseases. *Deutsches Arzteblatt International, 107,* 857–862.

Wigfield, A., Eccles, J., & Rodriguez, D. (1998). The development of children's motivation in school contexts. In P. Pearson & A. Iran-Nejad (Eds.), *Review of research in education* (Vol. 23, pp. 73–118.) Washington, DC: American Educational Research Association.

Wight, R. G., LeBlanc, A. J., & Badgett, M. V. L. (2013). Same-sex legal marriage and psychological well-being: Findings from the California Health Interview Survey. *American Journal of Public Health, 103,* 339–346.

Wilcox, A. J., Weinberg, C. R., & Baird, D. (1995). Timing of sexual intercourse in relation to ovulation: Effects on the probability of conception, survival of the pregnancy, and sex of the baby. *New England Journal of Medicine, 333,* 1517–1519.

Wilkinson, L., & Marrett, C. (Eds.) (1985). *Gender influences in classroom interaction.* Orlando, FL: Academic Press.

Wilkinson, R. (1996). *Unhealthy societies: The afflictions of inequality.* New York, NY: Routledge.

Williams, A., Khattak, A. Z., Garza, C. N., & Lasky, R. E. (2009). The behavioral pain response to heelstick in preterm neonates studied longitudinally: Description, development, determinants, and components. *Early Human Development, 85,* 369–374.

Williams, A. L., & Merten, M. J. (2009). Adolescents' online social networking following the death of a peer. *Journal of Adolescent Research, 24*(1), 67–90.

Williams, C., & Kimm, S. (1993). *Prevention and treatment of childhood obesity.* New York, NY: New York Academy of Sciences.

Williams, J. D., & Jacoby, A. P. (1989). The effects of premarital heterosexual and homosexual experience on dating and marriage desirability. *Journal of Marriage and the Family, 51,* 489–497.

Williams, P. M., Goodie, J., & Motsinger, C. D. (2008). Treating eating disorders in primary care. *American Family Physician, 77*(2), 187–195.

Willis, D. J., Holden, E. W., & Rosenberg, M. S. (Eds.). (1992). *Prevention of child maltreatment: Developmental and ecological perspectives.* New York, NY: Wiley.

Winfree, L. T., Backstrom, T. V., & Mays, G. L. (1994). Social learning theory, self-reported delinquency, and youth gangs. *Youth and Society, 26,* 147–177.

Winkler, I., Haden, G. P., Ladinig, O., Sziller, I., & Honing, H. (2009). Newborn infants detect the beat in music. *Proceedings of the National Academy of Science, 106,* 2468–2471.

Winters, K. C., & Arria, A. (2011). Adolescent brain development and drugs. *Prevention Researcher, 18*(2), 21–25.

Witherington, D. C., Campos, J. J., Harriger, J. A., Bryan, C., & Margett, T. E. (2010). Emotion and its development in infancy. In J. G. Bremner, & T. D. Wachs (Eds.), *The Wiley-Blackwell handbook of infant development* (pp. 568–591). Malden, MA: Wiley-Blackwell Publishing.

Wolf, D. (1993). There and then, intangible and internal: Narratives in early childhood. In B. Spodek (Ed.), *Handbook of research on the education of young children* (pp. 42–56). New York, NY: Macmillan.

Wolf, N. (1997). *The beauty myth.* New York, NY: Vintage Books.

Wolfe, D. A., McMahon, R. D., & Peters, R. D. (Eds.). (1997). *Child abuse: New directions in prevention and treatment across the lifespan.* Thousand Oaks, CA: Sage.

Wolff, P. (1966). The causes, controls, and organization of behavior in the neonate. *Psychological Issues, 5,* 1–105.

Wolfson, A. R., & Carskadon, M. A. (1998). Sleep schedules and daytime functioning in adolescents. *Child Development, 69,* 875–887.

Wolock, I. (1998). Beyond the battered child. *Readings: A Journal of Reviews and Commentary in Mental Health,* 4–9.

Wood, E., Senn, C. Y., Desmarais, S., Park, L., & Verberg, N. (2002). Sources of information about dating and their perceived influence on adolescents. *Journal of Adolescent Research, 17*(4), 401–417.

Woodburn, J. (1982). Social dimensions of death in four African hunting and gathering societies. In M. Bloch & J. Parry (Eds.). *Death and the regeneration of life* (pp. 187–210). Cambridge, UK: Cambridge University Press.

Woolfolk, A. (2013). *Educational psychology.* Upper Saddle River, NJ: Pearson.

Woolston, J. (1993). *Eating and growth disorders.* Philadelphia: Saunders.

Wootan, M., & Liebman, B. (1998). Ten steps to a healthy 1998. *Nutrition Action Health Letter, 25*(1), 1, 6–10.

Worden, J. W. (1996), *Children and grief.* New York, NY: Guilford.

World Bank. (1997). *Confronting AIDS: Public priorities in a global epidemic.* New York, NY: Oxford University Press.

World Health Organization (WHO). (2011). *WHO recommendations for induction of labour.* Retrieved from http://whqlibdoc.who.int/publications/2011/9789241501156_eng.pdf

World Health Organization (WHO). (2013). *Treatment of children living with HIV.* Retrieved from http://www.who.int/hiv/topics/paediatric/en/index.html

Wozniak, R., & Fischer, K. (1993). *Development in context: Acting and thinking in specific environments.* Hillsdale, NJ: Erlbaum.

Wright, P. H. (1987). Minority students: Developmental beginnings. *New Directions for Student Services, 38,* 5–21.

Wright, J. C., Huston, A. C., Truglio, R., Fitch, M., Smith, E., & Piemyat, S. (1995). Occupational portrayals on television: Children's role schemata, career aspirations, and perceptions of reality. *Child Development, 66,* 1706–1718.

Wright, K. (2000). Computer-mediated social support, older adults, and coping. *Journal of Communication, 50,* 100–118.

Wright, P. H. (1988). Interpreting research on gender differences in friendship: A case for moderation and a plea for caution. *Journal of Social and Personal Relationships, 5,* 367–373.

Y

Yacker, N., & Weinberg, S. L. (1990). Care and justice moral orientation: A scale for its assessment. *Journal of Personality Assessment, 56,* 18–27.

Yale School of Medicine. (2013). *Achondroplasia.* Retrieved from http://www.yalemedicalgroup.org/stw/

Yang, S., Yang, H., & Lust, B. (2011). Early childhood bilingualism leads to advances in executive attention: Dissociating culture and language. *Bilingualism: Language and Cognition, 14*(03), 412–422.

Yap, S. C., Anusic, I., & Lucas, R. E. (2012). Does personality moderate reaction and adaptation to major life events? Evidence from the British Household Panel Survey. *Journal of Research in Personality, 46,* 477–488.

Yarrow, M., & Waxler, C. (1978). The emergence and functions of prosocial behavior in young children. In M. Smart & R. Smart (Eds.), *Infants, development and relationships.* New York, NY: Macmillan.

Yeh, S. S. (2008). High stakes testing and students with disabilities: Why federal policy needs to be changed. In E. L. Grigorenko (Ed.), *Educating individuals with disabilities: IDEIA 2004 and beyond.* New York, NY: Springer.

Yeung, W. J., Sandberg, J. F., Davis-Kean, P. E., & Hofferth, S. L. (2001). Children's time with fathers in intact families. *Journal of Marriage and Family, 63,* 136–154.

Yoder, P., & Warren, S. (1993). Can developmentally delayed children's language development be enhanced through prelinguistic intervention? In A. Kaiser & D. Gray (Eds.), *Enhancing children's communication: Vol. 2* (pp. 35–62). Baltimore, MD: Paul Brookes.

Yonas, A. (1988). *Perceptual development in infants. Minnesota Symposium on Child Psychology: Vol. 20.* Minneapolis: University of Minnesota Press.

Yoshikawa, H., Aber, J. L., & Beardslee, W. R. (2012). The effects of poverty on the mental, emotional, and behavioral health of children and youth: Implications for prevention. *American Psychologist, 67*(4), 272.

Youniss, J. (1980). *Parents and peers in social development: A Sullivan-Piaget perspective.* Chicago: University of Chicago Press.

Youniss, J., & Smollar, J. (1985). *Adolescent relations with mothers, fathers, and friends.* Chicago: University of Chicago Press.

Yousefi, M., Karmaus, W., Zhang, H., Roberts, G., Matthews, S., Clayton, B., & Arshad, S. H. (2013). Relationships between age of puberty onset and height at age 18 years in girls and boys. *World Journal of Pediatrics, 9*(3), 230–238.

Yu, J. (2012). A systematic review of issues around antenatal screening and prenatal diagnostic testing for genetic disorders: Women of Asian origin in western countries. *Heath and Social Care in the Community, 20,* 329–346.

Yuan, A. S. V. (2012). Perceived breast development and adolescent girls' psychological well-being. *Sex Roles, 66,* 790–806.

Z

Zahn-Waxler, C., Radke-Yanow, M., & King, R. A. (1979). Child rearing and children's prosocial initiations toward victims of distress. *Child Development, 50,* 319–330.

Zahn-Wexler, C., Radere-Yanow, M. Wagner, E., & Chapman, M. (1992). Development of concern for others. *Developmental Psychology, 28,* 126–136.

Zampi, C., Fagioli, I., & Salzarulo, P. (2002). Time course of EEG background activity level before spontaneous awakening in infants. *Journal of Sleep Research, 11,* 283–287.

Zani, B. (1993). Dating and interpersonal relationships in adolescence. In S. Jackson, & H. Rodriguez-Tome (Eds.), *Adolescence and its social worlds* (pp. 95–119). Hillsdale, NJ: Lawrence Erlbaum.

Zarbatany, L., Hartmann, D. P., & Rankin, D. B. (1990). The psychological functions of preadolescent peer activities. *Child Development, 61,* 1067–1080.

Zhang, J., Himes, J. H., Guo, Y., Jiang, J., Yang, L., Lu, Q., Ruan, H., & Shi, S. (2013). Birth weight, growth and feeding pattern in early infancy predict overweight/obesity status at two years of age: A birth cohort study of Chinese infants. *PLoS ONE, 8,* 1–8.

Zigler, E. F., Taussig, C., & Black, K. (1992). Early childhood intervention: A. promising preventative for juvenile delinquency, *American Psychologist, 47,* 997–1006.

Zimmer-Gembeck, M. J., & Helfand, M. (2008). Ten years of longitudinal research on U.S. adolescent sexual behavior: Developmental correlates of sexual intercourse, and the importance of age, gender and ethnic background. *Developmental Review, 28*(2), 153–224.

Zimmerman, L., & McDonald, L. (1995). Emotional availability in infants' relationships with multiple caregivers. *American Journal of Orthopsychiatry, 65,* 147–152.

Zipfel, S., Wild, B., Groß, G., Friederich, H. C., Teufel, M., Schellberg, D., . . . & Burgmer, M. (2014). Focal psychodynamic therapy, cognitive behaviour therapy, and optimised treatment as usual in outpatients with anorexia nervosa (ANTOP study): Randomised controlled trial. *Lancet, 383*(9912), 127–137.

Zweig, J. M., Dank, M., Yahner, J., & Lachman, P. (2013). The rates of cyber dating abuse among teens and how it relates to other forms of teen dating violence. *Journal of Youth and Adolescence, 42,* 1063–1077.

Author/Name Index

Aber, J. L., 318
Abma, J. C., 413, 415
Abukabar, A., 122
Abu-Raiya, H., 325
Acebo, C., 356
Acock, A. C., 401
Adachi, P. J., 239
Adair, L., 185
Adolph, K. E., 119, 190
Ahadi, S., 163
Ahlberg, C., 252
Ahn, J., 250
Aiken, L., 288
Ainsworth, M. S., 52, 144, 163, 164, 165, 166, 169
Akande, A., 169
Alberts, A., 375
Alexander, A. W., 283
Alexander, G. M., 323
Alexander, K. L., 311
Allen, J. P., 386, 394
Allhusen, V. D., 159
Altenbaugh, R., 382
Amacker, A., 91
Amato, P. R., 312, 313, 314, 315
Ames, L. B., 217
Anastasi, A., 289
Anderson, A. M., 153
Anderson, B., 172
Anderson, J., 239
Anderson, L. M., 239
Andrien, M., 186
Angier, N., 68
Anglin, J., 285
Anthis, K. S., 389, 406
Apfel, N. H., 11, 417
Apgar, V., 107, 108
Arbeau, K. A., 305
Archer, S. L., 107, 389, 390
Archibald, A. B., 346
Archibald, J., 143
Arditti, J. A., 315
Arend, R. A., 167
Arguello, R., 188
Ariès, P., 11
Arliss, L., 212
Armenta, B. E., 233
Armour, S., 410
Armstrong, J., 421
Arnett, J. J., 343, 388, 392, 398, 406
Arria, A., 360
Arterberry, M. E., 115
Arthur-Banning, S., 270
Artiga, S., 187, 188
Asendorpf, J. B., 176
Ashley, K. B., 413
Ata, R. N., 358
Aureli, T., 155
Aviezer, O., 168
Ayers, T. S., 334
Ayscue, J. B., 325
Azmitia, M., 318, 319

Bachman, J. G., 384
Backx, F., 268
Bader, M., 324
Bagwell, C. L., 250, 326, 402
Baharudin, R., 308
Bailey, J. M., 412
Baillargeon, R., 138, 139
Baird, P., 68
Baker, B. L., 270

Baker, C., 210
Baker, J. E., 332
Bakermans-Kranenburg, M. J., 174
Balantekin, K. N., 267
Baldwin, D. A., 16
Balk, D., 349, 350
Balter, M., 412, 413
Bamford, F., 114
Bandura, A., 42, 43, 53, 237
Bank, L., 230
Banks Tarullo, L., 217
Barbaresi, W. J., 272
Barber, B. K., 312, 318
Barber, E., 99
Barlow, D. H., 174
Barness, L., 356
Barr, H. M., 87
Barr, R. G., 160
Barrett, H. C., 144
Barrett, K. C., 160, 161
Barry, H., 39
Barth, J. M., 296, 324
Bartholomew, K., 174
Bartick, M., 171
Bartolic, S., 238
Barton, E. E., 245
Bartsch, K., 366
Bat-Chava, Y., 390
Batenhorst, C., 233
Bates, J. E., 312
Bauman, K. E., 355
Baumrind, D., 227, 396
Baydar, N., 229
Beaman, J., 314
Bean, R. A., 312, 313, 318
Beardsall, L., 230
Beardslee, W. R., 318
Beauchamp, G. K., 116
Beck, D. M., 201
Becker, A. E., 267
Beelmann, A., 324, 325
Bègue, L., 20
Behrens, K. Y., 167
Behrman, R., 188
Bei, B., 24
Bell, K. L., 383
Bellamy, M. A., 308
Bellmore, A. D., 326, 404
Bellugi, U., 214
Belon, K., 356
Belsky, J., 154, 156, 157, 158, 164, 169, 170, 172, 173, 254, 255
Bem, S. L., 251, 253
Benatov, J., 325
Benedict, J. O., 245
Benenson, J. F., 247
Benner, A. D., 380
Benner, P., 372
Benoit, D., 174
Berg, E. C., 316
Berger, A., 161
Berger, R., 325
Berko, J., 208
Berlin, J. E., 290, 291
Berndt, T. J., 321, 322, 411
Bernhardt, J. S., 90
Bertrand, K., 355
Beydoun, M. A., 266
Bhavnagri, N., 250
Bialystok, E., 286
Bierman, K. L., 321, 322, 325
Bingham, C. R., 409, 410

Birch, L. L., 253, 266, 267
Black, M., 225
Black, M. C., 411
Blackman, J. A., 87, 89
Blair, J., 88
Blakemore, S. J., 321, 342, 359, 360
Blanchett, W. J., 291
Blanck, G., 48
Blashill, A. J., 347
Bleakley, A., 240
Blinn Pike, L., 398
Block, D., 166, 167
Bloom, D. A., 189
Bloom, L., 144
Boat, T., 355
Bock, R. D., 311
Boergers, J., 356
Bogdon, J. C., 94
Bohan, J., 304
Bohn, A., 304
Boivin, M., 235
Bojko, M., 325
Bolger, K. E., 318
Bollerud, K., 371
Bonnie, R., 355
Booth, D. A., 116
Booth, J. R., 280
Bornstein, M. H., 228
Bowen, N. K., 310, 311
Bowers, R., 374
Bowker, J. C., 322, 326
Bowlby, J., 52, 163, 164, 165, 254
Boyle, M., 298
Bradley, M., 96, 420
Branje, S. J. T., 322
Branstetter, W. H., 233
Brazelton, T. B., 107
Bredekamp, S., 217
Breiding, M. J., 411
Brendgen, M., 235
Brent, S. B., 333
Bretherton, I., 168, 169, 176, 177
Bridges, L. J., 156
Brim, O. C., 110
Brindle, J. A., 208
Brinsden, P., 72
Brislin, R., 381
Brody, G. H., 87, 312, 313, 319, 322
Bronfenbrenner, U., 8, 10, 47, 48, 53, 55, 399, 419
Bronner, F., 122
Bronstein, P., 153, 307
Brooks-Gunn, J., 176, 303, 343, 346
Brooten, D., 123
Broughton, D., 192
Brown, B. B., 320, 404, 408
Brown, G. L., 169, 170
Brown, J. R., 27
Brown, L., 230
Brown, R., 207
Brownell, C. A., 160
Bruchmüller, K., 271
Brumariu, L. E., 167
Bruner, J., 211
Bryant, B. K., 318, 320
Bryant, G. A., 144
Buck, K., 91
Buckley, K., 98
Bugental, D. B., 257
Buhrmester, D., 322, 401
Burd, L., 88
Burke, T., 356

Burnaford, S. M., 305
Burns, B. J., 257
Bury, M., 188
Bush, N. F., 419
Bushman, B. J., 20, 237
Buss, A. H., 233, 326
Buss, K. A., 161
Butler, A. B., 316
Buyse, E., 173
Byard, R., 112
Bye, K., 91
Byne, W., 412

Cain, K. M., 307
Cain, S., 404
Caine, D., 268
Cairns, R. B., 382
Calabrese, R. L., 399
Caliso, J., 255
Calkins, S. D., 231
Call, K. T., 407, 409
Callanan, M. A., 252
Callister, P., 171
Calvert, S. L., 238, 239, 240
Campos, J. J., 131
Campos, R., 18, 245
Camras, L. A., 160
Canfield, R., 131
Cannella, G., 12, 197
Cannon, J., 203
Caravita, S. C. S., 325
Card, N. A., 234, 235, 327
Carlo, G., 233
Carlson, C. I., 391, 394
Carlson, E. A., 163
Carlson, S. M., 201
Carlsson, M. A., 278
Carroll, J., 113
Carskadon, M. A., 356
Case, R., 45, 53, 139, 191, 203, 205, 279
Casey, B. J., 360
Caspi, A., 161, 163, 235
Cassidy, J., 158
Cassidy, S. B., 65
Caterall, J., 382
Caughey, A. B., 97
Cazden, C., 330
Cervantes, C. A., 252
Chadwick, A., 158
Chafel, J., 11
Chan, A., 248, 249, 250, 321, 322, 323, 324, 325
Chan, S., 74
Chandler, M., 308
Chang, A., 356
Chao, R. K., 225, 228
Chao, W., 401
Charman, T., 321
Chase-Lansdale, P. L., 90, 409, 414, 415, 416, 417
Chavajay, P., 45, 49
Chazan-Cohen, R., 217
Cheek, D., 346
Cheek, N. H., 346
Chen, J., 411
Chen, X., 266
Cheng, Y. W., 97
Cherkes-Julkowski, M., 272
Cherlin, A. J., 228
Cherry, F., 17
Chervin, R. D., 271, 273

Chess, S., 162
Chomsky, N., 210
Choudhury, S., 321
Christakis, D. A., 237, 239, 245
Christensen, K. Y., 345
Christodoulou, J., 292
Chung, A. E., 267
Cicchetti, D., 255, 419
Cicirelli, V. G., 156
Cillessen, A. H. N., 250, 326
Cinamon, R. G., 316
Clark, R., 170
Clarke, A. T., 237
Clarke-Stewart, K. A., 159, 170, 314
Clark-Pearson, K., 405, 406
Clegg-Kraynok, M. M., 111
Closson, L. M., 325
Coakley, J., 346
Coates, A., 191
Coates, J., 212
Coatsworth, J. D., 307, 308, 326, 328
Cobb, P., 205
Cogan, R., 96
Cohen, E., 296
Cohen, P. N., 296
Coie, J. D., 236, 325, 326
Coiro, M., 270
Colby, A., 15, 369, 371
Colby, S. L., 390
Coldwell, J., 319
Cole, M., 49
Cole, S. Z., 124
Coleman, J., 395
Coles, R., 191
Coley, R. L., 90, 311, 409, 414, 415, 416
Coll, C. G., 48
Collier, K. M., 239
Collins, W. A., 391, 394
Comer, J. P., 237, 238
Comstock, F., 240
Condry, J., 238
Cong, X., 160
Conger, R. D., 400, 401
Conklin, H. M., 280
Connell, S. L., 240
Connelly, K., 120
Connolly, J., 404
Connolly, S., 347, 349
Cooke, L., 186
Cooksey, E. C., 318
Copeland, L., 354
Copen, C. E., 309, 413, 415
Coplan, R. J., 326
Copple, C., 217
Coren, S., 113
Corley, C. J., 398
Corneal, D., 253
Corpus, J. H., 307
Corr, C. A., 349, 350
Corsini, R., 186
Costa, A., 400
Côté, S., 327
Countryman, J., 242
Covitz, L. M., 398, 400
Cowan, N., 173, 280
Cowan, P. A., 153
Cowart, B. J., 116
Cowell, J. M., 355
Cox, D. N., 403
Cox, M. J., 169, 170, 173
Coyne, J. C., 419

I-1

Coyne, S. M., 237, 239, 253, 327, 328
Crane, D. R., 312, 318
Creasey, G. L., 241
Crick, N. R., 234, 235, 327
Crnic, K., 156
Crockenberg, S. B., 162, 178
Crockett, L. J., 411
Crouter, A. C., 253, 318
Crow, S. J., 357
Cuffaro, H., 216
Cummings, E. M., 400
Cummings, J. L., 400
Currie, J., 256
Curry, G. D., 422
Czaja, S. J., 256

Dalglish, P., 19
Dalton, B., 212
D'Alton, M. E., 73
Dalton, S., 265
Damon, W., 14, 15, 303, 304, 305, 329, 387, 402
Daniels, K., 309
Danner, F., 356
Darling, N. E., 225, 227
Darwin, C., 12
Datar, A., 124
D'Augelli, A. R., 413
Davidson, R. J., 163
Davies, B., 193, 332
Davies, I., 115
Davies, K. M., 332
Davis, E., 84
Davis, J. N., 266
Davis, K., 292
Davis, M. M., 188
Davis-Floyd, R. E., 100
Dawson, G., 209
Deater-Deckhard, S., 236
Deaux, K., 193
DeBlassie, R. R., 411
DeCasper, A. J., 83, 153
DeCherney, A. H., 73
Deci, E. L., 307, 308
De Civita, M., 310, 311
Declercq, E., 97
De Goede, I. H., 322
De Jaeger, A. E., 305
DeJong, W., 357
DeKlyen, M., 235
Delamont, S., 296
Del Dotto, J., 282
Del Guidice, M., 141
DeLisi, M., 235
Delsing, M. J., 322
Demetriou, A., 376
Demo, D. H., 401
Denham, S., 321
Deniz, M., 167
Dennis, S., 205
Denson, N., 296
Dermer, A., 121
DeVries, C., 96
de Weerth, C., 250
DeWolf, D. M., 169
DeWolff, M. S., 169
D'Hondt, E., 193
Diamond, J., 67, 70
Diamond, L. M., 412, 413
Dickstein, S., 165
Dillon, J. A., 244, 341, 342, 343
Dillow, M. R., 314
Dishion, T. J., 404, 405, 421
Dodge, K. A., 235, 236, 238, 255, 312, 326
Doherty, D., 185
Dorius, C., 313, 314
Dorius, G. L., 410
Dornbusch, S. M., 397
Doumen, S., 173
Dovidio, J. F., 287
Downey, G., 419
Driscoll, D. A., 71
Druey, M. D., 225
DuBois, D. L., 324, 404
Duncan, D. T., 420
Duncan, G. E., 267
Dunham, P., 155

Dunkle, C. E., 389, 406
Dunn, J. F., 156, 230, 231, 244, 250, 319
Dunsmuir, L., 403
Durand, V. M., 174
Durbin, D. L., 404
Dusek, J. B., 402
Duursma, E., 230
Dweck, C. S., 307
Dyregrov, A., 332
Dyregrov, K., 332
Dziurgot, T., 245

Eakins, P. S., 95
East, P., 230
Ebbeling, C. B., 266
Eccles, J. S., 311, 343, 380, 391, 395, 419
Eckerman, C. O., 246
Eckstein, D., 231
Edelstein, W., 279
Edwards, C. P., 218, 233
Egeland, B., 255
Eisenband, J., 203
Eisenberg, N., 160, 161, 232, 233, 234, 235
Eisner, E., 324
Eklund., 297
Elbers, E., 203
Elder, G. H., 48
El-Dib, M., 117
Elkind, D., 278, 342, 374
Elliot, A. J., 307
Ellis, R., 156
Ellis, S., 320, 322
Emery, R. E., 237
Emes, C. E., 239
Emmerich, W., 251
Endres, J., 186
Engel, S., 244
Engelmann, T. G., 111
Engle, J. M., 159
Ennett, S. T., 355
Enriquez, E., 267
Ensminger, M. E., 228
Entwisle, D. R., 311
Erdley, C. A., 307
Erel, O., 230
Erikson, E. H., 34, 35, 37, 38, 40, 53, 152, 175, 178, 306, 329, 342, 387, 388, 389, 391, 392, 406
Evans, C. A., 155
Evans, E., 420
Eveleth, P., 185
Everly, G. S., 91

Fabes, R. A., 234, 235
Fabiano, G. A., 272
Fagioli, I., 115
Fagot, B. I., 158, 212, 251, 252
Fairburn, C., 358
Falbo, T., 231
Fangos, J. H., 332
Fantz, R., 130
Farrangy, P., 254
Farrant, B. M., 178
Farver, J. A. M., 233, 245
Fein, D., 209
Feinberg, M. E., 154
Feinbloom, R. I., 68, 71, 73, 98
Feld, S., 307
Fellowes, J., 192
Ferber, R., 114
Ferholt, J. B., 153, 254
Ferketich, S. L., 169
Fernald, A., 116
Ferrage, A., 186
Ferrer, B. M., 178
Fifer, W. P., 41
Fildes, A., 186
File, T., 238
Finch, B. K., 125
Finch, M. H., 383
Finders, M., 380
Findling, R. L., 272
Fine, G. A., 329

Finkelhor, D., 254, 257
Fischer, K., 45, 53, 205, 273, 304
Fish, M. C., 155, 246
Fitzgerald, H., 188, 271
Fivush, R., 323
Flanagan, C. A., 393
Flanders, J. L., 243
Flavell, J. H., 366
Fletcher, A. C., 395, 408
Flom, R., 132
Flor, D. L., 312, 313
Foehr, U. G., 239
Fomon, S. J., 108
Forrest-Pressley, D., 47
Forssberg, H., 120
Foster, S. L., 393
Fowler, C., 314
Fox, K., 347
Fox, N. A., 170
Frank, E., 110
Frank, M., 171
Franklin, A., 115
Fransson, P., 111
Fraser, A. M., 90
Fredricks, J. A., 382
Fredstrom, B., 322
French, D. C., 322
French, J., 379
Freud, S., 306
Friedlmeier, W., 233
Friedman, J., 50, 51
Frieze, I., 307
Froberg, K., 346
Fry, J., 349
Fuligni, A. J., 395
Fulkerson, J. A., 266
Furman, W., 319, 321, 322, 325
Furstenberg, F. F., 415
Futagi, Y., 116

Gabhainn, S. N., 351
Gable, C. J., 356
Gaesser, G., 265
Galambos, N. L., 318
Galassi, J., 380
Galinsky, E., 153
Gallagher, J., 290, 291
Gallagher, M., 382
Gallagher, S., 290, 291
Gallaway, C., 144
Galtry, J., 171
Gamble, J., 190
Garbarino, J., 8, 156, 255, 328, 419
Garcia, F., 228
Garcia, G., 41
Gardner, H., 72, 291, 292, 293, 378
Garland, A. F., 420
Garner, P. W., 230
Gathercole, S. E., 375
Ge, X., 394
Geary, D. C., 281, 282
Geddes, J. K., 406
Gee, J., 294
Geiger, B., 156
Gentile, D. A., 237, 240
George, C., 174
George, T. P., 321
Gerbasi, M. E., 267
Gerbner, G., 239
Gershoff, E. T., 175
Gesell, A., 12
Gestwicki, C., 217
Ge, J., 294
Gianino, A., 161
Giedd, J. N., 359, 360
Gilbert, S. P., 97
Gillies, R. M., 298
Gilligan, C., 27, 367, 372, 373, 390
Ginsburg, G. S., 307, 308
Ginsburg, H. P., 203, 205
Giordano, P. C., 403, 404
Glasgow, K. L., 394, 396
Glass, D. C., 110
Glass, J. C., 322
Glauser, B., 12, 18, 19
Gluszek, A., 287
Godfrey, K. M., 91
Gogtay, N., 360

Goldin-Meadow, S., 214
Goldman, L., 201
Goldman, S. E., 68
Goldsmith, H. H., 161
Goldson, E., 124
Goldstein, A. P., 421
Goldstein, S., 248
Goldwyn, R., 254
Golledge, R., 303
Golombok, S., 72, 321, 323, 412
Gondoli, D. M., 320
Gonzalez, A. L., 308
Gonzalez-Boto, R., 297
Goodnow, J. J., 15, 49, 218
Goosens, F. A., 173
Gopaul-McNicol, S., 213, 215, 218
Gordon, S., 372
Gorman, C., 87
Gorman, K. S., 187
Gornick, J. C., 316
Gortmaker, S. L., 357
Gottesman, I. I., 72, 73
Gottfried, A. E., 316, 317
Gottman, J. M., 247, 314
Gould, D., 297
Graber, J. A., 346, 357, 359
Gracia, E., 228
Graham, S., 328, 380
Gralinski, J. H., 177
Granier-Deferre, C., 153
Granrud, C., 130
Green, J. A., 160, 294
Green, R., 412
Greenfield, P., 16, 145
Greenhaus, J. H., 316
Greenleaf, C. A., 358
Greenson, J., 209
Gregg, M., 377
Griffiths, M., 333
Grisham, D. L., 212
Grolinck, W. S., 161
Gross, R., 124
Grossmann, K. E., 168
Grotpeter, J. K., 235, 327
Grundy, A. M., 320
Grusec, J. E., 225, 228, 232, 312, 313, 394, 407, 409
Grzywacz, J. G., 316
Guardo, C., 304
Guerra, N. G., 225
Gunnar, M. R., 163, 165
Gunnarsdottir, I., 123
Gupta, N. D., 316
Guralnick, M. J., 205
Guttmacher, A., 84
Guttman, A., 359

Hagan, R., 252
Hagerman, R. J., 67, 75
Haines, E. L., 193
Haith, M., 132
Häkkinen, I., 310, 311
Hakuta, K., 286
Halil, T., 160
Halim, M. L., 251, 252, 324
Hall, A. R., 404
Hall, D. W., 351
Halliday, J. L., 68, 69
Hallinan, M. T., 324
Halperin, J. M., 273
Ham, M., 343
Hamann, K., 232
Hamarta, E., 167
Hamburg, D. A., 343, 355, 422
Hamer, D. H., 412
Hamilton, B. E., 414
Hannon, E. E., 132
Hansen, D. J., 255
Hanson, M., 189
Hardy, J. B., 418
Hare-Mustin, R. T., 253
Hareven, T., 12
Harkness, S., 114, 168, 218
Harold, G. T., 310, 400, 401
Harrington, J. W., 123
Harris, P., 81, 82
Harrison, D., 116
Hart, B., 144

Hart, C. H., 227, 233, 244, 272, 395
Hart, D., 227, 303, 304, 305, 387
Harter, K. S. M., 178, 304, 305, 387
Hartup, W. W., 158, 163, 249, 250, 320, 321, 322, 326, 402
Hasan, Y., 20, 21
Haslett, B., 144, 145
Hastings, P. D., 312, 313
Hatzenbuehler, M. L., 420
Havekes, E., 324
Hay, P., 358
Hayenga, A. O., 307
Hayes, R., 233
Hayne, H., 129
Haynie, D., 410
Hayward, C., 314
Haywood, H. C., 48
Hazen, C., 392
Heal, D. J., 272
Heath, S., 212, 289
Hechtman, L., 273
Heffer, R. W., 308
Hegewisch, A., 316
Hegreness, R., 270
Heikamp, T., 225
Heine, S. J., 28
Heinmiller, B. M., 132
Hellström, A. L., 189
Helmerhorst, F. M., 72
Hendler, M., 277
Hendrick, H., 12
Hennessy, M., 240
Henrich, J., 28
Henry, B., 235
Hernandez, D. J., 48
Hernandez, H., 287
Hernández, M., 48, 287
Herrenkohl, R. C., 235, 255
Hersh, R. H., 367, 368
Hershberger, S. L., 413
Hespos, S. J., 138
Hesse, E., 167
Hesse-Biber, S., 358, 359
Hesser, J., 318, 319
Hetherington, E. M., 11, 243, 309, 311, 314, 315, 316, 393, 398, 399, 400, 401
Hildick-Smith, G. J., 355
Hill, D. A., 84, 279
Hills, A. P., 188
Hinduja, S., 406
Hines, M., 321, 323
Hinkley, T., 193
Hirsch, B. J., 324, 404
Ho, D., 145
Ho, E., 119
Hoare, C. H., 305
Hodapp, R. M., 68
Hodges, E. V., 236
Hodnett, E. D., 95
Hoeve, M., 227, 229, 235
Hoff, E., 208, 210, 212
Hoff-Ginsberg, E., 211, 230
Hoffman, L. W., 170, 307, 316, 317, 323, 324
Hoffnung, A., 96
Hoffnung, M., 245
Holden, C., 420
Holden, E. W., 420
Holmes, L. J., 97
Holzgreve, W., 71
Holzman, L., 204
Hooper, C. J., 280
Horgan, J., 69, 75
Hornor, G., 256
Horst, L., 186
Howe, N., 230, 244, 318, 319
Howes, C., 158, 159, 244, 245, 247, 248, 250, 324
Hoza, B., 321
Huang, B., 408
Huang, L., 225
Hubbard, R., 71
Hübner, R., 225
Hudley, C., 328
Huesmann, L. R., 237
Hughes, F. P., 246
Hunt, C., 112

Hurrelmann, K., 343
Huston, A. C., 237, 239, 240, 251
Hyde, J. S., 171, 231
Hyman, J. P., 153, 156
Hymel, S., 325, 326

Ianni, F., 380
Infante, M. A., 87
Inhelder, B., 201, 202, 365
Innamorati, M., 153
Insabella, G. M., 164
Insana, S. P., 111, 113
Iyer, S. N., 143
Izard, C. E., 160, 161

Jaccard, J., 415
Jacknowitz, A., 124
Jackson, A. W., 358
Jackson, M. F., 296, 324
Jackson, P., 330
Jacob, V., 188
Jacobvitz, D. B., 419
Jacoby, A. P., 412
Jadack, R., 371
Jaffee, S. R., 255
Jain, A., 156
James, J., 411
James, T., 242
James, W., 115
Jamison, R., 321
Jang, Y., 233
Jansson, U. B., 189
Jaworski, A., 243
Jenni, O. G., 356
Jensen, L. A., 388, 392, 398, 406
Jernigan, T. L., 109
Jimenez, R., 27, 286
Jin, M. K., 168
Johansen, R., 381
Johnson, D. W., 296, 325
Johnson, M. S., 256, 271
Johnson, P., 296
Johnson, S. P., 287
Johnson, V. E., 314
Johnson, W., 109
Johnston, L. D., 343, 352, 353, 354, 355
Jones, D. N., 296
Jones, R. P., 403
Jordan, A. B., 240
Jose, P. E., 151
Joshi, M., 22
Josselson, R., 349, 386, 387
Junaid, K. A., 192
Jusczyk, P. W., 132

Kadushin, F. S., 96
Kaestle, C. E., 351
Kagan, J., 129, 161, 163, 345, 347
Kaijura, H., 116
Kaiser, I., 84
Kaitz, M., 141
Kaloustian, G., 169, 173, 174
Kalter, N., 334
Kalverboer, A., 189, 190, 192
Kamii, C., 278
Kao, G., 26
Kaplan, L., 112
Karam, R. G., 273
Karpov, Y. V., 48
Katz, P. P., 314
Kaufman, M., 266, 412
Kavanaugh, R. D., 244
Kawaguchi, D., 317
Kaye, H., 41
Kazdin, A. E., 272
Keane, S. P., 231
Keating, D., 279, 363, 364, 378
Keefe, J., 379
Keefer, C., 114
Keehn, D., 227
Keller, M., 321
Kellman, P. J., 115
Kendall-Tackett, K. A., 255, 256
Kenney, G., 187
Kermoian, R., 131
Kerns, K. A., 167
Kerr, M., 162, 163

Keysers, C., 141
Kikas, E., 236
Kim, G., 176
Kim, J. Y., 318, 319
Kim, S. K., 233
Kimm, S., 123
King, K. M., 357
King, P. M., 378
King, V., 315, 316
Kingerlee, S., 119
Kirby, D., 351, 414
Kirjavainen, T., 310
Kirsh, S. J., 239
Kisilevsky, B. S., 83, 129
Kisler, T. S., 187
Kistner, J., 255
Kitchen, J., 290
Kitchener, K. S., 378
Kite, M. E., 193
Kitzinger, J., 12
Klahr, D., 45, 278
Klaus, M. H., 97
Klaus, P. H., 97
Kleinsorge, C., 398, 400
Klimes-Dougan, B., 255
Klinnert, M. D., 176
Knafo, A., 329
Knox, G. W., 422
Kochanska, C., 176, 177
Kochanska, G., 160, 225, 227
Koester, J., 381
Kohlberg, L., 367, 368, 369, 371
Kohler, P. K., 351
Kohn, M. L., 316, 396
Kolak, A. M., 156
Kool, R., 242
Kopp, C. B., 161, 162, 177
Korbin, J. E., 256
Kordi, A., 308
Koretz, D., 379
Kosciw, J. G., 412
Kostelny, K., 328
Kotloff, L., 218
Kovacs, D. M., 323
Kozol, J., 19, 328
Kramer, D. A., 332
Krans, E. E., 188
Krasnor, L., 244
Kringelbach, M. L., 194
Krishnakumar, A., 255
Kroger, J., 388
Kroonenberg, P. M., 166, 168
Krueger, J., 230
Krueger, W., 230
Kryger, M., 114
Krysan, M., 324
Kuczynski, L., 227
Kuhl, P., 116, 141
Kuhn, D., 364, 376
Kulb, N., 98
Kumari, N., 194
Kutaka, T. S., 218
Kutner, L., 237, 238
Kutz-Costes, B., 237

Ladd, G. W., 233, 244
Laditka, J. N., 416
Laditka, S. B., 416
Lafferty, W. E., 351
Lakoff, G., 366
Lall, D. I., 305
Lally, M. M., 358
Lamaze, F., 96
Lamb, J. A., 225, 227, 228
Lamb, M. E., 156, 169, 253
Lamborn, S. D., 226, 395, 397
Lamke, L. K., 253
Lammert, O., 346
Lang, C., 121
Lanham, J. S., 124
Lapsley, D., 375
Laris, B. A., 351
Larrabee, M., 373
Larson, R. W., 320, 343, 391, 392, 393, 394
Larzelere, R. E., 237
Lasley, J. R., 421

Latan, R., 296
Laughlin, L., 158
Lauricella, A. R., 240
Lave, J., 204, 293
Lawson, A. E., 90
Lawver, T., 242
Laybourn, A., 231
Leadbetter, B., 366
Leaper, C., 252, 296
Leckman, J., 52
Lee, F. R., 89
Lee, J. S., 310, 311
Lee, S. J., 237, 238
Lee, S. Y., 308
Lee, V. E., 380
Leggett, E. L., 307
Leidy, M. S., 225, 226
Leigh, B. C., 411
Leinbach, M. D., 251
Leinhardt, C., 377
Lens, W., 307
Lepage, J. F., 141
LePort, A. K., 46
Lerner, J., 281
Letourneau, N., 155
LeVay, S., 412
Levenson, R. W., 314
Levine, A. D., 406, 407
Levine, G., 17
LeVine, R., 120
Levitt, M. J., 404
Levy-Shiff, R., 153, 154
Lewis, C. T., 90, 156, 242
Lewis, D., 123
Lewis, J. A., 404
Lewis, J. M., 242
Lewis, M., 39, 160, 161, 175, 176, 303, 404
Lickona, T., 371
Lieber, C. S., 240
Liebman, B., 122
Liebmann-Smith, J., 72
Liem, D. G., 116
Liem, R., 318
Lightfoot, C., 348
Lightfoot, S. L., 350
Lillard, A. S., 216, 239
Lindblad-Goldberg, M., 226
Lindell, S. G., 96
Linder, J. R., 239
Linn, S., 87
Linney, J. A., 330
Lipsitt, L., 41
Litman, C., 178
Little, T. D., 163, 234, 327
Littleton, H. L., 91
Liu, H., 266
Livingston, G., 309, 310
Livingston, M., 96
Livson, N., 347
Lochman, J. E., 296, 324
Loeb, R. C., 228
Loeber, R., 328, 421
Lohnes, K. L., 334
Londerville, S., 167
Loprinzi, P. D., 193
Lord, H., 318
Lothian, J., 96
Louis, B., 380
Love, J. M., 173, 217
Lozano, P., 245
Lozoff, B., 91
Lucas-Thompson, R. G., 172
Luciana, M., 280
Ludden, A. B., 358
Ludwig, B., 355
Ludwig, D. S., 266
Luna, B., 359, 376
Lundy, B. L., 156
Luria, A. R., 49
Lust, B., 286
Luster, T., 422
Lustig, M., 381
Lynch, B., 355
Lynch, J. S., 281
Lyon, D., 283
Lyons-Ruth, K., 166, 167
Lytton, H., 252

Maccoby, E. E., 152, 225, 228, 252, 296, 323, 324
MacKinnon-Lewis, C., 327
MacLean, M., 22
Madden, M., 406
Maffulli, N., 268
Maggs, J. L., 318
Maguire, M. D., 250
Mahler, M., 164, 169
Mahoney, J. L., 318, 382
Main, M., 53, 163, 166, 167, 174, 233, 254
Maker, J., 291
Malatesta, C. Z., 160
Malina, R. M., 345, 346
Malinosky-Rummell, R., 255
Mallory, G., 219
Mancini, L. M., 111
Mandara, J., 225
Mandel, D. R., 132
Manera, V., 141
Manganello, J. A., 237
Mangelsdorf, S. C., 154, 165, 169
Manhart, L. E., 351
Manzi, C., 303
Marcia, J. E., 388, 389, 390, 391
Marcus, D., 303
Marcus, G., 208
Marecek, J., 253
Marentette, P., 143
Margolin, E. G. J., 290
Margolin, L., 290
Margraf, J., 271
Marini, M. E., 267
Markman, H. J., 96
Marlowe, B., 216
Marquez, S., 297
Marrett, C., 296
Marschark, M., 143, 214
Marsella, A. J., 328
Martin, B., 236
Martin, C. L., 251, 252, 253
Martin, J. A., 90, 99, 225, 228
Martin, S. B., 358
Martinez, G., 413, 415
Masapollo, M., 116
Masten, A. S., 307, 308, 326, 328
Mataix-Cols, D., 272
Matas, L., 167
Matheson, C. C., 244, 245, 247
Mathews, D., 290
Mayer, B., 233
Mayes, L. C., 52
Mazur, J., 128
McAdoo, H. P., 422
McCall, G. J., 398
McCall, R., 84, 129
McCloyd, V. C., 328, 390
McCluskey, K., 162
McCurdy, K., 187
McDaniel, D., 208
McDonald, M., 187
McGarell, E. F., 421
McGinley, M., 233
McGuffin, P., 64
McGuire, E. J., 189
McHale, S. M., 157, 253, 318
McKay, S., 93, 94
McKussick, V. A., 64
McLoyd, V. C., 393
McNamara, T., 281
McQuoid, Joan., 399
Measor, L., 296
Meehan, P. J., 420
Meesters, C., 318
Meeus, W. H. J., 322
Meilman, P., 389
Meins, E., 144
Mela, D., 357
Meltzer, L. J., 273
Meltzoff, A. N., 138, 141, 209
Ménard, L., 116
Menkes, J., 117
Mennella, J. A., 116
Mercer, P. W., 355, 356
Mercer, R. T., 69
Merenstein, G., 343, 345
Messer, D., 209, 211

Messinger, D. S., 160
Messner, M., 270
Mestre, M. V., 233
Metallinos-Katsaras, E., 187
Metz, K., 279
Michaels, S., 295
Michelsson, K., 111
Mickelson, K. D., 174
Mikaye, K., 168
Milevsky, A., 227, 228, 229
Miller, B., 421
Miller, P. H., 38, 43, 135
Milner, J. S., 255
Milteer, R. M., 245
Milunsky, A., 65
Minagawa-Kawai, Y., 132
Mindell, J. A., 273
Minino, A. M., 350
Miramontes, O., 213
Mishna, F., 285
Miyazaki, J., 317
Mogford, K., 210
Moilanen, K. L., 411
Monk, T. H., 153
Monsour, A., 387
Montemayor, R., 393
Montessori, M., 216
Montgomery-Downs, H. E., 111, 113
Moore, C., 155
Moore, D., 392
Moore, E. G. J., 311
Moore, M. K., 120
Moore, S., 351
Moorefield, B. S., 316
Moorehouse, M. J., 317, 324
Morrison, E. H., 99
Morrongiello, B., 132
Morrow, L., 216
Mortimer, J. T., 383, 407
Moscicki, A., 351
Moses, L. J., 176
Mosher, W. D., 309
Moss, P., 356
Munroe, R., 120
Murphy, L., 232
Myers, J., 366
Myhill, D., 296

Naaktgeboren, N., 72
Nagle, R. J., 357
Nakao, T., 272
Nathanson, A. I., 240
Nation, M., 327
Navarro-Rivera, J., 403
Neal, J. W., 326
Neff, C., 169
Neinstein, L. S., 315
Nelson, A. I., 351
Nelson, D. A., 239, 327
Nelson, K., 201
Nelson, S. E., 108
Netter, S., 227
Neulinger, J., 110
New, R., 219
Newcomb, A. F., 326, 402
Newman, F., 204
Newman, K., 383
Newman, R. S., 132
Nezworski, T., 172
Nicholson, J. M., 97
Nickerson, A. B., 357
Nickerson, B. G., 322
Nishina, A., 404
Noam, G., 367
Noboa, J., 399
Noddings, N., 372
Nolen-Hoeksema, S., 155
Noller, P., 156
Noppe, I. C., 156
Norbeck, J. S., 91
Norenzayan, A., 28
Norman, C., 310
Norman, R. E., 255
Nucci, L., 371
Nugent, J., 107
Nunes-Costa, R. A., 400

O'Brien, M., 31
O'Brien, S. F., 322

O'Callaghan, F. V., 88
O'Connell, E., 355
O'Connor, C., 382
O'Connor, M., 295
O'Donnell, J., 328
O'Donnell, K., 391
O'Hara-Devereaux, M., 381
Oiler, D. K., 143
O'Keefe, M., 196
O'Keeffe, G. S., 405, 406
Oldehinkel, A. J., 343
Olds, D. L., 90, 91, 418
Olsen, J. P., 326
Olsho, L., 133
Olson, K., 255
Oppenheim, D., 225
Orfield, G., 325
Orland-Barak, L., 295
Ormel, J., 343
Orr, M., 380
Ortman, J. M., 390
Orzech, K., 356
Osgood, D. W., 318
Oster, H., 160
Otis, N., 380
Overton, W., 303
Owen, M. J., 64
Owen, M. T., 169, 170, 173
Owens, D., 332
Owens, J. A., 356

Pagani, L., 310
Page, D. C. 64
Painter, J. E., 266
Pakiz, B., 328
Pallock, L. L., 226
Paniagua, F. A., 74
Pappas, S., 203
Pappert, A., 71
Paquette, D., 156, 243
Parente, M. E., 318
Parke, R. D., 156, 158, 165, 250
Parker, K. C. H., 174
Parkhurst, J., 247
Parkinson, S., 17
Parsons, C. E., 194
Parten, M., 245, 246, 247
Pasley, K., 316
Pasterski, V., 321, 322, 323
Patchin, J. W., 406
Patterson, C. J., 412
Patterson, G. R., 227, 238, 404, 405
Patterson, M. L., 133
Paulston, C., 381
Pavilanis, R., 245
Pawlak, D. B., 266
Pearson, D., 27
Pease-Alvarez, L., 286
Peets, K., 236, 238
Peipert, J. F., 415
Pelaez, M., 176
Penner, S., 209
Pennington, B. F., 282, 283
Perkins, D., 294, 297
Perrin, E. M., 433
Persaud, T., 120
Peskin, H., 347
Pesonen, A. K., 174
Peters, E., 250
Peterson, J., 239
Peterson, P., 380
Peterson, R. L., 282, 283
Petlichkoff, L., 269, 297
Petrie, T. A., 358
Pettit, G. S., 227, 312
Pettito, L., 143
Phillips, B., 356
Phinney, J. S., 390, 404
Phipps, M. G., 415
Piaget, J., 13, 34, 43, 44, 45, 47, 49, 53, 134, 135, 136, 137, 138, 139, 140, 184, 200, 201, 202, 203, 204, 205, 243, 244, 276, 277, 278, 279, 320, 364, 365, 366, 367
Pianta, R., 255
Pica-Smith, C., 403, 404
Pick, A. D., 132
Pihl, R. O., 243
Pike, A., 319, 398

Pilling, M., 115
Piotrowski, C., 224
Pipp, S. L., 45
Pisoni, D. B., 132
Pittard, W. B., 416
Pittman, J. F., 266
Pittman, T., 266
Plomin, R., 162, 233
Polka, L., 116
Pollitt, E., 122
Pomerantz, E. M., 308
Porter, C. L., 155
Porter, R. H., 116
Posada, G., 169, 173, 174
Posner, J. K., 318
Poulin, F., 248, 249, 250, 321, 322, 323, 324, 325
Poussaint, A. F., 237, 238
Powell, G. N., 316
Powell, M., 332
Powell, N., 324
Power, T. G., 241, 243, 244, 246, 247, 248, 250, 252
Pownall, T., 119
Poynton, T. A., 403, 404
Prause, J., 172
Prenovost, M. A., 324
Presaghi, F., 155
Price, R. H., 318
Primeau, M. R., 82
Prinstein, M. J., 420
Prinz, E., 214
Prinz, P., 214
Pritchett, L., 125
Proctor, C. P., 212
Pryor, D. W., 421
Puhl, R. M., 357
Purhonen, M., 152

Quan, J., 172
Queen, P., 121
Quinlan, J. D., 84
Quintana, S. M., 324

Raabe, T., 324, 325
Raby, K. L., 174
Radua, J., 272
Raffaelli, M., 411
Raikes, H., 217
Raker, C. A., 415
Raloff, J., 355
Ramanan, J., 318
Ramirez, O., 157, 226
Ramos, K. D., 392
Ramsey, P., 212
Raphael, D., 97
Rasmussen, E. E., 239, 240
Raver, C. C., 155
Rawlins, W. K., 321, 402
Reaves, J., 325
Recchia, H., 230, 318
Reeder, K., 211
Regalia, C., 303
Rege, M., 318
Reid, M., 401
Reimer, R. A., 240
Reinhold, A., 171
Reiser, J. J., 116
Remafedi, G., 412
Reynolds, A. J., 308
Rhode, D. L., 90
Rhodes, C., 379
Rice, J. C., 237
Richards, M. H., 110, 144, 391, 394, 403
Richio, L. J., 415
Richter, P., 89
Rickman, M. D., 163
Rideout, V. J., 239
Rieck, T., 358
Rieder, R. O., 409, 413
Rigsby, D. C., 415
Riksen-Walraven, J. M., 250
Riley, E. P., 87
Ritchey, M. L., 189
Rivkees, S. A., 114
Roberts, A., 325
Roberts, D. F., 239
Roberts, P., 357

Roberts, W., 327
Robertson, C., 91
Robin, A. L., 391, 393
Robins, R. W., 178, 179
Rochat, P., 176
Roche, K. M., 228
Rockwell, R., 186
Rodkin, P. C., 321, 322, 326
Roelofs, J., 318
Roggman, L. A., 172
Rogoff, B., 45, 48, 49, 204
Roland, A., 74, 305
Rolf, J., 328
Romaine, S., 285
Romig, J., 421
Romney, D. M., 242
Rooks, J. P., 95
Roopnarine, J. L., 245, 253
Rose, J., 190
Rosemary, S. L., 305
Rosenberg, B. G., 231
Rosenberg, M. S., 257, 304
Rosenheim, M. K., 414
Ross, H. S., 230, 318
Ross, P., 290
Rossell, C. H., 325
Rothbart, M. K., 161, 162, 163, 235
Rourke, B., 282
Rovine, M., 172
Rowe, M. L., 110
Rowland, T., 268
Rubenstein, J. L., 158, 420
Rubia, K., 272
Rubin, K. H., 244, 322, 324, 326
Ruble, D. N., 251, 252, 253, 324
Rudowitz, R., 188
Rudy, D., 228
Ruhm, C. J., 171
Ruiz-Primo, M. A., 279
Ruptic, C., 279
Russ, S. W., 244
Russell, K., 355
Rutter, M., 272
Ryan, A. M., 321
Ryan, C., 238
Ryan, J., 359
Ryan, R. M., 308
Rytz, A., 186

Sabo, D., 270
Sadovnick, A. D., 68
Sagi, A., 168, 174, 328
Sagi-Schwartz, A., 328
Salafia, E. H. B., 320
Saler, L., 334
Salguero, A., 297
Salisbury, C., 91
Salmivalli, C., 236
Salomon, G., 294, 297
Saltali, N., 167
Salzarulo, P., 115
Samper, P., 233
Samter, W., 145
Samuels, C. A., 278, 379
Samuelsson, I. P., 278
Sandler, I. N., 334
Sandnabba, N. K., 252
Sandrin, D., 116
Sanfilippo, J., 189
Santrock, J., 316
Saracho, O. N., 212, 241
Sarafino, E., 421
Sarver, M. D., 285
Sasse, D., 363, 378
Sato, D., 87
Sault, N., 267
Savage, J. S., 267
Savelsbergh, G., 118
Savin-Williams, R. C., 411, 412, 413
Sawalani, G. M., 234, 327
Sawin, D., 232
Scabini, E., 303
Scarr, S., 158, 172
Scharkow, M., 20
Schlecter, S., 227
Schlegel, A., 399
Schneider, S., 271
Schonert-Reichl, K. A., 391
Schoppe-Sullivan, S. J., 154

Schrader, D., 367
Schur, E. A., 267
Schwalberg, R., 415
Schwartz, D., 236
Schwartz, S. H., 329
Schweinhart, L., 22, 216, 422
Schweinle, A., 133
Scollon, R., 381
Scollon, S., 381
Scott, K. D., 97
Sebastián-Gallés, N., 286
Sedgh, G., 414
Seeley, W. W., 189
Seguin, J. R., 243
Seidel, H., 115
Seider, S., 292
Seidman, E., 330
Seidman, S. N., 409, 413
Seidner, L. B., 305
Seifer, R., 162
Seifert, K., 3, 12, 45, 278
Seiffge-Krenke, I., 343
Seitz, V., 11
Selekman, J., 67, 70
Selman, R., 304, 321
Shafer, M. B., 351
Shanahan, L., 231
Shanahan, M. J., 407
Shapiro, A. F., 153, 154
Sharp, S., 217
Shatz, M., 230
Shaver, P. R., 392
Shaw, S. F., 285
Sheehan, M. J., 238
Sheldon, S., 111
Shepherd-Look, D., 250
Sheppard, K., 251
Shin, Y. L., 245
Shmueli, A., 97
Short, J. E., 238
Shrum, W., 323, 324
Shultz, S., 116
Shure, M. B., 328
Silber, S. J., 72
Sillén, U., 189
Silva, P. A., 163
Silverman, P. R., 333
Silverstein, L. B., 170
Simkin, P., 95
Simons, B. L., 314, 401
Simpson, J. A., 174
Simpson, J. L., 71
Sinclair, D., 344
Singer, J. L., 244
Siska, E., 113
Sitterle, K., 316
Sizer, T., 382
Skinner, A. C., 267
Skinner, B. F., 209
Skolnick, A., 225
Skolnick, J., 225
Skolnick, N., 334
Slade, A., 167
Slater, A. M., 130
Slaughter, V., 333
Slavin, R. E., 297, 325, 379, 382
Slinger-Constant, A. M., 283
Slomin, M., 157
Slomkowski, C., 230
Sloper, P., 68
Small, S. A., 411
Smetana, J. G., 392, 393, 395
Smilansky, S., 243
Smith, A., 268
Smith, D., 194
Smith, D. E., 398
Smith, E., 131
Smith, N., 316
Smith, P. K., 242
Smith, S. L., 272
Smitherman, G., 398
Snidman, N., 161, 163
Snowling, M., 282
Soley, G., 132
Soli, A., 157
Soltis, J., 160
Solomon, J., 166, 167
Sommerville, J., 12
Soriano, F. I., 421

Sorkhabi, N., 225
Soto, L., 287
Sousa, C., 255
Spaccarelli, S., 257
Spassov, L., 114
Speece, M. W., 333
Spence, M. J., 153
Spencer, T. J., 272
Spergel, I., 422
Spetner, N., 133
Spitze, G. D., 231
Spivak, G., 328
Spodek, B. O., 212, 241
Sponseller, D., 243
Spurrier, N. J., 193
Sroufe, L. A., 167
St. James-Roberts, I., 140, 160
St. Peters, M., 250
Stacey, N., 188
Stackhouse, J., 282
Stake, J. E., 254
Stanger-Hall, K. F., 351
Statista., 406
Steele, H., 174
Steiger, C., 94, 96, 97
Stein, A., 194
Steinberg, L. D., 225, 227, 318, 360, 391, 394, 395, 396, 397, 406, 407
Steiner, G., 201
Steiner, H., 269
Steiner, J. E., 116
Steinhard, J., 73
Stern, D. N., 152, 153, 155, 169, 254
Sternberg, R. J., 72, 289, 290, 292, 293, 377
Stevens, N., 249, 250, 321
Stevenson, H. W., 308, 310, 311
Stevenson-Hinde, J., 167, 228
Stewart, R. B., 156
Stifter, C. A., 170, 171
Stiles, J., 109
Stipek, D. J., 176, 307
Stocker, C., 225
Stokes, G., 412
Stolberg, A. L., 314
Stone, M. R., 404
Stout, B. C., 86
Stouthamer-Loeber, M., 328, 421
Stratford, B., 67, 68
Strayer, J., 327
Streissguth, A. P., 87
Stucky, B. D., 234, 327
Suchodoletz, A. V., 225
Sue, D. W., 74
Sullivan, A., 372, 392
Sullivan, H., 320
Sullivan, J. L., 89
Sullivan, K., 392
Sullivan, S. J., 110
Sunderman, G. L., 380
Super, C. M., 168, 218
Susa, A. M., 245
Suzuki, Y., 116
Swain, M., 287
Swanson, H., 281
Swanson, S. A., 357
Swendsen, J., 357
Swinburn, B. A., 266
Sykes, P., 296

Tadmor, C. T., 325
Taffel, S. M., 99
Takanishi, R., 350
Takata, S., 421
Takei, W., 143
Tandon, P. S., 245
Tanner, J. M., 185, 346
Tardiff, T., 144
Tasker, F. L., 412
Taylor, C. A., 237
Taylor, J., 27, 372, 373
Taylor, M. J., 110
Teixeira, R., 324
Telkemeyer, S., 143
Telle, K., 318
Temple, J. A., 308
Terry, R., 283, 284
Tesman, J., 188

I-4 Author/Name Index

Testa, M. F., 414
Teti, D. M., 156
Théoret, H., 141
Thomas, A., 161, 162
Thomas-Presswood, T., 213, 215, 218
Thompson, R. A., 29
Thorsdottir, I., 123
Tilden, V. P., 91
Tillman, P., 354
Tobin-Richards, M. H., 347
Tomasello, M., 232, 233
Toribe, YH., 116
Toro, R. I., 225
Tortolero, S. R., 351
Toth, K., 209
Toth, S. L., 419
Tough, P., 378
Trainor, L. J., 132
Trawick-Smith, J., 245
Tremblay, R. E., 235, 310
Trent, K., 231
Trinke, S., 174
Triona, L. M., 278
Trommsdorff, G., 225, 233
Tronick, E. Z., 160, 161, 174
Tropp, L. R., 324
Trost, S. G., 193
Trzesniewski, K. H., 178, 179
Tuero, C., 297
Tur, A., 233
Turenshine, H., 110
Turiel, E., 371
Turkheimer, E., 72, 73
Turner, E. A., 308
Tzuk, K., 316

Ullal-Gupta, S., 83

Underwood, M., 327
Updegraff, K. A., 156
Urbano, R. C., 68
Urbina, S., 289
Uusitalo, R., 310

Valkenburg, P. M., 245
Vandell, D. L., 153, 154, 318
van den Boom, D. C., 162, 169
van den Broek, P., 281
van der Horst, K., 186
van der Voort, T. H. A., 245
van der Westerlaken, L. A., 72
Vandewater, E. A., 238, 240
van IJzendoorn, M. H., 155, 166, 168, 169, 173, 174
van Jaarsveld, C. H., 186
van Reek, J., 398
van Sleuwen, B. E., 120
Vansteenkiste, M., 307, 308
VanTassel-Baska, J., 291
Vaughn, M. G., 235
Ventura, A. K., 186
Ventura, S. J., 414
Verhulst, F. C., 343
Verner, M., 316
Verschueren, K., 167, 173
Vespa, J., 309
Vignoles, V. L., 303
Vissing, Y., 19
Vitaro, F., 235, 236, 310, 405
Volling, B. L., 156, 157, 169, 230
Votruba, M., 318
Vouloumanos, A., 116
Vygotsky, L. S., 45, 48, 49, 50, 53, 204, 211, 216, 244, 293, 321, 322, 329

Wadsworth, B., 200, 276, 277
Wadsworth, M. E. J., 110
Wagner, R., 290
Wahistrom, K., 356
Waite, E. B., 231
Waite-Stupiansky, S., 278
Wakschlag, L. S., 417
Walberg, H., 379
Walden, T. A., 176
Walk, R., 131
Walker, J. M., 329, 330
Walkerdine, V., 215
Walsh, D. A., 237, 240
Walsh, P., 314
Walter, J. L., 305
Wandersman, A., 327
Wang, M. T., 309
Wang, Y., 266
Ward, R. H., 90
Wardle, J., 186
Warneken, F., 232, 233
Warner, K. E., 355
Warnock, F., 116
Warren, K. R., 87
Warren, M., 343
Warren, S., 145
Wartella, E. A., 240
Waterman, A. S., 389, 390
Waters, E., 168
Watson, M. W., 238
Waxler, C., 232
Weikart, D., 422
Weinberg, M. K., 160
Weisberg, P., 277
Weisel, A., 316
Weisner, T. S., 324
Weiss, G., 273
Weiss, L. H., 394

Wells, M. S., 270
Werker, J. F., 133
Wertsch, J. V., 48, 49, 293
White, B., 146, 177, 178
White, R. D., 373
White, S. D., 411
Whiteman, S. D., 157
Whiting, J. W. M., 120, 233, 245
Whitson, J., 204
Widom, C. S., 256
Wigfield, A., 296, 329
Wiggins, G., 373
Wilcox, A. J., 80
Wilcox, T., 133
Wilhelm, S., 347
Wilkinson, J., 233
Wilkinson, L., 296
Wilkinson, R., 187, 188
Williams, A. L., 116
Williams, C., 123
Williams, R. A., 324, 412
Willis, D. J., 257
Willoughby, T., 239
Wilson, T., 321, 356
Wilson-Mitchell, J. E., 324
Winfree, L. T., 421, 422
Winkler, I., 132
Winters, K. C., 360
Witherington, D. C., 176
Witkow, M. R., 404
Wolf, D., 280
Wolfe, D. A., 257
Wolfson, A. R., 356
Wolock, I., 254
Wolters, C. A., 308
Wood, E., 411
Wood, P., 321
Woolfolk, A., 377

Woolston, J., 124
Wootan, M., 122
Worobey, J., 186
Wozniak, R., 205
Wren, T., 367
Wright, J. C., 239, 240
Wu, F., 324

Yang, H., 286
Yang, S., 286
Yarger, R. S., 280
Yarrow, M., 232
Yeh, S. S., 379
Yeung, S. E., 156
Ying, Y., 225
Yinon, H., 295
Yoder, P., 145
Yonas, A., 130
Yoshida, T., 381
Yoshikawa, H., 318
Youniss, J., 320, 322, 402
Yousefi, M., 185
Yu, J., 74
Yuan, A. S. V., 346, 347

Zampi, C., 115
Zane, N., 74
Zani, B., 411
Zarbatany, L., 322
Zevitz, R., 421
Zhang, J., 123
Zhou, C., 245
Zigler, E. F., 171, 420, 422
Zimmerman, F. J., 173, 237, 239
Zucker, K. J., 251, 412

Subject Index

Academic achievement, 310–311
Academic intelligence, 289
Accommodation, 44, 45, 135
Achieve, challenge to, 302
Achievement motivation, 307–308
    differences in, 307
    middle childhood in, 307–308
Achievement test, 288
Action-getting techniques, 156–157
Activity settings, 204
Acute illnesses, 270
Adaptation, 45
Adderall, 272
Additive bilingual education, 287
Adolescence
    brain development, 358–361
    clique, 405
    cognitive development, 363–384
    crowd, 405
    description of, 341
    displaced homemaker, 401
    health in, 349–361
        alcohol and tobacco, 354–355
        death, causes of, 349–350
        drug use, 351–354
        eating disorders, 357–358
        nutritional problems, 356–357
        sexually transmitted infections, 351
        sleep, 355–356
    homophobia, 412
    identity
        diffusion, 388
        versus role confusion, 387
        status, 388
    individuation, 386–387
    information processing of thoughts, 375–377
    juvenile delinquency, 420–422
    moral development, 367–375
        ethics of care, 373
        Gilligan's ethics of care, 372–373
        judgment, 367–370
        justice, issues in, 370–372
    negative identity, 388
    operational thinking, 364–367
        formal thought, 365–366
        implications, 366–367
        logical combination of ideas, 365
        possibilities *versus* realities, 364–365
        scientific reasoning, 365
    physical development, 341–361
        height and weight, 343–344
        psychological effects, 347–349
        puberty, 345–349
    school, influence of, 377–384
        cognitive effects, 378–380
        social effects, 380–384
    social aspects of, 343
    social cognition, development of, 373–375
    socioeconomic status (SES), 396
Adolescent egocentrism, 47, 373–374
Adolescent friendships, qualities of, 402
Adolescent pregnancy, and parenthood, 413–418
Adoption study, 73–74
Adult-focused activities, 184
Adulthood theories, normative-crisis model, 51
After-school care, 318
Age, peer group membership, 322
Aggression, 234–236, 327–328
    child-rearing styles and, 235–236

media influences on, 236–237
over life course, 328
peer influences on, 236
positive behavior methods, 238
spanking and punishment, 237–238
temperamental differences in, 235
Alcohol, adolescence, 354–355
Allele, 62
American Sign Language (ASL), 212
Amniotic sac, 82
Androgyny, 253–254
Anorexia nervosa, 357
Anticipation of visual events, 131–132
Anxious-avoidant attachment, 166
Anxious-resistant attachment, 166
Anxious-resistant infants, 167
Apgar Scale, 107
    score, 108
Approach behaviors, 164
Assessment, impact of, 296–298
    competitive goals, 297
    cooperative goals, 297
    individualized goals, 296
Assimilation, 44, 135
Assisted reproductive technology (ART), 72
Asthma, 271
Athletics, middle childhood and, 266–270
    physical effects of, 268–269
    psychological effects of, 268–269
    teamwork and competition, 269–270
    training in achievement motivation, 269
Attachment, 40, 51–52, 107
    behavioral system, 164
    differences in, 167
    long-term and intergenerational effects of, 174
    patterns, consequences of, 167
Attachment formation, 164–165
    effects of day care and multiple caregivers, 171–174
    effects of maternal employment, 170–171
    influences on, 167–174
    role of father, 169–170
    role of mother, 169
Attention deficit/hyperactivity disorder (ADHD), 43, 271–273
Attitudinal independence, 391
Authoritarian parents/parenting, 227–228, 394
Authoritative parents, 394
Authority parenting, 225–227
Autistic phase, 164
Autonomy, 34, 152, 174–179
Avoidance of closeness, 388

Babbling, 143
Balanced bilingual, 286
Basic operations of reasoning, 378
Basic trust, 175
Behavioral learning in infancy
    imitation, 140–141
    operant conditioning, 139–140
Behavioral learning theories
    classical conditioning (Pavlov), 40–41
    lifespan applications, 43
    operant conditioning (Skinner), 41–42
Behavioral styles, 163
Behavior exhibited between parents, 154
Behavior genetics, 71
Behaviorism, 139
Behavior modification, 43, 272
Behaviors, 410–411
Beliefs, 379

Bereavement, children with, 334
Bilingualism, middle childhood and
    cognitive effects of bilingualism, 286
    social effects of, 286–287
Binge eating disorder (BED), 357, 358
Birth
    childbirth settings and methods, 94–98
    family and, 100
    faulty passenger, 99–100
    fetal presentation (orientation), 91–92
    prenatal development and. *See* Prenatal development and birth
    problems during labor and delivery, 98–99
    stages of labor, 92–94
Blended family, 315–316
Blood transfusions, 70
Blood type inheritance, 64
Body mass index (BMI), 265
Brain development, 358–361
Breast milk, 121
Broad socialization, 398
Bronfenbrenner's ecological systems
    chronosystem, 8–9
    exosystem, 8–9
    macrosystem, 8–9
    mesosystem, 8–9
    microsystem, 8–9
Bulimia nervosa, 357–358

Caesarean section, 99
Canalization, 84
Cardinality, 203
Caregiver-infant relationships, 155
Caregiver-infant synchrony, 154–155
Caregiver-infant temperament, 155
Caregivers, 160
    multiple, 171–174
    speech, 145
Central nervous system, 109
Cephalic presentation, 91
Cephalocaudal principle, 117
Cephalopelvic disproportion (CPD), 99
Certified nurse-midwives (CNMs), 96
Child abuse, 254–257
Childbirth, preparing for, 93
Child maltreatment, 254–257
    causes of, 254–255
    consequences of, 255–257
    cultural differences and, 256
    overview of, 254
    punishment and, 237–238
    treatment and prevention of, 257
Child-rearing
    demands and responsibilities of, 154
    extended family supports for, 226
    private enterprise system of, 224
    styles of, 235–236
Children
    growth, impact on adults
        appearance effects, 194
        motor skills effect, 194–195
    health care, reforming, 188
    second chance to learn, 284
Child's weight problem, guidelines for responding, 266
Chromosomes, 60
Chronic illnesses, 270
Classical conditioning, 40–41
Classrooms, 294–295
Clique, 405
Codominance, 64

Cognition, 128
    infant, 129–133, 137–139
    and memory in infants, 128–129
    situated, 203–204
    social, development of, 373–375
Cognitive development, 363–384
    behavioral learning in infancy
        imitation, 140–141
        operant conditioning, 139–140
    cognition and memory in infants
        arousal and infants' heart rates, 128
        recognition, memory, and infant habituation, 128–129
    description of, 5
    domain of, 5–6
    end of infancy, 148
    infant perception and cognition
        auditory perception in infancy, 132–133
        coordination of sensory information, 133
        visual perception in infancy, 129–132
    language acquisition, 141–143
        influences of professional caregivers, 146–148
        parental influences, 144–146
        phonology, 143
        semantics and first words, 143–144
    Piaget's stage theory, 133–134
        of infant cognition, 137–139
        stages of sensorimotor intelligence, 134–137
    theories
        information-processing theory, 45–47
        lifespan applications, 47
        Neo-Piagetian, 45
        Piaget's, 44–45
Cognitive development, middle childhood
    conservation in, 276–279
    information processing skills, 279–285
        learning disabilities, 281–285
        memory capacity, 279–281
    intelligence, defining and measuring, 287–289
        Gardner's theory, 292–293
        information processing approaches, 289–294
        psychometric approaches, 287–288
        sociocultural approaches, 293–294
        triarchic theory, 289–293
    language development, 285–287
        cognitive effects of bilingualism, 286
        social effects of bilingualism, 286–287
    Piaget's theory and, 276–279
        assessment of student's progress, 279
        curriculum content, 278–279
        teaching methods, 278
    school influences, 294–298
        biases the affect learning, 296
        impact of assessment, 296–298
        participation structures, 294–295
Cognitive development, preschool children
    activity settings, 204
    conceptual development, 202–203
    early education, 216–219
    egocentrism, 201–202
    neostructuralist theories of, 205–206
    preoperational stage, 200–201
    from preschooler to child, 219

I-7

Cognitive development, preschool children (*continued*)
    situated cognition, 203–204
    social constructivism, 204
    symbolic thought, 201
    zone of proximal development (ZPD), 204
Cognitive theory, 243
Cohort, 22
    effects, 156
Collective autonomy, 74
Community context, 397
Competence, 177–179
Conception, 80
Concept of numbers, 203
Conceptual development, 202–203
Concrete operational thought, 364
Concrete operations, 276
Conditioned response, 41
Conditioned stimulus, 41
Conflictual independence, 391
Conservation, 276–277
    task, 203
    training, 277–278
Consolidation-of-self subphase, 387
Constructive play, 243
Content of moral beliefs, 371
Context of thinking, 290
Contextual developmental theories, 48–50
Contextual dialogue, 146
Contingent dialogue, 146
Continuity within change, 76
Contraception, decisions about, 414–415
Control group, 21
Control talk, 295
Conventional reasoning, 367
Conventions *versus* morality, 371
Cooperative learning experiences, 325
Cooperative reciprocity, 321
Coparenting, 154
Coregulation, 155
Correlation, 25–26
Crib death, 111, 112
Critical period, 85
Critical thinking, 378–379
    programs to foster, 379
Cross-cultural studies, 233
Cross-sectional study, 22
Crowd, 405
Cultural differences, 74, 305
Custody arrangements, 314–315

Dating, 411
Day care, effects on, 171–174
Deaf and hearing impaired, 213–215
Death, children's understanding of
    children with bereavement, 334
    developmental impact, 333–334
Decentration, 276
Decision-making authority, 224
Decisions about contraception, 414–415
Defense mechanisms, 36
Delinquency
    cultural views of, 398–399
    reducing and preventing, 421
Delivery
    medicinal methods during, 97–98
    problems during, 98–99
    process of, 94
Dependent variable, 20
Depression
    causes of, 419
    teenage, 418–419
Depth perception, 131
Development
    description of, 6
    ecological systems of, 8–9
    ethical constraints on studying, 27–29
    selected landmarks of, 6
Developmental diversity, 76–77
Developmental studies
    benefits, 10
    early precursors, 12
    ethical concerns, 27–29
    modern, 12–13
Developmental theories
    active or passive, 34
    classification, 33
    comparison, 52–54
    continuous or discontinuous, 33–34
    ideas and beliefs, 32

maturation or experience, 33
    qualities, 32–33
    value of, 50–51
Diet/dieting, 267
    and nutrition, 91
Differentiation subphase, 386
Difficult babies, 162
Diffusion of industry, 388
Diffusion of time perspective, 388
Direct-entry midwives (DEMs), 96
Directive *versus* nondirective authority, 74
Discourse, 294
Disorganized-disoriented attachment pattern, 166, 167
Displaced homemaker, 401
Dispositions, 379
Division of labor, 154
Divorce, 309, 400–401
    custody arrangements and, 314–315
    impact on
        adolescence, 400–401
        children, 309, 315–316
    negative effects of, 314
    parents with school-age children, 315
Domain, 5
Domain-specific knowledge, 378
Dominant gene, 62
Doulas, 96–97
Down syndrome, 68
Drop out of high school, 380–384
Drug abuse in adolescence, 351–354
Drug use, 351–354
Duos and telegraphic speech, 207–208
Dyslexia, 281

Early childhood
    average height and weight during, 184–185
    physical development. *See* Physical development, early childhood
    psychosocial development. *See* Psychosocial development, early childhood
Early-maturing boys, 348
Early-maturing girls, 348
Early-phase tasks, grieving, 332–333
Easy babies, 162
Eating disorders
    adolescence and, 357–358
    female athletes and, 359
Education, 216–219
Effacement, 92
Ego, 35
Egocentrism, 201–202
Embryonic stage, 80
Emergence, 174
Emotional independence, 391, 392
Emotional patterns between parents, 153
Emotional response to wrongdoing, 177
Emotions, 160–163
    expressions of, 160
    importance of, 152
Empathy, 232–233
Employment, 383–384
    maternal, 170–171
End of infancy, 148
Environmental deficiencies, 110
Environmental determinism, 75, 76
Erikson's theory, 34, 37–40, 175
Establish joint custody, 314
Estrogen, 346
Ethics of care, 373
Ethnicity and community, in family decision making, 397
Ethological theory, 51–52, 242–243
Ethology, 52
Eugenics, 71
Every Student Succeeds Act (ESSA), 380
Exosystem, 48
Experience base, 366
Experimental group, 21
Experimentation subphase, 386
Expertise, 376–377
Expressive style, 144
Extinction, 42
    burst, 42

Failure to thrive, 124
False self, 387

Families
    with authoritative parenting styles, 397
    effects of differences in, 195–197
    effects of work on, 316
    ethnic differences in, 396–397
    management of, 154
    modern, 309
Family life
    during middle childhood, 308–309
    quality of, 312–313
Family relationships, 391–401
    authoritarian parenting, 227–228
    authority parenting, 225–227
    challenge of, 302–303
    changes over time, 229
    divorce, remarriage, and single parenthood, 400–401
    indifferent parenting, 228–229
    only children, 231
    with parents, 391–398
    permissive parenting, 228
    siblings, 229–231
Father-infant interactions, 155–156
Father's role, 169–170
Fetal alcohol syndrome (FAS), 87
Fetal presentation, 91
Fetal stage, 80
Fine motor coordination, 191
    prerepresentational drawing, 191–192
    representational drawing, 192
Fixation, 36
Fluids, 70
Focalin, 272
Fontanelles, 107
Foreclosed individuals, 389
Formal curriculum, 378
Formal operational thought, 364
Freestanding birth centers (FBCs), 95
Freudian Theory, 35–37
Friendship, 247–250, 321, 401–404
    adolescence and, 401–404
    adolescent, 402
    interethnic, 403–404
Functional independence, 391
Functional play, 243
Functional relationships, 200

Games with rules, 244
Gangs, 420–421
Gardner's theory of multiple intelligences, 292–293
Gender, 250–254, 330–331, 402–403
    differences, 212
    influences, 250–251
    peer group membership, 322–323
Gender development, 250–254
    androgyny, 253–254
    concept, 250–251
    gender-role stereotypes, 251
    influences, 252–253
    learning gender schema, 251–252
Gender-role preferences, 390
Gender-role stereotypes, 251
Gene, 60
General ability test, biases of, 289
Genetic abnormalities chromosome disorders, 65–70
    dominant gene disorders, 68–69
    Down syndrome, 65–68
    due to abnormal genes, 68–70
Genetics, 59–60
    counseling, 70–71, 74
    determinism, 75, 76
    imprinting, 65
    structures, 60
Genetic transmission
    of eye color, 63
    looking back/looking forward, 76–77
    meiosis, 60–61
    mitosis, 60–61
    role of DNA, 60
Genotype, 61–62
Germinal stage, 80
Gifted students, 290–291
Gilligan's ethics of care, 372–373
Grandmothers/grandparents, 157
    involvement of, 417
Grasping, 118–119
Grieving, process of, 332–333
Gross motor development, 117–118

Group acceptance, 321
Growth spurt, 343

Hemophilia, 64
Heredity, 71–76
Heteronomous morality, 368
Holographic speech or telegraphic speech, 207–208
Homophobia, 412
Hope, 38
Hospital births, 95
Hostile attribution bias, 236
HTT gene, 69
Human agency, 48
Huntington disease, 69
Hydroxyurea, 70
Hyperactivity, 271
Hypothesis, 17
Hypothetical-deductive reasoning, 365

Id, 35
Identity
    development, theories of, 386–391
    diffusion, 388
    versus role confusion, 387
    search for, 391
    status, 388–389
Identity-achieved individuals, 389
Identity-diffused individuals, 389
Imaginary audience, 47, 374
Imitation, 42, 140–141
Independent variable, 20
Indifferent parents/parenting, 228–229, 394–395
Individual genetic expression
    dominant gene, 62
    genotype, 62
    phenotype, 62
    polygenic transmission, 64
    recessive gene, 62
    sex determination, 64–65
    transmission of multiple variations, 62–64
Individualism, 267
Individuation, 386–387
Industry
    versus inferiority, 306
    latency and crisis of, 306
Infancy
    auditory perception in, 132–133
        discriminating between sounds, 132
        localization of sounds, 132–133
    cognitive effects of, 145
    end of, 148
    support cognitive development during, 135
    visual perception in, 129–132
Infant-directed speech, 145, 211
Infant-mother attachment, 157
Infants. *See also* Piaget's stage theory
    arousal, 113–114
    attachment
        day care, effects on, 171–174
        definition, 163
        disorganized-disoriented attachment, 166
        father's role, 169–170
        intergenerational effects, 174
        long-term effects, 174
        maternal employment, 170–171
        mother's role, 169
        multiple caregivers, 171–174
        patterns, 167
        secure attachment, 163–165
        strange situation (SS), 165–166
        working models, 164
    attachment formation, 164–165
    auditory acuity, 115–116
    autonomy, 174–179
        competence, 177–179
        emergence, 174
        emotional response to wrongdoing, 177
        observational learning, 176
        operant conditioning, 175
        self-awareness, 177
        self-description, 177
        self-esteem, 177–179
        self-evaluation, 177
        self-recognition, 177
        social referencing, 176
    brain growth, 109–111
    breast milk *versus* formula, 121

cognition and memory in
  arousal and infants' heart rates, 128
  recognition, memory, and infant habituation, 128–129
cognitive development, 123–126
consequences for, 123–124
day-care program, 159
emotions and temperament, 160–163
emotions, development of, 161
failure to thrive, 124
growth curves for, 109
habituation, 128–129
heart rates, 128
lifespan themes, 179
low-birth-weight infants, 123–124
mortality rate, 124–126
motor development, 117–120
olfactory acuity, 116–117
overnutrition, 122–123
perception and cognition
  auditory perception in infancy, 132–133
  coordination of sensory information, 133
  visual perception in infancy, 129–132
physical growth, 108–109
poor nutrition, 121–122
sensory acuity, 115
sleep, 111–113
tactile, 116–117
taste, 116–117
thinking, 147
visual acuity, 115
Infer grammatical relationships, 208
Inferiority, 306
Informal curriculum, 378
Informal operational thinking, 47
Information processing
  approaches, 289–294
  of thoughts, 375–377
Information processing skills
  implications for elementary education, 281
  learning disabilities, 281–285
  long-term memory (LTM), 280–281
  memory capacity, 279–281
  working memory, 280
Information processing theory, 364
  definition, 45
  developmental changes, 46–47
  key principles, 46
  model of learning, 46
Informed consent, 28
Integrated care, 373
Intellectual performance, range of reaction for, 73
Intelligence, middle childhood and, 286–289
  biases of, 289
  Gardner's theory, 292–293
  information processing approaches, 289–294
  psychometric approaches, 287–288
  sociocultural approaches, 293–294
  triarchic theory, 289–293
Interethnic friendships, 403–404
Intergenerational effects, 174
Intermodal perception, 133
Interviews, 27
In vitro fertilization (IVF), 72

Joint parent-teen, 397
Juvenile delinquency, 420–422
Juvenile period, 321

Knowledge base, 47
Kohlberg's six stages of moral judgment, 367–370

Labor
  problems during, 98–99
  stages of, 92
Language acquisition, 141–143
  deaf and hearing impaired, 213–215
  deficits and differences, 215
  duos and telegraphic speech, 207–208
  gender differences, 212
  imitation and practice, 209
  infer grammatical relationships, 208
  influences of professional caregivers, 146–148

language acquisition device (LAD), 210–211
overgeneralizations, 208
parental influences, 144–146
parent-child interactions, 211–212
phonology, 143
regularities, 208
reinforcement, 209
semantics and first words, 143–144
socioeconomic differences, 212–213
syntactic rules, 206–207
syntax rules, 206
Language acquisition device (LAD), 210–211
Language development, 285–287
  cognitive effects of bilingualism, 286
  social effects of bilingualism, 286–287
Lanugo, 106
Late-maturing boys, 348
Late-maturing girls, 348
Late-phase tasks, grieving, 333
Latency, 306
Learning
  disabilities, 281–285
    causes of, 282–283
    children with specific, 283–285
  orientation, 307
  rules, limits of, 208–209
  theory, 242
Lifelong growth, 76
Lifespan
  effects of, 401
  perspectives, 391
  themes, 179
Lifespan development, 4
  changing meanings, 15
  continuity within change, 13–14
  diversity, 16
  lifelong growth, 14–15
  strength and limitations, 29
  vantage points, 15
Lifespan psychology
  case studies, 27
  experimental study, 19–21
  naturalistic studies, 24–27
  quasi-experimental studies, 21–24
  scientific methods, 16–18
Linkage and association studies, 75
Longitudinal study, 22
Long-term effects, 174
Long-term memory (LTM), 46, 280–281
Low birth weight, 123–124

Macrosystem, 48
Magnet schools, 325
Magnitude of numbers, 203
Male mortality rates, 350
Marcia's theory of identity status, 389
Marital conflict, 400
Matched guise technique, 287
Maternal employment, 170–171
  effects of, 316–317
Media
  effects of, 238–240
  influences, 236–237
Medicaid eligibility, 188
Meiosis
  process of, 61
  for sperm cells, 61
Memory, 128–129
  capacity, 279–281
  effects of, 138–139
Menarche, 345
Mental space, 45
Mesosystem, 48
Metacognition, 47, 376
Metacognitive knowledge, 378
Metalinguistic awareness, 286
Microsystem, 48
Middle childhood
  and athletics, 266–270
    physical effects of, 268–269
    psychological effects of, 268–269
    teamwork and competition, 269–270
    training in achievement motivation, 269
  health and illness, 270–273
    attention deficit hyperactivity disorder, 271–273
    sleep, 273
    social influence on, 271

height and weight, trends and variations in, 264–265
and motor development, 266–270
physical development, 264
Middle-phase tasks, grieving, 333
Middle school, 380
Midwife, 94
Mitosis, process of, 61
Mixed-pattern babies, 162
Modeling, 42
Modern families, changing nature of, 309
Modern midwives, 96–97
Moral development, 367–375
  ethics of care, 373
  Gilligan's ethics of care, 372–373
  judgment, 367–370
  justice, issues in, 370–372
Morality, 367
  conventions versus, 371
  gender differences in, 372
Moratorium individuals, 389
Moro reflex, 115
Morphemes, 206
Mortality, 270
Mother's role, 169
Motivational orientation, 308
Motor development
  cultural and sex differences in, 120
  middle childhood and, 266–270
  milestones of, 119
Motor skill development
  catching, 191
  definition, 117
  drawing, 191–192
  fundamental, 189
  jumping, 190
  running, 190
  throwing, 191
  variations, 193–194
  walking, 190
Motor versus cognitive limitations, 138
Multifactorial disorders, 70
Multiple caregivers, 171–174
Multiple intelligences, 292–293
Myelination, 110

Narrow socialization, 398
National Health and Social Life Survey (NHSLS), 410
Negative identity, 388
Negative reinforcement, 41
Neonate, 106
Neo-Piagetian theory, 205
Neostructuralist theory, 205
Neurons, 109
  anatomy of, 110
Newborn, physical development
  Apgar Scale, 106
  first few hours, 106–107
  size and bodily proportions, 107–108
Nighttime bladder control, 189
No Child Left Behind Act (NCLB), 379–380
Noncustodial fathers, 314
Noncustodial mothers, 314
Nonparental caregivers, 157–158
Non-REM sleep, 111
Normative crisis model, 51, 321–322
Normative transitions, 321
Norms, 13
Nutritional problems, adolescence and, 356–357

Obesity, 265
Object constancy, 130, 164
Observational learning, 42, 176
Olfaction, 115
Operant conditioning, 41–42, 139–140, 175
Operant learning, evidence of, 139
Operational thinking, 364–367
  formal thought, 365–366
  implications, 366–367
  logical combination of ideas, 365
  possibilities versus realities, 364–365
  scientific reasoning, 365
Opposite-sex companionship, 403
Ordinality, 203
Overgeneralizations, 208
Overnutrition, 122–123
Overt aggression, 234, 327
Ovum, 60

Pain medications, 70
Parent-adolescent conflict, 393
Parental expectations, 310–311
Parental influences, 144–146, 406–407
Parental unemployment, 317–318
Parent-child interactions, 211–212
Parent-child relationship, 224, 395
  authoritarian parenting, 227–228
  authoritative parenting, 225–227
  change over time, 229
  indifferent parenting, 228–229
  permissive parenting, 228
Parenthood, 413–418
  transition to, 153–154
Parenting
  goals, 312–313
  practices, 154
  quality of, 308–309, 312–313
  stresses and responsibilities of, 156
  styles, 394–395
Parent-teen communication, 415–416
Participation structures, 294–295
Paternal involvement, 154
Peer
  challenge of, 303
  conformity to, 328–329
  definition, 302
  influences, 236, 405–406
  interactions with, 158–160
Peer groups
  adolescence and, 404–407
  adolescent's choice of, 408
  structure of, 405
Peer relationships, middle childhood and, 320–331
  conformity to peers, 328–329
  functions of friends, 321
  functions of other peers, 322
  group membership, 322–325
  popularity and rejection, 325–328
  school influences on peer relations, 329–331
  theorists about
    Piaget, 320
    Sullivan, 320–321
Perceived popularity, 326
Perception, 128
  in infancy, 129–133
Perceptual masking, 281
Performance orientation, 307
Period of transition, 92
Permissive parenting, 228
Permissive parents, 394
Personal autonomy, 74
Personal fable, 47, 374–375
Phenotype, 62
Phonemes, 143
Phonology, 143, 206
Physical activity play, 242
Physical development, 184–185
  in adolescence, 353–354
  bladder control, 187–189
  description, 5
  domains, 5
  first two years, 106–107
  gender differences, 192–193
  genetic background, 185
  growth measurement, 184–185
  health and poverty, 186–187
  impact of children's growth on adults, 194–197
  influences on, 184–185
  middle childhood, 264
  motor skill development, 190–194
  nutritional needs during, 186
  socioeconomic status, 186
Physical maturation, 45
Piaget's preoperational stage, 200–201
Piaget's stage theory, 133–134
  of infant cognition, 137–139
  infant cognition according, 134
  stages of sensorimotor intelligence, 134–137
Piaget's theory, 276–279
  assessment of student's progress, 279
  of cognition, 44–45
  concrete operational skills, 276
  curriculum content, 278–279
  of education, 278
  influence on education, 278

Piaget's theory (continued)
    assessment of students' progress, 279
    curriculum content, 278–279
    teaching methods, 278
    middle childhood and, 276–279
        assessment of student's progress, 279
        curriculum content, 278–279
        education, influence on, 278–279
        teaching methods, 278
Placenta, 80, 81
Plasticity, 110
Play
    cognitive theory, 243
    constructive, 243
    ethological theory, 242–243
    functional, 243
    games with rules, 244
    learning theory, 242
    nature of, 241
    other influences, 244–245
    pretend, 244
    psychoanalytic theory, 241–242
    social levels, 245–247
Political philosophies, 390
Polymorphisms, 75
Poor nutrition, 122–123
Popular child, 325–326
Popularity, 321
Positive behavior methods, 238
Positive reinforcement, 41
Possibilities versus realities, 364–365
Postconventional moral judgment, 370
Postconventional reasoning, 367
Practice subphase, 386
Pragmatics, 206
Preconventional reasoning, 367
Pregnant teenagers, 417
    prevention and support programs, 418
Preimplantation diagnosis, 70
Prenatal counseling, 71
Prenatal development and birth, 80–84
    conception, 80
    embryonic stage, 81–82
    experience of pregnancy, 83–84
    fetal stage, 82–83
    germinal stage, 80–81
    stages of prenatal development, 80
Prenatal diagnosis, 70–71
Prenatal influences on child, 84–91
    environmental hazards, 89–90
    harmful substances, diseases, and environmental hazards, 85–86
    maternal age and physical characteristics, 90
    maternal diseases, 89
    medicinal drugs, 86–87
    nonmedicinal drugs, 87–89
    pediatric AIDS, 89
    prenatal health care, 90–91
Preoperational stage, 200–201
Prepared childbirth, 95–96
Preschool children, 184
    classification skills, 202
    cognitive development, 200–206
    concept of numbers, 203
    conservation task, 203
    egocentrism, 201–202
    language acquisition and variations, 206–212
    reversibility, 202–203
Preschoolers, 158
    effects of media, 238–240
    friendships, 247–250
    gender stereotypes, 250–251
    play activities, 240
Pretend play, 244
Primary-caregiver fathers, 156
Primary sex characteristics, 345
Professional caregivers, 146–148
Projection, 36
Prosocial behavior, 232–233
    development of, 232–233
    sources of, 233
Proximodistal principle, 117
Psychoanalysis, 35
Psychoanalytic theory, 241–242
Psychodynamic developmental theories
    Erikson's, 37–40
    Freudian, 35–37
    lifespan applications, 40

Psychodynamic theories, 306
Psychometric approaches, 287–288
    to intelligence, 288–289
Psychosexual stages, 36
Psychosocial crisis, 38
Psychosocial development, adolescence, 385–423
    family relationships, 391–401
        divorce, remarriage, and single parenthood, 400–401
        with parents, 391–398
    identity development, theories of, 386–391
    sexuality, 409–413
        and everyday life, 413
        sexual experience, 409–410
        sexual orientations, 412–413
    social relationships, 401–409
        friendship, 401–404
        peer groups, 404–407
    special problems, 413–422
        adolescent pregnancy and parenthood, 413–418
        juvenile delinquency, 420–422
        teenage depression and suicide, 418–420
Psychosocial development, description, 6
Psychosocial development, early childhood
    child abuse and maltreatment, 254–257
    gender development, 250–254
        androgyny, 253–254
        concept, 250–251
        gender-role stereotypes, 251
        influences, 252–253
        learning gender schema, 251–252
    play in
        cognitive theory, 243
        constructive, 243
        ethological theory, 242–243
        functional, 243
        games with rules, 244
        learning theory, 242
        nature of, 241
        other influences, 244–245
        pretend, 244
        psychoanalytic theory, 241–242
        social levels, 245–247
    relationships with family
        authoritarian parenting, 227–228
        authority parenting, 225–227
        changes over time, 229
        indifferent parenting, 228–229
        only children, 231
        permissive parenting, 228
        relationships with siblings, 229–231
    social world
        aggression, 234–236
        effects of media, 238–240
        empathy, 232–233
        prosocial behavior, 232–233
Psychosocial development, first two years
    attachment formation, 163–174
    autonomy, emergence of, 174–179
    early social relationships, 152–160
    emotions and temperament, 160–163
Psychosocial development, middle childhood, 301–336
    age of industry and achievement, 306–308
    challenges of, 302–303
    death, loss, and grieving during school, 332–334
    family relationships, 308–320
    peer relationships, 320–331
    sense of self, 303–305
    social support, sources of, 318–320
Psychosocial moratorium, 388
Puberty, 185, 343–349
    adolescents' reactions to onset of, 348
    hormonal changes, 346–347
    nonnormative effects of, 349
    primary sex characteristics, development of, 345
    secondary sex characteristics, development of, 345
        body hair, 346
        breasts, 345–346
        voice, 346
    timing of, 347–348
Punishment, 42

Random sample, 20
Range of reaction, 71–72
Rapprochement subphase, 387
Reaching, 118–119
Recall memory, 280–281
Recessive gene, 62
    disorders, 69
Reciprocal friend, 326
Reciprocity, 321
Recognition, 128–129
    memory, 280
Reconstituted family, 309
Recreational people, 410
Reflex, 117
Registered nurses (RNs), 96
Regularities, 208
Reinforcement, 41, 209
Relational aggression, 234, 327
Religious beliefs, 390
Remarriage, 315–316, 400–401
REM sleep, 111
Repression, 36
Resilience, 382
Reversibility, 276
Ritalin, 272

Same-sex friends, 403
Sample, 26
Schemes, 44, 45, 134
School
    challenge of, 303
    culture, 329–330
School-age children, 157, 270, 305
School influences, 294–298, 377–384
    biases the affect learning, 296
    classroom discourse, 294–295
    cognitive effects, 378–380
    impact of assessment, 296–298
    participation structures, 294–295
    social effects, 380–384
Scientific reasoning, 365
Secondary-caregiver role, 156
Secondary sex characteristics, 345
Secure attachment, 163–165
Segregation, patterns of, 324
Selective attention, 280
Self-awareness, 177
Self-concept, 303
Self-constancy, 304
Self-control, 395
Self-description, 177
Self-directed regulatory behaviors, 160–161
Self-esteem, 177–179, 316
Self-evaluation, 177
Self-recognition, 177
Self-regulation, phases of, 162
Self-reliance, 395
self, stability of, 304–305
Semantic relations, 207–209
Semantics, 143–144
Sense of self, 303–305
Sensitivity to transformations, 276
Sensorimotor intelligence, stages of
    combined secondary circular reactions, 136
    early reflexes, 135
    first symbols, 137
    primary circular reactions, 135–136
    secondary circular reactions, 136
    tertiary circular reactions, 137
Sensory information, coordination of, 133
Sensory memory, 46
Separation anxiety, 164, 165
Separation-individuation phase, 164
Sequential study, 23
Sex-linked recessive traits, 64–65
Sexual attitudes, 410–411
Sexual behavior, 415
Sexual experience, 409–410
Sexuality, 409–413
    in adolescence, 409–413
    and everyday life, 413
    sexual experience, 409–410
    sexual orientations, 412–413
Sexually transmitted infections, adolescence and, 351
Sexual-minority orientations, development of, 412
Sexual orientations, 412–413

Shame, 74
Shaping, 42
Short-term memory (STM), 46
Siblings
    interactions with, 156–157
    relationships, 229–231
    support, 318–319
Sickle-cell disease, 69, 70
Signaling behaviors, 164
Situated cognition, 203–204
Skills, 45
    base, 366
Sleep, 273
    adolescence and, 355–356
    requirements, developmental changes in, 112
Slow-to-warm-up babies, 162
Social activity, 203–205
Social biases, 296
Social class, differences in, 390
Social cognition, 373–375
Social cognitive learning theory, 42–43
Social constructivism, 204
Social conventions, 371
Social-economic status (SES), 350
Social-emotional consequences, 347
Social levels, 245–247
Social media, 405–406
Social patterns between parents, 153
Social referencing, 176
Social relationships, 401–409
    adolescence and, 401–409
    caregiver-infant synchrony, 150–151
    coparenting, 154
    father-infant interactions, 155–156
    friendship, 401–404
    grandparents, 157
    interactions with peers, 158–160
    interactions with siblings, 155–157
    with nonparental caregivers, 157–158
    peer groups, 404–407
    transition to parenthood, 153–154
Social status, 321
Social support, sources of
    beyond siblings, 319–320
    sibling support, 318–319
Social trajectories, 48, 49
Social transmission, 45
Social world behavior
    aggression, 234–236
    conflicts, 234–236
    empathy, 232–233
    prosocial behavior, 232–233
Sociocultural approaches, 293–294
Sociocultural perspective on intelligence, 293
Socioeconomic differences, 212–213
Socioeconomic status (SES), 396
Sociometric popularity, 326
Spanking, 237–238
Speed of processing, 376
Sperm, 60
Standardized tests, 288–289
Stay-at-home mothers, 310
Stepmothers, 316
Stereotypical family, 309
Stigma, 74
Stranger anxiety, 164
Strange situation (SS), 165–166
Strattera, 272
Street children, 49
Stress, and health, 91
Students, experience in classroom, 330–331
Stunting, 122
Sudden infant death syndrome (SIDS), 112–113
Suicide, 418–420
Superego, 35
Survey, 26
Swaddling infants, 120
Symbiotic phase, 164
Symbolic thought, 201
Symmetrical reciprocity, 321
Synaptic pruning, 110
Synaptogenesis, 109–110
Syntactic relations, 207–209
Syntactic rules, 206–207
Syntax, 206–207, 212
    rules, 206

I-10 Subject Index

Tactile acuity, 115
Teens/teenage, 405–406
    depression, 418–420
    parenthood, consequences of, 415–416
    pregnancy, causes of, 414
Temperaments, 51–52, 160–163
    developmental effects of, 163
    differences, 235
    experience and context on, 163
    importance of, 152
    original classification of, 162
    predictions of, 162–163

Teratogen, 85
Testis-determining factor, 64
Testosterone, 346
Toddlers, 158
    in day care, 158
Traditional people, 410
Transient exuberance, 109–110
Transition to parenthood, 153–154
Transverse presentation, 91
Triarchic theory of intelligence, 289–293
Trust, 152
Twin adoption study, 75
Twin study, 75

Umbilical cord, 82
Unconditioned response, 40
Unconditioned stimulus, 40
Unilateral friend, 326
Unilateral parent, 397
Unilateral teen, 397
Unpopular child, 326–327

Validity, 21
Values, 379
Vernix, 106
Vocational choice, 390

Walking, 119–120
Weight, changes in, 344
Working memory, 280
Working models, 164

Young children
    developmentally appropriate practices, 217
    fine motor coordination, 191–192

Zone of proximal development (ZPD), 48, 204, 211, 293
Zygote, 60, 79